DICTIONARY
OF
AMERICAN BIOGRAPHY

PUBLISHED UNDER THE AUSPICES OF
THE AMERICAN COUNCIL OF LEARNED SOCIETIES

The American Council of Learned Societies, organized in 1919 for the purpose of advancing the study of the humanities and of the humanistic aspects of the social sciences, is a nonprofit federation comprising forty-three national scholarly groups. The Council represents the humanities in the United States in the International Union of Academies, provides fellowships and grants-in-aid, supports research-and-planning conferences and symposia, and sponsors special projects and scholarly publications.

MEMBER ORGANIZATIONS
AMERICAN PHILOSOPHICAL SOCIETY, 1743
AMERICAN ACADEMY OF ARTS AND SCIENCES, 1780
AMERICAN ANTIQUARIAN SOCIETY, 1812
AMERICAN ORIENTAL SOCIETY, 1842
AMERICAN NUMISMATIC SOCIETY, 1858
AMERICAN PHILOLOGICAL ASSOCIATION, 1869
ARCHAEOLOGICAL INSTITUTE OF AMERICA, 1879
SOCIETY OF BIBLICAL LITERATURE, 1880
MODERN LANGUAGE ASSOCIATION OF AMERICA, 1883
AMERICAN HISTORICAL ASSOCIATION, 1884
AMERICAN ECONOMIC ASSOCIATION, 1885
AMERICAN FOLKLORE SOCIETY, 1888
AMERICAN DIALECT SOCIETY, 1889
AMERICAN PSYCHOLOGICAL ASSOCIATION, 1892
ASSOCIATION OF AMERICAN LAW SCHOOLS, 1900
AMERICAN PHILOSOPHICAL ASSOCIATION, 1901
AMERICAN ANTHROPOLOGICAL ASSOCIATION, 1902
AMERICAN POLITICAL SCIENCE ASSOCIATION, 1903
BIBLIOGRAPHICAL SOCIETY OF AMERICA, 1904
ASSOCIATION OF AMERICAN GEOGRAPHERS, 1904
HISPANIC SOCIETY OF AMERICA, 1904
AMERICAN SOCIOLOGICAL ASSOCIATION, 1905
AMERICAN SOCIETY OF INTERNATIONAL LAW, 1906
ORGANIZATION OF AMERICAN HISTORIANS, 1907
COLLEGE ART ASSOCIATION OF AMERICA, 1912
HISTORY OF SCIENCE SOCIETY, 1924
LINGUISTIC SOCIETY OF AMERICA, 1924
MEDIAEVAL ACADEMY OF AMERICA, 1925
AMERICAN MUSICOLOGICAL SOCIETY, 1934
SOCIETY OF ARCHITECTURAL HISTORIANS, 1940
ECONOMIC HISTORY ASSOCIATION, 1940
ASSOCIATION FOR ASIAN STUDIES, 1941
AMERICAN SOCIETY FOR AESTHETICS, 1942
METAPHYSICAL SOCIETY OF AMERICA, 1950
AMERICAN STUDIES ASSOCIATION, 1950
RENAISSANCE SOCIETY OF AMERICA, 1954
SOCIETY FOR ETHNOMUSICOLOGY, 1955
AMERICAN SOCIETY FOR LEGAL HISTORY, 1956
AMERICAN SOCIETY FOR THEATRE RESEARCH, 1956
SOCIETY FOR THE HISTORY OF TECHNOLOGY, 1958
AMERICAN COMPARATIVE LITERATURE ASSOCIATION, 1960
AMERICAN ACADEMY OF RELIGION, 1963
AMERICAN SOCIETY FOR EIGHTEENTH-CENTURY STUDIES, 1969

DICTIONARY
OF
American Biography

Supplement Six

1956–1960

John A. Garraty, *Editor*

WITH AN INDEX GUIDE TO THE SUPPLEMENTS

Charles Scribner's Sons
NEW YORK

The preparation of the original twenty volumes of the Dictionary was made possible by the public-spirited action of the New York Times Company and its president, the late Adolph S. Ochs, in furnishing a large subvention. The preparation and publication of Supplement 6 have been supported by the sale of those volumes and the preceding Supplements. Entire responsibility for the contents of the Dictionary and its Supplements rests with the American Council of Learned Societies.

COPYRIGHT © 1980 AMERICAN COUNCIL OF LEARNED SOCIETIES

Library of Congress Cataloging in Publication Data (Revised)

Main entry under title:

Dictionary of American biography.

    Includes index.
    Supplements 1–2 comprise v. 11 of the main work.
    CONTENTS: 3. 1941–1945.—4. 1946–1950.—5. 1951–1955.
      6. 1956–1960.
    1. United States—Biography. I. Garraty, John
Arthur, 1920–
E176.D563 Suppl.   920'.073   77-2942
ISBN 0-684-16226-1 (Suppl. 6)

5 7 9 11 13 15 17 19   V/C   20 18 16 14 12 10 8 6

Printed in the United States of America

American Council of Learned Societies Committee on the
Dictionary of American Biography

Editorial Staff

PREFACE

With this supplement, which contains biographies of 524 persons, written by more than 450 authors, the *Dictionary of American Biography* extends its coverage through December 31, 1960, and reaches a total of 17,084 sketches. As with earlier volumes, this one could not have been completed without the generous and unpaid cooperation of dozens of experts in various fields. These scholars have assisted both in deciding which persons to include in the supplement and in locating authors for the biographies. I wish to thank them most sincerely for their help.

As was the case with *Supplement Five*, the authors of the sketches have been asked to fill out data sheets for their subjects covering the following information: Section I: full date of birth and death; place of birth; full name of father; full name of mother; father's occupation; economic and social position of the family at the time of the subject's birth; education; institutions attended, dates, degrees earned; full name of spouse, or if never married mention of this fact; date of marriage; number of children, names of any of apparent historical importance; place of death. Section II: number of siblings, number of each sex; order of birth of subject, order among those of same sex; economic and social position of mother's family; names of close relatives who achieved distinction; nationality and time of migration to the United States of ancestors; religious affiliation of subject; religious affiliations of father and mother; religious affiliation of spouse; economic and social position of spouse at time of marriage; highest education of spouse; names and dates of birth of children; cause of subject's death; place of burial; date of spouse's death.

Authors were asked to include in their essays all the facts in Section I, but only such details from Section II as seemed relevant. The purpose was to gather the material in a form convenient for researchers, but to keep most of it out of the biographies themselves. The data sheets will be placed on file along with other *DAB* papers in the Library of Congress, so that sociologists, psychologists, and other researchers interested in collective biography can have access to them.

As with past volumes, we are much indebted to individuals and institutions that have provided help with our editorial task, particularly Louis Starr and Elizabeth Mason of the Oral History Collection, Columbia University; Rand Hoffman, the research assistant; Susan O. Thompson and Phyllis Dain of Columbia University; and Walter C. Allen of the University of Illinois. We are most grateful for the assistance of all these persons.

I wish also once again to thank the American Council of Learned Societies, its president, Robert Lumiansky, and the members of the council's board for the *DAB* for their many kindnesses and wise guidance.

JOHN A. GARRATY

DICTIONARY
OF
AMERICAN BIOGRAPHY

DICTIONARY OF

AMERICAN BIOGRAPHY

Abbott—Zuppke

ABBOTT, EDITH (Sept. 26, 1876–July 28, 1957), social worker, educator, and author, was born in Grand Island, Nebr., the daughter of Othman Ali Abbott and Elizabeth Maletta Griffin. Her father, a Civil War veteran, was a successful lawyer and the first lieutenant governor of Nebraska. Her mother came from a Quaker family and was a strong advocate of woman's rights and suffrage. Susan B. Anthony was one of the celebrities who visited the Abbotts during Edith's childhood. Although reared in relative affluence, Edith and her younger sister Grace, who also became a renowned social worker, considered themselves "children of the old frontier." "We were brought up," Edith recalled, "hearing the story of the making of a state in the prairie wilderness; and we knew the men and women of courage, ability and boundless energy who faced the difficulties of blizzards, droughts, and other hardships of the covered-wagon days."

Following five years at Brownell Hall, an Episcopalian boarding school in Omaha, Edith attended the University of Nebraska and graduated in 1901. She enrolled in the graduate school of the University of Chicago in 1902, received a fellowship in political economics in 1903, and took her Ph.D. in 1905 with a thesis on the wages of unskilled labor in the United States from 1830 to 1900. After postdoctoral study at the London School of Economics, where she came under the influence of the English social reformer Beatrice Webb, she taught political economics for one year at Wellesley College.

Abbott's career in social work began in 1908 when Sophonisba Breckinridge, her mentor at the University of Chicago, invited her to join the staff of the Chicago School of Civics and Philanthropy. For the next decade she lived with her sister at Hull House, Chicago's famous social settlement, and worked with her for protection of juveniles and immigrants and for improvement in housing and correctional institutions. During this period she published her first book, *Women in Industry* (1910), and collaborated with Breckinridge on *The Delinquent Child and the Home* (1912) and other studies of the social impact of compulsory education and child labor laws.

In 1920 Breckinridge and Abbott arranged to have the School of Civics and Philanthropy incorporated in the University of Chicago as the School of Social Service Administration. At their insistence it received graduate status. As Abbott explained, "We wanted to develop *not* a vocational school but a professional school with a broad educational program and an emphasis on research." She taught courses dealing with the history of English and American philanthropy, methods of social research, immigration, and public welfare administration. In 1924 Abbott succeeded Breckinridge as dean and served in that capacity until 1942. Under Breckinridge and Abbott's leadership, the School of Social Service Administration was unique among American schools of social work in its emphasis on the public, as opposed to voluntary, aspects of social service and on the training of public welfare administrators and policymakers.

Abbott was a member of an advisory committee on emigration of the International Labor Organization. She also served two terms as president of the National Association of Social Workers and in 1937 was president of the National Conference of Social Work. She founded (1927), edited, and contributed numerous articles, reviews, and notes to the *Social Service Review*. Her books on immigration (1924, 1926) and public assistance (1940) were documentary studies intended as casebooks for students of welfare policy. In her writing and teaching she paid close attention to history, not out of reverence for the past, but because she believed students must learn to examine "the legacy of an older age" in a critical spirit and with awareness of the changed conditions and needs of their own time.

A progressive Republican, Abbott admired Senator George Norris of Nebraska, supported Theodore Roosevelt in 1912, Herbert Hoover in 1928, and Franklin Roosevelt in the 1930's, and championed the women's suffrage, prohibition, and proposed child labor amendments to the U.S. Constitution. She was sympathetic to the New Deal but criticized inadequacies in its welfare policies and programs.

Although frail in appearance, Abbott was strong-willed and possessed the capacity for sustained and arduous work and the ability to express ~inions with precision and authority. She made important contributions to professional education for social work, to research on social problems, and to the expansion and improvement of social services on the local, national, and international scene. "The main drives in Edith's life," observed an admirer, Helen Cody Baker, in 1936, "have been toward broadening and strengthening our public welfare services and the adequate preparation of students to do the job."

Abbott never married. She continued to edit the *Social Service Review* after retiring from teaching and administrative duties and remained influential at the School of Social Service Administration until 1952. Her last years were spent in Grand Island in the imposing house that her family had occupied for seventy years.

[The Edith and Grace Abbott Papers in the Department of Special Collections, University of Chicago Library, contain twenty-two boxes of Edith Abbott's personal, academic, and professional papers. For a bibliography of her writing compiled by Rachel Marks, see *Social Service Review*, Mar. 1958. Among Abbott's publications not mentioned in the text are *Report on Crime and the Foreign Born* (1931); *Social Welfare and Professional Education* (1931; rev. and enl., 1942); *The Tenements of Chicago, 1908–1935* (1936); and *Some American Pioneers in Social Welfare* (1937).

See also Othman A. Abbott, *Recollections of a Pioneer Lawyer* (1929); Elizabeth Wisner, "Edith Abbott's Contribution to Social Work Education," *Social Service Review*, Mar. 1958; Helen R. Wright, "Three Against Time: Edith and Grace Abbott and Sophonisba Breckinridge," *ibid.*, Mar. 1954; and *Social Service Administration Newsletter*, Dec. 1957. For obituary and photograph, see the *New York Times*, July 30, 1957.]

ROBERT H. BREMNER

ABBOTT, ELEANOR HALLOWELL (Sept. 22, 1872–June 2, 1958), novelist and short story writer, was born in Cambridge, Mass., the daughter of Edward Abbott, a Congregationalist (later Episcopal) minister, and Clara Davis. Jacob Abbott, author of the Rollo books, was her paternal grandfather, and the popular clergyman Lyman Abbott, an uncle.

Abbott attended private schools in Cambridge. She disliked school and recalled that recess was her favorite part of the school day. Although she was at the bottom of her class in most subjects, her teachers encouraged her special talent for English composition. She filled notebooks with many stories but did not finish them. Later she took writing courses at Radcliffe College.

For a short time Abbott dabbled in free-lance advertising in Boston and considered the offer of a job as an advertising copywriter in New York. For four years she was employed as a private secretary and teacher of English composition at the state normal school in Lowell, Mass. Describing her literary background, she wrote that she was weaned on a bottle of ink and it was "only to be expected that I should take the earliest possible opportunity to try my hand at the various forms of imaginative writing." After much discouragement and many rejections, *Harper's Magazine* accepted two poems and *Lippincott's* and *Smart Set* published stories. Three of her short stories won prizes offered by *Collier's* and *Delineator*. Abbott wrote at night, after a day of other work, and initially used a pseudonym. Often she thought of a title and then fashioned the plot around it.

Abbott's best-known novel was *Molly Make-Believe* (1910). This two-year best-seller told the romantic story of a young man, wintering in Florida while recovering from a serious illness, and his fiancée, who perpetrates a good-natured deception on him for his diversion. Other novels included *The White Linen Nurse* (1913), *Little Eve Edgarton* (1914), *The Indiscreet Letter* (1915), *The Stingy Receiver* (1917), *The Ne'er-Do-Much* (1918), *Old Dad* (1919), *Peace on Earth* (1920), *Rainy Week* (1921), and *Silver Moon* (1923). Collections of short fiction were *Sick-a-Bed Lady and Other Stories* (1911), *Fairy Prince and Other Stories* (1922), *But Once a Year* (1928), and *The Minister Who Kicked the Cat and Other Stories* (1932). "Sick-a-Bed Lady" won a $1,000 prize offered by *Collier's* and established Abbott as a writer. During her career she frequently wrote about invalids and received many letters from them expressing gratitude for her sympathetic treatment.

Abbott's most enduring book, *Being Little in Cambridge When Everyone Else Was Big* (1936), first published in the *Ladies' Home Journal*, described Cambridge in the 1870's and 1880's. Her recollections, warm and emotional, were filled with the delights and disappointments of her conservative Boston childhood. She asserted that since childhood she had had a consciousness of the actual event of her birth and that throughout her life she never forgot any "emotionalized experience."

Abbott wrote with little regard for critics' appraisals. While some reviewers described her writing style as effusive and contorted, with strained syntax and excessive metaphors, others called it sincere, original, and refreshing—the expression of a vivid imagination. Her works, basically light fiction, had a wide following among readers who sought writing that was neither "literary" nor taxing.

In November 1908 Abbott married Fordyce Coburn, a physician; they had no children. After a brief period in Lowell, Mass., they moved to a farm near Wilton, N.H. Abbott enjoyed outdoor life, particularly fishing, hunting, hiking, gardening, and horseback riding. In later years she suffered from chronic arthritis. She died in Portsmouth, N.H.

[Abbott reminisced about her childhood associations in *Being Little in Cambridge When Everyone Else Was Big* (1936). See also Clara Savage, "Eleanor Hallowell Abbott," *Good Housekeeping*, July 1917; Mayetta J. Evans, "Author of Old Dad," in *Woman's Home Companion*, Oct. 1918; and "Some of Us," *Ladies' Home Journal*, Dec. 1924.]

MARY SUE D. SCHUSKY

ADAMS, ANNETTE ABBOTT (Mar. 12, 1877–Oct. 26, 1956), attorney and judge, was born in Prattville, Calif., the daughter of Hiram Brown Abbott, a merchant, and Annette Frances Stubbs. Following her 1897 graduation from the California State Normal School at Chico, she taught in California secondary schools for three years. She received the bachelor of law from the University of California at Berkeley in 1904, and then returned to teaching for two years. On Aug. 13, 1906, she married Martin H. Adams; they had no children. The following year Adams moved to educational administration and became one of the first women high school principals in California when she headed the Modoc County High School at Alturas.

Adams returned to the University of California in 1910 and received the doctor of jurisprudence degree in 1912, the same year in which she was admitted to the California bar. Determined that the field of the law should not remain an all-male domain, she pioneered in the formation of an all-woman law firm by entering into a San Francisco partnership with Marguerite Ogden in 1913. President Woodrow Wilson appointed her assistant United States attorney for the Northern District of California in 1914; during her four-year tenure she secured the conviction of associates of the German consulate in San Francisco who had collaborated to use the United States as a base to launch military expeditions against England. These activities had contributed to the precarious position of American neutrality in the months before the United States entered World War I.

On July 25, 1918, Wilson appointed Adams United States attorney for the Northern District of California. She was the first woman in the nation's history to hold this Justice Department post. On June 26, 1920, she became the first woman assistant attorney general, a position she held until August 1921, when she was replaced by a Harding appointee. During those years in Washington she argued successfully the government's position in *Dillon* v. *Gloss,* in which the United States Supreme Court upheld the validity of the Volstead Act and the constitutionality of the ratification procedures of the Eighteenth Amendment.

Adams returned to private law practice in San Francisco in 1921. During the 1920's she argued a number of extremely complicated water rights cases at a time when ranchers and power companies were in deep dispute over California's limited water supply. In several cases before the California Supreme Court she established a foundation for the riparian rights of plaintiffs for the use of water adjacent to their lands.

In 1932 Adams campaigned hard for the election of Franklin Roosevelt as president, heading a committee of women lawyers supporting him. The Democratic victory brought with it an intense effort led by Mary Williams Dewson, head of the Women's Division of the National Committee, to appoint more women to federal office. Dewson sought to persuade Roosevelt to surpass the record of his five immediate predecessors, who had appointed only twelve women in twenty-four years. In 1935 Roosevelt, perhaps as a result of Dewson's lobbying, selected Adams as a special assistant counsel to Attorney General Homer Cummings. She worked especially in the area of oil litigation cases, in which she applied her experience with the California natural resources suits. She was successful in recovering for the government the lands in the Naval Oil Reserve in Kern County, Calif.—territory which had been involved in the Elk Hills scandal of the 1920's.

Although Adams was successful in her work at the Justice Department, she was most interested in receiving an appointment to the federal bench for the Northern District of California. However, "the difficulties of appointing a woman" constituted a sufficient reason for the Democratic party male leadership to oppose her nomination to this post. Instead of confronting the party's opposition, Roosevelt, on July 22, 1940, appointed Adams special assistant to the U.S. attorney general in conducting proceedings to condemn Terminal Island in Los Angeles for use by the United States Navy. She resigned this post on Sept. 30, 1941.

Six months later Adams secured judicial appointment, but at the state rather than the federal level. California Governor Culbert L. Olson named her presiding judge of the Court of Appeals for the Third District of California in Sacramento. She was the first woman to hold this position and she was assisted by two male associate justices. On Nov. 3, 1942, California voters elected Adams to a twelve-year term on the appellate court. She held the judgeship for ten years, retiring on Nov. 30, 1952. She died in Sacramento, Calif.

[On Adams and her career, see Mary W. Dewson, "An Aid to the End" (memoirs, Schlesinger Library, Radcliffe College); Elsie L. George, "The Women Appointees of the Roosevelt and Truman Administrations" (Ph.D. diss., American University, 1972);

and the obituary notice in the *New York Times*, Oct. 27, 1956. For Adams' opinions in the California courts, see *California Appellate Reports*, 2nd series, 1942–1952.]

CAROL ELIZABETH JENSON

ADAMS, FRANKLIN PIERCE (Nov. 15, 1881–Mar. 23, 1960), journalist and radio personality, known as "F.P.A.," was born in Chicago, Ill., the son of Moses Adams, a dry-goods merchant, and Clara Schlossman; his parents were recently arrived German-Jewish immigrants. Adams attended the Douglas School and graduated from the Armour Institute of Technology in 1899. He attended the University of Michigan "and almost completed my freshman year." His academic record at Michigan was undistinguished, but he was introduced to the classical scholarship and other learning that he displayed throughout his adult life.

Adams worked for an insurance company as a clerk and then as a salesman before deciding to become a writer. On Feb. 22, 1901, on a sales call, he discovered humorist George Ade eating strawberries for breakfast at eleven o'clock. If writers lived like that, Adams decided, he would be a writer. In 1903 he began writing a column and daily weather article for the *Chicago Journal*, at a salary of $25 a week. A raise a year later to $30 was not enough to keep him from joining the *New York Evening Mail*, for which he wrote the column "Always in Good Humor." His erudite wit soon became apparent in such pieces as "Baseball's Sad Lexicon" (1908):

These are the saddest of possible words:
"Tinker to Evers to Chance."
Trio of Bear Cubs and fleeter than birds,
Tinker and Evers and Chance.
Ruthlessly pricking our gonfalon bubble,
Making a Giant hit into a double—
Words that are heavy with nothing but trouble:
"Tinker to Evers to Chance."

Living up to the title of the column, as his publisher, Henry L. Stoddard, demanded, proved too trying, so Adams left the *Evening Mail* for the *Tribune* in 1913. His farewell typified the extensive knowledge that he brought to his work. A phrase of Horace, "Exegi monumentum aere perennius," could be developed acrostically as "Read the *Tribune.*"

On Jan. 1, 1914, Adams began a new column, "The Conning Tower," in which writers, artists, dowagers, and debutantes discussed his epigrams. Latin professors entertained their classes with his versified translations of Horatian odes. In 1909 Adams had collaborated with O. Henry in writing the musical comedy *Lo;* during World War I he served in the intelligence service, occasionally turning out a column, "The Listening Post," for *Stars and Stripes.* Of his service record, he quipped: "I didn't fight and I didn't shoot, but, General, how I did salute!" Adams resumed his career at the *Tribune* after the war.

In January 1922 Adams moved to the *New York World,* and later that year he produced the Broadway show *The '49ers.* In February 1931, when the *World* ceased publication, Adams moved to the *New York Herald Tribune;* his column was subsequently syndicated in six newspapers. Although he was paid handsomely by publisher Ogden Reid, rumors spread that Reid did not appreciate his talents. In March 1937 Adams left the *Herald Tribune,* observing, "They [the publishers] just wanted me to work for less money, whereas I wanted to work for more." Two months later he resumed his column in the *New York Post.*

In May 1938 Adams became the first regular panelist on the radio quiz show "Information Please," installed as the grumpish yet nimble expert-in-residence on American and English literature and drama. Between 1939 and 1942 the best programs were made into movie shorts, offering millions the opportunity to see the man whom friends described as a cross between Groucho Marx and King Alfonso of Spain. Adams' reputation as a member of the radio "Brain Panel" grew so rapidly that he accepted his firing from the *Post* in September 1941 with relative equanimity. While on the air he smoked a large cigar and favored crimson neckties. According to the journalist Frank Sullivan, Adams had "a certain electric dash and affects a kind of leer which seems to madden women." The program left the air in 1948; an attempt to revive it for television in the summer of 1952 was unsuccessful.

Adams spent the last five years of his life in a New York City nursing home, where he died. In a 1957 interview he recalled his own lines:

Journalism's a shrew and scold—
I like her.
She makes you sick, she makes you old—
I like her.

Commenting on journalists, he added: "It's no use to advise them. They won't work."

Not working, Adams argued, produced a lack of originality and imagination—the very qualities that characterized his own columns for almost forty years. He gently chided mispronunciations and the "nice Nellies" of literature. In his casual, almost offhand judgments on books, he was among the first to recognize the merits of D. H. Lawrence, Ring Lardner, Somerset Maugham, and Sinclair Lewis.

In the period between the wars, acceptance by "F.P.A." as a contributor to "The Conning Tower" became a much sought-after honor. He even presented an annual award, The Conning Tower Watch, for the best contribution. These efforts combined with Adams' salty comments about the contemporary scene to produce a pungently personal picture of the United States. He crusaded, for example, against poor grammar, witless conversation, prohibition, and unrhymed, free verse ("prose masquerading as poetry"); and for crisp writing and crisp bacon, classical education, and Franklin Delano Roosevelt.

In June 1911, while working for the *Evening Mail,* Adams adopted the pattern of Samuel Pepys in the weekly Saturday feature "The Diary of Our Own Samuel Pepys." Years later he acknowledged that, at first, "I tried to be facetious, using the old adage of paraphrasing modern slang in archaic words. I wince now at reading it." By 1940, in a mildly seventeenth-century form, he told readers what he ate, who his opponents were in tennis and poker, what clothes he wore, and what friends he saw. "I cannot quite analyze its charm," said Deems Taylor. "It is a quality of complete, almost telegraphic simplicity, yet unerring in its points without seeming to go after them . . . it is so perfect that it looks effortless."

Adams' marriage to Minna Schwartze, on Nov. 15, 1904, ended in divorce; his second, on May 9, 1925, to Esther Sayles Root, the daughter of New York publisher Charles Towner Root, endured. Her air of calm and moderation complemented his waspish tendencies. They had four children.

A convivial and witty raconteur, Adams left no serious philosophical legacy, yet a comment on death tells much about him. "I fear the Reaper not at all, yet is this life, imperfect though it be, so sweet I am loath to quit, I am dizzy to think I may not see one hundred years hence."

[Beginning with *Tobogganing on Parnassus* (1911), Adams' verses and parodies were reprinted in *In Other Words* (1912); *By and Large* (1914); *Weights and Measures* (1917); *Something Else Again* (1920); *Overset* (1922); *So There!* (1922); *So Much Velvet* (1924); *Half a Loaf* (1927); *Christopher Columbus*

(1931); and *The Diary of Our Own Samuel Pepys* (1935). On his life and work, see R. Erwin, "F.P.A.: Work," *Editor and Publisher*, July 6, 1957; "Notes and Comment," *New Yorker*, Apr. 2, 1960; G. W. Johnson, "No Taste for Trivia," *New Republic*, Apr. 11, 1960; and the *New York Times*, Mar. 24 and 26, 1960.]

WILLIAM F. STEIRER

ADAMS, SAMUEL HOPKINS (Jan. 26, 1871–Nov. 15, 1958), author and journalist, was born in Dunkirk, N.Y., the son of Myron Adams, a Presbyterian minister, and Hester Rose Hopkins. His grandparents were distantly related to, but apparently not overawed by, the better-known Boston Adamses. He attended the Free Academy in Rochester, N.Y., and spent one semester at Union College, but received the B.A. in 1891 from Hamilton College in Clinton, N.Y.

Upon graduation Adams joined the *New York Sun* as a reporter and special writer, one of a generation of "gentlemen journalists"—Arthur Brisbane, Jacob Riis, Richard Harding Davis, Will Irwin, and David Graham Phillips—who were trained on that paper in the exacting traditions of its editor Charles A. Dana. On Oct. 19, 1898, Adams married Elizabeth Remson Noyes; they had two children. That marriage ended in divorce in 1909, and on Apr. 11, 1915, Adams married former stage actress Jane Peyton Van Norman Post.

In 1900 Adams was hired by S. S. McClure for *McClure's Magazine*. He was a staff member from 1903 to 1905, when the muckraking movement was at its height. Adams quickly made his own mark as a muckraking journalist with a series of articles for *Collier's Weekly* on patent medicine and medical quackery; together with such men as Harvey Wiley and Upton Sinclair he was credited with having inspired the passage by Congress of the Pure Food and Drug Act. For his exposé work he was made a lay associate member of the American Medical Association in 1913.

The A.M.A. also sponsored the publication of the *Collier's* articles as Adams' first book, *The Great American Fraud* (1906). Thereafter, except for a brief stint as editor of *Ridgeway's Weekly* (1910), Adams was a free-lance writer, producing some fifty books and numerous articles and short stories in the course of his career. His was a satisfying professional life, permitting "freedom of thought, action and mode of existence," he wrote in 1942, "and this in an era when individual choice, threatened as it is throughout an imperiled world, has never been so precious."

Few of Adams' works won lasting critical acclaim but almost all were commercially successful. He wrote mystery stories, historical romances, and novels about crusading newspapermen (*The Clarion*, 1914.) Under the pseudonym Warner Fabian he wrote the novel *Flaming Youth* (1923), whose title was quickly adopted as one of the labels for the 1920's. In 1926 he wrote *Revelry*, a melodramatic fictionalized account of Warren Harding's presidency; the book was condemned by several state legislatures, and banned in Philadelphia and Washington, D.C.—in the meantime selling 100,000 copies. Seventeen of Adams' novels and stories became motion pictures; in addition to *Flaming Youth*, these included *The Gorgeous Hussy*, starring Joan Crawford, for which he wrote the screenplay (1936); *It Happened One Night*, with Claudette Colbert and Clark Gable (based on his short story "Night Bus," 1934); and *The Harvey Girls* (1942).

Adams ventured into nonfiction with *The Godlike Daniel* (1930), a colorful but unreliable biography of Daniel Webster, and *Incredible Era* (1939), an account of the Harding administration. In the absence of Harding's presidential papers—then inaccessible—such a book necessarily had to be largely a matter of hearsay and conjecture, as the author acknowledged in his introduction. Nevertheless, it was accepted for many years as "indisputably the best book on Warren Harding and his administration." Historians have been less kind to *Incredible Era* than have literary people; Frederick L. Paxson attacked the book in the *American Historical Review* (1940), and Robert K. Murray, whose own research profited from the opening to scholars of the Harding Papers in 1964, stated that the Adams book had "all the trappings of scholarship but little of the substance." Murray recognized, however, that Adams and other writers on Harding who had personally lived through that era were of necessity influenced by its climate of opinion: "They reported history as they saw it and lived it."

In his later years Adams turned again to biography (*Alexander Woollcott: His Life and His World*, 1945), to juvenile historical fiction (*The Pony Express, The Santa Fé Trail, The Erie Canal*), and to family reminiscence, in a delightful series of *New Yorker* essays published as *Grandfather Stories* (1955). He remained active as a writer to the end of his long life but was reported to have said, "I'm damned if I want my last novel to appear posthumously." *Tenderloin*, a novel of turn-of-the-century Manhattan drawn from his observations in the 1890's as a reporter for the *Sun*, was in press when he died. It was promptly turned into a Broadway musical. Adams died in Beaufort, S.C.

[Adams' papers, including correspondence and typescripts, are located at Syracuse University and Hamilton College. See also Stanley J. Kunitz and Howard Haycraft, eds., *Twentieth Century Authors* (1942) and *First Supplement* (1955); and the obituary notice in the *New York Times,* Nov. 17, 1958. For literary assessments of Adams' work, see Robert K. Murray, *The Harding Era: Warren G. Harding and His Administration* (1969); and Serrell Hillman, "Samuel Hopkins Adams: 1871–1958," *Saturday Review,* Dec. 20, 1958.]

PAUL A. CARTER

ADAMS, WALTER SYDNEY (Dec. 20, 1876–May 11, 1956), astronomer, was born in the north Syrian village of Kessab, near Antioch, then a province of the Turkish Empire, the son of Lucien Harper Adams and Nancy Dorrance (Dora) Francis, missionaries working under the American Board of Commissioners for Foreign Missions. He received his early academic training from his parents, who raised their three children in an open but strongly religious atmosphere, providing them with a strong foundation in history and classical language. In 1885 the family returned to Derry, N.H., where Adams attended first a district school and then several private academies, graduating from Phillips Academy, Andover, in 1894. His interest in astronomy seems to have begun while he was still in Syria.

Adams graduated in 1898 from Dartmouth with the A.B. and upon the advice of his astronomy instructor, Edwin Frost, went to the University of Chicago's Yerkes Observatory to continue astronomical training. In 1900 he received the A.M. and, again with the encouragement of Frost, who was by this time also at Yerkes, went to Munich to study for the Ph.D. Within a year, however, he returned to Yerkes with an appointment from the director, George Ellery Hale, as a computer and general assistant. He held the post until 1904, when he left with Hale to establish the Mount Wilson Solar Observatory in California, where he was to spend the rest of his professional life.

Adams worked mainly with Hale and became involved in studying the spectra of sunspots by photography. It had long been known that sunspot spectra differed from normal solar spectra, although the exact differences and their interpretation were in dispute. Adams' photographic work with the large Mount Wilson solar telescopes and his subsequent experimental work with laboratory spectra helped to establish that the spectral differences' were due to temperature changes—spots being somewhat cooler than the general surface of the sun. Working with Hale and Henry Gale, he also found that spectral differences were produced by density changes.

Much of what Adams was finding out about solar spectra applied to problems in the classification of stars, another continuing interest of Hale's. Adams began to examine the highly detailed spectra of the brightest stars with the solar telescopes at Mount Wilson and soon found that stars redder than the sun had spectra similar to sunspots, allowing him to conclude that their temperatures were proportionally lower than that of the sun.

From 1910 to 1914 Adams worked with the Dutch astronomer J. C. Kapteyn, who, as visiting astronomer at Mount Wilson, engaged Adams in a search for evidence of interstellar absorption. Kapteyn suggested that Adams analyze similar spectra of pairs of stars at different distances from earth, on the same spectroscopic plate, so that they could be examined efficiently for spectroscopic evidence of absorption in the intervening space—the more distant star presumably showing the hoped-for effects more prominently. Adams, with Anton Kohlschütter, followed out this idea and indeed found differences, which both Hale and Kapteyn joyfully thought to be due to absorption. But Adams' experience in examining slightly dissimilar spectra, and his zeal for exactitude, led him to doubt this explanation. Eventually he found that the spectroscopic differences were far better interpreted as due to actual physical differences between the stars—primarily a luminosity difference. Thus came one of astronomy's most valuable empirical techniques for the determination of luminosities, and hence distances, of the stars—the method of spectroscopic parallaxes.

Adams' technique expanded the number of stars with determinable luminosities and came as a windfall, for just at that time the existence of giant and dwarf stars had been proposed by Henry Norris Russell and Ejnar Hertzsprung. Adams' technique established criteria by which giant and dwarf stars could be distinguished. Through this work Adams gained international prominence. In 1917 he received the Gold Medal of the Royal Astronomical Society, and the next year the Draper Medal of the National Academy of Sciences. He steadily advanced at the Mount Wilson Observatory, becoming acting director in 1910, assistant director in 1913, and director in 1923, holding this last position until his retirement in 1946.

On June 2, 1910, Adams married Lillian Maud Wickham. She died in 1920, and on June 15, 1922, he married Adeline L. Miller. They had two sons. His students and colleagues remember him as a methodical and tireless observer and administrator, who reflected his New England heritage in running the observatory. During his tenure at Mount Wilson, he became intimately connected with the design, construction, and maintenance of many of its major instruments, including the 200-inch telescope. Even while Hale was director, it was Adams who really ran the observatory, for Hale was frequently away in Washington or abroad, or was incapacitated on account of a recurrent disability.

In addition to his work in sunspots and spectroscopic parallaxes, Adams' research in spectroscopic astronomy included the determination of radial velocities, from the measurement of Doppler-shifted line spectra in stars. In 1925, using this method, he succeeded in the extremely difficult task of detecting and identifying a spectral displacement in the white dwarf star Sirius B due not to Doppler motion but to the relativistic effect of extreme density—an apparent reddening predicted by A. S. Eddington from Einstein's equations.

Another extremely difficult spectroscopic feat attempted by Adams in the 1920's and 1930's was the detection of oxygen and water vapor in the Martian atmosphere. This too had long been a controversial problem, with observations differing widely, since the Martian spectrum was heavily masked by terrestrial absorption. Even though Adams' results have been recently shown to have been illusory, and far too excessive, it is a tribute to his skill and a testimony to his reputation that the values he derived in 1928 were accepted for more than thirty years. He died in Pasadena, Calif.

[On Adams and his work, see Helen Wright, in *Dictionary of Scientific Biography* (1970), which contains detailed references to Adams' bibliography and to other biographical sources; W. S. Adams, "Autobiographical Sketch" (unpublished, National Academy of Sciences, 1954); Dinsmore Alter, "Walter Sydney Adams," *Griffith Observer,* Aug. 1956; and George Ellery Hale Papers, Microfilm Edition (1968.]

D. H. DeVorkin

ADLER, FELIX (June 17, 1897–Feb. 1, 1960), "King of Clowns," was born in Clinton, Iowa. At the age of nine he saw his first circus and was inspired by the tightrope walkers; he repeatedly broke his mother's clothesline in his attempts to learn the skill. He left home at an early age to become an acrobat, but his clumsiness in performing acrobatic feats made the audience laugh, so he decided to become a clown instead. His father agreed to let him stay with the circus if he promised to attend school and work with the circus only in the summer until he graduated from high school. His first job was as water boy for the elephants, but he soon became fascinated with the clowns, whom he observed closely, studying their mannerisms, techniques, and costumes. Upon graduation from high school, he wrote Charles Ringling for a job and was hired as a clown.

Adler was with the Ringling Brothers and Barnum and Bailey Circus from 1910 to 1959, during which time he became famous as a "producing clown," one who originates gags and props. His most famous props included a pair of spotted balloon trousers that inflated, a tiny hat with a long flower, and a red nose that lit up. Another costume he created was that of the Big Bad Wolf, for which he draped a coat and hat over his tights and held a miniature umbrella. But Adler was best known for his baby pig acts. He trained hundreds of baby pigs to climb ladders, glide down slides, drink from baby bottles, stand on their hind legs, prance around him, or follow on a leash. When asked the secret of his success, Adler replied, "The simpler the trick the better, so long as it contains an element of surprise."

Adler made so many appearances before presidents (Warren G. Harding, Calvin Coolidge, and Franklin D. Roosevelt) that he earned the title "White House Clown." He was also an author, radio performer, and the first clown to appear on television. In addition to his circus performances, he also entertained children in hospitals across the country.

On Mar. 6, 1948, Adler married Amelia Irwin; they had no children. She subsequently became the only woman clown with the circus. Although she loved the work, she admitted, "It's not in my blood, like with Felix." Adler loved the circus, but in May 1959, after bus and truck convoys had begun replacing the famous circus train, he decided to quit. He then signed a contract with the International Circus at Palisades Amusement Park. He died in New York City three months before he was to have opened in New Jersey. Throughout his long career, Adler was one of

8

America's best-known and most beloved clowns.

[Information on Adler may be found in John Durant and Alice K. Rand Durant, *Pictorial History of the American Circus* (1957); Douglas Newton, *Clowns* (1958); Esse Forrester O'Brien, *Circus: Cinders to Sawdust* (1959); Felix Sutton, *The Big Show: A History of the Circus* (1971); Rhina Kirk, *Circus Heroes and Heroines* (1972); and John H. Towsen, *Clowns* (1976). Photographs of Adler in his various costumes are in Charles Philip Fox and Tom Parkinson, *The Circus in America* (1969); and Peter Verney, *Here Comes the Circus* (1978). See also the following obituaries: *New York Times,* Feb. 2, 1960; *Newsweek,* Feb. 15, 1960; and *Time,* Feb. 15, 1960.]

SUE HABEL

ADRIAN, GILBERT (Mar. 3, 1903–Sept. 13, 1959), costume and dress designer known professionally by his first name only, was born Adrian Adolph Greenburg in Naugatuck, Conn., the son of Gilbert Greenburg and Helen Pollock, both of German-Jewish extraction. His parents, who operated a successful millinery shop, were competent artists, his father a local caricaturist, his mother a still-life painter.

Adrian demonstrated an early talent for drawing. His favorite subject, wild animals, remained a lifelong inspiration. An uncle, Max Greenburg, a Broadway scenic designer, stimulated his interest in design for the theater. Influenced by his older sister Beatrice, who was studying dance in New York, he enrolled in 1921 at the New York School of Fine and Applied Arts (now the Parsons School of Design). On the advice of his instructor, he transferred to the school's Parish branch, where he was influenced by Erté and Rosa Bonheur.

At the Beaux-Arts students' ball, Adrian's prizewinning costume attracted the attention of Irving Berlin, who commissioned him to design for his forthcoming *Music Box* revue. Starting as assistant costume designer, he designed for three successive *Music Box* revues as well as for the *Greenwich Village Follies* and *George White's Scandals.* In 1925 Adrian went to Hollywood to design costumes for *The Eagle,* starring Rudolph Valentino and produced by Valentino's wife, Natacha Rambova; and remained to design costumes for Valentino's next movie, *The Cobra.*

The following year Adrian was hired by Cecil B. DeMille to design the costumes for *The King of Kings.* He followed DeMille to MGM and in 1928 designed his first costumes for Greta Garbo,

in *A Woman of Affairs.* Over the next two years he did the costumes for *Love* (a silent film based on *Anna Karenina)* and *The Last of Mrs. Cheyney.* In 1930 he was lent to Twentieth-Century Fox to design the costumes for his future wife, Janet Gaynor, in *Daddy Long Legs.* That year Adrian became the chief designer at MGM and in the course of seven years and thirty-five films, designed costumes for Joan Crawford, Greta Garbo, Jean Harlow, Carole Lombard, Jeanette MacDonald, and Norma Shearer. He was one of the first to utilize strong contrasts of black and white and striking decorative motifs. He was lavishly underwritten by Irving Thalberg, production head of MGM, and no expense was spared on his designs. His only rival was Travis Banton, chief designer at Paramount.

Adrian was one of the movers of Hollywood society, particularly known for his lavish parties. In 1938 he spent several months in France gaining inspiration for the costumes for the film *Marie Antoinette.* In August 1939 he eloped with Janet Gaynor to Yuma, Ariz. They had one son. That year he also designed the clothes for *The Women* and costumes for *The Wizard of Oz.* In 1940 he left MGM and started his own business, where he designed the clothes for *The Philadelphia Story* and *Woman of the Year* with Katharine Hepburn.

In 1941, with his friend Woody Fuert, he founded Adrian Ltd., which produced both made-to-order and ready-made clothes. His clothes were taken up by Hollywood celebrities and the business prospered. The New York fashion establishment never fully accepted Adrian, however, and fashion magazines and arbiters rarely paid him the attention given New York and Paris designers.

Adrian was anxious to adapt his designs to the needs of American women and felt that the war in Europe offered an excellent opportunity for designers to assert themselves and to initiate a truly American school of fashion. In 1945 he won the Coty American Fashion Critics Award, but he was bitterly disappointed by the New York fashion world's return to Paris for inspiration as soon as World War II ended. He opposed Dior's sloping shoulder "new look" of 1947. The following year he brought his clothes to New York, where Gunther-Haikel reproduced a replica of his airy Beverly Hills salon; in 1949 he had a successful exhibit entitled "Paintings of Africa" at the Knoedler Galleries. A second show, "Paintings of Darkest Africa, Congo and Sudan," was mounted by Knoedler in 1951.

In 1950 Adrian built a ranch near Anapolis,

Brazil. After suffering a heart attack in 1952, he closed his business and retired there. He and his wife spent much of their time entertaining friends, farming, and painting landscapes.

In 1958 Adrian returned to Los Angeles as costume designer for the Los Angeles Civic Light Opera Company's production of *At the Grand,* a musical version of the film *Grand Hotel.* The show was not successful, but his costumes were favorably reviewed. As designer for the musical *Camelot* (1959), Adrian had the opportunity to indulge his interest in medieval costumes. While *Camelot* was still in production, he died of a second heart attack in Hollywood.

Adrian's fashion innovations include exaggerated wide shoulders on tailored suits, dolman sleeves, tapered waists, and huge ruffle-topped sleeves. His interests in color and design are demonstrated by his intricate use of pinstripe fabrics and set-in patches of color, dramatic animal prints on sinuous black crepe evening dresses, the use of checked gingham for lavish evening dresses, asymmetric lines, and diagonal closings.

[On Adrian and his work, see Quigley Publishing Corporation, *Motion Picture Almanac,* 1936–1938; the obituary notice, *New York Times,* Sept. 14, 1959; Charlotte Calasibetta, *Fairchild's Dictionary of Fashion* (1975); Robert Riley, "Adrian," in Sarah Tomerlin Lee, ed., *American Fashion* (1975); and Josephine Ellis Watkins, *Fairchild's Who's Who in Fashion* (1975).]

ARNOLD SCAASI

AKINS, ZOË (Oct. 30, 1886–Oct. 29, 1958), playwright, poet, and screenwriter, was born in Humansville, Mo., the daughter of Thomas Jaspard Akins and Sarah Elizabeth Green. According to her unpublished memoir, "Others Than Myself," her maternal grandfather (who claimed to be descended from the earl of Pembroke) had moved to Missouri from Washington, D.C. When Akins was twelve her family settled in St. Louis, where her father served as postmaster and worked with the Republican National Committee. She was educated at Monticello Seminary in Godfrey, Ill., and at Hosmer Hall in St. Louis.

Akins was tutored in etiquette by her socially proper mother, who also encouraged her interests in poetry and drama. When she was fifteen her poems and essays began to appear in *Reedy's Mirror,* and her first play was produced by classmates at Monticello. She was infatuated with

the theater and performed briefly with the Odeon Stock Company.

She was also infatuated with the prestigious editor of the *Mirror,* William Marion Reedy, who was twenty-four years her senior and who encouraged her literary pursuits. For a time they were engaged to be married, but Akins' family intervened and the plans were cancelled. The break made a strong impression, and references to their romance appear in several of her works, most notably the unproduced play "Sleeping Dogs," which was copyrighted in 1916.

Determined to make a career as an author, Akins moved to New York, where she had several failures and a bout with tuberculosis before *The Magical City* was produced by the Washington Square Players in 1916. A love triangle in free verse, the work demonstrated her skill with language but had limited popular appeal. She then abandoned verse in favor of a more realistic dialogue with *Papa* (1919), a comedy satirizing modern manners. After it failed, Akins turned to serious social melodrama in a bid for commercial success.

The result was *Déclassée,* which opened on Oct. 6, 1919, and ran for 257 performances at Frohman's Empire Theater. A starring vehicle for Ethel Barrymore, *Déclassée* traces the declining fortunes of an aristocratic English lady. Despite its awkward plot and excessive sentiment, it was a genuine hit. Lady Helen Haden was the first in a series of star roles that Akins created for prominent American actresses, including Tallulah Bankhead, Laurette Taylor, Billie Burke, and Judith Anderson.

Although her skill as a playwright inclined toward comedy of manners, the success of *Déclassée* prompted Akins to explore contemporary morals in a serious vein. In *Daddy's Gone A-Hunting* (1921) she dramatized a young artist's attempts to pursue an unconventional marriage and life-style. Despite its confusing resolution, it ran for 129 performances. Her other serious efforts, *The Varying Shore* (1921), *Thou Desperate Pilot* (1927), and *The Furies* (1928), were less successful.

Akins' early comedies, *The Texas Nightingale* (1922) and *A Royal Fandango* (1923), were not popular successes, but it was in these cosmopolitan and witty plays that she demonstrated her greatest skill. In 1930 she scored a triumph with *The Greeks Had a Word for It,* a wisecracking study of three former Ziegfeld girls, which became the basis—along with *Loco* by Dale Eunson and

Katherine Albert—for the screenplay of *How To Marry a Millionaire.*

Akins' work was easily adapted to the screen, and in 1930 she signed a contract with Paramount Pictures and moved to Hollywood. Her first film, *Sarah and Son,* starring Ruth Chatterton, continued the Akins tradition of creating strong female roles. She made—and spent—a fortune in Hollywood, earning as much as $2,000 a week. She cultivated glamorous people, gave elaborate parties, and bought a Pasadena estate that she named Green Fountains. She published a volume of poetry and wrote scripts for *Morning Glory* (1933), *Outcast Lady* (1934), *Lady of Secrets* (1936), *Camille* (1937), and *Zaza* (1939).

On Mar. 12, 1932, Akins married Hugh Cecil Levinge Rumbold, a scenic designer and stage director. Barely eight months after their marriage, Rumbold died of acute hepatitis. Three years after his death, Akins had her biggest success with an adaptation of Edith Wharton's novel *The Old Maid.* When the play was awarded the Pulitzer Prize, at the expense of such original works as *The Petrified Forest* and *The Children's Hour,* a controversy erupted that led the New York drama critics to inaugurate their own award (the Critics' Circle) the following season.

Akins' film work declined sharply in the 1940's, and she was forced to sell Green Fountains to pay back taxes. She was one of America's few successful women dramatists and a gifted writer of social comedy, but work was scarce. She suspected that her strong anti-Nazi sentiments were being perceived as pro-Communist, and during the era of the Hollywood blacklist she returned to the stage. But her last play, *The Swallow's Nest* (1951), did not survive its tryout production. Her enthusiasm and flamboyance were not exhausted, however, and she continued working on her memoirs and other projects until her death, in Pasadena, Calif.

[Akins' papers, including letters and manuscripts, are housed in the Huntington Library, San Marino, Calif. A good analysis of the major dramatic works is Ronald A. Mielech, "The Plays of Zoë Akins Rumbold" (diss., Ohio State University, 1974). Other sources include John van Doren, "Zoë Akins—a Playwright With Ideas," *Theatre,* Feb. 1922; Catherine Cranmer, "Little Visits With Literary Missourians," *Missouri Historical Review,* Jan. 1926; "Some Playwright Biographies," *Theatre Arts,* July 1927; and the obituary notice, *New York Times,* Oct. 30, 1958.]
                                    BARRY B. WITHAM

ALEXANDER, WILL WINTON (July 15, 1884–Jan. 13, 1956), authority on race relations, was born near Morrisville, Mo., the son of William Baxter Alexander, a farmer, and Arabella A. Winton, a former schoolteacher. After receiving the B.A. from Scarritt-Morrisville College in 1908, Alexander followed the family tradition of Methodism and studied theology at Vanderbilt University, where he received the Bachelor of Divinity in 1912. He had been ordained to the ministry of the Methodist Church, South, in 1911, and he held pastorates in Nashville (1911-1916) and Murfreesboro, Tenn. (1916-1917). In October 1914 he married Mabelle A. Kinkead; they had three sons.

Alexander's pastoral experience aroused his interest in the problems of race and poverty. In 1917 he left the ministry to work with the Young Men's Christian Association War Work Council in Georgia. In 1919 he took a leading part in founding the Commission on Interracial Cooperation with headquarters in Atlanta, Ga.; he served as director during its twenty-five-year existence. His object was to bring together the educated people of the South, both white and black, to consult on community affairs and to solve racial problems. The information on the activities of the revived Ku Klux Klan of the 1920's gathered by the commission in communities throughout the South, was turned over to the *New York World* and provided much of the evidence for that newspaper's nationally influential exposé of the Klan.

While still acting as executive director of the Interracial Commission, Alexander did much to initiate and guide the program of fellowships established by the Rosenwald Fund for talented young southerners, both black and white, for advanced study, usually outside the South. At the same time he took an interest in the colleges and universities for blacks in Atlanta, and he was one of the planners and the acting president of Dillard University in New Orleans during the early 1930's, when the modern university was being created.

The network of personal contacts and good will that Alexander and the Interracial Commission built up in communities throughout the South formed the basis of his strength. Yet he always found financial dependence on local communities constraining, and he was happiest and most effective when he gained the support of foundations—notably those associated with the Rockefeller, Carnegie, Rosenwald, and Stern families—for the organizations for which he worked.

Community effort and goodwill were not enough, as Alexander recognized in the desperate economic conditions in the 1930's. His concern for the tragic plight of southern tenant farmers and sharecroppers, both black and white, led him to look to Roosevelt's New Deal for help. In 1935 Alexander went to Washington as assistant administrator of the Resettlement Administration under Rexford Guy Tugwell. On Tugwell's resignation in 1936, he was appointed administrator and when the Resettlement Administration was succeeded by the Farm Security Administration (FSA) in 1937, Alexander became its first head. In the work of these agencies the interests and personalities of Tugwell and Alexander were complementary. An extraordinarily stimulating source of ideas, Tugwell was chiefly interested in the classification and long-term planning for the best possible use of all land. Alexander admired Tugwell's vision, but his own gift was for human relationships and his main concern was with the immediate problem of the rehabilitation of those farmers who were in the most desperate straits—in the Great Plains dust bowl as well as in the South—and to whom such major agencies as the Agricultural Adjustment Administration offered little help. Authorities differ on the actual roles of Alexander and Tugwell, and Tugwell himself has taken the view that his original ideas of the goals of the Resettlement Administration were much altered under FSA.

That the FSA remained viable during Alexander's administration was in part owing to his personality. He recognized that it was hopeless to expect support from most of the major farm organizations, but that their neutrality was essential to the FSA's survival. Edward A. O'Neal, the president of the powerful American Farm Bureau Federation, which began its major attack on the FSA in 1940, maintained that he could get along with Will Alexander but not with his successor. It was, however, the votes of a group of senators from the Midwest that finally killed the FSA. Alexander was never able to come to terms with this group, especially Senator Everett M. Dirksen of Illinois.

After his resignation from the FSA on June 30, 1940, Alexander became vice-president of the Rosenwald Fund (1940–1948), and advisor to various agencies of the federal government, especially on the problems of minorities.

Alexander's choice of Chapel Hill, N.C., as his home upon retirement is symbolic. Although he had come from the same milieu as the romantic, backward-looking Nashville agrarians, he had always encouraged and shared the lively interest in hard facts and the hopeful vision of the southern regionalists associated with the University of North Carolina. His aim in the Interracial Commission had been "to change the racial climate of the South." Other leaders were doubtless more influential in particular areas, but in the southern region as a whole, during the interwar period, probably no one accomplished as much as Alexander in creating a climate that would make changes in race relations possible. He died in Chapel Hill.

[Alexander's writings include "Overcrowded Farms," United States Department of Agriculture *Yearbook of Agriculture* (1940); "The Color Line Cracks a Little," *New Republic*, Sept. 22, 1941; "Our Conflicting Racial Policies," *Harper's*, Jan. 1945; and, with Charles S. Johnson and Edwin R. Embree, *The Collapse of Cotton Tenancy* (1945).

See also Christiana McFadyen Campbell, *The Farm Bureau and the New Deal: A Study in the Making of National Farm Policy, 1933–1940* (1962); Wilma Dykeman and James Stokeley, *Seeds of Southern Change: The Life of Will Alexander* (1962); Mark Ethridge, "About Will Alexander," *New Republic*, Sept. 22, 1941; R. G. Tugwell, "The Resettlement Idea," *Agricultural History*, Oct. 1959; the Oral History Collections, Columbia University (1952); and obituary notices in the *New York Times*, Jan. 14, 1956, and the *Raleigh News and Observer*, Jan. 15, 1956.]

CHRISTIANA McFADYEN CAMPBELL

ALLEN, FRED (May 31, 1894–Mar. 17, 1956), comedian, was born John Florence Sullivan in Cambridge, Mass. He was the son of John Henry Sullivan, a bookbinder, and Cecilia Herlihy. His mother died when he was three, leaving him in the care of her sister. While attending the Boston High School of Commerce, he worked at night in the Boston Public Library. Among the books he read there was one on the origin and development of comedy; he found it intoxicating and began to collect jokes. He taught himself to juggle tennis balls and tin plates and to balance feathers, broomsticks, and other objects on his chin and forehead. His juggling act, with comic asides, was a hit at a Christmas show given by the library employees; and as he was packing up his props, a girl in the audience said, "You're crazy to keep working here at the library. You ought to go on the stage!"

After graduating from high school in 1911,

Allen began on the vaudeville circuit, billed as Paul Huckle, European Entertainer. Soon afterward he became Freddy St. James, juggling for $25 a week in small New England theaters. Since he could keep only four balls in the air (an expert juggler could handle eleven), he astutely billed himself as "The World's Worst Juggler"—getting laughs by a line of patter that emphasized his ineptness.

In 1916 Allen toured Australia and New Zealand for eleven months. He juggled and played the banjo, but it was his monologue that captured audiences. He spent his spare time reading Shakespeare, Artemus Ward, Mark Twain, Finley Peter Dunne, and current British humorists.

On his return to the United States, he needed a new name to demand a higher salary for his new act, and as Fred Allen he became a star. *Variety* praised his running-fire comments as "probably the brightest talk ever heard on a vaudeville stage," and he was given top booking at the Palace Theater on Broadway. In musical revues such as *The Passing Show of 1922, The Greenwich Village Follies, The Little Show* (1929), and *Three's a Crowd* (1930) his deadpan, devastating standup patter stopped the show. He always wrote his own lines.

With the demise of vaudeville imminent in the early 1930's, Allen joined other leading comedians in turning to film and radio. He began on radio in October 1932 on "The Linit Bath Club Revue," a half-hour comedy program. To the new medium he brought his stinging, endearing observations of American life, his striking nasal intonation, and his partner and wife, Portland Hoffa, whom he had married in May 1927. Her personality on the air, as she fed him questions, sounded according to Allen "like a small E-flat Frankenstein monster."

In 1934 Allen began his own hour-long program, "Town Hall Tonight," redubbed "The Fred Allen Show" five years later. Novelist Herman Wouk, who worked for the show, said, "In Fred Allen, the voice of sanity spoke out for all Americans to hear during a trying time in our history, in the classic and penetrating tones of comic satire." In 1942 Allen introduced Allen's Alley, probably the program's best-known feature. The improbable street—never described but always left to the audience's imagination—was inhabited by such diverse characters as Falstaff Openshaw, the resident poet; Mrs. Pansy Nussbaum, a Jewish housewife from Brooklyn; the loudmouth Ajax Cassidy; the ageless and taciturn Titus Moody; and the Alley's star character, Beauregard Claghorn, a bombastic Southern senator.

Allen left the air in June 1949; his last guest, appropriately, was Jack Benny, with whom he had conducted a well-publicized radio "feud" for over a dozen years. Their rivalry was the subject of *Love Thy Neighbor* (1940), one of five films in which Allen appeared. In 1952 he was scheduled to begin a TV series when his first heart attack forced him into semiretirement.

Allen's wit—"the professor was a retired magician who had eaten his rabbit in the early days of his retirement"—and his glorious metaphors, such as his characterization of an overpraised radio performer as "the man with the barefoot voice," are preserved in *Treadmill to Oblivion* (1954), which chronicles his early years in radio; *Much Ado About Me* (1956), which deals with his early years in vaudeville; and his *Letters* (1965), edited by Joe McCarthy. He died in New York City.

[Sources on Allen and his career include Steve Allen, *The Funny Men* (1956); John Dunning, *Tune in Yesterday* (1976); and Maurice Zolotow, "Fred Allen: Strictly From Misery," in Frank Brookhouser, ed., *These Were the Years* (1959).]

EDWARD WEEKS

AMES, EDWARD SCRIBNER (Apr. 21, 1870–June 29, 1958), philosopher and clergyman, was born at Eau Clair, Wis., the son of the Reverend Lucius Bowles and Adaline Scribner Ames. He was reared in small towns in Illinois and Iowa, where his father served as a Disciples of Christ minister, in a household marked by plainness, stability, a devoutly religious spirit, and respect for education. In 1886 he entered Drake University, from which he received the B.A. in 1889 and the M.A. in 1891. In 1892 he received the B.D. from the Yale Divinity School and remained there for an additional two years of graduate study in philosophy. On July 6, 1893, he married a college classmate, Mabel Van Meter, of Van Meter, Iowa. They had four children. In 1895 Ames received the first Ph.D. degree in philosophy given by the newly founded University of Chicago. With the exception of three years (1897–1900) as professor of philosophy and religion at Butler College, he spent the remainder of his long life in association with the University of Chicago. In 1900 he became minister of the University Church of the

Disciples of Christ and remained in this pastorate for forty years, building a small and struggling congregation into a substantial and innovative church located on a strategic corner adjacent to the Chicago campus. From this pulpit his influence radiated widely. He was a university preacher at Harvard in 1912–1914, and became a leading advocate of modernism in his denomination, particularly through the Campbell Institute, an association of ministers whose publication, *The Scroll,* he edited from 1903 to 1951. From 1937 to 1945 he was dean of the Disciples Divinity House, a residential hall for ministerial students at Chicago. His published books of sermons and essays, as well as his numerous pamphlets and articles, found a national audience and made him one of the major voices of liberal religion in America.

Alongside Ames's career as a churchman should be placed his academic career as a philosopher of religion. In 1900 he joined the faculty of philosophy at the University of Chicago; at the time of his retirement in 1935 he was chairman of the department. His two major works—*The Psychology of Religious Experience* (1910), a pioneering work in its field, and *Religion* (1929), the book that perhaps best represents his thought—have earned him an enduring place among American philosophers of religion.

Tall and well-proportioned, Ames had a warm, genial manner and a delightful sense of humor. William Blakemore, who knew him well, believed that "humanistic theism" is the term that best describes his thought. In any event, some main themes are clear. As a student at Yale and Chicago the wonders and possibilities of the modern world had been opened up to him. Ames was especially impressed by the free spirit, the patient methodology, and the remarkable achievements of science. Embracing an evolutionary understanding of the world, he formed an essentially optimistic view of human life. He was not blind to the reality of evil; and while he did not suppose that progress was inevitable, he did believe that it was possible. The love of life and a sense of its worth and potentiality for good were fundamental to him.

At the same time, deeply influenced by the empirical and pragmatic philosophy of William James, Ames held to an essentially sympathetic view of religion and its aspirations. It arises, he believed, out of human experience, and evolves from lower to higher forms. Its proper function is not to prepare men for a life after death but to help them to discover the meaning and beauty to be found in life on earth. The modern world challenges religion to develop a new piety that does not flee the world but calls men to work with God in the creation of a more just, humane, democratic, and peaceful society. God was to Ames idealized and personified reality; yet his sense of wonder before the infinite mystery and unity of the universe suggests that God is more than can be expressed in purely rational terms. He revered Jesus as the embodiment of all that is highest and best in the human pilgrimage.

For Ames, salvation is not escape from sin but growth toward more abundant living. The value of religion is to be determined by the extent to which it serves to fulfill the potentialities of human nature. Thus a principal thrust in his lifework was the effort to combine the critical, adventurous spirit of science with the idealistic and inspirational life of religion; in short, to unite intelligence with love. He died in Chicago, Ill.

[A bibliography of Ames's works compiled by Edward A. Henry is in Winfred E. Garrison, ed., *Faith of the Free* (1940). See also his autobiography, *Beyond Theology* (1959), and *Prayers and Meditations of Edward Scribner Ames* (1970), both edited by Van Meter Ames. His sermons and essays include *The Divinity of Christ* (1911); *The Higher Individualism* (1915); *The New Orthodoxy* (1918); and *Letters to God and the Devil* (1933). On his relation to the Disciples Divinity House, see William Barnett Blakemore, *Quest for Intelligence in Ministry* (1970); for an appraisal, see Harvey Arnold, "A Religion That Walks the Earth," *Encounter,* Fall 1969.]

RICHARD M. POPE

ANDERSON, MAXWELL (Dec. 15, 1888–Feb. 28, 1959), playwright, was born in Atlantic, Pa., the son of William Lincoln Anderson, a Baptist minister, and Perrimela Stephenson. He got his schooling at the various places where his father held pastorates in Pennsylvania, Ohio, Iowa, and North Dakota. In 1911 he received the B.A. from the University of North Dakota and began teaching high school English. In the same year he married Margaret Haskett. They had three sons.

In 1913 he was granted a teaching fellowship at Stanford University where, a year later, he received an M.A. in English literature. For the next three years he taught at Polytechnic High School in San Francisco. In 1917 he joined the faculty of Whittier College, a Quaker institution in Southern California, but was discharged at the end of his first year for the forthright expression of anti-war views and for defending a student who had taken a stand as a conscientious objector. He turned for employment to journalism, where the expression of his independent views on controversial issues again went against the prevailing mood. He worked briefly in Grand Forks, N.D., for the *Herald* and in San Francisco for the *Chronicle* and the *Bulletin*. In 1918 he was invited to join the staff of the *New Republic,* to which he had been contributing verse.

For the next six years Anderson served on the editorial staff of the *New Republic,* the *New York Globe,* and the *New York World.* In 1921 he was one of the founders of *Measure,* a magazine of verse; and in 1925 he published a book of his early poetry, *You Who Have Dreams.*

In 1923 Anderson wrote his first play, *White Desert,* a verse tragedy. While not a box office success, it won the attention of Laurence Stallings, a reviewer for the *World,* with whom he collaborated on *What Price Glory?* (1924), which "presented war as it is, not as it has been lied about on the stage for centuries." It was an unqualified success; and Anderson, at the age of thirty-six, gave up journalism to devote himself exclusively to playwriting.

In 1925 he and Stallings produced two historical romances, *First Flight* and *The Buccaneer.* These were failures, and the writers parted company. In the same year, however, Anderson produced *Outside Looking In,* a successful dramatization of Jim Tulley's *Beggars of Life.* In *Saturday's Children* (1927), a romantic comedy, Anderson presented marriage as fatal to the love affair; *Gods of the Lightning* (1928) was a journalistic commentary based on the Sacco-Vanzetti case. Although Anderson was still pursuing his first love, dramatic poetry, his two poetic plays of this period, *Sea Wife* (1924) and *Gypsy* (1929), were not produced.

The achievement toward which the whole of Anderson's effort had been tending was *Elizabeth the Queen* (1930), a great romantic verse tragedy based on the love affair of Elizabeth I and the Earl of Essex. The play was a triumphant demonstration of the validity of Anderson's artistic principles: characters of heroic stature who act from conscious motives; an action, based on historical subject matter, treated so as to illuminate contemporary issues—the whole embodied in the style of blank verse. Audiences were delighted, especially those who, weary of realism, saw in the

work a promise of return to grandeur in the theater.

Encouraged by this success, Anderson wrote four more historical plays. Those that resembled most nearly the romantic treatment in *Elizabeth the Queen* were *Night Over Taos* (1932), *Mary of Scotland* (1933), *Valley Forge* (1934), and *The Masque of Kings* (1937). Anderson wrote no play in 1931, the year his first wife died. In 1933 he married Gertrude Maynard; they had one daughter.

Between *Elizabeth the Queen* (1930) and *Key Largo* (1939), Anderson wrote thirteen plays, the imaginative and technical resources of which seemed inexhaustible. He had another triumph with verse tragedy in *Winterset* (1935), based on the Sacco-Vanzetti case. The play centers not on miscarriage of justice but rather on love destroyed by the hero's having committed himself to settling scores with the past. It won the first New York Drama Critics' Circle Award.

The *Wingless Victory* (1936) presents an interesting story of racial conflict against a background of seventeenth-century New England Puritanism.

Several plays of this decade were satiric; *Both Your Houses* (1933), which won a Pulitzer Prize, presented American lawmakers as unscrupulous self-servers. In 1937 three highly successful plays were produced: *High Tor,* which won his second New York Drama Critics' Circle Award, *The Masque of Kings,* and *The Star Wagon,* a work of science fiction. There was also a one-act play for radio, *The Feast of Ortolans.*

Anderson had long resented the power of theatrical producers and literary critics over plays and playwrights. In 1938 a group of dramatists, including Anderson, Robert Sherwood, Elmer Rice, Sidney Howard, and S. N. Behrman, founded the Playwrights' Producing Company to enable playwrights to produce their own plays. There was a strong fraternal feeling among the members, and the venture was a great success. Anderson's plays for 1938 were *Knickerbocker Holiday,* a musical comedy written in collaboration with Kurt Weill; and another one-act play for radio, *Second Overture.* This period ended with *Key Largo,* a tragedy that nonetheless affirms life in its vision that man is destined for ultimate victory.

During World War II Anderson visited the troops at the various fronts. At the same time he continued to write plays: *Candle in the Wind* (1941), *The Eve of St. Mark* (1942), and *Storm*

Operation (1944)—plays in which he attempted to reestablish the heroic treatment of war that *What Price Glory?* had contributed so brilliantly to demolishing. *Journey to Jerusalem* (1940), although not one of them, had set the tone for these war plays. They were slight by comparison with the plays of the 1930's, but they reflected the reluctance with which America had entered World War II. Anderson once said, "I never wrote a play in which I did not try to say something of significance."

In his *Truckline Cafe* (1946), Anderson had "attempted to suggest the confusion in men's minds—and lives—as they try to find a way to live after the fantastic dislocation the war brought to nearly all of us." He failed, but tried again with a dramatization of the trial and death of Socrates, *Barefoot in Athens* (1951). Again he failed—or seemed to. But he had already done what he was striving to do. In *Joan of Lorraine,* produced in 1946, he was asking, like Socrates himself, "Why do you believe what you believe?" As one of his biographers put it, Anderson had been asking some version of this question since the first question in 1924, "What price glory?" Joan found her answer, as the hero of *Key Largo* found his. Both plays are tragedies, not because knowledge is poison, nor the desire for understanding a tragic flaw, but because both protagonists had made serious mistakes in their quests. The effort to rectify these mistakes cost them their lives—a new concept of tragedy.

Anderson's only work for 1947 was a volume of essays, *Off Broadway,* explaining his dramatic theory, a subject with which he had always been concerned. *Anne of the Thousand Days* (1948) was notable chiefly for its modern theatrical devices and the drama of its leading figures, Henry VIII and Anne Boleyn. *Lost in the Stars* (1949), with music by Kurt Weill, is a dramatization of Alan Paton's novel *Cry, the Beloved Country.*

In *Bad Seed* (1954) Anderson redeemed William March's interesting but poorly written novel, *The Bad Seed,* about a child criminal, based on the idea that a disposition to criminal behavior is hereditary.

During the 1950's his son Alan was working with him on the production of the "Omnibus" television series. In 1958 Anderson was represented on the New York stage as coauthor with Brendan Gill of *The Day the Money Stopped* and as author of *The Golden Six,* produced off Broadway. In thirty-five years Anderson produced thirty-three plays and at least as many articles. In 1953 Anderson's second wife died, and the following year he married Gilda Oakleaf. He died at his home in Stamford, Conn.

[On Anderson and his work, see Laurence Avery, *A Catalogue of the Maxwell Anderson Collection at the University of Texas* (1968), which lists published and unpublished works, contributions to books and periodicals, letters by and to Anderson, and diaries; and *Dramatists in America: Letters of Maxwell Anderson, 1912–1958* (1977). There is a small collection of manuscripts and memorabilia at the University of North Dakota. See also Martha Heasley Cox, *Maxwell Anderson Bibliography* (1958). For biographical and critical material, see Barrett H. Clark, *Maxwell Anderson: The Man and His Plays* (1933); John Gassner, "Introduction[s]" in *Treasury of the Theatre* (1935) and *Twenty-Five Best Plays of the Modern American Theatre* (1949); and Charles W. Cooper, *Whittier: Independent College in California* (1967), which includes an account of Anderson's dismissal from the faculty of Whittier College. Anderson discusses his principles of composition in *Off Broadway* (1947); the only critical work on the plays is Mabel Driscoll Bailey, *Maxwell Anderson: The Playwright as Prophet* (1957). See also John F. Wharton, *Life Among the Playwrights* (1974), a history of the Playwrights' Producing Company; and Harold Clurman, *All People Are Famous* (1974). The Columbia Oral History Collection contains a thirty-four-page memoir by the playwright done in 1956. There are other references to Anderson in the collection, especially in *The Reminiscences of Frank Ernest Hill.*]

MABEL DRISCOLL BAILEY

ANDERSON, VICTOR VANCE (Dec. 26, 1879–July 26, 1960), psychiatrist, author, educator, and physician, was born in Barbourville, Ky., the son of William Ballinger Anderson and Flora Herndon. He earned the B.A. from Union College in Barbourville in 1898 and moved on to the Hospital College in Medicine, now part of the University of Louisville, where he received the M.D. in 1903. Anderson practiced general medicine in Lynchburg, Va., from 1904 to 1911. In 1906 he married Clara Beaumont. They had one daughter.

Like many physicians of this era, Anderson's interests became increasingly specialized. In 1912 he received training in psychiatry at Boston's Psychopathic Hospital, and by 1913 he had become the psychiatrist and medical director of the City of Boston's Municipal Court, a post that he retained until 1918.

Anderson's subsequent career mirrored a significant shift in the concerns of the psychiatric profession toward applying the knowledge gained from treating the mentally ill to the problems and realities of society at large. In 1919 Anderson moved to New York City. Then he became a pioneer in the founding of America's first child guidance clinics, supported by public funds and devoted to the prevention and treatment of mental and emotional illness, and in helping to establish what is now known as the community mental health movement.

From 1918 to 1919 Anderson served as scientific advisor to the New York State Prison Commission, directing surveys and formulating recommendations that led to greatly needed prison reforms. In 1919 he became associate medical director of the federal government's National Committee for Mental Hygiene and retained this post until 1924. During his association with the group, Anderson established child guidance clinics in many communities throughout the United States. He also directed and wrote mental health reports for Cincinnati and St. Louis and for Georgia, West Virginia, Maryland, South Carolina, Kentucky, and Missouri. He was a founder of the American Orthopsychiatric Association (1924), serving as its first president, and a charter member of the American Academy of Child Psychiatry.

Anderson's move to New York also reflected another departure from a psychiatrist's conventional spheres of activity. From 1924 to 1930 he was psychiatrist and director of medical research for R. H. Macy and Co. In this capacity, he applied psychiatric theories and techniques to such problems as the selection of executives, the appropriate reaction to employees with problems of mental health, the screening of potential employees, and the application of psychiatric insights to the entire field of industrial management. In 1930, two years after the death of his first wife, Anderson married Margaret Cavender.

Two of Anderson's books, *Psychiatry in Industry* (1929) and *Psychiatry in Education* (1932), achieved large sales during the 1930's. They supplied specific recommendations in nontechnical language, applying psychiatric principles to the employment interview and to the problems of the elementary and secondary schoolteacher. Standard texts in many colleges and universities, these works were translated into several languages including Chinese.

Anderson's writings were bound to the period in which they were published. They reveal an almost total lack of awareness of the clinical findings of psychoanalysis, dynamic psychology, and post-Freudian ego psychologies as well as of the research of academic and educational psychologists who were then making seminal contributions to both psychiatric medicine and applied psychology.

As an educator and educational administrator, Anderson had long been interested in creating a controlled environment for the study of exceptional children in which his principles of child psychiatry could be tested and applied. He hoped to modify behavior patterns and personalities, the goal implicit in all psychotherapies. In 1924 he founded the Anderson School in Staatsburg, N.Y., and remained director until his death.

[On Anderson and his work, see the obituary notices in the *New York Times*, July 27, 1960; and *Journal of the American Medical Association*, Oct. 1, 1960.]

A. MICHAEL SULMAN

ANDREWS, ROY CHAPMAN (Jan. 26, 1884–Mar. 11, 1960), explorer, zoologist, and author, was born in Beloit, Wis., the son of Charles Ezra Andrews, a wholesale druggist, and Cora May Chapman. Even in grammar school Andrews wanted to be an explorer, and his life became the fulfillment of that ambition. He owned his first rifle when he was nine and soon learned to mount the birds and animals he shot. After graduating from Beloit Academy in 1902, he worked his way through Beloit College as a taxidermist, graduating in 1906 with the B.A.

That summer he began a thirty-five-year association with the American Museum of Natural History. Arriving in New York with only thirty dollars, he went to the museum and asked the director, Hermon C. Bumpus, for a job, expressing his willingness to scrub floors, if necessary. When Bumpus observed that college graduates should not scrub floors, Andrews replied "not any floors, but Museum floors are different." He was hired as a general assistant in the department of preparation, where he mixed clay and helped set up exhibits.

Endowed with enormous energy and ability, Andrews soon established a reputation in the field of cetaceans. Before the age of thirty, he was a leading authority on whales. One of his first assignments had been to obtain the skeleton of a whale washed up on Long Island. He had to work waist-deep in freezing seawater to retrieve the remains. Soon afterward, he helped overcome problems in the construction of the life-size model of a giant blue whale, one of the museum's most popular exhibits. He was appointed assistant in mammalogy in 1909 and assistant curator of the department of mammals in 1918.

Andrews sailed on expeditions to the Pacific Ocean, studying whales and the whaling industry. The museum sent him to British Columbia and Alaska in 1908, and in 1909–10 he was its representative aboard the U.S.S. *Albatross* on a voyage to the Dutch East Indies, Borneo, and the Celebes. In 1911–12 Andrews studied whales off Korea and Japan, sending back enough specimens to fill a large exhibit hall. He also found specimens of the California gray whale, which had been believed extinct. After returning to the United States, he received the M.S. from Columbia University in 1913, with a thesis on whales.

Thriving on adventure, Andrews stalked whales, dissected them, sketched them, and recorded their characteristics. He persisted despite almost constant torment from seasickness and a number of harrowing experiences. Shipwrecked on a Pacific island, he had to eat monkeys to survive. On the deck of a whaler, he escaped death by inches when the carcass of a whale slipped from a tackle, crushing the man standing beside him. Throughout his life he made light of the perils of exploration, claiming that he found it more dangerous to live in a modern city than in the wild.

On Oct. 7, 1914, Andrews married Yvette Borup, the sister of an explorer who had accompanied Admiral Robert E. Peary during his journey to the North Pole; they had two sons.

In 1916 Andrews shifted his fieldwork and research interest, setting out to test the theories of William Diller Matthew and Henry Fairfield Osborn that Asia was the place of origin and dispersal of some reptilian, mammalian, and primitive human life. With the support of Osborn, then director of the Museum of Natural History, and with funds raised personally from J. P. Morgan, John D. Rockefeller, and others, Andrews led a series of expeditions to Asia. In 1916–17 he made a reconnaissance trip to Burma and Tibet. In 1918 he worked briefly for United States Naval Intelligence in China, and in 1918–19 he led a survey party to northern China and Outer Mongolia.

Andrews led five major Central Asiatic expeditions, in 1922, 1923, 1925, 1928, and 1930. These represented a new type of exploration, for they brought together representatives from half a dozen sciences. Yvette Andrews recorded the adventure in both still photographs and motion pictures. These expeditions were the largest to leave the United States until that time; the 1922 caravan included forty persons, eight motorcars, and 150 camels.

Although the expeditions did not discover the earliest beings (such remains were found years later in Africa), they made major scientific findings that established Asia as one of the chief dispersal centers of animal life. They uncovered implements dating back 20,000 years, thereby proving that the Gobi Desert had been inhabited by dune dwellers who later migrated to China and Siberia. Their geological findings confirmed that Outer Mongolia had never had an ice age and was the oldest area of continuously dry land. The rich fossil fields that they discovered yielded specimens of many early mammals and dinosaurs. Among them were the largest carnivore, which was named the *Andrewarches* in honor of its discoverer, two skulls and other fragments of the largest known mammal, a species of rhinoceros called the *Baluchitherium,* which lived about thirty million years ago, stood eighteen feet high, and weighed twenty tons.

The most spectacular discovery, for which Andrews became world-famous, was of three nests containing two dozen dinosaur eggs, the first ever found. Discovered in the Gobi in 1928 and pictured in newspapers around the world, the nine-inch-long eggs of the duck-billed iguanodon, laid 100 million years earlier, had been perfectly preserved.

Andrews was responsible for much of the success of these expeditions. He conceived them, raised the funds, and led them through the perils of banditry in Mongolia and revolution and civil war in China. He was adept at obtaining publicity and at achieving prompt publication of scientifiic findings. During the early 1930's, civil war and the Japanese invasion of China made further exploration impossible, and Andrews returned to New York City. He was divorced from his first wife in 1931; and on Feb. 21 1935, he married Wilhelmina Anderson Christmas.

Andrews capped his career as vice-director (1931–34) and director (1935–42) of the American Museum of Natural History. In retirement he continued to write best-selling books conveying his enthusiasm for exploration, discovery, and science. Many of these, written in a terse, chatty style, became classics. Among his most popular publications were *On the Trail of*

Ancient Man (1926), *Ends of the Earth* (1929), *This Business of Exploring* (1935), *This Amazing Planet* (1940), and his autobiography, *Under a Lucky Star* (1943). He died in Carmel, Calif.

Filled with a zest for life, Andrews lived it to the fullest. He had a restless spirit, an ebullient personality, a determined will, and boundless energy. Fieldwork and exploration, not research, consumed him. Not content merely to see the world, he wanted to know its secrets. For three decades he was the popular ideal of the romantic explorer, combining scientific ability and the capacity to direct major expeditions and institutions with the showmanship necessary to obtain publicity and financial support. Andrews' significance lies both in his own findings and in the international attention he drew to the role and value of the explorer-naturalist and the large-scale modern scientific expedition.

[Many of Andrews' papers, including field journals for the Central Asiatic expeditions, are at the American Museum of Natural History, New York City. Andrews' autobiographical works, in addition to those mentioned in the text, include *The New Conquest of Central Asia* (1932) and *An Explorer Comes Home* (1947). Other works include *Meet Your Ancestors* (1945); *All About Dinosaurs* (1953); *All About Whales* (1954); and *In the Days of the Dinosaurs* (1959).

Jules Archer, *From Whales to Dinosaurs* (1976), is a new edition of the biographical *Science Explorer* (1968). Other accounts are D. R. Barton, "Gambler on the Gobi," *Natural History*, Feb. 1940; and obituaries in the *New York Times* and *New York Herald-Tribune*, Mar. 12, 1960.]

JOHN WHITECLAY CHAMBERS II

ANGLIN, MARGARET MARY (Apr. 3, 1876–Jan. 7, 1958), actress, was born in Ottawa, Canada, the daughter of Timothy Warren Anglin, speaker of the House of Commons, and Ellen A. McTavish. Raised a Catholic and educated at the Convent of the Sacred Heart, in Montreal, Anglin showed an early interest in theater, and by the time she was fifteen had decided to become a professional concert reader. Although her father did not approve of such a career, she evidently had the support of her mother, who secretly financed her way to New York City to study elocution. There, at seventeen, she became one of the first pupils in Nelson Wheatcroft's Empire Dramatic School.

Anglin got her first opportunity in theater from Charles Frohman. Having promised to engage the four most promising students of

Wheatcroft's school, Frohman found himself particularly pleased with Anglin and cast her as Madeline West in his production of Bronson Howard's *Shenandoah* at New York's Academy of Music in 1894. Eager for greater challenges, however, she left Frohman's management, frustrated by the trivial parts assigned her, and became a member of James O'Neill's company for the 1896–1897 season, playing Ophelia in *Hamlet*, Virginia in Sheridan Knowles's *Virginius*, and Mercedes in O'Neill's version of *The Count of Monte Cristo*. The following season she played Meg in *Lord Chumley*, co-starring with E. H. Sothern.

These were Margaret Anglin's apprentice years. When, in the fall of 1898, Richard Mansfield engaged her to play Roxane in Rostand's *Cyrano de Bergerac*, she began to attract attention. Within a year she was playing leading roles in Frohman's stock company, pleasing audiences with Mrs. Dane in Henry Arthur Jones's *Mrs. Dane's Defence* and as Dora in Sardou's *Diplomacy*. For the next four seasons she played in Henry Miller's stock company in San Francisco, most notably opposite Miller in *The Devil's Disciple* and *Camille*. During the 1905–1906 season she contracted with the Shubert organization and starred in the title role of Zira in a play adapted from Wilkie Collins' *The New Magdalen*.

By the first decade of the twentieth century American dramatists were beginning to extricate themselves from the tangle of spectacular melodrama and farce that had limited their creativity in the nineteenth century. Helping to bring America into the world of modern drama, William Vaughan Moody wrote *The Great Divide*, in which Margaret Anglin, as Ruth Jordan, co-starred with Henry Miller. A substantial acting success, their engagement opened in New York at the Princess Theatre on October 3, 1906, and ran through 1908. "Never," wrote the critic for the *New York Sun* (Oct. 4, 1906), had Miss Anglin "been more poignantly emotional."

During these years critics invariably described her as a powerful emotional actress with a voice that "throbs and sobs." The damp lace handkerchief of the anguishing heroine seemed always in her hands until suddenly, in 1909, after a very successful run of *The Awakening of Helena Richie*, Anglin announced that she wanted to play comedy. Within months willing playwrights deluged her with 420 comedies, one of which was *Green Stockings*, in which she starred in 1911.

On May 8, 1911, she married Howard Hull, an author and playwright who became her manager.

After showing a special aptitude for refined comedy in *The Importance of Being Earnest* and *Lady Windermere's Fan,* Anglin turned actress-manager in 1913 and presented Shakespeare in repertory: *The Taming of the Shrew, Twelfth Night, As You Like It,* and *Anthony and Cleopatra.* In 1915 she produced *Antigone* and *Electra* of Sophocles and *Iphigenia in Aulis* and *Medea* of Euripides at the Greek Theater of the University of California at Berkeley, appearing in the major female roles while directing and supervising the productions. Six years later she repeated the role of Clytemnestra in *Iphigenia in Aulis* in a memorable production at the Manhattan Opera House with Walter Damrosch conducting a musical accompaniment he had composed for the occasion.

Anglin had, according to one critic, "the witchcraft of simplicity," extracting that richness of interpretation which delighted audiences. She was also a strong woman with definite ideas and would stop a performance until a noisy audience quieted down. During a period of great turbulence in American theater history, when the Shuberts challenged the control of the Theatrical Syndicate, she was able to act for both agencies. When Actors' Equity voted to strike in August 1919, she opposed the action and supported the Actors' Fidelity League. Her last Broadway appearance was as Lady Mary Crabbe in *Fresh Fields* in 1936. Seven years later, after a forty-year career in which she estimated that she had acted in eighty plays, she gave her final performance in a road company production of *Watch on the Rhine.* Not strikingly beautiful but graceful and charming, she almost invariably received enthusiastic reviews, while friends enjoyed what has been described as "a warmth of human nature." She died in Toronto.

[See the obituary notice, *New York Times,* Jan. 8, 1958; Lewis C. Strang, *Famous Actresses of the Day in America* (1902); Forrest Izard, *Heroines of the Modern Stage* (1915); Thoda Cocroft, *Great Names and How They Are Made* (1941), written by her business manager; and William C. Young, *Famous Actors and Actresses on the American Stage* (1975).]

WALTER J. MESERVE

ARLEN, MICHAEL (Nov. 16, 1895–June 23, 1956), novelist and short story writer, was born Dikran Kouyoumdjian in Ruse, Bulgaria, the son of Sarkis Kouyoumdjian, an importer.

The family had fled Turkish persecution in Armenia in 1892 and in 1901 settled in Southport, England, where there was a large Armenian colony. Dikran was sent to Malvern College in Worcestershire to prepare for Oxford and a business career. He chose medical school at the University of Edinburgh instead, but after a few months in 1913 realized that it had been "a silly mistake." After a brief vacation in Switzerland, he moved to London, where he lived on a small allowance. Feeling exiled and lonely, he befriended writers, artists, and the young society people who frequented bohemian quarters.

In 1916 Dikran began writing for *Ararat* in support of Armenian causes and for *New Age,* a weekly subsidized by the Fabians and edited by Alfred R. Orage. He also published informal essays, book reviews, short plays, and—encouraged by Orage, D. H. Lawrence, and George Moore—romantic fiction. A series of sketches about his youth became *The London Venture* (1919), published under the pseudonym Michael Arlen, the name of one of his characters. He legally changed his name in 1922, when he became a naturalized British subject.

Combining a highly artificial manner with an essentially romantic spirit, Arlen's fiction quickly won the approval of the London café society that he mocked and admired. Such stories as "When the Nightingale Sang in Berkeley Square" and "Introducing a Lady of No Importance and a Gentleman of Even Less" suggest the extent to which manner, for Arlen, was all important. In 1924 he published his best-known work, *The Green Hat,* the cynical and sentimental romance of Iris March, "a young woman careening in canary-colored motor cars between Deauville and Nice," who leads a notoriously promiscuous existence but dies "for purity." Celebrated, parodied, attacked on both sides of the Atlantic, and translated into eight languages, the novel set a new standard for titillating indecency and earned its author a small fortune.

Arlen had always looked "spruce, elegant, debonair," as a friend observed; now he acquired a yellow Rolls-Royce and attracted such socialites as Nancy Cunard into his circle. His dramatic adaptation of the novel starred Katherine Cornell in New York and Tallulah Bankhead in London; Greta Garbo played Iris March in the film version, *A Woman of Affairs* (1928). On May 1, 1928, Arlen married Atalanta Mercati, a Greek-American countess. They had two children and lived in a villa near Cannes for the next decade.

After producing three more popular romances, Arlen wrote *Man's Mortality* (1933), a serious speculation about the state of the world in the year 1987. It was influenced in part by H. G. Wells, then a neighbor. "I'm through with women in love," Arlen said. "My new novel is about politics." Although it was not a popular success, the book was Arlen's best work, free of stylistic affectation yet characteristically witty and sometimes profound.

After returning to England in 1939, Arlen wrote a column in the *Tatler* for six months and then aided the war effort as public relations officer for the western Midlands region. When a question was raised in Parliament in January 1941 as to the suitability of a "foreigner" in that important post, Arlen resigned, deeply hurt. Having already sent his family to the United States, he left England, spending a few years in Hollywood as a screenwriter before settling in New York City in 1945 or 1946. Arlen kept in touch with a wide circle of writers and celebrities, but his writing dwindled to almost nothing. One of his last stories (1941), "Gay Falcon," was the basis for fourteen films and a popular radio series about a romantic rogue. Arlen became an American citizen in June 1952, four years before his death in New York City.

Although Arlen's fiction may still be enjoyed for its wit and charm, the significance of his career rests heavily on the role he created for himself, a role he sustained entertainingly and carefully, rivaling the most sophisticated and wealthy people of his day. Yet he was always conscious of being an exile and was never quite secure behind his brilliant mask. Some of his famous remarks about himself hint at this: "Every other inch a gentleman" and "a case of pernicious Armenia." D. H. Lawrence, who modeled the character of Michaelis in *Lady Chatterley's Lover* on Arlen, noticed in 1927 "something about him I rather like—something sort of outcast, [a] dog that people throw stones at by instinct, and who doesn't feel pious and Jesusy on the strength of it. . . ." Arlen himself alleged that "My mother taught me to think a distressed area should make the best of itself."

Arlen's numerous literary friendships included Richard Aldington, Osbert Sitwell, and Noel Coward in England, and William Saroyan, Thornton Wilder, and John O'Hara in the United States. Ernest Hemingway remembered that Arlen had introduced him to the Englishwoman who inspired the character of Brett Ashley in *The Sun Also Rises;* and F. Scott Fitzgerald, although he dismissed Arlen's fiction as "hurried" and "second-rate," knew the plots of all his works by heart.

Ten years after the publication of *The Flying Dutchman* (1939), his last novel, Arlen appeared to Geoffrey T. Hellman "poised, urbane, resplendent in a pin-striped blue suit . . . possessed by no demon whatever and apparently the world's best adjusted writer." Even for his detractors, Arlen came to represent the skillful professional who makes the most of his opportunities, never bewails his lot, and seldom takes his writing so seriously as to put it ahead of stylish living.

[Obituary notices in the *New York Times,* June 24, 1956, and London *Times,* June 25, 1956, outline Arlen's public career. Harry Keyishian, *Michael Arlen* (1975), contains a biographical summary, critical interpretation, and detailed bibliography. See also Alec Waugh, *My Brother Evelyn and Other Portraits* (1967), a more personal summary; and Michael John Arlen, *Exiles* (1970), an eloquent reminiscence. Interviews include Geoffrey T. Hellman, "Loller," *New Yorker,* Apr. 9, 1949; and William Saroyan, "The Armenian Who Almost Didn't Want to Be an Armenian," *Ararat* (New York), Autumn 1970.]

DEAN FLOWER

ARNOLD, EDWARD (Feb. 18, 1890–Apr. 26, 1956), actor, was born in a tenement in New York City, the son of Carl Schneider and Elizabeth Ohse, Lutheran immigrants from Germany. He was named Guenther Edward Schneider but changed it to Edward Arnold early in his career on the advice of Ben Greet, who headed the acting company with which he apprenticed.

At the age of eleven Arnold left school to help support his family. His father, a former U.S. Navy seaman and fur-cutter, died later that same year and within two years his mother died, leaving five children to fend for themselves. Arnold went to live with his Uncle "Hilmer," who played bass viol at Tony Pastor's Variety Hall on Fourteenth Street. Uncle "Hilmer" was Arnold's first professional contact with the world of show business.

A few years earlier Arnold had joined the Drama Club of the East Side Settlement House. There he had his first taste of public approbation when he played Lorenzo in *The Merchant of Venice* and was greatly encouraged by the director John D. Barry. (In 1940, when he wrote his memoirs, he remembered this early experience and entitled his book *Lorenzo Goes to Hollywood.*)

Arnold was fifteen when he joined the Ben Greet Players. Before this he worked at a series of odd occupations such as handy man to a jewelry manufacturer, newsboy, bellhop, grocery clerk, and janitor's helper. Later, when theatrical engagements became scarce, he sold insurance and tended the boiler at Columbia University.

At the age of seventeen Arnold was engaged as company juvenile and assistant stage manager for Maxine Elliott's touring company. This was followed by three seasons as juvenile with Ethel Barrymore's company, where he played in such vehicles as *Mid-Channel* and *Trelawney of the Wells.* He went on to appear with the Frohman Company, Maude Adams, Otis Skinner, and William Gillette, and with each successive venture his reputation grew as a reliable juvenile and second lead.

In 1915, while on tour, Arnold met and married Harriet Marshall in Richmond, Va. They had three children. They divorced in 1927, and two years later Arnold married Olive Emerson, a noted concert singer from Minneapolis, remembered for her performances on the Westinghouse Program on NBC radio. This marriage ended in divorce in 1948. Arnold married Cleo Patricia McClain in 1951.

In 1918 Arnold's career began to blossom, and in 1919 he made his first film appearance in Essanay's feature *Is Marriage Sacred?* He made several silent films, maintaining his stage career at the same time. It is believed that he appeared in over forty films for Essanay in Chicago, but there is no existing record of which films. He did appear in the 1927 classic *Sunrise—A Song of Two Humans.*

In 1920 Arnold appeared in Eugene O'Neill's first full-length drama, *Beyond the Horizon,* and continued his healthy stage career in such plays as *The Mad Honeymoon* (1922), *The Nervous Wreck* (1923), *Easy Come, Easy Go* (1924), *The Jazz Singer* (1928), *The Conflict* (1929), and *The Inkwell* (1929–1930), with Viola Dana. The previous season he also appeared in vaudeville with Dana.

During the 1930's there were major changes in Arnold's career. He worked for the Theatre Guild, supporting Alla Nazimova in *A Month in the Country* (1930) and was in *Miracle at Verdun* (1931). He then made his first appearance in a musical revue, receiving third billing in *The Third Little Show* (1932) opposite Beatrice Lillie. He left this to play Jacob Dillon in the melodrama *Whistling in the Dark,* which played on Broadway

and then toured to the West Coast, where Arnold became, once and for all, a movie actor.

In 1932 he made an auspicious double debut in *Okay America* at Universal and supporting all three Barrymores in *Rasputin and the Empress* at MGM, which became his home studio. In 1933 he repeated his stage role in *Whistling in the Dark.*

During the next twenty-three years Arnold played in ninety-three films, often portraying villains. As a screen "heavy" he weighed in at about 200 pounds. Weight did not prevent him playing heroes, however. Throughout his career he fluctuated between leading roles and cameo appearances. Among his most memorable characterizations are "Diamond Jim" Brady (essayed twice, first in the 1935 *Diamond Jim* and again, in 1940, in *Lillian Russell*), Barney Glasgow in Edna Ferber's *Come and Get It* (1936), Nero Wolfe (1936), Achille Weber in *Idiot's Delight* (1939), and the confused and beleaguered Judge Harry Wilkins in 1947's *Dear Ruth.* Other important films include *The White Sister, Sadie McKee, You Can't Take It With You, Meet John Doe, The Hucksters, Command Decision,* and *All That Money Can Buy* (also known as *The Devil and Daniel Webster*).

In 1947 he began an ABC radio series, "Mr. President," in which he portrayed a different first executive in each episode. In 1953 and 1954 he toured with a stage-lecture version of this series. He also made several television appearances.

Arnold was the originator of the "I Am an American" movement during the war and also campaigned against professional beggars in the United States. His charity work and personal involvement with various organizations, both professional and charitable, was well enough known for columnist Hedda Hopper to label him—along with James Cagney and Henry Fonda—one of the "three nicest men in Hollywood." He was a man known for his good and freely given advice. He died in Encino, Calif., and was buried at San Fernando Mission, Calif.

[The major biographical sources are Arnold's autobiography, *Lorenzo Goes to Hollywood* (1940), in collaboration with Frances Fisher Dubuc; Paul Michael, ed., *The American Movies Reference Book: The Sound Era* (1969); and Frank Buxton and Bill Owen, *The Big Broadcast* (1972). See also *Photoplay,* July 1935, May 1936, and Sept. 1941; *Time,* Aug. 12, 1935; *Motion Picture Magazine,* May 1937; *Lion's Roar* (MGM house organ), Nov. 1941–Feb. 1945; the clipping files of the Billy Rose Theatre Collection, Lincoln Center Library of the Performing Arts, New

York; and the obituary in the *New York Times*, Apr. 27, 1956. Good photographs of Arnold are in *Lorenzo Goes to Hollywood*, and Daniel Blum, *Pictorial History of the Talkies* (1958).]

J. PETER BERGMAN

ASTOR, WILLIAM VINCENT (Nov. 15, 1891–Feb. 3, 1959), financier, navy officer, sportsman, and public benefactor, was born in New York City, the son of John Jacob Astor IV and Ava Willing and the great-great-grandson of John Jacob Astor, the first of the name in the United States. Vincent was educated at the Westminster School, Simsbury, Conn., and at St. George's School, Newport, R.I. In 1910 his parents were divorced; his father then married Madeleine Talmadge Force.

After tutoring by the young newspaperman H. V. Kaltenborn, the six foot, four inch Astor entered Harvard College in the fall of 1911 but remained there for only seven months. He left in April 1912, shortly after his father, with whom Vincent had a very close relationship, went down on the *Titanic*. (The pregnant Madeleine Force Astor was a survivor of the sinking.) At twenty years of age Vincent was thrust into the business of managing the Astor estate and the family's various other interests.

Astor, nevertheless, found time for sports. He raced automobiles and lent his support to aviation; he was a pilot and Early Bird, who joined the Aero Club of America back in 1913. He was an enthusiastic yachtsman, cruising the seas in the *Noma* or in his later yacht, the *Nourmahal*. He was accompanied on his oceanic trips by friends and scientists who studied marine life. For the Bronx Zoo he brought back rare specimens from many climes.

With his knowledge of seamanship and navigation, it was only natural that he should volunteer for naval service in World War I. He gave *Noma* to the government, and it joined the U.S. mosquito fleet as a submarine chaser, on which Astor served. He also saw some service on the *Nourmahal*, another gift of his to the navy. He was stationed in France as a naval port officer, was transferred to the *Aphrodite*, and became its executive officer. Finally, he returned home in command of the captured German submarine *U-117*, a sabotaged U-boat filled with gas that made most of the American crew ill and injured Astor's lungs. It was a hazardous assignment in an unfamiliar craft.

During World War II, Astor rose to the rank of naval reserve captain, serving in naval intelligence and the eastern sea frontier. Again, there was an Astor *Nourmahal* in governmental service. He saw active duty in command of large convoys, crossing to England in 1944.

John Jacob Astor IV had left a $5 million trust fund for Ava Alice, Vincent's sister, and a similar fund of $3 million for his unborn child. The remainder of his vast estate, about $87 million, was bequeathed to Vincent. Approximately $63 million, the largest of the family investments, was in New York City real estate. The properties included the St. Regis and the Waldorf-Astoria hotels as well as many apartment and office buildings.

Astor's business method was to develop or improve the properties, always taking an active interest in the operations. Many of his inherited slum tenements, called "Astor Flats," he caused to be razed. Others he sold to New York's Municipal Housing Authority for little cash and long-term mortgages. Squalor was once a hallmark of Astor realty holdings. To offset this image, a new heading for his advertisements was devised—the smart "Vincent Astor Offers."

During the 1920's Astor sold about $40 million worth of his New York holdings. He reinvested $15 million of that sum in improvements and the erection of new buildings. "Every dollar is a soldier to do your bidding" was one of his rare quotations. He was interested in offshore oil development, was an investor in southwestern oil, and built the Illuminating Building in Cleveland. He made a profit of $371,000 on his share of the motion picture *Ben Hur*.

An independent in politics, Astor backed Franklin D. Roosevelt in the 1932 presidential campaign and strongly supported the New Deal in its early stages. Then, disenchantment came, although Astor remained personally friendly with Roosevelt. In February 1933, Astor and Roosevelt took an eleven-day cruise on the *Nourmahal*, going ashore in Miami, Fla., for a triumphal parade. It was there that an assassin's bullet, aimed at president-elect Roosevelt, killed Chicago's Mayor Anton J. Cermak.

Through politics, Astor became involved in the publishing business. In 1933, with brain truster Raymond Moley as editor, he became a partner in the creation of the magazine *Today*, an outlet for Moley's political theories. After Moley broke with Roosevelt, he became a vigorous critic of the president via *Today*. In 1937 the publication merged with *News Week* (later *Newsweek*) magazine; Astor remained its owner and chairman of the board until his death.

As time passed, Astor disposed of more and more of his properties, until he owned no real estate except the St. Regis, the *New York Times* annex, and his residences. The Captain, as he was known, had one notable failure—his projected $75 million Astor Plaza died in 1957 for lack of adequate financing. In 1958 the First National City Bank of New York took the project off Astor's hands and put up its own building on the location at Park Avenue and 53rd Street.

Astor was a member of twenty-nine clubs and a director of many corporations, including United States Trust, Great Northern Railroad, Chase National Bank, Western Union Telegraph, International Mercantile Marine, and the United States Lines. (Astor was an adherent of a strong American merchant marine.) He was a trustee of the New York Public Library (which grew largely out of a $400,000 bequest made by the first John Jacob Astor), a governor of New York Hospital, and a director of the New York Post-Graduate Medical School and Hospital. His varied philanthropies included the establishment of a $1 million playground in Harlem; the Astor Home in Rhinebeck (for disturbed children), given to the Catholic Church and run by the Sisters of St. Vincent de Paul; and a clubhouse for nurses.

In 1948 Astor established the Vincent Astor Foundation, with its slogan "the alleviation of human misery." The foundation has sought "to lift the sights, broaden the opportunities, and enrich the lives of the urban population." The organization has supported medical and surgical research, child care, as well as cultural and educational programs. It has clung to its two major principles of being "people-oriented" and spending its funds entirely in New York City. In 1973 the foundation allotted more than $55 million to some 280 grantees.

Astor was an Episcopalian; he served as senior warden of the Church of the Messiah in Rhinebeck. He married Helen D. Huntington on Apr. 30, 1914; they were divorced in 1940. He then married Mary B. Cushing on Sept. 27, 1940; they were divorced in 1953. In Bar Harbor, Maine, on Oct. 8, 1953, Astor married Brooke R. Marshall. There were no children from any of the marriages. Thus, Astor's death marked the end of the house of Astor on American soil. (There is an English branch.) Whereas John Jacob Astor had left only one-fortieth of his estate, $500,000, for the public weal, Vincent Astor chose another

path. He left $2 million outright to Mrs. Astor and a life interest in half of the estate, to do with as she chose. He made twenty-four smaller bequests totaling $800,000 and left the remainder of his fortune (between $100 million and $200 million) to various charities, chief of which was the Vincent Astor Foundation.

During much of his life, Astor broke with family tradition by keeping close personal watch over his holdings, investing part of his capital in fields other than real estate, having little enthusiasm for the kind of social life his ancestors enjoyed and taking an active part in social reform. He believed that the masses would be served best by an enlightened capitalism.

Roland L. Redmond, a Harvard classmate of his, summed up Astor in these words: "Vincent Astor was a man of strong character and decided views, but he was nevertheless modest and retiring. He never sought public acclaim or positions of prominence."

[There is no definitive biography. Chief sources on Astor and his career include John Alexander, "The Golden Spoon," in *Profiles From the New Yorker Magazine* (1938); Cleveland Amory, *Who Killed Society?* (1960); *Harvard College, Class of 1915's 25th and 45th Anniversary Reports; Vincent Astor Foundation Reports* (1973, 1976); Hans von Kaltenborn, *Fifty Fabulous Years, 1900–1950* (1950); Lucy Kavaler, *The Astors: A Family Chronicle of Pomp and Power* (1966); Harvey O'Connor, *The Astors* (1941); *Social Register of New York* (1973); John Tebbel, *The Inheritors* (1962); and personal communications with Mrs. Vincent Astor. There are many photos of Vincent Astor in the newspapers and magazines of his day. His likeness appeared as the cover picture on *Time*, Apr. 19, 1934. A very fine photo of him is to be found on the inside front cover of the *Vincent Astor Foundation XXV Anniversary Report* (1973).]

THEODORE L. MAYHEW

ATKINSON, HENRY AVERY (Aug. 26, 1877–Jan. 24, 1960), clergyman and foundation executive, was born in Merced, Calif., the son of Thomas Albion Atkinson, a Methodist minister, and Sarah Jane Yeargin. He received an A.B. from Pacific Methodist College in 1897 and attended Garrett Bible Institute. Doctrinal differences led to his abandonment of Methodism and his ordination as a Congregational minister in 1902. On May 29, 1901, he married Grace Olin; they had no children. He held pastorates in Albion, Ill. (1902–1904), Springfield, Ohio (1904–1908), and Atlanta, Ga. (1908–1911).

Atkinson preached in lumber camps in California, served as chaplain of a labor organization in Ohio, and taught sociology at the Atlanta Theological Seminary; his obvious concern with economic and social problems led to his service from 1911 to 1918 as secretary of the Department of Church and Labor of the Congregational denomination. A protégé of Washington Gladden, Atkinson stood in the vanguard of the social gospel tradition, encouraging acceptance of collective bargaining and strikes and educating churchgoers to workers' aspirations for a living wage and improved safety standards. From 1920 to 1932 he served as general secretary of the Universal Christian Conference on Life and Work.

In 1916 the Department of Church and Labor, renamed the Social Service Commission, moved to Boston, where Atkinson became involved in discussions about the postwar world when he joined the League to Enforce Peace and served as extension secretary to the branch there. This post brought him into contact with Hamilton Holt and Frederick Lynch, who had helped establish the Church Peace Union in 1914 with a gift of $2 million from Andrew Carnegie. The union sought to promote world peace by working with religious leaders of all denominations. In 1918 Atkinson directed the work of one of its affiliates, the National Commission on the Churches and the Moral Aims of the War. In December 1918 he became general secretary of the Church Peace Union and of its affiliate, the World Alliance for Promoting International Friendship Through the Churches. Thereafter, Atkinson found the focus of his lifework in seeking to enlist the world's religious leaders in the quest for peace. He traveled abroad nearly every year, meeting leaders in Europe, India, and the Far East; and by 1945 he had organized branches of the World Alliance in thirty-nine countries. At a conference at The Hague in 1919, Atkinson began an effort that led to meetings at Stockholm in 1925, at Lausanne in 1927, and at Oxford and Edinburgh in 1937. These conferences led to the establishment of the World Council of Churches in 1948. Although receiving credit as the organizer of that movement, Atkinson failed to achieve a congress of world religions in the 1930's despite a decade of detailed planning.

Atkinson became a foe of religious intolerance and an outspoken critic of anti-Semitism. He served as cochairman (1940–1956) of the Council Against Intolerance in America, and as chairman of the advisory board (1944–1956) of the Non-Sectarian Anti-Nazi League; and he supported the Zionist movement. A forest in Israel bears his name in recognition of his efforts to gain public acceptance of the partitioning of Palestine.

Atkinson possessed remarkable administrative and organizational ability, and while serving simultaneously as the head of several organizations or commissions was busily creating others. A pragmatist who appraised world conditions realistically, he responded at the opportune time to needs and established and maintained channels for constructive action. He believed that religious institutions cannot be divorced from the community, and that they can be positive forces to resolve problems and to set an example of how people can unite in a common cause.

Atkinson's reliance on positive responses on behalf of justice and right did not allow him to embrace pacifist doctrines. He endorsed United States participation in World Wars I and II and campaigned for an abandonment of neutrality between 1939 and 1941. He believed in a politically organized world—even one that could impose sanctions upon wrongdoers. He campaigned for United States membership in the League of Nations and the World Court and served as unofficial consultant to the State Department at the United Nations conference in San Francisco in 1945.

Atkinson made friends easily, holding their respect because of his dedication to causes, his belief in brotherhood and justice, and the integrity of his convictions. After the death of his wife in 1954, he married Marjorie Jefferson Weber on Apr. 12, 1955, the year in which he retired as general secretary of the Church Peace Union. He died in Baltimore, Md.

[Atkinson's papers are in the Church Peace Union, Council on Religion and International Affairs collection at Columbia University. His writings include The Church and the Peoples Play (1915); Men and Things (1918); Prelude to Peace: A Realistic View of International Relations (1937); and Theodore Marburg: The Man and His Work (1951). His activities are described in Roy M. Houghton, "Henry Avery Atkinson," Advance, July 1945; and in Charles S. Macfarland, Pioneers for Peace Through Religion (1946).]
WARREN F. KUEHL

ATTERBURY, GROSVENOR (July 7, 1869–Oct. 18, 1956), architect and town planner, was born in Detroit, Mich., the only child of Charles Larned Atterbury, a prominent New York City lawyer, and Katharine Mitchell Dow. He was educated at the Berkeley School in New

York and at Yale University, receiving a B.A. in 1891. From 1890 to 1893 he also studied painting with William Merritt Chase. But it was the six months he spent abroad in Europe and Egypt after his graduation that confirmed his intent to become an architect. Consequently, in 1892–93, he was a special student in construction at the Columbia University School of Architecture and, during 1892, also acquired experience with practical building in the office of McKim, Mead and White. His formal training was completed in Paris at the École des Beaux Arts, Atelier Blondel, in 1894–95.

Upon his return to New York City, Atterbury's enthusiastic intensity attracted the attention of many influential family friends and business associates, allowing him to establish a practice quickly. Primarily residential at the beginning, it included many large country houses on Long Island, where the Atterburys had a summer place at Southampton. Significant among these was the group of "Moorish" houses built in 1897 for Henry O. Havemeyer on Bayberry Point, Islip—imaginative in their use of stucco made from the sand on the site so as to blend buildings and setting. Robert W. De Forest's Cold Spring Harbor residence, "Wawapek" (1898), was a skillful fusion of Adirondack hunting lodge, shingle style, and Colonial revival. Less exuberant with their severely elegant mixture of motifs were his turn-of-the-century New York City town houses for John Williams Robbins at 33 East 74th Street (medieval and German) and John S. Phipps at 6 East 87th Street (Roman, Venetian, and French).

As an architect of philanthropic projects, Atterbury's compassion for the individual, of whatever social status, made his solutions particularly satisfying, as in the roof garden he placed on the first Phipps Model Tenement on East 31st Street near First Avenue in New York (1907), or in the attention to detail in the Psychiatric Clinic of Johns Hopkins Hospital in Baltimore (1915).

Atterbury received his most important commission in 1909 from the Russell Sage Foundation for Forest Hills Gardens, in Queens, one of the earliest model towns. On a curving street plan developed by Frederick Law Olmsted, Jr., Atterbury designed the railroad station, with its adjoining hotel and shops; row housing; and grouped and single houses—all in a consistent and emphatically textured Tudor-German style. Later additions to the scheme, by other architects,

had to be approved by Atterbury's office. The picturesque result became the archetype of American garden suburbs. Later, and less lavish, workingmen's housing was done by Atterbury in 1915–16 at Indian Hill in Worcester, Mass., for the Norton Company, and in 1916 at Erwin, Tenn., for the Holston Corporation.

Several of the housing units at Forest Hills Gardens were entirely constructed of large concrete sections, precast at a plant on the site. Since 1904 Atterbury had worked on the problem of simplifying cheap housing construction, which he was convinced would lead to the standardization of a relatively few parts made of one homogeneous material. His exhaustive research and experiments, backed by Phipps and then the Russell Sage Foundation, culminated in a series of "demonstrations" of constructed concrete houses, beginning in 1907, and continuing in Sewaren, N.J., in 1910 and at Forest Hills Gardens in 1913 and 1918. These constituted the earliest practical examples of such prefabrication in the country.

In the years just before America's entry into World War I, the range of Atterbury's commissions became ever wider, embracing churches for his town projects, the picturesque yet practical Parrish Art Museum at Southampton, L.I. (completed 1913), the continuing restoration of the New York City Hall, especially the freely interpreted cupola of 1917, and the nine-story, vigorously rusticated Russell Sage Foundation Building at Lexington Avenue and 22nd Street in New York City (*ca.* 1915). He was instrumental in the founding in 1910 of the National Housing Association, of which he became a director, and of the National City Planning Institute (now the American Institute of Planners) in 1917. He was president of the Architectural League of New York (1915–17).

Undertakings such as the inwardly complex 1922–24 American Wing of the Metropolitan Museum of Art in New York, the 1934 rustic Tudor model farm group for John D. Rockefeller, Jr., at Pocantico Hills, N.Y., and even the enormous Amsterdam Houses scheme (with Harvey W. Corbett and Thomas S. Holden) of 1949 for the New York City Housing Authority, attest to Atterbury's continuing attractiveness to patrons. He gradually became increasingly selective about accepting commissions, especially after his marriage to Dorothy Axtell Johnstone on Mar. 24, 1923. Greater time could thus be spent on each project, yet his styles tended to become more "correct" and his detail more ponderous, as in the heavy Tudor of the Aldus C. Higgins residence in Worcester, Mass. (1921–23). That new problems could still inspire ingenious solutions can be seen in the creative use of exterior display fountains to help cool the interior of the Florence L. Pond residence (1936), "Stone Ashley," near Tucson, Ariz. His real love remained the ongoing development of his patented precast units long after commerical firms had ceased showing interest. Indeed, he was still working on these, after retirement and after a partially paralyzing stroke, at the time of his death in Southampton, L.I.

Atterbury was personally and stylistically a conservative (he thought Frank Lloyd Wright an "exhibitionist"), who ran his office as if it were a Beaux Arts atelier. His major designers, first of all John Tompkins in the late 1910's and ultimately Frank Dvorak, invariably worked from Atterbury's thumbnail sketches and were always "associates," never partners. For all his conservatism, however, Atterbury's pragmatic approach to problem solving led him toward structural innovations that have not yet been adequately considered.

[Atterbury's literary remains are mostly in the form of addresses given to professional societies or reports to official and philanthropic organizations, the most important of which is the Russell Sage Foundation, New York City. One such report, that of the Regional Plan of New York and Its Environs of the Russell Sage Foundation, was published as *The Economic Production of Workingmen's Homes* (1930). More accessible are "Model Towns in America," *Scribner's,* July 1912, and "Bricks Without Brains," *Architecture,* Apr. 1936. On Atterbury and his career, see "The Work of Grosvenor Atterbury," *American Architect and Building News,* Aug. 26, 1908, and Sept. 2, 1908; "Forest Hills Gardens, Long Island, an Example of Collective Planning," *Brickbuilder,* Dec. 1912; and Fred Squires, "Houses at Forest Hills Gardens," *Concrete,* Jan. 1915.]
DONALD HARRIS DWYER

AVERY, SEWELL LEE (Nov. 4, 1874– Oct. 31, 1960), business executive, was born in Saginaw, Mich. He was the son of Waldo Allard Avery, a wealthy lumberman of old Boston stock, and of Ellen Lee. After attending Michigan Military Academy, Avery drifted into the University of Michigan Law School, where he received an LL.B. in 1894. His father was part owner of the Western Plaster Works, a medium-sized gypsum firm, and Avery went to work as manager of its plant at Alabaster, Mich. On Oct. 11, 1899, he married Hortense Lenore Wisner, with whom he lived modestly in a couple of rooms fronting Lake Huron (an indoor bathtub constituted their major extravagance). They had four children.

In December 1901 twenty-five midwestern gypsum companies, seeking to end internecine price wars, combined to form the United States Gypsum Company. Avery assumed charge of the new firm's Buffalo office and subsequently became sales manager for a larger district centered in Cleveland. The original trust organization of U.S.G. led to bitter intrafirm rivalry. After two corporate shakeups, Avery emerged in 1905 as president. He retained that position until 1937 and served as chairman until 1951; he and his brother Waldo figured also as the company's two largest stockholders.

Avery transformed U.S. Gypsum from a regional producer of plaster into the nation's dominant building materials firm. The concern grew steadily despite adverse conditions in the construction industry before World War I, and it rode the crest of the building boom in the decade after 1919. Sensing a downturn coming, Avery slashed expenses by laying off almost half the firm's employees in September 1929; he subsequently deployed a $35 million retained earnings surplus to expand horizontally and vertically in order to increase market share while competitors foundered in the depths of the Great Depression.

U.S. Gypsum spokesmen declaimed that they were "not running a benevolent society" for any class of employee and stood firm against pension and benefit plans well into the 1950's. From the shareholders' point of view, however, company strategy proved phenomenally successful. Even in the 1930's, pretax profits approached 20 percent of sales. Business circles hailed Avery's "genius for organization," and he was invited to join the boards of a list of corporations that read like a cross section of American business. He became a trustee of the University of Chicago and a stalwart of that city's charitable and cultural institutions. *Fortune* called him "the most important U.S. tycoon to make his reputation out of the depression."

In 1931 Avery caught the eye of Harry P. Davison, a J. P. Morgan partner who was seeking a management wizard to save Montgomery, Ward and Co. The nation's second largest mail-order house stood poised on the brink of disaster after a decade of business misjudgments. Avery was reluctant to take over Ward's, but the directors offered stock options that would be worth millions if the company recovered. He signed on as chief executive officer (while retaining his post at U.S. Gypsum) in November 1931.

Avery recruited the nation's best merchandising talent. He revamped the Ward catalog, wrote off unprofitable lines, tightened central controls, and unified product distribution to mail-order and retail outlets. Meanwhile, the personnel department monitored employee performance and disclosed the rankings on large screens; a major issue at Ward's became "keeping your picture off the bottom row." The treasurer compiled exhibits of losing operations for display in the chartroom where managers met. "We can always find something," he boasted, "to rub their noses in." Results came quickly. Of Ward's 35,000 employees, 22,000 left their jobs during the first three years of Avery's tenure. But company earnings recovered smartly, and so did Ward common: Avery's stock options were worth $1.8 million by 1934.

Avery's conservative stewardship involved no little irony, for sixty years earlier Aaron Montgomery Ward had founded the firm with the patronage of the populist-oriented National Grange. Mail order had helped rural folk overcome the monopoly of the country store, and Ward's retained its image as the farmer's friend. Avery conceded that the money pumped into agricultural areas through New Deal relief programs was largely responsible for the company's improved cash flow. Nevertheless, he opposed welfare measures as inflationary. He spurned the National Recovery Administration's "Blue Eagle" and denounced "impractical and dreamlike idealists" in the Roosevelt administration who, he thought, "like the dog on the bridge, lost what they had, trying to get what they saw in the water." He underscored these convictions by joining the American Liberty League and by serving on the Republican National Finance Committee.

During World War II, Avery engaged in a protracted dispute with the War Labor Board (WLB) and became a symbol of opposition to the extension of government economic controls. Seeking to prevent stoppages that would interfere with production, the WLB endorsed a "maintenance-of-membership" clause in labor contracts as a compromise between the closed and the open shop. Avery considered the compromise formula a disguised victory for the closed shop and for "union racketeers." Without such protection the United Mail Order, Warehouse and Retail Employees Union (CIO) might in fact have encountered difficulty in organizing Ward's sales staff. In April 1944, Avery repudiated a contract containing the offending provision and defied the WLB.

The 1943 Smith-Connally Act empowered the president to take over manufacturing plants useful to the war effort in case of labor disturbances. Whether a primarily distributive enterprise like Ward's fell within the purview of the act was unclear. But the director of war mobilization felt that the administration had to proceed in order to maintain its credibility with labor and to uphold the prestige of the WLB. Attorney General Francis Biddle flew to Chicago in the hope of effecting the seizure peaceably. "To hell with the government," said Avery in the confrontation at company offices, "I want none of your damned advice." Biddle ordered Avery ejected bodily; the latter replied with the most denigrating epithet he could muster: "You New Dealer!" The next day virtually every front page in the country featured a photograph of two soldiers carrying out the frail-looking septuagenarian. Sixty-one percent of those polled by Gallup supported Avery, and Republican newspapers attacked Roosevelt for following in the footsteps of Hitler. While litigation dragged on (the Supreme Court sidestepped a ruling on the president's general war powers in the case), Congress investigated. Avery appeared on Capitol Hill to excoriate the members of the WLB as "academics without experience, frequently . . . of a pink persuasion." Although the controversy receded in the public mind, army troops occupied Ward plants again between December 1944 and October 1945. Yet in the end Avery prevailed; he never did accept "maintenance of membership."

In the postwar decade Avery's fabled business acumen failed him. Other merchandising chains expanded rapidly to meet the surge in consumer demand. Ward's did not open a single new store and turned away business rather than carry excess inventory. Avery believed another depression close at hand and built up reserves to prepare for it. By 1954 Ward's had amassed almost as much in liquid assets as it registered in annual sales. But the opportunity to reapply the countercyclical strategy that had brought Avery renown a generation earlier never came. Three-quarters as large as Sears, Roebuck in 1941,

Ward's shrank to a shell one-fourth the size of the industry leader. Critics dubbed it the "bank with a store front." While competitors turned to increasingly sophisticated market-research departments, Avery kept the most trivial decisions in his own hands. His wife even exercised a veto power over styles in women's hats.

Avery had never welcomed criticism by subordinates. "When anybody ventures to differ with me," he once told stockholders, "I throw them out of the window." But now he discerned conspiracies everywhere and stalked through company headquarters proclaiming, "I'll show 'em who runs Ward's." He repeatedly purged top management; altogether four presidents and forty vice-presidents left the company. Finally Louis E. Wolfson, a Florida corporate promoter (later imprisoned for security act violations), mounted a widely publicized campaign to take over Ward's. Avery's forces met the proxy challenge successfully, but his disjointed rambling at the crucial stockholders' meeting shocked his own supporters, who forced his resignation as chairman in April 1955. Ward stock rose five points on the news.

Hortense Avery died in April 1956, and that month Avery relinquished his seat on the Montgomery Ward board. His successors hired a new management team away from Sears and spent the reserves that he had hoarded for store modernization and expansion. But they could not overcome Avery's legacy; they remained at a disadvantage in major markets where competitors had moved in ahead of them. By 1976 Ward's —having become a subsidiary of the Mobil Corporation—ranked only fifth among the nation's retailers. Avery himself proved no more adept in sheltering his assets from inheritance taxes than in accommodating to changes in mass merchandising; more than half his $20 million estate fell to the federal government, whose encroachments he had feared and so passionately fought. He died in Chicago.

[Accounts of Avery's stewardship at U.S. Gypsum and Ward's appear in *Fortune*, Jan. 1935, Feb. 1936, May 1946, Dec. 1952, Sept. 1955, May 1956, Nov. 1960, May 1970; *New Yorker*, May 21, 1955; and *Business Week, Time,* and *Newsweek* (frequent articles, 1932-1956). See also obituaries in the *New York Times*, Nov. 1, 1960; and in *Time* and *Newsweek*, Nov. 14, 1960.

On mass merchandising, see Boris Emmet and John E. Jeuck, *Catalogues and Counters: A History of Sears, Roebuck and Company* (1950); and Frank B. Latham, *1872-1972: A Century of Serving Consumers: The Story of Montgomery Ward* (1972). For Avery's political views and his conflict with the War Labor Board, see Francis Biddle, *In Brief Authority* (1962); John L. Blackman, Jr., *Presidential Seizure in Labor Disputes* (1967); Richard Polenberg, *War and Society: The United States, 1941-1945* (1972); Joel Seidman, *American Labor From Defense to Reconversion* (1953); Nancy Allen Hobor, "The United States vs. Montgomery Ward" (Ph.D. dissertation, University of Chicago, 1973); and U.S. Congress, House of Representatives, 78th Congress, 2nd Session, *Hearings Before the Select Committee to Investigate Seizure of Montgomery Ward and Co.*, and *Report of the Select Committee to Investigate Seizure of Montgomery Ward and Co.* (1944).]

STEPHEN A. SCHUKER

AYDELOTTE, FRANK (Oct. 16, 1880–Dec. 17, 1956), college president and foundation officer, was born in Sullivan, Ind., the son of William Ephraim Aydelotte and Matilda Brunger. His father was the prosperous proprietor of a wooden mill. After graduating from Indiana University in 1900 with the B.A., Aydelotte worked briefly as a reporter in Vincennes and then taught English for six months at the Southwestern State Normal School in California, Pa. In 1901–02 he taught at Indiana University and then took the M.A. in English at Harvard in 1903. He taught for two years at Louisville (Ky.) Boys' High School and in 1905 won a Rhodes Scholarship.

The Oxford experience was crucial in shaping Aydelotte's philosophy of higher education. On June 23, 1907, he married Marie Jeanette Osgood; they had one son. By the terms of the Rhodes Trust, Aydelotte was compelled to resign his scholarship after he married; but the couple remained at Oxford until late 1907, while he completed the requirements for the B.Litt. (1908). Four years later they returned to Oxford while he polished his *Elizabethan Rogues and Vagabonds* (1913). This is a durable product of great industry, sharp perspective, and good humor; but Aydelotte was drawn less to scholarly research than to seeking the most effective ways of teaching English literature and rhetoric to American undergraduates, whose motivation tended to be more vocational than intellectual. Aydelotte became associate professor of English at Indiana early in 1908 and was professor at the Massachusetts Institute of Technology from 1915 to 1921. By then he had established a reputation as a consultant, editor, and publicist.

From 1914 to 1921 Aydelotte was editor of the *American Oxonian,* and in 1917 he became American secretary of the Rhodes Trust. Widely known to educators and foundation executives, he was often sought as an officer. In 1921 he accepted the presidency of Swarthmore College, an institution of 500 students and fifty teachers that had been founded in 1864 by Hicksite Quakers.

Aydelotte found Swarthmore conventional and undistinguished; under his administration, it became known for its commitment to intellectual purpose. Impressed with the success of Oxford in its attention to the more talented and ambitious students, he persuaded faculty and trustees to institute, as an alternative to the pass degree, an honors program of exacting standards. Signally effective in obtaining gifts and grants, he was able to improve the quality of the faculty and, despite a growing enrollment, to reduce the ratio of students to teachers. Never burying himself in routine, or succumbing to complacency, he kept central the goal of making Swarthmore a citadel of excellence. Throughout his presidency he maintained his collateral interest in the Rhodes Trust Foundation, served on various foundation boards, and, beginning in 1924, formulated plans for the Guggenheim Awards and the Commonwealth Fellowships. Aydelotte was able to do so many things well because of his robust constitution, sanguine disposition, capacity to distinguish the essence from the miscellany, and unusual skill in personal relationships.

In 1940 Aydelotte left Swarthmore to become the second director of the Institute for Advanced Study at Princeton, N.J. He had been a trustee since its founding in 1930 and had known Abraham Flexner, the founding director, since their days as schoolteachers in Louisville. Flexner had ruled the institute autocratically; after his departure, staff and scholars insisted on greater voice in its administration.

Aydelotte's tenure at the institute was the least satisfying phase of his career. Financial constraints complicated the introduction of provisions for scaled compensation and for annuities after retirement, and the outbreak of World War II and personal conflicts among scholars created much unhappiness.

He retired in 1947 and was succeeded by J. Robert Oppenheimer. Widowed in 1952, Aydelotte declined in vigor in his last years but remained an enthusiastic devotee of golf almost to the last. He died in Princeton, N.J.

[Aydelotte's official papers are at Swarthmore College; his private papers are destined for deposit in the Friends' Historical Library at Swarthmore College. Frances Blanshard, *Frank Aydelotte of Swarthmore* (1970), is thorough, reliable, and sympathetic without being adulatory. *Swarthmore College Bulletin,* Feb. 1957, is devoted almost entirely to tributes. *An Adventure in Education: Swarthmore College Under Frank Aydelotte* (1941), by the Swarthmore College Faculty, includes one article by an outside examiner, various statistics, and an extensive bibliography.]

THOMAS LEDUC

BAADE, WILHELM HEINRICH WALTER (Mar. 24, 1893–June 25, 1960), astronomer, was born in Schröttinghausen, Westphalia, Germany, the son of Konrad Baade, a schoolteacher, and Charlotte Wulfhorst. From 1903 to 1912 Baade was a student at the Friedrichs-Gymnasium in Herford. He studied at the University of Münster from 1912 to 1913 and at Göttingen, where he was an assistant to the mathematician Felix Klein from 1913 to 1919. Shortly after passing his doctoral examination in July 1919 with a *sehr gut,* he became an assistant at the University of Hamburg's observatory in Bergedorf. There he began systematic observations of comets and asteroids; he reported the discovery of a comet in 1922 and of a minor planet (Hidalgo) in 1920 that turned out to have the largest orbit of any known asteroid. In 1929 Baade married Hanni Bohlmann, a calculator at the Hamburg Observatory; he later named one of "his" asteroids "Muschi"—the nickname he always used for her.

Inspired by the work of Harlow Shapley at the Mount Wilson Observatory, Baade, almost alone among European astronomers, embarked on an observational program of clusters and variable stars to delineate the structure of the Milky Way. Although handicapped by the comparatively small size of the Bergedorf reflector (one meter aperture), he soon demonstrated the existence of isolated cluster-type variables in the spherical space surrounding the disk of the Milky Way. Many years later, at the Mount Wilson Observatory, he was to use similar isolated variable stars to derive the distance to the center of the Milky Way.

His zeal and ability won him a Rockefeller fellowship in 1926, enabling him to visit the large telescopes at Mount Wilson, near Pasadena, Calif. Upon his return to Bergedorf in 1927 Baade was promoted to observer, but he failed in his attempt to have the one-meter telescope moved to a more favorable southern location, and when he was offered a staff position at Mount Wilson in 1931, he accepted immediately.

The first problem Baade undertook with the 60- and 100-inch telescopes was the improvement of brightness measurements for faint stars. Like many astronomers of the period before the establishment of photoelectric photometry, Baade was frustrated by the lack of a precise intensity scale. For many years he worked painstakingly with neutral half-filter photographic techniques, but he was not satisfied with the results. When it finally became apparent that photoelectric multipliers could provide the requisite accuracy, he guided several students into critical research problems in this area, never publishing his own laboriously achieved but still imperfect photographic magnitudes.

In the 1930's and 1940's Baade's major interest concerned the stellar content of various systems of stars. Analyzing two nearby dwarf galaxies that had recently been found by Harvard astronomers, Baade and Edwin P. Hubble discovered that these systems contained several globular clusters, numerous cluster-type variable stars, and a background of red giant stars. For the first time the components of the so-called elliptical galaxies were discerned, a revelation that eventually led to Baade's greatest contribution.

During World War II Baade was classed as an enemy alien. (Although he applied for American citizenship, the papers were lost in a move, and with characteristic scorn for bureaucracy, he never completed the naturalization.) He was nevertheless allowed to observe on Mount Wilson and, aided by the darkened skies associated with the Los Angeles blackout, continued his studies of the hitherto unresolved nuclear regions of the nearby galaxies in Andromeda. By choosing only the best nights, paying fastidious attention to the focus of the 100-inch telescope (which varied with temperature throughout the night), and by using specially sensitized red plates, he finally distinguished individual stars in the center of the Andromeda nebula and its companions.

The resolution of these galaxies into stars provided a key to the differing types of components of spiral galaxies on one hand, and elliptical galaxies and globular clusters on the other. Baade conceived of two discrete populations: Type I, characterized by the young, blue stars in the dusty arms of spiral galaxies; and Type II,

defined by the older, fainter red stars of ellipticals as well as in the nuclear regions of the spirals. The concept of stellar populations, although later considerably revised, proved remarkably fertile for the analysis of stellar systems.

Using the concept of stellar populations as a guide, Baade predicted the presence of cluster-type variable stars in parts of the Andromeda nebula, but they were too faint to be resolved with the 100-inch reflector on Mount Wilson. When the 200-inch Palomar telescope commenced operations in 1948, Baade resumed this research but soon realized (from the newly calibrated brightness of the red giant stars) that the cluster-type variables were still beyond his reach. This fact could be reconciled with other data only by recalibrating the scale of absolute luminosities of the cluster-type and of cepheid variable stars, a step that approximately doubled the accepted distance of virtually all the galaxies including the Andromeda nebula. Announced in 1952 at the International Astronomical Union, this result climaxed Baade's lengthy studies on the contents of stellar systems.

In the 1950's Baade and his longtime collaborator Rudolph Minkowski began a successful survey to identify the strongest radio sources with optical objects. Of particular importance were their identifications of the Cygnus A and Perseus A radio sources as distant galaxies, and Baade's demonstration that the light of the peculiar jet in the galaxy M87—identified with the radio source Virgo A—is strongly polarized. His detailed study of the polarization in the Crab nebula revealed the intricate structure of the magnetic field and of the synchrotron radiation in an exploded object.

Baade published very sparingly, but he freely communicated his results to a steady stream of visitors. His exuberance, infectious enthusiasm, and delight in practical jokes made him an unforgettable character in the astronomical fraternity. In the fall of 1958, after his retirement, he gave a brilliant lecture course at Harvard; published posthumously as *Evolution of Stars and Galaxies* (1963), it records many of the observations and ideas that he never took time to publish. In 1959 Baade accepted the Gauss professorship in Göttingen, where he died.

[Sources include Allan R. Sandage's notice, *Quarterly Journal of the Royal Astronomical Society,* June 1961; Sally H. Dieke, *Dictionary of Scientific Biography*

(1970); O. Heckmann, *Mitteilungen der Astronomischen Gesellschaft* 1960 (Hamburg, 1961), 5–11, with portrait and bibliography; John Jackson, "The President's Address on the Award of the Gold Medal to Dr. Walter Baade," *Monthly Notices of the Royal Astronomical Society,* 114 (1954), 370–383; and the obituary notice in the *New York Times,* June 28, 1960.]

OWEN GINGERICH

BAKER, WALTER RANSOM GAIL (Nov. 30, 1892–Oct. 30, 1960), electrical engineer, was born in Lockport, N.Y., the son of Ermin H. Baker, a merchant, and Mary Anna Keck. Baker worked as a telephone clerk before enrolling at Union College in Schenectady, N.Y., where he studied electrical engineering. He was awarded the B.E. in 1916 and the M.E.E. in 1919. Baker was persuaded by Charles A. Hoxie to decline a job with the telephone company and instead to go to work for the General Electric Company (GE). He joined the General Engineering Laboratory of GE in 1916 and was involved in the development and manufacture of radio apparatus for the Army Signal Corps and the navy during World War I. Baker married Naomi M. Longdyke on Aug. 30, 1919; they had no children.

In 1920 Baker became a member of the radio engineering department of GE, a position that involved him in the beginnings of the radio broadcasting industry. He was instrumental in the design of three of the first radio stations: WGY in Schenectady, KOA in Denver, and KGO in Oakland. During the early 1920's he wrote several technical papers describing radio transmitters manufactured at GE. In a paper presented at a meeting of the Institute of Radio Engineers (IRE) in 1923, Baker noted the dramatic growth of radio broadcasting since the war and listed the necessary characteristics of a transmitting station of the highest quality. He reported that GE had received 50,000 letters from listeners during the first twelve months of operation of WGY, and that its signal had been received as far away as Hawaii. In another paper published in 1922, Baker described experimental duplex (two-way) telephone experiments between a shore station and the S. S. *America.*

A significant change occurred in 1924 when Baker assumed administrative responsibility for radio products manufactured by GE. He remained in that capacity until 1929, when he was named to manage production of radio apparatus at the Radio Corporation of America (RCA) plant in Camden, N. J. He was promoted to a vice-president at RCA but returned to GE in 1935 as manager of the radio-television department in Bridgeport, Conn. He became a vice-president of GE in 1941. He was also selected as director of the engineering division of the Radio Manufacturers Association (RMA).

Baker played a major role in the advent of television. In an article published in 1939, he announced that television was "ready for public participation," and predicted that it would have a greater impact than radio. When the Federal Communications Commission (FCC) announced in May 1940 that commercialization of television would be permitted as soon as the industry could agree on necessary standards, Baker agreed to serve as chairman of the National Television System Committee (NTSC) to formulate standards. Nine panels were established with 168 experts from fifteen organizations, and a 600,000-word set of reports was produced by late 1940. The NTSC sent its final report to the FCC in March 1941, and its recommended standards were adopted in May. Commercial television was permitted after July 1, 1941.

Commercial television was delayed, however, by the outbreak of World War II. As head of the electronics division of GE, Baker helped expand the company's manufacturing facilities to cope with military needs for radio and radar systems. In 1943 he was named chairman of the Radio Technical Planning Board (RTPB), with a mandate to consider whether wartime technical developments would necessitate revision of the NTSC standards or frequency allocation. The RTPB followed the example of NTSC with thirteen panels comprising about 600 experts and arrived at what Baker characterized as a "democratic" set of recommendations.

In 1947 Baker was elected president of the IRE. In a speech the same year he reviewed the impact of broadcasting and credited it with having expanded the horizons of millions and having overcome barriers of distance, language, and custom. He felt that this achievement was largely due to the organized efforts of ordinary engineers rather than a few isolated geniuses.

In 1950 Baker was appointed chairman of a second NTSC committee to recommend standards for compatible color television. This committee required thirty-two months to complete its work—"an expenditure of effort unmatched by any industry technical committee in the peacetime history of this country." The FCC adopted the committee's recommendations and commercial broadcasting under the new standards was authorized after Jan. 22, 1954. Television station WRGB in Schenectady, named in honor of Baker, was used in one of the first experiments in broadcasting a program relayed from a remote location. Baker developed an interest in the educational potential of television and published a paper entitled "Educational Television—An Investment in the Future" in 1954. He argued that technological change had tended to overwhelm the American educational system and that television might be utilized to enhance retention because of its visual impact. Baker retired from GE in 1957 but remained active as vice-president of research at Syracuse University. He died in Syracuse, N.Y.

[A small collection of Baker's papers is located at the State Historical Society of Wisconsin. Baker's publications in *GE Review* include "Radio Communication," "Duplex Radio Telephone Transmitter With Special Reference to Tests on the S. S. *America*," and "Commercial Radio Telephone and Telegraph Transmitting Equipment," 25 (1922); "Radio Broadcasting Station WGY, General Electric Company, Schenectady, N.Y.," 26 (1923); "Television Now Ready for Public Participation," 42 (1939); "Planning Tomorrow's Electronic Highways," 50 (1947); and "Educational Television—An Investment in the Future," 57 (1954).

See also in *Proceedings of the IRE* "Commercial Radio Tube Transmitters," "Description of the General Electric Company's Broadcasting Station at Schenectady, N.Y.," 11 (1923); and "The Institute and the Radio Industry," 35 (1947); and the obituary notices in the *New York Times*, Oct. 31, 1960; and *Proceedings of the IRE*, 48 (1960).]

JAMES E. BRITTAIN

BALLANTINE, ARTHUR ATWOOD (Aug. 3, 1883–Oct. 10, 1960), corporate lawyer and Treasury official, was born in Oberlin, Ohio, the son of William Gay Ballantine, professor of Old Testament and later president of Oberlin College, and Emma Atwood. Ballantine graduated *summa cum laude* from Harvard College in 1904 and three years later took his law degree, also with honors, from the Harvard Law School. On June 19, 1907, he married Helen Bailey Graves; they had five children.

Ballantine joined the prestigious Boston firm of Gaston, Snow and Saltonstall in 1906 and became a junior partner six years later. He also taught part-time at the Harvard Law School and later at the Northeastern Law School. In 1914, with Joseph O. Procter and Robert E. Goodwin,

he established a new firm specializing in corporate matters. He entered his first government service as a "dollar-a-year man" in 1917, as a special advisor to the United States Commissioner of Internal Revenue on legal questions related to the war revenue measures. The following year he became solicitor of internal revenue, the Treasury Department's chief legal advisor on tax and revenue issues.

His work in that department, as well as his established legal reputation, brought him increasing corporate business after the war, and he found it necessary to leave Boston for New York in 1919. There he joined with other men he had known from law school days to form Root, Clark, Howland and Ballantine. Eventually he became senior partner in the successor firm, Dewey, Ballantine, Bushby, Palmer and Wood. At all times the firm devoted itself primarily to tax, corporate, and securities law.

During the 1920's Ballantine led a life typical of a successful Wall Street lawyer: membership in the right clubs, a country home at Oyster Bay on Long Island, directorships of large corporations and civic groups, and consultant positions on the tax committees of bar and business groups, including the United States Chamber of Commerce and the National Industrial Conference Board. He did little government work other than serving in 1927 as an advisor to the Joint Congressional Committee on Internal Revenue Taxation.

In 1931 President Herbert Hoover named Ballantine assistant secretary of the Treasury, and the following year he became undersecretary. It was a crucial position during the Great Depression, and few political appointees had as much knowledge of their fields as Ballantine did. Although, like Hoover, he favored reducing federal expenses, unlike the president Ballantine recognized the need for the government to take a more positive role in relief as well as to use federal influence and resources to shore up the economic system. He helped organize the Reconstruction Finance Corporation and was one of its first directors. As undersecretary of the treasury, he oversaw the spending of $700 million in government funds on federal building projects.

When the banking crisis reached its peak during the 1932–1933 interregnum, Ballantine found himself one of the key government officials. In February 1933 he led the team that tried to negotiate private loans and guarantees to keep open the Union Guardian Trust Company of

Detroit. When these talks collapsed, mainly due to Henry Ford's antagonism to both private banks and the national government, Ballantine worked with Michigan Governor William A. Comstock to arrange the statewide banking moratorium, a precursor to the national banking holiday that ushered in Franklin D. Roosevelt's administration.

Ballantine and Roosevelt had been classmates at Harvard; Ballantine was editor of *The Crimson* when Roosevelt had been a member of the staff. Ballantine assisted William Woodin, secretary of the treasury designate, and presidential counsel Raymond Moley, and agreed to stay on at the Treasury to help the new appointees during this critical period. Both Woodin and Moley later praised Ballantine, who served as liaison between the Hoover and Roosevelt administrations, for his "patriotism" and "indispensable" contributions.

Ballantine had been urging a banking moratorium for some time, and Roosevelt's understanding and acceptance of the idea gratified him. It was Ballantine who drafted the president's fireside chat of Mar. 12, 1933, which explained the banking holiday to the American people and did much to restore public confidence.

Ballantine stayed in office through May 1933 and devised the plan for reopening America's banks. But from the beginning he opposed New Deal programs based on deficit financing and large-scale government spending. He returned to New York and resumed his law practice, not to reenter government service until World War II. In June 1943, Secretary of the Navy Frank Knox appointed him to prepare a report on the organization, methods, and procedures of naval courts. In April 1946, Secretary of the Navy James V. Forrestal named him senior member of a board to update and implement naval court reform. For this work he received the Distinguished Public Service Certificate of Award from the navy in 1948.

After the war, Ballantine's law practice prospered, especially after former New York governor and Republican presidential candidate Thomas E. Dewey accepted his invitation in 1955 to join the firm. Popular and sociable, Ballantine had an inexhaustible store of Down East stories. In the words of a friend, "he skated well and played golf just well enough to be very popular." He died in New York City.

[On Ballantine and his career, see Harvard College Class of 1900, *Twenty-fifth Anniversary Report*

(1925) and *Fiftieth Anniversary Report* (1950); Arthur A. Ballantine, "When All the Banks Closed," *Harvard Business Review,* March 1948; *New York Times,* Oct. 12, 1960; Association of the Bar of the City of New York, *Memorial Book* 1961; and Susan Estabrook Kennedy, *The Banking Crisis of 1933* (1973).]

MELVIN I. UROFSKY

BARKLEY, ALBEN WILLIAM (Nov. 24, 1877–Apr. 30, 1956), U.S. representative, senator, and vice-president, was born in a log cabin near Lowes, Ky., the son of John Wilson Barkley, an impoverished tobacco farmer, and Electra A. Smith. He rose to prominence in a manner that exemplified the American success ethic. As a boy he combined his schooling with hard farm labor; after graduation from high school, he worked his way through Marvin College (B.A., 1897) and spent a year studying law at Emory College (1897–98). Most of his legal education was the product of reading and observation in the offices of prominent Paducah, Ky., attorneys for whom he worked. Admitted to the Kentucky bar in 1901, he still felt it necessary to spend a summer at the University of Virginia Law School in 1902. On June 23, 1903, he married Dorothy Brower; they had three children.

The young lawyer soon turned to politics. He was a first-rate speaker and a gregarious, energetic campaigner. In 1905 he was elected prosecuting attorney of McCracken County, Ky. Four years later he won office as county judge, essentially an administrative position in which his chief accomplishment was improvement of the rural roads. In 1912 he was elected to the House of Representatives as a Democrat.

As a congressman Barkley reflected the interests and aspirations of the rural progressive wing of the early twentieth-century Democratic party. He quickly became a follower of Woodrow Wilson, whom he described in 1954 as "the greatest statesman and greatest President under whom I ever served." A down-the-line supporter of the New Freedom, he was especially active in working for rural credit and highway aid measures. He was an equally strong backer of the president's foreign policy, including the decision for war in 1917, the subsequent Treaty of Versailles, and the League of Nations. His faith in Wilsonian internationalism remained steadfast for the rest of his life.

Barkley was, however, no ideologue. Above all a professional politician whose career rested upon his ability to persuade his constituency to elect him to office, he was willing to adjust his positions on specific issues. Like many rural progressives he supported prohibition, although he was personally skeptical of the dry crusade. As he recalled it, he strictly observed the Eighteenth Amendment, but he was happy enough to advocate its repeal in 1932 after national sentiment had swung against it. Like all good Wilsonians he was a low-tariff man, but he voted for high duties on coal, one of his state's most important products. After he sustained his only electoral defeat—a 1923 candidacy for governor of Kentucky—partly because he had offended powerful interests by advocating a tax on coal production, he reversed his position.

When Barkley was elected to the Senate in 1926 he was already something of a national figure. He had served as acting chairman during much of the 1924 Democratic convention, the first to be nationally broadcast. In 1928 a group of supporters unsuccessfully promoted him for the vice-presidency. Both before and after the 1928 convention he supported Alfred E. Smith; he was capable of bucking the prejudices of his constituents if he felt the issue was important enough. In 1932 he was one of the leading preconvention supporters of Franklin D. Roosevelt, who secured his designation as convention keynoter. Thereafter he was a major speaker at every Democratic convention through 1952, and he delivered keynote speeches again in 1936 and 1948. Later generations might find his addresses excessively partisan and bombastic; committed Democrats at the time found them both inspiring and entertaining. As a political orator, Barkley had few peers.

Easily reelected to the Senate in 1932, Barkley established himself as one of the most prominent supporters of Roosevelt and the New Deal. Democratic majority leader Joseph Robinson appointed him assistant majority leader in 1933. After Robinson's death in 1937 Barkley ran to succeed him. Aided by intensive White House support, he defeated Mississippi Senator Pat Harrison by one vote. Facing a serious primary challenge from Kentucky governor A. B. ("Happy") Chandler in 1938, he once again got strong backing from the administration. A small scandal surfaced when investigative reporters discovered that Works Progress Administration workers had been pressured to donate to the Barkley campaign, but the senator won rather handily.

Barkley's performance as majority leader drew mixed evaluations. Robinson had been one of the strongest leaders in the history of the Senate, and Barkley succeeded him just as the conservative coalition was beginning its twenty-five year dominance of the Congress. He not only faced difficulty with the Republicans but also suffered frequent obstruction from powerful members of his own party. He appears to have seen his job as one of conciliation between the conservatives on Capitol Hill and the militant New Dealers who formulated the White House legislative program.

Barkley's own policy positions were predominantly liberal, even to the extent of supporting civil rights legislation, but he usually counseled acceptance of whatever compromises could be put through the legislative process. Frequently criticized as weak and ineffective, he was nonetheless capable of ordering the Senate sergeant at arms to "arrest" absent members in November 1942, in an effort to compel their attendance to break a filibuster. The following year he defeated a conservative attempt to limit his powers. Unlike Robinson, Barkley retained his regular committee assignments and carried a heavy legislative workload on top of his leadership duties. But his record was ambiguous because his name was never attached to a major bill, although he was involved in every important congressional issue of his time.

After the outbreak of World War II in Europe, Barkley backed Roosevelt's program of aid to the anti-Axis forces. As permanent chairman of the 1940 Democratic convention, he presided over Roosevelt's third-term nomination. After Pearl Harbor he was especially vocal in support of a new international organization and of a Jewish homeland in Palestine. (Louis Brandeis had persuaded him of the merits of Zionism years earlier.)

The war years were personally and politically difficult. His wife, ill with heart disease, became an invalid requiring constant nursing care, and the senator had to supplement his salary with speaking fees; until Dorothy Barkley's death, on Mar. 10, 1947, he combined his congressional duties with an exhausting lecture schedule. Other disappointments came from the White House—Roosevelt passed him over for a Supreme Court vacancy in 1943 and for the vice-presidential nomination in 1944. The political rift between the president and Congress widened and made the Senate majority leader's position increasingly uncomfortable. In February 1944

Roosevelt issued a stinging veto of a revenue bill that Barkley had advised him to approve. The Kentuckian denounced the veto, resigned as majority leader, and was promptly reelected by fellow Democrats. The president quickly repaired their relationship, and a few months later at the Democratic convention Barkley placed Roosevelt's name in nomination for a fourth term.

Barkley was friendly with Roosevelt's successor, but Harry S. Truman appears to have considered the Kentucky senator a man of limited capabilities. After the Republicans gained control of Congress in the 1946 elections, Barkley, now Senate minority leader, was rarely asked to consult with the White House on legislative tactics. Truman dealt with other senators on foreign policy. Having no hope that the conservative Congress would pass his liberal domestic program, Truman requested it only to build a platform for the 1948 campaign. Barkley privately compared himself to a catcher in a night baseball game: he never knew what the pitcher was going to throw and the lights went out every time the ball was released. Nevertheless, after Supreme Court Justice William O. Douglas had turned the offer down, Truman selected Barkley as his vice-presidential running mate in 1948.

Barkley's vice-presidency (1949–53) was an active one. He lobbied for administration programs and was included in the decision-making process, but inevitably his major function was as an administration publicist and purveyor of goodwill, a role he handled well. He became known as the "Veep"—a title coined by his ten-year-old grandson. His personal life brightened considerably after his marriage on Nov. 18, 1949, to Jane Rucker Hadley, a Saint Louis widow some thirty years his junior. In 1952 he sought the Democratic presidential nomination. The outgoing Truman extended lukewarm support, but Barkley's advanced age cost him the backing of other key party leaders, and he withdrew.

After a brief semiretirement, Barkley was reelected to the Senate in 1954, defeating John Sherman Cooper. No longer a leader, he was considered a beloved elder statesman. He died of a heart attack while speaking to students at Washington and Lee College in Lexington, Va. For all his accomplishments, Barkley was perhaps best remembered as one of the last of the old-fashioned political orators. A friend, upon hearing the circumstances of his death, remarked fondly: "It is the way he would have wanted to go. He never could turn down a crowd."

[Barkley's papers are at the University of Kentucky. His only published memoir, *That Reminds Me* (1954), is based on a series of interviews with journalist Sidney Shalett. His wife describes their marriage in Jane R. Barkley (as told to Frances Spatz Leighton), *I Married the Veep* (1958). There is no biography; the most satisfactory treatment is Polly Ann Davis, "Alben W. Barkley: Senate Majority Leader and Vice-President" (Ph.D. diss., University of Kentucky, 1963).

See also C. A. Leistner, "The Political Campaign Speaking of Alben W. Barkley" (Ph.D. diss., University of Missouri, 1958); Glenn Finch, "The Election of United States Senators in Kentucky: The Barkley Period," *Filson Club Historical Quarterly*, 45 (July 1971); John H. Hatcher, "Alben Barkley, Politics in Relief and the Hatch Act," *ibid.*, 40 (July 1966); J. B. Shannon, "Alben W. Barkley: 'Reservoir of Energy,'" in J. T. Salter, ed., *Public Men In and Out of Office* (1946); and the obituary notice in the *New York Times*, May 1, 1956.]

ALONZO L. HAMBY

BARNES, JULIUS HOWLAND (Feb. 2, 1873–Apr. 17, 1959), industrialist and government adviser, was born in Little Rock, Ark., the son of Lucien Jerome Barnes, a banker, and Julia M. Hill. In 1883 the family settled in Duluth, Minn. Midway through Barnes's freshman year in high school his father died, and he left school to work as an office boy in the wheat brokerage firm of Wardell Ames. He steadily advanced in the company, which was one of the nation's largest wheat exporters, and on Ames's death in 1910 assumed the presidency. In 1914 he attained control of the firm and renamed it the Barnes-Ames Company. Barnes specialized in export trade and developed a solid knowledge of transportation systems.

The outbreak of World War I disrupted European trade routes and seriously threatened wheat trade. Large exporters on the Council of Grain Exchange accepted Barnes's plan to transact business collectively during the war, and Barnes was chairman of a council committee to handle exporting. Once the United States became involved in the conflict, Herbert Hoover, head of the newly formed Food Administration, impressed by Barnes's handling of the wheat problem, invited him to supervise the administration's Cereal Division through the Grain Corporation. Barnes accepted, and immediately divested himself of his grain interests. He did, however, retain presidency of the McDougall Shipbuilding Company of Duluth, which constructed vessels for Great Lakes traffic.

The Food Administration helped stimulate

the domestic production of foodstuffs and then distributed them overseas. Barnes believed this could best be accomplished through private management rather than government regulation. The government initially capitalized the Grain Corporation at $50 million and owned all the stock. The Corporation then formed agreements with producers to buy wheat at an established price, thereby ensuring stability and eliminating speculation.

In November 1918 the Food Administration became the American Relief Administration (ARA)—the American instrument for economic reconstruction and food distribution in Europe. The Grain Corporation became the United States Grain Corporation and acted as the ARA's purchasing agent. Barnes resigned from the presidency in June 1920 to return to private business. He reacquired the Barnes-Ames Company and also became president of Intercontinental Development Corporation. Another company, Klearflax Linen Looms, which Barnes served as board chairman, began to profit from his earlier invention of a procedure for manufacturing linen rugs from formerly discarded flax straw.

In 1920 Barnes took his first and only step into politics. He strongly admired Hoover and became one of a group of advisers who encouraged him to seek the Republican party presidential nomination. Barnes and other investors bought the *Washington Herald* to further Hoover's candidacy. Barnes also acted as Hoover's unofficial floor manager at the Republican National Convention. All these efforts proved futile, however, and Barnes developed little influence within the party power structure.

Throughout the 1920's Barnes devoted much attention to his business interests. In May 1922 he became president of the United States Chamber of Commerce. He served for two years, remaining on the board of directors until 1931. He was an ardent propagandist for the free enterprise system, extolling through speeches and articles the virtues of individualism and the business ethic. He shocked many in the corporate world by urging the hiring of "unemployables"—the chronically unemployed who many businessmen thought to be incapable of sustained employment—who demonstrated a willingness to work.

Economic realities of the early Great Depression days, however, doomed Barnes's plans. He lost more than $2 million in the October 1929 stock market crash. One month later President Hoover asked Barnes to head the newly created National Business Survey Conference, composed of key industrial leaders. The conference, which Hoover hoped would restore confidence in the business community, concluded that stimulation of the construction industry through increased private spending and voluntary agreements among trade associations would promote economic recovery. But it had no real authority, and could only attempt to reassure the public with periodic statistical reports purporting to show that prosperity was just around the corner. In his speeches and articles Barnes presented an optimistic view of the economy, but his viewpoint became untenable as the depression deepened. The conference was finally dissolved on May 6, 1931.

During the next decade Barnes increasingly turned his attention to his shipbuilding interests. As early as 1905 he had begun a crusade for a navigable water route connecting the Great Lakes with the Atlantic via the Saint Lawrence River. Such a waterway, he believed, would be an asset to the region and would help secure the nation's defenses. Barnes and a succession of lobbying groups emphasized these arguments, but encountered stiff opposition from railroad and Atlantic coast interests. From 1944 to 1948 he served as president of the National Saint Lawrence Association and testified numerous times before congressional committees. In May 1959, one month after Barnes's death, the Saint Lawrence Seaway was opened.

On June 30, 1896, Barnes married Harriet Carey; they had two children. Barnes devoted much time to his family and philanthropic interests. He sponsored the Duluth Boat Club and donated a natatorium to the Duluth Y.M.C.A. These philanthropies and money spent on the Saint Lawrence campaign exhausted his fortune, and he left only a $52,000 estate. He died in Duluth, Minn.

[The largest collection of Barnes's papers is at the Saint Louis County Historical Society in Duluth, Minn. The Herbert Hoover Presidential Library and the Hoover Institute at Stanford also have substantial materials. Barnes's correspondence during his years in the Food Administration are in the U.S. Grain Corporation records at the National Archives.

See also Gary Best, *The Politics of American Individualism: Herbert Hoover in Transition, 1918–1921* (1975); Carlton Mabee, *The Seaway Story* (1961); William C. Mullendore, *History of the U.S. Food Administration* (1941); Albert U. Romasco, *The*

Poverty of Abundance (1965); Frank M. Surface, *The Grain Trade During the World War* (1928); and the obituary notice in the *New York Times*, Apr. 18, 1959.]

CHARLES C. HAY III

BARRYMORE, ETHEL (Aug. 15, 1879–June 18, 1959), actress, was born in Philadelphia, Pa., the daughter of Maurice Barrymore and Georgiana Drew. Her father, whose real name was Herbert Blythe, was a matinee idol and "Beau Brummel" of his day; her mother was the sister of the noted actor John Drew, Jr. Barrymore's brothers, Lionel and John, also became leading theatrical and film stars. Barrymore began acting almost as soon as she could talk, performing *Camille* and other plays with her brothers in an old barn. She attended the Academy of Notre Dame, a convent school in Philadelphia, until 1894, when she joined her grandmother, Mrs. John Drew, who was touring Canada in *The Rivals*. Barrymore made her professional debut in this play in the minor role of Julia. She received her first important opportunity as Kate Fennell in *The Bauble Shop* (1894), written by her uncle, John Drew, and produced by Charles Frohman.

During the next few years, Barrymore gradually began to attract favorable attention. After appearing in New York City in a one-line role in Drew's *That Imprudent Young Couple* (1895), she made her London debut in *Secret Service* (1897) and toured in Henry Irving's melodrama, *The Bells* (1897). In 1901 Frohman engaged her for the starring role of Madame Trentoni in his New York production of Clyde Fitch's *Captain Jinks of the Horse Marines*. The public took Barrymore to heart, and a week after the play opened she rounded the corner to the theater to find her name in lights.

Other starring roles followed in a double bill of *A Country Mouse* and *Carrots* (1903), *Cousin Kate* (1903), and *Sunday* (1904), in which play, amid thunderous applause, Barrymore delivered the memorable line: "That's all there is, there isn't any more." She also played Mrs. Grey in James M. Barrie's *Alice Sit-by-the-Fire* (1905), Nora in Henrik Ibsen's *A Doll's House* (1905), and the leading role in W. Somerset Maugham's *Lady Frederick* (1908). By 1910 Barrymore had become a romantic idol, whose walk and plaintive, haunting voice were being imitated by women everywhere.

On Mar. 14, 1909, following rumors of her engagement to various men, Barrymore married Russell Griswold Colt, the son of the president of the United States Rubber Company. They had three children. After numerous separations and reconciliations, they were divorced in 1923.

Between 1914 and 1918 Barrymore appeared in thirteen films, having signed with Metro Pictures Corporation in 1915 to make four movies a year; she despised all but one, *The Awakening of Helen Ritchie* (1916). Returning to the stage, she starred in such drawing-room comedies as Zoë Akins' *Déclassée* (1919), in which she achieved one of her greatest successes, and in Maugham's *The Constant Wife* (1926), which she often performed in summer theaters. Other roles in her broad repertory included the somber peasant in Gerhart Hauptmann's *Rose Bernd* (1922) and a nun in G. Martínez Sierra's *The Kingdom of God* (1928), the play with which she opened the Broadway theater named for her and built by impresarios J. J., Lee, and Sam Shubert. Her many Shakespearean roles included Juliet in the Arthur Hopkins production (1922). In 1932 she returned to Hollywood to star with her brothers in *Rasputin and the Empress*—the only work in which the three Barrymores appeared together.

Having decided that the stage was entering a phase of atrophy, Barrymore announced her retirement on the Ben Bernie radio program in August 1936. But a year later she returned to Broadway in the Theater Guild production of Sidney Howard's *The Ghost of Yankee Doodle*. A series of rather flimsy vehicles followed, including *Whiteoaks* (1938) and *Farm of Three Echoes* (1939), in which she played aged but still vigorous characters, and Vincent Sheean's *International Incident* (1940). Finally, in Emlyn Williams' *The Corn Is Green* (1940), Barrymore was given a drama of substance and achieved one of her greatest triumphs in the impressive role of Miss Moffat, a Welsh schoolteacher. While on tour in the play she was persuaded to appear as a frumpy cockney with Cary Grant in *None But the Lonely Heart* (1944), adapted and directed by Clifford Odets. She received an Academy Award in 1944 for her portrayal.

Following her last Broadway appearance, in *Embezzled Heaven* (1944), Barrymore played in some of her better films—*Portrait of Jennie* (1949), *Pinky* (1949), *Kind Lady* (1951), *Young at Heart* (1954), and *Johnny Trouble* (1956), her last movie. Beginning in 1952 she made several television appearances and in 1956 was hostess of her own series, "The Ethel Barrymore Theater."

Barrymore was described by critic Harold

Clurman as possessing a naturally regal quality. Her classical profile and throaty, vibrant voice captivated audiences for over half a century. As an admirer once noted, her voice not only produced rich sounds, it echoed a wealth of experience. Critics have written of weeping from beginning to end of a play in which Barrymore appeared, completely forgetting to follow the plot. Barrymore's versatility as an actress enabled her to hold a central place in the hearts of theatergoers long after she had moved from glamorous roles to mature characterizations.

She died in Hollywood, Calif.

[On Barrymore and her career, see Isaac F. Marcosson and Daniel Frohman, *Charles Frohman* (1916); John Drew, *My Years on the Stage* (1922); John Barrymore, *Confessions of an Actor* (1926); Gene Fowler, *Good Night, Sweet Prince* (1944); Lionel Barrymore, *We Barrymores* (1951); Ethel Barrymore's autobiography, *Memories* (1955); Hollis Alpert, *The Barrymores* (1964); George Freedley and John A. Reeves, *A History of the Theatre* (1968); and Evelyn Mack Truitt, *Who Was Who on Screen* (1974). Other sources include interviews in the *New York Times*, Dec. 22, 1940, and Feb. 5, 1941; and obituary notices in the *New York Times* and *Chicago Daily Tribune*, June 19, 1959.]

L. MOODY SIMMS, JR.

BAUM, HEDWIG ("VICKI") (Jan. 24, 1888–Aug. 29, 1960), novelist, was born in Vienna, Austria, the only child of Herman Baum and Mathilde Donat. She was named Hedwig but called Vicki for Victor because her father wanted a boy. Although her family provided the creature comforts of a Jewish bourgeois home, her early life was oppressive. Her mother was institutionalized as a psychotic for much of Vicki's childhood; her father, a cold, overbearing bookkeeper, frequently returned to his parents' home. Vicki escaped into her own world of fantasy and read voraciously—at the risk of constant recrimination from her father. In her autobiography she recalled her childhood as "a hell too hot to bear."

Baum attended grammar school in Vienna and studied the harp at the Vienna Konservatorium from 1904 to 1910, making her first concert appearance at eleven. Her life revolved around an intimate group of young intellectuals who frequented the coffeehouses of Vienna, and her career as harpist centered at the Deutsches Theater and at the Vienna Konzert Verein (later the Vienna Symphony Orchestra). She also taught at the musical high school in Darmstadt, Germany.

In 1906 she married Max Prels, a poet. They enjoyed a casual Bohemian life, but constant financial troubles and the strain of launching an unsuccessful literary magazine ended the marriage four years later. During this period she published several short stories under her husband's name in *Monatshefte*, a popular German magazine. When she was only in her teens, she had published a short story under a *nom de plume* in *Muskete* ("The Musket"), a Viennese humorous weekly.

On July 17, 1916, at the height of her musical career, she married Richard Johannes Lert, conductor of the orchestra she played with in Darmstadt. The Lerts led a nomadic life, because of her husband's musical positions in Kiel, Hanover, Mannheim, and Berlin. She gave up her musical career to raise two sons and often wrote late at night while they slept.

During World War I two Baum books were published by Erich Reiss. One was the story of her childhood, *Frühe Schatten* ("Early Shadows," 1919), a partial attempt at self-analysis. Verlag Ullstein of Berlin published her first novel in paperback, *Der Eingang zur Bühne* ("Stage Entrance"), in 1920. She received 5,000 marks and first prize in a contest for *Der Weg* ("The Road," 1925); one of the judges was Thomas Mann. From 1926 to 1931 she edited magazines issued by Ullstein, the largest publishing house in Germany, and also contributed to Ullstein periodicals, including *Dame,* a woman's magazine similar to *Vogue*. Some of her early novels appeared in these magazines in serialized form.

After a fourteen-hour day of editing, Baum wrote late at night in quiet and solitude. At the time, Berlin was a city of intellectual ferment and cultural and political diversity. These were the "happiest, most interesting and most fruitful years" of her life. Her novel *Stud. chem. Helene Willfüer* ("Helen Willfur, Chemistry Student"), published in 1928, was the story of an innocent young girl's struggle in amoral Berlin of the 1920's and was adapted for the screen.

Baum's best-known novel, *Menschen im Hotel* ("Grand Hotel," 1929), was written in six weeks and first appeared in installments in the *Berliner Illustrierte Zeitung*. An immediate success, it was soon dramatized and initially produced under Max Reinhardt's auspices at the Theater am Nollendorfplatz in Berlin in 1929. Translated into English as *Grand Hotel,* it was a best-seller in the United States and a Book-of-the-Month Club selection. In November 1930 the play began a thirteen-month run in New York at the National Theater, grossing more than one million dollars. As a movie (1932) it starred Greta Garbo, Joan Crawford, John and Lionel Barrymore, Wallace Beery, and Jean Hersholt. Later it inspired the Hollywood musical *Weekend at the Waldorf* (1945) as well as the stage musical *At the Grand* (1958) starring Paul Muni.

At the height of her career Baum came to see a Broadway performance of *Grand Hotel.* She and her family soon moved to southern California, where she wrote film scripts for various movie companies, including Paramount and Metro-Goldwyn-Mayer, in addition to two unsuccessful Broadway plays, *Divine Drudge* (1933) and *Summer Night* (1939). Her husband became conductor of the Pasadena Symphony Orchestra. However, she considered her Hollywood screen writing a failure. In 1938 she became an American citizen. She died of leukemia in Hollywood, Calif.

Although Baum wrote approximately thirty novels, her reputation is based mainly on *Grand Hotel,* which greatly influenced other writers of the period. Within the setting of an elegant Berlin hotel, such diverse characters as an aging Russian ballet dancer (inspired by Pavlova), a nondescript, provincial clerk with a fatal illness, and a baron turned jewel thief were woven together, surrounded by the glamor and intrigue of the hotel.

Typical of her literary output in general, *Grand Hotel* displayed her gift for storytelling and her sentimental and uncomplicated style. Well aware that critics found her writing flamboyant, overblown, even banal and superficial, she once described herself as "a first-rate second-rate author." Nevertheless, her combination of romantic characters, exotic situations, and fast-moving plots provided readable, entertaining escape literature in an age dominated by the harsh realities of the Great Depression and World War II.

In an effort to free herself from the stigma of the reputation as the "girl who wrote the Grand Hotel" she sent a manuscript of *The Mustard Seed* (1953) to a publisher under a pseudonym. Considerably different from her other novels, this book about a faith healer in California discussed current social problems, including drug abuse, alcoholism, homosexuality, and neuroses.

Small and slight, Baum weighed less than one hundred pounds. She dressed stylishly, neither smoked nor drank, but loved to dance. Next to her family, gardening was her greatest joy.

[Written in German and translated into English, Baum's novels include *And Life Goes On* (1931); *Falling Star* (1934); *Men Never Know* (1935); *A Tale From Bali* (1937); *Shanghai '37* (1939); *The Ship and the Shore* (1941); *Marion Alive* (1942); *The Weeping Wood* (1943); *Hotel Berlin '43* (1944); *Headless Angel* (1948); *Danger From Deer* (1951); *Written on Water* (1956); and *Theme for Ballet* (1958). On her life and work, see "My Own Little Story," *Pictorial Review,* Sept. 1931; "I Discover America," *Good Housekeeping,* July 1932; Stanley J. Kunitz, ed., *Authors Today and Yesterday* (1933); Leonora W. Armsby, *Musicians Talk* (1935); *New York Times Book Review,* Oct. 11, 1953, p. 33; and *It Was All Quite Different* (1964), her memoirs.]

MARY SUE DILLIARD SCHUSKY

BEARD, MARY RITTER (Aug. 5, 1876–Aug. 14, 1958), historian and author, was born in Indianapolis, Ind., the daughter of Eli Foster Ritter, a Quaker turned Civil War colonel, and Narcissa Smith Lockwood. An intense, stubborn man, her father was a lawyer, a temperance advocate, and a founder of the First United Methodist Church of Indianapolis; her mother brought to the marriage the status of one of the major families of central Indiana.

Mary Ritter graduated from DePauw University in 1897. (Her father, her four brothers and her younger sister all attended DePauw.) She taught German briefly and in 1900 married a college friend, Charles Austin Beard. They went to England, where she was captivated by the excitement surrounding Ruskin Hall, a workingman's school Charles Beard helped to found in Oxford. During this time she worked closely with Emmeline Pankhurst and other militant suffragists.

When the Beards returned to the United States in 1902 they enrolled in graduate school at Columbia University. Charles Beard went on to receive a Ph.D., teach political science at Columbia, and launch his long and successful career. Mary Beard withdrew from graduate school, had two children, and threw herself into political activity. She became secretary of the legislative committee of the Women's Trade Union League of New York. A devoted suffragist, she edited *The Woman Voter,* a journal of the Woman Suffrage League of New York, organized Emmeline Pankhurst's visit to the United States, and helped put together the contingent of black women in the protest march in Washington, D.C., in 1913. According to her daughter, she soon had a reputation in the Columbia University community "at least as scandalous as that of her combative husband." In later years she made a strenuous effort to establish a world center for women's archives; she published and tried to initiate what would have been the first women's studies program in an American college; she established a group project to rewrite the *Encyclopaedia Britannica* from a feminist perspective; and she lectured widely and gave two nationwide broadcasts on the subject of women's history.

Above all Beard was a productive scholar and historian. She and her husband collaborated on eight books, including the influential two-volume *The Rise of American Civilization* (1927) and *The Basic History of the United States* (1944), which Charles Beard described as "our last will and testament to the American people." Alone she wrote six books and edited one; she coauthored another on women's humor. Except for two books, including *A Short History of the American Labor Movement* (1920), her more than forty years of productive work was devoted to analyzing the role of women in history.

From the appearance of *Woman's Work in Municipalities* (1915), to her most famous book, *Woman As Force in History* (1946), certain themes persisted. In her early activist years, she associated in England and the United States with the most radical wing of the woman's movement. She worked closely with Alice Paul in organizing the Congressional Union and later the Woman's Party. When she turned from activist to social analyst, her work became even more radical. She audaciously placed woman at the center of history and society and then insisted that the world look again from this perspective.

The core of everything Beard wrote and did was the conviction that women were a powerful force in the creation of civilization and culture and that history and politics were incomplete without that recognition. She devoted her life to trying to persuade women of their own vital historic past and their power to change the present. It was a crusade for women's minds, and it took many forms. In her long and serious books she tried to demonstrate, theoretically and historically, how false and tyrannical was the assertion that women throughout history have been a subject group. Her imaginative fifty-page syllabus for a women's

studies program, issued in 1934, offered a creative alternative to traditional education. Published by the American Association of University Women, it is not an "extension to women of men's education" because that "education is so rigid, so scholastic . . . that to parallel it with the same woman's education of herself . . . would count for very little." It is because women "enjoy the liberties of the disinherited" that their vision can be bold and new. In her writings on women's education, Beard argued against reliance on men for "ideological management." Women must take education, she insisted, and "socialize it . . . by stretching it beyond the privileged and idle services of a class . . . to make it . . . an agent of humanitarian evolution." Beard's five-year struggle to establish an international Women's Archive, an effort of awesome magnitude, was aimed at demonstrating the existence and force of a collective woman's world.

Beard's vigorous criticism of militant feminists stemmed from her belief that feminists should use their energies to create a better and more humane society, and not settle for an equal share in this one. Without support from the woman's movement, without a body of ideas upon which to build, without models of any kind to follow, alone, she boldly insisted upon the truth of her woman-centered view of history and her radical vision of a world where "enduring humanity" would prevail.

Charles and Mary Beard lived in New York City and in New Milford, Conn., dividing their time between an active social and intellectual life and their demanding work. Mary Beard's most productive years did not occur until her children were grown. After her husband's death in 1948, she continued writing. In 1955, at the age of seventy-nine, she published a lengthy essay, *The Making of Charles A. Beard*. She died in Scottsdale, Ariz.

[In addition to the works cited in the text, Beard wrote *On Understanding Women* (1931); *A Changing Political Economy As It Affects Women* (1934); and *The Force of Women in Japanese History* (1953). She collaborated with Charles A. Beard on *American Citizenship* (1914) and with Martha B. Bruère on *Laughing Their Way: Women's Humor in America* (1934); she edited *America Through Women's Eyes* (1933).

The DePauw University Library has a file, assembled by Charles and Mary Beard's children, Miriam Beard Vagts and William Beard, that contains speeches, newspaper clippings, articles, photographs, and data on the family. Articles and correspondence can be found in the Radcliffe College Library, which also holds transcripts of her two broadcasts—"The Woman—The Pioneer" and "What Nobody Seems To Know About Women"—and in the Sophia Smith Collection at Smith College. See also the obituary in the *New York Times*, Aug. 15, 1958.]

ANN J. LANE

BECHET, SIDNEY (May 14, 1897–May 14, 1959), musician, was born in New Orleans, La., the son of Omer Bechet, a shoemaker, and Josephine Mitchell. His paternal grandparents were slaves who had assumed their owner's surname. One of Bechet's brothers gave him his first clarinet, which he soon taught himself to play well enough to improvise alongside such renowned jazz trumpet players as Manuel Perez and Freddie Keppard. George Baquet, a clarinetist, heard him playing on the street and gave him lessons. But Bechet never learned to read music and retained the unorthodox fingering that he had devised. He later received further training from two other New Orleans clarinetists, Louis ("Big Eye") Nelson and Lorenzo Tio. After substituting for George Baquet and working in his brother Leonard's band, he gained enough of a reputation to play in some of the most popular dance and marching bands in New Orleans, including those of Jack Carey, Bunk Johnson, John Robichaux, Buddie Petit, and Henry Allen, Sr.

In 1914 Bechet left New Orleans in a traveling show along with the pianist and composer Clarence Williams. During the same year, he joined a touring carnival in Texas. After a few brief engagements in his hometown, including one with Joe ("King") Oliver, he left New Orleans for good in 1917 with another road show, arriving in Chicago later that year. There he worked with Lawrence Dehé, Joe Oliver, Freddie Keppard, and pianist Tony Jackson. For a short time he experimented with a curved soprano saxophone. Next, Bechet went to New York as a member of Will Marion Cook's Southern Syncopated Orchestra. The band toured Europe in June 1919. Bechet reputedly played before King George V, and he certainly scored a considerable personal success in London. It was there that he was heard at a concert in the Royal Philharmonic Hall by the Swiss conductor Ernest Ansermet, who called him an "artist of genius." Soon afterward Bechet bought his first straight soprano saxophone, which rapidly became his preferred instrument. In 1920 he worked in drummer Benny Peyton's band at two London clubs and at the Hammersmith Palais

de Danse, a popular ballroom, in between engagements in Paris with the Southern Syncopated Orchestra. Having been accused of rape by a prostitute—the charge was later dismissed—he nevertheless was deported from England in 1921 after what, in his own account, appears to have been a miscarriage of justice. Back in New York, he worked with the bands of Ford Dabney, Duke Ellington, and James P. Johnson, as well as with singer Mamie Smith. Ellington, who had heard him earlier in Washington, admired Bechet's "woody" clarinet tone and described him as "one of the truly great originals."

During the 1920's Bechet also toured in the musical shows "How Come?," "Black and White Revue," and "Seven Eleven," after which he formed a band for engagements at the Rhythm Club and a club named for him (Club Basha) in New York. He returned to France in 1925 with a band led by pianist Claude Hopkins, to perform in "La Revue Nègre," a show featuring Josephine Baker. The following year he toured Russia in a group led by Benton Peyton. Next he organized a fourteen-piece band in Berlin for a new edition of "La Revue Nègre," which had enjoyed a great success in Paris. After further engagements in Germany, Bechet joined Noble Sissle's band in Paris. He continued to work in Europe until 1929, when he was jailed for eleven months in Paris following a fight with another musician, in which a woman bystander was shot.

Bechet returned to New York in 1931, rejoined Noble Sissle, toured briefly with Duke Ellington, and then formed a band with the trumpet player Tommy Ladnier. They were a success at the Savoy Ballroom in Harlem, but the Great Depression was making itself felt in the jazz world. For a year he and Ladnier operated a tailor's shop. He rejoined Noble Sissle in 1934 and remained with him until 1938, when an upsurge of interest in the New Orleans jazz idiom helped restore him to prominence. In June 1935 he married Marielouise Crawford. He played at many clubs in the New York area, including Ryan's and Nick's, and at Eddie Condon's wartime concerts at Town Hall. Records made under his own name further enhanced his reputation.

After World War II, Bechet returned to Europe, eventually making France his permanent home. He married Elizabeth Ziegler, a friend for twenty-three years, on Aug. 17, 1951. Bechet soon became extremely popular in France, sometimes playing with visiting American musicians but more often with local bands such as

Claude Luter's, which enthusiastically simulated the New Orleans jazz style. Records, particularly his hit version of "Les Oignons," added to his popularity, which for a time probably surpassed that of any other jazz musician in France.

Although best known for his soprano saxophone playing, Bechet was unquestionably one of the greatest jazz clarinetists. His vibrato, phrasing, improvisation, tone, and execution were all remarkably convincing. His imperious saxophone sound dominated every ensemble, whether or not it included a trumpet. His broad vibrato to some extent accounted for his partial eclipse in the 1930's, when it was considered old-fashioned, but his inexhaustible flow of ideas and the unique rhythmic zest with which he expressed them eventually won him deserved recognition.

The most notable of Bechet's disciples was Johnny Hodges, whom he helped as a young man in Boston and at the Club Basha. Hodges established his reputation as an alto saxophonist with Duke Ellington, but during the 1930's he was the only musician to play the soprano instrument with comparable fluidity. On both instruments he revealed the debt to Bechet that he always acknowledged in speech. Both were outstanding in their constant ability to play the difficult soprano saxophone in tune.

Bechet liked to stress the importance both of "playing with the right people" and of "doing it your own way." He composed a number of attractive tunes and an extended work for ballet performance entitled "La Nuit est une sorcière" (1953). He died in Paris.

[Bechet's autobiography is *Treat It Gentle* (1960). Other sources are Frederic Ramsey and Charles Edward Smith, *Jazzmen* (1939); Hugues Panassié, *The Real Jazz* (1942); Nat Shapiro and Nat Hentoff, *The Jazzmakers* (1957); Martin Williams, *Jazz Masters of New Orleans* (1967); Gunther Schuller, *Early Jazz* (1968); Stanley Dance *The World of Duke Ellington* (1970); John Chilton, *Who's Who of Jazz* (1970); and Duke Ellington, *Music Is My Mistress* (1973).]

STANLEY DANCE

BEHN, SOSTHENES (Jan. 30, 1882–June 6, 1957), businessman, was born in St. Thomas, Virgin Islands. His father, William Behn, was Danish and served as French consul; his mother, Louise Monsanto, was French. Sosthenes—the word means "life strength" in Greek—was educated in St. Thomas; Ajaccio, Corsica; and at the Ste. Barbe College in Paris. In 1898 he came to New York City, where he worked as a clerk for

the International Express Company. He then moved to the Morton Trust Company (later Guaranty Trust Company) and soon rose to the post of foreign exchange manager. In 1904, with his brother Hernand, he established Behn Brothers, a sugar brokerage house in Puerto Rico.

In 1914 the firm purchased the Puerto Rican Telephone Company from a friend who had allegedly acquired it as payment for a bad debt. The system was connected to the United States mainland by submarine cables. In 1916 Behn Brothers acquired the Cuban Telephone Company and proceeded to negotiate a contract with the American Telephone and Telegraph Company (A.T.&T.) that provided for laying cable between Cuba and Key West, Fla. During World War I, Behn was commissioned captain in the Army Signal Corps. He served from June 1917 to February 1919, rising to the rank of lieutenant colonel and participating in the Château Thierry, St. Mihiel, and Argonne campaigns. On Mar. 31, 1921, he married Margaret Dunlap; they had three children.

On June 16, 1920, the Behn brothers initiated what was to be their most successful venture. Using as a nucleus their Puerto Rican and Cuban telephone companies, and their half-interest in the Havana–Key West cable, they incorporated in Maryland as the International Telephone and Telegraph Corporation (I.T.&T.), issuing 50,000 shares of stock at $68.50. It has been argued that the lofty title for the new venture was chosen primarily with the hope that the initials would be confused with the established and prestigious A.T.&T. In 1924 the firm was awarded a contract to rehabilitate and operate the Spanish telephone system. Behn's wartime contacts, knowledge of Spanish, residence in Madrid (1923), and diplomatic skill were probably instrumental in securing the contract against strong competition from Swedish and German firms. Although American engineers were brought over to do the work, operation of the system was ultimately left to Spanish nationals.

Aided by a $30 million loan from J. P. Morgan and Company, Behn Brothers in 1925 acquired the International Western Electric Company (later renamed International Standard Electric) from A.T.&T., thereby gaining manufacturing facilities in nine countries. Since that time, I.T.&T. has not faced competition from A.T.&T. outside the United States or challenged it within the United States.

I.T.&T. expanded rapidly throughout the

1920's as Behn built an international communications empire through negotiation, acquisition, and merger that reached into Argentina, Australia, Belgium, China, England, France, Italy, Japan, Norway, and Romania. I.T.&T. was essentially engaged in absorbing the world's communications systems. Between 1924 and 1930 the value of its plant and property increased from $26 million to $297.7 million, while total assets soared from $38.3 million to $535.2 million. In less than a decade I.T.&T. had grown from obscurity to the world's second largest communications corporation. This growth was facilitated to a large extent by Behn's skill in handling international currency.

The firm's international character was reflected in its New York City headquarters, at 67 Broad Street. Inside the thirty-three-story skyscraper, completed in 1928, Behn worked in a Louis XIV, oak-paneled chamber, and behind his desk hung a painting of Pope Pius XI. Banquets for 200, featuring French cuisine, were unmatched in other corporate headquarters. Behn delighted in entertaining guests by telephoning subsidiaries around the world and showing off his command of several foreign languages.

I.T.&T. was imperiled by the stock market crash of 1929, as its debt reached $122 million. Behn responded by cutting costs and instituting his "Shanghai formula": encouraging subsidiaries to go into their own money markets to raise funds to pay off the parent company's debt. In addition, some debt was eradicated in 1933 when the dollar went off the gold standard, thereby effectively raising the value of the foreign currencies in which most of I.T.&T.'s business was transacted.

The economic and political turmoil of the 1930's did little to dampen Behn's interest in acquisition. In 1930 he created a holding company in Germany, the Standard Elektrizitäts Gesellschaft, and three months later he purchased the Lorenz Company. These developments placed him in competition with Siemens and Ericsson, European giants in the fields of electrical equipment and telecommunications systems. In December 1931 he purchased 27 percent of Ericsson's stock shortly before Ivar Kreuger, the financier who controlled the Swedish telephone company, committed suicide rather than face charges of fraud uncovered by auditors. Behn and I.T.&T. were left with stock in the badly shaken firm.

Political complications on the Continent were particularly severe in Spain, where civil war raged from 1936 to 1939. I.T.&T.'s Spanish subsidiary, headquartered in Madrid, was caught in the middle during the siege of the capital in 1936. According to *Time*, "Telefonica headquarters was shelled 184 times by Franco gunners, while retreating Loyalists threatened to blow it up as a suspected spy center." Behn went to Madrid and temporarily resolved matters, but in April 1945 he was forced to sell the company to the Franco government and private Spanish investors for $88 million.

With the spread of Nazi influence in Europe, Behn developed a dual strategy. First, he transferred holdings, so that at the outbreak of World War II, 56 percent of I.T.&T.'s assets were in the United States and Latin America. Second, he pursued a policy of accommodation in an effort to protect those interests which could not readily be sold or relocated. Accommodation was in no way a departure for the company, as it had always been Behn's policy to get along with the government of any nation in which he had dealings. Stockholders had to be protected against the specter of nationalization, and profits frequently were dependent on rate structures for telephone service approved by the national governments.

How far was "getting along" carried? Detractors claim that accommodation included directions, as late as 1938, to Lorenz (a German subsidiary) to purchase a 28 percent interest in Focke-Wulf, a German firm that made bombers. I.T.&T. insists that the company lost all practical contact with their German subsidiaries years before they were eliminated from I.T.&T.'s accounts in 1939. During World War II the company made direction finders for American vessels, and Behn won the confidence of United States military intelligence by providing information that only an international communications network could offer.

In 1945 I.T.&T. opened a research and development facility known as International Telecommunications Laboratories, Incorporated. The following year Behn won acclaim for negotiating a cash settlement reportedly worth $95 million when Argentina nationalized I.T.&T. property. The firm's efforts to expand United States operations led to the purchase of Capehart-Farnsworth (radio and television sets) and Colderator (refrigerators)—acquisitions that proved unfortunate. In the late 1940's Behn worked to block the expropriation of property by Communist regimes in Hungary, Poland, East Germany, Czechoslovakia, and Yugoslavia.

These efforts may well explain the arrest and showcase trial of three I.T.&T. executives in Budapest in 1950. Whether Behn had encouraged them to spy, or United States intelligence used I.T.&T. as a front for spying operations, is unclear. In any case, Behn was unable to prevent the loss of the company's property in eastern Europe.

Faced by criticism and pressure from stockholders, Behn retired in June 1948 as president of I.T.&T. and became chairman of the board, a position from which he continued to exert influence until his retirement in May 1956. He earned the title of global businessman for building a $760 million worldwide communications empire. In leading one of the pioneering conglomerates and multinational corporations, he was guided primarily by the law of survival. The well-being of the firm was never subordinated to the concerns of any nation. Possessing an international information network second to none, Behn was frequently able to keep I.T.&T. and its properties one step ahead of imminent disaster. He died in New York City.

[There is no full-length study. See Anthony Sampson, *The Sovereign State of ITT* (1973), chapters 2–3, a scathing attack on the company's history; "I.T.&T.'s Nine Lives," *Fortune*, Sept. 1945; *New York Times*, May 24, 1956; the obituary notice, *New York Times*, June 7, 1957; "Global Operator," *Time*, June 17, 1957; and "I.T.&T. Rebuilds Empire on Overseas Manufacturing," *Business Week*, Aug. 9, 1958.]

THOMAS R. WINPENNY

BELL, BERNARD IDDINGS (Oct. 13, 1886–Sept. 5, 1958), clergyman, educator, and writer, was born in Dayton, Ohio, the son of Charles Wright Bell, a paper manufacturer, and Vienna Valencia Iddings. He received the B.A. in 1907 from the University of Chicago and then enrolled at the Western Theological Seminary in Chicago (later part of Seabury-Western Seminary), graduating with a Bachelor of Sacred Theology degree in 1912. In 1910 he became a deacon and priest of the Episcopal Church and vicar of St. Christopher's Church in Oak Park, Ill.

On Apr. 24, 1912, Bell married Elizabeth Wood Lee. They had one child. He was appointed dean of St. Paul's Cathedral Church in Fond du Lac, Wis., in 1913. During his five years there, Bell served as the examining chaplain to the bishop and as senior aide to the chaplain at the

Great Lakes Naval Training Station (1917–1919), and wrote two books, *Right and Wrong After the War* (1918) and *The Church's Work for Men at War* (1919).

In 1919 Bell was appointed warden of St. Stephen's College (now Bard College) at Annandale-on-the-Hudson, New York. Over the next decade at St. Stephen's he developed and guided a rigorously classical liberal arts curriculum where a small faculty-student community examined the original Greek and Latin classics. When St. Stephen's became a branch of Columbia University in 1930, Bell received a three-year appointment as professor of religion in the department of philosophy at Columbia.

From 1933 to 1946 Bell was the preaching canon at St. John's Cathedral in Providence, R.I., and also taught frequently at universities and colleges in the United States and England as visiting lecturer of religion. He returned to Chicago in 1946 as the honorary canon at the Cathedral of Sts. Peter and Paul and as an educational consultant to the Right Reverend Wallace E. Conkling, Protestant Episcopal bishop of Chicago. His duties involved chaplain service at the University of Chicago and other schools in the diocese.

Bell also taught religious education and preaching from 1946 to January 1948 at Seabury-Western Theological Seminary in Evanston, Ill. After resigning this position, he spent the last years of his life lecturing, preaching, and writing books, articles, and pamphlets. He was a frequent contributor to the *Atlantic Monthly, Living Church, Criterion,* and the *New York Times Magazine.* Bell's activities after 1955 were partially curtailed by blindness. He died in Chicago.

In *Right and Wrong After the War* (1918) and *The Church's Work for Men at War* (1919), Bell supported a limited social reform commitment for the church. Warning that the rich should not "live in idle luxury," he insisted that the Christian religion did not call for supine obedience to an ecclesiastical organization or compliance with legalistic formulas for conduct or the observance of "ancient, fixed, and formal liturgies, however beautiful."

Yet, this recognition of the church's task in social reconstruction was always modified, in his subsequent writings, by the admonition that a social gospel Christianity, in which the service of God became merely a vague humanitarian concern for the common good, distorted the essence of Christianity. For Bell was an unregenerate pessimist who subscribed to the maxim of the prophet Jeremiah, "Cursed is the man who has faith in man." He did not believe that changes in the social structure could appreciably alter the character of individuals. Since original sin was a symbolic representation of what occurs at each decisive moment of existence, human beings could endeavor to mitigate only the greatest evils.

Like Ortega y Gasset and T. S. Eliot, Bell lamented the passionate and pernicious politicization of modern life that threatened to substitute political action for all knowledge, wisdom, and religion. Vox populi, without the mediating influence of religion, was always vox diaboli. Collective social action drained people of solitude, intimacy, autonomy, and authentic community. Society represented a historical order, a protective structure of meaning, erected in the face of chaos. Only within a social order, nurtured by perennial Christian truths, did the life of the group and the individual make sense.

In more than twenty books published between 1918 and 1955, and in his many essays and sermons, Bell revealed a preoccupation with Christian apologetics and with having the church lead the work toward the recovery of permanent and universal moral values. "Over against Liberalism, whose god is me, and equally opposed to Communism, whose god is us," he wrote in *The Church in Disrepute* (1943), "stands Christianity and should be standing Christ's Church, to bid men to live and labor for the glory of that God who has revealed Himself."

Suffusing Bell's thought was a core of persistent themes: a tragic view of life; the problem of redemption; the ineluctable significance of original sin; and the rootless and fragmented nature of modern society dissevered from loyalties to family, church, and community. In opposition to the empirical, scientific, and materalist ethos he held responsible for the twentieth century's pervasive moral relativism, Bell attempted to interpose the enduring truths of Western Christian culture. In *Affirmations* (1938) he resolutely affirmed a faith that "is not primarily a matter of philosophy, but of entrustment to a God who reveals Himself." And to those propagators of a liberal Christianity determined to perfect men through collective governmental action, Bell responded that the crucial Christian message was to inform men that life involved uncertainty, insecurity, pain, and suffering. The Church should provide the courage to "live simply, honestly, bravely, joyfully in the midst of a difficult world."

This conviction about the irredeemably flawed nature of man led Bell to declare, in *A Catholic Looks at His World* (1936), that he was an "Anglo-Catholic" who regarded the Church "as Catholic rather than Protestant." He described himself in 1949 as "a qualified anti-statist" and demonstrated a strong animus to collective attempts to forge the good society. Decrying ideological thought, he wrote in 1936: "Most modern Utopias, all the way from those of the capitalistic individualist to those of Marx, Lenin, Hitler and Mussolini are based on Rousseau's presuppositions about man."

Bell's profound disaffection with the governing ideas of the contemporary world—relativism in philosophy and social thought, secularism and materialism in daily living, and romanticism and naturalism in literature—caused him to view education as the crucible through which the return to first principles could occur. His diagnosis and prescription for the improvement of society was the refurbishing of traditional classical education and the repudiation of John Dewey's educational views.

Dewey, in Bell's estimate, had been completely captivated by Rousseau. His "essentially romantic and unrealistic" philosophy was so triumphant in the public schools that "our children are in consequence being trained in a notion of man's nature so untrue as to make our temper hysterical and our culture increasingly fragile." Since Dewey and his disciples had been responsible for supplanting traditional normative values with a subversive secularism, their intellectual and institutional hegemony had to be challenged. "The religion of the public schools," he wrote in *Crowd Culture* (1952), "is a nontheistic and merely patriotic Secularism. The public schools, without its being generally perceived by those who direct the schools, have become, because of this monopoly advocacy, the most dangerous opponents of religious liberty on the American horizon."

Bell's solution to the crisis in American education was to admit first that our "exaggerated optimism about man" was "the chief cause of our decay" and then to cultivate "a democratic elite" that will exemplify excellence and "a more urbane and humane way of living." To think that the average person "can be entrusted without skilled critical leadership to run himself and society" was to create a "crowd culture" that celebrated mediocrity, contemporaneity, and triviality.

"The two things I like best to do," Bell once remarked, "are to say Mass and to preach." And throughout his life he affirmed in cogent and moving sermons and lectures, as well as books and essays, what seemed to him the very essence of Christianity: "the substance of things hoped for, the evidence of things not seen" (Heb. 11:1). He believed that the life of the soul is nourished by an openness toward God and that the agonies of human existence, the periods of doubt and pain, guilt and despondency, contrition and repentance, abandonment and hope, the silent stirrings of love and grace, constituted an inexorable cycle.

[For Bell's theological views, see *Beyond Agnosticism: A Book for Tired Mechanists* (1929); *Preface to Religion* (1935); *A Catholic Looks at His World* (1936); *God Is Not Dead* (1945); and *A Man Can Live* (1947). His critique of American education can be found in *Crisis in Education: A Challenge to American Complacency* (1949); and *Crowd Culture: An Examination of the American Way of Life* (1952). The Russell Kirk Papers, Clarke Historical Library at Central Michigan University, Mount Pleasant, Mich., contain a number of letters written by Bell. On his life and writings, see M. Whitcomb Hess, "Canon Bell: Crusader for Religious Education," *Catholic World* (May 1951), 98–104; and Nelson R. Burr, *A Critical Bibliography of Religion in America* (1961), p. 1149, which is vol. IV of a series, Religion in American Life. For an extreme right-wing attack upon Bell's early interest in having the Church attempt some social reform leadership and his intellectual leadership of St. Stephen's College, see Edgar C. Bundy, *Apostles of Deceit* (1966), 401–402. There are obituary notices in *Living Church* (Sept. 21, 1958), 11, 19; and the *New York Times* (Sept. 6, 1958), 17.]

FRANK ANNUNZIATA

BELL, DE BENNEVILLE ("BERT") (Feb. 25, 1894–Oct. 11, 1959), football player, coach, club owner, and commissioner of the National Football League (1946–1959), was born in Philadelphia, Pa., the son of John Cromwell Bell and Fleurette de Benneville Myers. Bell was expected to enter law, politics, or business. His father had been attorney general of Pennsylvania and his brother, John Cromwell Bell, Jr., was in turn lieutenant governor, governor, and a justice of the Pennsylvania Supreme Court. "Bert," a nickname he much preferred to de Benneville, played football, basketball, and baseball while a student at the Haverford prep school in Philadelphia. At the University of Pennsylvania, which he entered in 1915, he was a better than average quarterback and punter. Under his generalship the 1915 club upset a mighty Michigan team but lost to Oregon in the Rose Bowl. World War I interrupted Bell's education; in 1918 he served with a field hospital unit in France. He returned to captain the Pennsylvania team of 1919 but left the university in 1920 without a degree.

In the 1920's and early 1930's Bell dabbled in business and football coaching, although he devoted much of his time to heavy drinking, gambling, and courting chorus girls. Each fall from 1920 through 1928 he served as an assistant to first John Heisman and then Louis A. Young in coaching the backfield of the Pennsylvania football team; in 1930 and 1931 he was the backfield coach for Temple University. At Pennsylvania he gained notoriety for developing the "hidden ball" trick, now outlawed, in which the players wore patches at their elbows designed as footballs. In the 1920's he also managed hotels in which his father had an interest, first the St. James and later the Ritz Carlton in Philadelphia, and was a part owner of a brokerage house.

The stock market crash of 1929, in which he experienced heavy losses, checked Bell's taste for gambling. And Frances Upton, who starred in several Broadway musical comedies, persuaded him to give up drinking as a condition for her friendship. The couple married on Jan. 4, 1934; they had three children. Marriage and a family helped bring stability to Bell's chaotic life.

In 1933 he and six friends purchased the franchise of the Frankford Yellow Jackets of the National Football League (NFL) for $2,500. In honor of the Blue Eagle, the symbol of the New Deal's National Recovery Administration, they renamed the club the Philadelphia Eagles.

Investing in a professional football team in 1933 was risky. College football was far more popular and only a few NFL franchises were profitable. The Great Depression added to the woes of the league. The Eagles allegedly lost $80,000 between 1933 and 1936; in the latter year Bell acquired total ownership of the club for a mere $4,500. (Only a substantial inheritance from his father in 1935 saved Bell from financial ruin.) He served as club owner, general manager, and coach of the Eagles. Under his coaching the team won only ten games, lost forty-four, and tied two. Fewer than 5,000 fans usually attended home games. Following the 1940 season, in a complicated three-way transaction, Bell sold the Eagles and obtained half interest with Arthur J. Rooney, Jr., in the Pittsburgh Steelers. He served at various times as coach, general manager, and president of the Steelers until 1946, when he sold his interest in the club upon assuming the commissionership of the NFL.

Before Bell became commissioner, reasoning

that the league needed a system to equalize competition between the weaker and stronger teams, he persuaded the owners to accept a "draft" system. Starting in 1936 the teams chose college players in reverse order of their league standing at the close of the previous season. While the draft may not have functioned effectively as an equalizer of competition, it did serve the interest of owners in forcing prospective athletes to negotiate with only one club. After World War II professional baseball, basketball, and hockey copied Bell's system.

As commissioner, Bell made many important contributions to professional football. He spearheaded the passage of special sports antibribery laws in several states and also hired former Federal Bureau of Investigation agents to maintain surveillance of gamblers, players, owners, and NFL radio broadcasters. In order to reduce the advantages of professional gamblers who often had access to knowledge unavailable to the public, Bell required that teams announce at least forty-eight hours in advance of the games the names of players who were unlikely to appear in a contest.

Bell guided the NFL through a costly war with the All-America Conference, which was organized in 1946. Competition for talent drove up player salaries, costing the combined leagues an estimated $6 million. On Dec. 9, 1949, the All-America Conference "surrendered," but the Cleveland, San Francisco, and Baltimore franchises were taken into the NFL on favorable terms. When the owners were unable to agree upon a procedure for the division of the players made available by the dissolution of the rival conference, Bell assigned them to NFL clubs. He also reached an understanding with the Canadian Football League that sharply reduced player raids.

Television presented another challenge to Bell. Although it was a major force in destroying many minor-league professional baseball teams in the 1950's, it proved to be a boon to football. Bell persuaded the NFL owners to permit only road games to be televised. In 1951 the federal government filed an antitrust suit against the league for this policy but lost. By 1959 each club was receiving nearly $100,000 annually from television rights. Bell made sure that the radio and television commentators would be league boosters rather than critics; he insisted that announcers refrain from criticizing players, coaches, owners, or game officials.

Bell employed his authority broadly to prevent "any action detrimental to the welfare of the National Football League." He united the faction-ridden owners into a single economic cartel, a far stronger one than existed in any other professional team sport. A heavyset man, with twinkling eyes and a ready smile, Bell seemed to be able to disarm the most fierce antagonists. Despite his upper-class origins, he had a "common touch," being equally at ease with owners, reporters, players, and congressmen.

Under Bell's leadership professional football rose to new heights of popularity and financial stability. Average game attendance nearly doubled between 1946 and 1959; only two clubs reported profits in 1946, but only two lost money in 1959. By the late 1950's some 40 million fans regularly watched NFL games on television. While the players benefited from the league's prosperity, Bell and the owners tightly restricted their economic freedom. Testimony before a congressional committee in 1956 revealed that the "option clause" in player contracts was only a nominal right, for the owners apparently had a gentleman's agreement to blacklist any player who tried to exercise the option by signing with another club. Under pressure from the committee, Bell, without even consulting the owners, agreed to recognize the Players Association. Omens of a new era of professional football characterized by a three-way power struggle between the NFL, the Players Association, and the American Football League (organized in 1959) were already present when Bell died of a heart attack while watching a game between the Philadelphia Eagles and the Pittsburgh Steelers.

[Both the NFL office in New York and the Pro Football Hall of Fame in Canton, Ohio, have rich newspaper files on Bell. W. C. Heinz, "Boss of the Behemoths," *Saturday Evening Post*, Dec. 3, 1957; Al Hirshberg, "He Calls the Signals in Pro Football," *New York Times Magazine*, Dec. 23, 1958; and John Lardner, "A Czar's Ultimatum," *Newsweek*, Dec. 15, 1958, are especially valuable articles. See also hearings before the Anti-Trust Subcommittee of the Committee of the Judiciary, House of Representatives, *Organized Professional Team Sports*, 85th Cong., 1 sess. (Washington, 1957).]

BENJAMIN G. RADER

BELL, ERIC TEMPLE (Feb. 7, 1883–Dec. 21, 1960), mathematician, author, and educator, was born in Aberdeen, Scotland, the son of James Bell and Helen Jane Lindsay-Lyall. His father was in the merchant marine and the son of an eminent London mercantile family. Bell was educated by tutors and attended Bedford Modern School, where under the guidance of E. M. Langley he became interested in mathematics.

He immigrated to the United States in 1902—to avoid "Woolrich or the India Civil Service"—and in two years earned an A.B. from Stanford University. He worked as a mule skinner in Nevada, as a surveyor, and as a partner in a telephone company that went broke as a result of the San Francisco earthquake of 1906, then returned to academia to receive a second A. B. from the University of Washington in 1908. There followed a short sojourn as a teacher and worker in the lumber industry of northern California. On Dec. 24, 1910, he married Jessie Lillian Smith Brown, a widow. They had one son.

In 1912 Bell received his Ph.D. in mathematics from Columbia University, beginning a distinguished career as a teacher and scholar at the University of Washington (1912–1926) and as visiting professor at the University of Chicago (1924–1928) and at Harvard (1926). From 1926 until his retirement in 1953, he was professor of mathematics at the California Institute of Technology. Bell published nearly 300 articles and edited several professional journals. In 1921 he won the Boucher Award for "Arithmetical Paraphrases," a basic contribution to the theory of numbers (a branch of pure mathematics dealing with properties of integers). He was an authority in this as well as elliptic functions, finding solutions to important problems that had resisted solution for eighty years. Two books, *Algebraic Arithmetic* (1927) and *The Development of Mathematics* (1940), became standards in the field. He was president of the Mathematical Association of America from 1931 to 1933.

From 1930 Bell devoted much of his energy to popularizing mathematics for the layman. *Men of Mathematics* (1937) was devoted to relating the importance of mathematical discoveries to the men responsible. *The Development of Mathematics,* which brilliantly delineated the significant trends of mathematics, was filled with information and opinion without being tedious or encyclopedic. *Mathematics, Queen and Servant of Science* (1951) demonstrated the twin capacities of mathematics—the esoteric and the inescapably practical—and was his most sweeping attempt at popularization. *The Last Problem* (1961) was supposed to center around the life of the seventeenth-century French mathematician Pierre Fermat but was really an excuse for writing a history of the theory of numbers in a style that has

something to offer layman and specialist alike. Bell's style was lucid and easy-flowing for such usually abstruse materials, and his insights continue to stimulate mathematicians in spite of some criticism of his fanciful flights of imagination.

Under the name of John Taine, Bell published seventeen science fiction novels noted for their violence and exciting plots. *Before the Dawn* (1934), published under his own name, was his favorite. It concerned dinosaurs and was inspired by statues of dinosaurs near his boyhood home in Croydon Park, near London. Together with *The Time Stream* (1946), it ranks among the most popular science fiction works of its time. Bell excused his writing of science fiction by stating "that if this made money for publishers, some publishers might be interested in more serious works." Another statement in which he said that he wrote for recreation may be closer to the truth. He also produced a volume of poetry. After his retirement in 1953, Bell continued to be active in serious research. He died in Watsonville, Calif.

[There is no detailed biography. Stanley J. Kunitz, ed., *Twentieth Century Authors,* supp. 1 (1955), contains Bell's own insights. See also the obituary notice by T. A. A. Broadbent in *Nature,* Feb. 11, 1961; *Dictionary of Scientific Biography;* and the obituary notice, *New York Times,* Dec. 22, 1960.]

RONALD RIDGLEY

BELL, LAWRENCE DALE (Apr. 5, 1894–Oct. 20, 1956), aerospace pioneer and entrepreneur, was born in Mentone, Ind., the son of Isaac Evans Bell and Harriet Sarber. His father owned a small lumber mill until he retired in 1907 and moved to Santa Monica, Calif. Bell was already interested in aviation as a student at Santa Monica High School. In 1912 he became a mechanic for his brother Grover E. Bell and Lincoln Beachy, who were exhibition pilots. When Grover was killed in an accident, Bell quit the aviation business briefly before going to work for Glenn L. Martin. In 1913 he converted a Martin plane into a bomber for Pancho Villa. Within two years he had risen to the position of superintendent and persuaded Martin to hire an engineer, Donald Douglas, Sr., who had graduated from the newly established aeronautical program at the Massachusetts Institute of Technology. On July 17, 1915, Bell married Lucille Mainwaring. They had no children.

In 1917, when the Martin and Wright interests were merged, Martin went to Cleveland and took

Bell with him to start another company. Bell was soon promoted to vice-president and general manager. He left in 1928 to join Reuben Fleet at the Consolidated Aircraft Company in Buffalo, N.Y., and within a year he had become vice-president and general manager. In 1935 Consolidated moved to San Diego, Calif., but Bell remained in Buffalo. On July 10, he established the Bell Aircraft Corporation with the help of Ray P. Whitman and Robert J. Woods, who had raised $150,000.

The company at first took on subcontracts from other manufacturers and did experimental work. Bell, who had learned to fly many years before, was far more interested in design and engineering than in flying. Woods, a top aeronautical engineer, designed the XFM-1 Airacuda, the first American twin-engine multiplace fighter plane, which was first flown on Sept. 1, 1937. Bell received a small Air Corps contract for it the following year, but it went no further.

Meanwhile, in 1937, Bell had offered the Army Air Corps a single-seater design with the engine placed behind the pilot, and contracts followed for the widely used P-39 Airacobra. The company began to benefit almost at once from both the British need for planes and from President Roosevelt's expansion of the air corps—in 1939 Bell had 100 employees; by 1944, there were 55,000 employees at five Bell plants. During World War II, the P-39 was followed by the similar P-63. Bell also took over Boeing B-29 production contracts and turned out a bomber a day for 663 consecutive days at the Marietta, Ga., plant. To meet a threatened shortage of aluminum, Woods and his team designed the XP-77 fighter plane made almost entirely of molded Sitka spruce plywood. Late in the war Bell developed the pioneer jet fighter, the P-59 Airacomet.

In addition to supervising the company's wartime activities, Bell served as president of the National Aircraft War Production Council and on the Aircraft War Production Council, East Coast, Incorporated. Through these organizations he was instrumental in arranging for the exchange or transfer of key personnel to help speed production. In 1944 he was awarded the Daniel Guggenheim Memorial Medal for "achievement in design and construction of military aircraft and for outstanding contributions to the methods of production." After the war he was honored by the American Legion for his work in hiring the handicapped, who made up 5.5 percent of his work force in 1951.

Bell was always looking to the future. In 1941 he brought a young Princeton graduate with twelve years' helicopter experience into the firm, setting him up in a workshop well removed from the company's activities so that he would not be interrupted. The idea paid off handsomely, after Bell himself had devoted many hours to working with him, and in March 1946 Bell was awarded the first commercial license for helicopters by the Civil Aeronautics Board. Two years later the X-1 experimental plane was awarded the Collier Trophy, and in 1953 the X-1A raised the world's speed record from 967 to 1,650 miles per hour.

Earlier, Bell had directed his engineers to investigate remote control as a way of saving the lives of test pilots, and this led the company to guided missiles. In the early 1950's subcontract work for the B-47 and B-36 was moved from the main plant to Tonawanda, N.Y., and the helicopter division was relocated to Fort Worth, Tex. The move enabled the Buffalo headquarters to concentrate on guided missiles, a natural fusion of the remote control, supersonics, and rocketry in which Bell had become a leader. One of his bold moves in this connection had been to hire Walter Dornberger, the German general who had managed the Peenemünde experimental facilities where the V-2 rocket was developed. By 1952 Bell systems were being used to guide the weapons of other makers as well. By 1955 Bell was also engaged in VTOL (vertical takeoff and landing) designs and was a leader in maintaining American technical superiority over the Russians.

Motivated as much by dreams of flying as by profits, Bell assembled a team of engineers and analysts who could turn his ideas into hardware. The strain, however, provoked intermittent ulcer attacks. In 1954 he turned over the general management of the company to Leston P. Faneuf, after having suffered a mild heart attack the previous year. He resigned the presidency on Sept. 18, 1956, but remained chairman of the board. He died in Buffalo, N.Y. In 1960 the defense business of Bell Aircraft was acquired by Textron, and three operating divisions were established: Bell Aerospace Textron, Buffalo; Bell Helicopter Textron, Fort Worth, Tex.; and the Hydraulic Research Division, Valencia, Calif.

[Bell's papers are at Bell Aerospace Textron, Buffalo, N.Y. See also D. Seligman, "Barrier-breaking Bell Aircraft," *Fortune*, Mar. 1956; *Bell Aerospace Release*, June 1956, the most useful account; the obituary notice, *New York Times*, Oct. 21, 1956; Ray Wagner, *American Combat Planes* (1960); and *Rendezvous*, July 1975.]

ROBIN HIGHAM

BELLANCA, GIUSEPPE MARIO (Mar. 19, 1886–Dec. 26, 1960), aeronautical designer and manufacturer, was born in Sciacca, Sicily, the son of Andrea Bellanca, a miller, and Concetta Merlo. After attending local schools, he entered the Istituto Tecnico of Milan in 1904, from which he graduated four years later with a teaching certificate in mathematics. He then studied at the Milan Politecnico, which awarded him degrees in mathematics and engineering in 1910.

Bellanca's interest in aeronautics was aroused in July 1908, when he observed the flight of Léon Delagrange, pioneering French aviator, at Turin. With two associates he set to work on the design and construction of an aircraft. The first machine crashed during a test flight in September 1909. Bellanca's second aircraft never flew because he could not raise the money to purchase an engine.

Largely through the efforts of his brother August, who had emigrated earlier, Bellanca came to the United States in September 1912. While living in Brooklyn, he built a parasol/monoplane—a single-wing aircraft in which the pilot rode in an exposed structure below the wings—which he used to teach himself to fly. Bellanca opened a flying school at Garden City, N.Y., in 1914. His most famous student was Fiorello La Guardia, then a young lawyer.

Bellanca joined the aeronautical division of the Maryland Pressed Steel Company, Hagerstown, Md., in 1916; and during the next four years he designed two biplanes, essentially refinements of conventional designs. By 1920 he had gained confidence in his skill as a designer and was ready to move into other areas. Aware of the early wind tunnel experiments of Gustave Eiffel, Bellanca sought to design an aircraft with minimum drag and maximum lift. Plans for what later became known as the CF were completed late in 1920. Bellanca concluded an agreement with the Omaha Aircraft Company in 1921 for manufacture of the CF, but the company went bankrupt before the prototype was built.

Victor Roos, a motorcycle dealer in Omaha, agreed to provide funds to complete the machine, which was test-flown in June 1922. Experts soon hailed the CF as the most advanced aircraft of the time. A high-wing monoplane with an enclosed cabin for the pilot and four passengers, it had double the lift per pound of thrust and twice the glide angle of other aircraft. This advanced performance came from high-lift, low-drag wings incorporating the Bellanca "M" airfoil; the use of airfoil lifting struts (designed not only to provide support for the wings but also to supply additional lift); and other aerodynamic refinements. The CF won thirteen prizes for performance and efficiency at air meets during the summer of 1922, and Bellanca was nominated for the prestigious Collier Trophy. Although the CF was clearly superior to contemporary aircraft, Bellanca found no buyers for it because the market was saturated with inexpensive World War I surplus machines.

While in Omaha, Bellanca married Dorothy M. Brown on Nov. 18, 1922. They had one son. Bellanca became a naturalized American citizen about this time.

The next two years were lean ones. Bellanca received a contract to modify aircraft operated by the Air Mail Service of the Post Office Department. But the results, while technically rewarding, were not rewarding financially. In March 1925 he joined the Wright Aeronautical Company, charged with designing an aircraft to show off the company's new Whirlwind engine. Two prototypes resulted: the Wright-Bellanca (W-B) I and II. Although the W-B II, a further refinement and improvement of the basic CF concept, proved the most efficient aircraft of the time, Wright decided not to go into production, lest competition with airframe manufacturers hinder potential sales of the Whirlwind engine.

In December 1926, Bellanca founded the Columbia Aircraft Company in partnership with Charles A. Levine, an eccentric Brooklyn millionaire. The company purchased the W-B II prototype, modified it, and christened it *Columbia*. In March 1927, *Columbia* established an endurance record of fifty-one hours and thirty minutes. The aircraft's performance sparked the interest of Charles A. Lindbergh, who sought to acquire it for his proposed transatlantic flight. Although Bellanca came to favor the idea, Levine did not. Instead, *Columbia* was readied for a transatlantic flight with Clarence D. Chamberlin as pilot. Legal complications prevented the aircraft's departure until after Lindbergh's successful flight. Two weeks later, on June 4–6, 1927, Chamberlin flew *Columbia*, with Levine as passenger, from Roosevelt Field, Long Island, to Eisleben, Germany, a distance of 3,905 miles—301 miles farther than Lindbergh had flown.

This flight brought Bellanca both recognition and financial support. In December 1927 he signed an agreement with members of the du Pont family to build a factory at New Castle, Del. Bellanca aircraft demonstrated their superiority during the early 1930's in a series of long-distance flights, the most notable occurring in October

1931, when Clyde Pangborn and Hugh Herndon flew nonstop across the Pacific from Tokyo, Japan, to Wenatchee, Wash.

The 1930's marked a revolution in aircraft design. The future lay with multiengine, all-metal machines of monocoque (single-shell) construction, like the Douglas DC-3. Bellanca, however, clung to his basic design concepts of the 1920's. Between 1930 and 1950 he produced several successful single-engine aircraft, especially the Cruisair series, that were noted for their efficiency, reliability, and safety. But the Bellanca company never became a major aircraft manufacturer. As noted by the *New York Herald-Tribune* at the time of his death, "Most of Mr. Bellanca's friends saw him as an artist, indeed as a genius, though they deplored his lack of business acumen."

In 1955, Bellanca retired to his home in Galena, Md., where he devoted his last years to designing aircraft of fiberglass construction. He died in New York City.

[The papers of Giuseppe M. Bellanca, in the possession of his son, August, at Galena, Md., are the central source and comprise personal and business correspondence, newspaper clippings, designs, blueprints, photographs, and motion picture films. The pioneering CF aircraft is preserved at the National Air and Space Museum, Smithsonian Institution. The only reliable secondary source is Julius A. Zito, "G. M. Bellanca and His Contributions to the Field of Aviation" (unpublished senior thesis, St. Francis College, Brooklyn, N.Y., 1971), which used the Bellanca papers. See also obituary notices, *New York Times* and *New York Herald-Tribune* (both Dec. 27, 1960).]

WILLIAM M. LEARY, JR.

BENNETT, HUGH HAMMOND (Apr. 15, 1881–July 7, 1960), soil conservationist, was born in Wadesboro, N.C., the son of William Osborne Bennett and Rosa May Hammond. His father owned a 1,200-acre farm and supported his large family with homemade products, ranging from food to cloth. As the boy learned, the land had been exhausted by primitive methods of cultivation, and only strenuous labors gave the Bennetts their livelihood. He attended schools in Anson County and cut wood to earn money in order to enroll at the University of North Carolina in 1897. His studies were interrupted (1899–1901) by lack of funds, but he returned to receive the B.S. in 1903. That year he joined the Bureau of Soils of the U.S. Department of

Agriculture and began a lifetime study of soil types.

Bennett was a big, friendly man, with an endless store of anecdotes. During his crusade to save and develop land resources he conversed with countless people and with farm and professional assemblies. In time he was universally recognized as the embodiment of what became the soil conservation movement.

Bennett's early observations concerned soil erosion. For example, in 1905 he noted that sloping fields were especially liable to sheet erosion, and he contrived ways to inhibit or prevent runoffs which carried away the land's minerals. In 1906 he was appointed soil scientist by the bureau and was placed in charge of surveys that began in the East but ultimately took him nearly everywhere.

In 1909 Bennett became supervisor of soil surveys, a position he held until 1928. In 1909 he made the first of many visits abroad, studying under dangerous jungle conditions the agricultural possibilities in the Canal Zone. Bennett also made two trips through Alaska; in 1914 he studied the land on which the territorial railroad was to be constructed, and in 1916 he worked with the Alaskan Chugach National Forest Commission. Three years later Bennett was back in Central America—this time with a committee mediating a Honduras–Guatemala boundary dispute. Further visits to Central and South America in 1923–1924 took him to Ecuador, Venezuela, and Brazil to study rubber-producing soils.

Bennett's work in Cuba in 1925–1926 and in 1928 involved soil surveys and the efficient production of sugar. He recommended that workers be permitted to grow their own food on patches of land—a policy that helped keep previously transient labor dependably close to the plantations. Bennett's book *The Soils of Cuba*, prepared with Robert V. Allison (1928), was filled with observations that subsequently enriched Bennett's maturing soil conservation program.

In 1928, with William R. Chapline, Bennett published his landmark Department of Agriculture Circular No. 33, "Soil Erosion, a National Menace." The same year he persuaded congressmen of the need for erosion control; Congress appropriated $100,000 for the program. In his testimony before committees he often employed dramatic devices, such as pouring water on towels to demonstrate how water could soak into soil. He then removed the towels and poured water on the desk to show it running off to the floor. The Buchanan Amendment (1929) set up stations where soil agents could study local and regional conditions.

In 1933 Bennett became director of the Soil Erosion Service in the Department of the Interior and worked intensively with erosion and flood control projects of the depression era. His 1935 appeal to congressional legislators for a broader-based agency was timed to coincide with a dust storm that was sweeping over Washington. The phenomenon so impressed the Senate committee that it hurriedly passed Public Law 46, the first soil conservation act in history. Bennett was appointed chief of the new Soil Conservation Service, placed in the Department of Agriculture.

Bennett's work thereafter ranged from setting up what by 1946 became 1,700 soil conservation districts in the United States to leading in the creation of a science of conservation. This involved such elements as contour tillage to resist water runoffs and stubble mulch, which held the land down during windstorms. He wrote steadily on soil conservation and carried his message to high-level conferences and committees in America and abroad. Bennett received numerous honors and awards, and in 1948 the Inter-American Conference on Conservation of Natural Renewable Resources recommended that he be awarded the Nobel Prize "for services to humanity."

Bennett's vigor and heartiness impressed friends throughout his life. In 1907 he married Sarah Edna McCue, who died in 1909, leaving him a daughter. He married Betty Virginia Brown in 1921; they had a son. Bennett farmed his own acres at Eight Oaks near Falls Church, Va. He never relaxed his vigil against careless land policies. *Time* magazine called him a "gloomy soil saver," but many others emphasized his enduring faith in and influence on the public and its spokesmen. He died in Falls Church, Va.

[In addition to the works cited in the text, Bennett wrote *The Agricultural Possibilities of the Canal Zone* (1912); *The Soils and Agriculture of the Southern States* (1921); *The Cost of Soil Erosion* (1934); *Soil Conservation* (1939); and "Land in Peril," *Nation*, May 23, 1953. On his life and work, see Wellington Brink, *Big Hugh, the Father of Soil Conservation* (1951); Denton Harper Simms, *The Soil Conservation Service* (1970); and the obituary notice in the *New York Times*, July 8, 1960. Glimpses of Bennett appear in memoirs in the Columbia University Oral History Collection.]

LOUIS FILLER

BENSLEY, ROBERT RUSSELL (Nov. 13, 1867–June 11, 1956), anatomist, was born near Hamilton, Ontario, Canada, the son of Robert Daniel Bensley, a farmer, and of Caroline Vandeleur. He was educated at the University of Toronto, where he majored in classics. At the age of twenty-one, he suffered a gunshot wound in the leg. It had to be amputated, and during a long convalescence in Hamilton, he became keenly interested in the animals and plants around him. After receiving the B.A. degree from Toronto in 1889, Bensley entered the University of Toronto Medical School. He was awarded the M.B. degree in 1892. On Sept. 12, 1892, he married Cariella May; they had three children.

Bensley began to practice medicine in Toronto but also taught in the department of biology at the university from 1892 to 1901. In the latter year he was named assistant professor of anatomy at the University of Chicago, beginning a long career of research and teaching in that discipline.

Although Bensley always regarded himself as an anatomist, he is chiefly remembered as a cytologist. His first significant research at Chicago concerned the structure of the pancreas. He developed staining techniques with supravital dyes that made possible the differentiation of the structural parts, in particular the islets of Langerhans and acini. This work played an important role in the later discovery of insulin.

Bensley's most significant early work was the discovery of what are now called mitochondria. The discovery proceeded from a reading of a forgotten text by the histologist Richard Altmann, and was not at once accepted. Bensley developed special staining techniques to reveal the mitochondria that were based on a special formulation of the dye Janus green. This technique, still used, established him as a researcher of the first rank.

In 1905 Bensley became director of the Hull Laboratory of Anatomy at Chicago, retaining that position until his retirement in 1933. In the same year he became associate professor, rising to full professor in 1907. In 1918 he was president of the American Association of Anatomists. Bensley remained at Chicago for the rest of his career, except for a year (1930–1931) at Washington University, St. Louis. Bensley's research during his mature years covered a wide range of anatomical subjects: the gastric glands of mammals, the stomach and the pancreas, the kidney, and the salivary and thyroid glands. Usually his preferred tool was staining. In 1929, with H. B. Owens, he introduced osmic acid as a staining agent and used it for a study of the apparatus of Golgi. Osmic acid continues to be widely used as a stain, particularly for electron microscopy. Bensley also developed, in collaboration with students, two other techniques of great importance: centrifugation and freeze-drying. With N. L. Hoerr he showed that it was possible to break up cells by centrifuging and to collect mitochondria and other cellular constituents for subsequent chemical analysis. With Isidore Gersh he reintroduced the technique of freeze-drying (another contribution of Altmann's) as a method for preserving the topology of the cells as they had existed in vivo. These researches, both of the first rank in importance, were carried out when Bensley was close to retirement.

After his retirement Bensley continued to live in Chicago, where he died, but retained his Canadian ties. He spent his summers in Ontario, where he had a house in the Go Home Bay area. He remained interested in his field, delivering his last invited paper in Boston at the age of eighty-five. Although he did not receive the highest honors—which there is no reason to believe he particularly coveted—Bensley remains an important figure among the handful of men who brought the United States into the front rank of countries engaged in medical research during the years immediately before and after World War I.

[See the brief obituary in the *New York Times,* June 13, 1956; and E. V. Cowdry, "R. R. Bensley, Cytologist," *Science,* Nov. 16, 1956.]

C. G. B. GARRETT

BENTLEY, ARTHUR FISHER (Oct. 16, 1870–May 21, 1957), political scientist, philosopher, and sociologist, was born in Freeport, Ill., the son of Charles Frederick Bentley, a banker, and Angeline Alice Fisher. After attending public schools in Freeport and Grand Island, Nebr., he studied briefly at York College in Nebraska and at the University of Denver. He next worked for three years in his father's bank. In 1890 Bentley entered Johns Hopkins University and in 1892 was awarded an A.B. with high honors. His *The Condition of the Western Farmer as Illustrated by the Economic History of a Nebraska Township* was published in 1893 in the Johns Hopkins University Studies in Historical and Political Science.

Bentley spent the following three years in graduate work in economics and sociology—two at Johns Hopkins and one at the universities of

Berlin and Freiburg im Breisgau. At Berlin he gained insights from Adolf Wagner and Gustav Schmoller on the desirability of social and economic reform, and George Simmel inspired him to analyze the complex interactions of individuals and social groups. At Johns Hopkins, Bentley explored subjects ranging from the economics of competition and monopoly to the history of economic thought. In June 1895 he received his doctorate. His thesis, "The Units of Investigation in the Social Sciences," was published in *Annals of the American Academy of Political and Social Science.*

During the academic year (1895–1896) Bentley was lecturer in sociology at the University of Chicago and came to know John Dewey as a student in his seminars on logic and ethics. Having decided that his gifts were not in college teaching, Bentley spent the next fourteen years as a journalist—as a reporter and then an editorial writer for the *Chicago Times-Herald* (later the *Record-Herald*). As a newspaperman, he learned the facts of economic, political, and social life of that turbulent city. In 1899 he married Anna Harrison, a physician. Between 1896 and 1908 he wrote *The Process of Government* (1908), a classic work in which he laid a firm basis for the flourishing study in America of "pressure groups" or "group pressures." His subtle approach was not fully appreciated for almost thirty years, but beginning in the late 1930's political scientists began to apply Bentley's insights. His combination of tough-mindedness and open-mindedness made him the most devastating political realist of his time, and yet he escaped the limitations of both Charles A. Beard and Vilfredo Pareto. Bentley's candor in describing how all forms of government, including the despotic, respond to the pressures of various social groups exposed him to the charge of being an extreme relativist who might condone various forms of dictatorship or absolutism. Some critics failed to see that Bentley could insist on portraying the whole truth about political behavior while maintaining a genuine idealism and concern for improving the welfare of all exploited or underprivileged groups.

In 1911 Bentley left Chicago for a rural retreat in Paoli, Ind., where he devoted his energies to scientific research and writing. During World War I he helped organize Red Cross activities in Indiana. With the return of peace he became interested in the cooperative work of the Non-Partisan League in North Dakota. He then wrote a massive critical study of the American business and political scene entitled *Makers, Users, and Masters*. The original volume was rejected by several publishers, but a compressed version was published in 1969. Critics praised it as a penetrating analysis of the power exerted by the captains of business and finance over the American economy at the time of World War I.

During the early 1920's Bentley reformulated his ideas on a science of society. In *Relativity in Man and Society* (1926) he contended that sociologists should adopt Albert Einstein's method of viewing space and time as dimensions or integral phases of the events they describe. He urged them to introduce their own observational position in space-time and society as an essential factor in their reports on social events.

Bentley's first wife died in 1924. Six years later he married Susan W. Chipman, an old friend. She died in 1942, and in 1946 he married Imogene M. Shaw. After 1926 Bentley devoted himself to the philosophy of scientific inquiry. His *Linguistic Analysis of Mathematics* (1932) was a challenging study of the nature of meaning and postulates in mathematics and the other sciences. In trying to clarify the relations of ordinary language to mathematical signs and symbols, he anticipated the work of Ludwig Wittgenstein.

Three years later Bentley's views on the proper methods for studying human behavior were presented in *Behavior, Knowledge, Fact*. Rejecting the traditional dichotomies of mind and body, mind and object, man and society, and the organism and its environment, he stressed the need for sociologists to construct a relativistic "behavioral space-time." These two iconoclastic volumes were appreciated by only a small group of readers. Among them was John Dewey, who wrote that they had helped to clarify his ideas on some important problems in his treatise *Logic, the Theory of Inquiry* (1938). Dewey's interest in Bentley's insights led to their collaborating on *Knowing and the Known* (1949). In this work they proposed the "transactional" approach, which presents a total situation and process so that the constituent parts, human and nonhuman, can be seen as integrated phases of that situation and process. This approach was applied by research workers in biology, physics, political science, psychology, and sociology. In 1954 Bentley's major essays on language, logic, and scientific inquiry were collected and published as *Inquiry Into Inquiries*.

Bentley was a thinker of great originality and profound understanding of complex problems —an iconoclast who had become an internationally famous figure in at least three disciplines. He had the courage to advance hypotheses that challenged many dominant views and vested intellectual interests. His vigorous criticism of authorities and his revolutionary ideas for restructuring whole areas of scientific research antagonized many. But his ideas eventually influenced the work of such leading scholars as Charles A. Beard in history, John Dewey in the theory of logic and knowledge, Ludwig von Wiese in sociology, Karl Llewellyn in law, Adelbert Ames and Hadley Cantril in perceptual psychology, and Percy W. Bridgman in mathematics and physics. Bentley died in Paoli, Ind.

[Manuscripts of Bentley's writings and correspondence, as well as articles and books about him, are at the Lilly Library, University of Indiana; notes and varied materials are in the files of Sidney Ratner. Two important articles by Bentley not cited in the text are "Kennetic Inquiry," *Science*, Dec. 29, 1950; and "The Word 'Transaction,'" *Humanist*, Jan.–Feb. 1957.

See also Paul F. Kress, *Social Science and the Idea of Process: The Ambiguous Legacy of Arthur F. Bentley* (1970); Sidney Ratner, "Arthur F. Bentley," *Journal of Philosophy*, July 3, 1958; Sidney Ratner, Jules Altman, and James E. Wheeler, eds., *John Dewey and Arthur F. Bentley: A Philosophical Correspondence 1932–1951* (1964); Richard W. Taylor, ed., *Life, Language, Law: Essays in Honor of Arthur F. Bentley* (1957); "Paoli's Adopted Son," *Paoli Republican*, Mar. 26, 1957; and obituary notices in the *Paoli News*, May 21, 1957, and the *New York Times*, May 22, 1957.]

SIDNEY RATNER

BERENSON, BERNARD (June 26, 1865– Oct. 6, 1959), art historian and connoisseur, was born Bernhard Valvrojenski at Biturmansk, near Vilna, Lithuania, the son of Albert Valvrojenski and Julia Mieliszanski. His parents were Jewish and of humble circumstances; his father made his living in the timber trade, but like many of his coreligionaries in the Baltic provinces, he began to think of immigration to America. Before taking this step he changed the family name to Berenson. Bernard (the "h" was dropped at the time of World War I) received his earliest education in the school of the local synagogue, where he learned Hebrew. He was ten years old when the family moved to Boston, Mass., where his father became a dealer in scrap metal. In the new environment the attachment to Jewish orthodoxy weakened; the children remembered that their father used to read Voltaire to them, and he evidently inculcated a broadly tolerant religous view.

Berenson is said to have taught himself Greek, and his parents encouraged his omnivorous reading. He attended the local public school in South Boston and the celebrated Boston Latin School before entering Boston University in 1883. During his first year there, he heard the lectures of Charles Eliot Norton of Harvard University on the building of medieval churches in Italy. Norton was much impressed with Berenson's intellectual promise and arranged for his transfer to Harvard. There he received the B.A. in June 1887.

At Harvard Berenson studied languages and literatures, including Sanskrit, Arabic, and Medieval German. In a fellowship application at the end of his senior year he declared that he wished to devote every spare moment to literature and comparative religion. He hoped to find some place in the program for French and Italian art and architecture. Although he failed to win the scholarship, a group of friends, among whom was Isabella Stewart Gardner, decided to support his studies abroad. He spent the autumn and winter of 1887-1888 in Paris and London and also at Oxford University, where he absorbed particularly the aesthetics of Walter Pater and John Ruskin.

In the spring of 1888 he made his first trip to Italy and immediately felt that he had discovered his vocation in the study of Italian art. Accurately attributing medieval and Renaissance painting was then in its infancy, and as early as 1890 he described his determination to devote himself to connoisseurship:

> . . . nobody before us has dedicated his entire activity, his entire life, to connoisseurship . . . we are the first to have no idea before us, no ambition, no thought of reward. We shall give ourselves up to learning to distinguish between the authentic works of an Italian painter of the fifteenth or sixteenth century and those commonly ascribed to him *(Sketch for a Self-Portrait* [1949], p. 51).

The methods adopted by Berenson in proceeding with this task owed a good deal to the Italian art historian Giovanni Morelli, who had formulated what he called scientific criteria for determining attributions by the study of morphological detail. Berenson developed Morelli's principles in an essay, "The Rudiments of Connoisseurship" (1902). He cautioned against relying too much on documents, which could be forged. Even where signatures were genuine, a master might have signed a work painted by his pupils. Berenson emphasized the importance of concentrated observation to determine those characteristics that made the style of a given painter unique.

In portraits details like the ear or fingernails might be unconsciously repeated time after time and thus become a guide to an artist's style. In *The Study and Criticism of Italian Art* (1902), Berenson proposed the general principle that "details determine characteristics in proportion (a) as they are not vehicles of expression, (b) as they do not attract attention, (c) as they are not controlled by fashion, (d) as they allow the formation of habit in their execution."

In 1890 Berenson was in London studying Italian pictures in English collections; there he met a young Anglo-Irish lawyer, Frank Costelloe, and his wife, the former Mary Logan Smith. After Berenson had become acquainted with the Costelloes, and had spent some time at the Smiths' country house, Friday's Hill, Mary became captivated by his enthusiasm for Italian Renaissance art, and presently fell in love with the man as well as with the subject. In 1891 she left Costelloe and moved to Fiesole—Berenson maintained a separate establishment in Florence—where she remained for most of the decade. With her encouragement and collaboration Berenson brought out his *Venetian Painters of the Renaissance* (1894), followed soon after by *Lorenzo Lotto; An Essay in Art Criticism*. In 1896 came *Florentine Painters of the Renaissance* and in 1897 *Central Italian Painters of the Renaissance*. The attributions made in these lists established Berenson's authority as a connoisseur, and in 1897 he began work on his greatest scholarly enterprise, *Drawings of the Florentine Painters* (1903).

At the turn of the century international dealers found among American millionaires an ever-rising market for Italian medieval and Renaissance painting, and their clients increasingly depended on Berenson's authentication of a picture. In view of his belief that he should work "with no thought of reward," it is ironic that his connoisseurship had striking economic consequences. Berenson began by acquiring pictures for such collectors as Mrs. Gardner in Boston and Benjamin Altman in New York, receiving a substantial commission on each purchase. Soon, however, he found it more convenient to serve as consultant, for an annual retainer, to such international dealers as Martin H. Colnaghi and the

Duveen brothers. From 1905 to 1939 he was under contract to the Duveen firm, and received fees that sometimes amounted to $100,000 a year. Thus he acquired the fortune that enabled him first to rent and then to buy Villa I Tatti near Florence, to create his own collection and library, and to carry on his work at leisure.

Frank Costelloe died in 1899, and on Christmas day, 1900, Mary Costelloe and Berenson were married in a Catholic service in the chapel of Villa I Tatti. Berenson had left the Jewish faith and adopted Episcopalianism while in Boston. In 1895 he had converted to Roman Catholicism at the monastery of Monte Oliveto near Siena, but it is clear that his commitment to Rome was based more on the aesthetic appeal of the liturgy than on the authority of the dogma. His religious interests were directed more to art than to theology.

The villa was enlarged at intervals during the succeeding decades, chiefly to accommodate Berenson's ever-growing library. In this setting he organized for over fifty years a life that combined scholarship in art history with an elegant and discriminating hospitality. Among his notable friends who were frequent guests were Edith Wharton, Learned Hand, Henry Adams, Walter Lippmann, and Kenneth Clark.

During World War II, Berenson remained at the villa except when he went into hiding for the period of the German occupation after the fall of Mussolini. Mary Berenson, who had long been an invalid, died shortly after the war.

In his remaining years, Berenson had the constant support of his devoted secretary and companion, Nicky Mariano, the daughter of a church historian who had entered his household as librarian in 1918. He worked on the last of the many editions of the lists of Italian Renaissance painters, lavishly illustrated and published by Phaidon. There was also a series of critical essays and autobiographical works: *Aesthetics and History* (1948); *Sketch for a Self-Portrait* (1949); *Rumour and Reflection* (1952); and *The Arch of Constantine or The Decline of Form* (1954).

Berenson received the rare honor of citizenship in the commune of Florence and became a figure of world renown, enjoying the homage of friends and admirers of every nationality. He died at I Tatti in his ninety-fifth year. He bequeathed to Harvard the villa with its library and collections and his residuary estate. With this generous legacy, the university established the Harvard Center for Italian Renaissance Studies in Florence.

[The Berenson Archive at Villa I Tatti contains the manuscripts of his works, diaries, and a large portion of his correspondence. Several selections from the letters and diaries have been published: *The Bernard Berenson Treasury* (1962), selected and edited by Hanna Kiel; *Sunset and Twilight: From the Diaries of 1947–58* (1964), edited by Nicky Mariano; *The Selected Letters of Bernard Berenson* (1964), edited by A. K. McComb; and Umberto Morra, *Conversations With Berenson* (1965), translated by Florence Hammond.

Sylvia Sprigge, *Berenson: A Biography* (1960), contains material from the archive but is marred by a number of errors. See also Nicky Mariano, *Forty Years With Berenson* (1966); and Ernest Samuels, *Bernard Berenson: The Making of a Connoisseur* (1979). The Paul Sachs memoir in the Oral History Collection of Columbia University contains copies of the correspondence of the two men over a period of many years and abundant material about Berenson and I Tatti. See also the obituary in the *New York Times*, Oct. 8, 1959.]

MYRON P. GILMORE

BERGER, MEYER (Sept. 1, 1898–Feb. 8, 1959), reporter, columnist, author, known as Mike Berger, was born in New York City, where he lived throughout his life. He was one of eleven children of Ignace (or Ignatz) Berger, a Jewish immigrant tailor from what is now Czechoslovakia, and Sarah Waldman, who ran a small candy store. Their home on the Lower East Side was steeped in poverty, and Berger was selling newspapers on Broadway when he was only eight years old. In 1911, at the age of twelve, he was forced to quit school and go to work for $1.50 a week as a messenger boy for the *New York Morning World.* Chasing copy and running errands between the newspaper's Brooklyn office and its Park Row building, "Mike," as the enterprising youth was called, advanced until he was head office boy by 1917.

With the entry of the United States into World War I, Berger volunteered for the army but was rejected because of poor eyesight. Whether he memorized the test chart letters and so got through a second examination or posed as a musician eligible for a military band is unclear, but his persistence somehow won him eventual acceptance. He served in the 27th Division's 106th Infantry in France, where as a line sergeant he won a Purple Heart, the Silver Star, and the Conspicuous Service Cross.

After his discharge in 1919, Berger returned to the *World* as a police reporter in Brooklyn. In 1922 he joined the Standard News Association, where he was a district reporter in Brooklyn and a top rewrite man for five years. On Aug. 29, 1926, he married Mae Gamsu; they had no children. In March 1928 he became a reporter on the *New York Times*, thereafter his journalistic home, except for a year (1937–38) as a staff writer for the *New Yorker*.

On the *Times* Berger covered murders among Brooklyn gangsters and grew to be a specialist in the life and lore of the underworld. He reported the shootings of the racketeers and the lawlessness of the prohibition era. When Al Capone was tried in 1931 for income tax evasion, Berger produced from Chicago a series of sixteen articles so informative and graphic that they were nominated for a Pulitzer Prize. He also reported the widely followed similar trial of Dutch Schultz (Arthur Flegenheimer).

In 1942 Berger was sent to London to report the impact of World War II on the British people. His accounts were so vivid that after a few months he was brought back to describe the effects of the conflict on the home front—Manhattan and its metropolitan area. He was at his best in a daily by-line column, "About New York," that first appeared in 1939–40. This freed him to walk the city streets, stroll through parks, ride subways, and talk to taxi drivers, workmen, and saleswomen. It came to be a popular feature, sensitively presented. Many readers felt that they knew the author personally.

Berger was awarded a Pulitzer Prize in 1950 for his reporting of the killing of thirteen people in Camden, N.J., by Howard Unruh, a crazed veteran. Using shorthand, he interviewed fifty witnesses along the murderer's course and then "in two and a half hours pounded out 4,000 words which were printed in the first edition without a word changed by the editors." Few knew that he gave his $1,000 award to the killer's mother.

Representative columns, including humorous pieces about oddities at the 1939 World's Fair in Flushing Meadow, were collected in his first book, *The Eight Million* (1942), illustrated by his brother Henry. He collaborated with a Catholic priest, James Keller, on *Men of Maryknoll* (1943), a reflection of Berger's deep interest in the Maryknoll missionaries whom he frequently visited and for whom he prepared a handbook, "Notes on Missionary Writing" (1945), to assist evangels in reporting their experiences. In anticipation of the *Times* centennial, Berger was given a two-year assignment of writing *The Story of the New York Times,* completed in 1951. Although basically historical, his narrative was often anecdotal, "about the *Times*" in the way his column was

"About New York." *New York, City on Many Waters* was published in 1955.

Berger was tall, thin, and balding, with a long gentle face. He tended to shyness yet was almost immediately friendly, and always so to the unfortunate, handicapped, or deprived. A sufferer from stomach ulcers during much of his professional life, he had a gastrointestinal attack followed by a stroke early in 1959, and he died three days later in New York City.

The audience that Berger had written for with wit, humanity, tenderness, simplicity, originality, understanding, crispness, and accuracy had extended far beyond New York's boundaries. After his death a representative letter came from Austin, Tex.: ". . . many years since I have been so saddened by a death of a person unknown to me except through print." At the Columbia University Graduate School of Journalism, where he was a visiting lecturer, Mike Berger Awards were endowed for New York journalists who distinguished themselves in his tradition of reporting.

[Berger's writings, notebooks, and papers are at the Columbia University Graduate School of Journalism. On his career, see Turner Catledge, *My Life and the Times* (1971); J. C. Devlin, "The Most Unforgettable Character I've Met," *Reader's Digest*, Oct. 1959; Gay Talese, *The Kingdom and the Power* (1969); Stanley Walker, *City Editor* (1934); and the *New York Times*, Feb. 9–12, 1959.]

IRVING DILLIARD

BINGHAM, HIRAM (Nov. 19, 1875–June 6, 1956), explorer and U.S. senator, was born in Honolulu, Hawaii, the son of Hiram Bingham and Minerva Clarissa Brewster, missionaries to the Gilbert Islands who had been forced by ill health to retire to Hawaii. He attended the Punahou School in Honolulu from 1882 to 1892 and in preparation for a missionary career spent two years at Phillips Andover Academy and four years at Yale. At the university he tutored and did odd jobs to finance his education.

Upon graduation from Yale with the B.A. in 1898, Bingham returned to Honolulu and became superintendent at the Palama Chapel Mission. Unhappy with this work, he resigned after eight months and was employed briefly as a chemist for an American sugar company. At the same time he renewed his acquaintance with Alfreda Mitchell, the granddaughter of Charles L. Tiffany, founder of Tiffany and Company, who was making a

Pacific tour. The two quietly became engaged.

Turning to the study of history, Bingham enrolled in the graduate program of the University of California at Berkeley, from which he received the M.A. in 1900. On Nov. 20, 1900, he and Alfreda Mitchell were married; they had seven sons. Bingham accepted an Austin teaching fellowship at Harvard and, during the next five years, earned another M.A. and a Ph.D. in the then relatively unexplored field of South American history.

In 1905 Bingham became a preceptor in the tutorial program instituted by Woodrow Wilson at Princeton. He taught only one year, however. Ambitious and restless, he secured leave in order to follow the 1819 march of Bolívar across the northern coast of South America in preparation for a biography. The difficult and dangerous journey from Caracas to Bogotá was described in Bingham's first book, *The Journal of an Expedition Across Venezuela and Colombia* (1909).

Upon his return in 1907, Bingham took a position as lecturer in South American history and geography at Yale. He became assistant professor of Latin American history in 1910 and was professor from 1915 to 1924. The Binghams built an imposing mansion in New Haven.

Teaching at Yale did not quench Bingham's urge to explore. Secretary of State Elihu Root named him a delegate to the first Pan-American Scientific Congress, held at Santiago, Chile, from December 1908 to January 1909. Bingham used the opportunity to undertake a six-month trek, retracing the old Spanish trade route from Buenos Aires to Lima. He chronicled the adventure in *Across South America* (1911).

In 1911 Bingham organized and directed the Yale Peruvian Expedition to search for the last Inca capital and to map an uncharted area of the Andes. He found Vitcos, which he deemed the final Inca base, uncovered the magnificent ruins of Machu Picchu, a rich source of Inca civilization, and made the first ascent of 21,000-foot Mt. Coropuna. Yale and the National Geographic Society jointly sponsored further expeditions in 1912 and in 1914–15. The discoveries in Peru laid the foundation for a series of popular lectures, articles, and books, including "Vitcos, the Last Inca Capital" (1912), *Inca Land* (1922), *Machu Picchu, a Citadel of the Incas* (1930), and *Lost City of the Incas* (1948).

Soon after the outbreak of World War I, Bingham again left Yale. He joined the Connecticut National Guard as captain of artillery in 1916. Determined to learn to fly, he won his

pilot's wings the next year at the age of forty-two. Promoted to lieutenant colonel, he served as chief of the Air Personnel Division of the Air Service in Washington and with the Allied Expeditionary Forces in France. *An Explorer in the Air Service* (1920) recorded his experience as commanding officer of the Allied flying school at Issoudon.

After the war, Bingham turned to politics. In 1916 he had served as alternate at large at the Republican convention. In the early 1920's, however, he sought a more active political role. His commitment to states' rights, federal economy, high tariff, and strong defense made him a staunch Old Guard Republican. Whereas in 1913 he had advocated the repudiation of the Monroe Doctrine as an "obsolete shibboleth," in 1920 he reversed his position. Six feet four, silver-haired, a famous explorer, aviator, author, and speaker, Bingham seemed an ideal candidate to J. Henry Roraback, the conservative Republican chairman and undisputed "boss" of Connecticut. Aided by Roraback, Bingham secured the nomination as lieutenant governor in 1922 and was elected. In 1924, after the incumbent Republican governor had incurred Roraback's displeasure, Bingham was nominated for governor. On a ticket headed by Coolidge, he secured the highest plurality in Connecticut history. He served in that office for only one day, however. During the campaign, on October 14, Frank Brandegee, the Republican senator from Connecticut, had committed suicide. Two months later, a special election was held to fill Brandegee's unexpired term. Following Roraback's wishes, the Republicans nominated the governor-elect. While the first campaign of 1924 had been exciting for Bingham, the second was ugly. He won, but with less than one-third his previous majority. Two years later he ran for a full term and was elected handily.

During his eight years in the Senate, Bingham served on the President's Aircraft Board in 1925 and drafted the Air Commerce Act of 1926, the first attempt at federal regulation of civil aviation. He chaired the Committee on Territories and Insular Affairs, visited China, and headed the Samoan Commission.

In September 1929, when the Senate Finance Committee was drafting the Hawley-Smoot tariff, Bingham, a committee member and representative of a state with many protected industries, consulted Charles L. Eyanson, a lobbyist of the Connecticut Manufacturers Association, as a tariff expert. He placed Eyanson on the Senate payroll as a clerk and took him into closed sessions of the Finance Committee. When Eyanson's role was revealed, Bingham acknowledged misjudgment but neither wrongdoing nor malicious intent. A subcommittee of the Judiciary Committee, chaired by George Norris of Nebraska, investigated and submitted a resolution of censure. On November 4, after four hours of debate and the inclusion of an amendment exonerating Bingham of "corrupt motives," the resolution passed 54 to 22 with 18 abstentions. It condemned Bingham's behavior as "contrary to good morals and senatorial ethics" and as tending "to bring the Senate into dishonor and disrepute." Bingham's conservatism and lofty, sometimes combative style of speaking irritated his midwestern Progressive colleagues, and the vote divided along strict sectional and partisan lines. All the northeastern Republicans supported the Connecticut senator. Within two days Bingham rejoined the tariff debate on the Senate floor.

In the Democratic sweep of 1932 Bingham lost his seat to Augustine Lonergan. He remained in Washington, however. In 1937 the Binghams, who had long been estranged, were divorced, and Bingham married Suzanne Carroll Hill. He became a director of banks and corporations, served as president of the National Aeronautic Association (1928–34), and continued to write, including a biography, *Elihu Yale, the American Nabob of Queen Square* (1939). During World War II he lectured on the Pacific Islands at naval officer training schools. In 1951 President Truman invited Bingham, whose long absence from government had not made him less conservative, to head the Loyalty Review Board of the Civil Service Commission. At Bingham's suggestion the basis for dismissals was changed from a finding of "reasonable grounds" of "disloyalty" on the part of the employee to a finding of "reasonable doubt" of "loyalty." The shift produced a series of rulings unfavorable to employees and led to the controversial dismissals of John Stewart Service and John Carter Vincent from the State Department. With the inauguration of Eisenhower in 1953, Bingham lost his position. He died in Washington, D.C.

[The rich collection of manuscript material at the Sterling Library of Yale University includes the Bingham family papers, the papers of the Yale Peruvian Expedition, and the Mitchell-Tiffany papers. Biographical articles have appeared in collective biographies of the Yale class of 1898 issued in 1908, 1938, and 1948. Bingham attacked the Monroe Doctrine in *The Monroe Doctrine: An Obsolete Shibboleth* (1913); and reversed his position in "The Future of the Monroe

Doctrine," *Journal of International Relations,* Apr. 1920. On his contributions and claims as an explorer, see John Hemming, *The Conquest of the Incas* (1970); Jerry E. Patterson assesses his writings on Latin America in "Hiram Bingham: 1875–1956," *Hispanic American Historical Review,* Feb. 1957. On his ideology and relationship to Roraback, see Rowland W. Mitchell, Jr., "Social Legislation in Connecticut 1919–1939" (diss., Yale University, 1954), ch. 7; and Edwin M. Dahill, Jr., "Connecticut's J. Henry Roraback" (diss., Columbia University, 1971), chs. 9 and 10. See also Duff Cooper's highly critical "A Superior Person," *American Mercury,* Mar. 1930.]

ESTELLE F. FEINSTEIN

BIRDSEYE, CLARENCE (Dec. 9, 1886– Oct. 7, 1956), scientist and inventor whose process for quick-freezing foods in convenient packages made his name a household word and created a multibillion-dollar industry, was born in Brooklyn, N.Y., the son of Clarence Frank Birdseye, lawyer and legal scholar, and Ada Underwood. While quite young, he developed two lifelong interests–natural history and food. At the age of five, Birdseye gave his mother a mouse skin that he had dressed; and before he had reached his teens, his proficiency in taxidermy led him to insert an advertisement in a sporting magazine offering instruction in the art under the impressive rubric of the American School of Taxidermy. At Montclair, N.J., where he attended high school, his other enduring interest, food preparation, came to light when he enrolled in the cooking class.

Following a family tradition, Birdseye entered Amherst College with the class of 1910; his attendance was irregular, however, owing to financial difficulties, and he did not graduate. Among his imaginative schemes for meeting college expenses were the sale of frogs to the Bronx Zoo for snake food and the live-trapping of 135 specimens of the comparatively rare black rat for a Columbia University professor's breeding experiments.

From 1910 to 1912 Birdseye was a field naturalist for the Biological Survey of the United States Department of Agriculture, work that led to his publication of a short monograph entitled *Some Common Mammals of Western Montana in Relation to Agriculture and Spotted Fever* (1912). A successful venture in marketing western furs during this period took him in 1912 to Labrador, where he was associated for a time with the medical missionary Sir Wilfred Grenfell. Birdseye traded in furs in Labrador for the next five years.

During a visit to the United States, Birdseye married Eleanor Gannett on Aug. 21, 1915; they had four children. In 1916 he returned to Labrador with his wife and their infant son. His changed domestic circumstances drew Birdseye's attention to the problems of food preservation. The meat of rabbits, ducks, and caribou, if frozen quickly at a temperature -40° or -50° F., retained its freshness indefinitely. Fish caught through holes in ice during subzero weather also were as firm and fresh when cooked weeks later, as if they had just been caught. Further crude experiments confirmed that quick-freezing preserves the natural characteristics of food by preventing the formation of the large ice crystals that gather in slowly frozen foodstuffs and rupture their cellular structure—thus destroying their texture, flavor, and natural juices and reducing their vitamin content.

World War I interrupted Birdseye's search for a commercial application of his findings. After returning to the United States, he became purchasing agent for the United States Housing Corporation (1917–19) and assistant to the president of the United States Fisheries Association (1920–22). In 1923 he resumed his experiments with quick-freezing, establishing himself in the corner of an icehouse in New Jersey. His capital investment was $7 for an electric fan, buckets of brine, and cakes of ice. The first successful product was dressed fillets of haddock, frozen brick-hard in square containers made from old candy boxes. The scientific principle was already known; Birdseye's contribution was to devise a method of artificially freezing perishables by pressing them between belts (later between refrigerated metal plates) that allowed the heat exchange to be accomplished directly upon the foods. Birdseye's first freezer was not portable, but the second was, and thus vegetables could be prepared and quick-frozen at the source of supply.

In 1924, to be near a reliable source of fresh fish, Birdseye established laboratories for research and development at Gloucester, Mass. With a small group of associates and despite precarious financing of his small operation (called General Foods Company and General Seafoods Corporation), Birdseye perfected his process, coined the word "quick-freeze," and by 1928 was able to apply the technique to meat, poultry, fish, and shellfish in commercial quantities. The missing element, public acceptance, appeared after 1929.

In that year the Postum Company, skilled in the distribution of consumer food products, together with the Goldman Sachs Trading Corporation, acquired all patents and assets of Birdseye's company for a price in the range of $20 million to $23.5 million. Subsequently, the Postum Company purchased the Goldman Sachs interest and adopted the name General Foods, substituting "Corporation" for "Company." Within a few years quick-frozen foods had revolutionized food distribution, brought about sweeping changes in national eating habits, and effected fundamental improvements in American agriculture through stimulating the seed industry to refine varieties for quick-frozen products, introducing quality controls in field production, and stabilizing prices, which brought millions of acres into profitable use. Birdseye's name became a famous trademark. By 1976 hundreds of processors were producing quick-frozen foods with an annual value of nearly $17 billion.

Although his process made Birdseye wealthy, he continued to work. In the 1940's Birdseye invented a machine capable of quick-freezing loose vegetables individually, and a process for preserving foods by quick drying that he called the "anhydrous method." Neither was developed commercially. He also invented a reflector and an infrared heat lamp and a recoilless harpoon gun. His last project (1953–55) took him to Peru on an assignment to develop a new method of making paper stock from bagasse (crushed sugarcane stalks). While there he suffered a heart attack that he attributed to the high altitude. He died in New York City.

Birdseye was an inventor and cut-and-try experimenter in the tradition of Benjamin Franklin and Thomas Edison. Although untrained in any formal sense, he was an original thinker and investigator, gifted with keen powers of observation and an enormous curiosity. He was also a capable businessman who held some 300 American and foreign patents. His early interest in the natural world never flagged. Near the end of his life he was coauthor with his wife of *Growing Woodland Plants* (1951).

[Sources include *Amherst College Biographical Record* (1973); William H. Clark and James H. S. Moynahan, *Famous Leaders of Industry* (1955); Leicester H. Sherrill, "Quick Freezing of Filleted Fish," *Food Industries*, Oct. 1928; "Let Them Eat Cake," *ibid.*, Oct. 1934; "Quick-frozen Foods," *Fortune*, June 1939; Wambly Bald, "Lion Tidbit to Frozen Food Genius," *Quick Frozen Foods*, Sept. 1954,

Mar. 1960, and Feb. 1977. See also the obituary notices in the *Gloucester* (Mass.) *Daily Times,* Oct. 8, 1956; and the *New York Herald Tribune* and *New York Times,* Oct. 9, 1956. On the acquisition of the Birdseye process by the Postum Company, see "The Reminiscences of Edwin T. Gibson," Oral History Collections, Columbia University (1956).]

GERALD CARSON

BLOCH, ERNEST (July 24, 1880–July 15, 1959), composer, was born in Geneva. Switzerland, the son of Maurice Bloch, a shopkeeper, and Sophie Brunschwig. Although his father expected him to become a shopkeeper too, Bloch aspired from childhood to become a musician. When he was eleven he wrote out such a vow and placed it under a mound of rocks, around which he built a ritual fire. Unable to counter the force of such determination, Bloch's father permitted him when he was fourteen to begin the study of solfeggio with Émile Jaques-Dalcroze and of violin with Louis Rey. During this period Bloch completed several ambitious apprentice compositions, including the Oriental Symphony and an andante for string quartet. In 1896 he finished his academic training at the Geneva collège, and a year later he entered the Royal Conservatory of Music in Brussels, where he studied the violin with Eugène Ysaÿe and composition with François Rasse. He completed his musical training with Ivan Knorr in Frankfurt and Ludwig Thuille in Munich.

Bloch then settled in Paris, where he completed his first mature work, the Symphony in C-sharp Minor, in 1903. Two movements were performed in Basel the following year, but the work was not heard in its entirety until 1910, in Geneva. Financial reverses at home obliged Bloch to return to Geneva to work in his father's shop. On Aug. 13, 1904, he married Marguerite Schneider. Of their three children, Suzanne became a noted lutenist and scholar specializing in early music.

While attending to his father's business, Bloch continued to compose. Among his most noteworthy works of this early period are the symphonic diptych *Hiver—printemps* (1905); a song cycle for soprano and orchestra, *Poèmes d'automne* (1906); and *Macbeth*, a three-act opera first produced at the Paris Opéra-Comique on Nov. 30, 1910. The distinguished French musicologist Romain Rolland, impressed with the work, traveled to Geneva to meet the composer. When he discovered Bloch working in a shop, he persuaded him to abandon business for good and to devote himself exclusively to music.

From 1911 to 1915 Bloch taught composition and aesthetics at the Geneva Conservatory of Music, and during this period his music underwent a significant transformation. Turning from the post-Romantic and occasionally impressionistic style, he began writing music that was still romantic in its use of expansive melodic lines and lush harmonies but ethnic in subject matter and content. Bloch's desire was to reflect the history, culture, and ideals of the Jewish people. He wrote at the time: "I am a Jew. I aspire to write Jewish music not for the sake of self-advertisement, but because it is the only way in which I can produce music of vitality—if I can do such a thing at all." Rather than quoting authentic Hebraic melodies directly, Bloch exploited their intervallic and rhythmic patterns in an attempt to infuse his works with their mysticism, spirituality, and abiding melancholy. During this period he completed *Three Jewish Poems,* for orchestra (1913); two psalms for soprano and orchestra (1914); *Israel* (1916), a symphony in one movement inspired by the liturgy for Yom Kippur (the Day of Atonement); and *Schelomo,* for cello obbligato and orchestra (1916), a rhapsodic portrait of King Solomon which was the first composition to gain him international attention and is still one of his most frequently performed works.

In July 1916 Bloch came to the United States to conduct the orchestra for Maud Allan's touring dance group, which went bankrupt while on the road. Stranded, without money or a job, he almost starved during the next few months. His situation improved considerably in 1917, when he became the head of the theory department at the David Mannes School of Music in New York City. Significant performances of his compositions soon brought him into prominence, including the premiere of his String Quartet no. 1 (1916) by the Flonzaley Quartet and the world premiere of *Schelomo* by the New York Society of the Friends of Music, both in 1917. In 1919 he received the Elizabeth Sprague Coolidge Prize for his Suite for Viola and Piano, completed that year.

From 1920 to 1925 Bloch was director of the Cleveland Institute of Music and, from 1925 to 1930, director of the San Francisco Conservatory. His compositions from this period represent a temporary shift from Hebrew idioms toward a style often baroque in structure but reflecting the contemporary composer's consciousness of complex rhythmic procedures and dissonant harmonic writing. In the Piano Quintet no. 1 (1923) he experimented with quarter-tone-music; and in the Concerto Grosso no. 1 (1925), composed as a didactic exercise for his students at Cleveland, he demonstrated how music can be written in a neo-Baroque idiom and with classic simplicity while retaining a modern spirit. In the rhapsody *America,* which won first prize in a contest sponsored by *Musical America,* he paid tribute to his adopted land, having become an American citizen in 1924.

A grant from a patron in San Francisco enabled Bloch to give up teaching and to retire in 1930 to Roveredo Capriasco, Ticino, Switzerland, where he completed his most ambitious Hebraic work, the *Sacred Service* (1933), for the Sabbath morning prayers. The work symbolized for him "far more than a Jewish service," which "in its great simplicity and variety . . . embodies a philosophy acceptable to all men." The world premiere took place in Turin on Jan. 12, 1934, and Bloch conducted the American premiere three months later.

Bloch returned to the United States in 1938, and from 1943 until his death lived at Agate Beach, near Portland, Oreg., in a rambling and isolated house overlooking the Pacific. Each summer he taught composition at the University of California at Berkeley, devoting the rest of the year to his own music. He remained extraordinarily productive until his death, in Portland, of the cancer from which he had suffered for several years. Although he had abandoned Hebrew music, his later compositions retain much of its rhapsodic style, elemental rhythmic power, infusion of mysticism, and intervallic structure. His major works include the *Suite symphonique* for orchestra (1944); the String Quartet no. 2 (1945), which received the New York Music Critics Circle Award in 1945; and the *Concerto symphonique,* for piano and orchestra (1948).

In 1949 the League of Composers sponsored a three-day festival at the Juilliard School of Music in New York City, celebrating thirty-five years of Bloch's compositions; and in 1950, in honor of his seventieth birthday, a six-day festival of his music was held in Chicago, where the *Scherzo fantasque,* for piano and orchestra (1948), received its world premiere. In 1953 Bloch's String Quartet no. 3 (1952) and Concerto Grosso no. 2 (1952) both received the top award of the New York Music Critics Circle, the first time that first prizes were awarded in two categories to the same composer. His last works include the String

Quartet no. 5 (1955); the Symphony in E-flat Major (1955); and two suites for unaccompanied violin (1958), commissioned by Yehudi Menuhin. The world premiere of his Piano Quintet no. 2 (1957) was given at a memorial concert in New York City on Dec. 6, 1959.

[On Bloch's life and music, see Suzanne Bloch, "Ernest Bloch," *Musical America,* Feb. 15, 1956; Maria Tibaldi Chiesa, *Ernest Bloch* (1933); David Ewen, ed., *The New Book of Modern Composers* (1967); Irene Heskes and Suzanne Bloch, *Ernest Bloch: Creative Spirit* (1976); D. Newlin, "The Later Works of Ernest Bloch," *Musical Quarterly,* Oct. 1947; Paul Rosenfeld, *Musical Portraits* (1920); and Robert Strassburg, *Ernest Bloch: Voice in the Wilderness* (1977).]

DAVID EWEN

BOEING, WILLIAM EDWARD (Oct. 1, 1881–Sept. 28, 1956), aviation pioneer and business executive, was born in Detroit, Mich., the only son of Wilhelm and Marie Ortman Boeing. The family was wealthy and had substantial timber and mining property in Michigan and Minnesota. His father, who died when William was eight, was German-born and his mother Austrian. Boeing was educated in private schools in Europe and the United States, and he attended the Sheffield Scientific School at Yale for three years, leaving without a degree in 1902 in order to go into the lumber business in the Pacific Northwest. He was successful enough so that he decided in 1908 to settle permanently in Seattle. He retained extensive lumber and mining interests throughout his life.

About 1910 Boeing became interested in aviation. In August 1915 he learned to fly at Glenn L. Martin's flying school in Los Angeles and bought a Martin seaplane. At the same time he and a fellow enthusiast, Conrad Westervelt, an engineer officer in the United States Navy, undertook to build their own airplanes. For this purpose, in 1916 they organized the Pacific Aero Products Company, soon renamed the Boeing Airplane Company. This company built a few experimental seaplanes under the name B. and W. and during World War I was awarded a contract for Curtiss flying boats, but none was completed before the armistice. The abrupt cancellation of wartime contracts left the Boeing firm, like all other aircraft companies, in difficulties; in order to survive it built furniture and sea sleds and was fortunate in getting orders for reconditioning army planes. It achieved a firm footing in 1920 by winning a contract to build 200 Thomas-Morse MB-3 fighter planes, under a system that permitted aircraft manufacturers to bid on each other's designs in competition for military orders. The company also built a flying boat in 1919, the B-1, which carried mail for some years between Seattle and Vancouver, B.C., making it the first of the long line of Boeing transport planes. The competition of war surplus planes, however, discouraged further building of transports at this time.

On Sept. 27, 1921, Boeing married Bertha Potter Paschall, a widow; they had one child. Boeing's interests were now focused on the aircraft company. Its principal business through most of the 1920's was making fighter planes for the United States Army, but Boeing continued to believe in the potential of commercial aviation. His chance came in the latter part of the decade, provided first by the Kelly Air Mail Act of 1925, transferring the transport of air mail from the Post Office to private carriers, and second by the stimulation of public interest in aviation by Charles A. Lindbergh's transatlantic flight in 1927. In addition, the boom atmosphere of the period encouraged investment in speculative enterprises. In July 1927 Boeing Air Transport began flying mail and passengers between San Francisco and Chicago, using the M-40, designed by Boeing for this purpose.

Seeking an integrated combination of air transport and aircraft manufacturing companies, Boeing organized the Boeing Aircraft and Transport Corporation in Delaware late in 1927; it was renamed United Aircraft and Transport in February 1928. Boeing worked in close cooperation with two brothers, Fred B. Rentschler, president of the aircraft engine manufacturer Pratt and Whitney, and Gordon Rentschler, president of the National City Bank, which handled the financing. When completed, the United structure included the Boeing enterprises; other airlines providing access to New York, the Pacific Northwest, and San Diego; Pratt and Whitney; Hamilton Standard Propeller; and the Stearman, Chance Vought, and Sikorsky airframe firms. It was the most powerful and profitable aviation combine formed during this period.

United was materially aided by the high quality of Boeing planes. In particular the Monomail 200, first flown in 1930, introduced the all-metal, low-wing monoplane to American airways,

although its single engine limited its utility. Its successor, the twin-engine 247 brought into service in 1933, was the first genuinely modern transport airplane. It was so superior to any existing type that United's competitors had to match it to survive, and their search resulted in the Douglas DC series. The all-metal, low-wing design was also incorporated into Boeing's military aircraft, notably the B-9 bomber—which, however, was outmatched by the Martin B-10.

Boeing himself was a less active participant in aircraft design than he had been in his company's early days because his attention was necessarily absorbed by United Aircraft and Transport. During the Hoover Administration he was a somewhat reluctant participant in Postmaster General Walter F. Brown's plans for using airmail contracts to create a stable and financially sound system of air transport. Allegations of scandal in Brown's operations led Franklin D. Roosevelt to cancel all airmail contracts early in 1934, and a subsequent investigation by a Senate committee resulted in the Air Mail Act of 1934, which among other provisions required the separation of manufacturing and transport companies in aviation; United was divided into Boeing Aircraft, United Aircraft, and United Airlines.

Boeing had decided to give up active management in mid-1933, but he was so embittered by the outcome of the airmail controversy that in 1934 he withdrew from aviation altogether. In that year he was awarded the Guggenheim Medal for "successful pioneering in aircraft manufacturing and air transport." For the rest of his life he devoted himself to deep-sea cruising, fishing, and raising thoroughbred horses and cattle. For this last purpose he bought an estate, Aldarra Farms, in Fall City, Wash., in 1946 and gave his former home in Seattle to the children's Orthopedic Hospital. He had been in failing health for several years when he died aboard his yacht *Taconite* in Puget Sound.

[The most complete history, Harold Mansfield, *Vision* (1956), is undocumented and not indexed. On Boeing's career in aviation, see Charles J. Kelly, Jr., *The Sky's the Limit* (1963); John Bell Rae, *Climb to Greatness* (1968); and Henry L. Smith, *Airways* (1942).]

JOHN B. RAE

BOGART, HUMPHREY DeFOREST (Dec. 25, 1899–Jan. 14, 1957), actor and motion picture producer, was born in the affluent environment of fashionable Riverside Drive in New York City, the son of Belmont DeForest Bogart, an internist whose inherited wealth was vested in timber properties, and Maud Humphrey, a noted illustrator. (The "Maud Humphrey baby," a popular advertising figure, was a sentimentalized portrait of the infant Humphrey.) Bogart was educated at Trinity School in New York City and then at Phillips Academy in Andover, Mass. The circumstances of his leaving Andover have never been made clear, but his academic record was poor, and there were rumors of disciplinary infractions. In May 1918 he enlisted in the navy. It was while he was serving temporarily in the military police that a handcuffed prisoner, in an attempted escape, struck Bogart in the mouth with the cuffs, leaving him with a faint scar and the slight lisp that gave his distinctive vocal delivery its abrasive and sinister quality.

During the last years of the war the family investments had gone sour, and upon demobilization Bogart was forced to earn his livelihood on the stock exchange and then in the theater. He first became involved with the New York stage through the efforts of William A. Brady, a theatrical producer, neighbor of the Bogarts, and the father of Alice Brady, an actress who took a maternal interest in him. Working usually as a stage manager, taking bit parts as he was needed, Bogart soon won the juvenile lead in *Swifty* (1922) and then other ephemeral light comedies that echoed the brittle sophistication of the postwar years. He had some difficulty in finding subsequent roles, and the reviews of his early performances were not always kind.

On May 20, 1926, Bogart married Helen Menken, an actress well established on the stage; within a year divorce papers were filed. In April 1928 he married another actress, Mary Phillips, with whom he had previously played in a short-lived drama called *Nerves* in 1924.

Bogart made his first motion-picture appearance in a ten-minute film produced by Warner Brothers' Vitaphone Corporation in 1929, *Broadway's Like That*, featuring Ruth Etting and Joan Blondell. Fox Studios put him under contract for the following year, and he played supporting roles in six films showcasing such rising stars as Victor McLaglen and Spencer Tracy.

In the years that followed, Bogart moved from coast to coast in search of film and stage roles. He was playing on the stage in *Invitation to a Murder* in 1934, when he was spotted by Arthur Hopkins, the producer-director, who was casting for the Broadway production of *The Petrified Forest*. It was in this melodrama of desperate criminals and their hostages that Bogart, in the part of Duke Mantee—a feral, brooding murderer—made his mark. When Warner Brothers purchased the rights and approached Leslie Howard to recreate his leading role, Howard insisted that Bogart be contracted to play Duke Mantee in the film.

Bogart's box office appeal was established by this movie, and Warner Brothers added him to its stable of "tough guys," which included James Cagney, George Raft, and Edward G. Robinson. For six years he played in such pictures as *Bullets or Ballots* (1936), *The Great O'Malley* (1937), *Kid Galahad* (1937), *San Quentin* (1937), *Dark Victory* (1939), and *Brother Orchid* (1940). His belligerent last stands against the armed power of society became staple fare for movie audiences of the 1930's, and the climactic scenes of his death under fire held a peculiar fascination. The mythic allure of the Bogart-criminal culminated in *High Sierra* (1941), in which he portrayed not only the surface violence of a fugitive killer, but also tragic undercurrents of loyalty and tenderness.

It was, however, in *The Maltese Falcon* (1941), an adaptation of a Dashiell Hammett novel directed by John Huston, that the complexities of the "tough guy" stereotype began to challenge Bogart. As Sam Spade, a somewhat shabby and bitter private eye waging his own war against greed and mendacity, Bogart managed to convey both hardboiled disillusionment and an underlying integrity. This evolving character crystallized in *Casablanca* (1942), a tremendous success in which Bogart, playing with Ingrid Bergman, gained his first Academy Award nomination. The film, drawing upon wartime antipathy toward the Nazis, allowed Bogart to exploit the internal conflicts of the individual in a world torn by divided loyalties and confused values.

Bogart was fiercely committed to his craft. "I am a professional. I have a respect for my profession. I work hard at it." Despite his nightclub carousing and the heavy-drinking weekends on his yacht, he had a reputation for promptness and sobriety on the set and worked well with directors and fellow actors.

In August 1938 Bogart (now divorced from his second wife) married a character actress, Mayo Methot, whom he had met on the set of *Marked Woman* (1937). The couple became known because of their frequent public brawls as the Battling Bogarts, further enhancing his "tough guy" image. In 1949 Bogart founded his own studio, Santana Pictures, while remaining under contract to Warner Brothers. Acting in and directing his own films provided him with respite from the Warner Brothers fare. By the time Bogart met and fell in love with the model-actress Lauren Bacall, during the filming of *To Have and Have Not* (1944), the marriage had disintegrated. Their courtship in the full public eye, in Hollywood night spots and on his yacht, the *Santana*, reinforced his evolving image as the matured romantic leading man. They were married in May 1945 and had two children. Domestic life, to the amazement of many of his friends, brought deep satisfaction to Bogart. He also made a dramatic foray into politics, traveling to Washington in 1947 in support of actors, writers, and directors subpoenaed by the House Un-American Activities Committee. He actively supported the Democratic Party.

After World War II, Bogart took on a variety of demanding character roles. In John Huston's *The Treasure of the Sierra Madre* (1948) he played a prospector driven mad by greed. *The African Queen* (1951) gave him cobilling with Katharine Hepburn, and his characterization as Charlie Allnut, the tipsy riverboat captain, brought him an Academy Award. Other roles, such as Captain Queeg in the film version of *The Caine Mutiny* (1954), the middle-aged lover in *Sabrina* (1954), the leader of the fugitives who hold hostage a suburban family in *The Desperate Hours* (1955), and the simple rogue of *We're No Angels* (1955), all demonstrated his versatility. During the filming of *The Harder They Fall* (1956), his last movie, the effects of cancer were already being felt. He died at home in Beverly Hills, Calif., after months of treatment and one operation.

[See Richard Gehman, *Bogart* (1965); Alan G. Barbaur, *Humphrey Bogart: A Pyramid Illustrated History of the Movies* (1973); Nathaniel Benchley, *Bogart* (1975); and Allen Eyles, *Bogart* (1975).]
ALBERT F. McLEAN

BOOTH, ALBERT JAMES, JR. ("ALBIE") (Feb. 1, 1908–Mar. 1, 1959), football player, coach, and referee, was born in New Haven, Conn., the son of Albert James Booth, a gunmaker with the Winchester Repeating Arms Company, and Mary Louise Frank. He attended high school in New Haven and in 1928 entered the Sheffield Scientific School of Yale University, where he majored in applied economic science.

Described as one of Yale's greatest halfbacks and all-around athletes, Booth made national headlines with his exploits. He was captain of both the varsity football and baseball squads and won eight varsity letters in football, baseball, and basketball from 1929 to 1932. Of small stature—five feet, six inches tall, and weighing only 147 pounds—he acquired such appropriate nicknames as "Little Boy Blue" and "the Mighty Atom."

Booth first gained recognition as a sophomore halfback in the fall of 1929, when he scored twice in a 14–0 victory over Brown University. This performance was overshadowed later that year when Booth scored three dramatic touchdowns and dropkicked three extra points to beat a powerful Army team 21–13.

In his senior year Booth completed his athletic heroics by scoring three touchdowns in a 33–33 tie with Dartmouth, and by defeating archrival Harvard 3–0 with a field goal. (This was not the last time that Booth "singlehandedly" defeated Harvard. In the Commencement Day Baseball Game of 1932, in his last appearance in a Yale uniform he hit a grand-slam home run to win the game 4–3.)

A real-life embodiment of Frank Merriwell, Booth caught the imagination of a nation suffering through the early years of the Great Depression. His small size and elusive open-field running inspired spectacular newspaper stories, and he became one of the most popular American collegiate football heroes. Yet he was never selected as an All-American, although coach John Heisman considered him one of the best backs of the era.

During the Yale-Harvard game of 1931, Booth became ill and finished the game bundled up on the bench. The illness was first diagnosed as a cold or a mild attack of the grippe, and he was placed in the Yale infirmary. After an apparent case of pneumonia set in, Booth was transferred to New Haven Hospital. The final diagnosis was pleurisy with effusion. This serious illness ended his collegiate football career. Following a period of rest, Booth returned to Yale and finished his studies, although he did not graduate with his class. On July 4, 1932, he married Marion Gertrude Noble. They had two daughters. After graduating, Booth coached at Yale and at New York University, and later became a football referee. In 1932 he began a successful business career with the Sealtest Corporation, ultimately becoming general manager for the ice cream division in the southern

New England district. He died of a heart attack while returning by automobile from New York City, where he had attended a play with his wife.

[On Booth and his career, see Allison Danzig, *The History of American Football* (1956); Tim Cohane, *Sporting News*, Oct. 4, 1969; M. A. Stevens, "My Most Unforgettable Character," *Reader's Digest*, Nov. 1967; Yale University, Sheffield Scientific School, *Yearbook* (1932), 106–107, 555–560; and *Yale Alumni Weekly*, Dec. 4, 1931. Sealtest Corporation has a fifteen-minute film in its Hartford, Conn., office entitled *Little Boy Blue* and made in the early 1950's. See also the obituary and funeral notices, *New York Times*, Mar. 2 and Mar. 5, 1959.]

EDWARD PERSHEY

BORG, GEORGE WILLIAM (Oct. 24, 1887–Feb. 21, 1960), businessman and inventor, was born in West Burlington, Iowa, the son of Charles William Borg and Amelia Gustafson. (The names of both parents appear variously spelled in the record.) His father had emigrated from Sweden in 1882 and in 1894 went to work for Deere and Mansur Company, in Moline, Ill., manufacturers of agricultural implements.

Although the family was not poor, even in his earliest years George Borg appears to have been impressed with the possibility of poverty and later advocated the establishment of factories in rural areas so that his workers could fall back on agriculture during hard times. Shortly before graduation from public school, he was apprenticed to Deere and Mansur. He continued in the position after his father quit the firm to pursue his own inventions, the first of which was a woodworking machine that shaped wagon tongues (1904). In May 1904, Borg's father, in association with Marshall Beck, established Borg and Beck, manufacturers of woodworking machines; George subsequently moved over to the new firm. With the support of Beck, he was allowed to attend a business course at Augustana College, in Rock Island, Ill., a goal of some standing. After graduation he was able to help modernize and expand the business side of the partnership, previously run primarily by Beck.

The problems experienced by the Moline automobile firm, Velie Company, in manufacturing clutches led to expansion into that field. Stories differ on the crucial point of whether Charles Borg was the true inventor of the improved clutch or whether he opposed the scheme and George himself did the development. In either case the firm developed and then manufactured an improved disk clutch, designed not only to work better but to be easier to manufacture with relatively unskilled help. He was successful in introducing the clutch to the Jeffrey Company, which had a large truck order from the federal government for use in Mexico. As volume rose he induced the Tom Warner Company of Toledo to use his clutches in its transmissions. Similar agreements were concluded with other manufacturers. At the end of World War I he opened a factory in Chicago. In 1921 the partnership was purchased by a bank for $1.2 million and George Borg became head of the new company.

Eager to diversify, Borg soon established the Standard Parts Company and opened a chain of stores to sell automotive parts. In the late 1920's he also began an effort to merge with related firms, the first of which was the Warner Gear Company, soon joined by the Mechanics Universal Joint Company, the Marvel Carburetor Company, and others. Organized by banking interests, the new company was designed to withstand the trend among the largest automobile firms toward the manufacture of their own components. The new Borg-Warner Corporation was founded in 1928 with stock valued at $90 million. George Borg was president. By 1945 the firm had fifteen divisions, eight subsidiaries, twenty-seven plants, and more than eighty products including stoves, refrigerators, laundry equipment, and farm implements in addition to automobile components.

Meanwhile, Borg had established the George W. Borg Corporation, to manufacture automobile clocks. In 1940 he withdrew from direction of Borg-Warner to devote his attention to his own company, which by the mid-1950's was also producing electronic devices, precision instruments, and textiles and had a net operating income, after taxes, of $1.1 million.

Shortly before the war the Borg Corporation had purchased a bankrupt textile mill in Delavan, Wis. The mill operated on military contracts during the war, and shortly thereafter Borg and his engineers began to experiment with several of the knitting machines that had been used to make fleecy sweaters. The redesigned machines' first product was a round knit wool pad for polishing automobiles. Next they were used to make the paint rollers that were being pioneered by a neighbor, A. L. Touchet, and by 1954 about 90 percent of all rollers used Borg's new, thick-piled Dynel fabric. A variation, developed under the name of Borgana, was used for women's clothing.

Borg acquired ranch properties near Phoenix, Ariz., raising cotton, cattle, and grapes and, for a time, operating a luxury hotel called the Casa Blanca. He was a close friend of Peggy Warner Goldwater, wife of Senator Barry Goldwater of Arizona; she was related to the Warner family of Borg-Warner.

Borg married Florence Mary Wadsworth, from whom he was later divorced; they had two children. He then married Effie Task Brown; they had no children.

Borg died in Janesville, Wis. A man with an aggressive drive for accumulation, he slept little and restlessly investigated new avenues for the expression of his business talent. He dressed modestly, deprecated his own mechanical and inventive contributions, and was generous with his wealth, especially toward the educationally underprivileged. His money is now partly channeled through the George W. Borg Foundation.

[Robert J. Casey's popular biography *Mr. Clutch* (1948) should be balanced by the privately distributed sketch "Charles W. Borg," compiled by Malcome J. Bosse (n.d.). A sketch in *Business Week,* Sept. 25, 1954, concentrates on the textile years. See also the obituary notice, *New York Times,* Feb. 22, 1960.]

CARROLL PURSELL

BORI, LUCREZIA (Dec. 24, 1887–May 14, 1960), operatic soprano, was born Lucrezia Borja y González de Riancho in Gandía, Spain. She was the daughter of Vincenzo Borja Bonet and Concepción González de Riancho. Her father, a colonel in the Spanish army, was a descendant of the Borgia family of Italy. Bori was educated in a convent at Valencia. Although she had revealed a beautiful singing voice in childhood, and had received musical instruction at the Valencia Conservatory, for a long time no thought of her embarking on a professional musical career was tolerated, since a member of an aristocratic Spanish household did not commonly go on the stage. But her suppressed musical aspirations found support in her father. When she finished her schooling at the age of eighteen, he took her to Italy. There, in Milan, she studied voice for several months with Melchior Vidal. On Oct. 31, 1908, she made her debut at the Teatro Costanzi in Rome as Micaëla in *Carmen,* assuming the stage name of Lucrezia Bori.

Following several performances with the San Carlo Opera in Naples, Bori attracted the interest of the publisher Giulio Ricordi, who arranged for her to audition for Arturo Toscanini, Giacomo Puccini, and the general manager of La Scala in Milan, Giulio Gatti-Casazza. Their affirmative response led to her engagement at La Scala, where she appeared for two seasons between 1910 and 1912. One of her roles was Octavian in the Italian premiere of *Der Rosenkavalier* at La Scala in March 1911.

When the Metropolitan Opera Company of New York toured Europe in May 1910, Bori was invited to make a guest appearance in the title role of *Manon Lescaut* at the Théâtre du Châtelet in Paris. On Nov. 11, 1912, she made her American debut as Manon Lescaut at the Metropolitan Opera in New York City. During her three seasons there she was acclaimed for the elegance of her legato singing, her flawless intonation and diction, and the subtlety of her musicianship.

After Bori's third New York season, nodules in her throat necessitated an operation from which she emerged with seemingly permanent damage to her vocal cords. Over the next few years, during which she consulted numerous specialists and visited religious shrines, she never lost faith that she would be able to resume her career. She appeared in Monte Carlo in 1918, but her performance was far from acceptable. On Jan. 28, 1921, Bori returned to the Metropolitan Opera for her "second debut" there as Mimi in *La bohème.* The facility of her vocal production, the beauty of her sound, her musicianship, and her stage presence revealed that she had regained her form.

During the next fifteen years Bori remained one of the elect of that company and one of the world's preeminent interpreters of the principal soprano roles in the French and Italian repertory, notably Manon in the operas of Puccini and Massenet, Mélisande in *Pelléas et Mélisande,* Juliette in *Roméo et Juliette,* the title roles in *Louise* and *Mignon,* Mimi in *La bohème,* Suzel in *L'amico Fritz,* Magda in *La rondine,* Norina in *Don Pasquale,* Violetta in *La traviata,* and Fiora in *L'amore dei tre re.* She also was acclaimed as Maria in the world premiere of Deems Taylor's *Peter Ibbetson* (1931), Despina in *Così fan tutte,* Salud in Manuel de Falla's *La vida breve,* and Concepción in Ravel's *L'heure espagnole.*

Bori's last operatic appearance in New York took place on Mar. 21, 1936, in *La rondine* at the Metropolitan Opera. At a gala farewell concert there a week later, she received a twenty-minute standing ovation. Her farewell performance took place on Apr. 2, 1936, in *La bohème*, during a visit by the Metropolitan Opera to Baltimore. She had made 606 appearances with the company in twenty-nine roles.

When the Metropolitan Opera suffered a severe economic crisis in 1933, Bori became chairman of a fund-raising committee that, largely through her efforts, raised $300,000.

In 1925 Bori had been one of the first opera stars to broadcast on radio, appearing with John McCormack in a concert heard by an audience estimated at six million—the largest ever reached by a musical program at the time. Following her retirement she made several further appearances but, for the most part, she preferred a life of comparative seclusion in New York, devoting her time to the study of philosophy and to sculpting. In 1942 she became the first singer to serve on the board of directors of the Metropolitan Opera. Bori was elected chairman of the Metropolitan Opera Guild in 1942, and in 1953 she served as cochairman with George A. Sloan of a committee to raise $1.5 million to rehabilitate the auditorium of the Metropolitan Opera. She also held a permanent seat in the opera house (A-111). Bori, who never married, became an American citizen in 1943. She died in New York City.

[On Bori and her career, see John Francis Marion, *Lucrezia Bori of the Metropolitan Opera* (1962); Max De Schauensee, "Lucrezia Bori," *Musical America*, June 1960; William H. Seltsam, *Metropolitan Opera Annals* (1947); Robert J. Wayner, *What Did They Sing at the Met?* (1971); and R. R. Wile, "Edison Recordings of Lucrezia Bori," *Hobbies*, Aug. 1960.]

DAVID EWEN

BOVIE, WILLIAM T. (Sept. 11, 1882–Jan. 1, 1958), inventor and biophysicist, was born in Augusta, Mich., the son of William Bovie, a physician and farmer, and Henrietta Barnes Bovie. From his childhood Bovie was interested in natural science. He worked as a stenographer until he accumulated enough money to enroll in 1901 at Albion College, where he studied biology for three years and where, while still a student, he delivered a number of lectures in biology, advanced zoology, and geology. After transferring to the University of Michigan in the fall of 1904, Bovie completed his work for the B.A. the following spring, although he did not receive his diploma until 1908. From 1902 to 1904 Bovie was assistant biologist at Albion, and in 1905–1906 he was professor of geology and biology at Antioch.

In the fall of 1908 Bovie began work on a master's degree at the University of Missouri, where he met Martha Adams, an undergraduate. They were married on Sept. 15, 1909, and had one son.

While at Missouri, Bovie worked under George M. Read as an assistant and fellow in the department of botany. After receiving the A.M. in 1910, Bovie entered Harvard to work for a doctoral degree in plant physiology. Plant succession, the growth of plants, and the effects of ultraviolet light were his main interests. These pursuits led him to develop a precision auxanometer to measure plant growth (1912). The following year his two frequently cited papers on the coagulation of egg albumin by ultraviolet light appeared in *Science*.

In 1914 Bovie received the Ph.D. with a thesis entitled "The Action of Ultraviolet Light on Protoplasm." For the next six years he worked as a research fellow for the Cancer Commission at Harvard and eventually became director of the commission's biophysical laboratories. Here he continued his studies on the effects of ultraviolet light on protoplasm (1916) and on paramecia (1918–1919); he also made improvements in the quartz mercury-vapor lamp. In connection with his work on light, Bovie developed a direct reading potentiometer for measuring and recording reactions in chemical solutions (1915–1916). In the summer of 1916, working at the United Fruit Company Hospital in Santa Marta, Colombia, Bovie performed a series of experiments dealing with the action of extreme ultraviolet rays from tropical sunlight on blood serum in humans. When Harvard obtained a gram of radium bromide, Bovie and William Duane (who had studied with Marie Curie) experimented first with rabbits and then humans; Bovie designed and constructed the applicators used in these investigations. Bovie was the first in this country to put radium into a usable solution for treating cancer.

During discussions with Svante Arrhenius, who was then giving a course on physical chemistry at Harvard, Bovie worked out his concept of a new field, biophysics. In 1920 he became assistant professor of biophysics, a position he held until 1927. Bovie's report (1925) on the effects of light on growth patterns in chickens drew attention to the role of glass in filtering out some of the sun's beneficial rays. His pioneering research on the combined effects of heat and radiation led him in 1926 to his most important invention, the electrosurgical knife, or Bovie unit. This device was capable of cutting, coagulating, or desiccating tissue, depending on the type and power of the current selected. "Bloodless surgery" was first used for cancer of the breast, where it had the additional advantage of lessening the potential spread of malignant cells to other parts of the body. After having seen Bovie and his electrosurgical knife used against cancer, Harvey Cushing enlisted them both in brain surgery. His report (1928) of these 547 operations on brain tumors is a classic and includes Bovie's description of his new electrosurgical unit.

In 1927 Bovie became professor of biophysics and chairman of the newly created department at Northwestern University. To honor the invention of the electrosurgical knife, the city of Philadelphia awarded Bovie the John Scott Medal in 1928 and Albion College presented him with a D.Sc. degree in 1929. In June of that year Bovie resigned from Northwestern and moved back to New England. There he established a private research laboratory in Bar Harbor, Maine, which he ran for ten years. During this decade he did some pioneering work in the uses of microfilm. In 1939 Bovie became a lecturer in social technology at Colby College, in Waterville, Maine, where he remained until his retirement in 1948. As a consequence of his early work with radium, Bovie had lost a finger and suffered pains in his hands for the rest of his life. He died in Fairfield, Maine.

[On Bovie and his work, see Mrs. Kenneth J. Hollinshead ("Fidus Achates"), "Dr. William T. Bovie, 1905, Biophysicist and Inventer," *lo Triumphe* (Albion College Alumni Magazine), Sept. 1948; Alice Frost Lord, "Retired Genius of Electrical Surgery and Progressive Educational Theories Now Makes His Home in Fairfield," *Lewiston Journal* Magazine Section, Jan. 26, 1946; and the obituary notice, *New York Times*, Jan. 2, 1958. The largest collection of archival materials is at Harvard's Countway Library of Medicine in Boston. There is no known published list of Bovie's articles, which number at least thirty-seven.]

WILLIAM K. BEATTY

BOWEN, NORMAN LEVI (June 21, 1887–Sept. 11, 1956), geologist and petrologist, was born in Kingston, Ontario, the son of William Alfred Bowen and Elizabeth McCormick, English immigrants. He studied chemistry and mineralogy at Queen's University and received the honors degree of M.A. in 1907. For the next six summers Bowen worked in the field for the Ontario Bureau of Mines and the Canadian Geological Survey, most notably in British

Columbia with R. A. Daly in 1911. Bowen returned to Queen's University in 1907 to enter the School of Mining, receiving the B.S. in 1909. A lifelong association with the Geophysical Laboratory of the Carnegie Institution of Washington, D.C., began in 1910, when Bowen, who had entered the Massachusetts Institute of Technology the previous year, experimentally defined the conditions of crystallization for the pair of minerals nepheline-anorthite (expressed in the form of the phase-equilibrium diagram). On Oct. 3, 1911, he married Mary Lamont. They had one daughter.

The geophysical laboratory had been founded in 1906 under the direction of Arthur L. Day for the specific purpose of experimentally defining the physicochemical parameters governing geologic processes, particularly the formation of igneous rocks. In 1910, although a well-developed body of theoretical physical chemistry was at hand, almost nothing was known of the actual temperatures and pressures at which real rocks are formed. Classical methods of observation in the field and under the microscope were the basis for the inference of geologic processes, but their relation to the laws of physical chemistry was unknown. Harry Rosenbusch of Heidelberg headed the petrologic school that sought in the rock specimen itself the evidence of its origin and evolution; the method was essentially a posteriori. J. H. L. Vogt found artificially produced assemblages of silicate minerals in metallurgical slags. In his student paper "On the Order of Crystallization in Igneous Rocks" (1912), Bowen employed Rosenbusch's classical method even while disputing his conclusions. Bowen's early papers mention the influences of Vogt and the metallurgist Cecil H. Desch, as well as Alfred Harker and the petrologists Louis V. Pirsson and Joseph P. Iddings.

During the next forty-six years, alone and with other geologists and physical chemists—G. W. Morey, J. W. Grieg, F. C. Kracek, E. Posnjak, O. R. Tuttle and J. F. Schairer—Bowen established the phase diagrams for the principal components of igneous rocks and applied them to develop the modern magmatic theory of petrogenesis. In doing so he made Washington, with its twin laboratories of the Carnegie Institution and the U.S. Geological Survey, the world center of experimental petrology.

Bowen's first phase diagram, nepheline-anorthite, was the basis for his dissertation at the Massachusetts Institute of Technology in 1912.

Continuing as assistant petrologist at the geophysical laboratory, he undertook the study of the plagioclase feldspars, the most important mineral component of igneous rocks. In two months Bowen fused, quenched, and analyzed seventy-five separate silicate charges. He showed that the plagioclase feldspars were miscible in all proportions, and he established that the particular plagioclase (proportion of soda to lime) crystallizing out was determined solely by temperature. In melting silicate charges of a given composition, Bowen used the lowest temperature at which any glass could be obtained to determine the position of the melting-point curve (called the solidus) and the temperature of the first appearance of crystals in cooling down a silicate fusion to determine the freezing-point curve (liquidus). The results were checked against runs with natural crystals and against the newly published curves of Esper S. Larsen, Jr., for optical determination of the composition of plagioclase glass.

Bowen explained the plagioclase solid solution by using the crystal structure theory of William Barlow and William J. Pope, anticipating the first X-ray determination of any crystal structure by only months. In this classic paper of crystal chemistry, "The Melting Phenomena of the Plagioclase Feldspars" (1913), Bowen accounted for the association of different igneous rock types by proposing the separation of crystals and liquid at various stages of the crystallization of a magma. The work contained all the essential ideas of modern magmatic petrology. His Princeton lectures, published in 1928 as *The Evolution of the Igneous Rocks*, embodied a complete physicochemical theory of magmatic differentiation based on more than fifty of his articles that had been published since 1913, the majority being phase diagrams of silicate systems. No other twentieth-century work exerted a comparable influence on petrology.

In 1915 Bowen discussed laboratory and field evidence for crystallization differentiation in silicate liquids through the gravity settling of early-formed olivine crystals and the floating of silica minerals, a mechanism proposed also by Darwin. Preparation of ternary diagrams (three mineral components) by Bowen and Olaf Anderson extended the method from mineral pairs to complete, if ideal, rock systems. Also in 1915, Bowen published the complete theory as "The Later Stages of the Evolution of the Igneous Rocks," accounting for the differentiation of magmas by the process that he later named

"fractional crystallization." The assimilation of country rock by fusion with a magma, his laboratory results showed, would affect the quantities of various rocks produced but not their compositions. The temperature and composition of the final magma depended upon the events of its history, such as the settling, flotation, and filtration of early-formed crystals.

In 1917 Bowen explained the problem of monomineral rocks, such as the anorthosites, as segregations from a gabbroic melt. In the polemical "Crystallization-Differentiation in Igneous Magmas" (1919) he asserted the authority of the phase diagram over hypotheses derived from field studies and coined the term "filter-press" for processes that he considered in detail in "Differentiation by Deformation" (1920). In "The Reaction Principle in Petrogenesis" (1922) Bowen asserted that the two principal reaction series of silicate petrology, the continuous plagioclase and the discontinuous ferromagnesian series, together forced an order of crystallization confirming Rosenbusch's empirical order and contrary to that predicted by the law of mass-action. In "The Behavior of Inclusions in Igneous Magmas" (1922) he showed how the assimilation of foreign matter by a magma affects principally rates of crystallization and relative amounts rather than the mineralogy of the differentiates.

Bowen was professor of geology at Queen's University from 1918 to 1920 and professor of petrology at the University of Chicago from 1937 to 1947. The rest of his career was spent almost exclusively at the geophysical laboratory of the Carnegie Institution. He wrote 18 papers with J. F. Schairer, the last appearing in 1956. He was president of the Mineralogical Society of America in 1937 and of the Geological Society of America in 1946, and was a member of the National Academy of Sciences, the Royal Society of London, and the Accademia Nazionale dei Lincei. The "Bowen volume" of the *American Journal of Science* was dedicated to him in 1952 on his retirement. He died in Washington, D.C.

In addition to the intuitive understanding of the field geologist, Bowen had the ability to develop and apply a silicate physical chemistry to the intrusive rocks. The rare personal qualities that enabled him to surround himself with so many major collaborators and to lead the Carnegie Geophysical Laboratory to preeminence, coupled with his technical and intellectual virtuosity, gave rise to the modern magmatic school of petrology.

[Most of Bowen's papers were published in *American Journal of Science* and *Journal of Geology* beginning in 1910. His widely used Princeton lectures, *The Evolution of the Igneous Rocks* (1928), were reissued in 1956 with intro. by J. F. Schairer. Besides the papers mentioned above, Bowen's following articles are of major significance for the development of petrology: "The Binary System: $MgO-SiO_2$," *American Journal of Science,* 37 (1914), 487, written with Olaf Anderson and establishing peritectic behavior for orthopyroxene; "The Ternary System: Diopside-forsterite-silica," *ibid.,* 38 (1914), 207–264; "The Problem of the Anorthosites," *Journal of Geology,* 25 (1917), 209–243; "Diffusion in Silicate Melts," *ibid.,* 29 (1921), 295–317; "The Mineralogical Phase Rule," *Journal of the Washington Academy of Sciences,* 15 (1925), 280–284; "The Amount of Assimilation by the Sudbury Norite Sheet," *Journal of Geology,* 33 (1925), 825–829; "The Origin of Ultrabasic and Related Rocks," *American Journal of Science,* 14, 5th ser. (1927), 89–108; "The Problem of the Intrusion of Dunite in the Light of the Olivine Diagram," *16th International Geological Congress Report* (1933), 391–396, written with J. F. Schairer; "Progressive Metamorphism of Siliceous Limestone and Dolomite," *Journal of Geology,* 48 (1940), 225–274; and "Phase Equilibria Bearing on the Origin and Differentiation of Alkaline Rocks," *American Journal of Science,* 243–A (1945), 75–89. A complete bibliography of his work and portrait are in J. F. Schairer, "Memorial to Norman Levi Bowen (1887–1956)," *Proceedings. Geological Society of America* for 1956 (1957), 117–122. See also Cortland P. Auser, "Norman Levi Bowen," *Dictionary of Scientific Biography* (1970).]

CECIL J. SCHNEER

BOWERS, CLAUDE GERNADE (Nov. 20, 1878–Jan. 21, 1958), journalist, orator, historian, and diplomat, was born in Westfield, Ind., the son of Lewis Bowers, a merchant, and Juliet Tipton. He attended grade school in three Indiana communities—Whitestown, Lebanon, and Indianapolis—and in 1898 won the state high school oratorical contest and graduated from Indianapolis High School No. 1 (later Shortridge). There his formal education ended, but he continued his reading in history, biography, and literature.

An editorial writer on the Indianapolis *Sentinel* at twenty-one, Bowers moved to Terre Haute in 1903 as a reporter on the *Gazette.* Shifting to the Terre Haute *Star,* he wrote editorials and acquired a local reputation as a public speaker. In 1904 he received the fifth district Democratic congressional nomination. He lost then and again in 1906. From 1906 to 1911 he served on the

Terre Haute Board of Public Works, and in 1908 he was Indiana's youngest delegate to the Democratic National Convention at Denver. On Nov. 29, 1911, he married Sybil McCaslin in Indianapolis; they had one daughter.

When in 1911 John W. Kern entered the United States Senate, Bowers became his secretary. In 1913 Kern became the Senate majority leader, and Bowers was thus privy to confidential New Freedom developments. On weekends Bowers wrote *The Irish Orators,* which was published in 1916.

Bowers returned to Indiana in 1917 as editor of the Fort Wayne *Journal-Gazette.* He published *The Life of John Worth Kern* in 1918. A third book, *The Party Battles of the Jackson Period* (1922), and Bowers' trenchant pro-Democratic editorials led to a 1923–31 position in New York City as an editorial writer on the *Evening World.*

In New York Bowers produced not only thousands of editorials but also *Jefferson and Hamilton* (1925) and *The Tragic Era* (1929), both best-sellers. He presented Presidents Thomas Jefferson and Andrew Johnson in a highly favorable light; the earlier work contributed importantly to the Jefferson revival of 1925–50, and the latter popularized Reconstruction revisionism. Concurrently no other orator was more in demand for Democratic party love feasts. At the 1928 Jackson Day Dinner in Washington, Bowers rallied disparate Democrats in a spectacular performance. As temporary chairman and keynote speaker of the 1928 Democratic National Convention at Houston, he evoked ringing cheers and set delegates to parading in the aisles.

From 1931 to 1933, Bowers was a political columnist for the New York *Journal* and other Hearst papers. He was invited to nominate Franklin Delano Roosevelt at the 1932 Democratic National Convention in Chicago, but declined because William Randolph Hearst favored John Nance Garner. This is no sense chilled Bowers' relationship with Roosevelt; on platform and radio and in his columns he warmly supported the Roosevelt-Garner ticket. In April 1933, in recognition of party service, Roosevelt appointed Bowers ambassador to Spain.

Throughout the first three years of his mission, Bowers admired the slightly left-of-center Spanish Republicans, notably Manuel Azaña. Looking with skepticism upon Alejandro Lerroux and the "black biennium" (1933–35), he rejected rightist misgivings when in February 1936

Azaña's Republicans regained the Madrid ministry with Socialist assistance. In Bowers' opinion, the July rebellion under Francisco Franco and Emilio Mola would have quickly failed without intervention by Germany and Italy.

During the Spanish Civil War (1936–39), Bowers and most other ambassadors to Spain were located in southwestern France. From Saint-Jean-de-Luz he sent to Washington a stream of communications underscoring his Loyalist sympathies. The conflict, he insisted, was essentially a rehearsal for another world war. When the Loyalists lost, he sailed home and soon was named ambassador to Chile.

Bowers was in Santiago from 1939 to 1953. He worked resourcefully to induce Chile to sever relations with the Axis powers—the break occurred in January 1943. Economic and defense cooperation between Chile and the United States was his next principal concern. He countered post–World War II Soviet influences in Chile as assiduously as he had thwarted Axis maneuvers. Chilean socioeconomic development was another of his top priorities.

While a diplomat, Bowers wrote *Jefferson in Power* (1936), *The Spanish Adventures of Washington Irving* (1940), *The Young Jefferson* (1945), and *Pierre Vergniaud* (1950). Both *My Mission to Spain* and *Making Democracy a Reality* were published in 1954, followed by *Chile Through Embassy Windows* (1958) and *My Life* (1962).

While abroad Bowers discerned fundamental similarities relating Spanish Republicans and the Chilean Popular Front to his special hero Thomas Jefferson and to Roosevelt and Truman policies. Bowers did not speak Spanish in public, although the best evidence is that he read and understood it.

The son of financially disadvantaged parents, Bowers never forgot his humble origins, and no years proved happier than the ones in South America, when his lack of "side" endeared him to his Santiago neighbors. His sole regret of record was that he had not settled permanently in Chile. He died in New York City.

[Bowers' Papers are in the Lilly Library, Indiana University; his letters are found in the collections of Albert J. Beveridge, Josephus Daniels, William E. Dodd, and Cordell Hull, Library of Congress; and diplomatic dispatches and personal letters are in the Department of State Papers, National Archives, and Roosevelt and Truman libraries. The Columbia University Oral History Collection has a 149-page oral history memoir made by Bowers in 1954. See also Holman Hamilton and Gayle Thornbrough, eds., *In-*

dianapolis in the "Gay Nineties": High School Diaries of Claude G. Bowers (1964); *My Life: The Memoirs of Claude Bowers* (1962); and obituary notices in the *New York Times* and Washington *Evening Star,* both Jan. 22, 1958.]

HOLMAN HAMILTON

BOYLE, MICHAEL J. (June 11, 1879–May 17, 1958), labor leader, was born in Woodland, Minn., the son of Michael Boyle, a farmer, and Ann Kelly. He was educated in parochial schools and at the age of sixteen went to work as a lineman for various utility companies in Minnesota, Ohio, and Michigan before becoming an electrician for the Chicago Tunnel Company. A member of the International Brotherhood of Electrical Workers, in 1904 he transferred his card to Local 134, which had jurisdiction over "inside" electrical work in Chicago. In 1906, after a brief stint as statistician, Boyle became the union's business agent, a job he held intermittently until 1919, when he took the post of business manager and thereby formalized the position of personal dominance he had long since achieved over Local 134. In 1902 he married Minnie Alice Oberlin. They had three daughters. In 1936, four years after his wife's death, Boyle married Helen Kane.

At the time that Boyle embarked on his trade-union career, labor relations in Chicago construction were in flux. The famous lockout of 1900 had broken the stranglehold of the building trades, but thereafter the contractors' unity deteriorated, and the unions revived. Earlier abuses crept back in, and the vulnerability of individual contractors encouraged business agents to demand "strike insurance." The monopolistic relationship between unions and contractors' associations offered other opportunities for quick profit.

In 1909 Boyle, along with Congressman Martin B. ("Skinny") Madden, was indicted for extortion but not convicted. In 1914 indictments were returned against a number of electrical contractors, members of the Chicago Switchboard Manufacturers' Association, and officers of Local 134 for violation of the Sherman Antitrust Act. Boyle was charged with having agreed, in exchange for the closed shop, to exclude from the Chicago market switchboard equipment not produced by members of the Association. Testimony revealed, among other things, Boyle's financial interest in one of the firms and his acceptance of payments to permit the installation of non-Association switchboards. In 1917 he was fined $5,000 and sentenced to a year in jail. Boyle served four months in 1919–1920 before President Wilson commuted his sentence. In 1923, following his refusal to testify before a grand jury regarding allegations of jury-tampering in the acquittal of Illinois governor Len Small on charges of misappropriating public funds, Boyle received six months for contempt of court. His friend Governor Small commuted his sentence after he had served less than two months.

Boyle early developed a colorful reputation as "Umbrella Mike." It was said that his ever-present umbrella served as a convenient receptacle for contractors' payoffs while he held court at his unofficial headquarters at Johnson's saloon. In his first decade of union service Boyle amassed a considerable fortune, although how much derived from his union position, and how much from astute business and real-estate dealings, never became clear. When asked to explain how he had acquired so much money on a business agent's salary, Boyle remarked laconically, "It was with great thrift." Nor did he hesitate to exploit his union's strategic position in the city's power and rapid transit systems for collective-bargaining purposes. Although the Chicago *Tribune*, a bitter critic, accused him of "a reckless disregard of the public" (Jan. 23, 1937), only twice did he actually make good his threat to close down public services.

There was, in truth, a good deal more to Mike Boyle than met the public eye. The acumen that advanced his own fortunes was applied no less assiduously on behalf of the men he represented. A resourceful and tenacious negotiator, he compiled a remarkable record of gains for the Chicago electrical workers. The unemployment insurance plan he introduced served them well in the early years of the Great Depression. And Local 134, strongly organized and effectively administered, came through those disastrous years for Chicago construction better than most of the building trades. The loyalty that Boyle elicited from his labor constituency lasted throughout his life.

Boyle became, moreover, a force for stabilizing the labor relations of Chicago construction. As both sides organized themselves into industry-wide groupings and achieved a rough balance of power after 1911, the conditions emerged for ending the chaos and strife of earlier years. The Uniform Form of Agreement, adopted in 1915, invoked a set of basic principles on all participating employer associations and trade unions and put into effect a system of mediation and arbitration. Although Boyle broke away under wartime inflationary pressures to secure a special wage increase in July 1917 in violation of the union contract, he was thereafter an ardent supporter of the Uniform Agreement. In 1921 he was instrumental in saving the agreement after Judge Kennesaw M. Landis handed down an arbitration award bitterly disliked by the building trades. It was, of course, characteristic of Boyle that he had somehow managed to secure favorable treatment for the electricians in the award.

In his later years Boyle played an increasing role in the affairs of the International Brotherhood of Electrical Workers. A member of the executive board since 1914, Boyle in 1930 became vice-president for the sixth district, which covered the upper Midwest. Under the New Deal, he was notably successful at bringing electrical and utility workers into the IBEW and fending off the CIO. His highly organized district, encompassing 25 percent of all the IBEW membership, gave him a powerful voice in the national union, as was evident in 1947, when his support threw a contested election for the IBEW presidency to Daniel Tracy over Edward J. Brown, the incumbent president.

Boyle's career epitomized, for better or worse, major tendencies of American business unionism. When he died in Miami, Fla., after a period of semiretirement (he never relinquished his offices), he was widely and sincerely mourned within the union. But the Chicago *Tribune* barely noted his passing, which perhaps said something about the respectable turn Boyle's career had taken in later years.

[Boyle left no personal papers, although material by or concerning him may be found in the IBEW files and in the court records of the cases in which he was a defendant. Boyle's career may be followed in the IBEW convention proceedings; in the *Electrical Workers' Journal*; and in the Chicago press. The *New York Times*, May 19, 1958, contains a substantial obituary notice, as does the *EWJ*, May–June 1958, p. 20, which includes important biographical data, an assessment of Boyle by a colleague, and a photograph. Royal E. Montgomery, *Industrial Relations in the Chicago Building Trades* (1927), unravels the intricacies of the industrial-relations system and explains Boyle's part in it. Barbara W. Newell, *Chicago and the Labor Movement: Metropolitan Unionism in the 1930's* (1961), has some useful information on the later period, as does Harold Seidman, *Labor Czars* (1938), on the more disreputable side of Boyle's career.]

DAVID BRODY

BRECKINRIDGE, HENRY SKILLMAN
(May 25, 1886–May 2, 1960), lawyer and government official, was born in Chicago, Ill., the son of Joseph Cabell Breckinridge and Louise Dudley. A Civil War veteran, Breckinridge's father was a professional soldier who served as inspector general of the army from 1889 to 1903. Membership in a distinguished Kentucky family and his father's position in Washington enabled the young Breckinridge to mingle easily with politicians and diplomats. At the same time he was not pampered; he went to Europe as a cattle hand and earned his first money picking tomatoes for fifteen cents a bushel.

After a year at Bishop College in Lennoxville, Quebec, Canada, Breckinridge entered Princeton with the class of 1907. There he fell under the spell of Woodrow Wilson, became an early advocate of Wilson's presidential hopes, and turned his own life toward the law and politics. After graduation from Princeton, he attended Harvard Law School and received the LL.B. in 1910. On July 7, 1910, he married Ruth Bradley Woodman; they had two daughters. Moving to Lexington, Ky., in 1911, Breckinridge practiced law, served as a park commissioner, and battled the forces of Champ Clark to secure the state's delegation for Wilson at the 1912 Democratic convention. Kentucky went for Clark, but Breckinridge, although only twenty-seven, had some claims on the new administration. As a candidate for assistant secretary of war, he was, as he put it, "a dark horse and I think nobody would have bet me to show." But he impressed Wilson and Secretary of War Lindley M. Garrison, the opposition was weak, and he gained the post in April 1913.

Breckinridge moved easily in the official Washington circles that included his naval counterpart, Franklin D. Roosevelt. He organized a fencing club among his colleagues and was a member of the American team that placed third in the Olympic games of 1920. In 1928 he was also captain of the American Olympic team.

When World War I broke out in August 1914, Breckinridge headed a relief expedition on the battleship *Tennessee* to bring Americans back from Europe. He was struck by the magnitude and scope of modern warfare; the course that he saw European combat taking left him "impressed as never before with the necessity of adequate military preparations for the United States." He sided with Garrison on preparedness; in their view Wilson failed to push national defense with sufficient vigor. Differences over Kentucky pa-

tronage added to his disenchantment, and when Garrison resigned in February 1916 Breckinridge followed. Unhappy with Wilson but unsympathetic to the Republicans, he intended to sit out the 1916 election. Then an "indiscreet reference"—Breckinridge remarked to a traveling acquaintance that there had been a conciliatory postscript to a diplomatic protest to Germany about the sinking of the *Lusitania* in 1915—led to a controversy on that point between Massachusetts Senator Henry Cabot Lodge and Wilson in late October.

When the United States entered the war, Breckinridge joined the army. He served in France, primarily with the intelligence section of the Fifth Army Corps, and became a colonel. After the armistice he returned to Washington and was president of the Navy League from 1919 to 1921. He was instrumental in organizing the celebration of Navy Day.

In 1922 Breckinridge moved to New York. His first marriage ended in divorce in 1925, and on Aug. 5, 1927, he married Aida de Acosta Root, a benefactor of the blind and one of the first women aviators. Long interested in aviation himself, Breckinridge received his pilot's license at the age of forty-one. At about the same time he became Charles A. Lindbergh's attorney. He was an unsuccessful intermediary in the Lindbergh kidnapping case in 1932. The two men drifted apart over intervention in World War II, and in 1954 Breckinridge told the FBI, then making a security check on Lindbergh, who was being considered for an important government job, that Lindbergh was not fit for responsibility on important issues.

Breckinridge's public career became more active in the 1930's. He was Virginia Senator Harry F. Byrd's floor manager at the 1932 Democratic convention and served as counsel to a congressional investigation of dirigible disasters in 1933. As the New Deal developed, Breckinridge recoiled. In 1934 he ran as an independent from New York for the Senate, and two years later he opposed Roosevelt in several primaries as a member of the Association for Defense of the Constitution. "Four more years of this," he argued, "and we shall be boondoggled into bankruptcy." He supported Republican Wendell Willkie for president in 1940.

As World War II approached, Breckinridge championed American intervention. On radio and in the press he urged a declaration of war on the Axis powers. After Pearl Harbor he told a Canadian friend of his satisfaction at seeing the

United States in "this gigantic battle for the freedom of mankind." Too old for active military service, he sent ideas and encouragement to friends in government. Breckinridge had been separated from his second wife for three years before he divorced her in early 1947. On Mar. 27, 1947, he married Margaret Lucy Smith; they had one daughter. He remained an active attorney until the day of his death in New York City.

Breckinridge was tall and thin, with a nose that gave his face a distinctive sharp look. Among family and friends he was warm and captivating, but he could be a tart and articulate adversary in a public controversy. Drawn into public service by his background and the example of Wilson, Breckinridge found the evolution of the Democrats toward domestic liberalism unpalatable. In foreign policy he combined a devotion to a strong military posture with an abiding adherence to internationalism.

[The Breckinridge Papers in the Library of Congress and his "Reminiscences" in the Oral History Collection, Columbia University, are the basic primary sources. The Woodrow Wilson Papers, Library of Congress, and Charles A. Lindbergh Papers, Yale University, also have significant materials. Breckinridge's own works include *Report on Operations of United States Relief Commission in Europe* (1914); *Excerpts, 1935-1936* (1938); *". . . shall not perish . . ."* (1941); *Excerpts III, 1938-1941* (1944); "The Solving of the Hyphen," *Forum*, Nov. 1916; "The Valley of Decision," *Vital Speeches*, Mar. 23, 1936; "Nazis in Greenland," *Current History*, May 1940.

See also Stephen Hess, *America's Political Dynasties* (1966); E. D. Warfield, *Joseph Cabell Breckinridge, Jr.* (1898); and the obituary notice in the *New York Times*, May 3, 1960.]

LEWIS L. GOULD

BRENON, HERBERT (Jan. 13, 1880–June 21, 1958), motion picture director and producer, was born in Dublin, Ireland, the son of Edward St. John Brenon, a journalist and editor, and Frances Harris, a writer. Brenon grew up in London, where he attended St. Paul's School and King's College, University of London. In 1896 he immigrated to the United States and spent the next few years working in the theater in New York City and with touring groups. On Feb. 18, 1904, he married Helen Oberg, who took the stage name of Helen Downing when they toured as a vaudeville team. They had one son.

In 1906 Brenon operated a nickelodeon in Johnstown, Pa. Three years later he obtained a job in New York City as a scenarist-editor with Carl Laemmle's Independent Motion Picture Co. (IMP, forerunner of Universal). *All for Her* (1912), a one-reeler with George Ober, was the first film he directed. In 1913 Laemmle sent Brenon abroad with a small company that made several films in England, France, and Germany. *Neptune's Daughter* (1914), a seven-reel water spectacle starring Annette Kellerman, was filmed in Bermuda at great expense; it set attendance records. Brenon wrote most of his early films and frequently acted in them.

In 1914 Brenon left IMP and made one film with his own company, Tiffany Films. In 1915 and 1916 he made several films for William Fox, usually serving as his own scenarist and producer. He directed Theda Bara in four films in 1915, among them *The Two Orphans* (which also starred Jean Sothern and Brenon). By this time he was one of the most famous personalities in the film industry. Details of his production in Jamaica of *A Daughter of the Gods*, another "mermaid" extravaganza with Annette Kellerman, as well as of his consequent quarrel and lawsuits with Fox, were widely reported. Angered by the unprecedented amounts of time and money spent on the film, Fox removed Brenon's name from the credits of the film and had it reedited. When the movie was released in 1916, it was a huge success.

After his break with Fox, Brenon formed the Herbert Brenon Film Corp., which made six films, including *War Brides* (1916, an antiwar film, in which Alla Nazimova and Richard Barthelmess made their screen debuts); *The Lone Wolf* (1917, with Bert Lytell); *The Fall of the Romanoffs* (1917); and *The Passing of the Third Floor Back* (1918, with Sir Johnston Forbes-Robertson). *The Invasion of Britain (Victory and Peace)*, an ambitious propaganda film that Brenon directed for the British War Office in 1918, was a hapless project that was never publicly shown.

Brenon returned to the United States briefly in 1918 to obtain his final citizenship papers. Then he went to Europe again to make a series of movies with Marie Doro. In 1921 he was back in Hollywood directing three Norma Talmadge vehicles for Joseph M. Schenck. A group of films that he made for Fox in 1922 included *Any Wife*, with Pearl White, and three films starring William Farnum.

Between 1923 and 1927 Brenon directed seventeen films for Famous Players-Lasky (later Paramount). These were the most important years of his career. The highly acclaimed *Peter Pan*

(1924) had seventeen-year-old Betty Bronson in the title role and Ernest Torrence as Captain Hook. *A Kiss for Cinderella* (1925) continued the successful collaboration of James Barrie, Brenon, and Betty Bronson. Highlights of 1926 were *Dancing Mothers,* starring Clara Bow and Conway Tearle; *The Great Gatsby,* with Warner Baxter as Jay Gatsby; and *Beau Geste,* "one of the classic action-spectacles of the silent screen" (according to Geltzer), with a cast headed by Ronald Colman. Some of Brenon's other Paramount films were *The Spanish Dancer* (1923, starring Pola Negri, Antonio Moreno, and Wallace Beery; the first of nine Brenon films with photography by James Wong Howe); *The Woman With Four Faces* (1923, starring Betty Compson and Richard Dix); *Shadows of Paris* (1924, starring Pola Negri); and *The Song and Dance Man* (1926, starring Tom Moore). Brenon also produced many of his Paramount films.

In 1927 Brenon left Paramount to make *Sorrell and Son* on his own; this film, which starred H. B. Warner, was Brenon's favorite. Until 1933 he directed for several Hollywood studios— primarily RKO—usually producing his own work. *Laugh Clown, Laugh* (1928), with Lon Chaney and Loretta Young, was his last silent film. He reluctantly added "synchronized sound effects" (a music score) to *The Rescue* (1929, with Ronald Colman and Lily Damita), and made his first talkie, *The Lummox,* in 1930. Among the six other sound films that he made in Hollywood were *The Case of Sergeant Grischa* (1930, with Chester Morris) and *The Girl of the Rio* (1932, with Dolores Del Rio).

In 1935 Brenon went to England, where until 1940 he directed diverse films for British companies. These included *Housemaster* (1938, with Otto Kruger), which was the best received; *Yellow Sands* (1938, starring Marie Tempest and Robert Newton); and *The Flying Squad* (1940, with Sebastian Shaw, Jack Hawkins, and Phyllis Brooks), which was the last film Brenon made. He returned to the United States during World War II and retired. He died in Los Angeles.

In the silent film era Brenon was frequently grouped with Cecil B. DeMile and D. W. Griffith as one of the "Big Three" of filmmaking. Although less well-known, he is remembered as the creator of spectacular silent films and the director of numerous noted screen stars. Richard Koszarski wrote in 1976: "By the 20's Brenon had established himself at Paramount as a craftsman of the highest order. . . . Notable for their intel-

ligence and controlled sentiment, his films are especially strong in the richness of their performances."

[Brenon's published writings include "If Pictures Are Not Art, What Are They?" *New York Telegraph,* May 13, 1917; and "Opposition to Sound Film," *New York Times,* Oct. 21, 1928, IX:6. The only comprehensive and reliable source is George Geltzer, "Herbert Brenon," *Films in Review,* Mar. 1955. General sources are Richard Koszarski, *Hollywood Directors,* 1914–1940 (1976); obituary, *New York Times,* June 23, 1958, p. 23; Anthony Slide, *Early American Cinema* (1970): and Paul Spehr, *The Movies Begin* (1977). Also see Randolph Bartlett, "Brenon—The Man," *Photoplay,* Mar. 1918; Johnstone Craig, "The Face That Drives," *ibid.,* Nov. 1915; "Great Directors and Their Productions," *New York Dramatic Mirror,* July 15, 1916; "The King of Jamaica," *Photoplay,* July 1916; and Hugh Leamy, "Guiding the Stars," *Collier's,* Oct. 8, 1927. Sources on individual films include Gladwin Hill, " 'Peter Pan' of Brenon's Fond Memory," *New York Times,* Apr. 12, 1953, II:5; Clyde Jeavons, *A Pictorial History of War Films* (1974); and Adrian Turner, " 'Beau Geste,' " *Films Illustrated,* Aug. 1975.]

JUDITH DERISH

BROMFIELD, LOUIS (Dec. 27, 1896–Mar. 18, 1956), writer and experimental farmer, was born in Mansfield, Ohio (the unnamed setting of many of his novels), the son of Charles Bromfield, a banker, and Annette Maria Coulter. He was educated in the Mansfield public schools and briefly attended Cornell University (1914–1915), where he studied agriculture, and (for less than a semster) Ohio Northern University. He then transferred to Columbia University, where he was a journalism student until he enlisted in the United States Army Ambulance Service attached to the French army in 1917. Bromfield was awarded the Croix de Guerre and received his discharge in France. He returned to New York late in 1919.

Although his youthful ambition had been to restore the family farm to full productivity—from his father and grandfathers he had acquired a love of the land and a strong Jeffersonian democratic faith—Bromfield realized that the industrial society that had driven his family off the farm had made impossible the realization of his dream of a self-sufficient agricultural life. He therefore determined to be a writer, the career that his mother had urged on him.

In 1920–1922 Bromfield worked first for the

New York City News Service and later as a reporter and night editor for the Associated Press. He married Mary Appleton Wood on Oct. 16, 1921. Between 1922 and 1925 he worked as foreign editor and critic for *Musical America*, as assistant to producer Brock Pemberton, and as drama, art, and music critic for *The Bookman*, for which he wrote a monthly column, "The New Yorker." He also wrote music criticism for *Time* and became advertising manager for G. P. Putnam's Sons.

During this period Bromfield wrote a novel that was rejected by the publisher F. A. Stokes. By 1923 he had written and destroyed two more. Finally, *The Green Bay Tree* was accepted for publication by Stokes in 1924. The novel was well received and sold well, freeing Bromfield to write full time. As in the best of his later fiction, *The Green Bay Tree* drew upon his Ohio and family background, his dislike of industrialism, and his Jeffersonian convictions. He moved to Cold Spring Harbor, L.I., where he wrote *Possession* (1925). After the birth of a daughter, he took his family to France for a vacation. They remained for fourteen years, leasing an ancient *presbytère* near Senlis, where he wrote, gardened, and entertained. Two daughters were born in France.

The publication of *Early Autumn*, which received the Pulitzer Prize for 1926, established Bromfield as a leading American novelist; but, although he continued to publish an average of a book a year, by the end of the 1920's his reputation had begun to deteriorate. Some critics insisted that he had failed to reach his potential and had become too commercial. Marxist critics began to consider him reactionary. Nevertheless, his popularity remained high, and he published widely in popular magazines. In 1930 Bromfield worked briefly as a screen writer under contract to Samuel Goldwyn; and in 1933 he published *The Farm*, his most personal book. He spent that winter in America and began to talk of buying a farm in Ohio, but he returned to France. In 1932 Bromfield made the first of four visits to India, profound experiences that resulted in two novels, *The Rains Came* (1937) and *Night in Bombay* (1940).

In the late 1930's Bromfield served as president of the Emergency Committee for American Wounded in Spain. He also was made a chevalier of the Legion of Honor, and in the fall of 1938 he sent his family to Ohio. He followed some months later.

Upon his return to Ohio, Bromfield bought three rundown farms in Richland County; named them "Malabar Farm" in memory of India; and began to restore the property. Although he traveled to Hollywood and Brazil, among other places, during the next seventeen years, Malabar Farm remained his home. His major interest was in restoring the land through practices designed to correct the abuses of poor agricultural practice and to make the farm a productive, nearly self-sufficient unit, a goal he did not realize. He did, however, make substantial contributions to new farming techniques, including crop rotation, erosion control, and farm pond development.

During the last fifteen years of his life, Bromfield continued to write fiction—largely out of habit, as he commented; his convictions were reserved for his farming and the books that resulted from it: *Pleasant Valley* (1945), *Malabar Farm* (1948), *From My Experience* (1955), and *Animals and Other People* (1955). He died in Columbus, Ohio.

Although his literary reputation has not recovered from the decline that it suffered in the 1930's, Bromfield's early novels—*The Green Bay Tree, Possession,* and *Early Autumn*—rank high and *The Farm* is a fine interpretation of the coming of industrialism to the Midwest. His later nonfiction, particularly *Pleasant Valley, Malabar Farm,* and *Out of the Earth* (1950), are substantial contributions to the literature of agriculture and nature. Despite the veneer of sophistication that overlays much of his fiction, Bromfield was consistently a Midwesterner, an agrarian romantic, and a Jeffersonian Democrat. His work belongs in the mainstream of the literature produced in the Midwest in the first three decades of the twentieth century that dominated and directed American writing. Much of his work remains in print, and a number of his works have been made into successful motion pictures.

After Bromfield's death Malabar Farm became an experimental and model farm, the Louis Bromfield Ecological Center, supported by a private foundation. It is now owned and operated by the state of Ohio.

[Bromfield has been the subject of three books: Morrison Brown, *Louis Bromfield and His Books* (1956); Ellen Bromfield Geld, *The Heritage, a Daughter's Memories of Louis Bromfield* (1962); and David D. Anderson, *Louis Bromfield* (1964). *A Few Brass Tacks* (1946) and *A New Pattern For a Tired World* (1954) deal with his economic and social theories.]

DAVID D. ANDERSON

BROWN, GERTRUDE FOSTER (July 29, 1867–Mar. 1, 1956), suffragist and musician, was born in Morrison, Ill., the daughter of Charles Foster and Anna Drake. Her father earned a comfortable living as a trader in butter, eggs, and grain for the Chicago commodities market. Gertrude Foster's musical talent developed early, and at the age of twelve she was the organist of the local Presbyterian church. She convinced her parents to send her to the New England Conservatory of Music, from which she received a diploma in piano in 1885. She then went to study the piano with Scharwenka in Berlin and Delaborde in Paris. After returning to Chicago she began her career as a concert pianist, lecturer on Richard Wagner, and teacher. On Aug. 4, 1893, she married Raymond Brown, artist and newspaperman; and they moved to New York when he became art director for the Hearst newspapers and a group of magazines, including *Everybody's* magazine.

Until 1910 Brown pursued her musical career oblivious to the suffrage movement. Her introduction to that issue came at an otherwise dull dinner party on Long Island. A judge, the guest of honor, was asked by the hostess if he thought women ought to have the vote; and he declared, "Of course I do, and they would have voted years ago if they hadn't been such damn fools." Brown had never heard anyone mention woman suffrage, and her husband admitted that he had seen only an occasional newspaper squib about it. Together they sought to learn about the issue; and when they finally located the headquarters of the New York State Suffrage Association, they found a dreary place inhabited by one dowdy little woman in "very old fashioned clothes and frizzed grey hair." Gertrude Brown's professional friends knew little about suffrage; indeed, few had ever thought about it. Consequently, she invited a group of them to tea one afternoon to discuss the matter. Anna Howard Shaw, president of the National American Woman Suffrage Association (NAWSA), spoke to them. On the spot they organized the Suffrage Study Club, which grew rapidly.

The woman suffrage movement began expanding significantly about 1910, and the first suffrage parade was staged in New York City in May 1911. Three thousand women and eighty-nine men, including Raymond Brown, braved the jeers of the spectators. Two years later more than 40,000 people marched in the parade. Tall, attractive, energetic, and an able speaker and or-

ganizer, Brown was elected president of the New York State Woman Suffrage Association in 1913. She became a friend and associate of Carrie Chapman Catt, who headed the New York State Woman Suffrage Party. Catt managed the 1915 New York suffrage referendum campaign; and although defeated, the organization, tactics, and strategy that she developed promised victory in 1917. When Catt became president of NAWSA, the Woman Suffrage Party in New York was reorganized with Brown as vice-president and chairman of the organization committee. Catt mapped a national four-year plan, laid out month-by-month, to win suffrage in the states and ratification of the suffrage amendment to the Constitution. Success in New York was a crucial element, and Brown played a key role in the 1917 referendum victory. She then joined Catt in NAWSA as first vice-president.

With the entry of the United States into World War I, a group of women physicians and surgeons, organized by the New York Infirmary for Women and Children, offered their services to the government but were rejected. The French government, however, eagerly accepted them. NAWSA agreed to be responsible for the maintainence of the unit and raised nearly $135,000 to send seventy-four women to France. Brown went along as director of the Women's Overseas Hospitals. After the war, the unit was merged with other war relief agencies, and Brown returned to the suffrage campaign.

Following ratification of the Nineteenth Amendment in 1920, Brown helped launch the National League of Women Voters as the successor organization to NAWSA. She was asked to run for secretary of state of New York but declined. Instead, in February 1921, she became managing director of the *Woman Citizen*, which had superseded the *Woman's Journal* founded by Lucy Stone in Boston in 1870. Brown raised much of the money required to subsidize the magazine throughout the 1920's, but the Great Depression ended it in June 1931.

Brown then returned to her first love, music, which she practiced for her own pleasure and that of her friends, and spent summers traveling with her husband in Europe and North Africa. When World War II broke out, she and several of her former suffrage associates formed the Women's Action Committee for Victory and Lasting Peace. It supported the war effort and United States entry into the United Nations. After the war she retired entirely from community work to her music and travel. She made her last trip to Europe in 1952. She died in Westport, Conn.

[Brown's papers are being given to the Schlesinger Library at Radcliffe College and to the Sophia Smith Collection at Smith College by her niece Mildred Adams. Radcliffe has some correspondence and the minutes of the Woman Citizen Corporation (1917–1931). Smith has her unpublished version of the suffrage campaign, entitled "On Account of Sex." These materials and Brown's unpublished autobiography were used for Adams' account of Brown in *The Right to Be People* (1967).

Brown wrote *Your Vote and How to Use It* (1918), a manual for the newly enfranchised women voters of New York. Her husband anonymously published a brief, amusing, pro-suffrage book, *How It Feels to Be the Husband of a Suffragette* (1951), which adds his perspective and some detail to the story.]

J. STANLEY LEMONS

BROWNLEE, JAMES FORBIS (July 29, 1891–Oct. 12, 1960), business executive, was born in Oakland, Calif., the son of Malcolm Bruce Brownlee, a banker, and Myra Belle Forbis. He was educated in the public schools of Spokane, Wash., and at the Middlesex School in Concord, Mass. He graduated from Harvard University in 1913, with the B.A.

Brownlee's business career began in 1913, when he became a salesman for the American Sugar Refining Company in New York City. During World War I, he served as second lieutenant in the army and was stationed at Camp Hancock, Ga. He subsequently served in France as an ordnance officer. On March 10, 1917, he married Emeline Morley.

In 1925 Brownlee was promoted to general sales manager of American Sugar. He held that position until 1928, when he joined the General Foods Corporation as president of the Baker Associates Company, a marketing subsidiary responsible for the sale of half of General Food's products. He rose within the company and in 1932 was elected vice-president in charge of sales and advertising. He also became a director of General Foods but left in 1935 to become president of Frankfort Distilleries, a Louisville, Ky., corporation. He held that post until 1943, concurrently serving on several boards and councils and in several government positions. From 1936 until 1938, he was also president of the Jefferson Island Salt Company of Louisville.

Brownlee's government service began in 1937

with a two-year membership on the Washington-based business Advisory Council. In 1942 he served on the War Production Board, and, from 1942 to 1946, in the War Food Administration. From 1943 to 1945 he was deputy administrator in charge of price control for the Office of Price Administration, and in 1946 he was deputy director of the Office of Economic Stabilization. During his tenure with the O.P.A., Brownlee played a key role in the task of reconverting the country's economy to postwar conditions. His program involved industry-wide surveys of the ceiling prices of products with overall price increases where the ceilings proved to be restrictive.

After leaving full-time government service, Brownlee worked as a consultant to several corporations. From 1951 until his retirement seven years later he was a partner in the New York City investment firm of J. H. Whitney and Company. Also in 1951, Brownlee became chairman of the board and a director of the Minute Maid Corporation. From 1952 until 1956, he returned to part-time government service, serving as special adviser to the administrator of the Office of Defense Mobilization. He served as director of the Spencer Chemical Company of Kansas City, Mo., Pillsbury Mills of Minneapolis, and the American Express Company of New York City. His other postwar positions included that of director of the Chase Manhattan Bank and of the American Sugar Refining Company. In 1953 Brownlee was made a trustee of the Ford Foundation, and a year later he directed a business task force developed to study the problems of the soft coal industry and other facets of fuel supply. He died in Greensfield Hill, Conn.

HARVARD SITKOFF

BRYANT, LOUISE FRANCES STEVENS (Sept. 19, 1885–Aug. 29, 1959), social researcher and medical editor, was born in Paris, France, the daughter of Miriam Collins Nicholson and Charles E. Stevens. Her father, a civil engineer who spent most of his time working in South America, died of mountain fever while prospecting in Venezuela in 1888, leaving his wife with two daughters and a small fortune. Miriam Stevens, who had passed her husband's absences touring Europe, settled in New York after his death and led a fashionable life. The elder daughter shared her mother's sophisticated but nonintellectual interests, while Louise was studious and from an early age, bent on making her own life.

Louise attended public schools and planned to follow her sister to Smith College, but most of the Stevens' fortune was lost through corporate failures that forced the family to alter its way of life. Louise kept house for her mother during her older sister's senior year at Smith because there was not enough money to have both in college at once. She entered Smith in 1904, majored in philosophy, and graduated with the B.A. in 1908, but her sister's death in childbirth forced Louise to assume responsibility for the support of her mother over the next twenty-five years. Miriam Stevens often called men "an unworthy sex" after her husband's death and had restructured her life around her elder daughter. On learning of her death, Miriam remarked "Now I have nobody" and lived in mourning, a demanding and cold burden to her remaining child.

In 1903 Louise became engaged to Arthur A. Bryant, a Ph.D. candidate in philology at Harvard. They conducted their courtship mostly by mail during the next five years. By the time she graduated from Smith, she had begun to doubt whether she loved him enough to marry but gave in to his ardor. The marriage ended on her initiative after four years (December 1912), but she retained his name; and her status as "a married woman" was an important consideration when she was hired as an executive by an organization conducting sex research in 1927. After 1924 she shared a household with Lura Beam, a writer and editor, who also had a mother to support. They remained together until Bryant's death.

A zoology minor in college, Bryant obtained her first job as an assistant in the department of physiology and osteology at the American Museum of Natural History but left in April 1909 to become special agent in the Russell Sage Foundation's department of education. Bryant gained a national reputation as a social investigator through her studies of malnutrition among schoolchildren and advocacy of school feeding. Drawing on her own exhaustive research and on the work of such other Progressives as Robert Hunter, Bryant demonstrated that at least 10 percent of urban schoolchildren suffered from malnutrition and that the learning of many more was inhibited by poor nutrition. Although she linked malnutrition to poverty, she argued that school feeding programs need not be expensive and provided practical plans for administration. The Russell Sage Foundation usually published its studies but rejected *School Feeding* after a member of the editorial board complained that its recom-mendations would lead to socialism. The mono-graph was accepted by the commercial house of J. B. Lippincott, and before its publication in 1913 Bryant's research had been widely publicized through a syndicated article in 125 Sunday newspapers and through her presentations at professional conferences.

In 1911 Bryant moved on to graduate work at the University of Pennsylvania, where she earned the first Ph.D. in medical science in 1914. She supported herself by serving as head of the department of social service attached to Lightner Witmer's Psychological Clinic, a pioneering attempt to use social science in the identification and treatment of troubled children. Bryant's courses for social workers and her publications analyzing the clinic's records and methods provided a sympathetic interpretation of the deviant child, whose problems, she argued, were more often the result of disease or abuse than of hereditary defect. In September 1914 she became chief of the Women's Division of the Municipal Court of Philadelphia, where she was responsible for supplying judges with social data in domestic relations cases and became an advocate of the rights of unwed mothers and illegitimate children.

In 1918 Bryant became a statistician in the office of the Army Chief of Staff, where she prepared reports used in the mobilization effort. After the war, she turned down two government jobs in venereal disease control because she no longer wanted to work in the field of social pathology. She became Educational and Publications Secretary of the Girl Scouts of America, but four years of scouting provided enough respite from social pathology, and in 1923 she joined the New York Committee on Dispensary Development (CDD) as coordinator of research.

The CDD had been created by the United Hospital Fund of New York to study the problem of delivering medical care to the two-thirds of New York families whose incomes provided no surplus to meet the cost of serious illness. Bryant collaborated with Michael M. Davis on a series of monographs that analyzed the waste in the health care delivery system and recommended reforms.

When the CDD disbanded in 1927, Bryant became executive secretary of the National Committee on Maternal Health (NCMH). Robert L. Dickinson, a gynecologist, had organized the NCMH in 1923 to promote medical sex research because he was convinced that poor sexual adjustment was the primary cause of an apparent breakdown in stable family life.

Dickinson's work had been hampered by his lack of statistical skills and by the physician's characteristic focus on the individual case. Bryant provided quantitative expertise and a social scientist's perspective during the next eight years, and NCMH publications marked the emergence of sex research as an established field.

Bryant creatively edited a series of monographs that defined a new field of social biology and led to important changes in medical attitudes toward contraception and other aspects of sexual behavior. These studies included *Control of Conception* (1931), *A Thousand Marriages* (1931), *Human Sex Anatomy* (1933), *The Single Woman* (1934), *Human Sterility* (1934), and *Abortion: Spontaneous and Induced* (1936). Many of these volumes would not have been published during the Great Depression without the foundation subsidies raised by Bryant, the technical skills she provided, or the protection from vice-suppression zealots guaranteed by the committee's imprint.

Bryant left the committee in 1935, her health seriously affected by budgetary conflicts with Dickinson. Bryant was responsible for seeing that donor funds were spent on the projects for which they were given, but Dickinson's interest often shifted to a new project before others had been completed. By 1935 his focus had gone beyond "maternal health." Bryant's resignation followed an attempt by Dickinson to use a grant from the Rockefeller Foundation that had been allocated for a study of marriage counseling to pay the salaries of two homosexuals whom he planned to use as sources in a study of "inversion." Bryant spent a year convalescing after her resignation and never held another executive position. The last fifteen years of her working life were spent handling the clerical work for the American Association of University Women's art exhibits.

Bryant participated in two of the most important twentieth-century American social movements, the progressive search for social values and forms of organization appropriate to an industrial civilization and the attempt by women to establish themselves in the professions. Her career exemplified the successes and limits of both endeavors. Although she was a member of the Socialist party, Bryant's plainly written monographs avoided social comment and let the facts speak for themselves. By refraining from radical criticism in her investigations, she tacitly implied that piecemeal amelioration would work. Her feminism, like her politics, was nonstrident. She believed that woman's fight for equality had been

practically won by an earlier generation and that she could therefore concentrate upon her own work. Tragically, her conflict with Dickinson ended her professional career at the age of fifty. As a social reformer and woman professional she achieved a good deal, but she failed to realize fully her goals of social justice or equality for women. She died in Bronxville, New York, two days after her third coronary thrombosis, and was cremated.

[The ten boxes of Bryant Papers in the Sophia Smith Collection, Smith College, are well indexed and include reprints and photographs as well as personal and professional correspondence. Lura Beam's privately printed *Bequest From A Life: A Biography of Louise Stevens Bryant* (1963) is rich in detail and is a lyrical tribute to a friend and lover. On Bryant's early work, see also her *School Feeding* (1913); and "The Psychological Clinic," *Town Development*, Apr. 1916. On the Committee on Dispensary Development, see Ralph Pumphrey, "Michael M. Davis and the Development of the Health Care Movement, 1900–1928," *Societas*, Winter 1972; Louise Bryant, *Better Doctoring—Less Dependency* (New York, 1927); and Michael M. Davis, *Clinics, Hospitals, and Health Centers* (1927). James Reed provides a history of the National Committee on Maternal Health in Part III of *From Private Vice to Public Virtue: The Birth Control Movement and American Society Since 1830* (1978).]

JAMES REED

BRYSON, LYMAN LLOYD (July 12, 1888–Nov. 24, 1959), educator, radio broadcaster, and author, was born in Valentine, Nebr., the son of George E. Bryson, a druggist, and Nancy Melissa Hayes. His childhood was spent in a sparsely settled cattle-raising region. According to his own estimate, the "simple egalitarian democracy" of the frontier and his mother's "very deep implicit faith in the power of beautiful words to coerce . . . the social good" were the most significant influences in his early life. After completing high school in Omaha, Bryson entered the University of Michigan, where he wrote poetry, talked "great ideas," and read "in forty directions at once." After receiving the B.A. in 1910, he spent three years as a reporter for the *Omaha Daily Bee* (1910), the *Omaha Daily News* (1911), and the *Detroit Evening News* (1912–13). On Oct. 4, 1912, he married Hope Mersereau, an artist; they had one son. The following year he returned to the University of Michigan to study for the M.A., which he received in 1915. He was instructor, and then assistant professor, of rhetoric and journalism there from 1913 to 1917. During this period he also studied law; published a volume of poetry, *Smoky Roses* (1916); contributed verse to *Forum, Survey,* and *New Republic;* and had a one-act play, "The Grasshopper,"produced by the Arts and Crafts Theater of Detroit in 1917.

Except for the ten years (1918–28) when he traveled throughout the United States, Europe, and Asia doing administrative, organizational, and publicity work for the children's programs sponsored by the Red Cross, Bryson's subsequent career was devoted entirely to education in the broad, instrumental sense in which he used the term. He became a teacher by "a series of accidents," although his mother's belief that her son's "small lyric gift" would enable him to "get political power and do good" clearly affected his view of the teacher's function as midway between that of a poet and a statesman.

In 1928 Bryson became associate director of the San Diego Museum of Anthropology (he was made director in 1929) and professor of anthropology at San Diego State Teachers College. From 1929 to 1932 he was executive director of the California Association for Adult Education, and in 1931 and 1932 he also directed the University of California summer school in adult education. He left California to serve as the forum leader of the Des Moines adult education project (1932–34) and then went on to Teachers College, Columbia University, where he served initially as visiting professor (1934–35) and subsequently as professor of education (1935–53). Adult education, or the effort to make experience deliberately rather than accidentally educative "as a means of enriching and strengthening the lives of all men and women," had become Bryson's abiding vocation. In effect, his mature career consisted of efforts to harness the communications media to the educational needs of a democratic society.

During the mid-1930's, Bryson established a "readability laboratory" at Teachers College to determine how serious works on political, economic, and social questions could be made lucid, comprehensible, and appealing to a mass audience, and then to produce material that met these requirements. In 1938 he was appointed chairman of the adult education board of the Columbia Broadcasting System (CBS). Four years later he became director of education for CBS and, after World War II, counselor on public affairs. He was moderator of a number of radio and television discussion programs, notably "The

People's Platform," an informal analysis of current events; "Invitation to Learning," a review of the classics; "Time for Reason," a commentary on the background of current problems, including those of radio; and "Lamp Unto My Feet," a discussion of religious and ethical questions. Bryson also served as a lecturer and discussion leader of forums ranging from those sponsored by the New York Town Hall to the Jewish Theological Seminary Institute for Religious and Social Studies and Conference on Science, Philosophy, and Religion.

During World War II, Bryson was chief of the Bureau of Special Operations for the Office of War Information and thereafter became increasingly a social philosopher of scientific humanism. He sought to use "intelligence and experience" to create "conditions of freedom" beneficial both to the individual and to the social good. He wrote for both popular and scholarly journals—*Survey Graphic, House Beautiful, Saturday Review of Literature, Political Science Quarterly,* and *Business Week*—and his monographs were addressed to a wide range of audiences.

The fundamentals of his philosophy, however, remained constant. In *The Next America: Prophecy and Faith* (1952) Bryson stated that "the present battle for democracy, for the chance to develop as persons by the experience of choice and consequence, is between individuals and collectives," a view that placed him squarely in opposition to intellectuals who saw an alliance of government, labor unions, and schools as an antidote to the evils of a competitive, capitalist society. "Building a national culture in which there are to be, ultimately, no artificial barriers between any man and his own best self " was both the means and the end to which Bryson believed "the next America" should devote itself. Subsequently he wrote a number of articles and *The Drive Toward Reason* (1954), a series of lectures on the function of adult education in a democratic society. His wife died in 1944, and on May 11, 1945, he married Katherine McGrattan. He died in New York City.

[Bryson's major monographs include *A State Plan for Adult Education* (1934); *Adult Education* (1936); *Which Way America?* (1939); *The New Prometheus* (1941); *Science and Freedom* (1947); and *Time for Reason About Radio* (1948). He was editor of *The Communication of Ideas* (1948); *Facing the Future's Risks* (1953); and *An Outline of Man's Knowledge of the Modern World* (1960); and coeditor of a series published by the Jewish Theological Seminary's Conference on Science, Philosophy, and Religion. His autobiography is in Louis Finkelstein, ed., *American Spiritual Autobiographies* (1948); see also the obituary in the *New York Times*, Nov. 26, 1959. Bryson's papers are at the Library of Congress, except for a few in the possession of his widow. The Columbia University Oral History Collection has a 254-page memoir, done by Bryson in 1951, that deals particularly with his role in educational radio.]

ELLEN CONDLIFFE LAGEMANN

BUCKLEY, OLIVER ELLSWORTH (Aug. 8, 1887–Dec. 14, 1959), physicist and research engineer, was born in Sloan, Iowa, the son of William Doubleday Buckley, a lawyer and superintendent of public schools, and Sarah Elizabeth Jeffrey, a teacher. Buckley became interested in electricity and electronic communications at an early age. He read a five-volume set of books on electricity he found in his father's library; and when Sloan acquired a telephone exchange during his senior year of high school, he helped install it. As a student at Grinnell College, Buckley's greatest interests were mathematics and physics; and he taught there for a year after graduating in 1909 with the B.S. This led to a teaching assistantship in physics at Cornell University (1910), where Buckley received the Ph.D. four years later. Although Buckley was not considered a brilliant student, he was hardworking; and his dissertation adviser predicted a promising career. At Cornell, Buckley met Frank B. Jewett, of the Bell Telephone Laboratories. He was fascinated by Jewett's description of the interactions of science, engineering, and production at Bell; and in 1914 he obtained a position in the engineering department of the Western Electric Company (part of the Bell System). On October 14 of that year he married a Grinnell classmate, Clara Louise Lane. They had four children.

Buckley plunged into research on standard and wireless telephone systems, inventing and developing the ionization manometer, which became the best means for pressure measurements in extremely high vacuums. Prior to American involvement in World War I, he worked on submarine detection equipment; after American entry into the conflict, he served in France as a major, running a communications research section in Paris. The poor performance of underwater telegraph cable communications between France and America led him to launch

new research into the problem when he returned to Bell after the war.

By 1924, Buckley had developed a successful underwater telegraph cable system with a fourfold increase in capacity. At the same time he initiated work on a multichannel submarine cable for telephones, which was used over short distances by 1930. A great advance in the state of the art, it stimulated further research into long-distance transatlantic telephonic systems. The work required vacuum-tube amplifiers and other equipment with a trouble-free lifetime of at least twenty years in order for the system to be operationally and economically feasible—but no such components were available. By this time Buckley had other administrative duties; and World War II brought other research requirements, so that the submarine telephonic cable system was not activated until 1956.

In 1933 Buckley had become director of research at Bell Telephone Laboratories and executive vice-president in November 1936, reporting to Jewett, then president of Bell Laboratories. Responsibilities for operations and the organization of 4,500 scientists, engineers, and staff increasingly separated Buckley from the research that he enjoyed. Nevertheless, his contributions in the management of science paralleled those in science itself. In the late 1930's the new facilities of Bell Laboratories, at Murray Hill, N.J., became the first such complex planned to incorporate distinctive and functional research requirements. Buckley worked closely with the architects to determine the requisites of functional lab space. The resulting custom-built lab complex had features that have been copied by other laboratories. He succeeded Jewett as president of Bell Laboratories in 1940 and guided the complex through hundreds of military projects during World War II, including extensive work in radar. In recognition of his wartime contributions, Buckley was awarded the Medal for Merit and a presidential citation in 1946.

In the postwar era Buckley and Bell management agreed not to commit more than 20 percent of the resources of Bell Laboratories to military research and development. This was not an easy task, since Bell's competence and quality of work were highly valued by the armed services; and Buckley devoted considerable time to selecting military proposals that he deemed relevant to Bell Laboratories' capabilities. Significant projects included the Army's "Nike" anti-aircraft guided missile system and the atomic weapons program, carried out by a subsidiary, the Sandia Corporation. Meanwhile, Buckley launched vigorous programs in new communications technology and fundamental research that led to microwave radio relay systems and the invention of the transistor. Whenever possible, he left his office and prowled laboratories wherever exciting work was in progress. In 1950 he accepted a presidential appointment as chairman of the Science Advisory Committee. To do so, he resigned as president of Bell Telephone Laboratories, becoming chairman of its board of directors until his retirement in 1952. He died in Newark, N.J.

Most of Buckley's forty-three patents were issued prior to World War II, before administrative responsibilities claimed the bulk of his energies. Throughout his career he served on government advisory committees and prepared many papers and talks. In the 1940's and 1950's he did public service as a member of the General Advisory Committee of the Atomic Energy Commission and the National Multiple Sclerosis Society, of which he was chairman from 1953 to 1956.

Buckley was deeply admired for his creativity, leadership, judgment, and integrity. During his tenure at Bell Laboratories, support for fundamental research and scientific publication by its personnel maintained the respect of and contact with academic and government counterparts. During World War II, Bell Laboratories was in the forefront in developing the nascent art of systems engineering and, under Buckley's direction, became one of the nation's largest and most mature industrial laboratories.

[“Oliver E. Buckley Retires,” *Bell Laboratories Record,* Sept. 1952, includes several photographs. For an excellent summary of Buckley's career, including patents, publications, and honors, see Mervin J. Kelly, “Oliver Ellsworth Buckley,” in *Biographical Memoirs. National Academy of Sciences* (1964). Other sources include Prescott C. Mabon, *Mission Communications: The Story of Bell Laboratories* (1975), pp. 152–155; and obituaries in the *New York Times,* Dec. 15, 1959; and *Nature,* Mar. 5, 1960.]

ROGER E. BILSTEIN

BURDICK, USHER LLOYD (Feb. 21, 1879–Aug. 19, 1960), lawyer, congressman, and author, was born near Owatonna, Minn., the son of Ozias Warren Burdick, a farmer, and Lucy Farnum. In 1882 the family moved to a homestead northwest of Carrington, Dakota Territory, and in 1884 to Graham's Island, Benson County, Dakota Territory, where frontier farming experiences adjacent to the Fort Totten Sioux Indian reservation and a rural schoolteacher's influence provided important formative experiences. He became an expert marksman, acquired the ability to lasso, learned to speak a Sioux dialect fluently, and gained some knowledge of other Indian languages.

Burdick attended Mayville Normal School (now Mayville State College), intermittently teaching in rural and village schools until he graduated with a teaching certificate in 1900. His success in quieting unruly students in one school earned him appointment as deputy country superintendent of schools. He married Emma Rassmussen Robertson on Sept. 5, 1901; they had three children.

Burdick enrolled in the law department of the University of Minnesota, supporting his family by teaching classes in a business college. A large-framed man, standing 6 feet 2 inches and weighing 220 pounds, he participated in track—he ran the 100-yard dash in 10.5 seconds—and played right end on the Big Ten championship teams of 1903 and 1904. In 1904 he received the LL.B. and was admitted to the North Dakota bar. He combined law practice with employment in a bank in the village of Munich, N.Dak., a construction crew base for a Great Northern Railroad feeder (branch) line. Munich was home to seventeen illegal liquor establishments, a row of sporting houses along the railroad tracks, and a local reform movement that engaged Burdick's legal talents and physical prowess; he gained a county-wide reputation and was elected state representative from Cavalier County in 1906.

Theodore Roosevelt's books on western history and his reform image won Burdick's admiration. (He named his oldest son Quentin, after one of the president's sons.) He joined the coalition of liberal Republicans and Democrats that ousted the railroad-dominated Alexander McKenzie machine and elected a liberal Democrat, John Burke, as governor in what became known as the “North Dakota Political Revolution of 1906.” In the ensuing legislative sessions, Burdick became a leader, supporting anti-pass legislation—which made it a criminal act to give or receive free transportation on railroads for political purposes—primary elections, and popular election of senators.

Reelected in 1908, Burdick was chosen speaker

of the lower house. In 1910 he was elected lieutenant governor. The same year he transferred his law practice to Williston, N. Dak., near the Montana border, where he also dabbled in farming and ranching. In 1912 he declined the Progressive nomination for governor, sensing that a third-party ticket for state office and congressional seats in the 1912 general election could not result in his own election to office and would encourage Progressives who were Republican nominees to support Taft instead of Roosevelt. In 1914 he accepted the Progressive endorsement but was defeated by the incumbent conservative, L. B. Hanna. Two years later Hanna did not run and Burdick was again backed by the Progressives. Election seemed certain, but the emergence of the Nonpartisan League (NPL) diverted the protest vote and elected Lynn J. Frazier.

From 1913 to 1915 Burdick was state attorney and from 1915 to 1920 special prosecutor of Williams County, and from 1929 to 1932 he was assistant United States district attorney for North Dakota. During these years he helped organize and briefly led the North Dakota Farm Bureau. Later he was associated with the Farmers Union. Writing about western history, Indians, and the agrarian movement began to occupy much of his time. Roused by the hardships of his many farm clients, he denounced the Federal Reserve, the Agricultural Credit Corporation, the War Finance Corporation, and the Federal Intermediate Credit Banks as instruments of the "Twin City bank gang," and he supported Robert La Follette's 1924 presidential candidacy. As a consequence of cases he prosecuted as United States district attorney, he became an outspoken opponent of the Eighteenth Amendment.

Marital difficulties developed, ending in separation in 1920 and subsequent divorce. He then married Helen White, a secretary; they were divorced in 1926 or 1927. (According to Quentin Burdick, his father managed his second marriage and both divorces so carefully that the family did not know the time or place of the divorce proceedings.)

Burdick transferred his law practice to Fargo, N. Dak., and was not a major participant in North Dakota politics until farmer hardships caused him in 1932 to become North Dakota president of the Farm Holiday Association. Again he became a statewide figure. Without endorsement he ran unsuccessfully for Congress in 1932, but in 1934 his work with the Farm Holiday Association won him NPL endorsement, Republican party

nomination, and election. He was reelected four times. In 1932 Burdick had supported Franklin D. Roosevelt for president, but in 1936 he supported the Union Party presidential candidacy of William Lemke; as a consequence he lost his seniority rights in Congress.

Burdick's congressional career was that of an agrarian reformer and, until Pearl Harbor, an isolationist in foreign affairs. He consistently supported work relief, housing legislation, and assistance to debtor farmers. Although he customarily supported New Deal programs, he initially opposed social security, perhaps because of his adherence to the Townsend Plan. He opposed investigation of the sit-down strikes and refused to join in the attacks on Frank Murphy (who, as governor of Michigan, had supported the strikes) when Murphy was appointed attorney general. Burdick supported both the Ludlow Resolution, asking for a plebiscite before declaration of war, and the neutrality legislation sponsored by Senator Gerald P. Nye; he opposed big armaments, the draft, and lend-lease. After Pearl Harbor he vigorously supported the war effort and voted for the Fulbright Resolution, calling for a postwar international peacekeeping organization, a position he reversed during the postwar period.

In 1944, with NPL backing, he unsuccessfully sought the Republican nomination against the incumbent Nye. The senatorial effort cost Burdick his seat in the House of Representatives, and he returned to Williston, where he again practiced law and engaged in farming and ranching, specializing in breeding cattle and palomino horses.

Burdick defeated incumbent Charles Robertson for the Republican congressional nomination in 1948 and subsequently won in the general election. During his second congressional career, his interest in writing, the West, and Americana moved from avocation toward vocation. He spent much time browsing in antique shops for rare books; he established a library of some 12,000 volumes on his Maryland farm, where he specialized in raising milk goats.

As a congressman, Burdick did not sponsor any significant legislation; nor had he made a major effort on the Post Office, Civil Service, or Judiciary committees. But on the Indian Affairs and Pensions committees he sought to protect Indian interests, as well as those of his constituents.

Burdick served in Congress until 1959. Characterized as a "direct actionist"—an agrarian spokesman who brought voter pressure in support of farm legislation to bear upon his colleagues—he never forgot his pioneer roots, and he cultivated the image of a prairie, cowboy westerner, informal in personal appearance, who welcomed battle with the monopolistic eastern bankers and capitalists and thwarted their efforts to place American farmers in permanent thralldom.

A gregarious and convivial man, he was a powerful speaker and a colorful personality, known as a raconteur skilled in the use of dialects; he could entertain while persuading, whether in court or Congress, on the campaign trail, or in informal social groups. He tended to be the center of attention of any group.

His position on domestic policy did not change notably during his final ten years in Congress. On foreign policy he quickly reverted to an isolationist position and voted against arms for the North Atlantic Treaty Organization, opposed continued appropriations for the Marshall Plan, and advocated withdrawal from the United Nations. He pressed for legislation that would have prevented congressmen, judges, and other public officials from accepting fees for speeches, a position consistent with the anti-pass laws he sponsored when first elected to public office in 1906.

On July 31, 1956, he married a government employee, Mrs. Edna Bryant Sierson, who on Aug. 30, 1956, was accidentally killed while horseback riding on the Burdick ranch near Williston. On Feb. 28, 1958, he married another congressional employee, Mrs. Jean Rogers. Some marital difficulties ensued which may have influenced his decision not to run for reelection in that year.

The 1956 decision of the NPL to endorse candidates in the Democratic primary gave conservatives control of the North Dakota Republican party, and in 1958 they refused Burdick endorsement. He withdrew, influenced by the certainty that his NPL-endorsed son, Quentin, would be the Democratic general election candidate. He backed Quentin in the election, and his son became the first Democrat to be elected to the House of Representatives from North Dakota.

Burdick's final political action was to facilitate the development of North Dakota into a two-party state. He died in Washington, D. C., a few days after his son became United States Senator.

[The Usher L. Burdick papers are in the Orin G. Libby Historical Manuscript Collection, Chester Fritz Library, University of North Dakota. Burdick's works include *The Life of George Sperry Lofthus* (1939); *Tales From Buffalo Land: The Story of Fort Buford* (1940); *Jim Johnson Pioneer. A Brief History of the Mouse River Loop Country* (1941); *History of Farmers Political Action in North Dakota* (1944); *Recollections and Reminiscences of Graham Island* (1950); and *Some of the Old Time Cowmen of the Great West* (1957). See also "Should the United States Continue to Support the United Nations," *Congressional Digest*, Aug. 1952. On Burdick and his career, see Robert L. Morlan, *Political Prairie Fire: The Nonpartisan League, 1915–1922* (1955); and the obituary notice in the *New York Times*, Aug. 20, 1960.]

EDWARD C. BLACKORBY

BURLINGHAM, CHARLES CULP (Aug. 31, 1858–June 6, 1959), lawyer and civic leader, was born in Plainfield, N.J., the son of the Reverend Aaron Hale Burlingham and Emma Lanphear Starr. He received the B.A. from Harvard in 1879 and the LL.B. from Columbia Law School in 1881, and was admitted to the New York bar in September 1881. On Sept. 29, 1883, he married Louisa Weed Lawrence; they had three children.

In 1883, Burlingham began his lifelong association with the firm of Wing, Shoudy and Putnam. He became a member of the firm in 1889 and its head in 1910. His specialty was admiralty law, and by 1910 he was recognized as a leader of the admiralty bar. Burlingham established his reputation through the effective direction of litigation. Known as an able legal strategist, a skilled cross-examiner, and a persuasive pleader, Burlingham also contributed to improvements in the substance of the law. In 1909 and 1910 he served on the American delegation at the Brussels Conference on Maritime Law, and he was among the founders of the American Law Institute in 1923.

Burlingham also was involved in the affairs of New York City. He held only two public offices in his long career—member of the Board of Education from 1897 to 1902 and board president in 1902–03—but his influence on civic life was much greater than that of many who held high office. That influence was exercised through his leadership of the city bar, his many personal contacts, and his service on private reform committees and organizations.

Throughout his career, Burlingham's primary concern was the improvement of the city and state judiciary—the removal of judicial appointments from machine control, the elimination of corruption on the bench, and the appointment of competent, independent judges. In 1909 he used his influence with United States Attorney General George W. Wickersham to support the appointment of Learned Hand to the bench of the federal district court for southern New York. In 1913, as chairman of the Judicial Nominations Committee of the Fusion Committee of 107, he fostered the nomination and election of Benjamin Cardozo to the New York State Supreme Court. His advice on judicial appointments carried great weight with governors Alfred E. Smith, Franklin D. Roosevelt, Herbert Lehman, and Thomas E. Dewey. Roosevelt continued to consult Burlingham about possible judicial nominees while he was president.

Burlingham's concern with judicial corruption led him to work for political reform. In 1913 he supported John Purroy Mitchel, the successful fusion candidate for mayor who promised to end Tammany Hall's control of the courts. In 1921 he led an unsuccessful fusion movement to oppose Tammany mayoral candidate John F. Hylan.

In 1929 Burlingham succeeded Charles Evans Hughes as president of the Bar Association of the City of New York. Despite his age, he was one of the most effective presidents in the association's history; much of his activity was directed at cleansing the municipal judiciary of machine influence. In 1930 Burlingham requested an extensive investigation of the city magistrate courts; and that probe, conducted by his friend Samuel Seabury, resulted in removals and the exposure of widespread corruption in the administration of Mayor Jimmy Walker. Burlingham refused to accept a third term as president of the city bar in 1931 but continued his efforts for an independent judiciary. In October 1932 he played the central role in the creation of the Independent Judges Party, a special organization formed to oppose the two joint nominees of Tammany Hall and the Republican party for the New York State Supreme Court. Burlingham directed an unsuccessful campaign on behalf of his party's candidates, but the organization ceased to exist after the election.

In 1933 Burlingham served as chairman of the "harmony" committee that nominated Fiorello H. La Guardia and coordinated the efforts of independent fusion and Republican organizations to secure his election. From 1934 through 1945, when La Guardia refused to run for a fourth term, Burlingham was one of his most trusted advisors. An independent Democrat, Burlingham none-theless headed the 1937 election committee of Republican Thomas E. Dewey for Manhattan district attorney and supported his efforts to end corruption in city government.

Throughout his career Burlingham participated in liberal causes. During the 1920's he worked vigorously against the expulsion of five Socialists by the New York State Assembly and for a retrial for Nicola Sacco and Bartolomeo Vanzetti. During the 1930's he served as president of the Welfare Council of New York City, chairman of the executive committee of the Civil Service Reform Association, and national chairman of the Non-Partisan Committee for Ratification of the Federal Child Labor Amendment. In 1942 Burlingham ceased practicing law but retained the post of general counsel for his firm until his death in New York City. In 1953 he was awarded a special medal by the Bar Association of the City of New York for long and devoted service to his profession.

[There is no biography of Burlingham. The best introduction to his personality and activities is a memorial by Felix Frankfurter, reprinted in his *Of Law and Life and Other Things That Matter* (1965). The Columbia University Oral History Collection contains a valuable forty-five-page interview with Burlingham (1949); George W. Martin, *Causes and Conflicts: The Centennial History of the Association of the Bar of the City of New York, 1870–1970* (1970), provides useful information on Burlingham's tenure as president. *Felix Frankfurter Reminisces* (1960) includes an account of a conversation with Burlingham that provides insight into his personality. Charles Garrett, *The La Guardia Years* (1961); and Herbert Mitgang, *The Man Who Rode the Tiger: The Life and Times of Judge Samuel Seabury* (1963), include significant material. Burlingham's letters and articles in the *New York Times* are also useful. His correspondence was not preserved. There is an obituary in the *New York Times,* June 8, 1959.]

JEROLD SIMMONS

BURNS, BOB (Aug. 2, 1890–Feb. 2, 1956), radio and film star, was born Robin Burn in Greenwood, Ark., the son of William Robert Burn, a civil engineer, and Emma Needham. From a well-to-do family, Burns attended public school in Van Buren, Ark., and later the University of Arkansas, where he studied civil engineering.

Burns's interest in music began at an early age when he learned to play the mandolin, guitar, violin, cornet, and piano. At the age of fifteen he began playing the mandolin with the Van Buren City Queen Silver Cornet Band and at the same age created the instrument that was to bring him his first fame. While practicing with the band in a local plumbing shop, he put together two pieces of gas pipe and a whiskey funnel, blew, and thus was born the bazooka, an instrument resembling the trombone. The name "bazooka," which he copyrighted in 1920, was later adopted as the name for a weapon designed by the United States Army during World War II that looked like his musical instrument.

In 1907 Burns appeared with the Black Cat Minstrels playing the bazooka. It was with this group that he began his professional career in 1911, touring the South teamed with his brother, Farrar Burn, in a blackface number. Thereafter, with only a few breaks, Burns continued in the entertainment field. He toured in small-time vaudeville for ten years, ran his own carnival show, and was at times an orchestra leader. But he also worked as a river ferry pilot, hay and magazine salesman, peanut farmer, and advertising salesman. In 1913 he appeared as a $3 extra in a mob scene for the old Biograph motion picture studio in New York City.

Burns's career was interrupted by World War I, in which he served as a sergeant in the United States Marines. In 1919 he was awarded a gold medal as an expert rifleman. He also led the Marine Corps jazz band in Europe.

On Sept. 22, 1921, Burns married Elizabeth Fisher in Atlantic City, N. J. They had one son. From 1922 to 1930 Burns continued his career as an entertainer with Claude West in the team Burns and West.

In 1930 Burns moved to Hollywood, Calif., to make motion pictures. During 1930 he worked with John Swor, playing a blackface team called Black and Blue in the Fox picture *Up the River.* He appeared in several of Will Rogers' pictures, including *Young as You Feel.* In 1935 he appeared in *The Singing Vagabond.* The following year he played in *The Big Broadcast of 1937* and in *Rhythm on the Range,* with Bing Crosby and Martha Raye.

In 1936 Burns's first wife died. On May 31, 1937, he married Harriet Madelia Foster. They had three children.

The team of Burns and Raye proved such a comedy hit that they were teamed again in 1937 in *Waikiki Wedding.* During the same year he played in *Wells Fargo* and *Mountain Music.* In 1938 he played the title role in *Arkansas Traveler*

and also acted in *Tropic Holiday* and *Radio City Revels.* He subsequently appeared in *Our Leading Citizen* (1939), *I'm From Missouri* (1939), *Alias the Deacon* (1940), and *Comin' Round the Mountain* (1940). In 1942 he played the title role in *Hill Billy Deacon,* and three years later made *Belle of the Yukon.*

Running simultaneously with Burns's film career was an active career in radio. Beginning with comedy routines on local West Coast radio shows, in 1932 he made a name for himself as Soda Pop on the "Circus Radio Show." In 1935 Burns auditioned in New York City for "The Paul Whiteman Hour." An immediate success, Burns won a series of guest appearances on the "Rudy Vallee Music Hall." He began on the Vallee show with political talks in the style of Will Rogers. But when Rogers died and was elevated to a legend, Burns was forced to change his routine. He returned to his Arkansas origins and developed a hillbilly style that he was to continue on his own radio show.

In December 1935 Burns was signed for a twenty-six-week engagement to work with Bing Crosby on "The Kraft Music Hall"; Burns stayed for six years. In 1941 Burns began his own show, "The Arkansas Traveler," on which he popularized the character of the seedy hillbilly who wandered the countryside doing good deeds. Other characters he created for the show were Granpa Snazzy, Uncle Fud, and Aunt Doody. The program ran until 1947. From 1936 to 1940 Burns also wrote a syndicated column for Esquire Features entitled "Well, I'll Tell You."

In 1947 Burns retired from the entertainment business in order to devote his time to his ranch in Canoga Park, Calif. He made wise investments and was ranked among the richest people in Hollywood. He died in Encino, Calif.

[There is no biography of Burns. His obituary is in the *New York Times,* Feb. 3, 1956. On Burns's radio career, see John Dunning, *Tune in Yesterday: The Ultimate Encyclopedia of Old-Time Radio* (1976); and *Newsweek,* Dec. 14, 1935, and Sept 29, 1941. On Burns's film career, see *New York Times Film Reviews* (1973); Ray Stuart, *Immortals of the Screen* (1965); and *Time,* Oct. 31, 1938. Additional information on Burns is in the *National Cyclopaedia of American Biography,* XLII (1958).]

SUE HABEL

BYOIR, CARL ROBERT (June 24, 1888–Feb. 3, 1957), public relations counsel, was born in Des Moines, Iowa, the son of Benjamin

Byoir and Minna Gunyan. The elder Byoir had emigrated from Poland to the United States in 1875; he was an affectionate father but a poor provider whose business ventures—including running a restaurant and a clothing store—met with only marginal success. Carl Byoir therefore had to work from the age of ten. At fourteen, while still in high school, he became a reporter for the *Iowa State Register* and at seventeen was city editor of the *Waterloo* (Iowa) *Times-Tribune*. Entering the University of Iowa in 1906, Byoir negotiated printing contracts to publish thirty-seven college yearbooks, including Iowa's *Hawkeye*. He graduated in 1910 with all college expenses paid and savings of $6,500.

Byoir received the LL.B. from Columbia Law School in 1912 and was admitted to the bar but never practiced. While a senior at Columbia, he purchased the American rights to the kindergarten training methods of Maria Montessori, the Italian educator; he introduced the system to America and reportedly earned a profit of $63,000 from the franchise. In 1913, in association with Morgan Shepard, Byoir became publisher of *John Martin's Book for Children*, a read-aloud magazine for preschool children. After disposing of his interest in this venture, Byoir began to work for William Randolph Hearst in 1914, and in 1916 was promoted to circulation manager of *Cosmopolitan*.

When the United States entered World War I, Byoir was called to Washington by George Creel, chairman of the Committee on Public Information (CPI), to become an associate chairman of the group, which conducted the first massive wartime propaganda effort by the United States. Byoir was, in effect, the number-two man of the CPI; he developed new skills and insights into the techniques of influencing public opinion and acquired a wide and influential acquaintanceship. After the armistice, Byoir was sent by President Wilson to the peace conference at Versailles to help publicize American peace aims. For a short period after the war he was an adviser to President Thomas Masaryk of Czechoslovakia.

Byoir's immediate postwar activities included interests in an import-export business, several patent-medicine companies (whose advertising came under sharp criticism), and a company that made automobile parts. He married Grace Lancaster on Dec. 7, 1921; they adopted two nieces of Grace Byoir. Moving to Cuba in 1929 for health reasons, Byoir began a new career by leasing two English-language newspapers that he used to stimulate American trade and tourism. This led to a contract with the government to promote Cuba as a vacationland. Although Byoir denied any political orientation, he was a de facto supporter of the dictatorship of President Gerardo Machado. Carl Byoir and Associates was organized in 1930 to serve this account.

Byoir returned to New York in 1932 and took over the promotion and management of several Florida hotel properties. He rapidly accumulated a diversified list of corporate and trade association clients. Also in 1932, Byoir persuaded President Hoover that propaganda techniques could create jobs at no cost to the government by mobilizing public opinion in support of expanded production and the free enterprise system. He called the effort a "War Against Depression" and solicited the support of such powerful groups as the Association of National Advertisers, the American Federation of Labor, and the American Legion. This campaign, which he directed as a public service, was his only major failure; the economic problems of the Depression could not be solved by a public relations campaign. Byoir achieved national prominence as the creator and general director of the "Birthday Balls" celebrating the birthday of President Franklin D. Roosevelt. Organized in thousands of American communities, these fetes in 1934, 1935, 1936, and 1937 raised some $4 million to benefit research on infantile paralysis under the aegis of the Warm Springs Foundation.

Controversy swirled around Byoir in 1940 when a junior partner of the Byoir firm was accused of having handled (in 1934 and 1935) publicity in the United States for the German Tourist Information Office. Representative Wright Patman of Texas charged that Carl Byoir was a Nazi agent. Byoir demanded and got an investigation; he was cleared by the House Un-American Activities Committee and the Department of Justice, but the episode caused criticism of Byoir and of public relations practitioners in general. At the time, Byoir represented the Great Atlantic and Pacific Tea Company (A&P), which had successfully defeated anti-chain store legislation sponsored by Patman. A considerable segment of opinion agreed with a protest Byoir addressed to President Franklin D. Roosevelt regarding Patman's allegations: "Congressman Patman's attack," he wrote, "is born of malice."

In 1942 the A&P and Byoir were indicted on criminal charges of violating the Sherman Antitrust Act, and in 1946 Byoir was convicted and fined $5,000. Three years later a civil action was brought by the Justice Department seeking the dismemberment of A&P. Byoir presented the A&P position in large-space advertisements in some 2,000 newspapers. The suit was settled in 1954 by a consent judgment that left the food chain substantially intact.

The last legal clash between major economic powers in which Byoir was a figure occurred in 1953. The Pennsylvania Motor Truck Association brought a $250 million antitrust suit against the Eastern Railroad Presidents Conference and Carl Byoir and Associates. The railroads filed a counterclaim, each complainant charging the other with conspiring to injure its business. Beyond giving a pretrial deposition in behalf of the railroads, Byoir had only a limited connection with this case, which was ultimately decided by the Supreme Court in favor of the railroads.

Over the years Byoir counseled clients whose products ranged from ball-point pens to photographic supplies and greeting cards and influenced an estimated one hundred industries. "We will be judged by public opinion," he told his associates, "by the job we do." The judgment was that he was an imaginative, resourceful, tough-minded advocate and strategist for the businesses he served. He died in New York City.

The firm Byoir founded continued to flourish and in 1977 ranked third in size in the public-relations field. In March 1978, Carl Byoir and Associates merged with the advertising firm of Foote, Cone and Belding Communications, but continued to operate independently and retained its own name.

[There is no biography of Byoir. The Byoir Papers are located at Carl Byoir and Associates. See Robert James Bennett, "Carl Byoir: Public Relations Pioneer" (master's thesis, University of Wisconsin, 1968); George Creel, *How We Advertised America* (1920); James R. Mock and Cedric Larson, *Words That Won the War: The Story of the Committee on Public Information 1917–1919* (1939); Spencer Klaw, "Carl Byoir: Opinion Engineering in the Big Time," *Reporter*, June 10, 1952; Andrew Hacker, "Pressure Politics in Pennsylvania: The Truckers Versus the Railroads," in *The Uses of Power: Seven Cases in American Politics* (1962), edited by Alan F. Westin; Robert Bendiner, "The 'Engineering of Consent'—A Case Study," *Reporter*, Aug. 11, 1955; and obituary notices in the *New York Herald Tribune* and *New York Times*, both Feb. 4, 1957.]

GERALD CARSON

BYRD, RICHARD EVELYN (Oct. 25, 1888–Mar. 11, 1957), aviator and explorer, was born in Winchester, Va., the son of Eleanor Bolling Flood and Richard Evelyn Byrd. Harry Byrd, senator from Virginia, was his brother. His father was a lawyer who, with his wife's brother, established the Byrd political dynasty in Virginia. Byrd attended the Shenandoah Valley Military Academy, Virginia Military Institute (1904–1907), the University of Virginia (1907–1908), and the United States Naval Academy. While a midshipman he excelled in gymnastics, wrestling, and football.

Upon graduation (1912), Byrd was commissioned an ensign and was assigned to the battleship fleet. While on board the U.S.S. *Washington* he was decorated for twice saving men who were drowning. On Jan. 20, 1915, he married a childhood sweetheart, Marie D. Ames; they had four children.

After being noticed by Secretary of the Navy Josephus Daniels while teaching a religion class to sailors on the *Washington*, Byrd accepted Daniels' invitation to serve as his aide on the U.S.S. *Dolphin*, based in the Washington, D.C., navy yard. In March 1916, however, he was medically retired; an ankle, broken while at the Naval Academy, had never healed properly. He was recalled to active duty in May 1916 with the proviso that he not serve at sea. Ordered to Rhode Island, he organized that state's naval militia. When the United States entered World War I, Byrd was transferred to Washington, where he organized the Navy Department Commission on Training Camps and served as its secretary.

In 1917 Byrd convinced a medical board to allow him to enter flight training at the naval air station in Pensacola, Fla. He was designated naval aviator no. 608 in April 1918 and was ordered to Washington four months later to develop his proposal to fly the new NC-1 flying boat to France via the Azores, crossing the Atlantic for the first time. However, because of war pressures, he was instead made commander of the United States Naval Air Forces in Canada and ordered to establish naval air stations at Halifax and North Sidney, N.S., to patrol coastal waters for enemy submarines.

After the Armistice (November 1918), Byrd returned to Washington in order to develop the navigational methods and equipment for the attempted transatlantic flight of three NC flying boats. Navy regulations prevented him from accompanying the first successful transatlantic flight, but he flew as far as Newfoundland with the planes. Upon his return to Washington, he became an assistant to the director of naval aviation and a navy department liaison officer to Congress. He frequently argued the navy's case in the air power battle with the army, and was successful in developing support for legislation that established the Bureau of Aeronautics.

In August 1921 Byrd was sent to England to assist in navigating the British-built dirigible ZR-2 to the United States. Owing to a late train, he missed the trial flight during which the dirigible exploded and crashed, killing most of the men on board. He attended the Royal Air Force School of Aerial Navigation before returning to the United States in July 1922. On aviation duty with the Bureau of Navigation, he established naval reserve stations at Squantum, Mass., Rockaway Beach, Long Island, N.Y., and Chicago, Ill.

Byrd's initial involvement in polar work occurred in 1923, when he was assigned to assist in the development of a plan to fly the dirigible *Shenandoah* from Alaska over the North Pole to Spitzbergen. President Coolidge cancelled the flight in 1924, but the following spring Byrd organized and commanded the naval flying unit that accompanied the 1925 polar expedition of Donald B. MacMillan to Etah, Greenland. With three seaplanes Byrd's unit explored 30,000 square miles of northern Greenland and Ellesmere Island by air.

Later in 1925 Byrd was released from active duty as a lieutenant commander to seek private financial backing and to plan a flight to the North Pole. On May 9, 1926, he and Chief Machinist's Mate Floyd Bennett flew from Kings Bay, Spitzbergen, to the North Pole in the Fokker trimotor *Josephine Ford*, named after the daughter of Edsel Ford, a primary backer. For this successful flight Byrd and Bennett were awarded the Medal of Honor and Byrd also received the Distinguished Service Medal.

In June 1927 Byrd, Bert Acosta, Bernt Balchen, and George Noville flew the Fokker trimotor *America* from New York to France; demonstrating the feasibility of commercial transatlantic aviation, the flight carried a payload of 800 pounds of mail. But the venture was ill-starred. While flight testing the airplane, they crash-landed with Anthony Fokker as pilot. Byrd suffered a broken arm and Bennett, who was to pilot the *America* to France, was so seriously injured that he could not make the attempt. There was adverse weather throughout the transatlantic

flight, and when the plane arrived over Paris the weather prevented a landing. It flew back to the French coast, and Balchen landed the plane without injury in the surf at Ver-sur-Mer after a 39-hour-56-minute flight of about 4,200 miles.

Later that year Byrd began to organize an expedition to Antarctica. He planned to build a base on the coast, fly to the South Pole, and conduct scientific exploration by land and air. With the financial support of several wealthy businessmen, the American Geographical Society and the National Geographic Society, and hundreds of other contributors, he sailed south with forty-one men on two ships, with four airplanes, ninety-four dogs, materials for a small village, scientific equipment, and enough food and medical supplies for two years.

In December 1928 the expedition landed in the Bay of Whales, a huge natural harbor in the Ross Ice Shelf; they built a base, Little America, and after successfully passing the winter, Byrd, Balchen, Ashley McKinly, and Harold June flew to the South Pole (Nov. 28–29, 1929) and successfully returned to Little America. For this achievement Congress promoted Byrd to the rank of rear admiral and the navy awarded him the Navy Cross for extraordinary heroism.

The expedition discovered that part of west Antarctica now known as Marie Byrd Land, the Rockefeller and Ford mountain ranges, and the 10,000-foot La Gorce Mountain. Some 150,000 square miles of territory was photographed. In June 1930 the expedition returned to New York to a hero's welcome. Byrd undertook an extensive lecture tour and published *Little America* to pay off the expedition's debts.

In October 1933 Byrd left on his second expedition to Antarctica. He arrived at Little America in January 1934 with fifty-six men who would winter over. His goals were additional geographic exploration and the study of inland meteorological conditions in winter. He built a small hut in the ice more than 100 miles south of Little America and attempted to stock it with food and supplies for three men for the winter. When sufficient supplies were not stockpiled before the onset of winter, he decided to remain at "Bolling Advance Base" alone to conduct the meteorological observations.

During the winter Byrd almost died from carbon monoxide poisoning leaking from the stovepipe. but he was rescued on Aug. 11, 1934, by Dr. Thomas C. Poulter, his second-in-command, and three other members of a meteorite observation team, who set out when Byrd's messages became erratic and confused after five months in isolation. His book *Alone* (1938) is a record of his experience. Byrd returned to the United States in May 1935, again to a hero's welcome. Even President Franklin D. Roosevelt met his ship. That year he published *Discovery*, a record of the expedition.

The ordeal at Advance Base had a lasting effect on Byrd. In his diary he had written: ". . . if I survive this ordeal I shall devote what is left of my life largely to trying to help further the friendship of my country with other nations of the world." His friends organized Byrd Associates to work with him for international peace, and he became honorary chairman of the No-Foreign-War Crusade. In 1938 he made a radio broadcast to Europe calling for a moratorium on war. He also sought support for a third Antarctic expedition, which was forthcoming from President Roosevelt in 1939. The president recalled Byrd to active duty and appointed him commanding officer of the United States Antarctic Service (USAS), the first government-sponsored expedition to Antarctica since that led by Charles Wilkes in 1838–1842. Byrd was to establish a permanent United States presence in the Antarctic.

The expedition wintered at Little America and at Stonington Island, off the Antarctic Peninsula. Five new mountain ranges and five islands were discovered, and a comprehensive scientific program was conducted. About 700 miles of coastline were mapped, for the first time, using ships and planes in a technique that became a standard exploration practice.

When Byrd returned to the United States in 1941, he made many speeches calling for support of the president in the face of the threat of war. (With the onset of war the USAS was withdrawn from Antarctica and plans for colonization put aside.) During World War II he performed several secret missions in the Pacific and European theaters—exploring a new air route from the Panama Canal to Australia and studying the development of air support for ground troops in Europe. He was one of the first naval officers to land in Japan after the war, participating in the surrender ceremonies aboard the U.S.S. *Missouri* and investigating the effects of the atomic bombs dropped on Hiroshima and Nagasaki.

He served as a technical adviser on Arctic and Antarctic affairs for the chief of naval operations before assuming command in 1946 of the navy's operation Highjump, with 4,000 men, the largest

expedition ever to go to Antarctica. The massive expedition explored more than 1.5 million square miles of Antarctica, nearly half never before seen. Byrd continued his efforts to develop interest in Antarctica. He emphasized Antarctica's natural resources, its strategic location, and its importance in the development of southern hemisphere weather. He also prepared a study on Greenland that led to the establishment of Thule Air Base and defensive military activities. In 1949 he became founding chairman of the Iron Curtain Refugee Campaign of the International Rescue Committee, leading the national effort to assist refugees from Eastern Europe.

During the development of the plans for the International Geophysical Year in the 1950's, Byrd was influential in the American portion of an international Antarctic research program that included 500 scientific workers from thirteen countries at sixty locations in Antarctica. In 1955 President Dwight D. Eisenhower appointed him to his last command, that of officer in charge of United States Antarctic programs. He was responsible for the political, scientific, legislative, and operational aspects of the program, and he visited Antarctica for the fifth time from December 1955 to February 1956. Byrd received the Department of Defense Medal of Freedom in February 1957 in recognition of his work in the Antarctic program and for his humanitarian activities. He died in Boston, Mass.

The success of the Byrd and Bennett 1926 North Pole flight was initially doubted in Europe for nationalistic reasons; other nations were poised to send similar expeditions at the same time. Later doubts centered on the elapsed time reported by the newspapers. In his autobiographical *Come North With Me* (1958), Bernt Balchen questioned the figures claimed by Byrd and Bennett. (Balchen later claimed that Bennett confessed that they had not reached the North Pole before turning south to return to Spitzbergen.) In 1960 G. H. Liljequist, a polar meteorologist from the Norwegian-British-Swedish Antarctic Expedition (1949–1952), examined the meteorological records of May 1926 and concluded that the existence of the tail winds needed by Byrd to complete the flight in the reported time was highly improbable. But Byrd's Arctic success has been defended by aviation historians—John Grierson, Al Muenchen, and Henry M. Dater—and navigation and engineer experts—J. N. Portney and E. J. Demas.

Byrd demonstrated that airplanes were safe for

travel, invented navigational instruments, used the airplane as a tool scientifically to explore Antarctica, and assured himself a place in naval aviation history by his liaison work with the Congress in 1919–1923. Almost singlehandedly, he made the Antarctic part of the American consciousness.

[Byrd's private and public papers are held by his family in Boston, and the papers of many members of his expeditions are at the Center for Polar and Scientific Archives, National Archives and Records Service, Washington, D.C. In addition to the books listed in the text, Byrd wrote *Skyward* (1928) and *Exploring With Byrd* (1937). He joined thirty other polar explorers to coauthor *Problems of Polar Research* (1928) for the American Geographical Society. Firsthand recollections of Byrd appear in some memoirs of the Oral History Collection of Columbia University.

See also Charles J. V. Murphy, *Struggle* (1928); Russell Owen, *South of the Sun* (1934); Edwin P. Holt, *The Last Explorer* (1968); and the obituary in the *New York Times*, Mar. 12, 1957.]

PETER J. ANDERSON

CABELL, JAMES BRANCH (Apr. 14, 1879–May 5, 1958), novelist, essayist, and historian, was born in Richmond, Va., the son of Robert Gamble Cabell II, a physician, and Anne Harris Branch. The family was prominent in Richmond. After private schooling, Cabell attended the College of William and Mary, where he began writing poetry. In 1895 he composed an essay that was later revised and published in the *International Magazine* as "The Comedies of William Congreve" (1901). He mastered Greek and French well enough to teach these subjects as an upperclassman, and in 1898 he graduated with high honors.

After working briefly for the *Richmond Times*, Cabell went to New York in 1899 as a reporter for the *Herald*. He returned to Richmond in 1901, spent a year as a reporter for the *Richmond News*, then turned to free-lance writing. Over the next decade his stories appeared in such magazines as *Ainslee's*, *Smart Set*, and *Harper's Monthly*. Neither fact nor fantasy, these stories were enlivened by hints of sexual license that disturbed at least one of his magazine illustrators; Howard Pyle refused in 1907 to illustrate any more of them for *Harper's*. In 1906 Cabell was employed by his granduncle to research the family genealogy, a project that took him to England, Ireland, and France, and led to two privately

issued books, *Branchiana* (1907) and *Branch of Abingdon* (1911).

Collected in *The Line of Love* (1905), *Gallantry* (1907), and *Chivalry* (1909), Cabell's stories had eighteenth- and nineteenth-century settings; but his early novels—*The Eagle's Shadow* (1904) and *The Cords of Vanity* (1909)—dealt with contemporary life. None of these books sold well, and in 1911 he went to West Virginia to work for a coal company owned by an uncle.

For more than a decade Cabell spent his summers at Rockbridge Alum Springs, Va., enjoying his bachelorhood. In the summer of 1912 he met Priscilla Bradley Shepherd, widow of a lumber merchant and mother of five young children. She appealed to the unusual combination of irony and romance in Cabell's temperament, and gave it focus. They were married on Nov. 8, 1913, and had one son. Cabell said years later, without exaggeration, that she "entered into virtually everything I wrote." He settled into his wife's house at Dumbarton Grange, Va., and won the affection of her children. He finished *The Soul of Melicent* (1913), revised as *Domnei: A Comedy of Woman Worship* (1920), which he had begun in 1911, and began to map out the fictive realm of Poictesme, a medieval French province whose history from 1234 to 1750 he created over the next sixteen years. In his next genealogical work, *The Majors and Their Marriages* (1915), Cabell traced the distinguished ancestry of his wife, who was becoming a Richmond socialite and public figure.

Cabell's careers as novelist and genealogist prospered; indeed, they became interdependent. He was historian for the Virginia Society of Colonial Wars from 1916 to 1929, for the Virginia chapter of the Sons of the American Revolution from 1917 to 1923, and editor for the Virginia War History Commission from 1919 to 1926. Influenced by Guy Holt, his editor at McBride and Company, Cabell set down in *Beyond Life* (1919) the philosophy that reshaped all his writing about Poictesme.

Cabell's most famous novel, *Jurgen* (1919), told of a pawnbroker given a year of youth and allowed to spend it dallying in heaven and hell with numerous women of history and imagination. The lesson Jurgen learned was the vanity of youthful illusions, and he returned gratefully to his nagging wife. Luckily for Cabell's career, *Jurgen* was deemed indecent. On Jan. 14, 1920, the New York Society for the Suppression of Vice obtained a warrant and entered McBride and Company, seizing all plates and copies of the novel. Through the society's efforts, *Jurgen* disappeared from the bookshops, although it was to be had under the counter for prices of up to $50 per copy. Out of the ensuing *succès de scandale* Cabell won such admirers as H. L. Mencken, Hugh Walpole, V. L. Parrington, and Carl Van Doren. Recognizing a fellow satirist, Sinclair Lewis dedicated *Main Street* to him. Ellen Glasgow declared that only Cabell "survived the blighting frustration of every artist in the South." Walpole placed him above D. H. Lawrence, James Joyce, Virginia Woolf, and E. M. Forster.

While Cabell's reputation was being made, he remained aloof. (He was annoyed by frequent mispronunciations of his name—"Tell the rabble my name is Cabell," he would say.) From 1921 to 1924 he helped edit *The Reviewer,* a Richmond "little magazine." The eighteen-volume Storisende edition of his works (1927–30), hailed as "the most ambitiously planned literary work which has ever come out of America," comprised novels, stories, essays, and poems, all revised and prefaced. As if to mark the end of this era, he signed his subsequent work "Branch Cabell."

From 1932 to 1935 Cabell was one of the editors of *American Spectator.* He wrote three trilogies: *The Nightmare Has Triplets* (1934–37), *Heirs and Assigns* (1938–42), and *It Happened in Florida* (1943–49). Besides his collected essays on Virginia history, *Here Let Me Lie* (1947), he wrote two autobiographical works, *Quiet, Please* (1952) and *As I Remember It* (1955). His wife died in 1949 after prolonged suffering, leaving Cabell embittered. With his son's encouragement, however, he decided to court Margaret Waller Freeman, whom he had known while on the staff of *The Reviewer*, although she was many years younger than he. They were married on June 15, 1950; they had no children. At the time of his death in Richmond, Cabell had written more than fifty books.

Although Cabell continues to have defenders, the waning of his popularity that began in the 1930's has continued. At his best he could be charmingly skeptical and sardonic. "Writing," as he once defined it, was "a strategic retreat before unconquerable oblivion." Edward Wagenknecht described Cabell's manner as a "mixture of bleak disillusion and amused persiflage, with good sense and good humor persistently breaking in." But as Edmund Wilson observed of the style, "the arch preciosity of the nineties was learned early and has never been purged." Cabell was championed in the 1920's for his amoral reveling in pure fantasy and for his rejection of official American pieties. Yet behind the fantasy and satire was a conventional moralist, a novelist of compromise and acquiescence.

[No biography exists, but useful biographical sketches appear in the following critical works: Joe Lee Davis, *James Branch Cabell* (1962); and Desmond Tarrant, *James Branch Cabell: The Dream and the Reality* (1967). A selection of letters during the era of *Jurgen*'s celebrity, *Between Friends: Letters of Joseph Branch Cabell and Others* (1962), documents the period from 1915 to 1922. His autobiographical works, *Quiet, Please* (1952) and *As I Remember It* (1955), offer numerous but fragmentary memories. The most complete guide to his works is Frances Joan Brewer, *James Branch Cabell: A Bibliography of His Writings, Biography and Criticism* (1957). Full description of manuscripts and letters is in an addendum, Matthew J. Bruccoli, *James Branch Cabell: A Bibliography,* Part II: *Notes on the Cabell Collections at the University of Virginia* (1957). Useful criticism appears in Louis D. Rubin, *No Place on Earth* (1959); Edward Wagenknecht, *Cavalcade of the American Novel* (1952); Arvin R. Wells, *Jesting Moses* (1962); and Edmund Wilson, *The Bit Between My Teeth* (1965).]

DEAN FLOWER

CAHILL, HOLGER (Jan. 13, 1887–July 8, 1960), art authority, author, and national director of the Federal Art Project, was born Sveinn Kristján Bjarnarson in Snaefellsnessysla, Iceland, the son of Björn Jonsson and Vigdis Bjarnadottir. Shortly after his birth, the family immigrated to Canada. They later moved to North Dakota, where his father hoped to acquire land. Failing to do so, he worked at various jobs, with little success.

Cahill's childhood memories were of dire poverty and domestic strife. When he was eleven, his father deserted the family and his mother became seriously ill. Unable to look after him, she placed him with an Icelandic family some fifty miles away. But his guardians treated him badly, and two years later Cahill ran away to Canada, where he found temporary work as a farmhand. Most of Cahill's adolescence was spent wandering from job to job, trying to snatch whatever schooling he could, and always searching for his mother. She, in her own desperate need to support herself and her young daughter, had also become a wanderer. Cahill finally found her working on a North Dakota farm but soon had to leave her to look for employment. He did not see her again until 1947, when she was ninety-three.

Cahill subsequently worked as a cowpuncher

in Nebraska, a crewman on a Great Lakes ore boat, a dishwasher in several hotels, an office clerk for the Northern Pacific Railroad in Saint Paul, Minn., and an insurance salesman. At one point he shipped out to the Orient as a coal passer on the *Empress of China,* and jumped ship in Shanghai. A cholera epidemic there made his visit a short one—he returned on another ship bound for Vancouver—yet the city made a profound impression on him. He learned Chinese and spent many years reading widely on all aspects of Chinese culture.

In his late teens Cahill decided to pursue a writing career. With his savings sewn into his underwear, he hopped a series of freight cars until he reached New York City. While working at night as a short order cook, he attended courses in journalism at New York University. Having changed his name, he became a reporter for several suburban newspapers, then for about three years was editor of two weeklies, the *Bronxville Review* and the *Scarsdale Inquirer.* Returning to Manhattan, he became a free-lance magazine writer. He took courses at Columbia University (1915–1919), where he was impressed by John Dewey's definition of art as a mode of interaction between man and his environment. At the New School for Social Research (1921–1924) he became friends with Horace Kallen and Thorstein Veblen, from whom he learned to value handicraft as art. In 1919 he married Katherine Gridley; they had one daughter. The marriage ended in divorce in 1927.

Through his friendship with a number of artists who were his neighbors in Greenwich Village (among them John Sloan, Max Weber, George Bellows, and Robert Henri), Cahill developed a strong interest in modern art and began writing on the subject. In 1922 he joined the Newark Museum to assist its director, John Cotton Dana, an advocate of making art more accessible to the general public. Dana's faith in art as a means of popular communication, which reflected Dewey's theories on the subject, deeply influenced Cahill. At the Newark Museum, Cahill became largely responsible for its collection of modern art and also organized two significant exhibitions that dealt with the relatively new field of American folk art, "American Primitives" (1930) and "American Folk Sculpture" (1931).

By 1932, when Cahill moved to the Museum of Modern Art in New York as exhibitions director, he had achieved national eminence as an authority on American art. He served briefly as acting director, while the museum's director, Alfred H. Barr, Jr., was on leave; but his main contribution was organizing several important exhibitions, for which he prepared book-length catalogs. One dealt with the folk art collection of Mrs. John D. Rockefeller, Jr., now permanently installed in Colonial Williamsburg. Cahill's catalog for the exhibit, *American Folk Art* (1932), was the first major publication in that field. Another pioneering exhibition, in 1933, "American Sources of Modern Art" (Maya, Aztec, Inca), became a model for others. The following year he directed New York's First Municipal Art Exhibition. With Barr he edited *Art in America in Modern Times* (1934) and *Art in America: A Complete Survey* (1935), both standard texts for many years. In 1936 he published *New Horizons in American Art.*

Cahill also published several books of a more literary nature. His first novel, *Profane Earth* (1927), was followed by monographs on two American artists, *George O. "Pop" Hart* (1928) and *Max Weber* (1930). *A Yankee Adventurer* (1930) was the biography of Frederick Townsend Ward who, in the nineteenth century, organized the first modern Chinese army. Cahill also contributed short stories to *Scribner's Magazine* and *American Mercury* (1931–1932), and wrote a play about Wall Street, "Mr. Thousand."

In 1935, when Cahill had begun to devote full time to writing fiction, he was appointed national director of the Federal Art Project, part of the New Deal program to provide jobs for some 40,000 artists, writers, musicians, and theater people. A skillful administrator, Cahill understood how best to maintain and develop the talents of project workers while bringing art closer to the general public. Under Cahill's imaginative leadership, the art project created a significant impact on the nation's culture. Under its aegis hundreds of public buildings were decorated with murals, sculpture, paintings, prints, and photographs; it established art centers in more than a hundred communities; and it produced the superb Index of American Design, an outgrowth of Cahill's early interest in crafts and the decorative arts. The project also nurtured a generation of native artists, including most of the major painters and sculptors of the 1940's and 1950's, who shifted the art center of the world from Paris to New York. On Aug. 17, 1938, Cahill married Dorothy Canning Miller, who became senior curator of painting and sculpture at the Museum of Modern Art. While still director of the project, Cahill organized an exhibition, "American Artists Today," for the 1939 New York World's Fair.

When the Art Project became a casualty of World War II in May 1943, Cahill was finally able to devote most of his attention to writing fiction. His second novel, *Look South to the Polar Star* (1947), had a Chinese background; *The Shadow of My Hand* (1956) was set in the Midwest of his youth. He died in Stockbridge, Mass., while working on another novel, *The Stone Dreamer.*

[See Jerre Mangione, *The Dream and the Deal* (1972); William F. McDonald, *Federal Relief Administration and the Arts* (1969); Richard D. McKinzie, *The New Deal for Artists* (1973); and Francis V. O'Connor, ed., *The New Deal Art Projects* (1972); and *Art for the Millions* (1973), which includes Cahill's essay "American Resources in the Arts." Cahill's reminiscences are in the Columbia University Oral History Collection, New York.]

JERRE MANGIONE

CANNON, IDA MAUD (June 29, 1877–July 8, 1960), social worker and medical reformer, was born in Milwaukee, one of four children of Colbert Hanchett Cannon, an official of the Great Northern Railroad, and Sarah Wilma Denio. Walter Bradford Cannon, the physiologist, was her brother. Her mother, a former schoolteacher, died when Cannon was four. After she graduated in 1896 from St. Paul High School, Cannon began her professional education at the nurses' training school of City and County Hospital (St. Paul). She completed the program in 1898, and then organized and directed a hospital at the state school for the feebleminded in Faribault, Minn. Temporarily blinded while fumigating a room with formaldehyde, she returned to St. Paul in 1900. She took courses in sociology at the University of Minnesota (1900–1901). While a student, she heard Jane Addams speak in Minneapolis about tenement and factory conditions; the experience deeply moved her and made social work her life interest.

Cannon's next position, as a visiting nurse in the river wards of St. Paul, sharpened her awareness of the relationship between social conditions and sickness. She realized that she had already encountered many of the poor patients in her district as hospital cases during her nurse's training. After organizing a summer camp for children, she moved to Cambridge, Mass., where she lived with the family of her brother Walter while attending the Boston (Simmons) School of Social Work (1906–1907). Cannon never married. Her brother's family became her family, and she remained in his house for most of her life.

Through her brother, Cannon met Richard Clarke Cabot, who in 1905 had initiated a program in hospital social service at the Massachusetts General Hospital. She began work in 1906 as a volunteer in this program, generally considered the first of its kind in the nation. The following year she took up full-time duties at the hospital and in 1908 became head of social service, a post she retained until her retirement in 1945.

As developed by Cabot and Cannon, hospital social service was intended to compensate for shortcomings in patient care that were inherent in the institutional setting and were exacerbated by an emerging scientific medicine preoccupied with the human body as a physiological organism. The social worker was to provide the physician—who might see fifty cases while in the outpatient clinic—with information about the "whole person" that could lead to a better understanding of the disease process. With its holistic perspective, social work attempted to counter the depersonalization of the patient that was a consequence of specialization and germ theory, both of which fostered a narrow and technical medical practice. The social worker also was charged with ensuring that the therapy prescribed by the physician was carried out.

For many years social service at the Massachusetts General resembled the tea party in Lewis Carroll's *Alice in Wonderland;* Cannon pointed to the futility, for example, of prescribing rest as a treatment for exhaustion when the patient would have to resume the support of a family immediately after leaving the examining room. A patient's housing, occupation, and background could cause or complicate illnesses and defeat even the best treatment. Work with tuberculosis, industrial diseases, and industrial accidents—heavily represented in the early twentieth-century clinics of a metropolitan hospital—broadened Cannon's interests from patient care to social reform. She saw her work both in reform and in humanizing medical practice as part of the Progressive movement.

Although she was increasingly aware of psychodynamic explanations of human behavior, Cannon's medical social work remained very much social diagnosis. She resisted the recommendations of her medical sponsors at the Massachusetts General, Cabot and James J. Putnam, who were receptive to psychiatric principles. Psychiatric social work, initiated at the hospital in 1918, remained outside of Cannon's department during her career. Confronting over whelming environmental factors—and influential in directing the attention of medicine toward them—medical social work grew away from casework, which embraced psychoanalysis and developed in the 1920's as the mainstream of social work. As casework evolved outside of the hospital setting, the social worker became a primary therapist. But in medical social work Cannon insisted that therapy be left to physicians.

Cannon was instrumental in shaping the field of medical social work. In her first decades at the Massachusetts General, the hospital's social service department was a regular stop on the itineraries of physicians and social workers seeking to initiate hospital social work programs elsewhere. The teaching function of the department was institutionalized in 1912 with the introduction of a specialized medical social work curriculum offered jointly with the Boston School of Social Work, where Cannon held an adjunct teaching appointment. She also advised on new programs in other cities and in 1914 conducted a survey of hospital social service organization and needs for New York City. Her *Social Work in Hospitals* (1913; revised edition, 1923) became the seminal text in the field.

Cannon was a leader in founding the American Association of Hospital Social Workers in 1918, of which she was vice-president (1918–1919) and president (1920–1921). As a delegate to the White House Conference on Child Health and Protection (1930–1931), she chaired a subcommittee on medical social service. She was elected president of the Massachusetts Conference of Social Work (1932) and vice-president of the National Conference of Social Work (1938–1939).

Cannon retired in 1945. After suffering a stroke in 1957, she lived in a nursing home in Watertown, Mass., where she died.

[The fullest account is an autobiographical work, *On the Social Frontier of Medicine: Pioneering in Medical Social Service* (1952). The *Annual Reports* of the Social Service Department, Massachusetts General Hospital, span her professional life; also useful are her articles "Changes in Hospital Care Through Social Service," *Trained Nurse and Hospital Review*, Apr. 1938; "Some Clinical Aspects of Social Medicine," *New England Journal of Medicine*, Jan. 1946; and "Medicine as a Social Instrument: Medical Social Service," *ibid.*, May 1951. The Ida Cannon papers, in the Social Service Department Archives, Massachusetts General Hospital, contain correspondence, investigative studies, a short typescript biography by Mary K. Taylor, and a bibliography.

For the context of Cannon's work, see Patricia N. Drew, "Social Work Practice: An Historical Comparison" (Ph.D. diss., Washington University, 1972); and Roy Lubove, *The Professional Altruist: The Emergence of Social Work as a Career, 1880–1930* (1965). Obituaries are in the *Boston Herald*, July 9. 1960; and *Massachusetts General Hospital News*, Dec. 1960. A retirement eulogy is in *Bulletin of the American Association of Medical Social Workers*, July 1946.]

MORRIS J. VOGEL

CAPEN, SAMUEL PAUL (Mar. 21, 1878–June 22, 1956), educator, was born in Somerville, Mass., the son of Elmer Hewitt Capen, president of Tufts College, and Mary Leavitt Edwards. After receiving the A.B. and A.M. simultaneously from Tufts in 1898, he earned another A.M. from Harvard in 1900 and, following a year of study at Leipzig, received the Ph.D. in modern languages at the University of Pennsylvania in 1902. He then became instructor in modern languages at Clark College, an experimental undergraduate school affiliated with Clark University, in Worcester, Mass. On Mar. 25, 1908, Capen married Grace Duncan Wright, daughter of the president of the college; they had one daughter.

Capen's growing interest in pedagogy and educational administration led him to serve as president of the Worcester Public Education Association from 1908 to 1911 and as a member of the Worcester School Board from 1908 to 1914. He began taking courses in education and psychology at Clark University in 1909 and was lecturer in educational administration there from 1911 to 1914 while continuing as a professor at Clark College.

In 1914 Capen was hired by the United States Bureau of Education as a specialist in higher education. He reported annually on trends and conditions in higher education, prepared statistics, and investigated college and university problems. His surveys of institutions established a standard method for such endeavors. With United States entry into World War I, Capen became executive secretary of the Committee on Education of the Council of National Defense, charged with the task of coordinating university resources for the war effort. He also served on the Advisory Board of the Committee on Education and Special Training of the War Department. In 1919 Capen became the first director of the American Council on Education. Through his efforts the new organization launched a study of the role of the national government in higher education, of standardization in higher education, of the status and future of the arts and sciences, and of the costs of a college education. He also founded the quarterly *Educational Record*, and edited it from 1920 to 1922.

Capen accepted the position of chancellor of the University of Buffalo in 1922. Until the twentieth century, Buffalo had been a collection of professional schools, adding a liberal arts college only in 1913, in response to the Flexner Report's insistence on at least one year of liberal arts work for candidates seeking admission to medical school. Capen set out to strengthen undergraduate education by more selective admissions and by creating a curriculum allowing more independent study. His first major move, however, was to strengthen professional education by replacing part-time faculty and developing the relationships between the medical school and local hospitals. He strongly supported the teaching of dentistry as a medical specialty, and within five years the principal items of his plan were embodied in regulations drafted by the Regents of the University of the State of New York for the registration of dental schools.

Capen's major innovation in undergraduate education at Buffalo was the tutorial system, in which a student could pursue independent advanced study under the direction of a faculty member. By 1931 all upperclassmen were taking a combination of courses and independent work. Economic conditions after World War II forced some retrenchment in the program. To supplement the tutorial system, Capen extended the advisory system for underclassmen, introduced the elective system, and established comprehensive examinations with outside examiners. He was a strong executive whose efforts at centralization were undercut only by his own tendency to pay too little attention to the financial aspects of university management. Renowed for his unrelenting defense of academic freedom, he insisted that such freedom required that academics distinguish their personal role from their institutional role in commenting upon politics, a stance that enabled him to achieve excellent school-community relations. He retired in 1950.

Capen, an austere man devoted to plain living and high thinking, felt that he would have been at home in the eighteenth century. Aloof but considerate, elegant and courtly in his behavior, he was able to lead without dictating and to mobilize faculty, administrators, students, and the community to contribute to achieving his vision of academic excellence. He died in Buffalo, N.Y.

[The best appreciation of Capen is Julian Park, "Samuel P. Capen, 1878–1956," *University of Buffalo Studies*, Oct. 1957. Also consult Capen's "Undated Biography to 1922" in the archives of SUNY at Buffalo; Douglas Clarke Crone, "An Historical Study of the Development of the Educational and Administrative Ideas of Samuel Paul Capen" (D.Ed. diss., SUNY at Buffalo, 1967); Julian Park, "The Elective System and the Tutorial Plan at the University of Buffalo, 1923–1953," *University of Buffalo Studies*, Aug. 1953; "The Skipper: A Steady Hand at the Helm," *University of Buffalo Alumni Bulletin*, Mar. 1945. Park's biography reproduces the portrait of Capen by Wyndham Lewis that hangs at the University of Buffalo.]

JOSEPH M. MCCARTHY

CARLSON, ANTON JULIUS (Jan. 29, 1875–Sept. 2, 1956), physiologist, was born in Svarteborg, Sweden, the son of Carl Jacobson, a farmer, and Hedvig Andersdotter. His father died when Carlson was very young, and by the age of seven the boy was herding sheep during the summer to augment the family income. In 1891 he immigrated to the United States, where his older brother was working as a carpenter.

Initially, Carlson too worked as a carpenter, but by 1893 he had saved enough money to enroll at the Augustana Academy and College at Rock Island, Ill. There he trained for the Lutheran ministry, receiving the B.A. in 1898 and the M.A. in 1899. He became a naturalized citizen in 1896. On Sept. 26, 1905, he married Esther Sjogren; they had three children.

In 1899 Carlson accepted a call to Anaconda, Mont., as substitute minister in the Swedish Lutheran church there. In addition to that work, he taught classes in science and philosophy. But he was beginning to have doubts about the dogmas of the Lutheran Church and to envision a different career. Using money loaned by a friend in Anaconda, he enrolled at Stanford University as a graduate student in physiology.

By 1902, Carlson had completed work for the Ph.D. at Stanford and had published the results of his research jointly with his dissertation supervisor, O. P. Jenkins. From studies of the rate of nerve impulse in mollusks, Carlson concluded that the conduction of the nerve impulse takes place in a liquid rather than in a solid medium. This was the first step toward the elucidation of the mechanism of propagation of the nerve impulse by Alan Hodgkin and Fielding Huxley half a century later.

In 1903 and 1904 Carlson was a research associate at the Carnegie Institution in Washington, D.C. He also worked in the marine biological laboratory at Woods Hole, Mass., where he made his first major discovery. Working with *Limulus*, the horseshoe crab, he was able to demonstrate that the cardiac nerves initiate and coordinate the heartbeat. This discovery established Carlson's reputation in the physiological community. In 1904 he joined the department of physiology at the University of Chicago, where he remained until his retirement in 1940.

In 1908 Carlson's interest shifted from invertebrate to mammalian physiology. He was greatly assisted in these endeavors by an association with Arno B. Luckhardt, who had the clinical training in medicine that Carlson lacked. Together they began work on the endocrine glands. Carlson's particular interest was in the comparative physiology of the thyroid and parathyroid, in which he made a number of significant discoveries. Specifically, he observed that fatal tetany following surgical procedures on the thyroid was caused by the removal, whether intended or not, of the adjacent parathyroid. This work led to the subsequent discovery by Luckhardt and others of means for preventing fatal tetany following parathyroidectomy. Carlson and his students also clarified the role of the thyroid in the metabolism of ammonia by the liver. He and his students did important work on the pancreas; one of them came close to the discovery of insulin. Carlson also had a continuing interest in hunger in relation to the physiology of the stomach. He published a classic series of papers on the subject in *American Journal of Physiology* during 1912 and 1913.

Carlson became associate professor at Chicago in 1909, professor in 1914, and chairman of the physiology department in 1916. He was especially involved in the teaching of medical students and developed courses for them involving extensive experimentation on dogs and other mammals.

On the entry of the United States into World War I in 1917, Carlson enlisted as a major in the Sanitary Corps. He served for two years as an inspector of the food served in army camps and as an associate of the Hoover Commission. He left the Army in 1919 with the rank of lieutenant colonel. Upon his return to Chicago, he and Luckhardt began an intensive study of the visceral sensory nervous system.

After the discovery of insulin, Carlson launched his last major research effort, which sought to clarify the association of an overdose of insulin with the appearance of a sensation of hunger (1924). Carlson subsequently did little laboratory work of his own, although he supervised the work of graduate students until he retired. He continued to write and to speak out on public affairs. He pressed for free lunches for poor children in the public schools of Chicago and worked on committees to improve child health and to fight infantile paralysis. He agitated for control of the use of lead arsenate as an insecticide by fruit growers. He was an early opponent of fascism and a supporter of the American Civil Liberties Union. Particularly impatient with antivivisectionists, he said on one occasion: "If man isn't worth more than a dog, then our efforts to improve man are in error." In his last years he was much preoccupied with the social responsibilities of scientists. Carlson died in Chicago.

[The principal source, Lester R. Dragstedt's notice, *Biographical Memoirs, National Academy of Sciences,* 35 (1961), includes a bibliography of Carlson's writings. See also the obituary notice by Victor Johnson, *Science,* Oct. 19, 1956; and H.M. Sinclair, *Nature,* Dec. 15, 1956; and the *New York Times,* Sept. 3, 1956.]

C. G. B. GARRETT

CARNEGIE, HATTIE (Mar. 14, 1886–Feb. 22, 1956), fashion designer and retailer, was born Henrietta Kanengeiser, in Vienna, Austria. Her family immigrated to the United States in 1897. After attending New York public schools for two years, she went to work at Macy's department store as a messenger. Her first professional brush with fashion came when a neighborhood shopowner noticed her flair for dressing and gave her a wardrobe in exchange for promoting her merchandise.

In 1909 she opened her own business, "Carnegie-Ladies' Hatter," on East 10th Street in New York City with a friend, Rose Roth. Although unrelated to Andrew Carnegie, she adopted the name, which for her was a symbol of

American success. Roth made dresses and Carnegie designed and sold hats. It is legendary that she could not sew.

In 1913 the business was incorporated with a capital of $100,000 and moved to 86th Street and Broadway, then a fashionable center. Even at this time her clothes were expensive, starting at $75. Although short and slight, Carnegie displayed unbounded energy and was the best advertisement for her shop, wearing her own designs at popular meeting places of New York society—the smartest restaurants, the theater, and the opera. At the end of World War I, she bought out her partner and changed the emphasis of the business from the design and sale of solely American creations to the restyling and sale of Paris originals. In 1923 she opened the shop at 42 East 49th Street that was to become a haven for well-dressed matrons and their debutante daughters and the foundation of her fashion empire.

From her first trip to Europe in 1919 to the beginning of World War II, Carnegie made 142 buying trips to the European fashion market, returning with more than 100 original models each time. Her buying sprees soon made her one of the fabulous characters of the Paris market. She bought Paris originals without thought to cost, often not knowing where she would get the money to pay for them.

Carnegie was known for her ability to spot new talent and on a buying trip to Paris in the 1920's she is said to have discovered the designer Madeleine Vionnet, whom she launched on a career that eventually placed her at the top of Parisian haute couture. In her New York business Carnegie trained many young designers who were to become greats of the American fashion world, including Bruno, Jean Louis, Claire McCardell, and Norman Norell.

Carnegie had enormous influence on fashionably dressed affluent Americans. The "little Carnegie suit" became a status symbol of the 1930's and 1940's, and there is evidence that "the little black dress" beloved by women all over America was first adapted for them by Carnegie. In 1939 she won the Nieman-Marcus Award and, in 1948, the American Fashion Critics' Award for "consistent contribution to American elegance."

During World War II and into the 1950's her salon continued to prosper. Besides the made-to-order business, the corporation operated a wholesale dress business, a millinery business, and nationally distributed wholesale lines of jewelry, cosmetics, and perfume. She also operated retail shops in Southampton, N.Y., and Palm Beach, Fla.

Carnegie's second marriage, to Ferdinand Fleischman, ended in divorce in 1924. On Aug. 28, 1928, she married John Zanft, a motion picture executive. She died in New York City.

[On Carnegie and her career, see "Luxury, Inc.," *New Yorker*, Mar. 31, 1934; the obituary notice, *New York Times*, Feb. 23, 1956; and Josephine E. Watkins, *Fairchild's Who's Who in Fashion* (1975).]

ARNOLD SCAASI

CARNEGIE, MARY CROWNINSHIELD ENDICOTT CHAMBERLAIN (Mar. 15, 1864–May 17, 1957), hostess, was born in Salem, Mass., the daughter of William Crowninshield Endicott, a lawyer, and Ellen Peabody. She was a descendant of John Endecott, first governor of the Massachusetts Bay Colony. Her education, in a private school, was sketchy. In the spring of 1882 she accompanied her parents to Europe. In England they greatly enjoyed the social life of London. In September 1883 they returned to the United States, and in February 1885 her father became secretary of war in Grover Cleveland's cabinet. In November 1887, while living in Washington, she met at the British legation Joseph Chamberlain, who had come to attend a fisheries conference. Chamberlain was fifty-one and a widower for thirteen years, having lost two wives in childbirth. On Feb. 11, 1888, he proposed marriage and was accepted. The Endicotts were not enchanted but accepted the engagement on condition that it be kept secret until after the presidential election, lest the Irish vote against Cleveland for tolerating a cabinet member whose daughter would marry an Englishman.

The wedding took place in Washington on Nov. 15, 1888. In most Anglo-American marriages of the period, the man had the position and the wife the money; with the Chamberlains the roles were reversed. After a honeymoon in France and Italy, the Chamberlains lived in Birmingham and in London. Mary Chamberlain, who never had a child of her own, thus acquired two stepchildren: including twenty-five-year-old Austen, a future foreign secretary, and nineteen-year-old Neville, who would become prime minister. Although she spent the next sixty-nine years in England, she never lost touch with Massachusetts, for the Endicotts and Chamberlains visited each other frequently.

For the next eighteen years, Mrs. Chamberlain was absorbed in her husband's political career in the House of Commons and as colonial secretary. She accompanied him everywhere, listening rather than talking. Queen Victoria liked her. It was in no small part due to her that her husband progressed in the queen's view from "that dangerous radical" to her "favorite minister."

In July 1906 Joseph Chamberlain had a paralytic stroke that effectively ended his political career. After his death, eight years later, Mary Chamberlain settled in London. On Aug. 3, 1916, she married the Reverend William Hartley Carnegie, a widower with five daughters, who was rector of St. Margaret's Westminster, a canon of the abbey, and chaplain to the speaker of the House of Commons. She thus spent the next two decades in the higher circles of the Church of England. She made the canon's house in Westminster a hospitable center of Anglo-American relations. The brocade curtains that her grandfather had bought in Paris in 1844 for his Salem drawing room fitted the windows in Dean's Yard without alteration.

Canon Carnegie died in 1936 and was buried in the nave of Westminster Abbey. His widow bought a house at 41 Lennox Gardens and entered the third stage of her London life. Her stepson, Neville Chamberlain, became prime minister in 1937. The war that he had been unable to avert brought less change to Mary Carnegie's way of life than to most others. She had not the slightest intention of seeking refuge in the country or of returning to America: in London she had lived for fifty years, and in London she would stay. With food and servants in short supply, she kept a remarkable approximation of the style that she had created as a bride. Even during the blitz, she entertained and encouraged by welcoming at her table the numerous American and British relatives whose military and naval duties had brought them to London.

Beginning in 1947, Mrs. Carnegie returned to Boston each summer to visit her sister-in-law. Although her eyesight began to fail, her spirits never did. On her ninety-third birthday she went to the theater in London. When it was suggested that she might like to go home at the end of the play, she replied, "I should hate that! I want to be taken to a large, loud, gay restaurant for supper!" Until a fortnight before her death in London she gave dinner parties as usual.

[Diana Whitehill Laing, *Mistress of Herself* (1965), is a full biography. For details on the Salem family background, see William Crowninshield Endicott and Walter Muir Whitehill, *Captain Joseph Peabody, East India Merchant of Salem* (1962); and William Crowninshield Endicott, *A Memoir of Samuel Endicott* (1924).]

WALTER MUIR WHITEHILL

CARR, CHARLOTTE ELIZABETH (May 3, 1890–July 12, 1956), social worker, was born in Dayton, Ohio, the daughter of Joseph Henry Carr, a prosperous businessman, and Edith Carver. Her career in social work began upon graduation with the B.A. from Vassar in 1915, when she became a matron in a Columbus, Ohio, orphan asylum. She subsequently worked with delinquent and runaway children with the New York State Charities Aid Association and New York Probation and Protective Association and as a New York City policewoman, patrolling the streets from 6 P.M. to 6 A.M. During the next several years Carr held personnel positions with industrial enterprises, including assistant employment manager of the American Lithograph Company in New York City, employment manager of the Knox Hat Company (1921–1923) in Brooklyn, N.Y., and personnel manager of the Stark Mills (1923) in New Hampshire.

In 1923 Carr returned to the field of social work, serving under Frances Perkins as assistant director of the Bureau of Women in Industry of the New York State Department of Labor. In 1925 she started a similar bureau for Pennsylvania and was director until 1929, when she was dropped from the state payroll for refusing to pay political assessments. She returned under Governor Gifford Pinchot in 1931 as deputy secretary of labor and industry, subsequently serving as secretary from 1933 to 1934. In 1934, during the depths of the Great Depression, Governor Herbert Lehman of New York drafted her as an adviser on the problem of relief. Shortly thereafter, Mayor Fiorello La Guardia made her executive director of the Emergency Relief Bureau in New York City (1935–37), where she had under her supervision as many as 18,000 employees, a monthly budget of $9 million, and the welfare assistance of nearly one million people.

In 1937 Carr succeeded Jane Addams as head of Chicago's Hull House, serving until December 1942, when she resigned due to friction arising from her active support of President Franklin Delano Roosevelt's election campaign. From 1943 to 1945 she served as assistant to the vice-chairman of the War Manpower Commission. In 1945 she became the first director of the newly formed Citizens' Committee on Children of New York City, serving until her retirement in 1953. Under her leadership, public housing projects added health stations, kindergartens, and day-care centers. Advances and improvements were also made in police aid to juveniles and school truancy programs. A foster-home program in the welfare department was established.

Carr never married. She was a big, heavy woman who described herself as a "fat Irish-woman." She was genial, yet commanded attention and respect. A born storyteller, she could dominate a social conversation with witty anec-dotes and reminiscences. She was both politic and canny, intelligent and innovative. Above all, she was a skillful administrator and a superb mobiliz-er of people. Her lifelong struggle for the better-ment of life and work for the poorest third of the population was characterized by boundless en-ergy, vigorous action, the ability to work under pressure, practical idealism, and the talent to confer and negotiate with industrialists and busi-nessmen as well as with labor leaders and workers. Her prized nickname "Scarlet" was based on her tough, aggressive qualities. Early in her industrial relations work in Pennsylvania, she singlehan-dedly mediated for four hours with striking miners when her car was stopped at a roadblock, thus opening the way for a quick and peaceful settlement.

At Hull House, Carr refused blindly to pattern her leadership and programs on those of Jane Addams. When she arrived to take up her duties, she declined to be photographed with a group of neighborhood children called in for the occasion. "Those children never laid eyes on me before," she stated bluntly. "Why should they look up at me and smile?" At Hull House Carr formu-lated adult education programs and community centers, and conducted research on health ser-vices. She worked tirelessly to eliminate racial and cultural barriers at Hull House and in the neighborhood, and invited the distinguished black social worker Faith Jones into the Hull House family. In her view the slum problems of Hull House did not inherently make the neighborhood a problem community. Rather, she believed that the Hull House problems, like all similar social and economic problems, were community problems.

During the Great Depression, Carr ran New York's relief program efficiently and intelligently rather than—as she put it—"humanely." Under her leadership thousands of relief recipients found jobs in the federal WPA, thus moving off the relief rolls. Believing that work relief preserved self-respect, she considered domestic welfare fundamentally tragic. For efficiency as well as economy she cut administrative costs, while at the same time providing the right to organize and appeal employment grievances. She believed that some good things came out of the depression, such as old-age assistance, unemployment relief, and the right-to-earn and wage-hour regulations.

Carr was also interested in the problems of working women and children and of workers in hazardous jobs. She was a frequent contributor to social-work journals and throughout her career actively participated in a wide range of profes-sional meetings and conferences. The night before her death, in New York City, she had represented the New York Welfare Department at a housing rehabilitation meeting.

[MS material on Carr's years at Hull House is in the Jane Addams Memorial Collection, University of Il-linois, Chicago. See also George Britt, "Charlotte Carr at Hull-House," *Survey Graphic*, Feb. 1938; and Mil-ton S. Mayer, "Charlotte Carr—Settlement Lady," *Atlantic Monthly*, Dec. 1939. An obituary, including a photograph, appears in the *New York Times*, July 13, 1956. Henry L. McCarthy, former welfare commis-sioner of New York City, provided personal and professional information for this article.]

MARY SUE DILLIARD SCHUSKY

CARRINGTON, ELAINE STERN (June 14, 1891–May 4, 1958), magazine and radio scriptwriter, was born in New York City, the daughter of Theodore Stern, a merchant, and Mary Louise Henriquez. She received her education at St. Agatha's School and at Columbia University (1910–1911), and on Mar. 23, 1920, married a childhood schoolmate and lawyer, George Dart Carrington. They had two children.

Carrington developed her aspirations to write while an adolescent. Persisting in the face of nu-merous rejections, she had her first short story published in 1910; and the following year she won several short fiction and scenario-writing contests, including a $1,000 prize awarded by the *New York Evening Sun*. By the late 1920's she had become an established contributor of short fiction to such mass-circulation magazines as *Collier's, Pictorial Review, Harper's, Delineator,* and the *Saturday Evening Post*. Reviewing *All Things Considered* (1939), an anthology of these stories, the *New York Times* found a strain of sharp satire running through Carrington's writings, although their dominant tone was sentimental. Carrington was coauthor of the Broadway play *Nightstick* (1927), which became the basis for the movie *Alibi* (1929). She also published *The Gypsy Star* (1928) and a detective novel, *The Crimson Goddess* (1936).

Carrington achieved her greatest material success and public impact as the creator and writer of radio daytime serial dramas, or soap operas. In 1932, the National Broadcasting Company asked her to develop a radio script from a story that she had submitted. It went on the air in October as "Red Adams," broadcast three nights a week, later acquiring a sponsor and moving to daytime radio. With a change of title, characters, and plot, it emerged as "Pepper Young's Family" in June 1936. Drawing upon her own experiences, Carrington portrayed the trials, conflicts, and problems of a typical American middle-class family, as well as its warmth, understanding, and cohesiveness. The program, which at one time was heard daily on two networks, was still broadcast at the time of her death.

Carrington's success with this serial led to two other long-running soap operas, "When a Girl Marries," begun in May 1939, and "Rosemary," which went on the air in October 1944. Although they lacked some of the warmth and humor of "Pepper Young" and fit more closely the grief-ridden formula that still endures in television soap opera, both attracted large followings. At the height of her career in the 1940's and early 1950's, Carrington turned out approximately 38,000 words each week, earned an annual income well in excess of $200,000, and reached an average of about 2 million listeners with each broadcast. She was also responsible for "The Carrington Playhouse" during the mid-1940's, which produced the scripts of amateur writers with aspirations similar to those that she had nurtured as a young woman.

Among the artists and technicians of network radio in New York from the early 1930's to the late 1950's, Carrington was known as "Queen of the Soapers." With writers Irna Phillips and Frank and Anne Hummert, she "determined and defined what soap opera unalterably became." Tall, buxom, and gray-haired, she was often described as energetic and pleasant but fiercely independent in her relations with networks and sponsors. Her autonomy is illustrated by her introduction of such subjects as racial integration into her serials and in her work to help found the Radio Writers Guild.

A self-conscious popular artist, Carrington was anxious to defend her work against the attacks of critics—if not for its artistic value, then for its social role. She designed her programs to teach the importance of family life and to offer behavioral guidance and moral support in times of personal stress. Her belief that serials played a useful role was demonstrated by empirical studies of audiences beginning in the late 1930's. Research showed that serials gave many women psychological support in coping with personal difficulties, as they followed problem-solving stories on radio, and a positive self-image, as they observed heroines overcoming obstacles. In 1950 Carrington received an award from the National Conference of Christians and Jews for her radio achievement.

Carrington was not successful in television; the serial "Follow Your Heart" was canceled after a three months' run in 1954. She died in New York City.

[See Madeleine Edmondson and David Rounds, *The Soaps* (1973); Mary Jane Higby, *Tune in Tomorrow* (1968); Ruth Adams Knight, *Stand by for the Ladies!* (1939); James Thurber, "Soapland," in *The Beast in Me and Other Animals* (1948); and W. Lloyd Warner and William E. Henry, "The Radio Day Time Serial: A Symbolic Analysis," *Genetic Psychology Monographs,* 37 (Feb. 1948). There are obituaries with portrait in the *New York Times* and *New York Herald-Tribune,* May 5, 1958.]

ALAN HAVIG

CHAFEE, ZECHARIAH, JR. (Dec. 7, 1885–Feb. 8, 1957), law professor and civil libertarian, was born in Providence, R.I., the son of Zechariah Chafee and Mary Dexter Sharpe. After a comfortable childhood and attendance at Brown University (B.A., 1907), Chafee dutifully entered the family's iron business, first working in the shop, then becoming secretary and assistant to his father. Although he continued to be associated with the foundry's board of directors all his life, after three years he left the firm and entered the Harvard Law School. There he was greatly influenced by the theories on sociological jurisprudence advocated by Roscoe Pound and others. On July 20, 1912, he married Bess Frank Searle of Troy, N.Y.; they had four children. Chafee received the LL.B. in 1913, and entered a Providence law firm, but he left in 1916 to teach at the Harvard Law School. He rose from assistant professor to professor of law in 1919, to Langdell professor of law in 1938, and to a university professorship in 1950.

Until he began teaching, Chafee had no involvement in, or very much concern for, civil liberties, but in taking over the third-year equity course, he suddenly found himself interested by the ambiguities attendant to the classic doctrines of libel. When World War I broke out and judges across the land began issuing new and frequently arbitrary guidelines, Chafee realized that freedom of speech in the United States was undergoing a severe trial.

At Harold Laski's invitation, Chafee wrote an article for the *New Republic* analyzing the various district court decisions under the Sedition Act and their relationship to the First Amendment. "Freedom of Speech" appeared the week of the armistice, and it, along with the expanded version he wrote for the *Harvard Law Review* (June 1919) and his book *Freedom of Speech* (1920), established Chafee as one of the nation's leading civil libertarians. He argued that even in wartime the traditional doctrines of libel and sedition as propounded by Blackstone would have to be maintained in order to preserve free speech. While conceding that in emergency situations there might have to be some restraints, he maintained that liberty must be safeguarded in all cases. In the struggle between public safety and the search for truth, "the great interest in free speech should be sacrificed only when the interest in public safety is really imperiled, and not, as most men believe, when it is barely conceivable that it may be slightly affected."

Attempting to safeguard civil liberties in wartime was, at best, a difficult task, but it was compounded by the consideration that many of those whose rights were violated were political radicals. Chafee, the most conservative of men, labored diligently to make his argument acceptable and understandable to those who could not distinguish between civil libertarianism and radicalism. Throughout his book he referred to his own "traditional political and economic views," and his overall philosophy strongly reflected his own patrician background. He once declared that he could not understand why he "should be out mountain climbing and enjoying life while some other chap who started life with less money and gets a little angrier and a little more extreme should be shut up in prison."

The government's prosecution of Jacob Abrams, and the subsequent Supreme Court confirmation (with Holmes and Brandeis dissenting) of Abrams' twenty-year jail sentence for distributing leaflets opposing American intervention in Russia, was just the type of behavior Chafee abhorred. His criticism of the Abrams case led Austen G. Fox and twenty other conservative Law School alumni to petition the Harvard Overseers to inquire into Chafee's alleged radicalism. In May 1921, at a trial before a special committee in the Boston Harvard Club, Chafee defended himself against charges of radicalism and impropriety. "Gentlemen, I had no sympathy with the political and economic doctrines of these prisoners," he said. "My sympathies and all my associations are with the men who save, who manage and produce. But I want my side to fight fair. And I regard this Abrams trial as a distinctly unfair piece of fighting." According to Felix Frankfurter, Chafee's speech was the finest defense of liberty he had ever heard. When Harvard President A. Lawrence Lowell threw himself into the fight on Chafee's behalf, the committee dismissed all the charges against the Law School professor.

Although Chafee overnight became the hero of civil libertarians, he always downplayed his own role. "It did not take a great deal of courage," he said thirty years later, "because I could always have gone back to the practice of law if I had been forced to give up teaching." Yet throughout his life, Chafee found himself constantly involved in issues affecting the rights of his fellow citizens. In 1929 he headed a subcommittee of the Wickersham Commission that looked into police use of third degree and improper trial procedures. In 1938 he chaired the American Bar Association Commission on the Bill of Rights, which filed amicus briefs in the Flag Salute cases. During World War II, he served on the Commission on Freedom of the Press, and afterward performed similar duties for the United Nations.

Chafee, however, was never an absolutist; he believed that all rights had limits. In the 1950's he argued that while individuals, under the Fifth Amendment, need not testify against themselves, they did not enjoy the right to withhold information about others. Cooperation with the government was an underlying principle of the Constitution, and it did not give citizens the privilege of protecting their friends.

Chafee taught at the Harvard Law School for thirty-six years, during which time he published numerous books not only on questions of freedom but also on other legal problems. In fact, when anyone asked him what he regarded as his principal professional accomplishment, he unhesitatingly identified the Federal Interpleader Act of 1936, a complex piece of legislation that enabled multiple claims against the same person originating in different states to be resolved into one proceeding. In 1950, as one of Harvard's six university professors with the right to teach on any subject he desired, he chose Fundamental Human Rights, hoping to make students aware "of how dearly these rights were bought and of what they meant to the men who put them forever into our fundamental law." He retired in June 1956. His death, in Cambridge, Mass., according to Mark Howe and Archibald MacLeish, "was rightly reckoned by the best of his contemporaries as a loss not only to the University but to the country."

[The Chafee papers are located in the Harvard Law School Library. His books include *The Inquiring Mind* (1928); *Free Speech in the United States* (1941); *Some Problems of Equity* (1950); and *The Blessings of Liberty* (1956).
See also *Harvard Law Review* (1957); Arthur E. Sutherland, *The Law at Harvard* (1967); Jerold S. Auerbach, "The Patrician as Libertarian: Zechariah Chafee, Jr., and Freedom of Speech," *New England Quarterly* (1969); and the obituary notice in the *New York Times*, Feb. 9, 1957.]

MELVIN I. UROFSKY

CHANDLER, RAYMOND THORNTON

(July 23, 1888–Mar. 26, 1959), author, was born in Chicago, Ill., the son of Maurice Benjamin Chandler, an engineer, and Florence Dart Thornton. His parents were divorced when Chandler was seven, and his mother returned to her family in London. From 1900 to 1905 he attended Dulwich College, an institution whose classical curriculum and British "old school" code were formative influences. Chandler next studied in Paris and Munich for the British Civil Service examinations, which he took in 1907, having been naturalized a British subject. He placed third among 600 candidates, with top honors in classics; but after six months in the Admiralty, he resigned and turned to writing as a career. Following brief and unsuccessful stints as a reporter and the publication of some poetry and essays, he returned to the United States in 1912.

Chandler was working as an accountant in Los Angeles when he enlisted in the Canadian army in August 1917. He served in France for three months, returning to Britain as sole survivor of his company, then transferred to the Royal Air Force. His pilot's training was halted by the armistice, and he returned to California. On Feb. 6, 1924, he married Pearl Eugenie Hurlburt Porcher ("Cissy") Pascal, twice divorced and eighteen years his senior. At this time Chandler had been employed for two years by an oil syndicate, of which he was to become a top executive. Though called a genius in business, he became irritable and dominating, and drank heavily; in 1932 he was fired.

Chandler fell back on an earlier interest in writing fiction, and cast about for a salable mode. He had read contemporary slick magazines but was put off, he said, by "their fundamental dishonesty in the matter of character and motivation." Having also dipped into pulp magazines as a time killer, he was struck by the thought "that I might be able to write this stuff and get paid while I was learning." In five months Chandler produced a story accepted by the leading magazine in the field, *Black Mask*. Twenty more mystery tales appeared between 1934 and 1939. For his earliest work he had borrowed from Dashiell Hammett and Erle Stanley Gardner, among others; but by the time his first full-length novel, *The Big Sleep*, was published in 1939, the character of private detective Philip Marlowe and the taut, mannered language in which Marlowe expressed himself had evolved completely. Chandler drew from his earlier short fiction in several of his other novels: *Farewell, My Lovely* (1940), *The High Window* (1942), *The Lady in the Lake* (1943), *The Little Sister* (1949), *The Long Goodbye* (1953), and *Playback* (1958).

Although Chandler's novels sold relatively well and brought him critical approval, in 1943 he was happy to accept a screenwriting contract for greater financial stability. His initial script, of James M. Cain's *Double Indemnity*, was nominated for an Academy Award and made his Hollywood reputation. Chandler produced several other screenplays in the next three years—notably *The Blue Dahlia*—but withdrew from the production of his own *The Lady in the Lake*. The screenplay for another Chandler story, *The Big Sleep*, was written by William Faulkner, Leigh Brackett, and Jules Furthman. Chandler was pleased with the film, but by 1946 he was sick of Hollywood and the screen world.

During their Los Angeles years the Chandlers had led a nomadic existence; they now settled in La Jolla, Calif. Because of Cissy Chandler's advanced age and ill health, they had little social life. His work continued, but to some critics his last three novels seemed overwritten. The crispness of the earlier prose had given way to a more discursive style, in part because he was trying to incorporate criticism of the California way of life into his books.

In 1952 the Chandlers visited England and were feted by literary admirers. Cissy Chandler's health, however, continued to fail; and they returned to La Jolla, where she died in 1954, leaving Chandler desolate and suicidal. He went to England in 1955 and stayed abroad most of the following year. Upon his return to California, Chandler became embroiled in legal questions about his nationality (he had remained a naturalized Briton but regained his status as an American citizen in 1955) and about taxes he owed in Britain. Heavy drinking was now taking its toll; and though Chandler was able to go to New York in 1959 for installation as president of the Mystery Writers of America, he did not continue on to London, where he had planned to marry and settle with his literary agent, Helga Greene. Instead he returned to La Jolla, where he died of pneumonia contracted after a period of steady drinking.

Chandler's claims as a serious novelist have been upheld by writers as disparate as J. B. Priestley, Ronald Knox, Somerset Maugham, and Edmund Wilson. W. H. Auden echoed his subject's own credo when he commented that Chandler was interested in writing "not detective stories, but serious studies of a criminal milieu, the Great Wrong Place, and his powerful but extremely depressing books should be read and judged, not as escape literature, but as works of art" (*Harper's*, May 1948, p. 408).

[The standard biography, based upon hundreds of Chandler letters, is Frank MacShane, *The Life of Raymond Chandler* (1976); it includes portraits. MacShane also edited *The Notebooks of Raymond Chandler* (1976) and *English Summer* (1976), with hitherto unpublished writings. Matthew J. Bruccoli collected earlier works in *Chandler Before Marlowe* (1973). Critical evaluation appears in Philip Durham, *Down These Mean Streets a Man Must Go* (1963). Also see Matthew J. Bruccoli, *Raymond Chandler: A Checklist* (1968).]

J. V. RIDGELY

CHASE, EDNA WOOLMAN (Mar. 14, 1877–Mar. 20, 1957), magazine editor, was born in Asbury Park, N.J., the daughter of Franklyn Alloway and Laura Woolman. Her parents' early

divorce left her with no memory of her father. When her mother remarried and moved to New York City, Chase was brought up by her maternal grandfather and stepgrandmother in a warm and secure Quaker environment of a small New Jersey village. Chase attended a country school, and her grandfather tutored her in the evening. When her mother visited, Chase was fascinated by her fashionable clothes; and during silent Quaker meetings Chase imagined how her soberly attired relatives would look in such dress.

By 1895 Chase was living in her mother's small apartment. Chase's friend who worked for *Vogue* helped her find a temporary job addressing envelopes for the three-year-old weekly. She remained with *Vogue* for nearly sixty years, shaping it into the world's foremost fashion magazine. A petite woman with curly hair and sparkling brown eyes, she was described by a colleague as "the youngest young woman" he "had ever seen in an office." Since her mother's second marriage was floundering, Chase moved to a congenial boardinghouse soon after starting her job.

The informal *Vogue* office, staffed primarily with society people, became Chase's real home. Her work was varied and she absorbed editorial policies, particularly when she worked with the publisher Arthur Turnure. Chase warned him about deadlines and he asked for her opinion on layouts. In 1901, when Turnure's sister-in-law Marie L. Harrison became editor, she gradually delegated more authority to Chase. On Jan. 5, 1904, Chase married Francis Dane Chase, a handsome but irresponsible banker's son from Boston; they had one daughter. Their marriage ended in divorce.

Chase was among the employees Condé Montrose Nast retained when he purchased *Vogue* in 1909, three years after Turnure's death. She became a "human telephone system between publisher and editor" when a financial misunderstanding cooled Harrison's relations with Nast. By 1911 Chase was managing editor in all but name. Unwilling merely to report fashion and to picture the banal costumes worn at fancy dress balls, she commissioned *Vogue* artists to design special costumes. One prizewinning dress was copied by Florenz Ziegfeld for his *Midnight Frolic*.

When the *Ladies' Home Journal* tried to hire Chase, Nast made her editor of *Vogue* in 1914. Her "look of fragile prettiness," enhanced by prematurely gray hair, belied her innovative and aggressive spirit. Nast lacked her imagination, she lacked his urge to expand; but they both realized the importance of advertising. Neither viewed facile agreement as the road to success. She liked "nothing better than a sharp exchange of opposing views," and he "considered one son-of-a-gun in every department to be therapeutic." Together they shaped *Vogue* into a semimonthly periodical that was published in four countries and in three languages (English, French, and German).

In developing *Vogue*'s elegant format, Chase and Nast usually kept the magazine apolitical, but they could not avoid the issue of woman's rights. The editorial policy of *Vogue* was antisuffragist and stressed "important public work" that women could "perform without the ballot"; *Vogue*'s main concern was fashion. With the aim of sustaining the interest in fashion during war-time, Chase organized the first American fashion show on Nov. 4, 1914. To still the fears of the French couture over their newborn rival, she planned a New York show for them a year later. Knowing that buyers would not purchase a dress unless they could see its design, Chase insisted on precise illustrations. She complained when French designers tried to keep their models ex-clusive by presenting her with amateur sketches of inferior designs. She also objected when *Vogue* photographers forgot they were illustrating dresses—not merely shooting avant-garde pic-tures. "Show the dress," read a directive Chase hung in the studio, "and if that can't be done with art then art be damned." Spurred by publicity from the fashion shows and by Chase's striking application of photography and modern art to fashion illustrations, *Vogue*'s advertising soared.

On Nov. 22, 1921, Chase married Richard T. Newton, an English automotive engineer and inventor; he died in 1950. Since *Vogue* was primarily staff-written (with help from Frank Crowninshield of the Nast-owned *Vanity Fair*), Chase dominated every part of its production. In the thirtieth anniversary issue Nast paid tribute to her vision, clear thinking, "genius for organiza-tion, . . . practical knowledge of advertising and unfailing tact." By 1926 *Vogue* had the second highest annual income of all American magazines, even though its circulation was only 150,000. Chase was named editor in chief of all *Vogue* editions in 1929.

During the Great Depression, Chase coined the slogan "More Taste Than Money" and an-nually brought out an issue dedicated to that premise. She maintained high standards, refusing

to publish anything she considered tasteless or false. Aware that *Vogue* had a faithful following among buyers for large stores, advertisers con-tinued buying *Vogue* ads during the Depression. But Nast's *Vanity Fair* failed in 1936 and merged with *Vogue*, which became thereafter somewhat more literary. In 1938, for example, Chase con-ceived of an annual all-American issue, and Thomas Wolfe's "Prologue to America" made it memorable.

By the 1930's Chase was the doyenne of the fashion industry and was awarded the Legion of Honor from France in 1935. In overseeing the American, British, and French editions of *Vogue*, and for its short life, the German edition, Chase tried to include on each staff an editor with a flair for clothes, one linked to the artistic and literary community, and one who moved in high social circles. For each issue she recommended a plan-ning conference, another meeting "while it was in the works," and a "free-for-all" postmortem session.

In an era when few women had full-time ca-reers, Chase did not retire from active editing until 1952, when she became chairman of the editorial board. In 1954 she wrote a candid au-tobiography, *Always in Vogue*, with her daughter Ilka Chase, an actress and author. Chase admitted she had missed a good deal in the "one-goal" life she had led, but added, "I know too that every-thing else together could not have made up the sum of satisfaction I have derived from my job." She died in Sarasota, Fla.

[Chase's autobiography is the best source on her life and career. Also refer to Frank Luther Mott, *A History of American Magazines* (1957); and *Vogue*, Jan. 1, 1923; Oct. 15, 1954; and Apr. 15, 1957. See also "France Awards the High Priestess of Fashion a Ribbon," *Newsweek*, Aug. 24, 1935; "Stylocrats," *Time*, Aug. 18, 1947; A. Rogers, "Editor in a Lioness's Mane," *Saturday Review*, Oct. 30, 1954; "Fifty-nine Years in Fashion," *Life*, Nov. 8, 1954; and the obituary notices, *New York Times*, Mar. 21, Mar. 24, 1957.]

OLIVE HOOGENBOOM

CHENNAULT, CLAIRE LEE (Sept. 6, 1893–July 27, 1958), military leader and airline executive, was born in Commerce, Tex., the son of John Stonewall Chennault, a farmer, and Jessie Lee. He grew up in rural northeastern Louisiana and was a bright though reluctant student. In 1909–1910, while at Louisiana State University (where he took ROTC training), he applied for admission to both West Point and Annapolis, but decided against a military career. He did a brief stint of study at the State Normal School at Natchitoches and received a teaching credential in 1910. On Dec. 25, 1911, he married Nell Thompson; they had eight children.

For several years Chennault taught public school and held other jobs, but he knew he wanted to fly. He was repeatedly rejected for flight training after the United States entered World War I in April 1917, but was commissioned a first lieutenant in the infantry reserve. While stationed in San Antonio, Tex., he learned to fly at Kelly Field; he won his rating as a fighter pilot in 1919. Discharged from the army a year later, he farmed briefly in Louisiana, and on Sept. 24, 1920, was commissioned a first lieutenant in the new Army Air Service.

Chennault's subsequent assignments included service with the Ninety-Fourth Fighter Squadron at Ellington Field, Tex., and command of the Nineteenth Pursuit Squadron, stationed at Wheeler Field, Hawaii. He was promoted to captain in 1929, while serving at Brooks Field, Tex. From 1930 to 1937 he was at the Air Corps Tactical School, Langley Field, Va. (later moved to Montgomery, Ala.), first as a student then as instructor. While there he organized and led the Air Corps acrobatic exhibition team (popularly known as "Three Men on a Flying Trapeze"). During these years he developed the theories of air tactics he later applied against the Japanese in China; in 1935 he published them in a textbook, *The Role of Defensive Pursuit*.

Chennault attacked the fashionable theory that bombers could operate without escort by virtue of their speed and firepower; he perfected team combat tactics, experimented with airdrop supply and paratroop techniques, and crusaded for greater firepower and range in fighter aircraft. His vigorous public advocacy of these views made him unpopular with the dominant strategic bombing school in the Army Air Corps. In April 1937, suffering from overwork, chronic bronchial trouble, and partial deafness, he accepted retirement for physical disability with the rank of captain.

The day after retiring, Chennault left for the Far East to survey the Chinese air force for Mme Chiang Kai-shek. After the Japanese invasion in July, he became personal adviser to Generalissimo Chiang Kai-shek and supervised the training of the Chinese air force by American instructors at bases in southwestern China. Late in 1940 Chiang sent him to the United States to enlist support for an American-manned and -equipped air force. He faced bitter opposition, particularly from the Army Air Corps chief, General H. H. Arnold. But China had friends in high places, including President Roosevelt, Secretary of the Navy Frank Knox, and Secretary of the Treasury Henry Morgenthau. Chennault was able to recruit some 100 pilots and to buy the same number of new Curtiss-Wright P-40B fighters. By midsummer of 1941 his American Volunteer Group (AVG)—soon nicknamed the Flying Tigers from the tiger-shark teeth, tongue, and eyes painted on the noses of the aircraft—was training at a Royal Air Force base at Toungoo, Burma. After the Japanese invasion the main base was moved to Kunming in southern Yunnan, China.

From mid-December until its incorporation into the United States Army in July 1942, the AVG ran up a remarkable record. Chennault trained his men to fight in pairs, stressing accurate gunnery and hit-and-run tactics to exploit the P-40's firepower, ruggedness, and speed in diving and level flight against the fast-turning but fragile and lightly armed Japanese Zero fighters. His ground crews were drilled in rapid refueling and repair, and the virtually foolproof Chinese air-raid warning net protected his small force from surprise attack. With the RAF the AVG kept Rangoon and the Burma Road open for two and a half months in 1942; it was a key factor in defeating the Japanese invasion of Yunnan that spring, and it stopped enemy bombing of China's cities. At a cost of four pilots lost in air combat out of a total of twenty-six for all causes, it destroyed at least 299, and probably another 153, enemy aircraft. During the next three years, Chennault's expanded forces (China Air Task Force and, after March 1943, the Fourteenth Air Force) destroyed some 2,600 enemy aircraft and probably 1,500 more, sank 2,300,000 tons of enemy merchant shipping, and killed 66,700 enemy troops, losing about 500 aircraft in combat.

During most of the war Chennault was at odds with his American superiors, especially the China-Burma-India theater commander, Lieutenant General Joseph W. Stilwell. But Chiang Kai-shek's confidence in him never wavered, and he won the respect of Lieutenant General Albert C. Wedemeyer, who replaced Stilwell after his forced recall in October 1944. The Stilwell-Chennault feud transcended professional disagreement; each saw the other as personally un-principled, prejudiced, and power-hungry.

Late in 1942 Chennault was able, with the help of Wendell Willkie, to bring his strategic ideas to Roosevelt's attention. He asserted that with 150 fighters and smaller numbers of bombers, main-tained at full strength, he could cripple the Japanese air force in less than a year and then bomb Japan into submission. Stilwell's view, supported by most of the high command, was that Japan would react to such a threat by overrunning the American air bases in eastern China and that the Chinese armies could not stop them. Chen-nault rated Chinese capabilities higher. In May 1943 Roosevelt gave him a free hand and a six-month priority on tonnage flown over the "Hump" from India. After suffering heavy damage, the Japanese launched their offensive in 1944 and captured the main American bases, as predicted. The Fourteenth Air Force continued to operate with growing effect from other bases farther west.

By 1945 China had become a military back-water. In the spring Army Chief of Staff General George C. Marshall and General Arnold forced Chennault's ouster, on the basis of Stilwell's charges of insubordination. Chennault retired the following October with the rank of major general. Chiang Kai-shek awarded him China's highest honor, the Order of the White Sun and Blue Sky.

After the war Chennault became a leading champion of resistance to Communism in the Far East. In 1946 he retired to China and organized a civil airline, with himself as president, to carry relief supplies into the interior under contract to the Chinese Nationalist Relief and Rehabilita-tion Agency. CAT, as the airline was popularly known, was reorganized as Civil Air Transport in January 1948, and by the end of that year its expanding relief and commercial operations had made it one of the world's largest air cargo carriers. During the ensuing Chinese civil war CAT continued to work for the Nationalists, airlifting supplies to isolated garrisons and evac-uating troops and refugees before the ad-vancing Communists. As the first of the Cen-tral Intelligence Agency's commercial "pro-prietaries," CAT provided logistical support to CIA operations in Korea, Indochina, North Vietnam, Laos, and Tibet. CAT transports had a major supply role in the Korean War, and during the siege of Dien Bien Phu in 1954 kept the garrison supplied until it was overrun.

After divorcing his first wife in 1946, Chen-nault married Anna Chan, a Chinese journalist, on Dec. 21, 1947; they had two daughters. In July 1958, by Act of Congress, he was awarded the honorary rank of lieutenant general. He died later that month in New Orleans, La.

[Chennault's memoirs were published as Robert B. Hotz, ed., *Way of a Fighter* (1949). See also Hotz's wartime account, *With General Chennault* (1943); Anna Chennault, *Chennault and the Flying Tigers* (1963); Robert Lee Scott, Jr., *Flying Tiger* (1959); and Keith Ayling, *Old Leatherface* (1945). Theodore H. White, ed., *The Stilwell Papers* (1948), presents Stilwell's side of his feud with Chennault. For great-er detail, see vols. I. IV, and V of the official air force history, Wesley F. Craven and James L. Cate, eds., *The Army Air Forces in World War II,* 7 vols. (1948–1958); and the three-volume China-Burma-India Theater subseries by Charles F. Romanus and Riley Sunderland (1953, 1956, 1959) in the army official history, *U.S. Army in World War II.* The Oral History Collection at Columbia University contains much on Chennault, particulary in the memoir of Paul Frillman and in those of several Flying Tiger veterans.]

RICHARD M. LEIGHTON

CHESSMAN, CARYL WHITTIER (May 27, 1921–May 2, 1960), criminal and writer, was born in St. Joseph, Mich., the only child of Serl Whittier Chessman, an ambitious laborer who worked at a variety of jobs, and Hallie Cottle. Soon after Caryl's birth the family moved to Glendale, Calif., where Serl opened a gasoline station. In 1927 Caryl almost died of pneumonia. His aptitude for music was ended the following year by encephalitis, which left him tone deaf and possibly affected his personality. He became temperamental and occasionally capriciously cruel. An automobile accident in 1931 left Caryl's aunt dead, his mother paralyzed from the waist down, and Chessman with a smashed nose and distorted lower lip that marred his appearance for the rest of his life. Medical bills combined with the Great Depression, then at its worst, caused Serl to lose his gas station. After trying a series of oc-cupations he ended up on relief and attempted suicide.

At Glendale High School Caryl did not feel accepted, being nicknamed "Hooknose," still puny, weakened by diphtheria when fifteen, and humilated by his family's poverty and sickness. It was among the school's troublemakers that he gained approval by stealing automobiles, learning to drive with great skill and daring, and com-mitting burglaries. His antisocial behavior was deliberate and unremitting, and he dramatized himself as a challenger of the law enforcement authorities. Arrested at sixteen in 1937 for auto theft, he was to spend less than one and a half years of the remaining twenty-three of his life as a free man. During his brief periods of freedom, he committed robbery, burglary, and other crimes. Committed to reform school, roadwork camp, and prison in 1937, 1938, 1939, and 1941, each time Chessman's good behavior obtained early release or a chance to escape. A conviction in 1943 imprisoned him until the end of 1947. Twice he married girls who in vain hoped to reform him. The first marriage was annulled after a few months in late 1939. His second marriage in 1940 ended in divorce in 1947.

In January 1948, about a month after Chessman had been released on parole from Folsom Prison, there occurred in rapid succession a series of crimes in Los Angeles for which Chessman was held largely responsible. In some of the crimes a car with a red spotlight was used to impersonate police in approaching parked couples in lovers' lanes for robbery and sexual assault. On May 21, 1948, a jury in the superior court of Los Angeles found Chessman guilty of seventeen felonies, including two violations of California's "Little Lindbergh" kidnapping law of 1933, which allowed the death penalty. In the trial he insisted on acting as his own defense counsel, with some resulting disadvantages, although he was often skillful in the role. Acknowledging his criminal background, he maintained, however, that the sex crimes of the "red light bandit" were unlike any crime in his own past, that the evidence was faulty, and that the prosecution's insistence on the death penalty required a strained, technical application of the state's kidnapping law to what were essentially only robbery and sexual assault. The prosecutor was successful in blurring such distinctions, making the most of Chessman's reputation as a criminal and sex pervert to urge the death penalty.

Following his conviction, Chessman and a growing army of supporters fought for twelve years against his execution. While carrying on his legal battle from his cell, Chessman wrote four books, one of them fictional, all based on his experiences. They were widely read and acclaimed, bringing public sympathy and money for his costly litigation. *Cell 2455, Death Row* (1954) went through six printings by the end of 1955. It was translated into several languages and was the basis of a film produced in 1955. One avenue of

appeal was cut off in 1950 when the California Supreme Court upheld the kidnapping charge against Chessman's accomplice in some of the crimes. But Chessman demanded a new trial, claiming that his appeal could not be considered fairly because the court reporter's record of the trial was incomplete, inaccurate, and fraudulently affected by the prosecution. The reporter died shortly after the trial, and his notes were almost indecipherable. In 1959 both state and federal supreme courts decided that the revised transcript was sufficiently accurate and complete, largely because it was not much more imperfect than many other trial records of the time.

During the months preceding Chessman's execution, petitions poured in from many parts of the world asking that he be spared. Many of his supporters accepted his guilt but did not think he deserved the death penalty, while others opposed capital punishment on principle. At one point Governor Edmund G. Brown, the day before the execution date, granted a sixty-day reprieve and convened a special session of the legislature to consider abolishing capital punishment. But it failed to act. The execution was postponed eight times, but the ninth date was kept and Chessman died in the gas chamber at San Quentin.

The twelve-year delay was partly a result of the death of the court reporter, which gave Chessman his major legal issue and time in which to place his case before the public and raise money for litigation by his writing. The closer examination that the U.S. Supreme Court began to give the Chessman case in 1955 may have been partly on account of his public recognition. It has been said that the Court could and should have disposed of all aspects of the transcript controversy in 1950 when it first encountered it, but that it did not consider it fully until seven years later.

[Besides *Cell 2455, Death Row* (1954; enlarged ed., 1960), Chessman published *Trial by Ordeal* (1955) and *The Face of Justice* (1957), both of which are autobiographical; and also the novel *The Kid Was a Killer* (1960). The 1960 edition of *Cell 2455* has a chapter added by Chessman's literary agent. Sympathetic accounts include Milton Machlin and William R. Woodfield, *Ninth Life* (1961), a journalistic biography; and William M. Kunstler, *Beyond a Reasonable Doubt?* (1961), which is primarily a reconstruction of the trial record. See also "The Caryl Chessman Case: A Legal Analysis," *Minnesota Law Review*, Apr. 1960, which concludes that Chessman's rights were not violated. On Chessman himself, see Bernice Freeman Davis, *The Desperate and the Damned* (1961), 161–198,

207–225; Clinton T. Duffy, *88 Men and 2 Women* (1962), 142–154; and Byron E. Eshelman, *Death Row Chaplain* (1962), 187–215. For guidance to other books and articles on Chessman, see Andrew O. Largo, compiler, *Caryl Whittier Chessman, 1921–1960: Essay and Critical Bibliography* (1971).]

GALEN R. FISHER

CLARK, BOBBY (June 16, 1888–Feb. 12, 1960), entertainer, was born Robert Edwin Clark, in Springfield, Ohio, the son of Victor Brown Clark, a train conductor, and Alice Marilla Sneed. In the fourth grade he met Paul McCullough, four years his senior, who was to become his stage partner for many years. Together they practiced bugle blowing and tumbling at the local YMCA and began their career as performers at an Elks circus in Delaware, Ohio. They made their first professional appearance in June 1905, as comedy acrobats and bugle players with the touring Culhane, Chace and Weston Minstrels. Their engagement proved more instructive than profitable, for after twelve weeks the owner absconded, leaving them stranded. Their next engagement, with Kalbfield's Greater California Minstrels, ended similarly.

Undiscouraged, they joined the Hagenbeck-Wallace Circus and gradually transformed themselves into clowns. Clark's makeup—spectacles painted with burnt cork—became his trademark. Chomping on a cigar, he treated audiences to such bizarre comic turns as his impression of a young Bulgarian weasel calling its mate. McCullough slipped easily into the role of straight man. After touring Mexico with the Sells-Floto Circus, they joined the Ringling Brothers Circus in 1906, and soon afterward made their first appearance in New York City at Madison Square Garden.

After six years under the big top they turned to vaudeville, giving their first performance at the Brunswick, New Jersey, Opera House in December 1912. By then their stage personalities were well established. Clad in a short covert-cloth topcoat and porkpie hat, swinging his cane like a golf club, Clark would scuttle around the stage, leering, his voice a ribald gargle; while McCullough, in his checkered suit, bow tie, and ratty fur coat, beamed approval. Unlike most vaudeville comedians, they never resorted to dialect routines or blackface. Although they used many props, their routines were built around the simplest ideas—their comic inability, for example, to hoist a chair onto a table.

In 1917, while appearing at the Orpheum Theater in Boston, they were spotted by Jean Bedini, a leading producer of burlesque, who engaged them to appear in *Puss Puss* at the Casino Theater in Philadelphia. They had not been headliners in vaudeville, but in burlesque, then in its heyday, they found the ideal medium for their freewheeling style. Under the management of C. B. Cochran they appeared in London in *Chuckles of 1922,* scoring particularly well in a skit in which they made elaborate preparations for a tumbling act but never turned so much as a somersault.

Their London success led to their appearance in the 1922 and 1924 editions of Irving Berlin's *Music Box Revue,* sharing the honors with fellow comics Fanny Brice and Charlotte Greenwood. By then an established star, Clark on Sept. 28, 1923, married Angèle Gaignat, a chorus girl who had appeared with him in burlesque. Following an engagement in their first book show, *The Ramblers* (1926), Clark and McCullough moved to Hollywood, where they appeared in a dozen shorts for Fox Studios and in sixty more for RKO. Moviemaking did not appeal to them, however. With their uninhibited style they chafed at the discipline imposed by directors and scriptwriters and returned to Broadway musicals, most notably *Strike up the Band* (1930), *Here Goes the Bride* (1931), *Walk a Little Faster* (1932), and *Thumbs Up!* (1934).

McCullough's suicide in March 1936 ended their partnership. Clark was distraught but reestablished himself as a single performer in *The Ziegfeld Follies* (1936). He later enlivened a number of musicals such as *The Streets of Paris* (1939), *Star and Garter* (1942), and *Mexican Hayride* (1944), but his most notable appearances were in legitimate comedy. As Ben, the sailor, in a 1940 all-star revival of Congreve's *Love for Love,* he seemed on leave from Minsky's rather than the British Fleet, but he played the role with irresistible verve. He was no less irrepressible as Bob Acres in a 1942 production of Sheridan's *The Rivals,* prompting the director, Eva Le Gallienne, to observe, "I'll just try to keep the other actors out of your way." As Monsieur Jourdain in Molière's *Would-Be Gentleman* (1946), not content with rewriting his role, Clark interpolated such characteristic bits of business as flinging a snuffbox across the stage into his valet's pocket. After appearing in *As the Girls Go* (1948), he virtually retired from the stage. He occasionally appeared on television and starred in a 1956 tour of *Damn*

Yankees, but for the greater part of the time he lived quietly, listing as his avocations golf, bridge, boxing, music, opera, and Shakespeare. Like many comedians, offstage he was quiet, conservative in dress, and domestic in his habits. He died in New York City.

A performer in the great tradition of popular entertainment, Bobby Clark was experienced in every form of comedy. He created and perfected a unique persona, and his art was a continuing demonstration of that character's enduring theatrical vitality.

[Robert L. Taylor, "Comedian," *New Yorker,* Sept. 13, 20, and 27, 1947, and reprinted in his book *The Running Pianist* (1950) is the main source. See also *Who's Who in the Theatre,* 12th ed. (1957); and R. Dowring, "Minnie and Mr. Clark," in George Oppenheimer, ed., *The Passionate Playgoer* (1958).]

WILLIAM W. APPLETON

CLEGHORN, SARAH NORCLIFFE (Feb. 4, 1876–Apr. 4, 1959), reformer, novelist, and poet, was born in Norfolk, Va., the daughter of John Dalton Cleghorn and Sarah Chestnut Hawley. In 1877 the family moved to a small farm near Madison, Wis.; but John Cleghorn was not cut out for farming, and after five years he went into business in Minneapolis. Sarah's mother died when the girl was nine, and she and her younger brother were reared by two maiden aunts in Manchester, Vt. Cleghorn was to write lovingly of the people in this New England village and of its old houses, shops and offices, and cemetery, whose ponds made it the children's playground. Sojourns in Troy, N.Y., where her father had moved after his wife's death, figured in her upbringing, as did annual three-month interludes in New York City, where she visited with Audubon cousins, granddaughters of the naturalist.

Taught at home by her mother and then by her aunts, Cleghorn had no formal education until she entered the Burr and Burton Seminary in Manchester, where she studied Latin and Greek and experimented with verse. After graduating in 1895, she attended Radcliffe College for one year but withdrew for financial reasons. About this time she met Dorothy Canfield (later Mrs. John R. Fisher); they became devoted friends.

The "most sickening" event of Cleghorn's adolescence was her reading of "the burning alive of a Negro by his white neighbors somewhere in the South." The brevity of the report and its inconspicuousness shook her confidence "in the New York *Tribune* and in America." Disturbed to find the churches giving so little attention to the social unrest of the 1890's, she began to interest herself in labor problems and unionization. She had been writing short fiction for Elbert Hubbard's *Philistine* and other publications and had been contributing poetry to *Scribner's, Harper's,* and the *Atlantic.* She now turned to writing that expressed social concerns in the *American Magazine.* Increasingly an admirer of Eugene V. Debs, she joined the Socialist party in 1913 and felt ennobled by her affiliation with so active a political minority. Out of this experience came her most widely known verse. On a visit to South Carolina she observed young children at work in a cotton factory that stood at the edge of a golf course. Astounded by the juxtaposition of youthful mill hands and adult players, she wrote:

The golf-links lie so near the mill
That almost every day
The laboring children can look out
And watch the men at play.

After deciding against the expansion of her verse, she sent the quatrain to Franklin P. Adams, conductor of "The Conning Tower" column in the *New York Tribune,* where it appeared on Jan. 23, 1915, en route to countless reproductions and a permanent place in American literature.

One cause crowded another. Cleghorn's fervent belief that public ownership was better than unrestrained capitalism led to a friendship with the socialist leader Norman Thomas. She was a pacifist even before World War I. She worked within prisons for the rehabilitation of inmates, holding that punishment was not a corrective. She vigorously opposed social and political discrimination on the basis of race and sex. She became a leading antivivisectionist and an ardent protector of wildlife. She proclaimed the benefits of a vegetarian diet. Cleghorn took her causes to the newspapers through short, pointed, and informed letters to the editor and was regularly cheered by the response of unknown but intensely interested readers.

Cleghorn's life was simple. An intense interest in the workers' education movement led her in 1920 to begin teaching at the Brookwood Labor School, Katonah, N.Y. From 1922 to 1929 she taught dramatics and English at the Manumit School, near Pawling, N.Y. In 1929 she was substitute associate professor of English at Vassar. Her income from writing ranged from modest to nonexistent. Her first book, a novel, *A Turnpike*

Lady (1907), she called "a kind of daguerreotype in print." She never married, and characterized *The Spinster* (1916) as "one-third fiction and two-thirds a slightly arranged autobiography." The book was praised by William Dean Howells and went into a second edition.

Cleghorn was coauthor with Dorothy Canfield Fisher of *Fellow Captains* (1916), a collection of essays. Many of her poems appeared in *Portraits and Protests* (1917), divided into three categories: depictions of a disappearing New England way of life, expressions of mysticism, and "burning poems," such as "Comrade Jesus," about the evils of society. *Threescore* (1936), her warmly reviewed autobiography, was adorned with many poems. *The Seamless Robe,* her last book, was published in 1945.

In 1943 this disturber of the easy conscience moved to Philadelphia, where she died. Robert Frost called her a "saint." What was important to her, he said, was "not to get hold of both ends, but of the right end."

[See Katherine Woods's review of *Threescore,* Cleghorn's autobiography, *New York Times,* Mar. 29, 1936, VI:4; and Irving Dilliard, "Four Short Lines," *The Nation,* Apr. 10, 1976. For a list of Cleghorn's writings, see *Twentieth Century Authors* (1942), which also includes a portrait. Her papers, MSS, and books are at the Bailey Library, University of Vermont.]

IRVING DILLIARD

CLINE, GENEVIEVE ROSE (July 2, 1879–Oct. 25, 1959), lawyer and judge, was born in Warren, Ohio, the daughter of Edward B. Cline and Mary A. Fee. She followed a business program at Oberlin College and then worked for a manufacturing firm in Cleveland. When her mother became ill, she returned to Warren and helped manage the household. Cline's brother had a law office in Warren, and he encouraged her to read law. She enrolled at nearby Baldwin-Wallace College, receiving her LL.B. in 1921.

Shortly after Cline started her practice in Cleveland, President Warren G. Harding began seeking capable women to appoint to federal office. He named her appraiser of merchandise at the Port of Cleveland in 1922. She held this office for six years, winning the respect and confidence of many businessmen and lawyers.

Toward the end of 1927 there were rumors of an opening on the United States Customs Court. Cline's friends campaigned to enlist Ohio senatorial support for her nomination. Political leaders

throughout the state called on President Calvin Coolidge to name her to the federal bench. The president chose a man, but when there was a second opening a few months later, he sent Cline's name to the Senate.

Although confirmation would normally have been routine, Senator William H. King of Utah was reluctant to let a woman have such a political plum. He, as well as a committee representing the New York Customs Bar Association, questioned her qualifications. In response to this, Cline's supporters flooded the Senate Judiciary Committee with endorsements from lawyers and judges. Finally, the committee did not even call her to testify; the Senate confirmed her appointment on May 25, 1928.

Cline took the oath of office on June 6, 1928. At a small reception following the swearing-in ceremonies, she declared: "I do want to say not only for myself but in behalf of my sister members of the bar, I thank you and want to assure you that I shall meet all absolutely fairly as man to man in the court." She served on the Customs Court for twenty-five years, until her retirement in 1953. Cline, who never married, died in Cleveland, Ohio.

[On Cline and her career, see the *New York Times,* May 16 and June 7, 1928; C. Marshall, "A Lady Sits in Judgment," *Women's Journal,* Sept. 1928; *Cleveland Plain Dealer,* Oct. 26, 1959; and *Congressional Directory,* 81st Cong., 2d Sess. (1950).]

MELVIN I. UROFSKY

COBO, ALBERT EUGENE (Oct. 2, 1893–Sept. 12, 1957), businessman and mayor of Detroit, was born in Detroit, Mich., the son of August Cobo, a marine engineer, and Elizabeth Byrn. He attended elementary schools in Detroit and spent two years at Western High School. Thereafter he took night classes at the Detroit Business Institute (1912–1913) and later (1920–1922) a correspondence course at the Alexander Hamilton Institute. He went to work at the age of seventeen as an office boy, running errands for the Detroit Copper and Brass Rolling Mills. A year later, in 1911, he and his brother Edward began making candy and ice cream in a basement, and by World War I they were operating two confectionery stores. On June 3, 1914, he married Ethel Logan Christie; they had two daughters.

In 1918 Cobo became a junior salesman with the Burroughs Adding Machine Company. After his first year, he was promoted to senior salesman in charge of a district. In 1925 he left Burroughs to accept a position with the Sundstrand Adding Machine Company as a manager in the Detroit area. The next year he was placed in charge of establishing new factory branches for that company. When Sundstrand merged with the Elliot-Fisher bookkeeping machine company, Cobo was promoted to assistant manager for the central district. He remained with the consolidated firm until 1928 and then returned to Burroughs as a salesman. The following year he was made a sales executive in charge of governmental and utility accounts.

In the spring of 1933, when Detroit's financial affairs were in perilous condition as a result of the Great Depression, Burroughs lent Cobo to the city for six months. Cobo helped to avert a threatened bankruptcy by establishing policies for redeeming the scrip then paid to municipal employees and by helping to trim the city's annual budget. He also initiated a deferred tax-payment plan enabling thousands of Detroiters to retain their homes that otherwise would have been lost for nonpayment of taxes.

Cobo never returned to private business. He replaced the deputy treasurer of Detroit when he resigned in July 1933 and, upon the death of the city treasurer in April 1935, was appointed to complete a term that expired the following year. Beginning in 1937, Cobo was reelected biennially for seven consecutive terms, each time by overwhelming majorities. His political popularity was such that both the Democratic and Republican parties sought unsuccessfully to nominate him for state treasurer.

In 1949 Cobo entered Detroit's nonpartisan election as a candidate for mayor. He campaigned on the issues of the interests of the homeowner; the economies that he had practiced in the treasurer's office; and the savings realized through his judicious management of the city's bonded indebtedness. Backed by business and civic groups and the American Federation of Labor (AFL), Cobo was elected mayor in November by a landslide margin over George Edwards, who was supported by the United Auto Workers–CIO. Later, as mayor, Cobo would declare July 4, 1951, "Taxpayers' Day."

Cobo promised an "efficient, businesslike government" and sought top business leaders to solve the problem of the city-owned street railway system. He also authorized the expansion of Detroit's municipal hospital and pressed for slum clearance and urban renewal through the Federal Housing Act of 1949. In August 1950, during his first year in office, Cobo was confronted by a strike of the city's sanitation workers. He resolved the conflict by invoking the state's Hutchinson Act, which prohibited walkouts by public employees and under which strikers could be discharged with a loss of seniority and pension rights. In the fall of the same year, Cobo resorted to the courts to stop a strike threat by the AFL's Streetcar and Bus Operators Union, and again in April 1951, he took court action when transit employees conducted an unscheduled strike. Cobo's use of the Hutchinson Act did him surprisingly little damage politically, even in labor-oriented Detroit. He was reelected by a comfortable margin in 1951. The city voters also approved a charter amendment that lengthened the mayor's term of office from two to four years. Cobo was again reelected in 1953.

During his almost eight years as mayor, Cobo used his financial acumen and administrative talent to change the face of downtown Detroit. He played a major role in the construction of Detroit's modern expressway system and in the development at Detroit's core of a modern civic center, which included the Veterans' Building, the City-County Building, the Ford Auditorium, and the Exhibition and Convention Hall. One of his proudest achievements was the revenue bond financing plan, which made it possible to construct twenty miles of expressways in seven years instead of the fifteen it would have taken under a pay-as-you-go plan. Cobo accomplished this by borrowing against future motor vehicle tax receipts.

In 1956 Cobo entered his first partisan election as the Republican candidate for governor of Michigan, opposing the incumbent, G. Mennen Williams. Cobo was defeated. He did not plan to seek reelection to the mayor's office. Cobo died in Detroit less than four months before his last term would have ended.

[The mayoral years are covered by the Albert E. Cobo Papers at the Burton Historical Collection of the Detroit Public Library. Other important aspects of his career can be obtained from Albert E. Cobo, "Street and Traffic Management: A New Approach," *Traffic Quarterly,* Jan. 1952; "Interview With Mayor of Detroit, Albert E. Cobo," *U.S. News and World Report,* July 19, 1957; and the *New York Times,* Sept. 1, 6, 1950; May 12, 17, Nov. 7, 8, 1951; May 6, Nov. 7, 8, 1956; and the obituary of Sept. 13, 1957. Basic information on Cobo's life can be found in the biographical file in the Detroit Public Library; the *Detroit Free Press,* Aug. 11, 1956; and *Pathfinder,* Jan. 25, 1950.]

MELVIN G. HOLLI

COHEN, OCTAVUS ROY (June 26, 1891–Jan. 6, 1959), popular novelist, playwright, and screenwriter, was born in Charleston, S.C., the son of Octavus Cohen, a lawyer and editor, and Rebecca Ottolengui. At seventeen he graduated from the Porter Military Academy in Charleston and, in 1908, from Clemson College (with a B.S. in engineering). After working for the Tennessee Coal, Iron and Railroad Company as a civil engineer (1909–1910), he turned to journalism, working in the editorial departments of the Birmingham (Ala.) *Ledger,* the Charleston (S. C.) *News and Courier,* the Bayonne (N. J.) *Times,* and the Newark (N. J.) *Morning Star* during the next two years. He was admitted to the South Carolina bar in 1913 and practiced law in Charleston for two years. On Oct. 6, 1914, he married Inez Lopez of Bessemer, Ala. They had one son.

In later years Cohen delighted in citing the variety of youthful jobs that led him to writing, but his literary career was equally varied. Between 1917 and his death he published fifty-six volumes, works that included humorous and detective novels, plays, and collections of short stories. He wrote successful Broadway plays and radio, film, and television scripts; and he published hundreds of short stories and serials, many of them uncollected, in the *Saturday Evening Post, Collier's,* and other popular magazines.

Cohen published his first short story, "False Alarm," in *Colliers* (Apr. 17, 1915), and his first mystery novel, *The Other Woman* (1917), in collaboration with John Ulrich Giesy. In 1919 Cohen began a long, successful career as a playwright, writing *The Crimson Alibi* in 1919, *The Scourge, Come Seven,* and *Shadows* in 1920, and *Every Saturday Night* in 1921. *The Crimson Alibi* was produced on Broadway in 1919 and *Come Seven* in 1920.

Cohen's most successful literary creations were a series of innocent Southern blacks, among them the dignified Florian Slappey, lawyer Evans Chew, and the Pullman porter–philosopher Epic Peters, who appeared in 250 stories. He also created a popular detective, the fat, semiliterate Jim Hanvey, a favorite of the late "S. S. Van Dine" (pseudonym of Willard Huntington Wright). Together, these characters and others

populated Cohen's stories in *The Saturday Evening Post;* they were the subjects of many of his novels and collections of short stories in the 1920's and 1930's, and they remain his most original creations. Unfortunately they have been so frequently plagiarized in whole or in part that they seem less original than they otherwise would have seemed today.

Between 1920 and 1950, Cohen published at least one book almost every year (and, in some years, as many as three). His books include *Six Seconds of Darkness* (1921), *Jim Hanvey, Detective* (1923), *The Iron Chalice* (1925), *The Outer Gate* (1927), *The Backstage Mystery* (1930), *Transient Lady* (1934), and *Child of Evil* (1936), popular mysteries; and *Highly Colored* (1921), *Assorted Chocolates* (1922), *Florian Slappey Goes Abroad* (1928), *Epic Peters, Pullman Porter* (1930), and *Florian Slappey* (1938), all of which are adventures of his popular black characters. *Kid Tinsel* (1941) was the first in a series of sophisticated mysteries that constitute what will probably prove to be his most durable work; others include *Lady in Armor* (1941), *Sound of Revelry* (1943), and *Dangerous Lady* (1946). Many of these works were made into films. In 1945–1946 he was a writer for the popular "Amos 'n' Andy" radio series. *Borrasca* (1953), a historical novel set in Virginia City, Nev., during the Comstock Lode boom of the early 1870's, was his only major departure from his usual subject matters.

Cohen's popularity remained great throughout his writing career. He adapted to a succession of popular media, moving first to New York and then to Los Angeles. But much of his subject matter (particularly his stories of black life in the South and his detective fiction) was drawn from his South Carolina youth and his apprenticeship careers. However, it has lost its appeal in a more complex age than that between the world wars, and his stories of Southern blacks may be considered offensive, much in the way that Amos 'n' Andy, who entertained a more simplistic America for a generation, have been rejected in the course of black liberation. But Cohen's blacks, however stereotyped, were never viciously or maliciously portrayed. His treatment, if condescending, was always affectionate.

Cohen has received almost no serious critical treatment, although Birmingham-Southern College awarded him an honorary Litt. D. in 1927 for his services to Southern literature. There is little likelihood that his critical reputation will improve, although his work gives valuable insights into

American popular values and tastes during the first half of the twentieth century. He died in Los Angeles, Calif.

[Cohen's other works include *Romance in the First Degree* (1944); *Danger in Paradise* (1945); *Love Has No Alibi* (1946); *Don't Ever Love Me* (1947); *More Beautiful Than Murder* (1948); *My Love Wears Black* (1948); *A Bullet for My Love* (1950); and *Love Can Be Dangerous* (1955). There is no full-length study of his life or work. He wrote one autobiographical article, "The Woman Who Changed My Life," *American Magazine*, July, 1954. See also *Twentieth Century Authors* (1942); *Twentieth Century Authors Supplement* (1955); and the obituary notice, *New York Times*, Jan 7, 1959. There is a collection of his letters at the University of Oregon Library.]

DAVID D. ANDERSON

COHN, ALFRED EINSTEIN (Apr. 16, 1879–July 20, 1957), physician, was born in New York City, the son of Abraham Cohn and Maimie Einstein. His father was a wealthy tobacco merchant who, although his business interests were centered in Georgia, spent much of his time in New York. The family had literary, artistic, and intellectual interests; Cohn's younger brother, Edwin Joseph, became a distinguished chemist. Cohn was educated at Columbia University (A.B., 1900; M.D., 1904) and served a three-year internship at Mount Sinai Hospital in New York. From 1907 to 1909 he studied with Wilhelm Trendelenberg and Ludwig Aschoff in Freiburg, and with James Mackenzie and Thomas Lewis in London. Willem Einthoven's introduction of the string galvanometer had made electrocardiography an exciting new technique in medicine; Cohn helped Lewis set up a string galvanometer at University College in London.

The first electrocardiograph in the western hemisphere was that brought to New York by Cohn in August 1909 and was used by him at Mount Sinai Hospital until 1911, when he brought it to the Rockefeller Institute for Medical Research. It is now part of the George E. Burch Collection in New Orleans. The first string galvanometer for use in electrocardiography that was manufactured in the United States was made for Cohn in 1915, and is now in the Smithsonian Institution.

On Apr. 24, 1911, Cohn married Ruth Walker Price, the daughter of Edward A. Price, a prosperous New York merchant; they had no children. Cohn joined the staff of the Rockefeller Institute for Medical Research in 1911, became a member in 1920, and retired in 1944.

Besides being an early worker in the field of electrocardiography and an early specialist in diseases of the cardiovascular system, Cohn was even more influential as a teacher. Among the men influenced by him were Carl A. L. Binger, Robert L. Levy (with whom Cohn published important studies of quinidine), Harold J. Stewart, the physician and psychologist Henry A. Murray, J. Murray Steele, A. Garrod Macleod, Henry A. Schroeder, Alfred E. Mirsky, and George E. Burch. Burch said of Cohn that although he "did little electrocardiographic research, he influenced others to work in the field and helped to demonstrate to the medical public in this country the clinical usefulness of the electrocardiograph." Burch has told me in correspondence that Cohn was important both as one of the earliest American physicians to devote himself wholly to clinical research—"he began his work at the turn of the century when clinical research was non-existent"—and as a physician who could encourage young men to take up such research.

Throughout his career Cohn participated in medical organizations and in public affairs. He was an early member of the Association for Prevention of Heart Disease (later the New York Heart Association, which formed a model for the American Heart Association). He was active in the New York Tuberculosis and Health Association, and was for many years an adviser to the Carnegie Corporation, the China Medical Board of the Rockefeller Foundation, the Veterans Administration, and the New York Academy of Medicine. His interest in public health was reflected in an important study written with Claire Lingg, *The Burden of Diseases in the United States* (1950). In the 1930's and 1940's Cohn participated in many projects designed to help refugees, including the American Committee for Emigré Scholars, Writers and Artists (now the American Council for Emigrés in the Professions). That work brought him into close contact with many eminent figures, including Dr. George Baehr, Eleanor Roosevelt, and Edward R. Murrow. Cohn was also a longtime and close friend of Justice Felix Frankfurter.

In addition to his publications in scientific and medical journals, Cohn wrote essays on medicine and society, on the history of medicine, and on art and its relation to medicine and science. These essays were collected as *Medicine, Science and Art* (1931) and *No Retreat From Reason* (1948). A single long essay was published as *Minerva's Progress* (1946). Cohn was a collector of art and a bibliophile; his working collection of scientific and medical books and his large general library are preserved in the Cohn Library of the Rockefeller University. He died in New Milford, Conn.

[I have used material from George W. Corner, *A History of the Rockefeller Institute* (1964), and George E. Burch and Nicholas P. De Pasquale, *A History of Electrocardiography* (1964), which contains a portrait of Cohn. Aspects of Cohn's life and work were discussed with Walther Goebel, Rebecca Lancefield, and Maclyn McCarty of the Rockefeller University; with Mrs. Alfred E. Mirsky, librarian, and Ruth Sternfeld, archivist, of the Rockefeller University; and with George E. Burch, Tulane University. Cohn's papers, which are extensive and apparently intact, are preserved in the archives of the Rockefeller University.]

PAUL F. CRANEFIELD

COHN, HARRY (July 23, 1891–Feb. 27, 1958), motion picture producer, was born in New York City, the son of Joseph Cohn and Bella Hudesman. His father, a tailor, emigrated from Germany and his mother from a village in Russia. Cohn grew up in a four-room apartment in Manhattan with his parents, grandmothers, and three brothers. After leaving school at the age of fifteen, he worked as a pool-hall hustler, streetcar conductor, fur salesman, shipping clerk, and song plugger for a music publisher.

In 1913 Cohn entered the motion picture industry as producer of short films for music publishers and in 1918 was hired as West Coast secretary to Carl Laemmle, an early producer for whom his brother Jack worked. In 1920 he founded the C.B.C. Film Sales Corporation with Jack Cohn and Joe Brandt, and established a studio in Hollywood on Sunset Boulevard, an area known as "Poverty Row." They released a series of two-reelers called *Screen Snapshots* (1922–1923), short subjects showing movie stars in their leisure time, and *The Hall Room Boys,* based on a vaudeville routine and comic strip. With an investment of $20,000, Cohn produced C.B.C.'s first feature film, *More to Be Pitied Than Scorned* (1922); the investment returned $130,000. Tired of hearing the company referred to as Corned Beef and Cabbage, the proprietors changed the name to Columbia Pictures in January 1924. Cohn served as vice-president from 1924 to 1932 and as president from 1932 until his death.

Volatile and competitive, Cohn was a man of strong physical presence and dictatorial ways who typified the popular image of a movie mogul of the 1920's. He is credited with the phrase, "I don't have ulcers, I give them." Although many feared him as an abusive tyrant, he was nevertheless a man of parts. His defenders claimed that he could be surprisingly kind, citing chapter and verse. The screenwriter Dore Schary called him "brash, vulgar, and interesting." Throughout his career, Cohn maintained a concept of high quality in motion picture production. He placed particular emphasis upon the story as the foundation of the film. As a production manager he was imaginative, but he carefully employed cost-cutting techniques to reduce waste. Although instrumental in promoting many actors and actresses—including William Holden, Rita Hayworth, Kim Novak, and Jack Lemmon—to stardom, he did not have an expensive stable of stars. He frequently obtained a performer under a loan agreement with another studio. Cohn's first big success was *The Blood Ship* (1927). The same year he selected Frank Capra to direct *That Certain Thing* because his name was at the head of an alphabetical list of available directors. The picture was a financial success and marked the beginning of a mutually profitable relationship between Cohn and Capra.

Cohn assigned Capra to take over the direction of *Submarine,* an ailing sound production that had been budgeted at $150,000, a huge sum for Columbia at that time. The warm public reception for the film, which starred Ralph Graves and Jack Holt, increased Columbia's earnings from eighty-one cents per share in 1927 to $1.27 per share in 1928, and Cohn's personal share took him into the higher income brackets. Capra directed Jack Holt in *Flight* (1929) and *Dirigible* (1931), which followed the same pattern of adventure and suspense.

Cohn then gave Capra a loose rein in direction that resulted in a number of outstanding films. Among them were *Lady for a Day* (1933), a smash hit that received four Academy Award nominations, and *It Happened One Night* (1934), with Clark Gable and Claudette Colbert, which won five Academy Awards. After this extraordinary success, Cohn and Columbia were no longer considered a part of Poverty Row. Other Cohn and Capra pictures were *Mr. Deeds Goes to Town* (1936), starring Gary Cooper and Jean Arthur, *Lost Horizon* (1937) with Ronald Colman, and *You Can't Take It With You* (1938) and *Mr. Smith Goes to Washington* (1939), both starring James Stewart and Jean Arthur. Capra said of Cohn, "He was the toughest man I ever met," but in each of these productions Cohn stood behind Capra and risked his money and reputation. Cohn also attracted other first-rate directors. Among them were John Ford (*The Whole Town's Talking* [1935]), Leo McCarey (*The Awful Truth* [1937]), and George Cukor (*Holiday* [1938]). In July 1941 Cohn divorced Rose Barker Cromwell, whom he had married on Sept. 18, 1923, and married Elizabeth Miller, an actress known as Joan Perry; they had three children.

Since Columbia had never owned theaters, it was not hampered by unprofitable real estate investments when television began to pose a serious threat to the motion picture industry after World War II. Cohn continued to produce successful films, resisting coarseness, nudity, and revealing costumes. He had refused to spend vast sums of money on musical extravaganzas, but changed his policy with the advent of color film in the 1940's. Among Columbia's later productions were *You Were Never Lovelier* (1942) with Fred Astaire and Rita Hayworth, *Picnic* (1956), and *The Bridge on the River Kwai* (1957). Despite Cohn's autocratic management, the atmosphere at Columbia was less structured than that of larger studios and there was less fragmentation of duties, a policy that apparently stimulated creativity. A skillful judge of stories, stars, and directors, Cohn built Columbia Pictures amid fierce competition to become a respected multimillion-dollar motion picture company. He died in Phoenix, Ariz.

[See Frank Capra, *The Name Above the Title* (1971); Rochelle Larkin, *Hail Columbia* (1975); Bob Thomas, *King Cohn* (1967); and Norman Zierold, *The Moguls* (1969).]

ERNEST A. MCKAY

COLMAN, RONALD CHARLES (Feb. 9, 1891–May 19, 1958), actor, was born in Richmond, Surrey, England, the son of Charles Colman, a silk importer, and Marjory Read Fraser. Colman grew up in a large and fairly prosperous family and prepared for Oxford at the Hadley School at Littlehampton, Sussex. He dreamed of being an engineer and was active in school theatricals; but all thoughts of university ended in his sixteenth year with the sudden death of his father, which cut off much of the family's income. He went to work for a London steamship company and rose quickly from office boy to junior accountant while establishing himself as a performer

with the Bancroft Amateur Dramatic Society and occasionally playing the banjo with a "concert party." At the age of eighteen, he completed this portrait of an Edwardian young man by joining an exclusive regiment, the London Scottish Regional Guards (his mother was Scottish).

Colman's brigade of volunteers was among the first British Expeditionary Forces sent into France in 1914. Out of England only two months, he saw action at Ypres, was wounded at Messines, and was decorated and medically discharged in May 1915. Although he rarely talked of his experiences in the war, they influenced some of his best screen performances.

Back in London, Colman discussed a post in the Orient with an uncle in the Foreign Service, but, while waiting for the appointment, he was cast in his first professional part—mute and in blackface—as an Indian herald, waving a flag and blowing a trumpet, in *The Maharani of Arakan*. Next, he was given a bit part by Gladys Cooper in *The Misleading Lady* (1916); and despite some embarrassing clumsiness in rehearsals, he was encouraged enough by a review to decide against a diplomatic career.

His first success, the following year, was as the young syphilitic husband in *Damaged Goods*. This first, daring discussion of the subject on the London stage packed the house for several months before it was closed by German zeppelin bombings. A number of minor plays and not very satisfying films followed. In several of these Colman was cast in Jewish parts, as his dark appearance continued to register as "foreign."

On Sept. 18, 1920, he married the actress Thelma Raye, with whom he had been living. Having decided to try the Broadway stage, he sailed for New York a month later. He survived on "dishwashing jobs and a diet of soup and rice pudding" until his first walk-ons. He then played a bit part in the Philadelphia run of George Arliss' highly successful *The Green Goddess*, but was replaced after only one week on Broadway. In 1922 he toured for seven months in Fay Bainter's hit *East Is West* and was cast—and then dropped—from Somerset Maugham's *East of Suez*. His appearance as the "other man" in Ruth Chatterton's production of Bataille's *La Tendresse* (1922) was his first and last major role in a Broadway hit.

Film director Henry King offered Colman the role of Lillian Gish's lover in her first independent production, *The White Sister,* to be filmed in Italy. On location Thelma Colman seemed unable to cope with her husband's sudden success, and quarrels led to a separation that lasted until 1935, when they were divorced.

The White Sister (1923), a brilliant success, led Samuel Goldwyn to cable a contract offer to Colman, on location again in Italy with King and Lillian Gish. Upon the completion of *Romola* (1925), Colman came to Hollywood. From his arrival in mid-1924 to the end of 1925, he made nine films, including *The Dark Angel*, his first starring vehicle and the first in a series of love stories in which he was paired with Goldwyn's Hungarian discovery, Vilma Banky. The 1925 list also includes *Stella Dallas* and Ernst Lubitsch's version of *Lady Windermere's Fan*—wordless Oscar Wilde! There were only three Colman films in 1926, including the classic *Beau Geste*. From then on, he would make only one or two films annually.

The transition to sound was easy for Colman, and his first "talkie" was *Bulldog Drummond* (1929). Notable among his subsequent films were *Arrowsmith* (1931) with Helen Hayes, which Colman long regarded as his finest, and a series in which his special personality appeared most fully: *A Tale of Two Cities* (1935), *Lost Horizon* and *The Prisoner of Zenda* (1937), *If I Were King* (1938), *The Light That Failed* (1939), and *Random Harvest* (1942). *The Late George Apley* and an Academy Award for best actor in *A Double Life* came in 1947. His last full-length role was in *Champagne for Caesar* (1950).

Colman married Benita Hume on Sept. 30, 1938; they had one daughter. In 1950 the Colmans starred as a college professor and his wife in a popular radio series, *The Halls of Ivy*, which ran two years. A 1955 attempt at a television version lasted only one season. One of his last film appearances, ironically, brought him back to his beginnings: in *Around the World in 80 Days* (1956) he played a cameo role as an Indian train conductor. He died in Santa Barbara, Calif.

Colman's most memorable performances gained depth and resonance from his own experiences. In *The Dark Angel* as a blinded soldier and in *Random Harvest* as a shell-shocked amnesiac, the veteran of the British Expeditionary Force created poignant portraits of soldier-victims of his generation. In *Lost Horizon* the actor who had once contemplated a diplomatic career personified for all time the unique scholar-diplomat-adventurer chosen to rule Shangri-La. To *Beau Geste, A Tale of Two Cities,* and *The Prisoner of Zenda* he brought Edwardian convictions about

honor and *noblesse oblige* tinged with just enough ironic humor to make those old-fashioned notions acceptable. This ability to create memorable characters who were also unique reflections of himself was epitomized by *A Double Life,* in which he realistically portrayed an actor who actually became the characters he played. The role was a metaphoric image of Ronald Colman's art.

[Juliet Benita Colman, *Ronald Colman, A Very Private Person* (1975), his daughter's well-researched and affectionate biography, includes insights not available elsewhere and photographs from all stages of Colman's career.]

DANIEL S. KREMPEL

COMISKEY, GRACE ELIZABETH REIDY (May 15, 1893–Dec. 10, 1956), owner of the Chicago White Sox baseball team, was born in Chicago, Ill., one of three daughters of Elizabeth and Thomas Reidy, a route supervisor for the Chicago Rapid Transit Company. All the daughters married executives of the Chicago White Sox. After graduating from high school, she worked as a dental technician until 1913, when she married John Louis Comiskey, the son of Charles Albert Comiskey, a celebrated baseball player who owned the Chicago White Sox. The couple honeymooned as members of the 1913–1914 world-touring White Sox and New York Giants baseball expedition organized and led by the elder Comiskey and by John McGraw.

As heir apparent to the Comiskey franchise, Grace's husband long labored in the shadow of his famed father. His duties included running a soft-drink bottling plant under a wing of the grandstand at Comiskey Park and handling sales during games. From 1913 to 1920 the elder Comiskey ran the club, sharing administrative duties with Harry Grabiner. The White Sox were a power in the American League until the "Black Sox" scandal of 1920 ended their reign and, by banning players under suspicion, reduced them to second-rate status. From then until the elder Comiskey's death in 1931, the White Sox were a pinchpenny club of flagging fortunes.

In 1931 J. Louis Comiskey became owner and attempted to restore the club's fortunes by purchasing star players. But he was corpulent and ailing and delegated decision-making to Grabiner and to the team manager, Jimmy Dykes. Comiskey's major achievements were rebuilding the team into a contender and equiping Comiskey Park for night games.

While her father-in-law and husband lived, Grace Comiskey had little to do with club operations. She had three children, one of whom, Dorothy, served as club secretary beginning in 1937 and became club treasurer two years later. Dorothy married White Sox pitcher John Rigney, who retired from active play in 1947 and joined the front office, rising to vice-president.

J. Louis Comiskey died in 1939, and Grace Comiskey became the first woman club owner in American league history and the second in major league baseball history. "There must always be a Comiskey at the head of the White Sox," she said. "My son Charley, grandson of the founder of the White Sox, will be fully fitted to operate the franchise when he reaches the proper age."

But keeping the team in the family was no easy task, since her husband had not authorized her to take over management. In 1940 she went to court to challenge the right of the First National Bank of Chicago, trustees of her husband's will, to sell the club, which it considered a poor investment. When Grace Comiskey blocked a forced sale, the bank withdrew, and in 1941 she gained control on behalf of her children.

In 1945 Grace Comiskey ousted general manager Grabiner after he and Bill Veeck sought to purchase the club. When Grabiner's replacement resigned after a brief tenure, she brought in Frank Lane as general manager. Lane's successful trades boosted the team's performance and increased attendance. Although the White Sox won no championship during Grace Comiskey's tenure, hers was a profitable, contending franchise. And, unlike a new breed of baseball owners whose lucrative outside business interests supported their baseball ventures, she depended entirely on baseball income. During her tenure the club was valued at $3 million.

Harassed by her son's impatient demands to take full control, Grace Comiskey determined to place the club in the hands of her daughter, Dorothy, who had twenty years' experience in its administration. This strategy was accomplished by her bequeathing 500 shares of club stock to Dorothy, before dividing the bulk of the stock equally between Dorothy and Charles.

Grace Comiskey died in Chicago. Her will, which gave 54 percent ownership to her daughter, was contested by her son in a series of lawsuits. In 1958, wearied by her brother's continuing opposition, Dorothy sought to sell him the club, but

his offer of $1.7 million was exceeded by a $2.7 million offer from a syndicate headed by Bill Veeck, Hank Greenberg, and Arthur Allyn, Jr. When Charles failed to match the higher offer, Dorothy sold her shares to the Veeck syndicate on Mar. 10, 1959. That year, under Veeck's dynamic leadership, the White Sox won their first pennant in forty years. But it was not a Comiskey triumph. In 1962 Charles Comiskey sold his stock to an outsider, Arthur Allyn, Jr., who earlier had bought out Veeck. Control of the White Sox then passed out of Comiskey hands.

[No biography of Grace R. Comiskey or her husband John Louis Comiskey exists. An extensive clipping file on the Comiskeys and on the White Sox, including photographs and major obituaries, is in the Baseball Hall of Fame Library at Cooperstown, N.Y. Dave Condon's *The Go Go Chicago White Sox* (1960), dedicated to Grace Comiskey, offers a limited account of her career as White Sox owner. More candid glimpses into the Comiskey era of club ownership may be found in two books by Bill Veeck (written with Ed Linn): *Veeck As in Wreck* (1962), which covers the Comiskey era, detailing how the family lost control; and *The Hustler's Handbook* (1965), in which the completion of Arthur Allyn's purchase is described.]

DAVID QUENTIN VOIGT

COOKE, MORRIS LLEWELLYN (May 11, 1872–Mar. 5, 1960), consultant engineer in scientific management and progressive reformer, was born in Carlisle, Pa., the son of William Harvey Cooke, a doctor, and Elizabeth Richmond Marsden. He attended Lehigh Preparatory School and Lehigh University, graduating in 1895 with a degree in mechanical engineering. After an apprenticeship at Cramp's Shipyard in Philadelphia and work in various companies—interrupted by a term in the navy during the Spanish-American War—he rose to executive positions, primarily in printing firms, and practiced as a management consultant.

On June 16, 1900, he married Eleanor Bushnell Davis; they had no children. With her encouragement Cooke threw his energy into a variety of projects, in which he sought to fulfill what he regarded as the duty of all engineers—to utilize their knowledge for the public welfare. He found inspiration in the principles of scientific management developed by Frederick W. Taylor. "There is a philosophy and an art and a science of human labor," he wrote in 1913. Engineers were to organize effort towards greater production, for only an economy of abundance would permit humanity to move toward social justice and moral advancement. Like Robert O. Valentine and Harlow S. Person, Cooke developed a progressive interpretation of scientific management. He came to believe that collective bargaining was a necessity; and he sharply distinguished business from engineering. Although never an advocate of public ownership, he insisted that government must direct the uses of science and technology for the benefit of all.

Cooke, a Progressive Republican, served in the Blankenburg reform administration of Philadelphia (1911-1915), as director of public works; he led a fight against the Philadelphia Electric Company, which focused his attention on the issue of electric rates and monopoly power.

After serving on the United States Shipping Board during World War I, Cooke campaigned to develop further uses of electricity and to control the utility holding companies. In 1925, for Pennsylvania Governor Gifford Pinchot, he formulated a "Giant Power" plan for a state-directed reorganization of the electric industry, providing for mine-mouth generating plants, long-distance transmission lines, rural electrification, and continuing oversight by public boards. After Governor Franklin D. Roosevelt appointed him to the Power Authority of the State of New York in 1931, he became a strong supporter of Roosevelt.

During the New Deal, Cooke advised the Tennessee Valley Authority, organized conferences, and chaired study committees. When Roosevelt appointed him to head the Mississippi Valley Committee, in the Public Works Administration, he tried to order the task so that "as it goes forward it should secure the outlines of an ultimate planning agency for the nation as a whole." In its report in December 1934, the committee proposed that the federal government establish a many-faceted program for the watershed, dealing with soil erosion, public works, hydropower, and rural electrification. Cooke also favored federal reforms of land use (1936).

In 1934 Roosevelt appointed him to a national power policy committee that was to draw up legislation on holding companies. Although it outlined what became the Public Utility Holding Company Act of 1935, the group, to Cooke's disappointment, never formulated a general policy.

Perhaps Cooke's most significant achievement came in 1935, when he prevailed upon Roosevelt to set up the Rural Electrification Administration (REA). As director, Cooke was to lend money to groups that would construct lines and distribute current. At first it was unclear who these recipients should be, but rural cooperatives emerged as affective agencies, and REA successes stimulated the electric companies to extend their own lines to the countryside.

As administrator Cooke sometimes lacked decisiveness. His faith in technology led him to take an apolitical stance that disturbed those fellow liberals who, like his successor John Carmody, regarded private utility officials as "skunks on principle." Yet it was Cooke, more than any other individual, who created the REA. He resigned his post in March 1937.

During World War II, Cooke negotiated the settlement of an oil dispute with Mexico. He also headed a mission to survey the resources of Brazil. In 1950 President Harry S. Truman appointed him chairman of the President's Water Resources Policy Commission. Its report (1950) called for national watershed planning, to be coordinated by an overall board of review, but Truman rejected the highly controversial recommendations. This was Cooke's last official post. He died in Philadelphia, Pa.

Like many other Progressives and New Dealers, Cooke believed deeply in the benefits of technology and of government planning. He was primarily a disseminator of ideas, but in the long run he greatly contributed to the movement for public control of resources and of the environment.

[The Cooke Papers are in the Roosevelt Library, Hyde Park, N.Y. Cooke's works include *Our Cities Awake* (1919); "On Water Planning for the Nation," *Journal of the American Water Works Association,* 27 (Aug. 1935); "Professional Ethics and Social Change," *Advanced Management,* 11 (Sept. 1946); "Plain Talk About a Missouri Valley Authority," *Iowa Law Review,* 32 (Jan. 1947); "The Early Days of the Rural Electrification Idea: 1914–1936," *American Political Science Review,* 42 (June 1948); and, with Philip Murray, *Organized Labor and Production: Next Steps in Industrial Democracy* (1940).

There are two biographies: Kenneth E. Trombley, *The Life and Times of a Happy Liberal: A Biography of Morris Llewellyn Cooke* (1954); and Jean Christie, "Morris Llewellyn Cooke: Progressive Engineer" (Ph.D. diss., Columbia University, 1963). See also Jean Christie, "The Mississippi Valley Committee: Conservation and Planning in the Early New Deal," *Historian,* 32 (May 1970) and "Giant Power: A Progressive Proposal of the Nineteen-Twenties,"

Pennsylvania Magazine of History and Biography, 96 (Oct. 1972); and the obituary notice in the *New York Times,* Mar. 6, 1960.]

JEAN CHRISTIE

COOKE, ROBERT ANDERSON (Aug. 17, 1880–May 7, 1960), physician, was born in Holmdel, N.J., the son of Henry Gansevoort Cooke, a third-generation physician, and Maria Cowdrey. His early education was provided at the family farm in Holmdel by a governess. He then attended Rutgers Preparatory School in New Brunswick and received the A.B. in 1900 from Rutgers College. In 1904 he earned the M.D. from the College of Physicians and Surgeons, Columbia University, and the A.M. from Rutgers. He was awarded a D.Sc. in 1925 by Rutgers.

Cooke had suffered from allergy since childhood. On the farm he had severe asthma attacks after contact with horses or other animals. During his internship at Presbyterian Hospital in New York (1905–07), his own condition focused his attention on allergy problems. Assigned to ride horse-drawn ambulances, he suffered an asthmatic attack after each call. In 1908, having been exposed to diphtheria, he received a shot of antitoxin produced in horse serum. He immediately felt hot and dizzy, his face and arms swelled, and he gasped for breath. Only prompt Adrenalin injection saved him from death by anaphylactic shock.

By 1910 Cooke had decided to devote his career to the study and treatment of allergy. At that time allergic reactions were believed due to poisons in the substances to which the individual had been exposed, and no treatment was available. Cooke rejected this view, observing that some persons reacted to horse serum extracts, pollens, certain foods, or other substances, while others were not sensitive to them. In his practice he sought patients suffering from asthma and hay fever. He developed methods of testing for allergy and treated symptoms by neutralization of allergic reactions.

In February 1919 Cooke founded and directed the first clinic for allergic diseases at New York Hospital. From 1920 to 1940 he was assistant professor of immunology and then of clinical medicine at Cornell University Medical College. In 1932 he moved his allergy clinic, by then world-renowned, to Roosevelt Hospital, where he became director of the Department of Allergy. In 1949 Cooke assumed directorship of the new

Robert A. Cooke Institute of Allergy, named in honor of his outstanding work in the field.

Beginning with an early published paper, "The Treatment of Hay Fever by Active Immunization" (1915), Cooke engaged in basic research and experimentation in immunology, making important contributions to knowledge of the nature and treatment of allergies. While pursuing his interest in hay fever and asthma, he also dealt with such other aspects of hypersensitivity as allergic reactions to specific foods.

Cooke developed the first treatment for desensitization for hay fever. He believed that multiple shots of desensitizing extracts created immunity, and he was the first to demonstrate the development of a blocking antibody after desensitization. As physicians began treating allergies, Cooke tackled the problem of standardizing dosage. Practitioners agreed that the higher the dose administered, the better the results; but in the early years of allergy treatment, doses were not uniform in strength, and it was unsafe to administer greater quantities. Cooke promoted the view that doses of extract should be standardized and was responsible for the protein nitrogen unit used in such standardization. His studies of family incidence of hay fever showed the importance of hereditary factors in allergy. He also sought to understand nonallergic asthma and demonstrated that some cases were not caused by substances revealed by skin tests.

Some of Cooke's findings were controversial and were disputed by other investigators. Cooke and Mary Loveless demonstrated antibody development after multiple shots but disagreed over the nature of the antibody. Allergists accepted Cooke's view on the importance of standardizing doses for desensitization, but not all agreed with him on the proper size of a standard dose. While Cooke favored the use of interdermal skin tests to determine hypersensitivity, others preferred scratch tests. In his basic research on the nature of allergy, Cooke established rigorous scientific principles in a newly emerging field. He published more than 120 articles and essays. His book, *Allergy in Theory and Practice* (1947), was long the standard text.

Cooke worked to establish the field of allergy as a medical specialty. In 1923 he founded the American Society for the Study of Allergy and Allied Conditions (now the American Academy of Allergy) and was its first president. He was founder and chairman, in 1938, of the Association of Allergy Clinics of Greater New York.

Beginning in 1930 he was active in the American College of Physicians as governor, regent, and vice-president successively, and was elected fellow and master. He was also elected a fellow of the American Medical Association and of the New York Academy of Medicine. He trained a generation of allergists who demonstrated their high esteem and respect for him when they established the Robert A. Cooke Institute of Allergy Alumni Association in 1958. This group sponsors an annual memorial lecture given at the meeting of the American Academy of Allergy.

Cooke married Florence Rogers in 1916. They had one son before their divorce in 1926. Cooke married A. Louise Hegan on Apr. 18, 1929; she died in 1947. In 1950 he married Marie McNally Salman. He was able to treat his own allergy sufficiently so that he could raise purebred Angus cattle at Hockhockson Farm in Colts Neck, N.J., a family property since 1789. He applied the same high standards of achievement in this endeavor as in medicine, founding the New Jersey Aberdeen-Angus Breeders Association in 1938.

[Many of Cooke's articles are cited in his *Allergy in Theory and Practice* (1947); see also *Index Medicus*. On his life and work, see *Time*, Mar. 10, 1958; *Journal of the American Medical Association*, July 2, 1960; and Max Samter, ed., *Excerpts From Classics in Allergy* (1969).]

ADELE HAST

COOLIDGE, THOMAS JEFFERSON (Sept. 17, 1893–Aug. 6, 1959), financier and government official, was born in Manchester, Mass., the son of Thomas Jefferson Coolidge and Clara Amory. He attended St. Mark's School in Southborough, Mass., and Harvard College, from which he was graduated with the B.A. in 1915 *magna cum laude* in mathematics. As an undergraduate he combined athletics and scholarship; in November 1914 he was elected to Phi Beta Kappa shortly after he had run ninety-eight yards for a Harvard touchdown in the first Harvard-Yale game to be played in the Yale Bowl.

In 1916 Coolidge served for a few months on the Mexican border as a sergeant with the Headquarters Company of the 101st Massachusetts Field Artillery. When the United States entered the war, he was transferred to the Plattsburgh, N.Y., Training Camp and commissioned captain. He served in France as battery commander and regimental adjutant in the 302nd Field Artillery and was promoted to major.

After returning to Boston, he joined the Old Colony Trust Company (founded by his father in 1890 and merged in 1929 with the First National Bank of Boston), of which he became chairman of the trust committee in 1940. He was for a time chairman of the board of the United Fruit Company, a director and member of the executive committee of the Boston Edison Company, and a director of the First National Bank of Boston and the New England Mutual Life Insurance Company.

In 1921 Coolidge became a trustee of the Boston Museum of Fine Arts; when he was elected president of the board in 1925 he was the youngest ever to hold that office. During his nine-year administration a wing for European decorative arts was added and a new building constructed for the museum school. He was averse, however, particularly during the Great Depression, to making further additions to the plant, for he was more concerned with improving the quality of the collections than adding to the number of exhibits. On Aug. 20, 1927, Coolidge married Catherine Hill Kuhn of San Mateo, Calif. They had three children.

Coolidge was called to Washington in March 1934 as special assistant in charge of fiscal affairs to Secretary of the Treasury Henry Morgenthau, Jr. In October of that year, when he became undersecretary of the treasury, he resigned as president of the Museum of Fine Arts. His mastery of foreign exchange, reserves, refunding operations, and the like made him invaluable in that post, but he was not happy with the New Deal and resigned fifteen months later. In his twenty-fifth anniversary Harvard class report he wrote: "In political beliefs I am a very old-fashioned liberal, not recognized today, who believes that government powers should not be centralized in Washington and that the country will be happier, more prosperous and will better retain its democratic form of government if the individual affairs of the citizens are managed locally under State laws with the Federal government handling the foreign affairs with wisdom." Some of Coolidge's friends would have categorized him as an "arch conservative" rather than an "old-fashioned liberal" and felt that, notwithstanding his great admiration for his ancestor Thomas Jefferson, he might on occasion have agreed with the views of Alexander Hamilton.

Despite his disagreements with the New Deal, in October 1937 Coolidge was appointed United

States representative on the financial committee of the League of Nations by Secretary of State Cordell Hull. A decade later he was named chairman of the Committee on Federal-State Relations of the Hoover Commission on Organization of the Executive Branch of the Government.

Coolidge served as an overseer of Harvard from 1926 to 1932. He was a trustee of the Isabella Stewart Gardner Museum and of the Peter Bent Brigham Hospital, to which he gave $1 million shortly before his death, with the request that it be kept anonymous. In 1958 he gave the Massachusetts Historical Society 282 manuscripts to be added to the Thomas Jefferson Papers that his grandfather had given in 1898.

Although tall and extremely handsome, Coolidge was modest and shy. He did not say much unless he fell into discussing a subject on which he had strong opinions. After his death, in Beverly, Mass., Arthur Krock of the *New York Times* wrote: "He was a rock of basic constitutional principles as Jefferson conceived them to be in the structure of this Republic. His integrity was flawless; his moral and physical courage unwavering; his personal loyalties discriminating but abiding; his charm and humor as exceptional as his good looks; his intelligence high, his capacity great for any task he assumed; and his companionship a source of joy to those privileged to have it. Moreover, he had the rare quality of objective self-analysis, the more unusual because his prejudices were strong. In me he inspired one of the greatest affections and admirations I have ever felt for anyone."

[Memoir by Frederick J. Bradlee in Massachusetts Historical Society, *Proceedings*, LXII (1957–1960), 373–378. Reports of the Harvard class of 1915; Walter Muir Whitehill, *Museum of Fine Arts Boston: A Centennial History* (1970).

Coolidge published "We Are a Fortunate People," *Saturday Evening Post*, Sept. 19, 1936, and in 1941 privately printed a series of speeches and articles arguing against centralization of power under the title *Why Centralized Government?*]

WALTER MUIR WHITEHILL

COOPER, (LEON) JERE (July 20, 1893–Dec. 18, 1957), congressman, was born on a farm in Dyer County, Tenn., the son of Joseph William Cooper and Viola May Hill. The family moved to Dyersburg, the county seat, where his father was employed in the cotton-oil mill. A good student, Cooper worked his way through high school as a grocery delivery boy and clerk and as an apprentice butcher.

In 1914 Cooper received the LL.B. from Cumberland University, a law school in Lebanon, Tenn., requiring a one-year course of study for the degree. He was admitted to the Tennessee bar in 1915 and began to practice in the Dyersburg law office of Ewell Weakley. On June 23, 1917, Cooper enlisted in the Second Infantry Regiment of the Tennessee National Guard. He was commissioned a first lieutenant and transferred, with his company, to Company K of the 119th Infantry, 20th Division of the United States Army, where he saw action in France and Belgium. He was promoted to captain in July 1918 and was discharged on Apr. 2, 1919.

Cooper's political interests were heightened when he returned to resume his law practice. His organization of the local American Legion post led to involvement in state and national Legion affairs. In 1921 he was elected state commander of the Tennessee American Legion, and the following year he served on the National Executive Committee. He was also elected to the Dyersburg City Council and was appointed to the school board. In 1920 he began an eight-year term as city attorney, and in 1924 he managed the successful senatorial campaign of General Lawrence D. Tyson.

In 1928 Cooper trounced four Democratic primary contenders for the ninth District congressional nomination; he went on to defeat his Republican opponent in the November election by 16,967 votes. Cooper represented the ninth District (later the eighth) from 1929 until his death in 1957. As a freshman congressman he was assigned to the Flood Control Committee and later served on the elections and veterans affairs committees.

Cooper married Mary Lucille Rankley, a history teacher, on Dec. 30, 1930; they had one son, who died when he was sixteen. Cooper's wife died on Oct. 2, 1935, and he never remarried.

A vacancy on the House Ways and Means Committee in 1932 led to Cooper's appointment over several senior members. The *New York Times* later described his record as one of "fairly consistent support for New and Fair Deal Measures." He was at the time, however, much less in favor of reform. When the House heard testimony in 1935 on the Rayburn-Wheeler holding bill, which was opposed by the power companies, Cooper charged that the TVA was "distributing propaganda among the schools." He later reversed his position.

In March 1939 Cooper was appointed by Chairman Robert L. Doughton of North Carolina to a special Ways and Means Subcommittee on tax legislation. As the committee's "tax-brain," he persuaded it to adopt a "pay-as-you-go" tax measure. In 1945, as vice-chairman of the congressional committee to investigate the Pearl Harbor disaster, he traveled to Hawaii. In the 81st Congress (1949–1951), he supported the subversive activities control bill; in 1948, and again in 1950, he supported the tidelands oil bill.

Cooper's quiet, careful demeanor led reporters to call him the "Sphynx." *Newsweek* described him as "another party wheelhorse whose slow, verbose questioning of witnesses often resembles a filibuster." Nevertheless, House Speaker Sam Rayburn relied heavily on Cooper as a "Democratic trouble shooter."

On Aug. 10, 1953, President Dwight D. Eisenhower appointed Cooper to a seventeen-member bipartisan committee on foreign economic policy. A month later he urged that the United States move "swiftly to liberalize . . . trade policies and to seek reduction of trade barriers throughout the free world generally to ease the dollar gap." During a 1954 television appearance with leading Democrats, Cooper responded to a plea by Eisenhower for passage of the pending tax law by pledging to seek elimination of a provision giving special advantages to "those fortunate enough to own corporation stock." In the 84th Congress (1955–1957) Cooper rose to Ways and Means chairman and also became chairman of the Democratic Committee on Committees, in which post he influenced the selection of Democrats to serve on other committees. As chairman of the Ways and Means Committee, Cooper fought for a three-year extension of the Reciprocal Trade Program, of which he was a long-time supporter, by advocating the Hull Reciprocal Trade Agreements Act. He also drafted a bill to extend trade agreements and to increase presidential power in tariff regulation.

Cooper died in Dyersburg and was succeeded as chairman of the Ways and Means Committee by Democrat Wilbur D. Mills of Arkansas.

[There is no full-length biography. On his congressional career, see *Time*, May 3, 1943; *New York Times*, Jan. 5, 1955; *Saturday Evening Post*, Jan. 8, 1955; the obituary notice in the *New York Times*, Dec. 19, 1957; and U.S. Congress, *Memorial Services Held in the House of Representatives . . . With Remarks . . . in Eulogy of Jere Cooper* (1958).]

HARVARD SITKOFF

CORI, GERTY THERESA RADNITZ (Aug. 15, 1896–Oct. 26, 1957), biochemist, was born in Prague, Czechoslovakia, the daughter of Otto Radnitz, a sugar refinery operator, and Martha Neustadt. She attended secondary schools in Prague and Tetschen before becoming a medical student at the German University of Prague (Ferdinand University), from which she received an M.D. in 1920. In August of that year she married Carl Ferdinand Cori, a classmate, thus assuring the continuation of a productive scientific collaboration that had started in medical school as a joint research project in immunology. After two years as an assistant at the Karolinen Children's Hospital in Vienna, she joined her husband at the New York State Institute for the Study of Malignant Diseases in Buffalo, where she was assigned first to the pathology department. In 1928 the Coris became American citizens. In 1936 they had a son.

While at Buffalo the Coris concentrated on studying the absorption of sugars from the intestine and the effects of insulin and epinephrine on the fate of the absorbed carbohydrates and on glycogen formation and degradation. Initially, rats were the test animals and observations were made with whole animal preparations. The quantitative care with which the measurements were carried out led to the recognition that lactate produced from glycogen in the muscle could be converted to glucose in the liver, released, and taken up from the blood by the muscle, to be reconverted to glycogen—a phenomenon known as the Cori cycle.

In 1931 Carl Cori was appointed professor of pharmacology at Washington University School of Medicine in Saint Louis, Mo.; Gerty Cori was named research fellow and associate in pharmacology and biochemistry. In 1943 she was appointed associate professor of research and, in 1947, professor of biological chemistry, a position she held until her death.

Before leaving Buffalo the Coris had begun to use isolated muscle preparations and tissue extracts, and had developed a method for the analysis of hexosemonophosphates as barium salts. Because the products were analyzed by two independent means ("reducing power" and organic phosphate), a new phosphorylated intermediate was discovered in 1936, glucose 1-phosphate (the Cori ester). In 1938 they demonstrated the enzymatic conversion of glucose 1-phosphate to glucose 6-phosphate. The enzyme (phosphorylase) that forms the 1-ester from glycogen was discovered and crystallized in 1942. For these studies the Coris were awarded half of the Nobel Prize in physiology and medicine in 1947.

In her Nobel address Gerty Cori pointed out the need to work with extremely pure enzyme preparations if one is to understand an enzyme mechanism and to unravel the events occurring in the whole animal in response to physiological changes. As an example she described the recognition that muscle phosphorylase exists in two forms, a comparison of the distinguishing properties of the two forms, and the in vitro conversion of the active form into the inactive form as well as the in vivo coversion during muscle contraction in animals. Experience gained with muscle was then applied to studies with dialyzed extracts of liver to show that adding glycogen and phosphate to such extracts led to an accumulation of hexosephosphate and glucose, the glucose resulting from a specific glucose 6-phosphatase present in the liver and not in muscle.

The Coris had recognized that a "branching enzyme" was required for the formation of normal glycogen and that a "debranching enzyme" participated with phosphorylase in the complete degradation of tissue glycogen. Attention was turned to a biochemical investigation of the tissues of children storing excessive amounts of glycogen and to the structure of the stored polysaccharide. One group of patients who accumulated large amounts of normal glycogen in the liver was shown to be deficient in glucose 6-phosphatase. The report on this subject (1952) was the first description of an inborn error of metabolism due to the lack of a known tissue enzyme. Since that time several hundred heritable metabolic diseases have been demonstrated, each due to a deficiency of a specific enzyme. A companion paper reported the results of structural studies on glycogen isolated from the livers of ten children with glycogen storage disease. In eight of the cases no abnormality of structure was noted, but the other two cases contained polysaccharides deviating from normal. One was poorly branched and led to a prediction of a deficiency of the branching enzyme; the other polysaccharide resembled a phosphorylase limit dextrin and suggested a deficiency of the debranching enzyme. Both predictions were correct. Glycogenesis due to a

lack of debranching enzyme is frequently called Cori's disease.

Throughout her life Gerty Cori maintained interests in gardening, art, music, and reading, particularly history and biography. She frequently spent summer vacations in the mountains. On such a trip in 1947, to Colorado, she experienced unusual physical difficulty in climbing. It became apparent that her health was impaired. The severe anemia revealed in this way persisted for a decade, during which time she continued work until her death in Saint Louis.

[Cori's writings include a series of scientific papers entitled "The Fate of Sugar in the Animal Body," *Journal of Biological Chemistry* (1925–1928); "Crystalline Muscle Phosphorylase," *ibid.* (Nov. 1943), written with Arda A. Green and Carl F. Cori; "Glucose-6-Phosphatase of the Liver in Glycogen Storage Disease," *ibid.* (Dec. 1952), written with Carl F. Cori; "Glycogen Structure and Enzyme Deficiencies in Glycogen Storage Disease," *Harvey Lectures* (1952–1953); "Amylo-1, 6-Glucosidase in Muscle Tissue in Generalized Glycogen Storage Disease," *Journal of Biological Chemistry* (Jan. 1956); and "Biochemical Aspects of Glycogen Deposition Disease," *Modern Problems in Pediatrics* (1957). On her life and work see B. A. Houssay, "Carl F. and Gerty T. Cori," *Biochimica et biophysica acta* (Apr. 1956); S. Ochoa and H. M. Kalckar, "Gerty T. Cori, Biochemist," *Science* (July 4, 1958); and Carl F. Cori, "The Call of Science," *Annual Review of Biochemistry* (1969).]

BARBARA ILLINGWORTH BROWN

COSTELLO, LOU (Mar. 6, 1906–Mar. 3, 1959), comedian, was born Louis Francis Cristillo in Paterson, N. J. He was the son of Sebastian Cristillo, a weaver in a silk mill and later an insurance salesman, and Helen Rege. Costello's unspectacular school career disappointed his father, but it demonstrated his talent for athletics and comedy. Costello was skilled in basketball, baseball, and later in boxing, which he gave up after fourteen fights. One Halloween he won a prize for impersonating Charlie Chaplin. He was often forced to stay after school and write on the blackboard "I'm a bad boy," a catch phrase that he later incorporated into his radio show.

Costello quit high school and worked in a haberdashery, slaughterhouse, and prize ring, but his restless nature drove him to the West Coast. In 1927, accompanied by a friend, Gene Coogan, he arrived in Hollywood and made the rounds of the studios. He worked as a laborer and then as a studio stunt man, doubling for Dolores Del Rio, in *The Trail of '98*. But while jumping from the second story window of a burning building he was injured, and he decided to further his career in a less dangerous manner. On the way back to the East Coast he appeared in his first comic role, playing a Dutch dialect comedian in St. Joseph, Mo. In the early 1930's Costello traveled the vaudeville circuit, perfecting this routine. He developed his trademarks of a tiny bowler hat; an oversized, unpressed suit; a long jacket that stretched to his knees; and a tie that hung even lower.

The exact date of Costello's meeting with Bud Abbott is not known, but in the early 1930's, John Grant, the producer of Costello's New York City show, suggested Abbott as a new straight man. The two worked well together; Abbott's dapper figure and flat, withering sarcasm was the perfect foil to the stocky Costello, whose shrill cries suggested complete ineptitude. They toured the leading vaudeville theaters, attempting old-fashioned farce and buffoonery. On Jan. 20, 1934, Costello married Anne Battler, a Broadway dancer; they had four children.

Abbott and Costello made the transition to radio in 1938, appearing on the Kate Smith Radio Hour. Their ten-minute guest spot became a regular for the next eighteen months. They acquired their own show in 1941. Abbott and Costello managed to transfer old-style vaudeville slapstick to the radio. They could work without a script by capitalizing on each other's verbal quickness. They developed the successful baseball routine, "Who's on First?" earning as much as $15,000 for a single performance.

The first of Abbott and Costello's thirty-six films was *One Night in the Tropics* (1940), and with their next film, *Buck Privates* (1941), they became a national phenomenon. This film grossed over $10 million, the largest amount earned by Universal Films up to that date.

During the war years their careers reached an apogee, but they continued to make films until 1956. According to Jim Mulholland, author of *The Abbott and Costello Book* (1975), they were the most successful comedy team in motion picture history. In December 1952 they moved to television with the *Abbott and Costello Show*, which ran two seasons on CBS.

Abbott and Costello personally maintained a friendly rivalry, but on several occasions it threatened to end the partnership. They first split up in 1945, but their lawyers prompted a reconciliation. The final breakup came in 1957 because Costello wanted to branch out on his own into dramatic roles.

There is evidence that Costello was never completely satisfied with his image as a clumsy fall guy. He stated that his favorite motion picture role was as Benny Miller in *Little Giant* (1946), because it was the "first time in the story they actually let me win the girl. In all my other pictures my love pretensions were regarded as ridiculous." *Little Giant* is notable because Abbott and Costello attempted to work separately; the film was not a success. Costello also complained that comedians never win Academy Awards: "The best they get is a chance to work for free to liven up the Academy shindig."

Costello had a chance to play a dramatic role when he appeared on television in a *Wagon Train* episode (October 1958), playing the part of a drunken derelict accused of murder. In 1959 his only film without Abbott was released, *The Thirty-Foot Bride of Candy Rock*.

Despite his financial success, Costello claimed that he was not able to save anything. He was plagued by a tax suit, lived lavishly, and gave generously to charity. He and Bud Abbott founded the Lou Costello Jr. Youth Foundation in memory of Costello's only son, who drowned in 1943. Costello died in Los Angeles.

Costello demonstrated a mastery of popular comedy, and he was able to touch the vulnerabilities of a mass audience. Carol Burnett wrote that "Lou Costello is the most underrated comedian of all time."

[On Costello, see articles in the *Saturday Evening Post*, Sept. 28, 1946; the *Los Angeles Daily News*, June 20, 1953; and the *Los Angeles Examiner*, Mar. 4, 1959. Alvin H. Maril's retrospective on the Abbott and Costello partnership is in *Screen Facts*, 1970. See also John T. Weaver, *Forty Years of Screen Credit* (1970); Leslie Halliwell, *Filmgoer's Companion* (1971); Richard J. Anobile, *Who's on First?* (1972); John Dunning, *Tune in Yesterday* (1976); and Bob Thomas, *Bud and Lou* (1977). Clippings of Costello's career and obituary notices are at the Motion Picture Academy of Arts and Sciences, Beverly Hills, Calif.]

STEPHEN O. LESSER

COX, JAMES MIDDLETON (Mar. 31, 1870–July 15, 1957), publisher and politician, was born in Jacksonburg, Ohio, the son of Gilbert Cox, a farmer, and Eliza Andrews. The youngest of a family of seven children, Cox worked on the farm, was a janitor in the public school, and served as a sexton in the United Brethren Church which his family attended. (He later joined the Episcopal Church.) Cox left school at fifteen, moved to Middletown, Ohio, and, tutored by his brother-in-law, at age seventeen passed an examination for teacher certification. Subsequently he taught school for a few years prior to entering his lifelong field, journalism. Working in all capacities on his brother-in-law's paper, the Middletown *Signal*, in 1892 Cox scored a major scoop about a train wreck—he monopolized the only available telegraph line—that led to a position on the Cincinnati *Enquirer*. Two years later he accompanied Paul J. Sorg, a wealthy tobacco manufacturer and newly elected congressman, to Washington as private secretary. After Sorg's defeat in the next election, Cox returned to Ohio; in 1898, backed by funds provided by Sorg, he purchased the Dayton *Daily News*.

As a publisher Cox added a woman society editor, stopped the practice of accepting prepared pages furnished by certain firms, adopted wire services for national and world developments, used photography and marketing services, and charged all advertisers uniform rates. He combined editorial sense and business acumen.

Short and stocky, the bespectacled Cox resembled both Napoleon and Theodore Roosevelt, whose pictures hung on his walls. By the age of twenty-eight he had a reputation for aggressive reform journalism; he took pride in the $1 million in lawsuits against his Dayton *Daily News,* all of which were later dropped. (In 1927 his Canton [Ohio] *News* was awarded the Pulitzer prize for its fight against corruption in the municipal government.

In 1908 Cox plunged into politics, easily winning election to Congress on the Democratic ticket. A liberal and progressive politician, he was reelected to the House in 1910, and in 1912 he was elected governor of Ohio. His victory in this contest in large part resulted from the split within the Republican ranks between President William Howard Taft and Theodore Roosevelt.

Cox's record as governor was impressive. Honest and efficient, he was probably proudest of his accomplishment of school reforms. He completely reorganized the Ohio school system, consolidating school districts and increasing salaries and training for teachers. He also in-

troduced a workmen's compensation act, the initiative and referendum, and a minimum wage and a nine-hour-day law for women. He launched a new state highway construction program, pioneered in prison reform, and supported a new measure regulating banks, a fairer tax system, and municipal home rule. Other measures included laws that provided for mothers' pensions and a more efficient state budgeting procedure. For responding to the devastating Ohio River flood of 1913 with extraordinary executive vigor, Cox received the Red Cross Gold Medal of Merit.

Cox was defeated in the 1914 gubernatorial election, but he ran again successfully in 1916. Reelected in 1918—the only major Democrat in the state to win election that year—Cox became the first Ohio Democratic governor to serve three terms. Consequently he occupied an excellent position for the 1920 presidential nomination, representing as he did a crucial swing state.

In 1893 Cox married Mayme L. Harding of Cincinnati; they had three children. They were divorced in 1910, and on Sept. 15, 1917, Cox married Margaretta Parker Blair of Chicago. They had one child. His divorce and remarriage had no effect on his political career.

At the 1920 Democratic national convention in San Francisco, Cox was nominated on the forty-fourth ballot, defeating such opponents as William G. McAdoo and A. Mitchell Palmer. The New York *Tribune* attributed his nomination to his being a wet candidate, to his not being identified with the Wilson administration, and to his being from Ohio. Franklin Delano Roosevelt was selected as his running mate. Ignoring cautious advisers, Cox courageously endorsed the League of Nations, basing his campaign on that issue and calling it the supreme test. This stance contributed to his defeat. Warren G. Harding, the Republican candidate, campaigned for a return to normalcy, and the voters, weary of reform at home and crusades abroad, elected him by a wide margin—404 to 127 in the electoral college. Cox never again ran for public office.

In 1933 Cox accepted appointment by President Frank D. Roosevelt as a member of the American delegation to the London World Monetary and Economic Conference, which was called to try to halt the ravages of the spreading world depression. Although Roosevelt was responsible for the failure of the conference to reach a common approach, Cox defended the president's policy in his memoirs, *Journey Through My Years* (1946).

After 1933, Cox repeatedly refused administration offers, ranging from head of the Federal Reserve System to ambassadorships. He was an avid baseball fan, a passionate golfer, and an inveterate reader—biography and history were his favorites—and an enthusiastic fisherman and hunter. He maintained a fishing shack in the woods of upper Michigan peninsula and earned a reputation as a gourmet cook on recreational expeditions. While keeping close control over his newspapers, he left much leeway to his editors in the belief that the individuality of his outlets could thus be preserved. By the time of his death Cox owned a chain of flourishing newspapers and numerous radio and television stations in Ohio, Georgia, and Florida. He died in Dayton, Ohio.

[There is no biography of Cox. See Irving Stone, "James Middleton Cox," in *They Also Ran: The Story of the Men Who Were Defeated for the Presidency* (1966);"Cox in Wilson's Shoes," *New Republic,* July 21, 1920; " 'Jimmy' Cox, Before and After Nomination," *Literary Digest,* July 24, 1920; "The New Democracy and Its Banner-Bearers" and "The League of Nations as the Dominant Issue," both in *Current Opinion,* Aug. 1920; "Governor Cox and the Ohio Budget," *Review of Reviews,* 62 (1920) 46–48;"How Not to Be President," *Newsweek,* Dec. 9, 1946; "Then There Was One," *ibid.,* Jan. 17, 1949; and obituary notices in *Time* and *Newsweek,* both July 29, 1957; and the *New York Times,* July 16, 1957. Also see the James P. Warburg memoir in the Columbia University Oral History Collection; other memoirs in the collection also have material about Cox.]

DANIEL M. SMITH

CRAIG, WINCHELL McKENDREE (Apr. 27, 1892–Feb. 12, 1960), neurosurgeon, was born in Washington Court House, Ohio, the son of Thomas Henry Craig, a dry-goods merchant, and Eliza Orlena Pine. After attending public school in Washington Court House and Culver Military Academy, Craig in 1915 received the B.A. degree from Ohio Wesleyan University. In 1919 he was graduated with the M.D. from Johns Hopkins University. From 1919 to 1921 he served internships at New Haven (Conn.) Hospital and Roosevelt Hospital in New York City and a residency in surgery at Saint Agnes Hospital in Baltimore. During the next three years he was a fellow in surgery at the Mayo Foundation for Medical Education and Research, in Rochester, Minn. He joined the staff of the Mayo Clinic in 1926 as a neurosurgeon. On Feb. 16, 1928, Craig married Jean Katherine Fitzgerald. They had four children.

Craig became instructor in neurologic surgery at the Mayo Foundation Graduate School in 1927, assistant professor in 1929, associate professor in 1932, and professor of neurosurgery in 1937. He was head of the section of neurologic surgery of the Mayo Clinic from 1946 to 1955 and subsequently senior consultant until his retirement in 1957. From 1946 to 1959 he was director of civil defense for Rochester and Olmsted County; he then became field representative of the American Medical Association's Council on Medical Education and Hospitals. He resigned this position in November 1959 to accept appointment by President Eisenhower as special assistant for health and medical affairs to Arthur S. Flemming, United States secretary of health, education, and welfare.

During World War I Craig served as a member of an emergency corps recruited at Johns Hopkins to fight influenza at Camp Meade, Md. In 1927 he organized the Mayo Clinic medical specialists' unit of the United States Naval Reserve in which he served until 1941 with the initial rank of lieutenant and subsequently that of commander. He was called to active duty in the navy in 1941 and took his unit (Fifty-fourth Medical Specialists' Unit) to the United States Naval Hospital in Corona, Calif., where he became chief of surgery. Advanced to captain in 1942, he was transferred to the National Naval Medical Center at Bethesda, Md., where he served as chief of surgery until 1945. He was promoted to rear admiral in 1943 and was transferred to the Bureau of Medicine and Surgery in Washington, D.C., to direct the graduate training program. Craig was the first civilian physician in the history of the navy to reach the grade of rear admiral. He was awarded the Legion of Merit, the Naval Reserve Medal, and the Bronze Star; he returned to civilian life on Jan. 31, 1946.

After the war Craig served as a reserve consultant to the surgeon general of the navy, as a civilian consultant to the Veterans Administration, and as a member of the Naval Research Division of the National Research Council. In 1949 Craig was appointed by Secretary of Defense Louis A. Johnson to a special task force to study the relations between officers in the regular medical services of the armed forces and those in the civilian components or reserve corps. In 1955 and 1957, he lectured to naval personnel stationed at medical installations in the Far East.

Craig's intention when he first came to the Mayo Foundation in 1921 was to become a general surgeon; in fact, his graduate training was concentrated on general surgery, surgical pathology, general medical and surgical diagnosis, and postoperative treatment. Subsequently he served in turn as resident physician at the Colonial Hospital, first assistant in neurology, associate in surgery, and associate in neurosurgery. His master's thesis was on tumors of the spinal cord, and in 1930 he received the M.S. degree in surgery from the University of Minnesota. Thereafter, Craig's prime interest in practice, research, and publication was neurologic surgery. He became widely known for his works on surgery of the sympathetic nervous system, the surgical treatment of hypertension, and the classification of tumors of the brain and spinal cord. The Craig headrest, which he described in 1935, is still widely used in ventriculography and other neurosurgical procedures.

When Craig entered neurosurgery, most surgeons were extremely reluctant to operate on the brain or spinal cord because of the seemingly insurmountable technical and physiological problems. Craig and his contemporaries persisted with unremitting effort to evolve this complex and difficult branch of surgery into a distinct and respected specialty. He was responsible for more than 300 contributions to the medical and surgical literature.

Craig had none of the irascible or tempestuous temperament that tradition has accorded the neurosurgeon. Even under the most exasperating stresses of the operating room, he remained calm and quiet, master of the situation and unfailingly considerate of the younger surgeons under his direction. His vast experience and basic intuition helped form Craig as a master diagnostician.

Tribute to Craig's renown were several memorable experiences involving famous patients. During the Quebec Conference (1943), Winston Churchill called the attention of President Roosevelt to the fact that his chief cartographer, Richard Pim, was suffering greatly from sciatica and pain in the lower back. Roosevelt had Rear Admiral Ross T. McIntire, his personal physician, see Pim, and a diagnosis of protruded intervertebral disk was immediately made. Pim was flown to Washington, and Craig removed a large herniated disk found to be lying free in the vertebral canal. Immediate relief was effected.

In January 1944, Craig was invited by McIntire to see President Franklin D. Roosevelt, who was complaining of a knot on the back of his head that seemed to be increasing in size. On Feb. 4, 1944, at the United States Naval Hospital, Craig removed a benign epidermoid cyst from the president's head. Also in 1944, Craig removed a grade 4 astrocytoma from Senator Charles McNary of Oregon. McNary was able to return to the Senate briefly but knew from a discussion with Craig that he only had a short time to live. He got his Senate affairs in order and before he died wrote Craig that he greatly appreciated his frankness and help.

Craig gave the William J. Mayo Lecture at the University of Michigan in 1940 and the first W. J. and C. H. Mayo Memorial Lectureship at Dartmouth Medical School in 1942. In 1946 he was elected president of the Society of Neurological Surgeons, in 1948 president of the Harvey Cushing Society, and in 1953 president of the Association of Military Surgeons of the United States. In 1957 he delivered the George M. Kober Memorial Lecture at Georgetown University.

Craig died in Rochester, Minn.

[Craig was author of *The Craig Family: Genealogical and Historical Notes About the Craigs of America* (1956); and *History of the Development of the Section of Neurologic Surgery at the Mayo Clinic* (1958). On his life and work, see the Craig biographical file at the Mayo Clinic section of communications; the Mayo Clinic Library Collection's reprints of Craig material published between 1923 and 1958; Mayo Clinic, *Physicians of the Mayo Clinic and the Mayo Foundation* (1937); and obituaries in major medical and surgical journals, including the *Journal of the American Medical Association, Transactions of the American Surgical Association, Transactions of the American Neurological Association,* and *Journal of Neurosurgery.*]

JACK D. KEY

CROSSER, ROBERT (June 7, 1874–June 3, 1957), United States congressman, was born in Holytown, Bothwell Parish, Lanarkshire, Scotland, the son of James Crosser, a physician, and Barbara Crosser. In 1881 the Crosser family immigrated to the United States, settling first in Cleveland, Ohio, before moving later that year to Salineville, Ohio, where Crosser practiced as a country physician. In 1893 Robert Crosser graduated from high school in Salineville. After studying the prerequisite Latin and Greek, he was admitted to the classical course at Kenyon College in Gambier, Ohio, where he graduated with a B.A. degree in 1897.

Crosser then enrolled at the law school of Columbia University. Financial circumstances forced his withdrawal after less than a year's attendance, and in the fall of 1898 he entered the Cincinnati Law School, where William Howard Taft was one of his professors. He received his LL.B. degree in 1901 and in September, after being admitted to the bar of the Supreme Court of Ohio, he began private practice in the Cleveland offices of Ford, Snyder, Henry and McGraw —the first of three law firms with which he would be associated during his lifetime. During these early years, Crosser also served as professor of the law of torts at Baldwin-Wallace University Law School (1904–1905). On Apr. 18, 1906, he married Isabelle Dargavel Hogg. They had four children.

In addition to the law, Crosser also manifested a keen interest in politics. He endorsed the "gas and water socialism" of Cleveland's progressive mayor, Tom L. Johnson. In 1908 he campaigned in the Ohio presidential contest for William Jennings Bryan against his old law professor, Taft. Two years later Crosser was elected to the Ohio legislature, and in 1912 he served as a delegate to the Fourth Constitutional Convention of Ohio. Elected chairman of the initiative and referendum committee, he was largely responsible for the inclusion of these direct-democracy amendments into the Ohio Constitution.

With his prestige enhanced, Crosser successfully captured a congressional seat as a Democratic representative-at-large from Ohio in 1912. In 1914 and 1916 he was reelected representative of the Twenty-first Ohio District, consisting of several wards of the city of Cleveland. Crosser enthusiastically supported most of President Woodrow Wilson's domestic reform legislation, especially the Federal Reserve Act. In 1916 he was instrumental in securing passage of the Adamson Act, limiting working hours of railroad employees to eight hours a day. This effort was the first of Crosser's tireless endeavors as a champion of the rights of labor. In addition, he advocated government ownership of railroads, municipal ownership of public utilities, and a comprehensive program of reforestation and flood control.

American participation in World War I temporarily interrupted Crosser's congressional ca-

reer. He was one of twenty-four congressmen to oppose Wilson's conscription bill; he attempted to amend the president's espionage bill to offer greater protection for conscientious objectors and philosophical anarchists; and he proposed the imposition of a national single tax to finance the war. These unpopular measures earned him the enmity of the Wilson administration and his local Democratic organization. Consequently, he was defeated for renomination in the 1918 primaries and again in 1920. With wartime hysteria somewhat abated, he was elected in 1922 and resumed his old seat on Mar. 4, 1923, beginning thirty-two years of uninterrupted service. The GOP administrations of the 1920's were not receptive to Crosser's incessant pleas for reform legislation in the areas of labor, agriculture, and transportation. Nevertheless, according to Crosser's friend, Representative Charles A. Wolverton of New Jersey, he "blazed the trail for much of the social-welfare legislation during Franklin D. Roosevelt's administration."

When the Democratic party regained control of Congress in March 1933, Crosser became the first chairman of the House Democratic Steering Committee—a position he would hold again in the Seventy-eighth Congress (1943–1944). He was an ardent supporter of most New Deal measures; his work for the Federal Deposit Insurance Corporation Act and the Society Security Act was especially important.

It was as a member of the House Committee on Interstate and Foreign Commerce, however, that Crosser particularly distinguished himself. In that capacity he was coauthor of the Railroad Labor Act of 1934, which established the right of railroad workers to organize and bargain collectively. He also helped draft the Railroad Retirement Acts of 1934 and 1935 and was instrumental in obtaining congressional approval of the Railroad Unemployment Insurance Act.

Crippling arthritis forced Crosser into a wheelchair in 1937, but he continued to discharge his legislative duties. He served as chairman of the House Committee on Interstate and Foreign Commerce throughout the Eighty-first and Eighty-second Congresses (1949–1952). During World War II and thereafter, Crosser's commitment to New Deal liberalism continued undiminished. He was also a consistent proponent of the Cold War policy of containment. In 1952, a "Republican year," the veteran Ohio congressman scored his most satisfying victory. Despite only token support from the Cuyahoga County

Democratic organization, he received a majority of 99,520 votes to 49,947 for his opponent. "Today," declared the *New York Times*, "he stands as one of the nation's political marvels—a man who cannot be beaten." But two years later, old age and an aggressive young opponent, Charles A. Vanik, combined to defeat him in the primaries. He died in Bethesda, Md.

[Crosser's papers are at the Ohio Historical Society, Columbus. On his life and career, see the *New York Times*, Nov. 16, 1952; the *New York Times* and *Cleveland Plain Dealer*, June 4, 1957; Hoyt L. Warner, *Progressivism in Ohio, 1897–1917* (1964); and *Biographical Directory of the American Congress, 1774–1971* (1971).]

RONALD A. MULDER

CROTHERS, RACHEL (Dec. 12, 1878–July 5, 1958), playwright, was born in Bloomington, Ill., the daughter of Eli Kirk Crothers, a physician, and Marie Louise de Pew. Abraham Lincoln, a friend of the family, defended her father in a malpractice lawsuit at Bloomington in 1857–1858. Her mother began to study medicine at the age of forty and became the first woman doctor to practice in central Illinois.

Crothers graduated from the Normal University High School at Normal, Ill., in 1891. Although her elders viewed her theatrical aspirations with some skepticism, a year later she went to Boston to study elocution under Henry Addison Pitt. She returned to Bloomington to teach elocution for two years, then, determined to become an actress, traveled to New York to enter the Stanhope-Wheatcroft School of Acting. Within three months she became an instructor there. Crothers remained at Stanhope-Wheatcroft for four years, writing and producing a number of one-act plays for the students. She left the school to spend three seasons on the professional stage.

Crothers' first full-length play was *The Three of Us,* produced in 1906. An immediate success, it announced the arrival of the liberated woman on the American stage. From then until 1937, when she ended her career with *Susan and God,* a new Crothers play appeared on Broadway almost every year. At a time when 100 consecutive performances constituted a hit, the majority of her plays were successes.

More than half of Crothers' plays chronicled the journey of the New Woman through modern America. *The Three of Us, The Coming of Mrs. Patrick* (1907), *A Man's World* (1910), and *Ourselves* (1913) attacked the double standard of sexual morality and constituted the first group of plays in what she called her "Dramatic History of Women." *Young Wisdom* (1914), *Nice People* (1921), and *Mary the Third* (1923), plays that exploited the revolution in manners and morals, continued the cycle. *He and She* (1920), *Let Us Be Gay* (1929), *As Husbands Go* (1931), *When Ladies Meet*(1932), and *Susan and God* (1937) examined divorce, the aftermath of the revolution.

The Three of Us, Nice People, Mary the Third, Let Us Be Gay, As Husbands Go, When Ladies Meet, and *Susan and God* were all Broadway hits. Among Crothers' other successes were *Old Lady 31* (1916), *A Little Journey* (1919), *39 East* (1919), *Expressing Willie* (1924), and *A Lady's Virtue* (1925). Less successful were *The Coming of Mrs. Patrick, Myself, Bettina* (1908), *A Man's World, Ourselves, Young Wisdom, The Heart of Paddy Whack* (1914), *Mother Carey's Chickens* (1917), *Once Upon a Time* (1918), *He and She, Everyday* (1921), *Venus* (1927), and *Caught Wet* (1931).

Crothers also directed *The Book of Charm* by John Kirkpatrick (1925), *Thou Desperate Pilot* by Zoë Akins (1927), and *Exceeding Small* by Caroline Francke (1927). The failure of *Thou Desperate Pilot* plunged her deeply into debt, but the royalties from *Let Us Be Gay* restored her financial security.

In Hollywood, Crothers adapted A. E. Thomas' *No More Ladies* for Irving Thalberg but, disgusted with the constant readaptations, asked Metro-Goldwyn-Mayer to remove her name from the screen credits. Samuel Goldwyn brought her back to Hollywood to adapt her own *House of Lorrimore,* which became the film *Splendor,* starring Miriam Hopkins.

Crothers never married, having instead a lifelong affair with the theater. In 1917 she founded and became the first president of Stage Women's War Relief. During the Great Depression she helped form the United Theater Relief Committee, which created the Stage Relief Fund to help needy theater people; she was its president from 1932 to 1951. In January 1940 she helped found and direct the British War Relief Society's American Theatre Wing, which became best known for its Stage Door Canteens.

Crothers was responsible for the direction,

staging, and casting of all but her first two plays. Her casts included Carlotta Nillson, Maxine Elliott, Mary Mannering, Chauncey Olcott, Cyril Keightley, Emma Dunn, Estelle Winwood, Constance Binney, Henry Hull, Francine Larrimore, Tallulah Bankhead, Katherine Cornell, Chrystal Herne, Lily Cahill, Frieda Inescort, Walter Abel, Selena Royle, Paul McGrath, Nancy Kelly, and Gertrude Lawrence—a veritable *Who's Who* of the modern American theater.

Although not without its failures, Crothers' career was one of the most successful in the history of the American drama. She found her own formula, successfully combining sex, sentimentality, and sensationalism. Her plays explored the double standard, trial marriage, the Jazz Age, Freudianism, and divorce. Critical, often satiric, but always opting for sanity, they accurately reflect and record the first four decades of twentieth-century American social history.

Crothers was a professional, completely attuned to her audience, her subject, and her craft. Deeply devoted to the theater, she knew its faults, but she never lost her belief that "one of the most delightful things in all the world is a good play well acted," nor her conviction that the drama is "the greatest of all arts." She died in Danbury, Conn.

[The most complete treatment of the subject is Irving Abrahamson, "The Career of Rachel Crothers in the American Drama" (Ph.D. diss., University of Chicago, 1956). Clippings and other memorabilia are in three volumes of scrapbooks assembled by the author of this article, covering 1906 to 1918; 1912, 1917–1918, 1930–1935 (scattered clippings); and 1919–1932. Microfilm copies are on file at the University of Chicago Library; the originals are at the Illinois State Normal University Library, Normal, Ill. The best statement by Crothers of the theory behind her work is her essay "The Construction of a Play," in *The Art of Playwriting* (1928).

The best quick reference for information concerning her plays is Burns Mantle and Garrison P. Sherwood, eds., *The Best Plays of 1899–1909* (1944); also see their *The Best Plays of 1909–1919* (1933) and the following volumes in the series. An insightful appreciation by a contemporary is Bayard Veiller, *The Fun I've Had* (1941). An obituary is in the *New York Times,* July 6, 1958; also see letter by Sherman Day Wakefield, *ibid.,* July 12, 1958.]

IRVING ABRAHAMSON

CULBERTSON, JOSEPHINE MURPHY (1899–Mar. 23, 1956), contract bridge

expert, was born Josephine Murphy in Bayside, N.Y., the daughter of a mechanical engineer. After graduating from Morris High School in the Bronx, she took business courses at a convent. Her first job was as secretary to Pat Powers, a promoter of six-day bicycle races, then much in vogue. In 1919 she married Charles Dillon, who committed suicide a few months later.

In 1920 Culbertson became secretary to Wilbur Whitehead, a well-known auction bridge player, writer, and teacher, although she knew nothing about cards. Young and attractive, she quickly became a center of masculine attention on the highest levels of the New York bridge scene; and the excellent instruction she received enabled her to become a very strong player within a short time. She soon became a regular participant in the high-stakes games played on the third floor of the Knickerbocker Whist Club, where most of the better players in the New York area congregated. It was there in 1922 that she met Ely Culbertson, the son of an American petroleum engineer and a Cossack princess.

Ely Culbertson earned his living as a professional card player while striving to perfect a system of bridge bidding that would be vastly superior to those then in common use. Their card-table acquaintance blossomed into romance. They married on June 11, 1923, and continued their respective careers in bridge, Josephine as one of the most successful teachers of her time and Ely as a player in high-stakes games and, gradually, as a teacher in his own right. They had two children.

In the summer of 1927 the Culbertsons, while on a tour of California, were introduced to contract bridge, a recently invented variation. Ely at once appreciated its virtues and began to concentrate his efforts on adapting his auction bidding system to the new scoring table. Josephine, who had become an excellent theoretician in her own right, contributed amply to this work. The couple soon established themselves as leading authorities on contract. In 1929 they founded *Bridge World* magazine, the first enterprise in a growing bridge empire. Josephine's principal contribution was a question-and-answer column called "Pro et Contra" that proved to be one of the most popular features in the magazine. She conducted it for more than twenty-five years.

In 1930 the Culbertsons and their teammates, Theodore Lightner and Waldemar von Zedwitz, embarked on a tour of England. Their decisive defeat of all opposition caught the popular imagination on both sides of the Atlantic. Ely's *Contract Bridge Blue Book* (1930), edited by

Josephine (as were all of his writings during their marriage), became a best-seller, and the Culbertson name was known to millions. Their reputations were solidified by success in various matches; one, in 1931-1932, known as the Bridge Battle of the Century, against Sidney Lenz and his partners, established their superiority to the older generation of experts. A second, in 1935, against another husband-and-wife partnership, P. Hal and Dorothy Sims, disposed effectively of aspiring rivals to popular acclaim.

Josephine's role in the couple's rapidly expanding business was as great as that of her husband. From 1931 she conducted a syndicated newspaper column. She appeared on numerous radio shows and in films, and published several books—"largely prepared by the *Bridge World* technical staff," according to friend and business associate Albert Morehead. Apart from play on her husband's team (on which her favorite partner was not Ely but von Zedwitz), she appeared infrequently in serious competition. But she did score some notable successes, including the National Open Pairs in 1928, the Life Master Pairs in 1930, and the National Women's Pairs in 1935.

The Culbertsons were divorced in 1938, but they remained business partners. During her last years Culbertson's activities, especially competitive bridge, were restricted by poor health. She died in New York City.

It is difficult to assess Culbertson's role in the development of contract bridge because many of her best ideas appeared over her husband's signature. Ely often claimed to the press, for purposes of publicity, that his wife was the better player. Contemporaries are unanimous that this was not so. Whatever her true status among the players of her era, it is plain that her most lasting contribution to the game was to show countless women that they too had a place in an activity that until then had been largely a man's province.

[Culbertson's writings, wholly technical, include *Contract Bridge for Beginners* (1938); and *Calypso, the Four-Trump Game* (1955). Information about her early life is not abundant. Ely Culbertson's autobiography, *The Strange Lives of One Man* (1940), is useful. Her obituaries in the *New York Times*, Mar. 24, 1956, and *Bridge World*, May 1956, as well as the article in Richard L. Frey, ed., *Encyclopedia of Bridge* (1964), deal mostly with her professional career.]

DAVID I. DANIELS

CULLEN, HUGH ROY (July 3, 1881–July 4, 1957), oilman and philanthropist, was born in Denton County, Tex., the son of Cicero Cullen, a cattle buyer, real estate broker, and insurance salesman, and Louise Beck. Cullen's parents separated when he was quite young, and he was raised by his mother in San Antonio. His education was limited to elementary school, which he left at the age of twelve in order to work as a packer in a candy factory. Five years later he secured employment with a cotton-buying firm and in 1904 opened his own cotton-buying agency, which operated throughout Oklahoma and Texas. On Dec. 29, 1903, he married Lillie Cranz, the daughter of a prominent Schulenburg, Tex., merchant. They had five children.

Since cotton trading remained depressed after the Panic of 1907, Cullen moved his family to Houston in 1911. With substantial federal assistance, Houston had been dredging a ship channel that would convert the city to a major port. Cullen's father-in-law owned an attractive parcel of land that fronted on the new channel, and shortly after arriving in Houston, Cullen bought the land. When he later sold this property, Cullen became involved with other real estate transactions and city politics. He played a major role in raising Houston's share of the funds for the channel. He also fought vigorously to prevent another better-established real estate operator, Jesse H. Jones, from diverting the project nearer to sites in which Jones was interested. Cullen won this battle and saw much of his career as being a rivalry with Jones.

Cullen had a talent for enlisting the support of older men with capital to invest; he could also spot the most influential man in a group and negotiate successfully with him. In 1917 Jim Cheek, a Houston realtor who had benefited from Cullen's work for the channel, asked Cullen to become his agent for acquiring oil leases in western Texas. Cullen accepted on condition that he be taken in as a partner, and he quickly learned how to lease land and to drill for oil.

Cullen had an uncanny knack for finding oil. He claimed to have mastered "creekology," the "wildcatter's natural sense of surface geology." From the pattern of surface contours and the location and shape of the streams, he said he divined where the underground pools of oil were to be found. During the next fourteen years, he discovered oil fields in Texas worth billions of dollars. These included the fields at Pierce Junction, Blue Ridge, Rabb's Ridge, and, in 1934, the biggest one of all—Tom O'Connor's. Cullen drilled deep, substituted water for mud in certain critical stages of the drilling, and employed a new but simple technique for getting through "heaving" or "Jackson shale," a brittle rock formation that had been clogging the drilling taps for over a quarter of a century. His last technique was discovered under the aegis of Quintana Petroleum Company, which he had formed in 1932.

By developing wealth and reliable associates, Cullen was able to shift even more of his attention to public affairs. When Jones brought the Democratic national convention to Houston in 1928 and ardently supported its nominee, Al Smith, Cullen naturally switched to the Republicans and Herbert Hoover. Four years later, when Jones joined Franklin D. Roosevelt's entourage, Cullen continued to back Hoover. Thereafter, he supported Republican and conservative causes.

In 1947 Cullen again opposed Jones over the latter's proposed zoning program for Houston. Cullen denounced his opponent as the agent of those who, on second thought, he described as "New York merchants." Nevertheless, the overwhelming majority of the Houston voters agreed with Jones and with apparently no major ill effect on the later orderly development of the city.

In the 1952 presidential campaign, Cullen helped stall the candidacy of Senator Robert A. Taft and actively promoted the nomination of Dwight D. Eisenhower. He helped organize conservative Democratic support throughout the South for the Republican ticket, and he provided funds for Republican senatorial and congressional candidates in several states.

Shortly after a tragic accident that killed his only son in 1936, Cullen became interested in philanthropy and contributed a building in his son's memory to the small and struggling University of Houston. The school's concern with educating children of "working people" and providing practical evening courses for adults had attracted Cullen's attention. His donations (eventually totaling over $30 million) and leadership converted the university into a major institution. Texas hospitals also benefited from his generosity. During one week in 1945, he gave over a million dollars to each of four hospitals. He contributed an even greater sum to the Texas Medical Center. In 1947 he organized his major philanthropies under the Cullen Foundation, to which he transferred title for oil-producing fields valued at over $160 million. It became the third largest foundation in the United States. In 1955 Cullen estimated that he had given away 93 percent of his wealth.

Cullen was the archetypal Texas oil millionaire. He loved fancy clothes, good cigars, and liquor, and was also a rough-mannered man ready to bet $50,000 that he would strike oil on his next try. He never forgot the uncertain means by which he had acquired his fortune, consequently he was anxious that no one, especially "outsiders" (including the federal government), would despoil him or his descendants of it. He was equally proud of his membership in the Musicians' Protective Association of the American Federation of Labor and of his reputation as a staunch supporter of fair labor practices. During the 1930's and 1940's, he tried to promote the Scandinavian program of bringing industrial workers into the ranks of stockholders so that labor would "sit on the same side of the table with capital." Cullen remained politically conservative, and during his last years he was determined to protect America and its economic system against European and Asian Communism and "internal subversion." One observer noted that he was "by turns impulsive, sentimental, opinionated, gentle, sharp-tongued and folksy, and as tactful as a Texas steer stampeding through a glass works." But all of these adjectives pale, the observer added, "in favor of one word: generous." Cullen died in Houston, Tex.

[See the *New York Times,* Mar. 29, 1947, p. 17; *Christian Science Monitor,* May 7, 1947, p. 11; "Words of Wrath," *Newsweek,* Feb. 9, 1948; "A Man So Rich," *Time,* Apr. 7, 1948; George M. Fuermann, *Houston: Land of the Big Rich* (1951); Edward W. Kilman and Theon Wright, *Hugh Roy Cullen: A Story of American Opportunity* (1954); Theodore H. White, "Texas: Land of Wealth and Fear," *The Reporter,* May 25, 1954, an interesting summary of Texas oil; "A Man Who Likes to Give Away Millions," *U.S. News & World Report,* Feb. 11, 1955; Cleveland Amory, "Oil Folks at Home," *Holiday,* February 1957; *New York Times* obituary, July 5, 1957; David G. McComb, *Houston, the Bayou City* (1969); and Richard O'Connor, *The Oil Barons* (1971).]

NICHOLAS VARGA

CUMMINGS, HOMER STILLÉ (Apr. 30, 1870–Sept. 10, 1956), U.S. attorney general, was born in Chicago, Ill., son of Uriah C. Cummings, manufacturer and authority on cement, and Audie Schuyler Stillé. Homer graduated from the Heathcote School in Buffalo, N.Y. He received the Ph.B. degree from the Sheffield School of Yale University in 1891 and the L.L.B. from Yale Law

School in 1893. He then practiced law in Stamford, Conn., and in 1909 joined with Charles D. Lockwood to form Cummings and Lockwood. He remained a partner in this firm until 1933.

Cummings entered politics almost immediately. In 1896 he supported William Jennings Bryan, and Connecticut Democrats nominated him for secretary of state. The decision for Bryan rested on his conviction that government, law, and the Democratic party were the instruments for the achievement of social justice in America. His progressive sensibility was reinforced by his gifts as an orator. He was an incisive, dramatic trial lawyer and an astute, imperturbable, and loyal political manager.

In 1900, 1901, and 1904, Cummings was elected mayor of Stamford, where he instituted a progressive municipal program. He constructed and improved streets and sewers, reorganized the police and fire departments, and secured a shorefront park, later named for him. He was nominated for congressman-at-large in 1902 and for U.S. senator in 1910 and 1916. Each time he lost narrowly. He served as state's attorney for Fairfield County from 1914 to 1924. During Cummings' last year as county prosecutor, a vagrant, Harold Israel, was indicted for the murder of a popular parish priest on a street corner in Bridgeport. The evidence, including a confession, appeared overwhelming, but Cummings, after scrupulous investigation, became convinced of Israel's innocence. In a gripping courtroom scene he asked for and secured dismissal of the charge. In 1931 the National Commission on Law Observance and Enforcement (the Wickersham Commission) praised this act, and a film, *Boomerang* (1947) dramatized the affair.

Cummings began his association with the national Democratic party in 1900, when he was named committeeman from Connecticut, a post he held until 1925. He was a delegate-at-large to the 1900 Democratic convention, the first of many conventions he was to attend. In the 1912 campaign he directed the Democratic speaker's bureau from Washington, D.C. He served as vice-chairman of the national committee from 1913 to 1919 and as chairman from 1919 to 1920. Cummings greatly admired Woodrow Wilson and delivered a passionate keynote address at the 1920 convention in praise of the stricken president.

Cummings vainly attempted to calm the bitterly divided Democratic convention of 1924. As chairman of the Committee on Resolutions, he tried to formulate a compromisé plank on the controversial issue of the Ku Klux Klan. Unlike most Northeasterners, however, he supported William G. McAdoo over Alfred E. Smith for the presidential nomination. For the rest of the decade his political activity was restrained.

Cummings married four times. His marriage to Helen W. Smith in 1897 ended in divorce in 1907. They had one son. His 1909 marriage to Marguerite T. Owings was dissolved in 1928. The marriage to Mary Cecilia Waterbury in 1929 was happy; she died ten years later. He published a memoir, *The Tired Sea* (1939), as a tribute to Cecilia. In 1942 he married Julia Alter, who died in 1955.

With the coming of the Great Depression, Cummings reentered politics. In 1932 he helped persuade twenty-four senators and numerous congressmen to announce their support for Franklin D. Roosevelt. At Chicago he planned strategy, operated as floor manager, and delivered a resounding seconding speech. Following the election, Roosevelt chose Cummings as governor-general of the Philippines. However, when Senator Thomas Walsh, who had been designated attorney general, died on Mar. 2, 1933, Roosevelt named Cummings to lead the Justice Department on Mar. 4. Cummings accepted the post on a temporary, emergency basis, and then, a few weeks later, permanently. He served almost six years as attorney general; only William Wirt served longer (1817–1829).

Cummings transformed the Department of Justice. He established uniform rules of practice and procedure in federal courts. Appalled by the crime waves of the Prohibition era, he secured the passage of twelve laws that buttressed the "Lindbergh law" on kidnapping, made bank robbery a federal crime, cracked down on interstate transportation of stolen property, and extended federal regulations over firearms. He strengthened the Federal Bureau of Investigation, called a national crime conference, supported the establishment of Alcatraz as a model prison for hardened offenders, and reorganized the internal administration of the department. In 1937 Cummings published *We Can Prevent Crime,* and, with Carl McFarland, an assistant attorney general, *Federal Justice,* a comprehensive departmental history. *The Selected Papers of Homer Cummings* (1939), edited by Carl B. Swisher, supplemented the history.

Cummings' path as protector of New Deal programs was thorny. During his first week as attorney general, he advised Roosevelt that the Trading with the Enemy Act of 1917 permitted the president to close banks and regulate gold hoarding and export. Cummings personally argued the right of the government to ban gold payments before the Supreme Court and won the "gold clause" cases. The department's defense of subsequent administration measures was notoriously unsuccessful, however. During 1935–1936, the Court, frequently by 5-to-4 votes, overthrew eight key statutes, including the National Industrial Recovery Act (NIRA) and the Agricultural Adjustment Act (AAA).

The obtuseness of the conservative Court majority rankled. Cummings was eager to expand the judiciary and was outraged by the proliferation of lawsuits and injunctions against the government. After the election of 1936, Roosevelt instructed him to draft legislation for court reform. Neither wished to alter the Constitution. Both were attracted by an idea, proposed earlier by conservative Justice James McReynolds, to add a judge for every judge who refused to retire at age seventy at full pay. Such a measure might give the president the opportunity to appoint fifty new judges, including six to the Supreme Court. Roosevelt launched the proposal, prepared secretly by Cummings, on Feb. 5, 1937. The uproar that confronted the "court-packing plan" is well known. After 168 days the Senate killed the bill by returning it to committee.

Cummings retired on Jan. 2, 1939. He entered private law practice in Washington and instituted a spring golf tournament that annually brought executives, lawyers, and politicians together. He also retained his interest in the Connecticut Democratic party, along with a residence in Greenwich, and served on the Greenwich Town Committee until 1951. He died in Washington, D.C.

[Over 130,000 items of Cummings' manuscripts and other material are in the Alderman Library of the University of Virginia. A series of lectures, which he delivered at the University of Virginia, is printed under the title *Liberty Under Law and Administration* (1934). The brief of the Israel case appears in *Journal of the American Institute of Criminal Law and Criminology*, Nov. 1924. There is no full-length or recent biographical treatment of Cummings. Brief and incomplete sketches are in George Creel, "The Tall Man," *Collier's*, Jan. 4, 1936; *Encyclopedia of Connecticut Biography*, II (1917); William A. Kelly, "Honorable Homer Cummings, Attorney General of the United States—A Biographical Sketch," *Bulletin of the New Haven County Bar Association*, Jan. 1934; and Samuel J. Woolf, "Cummings Sees the Law as a Living Thing," *New York Times* magazine, Sept. 3, 1933. The obituaries in the *Stamford Advocate* and *New York Times* of Sept. 11, 1956, are full. A photograph and a short biography are included in *Selected Papers*. Insights into Cummings' political role appear in Ray S. Baker, *Woodrow Wilson*, VIII (1939); Frank Freidel, *Franklin D. Roosevelt* (1956); Harold Ickes, *The Secret Diary of Harold Ickes*, I (1953) and II (1954); and Robert K. Murray, *The 103rd Ballot* (1976). The court-packing crisis is detailed in Joseph Alsop and Turner Catledge, *The 168 Days* (1938). David L. Mazza has written a Ph.D. diss. on "The Political Contributions of Homer S. Cummings From Bryan Through Wilson, 1896–1925," St. John's University, New York (1978). Several reminiscences in the Columbia University Oral History Collection have substantial material on Cummings, particularly those by Justice Robert H. Jackson and Frances Perkins.]

ESTELLE F. FEINSTEIN

CURLEY, JAMES MICHAEL (Nov. 20, 1874–Nov. 12, 1958), politician, was born in Boston, Mass., the son of Michael Curley, a hod carrier, and Sarah Clancy, both of whom emigrated from Galway, Ireland, in 1864. When James was ten his father died. His mother worked as a scrubwoman, his older brother worked in a grocery store, and he sold newspapers; but their combined incomes barely met their basic needs in the sordid slums of Ward Seventeen. Curley graduated from the Dearborn Grammar School in 1886. For a time he attended classes at the Boston Evening High School, but he never graduated. His education came from haunting public libraries, and it served him well in building a reputation as one of the most polished and exciting political orators of his generation. Tall and strongly built, though nonathletic, Curley was a cigar-smoker but a teetotaling Sunday school teacher, who was well dressed, courteous, and shy with women. He was the ideal Irish club organizer, the tireless worker who carefully cultivated his popularity and political friendships. Unlike most politicians, from the outset Curley proclaimed politics his chosen career. When he became eligible to vote in 1896, he enlisted as a canvasser against the inept boss of his ward. Although his candidate was defeated, Curley gained prestige for his willingness to buck the system, a distinguishing trait.

Curley first ran for the Boston common council in 1898. Although he won by some 500 votes, the party bosses "counted him out" in the ward room to punish him for his earlier disloyalty. From every available rostrum Curley trumpeted the details of his loss, reminding the public about crooked deals. He challenged the boss system for selfish reasons, but the attack increased his popularity and when he piled up an even larger majority in 1899, the machine could not risk jobbing him again. The following year he also secured election as ward boss, the youngest in Boston.

He entered the council in 1900 when, for the first time, the Irish dominated it. Over the next half century, through personal magnetism and occasional chicanery, Curley wooed and won the Irish, who in turn controlled Boston. His techniques were conventional in big-city politics—personal and practical, concerned not with ideology but with getting things done. In 1902 he founded the Roxbury Tammany Club, a social welfare agency and political club modeled on New York's Tammany Hall, but without that organization's hierarchical structure. Curley counted on maintaining a high level of popularity without depending upon subordinates or alliances with other bosses.

In 1902 Curley was elected to the Massachusetts state legislature, where his only consistent voting record was prolabor.

In 1903 he ran for Boston alderman. During the campaign occurred the first of several brushes with the law. Impersonating two constituents seeking postal jobs, Curley and a co-worker took the civil service examination for them. In his defense Curley argued (correctly) that the law did not expressly prohibit proxies, but he was found guilty and sentenced to ninety days in jail. While in prison he continued his campaign, aroused public sympathy for pursuing a "just end" even by suspect means, and won in a landslide. He served as alderman from 1904 to 1909. To supplement his $750-a-year salary, he joined his brother in opening an insurance agency that prospered because of his political connections. On June 27, 1906, he married Mary Emilda Herlihy, like himself a product of the Roxbury streets. They had nine children.

In 1909 the Boston city government underwent major restructuring. Despite the abandonment of the ward system, Curley won election to the new at-large city council. In 1910 he was elected to Congress from the Twelfth District, in a campaign that he labeled "hippodrome at its finest." In Congress he cast his lot with Speaker of the House Champ Clark, becoming Clark's New England manager in his bid for the 1912 presidential nomination won by Woodrow Wilson. Curley distinguished himself by becoming House minority whip after only one year and by leading the successful House fight against a proposed immigration restriction bill. He did not finish his second term in Congress, deciding instead to run for mayor of Boston in 1914.

He ran against the Democratic incumbent, John F. ("Honey Fitz") Fitzgerald, boss of the North End, who had strong ties to Patrick J. Kennedy, boss of East Boston. (Kennedy's son, Joseph P., was courting Fitzgerald's daughter Rose.) The powerful Democratic city committee opposed Curley, who campaigned against the boss system. Fitzgerald withdrew from the race midway in the campaign, and Curley defeated the substitute candidate. Upon taking office he immediately began centralizing power in himself by refusing to give any patronage to other bosses. He turned City Hall into a job and social service workshop similar to the old Roxbury Tammany Club. Many of the city's jobless were put to work on one of the numerous public works projects that Curley initiated. To fund his programs, Curley drained the treasury, greatly increased the valuations of business and financial properties, and convinced a hostile state legislature to allow deficit spending. Six months after he assumed office World War I broke out; Curley guided the city through a year of depression to heightened prosperity by the end of 1915.

"Curleyism," the creation of a city-wide machine based on public service and public works, depended in part on the economic distress of voters and upon misgovernment by the previous administration. When all of his enemies combined against him in the 1917 mayoral campaign, he lost; after eighteen years of continuous employment in politics, Curley had to find a job. He displayed an amazing lack of business sense, being conned into swindles that cost him nearly all his savings. This business ineptitude by a political administrative genius characterized most of his private ventures over the rest of his life.

In 1918 Curley ran an unsuccessful campaign to return to Congress. He then bided his time until 1921 when he sought another term as mayor of Boston. Although he again faced the united opposition of Democratic bosses and Republicans, he capitalized on the corruptness of the incumbent administration and ran as a reform candidate. In a vicious campaign, both his opponents and Curley followed a basic law of politics: "Do others before they do you." Curley was elected, and he immediately plunged into a massive public works program that mounted to more than $24 million before his opposition had time to regroup. Welfare rolls shrank as he vastly expanded the public payroll to a point that found the treasury so depleted he could not pay city employees. Curley tried to borrow the money from one of the city's largest banks; when the president refused, Curley threatened to open water-main floodgates beneath the bank. He used similar tactics throughout his career. Still, most voters applauded his programs. Later, he claimed justifiably that he was at least ten years ahead of the New Deal in social legislation.

During Curley's second term (1922–1926), his enemies pushed through the legislature a bill prohibiting a Boston mayor from succeeding himself. In 1924 Curley therefore mounted a drive for the governorship. He made the resurgent Ku Klux Klan his major issue (even having some of his followers burn crosses as evidence of the danger), but his lack of an effective statewide organization and the popularity of presidential candidate Calvin Coolidge swept his Republican opponent into office. His enemies crowed about Curley's demise, but in 1929 he was elected to a third term as mayor. Shortly after he assumed office his wife died, followed six months later by his son, James Michael, Jr., whom Curley had been grooming to follow in his footsteps. Shaken, he took a European tour. In Italy he met with Mussolini and convinced him to abandon his struggle with the Vatican over the conscription of young men in the Catholic Boy Scouts and Catholic Action groups. It was one of Curley's proudest moments.

With the presidential campaign of 1932, Curley incurred a new set of enemies by dropping his earlier support of Al Smith, a hero in Massachusetts, and announcing for Franklin D. Roosevelt. Denied a seat in the state delegation to the Chicago convention, he got himself appointed as an alternate delegate from Puerto Rico. Working furiously behind the scenes, he played upon his friendship with William Randolph Hearst to gain the crucial California support, and as "Don Jaime Miguel Curleo" he announced Puerto Rico's vote for Roosevelt. For the national campaign Curley made a masterful movie short that was shown to more than 25 million people throughout the nation. At his own expense he stumped the country, giving 140 speeches in forty-one days, covering twenty-three western and midwestern states.

After the election Curley asked as a reward the ambassadorship to Italy, but instead Roosevelt offered the post in Poland. Curley refused and never forgave Roosevelt for what he considered a breach of promise.

Still their relationship remained strong enough that federal government funds helped Boston weather the early years of the Depression better than most major cities. Curley won the governorship in 1934 and instituted state public works programs similar to those he had undertaken as mayor, and he pushed much social legislation through an antagonistic legislature. With some cause he claimed that his administration was the most progressive and the most economical in the Commonwealth's history, although his enemies compared it to that of Louisiana's Huey Long.

Curley campaigned for the U.S. Senate in 1936, but lost to Henry Cabot Lodge, Jr. He remarried on Jan. 7, 1937, taking as his second bride a widow, Gertrude Casey Dennis. In that year he ran unsuccessfully for a fourth term as mayor and in 1938 was defeated for governor by Leverett Saltonstall. He lost another mayoral contest in 1940 to a former protégé, but was returned to Congress in 1943 and reelected in 1944. He did not serve out his term, but chose instead to run again for mayor. He served a fourth term from 1945 to 1949, then lost three attempts in a row to continue as mayor (under a changed state law) in 1949, 1951, and 1955. His last public position was a 1957 appointment to the State Labor Commission.

Throughout his career Curley's enemies repeatedly charged him with corruption but proved their cases only twice. The General Equipment Corporation affair began in 1933 and culminated in 1937 during his race against Saltonstall. Curley was charged with receiving a bribe for helping to settle out of court an insurance company claim against the city. Although the chief witness was an admitted perjurer who changed his story each time he told it, the court found Curley guilty and ordered him to repay the city $42,629 at the rate of $500 per week. Unable to pay, he faced jail; but thousands of Boston citizens contributed to a fund, and after three years and thirty-four continuances he paid the sum in full. His second conviction also appeared to be a trumped-up charge. Several months before Pearl Harbor, Curley accepted the presidency of Engineers Group, Inc., a firm organized to secure war contracts. His name topped the letterhead, but he received no compensation, never interceded with any government officials in its behalf, and resigned after about six months. Four years later, while Curley was in Congress, the Justice Department indicted Curley for conspiracy and charged him with having received more than $60,000 to peddle influence. The scandal actually helped his mayoral campaign in Boston, but after his election he was brought to trial and in a bizarre jury deliberation was found guilty of using the mails to defraud. He was sentenced to eighteen months in prison, and on June 27, 1947, all appeals exhausted, the sick seventy-two-year-old man entered jail. He served but five months, being released through executive clemency by President Harry S. Truman. He returned triumphant to Boston to resume his duties as mayor. In 1950 Truman granted him a full pardon.

Few political figures of the twentieth century were more controversial, more resilient, or more colorful than Curley. Edwin O'Connor fictionalized his life in the best-selling *The Last Hurrah* (1956), perhaps the best novel about politics yet written in the United States. However, incensed by what he felt were inaccuracies, Curley responded by writing his autobiography, *I'd Do It Again* (1957), which stands alongside *The Autobiography of Lincoln Steffens* (1931) as one of the most insightful inside accounts of municipal politics. When he died, newspapers predictably headlined him "the last of the big city political bosses." Several hundred thousand came to pay their last respects at the Massachusetts State House where Curley lay in state for three days. His probated will left but slightly over $20,000; he had not grown rich in his more than half-century in politics. Perhaps his most fitting eulogy came from a longtime bitter opponent who noted that "he's been criticized a lot, but the city would be a shabby place today without having had him." His life exemplified Curley's own political motto: "Work harder than anybody else. Preserve your self-respect and keep your word."

[A candid although generally approving biography is Joseph F. Dinneen, *The Purple Shamrock: The Honorable James Michael Curley of Boston* (1949). See also Michael E. Hennessy, *Four Decades of Massachusetts Politics, 1890–1935* (1935); J. Joseph Huthmacher, *Massachusetts People and Politics, 1919–1933* (1959); Raymond Moley, *After Seven Years* (1939); and Charles H. Trout, *Boston, the Great Depression, and the New Deal* (1977).

Important obituaries include *New York Times*, Nov. 13, 15, 16, 1958; *Christian Science Monitor*, Nov. 12, 13, 15, 1958; *Newsweek*, Nov. 24, 1958; *Time*, Nov. 24, 1958; and *Economist*, Nov. 22, 1958.]

STANLEY K. SCHULTZ

CURRAN, THOMAS JEROME (Nov. 28, 1898–July 29, 1958), lawyer and politician, was born in New York City, the son of Daniel Jerome Curran and Margaret Mary Connors. Both parents had emigrated from County Kerry, Ireland. When Tom Curran was twelve, his father, a stevedore, died in a pier accident. In later years he often related the incident to assure audiences that Republicans did not lack sympathy with the working classes. Curran graduated from Xavier High School in 1916. He interrupted his studies at Fordham University in 1918 to serve as an army instructor with the rank of second lieutenant. After receiving the B.A. from Fordham in 1920, Curran taught at Xavier while earning an L.L.B. at Fordham (1923). (In 1935 he received the J.S.D. degree from St. John's University.) After being admitted to the New York bar in 1924, he worked for the State Insurance Fund for two years. On June 26, 1926, he married Margaret Frances Farley; they had two sons.

In 1928, Curran became an assistant United States attorney for the Southern District of New York, in which post began a lifelong friendship with a young colleague, Thomas E. Dewey. During three years of federal service, Curran prosecuted two important cases: the Dachis case, dealing with arson and mail fraud, and the Cotter-Butte Mines mail-fraud case, which helped spark the Seabury investigations of 1930 and 1931 that dethroned Mayor James J. Walker and rocked the foundations of Tammany Hall. In 1931 Curran returned to private practice, became a partner in Blake, Stim, and Curran, and embarked upon his political career.

Curran was an anomaly in New York City and New York County politics, a first-generation, working-class Irish Catholic who was a Republican. While at Fordham he had predicted that he would succeed Charles Francis Murphy as leader of Tammany Hall, not an unreasonable expectation for a dedicated young man raised in the Irish political fiefdom of Greenwich Village. Yet when he first ran unsuccessfully for the Board of Aldermen from the Tenth Aldermanic District in 1931, it was as a Republican. Perhaps the timing was crucial in his choice of parties. Murphy's successor in Tammany was George W. Olvany, a Greenwich Village politician whose public pronouncement—"The Irish are natural leaders .... Even the Jewish districts have Irish leaders. The Jews want to be ruled by them"—did not sit well with the Jews, Italians, and others in the city, and embarrassed many Irish as well. Olvany's tenure came to a forced end in 1929, an occurrence that signaled internal revolt within Tammany. The Seabury investigations exposed the corruption of Tammany, and Governor Franklin D. Roosevelt's attack on Walker and on Tammany threw the organization into further disarray.

In any case, Curran ran again, successfully, for alderman in 1933 and in 1935 became minority leader of the Board of Aldermen. He served until 1937. In 1940 he assumed leadership, as president and executive chairman, of the New York County Republican Committee, a powerful post he held until his death. County leaders dominated state nominating machinery, distributed much of the patronage, and exerted considerable authority in delegations to the presidential nominating conventions. Curran proved an able guide through the thicket of conciliation politics that characterized relationships between Democrats and Republicans in city and county affairs.

Like his counterparts at Tammany Hall (most notably Carmine De Sapio, with whom he often cooperated), Curran usually put the interests of his organization ahead of ideology. In 1945, for example, having vigorously supported Fiorello La Guardia for mayor four years earlier, he worked just as hard to wilt the "Little Flower." Noting that most district leaders opposed La Guardia as an ingrate, Curran denounced him as the "most artful political dodger" the city ever had known. He supported instead Judge Jonah J. Goldstein, a Tammany Democrat, until almost the eve of the nomination.

While continuing as county leader, Curran served from 1942 through 1954 as secretary of state during the governorship of his old friend Dewey. He rationalized state regulatory legislation, especially in the licensing of various professions, and pioneered the first statewide committee to oversee real estate brokerage and sales transactions.

In 1944, Curran made his only bid for national office, challenging Robert F. Wagner, the popular incumbent, for the Senate. Long known for his anti-Soviet stance, Curran tried to paint Wagner as an out-of-date "stooge of the New Deal" and a dangerous radical. Running as much against the Political Action Committee of the Congress of Industrial Organizations (CIO) and communism as against Wagner, Curran lost

badly after a campaign tainted by ethnic and religious overtones. Few questioned Curran's basic integrity, although some doubted his statesmanship. La Guardia praised him as a "good alderman" but supported Wagner, a "great United States Senator." With less charity a local newspaper supporting Dewey for president criticized the bespectacled, scholarly-looking Curran as "one who is personally as colorless as dishwater, and whose political record of achievement matches that dubious distinction."

Curran was elected commissioner of the New York City Board of Elections in 1956. Shortly before his death he faced mounting opposition to his county leadership role, signified particularly in his failure to keep the party from endorsing Adam Clayton Powell, Jr., whom the Democrats had refused to support for Congress. Curran died in New York City.

An inveterate joiner of clubs, a staunch supporter of community (he helped found the Greenwich Villager Association) and church, Curran was the personification of the "organization man." Although he never achieved national prominence, his staying power as a city and state leader of the Republicans, a party notorious for internal shifts and shambles, attested Curran's aptitude as a professional politician.

[Curran correspondence on New York state politics is in the Edward Corsi papers, 1918–1965, in the Syracuse University Library. There are no biographies of Curran. Aspects of his career and of city and state politics during his life are discussed in Warren Moscow, *Politics in the Empire State* (1948); Lynton K. Caldwell, *The Government and Administration of New York* (1954); Newbold Morris and Dana Lee Thomas, *Let the Chips Fall* (1955); Wallace S. Sayre and Herbert Kaufman, *Governing New York City* (1960); Allan Nevins, *Herbert H. Lehman and His Era* (1963); Louis Eisenstein and Elliot Rosenberg, *A Stripe of Tammany's Tiger* (1966); Warren Moscow, *What Have You Done for Me Lately?* (1967); J. Joseph Huthmacher, *Senator Robert F. Wagner and the Rise of Urban Liberalism* (1968); Warren Moscow, *The Last of the Big-Time Bosses* (1971); and Robert Caro, *The Power Broker* (1974). The Columbia University Oral History Collection, Butler Library, contains two useful sources on Republican politics: Alger B. Chapman, "Reminiscences," and Frederick M. Davenport, "Reminiscences."]

STANLEY K. SCHULTZ

CURTIS, CHARLES PELHAM (May 8, 1891–Dec. 23, 1959), lawyer and author, was born in Boston, Mass., the son of Charles Pelham Curtis, who occasionally practiced law, and Ellen

Amory Anderson. The scion of a prosperous and well-established family, he graduated from the Groton School and enrolled in Harvard in 1910. He completed the required course work in three years, and spent his senior year in Paris at the École des Sciences Politiques. On July 17, 1914, he married Edith G. Roelker; they had five children.

Curtis proceeded through Harvard Law School with as brilliant an academic record as he had compiled at Harvard College, where he had been elected to Phi Beta Kappa. Upon graduation in 1917, he was elected to the Massachusetts Constitutional Convention; and when that body completed its work, he entered the naval reserve program at Annapolis. During World War I he served as a gunnery officer on the U.S.S. *Duncan*.

After the war Curtis joined the old-line Boston law firm of Choate, Hall and Stewart, but after two years he left to accept an appointment as special assistant United States attorney for Massachusetts. In 1923 he and his brother Richard Cary Curtis opened a law office. They soon built up a prosperous practice. Curtis was a director of a number of banks and corporations. In 1930 he merged his firm with Choate, Hall and Stewart, and eventually was named senior partner. During these years he became interested in labor law, helping to draft the Massachusetts arbitration statute and serving as chairman of the state commission that revised the workmen's compensation law.

Curtis was involved in the affairs of Harvard College, and at the age of thirty-three was the youngest graduate ever elected a member of the Harvard Corporation, on which he served from 1924 to 1935. He taught at Harvard College on an adjunct basis, and with George C. Homans wrote *An Introduction to Pareto, His Sociology* (1934). Curtis also wrote on other topics, including lion-hunting (an account of a family trip), investment, and philosophy; but his two most widely noted books dealt with the Supreme Court and the J. Robert Oppenheimer case.

In *Lions Under the Throne* (1947) Curtis tried to explain the workings and power of the Supreme Court in simple, nontechnical language; several reviewers suggested that this was one of the best introductions to the institution of the court yet written. In *The Oppenheimer Case: The Trial of a Security System* (1955), Curtis pieced together lengthy quotations from the hearings transcript to fashion an indictment of the federal security program.

On Feb. 27, 1936, a year after divorcing his first wife, Curtis married Frances Woodward Prentice of Stonington, Conn. Although he had been a lifelong Republican (and remained so in state politics), he supported the New Deal; and in 1941 he served for several months as special assistant to Undersecretary of State Sumner Welles. After the war Curtis took the lead in drafting the Massachusetts Fair Employment Act and led the campaign for its passage in 1946.

For the rest of his life Curtis was a successful attorney. He also was well-known as a sportsman and aviator in the Boston area, and a member of sailing and athletic clubs, as well as social clubs and bar associations. He continued to write books and pamphlets, and in 1952 caused a minor furor in legal circles when he published an article in the *Stanford Law Review* claiming that a lawyer had a right to lie for his clients. He died at Boston, Mass., from burns suffered in a fire at his Stonington home.

[Curtis' writings include *Hunting in Africa, East and West* (1925), written with Richard C. Curtis; *The Practical Cogitator* (1945), written with Ferris Greenslet; *It's Your Law* (1947); *The Modern Prudent Investor* (1955); and *A Commonplace Book* (1957).

Biographical information is in obituaries in the *Boston Traveler*, Dec. 23, 1959, and the *New York Times*, Dec. 24, 1959; and in Harvard College Class of 1914, *Twenty-Fifth Anniversary Report* (1939) and *Fiftieth Anniversary Report* (1964).]

MELVIN I. UROFSKY

DALY, REGINALD ALDWORTH (May 19, 1871–Sept. 19, 1957), geologist and petrologist, was born on a farm near Napanee, Ont., the son of Edward Daly, a tea merchant, and Jane Maria Jeffers. After attending the public schools of Napanee, Daly entered Victoria College of the University of Toronto, where he won prizes in English literature and astronomy, a silver medal in science, and a gold medal for general proficiency. He received the B.A. in 1891, the B.S. in 1892, and during the year 1891–1892 was also instructor in mathematics.

Daly's interest in geology was aroused when A. P. Coleman held up a piece of granite and remarked, "This is made of crystals." Encouraged by interviews with Nathaniel S. Shaler and J. D. Whitney, Daly entered Harvard for graduate study in geology; he obtained the M.A. in 1893 and the Ph.D. in 1896. He was assistant to Shaler in 1894–1895. A Parker traveling fellowship enabled him to spend 1896–1897 at Heidelberg, where he learned the techniques of microscopic analysis taught by Harry Rosenbusch; and the following year he studied with Alfred Lacroix in Paris. He then returned to Harvard, where he was instructor in physiography from 1898 to 1901.

From 1901 to 1907 Daly was employed by the Geological Survey of Canada doing geological reconnaissance along the Forty-ninth Parallel Boundary. In six field seasons Daly mapped a swath from the Strait of Georgia to the Great Plains, 400 miles long and from five to ten miles wide. He was accompanied only by a mountaineer, although parties of axemen were required to clear trails through the wooded areas. Daly brought back 1,500 rock specimens and studied 960 thin sections; sixty chemical analyses were made for him. He took 1,300 photographs, sounded lakes, and reported on the stratigraphy, structure, petrology, mineral resources, glacial geology and physiography. His three-volume report was published by the Geological Survey of Canada only five years after completion of the fieldwork. Although mainly descriptive, this work contained Daly's initial attempt to explain the variety of the igneous rocks, a subject that remained his primary interest and led him deep into geochemistry and geophysics.

On June 3, 1903, Daly married Louise Porter Haskell, of Columbia, S.C., whom he had met in Cambridge. A Radcliffe College graduate, she first taught at, then acquired and directed, a school for young women in Boston. Her aid in Daly's many writings was substantial and freely acknowledged, and she accompanied him on his travels and occasionally in the field. Their only child died in infancy. In 1907 they returned to Cambridge, where Daly became professor of physical geology at the Massachusetts Institute of Technology. He became an American citizen in 1920.

At MIT Daly lectured mainly on the origin of igneous rocks. He spent two more field seasons in the Rockies, along the route of the Canadian Pacific Railway; his field assistant was one of his students, Norman L. Bowen, also a Canadian, who was to pioneer in the study of rock differentiation.

In 1912 Daly succeeded William Morris Davis as Sturgis-Hooper professor of geology at Harvard and also became chairman of the department of geology and geography, a post that he held for thirteen years. He first took over the celebrated course in elementary physical geology originated by Shaler and then introduced a new one on the igneous rocks, which evolved into a wide-ranging treatment of geological and geo-physical topics. His summers were devoted to fieldwork; he recorded that he crossed America twenty-four times and the Atlantic fourteen. He retired in 1942.

Daly's publications include some 150 papers and seven books. The earliest works were concerned mainly with the igneous rocks: *Igneous Rocks and Their Origin* (1914) developed his petrological theory; a revised version, *Igneous Rocks and the Depths of the Earth* (1933), took into account later progress in geophysics and geochemistry. Daly's theory was eclectic—as he acknowledged. His basic assumption was the existence of an eruptible substratum of basaltic composition, available nearly everywhere and at all times. Under favorable conditions this material (magma) could be injected along deep fissures and, moving upward, might surround large blocks of the crust which would then founder into the depths. These blocks might then dissolve in the magma, changing its composition and giving rise to the varieties of igneous rocks. In his search for evidence of petrological differences between continental and oceanic rocks, Daly studied the islands of Ascension, Saint Helena, Tutuila, and Hawaii. He rejected the concept of distinctly different "Atlantic" and "Pacific" rock types and emphasized the uniformity of basaltic rocks wherever found.

Oceanic problems of a different sort also engaged Daly's attention. During early expeditions to Newfoundland and Labrador he had become acquainted with raised beaches and other shore-line phenomena, and in 1910 he proposed the glacial control theory of coral reefs to explain a remarkable accordance of lagoon depths at about thirty fathoms. He expounded this and other ideas in *The Changing World of the Ice Age* (1934). He proposed that atolls were eroded to sea level during the time of the great ice sheets, when sea level was some thirty fathoms lower than its present height; the fringing reefs of coral grew again as the water returned to the seas on deglaciation. Thought at first by many to be highly improbable, Daly's theory on the origin of submarine valleys held that these valleys were excavated by submarine currents of silt-laden water pouring down the continental shelf. In recent years this concept of turbidity currents has been confirmed. With much other material, it is presented in *The Floor of the Ocean* (1942).

The discovery by Vening Meinesz of the Indonesian belt of gravity anomalies drew Daly's attention to these geophysical measurements. He had argued—based upon the generally accepted idea of isostatic equilibrium—that the substratum, where compensation was believed to take place, must be mechanically weak; and this he found in harmony with his conception of an earth shell of eruptible basalt. This subject was discussed in *Strength and Structure of the Earth* (1940).

Probably no other American geologist has been more widely read or more generously recognized by American and foreign scientific societies. In 1932 Daly was elected president of the Geological Society of America, and in 1935 he received the Society's Penrose Medal. Other awards included the Hayden Medal of the Academy of Sciences of Philadelphia, the Wollaston Medal of the Geological Society of London, and the Bowie Medal of the American Geophysical Union. He was elected to the American Academy of Arts and Sciences in 1909, the American Philosophical Society in 1913, and the National Academy of Sciences in 1925. He was a member or correspondent of nearly every European geological society, the Geological Society of South Africa, and the Indian Academy of Science. Until his death he was an associate editor of the *American Journal of Science,* and before World War II he edited *Gerland's Beiträge zur Geophysik* and *Tschermaks mineralogische und petrographische Mitteilungen.* He died in Cambridge, Mass.

[Biographies of Daly include those of Marland P. Billings, *Proceedings. Geological Society of America, 1958* (1959); Francis Birch, *Biological Memoirs. National Academy of Sciences* (1956); and Kirtley F. Mather, *Dictionary of Scientific Biography* (1971). See also the notices in the *New York Times,* Sept. 20, 1957; and *Science,* Jan. 3, 1958.]

FRANCIS BIRCH

DAMON, RALPH SHEPARD (July 6, 1897–Jan. 4, 1956), airline executive, was born in Franklin, N.H., the son of William Cotton Damon and Effie Ives. Receiving the B.A. *cum laude* from Harvard in 1918, he planned to study astronomy, but service as an air cadet during World War I converted him to a lifelong career in aviation. He learned to fly before he learned to drive a car, but opportunities in the infant aviation industry were limited, and for a time he earned a living as a millwright. On Oct. 14, 1922, he married Harriet Dudley Holcombe; they had four children. That same year he won a job at the struggling Curtiss Aeroplane and Motor Co., where he soon became factory superintendent. In

the next decade he helped develop such well-known Curtiss airplanes as the Robin, the Thrush, and the first air transport with sleeping accommodations, the Condor. In 1935 he became president of the company.

By 1936 the Douglas DC-2 (soon to be followed by the DC-3) had taken the passenger aircraft market away from Curtiss. Damon left Curtiss and joined the rapidly growing American Airlines as vice-president in charge of operations and helped build the carrier into a leading coast-to-coast airline by World War II. In 1941, with the pressing need for greatly improved military pursuit aircraft, General H. H. Arnold of the Army Air Corps persuaded Damon to take charge at Republic Aviation Corporation and put the P-47 Thunderbolt into mass production. In 1943, with 450 P-47's a month coming off the line, he returned to American Airlines and in 1945 became president under C. R. Smith, chairman of the board.

Damon was convinced that international commercial aviation would grow rapidly after the war, that the United States would dominate it for years, and that there was a place in it for American Airlines. Juan Trippe of Pan American Airways, United States pioneer in international aviation, pressed Congress in 1945 to give exclusive rights to a single "chosen instrument," a "community airline," to develop the international field on behalf of the United States. Damon, whose company's subsidiary, American Export Airlines, was struggling to gain a foothold, acted as spokesman for seventeen domestic carriers that opposed Trippe's monopoly plan. There was enough potential traffic for several international United States carriers, he asserted, and experience and efficiency would more than outweigh subsidies that foreign lines would receive. He warned that a monopoly airline would soon grow "fat and complacent" and lose its cost advantages. "Airlines should be lean and hungry," he concluded, and Congress agreed, rejecting Trippe's plan and granting certificates to Pan American, American, and Transcontinental and Western Airlines (TWA).

By 1949 Pan American, with vastly greater experience and prestige, had garnered most of the still small, premium business of overseas aviation; TWA and American were lean and hungry. Without telling Damon, Smith opened negotiations with Pan American to sell American's international subsidiary. Hours after the deal was announced Damon resigned. Several offers of jobs arrived immediately, but Damon telephoned Howard Hughes, who controlled TWA, and was accepted for the presidential post that Jack Frye had stormily vacated less than two years before.

"I've always had the good fortune to join a winning team just as it is starting to win," Damon said in 1953, by which time TWA's three-year accumulated $18.6 million deficit of 1949 had been converted to annual profits of $28 million. Air traffic boomed after 1949, and Damon's predecessor had already worked out a consolidation of two maintenance centers that saved $2 million a year, but the rejuvenation of TWA was primarily due to Damon's efforts. For the first year he traveled almost constantly. An unprepossessing, cigar-smoking, hawknosed man in a battered hat and rumpled suit, he talked to passengers, mechanics, flight attendants, and pilots whenever he could, thereby boosting employee morale while cutting away deadwood. He sold TWA's old Boeing Stratoliners, bought forty-three Lockheed Constellations for the booming coast-to-coast service, and acquired fifty-two short-haul Martin aircraft for TWA's expanded network of routes. In 1949 Damon introduced air coach travel, which opened up flying to a mass market. By 1956 passengers were flying nonstop across the continent for $99 plus tax. In that year, at the height of pre-jet aviation's golden age, Damon died in Mineola, N.Y.

[On Damon and his career, see Ralph S. Damon, " 'TWA,' Nearly Three Decades in the Air," speech, Dec. 4, 1952, before the Newcomen Society, N.Y.C., *Newcomen Society* (1952); and articles in *Fortune*, July 1949; and *Time*, Apr. 23, 1945, Jan. 31, 1949, and Feb. 16, 1953. See also the obituary notice in the *New York Times*, Jan. 5, 1956.]

ALBRO MARTIN

DAVIES, JOSEPH EDWARD (Nov. 29, 1876–May 9, 1958), lawyer, diplomat, and author, was born in Watertown, Wis., the son of Edward Davies and Rahel Paynter. His father, who had emigrated from Wales, was a successful wagonmaker; his mother had been a prominent poet under the pen name Rahel o Fôn and a minister in the Welsh Congregationalist church. Davies was valedictorian at Watertown High School, and in 1894 enrolled at the University of Wisconsin, where he played football, was a student instructor in gymnastics, and was elected to Phi Beta Kappa. He received the A.B. *cum*

laude in 1898 and the LL.B. from the university's law school in 1901, and was admitted to the Wisconsin bar that year. Returning to Watertown, Davies was a state prosecutor for Jefferson County from 1902 to 1906. On Sept. 10, 1902, he married Emlen Knight, the daughter of a wealthy lumberman. They had three daughters.

In 1906 Davies moved to Madison, where he became prominent both as a trial lawyer and in the state Democratic party. In 1910 he was appointed secretary of the Wisconsin branch of the Democratic National Committee. In 1912 he worked for the presidential nomination of Woodrow Wilson throughout the state and in Chicago as chief of the Democratic party's western headquarters.

As one of "Wilson's Young Men," a small group that included Franklin D. Roosevelt, Davies was appointed commissioner of corporations in 1913. While head of that weak investigative bureau, he helped draft the Federal Trade Commission Bill but was displeased with the final version. Although an opponent of monopolies, Davies was a lifelong believer in the fundamental soundness of capitalism and was wary of unnecessary government intervention. His relatively conservative approach became manifest when he served as the first chairman of the Federal Trade Commission (1915–1916), a position from which he was ousted by more activist commissioners. After serving briefly on the War Industries Board, Davies resigned in 1918 to run in a special senatorial election in Wisconsin. He lost by fewer than 5,000 votes to Republican Irvine L. Lenroot. It is probable that he lost because of the emotional La Follette issue—when both candidates were asked how they would vote on a pending senatorial inquiry on La Follette's statements about American involvement in World War I, Lenroot was noncommittal, while Davies publicly castigated the respected senator.

After accompanying Wilson to the Versailles peace conference, Davies resigned from government service in 1920 to establish a private law practice in Washington. His firm, which specialized in antitrust and international law, soon became one of the most prominent in the capital. In the celebrated Ford Stock Valuation Tax Case of 1927–1928, Davies was reputed to have earned $2 million, one of the largest fees in history, for winning a $30 million tax refund from the United States Board of Tax Appeals for a group of former Ford stockholders. In addition, during the 1920's and early 1930's he was counsel to governments and businesses in Mexico, Peru, the Netherlands, Greece, and the Dominican Republic. Davies made headlines in September 1935 when he divorced his wife and three months later married Marjorie Merriweather Post Hutton, heiress to the General Foods fortune, known as "Lady Bountiful of Hell's Kitchen" for her charity work. They were divorced in 1955.

A vice-chairman of the Democratic National Committee during Roosevelt's second presidential campaign, Davies was offered the post of ambassador to the Soviet Union, which he agreed to take on only a short-term basis late in 1936. Charming, poised, and worldly, Davies was without pretensions and lax in the niceties of diplomatic etiquette. He was resented by such professionals as George F. Kennan and Loy Henderson, who served under him and generally disagreed with his evaluation of the Soviet system. In addition to negotiating the renewal of a trade agreement, Davies prepared detailed reports on the Soviet economy. After an extensive tour of the country, he discovered industrial strength and vitality where others saw only an inefficient and repressive society.

Davies was one of the few members of the western diplomatic corps to witness the Soviet purge trials. He was one of even fewer westerners to believe that such eminent old Bolsheviks as Radek, Bukharin, and Zinoviev were guilty of conspiring with supporters of the exiled Leon Trotsky and with agents of Germany and Japan. Although a concealed microphone was discovered in his embassy study, he maintained the opinion that the Russians were potential friends. Thus, he advocated collective security and American support for a London–Paris–Moscow alliance to challenge the Berlin–Tokyo–Rome axis. Such views made him somewhat suspect in Washington, but popular in Moscow. Thus, before leaving Moscow in June 1938 to assume the post of ambassador to Belgium and minister to Luxembourg, his devotion to the cause of Soviet-American amity was acknowledged by an unprecedented private farewell audience with Josef Stalin.

After returning to the United States in the spring of 1940, following the fall of Belgium, Davies continued to serve Roosevelt, most notably as chairman of the President's War Relief Control Board. When Germany invaded the Soviet Union in June 1941, he was one of the few presidential advisers to express confidence in the staying power of the Red Army. With the president's blessing, Davies published his frank and chatty memoirs, *Mission to Moscow,* late in 1941. A best-seller, this extremely favorable account of the Soviet Union during the purges was made into a major movie (1943). That year Davies met with Stalin to lay the groundwork for the Teheran Conference.

Throughout the war he was an indefatigable and, to some degree, controversial propagandist for Soviet-American friendship. In May 1945 he was President Harry S. Truman's special emissary to Winston Churchill and two months later was one of the inner circle of presidential advisers at the Potsdam Conference. In 1946 President Truman awarded him the Medal for Merit, the nation's highest civilian honor.

Although he was sent by Truman to Latin America in 1951 to work on proposed Organization of American States treaties concerning nationalization, Davies spent most of his last years in private law practice. He died in Washington, D.C. His ashes were placed next to those of Woodrow Wilson in the National Cathedral.

The controversial and colorful Davies was an unusual American businessman-diplomat. He was a millionaire who supported presidents Wilson and Roosevelt in their attempts to regulate American capitalism. Although other businessmen also believed that the salvation of the American system depended on the establishment of a welfare state, few agreed with him about both the desirability and the possibility of Soviet-American cooperation in world affairs. For those who believe that American misconceptions of Russian policies at the end of World War II contributed significantly to the creation of the Cold War, Davies stands as a statesman of singular vision.

[Davies' papers are at the Library of Congress and include an unpublished autobiography, "In the Days of Their Power and Glory," and "Biographical Notes." There is no full-length study. The best accounts are "Ambassador Davies," *Fortune,* Oct. 1937; Richard H. Ullman, "The Davies Mission and United States–Soviet Relations, 1937–1941," *World Politics,* Jan. 1957, a brief critical account; and Keith D. Eagles, "Ambassador Joseph E. Davies and American-Soviet Relations" (Ph.D. diss., University of Washington, 1966). A number of references to Davies appear in oral history memoirs in the Columbia University Oral History Collection, especially that of George Rublee.]

MELVIN SMALL

DAVIS, ELMER HOLMES (Jan. 13, 1890–May 18, 1958), news commentator and writer, was born in Aurora, Ind., the son of Louise Severin, a former high school teacher, and Elam Holmes Davies, a bank cashier. In the fall of 1906 he entered Franklin (Ind.) College, where he edited the school paper, wrote plays, and graduated *magna cum laude* with the B.A. in 1910. Davis won a Rhodes Scholarship to Queens College at Oxford University, where he studied Greek language, literature, and history. He received the B.A. with a second place in 1912, despite shortening the normal reading period by a year. He then traveled extensively on the Continent.

After the death of his father in 1913, Davis returned to the United States to become a writer. After working on *Adventure* magazine for several months, he was offered a job as cub reporter with the *New York Times* early in 1914. The following year, his sardonic wit won him the chance to cover one of the more whimsical stories of the decade, the voyage of Henry Ford's Peace Ship, aimed at ending the war in Europe. On Feb. 5, 1917, he married Florence MacMillan; they had two children. In 1920 Davis created columnist Godfrey M. Gloom, a character reminiscent of Finley Peter Dunne's "Mr. Dooley," whose acerbic political commentary appeared in most presidential campaigns until he was laid to rest in 1936. Davis also published an official history of the newspaper (1921).

While with the *Times,* Davis began to write the articles, stories, and novels that enabled him to strike out on his own as a free lance on Dec. 31, 1923. With two moderately successful novels behind him, and one already accepted for publication, he began contributing regularly to the *New Yorker,* the *Saturday Review of Literature, Harper's, New Republic,* and *Collier's.* By 1935 he had published nine novels.

But Davis always retained an interest in European politics, and after Hitler's reoccupation of the Rhineland in 1936, he turned decisively to foreign affairs. A series of perceptive articles analyzing the political situation in Europe appeared in *Harper's* in 1937 and 1938. Largely on the strength of these, in August 1939 he was asked by the Columbia Broadcasting System to become a radio news analyst replacing H. V. Kaltenborn, who was being transferred to Europe. Davis soon won a nationwide reputation with his brief but pertinent broadcasts mixing news and commentary. Millions of listeners grew to trust the man with the unemotional midwestern twang who refused to sugarcoat the news.

This reputation for truthfulness led President Franklin D. Roosevelt in June 1942 to appoint Davis head of the newly created Office of War Information (OWI). Although he believed his main task was simply to persuade the armed services and government agencies to release more war-related news, he soon discovered that it was impossible to coordinate and disseminate information about the president's programs without appearing to be an administration propagandist and thus incurring congressional hostility. Davis' talents were useless here, but he remained in the OWI in order to serve Roosevelt, who, he believed, embodied the best interests of the nation. By late 1943 he had succeeded in freeing the flow of military news; but as he later observed, "It certainly helped that from then on we had nothing but victories to report."

In September 1945 Davis wrote OWI's final report, and three months later he joined the American Broadcasting Company radio network. His twice-weekly broadcasts (increased to five in 1947) maintained the kind of good sense and fairness that had first won him a large audience. During the late 1940's, despite his opposition to communism, he tried to clarify the difference between external aggression, as represented by Soviet intervention in Czechoslovakia, and popular revolution, as exemplified by the Chinese communist revolution. At a time when such views were unpopular, he attacked the House Un-American Activities Committee for its persecution of individuals, and he attempted to place the highly charged issue of subversion in government in a rational perspective. In 1950, shocked by the anticommunist hysteria fostered by Senator Joseph McCarthy, Davis began to speak out against the excesses of the times, voicing support for besmirched public servants and academics. His strong defense of civil liberties won him the George Foster Peabody Radio Award in 1951. The citation observed that "in a year of great anxiety and bitter partisanship it has been reassuring and edifying to hear the sanity, the horse sense, and the dry Hoosier wit with which Mr. Davis contemplates a troubled world."

Acting on his conviction that ethics and principles should apply to one's political as well as one's personal life, Davis traveled throughout the United States in 1953, speaking on the need to defend freedom of thought. "Don't let them scare you" was the theme of his speeches, which were published the following year as *But We Were Born Free*. In 1955 *Two Minutes Till Midnight*, dealing with the threat of thermonuclear war, appeared. Soon afterward, advanced heart disease forced Davis to give up broadcasting. He died in New York City.

[Roger Burlingame, *Don't Let Them Scare You* (1961), is the only biography. Davis' papers are at the Library of Congress, manuscripts of his radio broadcasts are at the New York Public Library, and his OWI records are at the National Archives. Collections of his articles and speeches include *Not to Mention the War* (1940); *But We Were Born Free* (1954); *Two Minutes Till Midnight* (1955); and *By Elmer Davis* (1964). His OWI experience is recounted in "The Office of War Information Report to the President," available on microfilm. His novels include *The Princess Cecilia* (1915); *Times Have Changed* (1923); and *White Pants Willie* (1932). Davis' account of the Ford Peace Ship was obtained by the Columbia University Oral History Collection in 1955; he also is mentioned in memoirs by others.]

SYDNEY STAHL WEINBERG

DAVIS, OWEN GOULD (Jan. 28, 1874–Oct. 14, 1956), playwright, was born in Portland, Me., the son of Owen Warren Davis and Abigail Augusta Gould. His father was in the iron-manufacturing business in Bangor, Me., where Owen attended public school but did not finish high school. When he was fifteen his family moved to Middlesborough, Ky., and in 1889 he entered the University of Tennessee as a "sub-freshman" but left after a year "on my father's wishes that I should go to a northern school." He was admitted to Harvard as a special student in 1890, and two years later he enrolled in the Lawrence Scientific School of the university, where he specialized in geology. He left Harvard in 1893, without taking a degree, to work as a geologist and mining engineer.

He became disillusioned with the coal-mining business, however, and in 1895 he left Cumberland Gap, Tenn., for New York and a career in the theater. Davis had written plays as a youngster and had attended the theater regularly in Cambridge, so he was not totally unprepared for his new occupation. He worked at a variety of jobs until 1897 when, after seeing a production of *The Great Train Robbery*, he wrote a spectacular melodrama, *Through the Breakers*, produced in New York City on Jan. 30, 1899. Its success encouraged him to continue writing, and by the

time of his death he was credited with approximately 200 plays. (The exact number is obscured by his liberal use of pseudonyms.) From 1901 to 1934 there was at least one Davis production in New York City every season.

His early reputation was made in the "ten-twenty-thirty" melodrama—so called from the price, in cents, of seats—popular entertainment that relied heavily on sensational scenic effects and thrilling escapes. Davis became so famous in the popular theater that in 1905 he signed an exclusive contract with the producer Al Woods to deliver at least four "mellers" every year until 1909. In addition Woods guaranteed to revive four of the previously produced plays each season. Some of their most famous productions were *Confessions of a Wife* (1905), *Nellie, the Beautiful Cloak Model* (1906), and *Edna, the Pretty Typewriter* (1907).

In the summer of 1901 Davis leased the Baker Theater in Rochester, N.Y., and organized a stock company for the production of his plays. In that company was a twenty-year-old soubrette, Elizabeth Drury Breyer, whom Davis married sometime between March 1901 and May 1902. They had two children, both of whom pursued theatrical careers. Donald, a writer, coauthored with his father dramatizations of *The Good Earth* (1932) and *Ethan Frome* (1936) and wrote for television and films. Owen, Jr., an actor and television producer, was drowned accidentally in Long Island Sound on May 21, 1949.

By 1909 Davis had grown weary of "cheap" melodramas and began writing plays aimed at the more sophisticated Broadway audience. He was influenced by Eugene Walter's *The Easiest Way*, which he considered a great play. He had some success in 1913 with his social melodrama *The Family Cupboard*, and in 1915 *Sinners* ran for 220 performances. *Forever After* (1918), a sentimental war story starring Alice Brady, brought him additional recognition, as did *At 9:45*, a successful mystery play produced the following year.

But Davis' transition to the Broadway theater was not complete until 1921 when, under the influence of Eugene O'Neill, he wrote *The Detour*, a somber study of life on a Long Island truck farm. The play ran for only forty-eight performances, but its realistic characters and naturalistic dialogue earned him the critical praise that he had been seeking. Two years later *Icebound*, written in the same vein, won the Pulitzer prize, and Davis was elected to the National Institute of Arts and Letters.

In addition to serious dramas Davis also wrote Broadway comedies: *The Haunted House* (1924), *Easy Come, Easy Go* (1925), and *The Nervous Wreck* (1923), which was made into a musical with Eddie Cantor *(Whoopee,* 1928) and a film with Danny Kaye *(Up in Arms,* 1944). He dramatized *The Great Gatsby* (1926) and adapted *The Insect Comedy* as *The World We Live In* (1922). His mystery plays included *The Donovan Affair* (1926) and *The Ninth Guest* (1930).

As his prestige grew Davis joined his colleagues in the fight to expand copyright protection for American playwrights. He was instrumental in negotiating the crucial minimum basic contract between the Managers Protective Association and the Dramatists Guild in 1926, and he was active in the play jury schemes to prevent state censorship of the theater. In the summer of 1926 he was offered a chair in dramatic literature by the University of Michigan.

To the end, however, Davis was a commercial writer, and in spite of his honors and accomplishments he always returned to the popular stage. He spoke repeatedly of the "great play" that he wanted to write, but his gift was the capture and reflection of the changing public taste. He was most effective in melodrama and farce, and in the 1930's he wrote film scripts for Will Rogers (*They Had to See Paris,* 1929, and *So This Is London,* 1930) and radio scripts for "The Gibson Family" (1934). His Broadway efforts included *Jezebel* (1933) and *Mr. and Mrs. North* (1941). But failing eyesight and recurrent stomach disorders slowed his pace. *No Way Out,* a failure in 1944, was the last production of his prodigious career, which spanned the theater from Bronson Howard to Tennessee Williams and earned him the reputation of America's most prolific and most produced playwright. He died in New York City.

[Davis' papers and MSS are controlled by his son Donald Davis, but have not been available for examination. There are, however, some scripts at the New York Public Library and the Library of Congress. Two autobiographies, *I'd Like to Do It Again* (1931) and *My First Fifty Years in the Theater* (1950), are chatty and informative but sometimes inexact with regard to dates and events. Biographical sketches (which sometimes reprint Davis' own faulty recollections) appear in *Who's Who in the Theatre,* 10th ed. (1947); *Twentieth Century Authors* (1950); and the obituary notice, *New York Times,* Oct. 15, 1956. See also Frank Rahill, "When Heaven Protected the Working Girl," *Theatre Arts,* Oct. 1954; Lewin Goff,

"The Owen Davis-Al Woods Melodrama Factory." *Educational Theatre Journal,* Oct. 1959; and Barry B. Witham, "Owen Davis: America's Forgotten Playwright." *Players,* Oct.–Nov. 1970.]

BARRY B. WITHAM

DAVISSON, CLINTON JOSEPH (Oct. 22, 1881–Feb. 1, 1958), physicist and codiscoverer of the wave nature of the electron, was born in Bloomington, Ill., the son of Joseph Davisson, a painter and paperhanger, and Mary Calvert. Davisson was frail from childhood, never weighing much more than a hundred pounds throughout his life. He did not start school until the age of seven and lost an additional year through illness, graduating from Bloomington High School at the age of twenty. Davisson achieved scholastic distinction despite his limited physical resources and the need to work at night as an operator at the McLean County Telephone Company. Upon graduation he received a one-year scholarship for proficiency in physics and mathematics to the University of Chicago, which he entered in the fall of 1902.

Davisson immediately came under the influence of Robert A. Millikan, who received the Nobel prize in physics in 1923 for his researches on the elementary charge of the electron and the photoelectric effect. Davisson's first course with Millikan was crucial; he was "delighted to find that physics was the concise, orderly science [he] had imagined it to be, and that a physicist could be so openly and earnestly concerned about such matters as colliding bodies." It was fortunate that this early exposure was so positive, for at the end of his freshman year Davisson had to leave the university for lack of funds. He obtained temporary employment at the telephone company in Bloomington until January 1904, when he obtained, upon Millikan's recommendation, a temporary position as assistant in physics at Purdue University. By June he was able to return to the University of Chicago, where he continued his studies until August 1905. Forced to leave again for lack of money, Davisson was appointed part-time instructor in physics at Princeton, again upon Millikan's recommendation; he held this post until 1910. He returned to Chicago during the summers of 1906, 1907, and 1908, and finally obtained the B.S. in August 1908.

While at Princeton, Davisson had come under the influence of Owen W. Richardson. This electron physicist from England received the Nobel prize in physics in 1928 for his work on the thermionic emission of electrons. Davisson later credited his own success to having caught "the physicist's point of view—his habit of mind—his way of looking at things" from Millikan and Richardson rather than to any sequence of courses. His Ph.D. dissertation at Princeton (1911) was an extension of research initiated by Richardson on the positive ions emitted from alkaline metal salts, a topic of many of his later studies. On Aug. 4, 1911, Davisson married Richardson's sister, Charlotte Sara, who had come from England to visit her brother. They had four children.

In the fall of 1911 Davisson joined the Carnegie Institute of Technology in Pittsburgh as an instructor in physics. His eighteen-hour teaching load left him little time for research, and during his six years there he published only three short theoretical notes. In the summer of 1913 he visited the Cavendish Laboratory in Cambridge, England, where he worked with J.J. Thomson, who had been awarded the Nobel prize for physics in 1906. After the entry of the United States into World War I, Davisson attempted to enlist in the military service but was refused because of his frail health. He therefore took a leave from Carnegie Tech to work in military telecommunications research with the engineering department of the Western Electric Company Laboratories in New York City. His work involved supervising the development and testing of an oxide-coated nickel filament to substitute for the platinum filament then in use. After the war he accepted a permanent research position at Western Electric.

Relieved of the responsibility of supervising routine filament tests, Davisson turned to a program of basic research in oxide-coated cathodes. Western Electric was interested in these devices because of the need to supply the parent Bell Telephone Company with reliable signal amplifiers. As an offshoot of this work, Davisson and his assistant, Charles H. Kunsman, discovered late in 1920 that electrons directed at a clean nickel target in a vacuum were reflected with virtually no loss in energy, that is, they were elastically scattered. Realizing that these "billiard ball" electrons might serve as a tool for exploring the extranuclear structure of target atoms, Davisson and Kunsman developed an extensive program of scattering electrons from different materials. Despite considerable experimental and mathematical ingenuity, they failed to achieve a correlation between their findings and theoretical predictions. They abandoned the project late in

1923, at which time Kunsman left the company.

A year later, joined by Lester H. Germer, Davisson resumed the electron-scattering project. On Feb. 5, 1925, while the electron tube was being reactivated, an accident occurred that eventually changed the character of the investigation. The experimental tube cracked for some unknown reason, and the inrushing air badly oxidized the hot nickel target. The ensuing repairs involved extensive heating of the target in hydrogen and in a vacuum; when the experiments were resumed, the results obtained were markedly different from those noted by Davisson and Kunsman. The resulting shift in the experimental program, in which the polished nickel target was replaced by a specially prepared single crystal of nickel, took more than a year to prepare. The experimenters hoped that the new experiments would show how the electrons were scattered by the various crystal planes of the target, but again the results were inconclusive.

In the summer of 1926, Davisson and his wife took a vacation trip to England. He brought along some of the results of his recent experiments, which he showed to friends and colleagues at the Oxford meeting of the British Association for the Advancement of Science. Considerable interest was shown in these results, which the European physicists interpreted as possible evidence for the new wave theory of the electron then being discussed. (This idea, introduced by Louis de Broglie in 1923, had been extensively developed by Erwin Schrödinger early in 1926.) On his trip home Davisson studied the new wave mechanics with great excitement.

Davisson and Germer then embarked upon the final phase of their work, which was based on the assumption that their scattering experiments might enable them to learn something about the electron rather than about the target. Using the known properties of single crystals rather than of billiard-ball electrons, they experimentally substantiated essentially all the new features of the new wave theory of the electron. In a series of exhaustive experiments and comprehensive papers published from 1927 to 1929, they demonstrated that electrons, like light, have the dual properties of particles and waves. For this work Davisson shared the Nobel prize for physics in 1937 with George P. Thomson, who had come to the same conclusion—in an entirely different way—soon afterward.

Davisson did not pursue this new field of electron diffraction much beyond 1930, by which time his interests had shifted to electron optics. With his colleagues at Bell Telephone Laboratories (Western Electric had reorganized their research department under this name in 1925) he made fundamental contributions to electron lenses, electron microscopes, and early versions of a television receiver. After retiring in 1946 he became visiting professor of physics at the University of Virginia. He retired in 1954 and died in Charlottesville, Va.

Although neither impetuous nor innovative, Davisson could pursue any idea or shred of evidence to its conclusion. This careful approach enabled him to achieve unique results in the demanding field of high-vacuum electron beam tubes. Shy, modest, and reserved, he was ill at ease with the fame that his accomplishments brought him; yet his friends and family testify to his warmth, sparkle, and wit.

[There is an extensive collection of Davisson's personal papers at the Library of Congress; the Owen W. Richardson Papers, available on microfilm at the American Institute of Physics, New York City, contain much valuable correspondence. The records of his research are in the notebooks of L. H. Germer, C. H. Kunsman, and C. J. Calbick at the Bell Telephone Laboratories, May Hill, N.J. A nearly complete bibliography of his works follows Mervin J. Kelly's sketch, *Biographical Memoirs. National Academy of Sciences,* 36 (1962); his most important paper is "Diffraction of Electrons by a Crystal of Nickel," *Physical Review,* Dec. 1927, written with L. H. Germer. A comprehensive study of their discovery is Richard K. Gehrenbeck, "C. J. Davisson, L. H. Germer, and the Discovery of Electron Diffraction" (Ph.D. diss., University of Minnesota, 1973.]

RICHARD K. GEHRENBECK

DAWLEY, ALMENA (1890–Dec. 12, 1956), sociologist and educator, was born in Silver Creek, N.Y., the daughter of Frank Dawley, a civil servant, and Jennie Smith. In 1908 Dawley enrolled at Oberlin College, where she was exposed to the possibilities of a life of social service. After graduating in 1912 with a B.A., she attended the University of Chicago, from which she received an M.A. in commerce and administration in 1915. Her dissertation, "A Study of the Social Effects of the Municipal Court of Chicago," is generally regarded as a cornerstone of research in the field of social work. In it she suggested a humane but paternalistic approach toward those whom she regarded as the victims of society: "Very often, it is not a fine, not impris-

onment, nor even probation that an offender needs, but treatment in a hospital for his diseased or backward mind." Dawley saw possibilities for altruism and education in social institutions: ". . . the court should make the most of its opportunity of having before it human material which may be molded into better stuff."

Appointed supervisor of the department of social investigation for the Pennsylvania School for Social Service in 1920, Dawley took charge of reform investigations of the women's penal institutions, Bedford and Auburn, in New York State. Together with Mabel Ruth Fernald and Mary Holmes Stevens Hayes, she issued an influential report, *A Study of Women Delinquents in New York State* (1920).

Dawley's commitment was to the modernization and humanization of public institutions and to the training of health professionals to service them. Ever insistent on maintaining a balance between theoretical and practical training for the professional social worker, she spoke forcefully on the value of clinical training. She was one of the first researchers to raise child guidance and social work to the professional level. Her life demonstrated the effectiveness of coupling academic and practical commitments. She taught, first at Bryn Mawr from 1928 to 1936, and then at the University of Pennsylvania. In 1925 she and Frederick H. Allen founded the innovative Child Guidance Clinic in Philadelphia, which specialized in working with entire families as well as with children in clinical situations.

Dawley was a consultant to the surgeon general of the army and to the United States Public Health Service; she helped to establish the classification of psychiatric social workers in the army and air force. She never married. She died in Flourtown, Pa., shortly after retiring as associate director of the Child Guidance Clinic.

[Dawley published "Contribution of Mental Hygiene to the Theory and Practice of Case Work." *Proceedings of the National Conference of Social Work,* 55 (1928); and "Coordination of Effort in Mental Hygiene," *ibid.,* 56 (1929). See also the obituary notice, *New York Times,* Dec. 13, 1956.]

ANNETTE NIEMTZOW

DAY, ARTHUR LOUIS (Oct. 30, 1869– Mar. 2, 1960), geophysicist, was born in Brookfield, Mass., the son of Daniel Putnam Day and Fannie Maria Hobbs. After two years of tutoring by an energetic high school teacher, he entered

Yale and in 1892 graduated from the Sheffield Scientific School of the university with the B.A. He was then appointed Sloane fellow in physics and earned the Ph.D. in 1894. While at Yale, Day became acquainted with Josiah Willard Gibbs, who greatly influenced the scientific focus of his career. He taught for three years at Sheffield, then sought a wider experience at the Physikalisch-Technische Reichsanstalt in Berlin, then one of the best-equipped physics laboratories in the world. After a few months as a volunteer assistant he became a member of the staff, a remarkable feat for a non-German. On Aug. 20, 1900, Day married Helene Kohlrausch, daughter of the director of the Reichsanstalt. They had four children.

When the need for more physical chemistry in geology was recognized, the United States Geological Survey established a physical laboratory in 1900; and Day, persuaded by Carl Barus, who was then at Brown University, accepted a temporary appointment as physical geologist that fall. The physical laboratory was supported by supplemental funds from the newly established Carnegie Institution of Washington, and special grants were made to Day for his research during 1904–1906. On Jan. 1, 1907, he was appointed the first director of the Geophysical Laboratory of the Carnegie Institution of Washington, retaining the position, except for a leave of absence from 1918 to 1920, until his retirement in 1936. During World War I his marriage was severely strained, presumably by his wife's outspoken pro-German sentiments. When the war ended she returned to Germany; they were divorced in 1931. Day married Ruth Sarah Easling, his secretary, on Mar. 27, 1933. They had no children.

Three major scientific investigations were pioneered by Day at the United States Geological Survey. The first was the extension of the standard thermometer scale from 1200° to 1600°C., a task that he started at the Reichsanstalt, mainly with Ludwig Holborn. The nitrogen gas thermometer scale remains the thermodynamic standard and is still in use at the Geophysical Laboratory. The scale was essential for progress in studying the thermal behavior of common minerals that melt at very high temperatures.

In a second investigation Day, with the help of Eugene T. Allen and Joseph P. Iddings, measured the thermal stability of the major feldspar solid-solution series, albite-anorthite, using the cooling-curve method. The feldspars constitute 60 percent of the igneous rocks in the earth's crust. That classic study, reconfirmed several times with only relatively minor changes, contained a wealth of detailed observations on crystal growth.

The third investigation was the initiation of a major plan to study the physicochemical behavior of phases in systems of important oxides in the earth's crust. The first of these systems was calcium oxide-silica, which was expanded in 1911 to include alumina, the portland cement system. These major oxide systems now constitute a major source of fundamental information important not only to geology but also to the steel, cement, and glass industries.

After the completion of the Geophysical Laboratory in June 1907, and prior to World War I, Day set up a program, mainly with R. B. Sosman, of measuring the melting points of minerals on the gas thermometer scale; the physical properties of important end-member minerals also were measured. He next turned his attention to the nature and importance of volcanic gases, and joined Ernest S. Shepherd in the collection and analysis of gas samples from lava. They found water vapor to be the principal volcanic gas, thereby disproving the existing notion that such gases were anhydrous. Day took part in the physical and chemical studies of Kilauea (Hawaii), Mount Lassen (California), Mount Pelée (West Indies), the volcanoes of Guatemala, the geysers and hot springs of Yellowstone (Wyoming), and the fumaroles of the Valley of Ten Thousand Smokes (Alaska). His great breadth of interests led to the initiation of innovative programs for quantitative geological research, such as high-pressure phase chemistry, silicate calorimetry, spectral mineralogy, and hydrothermal mineral synthesis.

Because of their experience in the Geophysical Laboratory on the melting behavior of silicates, the staff members were called upon to help expand the fledgling optical glass industry when supplies from Germany were cut off by World War I. Day had been a research consultant for the Corning Glass Works, Corning, N.Y., since 1905 and was active in expanding its research. In 1918 he took a leave of absence from the Geophysical Laboratory to become vice-president in charge of manufacturing. He resumed the directorship of the laboratory in 1920, continuing as vice-president at Corning with less active participation. One of his earliest papers (1906) was on so-called quartz glass; his principal contribution was in placing the glass industry on a systematic scientific basis instead of relying on secretive "cookbook" methods arrived at by trial and error.

In 1921 Day was appointed chairman of the new Advisory Committee in Seismology of the Carnegie Institution of Washington. With his flair for organization, he mobilized one of the largest cooperative efforts in American science to study the earthquakes in southern California. The high level of seismology in the United States can be attributed in large measure to his efforts.

Day's organizational ability was recognized by his fellow scientists. He served as president of the Philosophical Society of Washington (1911), the Washington Academy of Sciences (1924), and the Geological Society of America (1938). He was elected to the National Academy of Sciences in 1911 and served as home secretary (1913–1918) and vice-president (1933–1941). An entire volume of the *American Journal of Science,* containing twenty-three papers on geophysics and geochemistry, was dedicated to him in 1938.

Recognizing the valuable stimulus of such honors, Day established a fund in 1948 for an Arthur L. Day Medal to be awarded annually by the Geological Society of America in recognition of "distinction in the application of physics and chemistry to the solution of geological problems." He also left a bequest of nearly $1.4 million to the National Academy of Sciences "for the purpose of advancing studies of the physics of the earth."

Day was a formal yet cordial person of great charm and dignity. His co-workers described him as shy and sensitive. Many associates recalled his help and kindness, especially during the Great Depression. He was a polished lecturer whose talks were usually based on firsthand observations and were documented with hand-colored photographic slides. As an administrator he gave his staff members complete freedom to do their research provided they were willing to accept the responsibilities of scientific leadership. A leader of scientists, he attracted an illustrious staff and established an environment of sound scholarship. He died in Bethesda, Md.

[The Carnegie Institution of Washington has a "Biography" of Day dated Mar. 25, 1922. See "American Contemporaries: Arthur Louis Day," *Industrial and Engineering Chemistry. News Edition,* Sept. 10, 1936; Robert B. Sosman, "Arthur Louis Day," *Yearbook. American Philosophical Society* for 1960, which contains a complete bibliography of Day's writings; "Memorial to Arthur Louis Day," *Bulletin of the Geological Society of America,* Nov. 1964; F. W. Preson, "Debt of Glass Technology to Geologists," *Ceramic Bulletin,* 44 (1965); and Philip H. Abelson, "Arthur Louis Day," *Biographical Memoirs. National Academy of Sciences,* 47 (1975), with bibliography of his works.]

H. S. YODER, JR.

DAY, GEORGE PARMLY (Sept. 4, 1876–Oct. 24, 1959), financier, publisher, and university executive, was born in New York City, the son of Clarence Shepard Day, a Wall Street broker, and Lavinia Elizabeth Stockwell. His boyhood traits of punctuality and salesmanship were humorously described by his older brother Clarence in *Life With Father* (1935), a best-selling memoir of the Day household. After attending Columbia Grammar School in New York City and St. Paul's School, Concord, N.H., Day entered Yale University, from which he graduated with a B.A. in 1897.

That same year Day joined the brokerage house of Clarence S. Day and Company as a clerk. In 1899 be became a partner in the firm, which was reorganized in 1903 as Day, Adams and Company. To a successful Wall Street career he added, in 1907, an innovative venture into academic publishing. With two other Yale graduates, his brother Clarence, and Edwin Oviatt, Day established the Yale Publishing Association to publish the *Yale Alumni Weekly,* the *Yale Review,* and other university-related publications. The following year, after consultation with Yale authorities, he founded the Yale University Press, which became, under his direction, one of the major scholarly presses in the world.

At first the entire staff of the press consisted of Day and his wife, Wilhelmine Octavia Johnson, whom he had married on Oct. 11, 1902. The first volume to appear under the Yale imprint was Benjamin W. Bacon's *Commentaries on the Gospel of St. Mark* (1909). A year later the press issued its first catalog, with a listing of twenty titles. In 1910 Day resigned from his brokerage firm to become treasurer of Yale University and moved the offices of the press from New York to New Haven.

In two influential addresses delivered in 1914, Day outlined his views on the function of a university press. Institutions of higher learning, he observed, were playing an increasingly active role in community affairs, and university presses must broaden their horizons accordingly. It was no longer sufficient for a press to serve the needs of a scholarly elite. Besides soliciting manuscripts from professors in rival institutions around the globe, a university-sponsored enterprise should publish a substantial number of important non-technical works that would attract the intelligent lay reader. Only in this way might a scholarly press fulfill its proper mission, which Day described as "university extension work of the finest kind."

Day's interest in broadening the scope and appeal of university publications found a practical expression in the Chronicles of America Picture Corporation, a New York enterprise that he organized in 1923 to produce a series of films dealing with critical periods in American history. Prominent historians served as advisers for the project, which partly was designed to popularize the press's *Chronicles of America* series. When Day resigned as president of the Yale University Press in 1944, its publications included some 1,800 titles in virtually every field except fiction and school textbooks.

Day's innovative publishing ideas also extended to problems of distribution. In 1914 he called upon the directors of other university presses to join in a cooperative marketing effort, and two years later he and Chester Lane established the University Press Association, which maintained a joint sales agency for its members in New York City. The association received little support from most presses, however, and collapsed after several years. Not until 1946, with the creation of the Association of American University Presses, was Day's farsighted vision fully realized. He was more successful in negotiating a foreign marketing arrangement with Oxford University Press, which agreed to distribute Yale publications abroad.

As treasurer of Yale University from 1910 to 1942, Day became celebrated for his effective fund-raising efforts. When he took office, the university's endowments totaled $12 million. By the time of his retirement this figure had risen to $101 million. Some of these funds were earmarked for the use of the press, which was able to install its own printing plant in 1919 as a result of alumni generosity. Day also served as treasurer of the Yale Athletic Association (1916–1932), chairman of the President's Committee on University Development (1938–1941), and director of the Yale Alumni Fund (1942–1959).

Dignified and somewhat forbidding in appearance, Day displayed little of his brother Clarence's whimsicality. But the ties of kinship

were evident in Day's penchant for fugitive verse. He wrote the lyrics for several college songs, including "The Wearers of the Green," the official song of Dartmouth College, and the humorous "Goodnight, Poor Harvard," which long remained a favorite with Yale undergraduates. A collection of his occasional poems, *Rhymes of the Times,* was published by Yale University Press in 1956.

Despite a crowded schedule, Day participated in local civic and philanthropic enterprises. Although he had no children of his own, he took a special interest in the work of the Connecticut Junior Republic, a juvenile rehabilitation agency that he, Irving Fisher, and other Yale figures helped to found at Litchfield in 1904. The Connecticut organization was an offshoot of William R. George's celebrated Junior Republic of Freeville, N.Y. (1895), one of the most successful reform efforts of the Progressive period. Day served as president and trustee of the Connecticut Junior Republic. He died in New Haven.

[Unpublished letters from Day are in the Charles Parsons Papers at Yale University and in the Records of the George Junior Republic at Cornell University. Day's contribution to the Junior Republic movement may be traced in Jack M. Holl, *Juvenile Reform in the Progressive Era* (1971). Day explained his approach to publishing in *The New Era of Publishing at Yale* (1914); *The Function and Organization of University Presses* (1915); *The Yale University Press* (1917); and *Yale Publishing As University Extension Work* (1922). On the early years of the Yale University Press, see Clarence Shepard Day, *The Story of the Yale University Press Told By a Friend* (1920); and Chester Kerr, *A Report on American University Presses* (1949). Campus politics during Day's tenure as treasurer are analyzed in George Wilson Pierson, *Yale: College and University, 1871–1937* (1955). See also Day's obituary notice, *New York Times,* Oct. 25, 1959.]

MAXWELL BLOOMFIELD

DEAN, GORDON EVANS (Dec. 28, 1905–Aug. 15, 1958), lawyer and business executive, was born in Seattle, Wash., the son of the Reverend John Marvin Dean, a Baptist minister, and Beatrice Alice Fisken. He attended public schools in Chicago, New York City, and Pasadena, Calif.; received the B.A. at the University of Redlands in 1927; and attended law school at the University of Southern California, graduating with the J.D. in 1930. On Aug. 9, 1930, Dean married Adelaide Williamson; they had two children.

Dean accepted a position as assistant dean and instructor of law at the Duke University Law School in Durham, N.C., in 1930. During his four years there, he gained admission to the bars of California (1930) and North Carolina (1931), and earned the master of laws at Duke (1932).

In 1934 Dean left Duke with Justin Miller, dean of the law school, to undertake a special study for the Department of Justice. They were to devise a more uniform system of probation, parole, and pardon in federal and state jurisdictions. This assignment brought Dean into the criminal division under Assistant Attorney General Brien McMahon. There Dean helped carry out the widespread reforms launched in the Justice Department by Attorney General Homer S. Cummings during the Roosevelt administration. He helped organize the National Crime Conference in December 1934 and drafted legislation for implementing Cummings' twelve-point program to broaden federal authority in prosecuting racketeers, bank robbers, kidnappers, and other felons who were taking advantage of the limitations of state laws. Dean also tested these laws by trying several key cases in United States district courts. He was admitted to practice before the United States Supreme Court in 1935, and, as chief of the appellate section in the criminal division, he argued a number of cases before the Supreme Court during the next three years.

Dean's outstanding work in the criminal division led Cummings to appoint him as special executive assistant to the attorney general in 1937. He was in charge of public affairs for the Department of Justice, and he advised the attorney general on the public relations aspects of all policy decisions in the department. He served in a similar capacity under Attorney General Robert H. Jackson. During this same period he also taught jurisprudence at the American University in Washington, D.C., and was a special lecturer on the American legal system at the Department of State.

In April 1940 Dean joined two former Justice Department associates, Brien McMahon and Walter E. Gallagher, in private law practice in Washington. During the next three years he handled several large accounts and a number of antitrust cases for the firm. In 1940 Chief Justice Charles Evans Hughes appointed him to an advisory committee to draft rules of procedure for the federal courts. Dean served on the committee until the new rules were adopted by the Congress and the Supreme Court in 1944.

Late in 1943 Dean joined the navy as an intelligence officer. In May 1945, while still serving in the navy, he was selected by Jackson, now an associate justice of the Supreme Court, to serve as his assistant in prosecuting major Nazi war criminals in Germany. Dean assisted Jackson in drafting the plan for establishing the International Military Tribunal during the summer of 1945 and then was largely responsible for collecting and organizing the massive compendium of documents to be used as evidence in the prosecutions. He resigned his navy commission in September 1945, and after the conclusion of the Nuremberg trials in 1946 he returned for health reasons to California, where he became professor of criminal law at the University of Southern California. At the same time he was also engaged in a private law practice and owned and operated an avocado and citrus ranch in Vista, Calif.

In the spring of 1949, at the suggestion of McMahon, who was now a United States senator from Connecticut and chairman of the Joint Committee on Atomic Energy, President Harry S. Truman appointed Dean to the Atomic Energy Commission. Dean and Commissioner Lewis L. Strauss sparked the successful effort to reverse the commission's recommendation against development of the hydrogen bomb. Dean's effectiveness and close ties to McMahon led to his appointment as chairman of the commission by Truman in July 1950. During the following three years Dean led the commission through a challenging period in which a vast expansion of facilities for producing special nuclear materials and weapons was undertaken. A sound administrator with an unerring sense of Washington politics, he continued to serve as chairman under President Eisenhower until the completion of his term on June 30, 1953. By this time Dean's first marriage had ended in divorce. On Dec. 19, 1953, he married Mary Benton Gore. They had two children.

With the assistance of Strauss, who succeeded him as the AEC chairman, Dean joined the investment banking firm of Lehman Brothers in New York City. He was especially interested in stimulating private development of nuclear power for civilian purposes. He organized and became the first chairman of the board of the Nuclear Science and Engineering Corporation, which he merged with the General Dynamics Corporation in 1955; he was senior vice-president and director until his death in an airplane accident at Nantucket, Mass.

[There are no biographies of Dean. In addition to

numerous speeches, he wrote *Report on the Atom: What You Should Know About the Atomic Energy Program of the United States* (1953). Firsthand recollections appear in some memoirs of the Oral History Collection of Columbia University. The files of the Atomic Energy Commission, now held by the United States Energy Research and Development Administration, Washington, D.C., contain a great deal of material on Dean, including his daily office diaries for the entire period of his service as commissioner and chairman.

See also Richard G. Hewlett and Francis Duncan, *Atomic Shield, 1947–1952* (1969); *Hearings on the Confirmation of Gordon E. Dean and Henry de Wolfe Smyth as Members of the Atomic Energy Commission* (1949); Carl B. Swisher, ed., *Selected Papers of Homer Cummings* (1939); and the obituary notice in the *New York Times,* Aug. 16, 1958.]

RICHARD G. HEWLETT

DELANO, WILLIAM ADAMS (Jan. 21, 1874–Jan. 12, 1960), architect, was born in New York City, the son of Eugene Delano, a merchant and banker, and Susan Magoun Adams. In 1880 Eugene Delano joined the Philadelphia branch of Brown Brothers and Company and in 1894 became a partner in the firm. The only skyscraper William Delano ever designed is the building at 59 Wall Street that houses the New York offices of Brown Brothers and Company (after 1930, Brown Brothers Harriman and Company).

After graduating from Yale in 1895 with the B.A., Delano studied for two years at the Columbia University School of Architecture. In 1897 he was hired as a draftsman by the firm of John Merven Carrère and Thomas Hastings, which was then competing for the commission of the New York Public Library; Delano was put to work on the competition drawings. While at Carrère and Hastings he became friends with Chester Holmes Aldrich, who was responsible for the firm's prizewinning renderings of the New York Public Library. He and Delano later formed an enduring partnership. Both Carrère and Hastings, as well as many of their draftsmen, had studied at the École des Beaux-Arts in Paris, and no doubt influenced by this Delano left for France in late 1898 and was admitted to the school in early 1899. He also studied with Victor Laloux, then the best-known architect in France. After receiving his diploma in 1902, Delano returned to New York City, where he and Aldrich opened an office in November 1903. From 1903 to 1910 Delano taught design at the Columbia University School of Architecture; in 1908 he received the

B.F.A. from Yale. On May 23, 1907, he married a widow, Louisa Potter Sheffield, daughter of the architect Edward Tuckerman Potter; they had one son.

McKim, Mead and White's Renaissance, Georgian, and classical revival work of the 1880's and 1890's and the Chicago World's Columbian Exhibition of 1893 initiated an academic trend in American architecture. Delano and Aldrich were among its foremost twentieth-century exponents. Although their production spanned a wide architectural range, including institutional and public buildings, their chief works were large city and country residences, most of which were situated in the northeastern United States. Delano appears to have brought in the majority of the firm's commissions, including its first important one, the Walters Art Gallery in Baltimore (1905). His mature work owed more to English and American sources than to French beaux-arts precedents, but his plans—uncomplicated, coordinated, and easily understood—reflected his rigorous training in Laloux's atelier.

Characteristically, Delano's designs were free interpretations or modifications of the more severe Georgian styles; they were chaste, sometimes austere, and always in good taste. He was greatly influenced by his father's house at 12 Washington Square North, part of the famous Greek Revival row. This influence is strongly felt in the red brick, stone- or marble-trimmed neo-Federal and neo-colonial houses and club buildings for which his firm is best known. These include the Knickerbocker (1914) and Brook (1925) clubs and the Willard D. Straight (1915) and William Sloane (1919) townhouses in New York City, and the James A. Burden residence (1916) in Syosset, L.I.

By the 1920's the firm was prospering. Delano created a series of memorable country houses, including the elaborate French château of Otto H. Kahn in Cold Spring Harbor, L.I., and the classical revival residence of Bertram G. Work in Oyster Bay, L.I. In contrast to the formality of these estates, he also did several houses in the casual English country-house tradition.

From 1924 to 1928 Delano was a member of the National Commission of Fine Arts; he served on the United States Treasury's Board of Architectural Consultants from 1927 to 1933; and from 1929 to 1946 he was a member of the National Capital Park and Planning Commission. In 1928 he helped design the general plan for the Federal Triangle in Washington, D.C., including the unfinished Circular Court and the Post

Office Building (1930) facing it. He also designed the Japanese Embassy in Washington, D.C. (1931), and the American Embassy in Paris (1933), which was styled to harmonize with Gabriel's eighteenth-century Place de la Concorde structures. Delano was on the board of design of the 1939 New York World's Fair, and in that year he became a member of the Art Commission of New York City; he was elected chairman in 1947. In 1948, at the request of President Harry S. Truman, he designed the controversial second-story balcony in the south portico of the White House, and from 1949 to 1952 he was consulting architect to the Commission on the Renovation of the Executive Mansion.

Delano and Aldrich was responsible for several air terminals, including stations for Pan American Airways at Miami, Fla. (1929), and in the Pacific Islands, and the New York Municipal Airport, La Guardia Field, New York City (1937–1943). Delano's Marine and Land Terminals at La Guardia represent an interesting amalgamation of the so-called style moderne —exceptional in his work—with a beaux-arts adeptness at handling problems of passenger circulation.

Delano espoused a traditionalist philosophy during the period when modernism was ascendant. At a time when it seemed to him that the functionalist, engineering element dominated the artistic in contemporary buildings, he argued that architecture was a fine art and the architect an artist. The developer and the promoter, he believed, had eclipsed the architect. However, he welcomed "the tendency today to create new forms rather than copy old ones" and rejoiced "in the many new materials, which give wider scope to the designers' imagination."

Delano was a member of numerous professional organizations, including the American Institute of Architects and the Society of Beaux-Arts Architects. He was a member of the National Institute of Arts and Letters, which awarded him its Gold Medal in 1940, and the American Academy of Arts and Letters. In 1953 he received the AIA Gold Medal, the institute's highest honor. Sociable and genial, Delano had an attractive personality that endeared him to many of his contemporaries. In 1950 he retired as senior partner of Delano and Aldrich (Aldrich had died in 1940) but continued to serve as consulting architect until his death in New York City.

[Delano's letters are in the Yale University Library, and William Potter Delano has Delano's unpublished autobiography (1944). Delano's articles include "My Architectural Creed," *Progressive Architecture*, Mar. 1932; "Further Thoughts on Contemporary Architecture," *ibid.*, July 1932; "Architecture Is an Art," *Architectural Forum*, Apr. 1940; "The Architect: Forgotten Man?", *New York Times Magazine*, Apr. 21, 1940; "A Marriage of Convenience," *Journal of the AIA*, May 1944; "Memoirs of Centurian Architects," *ibid.*, July–Oct. 1948; and "Perspectives," *Architectural Record*, May 1953.

On his life and work, see William L. Bottomley, "A Selection From the Works of Delano and Aldrich," *Architectural Record*, July 1923; Royal Cortissoz, *Portraits of Ten Country Houses Designed by Delano and Aldrich* (1924); "The Reminiscences of William Adams Delano," Oral History Collection, Columbia University (1950); "Talk of the Town," *New Yorker*, Apr. 5, 1958; and obituary notices in the *New York Times* and *New York Herald-Tribune*, Jan. 13, 1960; and in *Journal of the AIA*, Mar. 1960.]

SARAH BRADFORD LANDAU

DeMILLE, CECIL BLOUNT (Aug. 12, 1881–Jan. 21, 1959), actor, playwright, motion picture producer, and director, was born in Ashfield, Mass., the son of Henry Churchill DeMille, a playwright and lay preacher, and Matilda Beatrice Samuel. Reared in an atmosphere of spartan piety, he was educated at the H.C. DeMille Memorial School in Pamlico, N.J., and at the Pennsylvania Military College. At the outbreak of the Spanish-American War he ran away to enlist in the army but was rejected because of his youth. He graduated from the American Academy of Dramatic Arts in New York City in 1900 and made his stage debut on Broadway in *Hearts Are Trumps* that year. On Aug. 16, 1902, he married Constance Adams. They had one daughter and adopted three children.

DeMille toured the United States with his wife and E. H. Sothern in *If I Were King* (1902–1903) and appeared in *Lord Chumley* (1905), of which his father was coauthor. His first produced play, written with his brother William, was *The Genius* (1904), a three-act spoof of Greenwich Village artists. Their subsequent collaborations included *The Royal Mounted* (1908) and *After Five* (1913). DeMille was also coauthor, with David Belasco, of *The Return of Peter Grimm* (1911).

DeMille's friendship with Samuel Goldfish (later Goldwyn) and Jesse L. Lasky, a former glove salesman and show booker, respectively, led to their formation in 1913 of the Jesse L. Lasky Feature Play Company. Their first production was *The Squaw Man* (1914), based on Edwin M. Royle's stage hit. Directed by Oscar Apfel and starring Dustin Farnum, it was one of the first feature-length films to be shot in Hollywood and was an enormous success. In 1915 Adolph Zukor joined the company, and the Famous Players–Lasky Corporation was formed, with DeMille as director general.

That year, when the industry switched to a policy of filming stage plays with famous Broadway stars, DeMille promptly put into production a version of *Carmen* starring the noted opera singer Geraldine Farrar—and, for good measure, Wallace Reid, a movie favorite. The film established DeMille as a "name" director. With war clouds gathering, he deftly turned out a series of stirringly patriotic films, including *Joan the Woman* (1916), *The Little American* (1917), and *The Whispering Chorus* (1918), powerful expressions of his and cameraman Alvin Wyckoff's mastery of visual effects.

But even before the Armistice, DeMille sensed that the demand for such films would quickly be over. Casting about for a new popular subject, he released in quick succession a series of films in sharply different styles and carefully noted the public reaction to each. The trend, he decided, was toward a more sophisticated approach to sex. In a series of comedies he catered to the postwar vogue for higher living and looser morals, opening up to middle-class audiences the fashions and foibles of the fabulously rich in such movies as *Male and Female* (1919), *For Better, for Worse* (1919), *Don't Change Your Husband* (1919), *Why Change Your Wife?* (1920), and *Adam's Rib* (1923). In 1922 he established Cecil B. DeMille Productions, Incorporated, and served as president until its dissolution in 1951.

But the strident voice of reform was resounding in opposition to the sex and sin that flickered on movie screens. Realizing that flagrant immorality might not always sell, DeMille solved the dilemma in *The Ten Commandments* (1923), by merely concealing the sex and melodrama behind a biblical façade. It remained among the top-grossing films for many years. Like *The King of Kings* (1927), the story of Christ, the film epitomized the superspectacular genre and is often revived.

DeMille's attempt to set up his own studio (in Thomas Ince's replica of Mount Vernon at Culver City, Calif.) collapsed following two ambitious features, *The Road to Yesterday* (1925) and *The Volga Boatman* (1926). Reluctant to enter talking films, he became a producer-director for Metro-Goldwyn-Mayer in August 1928. He seemed to be finished in the industry until he went to Paramount as an independent producer with *The Sign of the Cross* (1932). A mélange of piety, sex, and luxurious sets and costumes, it became a Depression escapist hit. *Cleopatra* (1934) was another happy marriage of sex and sensationalism and proved equally popular. After years of stumbling, DeMille had again hit his stride, offering spectacular epics of unrivaled narrative drive, opulence, and—according to many critics—the nadir of bad taste.

DeMille's reign at Paramount continued uninterrupted despite the presence on the board of his old rival Adolph Zukor and the downfall of his friend Lasky. His epic Westerns, such as *The Plainsman* (1937), *Union Pacific* (1939), and *Northwest Mounted Police* (1940), retained the sweeping landscapes, grandiose scale, and larger-than-life acting of his earlier work. Despite scripts that sometimes limped like late-nineteenth-century pulp novels, and the frontal assaults of critics, his popularity continued unabated, and audiences flocked to the cinematic bread and circuses that he consistently delivered—*The Unconquered* (1947) and *Samson and Delilah* (1949) being prime examples.

DeMille was at his most abandoned in his sea stories, such as *The Buccaneer* (1938) and *Reap the Wild Wind* (1942), which, like his other works, offered leaden dialogue, dashing action sequences, and screen frescoes inspired by the work of such painters as Lawrence Alma-Tadema. DeMille provided his own thunderous prologues or previews for each of his films, unstintingly praising himself from behind a presidential desk.

From 1936 to 1945 DeMille was host of "The Lux Radio Theater," a weekly broadcast of adaptations of screenplays featuring well-known stars. He quickly became an institution on the show, with his behind-the-scenes stories of Hollywood, his intermission interviews, and his curtain-call chatter with the show's stars. Notwithstanding the impression he created, DeMille never directed the program and was producer in name only. A bitter dispute with the American Federation of Radio Artists, of which he was a member, ultimately forced him off the air.

The loser in a lengthy legal battle that he pushed to the Supreme Court, DeMille faced the inevitability of paying a one-dollar assessment levied against union members to defeat a proposed amendment to the California constitution that the union considered antilabor. The alternative was to leave the air and DeMille did so in January 1945. Suspended from the union, he was prohibited from further radio activity.

In 1949 the Academy of Motion Picture Arts and Sciences honored DeMille with a special award for his thirty-five years of pioneering in the industry. He made a brief screen appearance—as Cecil B. DeMille—in *Sunset Boulevard* (1950), starring Gloria Swanson, whose career he had been instrumental in developing. His skillful circus extravaganza, *The Greatest Show on Earth* (1952), best exemplifies the style of his last works and received an Academy Award for best film. DeMille's last movie, *The Ten Commandments* (1956), a remake of his earlier version, brought him full circle. Filmed on location, it typified his approach to lavish filmmaking. It employed as many as 25,000 extras in one scene and cost over $13 million to make—an exorbitant sum at the time. It was his greatest box-office success.

In his later years DeMille proved to be staunchly right wing, actively anti-Communist, and representative of all that was rearguard in conservative California. Because of his reactionary and somewhat anti-intellectual attitudes, his work has not enjoyed a critical revival since his death, in Hollywood. Although critics have never acknowledged his artistic merit, DeMille was a trailblazer in the industry and created a new genre, the epic film. During a career in which he produced and directed about seventy feature films, DeMille made more movies at greater cost, larger profits, and over a longer period that any other producer or director in Hollywood. Knowing that the movie public wanted entertainment, he gave them the ultimate in screen spectacle, like his peers in showmanship, P. T. Barnum in the circus and David Belasco in the theatre.

DeMille also made many contributions to the technique of filmmaking. He was a pioneer in lighting effects and in the use of color film. He introduced the megaphone on the set and later was the first to use a loudspeaker to address his players. He helped develop the use of the camera boom and movable sound camera, and he initiated the practice of shooting each scene twice to guard against loss of the negative. In his wide-brimmed hat, open-throated shirt, riding breeches, and leather puttees, he was the quintessential Hollywood director.

[DeMille is represented in the Oral History Collection of Columbia University. His *Autobiography*, edited by Donald Hayne (1959), is the principal source. The standard biography is Charles Higham, *Cecil B. DeMille* (1973). See also "Goodnight, C. B.," *Esquire*, Jan. 1964, by his niece, Agnes DeMille; Gabe Essoe and Raymond Lee, *DeMille: The Man and His Pictures* (1970); Phil A. Koury, *Yes, Mr. DeMille* (1959); and Gene Ringgold and DeWitt Bodeen, *The Films of Cecil B. DeMille* (1969).]

CHARLES HIGHAM

DENNY, GEORGE VERNON, JR. (Aug. 29, 1899–Nov. 11, 1959), educator and broadcaster, was born in Washington, N.C., the son of George Vernon Denny and Carrie Ricks Cobb. He received the B.S. in commerce from the University of North Carolina in 1922, although by then the theater had become his major interest. A member of the Carolina Playmakers as a student, Denny remained with the troupe after graduation; and from 1924 to 1926 he taught dramatic production at the university. On June 12, 1924, he married Mary Traill Yellott, an actress with the Playmakers; they had three children.

In 1926 Denny moved to New York City to act professionally and appeared in two short-lived Broadway productions. The following year he became manager for the W. B. Feakins Lecture Bureau; and in 1928 he was named director of the Columbia University Institute of Arts and Sciences, where he also managed a program of public lectures and concerts. His growing experience in the field of adult education led to Denny's appointment as associate director of the League for Political Education in 1931. The organization, founded in 1894 by a group of suffragists, had long worked to encourage better citizenship through a more thorough knowledge of public issues. Since 1920 the league had sponsored lectures, short courses, and discussion groups in its headquarters at Town Hall, in New York City. When the director of the league, Robert E. Ely, retired in 1937, Denny was named his replacement. In 1938 the organization was renamed Town Hall, Inc., and Denny became president, a position that he held until 1951.

Under Ely, Denny had initiated what would become his most notable achievement, the radio program "America's Town Meeting of the Air."

Disturbed at a neighbor's refusal to listen to Franklin D. Roosevelt's Fireside Chats because he bitterly opposed the president's policies, Denny conceived the idea of a radio program that would offer listeners diverse viewpoints on important, controversial national issues. Denny interested the National Broadcasting Company in an experimental series of programs that, "through the miracle of radio, was a nation-wide adaptation of the New England town meeting and a vast extension of the League's work." The series of six trial programs began on May 30, 1935, with Lawrence Dennis, A. J. Muste, Norman Thomas, and Raymond Moley discussing the question "Which Way America—Fascism, Communism, Socialism, or Democracy?" (Dennis took the fascist view, Muste the communist, Thomas the socialist, and Moley spoke for democracy.) Impressed with the program and its audience response, the network agreed to carry "Town Meeting" for the 1935–1936 season as a sustaining (noncommercial) program. Reluctant to accept sponsors who might compromise the program's impartial and educational nature, Denny broadcast on a sustaining basis except in 1944, when *Reader's Digest* became sponsor. "Town Meeting" remained on the air until June 1956.

Denny's role as moderator was central to the program's success. A former actor with an ebullient personality, he was able to mix a sufficient amount of showmanship with academic respectability, thus interesting a mass audience in serious issues. Indeed, Denny believed that the entertainment component of the program ensured fulfillment of its serious intent. His flair for the dramatic emerged after the evening's speakers had completed their opening statements. Taking center stage in Town Hall, or in auditoriums around the country and abroad when the show went on the road, he directed questions from an audience ranging from 1,000 to 1,500 people, many of whom were highly agitated and hostile toward one or another of the speakers. Denny's was the first radio program to so involve the studio audience.

Among the hundreds of persons who appeared on the program were Eleanor Roosevelt, Wendell Willkie, Harold Ickes, Robert A. Taft, Dorothy Thompson, Frances Perkins, Carl Sandburg, and Pearl Buck. At the height of "Town Meeting's" success in the 1940's, the speakers and topics arranged by Denny and his staff attracted an estimated audience of ten million listeners for each broadcast on approximately 170 stations of the NBC Blue network (later ABC). The program stimulated the organization of hundreds of discussion groups throughout the nation that, after listening to the broadcast, considered the issues in living room "town meetings." Denny's program was also one of the first to originate simultaneously from two or more locations. In 1943, for example, audiences in New York and London quizzed representatives of the American and British governments on postwar policies.

In Denny's opinion, "Town Meeting" played a vital role in the American political system. Democracy could survive threats to its existence only if citizens, especially political independents, carefully weighed the pros and cons of significant issues. And in a vast, technological society, only radio could transform the town-meeting concept of citizen involvement into a twentieth-century reality. The program was also noteworthy as the best example, during its era, of noncommercial, public service broadcasting, which attempted to inform listeners—not merely entertain them. "Town Meeting" was also one of the few public affairs programs aired in prime time, a fact that reflects its widespread popularity.

Denny left the program in February 1952 in a dispute over its management, believing that it had lost its vitality and sense of controversy. On Apr. 2, 1944, he had married Jeanne Sarasy (his first marriage had ended in divorce the previous year). In 1954 he built the Covered Bridge Shopping Area in West Cornwall, Conn. He also organized and served as president of International Seminars, Inc., and under its sponsorship conducted "town meeting" seminars in South America in 1958. He died in Sharon, Conn.

[Denny's papers are in the Manuscript Collection of the Library of Congress. He was author of *Town Meeting Discussion Leader's Handbook* (1940); and wrote the introduction and postscript to *Faith for Today* (1941), an anthology; and "Town Meetin' Tonight!", *Atlantic Monthly*, Sept. 1942. *Town Meeting* (1935–1956), the bulletin of the radio program, includes a transcript of the discussion; also see Harry A. Overstreet and Bonaro W. Overstreet, *Town Meeting Comes to Town* (1938). Other sources include S. J. Woolf, "The Umpire of the Town Meeting," *New York Times Magazine,* June 6, 1943; and an obituary notice, *New York Times,* Nov. 12, 1959.]

ALAN HAVIG

DENSMORE, FRANCES (May 21, 1867– June 5, 1957), ethnomusicologist, was born in

Red Wing, Minn., the daughter of Benjamin Densmore, a surveyor and civil engineer, and Sarah Greenland. She attended the Oberlin Conservatory of Music from 1884 to 1886. Individual study of the piano followed under Carl Baermann in Boston; and in 1889 and 1890 she studied counterpoint at Harvard with John K. Paine. Although she again studied piano, with Leopold Godowsky in 1898, she ended formal performances in 1893 for the study of American Indian music.

Densmore's first memory of Indian music dated from her childhood, when Sioux Indians sang and drummed nearby well into the night. Her mother encouraged an appreciation of the music, which many considered simply as noise. In 1895 Densmore began lecturing in St. Paul, Minn., on Indian music using the material of Alice Fletcher, who later helped shape her career. Densmore undertook systematic recording, traveling in 1904 to the St. Louis Exposition to record Philippine music. A tune hummed by Geronimo caught her interest, and she recorded it and other Indian music. The experience led her to the Chippewa of Minnesota and the recording of their music. She was first paid for such work in 1907, when William Henry Holmes of the Bureau of American Ethnology purchased her recordings. She was to become a lifelong collaborator for the bureau, starting with wax cylinders and continuing to tapes.

Her first work was among the Chippewa, whose music she described in two volumes (1910–1913) published by the bureau. Between 1911 and 1915 she traveled to the Dakotas to collect music of the Mandan, Hidatsa, and Sioux. She recognized from the beginning that music must be placed in a cultural context, and her description of Sioux religion, mythology, and social life makes *Teton Sioux Music* (1918) one of the best ethnographies of the Sioux.

Nearly every summer between 1920 and 1930, Densmore was recording on a different reservation. She worked among the Northern Ute, Pawnee of Oklahoma, Papago of Arizona, Indians of Washington and British Columbia, Winnebago and Menominee of Wisconsin, Pueblo Indians of the Southwest, and even the Tule of Panama. In addition to eight monographs published during this period, she found time for *The American Indians and Their Music* (1926), which brought her attention from a wider audience. Besides her technical analysis she described aspects of Indian music for journals ranging from the *American Anthropologist* to the more popular *Nation* and *Christian Science Monitor.*

The 1930's were no less productive for Densmore. The Southwest Museum and the Bureau of American Ethnology published her monographs on the Menominee, Yuman and Yaqui, Cheyenne and Arapaho, Santo Domingo, and Nootka and Quileute. She also worked among the Seminole in 1931 and Gulf State Indians in 1932. The following year she recorded Navajo and Sioux music at the Chicago World's Fair and later returned to the Southwest. In between she continued her study of Indians in Minnesota and Wisconsin.

In 1943, after fifty years of study, Densmore reduced her fieldwork but remained as active as ever, cataloging the songs and instruments she had collected. A major task was to ensure preservation of her recordings, and a $30,000 grant from Eleanor Reese enabled her to oversee the proper transcription and transfer of the Densmore-Smithsonian collection, first to the National Archives and finally to the Library of Congress, the only organization adequately equipped to transfer music from her perishable cylinders to service disks.

As a pioneer student of Indian music Densmore had to overcome a number of stereotypes. Initially she was much concerned simply to demonstrate that Indian music was as accurate as Western music in pitch, melody, and tempo. (As a musician she had intuitively recognized these factors, but she was also able to prove their validity by laboratory analysis using tone photographs taken with a phonodisk.) Likewise, she was among the first ethnomusicologists to realize that music must be understood in its cultural context. Although her later volumes tend to document cultures less well than her classic *Teton Sioux Music,* she developed a standard presentation that included an introductory history, ethnography with emphasis upon folklore and religion, and her own photographs. She continually compared her new recordings with former ones, and the monographs contain numerous tables of comparative analysis, especially by tone, interval, and melodic progression.

While recording and transcribing music across the North American continent, Densmore never allowed her need for time to interfere with her relationships with informants. She took pains to ensure they were treated fairly and that they understood her goal of preserving part of their heritage. She was usually accompanied in the field by her sister, Margaret. It was most unusual for white women to reside among Indians for a month or more at that time, yet Densmore seldom mentioned any hardships and never complained of the difficulties that she must have encountered. She "heard an Indian drum" at an early age and set out to preserve that music with notable determination.

Densmore had enormous energy and enthusiasm. *Seminole Music* (1956) appeared in her eighty-ninth year, *Music of Acoma, Isleta, Cochiti and Zuñi Pueblos* the next year, and *Music of the Maidu Indians of California* (1958) posthumously. Densmore never married. She died in Red Wing.

[There are a portrait and candid photos in *Frances Densmore and American Indian Music* (1968), edited by Charles Hofmann, which also contains her bibliography, some correspondence, examples of her work, and annotated reports from the Bureau of American Ethnology. Nancy O. Lurie provides a short biography in "Women in Early American Anthropology" in June Helm MacNeish, ed., *Pioneers of American Anthropology* (1966).]

ERNEST L. SCHUSKY

DE PALMA, RALPH (1883–Mar. 31, 1956), racing car driver, was born in Troia, Italy. His parents immigrated to New York City in the 1890's, and De Palma always considered New York City to be his home. Although christened Raffaele, De Palma Americanized his first name to Ralph at an early age. He graduated from high school and then attended Stevens Institute in Hoboken, N.J., but did not graduate. As a youth De Palma was interested in all kinds of racing. He was a quarter-mile runner on a National Guard track team. Later he became a bicycle mechanic and then a bicycle racer. He won half a dozen races as an amateur and finished second in a six-day race. He then became interested in motorcycle racing for a couple of years, winning most of the races he entered. About 1902 De Palma entered and won a bicycle race under an assumed name, was discovered, and was suspended from all athletic competitions for five years.

The lifting of the suspension coincided with De Palma's entry into motor racing. His involvement in motor racing occurred by accident. He was working as an automotive mechanic when, two days before the Briarcliff road race in April 1907, one of the drivers was hurt. De Palma volunteered to replace him and drove in the race. Although he did not win, his career as a driver had begun. Between 1907 and his retirement in 1934 he drove in 2,889 races, winning 2,557. Both his percentage of victories and total number of victories were probably all-time records. He was the greatest driver of his era, surpassing the exploits of such legendary figures as Barney Oldfield and Eddie Rickenbacker. He won approximately $1.5 million during his career.

De Palma's first major victory was in Philadelphia in 1908 at the Old Point Breeze Race Track when he drove a mile in less than sixty seconds, then a world's record for that kind of track. His earliest successes were as a member of the Fiat team. He toured the country in 1909 racing on dirt tracks. He won the National Dirt Track Championship in 1908, 1909, 1910, and 1911. He was the American Automobile Association national champion in 1912 and 1914, the winner of the Vanderbilt Cup in 1912 and 1915, and the winner of the Elgin National Road Race in 1912, 1914, and 1920. His triumph in the 1914 Vanderbilt Cup Race was especially gratifying, since he defeated his bitter rival Barney Oldfield. De Palma's cautious driving reflected his personality. He was the opposite of the publicity seeking, flamboyant, and foolhardy Oldfield. De Palma was never seriously injured in a race, although he did break a leg in 1909 at Danbury, Conn., and in 1912 in Milwaukee his car collided with another racer, went out of control, and overturned in a cornfield. Two cornstalks penetrated his thigh and abdomen, and he was hospitalized for eleven weeks.

Although De Palma considered his victory in the 1915 Indianapolis 500 Speedway Race his greatest triumph, his most famous race was the 1912 Indy. During that race he was leading by five laps when on the one-hundred-ninety-fifth lap a connecting rod in his Mercedes broke and the car began losing oil and power. The car came to a stop approximately a mile from the finish. He and his mechanic, Rupert Jeffkins, then pushed the car across the finish line to a standing ovation from the crowd. De Palma's unusual finish was naturally disallowed and the record book lists De Palma as having come in eleventh, even though his car was the second one across the finish line.

De Palma's Mercedes experienced the same mechanical difficulty at the same stage of the race in the 1915 Indy, but he was able to nurse it home just ahead of Dario Resta's Peugeot to capture the $25,000 first prize. His average speed of 89.94

miles per hour set a record for the Indy that was not surpassed until Jimmy Murphy's 94.48 miles per hour in 1922. De Palma never won the Indianapolis 500 again, although at his death he held the record of 613 for laps being in the lead.

De Palma was involved in the mechanical as well as the racing aspects of the automobile. In 1914 he became interested in engineering and research and went to work for the Packard Motor Car Company. Two years later he established the De Palma Manufacturing Company in Detroit for the production of racing cars and engines. He was responsible for many engineering advances, which he often used while racing. He was the first person to road-test four-wheel brakes in the United States.

With American entry in World War I, De Palma sold his business and enlisted in the Air Service. He earned a captain's commission and became director of flying at McCook Field, Dayton, Ohio. After World War I, De Palma rejoined the Packard Motor Car Company and resumed his driving. He persuaded Packard officials to go after the world's speed record and in 1919 at Daytona Beach, Fla., driving a Packard with a 905cc engine, De Palma set a world speed record of 149.875 miles per hour, breaking the old record by 8 miles per hour. He appeared in the major American and international races. He finished fifth in the 1920 Indy 500, fourth in 1922, and seventh in 1925. He finished second in the French Grand Prix in 1921, the first one held after World War I, and won the Canadian Championship in 1929. De Palma was elected to the Racing Hall of Fame in 1954 and to the Helms Hall of Fame.

After his retirement from racing De Palma worked for the Ford, Studebaker, Cadillac, and Ranger Aircraft companies. From 1946 to 1956 he was employed by the General Petroleum Corporation, officiating at economy road runs and lecturing on safe driving before high school audiences. He died in South Pasadena, Calif.

[On De Palma's early career, see his "Motor Racing Men," *Collier's*, Jan. 10, 1914. Accounts of DePalma's loss in the 1912 Indy and his victory in the 1914 Vanderbilt Cup Race are in Ross R. Olney, *Great Moments in Speed*, which also contains a photograph of the racer. De Palma's record at the Indianapolis 500 is found in Jack C. Fox, *The Illustrated History of the Indianapolis 500* (1975). Descriptions of De Palma's career are briefly touched upon in *Outing*, Jan. 1920, and *Hobbies*, July 1941. See also the obituary in the *New York Times*, Apr. 1, 1956.]

EDWARD S. SHAPIRO

DIAT, LOUIS FELIX (May 5, 1885–Aug. 29, 1957), chef and author, was born in Montmarault, France, the son of Louis Denis Diat, a shoemaker, and Anne Alajoinine. A rather shy and awkward boy, often disciplined and ridiculed in school because he was left-handed, Diat was happiest when helping his mother and grandmother prepare hearty soups, stews, and pastries. This experience gave him the desire to become a professional chef. When he was fourteen his father purchased an apprenticeship for him in the Maison Calondre, a catering firm in Moulins, near Vichy. After two years of rigorous training, followed by tours of duty in the kitchens of the Hôtel Bristol and the Hôtel du Rhin in Paris, Diat rose rapidly in the staid and hierarchical French culinary world. In 1903 the Hôtel Ritz in Paris, one of Europe's most exclusive and fashionable hotels, appointed him *chef potager*, and three years later he became an assistant *saucier* at the elegant new Ritz Hotel in London. There under the tutelage of the *chef de cuisines,* Émile Malley, whose impeccable attire and gentlemanly demeanor he emulated as his professional ideal, Diat refined his skills, expanded his repertoire, and caught the eye of the celebrated chef Auguste Escoffier. In 1910 William Harris and Robert W. Goelet built the Ritz-Carlton Hotel in New York City. On Escoffier's recommendation they chose Diat to organize its kitchens. Diat arrived in the United States on Oct. 8, 1910, applied for citizenship that November, and was naturalized in 1916. On Jan. 20, 1913, he married Suzanne Clemence Prudhon; they had one child.

Diat considered his mission to establish a level of cuisine at the Ritz-Carlton equal to that of the finest European hotels. With the full backing of the hotel's manager, Albert Keller, Diat spared no expense in his quest for culinary excellence. Unable to procure certain vegetables on the wholesale market, he asked local farmers to grow them and subsidized their output. Unhappy with the quality of the available cream, he eventually discovered, on a farm in Vermont, cream comparable to that produced in Normandy; it was shipped to the hotel daily. Diat had huge tanks built to hold trout and lobsters; he installed a French bakery oven and imported a Parisian *boulanger* to run it. Diat's domain covered two floors of the hotel basement and eventually included an ice cream plant, huge coffee roasters, a *pâtisserie*, and a fully equipped candy factory. He supervised a staff of over 100 trained to the most exacting standards.

The Ritz-Carlton had an aura of Old World

luxury and elegance that made it the ideal back-drop for visiting European royalty, debutante balls, and society parties. A string ensemble played in the beautifully decorated Palm Court; and ducks paddled around a water-lily pond in the rooftop Japanese garden. The Ritz quickly became the favored dining spot of New York's rich and powerful. The main reason for the hotel's success, however, was "Monsieur Louis," as Diat was known to co-workers and gourmets, who turned it into a temple of French cuisine. Nowhere in the United States could one dine on a more dazzling array of classic dishes, prepared with such skill and flair. The best foie gras was used lavishly, truffles were sliced by the hour, and the finest cognacs and madeiras laced sauces and soups. Many of the most popular creations were Diat's own, such as Breast of Guinea Hen Jefferson (guinea hen with ham, creamed tomatoes, rice fritters, and a whiskey sauce) and Lobster Albert (stuffed lobster *gratiné*, with mushrooms and a sauce half *Américaine* and half *Mornay*). But among the hundreds of dishes Diat invented, none received greater acclaim than *crême à la vichyssoise*, a simple but refined cold soup based on his mother's leek and potato soup. Named after the famous spa near Diat's hometown, the soup first appeared on the Ritz menu in the summer of 1917 to stimulate appeties dulled by New York's heat. It instantly became an all-weather American favorite.

For forty-one years Diat's life was inseparable from that of the Ritz-Carlton. A tireless worker, a perfectionist obsessed with maintaining the highest standards, yet always patient and soft-spoken with his staff, he regularly put in fourteen-hour days, six days a week. From 1916 to 1929, while living in New Rochelle, N.Y., he used to come to the Ritz on Sunday morning, return home for lunch, and then come back to his job for dinner. Still, he gave radio and newspaper interviews, lent his name and energy to countless efforts designed to improve the quality of American food, and wrote *Cooking à la Ritz* (1941), *Louis Diat's Home Cookbook: French Cooking for Americans* (1946), and *Sauces, French and Famous* (1951). Unlike other great chefs of the era whose books were geared mainly to professionals, Diat sought to demystify French cuisine and explain it so that ordinary home cooks could understand and duplicate it. Through his example, his writings, and the hundreds of chefs he trained, Diat played a major role in initiating the nation's interest in good food.

On May 2, 1951, the Ritz-Carlton was forced to close, a victim of spiraling costs, rising real estate values, and its own undiminished luxury. To the end Diat refused to compromise standards. When auditors advised him to cut expenses by using less cream and butter, he threatened to leave unless quality was maintained. It was. As late as December 1950, $47,000 a month was spent on provisions from more than fifty dealers, and the Ritz's kitchen staff of seventy-seven was one of the highest paid in the country. Although crushed by the demise of the Ritz, Diat remained active. He turned to writing about food and cooking, and, in collaboration with Helen Ridley, a home economist, he reached an ever-growing audience in the pages of *Gourmet* magazine. He was at work on his magnum opus, *Gourmet's Basic French Cookbook* (1961), when he died in New York City.

[A small but essential collection of Diat's scrapbooks, letters, and menus is in the possession of his daughter, Mrs. Suzette Lawrence, of Rhinebeck, N.Y. See also *Collier's*, May 3, 1945 (which contains a portrait); the *New York Times*, May 21, 1947; "Diat," *New Yorker*, Dec. 2, 1950; and the *New York Times* obituary, Aug. 30, 1957.]

JEROME L. STERNSTEIN

DILLE, JOHN FLINT (Apr. 27, 1884–Sept. 10, 1957), newspaper syndicator and originator of the "Buck Rogers" comic strip, was born in Dixon, Ill., the son of Jesse Brooks Dille, an educator who founded Dixon College, and of Florence Flint. He attended the University of Chicago, from which he received the Ph.B. in 1909. He then entered the advertising business in Chicago and in 1917 founded a feature syndicate, the National Newspaper Syndicate, of which he was president.

Through his syndicate Dille helped to popularize the commentaries and creative efforts of Lady Astor, Harry Lauder, Jr., Josephus Daniels, Walter B. Pitkin, and Albert Edward Wiggam by making their work available to newspaper clients at a relatively low unit cost. Undoubtedly, however, the most notable accomplishment of the syndicate was the science fiction comic strip "Buck Rogers." Dille was credited with originating adventure comic strips as an entertainment medium.

The "Buck Rogers" strip and its development illustrated Dille's entrepreneurial and managerial skills. The idea for the strip came from Philip Nowlan's short novel *Armageddon 2419 A.D.*, in the August 1928 issue of *Amazing Stories,* a science fiction magazine. The work described how a twentieth-century American pilot named Anthony Rogers was overcome by toxic gas that put him in suspended animation for five centuries. It was a great success and Nowlan wrote a sequel, *The Warlords of Han,* in March 1929. The two works were combined and published as *Armageddon 2419 A.D.* The book came to the attention of Dille, who was searching for new material and new ideas for his syndicate.

Dille contacted Nowlan and urged him to adapt his idea to a comic strip form. Skeptical at first, Nowlan agreed to do continuity writing for the strip, which was drawn by Richard W. Calkins, a World War I army pilot who worked for Dille. Getting Calkins to cooperate also took some persuasion, for he preferred to draw comic strips set in prehistoric times. But Dille, believing that "the future, which was unknown, was more fascinating than the past, which was known," felt that a futuristic comic strip was more salable to newspapers. The strip first appeared on Jan. 7, 1929. At its peak, it was carried by 287 newspapers although this number dwindled to twenty-eight when the strip was discontinued in 1968.

Dille's role in originating the strip did not end when he introduced Nowlan and Calkins. Active in alumni affairs at the University of Chicago, he frequently consulted leading scientists and tried to include accurate scientific information in the strip. For example, scientists were asked to speculate about such things as the construction of space suits and ways to prevent the moon from being infected by germs carried by astronauts. Among the prophetic information that did not come from scientists was the idea of an atom bomb, which appeared in the strip in 1938. Much of the strip, of course, was fanciful and many of the technical details less than accurate. Of the strip, Stephen Becker wrote in 1959: "It was the straight, raw stuff: men and women in space suits, with paralysis-ray guns and anti-gravity belts; oddly-shaped space ships and oddly-shaped villains; a hero and his girl, and a villain and his girl, and a young boy to keep juvenile interest fresh. Some of the science was simple: Rogers might be seen frisking about the surface of a planetoid, taking thirty feet at a stride because gravity was low. Some of it verged on the complex, with talk of orbits and airlocks and asteroids. But all of it was fascinating."

Although not particularly distinguished for draftsmanship or plot, "Buck Rogers" was a pioneer, the first of the science fiction strips. It also inspired a Buck Rogers craze; Buck Rogers dolls, "moon pistols," and rockets became popular toys, especially during the 1930's. Science fiction writer Ray Bradbury claimed that as a boy he was stimulated and inspired by "Buck Rogers" when the strip "burst upon our vision like some grander July Fourth, full of rockets celebrating tomorrow." The strip was translated into eighteen languages and published in forty countries; it was also the basis for a radio serial. Like other popular culture phenomena, "Buck Rogers" had several imitators, including the strip "Flash Gordon," which began in 1934.

In addition to his work on "Buck Rogers" and his feature syndicate responsibilities, Dille served as a director of the alumni foundation of the University of Chicago, president of the Chicago alumni chapter of Phi Gamma Delta, and president of the alumni association.

On June 14, 1911, Dille married Phoebe M. Crabtree; they had two sons, one of whom, Robert Crabtree Dille, succeeded his father as president of the National Newspaper Syndicate and edited *The Collected Works of Buck Rogers in the 25th Century,* which contained twelve "Buck Rogers" adventures from 1929 to 1946. Dille died in Chicago.

[Obituaries are in the *New York Times,* Sept. 12, 1957; *Editor and Publisher,* Sept. 14, 1957; and *Chicago Tribune,* Sept. 11, 1957. There is also a brief entry in *Who Was Who, 1951–1960.* See also Stephen Becker, *Comic Art in America* (1959), pp. 225–226; Maurice Horn, ed., *The World Encyclopedia of Comics,* III (1976); and Reinhold Reitberger and Wolfgang Fuchs, *Comics: Anatomy of a Mass Medium* (1971), pp. 68–69.]

EVERETTE E. DENNIS

DOCK, LAVINIA LLOYD (Feb. 26, 1858 Apr. 17, 1956), nurse and social reformer, was born in Harrisburg, Pa., the daughter of Gilliard Dock, a well-to-do landowner, and Lavinia Lloyd Bombaugh. After graduating from a private school in Harrisburg, she lived at home until her mid-twenties. Then an article on nursing in *New Century* suggested a career to her. Although nursing was not considered "ladylike" for a woman of her social background, Dock enrolled in Bellevue Training School for Nurses in New York City; she graduated in 1886. (At that time her brother, George, who became a professor of medicine, was studying medicine in Europe.)

Dock's first job was with United Workers, an organization that provided trained nurses in Norwich, Conn. She then volunteered to serve in Jacksonville, Fla., during a yellow fever epidemic and later joined other disaster services. In 1889, while helping victims of the Johnstown, Pa., flood, she met Clara Barton, founder of the American Red Cross. Years later, Dock collaborated on *The History of American Red Cross Nursing* (1922). She also was a visiting nurse for the New York City Mission and a night supervisor at Bellevue Hospital.

Dock contributed to the professionalization of nursing in many ways. Her *Materia Medica for Nurses* (1890) was a convenient reference work containing information about the proper doses of drugs and the best manner of administering them. Since the publisher anticipated a loss, Dock's father had to advance money for the printing. The book eventually went through eight editions and sold more than 150,000 copies.

The same year that *Materia Medica* appeared, Dock became assistant director of the new school of nursing at Johns Hopkins Hospital. Three years later she was made head of the Illinois Training School for Nurses at Cook County Hospital, Chicago. She left this position and nursing education as well in 1896, giving her lack of skill in dealing with people as the reason. In 1893 Dock became the secretary of the American Society of Superintendents of Training Schools for Nurses, the first national nursing association. The organization later spawned the American Nurses' Association. The first issue of the association's journal, the *American Journal of Nursing* (October 1900), contained Dock's article "What We May Expect From the Law." This article was the opening shot in the fight to get state registration for nurses. Dock herself received the "Registered Nurse" title in New York in 1902.

In 1898 Dock moved to the Henry Street Settlement House on New York City's Lower East Side. Henry Street was unique among settlements in having a visiting nurse service, and Dock became a lifelong friend and confidante of its nurse and social worker–founder, Lillian Wald. The settlement environment not only encouraged Dock to continue her contributions to nursing but also stimulated her involvement in social reforms.

Dock was an ardent pacifist, which influenced her efforts to make nursing an international profession. She was one of the founders and the first secretary (1899–1922) of the International Council of Nurses, serving without salary and traveling to Europe a number of times at her own expense. Because of her pacifist principles, Dock permitted no mention of World War I in the section of the *American Journal of Nursing* that she edited.

While at Henry Street, Dock became a militant suffragist. In 1912 at the International Council of Nurses conference in Cologne, Germany, her resolution endorsing women's suffrage passed unanimously. Upon her return to the United States, Dock became a member of the Woman's Party, picketed the White House and as a result was sentenced to thirty days in the workhouse. The episode got considerable publicity in the November 1917 issue of the *American Journal of Nursing*. On another occasion she was arrested for creating a disturbance at the polls. Altogether, Dock was jailed three times. She also advocated birth control and joined the movement for stricter antiprostitution laws.

In 1900 Dock published *Short Papers on Nursing Subjects*. Shortly afterward she began her collaboration with Mary Adelaide Nutting on the four-volume *History of Nursing* (1907–1912). With Isabel Maitland Stewart she condensed the four volumes into *A Short History of Nursing* (1920), which went through four editions. Her *Hygiene and Morality: . . . An Outline of the Medical, Social, and Legal Aspects of Venereal Diseases* (1910) showed moral courage for the time.

Prolonged illness in Dock's family forced her in 1922 to give up her organizational activities and retire with her four sisters to the family farm in Pennsylvania. She died at Chambersburg, Pa. Dock, who never married, was a woman of strong convictions, high standards, and selfless energy who made major contributions to the development of the nursing profession.

[Some of Dock's correspondence with Lillian Wald is among Wald's papers in the New York Public Library. In addition to her books, all of which are listed in the text, Dock wrote articles that include "Experiment in Contagious Nursing," *Charities,* July 4, 1903; and "Nursing Education," *ibid.,* Jan. 26, 1907. An excellent biographical sketch of Dock is Mary M. Roberts, "Lavinia Dock—Nurse, Feminist, Internationalist," *American Journal of Nursing,* Feb. 1956, with photographs. Some information on Dock is in books by and about Lillian Wald, including R. L. Duffus, *Lillian Wald: Neighbor and Crusader* (1938); Beryl Williams Epstein, *Lillian Wald: Angel of Henry Street* (1948); and Lillian Wald, *Windows on Henry Street* (1934). See also Helen E. Marshall, *Mary Adelaide Nutting: Pioneer of Modern Nursing* (1972). "The Reminiscences of Isabel Stewart," in the Columbia University Oral History Collection, has much of value on Dock's career.]

JUDITH ANN TROLANDER

DOLE, JAMES DRUMMOND (Sept. 27, 1877–May 14, 1958), founder of the Hawaiian pineapple industry, was born in Jamaica Plain, Mass., the son of Charles Fletcher Dole, a Unitarian minister and author, and Frances Drummond. He attended Roxbury Latin School and Harvard University. After graduating from Harvard in 1899, he headed for Hawaii with $1,500 and an interest in agriculture. His ancestors had been traders and missionaries to Hawaii in the eighteenth century and his father's cousin, Sanford Dole, was about to become the first governor of the new United States territory. In 1900 Dole bought a government homestead of sixty-four acres at Wahiawa and began to grow vegetables and pineapples. Previous attempts to grow pineapples commercially had failed because a pineapple picked green is sour and tough, and will not ripen, whereas a ripe pineapple would spoil before reaching markets on the mainland. Dole decided to pick the fruit ripe, can it on the island, and ship it to the mainland.

In the spring of 1901, Dole planted 75,000 pineapples, and in December of that year he organized the Hawaiian Pineapple Company. The first pack, canned in 1903, consisted of 1,893 cases. The next year the cannery packed 8,810 cases, and the next 25,022. In 1906 the company earned $30,489. Then came the panic of 1907, and the market for pineapple dried up. The Hawaiian pineapple industry, which by then consisted of eight packers, began 1908 with the prospect of a large, unmarketable surplus. Under Dole's leadership the members of the industry formulated a marketing plan unique in American business at the time—an industry-wide advertising campaign, without regard to brand. Within eighteen months the consumption of Hawaiian pineapple quadrupled.

In 1911 Dole hired Henry Ginaca to design a high-speed peeling and coring machine. Within a year Ginaca developed a machine that could size, peel, core, and cut the ends from 100 pineapples per minute. This made possible mass production of canned pineapple. Dole continued to seek ways to improve production and quality, and each new machine or technique was shared with the entire industry. Motor trucks, Caterpillar tractors, iron sulfate spray, and paper mulching were innovations he brought to pineapple growing. By 1916 he had leased 3,676 acres of land from the Waialua Agricultural Company. Needing still more land, in 1922 Dole bargained with Waialua for 12,000 acres on a seventeen-year prepaid lease with the right of renewal. For the lease and $1.25 million in cash he gave Waialua one-third ownership of his Hawaiian Pineapple Company. With the cash he bought the island of Lanai for $1.1 million. This cactus-covered land proved ideal for growing pineapples. Dole built a harbor, roads, and a town. Soon his company was producing 35 percent of Hawaii's pineapples. Although not yet using his name as a brand, Dole was fast becoming the king of the pineapple industry.

When Charles Lindbergh made his historic flight across the Atlantic in 1927, Dole became excited about the possibility of air service from Honolulu to the mainland. The Honolulu *Star-Bulletin* suggested an air race from California to Honolulu, and Dole offered $35,000 as prize money. In August 1928, Art Goebel and William V. Davis, Jr., won first prize. Because seven lives were lost in the effort, Dole was criticized for inspiring a dangerous stunt; but federal authorities, not Dole, had established the rules governing the flight.

As a result of the Great Depression, the Hawaiian Pineapple Company lost $5.4 million in operating income in the first nine months of 1931 and was on the verge of bankruptcy. Dole had recently perfected new methods of manufacturing a better pineapple juice and hoped this would rescue his company; but time and money for promotion were lacking. When the company's board met in late 1932, it appointed a committee including three executives of Castle and Cooke, a corporate conglomerate that owned a substantial interest in the Waialua Agricultural Company, to work out a plan for reorganization. The plan they formulated resulted in the creation of a new Hawaiian Pineapple Company in which Castle and Cooke held 21 percent interest and Waialua held 37 percent. In December 1932 Castle and Cooke took over management of the new company. Dole was made chairman of the board, an honorary position that left him without effective authority. He naturally was dissatisfied with the arrangement and pointed out that at the same time his authority in the company ended, the Dole name first appeared on every can produced by the company.

In 1933 Dole served briefly in Washington as chief of the Food Products Section of the Agricultural Adjustment Administration (AAA). Disillusioned with New Deal attempts to manage the economy, he resigned in January 1934, and in a series of articles condemned the inefficiency and conflicting authority he had found in the AAA.

Dole then moved to San Francisco, keeping his home in Hawaii primarily for vacations. He launched a series of successful new business endeavors with various partners. In 1936 he organized the Chemical Process Company to manufacture ion exchange materials for improved sugar purification. This company became a leader in its field and merged profitably into the Diamond Shamrock Company. Two years later Dole acquired the Schwarz Engineering Company, later renamed the James Dole Corporation, to develop food-processing equipment and techniques. A joint venture of this company and S&W Fine Foods resulted in a new product called Liquid Apple.

Dole resigned as chairman of the board of the Hawaiian Pineapple Company in 1948. He continued, however, to receive remuneration for the use of his name.

On Nov. 22, 1906, Dole married Belle Dickey; they had five children. He died in Honolulu. By the time of his death, pineapple was contributing $116 million a year to the Hawaiian economy and the islands were producing 72 percent of the world's supply.

[The largest collection of Dole papers is in the offices of Castle and Cooke, Honolulu. A few scrapbooks containing letters and articles are in the possession of Mrs. Hebden Porteus, Honolulu. George F. Nellist, ed., *Men of Hawaii*, V (1935); "James D. Dole," a summary prepared by the Honolulu Newspaper Agency (Sept. 25, 1956); and both the "Twenty-fifth ..." (1924) and "Fiftieth Anniversary Report of the Harvard Class of 1899" (1949) contain important biographical information. The best brief biographical sketches are obituaries in the *New York Times*, May 16, 1958; and *Newsweek*, May 26, 1958. The most detailed are Henry A. White, *James D. Dole: Industrial Pioneer of the Pacific* (1957); and Frank J. Taylor, Earl M. Welty, and David W. Eyre, *From Land and Sea, the Story of Castle and Cooke of Hawaii* (1976). In "The Ripening of Pineapples," *Nation*, Nov. 16, 1911, Dole

described the growing and canning of pineapples. Other articles on the pineapple industry include Tom White, "Pioneering in 'Pines,' " *Sunset*, Oct. 1927; "Hawaiian Island Transformed Into a Vast Pineapple Farm," *New York Times*, Apr. 12, 1931; "Pineapples Straight," *Time*, Oct. 28, 1935; Ernest R. May, "Hawaii's Man-Made Paradise," *Travel*, May 1945; and Frank J. Taylor, "The Billion-Dollar Rainbow," *Reader's Digest*, Dec. 1954. Earl C. May, *The Canning Clan, a Pageant of Pioneering Americans* (1938); and Sterling G. Slappey, ed., *Pioneers of American Business* (1973), both contain sections on Dole. For the Dole-sponsored air race, see *New York Times*, May 26–Sept. 18, 1927, and Lesley Ford, *Glory Gamblers* (1961). On Dole's government service, see his "Impressions of Five Months in Washington, August, 1933, to January, 1934," *New York Times*, Apr. 1934.]

MELBA PORTER HAY

DONOVAN, WILLIAM JOSEPH (Jan. 1, 1883–Feb. 8, 1959), lawyer, soldier, and diplomat, was born in Buffalo, N.Y., the son of Timothy Patrick Donovan, a railroad yard superintendent, and Anna Letitia Lennon. He entered Niagara University in 1901 to prepare for the priesthood, but transferred to Columbia University in 1904 to study law. After receiving the B.A. in 1905 and the LL.B. in 1907, Donovan returned to Buffalo to practice law; in 1912 he merged his firm, Donovan and Goodyear, with the leading law firm in Buffalo, O'Brian and Hamlin. On July 15, 1914, Donovan married Ruth Rumsey; they had two children.

After serving with the New York National Guard on the Mexican border in 1916, Donovan became a battalion major and subsequently a colonel in the New York 69th Regiment, one of the first American units to see action in France during World War I. He was wounded three times in combat and won the Distinguished Service Cross, the Distinguished Service Medal, and the Congressional Medal of Honor. After several special assignments both overseas and in Washington, Donovan returned to his law practice as a national war hero.

In 1922 Donovan became United States attorney for western New York, and later that year he accepted the Republican nomination for lieutenant governor. Victory went to the Democratic ticket headed by Alfred E. Smith, but Donovan ran far ahead of the other Republican candidates. Attorney General Harlan Fiske Stone, Donovan's former professor, appointed him chief of the Criminal Division in 1924; the next year, Donovan rose to assistant to the attorney general for the Antitrust Division. During four years in this post, he endeavored to avoid needless antitrust litigation by previewing, and offering his opinion on, proposed mergers. Donovan thus helped to implement the Coolidge-Hoover policy of cooperating with big business and deemphasizing antitrust actions.

In 1928 Donovan worked on behalf of Herbert Hoover, whom he had met during World War I, by helping in the Republican party's effort to line up votes among Catholics. When Hoover did not name him attorney general, the disappointed Donovan opened a law practice in New York City. Still politically ambitious, he unsuccessfully opposed Herbert H. Lehman for governor of New York in 1932. Throughout the 1930's Donovan practiced corporation law and was a sharp critic of the New Deal.

Donovan also spoke in favor of military preparedness. Several of his trips overseas, after which he reported to American officials, attracted much publicity because of their air of mystery and called attention to his ability to obtain and analyze intelligence data. In 1935 Donovan persuaded Benito Mussolini to let him observe Italian forces in Libya and Ethiopia; in 1938 he visited Spain. Two years later, after the outbreak of World War II, Secretary of the Navy Frank Knox asked Donovan to assess the British war effort firsthand, and upon his return Donovan published a number of influential newspaper articles on German subversion. He made a secret mission to southeastern Europe and the eastern Mediterranean in late 1940 and early 1941; on this trip he appraised British strengths and needs, and encouraged local officials to resist the Germans.

As American involvement in the war approached, Donovan, who had become convinced of the power of propaganda and the need for counterpropaganda and subversion during war, advocated the creation of a central American intelligence agency. President Franklin D. Roosevelt asked him to head an agency that would collect and analyze strategic intelligence as well as engage in counterpropaganda and clandestine operations; Donovan became coordinator of information on July 11, 1941. He and the staff that he assembled quietly began gathering information, studying everything from the economic structure of Germany to the personalities of world leaders, shaping American propaganda, monitoring foreign radio broadcasts, and—in a limited way at first—directing "special operations" (subversion, sabotage, and counterintel-

ligence) overseas. These activities greatly expanded between 1941 and 1945, until the organization had 30,000 employees and a nearly unlimited (and secret) budget.

When President Roosevelt restructured intelligence functions on June 13, 1942, Donovan became head of the new Office of Strategic Services (OSS), which was charged with conducting nonmilitary action against the enemy as well as with gathering and analyzing strategic information. OSS specialists (including many scholars) collected and evaluated a massive body of data that formed the foundation for decisions of policy and tactics. The public, though, was more interested in the glamorous covert activities of OSS agents abroad, mainly in occupied Europe: espionage, guerrilla warfare, assistance to underground groups, and the rescue of Allied soldiers. The OSS also operated in neutral countries, where it fought shadowy battles with Axis agents. It was less active in the Pacific Theater of Operations, in part because General Douglas A. MacArthur did not welcome OSS activities.

Donovan guided the OSS through the jealousy of other American (and Allied) intelligence agencies; the skepticism of the Joint Chiefs of Staff, to whom the OSS reported; occasional inappropriate use of OSS agents in the field; attempts to undermine the independence of. the OSS; the ridicule of Americans who regarded a "spy agency" as unnecessary or inconsistent with American ideals; and some resentment of his personal domination of the OSS. Opposition even to military rank for Donovan prevailed until 1943, when he was made a brigadier general.

Late in 1944, Donovan recommended to Roosevelt that a peacetime intelligence agency modeled on the OSS be established. On Aug. 25, 1945, Donovan (now a major general) resigned in order to demonstrate that his recommendation, which had been leaked to the press, was not motivated by ambition to head such an agency. On September 20, President Harry S. Truman dissolved the OSS. From his New York law office Donovan continued to advocate a permanent intelligence agency. When the Central Intelligence Agency was created, he was regarded as a possible director, especially after Dwight D. Eisenhower—whom Donovan had supported for the Republican nomination in 1952—became president. Donovan wanted the position, but Allen W. Dulles was the new president's choice. Eisenhower did ask Donovan, a vocal foe of communism, to become ambassador to Thailand, where he served in 1953–1954. He then returned to his law practice, but ill health increasingly limited his activities until his death in Washington, D.C.

Although Donovan's nickname, "Wild Bill," bespoke his colorful public reputation, he actually was a gentle, unassuming, intensely private man who gave the appearance of aloofness. He had few close friends. His most striking qualities were his inexhaustible energy, iron discipline, and self-control in any crisis.

[Donovan's papers are privately held. The articles that he wrote with Edgar A. Mowrer after his trip to England were published as *Fifth Column Lessons for America* (1940). The only biography is Corey Ford, *Donovan of OSS* (1970), by a former OSS staff member; it is neither critical nor particularly penetrating. See also Corey Ford, *Cloak and Dagger: The Secret Story of OSS* (1946), a semiofficial account; and R. Harris Smith, *OSS* (1972), a more scholarly account. Other works of value are Stewart Alsop and Thomas Braden, *Sub Rosa* (1964); and William Stevenson, *A Man Called Intrepid* (1976). Articles on Donovan include Henry F. Pringle, "Exit 'Wild Bill'," *Outlook*, Jan. 9, 1929; William G. Shepherd, "Today's Trust Busters," *Collier's*, Feb. 23, 1929; Elizabeth R. Valentine, "Fact-Finder and Fighting Man," *New York Times Magazine*, May 4, 1941; and Frederic Sondern, Jr., "Our Wartime Spymaster Carries On," *Reader's Digest*, Oct. 1947. Donovan appears in many oral history memoirs in the Columbia University collection, particularly in those of Justice Robert H. Jackson and of Sidney Alderman.]

DONN C. NEAL

DORAN, GEORGE HENRY (Dec. 19, 1869–Jan. 7, 1956), publisher, was born in Toronto, Canada, of Irish Presbyterian parents. Reared in a staunchly Calvinist atmosphere, he began his publishing career at fourteen, when he left school to work for the Willard Tract Depository of Toronto. Under the tutelage of S. R. Briggs, the firm's smug but commercially adept founder, Doran became familiar with every aspect of the religious book trade during the next seven years. In 1892 he decided that publishing opportunities were too circumscribed in Canada and moved to Chicago, where he joined Fleming H. Revell and Company, a house that catered to the publishing needs of the lesser evangelical denominations.

Doran's energetic salesmanship and personal charm soon brought new accounts to the company, and at the age of twenty-four he became a vice-president. Like other religious publishers of the late nineteenth century, Revell was cautiously expanding its lists to include more general offerings. This secularizing trend met with Doran's enthusiastic approval, and he was instrumental in adding such popular authors as Roswell Field and Charles W. Gordon ("Ralph Connor") to Revell's list. But despite these changes, the company remained essentially a publisher of religious books, and Doran grew progressively disenchanted with its inhibiting conservatism. In 1908 he returned to Toronto to establish his own firm, George H. Doran Company, Limited, in partnership with Hodder and Stoughton, English religious publishers who agreed to supply him with their extensive list of fiction, art, and children's books for distribution in the United States and Canada.

The following year he moved his headquarters to New York City, as he had planned from the start. He had become a naturalized American citizen in October 1896, and his American attachments had been further strengthened by his marriage in 1895 to Mary Noble McConnell of Evanston, Ill. Doran's intuitive grasp of the public taste and his willingness to take chances on new authors enabled him immediately to make relatively large profits. His first widely popular publication was Ralph Connor's novel, *The Foreigner*, which sold 125,000 copies in 1909. That same year Doran also gambled successfully on an obscure English novelist, Arnold Bennett, whose *Old Wives' Tale* he brought out at the urging of his wife. The publication of this work established Bennett's vogue in America and led to an enduring friendship between the author and Doran, who became Bennett's exclusive American publisher. Bennett also helped him to obtain contracts from such rising English literary figures as Hugh Walpole and Frank Swinnerton.

Doran's transatlantic connections were further enlarged through his purchase in 1910 of A. C. Armstrong and Son, a New York firm that was the American distributor of Hodder and Stoughton's religious titles. To keep abreast of literary fashions abroad, he made frequent trips to England, where his rooms at London's Hotel Savoy became a favorite meeting place for writers and agents. His British sympathies during World War I led him to publish propaganda for the British Ministry of Information, along with the writings of Theodore Roosevelt, Mary Roberts Rinehart, and other advocates of American intervention. Besides adding another popular novelist to his lists, Doran's wartime association with Mrs. Rinehart produced unexpected personal results: in 1919 her son Stanley married his only child, Mary, and joined the Doran firm.

Influenced by such able young editors as Eugene Saxton and John Chipman Farrar, Doran continued to publish new and unconventional authors of promise in the 1920's, including Stephen Vincent Benét, Du Bose Heyward, Hervey Allen, Michael Arlen, W. Somerset Maugham, and Aldous Huxley. In September 1918 the firm acquired *The Bookman* from Dodd, Mead and Company and brought that prestigious but commercially unprofitable journal to new heights of literary excellence under Farrar's editorship (1921–1927). Yet Doran never completely outgrew his fundamentalist background: "I would publish no book which destroyed a man's simple faith in God without providing an adequate substitute," he asserted in his autobiography. "I would publish no book which would destroy the institution of marriage without providing a substitute order of society which would be protective of the younger generations. All else I would cheerfully publish."

A Victorian gentleman in spite of himself, Doran was repelled by the nihilism of the most creative postwar writers, whose use of earthy language and often shocking themes he considered a betrayal of a socially responsible literary tradition. Deploring the acquiescence of younger publishers in what he considered the debasement of public taste, Doran later recalled that he had personally expunged certain "obscene" passages from John Dos Passos' *Three Soldiers* (1921) and had "flatly rejected" works by Hemingway, D. H. Lawrence, and "that ruffian Dreiser."

In 1925 Doran bought out his English partners, and two years later his firm merged with Doubleday, Page and Company. The new house, Doubleday, Doran and Company, was the largest trade publisher in the United States. But the union was short-lived; personality clashes and policy disagreements led Farrar and Stanley Rinehart to withdraw in June 1929 to found their own company, and Doran resigned the following year. After employment as a traveling representative of William Randolph Hearst's Cosmopolitan Book Corporation, he retired from publishing in 1934 to write his memoirs. Many of his later years were spent on an Arizona ranch, from which he moved back to Toronto as his eightieth birthday approached. Still vigorous and flamboyant, he took up residence in the Royal York Hotel, where he

enjoyed celebrity status as "the last of the impresario publishers" until his death.

[Doran's impressionistic and often unreliable *Chronicles of Barabbas* (1935, 1952) remains the best source concerning his publishing career. Other useful details are provided by obituary notices in the *New York Times*, Jan. 8, 1956; and the *Globe and Mail* (Toronto), Jan. 9, 1956. For Doran's outspoken comments on modern literary trends, see "People Who Read and Write," *New York Times Book Review*, Sept. 26, 1948. Charles A. Madison, *Book Publishing in America* (1966), assesses Doran's achievements within the framework of the publishing industry. There are unpublished letters from Doran in the Aldous Leonard Huxley Papers at Stanford University.]

MAXWELL BLOOMFIELD

DORSEY, THOMAS FRANCIS ("TOMMY") (Nov. 19, 1905–Nov. 26, 1956), a trombonist who led one of the most successful and long-lived swing bands from the mid-1930's to the mid-1950's, was born in Shenandoah, Pa., the son of Thomas Francis Dorsey, a miner and self-taught musician who led a band in his spare time, and of Theresa Langton. The father was determined that Tommy and his older brother, Jimmy, would not follow him into the mines. He saw music as their means of escape and began giving them lessons on the cornet as soon as they could blow a horn. Both boys were soon playing in their father's band; and by the time Tommy was sixteen, they had a band of their own, Dorsey's Wild Canaries.

The following year they joined the Scranton Sirens; and in 1924 they moved on to Jean Goldkette's big jazz band in Detroit, where they played with such celebrated musicians as Bix Beiderbecke, Joe Venuti, and Eddie Lang. By that time Jimmy had added the saxophone and clarinet to his instruments and Tommy was playing trombone.

The Dorsey brothers joined Paul Whiteman's orchestra briefly when Whiteman hired all of Goldkette's stars in 1927. For the next seven years they were among the busiest musicians in New York, playing radio and recording dates as accompanists to such singers as Bing Crosby and the Boswell Sisters and making their own records as the Dorsey Brothers Orchestra.

Temperamentally, the brothers were exact opposites. "Jimmy was always the level-headed one," Bill Rank, a trombonist in the Goldkette band, remembered. "Tommy was impulsive and aggressive. They used to fight like cats and dogs, but no one had better say anything about either one of them because, down deep, they loved each other." While the Dorseys were with the Goldkette band, in the mid-1920's, Tommy married Mildred Kraft; they had two children. Jimmy broke down and cried on Rank's shoulder, lamenting the loss of his roommate.

The brothers' differences stemmed largely from the fact that "Tommy was always a great one for pushing," as their mother recalled, "and Jimmy for taking his own sweet time." Their most celebrated battle occurred at the Glen Island Casino in New Rochelle, N.Y., on May 30, 1935. The year before, at the urging of Glenn Miller, the Dorseys had formed an eleven-piece orchestra for which Miller wrote most of the arrangements. The band caught on immediately and, on Memorial Day weekend 1935, they were playing at the packed Glen Island Casino when Tommy beat the tempo for "I'll Never Say 'Never Again' Again."

"Isn't that a little too fast?" asked Jimmy. "Let's do it right or not do it at all."

"All right!" exclaimed Tommy. "We won't do it at all." With a derisive blast on his trombone, he walked off the bandstand. For the next eighteen years the brothers went their separate ways, each leading his own band and rarely speaking to the other.

Jimmy continued to lead the Dorsey Brothers Band while Tommy took over a band from Joe Haymes. It first continued the "Dixieland" style that Glenn Miller had given the Dorsey Brothers Orchestra; but Tommy did not think highly of his talents as a jazz musician. He was a superb technician, a master of intonation and phrasing. As a result the band's arrangements gradually shifted to a more tightly knit, richly harmonized, melodic style.

Tommy was a perfectionist so far as his own playing was concerned and, because he expected the same from his sidemen, there was a great deal of turnover in the band. But by 1940 he had developed an orchestra that brought popular dance music to one of its high points. At the beginning of the decade, Dorsey's vocalists were Frank Sinatra and Connie Haines. Later, Jo Stafford was a featured singer. Sy Oliver, whose arrangements had helped establish the unique sound of Jimmie Lunceford's band in the 1930's, joined Dorsey to give the band harmonic and rhythmic depth. The sidemen included Bunny Berigan, Buddy Rich, Ziggy Elman, and, later,

Buddy De Franco, Charlie Shavers, Terry Gibbs, and Louis Bellson.

After World War II, the "name" bands that had flourished for more than a decade began to disappear, but Tommy Dorsey's orchestra survived. However, there were changes in his personal life. In 1941 he was divorced and on Apr. 8, 1943, he married Pat Dane. That marriage also ended in divorce. On Mar. 27, 1948, he married Jane New; they had two children.

There was also a change in his relationship with his brother. Jimmy Dorsey found it hard going after World War II, and in 1953 he gave up his orchestra, was reconciled with Tommy, and joined his band, which became known as Tommy Dorsey and His Orchestra, Featuring Jimmy Dorsey. After Tommy's sudden death in Greenwich, Conn., Jimmy took over the band; but within seven months he too was dead.

[An obituary is in the *New York Times,* Nov. 27, 1956. Also see Herb Sanford, *Tommy and Jimmy: The Dorsey Years* (1972); John S. Wilson's annotation on the record album "The Incomparable Tommy Dorsey" (1969); and Richard English, "The Battling Brothers Dorsey," *Saturday Evening Post,* Feb. 1946.]

JOHN S. WILSON

DRAPER, RUTH (Dec. 2, 1884–Dec. 30, 1956), monologuist, was born in New York City, the daughter of William Henry Draper, a physician, and Ruth Dana. Reared in a world of privilege and comfort, she showed a special knack for impressions as a child and was frequently called on by her family to perform for others. At the time there was no thought of a professional career, since those of her social class did not become theatrical performers. Draper's independent temperament led to her withdrawal at the age of eleven from Miss Spence's School, after only a year's attendance. Thereafter, she was privately educated. Her tutor, Hannah Henrietta Hefter, profoundly influenced her appreciation of art and literature; and years later, Draper praised her for having "lit the spark."

In 1903 Draper made her formal debut in society and for the next ten years exchanged visits with friends, attended charitable functions, and traveled. She wrote poetry and published "Winter Flowers" in *Scribner's Magazine* (March 1913). The verse, which was entirely conventional, showed none of the individuality that was to emerge in the scripts she prepared for her dramatic and humorous monologues. At parties Draper was frequently asked to perform her characterizations, and by 1910 she was well enough known in social circles to be included on bills for charity benefits and private performances. In 1913, while visiting London, she performed at a party attended by George V and Queen Mary. The latter became an ardent follower of her career and invited her to perform at Windsor Castle. Henry James was impressed by Draper in London and wrote a monologue for her. It was about an American, nouveau riche social climber in English society. James was a friend of the Draper family, and her inability to work with his material caused her considerable distress. But this pattern was consistent with her artistic development. She simply could not satisfactorily realize characterizations other than those she prepared herself.

At the outbreak of World War I, Draper was making appearances for various charities throughout the United States. After seeing her perform, the English actress Marie Tempest offered her a small part in *A Lady's Name,* which ran on Broadway for two months in 1916. It was one of the two times that she appeared other than as a solo performer. Toward the end of her career, she appeared in New York City with her nephew, Paul Draper, the classical tap dancer.

The Polish pianist Ignace Paderewski had known Draper since 1891, when he made his American debut and had encouraged her to become a professional. On Jan. 29, 1920, at the age of thirty-five, she gave her first professional appearance in Aeolian Hall, in London. The following year the French producer Aurélien Lugné-Poe presented her in Paris. Max Reinhardt sponsored her in Germany, and she toured Europe with conspicuous success. By the end of the decade she was able to have a nineteen-week season on Broadway.

Draper held a special affection for England, where her regular appearances made her something of a national institution, a status confirmed when she was made a Commander of the Order of the British Empire in 1951. She encountered the great and near great in many fields, from the theater to politics. Sarah Bernhardt encouraged her to do comedy; Eleonora Duse advised her against it. As ever she followed her own instincts and included both humorous and dramatic pieces in her programs. Although she never married, she had one great passionate friendship. While in Italy she met Lauro de Bosis,

a writer and opponent of fascism, and became involved in his struggle. After he died in 1931, while strewing propaganda leaflets on Rome from an aircraft, she endowed a lectureship at Harvard in his name. By 1935 Draper had brought her art as far as India and Ceylon (Sri Lanka). Praised extensively by the critics of her day, she lived to see herself rediscovered in the 1950's by a new generation.

Draper's performances were models of concision. She could convey the impression of a crowded room merely by her intonation and bearing. Her stage props were minimal—usually no more than a chair, table, or bench, and her lighting effects were equally simple. Wearing a dress of muted color, she transformed herself by means of voice, gesture, and accessories into a clubwoman, an immigrant, or a Greek dancing teacher. In addition to her skill with dialect, she was fluent in French and performed several pieces in that language. German, Spanish, and Italian phrases often turned up in her monologues. In "Five Imaginary Love Songs" she convincingly vocalized nonsense words in the manner of such languages as Arabic, Swedish, and Russian, which she did not know.

Draper did not originate the serious monologue, but her dramatically sophisticated characterizations considerably increased its impact. She created 35 monologues, portrayed 54 characters, and evoked the presence of more than 300 others. She was, in effect, a one-woman repertory company. She died in New York City, after having completed a performance.

[Draper translated Lauro de Bosis' *Icaro* from Italian (1933). On her life and art, see *The Art of Ruth Draper; Her Dramas and Characters* (1960), which includes a biographical memoir by Morton D. Zabel and the scripts of thirty-five monologues. Her extensive correspondence was published as *The Letters of Ruth Draper* (1979), Neilla Warren, ed.]

DON McDONAGH

DRINKER, CECIL KENT (Mar. 17, 1887–Apr. 14, 1956), experimental physiologist and educator, was born in Philadelphia, Pa., the son of Henry Sturgis Drinker, an engineer, lawyer, and president of Lehigh University, and Aimee Ernesta Beaux. Drinker attended Haverford School and Haverford College, graduating with a B.S. in 1908. He married Katherine Livingston Rotan on Sept. 7, 1910. They had two children.

Drinker and his wife both obtained the M.D. degree, he from the University of Pennsylvania in 1913 and she from the Women's Medical College of Pennsylvania in 1914. He ranked at the head of his class for each of the four years. After receiving the M.D., Drinker did research from 1913 to 1914 in the laboratory of Alfred Newton Richards at the University of Pennsylvania. Richards' catheterization of the kidney glomerulus probably stimulated Drinker's later research in catheterizing the lymphatics.

In 1914 Drinker took a fourteen-month residency at Peter Bent Brigham Hospital in Boston. This clinical experience was valuable in broadening his outlook for later research. He spent the winter of 1915–1916 in the department of physiology at Johns Hopkins, and then joined the department of physiology at the Harvard Medical School as an instructor. Drinker was acting head of the department in 1917–1918, while Walter B. Cannon did war work. Promotions followed, and he was appointed professor in 1924.

In 1921 President A. Lawrence Lowell of Harvard named Drinker to the committee planning the departmental composition and curriculum of the new school of public health at the university. The following year Drinker became acting head of the department of physiology there. For the next two decades he divided his efforts between applied physiology and administration at the school of public health and pure physiology at the medical school.

Drinker and several of his colleagues performed health surveys in various industries, and their reports on poisoning from manganese, radium, and carbon monoxide were pioneering efforts that became accepted as standards throughout the country. In 1926–1927 Drinker took a sabbatical leave to work in Copenhagen with August Krogh. He served as acting dean of the school of public health in 1930–1931, and in 1935 he became dean.

During World War II, Drinker was involved in projects to develop the high-altitude oxygen masks that were vital for the army and navy bombing programs. The work on these masks was a natural outgrowth of his earlier investigations of respiration during the 1920's that had led the navy to send its ablest research physicians to work with Drinker on oxygen poisoning and decompression sickness. Drinker continued this relationship with the navy after the war, serving as consultant physiologist to the Naval Medical Research Institute in Bethesda, Md., from 1948 to 1954.

In 1942 Drinker resigned from the deanship because of ill health, and in 1948 he retired completely from Harvard. He and his wife then moved to Falmouth, Mass. During 1948–1949 he lectured on physiology at the Cornell University Medical College in New York City. He died in Falmouth, Mass.

Between 1912 and 1950, Drinker wrote more than 250 scientific articles and books, several of which became classics. His articles on asphyxia and resuscitation were widely known. Three of his books were major contributions: *Lymphatics, Lymph, and Lymphoid Tissue* (1941), written with Joseph M. Yoffey; *Pulmonary Edema and Inflammation* (1945); and *The Clinical Physiology of the Lungs* (1954), which described his innovative experiments on anesthetized dogs. In 1919 Drinker helped to found the *Journal of Industrial Hygiene,* the first English-language journal in that field. He served as managing editor (1919–1932) and associate editor (1932–1948).

[Collections of archival materials are at the Countway Library of Medicine in Boston and the Harvard University Archives in Cambridge, Mass. On Drinker and his work see Catherine Drinker Bowen, *Family Portrait* (1970); Jean Alonzo Curran, *Founders of the Harvard School of Public Health* (1970); and Henry K. Beecher and Mark D. Altschule, *Medicine at Harvard* (1977). Obituary notices include *New York Times,* Apr. 16, 1956; *Journal of the American Medical Association,* June 16, 1956; J. H. Means, *Transactions of the Association of American Physicians,* 1956; and the unsigned notice in *AMA Archives of Industrial Health,* Jan. 1957.]

WILLIAM BEATTY

DUGGAR, BENJAMIN MINGE (Sept. 1, 1872–Sept. 10, 1956), botanist and plant pathologist, was born in Gallion, Ala., the son of Reuben Henry Duggar, a physician, and Margaret Louisa Minge. At the age of fifteen he matriculated at the University of Alabama, transferring after two years to the Mississippi Agricultural and Mechanical College (now Mississippi State College), where in 1891 he was awarded the B.S. with first honors. In 1892 he received the M.S. from the Alabama Polytechnic Institute at Auburn for a study of the germination of the teliospores of *Ravenelia*. While at Auburn he worked as assistant to George F. Atkinson in mycology and plant pathology.

From 1892 to 1893 Duggar was assistant director of the Alabama Experimental Station at Uniontown. The next year he enrolled at Harvard, where he earned the B.A. in 1894 and the M.A. in 1895. While at Harvard he worked with W. G. Farlow and Roland Thaxter in cryptogamic botany and was also assistant in botany at Radcliffe College. Duggar subsequently served for one year as assistant botanist at the State Laboratory of Natural History in Urbana, Ill., under Stephen A. Forbes, an entomologist.

Duggar enrolled at Cornell University in 1896 to begin his doctoral studies under the direction of Atkinson, who had moved to Cornell. Although interrupted several times, Duggar's association with Cornell extended over a sixteen-year period. While working on his Ph.D., he was employed as instructor in plant physiology at the university and as a cryptogamic botanist at the Experimental Station. During this period he began his research into the physiology of plants with a study of the germination of fungus spores. He continued this investigation in Europe with Wilhelm Pfeffer at Leipzig and George Klebs at Halle. In 1898 he was awarded the Ph.D. in mycology and cytology with a dissertation on the development of the pollen grain and embryo sac in *Bignonia, Symplocarpus,* and *Peltandra*.

In 1900 Duggar was appointed assistant professor of plant physiology at Cornell. He married Marie Livingston Robertson on Oct. 16, 1901; they had five children. He joined the U.S. Department of Agriculture in 1901 as a plant physiologist in the Bureau of Plant Industry. While there, he studied diseases of cotton and methods of mushroom culture. He continued his research in both areas after he had moved to the University of Missouri as chairman of the botany department (1902). His exhibit on the culture of mushrooms and other fungi won a grand prize at the 1904 World Exposition in St. Louis. He also discovered the sporulating stage and corrected the taxonomic classification of the fungus that causes cotton root disease.

During 1905 and 1906 Duggar spent several months in botanical laboratories in Germany and France, and in 1907 he returned to Cornell as chairman of the department of plant physiology. He completed the first American textbook on plant pathology, *Fungous Diseases of Plants,* in 1909 and a second textbook, *Plant Physiology,* in 1911. In 1912 he left Cornell and returned to Missouri as research professor of plant physiology in the Henry Shaw School of Botany at Wash-

ington University and the Missouri Botanical Garden in St. Louis. Here he conducted research into diverse areas of plant physiology and pathology, including nitrogen fixation and virus diseases of plants. In 1922 his wife died, and on June 6, 1927, he married Elsie Rist; they had one daughter.

Shortly after his second marriage, Duggar joined the faculty of the University of Wisconsin at Madison. Although his primary teaching duties were in plant physiology and economic botany, he also advised students in plant pathology. His major area of research involved a study of the effects of radiation on plant viruses and bacteria. This research led to his appointment to the Committee on Effects of Radiation on Organisms in the division of biology and agriculture of the National Research Council. He was chosen to edit *Biological Effects of Radiation* (1936), a book sponsored by the committee. With chemistry professor Farrington Daniels, he investigated quantum relations in photosynthesis in the alga *Chlorella*.

After retiring in 1943, Duggar accepted an appointment with Lederle Laboratories as a consultant in mycological research and production. From 1944 to 1948 his large-scale search for antibiotic-producing fungi resulted in the isolation and commercial production of the antibiotic Aureomycin (chlortetracycline).

Between 1892 and 1954 Duggar published more than 100 articles covering a wide range of scientific disciplines. Much of his early work was published in connection with the various state agricultural experiment stations, and he was representative of a large group of American scientists who contributed to the increase in agricultural productivity and efficiency that took place in the first half of the twentieth century. He also engaged in team research, often involving interdepartmental and interdisciplinary cooperation. Although Duggar pioneered in the study of viral diseases of plants and contributed to knowledge of the nature of the tobacco mosaic virus (1921–1937), his greatest achievement was in plant physiology and pathology. He died in New Haven, Conn.

[On Duggar and his work, see Morris H. Saffron, *Dictionary of Scientific Biography* (1971); John C. Walker, *Biographical Memoirs. National Academy of Sciences* (1958), with bibliography; *American Men of Science* (1955); and the obituary notice, *New York Times,* Sept. 11, 1956. Additional materials are in the unofficial archives of the botany department, University of Wisconsin, Madison.]

DIANE JOHNSON

DULLES, JOHN FOSTER (Feb. 25, 1888–May 24, 1959), lawyer and diplomat, was born in Washington, D.C., the son of the Reverend Allen Macy Dulles, a Presbyterian minister, and Elizabeth Foster. He was named after his maternal grandfather, John Watson Foster, who had served as secretary of state under President Benjamin Harrison, and his paternal grandfather, John Welsh Dulles, a prominent missionary. Diplomatic and missionary influences came to Dulles from both sides of the family; he could count among his relatives a minister to Great Britain, John Welsh, and another secretary of state, his uncle Robert Lansing.

Dulles spent his childhood in Watertown, N.Y., and attended public schools, except for a six months' stay in Lausanne, Switzerland, where he concentrated on learning French and German. He entered Princeton University in 1904. During his junior year he accompanied his grandfather, John Foster, to the Second Hague Peace Conference of 1907. Foster represented the Chinese government at that conference, and Dulles, a nineteen-year-old undergraduate, became secretary to the Chinese delegation.

This experience caused Dulles to think about a career other than the ministry, his original professional intention. After graduating from Princeton in 1908, and following a year of study at the Sorbonne in Paris, he studied law at George Washington University. He passed the bar examination in 1911 without completing the formal requirements for a degree, and entered the New York firm of Sullivan and Cromwell as a clerk, at fifty dollars a month. On June 26, 1912, Dulles, who was able to draw upon a $20,000 inheritance, married Janet Pomeroy Avery. They had three children. Dulles' legal career flourished as he became expert in the problems of international law, a field of increasing value to Sullivan and Cromwell. The firm was counsel to a number of foreign clients as well as to several American companies with overseas holdings.

It was on a trip to British Guiana for one of these latter clients that Dulles contracted malaria. Heavy quinine dosages saved his life, but damaged his optic nerve, impairing his vision slightly and leaving him with a noticeable tic in his left eye. As he grew older, this contributed to his generally dour countenance, even when he was in the best of spirits.

As American entrance into World War I neared in early 1917, Dulles received a special assignment in Central America from President Woodrow Wilson. His mission was to make sure that the governments of Panama, Costa Rica, and Nicaragua would fall in line for defense of the Panama Canal by declaring war on Germany when Congress did. Dulles was thus successfully launched on a career of public service that would eventually lead to his stewardship of the nation's affairs as secretary of state.

Barred from combat service because of his weak eyesight, Dulles received a direct commission in the army and was ordered to Washington for duty on the War Trade Board. By the end of the war he had been promoted from captain to major and was highly regarded by some of Wilson's closest advisers. On their recommendation he was appointed as counsel to the reparations section of the American Commission to Negotiate Peace (1919). In that capacity he argued the American case for a reparations policy based on a reasonable estimate of Germany's ability to pay. At Wilson's request he remained in Europe, long after the heads of state had departed, to handle matters connected with the problem of reparations from Germany's wartime partners, Austria, Hungary, and Turkey.

Proximity to the Allied statesmen did not improve Dulles' estimate of their ability to construct a lasting peace. Like Secretary of State Lansing, and his brother Allen Dulles, now also beginning a career in foreign relations, he returned from Versailles disillusioned by the failure of the peace commission to achieve a world made safe for democracy.

Unlike Lansing, who doubted the basic Wilsonian premise that a League of Nations could ensure peace, Dulles feared the inability of European democracy to meet the challenges of dissatisfied powers. He felt that the Treaty of Versailles would only increase these dangers. But from a personal point of view, Versailles was a great success for Dulles. Advanced to a partnership in Sullivan and Cromwell at the age of thirty-one, he brought the firm new clients from among the powerful acquaintances he had made while on the peace commission.

Over the next several years Dulles represented or advised several foreign financial and industrial interests, including service as special counsel to the bankers who drew up the Dawes Plan of 1924

177

for stabilizing German finances. He had few illusions, however, about the ultimate success of any plan that, without setting a final figure that Germany would have to pay, relied upon American loans to enable the German government to pay British and French claims. In 1927, the year he became the senior partner in Sullivan and Cromwell, Dulles represented the Polish government in negotiations to stabilize that country's finances.

The Great Depression all but destroyed these efforts to restructure the financial system of Europe. At several Berlin conferences in the early 1930's, Dulles represented American clients who were trying to salvage something from the wreckage of the Dawes loans and other investments in Germany. His association with these creditors, and the continuing association of Sullivan and Cromwell with German interests, led to criticism during World War II, much of it politically inspired, that Dulles was an appeaser.

As the "decade of despair" in Europe moved on, each year bringing the world closer to war, Dulles spent more and more time pondering America's role in this new stage of the struggle between "the dynamic and the static—the urge to acquire and the desire to retain." This was the central theme of his first book, *War, Peace and Change* (1939). Dulles had been concerned with this question since his experiences at Versailles, and it continued to trouble him after World War II, when he sought to counter the appeal of communism to newly independent and developing nations during the Cold War.

Like other Wall Street Republicans, Dulles was critical of Franklin D. Roosevelt's New Deal. He was not closely associated with the internationalist wing of the Republican party until the Japanese attack on Pearl Harbor (1941) plunged the United States into full participation in the war. Only a few months before Pearl Harbor he was still arguing that America should stay out of the struggle, and he criticized Churchill and Roosevelt for trying to re-create the very conditions that had produced World War I.

Soon after Pearl Harbor, however, Dulles was deeply immersed in postwar planning. This work grew out of his interest in the possibility of mobilizing church opinion behind an international peace program. As a delegate to several international meetings and conferences of church leaders, he had been impressed by the spirit of unity that prevailed at such gatherings, and he seemed to believe that only the Christian church could dispel the worship of sovereignty. In 1940

he became chairman of the Commission on a Just and Durable Peace established by the Federal Council of Churches. Besides speaking frequently on behalf of a postwar world organization, Dulles traveled to Great Britain to stress the importance of sound postwar planning; he also put together a pamphlet, *Six Pillars of Peace* (1943), which summarized the commission's proposals.

By 1944 Dulles was regarded as a leading Republican spokesman on foreign affairs, destined to play a large role in postwar foreign policy. At the outset of the Cold War, the administration of Harry S. Truman hoped to pursue a bipartisan foreign policy and Dulles often served on special delegations to assist the secretary of state at meetings of the Council of Foreign Ministers. Never a yes-man, Dulles made suggestions and occasionally took an independent line, but generally supported the president's policy. He was not known as a hardliner in those early years of the Cold War; his philosophic bent of mind sometimes led him to oppose not only the demands for stronger action against the Soviet Union put forward by other Republicans, but also some of the ideas presented within administration policymaking circles.

When Thomas E. Dewey lost the 1948 election to Truman, it seemed that Dulles had lost his chance to become secretary of state. Dewey appointed him to serve out the term of the late New York Senator Robert F. Wagner in 1949, but Dulles was defeated in a bid for election on his own the following November. Having time to reflect on the changed state of the world—and perhaps on his own apparently declining role—he wrote a second book, *War or Peace* (1950). Although he had often stressed the importance of moral considerations in conducting a successful foreign policy, the tone of this book was far more self-righteous and critical of American foreign policy. For the first time Dulles presented himself as a critic of the containment policy, although he had not yet found a suitable alternative.

His meditations were interrupted when President Truman asked him to undertake the negotiation and drafting of a peace treaty with Japan. Dulles accepted, although he must have been aware that he was given the assignment in large part because the administration needed someone to blunt Republican criticism of its Far Eastern policy. Before he left for Tokyo, Dulles urged Truman to take a stand in Asia against the spreading wave of communism.

The North Korean attack across the Thirty-eighth Parallel came while Dulles was in Japan.

With General Douglas MacArthur, Dulles cabled Washington, calling upon the administration to offer aid to South Korea. The Korean War was still going on in 1952, when the Republicans nominated Dwight David Eisenhower for the presidency. Dulles drafted the foreign policy planks of the Republican platform, denouncing containment as a negative, futile, and immoral policy "which abandons countless human beings to a despotism and godless terrorism." The Republicans, Dulles promised, would revive "the contagious, liberating influences which are inherent in freedom."

Eisenhower warned Dulles that whenever he discussed "liberation" he wanted to make sure that the qualifying phrase "by all peaceful means" was in the same sentence. Dulles never intended that the United States undertake a military campaign to roll back Soviet power from Eastern Europe. This became apparent almost immediately when the Eisenhower administration did not intervene during the 1953 bread riots in East Germany; and any lingering doubts disappeared when the United States did nothing more than condemn Soviet actions in crushing the 1956 Hungarian attempt at revolution.

When Dulles assumed office as secretary of state in 1953, he was convinced that containment was the very policy that the static powers had pursued in the 1930's and that had led to war. He was equally convinced that the United States had to adopt a dynamic policy to counteract the ideological force being exerted by the communist powers. To a degree, therefore, liberation really meant separation from dependence on Great Britain and France and from the policies of once-great powers now in decline.

In Europe this would mean disassociation of American policy from any tendency to accommodate Soviet pretensions to the control of Eastern Europe and any recognition of a so-called sphere of influence. Thus he opposed summit diplomacy as reminiscent of wartime Big Three meetings (particularly Yalta), at which Russian demands were given an air of legitimacy. He was suspicious of British and French willingness to bargain about anything, especially if thereby they could maintain the remnants of their past glory and colonial empires. Dulles' criticism of Anglo-French policies and his penchant for stating the Eisenhower administration's position in dramatic sweeping phrases like "massive retaliation" and "agonizing reappraisal" alarmed critics; they began to consider him an inflexible moralist whose views hindered the nation's ability to deal with an increasingly complex and rapidly changing world.

Dulles shrugged off such complaints, convinced that the United States could not afford to lose sight of moral and ideological questions in foreign policy. He regarded his greatest achievement to be the Southeast Asia Treaty Organization (SEATO), which, he felt, had saved South Vietnam and turned the tide against communism throughout that area. No doubt his greatest disappointment came in the Middle East, where, despite three years of constant effort, he failed to realign Arab nationalism into a workable relationship with Israel and American policy.

The Anglo-French-Israeli attack on Egypt in the fall of 1956 was a political embarrassment for Eisenhower, coming as it did near the climax of the presidential campaign; but for Dulles, Suez was a nightmare, destroying all hope of reconciling emerging anticolonial forces with America's reinvigorated anticommunism. In his last years, Dulles apparently gave more and more thought to a different sort of reconciliation in Europe. While he remained adamant against any reunification of Germany that did not permit the Germans to participate fully in the West's defense arrangements, he seemed willing to consider a *modus vivendi* that would help both East and West—and the Germans—to live together in Europe.

Eisenhower supported Dulles at every juncture and over the years their relationship seemed to grow stronger and stronger. Seriously ill with cancer, Dulles resigned on Apr. 15, 1959. He died in Washington, D.C.

Dulles became a symbol for hard-line Cold War policies. It is ironic, however, that the same Democrats and liberals who voiced the strongest criticisms of his foreign policies were often found among those criticizing Eisenhower's military policies as being too "soft" toward the Soviet Union. Critics further suggest that Dulles set the United States on the road to confrontation with powerful nationalistic forces in the Third World by virtue of his insistence that "neutralism" was an immoral policy in the era of the Cold War and by his support for reactionary leaders in Southeast Asia and Latin America. A powerful secretary of state, Dulles will be remembered as a controversial statesman.

[The Dulles Papers and Dulles Oral History Collection are located at Princeton University. Other papers are in the Dwight D. Eisenhower Library, Abilene, Kans. References to Dulles as secretary of state, as well as his own brief account of his New York senatorial campaign in 1949, are found in the Oral History Collection of Columbia University. In addition to the works cited in the text, Dulles wrote "Thoughts on Soviet Foreign Policy and What to Do About It," *Life*, May 3 and 10, 1946.

The standard reference is Louis L. Gerson, "John Foster Dulles," in Robert Ferrell, ed., *The American Secretaries of State and Their Diplomacy*, XVII (1967). Favorable accounts include John Robinson Beal, *John Foster Dulles* (1957); Roscoe Drummond and Gaston Coblentz, *Dulles at the Brink: John Foster Dulles's Command of American Power* (1960); Richard Goold-Adams. *The Time of Power: A Reappraisal of John Foster Dulles* (1963); Eleanor Lansing Dulles, *John Foster Dulles: The Last Year* (1963); and Michael Guhin, *John Foster Dulles: A Statesman and His Times* (1972).

Critical works include Emmet J. Hughes, *The Ordeal of Power: A Political Memoir of the Eisenhower Years* (1963); Herman Finer, *Dulles Over Suez: The Theory and Practice of His Diplomacy* (1964); Kennett Love, *Suez: Twice Fought War* (1970); and Townsend Hoopes, *The Devil and John Foster Dulles* (1973). See also the obituary notice in the *New York Times*, May 25, 1959.]

LLOYD C. GARDNER

DUNBAR, (HELEN) FLANDERS (May 14, 1902–Aug. 21, 1959), psychoanalyst, Dantean scholar, and leader in the American psychosomatic and clinical pastoral education movements, was born in Chicago, Ill. She was the daughter of Francis William Dunbar, a consulting engineer and patent expert, and Edith Vaughan Flanders, a genealogist. As a child she suffered from pseudo infantile paralysis, a rachitic disorder related to nursing problems. At the age of eight, because public school had proved disastrous, she began attending private classes at the University of Chicago's Laboratory School, where she continued for four years. Around 1912 her father became involved with extensive patent litigation on behalf of his employer, who nonetheless sold the defended rights. As a result, Mr. Dunbar withdrew and retired at age forty-six, moving the family to Manchester, Vt., where Helen's mother ran the household, with the help of an ever-present aunt and a grandmother. While Helen never lacked models for becoming a strong, steadfast woman, she grew up as a lonely, overprotected child, more at home with books than with people.

After three years with tutors in Vermont, Dunbar spent the spring term of 1917 at the Bishop's School in La Jolla, Calif.; the trip west was prompted by a "metabolic disturbance" for which her physician prescribed a meat-free diet and travel. The following fall she enrolled at the Brearley School in New York City, from which she graduated in 1919; she then went to Bryn Mawr. Though brilliant, Dunbar appeared shy and unsophisticated during her school and college years. She studied psychology, mathematics, and premedicine, but her increasing absorption in the writings of Dante Alighieri led her, upon receiving the B.A. in 1923, to begin graduate studies in philosophy at Columbia University. There she became a student of Dantean scholar Jefferson B. Fletcher, and completed her master's thesis in 1924. Dunbar continued on at Columbia, and also enrolled at Union Theological Seminary, where she received her Bachelor of Divinity degree *magna cum laude* in 1927. During 1926–1927 she also finished her first year at Yale University School of Medicine.

Dunbar's dissertation, *Symbolism in Medieval Thought and Its Consummation in the Divine Comedy* (1929; reprinted 1961), earned her lasting prestige as a Dantean scholar, while her divinity thesis won her the Ely-Eby-Landon Traveling Fellowship, which she used from July 1929 to March 1930 in Europe. Having served a subinternship in medicine and obstetrics (1928–1929), she received her M.D. in 1930. Dr. H. Flanders Dunbar, as she now called herself, spent her fourth year of medical school at the General and Psychiatric-Neurological Hospital in Vienna, at the Burghölzli Psychiatric Clinic in Zürich, and at the healing shrine of Lourdes, where she investigated the role of "religion as a unifying power in personal life."

Beginning in 1925, Dunbar spent summers at Worcester (Mass.) State Hospital studying the symbolistic functions of schizophrenia, and also worked with what was later to become the Council for the Clinical Training of Theological Students. After her return from Europe, she served from September 1930 to August 1937 as medical director of the council. At about the same time she also began research at New York's Columbia-Presbyterian Hospital as a psychiatrist assigned to the department of medicine.

In 1931 Dunbar was appointed director of the Joint Committee on Religion and Medicine of the Federal Council of Churches and the New York Academy of Medicine. During her directorship, which lasted until May 1936, Dunbar integrated the council into the Joint Committee's Department of Education, and her psychosomatic research program at Columbia into the Joint Committee's Department of Research. Thus she simultaneously provided support for both the clinical pastoral education and the American psychosomatic movements.

A direct outcome of Dunbar's research at Columbia, which included a pioneering psychiatric study of 1,600 serial admissions to a general hospital, was the publication of three classic books. From *Emotions and Bodily Changes: A Survey of Literature on Psychosomatic Interrelationships: 1910–1933* (1935) she compiled the dissertation for her doctorate of medical sciences, which she received from Columbia in 1936. *Psychosomatic Diagnosis* was published in 1943, followed by *Mind and Body: Psychosomatic Medicine* (1947). A promised sequel to *Emotions and Bodily Changes,* "on the relation of religion to health and . . . [the role of] religion . . . in directing and controlling emotion," never appeared.

Dunbar married psychiatrist Theodor Peter Wolfensberger (later Theodore P. Wolfe, Wilhelm Reich's translator and editor) on Oct. 6, 1932; they were divorced on Dec. 12, 1939. Eighteen days later Dunbar's father died, and the double loss affected her profoundly. Although Flanders Dunbar, as she now called herself, founded and edited the journal *Psychosomatic Medicine* from 1939 to 1947, and wrote eight books and twice as many articles over the next twenty years, her public career effectively ended after 1939. During the 1940's and 1950's, she increasingly devoted her time to private practice.

On July 13, 1940, Dunbar married George Henry Soule, an economist and editor of *The New Republic;* they had one child, Marcia Winslow Dunbar-Soule. (She did not marry obstetrician Raymond Roscoe Squier, as alleged in his suicide note published in 1951.)

On Aug. 21, 1959, the day her last and perhaps best book, *Psychiatry in the Medical Specialties,* came from the press, Dunbar was found floating face down in her swimming pool in South Kent, Conn. Despite suggestive comments in the obituaries, an autopsy did not reveal any conditions contributory to death other than drowning.

Dunbar's work, growing out of her studies in medieval symbolism and her interest in the unifying power of religion, clearly falls within the "organismic" tradition in American psychology and medicine, the "psychobiological" tradition in American psychiatry, and the "character analytic" tradition in psychoanalysis. But her holistic theories, focusing upon methods of observation,

prevention, and effective intervention, rather than upon psychodynamic etiology or specificity, were little appreciated during the three decades after 1939.

[There are no Dunbar Papers. In addition to the works mentioned in the text, Dunbar wrote *Your Child's Mind and Body: A Practical Guide for Parents* (1949); and *Your Pre-Teenager's Mind and Body* (1962), and *Your Teenager's Mind and Body* (1962), both edited by Benjamin Linder. A more extensive biographical sketch is Robert C. Powell, "Healing and Wholeness: Helen Flanders Dunbar (1902–1959) and an Extra-Medical Origin of the American Psychosomatic Movement, 1906–1936" (Ph.D. diss., Duke University, 1974).

See also Robert C. Powell, *CPE: Fifty Years of Learning, Through Supervised Encounter With Living Human Documents* (New York, 1975); and the obituary notice in the *New York Times,* Aug. 23, 1959.]

ROBERT CHARLES POWELL

DURAND, WILLIAM FREDERICK (Mar. 5, 1859–Aug. 9, 1958), pioneer mechanical and aeronautical engineer, was born in Bethany, Conn., the son of William Leavenworth Durand and Ruth Coe. He grew up on a farm near Derby, Conn., and as a boy showed unusual aptitude for mathematics and a fondness for working with tools. Because of these qualities he was encouraged to seek entrance to the United States Naval Academy; he graduated in 1880, ranking second in his class.

Durand's first professional assignment was on the U.S.S. *Tennessee,* the flagship of the Atlantic fleet, and the largest ship in the United States Navy. He was to look after the full-rigged wooden ship's small steam engine that was used for auxiliary power. After three years of sea duty, and a short tour of duty in the designing room at the Bureau of Steam Engineering, which at the time was involved in the design of the machinery for the first ships of the new steel navy, Durand was sent by the navy to Lafayette College to give instruction in steam engineering and iron ship building. On Oct. 23, 1883, he married Charlotte Kneen, a high school classmate; they had one son.

The exposure to academic life at Lafayette (1883–1885) was a turning point in Durand's career. In 1887 he resigned from the navy to accept a position at Michigan State College (now Michigan State University) to organize a new department of mechanical engineering. In 1891 he went to Cornell as head of the new postgraduate program of naval architecture and marine engineering that was being organized by Robert Thurston in Cornell's Sibley College.

Cornell provided Durand with his first real opportunity to contribute to the advancement of the then fledgling field of engineering. He conducted studies there that for the first time made it possible to design a ship propeller to meet any proposed condition of operation. Other enduring contributions made at Cornell include the invention of the radial planimeter for averaging the ordinates of a diagram plotted on a polar chart, and the introduction of logarithmic cross-section paper. As late as 1936 the general catalog of Keuffel and Esser Company listed logarithmic paper as Durand's Logarithmic Paper.

In 1904 Durand became head of the department of mechanical engineering at Stanford University, where he quickly became involved with the water and power problems of the west. Over the years he served as consultant to the Hetch Hetchy project of the City of San Francisco, and to the Metropolitan Water District of Los Angeles County. As an outgrowth of these activities he did significant research on hydraulic machinery, the hydraulics of pipelines, and the theory of the surge chamber.

With the development of the airplane Durand became interested in aeronautics. In 1914 he wrote an extensive paper, "The Screw Propeller; With Special Reference to Airplane Propulsion." The following year, upon the establishment of the National Advisory Committee for Aeronautics (NACA), now known as NASA, he was appointed by President Woodrow Wilson as one of the five nongovernmental members. At the first meeting of NACA, Durand set forth the need for research on the air propeller and proposed a study using models as he had done earlier with the ship propeller. This led to a series of studies, directed by Durand over a fifteen-year period, that for many years established the procedures by which air propellers were designed.

At the second meeting of NACA (1916), Durand was made its chairman and held this vitally important position when the United States entered World War I. He initiated the development of the first airplane supercharger and through NACA also sponsored the Liberty engine, established the first ground training schools for aviators, and negotiated a cross-license agreement that pooled airplane patents for the period of the war. The cross-licensing ended the bitter patent litigation between the Wright brothers and Glenn Curtiss that had hindered the progress of aviation. Durand continued as a member—although not chairman—of NACA until 1933, and again served during World War II, from 1941 to 1945.

In 1917 Durand was elected to the National Academy of Sciences and the American Philosophical Society. Shortly thereafter he took charge of the Washington activities of the engineering division of the National Research Council, concurrently with his chairmanship of NACA. In December 1917 Durand established a scientific liaison office in Paris. Among his staff on this assignment was a young naval aviator, Harry F. Guggenheim, who with his father later founded the Daniel Guggenheim Fund for the Promotion of Aeronautics, which was so important in developing the science of aeronautics and civil aviation during the 1920's and 1930's. Durand served as a trustee of this fund for many years.

Durand's retirement from Stanford (1924) changed the character of his activities but not their tempo. In 1925 he served as president of the American Society of Mechanical Engineers. The same year President Calvin Coolidge appointed him to a board of aeronautic inquiry set up in response to the public uproar created when General Billy Mitchell charged the military services with neglecting and suppressing aviation in national defense. When the board organized, financier Dwight Morrow became chairman and Durand secretary. Its report, drafted largely by Durand and Morrow, outlined a general plan for the development of military aircraft and also recommended the creation of the offices of assistant secretary of war for air and assistant secretary of navy for air. Its recommendations were promptly implemented and remained in effect until after World War II when the Department of Defense was established.

In 1927 Secretary of Interior Hubert Work made Durand a member of a five-man board of advisors to study the many problems associated with the development of the Colorado River. He contributed a report covering the engineering and economic problems involved in what is now known as the Hoover Dam, and he was subsequently appointed secretary of a board of consulting engineers that advised on this project. This service led to his involvement in a consulting capacity with a number of other great dams, including the Grand Coulee, Shasta, and Friant dams.

In 1935, after the loss of the airships *Akron* and *Macon*, the secretary of the navy appointed Durand as chairman of a special committee on airships to study technical and policy questions. The following year Durand served on a committee appointed by Secretary of Interior Harold L. Ickes to look into what had become a lively political issue, the question of tidal power at Passamaquoddy Bay, Maine. The resulting report quietly buried the proposal by showing that although the project was feasible as an engineering undertaking, it was clearly uneconomic as a source of power.

From 1929 to 1936 Durand devoted much of his time to organizing and editing a monumental six-volume encyclopedic work, *Aerodynamic Theory*. Sponsored by the Daniel Guggenheim Fund, this project gathered together for the first time the fundamental core of fluid mechanics theory that was applicable to aeronautic problems. As one of the twenty-five contributing authorities, Durand wrote three of the twenty divisions himself. It was still a major reference work at the time of his death.

In 1941 Durand was called to Washington by Vannevar Bush, then chairman of NACA. His new assignment, taken on at the age of eighty-two, was to chair a newly formed NACA committee instructed to study the possibilities of jet propulsion for application to aircraft. In his history of aircraft engines, Robert Schlaifer states that "it was apparently owing in large part to Durand, who was an especially energetic chairman, that jet propulsion was very seriously considered. . . . Until this time engineers had tended to think of the gas turbine purely as a substitute for the reciprocating engine in driving a propeller."

In 1941 Durand became chairman of the engineering division of the National Research Council. He also served as a member or chairman of numerous special ad hoc committees, as well as chief of Section 12.1 of the National Defense Research Committee.

At the end of the war, Durand resigned from all of his activities and actually retired. The next five years passed quietly, punctuated by such events as receipt from the hands of General Spaatz in 1946 of the Presidential Medal for Merit for his services in World War II. After his wife's death in 1950, he moved to an apartment hotel in Brooklyn, N.Y., a short walk from the home of his son and not too distant from various grandchildren. He died only a few months before his one hundredth birthday.

Durand had an extraordinary ability to grasp and retain ideas dealing with a great diversity of subjects. He further had an exceptional gift for both verbal and written expression and the ability to see all sides of a question. As a consequence, in a committee he was commonly the man who was asked to draft the report. The period during which he was highly productive was most unusual. If his life had ended upon retirement in 1924 at the age of sixty-five, he would have been considered as having had a distinguished career. On the other hand, if his lifework had consisted only of those things carried on after sixty-five, he would have been equally, if not more, distinguished.

[Durand's autobiography, *Adventures*, was published in 1953. Additional information can be found in the archives of the National Academy of Sciences, the Stanfordiana Collection of the Stanford Library, and the files of Stanford's Department of Aeronautical Engineering. See also Frederick Emmons Terman, "William Frederick Durand," *Biographical Memoirs. National Academy of Sciences* (1976); Robert Schlaifer and S. D. Herron, *Development of Aircraft Engines and Fuels* (1950); and the obituary notice in the *New York Times*, Aug. 10, 1958.]

FREDERICK EMMONS TERMAN

DURANTY, WALTER (May 25, 1884–Oct. 3, 1957), journalist, was born in Liverpool, England, the son of William Steel Duranty, a merchant, and Emmeline Hutchins. He attended Harrow and Bedford, and took a degree in classics with first-class honors from Emmanuel College, Cambridge, in 1906. Duranty did not launch his literary career as quickly or as successfully as his classmate Hugh Walpole. For seven years after graduation he traveled, lived a Bohemian life in Paris, and did tutoring whenever his money ran out.

At the age of twenty-nine Duranty took samples of his writing to the Paris bureau of the *New York Times* and was told that he "had no sense of journalism." Thereafter "he called every day," the bureau chief, Wythe Williams, noted, "his eyes always shining as he asked questions about what made up the news. . . . He finally talked himself into a position because he talked so much I could no longer refuse him. . . ." During his first year at the Paris bureau, the start of World War I gave Duranty a chance to prove he had learned his craft. He was attached to the French army, and during the summer of 1918 his dispatches from the battlefield were sent at the "double urgent" cable rate of seventy-five cents a word—the final measure of the *New York Times's* estimate of his importance.

After the Versailles Peace Conference, Duranty covered the famine and political unrest in the Baltic States and also gathered news about the Soviet Union (then closed to the "capitalist" press). Like most correspondents in Riga, Duranty was influenced by Russian émigrés and denounced the new Soviet state across the border. In 1920 he returned to the *Times* Paris bureau. He managed to enter the Soviet Union during the following year with Herbert Hoover's American Relief Association. In the spring of 1922 Duranty's pleas to the *New York Times* and to the Soviet government succeeded, and he became a Moscow correspondent. He learned to speak Russian during his first three years on the job. From this post he wrote about every major event in the Soviet Union for the next nineteen years (between 1934 and 1941 he was a traveling correspondent, returning to Russia for four or five months each year).

Duranty became well-known for "firsts" and "exclusives," and for personally influencing the course of Soviet-American relations. He realized that Josef Stalin was the man of destiny in the Kremlin as early as 1923, and he obtained two private interviews with the Soviet leader in the early 1930's. Duranty won the Pulitzer Prize in 1932 for articles on the Soviet Five-Year Plan. He worked for American recognition of the Soviet Union, and accompanied Maxim Litvinov to Washington in 1933 for the negotiation of the agreement. At the culmination of the Moscow purge trials (1936–1938), Ambassador Joseph E. Davies relied on Duranty for guidance.

Duranty was amused by the Soviet censors and agents who watched his work; he did not even complain publicly about the colleagues who questioned his integrity or about the editors who frequently buried his stories in the back pages of the *New York Times*. Indeed, he frequently seemed to be challenged by adversity. Friends noted that his "strangely charming pip-squeak voice" and his wooden leg (he lost a leg in a wreck of the Paris-Havre Express) made him seem debonair. Duranty married Jeanne Sheron in 1925; a separation soon followed, as did comments from his male colleagues about his success with women. Although Duranty did not pose for photographers in a trench coat, he was recognizable as the sort of romantic foreign corre-

spondent glamorized by Hollywood and envied by other journalists.

Duranty's strength was the orderly and vivid description of people who faced death because of a natural or political disaster. His World War I battlefield interviews toughened him for the job of describing the famines and purges of eastern Europe. This stoicism served him well in his reports on starvation in the Volga cities. Much of his chronicle of the liquidation of kulaks and Stalin's personal enemies gave sharp impressions of collective farms and courtrooms that both pro-Stalinists and anti-Stalinists found trustworthy. Although the emotional restraint of his reports frequently aroused the reader's sympathy for the condemned, Duranty was rarely concerned with the morality of government policy. "I am a reporter, not a humanitarian," he insisted.

Moral detachment did not sharpen Duranty's political analysis. He failed to understand how Stalin ruled. "Stalin is not an arrogant man," he wrote at the end of his career in Moscow, and added that the Soviet leader had been "remarkably long-suffering in his treatment of various oppositions." Duranty defended the verdicts of the major Moscow purge trials of the 1930's on the ground that the accused were trusted friends and advisers to Stalin, and would not have been prosecuted unless there was overwhelming evidence of crime. He interpreted the suicides and confessions of the accused as convincing signs of guilt, and cited the approval of the verdicts by the Soviet bureaucracy as proof that the prosecutions were justified. In one case Duranty simply accepted the word of the Soviet ambassador to the United States. By insisting that Stalin acted in response to a conspiracy of his disloyal subordinates, he misreported the biggest story he covered.

Duranty's failure as a political analyst was not a simple matter of bias. He wrote approvingly about shifts in Kremlin policy that made his life in Moscow more difficult (such as restrictions on social life and consumer goods brought on by Stalin). He was not a man of the left. He took up his Moscow assignment feeling that the Bolshevik government was "a compound of force, terror, and espionage, utterly ruthless in conception and in execution." Neither did Duranty advocate communism for the West: "An ugly, harsh, cruel creed this Stalinism," he warned his readers, and he publicly condemned an editorial in the *Times* that seemed to him too charitable in interpreting Stalin's plans for the kulaks.

But if Duranty always suspected that Stalin was

ruthless, as he worked on his story he usually found himself able to see Stalin's point of view. He developed the habit of finding a logic to the harshest measures and of seeing how Stalin aimed for the greater good of the Soviet Union. This was the problem; Duranty reported on Stalin so long that he began to sympathize with his struggles and solutions. "I had tried to make myself think like a true-blue Stalinist in order to find out what true-blue Stalinists were thinking, and had succeeded only too well," Duranty admitted in 1935. It was, however, a habit he could not break in his final fifteen years of writing about the Soviet Union.

Duranty's detailed and serious dispatches helped earn the *New York Times* a distinguished reputation for foreign coverage; but by leaving him on this assignment so long, the newspaper ensured that his point of view would become inadequate to cover the Soviet Union.

Duranty lived in southern California and in Florida after he left Europe in 1941. He married Anna Enwright in a hospital in Orlando, Fla., seven days before his death.

[The most important collection is *Duranty Reports Russia* (1934), with a profile of the journalist by Alexander Woollcott. Duranty told the story of his career in *I Write as I Please* (1935). His view of European politics and analysis of the Kremlin can be followed in *Red Economics* (1932); *Europe; War or Peace?* (1935); *The Kremlin and the People* (1941); *U.S.S.R.: The Story of Soviet Russia* (1944); and *Stalin & Co., the Politburo, the Men Who Run Russia* (1949). *Search for a Key* (1943) is an autobiographical novel. Duranty drew on his observations of Russian life to write a novel, *One Life, One Kopeck* (1937), and many short stories: *The Curious Lottery and Other Tales of Russian Justice* (1929); "The Parrot" in *Babies Without Tails* (1937), which won the O. Henry Memorial Award in 1928, and *The Gold Train and Other Stories* (1938). In 1945 he wrote a novel with Mary Loos: *Return to the Vineyard.*

There is important information on Duranty's career in Meyer Berger, *The Story of the New York Times, 1851–1951* (1951); Wythe Williams, *Dusk of Empire* (1937); Joseph E. Davies, *Mission to Moscow* (1941); and Robert St. John, *Foreign Correspondent* (1957). I have judged Duranty's reporting against the record documented by Robert Conquest, *The Great Terror: Stalin's Purge of the Thirties* (rev. ed., 1971). The Alexander Gumberg Papers, the State Historical Society of Wisconsin, show that from 1926 to 1931 Duranty was in contact with businessmen eager to expand Soviet-American trade.]

THOMAS C. LEONARD

DWIGGINS, WILLIAM ADDISON (June 19, 1880–Dec. 25, 1956), calligrapher, book and type designer, and author, was born in Martinsville, Ohio, the son of Moses Frazer Dwiggins, a physician, and Eva Siegfried. He attended school in Richmond, Ind., and Zanesville, Ohio, and in 1899 graduated from high school in Cambridge, Ohio. He then entered the Frank Holme School of Illustration in Chicago, where he studied lettering with Frederic W. Goudy and illustration with Frank X. Leyendecker and Joseph C. Leyendecker, illustrators for the *Saturday Evening Post*. Within two years Dwiggins had become an accomplished draftsman, and began free-lancing in Chicago. In 1902 he collaborated with Goudy on the design of *In a Balcony* for the Blue Sky Press. The following year Dwiggins returned to Cambridge to establish the Guernsey Shop, a small press producing illustrated books. On Sept. 8, 1904, he married Mabel Hoyle; they had no children.

Dwiggins subsequently moved to Hingham, Mass., where Goudy had relocated his Village Press. After Goudy moved the press to New York City, Dwiggins stayed on in Hingham, commuting to his Boston workshop and eking out a living by doing "potboilers" such as labels for cans and drawings of furniture for use in newspaper advertisements. He also designed motto cards and calendars for the publisher Alfred Bartlett. At a meeting of the Society of Printers in Boston, Dwiggins met Daniel Berkeley Updike, who obtained a grant for him to go to Europe in 1908; it was Dwiggins' only trip abroad.

Although Dwiggins was becoming successful in advertising and was amassing an impressive list of clients, his chief interest was bookmaking. In 1910 he bought a hand press and produced occasional bulletins under the imprint of The White Elephant Press. With his cousin Laurance Siegfried, and operating under the device of "Thedam Püterschein's Sons," Dwiggins published the first of three issues of *The Fabulist*, a serio-comic magazine, in the fall of 1915. The name originated in a rare moment of irritation, when Siegfried overheard him say, "I can't make the damn pewter shine." An entire imaginary family soon emerged: the learned, pedantic Dr. Herman Püterschein; his brother Jacob; and three sisters, Elsa, Henrietta, and Hedwig. Later, a "Mwano Masassi" appeared in *The Fabulist*, the last issue of which appeared in the fall of 1921.

During this period Dwiggins founded the imaginary Society of Calligraphers. Under the guise of being part of a special committee established by the "society," he and Siegfried published a satiric, tongue-in-cheek attack on existing standards of book production. Entitled *Extracts From an Investigation Into the Physical Properties of Books* (1919), the pamphlet concluded that "all books of the present day are badly made." The work was widely circulated, and its impact was great. Summing up its influence, Paul M. Hollister wrote: ". . . publishers either sent for Dwiggins, or set their designers to imitating him or . . . branched out along the lines of his principles. Take any fifty 'trade books' of 1937 . . . and you will see how often today's books echo his innovations."

In 1923, having learned that he had diabetes (then potentially fatal), Dwiggins decided to leave the advertising field. "I will produce art on paper and wood after my own heart," he wrote, "with no heed to any market." Chester Lane, director of the Harvard University Press, encouraged him to try to get more work from book publishers and gave him letters of introduction to several New York firms. During the next five years he worked on twelve books for eight publishers. Willa Cather's *My Mortal Enemy* (1926) was his first book for Alfred A. Knopf, the house for which he was consulting designer for almost thirty years.

By 1930 Dwiggins was designing bindings and wrappers for Knopf and, by 1936, entire books. He helped to establish the influential Knopf style and to make books produced by the company among the most physically attractive of the time. His designs were initially made with small, inked, wooden blocks. Finding this limiting, he devised a stencil technique, cutting and combining celluloid elements and stenciling them with brush and india ink, or with watercolors. Bold and unusual color combinations were characteristic of his work, and his stencil designs went well with the book type. His bindings for Knopf, usually of cloth stamped in gold or color on the back and often blind on the cover, had hand-lettered spines.

In *Layout in Advertising* (1928), which became a classic in the field, Dwiggins evaluated the legibility of certain typefaces and decried the lack of good design in advertising. In response Chauncey H. Griffith of the Mergenthaler Linotype Company asked Dwiggins to design new typefaces, and in the spring of 1929 he began a twenty-seven-year association with the company. Using the stencil method, Dwiggins designed eleven typefaces, in addition to five experimental faces and three Greek fonts. In 1929

the American Institute of Graphic Arts honored him with its gold medal for his accomplishments and held a comprehensive exhibition of his work in New York City.

Dwiggins' belief in a "balanced life" was reflected in the diversity of his interests, which included writing plays; designing kites and weathervanes; making woodcuts, watercolors, and murals; fashioning his own tools; and whittling marionettes. In addition to *Marionette in Motion* (1939), in which he explained the construction of his marionettes, Dwiggins published three marionette plays.

In 1937, Philip Hofer, of the Houghton Library at Harvard, put together the second show of Dwiggins' work, for the American Institute of Graphic Arts. In 1947, Dwiggins set up a press in his Hingham studio with Dorothy Abbe, a typographical designer, who became his working partner. The following year the Boston Book Builders presented an exhibit of his work at the Boston Public Library.

Described by his associates as gentle, humorous, and urbane, Dwiggins was devoid of professional jealousy and always willing to share his knowledge. His clarity and ironic wit were reflected in his conversation and literary style. He died in Hingham, Mass.

[Dwiggins' correspondence with Chauncey H. Griffith is in the Margaret King Library at the University of Kentucky. Collections of his papers, books, and other materials are in the Victoria and Albert Museum and the St. Bride Printing Library, London, and the Boston Public Library. His writings include "A Primer of Printer's Ornament," *Direct Advertising* (1920); "The Rebirth of Typographic Art," *Saturday Review of Literature* (1924); "D. B. Updike and the Merrymount Press," *Fleuron* (1924); "Counterbalanced Marionettes," in *Puppetry* (1935); "Twenty Years After," *Publishers Weekly* (1939); "The Five Hundred Years: A Time Problem and Its Solution," *Print* (1940); and "Trade Book Design," in *Graphic Forms* (1949). On Dwiggins and his work see Paul M. Hollister, *Dwiggins, a Characterization* (1929); "Check List of the Work of W. A. Dwiggins," *Dolphin* (1935); Paul M. Hollister, "Note to Be Filed in a Cornerstone," in catalog of American Institute of Graphic Arts show of Dwiggins' work (1937); Society of Printers, *W. A. Dwiggins . . . To Celebrate a Life* (1957); and Paul A. Bennett, ed., *Postscripts on Dwiggins* (1960).]

EUGENE M. ETTENBERG

EDGE, WALTER EVANS (Nov. 20, 1873–Oct. 29, 1956), governor of New Jersey, United States senator, and ambassador to France during the Hoover administration, was an archetypal Republican businessman-politician of the Progressive period and of the era between the two world wars. He was born in Philadelphia, Pa., the son of William Edge, an employee of the Pennsylvania Railroad, and Mary Evans. He grew up in Pleasantville, N.J., near Atlantic City. He left school at fourteen, started in the newspaper business as a printer's devil, and later published his own newspapers, the *Atlantic City Daily Press* and the *Atlantic City Evening Union.* Edge married Lady Lee Phillips on June 10, 1907. She died in 1915; they had one son. His second marriage was to Camilla Loyall Ashe Sewall on Dec. 9, 1922; they had three children.

Early in his life, Edge determined to make his fortune, then enter public service. Both ambitions were fulfilled. He was a self-made man, and his career was distinguished by dedication to efficiency and economy in government and to the development of New Jersey and national commercial and business interests. At the age of sixteen he was employed by the Dorland Advertising Agency in Atlantic City; he took over the firm before he was twenty and quickly built it into a multimillion-dollar enterprise. Under Edge's management, Dorland moved beyond the promotion of the New Jersey resort to resort and travel advertising and promotion in the United States and Europe.

Edge entered politics as journal clerk of the N.J. State Senate (1897–1899), and then served as senate secretary from 1901 to 1904. Elected to the state assembly in 1909, he was chosen its Republican leader in 1910. He served in the state senate for two terms (1911–1916), and as senate majority leader (1912) collaborated with Governor Woodrow Wilson in the passage of a workmen's compensation law. He was senate president in 1915 and the next year chaired an economy and efficiency commission that consolidated state boards and departments, and sponsored a state budget bill designed to centralize purchasing and place fiscal responsibility in the governor's office.

In 1916 Edge campaigned successfully for the governorship as "A Businessman With a Business Plan," winning a three-year term (1917–1920). In his inaugural address he promised to convert the state government into a modern business corporation. The governor was to be a kind of business manager, the state legislators corporate directors, and the citizenry stockholders.

Scandals in the state prison system allowed Edge to institute major reforms in the adminis-

tration of penal and charitable institutions. A prison inquiry commission, headed by Dwight Morrow, and a parallel commission to investigate state charitable institutions, led by Ellis B. Earle, were created to promote more efficient operation and more professional and humane treatment. In 1918 the New Jersey Plan centralized the state penal and welfare services under the supervision of volunteer citizen boards that hired expert directors. According to James Leiby, however, the widely hailed Edge reforms were ineffective. Edge, Morrow, and Earle, progressive-minded businessmen-financiers, focused almost exclusively on administrative improvements as opposed to an inquiry into "what was actually happening to the people in the institutions."

Other undertakings of the Edge administration, concluded by his successors, embraced plans for a vehicular tunnel under the Hudson River to New York City (Holland Tunnel), a bridge linking Camden, N.J., and Philadelphia, and interstate development of the facilities of New York port (The Port of New York Authority, 1921). Edge's administration was a paradigm of the businessman in government, dedicated and assured in his pursuit of New Jersey's commercial potential.

Edge was elected to the United States Senate in 1919 and again in 1924. Eager to expand the nation's export trade, in 1919 he sponsored legislation to amend the Federal Reserve Act by liberalization of credits on the export of American goods. He also proposed a joint resolution that led to the Budget and Accounting Act of 1921. A bureau of the budget, he explained, would introduce "real business control and management of our national responsibilities." The plan also reflected the business and financial community's concern with swollen federal expenditures and an expansion of federal functions in wartime and the postwar period.

An internationalist, Edge joined with the "mild reservationists" who favored United States adherence to the League of Nations subject to protection of national sovereignty. In the 1920's he was associated with the promotion of a Nicaraguan canal, the development of the Virgin Islands, improved salaries for postal employees, and the repeal of prohibition.

On Nov. 21, 1929, President Herbert Hoover appointed Edge ambassador to France. As was characteristic of the State Department under Hoover, Edge was kept tightly reined; diplomatic decisions were made in Washington by the president, Secretary of State Henry L. Stimson, and Treasury Under Secretary Ogden L. Mills. The Hoover Moratorium, a unilateral declaration that provided for postponement of reparations owed France by Germany as well as the wartime debts owed to the United States by its former allies, caught Edge as well as the French government by surprise. He sympathized with France's insistence on a *quid pro quo* for concessions to Germany on reparations and arms parity to consist of Anglo-American guarantees of her security. The onset of the Great Depression and the intensification of French nationalism, inspired by fear of a renascent Germany, further marked his tour in France.

The election of Franklin D. Roosevelt in 1932, and the Democratic landslides of the 1930's, seemed to have ended Edge's political career. While he conceded the necessity of many of the New Deal's reforms, he deplored its fiscal policies and Roosevelt's alliance "with groups strange to American democracy." But as a result of a Republican split in New Jersey in 1943, Edge was nominated for governor as a means of healing party differences. He was elected for the 1944–1947 term. Wartime and postwar problems, including major strikes, pressure for civil rights legislation, and the strains of demobilization, were complicated by a bitter struggle between Edge and Democratic mayor Frank Hague of Jersey City. At issue was Edge's quest for passage of a modernized state constitution to replace that of 1844. Hague probably feared the strengthening of the governor's fiscal and investigatory functions, and the proposal was defeated at the polls in 1944. A new constitution was secured by Edge's successor in office, Alfred E. Driscoll, in 1947. Edge's final legacy to his state was the deeding of the historic Princeton estate, Morven, as the governor's mansion following his death. He died in New York City.

[The most valuable manuscript sources are the Walter E. Edge Papers, containing correspondence, personal files, and scrapbooks, 1916–1956, at the New Jersey Historical Society, Newark, N.J.; Edge's dispatches to Washington, Foreign Affairs File, Herbert Hoover Presidential Library, West Branch, Iowa; and *Newark Evening News* clippings file and other items and photographs, New Jersey Division, Newark Public Library. Walter Evans Edge, *A Jerseyman's Journal: Fifty Years of American Business and Politics*, (1948), is informative and contains an excellent photograph.

See also James Leiby, *Charity and Correction in New Jersey: A History of State Welfare Institutions* (1967);

Duane Lockhard, *The New Jersey Governor: A Study in Political Power* (1964); the *Newark Sunday News*, pub., *The Governors of New Jersey* (n.d.); and obituaries in the *Newark Evening News* and *New York Times*, Oct. 30, 1956.]

ELLIOT A. ROSEN

EDWARDS, RICHARD STANISLAUS (Feb. 18, 1885–June 2, 1956), naval officer, was born in Philadelphia, Pa., the son of Richard Stanislaus Edwards and Lucy Brooke Neilson. He studied at the Episcopal Academy in Philadelphia from 1896 to 1903 and at the United States Naval Academy, from which he graduated in 1907. After eighteen months at sea as a midshipman, he was commissioned ensign in 1909.

Edwards' early service was on battleships and destroyers; but in 1912, as a lieutenant (j.g.), he took submarine training. In 1913 he took command of the submarine *C-3* with additional duty as commander, First Group, Submarine Flotilla, Atlantic Fleet. In July 1914 he was promoted to lieutenant. On Aug. 11, 1914, he married Hallie Ninan Snyder. That summer he was ordered to the Naval Academy, where he taught marine engineering and naval construction for two years.

Edwards spent World War I on battleships operating in the Atlantic; he was commissioned temporary lieutenant commander in 1917 and temporary commander the next year. In July 1919 he became aide and gunnery officer on the staff of Vice Admiral Clarence S. Wilkins, commander of a battleship squadron of the Pacific Fleet. After two years in that duty Edwards was named naval inspector of ordnance in charge of the naval ammunition depot at Kuahua, Hawaii.

In July 1924 Edwards took command of the destroyer *Wood* with such success that he received a letter of commendation in which President Calvin Coolidge noted that the ship had "received the highest combined merit in gunnery exercises and engineering performances for the year ending June 30, 1926, while in competition with all destroyers in our Navy in commission." After another tour of shore duty at Kuahua, Edwards in 1928 became executive officer of the battleship *Texas,* which won the battle efficiency pennant and the gunnery trophy in both 1928–1929 and 1929–1930. In 1930–1932 he was aide and fleet gunnery officer on the staff of Admiral Frank H. Schofield, commander in chief, Battle Fleet.

In the summer of 1932, Edwards joined the staff

of the army's Command and General Staff School, Fort Leavenworth, Kans., where he remained until the spring of 1934; in 1933 he was promoted to captain. He then spent a year studying at the Naval War College in Newport, R.I. In 1935–1937 he was commander, Submarine Squadron Six, based at San Diego, Calif., before returning to the Atlantic to command the submarine base at New London, Conn.

When the submarine *Squalus* sank in May 1939, Edwards' part in the rescue and salvage operations won him the Navy Cross and a commendation from President Franklin D. Roosevelt. In 1940 Edwards was ordered to the Pacific to command the battleship *Colorado*, but after less than four months was called back to New London, where on Dec. 7, 1940, he assumed duty as commander, Submarines Patrol Force, with the rank of rear admiral. Ten days later Admiral Ernest J. King became commander, Patrol Force, which was soon redesignated Atlantic Fleet. Thus began an association that was to be of profound significance in World War II.

On Dec. 20, 1941, King was designated commander in chief, United States Fleet, with headquarters in the Navy Department. Because a staff had to be assembled almost overnight, King drew heavily on tried associates from the Atlantic Fleet. Edwards became deputy chief of staff.

Edwards combined penetrating intellectual abilities with an immense capacity for hard work. By his ability to get to the core of complex problems quickly, he greatly lightened King's burdens. Edwards was selfless, with no concern for personal popularity or reputation, desiring only to aid King. Although he earnestly desired to return to sea, the state of his health would not permit it; he therefore remained in Washington throughout the war as King's principal assistant.

In August 1942 Edwards was promoted to vice admiral, and on Sept. 1 he became King's chief of staff. In September 1944 he assumed the new post of deputy commander in chief, United States Fleet–deputy chief of naval operations, in order (in King's words) "to attend to matters of *military policy* for me, whether derived from the business of the Navy Department, the Joint Chiefs of Staff, the State Department or the several war agencies." In April 1945 Edwards was promoted to admiral.

With the end of hostilities King took steps to abolish the wartime billet of commander in chief, United States Fleet, because of his view that the chief of naval operations should be the top man in the navy. When this was accomplished on Oct. 10, 1945, King continued as chief of naval operations and Edwards became vice chief of naval operations. He continued in that office until Mar. 1, 1946, when he went to San Francisco. He retired in March 1947 and spent the rest of his life in San Francisco. He died at the Naval Hospital in Oakland, Calif.

For his wartime service Edwards received the Distinguished Service Medal and high awards from the British, French, Polish, and Chinese governments. Although his name is hardly known to the American public, he was one of the outstanding flag officers of the navy. One could apply to him the words that Julian Corbett wrote of Lord Barham in *The Campaign of Trafalgar:* "Unseen and almost unnoticed he was gathering in his fingers the threads of the tradition which the recurring wars had spun, and handling them with a deft mastery to which the distant fleets gave sensitive response."

[Information on Edwards is available at the Division of Naval History, Navy Department.]

WALTER MUIR WHITEHILL

ELMAN, ROBERT (Nov. 9, 1897–Dec. 23, 1956), surgeon and medical educator, was born in Boston, Mass., the son of Samuel Elman, a merchant, and Bessie Marian Schmidt. He received his early education in public schools in Syracuse, N.Y., to which the family had moved. In 1918 he graduated from Harvard College with a B.S. (*cum laude*) and enrolled in the Johns Hopkins School of Medicine. While a fourth-year student he conducted research with Lewis H. Weed and George B. Wislocki that resulted in a creditable publication on the spinal arachnoid granulations with special reference to the cerebrospinal fluid. In 1922 he received the M.D. and was appointed an assistant in surgery by William S. Halsted; he worked in the Hunterian Surgical Laboratory primarily under the direction of Walter E. Dandy.

Elman had wanted to obtain further surgical training with Evarts A. Graham at Washington University in St. Louis, but since no position was available he spent the next two years, 1923–1925, as an assistant in pathology at the Rockefeller Institute, working with Peyton Rous and Philip D. McMasters; his research with McMasters led to a lifelong interest in pancreatic function. In 1926 he joined the staff at Washington University as an assistant in surgery and soon impressed

Graham with his research talents. Elman remained at Washington University in spite of paternal efforts to encourage his return to Syracuse and private practice. He completed his training and in 1947 rose to the position of professor of clinical surgery. In 1928 he married Minna Kreykenbohm of New York City; they had no children.

Elman's research on the loss of serum protein in patients with severe burns, first published in 1936, was an important factor in the adoption of the technique of administering blood plasma in such cases. It also led to his most important contribution, clinical and experimental studies of intravenous feeding with the amino acids of hydrolyzed protein. Beginning in 1937, he published a series of studies on protein nutrition in surgical patients with particular emphasis on parenteral administration of amino acid mixtures. This work was awarded the Samuel D. Gross Prize of the Philadelphia Academy of Surgery in 1945 and led to the publication of *Parenteral Alimentation in Surgery, With Special Reference to Proteins and Amino Acids* (1947).

Elman also contributed significantly to knowledge of pancreatic function and disease. He gave particular attention to the study of acute pancreatitis and the use of the serum amylase test in the diagnosis of this condition. He also did research on surgical shock, the regulation of gastric acidity, and urobilin physiology.

Elman's interest in surgical care and convalescence was sharpened by his World War II work with the National Research Council Committee on Convalescence and Rehabilitation. This project led to *Surgical Care: A Practical Physiologic Guide* (1951), which outlined a positive program of preoperative and postoperative care that differed from the traditional policy of "letting nature take its course." Between 1936 and 1952 six editions of his *Textbook of General Surgery* (written with Warren H. Cole) were published.

Elman was the second surgeon to be president of the American Gastroenterological Association. A stimulating teacher, he was not the type of surgeon who lorded over the other members of the medical-care team; anesthesiologists, internists, house staff, nurses, and medical students were all respected for their contributions. From 1951 to 1956 Elman was chief of staff and director of surgical service of the Homer G. Phillips Hospital in St. Louis. Here he trained many black physicians in an era of segregated residency, and he fought for the end of racial segregation in public hospitals and medical schools. He died in St. Louis, Mo.

[There is much information on Elman in the Evarts A. Graham papers, Washington University School of Medicine Library, St. Louis. A microfilm copy of this collection is in the History of Medicine Division, National Library of Medicine, Bethesda, Md. A portrait appears with the obituary notice, *Transactions of the American Surgical Association,* 1957.]

PETER D. OLCH

ELY, HANSON EDWARD (Nov. 23, 1867–Apr. 28, 1958), army officer, was born in Independence, Iowa, the son of Eugene Hanson Ely, a county superintendent of schools and a regional representative for Lippincott and Company, a schoolbook publisher, and Julia Lamb, the daughter of a Congregationalist missionary to the western Indians. A large, strong, athletic youth, Ely attended public schools in Iowa and did farm work during the summers before becoming a rural schoolteacher at seventeen. Winning appointment by competitive examination from the Second District of Iowa, he entered West Point in 1887. Ely compensated for a poor academic and disciplinary record—he graduated sixty-third among the sixty-five members of the Class of 1891—by becoming captain of the football team, a varsity boxer, and a member of the academy color guard.

After graduation Ely watched the closing of the American frontier from a series of western posts as a lieutenant in the Twenty-second Infantry Regiment. In 1897, shortly before his promotion to first lieutenant, he was assigned as the professor of military science and tactics at the State University of Iowa. His transfer to Iowa City was welcome since the town was the home of his wife, Mary Eliza Barber, whom he had married in 1891. They had four children.

When the war with Spain began in 1898, Ely volunteered the University of Iowa cadet corps for federal service, but his offer was refused. He then served as federal mustering officer for Iowa and Mississippi. In 1899 Ely rejoined the Twenty-second Infantry Regiment when it sailed for the Philippines. During the Philippine Insurrection (1899–1902), he served as regimental quartermaster, regimental commissary, and company commander. He so impressed Brigadier General Frederick Funston that he was appointed commander of Funston's special mounted scouts, an elite unit that performed reconnaissance duties in northern Luzon. For his service Ely later received a Silver Star Medal. While in the Philippines, he was promoted to captain in the Twenty-sixth Infantry; he also served as regimental adjutant and as an adjutant general for the Third District, Department South Luzon, as well as a depot commissary.

After his return from the Philippines in 1903, Ely alternated between duty with the Twenty-sixth Infantry and officer training. As a troop officer he performed effectively as a company commander, rifle instructor, and team marksman. In 1905 he was an honor graduate of the Infantry and Cavalry School at Fort Leavenworth and was rewarded by further assignment to the Staff College, from which he graduated in 1906. He then spent six months' leave in Germany observing maneuvers before returning to his regiment. In 1907 his wife died following the birth of their fourth child.

In 1908 Ely volunteered to return to the Philippines as a major in the Philippine Scouts, a native regiment in the United States Army. He served in the islands until 1912. On July 6, 1910, he married Eleanor Ashton Boyle. They had three children.

After brief service as a company commander in the Nineteenth Infantry, Ely was promoted to major, Seventh Infantry, in 1913 and served with the regiment in Texas. Like much of the army, Ely's regiment was deployed to protect the border settlements from Mexican raids and to train for a possible invasion of Mexico. In 1914 Ely participated in the occupation of Veracruz as acting commander of his regiment. He then served as a staff officer and inspector-instructor of the Indiana National Guard during the National Guard mobilization of 1916. He also attended the Army War College in 1915-1916.

America's entry into World War I provided Ely, then a major, with further opportunity for military advancement. Promoted to lieutenant colonel in May 1917, he commanded an officer training camp in Texas, but the War Department soon assigned him to observe the Allied armies on the Western Front. A temporary colonel and member of the General Staff, he joined General John J. Pershing's American Expeditionary Force (AEF) headquarters in July 1917, and was made AEF provost marshal. In September 1917 he was appointed chief of staff, First Division.

Ely's temperament and division problems shortened his service as chief of staff, but he made his reputation as a combat commander in the First Division's Twenty-eighth Infantry Regiment. After trench combat along the St. Mihiel salient in the winter of 1918, the division deployed to Picardy in April to meet one of a series of German offensives. On May 28, 1918, Ely's regiment made the first major attack mounted by the AEF, the assault on the town of Cantigny. Although Cantigny was not strategically important, its capture and defense against six German counterattacks heartened the entire AEF and French high command because it proved the effectiveness of American troops in heavy combat. For his dogged command of his regiment in the face of heavy casualties, Ely was promoted to temporary brigadier general and transferred to the Third Brigade, Second Division, in July 1918.

As an AEF brigade commander, Ely won a Distinguished Service Cross for heroism in the capture of Vierzy during the Second Division's July 1918 attack at Soissons—the first major Allied counterattack against the Germans. He then led the brigade in successful attacks at St. Mihiel and Mont Blanc as the Allied-American armies hammered the Germans back toward the Rhine. Promoted to temporary major general in October 1918, Ely commanded the Fifth Division in the later stages of the Meuse-Argonne offensive, the largest action by the AEF. At the time of the Armistice, Ely's division was one of the most effective organizations in the First Army and was severely punishing the Germans along the Meuse River. For his "rare qualities of leadership" as a regiment, brigade, and division commander, Ely won a Distinguished Service Medal and five Croix de Guerre. He then served on occupation duty in Luxembourg and Germany until his return to the United States in 1919.

Ely returned to less dramatic duties and reduced rank with the demobilization of the AEF, but his wartime achievements assured his promotion and significant assignments in the postwar army. In 1920 he became a permanent colonel and then brigadier general while commanding the Third Brigade, Second Division. In recognition of his achievement as an infantry commander and for his interest in army education, Ely became commandant of the Army General Service School at Fort Leavenworth (1921-1923), and of the Army War College in Washington, D.C. (1923-1927), where he emphasized the education of future combat commanders and the study of strategy and international relations. He finished his career as a major general in command of the Second Corps Area in the eastern United States until his retirement in 1931. During the postwar period, Ely was an outspoken advocate of military preparedness. In 1930 he was a dark-horse candidate for army chief of staff.

During his long retirement, Ely did not take a civilian job, but remained in touch with the army through his three army officer sons and former subordinates, and he often appeared as a speaker at veterans' reunions and patriotic meetings.

Ely was a strong disciplinarian, but would do anything to provide for his troops. He was contentious, ambitious, and candid with his fellow officers, whom he sometimes intimidated with his physical size and appearance and his "will, force, and fighting disposition." Diplomatic and conciliatory when he had to be, Ely could not abide self-serving and slipshod performance, and his criticism of slack performance made him seem "strong and tempestuous" to his peers and superiors. He had served in the United States Army during its transition from frontier constabulary to the nucleus of a wartime mobilized army of citizen-soldiers. His career reflected that change, culminating in high command in the American Expeditionary Force in World War I. He died in Atlantic Beach, Fla.

[On Ely and his career, see Hanson E. Ely, "Vital Statistics Questionnaire," 1940 and 1950, archives of the Association of Graduates, U.S. Military Academy, West Point, N.Y.; John A. Ely, "Hanson Edward Ely," *Assembly* (Spring 1959); Edward S. Holden, ed., *Register of the Officers and Graduates of the U.S. Military Academy, Supplement IV* (1901), *Supplement V* (1910), *Supplement VI* (1920), and William H. Donaldson, ed., *Supplement VII* (1930); Robert L. Bullard, *Fighting Generals* (1944); John Ely Briggs, "Hanson Edward Ely," *The Palimpsest*, Apr. 1930; and Louis B. Ely, "Official War Records of Major General Hanson E. Ely," privately published, n.d. See also correspondence from Col. John A. Ely, USA (ret.), Col. Louis B. Ely, USA (ret.), and Mrs. Judy E. Glacker; and the obituary notice in the *New York Times*, Apr. 29, 1958.]
ALLAN R. MILLETT

EMERSON, HAVEN (Oct. 19, 1874–May 21, 1957), public health educator and statesman, was born in New York City, the son of John Haven Emerson, a prominent physician, and Susan Tompkins. After attending private schools, Emerson entered Harvard in 1893 and completed the four-year course in three years. He received the B.A. in 1896, then enrolled in the College of Physicians and Surgeons, at Columbia University, where he combined extra research in physiology with his medical course work and was awarded both an M.A. and an M.D. in 1899. Following a residency at Bellevue Hospital, Emerson married Grace Parrish on June 15, 1901; they had five children. In 1902 he was made an associate in physiology and medicine in the College of Physicians and Surgeons. His growing reputation as a practitioner and teacher led to his appointment as assistant visiting physician at Bellevue Hospital in 1906.

Although he professed no religion, Emerson was a Puritan at heart, and his strong social consciousness reflected the Quaker and Unitarian background of his family. An early article entitled "Carious Teeth in the Tenement Population of New York City" (1908) demonstrated his concern for his fellowman, a concern that led him into the public health movement.

In 1914 Sigismund S. Goldwater became health commissioner of New York City. He selected Emerson as sanitary superintendent and assistant commissioner. Emerson's introduction to organized public health could scarcely have come under more propitious circumstances, for Goldwater, during his tenure of less than two years, reorganized the department, established an excellent rapport with both medical and civic groups, revised the Health Code, created the Bureau of Health Education, and established the first health district with a health center. A man of abundant energy, Emerson happily collaborated in these reforms; when Goldwater resigned to concentrate upon hospital administration, he was the logical replacement.

On assuming the office of health commissioner on Nov. 1, 1915, Emerson found himself in charge of a well-run and effective agency. His major contribution was to extend the health district plan to the entire borough of Queens and to broaden the activities carried on at the health centers. By involving local community groups and the New York Academy of Medicine in the work, he gained wide support for the health centers.

The most dramatic event in his administration was a poliomyelitis epidemic in 1916 that resulted in approximately 9,000 cases and 2,449 deaths. Emerson mobilized city, state, and federal resources in an effort to bring the outbreak under control and to learn something about the disease.

But a Democratic party victory in November 1917 resulted in his dismissal the following January, closing an era in which New York City had stood preeminent in public health. During his term as health commissioner Emerson called for treating alcoholism as a disease, began an educational program on heart disease, and started work on one of his most important publications. As chairman of the Committee on Control of Communicable Diseases of the American Public Health Association (APHA), he was largely responsible for its first report, *Control of Communicable Diseases in Man* (1917). During his thirty-five-year service on the committee, this report was gradually expanded and revised; it went through seven editions by 1950 and was translated into more than a dozen languages, becoming one of the most widely used public health documents in the world.

In 1918 Emerson was commissioned a colonel in the American Expeditionary Force and served overseas for eighteen months as chief epidemiologist of the army. From this experience came another of his major publications, *A General Survey of Communicable Diseases in the A.E.F.* (1919).

On his return to the United States, Emerson assumed the directorship of the Cleveland Hospital and Health Survey, the first of more than twenty similar surveys he was to make. In 1922 he became professor of public health practice and director of the Delamar Institute of Public Health, the forerunner of the Columbia University School of Public Health. By the time he retired in 1940, the Columbia School of Public Health ranked among the top institutions in the field.

After his retirement Emerson served on many health councils and committees. He also concentrated on one of his major aims—investigating the level of health services available throughout the United States. As chairman of the APHA subcommittee on local health units, he was responsible for *Local Health Units for the Nation* (1945). This study, now a standard work, provided detailed information on local health organizations within the United States and established the basic principles for the administration of local health services. For this work Emerson received a special Lasker Award for public service in 1949. For the last twenty years of his life he was a member of the New York City Board of Health.

Emerson never used alcohol, tea, coffee, or tobacco. He had little tolerance for stupidity, but his strong desire to improve the health of his fellowman and his personal warmth made him liked and respected by his associates. It was characteristic that shortly before his death at Southold, N.Y., he denounced the "fuzzy-minded nitwits" who opposed the fluoridation of the New York City water supply.

[Emerson's works, 1907–1955, including published papers and typed drafts with holograph amendments and corrections, were collected in four volumes (1962). Manuscripts are in possession of a daughter, Dr. Ethel Wortis, Southold, N.Y. Emerson contributed a memoir to the Columbia University Oral History Collection in 1950. See also *American Journal of Public Health*, Dec. 1949; *Journal of the American Medical Association*, June 22, 1957; *Lancet*, June 1, 1957; *American College of Preventive Medicine Newsletter*, Apr. 1965; and John Duffy, *A History of Public Health in New York City, 1866–1966* (1974).]

JOHN DUFFY

EPSTEIN, JACOB (Nov. 10, 1880–Aug. 19, 1959), sculptor, was born in New York City, the son of Max Epstein and Mary Solomon, prosperous Russian Jewish immigrants. He grew up in a large Orthodox family and attended public school until the age of thirteen. Although his father disapproved, Epstein resolved at a very early age to become an artist. He attended life drawing classes at the Art Students League, but in the spring of 1900 he decided to concentrate on sculpture. Shortly thereafter he entered a foundry to learn bronze casting and enrolled in New York's only school of sculpture, George Grey Barnard's night classes in modeling at the Art Students League. He continued to draw, however, and partly supported himself by selling his sketches. Hutchins Hapgood, who was acquainted with Epstein's drawings, invited him to illustrate his *Spirit of the Ghetto* (1902). With the proceeds from this commission, Epstein booked passage to Paris, then the mecca for serious art students.

Although he knew only a few words of French, Epstein applied to the École Nationale des Beaux-Arts and, after an entrance examination, was accepted. "Ce sauvage américain," as he soon became known, concentrated with fanatic zeal on the study of modeling. Foreigners were not popular at the school, however; and after six months Epstein transferred to the Académie Julian, where he studied until 1904. He also spent many hours in the Louvre, studying the old masters as well as early Greek, Cycladic, and Egyptian sculpture.

In 1904 Epstein began working on his own, and the following year he settled in London. Still considering himself a student, he frequented the British Museum, mentally comparing his own work with the masterpieces on exhibition. After several visits Epstein destroyed all his work.

In 1906 Epstein married Margaret Gilmour Dunlop, a Scotswoman and the driving force behind his career. They had two children. In 1907 he became a British subject and was introduced to the architect Charles Holden, who had recently designed a new building in the Strand for the British Medical Association. Holden commissioned Epstein to create eighteen more-than-life-size figures to decorate the exterior. Epstein was delighted and immediately set to work. "I had been like a hound on leash," he recalled, "and now I was suddenly set free."

In a little more than a year Epstein completed the eighteen nude figures, emulating the metopes of the Parthenon and representing "man and woman in their various stages from birth to old age." All went well until the scaffolding was removed from the first four figures. Then, on June 19, 1908, an attack of unexpected and unprecedented fury—based upon the nudity and lack of idealization of the figures and upon Epstein's *Jewishness*—was launched by the *Evening Standard and St. James Gazette,* and other publications joined the attack. Many artists and writers rose to Epstein's defense. According to Richard Buckle, his principal biographer, this controversy "set in motion a campaign of denigration which was to reopen with nearly every monumental work carved by Epstein until his old age: a campaign which would embitter the vulnerable and child-like artist, endanger his livelihood, deprive London of noble adornment, and indirectly hasten the sculptor's end."

Despite the controversy, Robert Ross, the literary executor of Oscar Wilde, commissioned Epstein in 1908 to design a tomb for Wilde. Epstein chose a twenty-ton block of stone, into which he carved a streamlined figure reminiscent of the great Assyrian winged bulls in the British Museum. The carving was completed in the spring of 1912 and was favorably received by London critics. When unveiled at the Père Lachaise cemetery in Paris, however, it evoked a torrent of protest. The genitals of the figure apparently offended certain Parisians and friends of the deceased. As a result, despite the efforts of

such intellectuals as George Bernard Shaw, the tomb remained covered with a tarpaulin until World War I.

While in Paris in 1912 to oversee installation of the tomb, Epstein met Pablo Picasso and Constantin Brancusi and became acquainted with Amedeo Modigliani, who shared Epstein's enthusiasm for African carvings. After returning to England, Epstein began experimenting with abstraction; and in 1913, with the precocious young artist Henri Gaudier-Brzeska, he formed a London chapter of the vorticist group. As indicated by their short-lived journal, *Blast,* the vorticists saw themselves as England's answer to France's cubists and Italy's futurists. Vorticist ideals were well summarized by Epstein's *Rock Drill* (1913), a geometrized robot figure with the visage of a primitive mask, originally mounted on a piece of machinery. Along with other contemporaneous semiabstract works, *Rock Drill* ranks among his most significant achievements.

After his scandalous tomb for Oscar Wilde, Epstein was given only two major public commissions until his old age, the William Henry Hudson Memorial in Hyde Park, London (1924), and the decoration of the London Underground Railway Headquarters building in Westminster (1928). Renouncing his experiments in abstraction, he turned to portraiture as a means of livelihood. By the 1920's his reputation had become established, and during the next three decades he created hundreds of portraits of friends, relatives, government officials, artists, and intellectuals. Typically they had rough, furrowed surfaces suggestive of the clay forms from which they were cast. Facial features were exaggerated; huge hollowed-out pupils, deep eye pouches, and patterned, wiglike hair enhanced the expressionist impact of the heads.

In his late years Epstein became a celebrated English institution. In 1954 he was knighted; and his large retrospective exhibit at the Tate Gallery (1955) was attended by 30,000 people in three weeks. Epstein's first wife died in 1947, and on July 8, 1955, he married Kathleen Garman, his longtime companion and mother of three of his children. While working at his first series of major public commissions since the 1920's, Epstein died in London.

Reviewing Epstein's career, the British sculptor Henry Moore noted that "He took the brickbats, he took the insults, he faced the howls of derision with which artists since Rembrandt have learned to become familiar. And as far as sculpture in this century is concerned, he took them first.... His warmth and his vitality and his courage will not be quickly forgotten. We have lost a great sculptor."

[Epstein was author of *The Sculptor Speaks* (1931), written with Arnold L. Haskell; and *Let There Be Sculpture* (1940), revised as *Epstein, an Autobiography* (1955). Richard Buckle, *Jacob Epstein, Sculptor* (1963), catalogs all his known works. Epstein's works are at the Museum of Modern Art and the Metropolitan Museum of Art, New York City. A large group of five figures, *Social Consciousness* (1951–1952), is in Fairmont Park, Philadelphia, Pa.]

PATRICIA FAILING

ERDMAN, CHARLES ROSENBURY (July 20, 1866–May 9, 1960), educator and theologian, was born in Fayetteville, N.Y., the son of the Reverend William Jacob Erdman and Henrietta Rosenbury. His father was a Presbyterian minister and participant in the Bible Conference movement. During the elder Erdman's pastorate in Jamestown, N.Y. (1878–1885), Charles joined the Presbyterian Church and received his preparatory education privately at home and at the Jamestown Collegiate Institute. He then enrolled at Princeton University, graduating in 1886.

Erdman then was an instructor at the Franklin School of Germantown, Pa., but returned to Princeton in 1887 to study at the theological seminary. He traveled abroad between his last two years and earned his seminary degree and his ministerial license and ordination in 1891. He married Mary Estelle Pardee on June 1, 1892. They had four children. From 1891 to 1897 he served as the minister of the Overbrook Church in Philadelphia. He then returned to Germantown as the Presbyterian minister. In 1906 he accepted the newly created chair of practical theology at the Princeton Theological Seminary.

At Princeton, Erdman was very popular with the ministerial students, who appreciated his clear exposition, inspiration, wit, and personal concern. The skills that made him effective as a teacher also characterized his preaching. His sermons were lucid, engaging, and practical. The same Bible Conference crowds that had gathered to hear his father eagerly attended his services also. His most prestigious pulpit ministry was as pastor of the First Presbyterian Church of Princeton from 1924 to 1934; he also maintained his position at the seminary. During his life he preached over 10,000 sermons.

Erdman also produced thirty-five books, most of which were expositions of books of the Bible; like his sermons they were clear and flowing essays written in a loving spirit and designed to both edify and instruct. Many of his New Testament works were translated into other languages. He also wrote a biography of Dwight L. Moody, whom Erdman knew and in whose Chicago church his father had served as pastor for three years.

The most sensational part of Erdman's career occurred in the 1920's, when Princeton Seminary was one of the major centers of the Modernist-Fundamentalist debate. He was one of the prominent figures in the struggle both at the seminary and in the Presbyterian church. Erdman held and promoted conservative theological views. Both he and his father contributed to *The Fundamentals* (1910–1915), and they served as editorial consultants for the dispensationalist *Scofield Reference Bible* (1909). Later, when standing for moderator of the Presbyterian General Assembly, Erdman declared, "I have always been a Fundamentalist in my beliefs.... The platform on which I stand is that of old-fashioned orthodoxy and Christian spirit...."

Despite his theological views, Erdman favored a denomination and seminary that would accommodate a liberal as well as an orthodox Christianity. For him organizational disunity represented a greater threat than theological heterodoxy. Partly because of his inclusivist views and gentle spirit, the liberal element of the church selected him as their candidate for moderator in 1924 and 1925. The exclusivists, who favored doctrinal purity (adherence to the Westminster Confession) more than organizational unity, were led by William Jennings Bryan, who had lost the 1923 election; John Gresham Machen, the articulate New Testament professor at Princeton Seminary; and Clarence E. Macartney, a member of the board of directors of the seminary. Macartney narrowly defeated Erdman for moderator in 1924, but Erdman reversed that result a year later.

At the seminary Erdman and President J. Ross Stevenson led the inclusivist faction against the majority puritan group headed by Machen. Erdman argued that at the seminary "no . . . division exists on points of doctrine [but only] . . . as to spirit, methods, or policies." Machen disagreed: "There is between Dr. Erdman and myself a very serious doctrinal difference indeed. It concerns the question not of this doctrine or that, but of the importance that is to be attributed to doctrine as such. . . ."

Erdman loved people ("I have always had a passion for friendships") and possessed a giving character ("I have always rendered any service which I was requested and always filled any possible engagement where I felt I could be of help"). He died in Princeton.

[The Erdman Papers are in the Speer Library, Princeton Theological Seminary. Erdman's "Personal Preparation for the Christian Ministry," *Princeton Seminary Bulletin,* November 1907, is suggestive of the author's emphases as a professor and counselor at the seminary. There is no full-length biography; see "Pen Portraits of Church Leaders," *Christian Herald,* November 1926, written about Erdman at the peak of his career; and Charles T. Fritsch, *et al.,* "In Memoriam," *Princeton Seminary Bulletin,* November 1960. On Erdman's role in the Fundamentalist controversy, see Edwin H. Rian, *The Presbyterian Conflict* (1940), Lefferts A. Loetscher, *The Broadening Church* (1954); and Ernest R. Sandeen, *The Roots of Fundamentalism* (1970).]

WILLIAM C. RINGENBERG

FARRAND, BEATRIX CADWALADER JONES (June 19, 1872–Feb. 7, 1959), landscape architect, was born in New York City, the daughter of Frederick Rhinelander Jones, gentleman of leisure, and Mary Cadwalader Rawle. As a child she became interested in gardens at her grandparents' country house in Newport, R.I., and at Reef Point, her parents' residence in Bar Harbor, Me., where, at the age of eleven, she participated in designing new plantings for the grounds. Her aunt, the novelist Edith Wharton, an expert in gardening and an amateur historian of landscape architecture (she had written *Italian Villas and Their Gardens),* may have played an important role in awakening Jones's interest in horticulture and landscape architecture. In any case, Wharton definitely served as a role model for her niece at a time when most well-to-do women did not pursue careers.

After her parents' divorce Jones lived with her mother. Mary Jones was said to have presided over a salon attended by society figures and friends, including Henry James, Theodore Roosevelt, and, of course, Edith Wharton, for whom she was agent and bookkeeper.

As a young woman Jones was a pupil of Charles Sprague Sargent, botanist and first director of the

Arnold Arboretum in Boston. Sargent suggested that she study landscape gardening and provided her first clients. As a supplement to her horticultural training, he urged her to study European garden design and landscape painting, and to observe and analyze natural beauty. Years of travel and independent study helped prepare Jones for professional practice. (At the time, there were no schools of landscape architecture.) She visited and studied the great gardens and landscapes of Italy, France, Germany, Holland, England, and Scotland. During these years the most important influence on her development was her discovery of the work of Gertrude Jekyll, the English landscape gardener one generation her senior. Jekyll had synthesized the formal and informal schools of English garden design. Gardens that changed gradually from formal architectonic extensions of the house to informal woodland gardens and herbaceous flower borders of delicately blended colors were her trademarks. Jones visited many of Jekyll's gardens, adopted many of her techniques, and eventually purchased her landscape plans and drawings.

In 1897 Jones opened a landscape architectural practice in Manhattan. Throughout her career she devoted herself mainly to garden design, the layout of private estates, and campus planting design. In 1899 she was a founder of the American Society of Landscape Architects. Of the eleven charter members, she was the only woman and the only one to have signed plans and drawings "landscape gardener." The word "architect," she maintained, should be reserved for designers of buildings.

Her social standing provided Jones with instant recognition and a ready supply of famous and wealthy clients, including John D. Rockefeller, Jr., J. P. Morgan, and Mrs. Woodrow Wilson, for whom she designed a flower garden at the White House in 1916. Her large-scale projects, concentrated in the Northeast and particularly in Long Island, N.Y., and Bar Harbor, Me., were designed and built mainly between 1910 and 1930. Her work is characterized by thoughtful siting and arrangement, sensitivity to proportion and detailing, and an approach to planting design characterized in part by the use of native species and the application of ecological principles in the development of plant schemes for special site conditions.

In 1912 a chance meeting with Mrs. Moses Taylor Pyne led to Jones's first campus consulting work at Princeton. Yale, Vassar, Hamilton, and the University of Chicago were among the colleges and universities that subsequently commissioned her work.

On December 17, 1913, she married Max Farrand, an American history professor at Yale. After his appointment as director of the Huntington Library in San Marino, Calif., they lived for twelve years in that state; she frequently traveled to the East and to England to work on the reconstruction of the grounds of Dartington Hall.

In 1922, commissioned by Mildred Bliss, Farrand began work on the gardens at Dumbarton Oaks in Washington, D.C. She later described this project as "the most deeply felt of a fifty years' practice." Her design ability was matched by broad knowledge of the literature of the field, and she was retained by Mrs. Bliss to assemble a collection of rare books for the garden library at Dumbarton Oaks.

In the 1940's the number of her commissions decreased and she served as landscape consultant to the Santa Barbara Botanic Garden and the Arnold Arboretum, as well as dedicating herself to the development and management of Reef Point, her family's summer home, as a botanical garden and library open to the public. In 1945, after her husband's death, she established the Max Farrand Memorial Fund to help carry out her work. One explanation for her efforts to ensure a permanent future for Reef Point was her disillusionment with the lack of knowledge of plant materials among the new generation of landscape architects. The project was abandoned in 1955, partly because of a lack of students in landscape design in the vicinity of Reef Point. Farrand died at Bar Harbor.

[The most important source, consisting chiefly of her landscape plans and drawings and unpublished manuscripts, is the Beatrix Farrand Collection on Landscape Design, housed in the University of California, Berkeley, College of Environmental Design Documents Collection. Biographical data are in Robert Patterson, "Beatrix Farrand 1872-1959: An Appreciation of a Great Landscape Gardener," *Landscape Architecture,* Summer 1959; *Reef Point Gardens Bulletins;* H. L. Vaughan, "Library Gift to California," *Landscape Architecture,* Oct. 1956; and Louis Auchincloss, *Edith Wharton: A Woman in Her Time* (1971). For analyses of her design work, see Georgina Masson, *Dumbarton Oaks: A Guide to the Gardens* (1968); and Beatrix Farrand, "Landscape Gardening at Yale," *Yale Alumni Weekly,* June 12, 1925; "Princeton Landscape Gardening," *Princeton Alumni Weekly,* June 9, 1926; and "Landscape Gardening at Princeton," *ibid.,* May 29, 1931. Photographs of Beatrix Farrand are in Louis Auchincloss, *Edith Wharton: A Woman in Her Time;* and in *Reef Point Gardens Bulletins.*]

MARLENE SALON

FARSON, NEGLEY (May 14, 1890–Dec. 12, 1960), journalist, was born James Scott Negley Farson in Plainfield, N.J., the son of Enoch Farson and Grace Negley. He was raised in an atmosphere of precarious gentility. His father was president of a struggling manufacturing company that bore his name, but he devoted most of his attention to yachting. Farson was raised by his grandparents. Major General James Scott Negley, a veteran of the Mexican and Civil wars, awed his grandson and attempted equally to awe his numerous creditors. Upon his death a cynical man who had lost his fortune on Wall Street was appointed Farson's guardian. He always tried to make a showplace of his estate, in an attempt to impress financiers. Farson remembered shooting ducks so that his guardian could put food on the table.

At the age of fifteen Farson was expelled from Phillips Andover Academy for helping to throw a Latin professor into the campus lake. He left his studies in civil engineering at the University of Pennsylvania in 1912, after his parents insulted his girl friend, who was an actress.

A search for money and adventure preceded Farson's writing career. After leaving college he sold oil in New York, chains in Manchester, England, arms in Moscow, and trucks in Chicago. He volunteered to fight with the United States and France in World War I, but he ended up with a commission in the Royal Flying Corps. Farson flew a scout plane in Egypt. In 1918 his plane crashed near Cairo, and he spent two years recuperating on a houseboat in British Columbia. On Sept. 22, 1920, he married Eve Stoker; they had one child.

Farson did free-lance writing after returning from the war. In 1924 he took a riverboat across Europe and wrote regularly for the *Chicago Daily News.* This assignment, like so many that followed, allowed him to express his interests in travel and fishing. Farson was a foreign correspondent for the *News* for eleven years. He spent about half of this time in England, and from 1933 to 1934 he was president of the London Association of American Newspaper Correspondents. He also reported extensively from western Europe, the Soviet Union, Egypt, and India.

During the isolationist 1920's and 1930's, Farson made foreign news exciting to Americans by offering an exotic travelogue interrupted by human interest stories about ordinary citizens and great leaders. He made fewer judgments about European politics than colleagues such as Walter Duranty, John Gunther, and Vincent Sheean. Like these journalists Farson wrote a best-selling memoir, *The Way of a Transgressor* (1936), which glamorized the role of the foreign correspondent: "I watched the world come to bits.... I talked with Dictators, I shot the great fin-whale with the dean of Norwegian gunners, I sat with Gandhi under his mango tree at Karadi, and I went up to Lossiemouth, to talk with Ramsay MacDonald.... I made a trip back to my own country, to sit with the strikers, listen to the wails of my taxable friends, talk with the drought-stricken farmers and cowboys of the Dakotas, to see if America was really getting a new sense of values under Roosevelt. I talked with Roosevelt in the White House and had a private view of John Dillinger, naked on the slab, after he had been shot. I watched Stalin review the Red Army in the Red Square." Farson wrote with the same enthusiasm about the hospitals in these countries, where emergency surgery often interrupted his coverage of the news.

Farson wrote much about human disasters, providing little in the way of analysis; and this style was probably the key to his popularity. His readers preferred a vivid record of personal experience to abstractions. Few readers of Farson could feel sorry for themselves, so briskly did he parade the misfortunes of other peoples and his own injuries. This approach often produced good reporting. Farson's political commitments did not color his vision. He defended the Soviet Union but wrote as appreciatively about czarist officials as about Lenin's bureaucracy. An anglophile, he covered the blitz but did not overlook the ignoble behavior of some Londoners under the bombs.

Farson's detachment and love of adventure were displayed in books about his travels in South America, Africa, and the Caucasus. The writing in the travel books is uneven, and in his second volume of memoirs Farson tried to explain why. He confessed that the pressure of daily reporting in the 1930's had been unbearable. Often, Farson recalled, he had only "an hour to write a dispatch of some 800 words or more, which in a few hours was going to be read by the State Department, the diplomats in Washington and the university professors ... nearly every word of those cables was written with nerves taut as a tuned-up violin." Farson began to drink heavily. He discovered, though, after leaving the *Chicago Daily News* in

1935, that the daily schedule was not the problem. It was the job of foreign correspondent itself: "I know of no profession more calculated to kill one's enthusiasm for the human race."

Farson found no simple path away from alcoholism, nor could he define a better role for the journalist. He contributed regularly to the *London Daily Mail* and continued to defy authorities who thought they knew better how to live: "I sometimes think that if life has taught me anything, it is not to believe all these people who make it their business to tell you how to live," he wrote in *Mirror for Narcissus* (1956). Farson died near Georgeham, North Devon, where he had fished and written during the last two decades of his life.

[Additional works by Farson, which include details of his life, are *Sailing Across Europe* (1926); *Black Bread and Red Coffins* (1930); *Transgressor in the Tropics* (1937); *Behind God's Back* (1940); *Bomber's Moon* (1941); *Going Fishing* (1943); *Last Chance in Africa* (1949); and *Caucasian Journey* (1951). Farson also published four novels. See also Philip Rahv, "The Cult of Experience in America," *Partisan Review*, Nov.–Dec. 1940; obituaries in the *New York Times*, Dec. 14, 1960, and in *Newsweek*, Dec. 26, 1960; and William Stott, *Documentary Expression and Thirties America* (1973). Shortly before his death Farson taped a program for British television (ITV) with his son.]

THOMAS C. LEONARD

FEININGER, LYONEL (CHARLES LÉONELL ADRIAN) (July 17, 1871–Jan. 13, 1956), painter, was born in New York City. His father's father, Alois Adolph Michael Feininger, had left Germany after the disturbances of 1848 to settle in Charleston, S.C.; his maternal forebears had also emigrated from Germany in the middle of the nineteenth century and his maternal grandfather served as a captain in the Union army. Feininger's own father, Charles (or Karl Friedrich Wilhelm) Feininger, was a concert violinist, composer, and violin teacher, while his mother, Elizabeth Cecilia Lutz Feininger, was a singer who also taught piano and organ. The family felt closer to an aristocratic and cosmopolitan than to a middle-class American style of life. Feininger himself was twice married, first in Berlin, to Clara Fürst, by whom he had two daughters, then, following their divorce, to Julia Berg Lilienfeld, in London in 1908. All three sons of his second marriage pursued artistic careers.

Feininger grew up speaking both English and German. He had his first violin lesson from his father when he was nine years old, and gave his first public violin performance when he was twelve. During his youth he also made maps of fantasy kingdoms and drawings of locomotives and boats, together with musical caricatures; he tinkered with machinery, and became an expert carver and builder of models of both historical and modern sailing ships. After attending grammar school in New York, Feininger went to Germany in 1887. He had intended to study music at the Leipzig Conservatory, but instead enrolled in the Hamburg School of Applied Arts. From 1888 until 1890 he studied at the Royal Academy of Art in Berlin; then, the following year, he attended the Collège St. Gervais in Liège, Belgium. Having spent 1892 mastering life drawing at the atelier Colarossi in Paris, Feininger returned to Berlin to begin a career as a graphic artist. He was notably successful as a caricaturist, and contributed to *Young People* and the *Chicago Tribune* in the United States, to *Ulk, Lustige Blätter,* and *Narrenschiff* in Germany, and to the *Témoin* in France.

It was in Paris, in 1906, while Feininger was working on two comic strips for the *Chicago Sunday Tribune,* the "Kin-Der-Kids" and "Wee Willie Winkie's World," that he turned from caricature to explore the new freedom offered by modern painting. (The whimsical humor of his comic drawings would reappear, however, in the sailboats, balloons, and locomotives, and in the stylized figures and landscapes of his late works.) Feininger's first paintings in oil, completed mostly in the open air during the spring of 1907, were impressionist in manner. He then began to fall back upon the vocabulary of his cartoons—the flat, decorative patterns in brilliant colors, the use of acute angles and diversified textures, the exaggerated proportions of figures and the amusing contrasts between tall and tiny figures—to reach his own highly individualistic style. In his paintings of 1907–1911 (such as *Der Weisse Mann* and *Das Kanalisationsloch I,* both estate of the artist) these characteristics are apparent, although Feininger's colors, while still bright, are more subtly applied. His coloristic concerns are also demonstrated in his watercolors of this period; in his student years in Berlin, Feininger had admired the freedom of J. M. W. Turner's brushwork in that medium, and had tried to achieve Turneresque effects of rainbow-like iridescence.

During the spring of 1911 Feininger was attracted by the art of the cubists and, especially, by that of Robert Delaunay, founder of orphism. Delaunay's study of prismatic light had much in common with Feininger's own brand of facet-cubism, which Feininger, however, preferred to call "prismism." Returning to Berlin, Feininger drew closer to the artists of the former *Brücke* group, including Karl Schmidt-Rottluff, who painted his portrait, and Erich Heckel. Alfred Kubin, the Austrian draftsman of macabre scenes, introduced him to Franz Marc, one of the authors of the *Blaue Reiter* ("Blue Rider") "almanac," and he also came to know Herwarth Walden, publisher of the radical magazine *Sturm* and director of the Sturm gallery, which promoted avant-garde exhibits.

In 1913 Marc invited Feininger to join the informally organized Blue Rider group in an exhibition in Walden's first German Salon d'Automne. Feininger had another show, with the expressionist painter Felix-Mueller, at the Sturm gallery in 1916, in which he displayed works (among them *Radrennen* and *Hafenmole,* both in private collections) that revealed his indebtedness to the Italian futurists, whose multiple images of rapid motion, interpenetrations of planes, and glorification of the machine had impressed him deeply.

In 1917 Feininger was subjected to semi-internment, since the United States had entered World War I, and he refused to give up his American citizenship. His first woodcuts were published in *Sturm* during the turbulent months of 1918 that saw the overthrow of Wilhelm II, whom he had often attacked in cartoons. After the revolution in November of that year, Feininger joined the progressive "November Group" of artists and writers, among whom he met the architect Walter Gropius, who was organizing a faculty for his new Weimar school, the Bauhaus. Gropius invited Feininger to teach there, in what was to be a radically new teaching institution, centered around architecture and the applied arts. Feininger became one of the first members of the staff, arriving in Weimar in May 1919. He taught there from 1919 to 1924, as "Form Meister" in charge of the graphics and print workshop. His woodcut *Die Kathedrale* decorated the cover of the first Bauhaus *Manifesto* in 1919. In 1924 he was exhibited by the art dealer Galka Scheyer as one of the "Blue Four," the others being Wassily Kandinsky, Paul Klee, and Alexi von Jawlensky; some of their works, part of the former Galka Scheyer collection, are now in the Pasadena Museum of Art, Pasadena, Calif.

After 1925, when the Bauhaus moved to Dessau, Feininger was relieved of his teaching duties and remained as a much-honored artist-in-residence. His reputation was well established, and his paintings and graphics were purchased by leading German museums. (The Detroit Institute of Arts became the first American museum to own one of his works when it bought his oil painting *Sidewheeler II* in 1921.) In 1933, however, the Bauhaus, which had just moved to Berlin, was closed by the Nazis and in 1937 Feininger, whose art had been defamed by its inclusion in the Munich show of "degenerate art," left Germany to return to the United States. He conducted a summer course at Mills College, in Oakland, Calif., that same year, and in the summer of 1945 taught at Black Mountain College in North Carolina.

Feininger's art had always had deep roots in the experiences of his New York youth. Now, as he returned to that city at the age of sixty-seven, almost unknown as an American painter, he again began to depict the sidewheelers, frigates, and locomotives—complete with diamond-shaped smokestacks and cowcatchers—that had marked his earlier work. But at the same time the grotesque humor of his caricatures had been transformed into ethereal fantasy. In his last paintings strange lights illuminate the stovepipe-hatted gentlemen of his imagination, while rickety toy trains clack across viaducts, phantom ships sail the oceans, and luminous stars shine over the deserted canyons of Mana-Hatta.

Feininger's life and art may thus be seen as a triptych of which his fifty years in Germany (1887–1937) represents the central panel, flanked by the narrower wings of his early years in New York (1871–1887) and his American ripe old age (1937–1956). He died in New York City.

[Some of the Feininger papers, partly on microfilm (Churchill and Kortheuer correspondence, clippings, and original drawings), are in the Smithsonian Institution Archives of American Art, Washington, D.C.; his sketchbooks are preserved in the Busch-Reisinger Museum, Cambridge, Mass. See also Hans Hess, *Lyonel Feininger* (1961); Ernst Scheyer, *Lyonel Feininger, Caricature and Fantasy* (1964); and Leona E. Presse, *Lyonel Feininger. A Definitive Catalogue of His Graphic Works, Etchings, Lithographs, Woodcuts* (1972). *Lyonel Feininger, Die Stadt am Ende der Welt* (1965) has text by his son Theodore Lux Feininger and photographs by his son Andreas Feininger.]

ERNST SCHEYER

FEUCHTWANGER, LION (July 7, 1884–Dec. 21, 1958), author, was born in Munich, Germany, the son of Sigmund Feuchtwanger, owner of a margarine factory, and Johanna Bodenheim. The youngest of nine children, he spent an unhappy childhood in an emotionally barren home where the strict Jewish orthodoxy was oppressive. Feuchtwanger attended the humanistic Wilhelms Gymnasium and then studied philology and philosophy in Munich and Berlin. He rejected a parental stipend, supported himself by tutoring, and lived in a garret amid the city's Bohemians. In 1907 he completed his doctoral thesis on Heinrich Heine's *The Rabbi of Bacharach*. He briefly published a semimonthly literary magazine to which Thomas Mann contributed. His writing career began with frequent theater reviews in the *Schaubühne*. Feuchtwanger's first novel, *Der tönerne Gott* ("The Earthen God," 1910), is justly forgotten.

In 1912 the shy, introverted, unhappy Feuchtwanger married the beautiful Marta Loeffler, who gradually imbued him with the confidence he was lacking. A two-year honeymoon trip through France, Italy, and North Africa ended in Tunis with the outbreak of World War I. Interned as a German in a French country, he managed a harrowing escape on an Italian steamship. The experience with frenzied French nationalism in Tunisia was matched by German war frenzy upon his return to Munich. With his poem "Lied der Gefallenen" ("Song of the Dead Soldiers") and a series of plays, he expressed his opposition to the war, his distaste for anglophobia, and the inhuman treatment of prisoners of war. Several of his plays also reflected his belief that Oriental contemplation and passivity would replace Western activism and power.

In 1918–1919 Feuchtwanger wrote his "dramatic novel" *Thomas Wendt* (later retitled *1918*). It signaled his transition from aestheticism to social involvements, his mounting concern with themes of revolution, and the polarity between contemplation and action. In 1920–1921 he recast an earlier play, *Jew Suess*, into a novel of the same title (in the American edition, *Power*). Because of the anti-Semitic climate, publication was postponed until 1925. This story of a controversial eighteenth-century court Jew at once catapulted Feuchtwanger to the top rung of European novelists. (The work was translated into thirty languages.) He continued to write plays, including *The Life of Edward the Second of England*, with Bertolt Brecht, whom Feuchtwanger had discovered in 1919.

In 1925, depressed by the growing Nazism in Munich, Feuchtwanger moved to Berlin. Two years later he began writing *Erfolg* ("Success," 1930), which dealt with the beginning of the Nazi movement in Bavaria. The Nazis never forgave him for his satire of Hitler in the character of Kutzner. Luckily Feuchtwanger was on a lecture trip in the United States when Hitler came to power. (He never returned to Germany.) In his absence the Nazis ransacked his home, destroying his library. *Josephus*, the first novel of his trilogy about the Roman-Jewish historian, was published only weeks before Hitler's assumption of power and received little attention.

In 1933 Feuchtwanger settled in Sanary sur Mer in southern France; he built a second library and continued his anti-Nazi activities. In one way or another, his next series of books—*The Oppermanns* (1934); the second Josephus novel, *The Jew of Rome* (1935); *The Pretender* (1936); and *Paris Gazette* (1939)—dealt with the Nazis, their leaders, and their victims. His works revealed a steady march leftward, which culminated in Feuchtwanger's 1937 trip to the Soviet Union and his interview with Stalin. His book *Moscow 1937* reported favorably on both experiences. As a German in France, Feuchtwanger was twice interned in 1939-1940. He was rescued from certain death only through the skilled intervention of his wife, and courageous American officials and citizens. His adventurous escape was recounted in *The Devil in France* (1941). He arrived in the United States on Oct. 5, 1940.

Feuchtwanger was bitterly attacked as a Communist or fellow traveler in *Time* magazine. He was also troubled to learn that the Nazis had used *Jew Suess* (the novel) as the basis for a vitriolically anti-Semitic film. He was glad to leave the hostile eastern climate for Los Angeles where, as in Sanary, a small community of refugees-in-exile had established itself. Feuchtwanger was happy in California despite a somewhat troubled relationship with his host country. Some had not wholly forgiven his satire of Babbittry in *Pep* (1929), translated by Sinclair Lewis and Dorothy Thompson. Others were displeased with his pro-Communist reputation. His application for American citizenship was never granted. In his play *The Devil in Boston* (1948), about the Salem witch-hunts, he expressed his fear of the type of oppressive climate that the McCarthy years were to represent. Yet he remained an optimist, as is demonstrated by the best of his novels written in America: *Josephus and the Emperor* (1942); *Proud Destiny* (1947), a sympathetic treatment of Benjamin Franklin's efforts to secure arms for American revolutionaries; *This Is the Hour* (1951), the unfolding of Goya's talents in conjunction with his growing social awareness; and *'Tis Folly To Be Wise*

(1953), about the French Revolution. His final novel was *Jephta and His Daughter* (1957). An extensive treatise on the historical novel *The House of Desdemona* (1963) was only partly completed by Feuchtwanger himself. He died in Pacific Palisades, Calif.

[The principal biographical and bibliographical source in English is Lothar Kahn, *Insight and Action* (1975), which provides the main secondary sources in English and German to 1975. The finest critical work is John Spalek, ed., *Lion Feuchtwanger* (1972), which includes a complete bibliography of Feuchtwanger's works, a chronology, a brief biographical account, and several noteworthy essays. For Marxist views of Feuchtwanger, see Hans Leupold, *Lion Feuchtwanger* (1967), a pictorial biography; and Joseph Pischel, *Lion Feuchtwanger* (1976), both in German.]

LOTHAR KAHN

FIELD, MARSHALL, III (Sept. 28, 1893– Nov. 8, 1956), newspaper publisher and philanthropist, was born in Chicago, Ill., the son of Marshall Field II and Albertine Huck; he was the grandson of Marshall Field, the eminent nineteenth-century merchant. Field was educated by private tutors and at the Colter School in Chicago. In 1906, following the deaths of his father and grandfather, the family moved to England. He attended Eton College from 1907 to 1912, when he matriculated at Trinity College, Cambridge. While he was in the United States in the summer of 1914, preparing to assume the inheritance (one of the world's great fortunes) and responsibility that would be his on his twenty-first birthday, World War I broke out. On Feb. 8, 1915, he married Evelyn Marshall; they had three children. When the United States entered the war, Field joined the First Illinois Cavalry as a private. Shipped overseas in March 1918, he saw combat as a lieutenant in the artillery at St. Mihiel and Verdun, and was awarded the Silver Star for gallantry under fire.

Discharged in February 1919 with the rank of captain, Field settled in Chicago, explored investment banking, and devoted his efforts to the family trust established by his grandfather. He joined the banking firm of Glore, Ward and Company, which became Marshall Field, Glore, Ward and Company in 1921. That year the Fields moved to Caumsett, their newly completed estate on Long Island. (The estate is now, at the family's wish, a state park.) In 1930 he divorced his wife and on August 18 married Audrey James Coats.

Field grew increasingly unhappy with the failure of his class—the stewards of American wealth—to foresee or cope with the Great Depression. By 1934, when his second marriage ended in divorce, he was openly questioning the values of his peers; and although he had backed Herbert Hoover in 1932, by 1936 he had become a serious liberal and New Dealer. Between 1932 and 1937 Field resigned twenty-three directorships, five finance committee memberships, and two trusteeships. On Jan. 15, 1936, he married Ruth Pruyn Phipps, of an old New York family prominent in public service; they had two children. In 1935 Field became active in child welfare, serving as president of the Child Welfare League of America. In October 1940 he established the Field Foundation, which concentrated on child welfare, social, and interracial problems; and in 1942, with Eleanor Roosevelt, he founded and was chairman of the U.S. Committee for the Care of European Children.

As a publisher, Field launched the New York tabloid newspaper *PM* on June 18, 1940; in October he formed a new corporation and bought out the other seventeen original backers. Unashamedly liberal, *PM* was greeted with cheers, insults, picket lines, and criminal restraint by other publishers. The newspaper accepted no advertising and hence was dependent solely on circulation for its revenue; but it never attracted a sufficiently large readership to survive without Field's financial backing. It did, however, earn him a serious reproof still remembered: as its publisher he was called "a traitor to his class" and was regularly attacked by conservatives.

The experience taught Field much about newspaper publishing and politics. In 1941 he decided to found a liberal but more conventional morning newspaper in Chicago, which had been virtually monopolized for decades by the isolationist and reactionary *Tribune*. On Dec. 4, 1941, the first issue of the *Chicago Sun* appeared. Philanthrophy, Field believed, was one thing; but if a commercial enterprise could not earn money it was not properly responsive to the public's needs. *PM* had shown no profit by June 1948, when it became briefly the *New York Star;* it ceased publication in January 1949. In September 1947 Field had bought the *Chicago Daily News,* an afternoon tabloid; in 1948 the *Chicago Sun* merged with the *Chicago Times,* and the morning *Sun-Times* has remained a major influence.

From 1942 to 1945 Field fought the refusal of the Associated Press to admit the *Sun* to membership, finally winning a landmark case in the United States Supreme Court. In 1944 he con-

solidated his communications and publishing ventures as Field Enterprises, comprising Simon and Schuster, Pocket Books, World Book Encyclopedia, the weekly pictorial supplement *Parade,* and two radio stations. In 1945 he published *Freedom Is More Than a Word,* in which he expounded his views on the press, society, liberalism, and freedom. He supported the work of such reformers as Aubrey Williams and Saul Alinsky, remained a force in child welfare, helped to found Roosevelt University in Chicago, and stoutly resisted the political hysteria of the 1950's, vigorously defending dissidents. He died in New York City.

Character, intelligence, and deep human sympathy led Field to assume the obligations of privilege. He gave greatly of himself to homeless children, sharecroppers, migrant workers, and blacks. In his fight against poverty, disease, and prejudice, his goal was freedom and a full life for all—not merely the lucky few.

[See Stephen Becker, *Marshall Field III* (1964); Marshall Field III, *Freedom Is More Than a Word* (1945); and John Tebbel, *The Marshall Fields* (1947).]

STEPHEN BECKER

FISHER, DOROTHEA FRANCES CANFIELD (Feb. 17, 1879–Nov. 9, 1958), author and moralist, was born in Lawrence, Kans., the daughter of James Hulme Canfield, a professor at the University of Kansas, and Flavia A. Camp, a schoolteacher. Her mother took her to Paris in 1890, and thereby awakened her interest in French culture. The family feared that James Canfield's outspoken endorsement of free trade and women's rights would cost him his job. Hence Fisher cherished the security of bucolic Arlington, Vt., where she spent many childhood summers with older relatives. She described the tensions of academic life in *The Bent Twig* (1915), and her Vermont vacations were fictionalized in the juvenile work *Understood Betsy* (1917), probably her best-selling story.

Dorothy, as she called herself when she entered the University of Nebraska in 1894, intended to pursue a musical career; but deafness forced her to turn to literature. She transferred in 1895 to Ohio State University, from which she graduated with the Ph.B. in 1899. After a year at the Sorbonne and four years in New York, she earned the first Ph.D. in Romance languages awarded by Columbia University to a woman. Her dissertation was published as *Corneille and Racine in England* (1904). Her first magazine story had appeared the year before. After teaching for a year at the Horace Mann School in New York City, she decided to concentrate on writing, and found it brought her a comfortable living.

On May 9, 1907, she married John Redwood Fisher. Her husband dropped out of law school to do editorial work when they married, and agreed to settle in Arlington, Vt., where her family owned farms and timberland. He also accepted the obscure role of consultant and first reader to his wife.

In 1911–1912 Fisher worked for five months with Maria Montessori in Rome, an experience that resulted in four books on child development (1912–1916) that were drawn also from her experience with her two children. Education remained her primary interest, expressed in her writing and in her service on the Vermont State Board of Education (1921–1923) and on the American Youth Commission (1935–1941).

Dorothy Fisher was an anti-imperialist and an antimilitarist, yet she fervently wanted the United States to join the Allies in 1914. Her husband volunteered for ambulance service in April 1916, and in August the family moved to Paris, where she organized the printing of books in braille for blinded soldiers, ran the commissary for her husband's training camp, and during the last year of the war ran a home for refugee children at Guéthary, Basses-Pyrénées. Writing in brief bursts, she completed two volumes of stories about wartime France. Fisher returned from the war profoundly depressed, but rebounded through intense work and produced her best, most popular writing in the 1920's. (Her husband, however, after being in charge of significant war work, had difficulty adjusting to the role of helpmate.)

The Brimming Cup (1921) was a best-seller. Fisher's translation of Giovanni Papini's *Life of Christ* (1923) sold 350,000 copies. Movie rights were sold for *The Home-Maker* (1924). *Her Son's Wife* (1926), which was serialized, reflected her early reading of Freud. *The Deepening Stream* (1930), which expressed her feelings about World War I and family life, sold more than 150,000 copies during its first three years. (Her fiction was published under her maiden name.) Fisher was also a member of the selection committee for the Book-of-the-Month Club (1926–1950), in which capacity she read some 150 books a year.

Gradually Fisher's output shifted toward nonfiction. She was elected president of the Adult Education Association in 1934. Her interest in the aims of the association, especially for women, was expressed in *Why Stop Learning?* (1927) and *Learn or Perish* (1930). Fisher's last novel, *Seasoned Timber* (1939), expressed her faith in education and in the ultimate triumph of freedom over fascism. Her personal war contribution was to assist refugees. In 1940 she organized the Children's Crusade for Children, which raised $130,000 in pennies.

Vermont Tradition (1953), Fisher's last major work, skillfully used local lore to illustrate her outlook on life. She continued dictating craftsmanlike copy almost until her death in Arlington, Vt.

[Fisher's correspondence, drafts, working papers, and photographs are in the Wilbur Collection at the University of Vermont, described in a memorial issue of *Vermont Historical Society News and Notes,* Dec. 1958. Elizabeth Yates, *Pebble in a Pool* (1958), the second edition of which is entitled *Lady From Vermont* (1971), is the only published book-length biography; but there are several studies in typescript, available through the University of Vermont. See also Bradford Smith, "Dorothy Canfield—the Deepening Stream," *Vermont History,* July 1959. Fisher's 129-page oral history memoir, done in 1955, is part of a series on the Book-of-the-Month Club in the Oral History Collection of Columbia University.

Fisher's novels not mentioned in the text are *Gunhild* (1907). *The Squirrel Cage* (1912), *Rough Hewn* (1922), and *Bonfire* (1933); collections of short stories are *Hillsboro People* (1915), *The Real Motive* (1916), *Home Fires in France* (1918), *Raw Material* (1923), *Basque People* (1931), *Fables for Parents* (1937), *Four Square* (1949), and *A Harvest of Stories* (1956). Her juveniles include *Made-to-Order Stories* (1925) and *A Montessori Mother* (1912; 1926).]

T. D. SEYMOUR BASSETT

FLAGG, JAMES MONTGOMERY (June 18, 1877–May 27, 1960), illustrator and writer, was born in Pelham Manor, N.Y., the son of Elisha Flagg, a businessman, and Anna Elida Coburn. His "all-happy" boyhood was spent in New York City. After attending public schools, Dr. Chapin's School (1889–1891) and the Horace Mann School (1891–1893), he left school to pursue a career in art. Flagg had drawn since early boyhood, and a page of his cartooned Latin axioms had appeared in the September 1890 issue of *St. Nicholas.* In 1893 he was sent by that magazine to report on the World's Columbian Exposition at Chicago. By then he was contributing also to *Judge* and *Life*.

Between 1894 and 1898 Flagg studied at the Art Students League under John H. Twachtman and J. Carroll Beckwith, and in 1898 attended Hubert Herkomer's Art School in Bushey, Hertfordshire, England. On Feb. 22, 1899, he married Nellie McCormick, eleven years his senior and the daughter of a St. Louis industrialist. They went to London, then moved to Paris, where Flagg's portrait of Victor Marec, whose Atelier de Peintre he attended, was hung in the Salon of 1900. Through the ensuing four years they traveled extensively in the United States and abroad before settling in New York City.

Flagg had intended to be a portraitist, and he continued to paint and draw portraits throughout his career. But his deft drawings were increasingly in demand, and he became one of the outstanding American illustrators of his time. Flagg's pen technique, featuring a skillful use of open hatching, was as personalized as the printed full signature that became his hallmark about 1908. Flagg was employed by most of the country's popular periodicals, contributing painted covers as well as drawings in pen and wash. He also illustrated books. Since he commonly produced a drawing a day, his annual income rose to $75,000. He also contributed articles, columns, and letters to magazines and newspapers. Between 1900 and American entry into World War I, Flagg published nine pictures-with-text books of his own, beginning with *Yankee Girls Abroad* (1900) and concluding with *The Mystery of the Hated Man* (1916).

Flagg was a confirmed urbanite, a habitué of the city's entertainment spots, a founder of the Dutch Treat Club, and a member of the Lambs and Lotos. Gregarious, ready-witted, and outspoken, he reveled in the company of notables, particularly those from the theatrical world, and of beautiful women.

Flagg vigorously supported America's involvement in both world wars. In 1917 Governor Charles S. Whitman appointed him New York state military artist, and an important segment of his work consisted of forty-six war posters that he produced between 1917 and 1919. One of these, captioned "I Want YOU/for U.S. Army," embodied Flagg's original conception of Uncle Sam. Some 4 million copies were printed then and 400,000 more during World War II, making it undoubtedly the best-known American poster.

Flagg's theatrical interests drew him into motion pictures. Official movies were written for the Red Cross and the Marines; and by 1920, under the sponsorship of Jack Eaton and Eltinge Warner, he had written scripts and participated in the making of twenty-four humorous short films. In the 1920's and 1930's Flagg celebrated the glamour of Hollywood in uncounted drawings and paintings of its stars.

After the death of his first wife in 1923, he married Dorothy Virginia Wadman, who had been his model, on May 10, 1924; they had one daughter. His book *Boulevards All the Way—Maybe* (1925) described their coast-to-coast honeymoon by automobile. Flagg, however, came to regard this marriage as a "mistake." "The great love of my life," he later explained, was Ilse Hoffman, a German-born model.

Flagg remained a public figure into the 1940's: artist, writer, and frequently speaker in public or on radio. He made posters for the United States Department of Forestry, for the later election campaigns of Franklin D. Roosevelt, and for patriotic causes during World War II. His last book was an autobiography, *Roses and Buckshot* (1946). It drew criticism as "a hectically candid effusion," but revealed much of his ebullient personality.

Flagg was vehement in condemning modern art: his own taste apparently never progressed beyond Claude Monet and John Singer Sargent. His declining years were made difficult by failing eyesight and by a sense of separation from the world. He died in New York City.

[Flagg's lively autobiography, *Roses and Buckshot* (1946), is carefree as to dates and hard facts, but effective as an exposure of his personality. *Boulevards All the Way—Maybe* (1925) is a travelogue of a transcontinental motor jaunt. Indicative of a current renewal of interest in Flagg is Susan E. Meyers, *James Montgomery Flagg* (1974), with a concise text, photographs, and plates covering all phases of his work. The article on Flagg in *National Cyclopedia of American Biography* is informative up to 1938, the date of its publication. Louis H. Frohman, "Flagg, Born Illustrator," *International Studio*, Aug. 1923, is an informal interview with the subject. An obituary is in the *New York Times*, May 28, 1960.]

HAROLD E. DICKSON

FLEMING, JOHN ADAM (Jan. 28, 1877–July 29, 1956), geophysicist and science administrator, was born in Cincinnati, Ohio, the son of Americus Vespucius Fleming, an inspector of stationary engineers for the city of Cincinnati, and of Katherine Barbara Ritzmann. He attended Hughes High School and the University of Cincinnati (1895–1899), majoring in civil engineering and chemistry. He received the B.S. in civil engineering "with highest distinction." Following graduation Fleming was employed as assistant engineer for the redesigning of the Sängerbund Society Convention Building at Cincinnati.

Fleming was an aide to Louis A. Bauer, chief of the Division of Terrestrial Magnetism of the U.S. Coast and Geodetic Survey, from 1899 to 1903. He resigned to become a partner and superintendent of the Vulcan Copper Works in Cincinnati, where he designed a special chemical apparatus for continuous distillation and manufacture of refined chemical products. He was also a building contractor with his brother. Fleming returned to part-time employment with the Coast and Geodetic Survey from 1904 to 1910.

During his service with the Coast and Geodetic Survey, Fleming developed and designed nonmagnetic observatory buildings, including the aboveground type of constant temperature observatory adopted for the survey's magnetic observatories at Cheltenham, Md.; Sitka, Alaska; and Honolulu, Hawaii. He looked after construction of the Cheltenham and Honolulu observatories and took part in the survey's magnetic survey of the United States, Hawaii, and Alaska, and in the reductions and compilations of magnetic data.

On June 17, 1903, Fleming married Henrietta Catherine Barbara Ratjen; they had one daughter. His wife died in 1912, and on Oct. 30, 1913, he married her sister, Carolyn Ratjen.

The Carnegie Institution of Washington organized its Department of Terrestrial Magnetism in 1904, with Bauer as its first director. Although still active with the Coast and Geodetic Survey, in 1904 Fleming became the chief magnetician and principal assistant to Bauer. During the next few years, Fleming took a major role in organizing and planning the expeditions for the magnetic and electric surveys of the earth that constituted the chief activities of the Department of Terrestrial Magnetism. In the early 1900's there were few magnetic measurements on land, and practically none on the oceans. Existing standards for the accuracy and intercomparability of observations were inadequate. Fleming designed and constructed improved instruments for use on land and especially at sea. Fleming was acting director of the Department of Terrestrial Magnetism from

1929 to 1934 and was director from 1935 to 1946. He directed the planning for more than fifty major land magnetic survey expeditions to all continents. He also supervised three cruises of the *Galilee* (a wooden sailing vessel chartered by the institution) and seven cruises of the *Carnegie* (a nonmagnetic sailing vessel built under the supervision of the Department of Terrestrial Magnetism). His men participated in polar expeditions led by others, even traveling by zeppelin and submarine. Fleming also directed what was probably the most extensive program in physical and biological oceanography during the first quarter of the twentieth century. Among the major contributions were the improved description of the geomagnetic field, the first isomagnetic world charts designating the major patterns of secular magnetic change, and the discovery of the diurnal variation of the atmospheric potential gradient on universal time.

Fleming planned and supervised the construction of almost all the buildings on the grounds of the Department of Terrestrial Magnetism. He designed a number of magnetic instruments, including the theodolite-magnetometer, universal magnetometer, magnetometer-inductor, and galvanometer for field use, and improved the design of instruments used in fieldwork.

The department's field station at Kensington, Md., was also designed by Fleming. Fundamental magnetic research was done there, and unique ionospheric equipment was installed. Fleming also participated in the Department of Terrestrial Magnetism's field magnetic surveys in the western hemisphere.

Fleming designed magnetic observatories in Peru and Australia. He selected the site of the Huancayo Magnetic Observatory, near Lima, Peru (11,000 feet above sea level), supervised its construction, and organized its activities. After its completion in 1922, solar and lunar magnetic diurnal variations nearly three times as intense as observed elsewhere were discovered. The other observatory, located 800 feet above sea level near Watheroo, Western Australia, at the focus of the systems of currents that cause the daily magnetic variations, began operation in 1919.

During World War I, Fleming assisted Edward L. Nichols at the Department of Terrestrial Magnetism in perfecting a magnetic underwater mine that was used extensively in the North Sea. Fleming was also the chief developer of a special gimbal-ring support for mounting a submarine detection device.

During World War II, Fleming was in charge of all work of the Carnegie Institution concerned with the proximity fuse and other ordnance devices, radio-wave and communications improvement, magnetic compasses and odographs, and uranium and ionospheric studies. Also, during that period, the department undertook the task of preparing new isomagnetic and iosporic charts. The results of voluminous surveys on land and sea, made over many years by the Department of Terrestrial Magnetism and other agencies, were used to improve the description of the earth's main field and its secular change.

Fleming's own scientific research included cosmic relations of geomagnetism and the detailed study of magnetic data accumulated during 1903–1945 in the discussion for and preparation of world magnetic charts for the epoch 1942.5.

Fleming had a cardinal role in the growth of the American Geophysical Union. In 1920, a year after its organization, he became secretary of the Section of Terrestrial Magnetism and Electricity, a post he held until 1929. From 1925 to 1947 he was general secretary of the American Geophysical Union, and was elected honorary president for life in 1947. During his years as general secretary, he was practically sole editor of its *Transactions.*

Fleming's work was his life and his hobby. He possessed great skill in judging the future capabilities of the young men he chose as his associates. His influence was significant upon the lives of many of his scientific colleagues, but he was so self-effacing that only those who knew and worked with him could properly assess and testify to what he did for geophysics in the United States and in the world at large. He died in San Mateo, Calif.

[Fleming published more than 130 scientific articles. He was a principal author of six volumes of *Researches of the Department of Terrestrial Magnetism,* published during 1915–1947. From 1928 to 1948 he was the editor and publisher of *Journal of Terrestrial Magnetism and Electricity* (now *Journal of Geophysical Research*). Important books prepared under his editorship include *Terrestrial Magnetism and Electricity* (1939) and *Scientific Results of the Ziegler Polar Expedition of 1903–1905* (1907). A complete bibliography is in *Biographical Memoirs. National Academy of Sciences* (1967).]

PHILIP H. ABELSON

FLETCHER, HENRY PRATHER (Apr. 10, 1873–July 10, 1959), diplomat, was born in Greencastle, Pa., the son of Lewis Henry Clay Fletcher, a bank cashier, and Martha Ellen Rowe. His mother died in 1882, and Fletcher was raised by his older sisters; his later humor, grace, and warmth may perhaps be attributed to their gentle discipline. Fletcher attended local public and private schools until 1884, when his father became auditor for the Cumberland Railroad in Chambersburg. He completed his basic education in 1889 at the Chambersburg Academy. (Fletcher later lamented his failure to attend Princeton; and the lack of college credentials remained a psychological—if not a real—impediment to his career.) At the age of eighteen, he became a district court reporter and began to read law with his uncle, Judge D. Watson Rowe. He passed the bar examination in 1894, entered partnership with his uncle, and became an active member of the Republican Party.

The Spanish-American War propelled Fletcher into a new direction. Through bounding enthusiasm, political pressure, and a convincing letter from Senator Matthew Quay, he gained entry into Theodore Roosevelt's Rough Riders. Fletcher went to Cuba as part of K Troop, First United States Cavalry, but saw no action. He then accepted a temporary commission as first lieutenant and stayed in the army long enough for a tour of duty in the Philippines, where he served as an adjutant and then as a revenue officer (1899–1901). He enjoyed a relatively peaceful army life, and his position in the army of occupation also helped form the conservative paternalism so characteristic of his mature philosophy. After leaving the army, Fletcher obtained an appointment from President Theodore Roosevelt as second secretary in the new Havana legation. He served in Cuba (1902–1903), China (1903–1905), and as secretary to the American legation in Portugal (1905–1907), before returning to Peking as chargé d'affaires—and as a seasoned diplomat with skills in Mandarin as well as Spanish.

Dollar diplomacy found no greater champion than Fletcher. Although he disapproved of political meddling, he sincerely believed that China benefited from American economic involvement. Along with his friend and associate, Willard Straight, American consul in Mukden, Fletcher protected U.S. treaty privileges, secured American concessions, and advanced Secretary of State Philander Knox's plan to neutralize Manchurian railways. He developed a solid reputation with his superiors and acquired other advantages from his China post. Straight provided him with Wall

Street connections, such as Edward H. Harriman, Thomas W. Lamont, and J. P. Morgan. These ties, which Fletcher used later to open Latin American markets, led to his meeting socialite Beatrice Bend. Their eight-year courtship ended in marriage on July 25, 1917, when Fletcher thought he was wealthy enough to provide his bride with the luxuries he felt she required. They had no children.

President William H. Taft appointed Fletcher minister to Chile in December 1909. After Wilson's election he survived the advent of the new administration and Secretary of State William J. Bryan's purge of mission chiefs by traveling to Washington to plead his case. Through his Wall Street friends, he received the support of presidential adviser Edward M. House, which also helped. A year later (1914), the Santiago post was elevated to embassy level and Fletcher became the first ambassador, heralding the trend toward professional and linguistically competent diplomats that culminated in the Rogers Act of 1924.

Between 1909 and 1916 Fletcher ably assisted American investment in Chile. By the time he departed, Guggenheim interests were prominent in Chilean copper, and Bethlehem Steel dominated Chile's iron ore industry.

Fletcher's appointment as ambassador to Mexico in 1916 brought a breath of fresh air to fouled United States–Mexican relations. As usual, he urged political restraint and advanced American economic interests. He pushed for an end to the United States arms embargo and strove to introduce more United States capital into revolution-torn Mexico. However, the subsoil mineral rights that Mexico claimed in its new constitution created immense friction and, over a period of time, the accumulated frustrations Fletcher experienced led him to recommend aggressive measures. His position stood in direct contrast with President Wilson's desire for caution, and Fletcher resigned on Jan. 20, 1920, four days after a patchwork truce had been arranged between the Carranza regime and oil producers.

During the next decade Fletcher served briefly as under secretary of state (1921–1922) and as ambassador to Belgium (1922–1924) and Italy (1924–1929). The treasured post, Great Britain, eluded him despite his active candidacy in 1923, 1928, and 1932. This was his greatest disappointment. In the midst of other assignments, he led the United States delegation to the Fifth Pan-American Conference (1923) and joined the United States delegation to the Sixth (1928). At both meetings he worked to stave off political challenges to the principle of United States intervention in Latin American affairs. He also headed the delegation to the International Conference for the Protection of Literary and Artistic Property, which met in Rome in 1928. After he left the Italian post in June 1929, he served on the Forbes Commission to Haiti (1930) and chaired the United States Tariff Commission (1930–1931). He headed the Republican National Committee (1934–1936) and remained a member and counselor to its executive body until 1944. Recalled to public service, Fletcher became a special adviser to the secretary of state in 1944 and participated in the Dumbarton Oaks Conference. He retired in 1945 and died in Newport, R.I.

[Primary sources include the Henry P. Fletcher Papers, Library of Congress, which contain 6,500 items covering the period 1898–1958; National Archives, Record Group 43 (Records of International Conferences, Commissions, and Expositions) and 59 (General Records of the Department of State); and *Papers Relating to the Foreign Relations of the United States*. The most complete study is Olivia Frederick, "Henry P. Fletcher and United States–Latin-American Relations, 1910–1930" (Ph.D. diss., University of Kentucky, 1977). See also Henry M. Wriston, *Executive Agents in American Foreign Relations* (1929); Graham H. Stuart, *The Department of State* (1949); and Graham H. Stuart, *American Diplomatic and Consular Practice*, 2nd ed. (1952).]

JAMES K. LIBBEY

FLEXNER, ABRAHAM (Nov. 13, 1866– Sept. 21, 1959), educational reformer, was born in Louisville, Ky., the son of Moritz Flexner and Esther Abraham, Jewish immigrants who had built a successful wholesale hat business, then been reduced to poverty by the panic of 1873. He always professed the highest respect for the ideals of his parents, even though, like most of his brothers and sisters, he drifted away from the observances and beliefs of their religion. Flexner entered Johns Hopkins University in 1884 with the assistance of a $1,000 loan from his oldest brother, Jacob, and received the B.A. in 1886. Throughout his career he was impressed with the Hopkins system of education, which was based on the German university system, and advocated the restructuring of American higher education along its lines.

Returning to Louisville in 1886, Flexner taught for four years in the local high school. Then, seeing a need for private tutoring to educate wealthy but unruly boys for eastern colleges, he founded a school that prepared students for college through brief but intensive work. His graduates performed so well that President Charles W. Eliot of Harvard asked Flexner to write an article describing his methods. It appeared in *Atlantic Monthly* under the title "The Preparatory School" (1904).

In 1898 Flexner married Anne Laziere Crawford, who became a successful playwright; they had two daughters. With his wife's encouragement he left Louisville in 1905 for graduate study in psychology at Harvard. The following year, after receiving the master's degree, his interest in German universities led him to study comparative education at the University of Berlin. There he reinforced his earlier notion that America should emulate German universities, in his opinion the best in the world. In 1908 Flexner published a critique of American higher education, *The American College*. Written from the viewpoint of a preparatory school administrator, the book called for more attention to intellectual matters within colleges and less to extracurricular activities.

This book proved decisive in Flexner's career, for it attracted the attention of Henry S. Pritchett, head of the Carnegie Foundation for the Advancement of Teaching. The foundation was about to initiate a major study of medical education in the United States and Canada, and Pritchett chose Flexner to make the study. (Flexner was quite surprised, thinking at first that Pritchett had mistaken him for his older brother Simon, then beginning a distinguished medical career as director of the Rockefeller Institute for Medical Research in New York City.)

Flexner's report, *Medical Education in the United States and Canada* (1910), was based on two years of extensive research. He visited all of the 155 American and Canadian medical schools and described each in detail. The data presented were shocking. Many teaching hospitals were antiquated and unsanitary; some he called death traps. Too many medical schools were proprietary institutions existing solely for the profit of their owners. Students who had not graduated from high school could readily gain admission to a medical school and were virtually guaranteed graduation if they paid the tuition. Even medical schools sponsored by reputable universities often lacked the most rudimentary clinical facilities. Flexner recommended that 120 medical schools be closed. Within the next few years, most of them were.

This report and one following it in 1912, *Medical Education in Europe*, made the front pages of leading newspapers around the world and established Flexner's reputation as an authority on medical education. In 1913, largely as a result of these investigations, John D. Rockefeller, Jr., asked Flexner to join the permanent staff of the General Education Board, which the Rockefellers had established to raise the level of education throughout the United States. For fifteen years Flexner worked there as assistant secretary, as secretary, and finally as head of its Division of Studies and Medical Education. He was author or coauthor of a number of reports, including *Prostitution in Europe* (1914), *Public Education in Maryland* (1916), *The Gary Schools* (1918), *Public Education in Delaware* (1919), and *Medical Education: A Comparative Study* (1925). His celebrated essay, "A Modern School" (1916), later reprinted in *A Modern College and a Modern School* (1923), led directly to the founding of the Lincoln School at Teachers College, perhaps the outstanding progressive school of the time. During his last two years at the General Education Board, Flexner spent most of his time with the awarding of grants to stimulate research in the humanities, an area he thought needed more attention.

Despite the diversity of his interests, Flexner's work on the General Education Board focused primarily upon medical education. He was especially concerned with establishing full-time research faculties in the basic sciences at medical schools, and during his tenure he guided the disbursement of the $50 million that the Rockefellers put into medical education. Flexner estimated that the original grants eventually led to something on the order of $600 million in new resources for American medical schools. He effectively used the Board's leverage to see most of his recommendations widely adopted before his retirement in 1928.

Also in 1928 Flexner delivered the Rhodes Trust memorial lectures at Oxford. In these three lectures, published in revised and expanded as *Universities: American, English, German* (1930), he stressed again his long-held notion of the superiority of German universities. The Germanic stress upon conceptual research and graduate training along the lines followed at Johns Hopkins continued to appeal immensely to him.

American educational leaders remained generally unresponsive to Flexner's call for reform, but his ideas found partial realization when Louis Bamberger and his sister, Mrs. Felix Fuld, gave

Flexner $5 million to establish the Institute for Advanced Study at Princeton. In 1930 he became its first director, and held the post until his retirement in 1939. He brought a small number of brilliant scholars to the institute and gave them complete freedom to pursue conceptual research. Attracting Albert Einstein was an early coup; and as he added noted men such as John von Neumann, the institute's fame spread. It remains a leading scholarly center.

After Flexner left the institute, he wrote an autobiography, *I Remember* (1940); two biographies, *Henry S. Pritchett* (1943) and *Daniel Coit Gilman* (1946), and a historical and contemporary analysis of foundations, *Funds and Foundations* (1952). Later he revised his autobiography, published posthumously as *Abraham Flexner: An Autobiography* (1960).

His wife died in 1955; and in 1957 Flexner moved from New York City to Falls Church, Va., where he died. His life was a tribute to the pursuit and attainment of excellence in education.

[For a more extended analysis of Flexner's educational ideas, see Michael R. Harris, *Five Counterrevolutionists in Higher Education* (1970); Robert Ulich's (1967) and Clark Kerr's (1968) introductions to Flexner's *Universities: American, English, German;* and Franklin Parker, "Abraham Flexner, 1866–1959," in *History of Education Quarterly,* 2 (1962). Carleton B. Chapman, "The Flexner Report," *Daedalus,* 103 (1974), offers more detail about the effect of the report on medical education; and Raymond F. Fosdick, *Adventure in Giving, the Story of the General Education Board* (1962), places Flexner's career with the Board in context. The reviews of *Universities: American, English, German* in *Journal of Higher Education,* 2 (1931), are a good indication of the kind of criticism the book encountered from leaders of American universities. Flexner's personal papers are in the Library of Congress. In addition to Flexner's memoir, done in 1954, the Oral History Collection at Columbia University contains many references to him.]

MICHAEL R. HARRIS

FLYNN, ERROL LESLIE (June 20, 1909– Oct. 14, 1959), actor, was born in Hobart, Tasmania, Australia, the son of Theodore Thomson Flynn, a marine biologist, and Marelle Young. He attended St. Paul's School in London and Southwest London College from 1921 to 1924 before returning to Sydney. A high-spirited, athletic boy, Flynn did not distinguish himself academically, and his formal education ended at seventeen. He worked briefly as a clerk in a Sydney shipping company but, bored by the prospect of a business career, accepted a position in New Guinea in 1927 as a cadet in government service. For the next six years, if we can credit his autobiography, he led a life of adventure equal to that of any of the picaresque heroes he later played on the screen. Flynn's account, however, has been much disputed; even the Warner Brothers publicity department blanched at some of his tall stories. Drawing on information from many of Flynn's contemporaries, John Moore describes his autobiography as a tissue of fact and fiction.

From 1927 to 1929 Flynn was an overseer on a copra plantation and then tried his luck as a prospector in the goldfields of New Guinea. After returning briefly to Sydney, he sailed back to New Guinea on a cutter, a voyage he described in *Beam Ends* (1937). Following an unsuccessful attempt to manage a tobacco plantation, he again returned to Sydney, where his good looks led to his appearance as Fletcher Christian in *The Wake of the Bounty* (1933), a modest Australian-made precursor to the famous MGM film. After a brief interlude as a sheep farmer and another foray into the goldfields, Flynn decided to carve out a career in England.

The circumstances under which he left Australia are mysterious—Flynn's own account includes his adventures as a diamond smuggler and numerous amorous episodes. In any event, he arrived in England in the spring of 1933 with almost no money. For a year and a half he worked in the Northampton Repertory Company as a utility actor, playing every sort of role. During a brief London engagement in John Drinkwater's *A Man's House* he was spotted by a talent scout and given a small part in *Murder at Monte Carlo* (1935), filmed at Warner Brothers' Teddington Studio. It led to an offer of a contract at $150 a week from Warner Brothers in Hollywood. Flynn accepted at once.

He began his career there as a corpse in *The Case of the Curious Bride* (1935). "Some say it was my best role," Flynn characteristically observed. On May 5 of the same year he married the French actress Lili Damita. His first real screen opportunity was as a replacement for Robert Donat in the title role of *Captain Blood*. His portrayal of a genteel buccaneer set the pattern for his swashbuckling epics and established him as the most dashing leading man since Douglas Fairbanks. Flynn disliked the comparison and tried to avoid typecasting, but the public proved indifferent to him in light comedy and straight drama, preferring him as the romantic man of action in such films as *The Charge of the Light Brigade* (1936),

The Adventures of Robin Hood (1938), and *Dodge City* (1939).

By 1941 Flynn's career had peaked. He was rejected for military service in World War II (Flynn became an American citizen in August 1942), broke with his director, Michael Curtiz, and divorced his wife. In February 1943 he was acquitted of the charge of statutory rape of two teenage girls. Soon, however, his popularity revived, and the phrase "in like Flynn" came into national usage. But Flynn, who had married Nora Eddington in 1943, was becoming bored with the routine of filmmaking and turned increasingly to drugs and alcohol. Audiences began to find his films less appealing. The derring-do of *Objective Burma* (1945) excited more derision than enthusiasm, and even *Adventures of Don Juan* (1949), tailored to Flynn's reputation, fell short of expectations.

In 1949 his career entered its final phase. Flynn left Warner Brothers to star at MGM in *That Forsyte Woman,* and for the rest of his life shuttled between Hollywood and Europe, making occasional films. Nora Eddington divorced him in 1949, and he married Patrice Wymore in 1950. He suffered serious financial reverses. He lost money backing a never-completed film, he was fleeced by his agent, and he was billed by the government for nearly a million dollars in tax arrears. Most of his last pictures were of little interest, but in *The Sun Also Rises* (1957) he gave a memorable performance as the ingratiating alcoholic, Mike Campbell. Flynn's last movie, *Cuban Rebel Girls* (1959), an amateurish semi-documentary starring Flynn and Beverly Aadland, his teenage companion during the last two years of his life, was a pathetic epitaph to his screen career. Old beyond his years, he died of a heart attack in Vancouver, B.C. He left four children.

"I was hoaxed by life," Flynn wrote in his autobiography. And perhaps he was the victim of his own legend. Nevertheless, he gave pleasure to millions of moviegoers. As Jack Warner, who described him as "charming and tragic," put it: "To the Walter Mittys of this world, he was all the heroes in one magnificent, sexy, animal package."

[Flynn wrote *Beam Ends* (1937); *Showdown* (1946); and *My Wicked, Wicked Ways* (1959). On his life and career, see John Hammond Moore, *The Young Errol: Flynn Before Hollywood* (1975); Tony Thomas, Rudy Behlmer, and Clifford McCarty, *The Films of*

Errol Flynn (1969); and Jack Warner, *My First Hundred Years in Hollywood* (1965).]

WILLIAM W. APPLETON

FORBES, WILLIAM CAMERON (May 21, 1870–Dec. 24, 1959), governor-general of the Philippines and investment banker, was born in Milton, Mass., the son of William Hathaway Forbes, president of the Bell Telephone Company, and of Edith Emerson, a daughter of Ralph Waldo Emerson. His grandfather, John Murray Forbes, was one of Boston's leading China merchants and railroad developers. Forbes received his early schooling at Milton Academy and Hopkinson's School in Boston. He graduated from Harvard College in 1892.

Competitive by nature, Forbes initially devoted himself to sports and business. He coached Harvard's freshman football team in 1894 and 1895, and its varsity in 1897 and 1898. His first love, however, was polo. A player of international caliber, he remained active into his eighties; and his book *As to Polo* (1911) went through six editions and many translations. Beginning in business as an unpaid clerk in the Boston brokerage firm of Jackson and Curtis (1894–1895), at age twenty-seven he became chief of the financial department of Stone and Webster, a utilities holding company and electrical engineering firm. In 1899 he was named a life partner in the family investment house, J. M. Forbes and Company.

Forbes grew restless in business, however, and turned to public administration. An unsuccessful bid for a seat on the Panama Canal Commission led in 1904 to a presidential appointment as secretary of commerce and police in the Philippines, with a seat on the governing Philippine Commission. Promoted to vice-governor in 1908, Forbes was appointed governor-general by William Howard Taft in 1909.

The Philippines, Forbes later wrote, were "the big central thing" in his life. Believing fervently in progress, efficiency, and modernity, he easily adopted the insight of William Howard Taft that Americans and Filipinos shared an interest in developing the economy of the islands. He reasoned that development—desirable in itself as a stimulus to prosperity—might also neutralize the political demand for independence. Accordingly, he concentrated upon infrastructure, extending and improving road, rail, and water transportation. He also sought, although less successfully, to create effective land registration and irrigation systems, to deal with animal disease, and to promote foreign investments. In order to facilitate political accommodation between Americans and Filipinos, he befriended Sergio Osmeña and Manuel L. Quezon, leaders of the rising Nacionalista party, and consulted them when filling government offices.

Although popular and constructive, this policy of "attraction" failed politically. Investment and infrastructure grew slowly, and in the meantime Forbes's rigid public opposition to independence and his subordination of education and other popular causes to economic growth alienated many Filipinos. Racial tensions beyond his control deepened divisions between Americans and Filipinos. Exhausted and seriously ill for much of 1911 and 1912, Forbes was unable even to maintain the administrative efficiency of his government. Following the inauguration of Woodrow Wilson in 1913, Filipino leaders reluctantly joined American anti-imperialists to secure a new governor-general more sympathetic to independence. President Woodrow Wilson released the name of Forbes's successor to the press and then requested a prompt letter of resignation.

Deeply embittered by his removal, Forbes tried unsuccessfully to renew his interest in business. Intermittently a consultant to Stone and Webster, receiver of the Brazil Railway Company from 1914 to 1919, and director of many firms, he also deepened his backstage role in Republican politics. But the Philippines remained uppermost in his mind. In 1921 President Warren G. Harding chose Forbes and General Leonard Wood to lead a mission to investigate American administration of the Philippines and also the performance of Filipinos in the wide range of posts they filled under Wilson and his governor-general Francis Burton Harrison. Its report, urging retention of the colony to consolidate past reforms, was the basis of Philippine policy in the Harding and Coolidge administrations. In 1928 Forbes published *The Philippine Islands*, a political and developmental history of the American period; and five years later he intervened in the revision of the Hare-Hawes-Cutting bill to strengthen the powers reserved to the American high commissioner and auditor in the proposed Philippine commonwealth.

In 1930 Forbes was appointed by Herbert Hoover to head the President's Commission for Study of Conditions in Haiti. The commission criticized the racial and cultural insensitivity of American rule and, in accordance with Hoover's predilections, recommended "Haitianization" of government offices and a phased withdrawal of American marines. Pleased with this outcome, Hoover named Forbes ambassador to Japan, a post he held from June 1930 until April 1932.

It was an unhappy choice. Despite private warnings, Forbes was unprepared for the outbreak of fighting between Japan and China in Manchuria on Sept. 18, 1931. He sailed for a planned leave in the United States the following day. Moreover, his analysis differed from that of Secretary of State Henry L. Stimson. Like most of the professional staff at the Tokyo embassy, Forbes believed that foreign pressure would unite the Japanese behind the military and would compromise the liberal foreign policy of Shidehara Kijūrō. Uncomfortable at delivering Stimson's harsh protests and embarrassed by the secretary's unwitting exposure of confidential exchanges between Forbes and Shidehara, Forbes became openly critical of American policy. Stimson, finding Forbes's reports obscure and his sympathies alien, accepted his standing offer to resign.

During the 1930's Forbes was chairman of the executive committee and the board of trustees of the Carnegie Institution of Washington. In 1935 he headed the American Economic Mission to the Far East, a study group sponsored by the National Foreign Trade Council. Forbes, who never married, died in Boston.

Like his political patrons Theodore Roosevelt and Henry Cabot Lodge, Forbes was wealthy, intelligent, willful, and energetic. Although proud of his family's past, he sought an independent career, free of his ancestors' shadows, in which to equal their achievements. His Emersonian inheritance and a certain complacency dissuaded him from seeking that career in business or a profession; and although generous and witty with a few friends, he was too private and arch for electoral politics. The fresh challenge and broad executive powers of a Philippine proconsulship suited both his temperament and his talents, and drew from him a creative response and a unique personal commitment. Deprived of this career, "my life's work," at the age of forty-three, Forbes remained a willing public servant and a gentleman dilettante in the age of professional expertise.

[Forbes's papers are in the Houghton Library, Harvard University; copies of his annotated journal are at the Library of Congress and the Massachusetts

Historical Society, Boston. A fanciful autobiography, *Fuddlehead by Fuddlehead* (1935), is at the Massachusetts Historical Society, Boston. Forbes wrote *The Romance of Business* (1921); "American Policies in the Far East," *Proceedings of the American Academy of Arts and Sciences,* Jan. 1939; and "A Survey of Developments in the Philippine Movement for Independence," *Proceedings of the Massachusetts Historical Society,* 1932–1936.

Forbes's Philippine career is analyzed in Peter W. Stanley, *A Nation in the Making: The Philippines and the United States, 1899–1921* (1974); Rev. Camillus Gott, "William Cameron Forbes and the Philippines, 1904–1946" (Ph.D. diss., Indiana University, 1974); and Theodore Friend, *Between Two Empires: The Ordeal of the Philippines, 1929–1946* (1965). Forbes's ambassadorship to Japan is discussed sympathetically in Gary Ross, "W. Cameron Forbes: The Diplomacy of a Darwinist," in R. D. Burns and E. M. Bennett, eds., *Diplomats in Crisis* (1974). Robert H. Ferrell, *American Diplomacy in the Great Depression: Hoover-Stimson Foreign Policy,* 1929–1933 (1957); and Armin Rappaport, *Henry L. Stimson and Japan, 1931–1933* (1963), are highly critical. See also James B. Crowley, *Japan's Quest for Autonomy* (1966).]

PETER W. STANLEY

FOSHAG, WILLIAM FREDERICK (Mar. 17, 1894–May 21, 1956), geologist, was born in Sag Harbor, N.Y., the son of William Frederick Foshag, a tailor, and Joanna Eva Riegler. During Foshag's boyhood the family moved to California, where his father became a citrus grower. He attended the University of California at Berkeley, receiving a bachelor's degree in chemistry in 1919 and a Ph.D. in geology in 1923. In 1917–1918 he had worked as a control chemist for the Riverside Portland Cement Company; and throughout his career he remained on cordial terms with officials of similar firms, such as the American Potash and Chemical Company, which forwarded unusual mineral specimens and told him about mining sites of geological interest.

In 1919 Foshag joined the staff of the geology department of the National Museum (part of the Smithsonian Institution), where he spent the rest of his professional career as assistant curator (1919–1929), curator (1929–1948), and head curator (1948–1956). During World War II, Foshag served as liaison between the United States and Mexico on the development of mineral resources for military purposes. He married Merle Crisler on Sept. 5, 1923; they had one son.

Foshag's work as an administrator had considerable influence on the development of the National Museum as a center for American research on gems and minerals. It was, however, in acquiring collections for scientific mineralogy, rather than gems, that he made the greatest advances. In part through Foshag's and Earl V. Shannon's professional friendships with the owners, the Roebling and Canfield collections (25,000 specimens) came to the museum in 1926, along with endowments ($200,000) for additional acquisitions. These collections not only provided the Smithsonian with samples of virtually every mineral species but also yielded quality materials for research on the chemistry, crystallography, and origin of minerals. Over the next three decades Foshag augmented the National Museum collections by frequent field expeditions to Mexico and the American Southwest. Besides using the Smithsonian collections in his own research, he encouraged others to study these materials. His most notable protégé was Harry Berman, an aide in the geology department of the Smithsonian in 1922–1924 who became a distinguished mineralogist.

Foshag also published many scholarly papers on mineralogy, some purely descriptive and others more theoretical. His earliest writings (mainly 1918–1924) were laboratory and field reports on the borates and their associated minerals from desert terrains in the Southwest. During 1924–1936 he published several papers dealing with specimens from the mineralogically complex site of Franklin Furnace, N.J. In 1926 he became interested in mineral deposits of Mexico, especially metallic ores; this work culminated in 1942 with a U.S. Geological Survey *Bulletin* on Mexican tin deposits, written with Carl Fries, Jr. In 1938–1942, Foshag published papers on the chemistry and petrology of meteorites, and during the 1950's he worked on Central American jade, contributing geological analysis to what had been mainly an anthropological subject.

Foshag's knowledge of chemistry led him to include quantitative chemical analyses in nearly all of his mineralogical papers. He employed concepts of physical chemistry, such as phase relationships, to study rock and mineral origins. He also used goniometers to measure crystallographic variables, and he developed competence in microscopic petrography. Foshag's papers proposed revisions in existing schemes of mineralogical classification, offered chemical and optical determinations that led to a more exact understanding of mineral composition or crystal structure, and reported new localities for minerals that had been poorly studied for lack of specimens.

Some dozen minerals that he described as new are still accepted as independent species.

In addition to his achievements as a mineralogist, Foshag had virtually a second scientific career as a volcanologist. He had been interested in minerals associated with volcanic phenomena for some time before the volcano Paricutín suddenly appeared in a Mexican cornfield in February 1943. Foshag had become fluent in Spanish as a result of his work on Mexican minerals. Within a month of its appearance, he had observed Paricutín; and he returned frequently to chart its course, collaborating with scientists of the Instituto de Geologia (particularly Jenaro González Reyes) to gather accounts of its inception and to monitor the daily notes of an observer stationed nearby.

Foshag and González's primary concern was to leave a factual account of the volcano's history as free of interpretation as possible for the use of other scientists, a goal embodied in their monograph *Birth and Development of Paricutín Volcano* (1956). Foshag also saw to it that the photographic record on Paricutín was very full, at one point persuading the United States Army to fly a helicopter near the rim while scientists took color movies of the volcano's outbursts. In addition, he published valuable analytic papers based on data from Paricutín, especially in regard to its aqueous and gaseous emanations. By the time Paricutín slipped into quiescence in 1952, Foshag had enough field data and samples backlogged to continue publishing on the topic until his death at Westmoreland Hills, Md.

[Foshag's papers in the department of mineral sciences of the National Museum consist mainly of his photographs and notes on Paricutín. The Smithsonian Institution Archives houses his correspondence (1948–1956); additional letters and reports appear throughout other records there. The two fullest biographies include nearly complete lists of Foshag's publications—W. T. Schaller, "Memorial of William Frederick Foshag," *American Mineralogist*, 42 (1957); and Clarence Ross, "Memorial of William Frederick Foshag (1894–1956)," Geological Society of America *Proceedings* for 1956 (1957). Only one important citation should be added to their lists: Foshag's "Mineralogical Studies on Guatemalan Jade," *Smithsonian Miscellaneous Collections* 135, no. 5 (1957).

Edward Kraus, "Presentation of the Roebling Medal . . . ," *American Mineralogist*, 39 (1953), 293–295, provides additional biographical data. Brian Mason, "Mineral Sciences in the Smithsonian Institution,"

Smithsonian Contributions to the Earth Sciences, 14 (1975), is useful on Foshag's administrative work.]
                                    MICHELE L. ALDRICH

FOWLER, GENE (Mar. 8, 1890–July 2, 1960), author and journalist, was born Eugene Parrott Devlan on the "west bank of Mullen's Mill Ditch" in Denver, Colo., the only child of a brief marriage between Charles Francis Devlan and Dora Grace Wheeler. Two months before Fowler was born, his father walked out in an argument over a cup of coffee and deserted his family for a hermitlike life as a logger on Squaw Mountain, Colo. Fowler did not meet him until 1920. After divorcing Devlan, Fowler's mother in 1894 married Frank Dennis Fowler, who subsequently adopted Gene. Despite the adoption, the boy was raised mainly by his maternal grandmother, Elizabeth Wheeler.

Fowler graduated from West Denver High School in 1911, although much of his attendance was rather spotty. To supplement his grandparents' shaky finances, he often took odd jobs. At ten, for example, he left school to work as a taxidermist's helper, an experience that led to his becoming a vegetarian. Later, after he had returned to school, he worked as a printer's devil and then in his uncle's produce business, as a wagon driver delivering groceries to Denver's red-light district.

It was from such experiences that Fowler acquired his zest for the offbeat story and the salty, two-fisted language that came to mark his later writing. Fowler also contributed to and edited for two years his high school magazine, whereupon several of his teachers urged him to pursue a writing career. Although unconvinced, Fowler nevertheless decided to attend the University of Colorado. Except for the influence of Jim Lockhart, his journalism teacher, Fowler found academic life unrewarding and left after one year.

After returning to Denver, Fowler became a night signal clerk for the American District Telegraph Company. Also in 1912, he was hired as a cub reporter on the *Denver Republican*. In October 1913 he became a reporter for the *Rocky Mountain News* when that paper bought the *Republican*. The following year Fowler moved to the *Denver Post* and subsequently became assistant sports editor. On July 19, 1916, he married Agnes Hubbard, a clerk in the Denver Health Department. They had three children.

In 1918 Fowler left Denver for a position with the *New York American*. His New York journalistic career was sensational, both for his success and his legendary hijinks. His quick temper often caused him difficulties with newspaper owners, especially the dictatorial William Randolph Hearst. Once, dismayed at news of a recent Fowler exploit. Hearst remarked that he wished Fowler would take a long trip. Fowler, angered upon learning of the comment, immediately packed his bags and left on an ocean voyage with his family. Two days out, he wired Hearst a message reading, "On my way to Egypt. Is this far enough?" However, despite his irrepressible spirit, Fowler's rapid rise in the newspaper business to become at only thirty-four the managing editor of Hearst's *American* is ample testimony to his success. While with the *American*, Fowler interviewed John Barrymore, initiating a lifelong friendship with the actor and providing the introductory piece for his later biography. In 1924 Fowler became sports editor of the *Daily Mirror*, only to return the following year to the *New York American* as managing editor. His newspaper career came to an end in 1931. As managing editor of the *Morning Telegraph*, he had assembled a first-rate reporting staff by paying outrageously high salaries. His publisher was furious when he discovered the size of Fowler's payroll, and promptly fired him. Thereafter, Fowler turned principally to movie script and free-lance writing.

As a scriptwriter, Fowler achieved notable success. Among his major credits, as coauthor or collaborator, were the scripts or screenplays for the following films: *State's Attorney* (1932), *What Price Hollywood?* (1932), *Union Depot* (1932), *The Mighty Barnum* (1934), *Call of the Wild* (1935), *A Message to Garcia* (1936), *White Fang* (1936), and *Billy the Kid* (1941). Fowler also wrote the original stories for *Career Woman* (1936), *Earl of Chicago* (1940), and *Billy the Kid* (1941). In 1957 his biography *Beau James* was made into a movie. Fowler's Hollywood achievements made him wealthy, but his lasting fame rests upon the books that began to appear in the 1930's, his most productive decade.

Fowler proved to be a facile and prolific free-lance writer. *Trumpet in the Dust* (1930) offered an insider's look at the newspaper industry. It was followed by the fictional *Shoe the Wild Mare* (1931). His first biography, *The Great Mouthpiece* (1931), detailed the life of William J. Fallon, a New York City lawyer "mouthpiece" for the criminal underworld. Then, in collaboration with Ben Hecht, Fowler wrote a play, *The Great*

Magoo (1932), which had an unsuccessful Broadway run. *Timber Line* (1933) was both a biography of the two owners of the *Denver Post* and a tale of newspaper escapades; *Father Goose* (1934), the life story of Mack Sennett; *Salute to Yesterday* (1937), a sentimental reminiscence of his Denver years; and *Illusion in Java* (1939), a romance.

In the 1940's Fowler wrote *The Jervis Bay Goes Down* (1941), an epic poem; *Good Night, Sweet Prince* (1944), a biography of John Barrymore; *A Solo in Tom Toms* (1946), an autobiography; and *Beau James* (1949), a biography of New York mayor Jimmy Walker. *Good Night, Sweet Prince*, Fowler's most successful biography, was critically acclaimed and became a best-seller.

[On Fowler's life and career, see his autobiographical *A Solo in Tom Toms* (1946) and *Skyline* (1961); Lucius Beebe, "Gene Fowler," *Holiday*, May 1959; the valuable obituary notice, *New York Times*, July 3, 1960; and Will Fowler, *The Young Man From Denver* (1962).]

PETER P. REMALEY

FOWLER, RUSSELL STORY (May 1, 1874–Jan. 5, 1959), surgeon, was born in Brooklyn, N.Y., the son of George Ryerson Fowler, a surgeon, and Louise Rachel Wells. After graduating from the Brooklyn Polytechnic Institute in 1891, he entered the College of Physicians and Surgeons of Columbia University, from which he received the M.D. in 1895. Although he passed the internship examination with highest honors at St. Mary's Hospital, Brooklyn, where his father was an attending surgeon, Fowler decided not to accept the appointment in order to avoid any suggestion of nepotism. By 1895 he was adjunct to the surgeon in chief at Brooklyn Hospital, and he soon became affiliated with Methodist Episcopal Hospital and German Hospital (later Wyckoff Heights Hospital), remaining on the staff of the latter institution in various capacities for the rest of his life. From 1896 to 1900 he was connected with the New York Polyclinic Medical School, first as clinical assistant and later as instructor in surgery, but the increasing demands of his practice prevented a continuation of his career as a teacher.

It was during these years, when Fowler was assisting his father in major surgery, that he adopted the procedure, following an operation, of raising the head of the bed about eighteen to twenty inches, a position that employed the force of gravity to help restore normal peristalsis and prevent peritonitis. His father gave equal credit to Fowler for the concept of "the elevated drainage posture" (commonly known as the Fowler position), which resulted in the saving of innumerable lives in the era before antibiotics, when septic peritonitis was almost invariably fatal. Fowler was also commended for improving gallbladder surgery and for the successful extirpation of large portions of the liver when such a procedure was considered quite hazardous.

In 1900 Fowler took a sabbatical to study at the Allgemeines Krankenhaus in Vienna, where the surgical tradition of Theodor Billroth was maintained by his favorite pupil, Karl Gussenbauer. Two years later Fowler again visited Europe, this time touring the principal hospitals in order to absorb the recent advances in abdominal surgery. After his return to America, he collaborated with his father in the preparation of the latter's *A Treatise on Surgery* (1906). By the age of thirty-two, Fowler was a central figure in the medical life of Brooklyn and Long Island. In addition to the hospitals already mentioned, he later served on the staffs of the Huntington, Beth Moses, and Bay Ridge hospitals, and as consultant to the Hebrew Orphan Asylum. By 1913, Fowler was recognized as one of the outstanding surgeons in North America. He was invited to become a founder of the American College of Surgeons, of which he served several terms as governor. Fowler also was a member of the licentiate (founders' group) of the American Board of Surgery.

During World War I, Fowler was a member of the New York State Committee of the Council of National Defense, and served as chairman of the Auxiliary Medical Defense Committee of Kings County. As organizer of the Kings County and Long Island medical advisory boards, he encouraged younger doctors to volunteer for active duty. From 1925 to 1929 he served on the Joint Committee on Graduate Education of the Kings County Medical Society and the Long Island Medical College. He was also a member of the New York Academy of Medicine, the Medical Editors' and Authors' Association, the Harvey Society, the Société Internationale de Chirurgie, and the Deutsche Aertze Verein.

An innovative and highly successful surgeon, Fowler was also a voluminous writer and an excellent speaker and discussion leader at surgical conferences. He wrote chapters for three systems of surgery; and his own book, *The Operating Room and the Patient* (1906), ran through several reprints and three editions.

Aside from his medical work Fowler loved nature and the outdoor life. He was an expert horseman and big-game hunter who spent vacations in Canada. Liberal in his view of a changing society, he took great pleasure in encouraging talent in younger men and in advancing their careers.

Fowler married three times. His first wife was Eleanor S. White, whom he married on Dec. 26, 1894; they had one son. The second was Sophie Conrad: they had one son. The third was Rose Blanche Beauchesne, whom he married on Aug. 11, 1933; they had two children. He died in Brooklyn, N.Y.

[A full bibliography of Fowler's writings is in *Author Catalog of the Library of the New York Academy of Medicine*, XIII (1969). Fowler's role in the development of "the elevated drainage posture" (the Fowler position) is discussed in George R. Fowler, "Diffuse Septic Peritonitis, With Special Reference to a New Method of Treatment," *Medical Record* (1900); and his work in liver and gallbladder surgery, in George R. Fowler, "Historical and Critical Observations Upon the Surgery of the Liver and Biliary Passages," *Brooklyn Medical Journal* (1900). See also *Bulletin of the American College of Surgeons* (1959); and John Shrady, *The College of Physicians and Surgeons of the City of New York*, II (1903).]

MORRIS H. SAFFRON

FRANK, JEROME (Sept. 10, 1889–Jan. 13, 1957), judge, legal philosopher, and author, was born in New York City, the son of Herman Frank, a lawyer, and of Clara New. The family later moved to Chicago, and Frank received the Ph.B. at the University of Chicago in 1909. He became secretary to Charles E. Merriam, his political science teacher at the university, when Merriam was elected a reform alderman (1909–1911). In 1912 Frank graduated from the University of Chicago Law School with highest honors. Two years later he married Florence Kiper, a poet and playwright. They had one daughter.

Frank specialized in corporate reorganization law in Chicago from 1912 to 1929. In the latter year he joined the New York law firm of Chadbourne, Stanchfield and Levy. On Felix Frankfurter's recommendation he was appointed general counsel to both the Agricultural Adjustment Administration (AAA) and the Federal

Surplus Relief Corporation in May 1933. Because of a policy disagreement—his group interpreted the tenant provisions of the AAA contracts with farmers liberally, in order to protect the interests of the hard-pressed southern sharecroppers—Frank and his staff were fired in 1935. President Franklin D. Roosevelt immediately appointed Frank as special counsel to the Reconstruction Finance Corporation. He prepared for Secretary of the Interior Harold Ickes the government's case in behalf of the Public Works Administration against the Alabama Power Company. The government sought approval for federal construction of electricity distribution systems, and was upheld by the Supreme Court. The low government salary led Frank to resume the private practice of law in 1936. He helped reorganize the Union Pacific Railroad, for which he earned a fee of $38,000. In 1937, at the request of William O. Douglas, chairman of the Securities and Exchange Commission (SEC), he became a commissioner. When Douglas was appointed to the Supreme Court in 1939, Frank became chairman of the SEC for two years. In 1941 he was named a judge of the U.S. Circuit Court of Appeals for the Second Circuit, comprising New York, Connecticut, and Vermont. He served on the court until his death.

In 1930 Frank attained fame as a legal philosopher and exponent of the school of "legal realism" through the publication of *Law and the Modern Mind*, an attempt to psychoanalyze the law. In 1932 he was appointed a research associate at the Yale Law School, and after 1946 was a visiting lecturer. In 1931 and again in 1946–1947 he was a visiting lecturer in law and anthropology at the New School for Social Research in New York City.

In the history of jurisprudence there have been four major schools of thought: the natural law, the historical, the analytical or positivist, and the sociological, of which legal realism was an offshoot. In the 1930's and 1940's legal realism was the dominant school in American jurisprudence, and Frank was one of its main spokesmen. He sought to analyze the decisional process on a psychological basis as a necessary corrective to the false picture often painted of the law as a strictly legal process. The sociological school (the outstanding exponent of which was Roscoe Pound of the Harvard Law School) emphasized the socioeconomic forces shaping the law. The legal realists used various approaches to the study of the law in action, and Frank was the

articulate artificer of its psychological wing. The legal realists, even more than the sociological school, deemphasized the preeminence of logic in the law. Frank in particular added a new dimension by emphasizing the psychological forces that produce an element of uncertainty in the law. The gospel of both Pound and Frank was that the jurist has an imperative duty to study empirically how law functions in society. Their principal protest was against analytical positivism, which posited a closed system of legal logic, a mechanistic approach holding that the judge never makes or invents new law through interpretation but only discovers it.

Before becoming a judge, Frank had assigned a "subordinate role" to rules. He later changed their status to a "significant" one. In his later writings he realized that he had previously exaggerated the extent of uncertainty in legal rules. It is easier to be a revolutionary in theoretical discussions than when deciding actual cases. But he was right in considering rules as only one of the factors entering into judicial decision-making, which frequently involves individualization. Frank was wrongly accused of being an extreme nominalist who refused to believe in any rules. On the contrary, he spoke of a "profound respect for the utility of syllogistic reasoning linked with an insistence upon recurrent revisions of premises based on patient studies of new facts and new desires. . . ."

Over time Frank shifted his emphasis from rule skepticism to fact skepticism. To him the individual traits of judges—deeply buried personal biases—often loomed larger than their socioeconomic biases. He was haunted by the specter of uncertainty about facts and resulting wrong decisions caused by the fallibility of judges, juries, and witnesses. He therefore suggested a number of reforms. He was an enthusiastic advocate of the inclusion of social studies in the law school curriculum. His opinion in *U.S.* v. *Roth*, 237 F.2d 796 (2d Cir. 1956), an obscenity case, has been called a classic. In it Frank supported his conclusions by research into social, scientific, psychological, and economic information. He wrote that social ideals must direct the thought of legal thinkers. He also championed the "scientific spirit"—"the discipline of suspended judgment."

Frank believed that a society's treatment of the weak and powerless was "the test of the moral quality of a civilization." He wrote in a dissenting opinion in *U.S.* v. *Johnson*, 238 F.2d 565 (1956), later upheld by the Supreme Court in 352 U.S.

565 (1957): "But I, for one, cannot sleep well if I think that, due to my judicial decisions in which I join, innocent destitute men may be behind bars solely because it will cost the government something to have their appeals considered." To him, "Justice is as justice does." He died at New Haven, Conn.

[Frank's published books include *Save America First* (1938); *If Men Were Angels* (1942); *Fate and Freedom* (1945); *Courts on Trial* (1949), his chef d'oeuvre; and *Not Guilty* (1957), written with Barbara Frank Kristein, his daughter.

Full-length works on Frank's life and philosophy are Julius Paul, *The Legal Realism of Jerome N. Frank* (1959); J. Mitchell Rosenberg, *Jerome Frank: Jurist and Philosopher* (1970), which includes lists of articles and reviews by Frank, of reviews of his books, and of cases in which he presented his leading legal opinions; and Walter E. Volkomer, *The Passionate Liberal: The Political and Legal Ideas of Jerome Frank* (1970). A study of legal realism is Wilfrid E. Rumble, Jr., *American Legal Realism* (1968). Also of value is the collection prepared by Barbara Frank Kristein, *A Man's Reach—The Selected Writings of Judge Jerome Frank* (1965). In 1952 Frank recorded a 194-page memoir for the Oral History Collection of Columbia University. In addition, many other memoirs in the collection—notably those of Henry Wallace, Gardner Jackson, and M. L. Wilson—have significant material about Frank. Information on Frank's government service can be found at the Franklin D. Roosevelt Memorial Library, in Hyde Park, New York. Memorial tributes are in *Yale Law Journal*, May 1957; *University of Chicago Law Review*, Summer 1957; *Journal of Legal Education*, 10 (1957); and *Yale Law Report*, 3 (1957).]

J. MITCHELL ROSENBERG

FRENCH, PAUL COMLY (Mar. 19 1903– June 3, 1960), executive director of CARE (Cooperative for American Remittances to Everywhere), was born in Philadelphia, Pa., the son of Harry S. French, a farmer and mechanic, and Gertrude Comly. He was reared in the tenets of the Society of Friends, which emphasized service to others as the only proper and right way of life. He left Northeast High School in Philadelphia in 1922 and for twelve years was a reporter with the former *Philadelphia Record* and the United Press. On Oct. 18, 1925, French married Marie Ann Kerr. They had two children. From 1937 to 1941 he served as Pennsylvania director of the Federal Writers' Project of the Works Progress Administration (renamed the Works Projects Administration in 1939).

Committed to pacifism, upon the outbreak of World War II French edited *Common Sense Neutrality* (1939). The following year he wrote *We Won't Murder*. Both books helped present the viewpoint of conscientious objectors. In the fall of 1940 French organized—under the aegis of the Society of Friends and several other churches —the National Service Board for Religious Objectors, of which he was named executive secretary (1940–1946). During the war he worked closely with top selective service officials and organized and administered various work projects—forestry operations, service in mental and general hospitals—for conscientious objectors. His pamphlet *Civilian Public Service* (1943) describes the work of the National Service Board for Religious Objectors.

In October 1946 French was requested to make a survey for CARE's board of directors, who were seeking ways to make the new agency's services more effective. His excellent recommendations for the streamlining of operations led to his appointment as CARE's second executive director on Mar. 31, 1947. On Nov. 2, 1946, two years after his wife's death, French married Dorothy Felton. They had two children.

CARE, then the Cooperative for American Remittances to Europe, had been organized in the fall of 1945 to provide a channel for aid to European war victims. Twenty-six American welfare organizations formed a nonprofit agency through which food packages could be sent to recipients in Europe. When French joined CARE, it was offering only army ration surpluses. Under his supervision, CARE began assembling its own packages with contents ranging from textiles, food, and books, to farming and hand tools. He developed a broader general relief program in addition to deliveries for designated relatives or friends of donors. He expanded the delivery area from Europe to Asia, the Far East, Latin America, the Caribbean and Africa, thereby changing the *E* of CARE to signify "Everywhere." To increase public support, French set up local CARE offices in major American cities and opened donor facilities in Canada as well as in Europe and Latin America. CARE became truly an international program. In the closing years of his administration French spurred development of CARE's self-help programs, which enabled improverished peoples to improve their living conditions.

French visited more than fifty countries and talked and consulted with countless people regarding CARE programs. In a letter to the *New York Times* (Aug. 18, 1950) he wrote: "I am convinced that the world cannot have peace and security while people are hungry." He twice testified before the Agricultural Committee of the House of Representatives, urging that farm surpluses be made available to American private relief agencies for use overseas. Although he took pride in the efficiency with which CARE did its job and the recognition it won him, French's real interest lay in the humanitarian aspect of the organization. His overriding concern was to get aid and the means of reconstruction to the people who needed it most.

A tennis player in early life, French later relaxed by reading biographies and history. He once stated that he had two "extravagances," books and tobacco. French claimed that he bought about three books a week and that he smoked a pipe and approximately six cigars a day. In 1955 French retired to his home in Yardley, Pa., where he died.

[All of French's papers and correspondence are at Swarthmore College. See also a three-page biographical news release from CARE, undated; an interview, with photograph of French, in *New York Post Magazine*, July 23, 1947; and the obituary notice, *New York Times*, June 4, 1960, p. 23.]

JOSEPH C. KIGER

FREY, JOHN PHILIP (Feb. 24, 1871–Nov. 29, 1957), labor leader, was born in Mankato, Minn., the son of Leopold Frey, a former army officer and small manufacturer, and Julia Philomen Beaudry. Frey attended public school in Mankato until he was fourteen and then worked in a lumber camp near Ottawa, Canada, for eighteen months. He then moved to Worcester, Mass., where he clerked in a grocery store before becoming an apprentice iron molder in 1888. Upon completion of his training in 1891, he quickly secured a job in a local foundry. On June 10, 1891, he married Nellie Josephine Higgins, the daughter of a wire worker. They had three children.

As a young journeyman, Frey gave other activities priority over unionism, and he did not join the International Molders and Foundry Workers Union until 1893. Yet, once a member, he quickly rose through the ranks, becoming president of his local within three months. In 1898 he resigned this post to become treasurer of the New England conference of molders; in 1899 he advanced to

vice-president of the Massachusetts State Federation of Labor; and in 1900 he began his fifty-year tenure as a vice-president of the Molders' Union. When in 1903 he assumed the editorship of the *Iron Molders' Journal,* a post held until 1927, he moved his family to Cincinnati, where the union had its headquarters.

Finding further advancement in the Molders' Union blocked, Frey gave most of his energy to the American Federation of Labor (AFL), becoming one of Samuel Gompers' more important lieutenants. For instance, as secretary of the Committee on Resolutions from 1909 to 1927, Frey ensured that most of Gompers' policies would be upheld by AFL conventions. After 1914, when Gompers' attention increasingly focused on foreign affairs, so did Frey's. During World War I, Frey went on two labor missions to Europe in order to promote greater support for the war among allied trade unionists. In 1919 he served as chairman of an AFL committee on European reconstruction, and in 1921 and 1924 he traveled to Mexico City as an AFL delegate to the Pan American Federation of Labor. The aging Gompers successfully pushed Frey for the presidency of the divided Ohio State Federation of Labor in 1924; this was an effort to strengthen the traditional craft unionists against more progressive forces. Frey held that post until 1928.

Gompers' death in late 1924 led Frey to forge new bonds of allegiance with the conservative craft unionists on the AFL executive council, most particularly Daniel J. Tobin of the teamsters, William L. Hutcheson of the carpenters, and Arthur Wharton of the machinists. In order to enable Frey to watch out for their interests within the federation while they governed their own unions, in 1927 these leaders made him secretary of the AFL Metal Trades Department in Washington and elevated him to president in 1934. Frey also became the leading intellectual spokesman for the federation and spent much of his time lecturing, writing, and serving on various government advisory committees. In the mid-1920's he was labor's loudest critic of scientific management, and in the early 1930's he lobbied vigorously to outlaw labor injunctions. As an arch-Republican and a defender of the AFL's voluntaristic political tradition, Frey opposed much of the New Deal's social legislation.

Frey's most significant defense of craft union "purity," however, came with his opposition of organizing mass production workers. At the 1934 AFL convention, he spoke for those interests adamantly opposed to industrial unionism, and throughout 1935 he tried to provoke a showdown between the two forces. In 1935 John L. Lewis established the Committee for Industrial Organization (which changed its name in 1938 to Congress of Industrial Organizations) to work for industrial unionism within the AFL. The following year Frey guided through the AFL executive council (of which he was not even a member) the suspension of all CIO unions from the federation. Having done much to split the labor movement, Frey became the most active strategist in the AFL's war against the CIO. Acting out of passion more than reason, he encouraged the federation to support antilabor politicians because the CIO had endorsed their prolabor opponents. And he used the newly established House Un-American Activities Committee to propagate his view that the CIO was little more than a communist front. During World War II, while serving on the War Production Board's shipbuilding stabilization committee and the Committee on Apprenticeships, Frey continued to snipe at the CIO. Indeed, his retirement as president of the Metal Trades Department in 1950 seemed necessary before a merger of the two organizations could be honestly explored. In 1955 the AFL and the CIO merged.

The slightly built, conservatively dressed Frey sought to project the image of moderation and scholarly attainment. He wrote *An American Molder in Europe* (1911), *The Labor Injunction* (1922), *Craft Unions of Ancient and Modern Times* (1944), and several pamphlets. In most of his writing he simply rehashed the tenets of craft unionism formulated by Gompers. A dogmatic person, Frey held unskilled workers in disdain and inflated his own importance—even flaunting his rank of colonel in the Special Army Reserves that he received for lecturing in 1928 at the Army Industrial College. He constantly worried that he was not receiving the respect he deserved or that others were plotting to undermine him. Such conspiratorial visions also shaped his conception of society, which he felt was being secretly controlled by socialists, bankers, or communists, depending on the temper of the times. Frey died in Washington, D.C.

[Discussions of Frey's activities within the AFL can be found in Irving Bernstein, *Turbulent Years* (1970); Melvyn Dubofsky and Warren Van Tine, *John L. Lewis: A Biography* (1977); and Philip Taft, *The A.F. of L. From the Death of Gompers to the Merger* (1959).

The Frey papers in the Library of Congress contain an unpublished history of the labor movement with some autobiographical material. See also the obituary notice, *New York Times,* Nov. 30, 1957. Frey completed his reminiscences for the Oral History Collection of Columbia University in 1955; other memoirs in the collection have references to him.]

WARREN R. VAN TINE

FROMM-REICHMANN, FRIEDA (Oct. 23, 1889–Apr. 28, 1957), psychiatrist and psychoanalyst, was born in Karlsruhe, Germany, the daughter of Adolf Reichmann, an Orthodox Jewish merchant, and Klara Simon. She grew up in Koenigsberg, East Prussia (now Kaliningrad R.S.F.S.R.), where her father had become a bank director.

The Reichmann family was close-knit. Much was expected of the children, and careful attention was paid to both the ethical precepts and formal practice of Orthodox Judaism. The spirited, progressive Klara Simon was the dominant figure in the household and a major force in Fromm-Reichmann's life. It was her gentle, kindly father, however, who insisted that she study medicine rather than languages, which were a major interest. He argued that medicine offered better opportunities at a time when there was considerable job discrimination against Jews.

Fromm-Reichmann's preparation for university entrance had taken place privately; girls were not yet permitted to attend German high schools (Gymnasiums). When she entered the medical school of the Albertus University in 1908, this diminutive young woman, who stood little more than four feet, ten inches tall, was a pioneer in a field still completely dominated by men.

Early in her studies, Fromm-Reichmann became aware of her gift for communicating with severely disturbed mental patients. After completing medical school in 1913, she engaged in postgraduate studies in neurology and psychiatry under Kurt Goldstein, who was one of the major influences on her professional development. She studied brain physiology and pathology and became interested in the emotional effects of brain injuries. A number of scientific papers resulted from her collaboration with Goldstein.

World War I created new opportunities for talented women. In 1916 Goldstein chose Fromm-Reichmann to organize and manage a 100-bed hospital for brain-injured soldiers. After the war, she followed Goldstein to Frankfurt am Main for two additional years of study. In 1920 she began a four-year period on the psychiatric staff of the Sanatorium Weisser Hirsch in a Dresden suburb. It was during this time that she first became familiar with the writings of Sigmund Freud and began psychoanalytic training, first with a Dr. Wittenberg in Munich, later with Hanns Sachs in Berlin.

Fromm-Reichmann's encounter with the psychoanalytic movement was a turning point in her life. She became so enthusiastic about this revolutionary new method that she believed for several years that it could not only alleviate individual human suffering, but might also become a tool for social change. With Erich Fromm she opened a progressive psychoanalytic sanatorium in Heidelberg in 1924. She married Fromm in 1926. He was almost eleven years her junior. The couple had no children. Their life together ended in the early thirties, although they were not divorced until 1942 and remained thereafter on friendly terms.

After the closing in 1928 of the sanatorium, which had drained her energies and remained financially unsuccessful, Fromm-Reichmann concentrated on the full practice and teaching of psychoanalysis. At this time, she was deeply influenced by Georg Groddeck, a charismatic and unorthodox pioneer in the treatment of psychosomatic illness through psychoanalysis. With Fromm and Groddeck, she became one of the founders of the South-West German Psychoanalytic Institute at Frankfurt am Main in 1929.

In 1933 the threat of Nazi persecution caused her to flee to Strasbourg, France, where she was joined by many of her analytic patients. From France she went briefly to Palestine. She then migrated to the United States, arriving in April 1935. By June, she was working at Chestnut Lodge, a private, psychoanalytically oriented psychiatric hospital on the outskirts of Washington, D.C. Here the director, Dexter Bullard, Sr., provided a sympathetic environment. She was to remain on his staff for the rest of her life.

During the late 1930's and throughout the 1940's, Reichmann became closely associated with Harry Stack Sullivan, who shared her interest in the treatment of psychotic patients. Both developed a growing understanding of the importance of interpersonal factors on the behavior of the mentally ill. The Washington School of Psychiatry of the William Alanson White Foundation became a forum for the dissemination of their ideas.

In spite of her charm and vivaciousness, Fromm-Reichmann maintained considerable reserve. She found it difficult to lean on others. Her personal life was overshadowed by the demands of her profession. Few of her friends knew how large a share of her income and energies was devoted to helping family members, friends, and strangers who were victims of fascism in Europe. Although her last years were troubled by increasingly poor hearing, a hereditary ailment, she continued to make extraordinary demands on herself, working simultaneously as therapist, administrator, teacher, lecturer, and author of scientific papers.

Fromm-Reichmann's extraordinary empathic gifts enabled her to unlock many aspects of schizophrenic communication, both verbal and nonverbal. Joanne Greenberg's autobiographical novel, *I Never Promised You a Rose Garden* (1964), portrays Fromm-Reichmann in the character of Dr. Fried and captures vividly her respectful and sensitive approach.

Fromm-Reichmann was a pioneer in the treatment of severe mental illness through psychoanalysis. Through her work with psychotic patients at Chestnut Lodge, she demonstrated the effectiveness of her approach. She called her method "psychoanalytically oriented psychotherapy," indicating that some modification of the classical method was necessary to treat schizophrenics and other severely disturbed individuals. In *Principles of Intensive Psychotherapy* (1950) she set down her ideas in a manner so lucid and accessible that it remains a classic. By convincing the psychiatric establishment that intensive psychotherapy could reach and heal severely disturbed patients, she encouraged a more hopeful therapeutic approach to this large and often neglected group.

[On Fromm-Reichmann and her work, see Edith Weigert, "In Memoriam: Frieda Fromm-Reichmann," *Psychiatry,* Feb. 1958; Douglas Noble and Donald Burnham, *History of the Washington Psychoanalytic Society and the Washington Psychoanalytic Institute* (1969). A selection of Fromm-Reichmann's papers was edited by D. M. Bullard, Sr., and published as *Psychoanalysis and Psychotherapy* (1959).]

SYLVIA G. HOFF

FRYE, WILLIAM JOHN ("JACK") (Mar. 18, 1904–Feb. 3, 1959), airline and manufacturing executive, was born near Sweetwater, Tex., the son of William Henry Frye, a rancher, and Nellie Cooley Frye. At the age of fourteen he was awestruck by the sight of a United

States Army plane—its pilot having lost his bearings—that landed in their pasture, and resolved to become a flier. After graduating from high school in 1923, Frye headed for Los Angeles, where he worked as a soda jerk. He spent his earnings on flying lessons and soon was teaching others to fly. With a partner, Paul Richter, who had a little capital, he bought the Burdett Flying School. Soon they were making more money by doing stunt flying for motion picture producers, among them Howard Hughes, who was shooting *Wings*. In 1927 Frye and Richter bought a single-engine Fokker and established Standard Airlines, a flying service between Los Angeles and Phoenix. They sold it in 1930 to Western Air Express, of which Frye later became president.

Commercial aviation barely existed in 1930, but the government was anxious to establish reliable airmail service, which, highly subsidized, could keep an infant airline alive. In 1930 Postmaster General Walter F. Brown, using airmail contracts as bait, pressed Western Air Express to merge with Transcontinental Air Transport, which had been formed in 1927 by W. W. Atterbury of the Pennsylvania Railroad, Charles A. Lindbergh, and others, to form one of several lines providing coast-to-coast service. Frye was in charge of operations of Transcontinental and Western Air (TWA), as the new company was called, and became president in 1934.

Frye's chief contribution to the rise of commercial aviation was his concentration on fast, comfortable, modern equipment and on devices that made all-weather operation much safer than in the past. He encouraged plane builder Donald W. Douglas to put into production a sleek, low-wing, twin-engine aluminum airplane and bought the first one for TWA in 1934. This DC-2, modified and designated DC-3, became the symbol of the new air age in the 1930's, when the craft was the chief workhorse of commercial aviation. Frye made TWA the first airline to use the Sperry automatic pilot, wing and propeller deicers, and wing flaps to make landings safer. His pilots were the first to receive training in celestial navigation. In marketing air travel, however, Frye was less successful until Mrs. Cornelius Vanderbilt, Jr., told him at a cocktail party that less emphasis on safety and more on the romance of flying was needed. After Mrs. Vanderbilt divorced her husband, she and Frye were married on Jan. 1, 1941.

The severe recession of 1937–1938 wiped out the slender profit margin that TWA had managed to attain and its chief owners, the banking firm of Lehman Brothers and Chicago taxi magnate John D. Hertz, demanded greater emphasis on profit and less on innovation. Frye and Richter turned to their old friend Howard Hughes, who was growing richer every day from the oil tool business left him by his father.

Hughes had always been fascinated by aviation; he made a record-breaking round-the-world flight in 1937. Hughes put up the money, and the three gained control of TWA in 1939. Turning his attention to securing secondary routes to feed traffic to the main line, Frye soon made TWA the third largest airline, after American and United, in the United States.

But it was high-speed, high-altitude, all-weather flying in which Frye and Hughes were interested. Turning this time to Lockheed, Frye and that company's Robert E. Gross developed a four-engine, three-rudder airplane, much bigger than anything then carrying passengers and capable of flying 400 miles an hour. In the spring of 1944 Hughes and Frye flew the first Constellation, as the new plane was called, from coast to coast in six hours and fifty-eight minutes. Until Douglas developed his DC-6, the Constellation was the plane on which the postwar commercial aviation industry depended.

TWA had been the first air carrier to sign a military transport contract with the government, flying around the world to places that had seldom seen an airplane before the war. With this experience, and with the "Connie," as the new plane was immediately nicknamed, Frye proposed to challenge Pan American Airways, the veteran United States overseas airline, for what he expected would be a rich postwar market in international air travel. But the market did not develop quickly, and despite increasingly expensive promotion by TWA, Pan American got most of it. The Constellation developed problems that required it to be grounded. What was worse, Hughes never shared Frye's enthusiasm for international aviation. When TWA needed large amounts of additional capital, Hughes was slow to respond and insisted on protecting his share of the company. Frye arranged a $100 million line of credit that called for Hughes to place his stock in a voting trust. Angered, Hughes planned to fire Frye in February 1947; Frye, however, was warned and resigned. He accepted the presidency, and later the chairmanship, of the General Aniline and Film Corporation, positions that left him time to enjoy his Arizona ranch.

Standing over six feet tall and weighing more than 200 pounds, Frye looked the part of the western rancher; yet he also spent much time reading and writing. In 1950 he divorced his wife and married Nevada Smith; they had one daughter. By the mid-1950's he was ready to return to the aviation business, and he and his associates formed the Frye Corporation to manufacture executive aircraft (1955). He was killed in an automobile accident in Tucson, Ariz.

[An obituary with portrait is in the *New York Times*, Feb. 4, 1959. Also see *Fortune*, April 1945; and *Time*, Oct. 1, 1945; Jan. 20, 1947; and Mar. 3, 1947.]

ALBRO MARTIN

FRYER, DOUGLAS HENRY (Nov. 7, 1891–Dec. 24, 1960), industrial psychologist, was born in Willimantic, Conn., the son of Henry Fryer and Nellie E. Finley. After graduating from Springfield College in Massachusetts in 1914, he attended Brown University for a year and then Clark University, from which he received his M.A. in 1917 and his Ph.D. in psychology in 1923. During World War I, Fryer was a psychological examiner and morale officer. In 1924 he was an assistant professor at the University of Utah. The remainder of his academic career was spent at New York University, where he started as an assistant professor in 1924 and became an associate in 1928. During the years 1925–1940 he was administrative chairman of the University Heights Department of Psychology, where he organized an experimental laboratory and became its first director of industrial training in 1949. He became the first president of the Association of Consulting Psychologists in 1930.

Fryer wrote his major book, *Measurement of Interests in Relation to Human Adjustment*, in 1931. Its aim was "to include between the covers of one book all that is of quantitative value" concerning subjective and objective measurement of educational and vocational interests. One of his conclusions was that objective measures were superior to subjective measures. The book was used as a text and remains an interesting historical record of the early development of what is today an important area of applied psychology.

Fryer married Katharine Homer on Aug. 25, 1934; they had five daughters. In 1937 he was elected president of the American Association for Applied Psychology. During the years 1936–1946 Fryer was a collaborator of the Forest Service of the Department of Agriculture. During World War II, he was first a research investigator for a committee on the selection and training of aircraft pilots (1940–1942). From 1943 to 1945 he was chief of personnel research in the War Department. In 1945 he became one of the founding directors of Richardson, Bellows, Henry and Company, a firm of consulting psychologists. From 1945 to 1947 he worked on personnel research in the Adjutant General's Office. In 1949–1950 he served as vice-president of the American Association for the Advancement of Science and as chairman of its psychology section. In 1950 he helped the Arabian Oil Company set up industrial training programs in the Middle East. Fryer became an adjunct professor at New York University in 1952.

Interest and morale were the focus of Fryer's research. He said that "a social organization exists only because of the morale of its members. A nation, a labor union, a social group, a social class, an army, a gang, a university exists because of its morale. Buildings, orders, authority, rules, laws, ownership, materials, books, etc., are but tools for the expression of well-being and a zest for social living." A zest for social living was reflected in Fryer's own career. He was not only a trainer and teacher but also a university administrator, consultant, collaborator, army officer, and editor. Several years before his death, former graduate students set up a fund in his name providing an annual stipend for leading doctoral candidates in the field of industrial psychology. Fryer died in Rye, N.Y.

[Fryer's works include *Vocational Self-Guidance: Planning Your Life Work* (1925); *General Psychology* (1927), a students' study syllabus; *Elementary Experiments in Psychology* (1927), a lab manual; *An Outline of General Psychology* (1936); and *Fields of Psychology* (1940). Fryer and Edwin R. Henry edited *Handbook of Applied Psychology* (1950); Fryer coauthored *Developing People in Industry* (1956).]

HENRY CLAY SMITH

FULTON, JOHN FARQUHAR (Nov. 1, 1899–May 29, 1960), neurophysiologist, medical historian, bibliophile, and author, was born in St. Paul, Minn., the son of John Farquhar Fulton, a physician, and Edith Stanley Wheaton. After graduating from Central High School in St. Paul and spending a year at the University of Minnesota (1917–1918), he entered Harvard University, from which he received the B.S., *magna cum laude*, in 1921. Fulton attended Magdalen College at Oxford University for two years as a Rhodes scholar and for another two years as Christopher Welch scholar and demonstrator in physiology. Oxford awarded him the B.A. with first-class honors in 1923, and the M.A. and D.Phil. in 1925. On Sept. 29, 1923, Fulton married Lucia Pickering Wheatland. They had no children.

During these years three men exerted a strong influence on Fulton and became lifelong friends: Edward Mark, professor of biology at Harvard; Charles Sherrington, professor of physiology at Oxford; and Harvey Cushing, eminent pioneer in brain surgery and book collector, who was then writing *The Life of Sir William Osler*. Osler also influenced Fulton through his writings and his magnificent library, where he was made welcome by Lady Osler and Osler's nephew, William Francis, who was preparing a catalogue of the library.

Access to this rich educational resource inspired Fulton to collect his own library in the history of physiology, and henceforth humanism and history were indissolubly combined with medicine in his perspective, teaching, and writing. Drawing on omnivorous reading, phenomenal luck, and the help of several book dealers, he amassed, despite limited funds, a library of most of the important works in physiology—between 7,000 and 8,000 volumes—in less than ten years. One of his purchases was a "lot" of twenty-two books by the seventeenth-century chemist Robert Boyle, for about $60. In 1965 a copy of one, *The Sceptical Chymist*, sold at auction at Sotheby's for $13,440. In 1930 he published *Selected Readings in the History of Physiology*, drawn entirely from his own collection.

The research Fulton undertook for the D.Phil. degree was an analysis of muscular contraction and its reflex control. He published his findings as *Muscular Contraction and the Reflex Control of Movement* (1926). After receiving the M.D. from Harvard in 1927, he served as associate in neurosurgery under Cushing in 1927–1928 at Peter Bent Brigham Hospital in Boston. He was involved in several research projects during this period and with Jaime Pi-Suñer made the now-classic distinction between the in-parallel position of muscle spindles and the in-series position of tendon organs relative to muscle stretch and contraction.

In his clinical work Fulton was a staunch exponent of Cushing's detailed study of patients and meticulous record keeping; he also developed a peerless surgical technique and a keen interest in patients, and showed promise of becoming a clinician. Nevertheless, he decided on a career in physiology when invited to return to Oxford as a fellow of Magdalen College in 1928. In 1930 he joined the faculty of the Yale University School of Medicine as Sterling professor of physiology and chairman of the department (1931).

The interest in the functions of the brain that he had developed under Sherrington and Cushing prompted Fulton to establish at Yale the first primate colony in America for the purpose of studying the correlations between cerebral physiology in apes and human neurological disorders. The nature of cerebral control of muscle movement was one of his earliest interests, and with Margaret Kennard he carried out experiments involving removing the motor and premotor areas of the cerebral cortex from chimpanzees and orangutans, then delineating the roles of the removed areas in spasticity, loss of skilled movements, and changes in reflex status. This work, reported in *The Sign of Babinski*, written with Allen D. Keller (1932), contributed importantly to the understanding of pyramidal and extrapyramidal motor systems.

While still at Oxford, Fulton had begun experimenting with Franc Ingraham on surgical approaches to the frontal and basal regions of the brain. At Yale this led to studies of the effects of cerebral lesions on autonomic functions. The representation of these functions in the frontal lobes of the brain was documented in the Beaumont Foundation lectures (1934). In 1935, Fulton and Carlyle Jacobsen reported on the behavioral effects of extirpation of the anterior association areas of the frontal lobes. They noted profound alterations in mood produced by these lesions in one of their chimpanzees. Their initial report prompted Antônio Caetano de Abreu Freire Egas Moniz to develop prefrontal lobotomy as an operation for relief of psychosis in mental patients, for which he shared the Nobel Prize in medicine or physiology in 1949. Apart from its dramatic and controversial, clinical applications, this line of work was, in terms of basic physiology, one of Fulton's most fruitful pursuits; subsequent investigations in his laboratory laid the basis for new concepts of the limbic system and its importance for behavior.

Fulton's enormous vitality, energy, and outgoing personality created an atmosphere in the laboratory that encouraged independence of thought. He enjoyed teaching and freely gave time, encouragement, and credit. His whole-hearted dedication to the work at hand some-times provided more push than was welcomed. Hebbel Hoff, a member of the faculty, later wrote: "The Laboratory of Physiology at Yale under Fulton was one of the rare places where full and free communication among the special-ists was a reality, and this global concept of med-icine has been remembered and practiced wherever his pupils have gone and whatever their specialities have been" (*Journal of the History of Medicine.* . . , Jan. 1962).

During World War II, decompression studies important to aviation safety were carried on in Fulton's laboratory. He also gave much time to the Committee on Aviation Medicine and other committees of the National Research Council. His friendships with British scientists were in-valuable in the joint planning between Britain and the United States. He helped Howard Florey to make the American connections that made pos-sible the large-scale production of penicillin.

In 1933, Fulton was instrumental in persuading Cushing to return to Yale after retiring from Harvard. When Cushing proposed that he and a friend, Arnold C. Klebs, join him in giving their books to Yale, Fulton became the motivating force in planning and establishing in 1941 an outstanding collection of books in the history of medicine at the Yale Medical Library. Also in 1941 he received a doctorate of science from Oxford. Ten years later Fulton became Sterling professor of the history of medicine and chairman of a new department, the third in the United States. In 1960, just before his death, the faculty was enlarged, the department was expanded to include the history of science, a graduate program was established, and instruction was extended to undergraduates as well.

The range of Fulton's interests and his pro-ductivity are reflected in his bibliography of 520 entries. Two works were widely used text-books. His *Physiology of the Nervous System* (1938), written to help students unite neuro-physiology with clinical neurology, was trans-lated into five languages. He was the editor of, and large contributor to, *Howell's Textbook of Physiology*, which he took over in 1942 and saw through three more editions: 15th ed. (1946), 16th ed. (1949), and 17th ed. (1955). He was co-founder of the *Journal of Neurophysiology* in 1938 and editor until 1960. He edited the *Journal of the History of Medicine and Allied Sciences* from 1952 to 1960.

Fulton also published *A Bibliography of the Honourable Robert Boyle* (1932)— he owned one of the finest collections of Boyle's works—and *The Great Medical Bibliographers* (1951). He col-laborated on several useful technical bibliogra-phies issued during the war at the request of the government.

As a biographer Fulton was at his best. His greatest achievement was *Harvey Cushing* (1946). He was also co-author (with Elizabeth H. Thomson) of a biography of Benjamin Silliman (1947), Yale's first professor of chemistry and geology.

Many honors acknowledging his contributions to physiology and the history of medicine came to Fulton in the form of distinguished lectureships as well as eighteen decorations and honorary de-grees, including a D.Litt. from Oxford in 1957. His activities in his last years were severely cur-tailed by ill health. He bore this without com-plaint, working steadily until his brief final illness. He died in Hamden, Conn.

[The Fulton Papers at the Yale Medical Library include his publications, correspondence, memora-bilia, and forty-six volumes of unpublished diaries, 1921–1922, 1927–1960. Works by Fulton include *Physiology* (1931); "A Bibliography of Two Oxford Physiologists: Richard Lower (1631–1691) and John Mayow (1643–1679), *Proceedings of the Oxford Bib-liographical Society* (1935); *Sir Kenelm Digby* (1937); *Aviation Medicine in Its Preventive Aspects* (1948); *Functional Localization in the Frontal Lobes and Cer-ebellum* (1949); *Humanism in an Age of Science* (1950); *Frontal Lobotomy and Affective Behavior* (1951); and *Michael Servetus, Humanist and Martyr* (1953), written with Madeline E. Stanton. There is a Fulton memorial number of *Journal of the History of Medicine and Allied Sciences*, Jan. 1962. Also see Arnold Muirhead, "Portrait of a Bibliophile," *Book Collector*, Winter 1962; and G. J. Dohrmann, "Fulton and Penicillin," *Surgical Neurology*, May 1975. Obituaries include Paul Bucy, *Archives of Neurology*, Nov. 1960; G. E. Hutchinson, *Yearbook of the American Philo-sophical Society*, 1960; P. D. MacLean, *Yale Journal of Biology and Medicine*, Oct. 1960; H. E. Hoff, *American Oxonian*, Jan. 1961; and L. G. Stevenson, *Bulletin of the History of Medicine*, Jan.–Feb. 1961. Dr. Gordon Shepherd graciously provided an assessment of Fulton's achievements.]

ELIZABETH H. THOMSON

GABLE, (WILLIAM) CLARK (Feb. 1, 1901–Nov. 16, 1960), actor, was born in Cadiz, Ohio, the son of William H. Gable, an oil driller and farmer, and of Adeline Hershelman. His mother died when he was seven months old, and he was left in the care of his maternal grandparents. After William Gable remarried in 1903, Clark joined his father and stepmother, Jennie Dunlap, in Hopedale, Ohio. After completing two years at Edinburg High School, he went to Akron, Ohio, with a friend. While working at an Akron tire factory, he saw a play, *The Bird of Paradise,* and was so fascinated by the scenery and costumes that he decided to become an actor. Not long thereafter he took an unsalaried position as a backstage callboy with a local stock company.

After his stepmother died in 1919, Gable reluctantly joined his father in the Oklahoma oil fields. In 1922 he became a member of a traveling troupe, the Jewell Players. The company folded two months later in Montana and Gable, almost penniless, hitchhiked to Oregon. In 1924, after working at various odd jobs, he joined a Portland, Oreg., theater group directed by Josephine Dillon. "For the first time," he later recalled, "I learned about acting."

On Dec. 13, 1924, Gable married Josephine Dillon. After working as a film extra in Hollywood, he appeared in a touring production of *Romeo and Juliet* and played the juvenile lead in Lionel Barrymore's production of *The Copperhead.* He then headed for Broadway. The virile charm he exhibited in Sophie Treadwell's play *Machinal* (1928) won him good reviews and a favorable audience reaction. In 1930 Gable's marriage ended in divorce; the same year he married Rhea Langham, a wealthy Texas socialite.

Returning to the West Coast in 1930, Gable won acclaim for his portrayal of Killer Mears in the Los Angeles stage production of *The Last Mile.* This led to a movie role, again as a "heavy," in *The Painted Desert,* starring William Boyd (1931). Gable made his debut as a leading man opposite Joan Crawford in *Dance, Fools, Dance* (1931). With Norma Shearer in *A Free Soul* (1931), he was described by one critic as "a fascinating villain" who had convinced the female customers that he was "naughty but nice."

Making a dozen films in 1931 alone, Gable went from an unknown extra to a star. His performances (mostly for Metro-Goldwyn-Mayer) in such films as *Susan Lennox—Her Rise and Fall* (1931), *Possessed* (1931), *Hell Divers* (1931), *Polly of the Circus* (1932), *Strange Interlude* (1932), *Red Dust* (1932), *No Man of Her Own* (1932), *The White Sister* (1933), *Hold Your Man* (1933), *Night Flight* (1933), and *Dancing Lady* (1933) were opposite such leading ladies as Marion Davies, Greta Garbo, Norma Shearer,

Jean Harlow, Carole Lombard, Helen Hayes, and Joan Crawford. A victim of typecasting, Gable was often given the role of a "heavy" with redeeming traits.

After finishing *Dancing Lady,* Gable was hospitalized for exhaustion. When he refused to play another "gigolo role," as he called them, the MGM authorities decided to discipline him by loaning him to Columbia for a Frank Capra comedy, *It Happened One Night* (1934). In this film Gable, relaxed and casual, established himself as a fine comedian. Both he and his leading lady, Claudette Colbert, won the Academy Award for their performances. Having escaped the typecasting net, Gable was now offered a wider range of parts. Back at MGM, he gave another outstanding performance as Fletcher Christian in *Mutiny on the Bounty* (1935).

From 1935 to 1940 Gable was at his peak. As one of MGM's top stars, he appeared in a series of major films: *Call of the Wild* (1935), *San Francisco* (1936), *Test Pilot* (1938), *Too Hot to Handle* (1938), *Idiot's Delight* (1939), and, finally, as Rhett Butler in *Gone with the Wind,* the Civil War epic that has become a screen classic. Released in 1939, *Gone with the Wind* was his greatest film; it made Gable the "King of Hollywood." To millions the tall, handsome man with the moustache, broad shoulders, gray eyes, and brown hair was a romantic idol and the symbol of masculinity.

On Mar. 29, 1939, following his second divorce, Gable married actress Carole Lombard. Less than three years later she was killed in a plane crash while returning to Hollywood from a war-bond-selling tour. Shortly after her death Gable announced that as soon as production of his current film—ironically titled *Somewhere I'll Find You* (1942)—was finished, he would join the Army Air Forces as a private. Forty-one years old at the time of his enlistment, he flew on five bombing missions over Germany and made a training film on aerial gunnery. Before his discharge in June 1944, he rose to the temporary rank of major.

Gable immediately resumed his movie career. His first postwar film was *Adventure* (1945), with Greer Garson. Although a forgettable romance, the film made money because millions of filmgoers were eager to see Gable again. The momentum of his great days in the 1930's and early 1940's carried him through a new series of MGM films, many of which were undistinguished—*The Hucksters* (1947), *Homecoming* (1948), *Command Decision* (1948), *Key to the City* (1950), *Across the Wide Missouri* (1951), *Lone Star* (1952), *Never Let Me Go* (1953), and *Mogambo* (1953). On Dec. 20, 1949, Gable married Lady Sylvia Ashley; they were divorced in 1952.

Gable left MGM in 1954 and at once became the most expensive free-lance actor in the industry. *Soldier of Fortune* and *The Tall Men*, both made for 20th Century-Fox in 1955, helped restore his image, which had become rather faded during the past decade. On July 11, 1955, he married Kay Williams Spreckels, whom he had known since the mid-1930's. They had one son. Then followed such films as *Run Silent, Run Deep* (1958), *Teacher's Pet* (1958), *But Not for Me* (1959), and *It Started in Naples* (1960). The last three of these, comedies made for Paramount, were reminiscent of the glossy humor of his movies with Myrna Loy and Claudette Colbert in the 1930's. Two days after the completion of his last film, *The Misfits*, in which he gave one of his finest characterizations, Gable suffered a heart attack. He died in Hollywood, Calif.

Gable appeared in sixty-seven motion pictures. From 1932 through 1942, he was among the top ten money-making stars in each of the annual surveys made by *Motion Picture Herald*. In 1945, after his three-year absence from the screen, he was still among the top ten male favorites in a *Boxoffice* poll. For a quarter of a century, his persuasive charm drew moviegoers by the millions. He had something for everyone—for women he was the great lover, and for men he was a man's man. During his heyday theater marquees had only to announce: "This week: Clark Gable."

[See Dan C. Fowler, "Clark Gable," *Look,* July 8, 1947; Carlos Clarens, "Clark Gable," *Films in Review,* Dec. 1960; George Carpozi, Jr., *Clark Gable* (1961); Jean Garceau, with Inez Cocke, *Dear Mr. G.* (1961); Charles Samuels, *The King* (1962); Gabe Essoe and Ray Lee, comps., *Gable* (1967); Gabe Essoe, *The Films of Clark Gable* (1970), with photographs; James Robert Parish and Ronald L. Bowers, *The MGM Stock Company* (1970), pp. 223–232; Alexander Walker, *Stardom* (1970), pp. 298–311; René Jordan, *Clark Gable* (1973), with photographs; Gavin Lambert, *GWTW* (1973); Warren G. Harris, *Gable and Lombard* (1974); and Lyn Tornabene, *Long Live the King* (1976).]

L. MOODY SIMMS, JR.

GANNETT, FRANK ERNEST (Sept. 15, 1876–Dec. 3, 1957), journalist and publisher, was born in Bristol, N.Y., the son of Joseph

Charles Gannett, a farmer who later became proprietor of several hotels, and Maria Brooks. He won a scholarship to Cornell University, where he worked on the college newspaper but in his junior year concentrated on a paying job as the campus correspondent for the *Ithaca Journal*. During the summer following his junior year, he worked for the *Syracuse Herald*.

Gannett graduated from Cornell with the B.A. degree in 1898. The following year he served as secretary to Cornell president Jacob G. Schurman, chairman of the first Philippine Commission (1899). Gannett was asked to serve as secretary to William Howard Taft, chairman of the second Philippine Commission, but instead became editor of the *Cornell Alumni News* (1900). In the same year he was hired as city editor of the *Ithaca Daily News*, and shortly afterward was named managing editor and business manager. For some months he served as editor of the *Pittsburgh Index,* then became part owner of the *Elmira* (N.Y.) *Gazette* (1906), which subsequently merged with the *Elmira Evening Star*.

In 1912 Gannett purchased the *Ithaca Journal*, which he consolidated with the *Ithaca News* in 1919. With his associates from the *Elmira Star-Gazette* he bought the *Union and Advertiser* and the *Evening Times* of Rochester, N.Y., which became the *Rochester Times-Union*. In 1921 the group purchased two Utica papers that merged as the *Utica Observer-Dispatch*, and two years later they acquired the *Elmira Advertiser* and its Sunday edition, the *Elmira Telegram*. By 1924 Gannett had purchased the interests of his associates and, mainly in the next decade, acquired many more papers, largely in upstate New York (Newburgh, Olean, Ogdensburg, Albany, Malone, Saratoga, Massena, Niagara Falls) but also downstate (Brooklyn) and in New Jersey, Illinois, and Connecticut. Over a period of forty years he acquired twenty-seven newspapers and tried, unsuccessfully, to buy others, including the *Indianapolis News*, the *Detroit Free Press*, the *Washington Post*, the *Philadelphia Inquirer*, the *Cleveland Plain Dealer*, the *Boston Herald*, and the *Chicago Daily News*. However, he never founded a newspaper.

On Mar. 25, 1920, Gannett married Caroline Werner; they had two children. He made Rochester, N.Y., the headquarters for his chain, and the *Rochester Times-Union* became the paper to which he devoted most of his time. Although Gannett kept an eye on all of his papers, he was prone to leave management and editorial policy largely to the local staff—at least when they did not stray too far from his standard of efficiency and his own editorial policy.

At first Gannett was not warmly received in Rochester. He was frequently viewed as too vigorous—even brash. He supported the Democratic position on the League of Nations in 1920 and the Democratic candidate for president, James M. Cox. Also, he frequently took on Rochester's Republican boss, George W. Aldridge. In addition, Gannett supported labor unions and public ownership of utilities. His eventual acceptance by the city leaders, including George Eastman, probably was influenced by his vigorous stand in favor of Prohibition and particularly by his purchase of the *Rochester Democrat and Chronicle* before it was snapped up by the Hearst chain of newspapers. Gannett was one of the first in Rochester to back pioneer radio. He devoted much of his time to the development of Rochester's Unitarian Church.

Although Gannett and his papers were normally Republican, he praised the New Deal in its first months (and lamented the intransigence of Republican opposition). In time, however, he turned against the New Deal, especially its labor and agriculture policies. When President Franklin D. Roosevelt attempted to pack the Supreme Court in 1937, Gannett opposed him strongly. He organized the Committee to Uphold Constitutional Government, which probably was the foremost pressure group in the nation that successfully opposed the plan. Gannett further used the organization to oppose Roosevelt's national government reorganization plans in 1939. Throughout the New Deal years he criticized the alleged Keynesian influence on the administration in Washington.

Bitten by the political bug, Gannett deluded himself into seeking the Republican nomination for president in 1940. In the process he garnered the support of Congressman James W. Wadsworth, of his congressional district, who nominated him at the national convention. When the convention selected Wendell Willkie, however, Gannett and most of his papers supported him. For a short time in 1942, Gannett served as vice-chairman of the Republican National Committee.

Gannett died in Rochester, N.Y. He left a legacy of vigorous newspaper management marked by efficiency and professionalism. Although his papers lacked the élan of big city publications, they did bring to their readers the wire services and syndicated columns of the large metropolitan areas. His professionalism was felt beyond his own newspapers, for he served as a director of the Associated Press and president of the New York State Publishers Association, New York Associated Dailies, and New York Press Association. The Frank E. Gannett Newspaper Foundation upon his death became the controlling stockholder of the Gannett Company, continued the publication of the Gannett papers, and allocated a portion of its profits for education and philanthropic organizations.

[Gannett wrote *Industrial and Labor Relations in Great Britain* (1939), *Britain Sees It Through* (1944), *The Fuse Sputters in Europe* (1946), and *Winging Round the World* (1947). Also see Samuel T. Williamson, *Frank Gannett, a Biography* (1940); Blake McKelvey: *Rochester, the Quest for Quality, 1890–1925* (1956), pp. 313–373, *passim.*; *Rochester, an Emerging Metropolis, 1925–1961* (1961), *passim.*; *Rochester on the Genesee, the Growth of a City* (1973), pp. 166, 169, 184, 200, 202, 210, 247; and an obituary in the *Rochester Democrat and Chronicle*, Dec. 4, 1957.]

MARTIN L. FAUSOLD

GARRETT, FINIS JAMES (Aug. 26, 1875–May 25, 1956), legislator and federal judge, was born near Ore Springs, Weakley County, Tenn., the son of Noah James Garrett, a farmer, and Virginia Baughman. He attended rural public schools, Clinton Academy, Clinton, Tenn., and Bethel College, McKenzie, Tenn., from which he graduated with the A.B. in 1897. While a student he learned the printer's trade, and became editor of the *Weakley County Democrat* and the *McKenzie Herald*. Between 1897 and 1899 he served as principal of Como (Tenn.) High School, taught in Milan, Tenn., and read law to prepare for the Tennessee state bar examination. For the next five years he practiced law in Dresden, Tenn., and was master in chancery. Garrett married Elizabeth Harris Burns on Nov. 27, 1901; they had two children.

In 1905 he was elected to the United States House of Representatives for the Ninth Congressional District of Tennessee on the Democratic ticket, and held that seat for the next twenty-four years. While serving on the Rules, Insular Affairs, and several select committees, Garrett voiced opinions on many governmental concerns. His crusade for Philippine independence was an issue he kept before the public. Fiscal conservatism appealed to him, and he worked to obtain sound budgets. He voted the party line on such national issues as woman suffrage, the World War I bonus, child labor legislation, the Fordney-McCumber tariff of 1922, and anti-lynching laws, as well as military appropriations. A stalwart defender of Woodrow Wilson's philosophy, he favored United States involvement in the League of Nations. Wilson once described him as "the strongest man in our ranks."

After World War I, Garrett spoke throughout the nation, promoting the idea that the Democratic party was the only party that could provide the leadership needed in the future. In 1921 Garrett was appointed as a federal judge for western Tennessee, but the Republican-controlled Senate Judiciary Committee refused to grant approval. As the acting House minority leader in 1921, he spoke vigorously and often against the Republican voting record, which he termed a "disgraceful and distressing failure."

During the administrations of Warren Harding and Calvin Coolidge, Garrett continued his attacks in Congress and at Democratic party rallies, emphasizing the need for national rather than sectional growth of the Democratic party. His speeches, although at times lengthy and referring to matters other than politics, were scathing commentaries on Republican failures to solve national problems. He strongly believed, however, that there should be a halt in the mad rush toward "centralization of governmental functions." A states' righter, Garrett felt that federal control of state obligations would lead to excessive dependence on Washington's ability to provide equally for all local needs.

During the 1926 Congressional campaign, in which he expressed opposition to Gilbert N. Haugen's bill for farm relief, Garrett's usually safe majority was cut to several hundred votes. Two years later he challenged the incumbent senator, Kenneth McKellar, a popular vote-getter, especially with labor. Garrett was defeated in the primaries, and his supporters claimed that party machine activity and voting frauds in Memphis and in Shelby County on behalf of his opponent were the deciding factors in the contest.

Shortly before he was to leave office in 1929, President Coolidge offered Garrett the post of associate judge on the Federal Court of Customs and Patent Appeals. He was formally appointed on Mar. 5, 1929, and served in this capacity for the next twenty-six years. When he was not occupied with judicial duties, he lectured on such nonpartisan issues as fiscal responsibility, the importance of democracy, and patriotism. On Dec. 9, 1937,

President Franklin D. Roosevelt elevated Garrett to presiding judge, a post he retained until his retirement in 1955. He died in Washington, D.C.

A man of gentle wit who showed fairness toward all parties, Garrett was appreciated for his contributions to the making and the enforcement of the law. His great regret was that more people were not aware of the importance of the branch of the federal judiciary in which he had served.

[Private papers and correspondence of Garrett are on microfilm in the library of Bethel College, McKenzie, Tenn. Scattered articles about him are in the *New York Times*, 1917–1956 (esp. 1917–1929). Major sources of information are the cumulative *Congressional Directory*, 1905–1929; the *Congressional Record* of the same period; and the reports of the United States Court of Customs and Patent Appeals, 1929–1955, with a special section devoted to the retirement ceremony and a dedicatory page at the time of Garrett's death.]

JOSEPH P. ZACCANO, JR.

GASTON, HERBERT EARLE (Aug. 20, 1881–Dec. 7, 1956), journalist, government official, and banking executive, was born in Halsey, Oreg., the son of William Hawks Gaston, a merchant and farmer, and Maria Glasgow Irvine. He attended schools in Tacoma, Wash., and studied at the University of Washington (1903–1904) and the University of Chicago (1904–1906). While in high school, Gaston began a career in newspaper work that was eventually to provide him with an entrée into the political arena. His first jobs were on papers in Tacoma, Seattle, and Chicago as reporter, printer, and as assistant city editor on the *Tacoma Tribune*. Between 1898 and 1910 Gaston was employed as well by the *West Coast Trade* (Tacoma), the *Seattle Times*, the *Tacoma Ledger*, and the *Chicago Record-Herald*. On Oct. 16, 1907, he married Ethel Bell. They had two children.

From 1910 to 1916 Gaston was assistant editor of the *Spokane Chronicle*. He was then hired as editor of the *Nonpartisan Leader* in Fargo, N.D. The following year he edited the *Fargo Courier-News* and then continued work with the Nonpartisan League from 1918 to 1920. He helped to establish the *Minneapolis Star* and became its first editor and publisher in 1920. Later that year he published his only book, *The Nonpartisan League*. His departure, two years later, from the league and the *Star* resulted from a rift with members who criticized his attack on gambling interests in the Twin Cities.

Gaston subsequently moved to New York City, where he became a staff member of the *New York World*, remaining with the paper until it ceased publication in 1931; from 1929 until its closing he was night editor. Among those who noticed his work on the *World* was Henry Morgenthau, Jr., who was then New York State commissioner of conservation. After the newspaper folded, Gaston went to work for Morgenthau as secretary of the New York State Conservation Department. He was appointed deputy commissioner of the department within a year. In his study of the Morgenthau diaries, John Morton Blum wrote that Gaston, along with Morgenthau's general counsel Herman Oliphant, was considered "the most dependable of Morgenthau's subordinates."

From state service Gaston went on to hold several posts within the federal government, beginning as secretary of the Federal Farm Board and deputy governor of the U.S. Farm Credit Administration, both before the end of 1933. In November of that year he was appointed special assistant to Morgenthau, in which post he handled matters of public relations. At that time Gaston was characterized in *The New Dealers* as having a political pedigree that "suggests the real lineage of the New Deal. He was a Roosevelt Republican under 'Teddy,' a Bull-Mooser in 1912, then a Wilsonite, then a Socialist, then a LaFollette independent in 1924, an Al Smith man in 1928, and finally a Roosevelt Liberal. . . . Morgenthau leans on him heavily in matters of public policy as well as public relations."

In 1939 Gaston became assistant secretary of the treasury under Morgenthau, with jurisdiction over the coast guard, the Secret Service, and the Bureau of Narcotics. Also that year he served as delegate to the first Conference of American Treasuries in Guatemala. He remained in the Treasury Department until 1945, when he became vice-chairman and director of the Export-Import Bank. Gaston succeeded William McChesney Martin, Jr., as bank president and chairman in 1949, retaining both posts until his retirement from government service in 1953.

Gaston had a variety of other positions on government boards and committees. From 1940 to 1945 he was a member of the Interdepartmental Committee on Cooperation With American Republics. At this time President Roosevelt was beginning to concern himself with hemi-spheric defense against the Axis powers. One of Gaston's recommendations resulted in the extension of gold loans to strengthen the monetary systems of Latin American countries. His background in journalism led to a position as secretary of the Board of War Communications (1941–1945). From 1942 to 1947 he presided over the Interdepartmental Committee on Employee Investigation, and in 1946 he was an alternate member of the Cabinet Committee on Palestine in London. He died in Los Angeles, Calif.

[See John Franklin Carter, *The New Dealers* (1934); the obituary notice, *New York Times*, Dec. 9, 1956; and John Morton Blum, *Years of Urgency, 1938–1941, From the Morgenthau Diaries* (1964).]

HARVARD SITKOFF

GAUSS, CLARENCE EDWARD (Jan. 12, 1887–Apr. 8, 1960), career diplomat, was born in Washington, D.C., the son of Herman Gauss (pronounced "Goss"), a government official, and Emilie Julia Eisenman. He graduated from Business High School in Washington and received private tutoring before becoming a clerk in the law firm of John M. Thurston (1903–1906). He also worked as a stenographer for the Invalid Pensions Committee of Congress (1903–1905). On Aug. 2, 1906, Gauss began his diplomatic career as a clerk in the Department of State with an annual salary of $900.

Gauss's diplomatic service abroad began and ended in China. He was first assigned as a deputy consul general at Shanghai (1907–1909), although he could not (and never did) communicate in Chinese. In 1912, after duty at the consular school in Washington and after passing his Foreign Service examinations, he returned to the consulate in Shanghai. In four years at that post he sought to protect and extend American economic interests. In 1913 Gauss earned an "excellent" rating from a State Department inspection team that found him to be a "tireless worker." Thereafter he was stationed at Tientsin (consul, 1916), Amoy (consul, 1916–1919), Tsinan (consul, 1919–1923), Mukden (consul general, 1923–1924), Tientsin (consul general, 1924–1926, 1927–1931), and Shanghai (consul general, 1926–1927). On Feb. 3, 1917, he married Rebecca Louise Barker; they had one son. An inspection report for Gauss in that year rated him "excellent" (96 of 100 points) and described him as one of the "ablest" and "most efficient" officers in the consular service, noting his high standing in "force, decision, discretion, and dignity."

After a two-year stint at the State Department (1931–1933), Gauss served as counselor of the legation at Peiping (1933–1935). For much of 1935 he held the post of consul general and counselor of the embassy in Paris. His next assignment, as consul general in Shanghai and counselor of the embassy in China (1935–1940), enhanced Gauss's reputation as an efficient and tough-minded diplomat. They were exhausting years, for he lived in the path of Japanese expansion. Bombs exploded perilously close to his quarters, and in 1937 he often toiled eighteen hours a day to evacuate hundreds of Americans to Manila. Gauss argued vigorously and sometimes successfully with Japanese officials who abused Americans or seized American property. He became president of the Court of Consuls and the recognized leader of Shanghai's besieged International Settlement.

His appointment as the first minister to Australia was an appreciated respite (1940–1941). Hardly settled in Canberra, however, Gauss was sent as ambassador to China in February 1941. Until his controversial retirement from that position in November 1944, he struggled to keep a divided China fighting against Japan and to unite the warring factions: the nationalists of Chiang Kai-shek and the communists of Mao Tse-tung. It was an embittering experience fraught with problems that stemmed from Gauss's personal style, the corruption and arrogance of the Chiang regime, the civil war, the war against Japan and the ambassador's relations with the American military, and President Franklin D. Roosevelt's conduct of foreign affairs by special emissaries in China.

Although respected for his professional skills, Gauss impressed most people as chilly. He was a formidable figure—in charge of the facts, meticulous, demanding, frank, and incorruptible—but he was sometimes cranky and never comfortable in relaxed conversation; when he spoke, he did so precisely and briefly. Far Eastern expert Stanley K. Hornbeck said Gauss was "hard to fool." Among those who worked with him, John Service commented on his "soldier's sense of duty," and John Paton Davies described him as "an intense man, shoulders humped forward from years of leaning over a desk, thin mouth turned down at the corners in near sneer, eyes a prismed blur as they peered out through thick lenses." Lacking the college education and social standing of many of his Foreign Service colleagues, Gauss felt uneasy at social gatherings and entertained infrequently. He seemed also to have placed a wall between himself and the Chinese.

Davies recalled the atmosphere surrounding one luncheon with Gauss as "gloomy" and "carping." There were good reasons. Many Chinese government officials were notoriously corrupt, and paid little attention to such serious problems as land reform and inflation. Gauss did not conceal his criticism of Chiang's mismanagement, nor did he indulge in the flattery Chiang desired. He often warned Washington against Chiang's propaganda, especially his exaggerated claims of success against the Japanese.

When China asked the United States for a $500 million loan in December 1941, Gauss favored a smaller amount, advising that Chiang would misuse funds unless they were tied to specific projects. Too much of the money, he predicted, would be pocketed by "self-seeking" elements. Washington granted the loan, however, without restrictions. In mid-1942 Chiang issued his "Three Demands" for an increase in American military aid, hinting that he might sign a separate peace with Japan. Gauss considered this a bluff, but Washington took the matter more seriously. Against Gauss's advice, Secretary of State Cordell Hull ended America's special right of extraterritoriality in 1943. Late in 1943 Chiang demanded a loan of one billion dollars. Gauss wrote to Washington: "We should maintain a firm position declining to be coerced by petulant gestures or threats." Secretary of the Treasury Henry Morgenthau, Jr., agreed and the loan request was rejected. The animosity between Gauss and Chiang grew. In August 1944, Gauss suggested to Chiang that he make a start toward broadening his government by including communists in a coalition war council. Chiang rejected the idea, and Gauss sadly reported that the Chinese leader was more interested in disposing of his opposition than in reconciling it. Gauss astutely foresaw the steady disintegration of Chiang's regime and the communist assumption of power. Yet, like most Americans, he did not welcome the prospect of a communist China, which he believed might become aligned with the Soviet Union. He thus reflected the American dilemma in China: he wanted neither Chiang nor Mao.

President Roosevelt helped further undermine

what little influence Gauss had in Chinese-American relations. The special presidential missions of Lauchlin Currie, Wendell Willkie, Henry Wallace, Donald Nelson, and Patrick Hurley bypassed Gauss's embassy and often failed to provide diplomatic information to the ambassador, thus stimulating rumors that Gauss would be replaced. Gauss complained that Gen. Joseph W. Stilwell, Chiang's American chief of staff, frequently encroached upon his diplomatic responsibilities. As Davies noted, Roosevelt "behaved as if Gauss scarcely existed." Gauss resented his diminished authority and the confusion in decision making, especially when the headstrong Hurley arrived in the fall of 1944. In November Gauss submitted his resignation. It was a sour parting for this career diplomat who recognized that he had been humiliated for years. Yet, loyally, he never protested publicly. Gauss was also tired and ill; in 1943 he had to return home for medical treatment, and an eye infection blinded him for several months after he left China in 1944.

Despite Gauss's appeal for another assignment early in 1945, Roosevelt offered him retirement from the Foreign Service. He retired quietly on May 31, 1945. That December, President Harry S. Truman appointed him, as a nominal Republican member, to the board of the Export-Import Bank, an important instrument of United States Cold War diplomacy. He held this post until mid-1952. During this period he testified on Sino-American affairs before congressional committees, holding firm to his anticommunist views and to his argument that Chiang must reform his government as a prerequisite for American aid. In 1950, in answer to right-wing charges, he defended Foreign Service officer John Service as a competent reporter and analyst of Chinese affairs. Gauss also boldly called Hurley's claims that Service sought Chiang's collapse "a figment of an imagination which is seeking its own glorification. . . ."

Gauss was not an innovator, and he left no diplomatic monuments. Not a significant force in Chinese-American relations, he is remembered as an efficient, self-effacing, intelligent functionary who mastered his assignments, and a person of energy and integrity who did not seek headlines (seldom holding press conferences, for example). Gauss defended American interests in China but did not share the opinion of some that China could be elevated to great power status under Chiang. Many scholars agree that his prognostications and

proposals were correct. He ultimately perceived what many Americans did not: that China under Chiang was a problem the United States could not solve.

[Papers pertaining to Gauss are in the Stanley K. Hornbeck Papers (Hoover Institution on War, Revolution and Peace, Stanford, Calif.), Nelson T. Johnson Papers (Library of Congress), Department of State Records (National Archives), and Department of State, *Foreign Relations of the United States* series (volumes by year and subject). The Department of State Records also contain inspection reports on the posts to which he was assigned. For an outline of Gauss's career, see James L. Durrence, "Ambassador Clarence E. Gauss and United States Relations with China, 1941–1944" (Ph.D. diss., University of Georgia, 1971). References to Gauss are in Department of State, *United States Relations with China* (1949); John Paton Davies, *Dragon by the Tail* (1972); John S. Service, *The Amerasia Papers* (1971); Barbara Tuchman, *Stilwell and the American Experience in China, 1911–45* (1971); and John Carter Vincent, *The Extraterritorial System in China: Final Phase* (1970).]

THOMAS G. PATERSON

GAUVREAU, EMILE HENRY (Feb. 4, 1891–Oct. 15, 1956), newspaper editor, was born in Centerville, Conn., the son of French-Canadian immigrants, Alphonse Gauvreau, who worked in an arms factory, and Malvina Perron.

When Gauvreau was six, his right leg was crippled in a traumatic incident. He later credited the handicap with turning his interests toward literature and music. For a time the family returned to Canada and he was educated at the Jesuit-run Provencher Academy in Montreal. When the Gauvreaus returned to the United States, he entered public schools.

At the age of eighteen, Gauvreau abandoned both high school and study as a flutist to work on the New Haven *Journal-Courier*. As a cub reporter he evinced tenacity and a talent for developing sensational news. He exposed officials who were taking graft from prostitutes, and later solved a murder that had baffled the police. The latter achievement won him a standing offer from Clifton L. Sherman, managing editor of the *Hartford Courant*; and in August 1916, Gauvreau moved to that city. Before leaving New Haven he married Sarah Welles Joyner, the *Journal-Courier* society editor. They had three children and were divorced in 1936.

Gauvreau's tenure at the *Courant* was spotted with controversy. As a reporter, the *Courant* historian has written, he "attracted off-beat news as a magnet attracts iron filings." With many exclusives to his credit, he rose to assistant managing editor and, following Sherman's resignation in September 1919, to managing editor. His vigorous, somewhat sensational news policies placed him in conflict with Charles Hopkins Clark, majority stockholder and editor in chief. When Gauvreau refused to terminate a series of stories about a traffic in fake medical diplomas, Clark forced him to resign.

Gauvreau then went to New York and, almost by chance, was hired by physical culturist and publisher Bernarr Macfadden to organize a daily newspaper, which appeared on Sept. 15, 1924, as the *New York Evening Graphic*. The *Graphic* was bizarre even in the "jazz journalism" era; its tone was lurid and it employed such techniques as the "composograph," a manufactured illustration that looked like a photograph. Gauvreau struggled for five years to put the *Graphic* on a high-circulation, profitable basis, but it was a losing battle.

He left the *Graphic* long before its 1932 closing, hired away by William Randolph Hearst in 1929 to work on the *New York Mirror*. As managing editor, Gauvreau found himself again in a circulation contest against the more successful *New York Daily News*. As a result, the *Mirror* paid less attention to news than to scandal, racing information, and promotional contests; its star was the Broadway columnist Walter Winchell, with whom Gauvreau was not on speaking terms, and about whom he wrote a novel, *The Scandal Monger*. Nor did he work smoothly with Arthur Brisbane, whom Hearst installed as editor in 1934. In 1935 Gauvreau published *What So Proudly We Hailed*, which contrasted the Soviet Union, as he had seen it as an observer on a congressional mission in 1933, and America. Hearst mistakenly believed the work to be procommunist, and Gauvreau was fired.

A friend, Representative William I. Sirovich of New York, then obtained Gauvreau a position as staff investigator for the House Committee on Patents. One assignment dealt with patent pooling in the aircraft industry; this inquiry led to his acquaintance with and admiration of General William Mitchell, the advocate of air power who had been court-martialed for expressing his opinions. Gauvreau was coauthor of a biography of Mitchell (1942), who died in 1936.

Late in 1936, Gauvreau went to work at the *Philadelphia Inquirer*, which had been acquired by the racing-news magnate Moses Annenberg.

Placed in charge of the rotogravure section, Gauvreau produced features in the gaudiest Sunday-supplement tradition. In 1938 Annenberg named Gauvreau editor of *Click*, one of many picture magazines founded in the late 1930's. Underpaid and overloaded with assignments, he resigned in 1940, following a conflict with management over his secretary's wages.

After his divorce from his first wife, Gauvreau married Winifred C. Rollins, who had been his secretary at the *Mirror*, on Dec. 5, 1936. In his later years he was handicapped by a deteriorative brain condition. He died in Suffolk, Va. In his autobiography Gauvreau wrote that he was one of those "spending their lives doing things they detest." He might have held his work in less contempt had he not been employed by a succession of irresponsible publishers. Nevertheless, he established a reputation as a skilled practitioner of a flawed trade.

[Gauvreau's autobiography, *My Last Million Readers* (1941), is the chief source for his life. His other writings include two novels, *Hot News* (1931) and *The Scandal Monger* (1932); *What So Proudly We Hailed* (1935); *Billy Mitchell* (1942), written with Lester Cohen; *The Wild Blue Yonder* (1944); and *Dumbbells and Carrot Strips—The Life and Times of Bernarr Macfadden* (1953),written with Mary Macfadden. His newspaper work is described in John Bard McNulty, *Older Than the Nation; The Story of the Hartford Courant* (1964), pp. 164–173; and Lester Cohen, *The New York Graphic* (1964). An obituary, with a portrait by James Montgomery Flagg, appears in the *New York Times*, Oct. 17, 1956.]

JAMES BOYLAN

GEDDES, NORMAN BEL (Apr. 27, 1893–May 8, 1958), theatrical and industrial designer, was born Norman Melancton Geddes in Adrian, Mich. He was the son of Clifton Terry Geddes, a businessman, and Flora Luella Yingling. In 1899 the family moved to Pittsburgh, where Clifton Geddes had invested in real estate; however, by 1901 he lost all of his money and they moved back to the Midwest. When Clifton Geddes left his wife, she and young Norman moved to Newcomerstown, Ohio, to live with her parents. Norman sold newspapers and worked in his uncle's grocery store. When his mother was able to rent a small house, he set up a studio in an attic room and began to paint.

Geddes was expelled from Newcomerstown High School at the age of fourteen for having drawn a caricature of the principal. When he later moved to New Philadelphia, Ohio, where his mother had moved, he was again expelled for sketching caricatures of school officials. A newspaper cartoonist, James H. Donahey, who had been through a similar experience at the same school, heard of the incident and invited Geddes to Cleveland, where he enrolled him in the Cleveland School of Art. Geddes remained in Cleveland for a few months and later attended the Art Institute of Chicago for about two months. In Chicago he first became familiar with the work of Matisse, Picasso, Cézanne, and Van Gogh. He also studied portraiture with the Norwegian Hendrick Lund.

After high school Geddes worked during the summer as a bellboy on a Lake Erie steamer, where he was taught magic by Howard Thurston, a professional magician. In 1913 he toured the Sun Gus Vaudeville Circuit as "Zedsky the Boy Magician"; and in 1914–1915 he toured the same circuit as Bob Blake, the "Eccentric Comedian." These brief forays were the full extent of his career as a performer.

In 1912 Geddes became an apprentice at the Peninsular Engraving Co. in Detroit. He won several design awards and was named director of the art department. He became general manager of Barnes Crosby Company, an advertising firm, in 1914. His work failed to satisfy his creative ambitions, so he wrote a play, *Thunderbird*, and went to New York City to try to get it produced. Producer David Belasco turned Geddes away, but referred him to Aline Barnsdall. She bought the play, and in 1915 Geddes quit his job in Detroit and moved to Los Angeles, where he planned to assist in the play's production. On Mar. 9, 1916, Geddes married Helen Belle Sneider; in order to celebrate the union Geddes changed his name to Norman Bel Geddes. They had two daughters, one of whom, Barbara, became the well-known actress. This marriage ended in divorce.

In Los Angeles Geddes worked with Barnsdall's Little Theater. Although *Thunderbird* was never produced, Geddes designed scenery, costumes, and lighting, and was able to put some of his innovative ideas into practice. His new techniques for stage lighting included eliminating footlights and installing high-intensity bulbs on the front of the theater balcony, a method that later became standard.

In 1917 Geddes heard about Otto Kahn, the wealthy banker who often financed promising young artists. He spent $4.80 of his last $7.00 to wire Kahn and ask for a $200 loan. Geddes used the money he received from Kahn for a trip to New York City. On Kahn's recommendation, Geddes was hired by the Metropolitan Opera Company the following year to do the costumes and scenery for *Shanewis*, an American opera by Charles W. Cadman. During the next twenty years Geddes designed about a hundred operatic, dramatic, and musical comedy productions. Some of his early productions included *Erminie* (1920); *The Truth About Blayds* (1921), starring Leslie Howard; and *The Rivals* (1922). Geddes' lighting for these productions was so successful that he was commissioned to redesign the electrical system of the Little Theater and the Booth Theater, both in New York City. He installed 1,000-watt lights in each house and hung some of his lamps on the front of the balcony. Despite some battles with older actresses who preferred the more flattering glow of footlights, Geddes continued with his innovative lighting. Historian Sheldon Cheney called his work "daring, inventive and flamingly imaginative." Along with Robert Edmond Jones and Lee Simonson, Geddes revolutionized the American theater by using costumes, scenery, and lighting to intensify the mood rather than merely to decorate the set. In 1923 Geddes collaborated with Max Reinhardt to stage *The Miracle*. For that vast production he converted the Century Theater into the likeness of a great cathedral, which the *New York Times* called "indescribably rich in color, unimaginably atmospheric in its lofty aerial spaces."

Around 1927 his interest turned to industrial design and by 1932 he had established Norman Bel Geddes & Co.—one of the first of such firms. He designed streamlined automobiles, passenger trains, and yachts; a vacuum cleaner; and a gasoline pump that registered prices. His philosophy was that function should determine form; as with his theatrical work, design effects were not merely decorative. By 1929 Geddes was also involved with architectural and landscape design. He designed about twenty-eight theaters in America and Europe and advised architects on exterior illuminations of buildings and grounds. Geddes' autobiography, *Horizons* (1932), illuminates his design theories.

On Mar. 3, 1933, he married Frances Resor Waite. Two years later he went into partnership with the architect George Howe. Also in 1935 Geddes produced the play *Dead End*, creating a starkly realistic set of a New York City street leading into the East River. A pier was constructed on the stage, and the orchestra pit was filled with water. This was his most commercially successful production.

In 1938 General Motors had Geddes design its 1939 New York World's Fair exhibit, which contained "Futurama," a futuristic design model of superhighways and cities. In the years 1940–1942, he modernized equipment and designed a tent without poles for the Ringling Brothers and Barnum and Bailey Circus, and his architectural firm designed a building for the Hayden Planetarium in New York City.

During World War II Geddes designed equipment for the Armed Forces and served on the National Inventors Council. On Dec. 20, 1944, he married Ann Howe Hilliard; they were divorced in 1950. On June 7, 1953, he married Edith Addams Lutyens Taylor. These two marriages were childless. A restless, gregarious individual, Geddes worked continually. He died in New York City.

[For more information, see Geddes' *A Project of a Theatrical Presentation of the Divine Comedy of Dante Alighieri* (1923); "Streamlining," *Atlantic Monthly,* Nov. 1934; *Magic Motorways* (1940) and *Miracle in the Evening* (1960); Lee Simonson's *Part of a Lifetime* (1943) and *The Art of Scenic Design* (1950); Sheldon Cheney, *The Theatre; Three Thousand Years of Drama, Acting and Stagecraft* (1952); Jo Mielziner, *Designing for the Theatre* (1965). See also the *New York Times:* review of *The Truth About Blayds*, Mar. 15, 1922, and of *Dead End,* Oct. 29, 1935; and obituary May 9, 1958.]

ELLIOT NORTON

GEORGE, WALTER FRANKLIN (Jan. 29,1878–Aug.4,1957), judge and U.S. senator, was born on a farm near Preston, Ga., the son of Robert Theodoric George and Sarah Stapleton. He received a bachelor's degree at Mercer University in 1900 and a law degree at Mercer the following year. He established a law practice at Vienna, Ga., in 1901 and maintained a residence there for the rest of his life. On July 9, 1903, he married Lucy Heard. They had two children. In 1907 George became solicitor general and, in 1912, judge of the Superior Court for the Cordele Judiciary Circuit of Georgia. In January 1917 he became judge of the Georgia Court of Appeals but resigned in October to become an associate justice of the Georgia Supreme Court. In 1922 he resigned his position and in November won his campaign to fill an unexpired term in the United

States Senate. Thereafter between 1926 and 1950 he was reelected five times.

George entered Congress as an old-fashioned Democrat, determined to defend the interests of the South. He favored stronger prohibition measures and opposed every effort on behalf of racial equality, including all antilynching laws. With the gracious manner of a Southern aristocrat—which he was not—and a resonant, compelling voice, he quickly emerged as one of the Senate's leading orators. He spoke seldom, but always with careful preparation and moving eloquence, and eventually became the country's leading exponent of the Southern congressional style. Friendly yet aloof, George was known from the beginning for his integrity and independence; his friends often designated him "the conscience of the Senate." Throughout his career he remained a conservative, and in time the Senate regarded him as its leading constitutional authority. After 1926, as a member of the tax-writing Finance Committee, he became the Senate's tax expert, leaving his imprint on every tax measure.

In 1928 George attended the Democratic National Convention at Houston as Georgia's "favorite son" candidate in opposition to New York's Alfred E. Smith. He opposed the liberal Franklin D. Roosevelt's nomination in 1932 but backed him during the campaign.

George supported much of the early New Deal but rebelled at some of its economic heresies, especially those that contributed to the power of labor. He opposed the wage-hours bill and denounced the industrial warfare of 1936 and 1937 as evidence of a declining respect for the law. His veneration for the Supreme Court compelled him to attack Roosevelt's court-packing plan of 1937. By 1938 he had piled up so extensive a record of resistance to the president's program that Roosevelt entered Georgia to campaign against George's reelection—an invasion that George termed "the second march through Georgia." Roosevelt met George at Barnesville, where he described him as a friend, a scholar, and a gentleman; but, he added, no liberal. Defending his allegiance to the Democratic Party, George accepted the challenge and conducted the campaign with his usual dignity and style. He won easily.

George favored the early neutrality legislation. In July 1939 he cast the deciding vote in the Foreign Relations Committee to terminate any further Senate consideration of Roosevelt's request for cash-and-carry sales to the European democracies in case of war. With Hitler's invasion of Poland less than two months later, George changed his mind on the question of aid, symbolizing the shift of conservative Southerners who had harassed the New Deal before 1938 to vigorous support of Roosevelt's post-1939 interventionist policies.

Following the death of Key Pittman in 1940, George became chairman of the Senate Foreign Relations Committee. In this role he backed Roosevelt's program of aid to Europe short of war. In 1941, before Pearl Harbor, George succeeded Pat Harrison of Mississippi as chairman of the Senate Finance Committee. Thereafter he managed the major wartime tax measures, including the pay-as-you-go income tax. Retaining his leadership role in foreign affairs, George supported the Connally Resolution of 1943, in which the Senate expressed its approval of general postwar international cooperation. As a member of the bipartisan Senate Committee of Eight, he urged Secretary of State Cordell Hull to continue his negotiations with foreign leaders on the creation of a postwar peace organization.

After the war George's concept of an honorable peace demanded opposition to Stalin, just as earlier it had required a war against Hitler. George supported NATO, but, in opposition to President Harry Truman, he insisted that the United States could not send troops to Europe without specific congressional approval. George's strong internationalism helped to shape the postwar world by assuring Senate support for the country's basic postwar international policies.

Like most conservative Southerners, George found his relations with Republican President Dwight D. Eisenhower far more harmonious than those with liberal Roosevelt and Truman. With the Democratic resurgence of 1954, he resumed the chairmanship of the Foreign Relations Committee, permitting his friend, Senator Harry F. Byrd of Virginia, to chair the Finance Committee. George helped to forge the strong bipartisan approach to foreign policy that characterized Eisenhower's first term. Secretary of State John Foster Dulles met privately with George at breakfast at least once a week to discuss foreign affairs. George prodded Eisenhower to attend the Geneva summit conference of 1955. His support of the administration's China policy was crucial. On Jan. 24, 1955, the administration had asked Congress for authorization to use

American forces to protect Formosa, if necessary, by defending the offshore islands against an assault from the mainland. Senator Hubert Humphrey of Minnesota attached an amendment to restrict the grant of authority to the more distant Formosa. George crushed the Democratic revolt by placing his prestige behind the administration's request. The president signed the Formosa Resolution on January 29. When George arrived for the ceremony, those present used the occasion to celebrate his seventy-seventh birthday.

Senate Democrats condemned George for denying them an independent role in the formulation of foreign policy. George was instrumental in inaugurating talks with Peking in 1955 by reminding Dulles that he could not satisfy those domestic groups that insisted on a Nationalist Chinese presence and still maintain United States leadership of the noncommunist world. In January 1956, George broke with the administration for the first time on the question of long-term foreign aid—largely because the issue was not popular in Georgia. Thereafter Dulles failed to gain his support for his Middle East policies. George believed the issues in that region too confused to identify a clear United States interest or to win the needed congressional support.

By the mid-1950's George had achieved a preeminent position in American political life. As president pro tempore of the Senate he could command any of that body's offices. Despite his independence, his colleagues regarded him as a good party man. On such critical issues as the Taft-Hartley Act he always supported the traditional Democratic stance. Nevertheless, as the 1956 senatorial campaign approached, George's friends warned him that he could not defeat the younger, more energetic, and more segregationist Governor Herman Talmadge. George had joined ninety-five other Southern members of Congress in pledging resistance to the Supreme Court's 1954 school desegregation decision, but he was growing more moderate on racial issues. His national leadership role, moreover, had weakened many of his ties to Georgia; one banker complained that he had not visited his country in eighteen years. Finally, in May 1956, George announced his retirement, declaring that another campaign would be too taxing. To prolong George's bipartisan role in foreign policy, Eisenhower appointed him ambassador to NATO, with headquarters in Washington. In

March 1957, George attended the Bermuda Conference between the president and British Prime Minister Harold Macmillan. He died in Vienna, Ga.

[As yet no biography or major study has appeared; still, during his lifetime George created a public record that, except for details, is scarcely hidden from view. *Current Biography Yearbook* for 1955 offers an excellent summary. *Who Was Who in America* contains vital statistics, as does the obituary notice, *New York Times*, Aug. 6, 1957. His congressional activity is recorded in the *Congressional Record*. The Columbia University Oral History Collection has a number of memoirs on George. See also *Newsweek, Time, Business Week,* and *U.S. News and World Report* (1953–1957).]

NORMAN A. GRAEBNER

GIBBS, (OLIVER) WOLCOTT (Mar. 15, 1902–Aug. 16, 1958), drama critic, author, and editor, was born in New York City, the son of Lucius Tuckerman Gibbs, an electrical engineer and inventor, and Angelica Singleton Duer. The direct descendant of Martin Van Buren and of Oliver Wolcott, Gibbs was born to social prominence and economic comfort but grew up in domestic chaos. His father died when he was six, and his mother, an alcoholic, lost custody of him and his only sister. The unhappy children were passed among relatives including their uncle George Gibbs, a distinguished electrical engineer, but a stern bachelor.

Gibbs attended Riverdale Country School, Bronx, N.Y., and the Hill School, in Pottstown, Pa. (1916–1919). A mediocre student, he was expelled for smoking in the chapel and in a "nearby cemetery." Gibbs remembered being an opinionated youth "substantially impossible to teach." To his later chagrin, he never went to college but drifted in and out of numerous jobs. He was an unpaid apprentice draftsman in the architectural firm of McKim, Mead, and White, an insurance clerk, a chauffeur, a timekeeper, and in 1923 a "gentleman brakeman" on the Long Island Railroad. To the horror of his family, Gibbs also drifted into a short-lived marriage with a railroad man's daughter. In 1924 he became a sports reporter for the Griscom chain of Long Island newspapers, where an important part of his job was playing tennis with the owner's weekend guests. By 1925 he was associate editor of the *East Norwich* (N.Y.) *Enterprise*. His odyssey ended in 1927, when his cousin, the novelist Alice Duer Miller, secured him a copyreading job on the

two-year-old *New Yorker*, where he remained until his death.

Gibbs became an associate editor in 1928 and along with the editor Harold W. Ross, James Thurber, and Katharine and E. B. White determined the young magazine's character, quality, and success. Gibbs's stern, sound, and witty judgments "helped form the magazine and shape its course." Thurber pronounced him "the best copy editor the *New Yorker* . . . ever had." In August 1929 Gibbs married Elizabeth Crawford, a promotion writer from the *New Yorker*'s advertising department—although his family thought she, too, was beneath his station. On Mar. 31, 1930, two days after seeing *Death Takes a Holiday* and after morbidly discussing that play, she jumped to her death from their seventeenth-floor apartment. Severely shocked by her suicide, Gibbs obtained psychiatric help and returned to the *New Yorker* "with a darker view of life" and "less confidence in himself."

Gibbs was a high-strung man at war with the world, a tortured soul with "a hard ball of panic in his stomach" who cultivated rudeness to rebuff all but a few select friends, among whom he was closest to the novelist John O'Hara. Although his marriage on Oct. 14, 1933, to Elinor Mead Sherwin, the daughter of a prosperous architect, and the subsequent birth of two children, brought Gibbs domestic stability, the nervousness and rudeness remained.

"Maybe he doesn't like anything," Ross once admitted, "but he can do everything." Over a thirty-year span, Gibbs contributed more words to the *New Yorker* than any other writer, filling its pages with satirical sketches, profiles, parodies, reminiscences, and comments as well as poems, stories, and reviews. Promoted to editorial writer, Gibbs from 1937 to 1942 turned out amusing, urbane, and humane weekly "Notes and Comments." He also contributed semiautobiographical short stories, collected as *Season in the Sun* (1946), celebrating Fire Island, a summer resort with which he had fallen "desperately in love." At his best as a parodist, Gibbs chose targets ranging from Ernest Hemingway to *Time* magazine. His superb ear for the style of others and his command of language enabled him to distinguish what he described as "the hairline that separates stylized wit from labored perversity." Although Gibbs denied that there was a *New Yorker* style, his own witty, clear, rhythmic, seemingly effortless prose, which he diligently labored to perfect, helped make the *New Yorker* famous for its polished writing.

In February 1940 Gibbs succeeded Robert Benchley as the *New Yorker* drama critic, and from December 1944 to July 1945 he was also its movie critic. Though he could be positive (he adored Helen Hayes), he was an acerbic critic, who admitted to writing "more disagreeably than most." He delighted his readers but often offended playwrights and actors and sometimes left the theater after a disastrous first act. In 1950 Gibbs became the first major American drama critic to write a successful Broadway play. His fear that his colleagues "were going to be rough" proved unfounded. They found *Season in the Sun*, based on his Fire Island stories, humorous, original, and intelligent. Running for 367 performances, it paid Gibbs, who was not wealthy, a welcome $2,000 a week in royalties. In his hour of triumph, Gibbs was modest to the point of diffidence. He deprecated his role as a critic ("a silly occupation for a grown man"), confessed that "more than anything" he wanted to write a novel but did not feel "capable of writing a good one," and predicted that his playwriting experience would make him "a more benign critic." His detractors, however, saw little in his subsequent reviews to change their belief that Gibbs "fed on his own typewritten venom." Indeed, on opening nights "Gibbs seemed as he slid down in his seat, dour face pressed against his hand, the congenital dyspeptic."

A natty dresser, Gibbs was small, gaunt, and handsome with light brown hair and a wispy mustache. During summers on Fire Island, he went barefoot, wore dirty dungarees and a sweatshirt, tanned himself until he looked "like a photographic negative," fished, played poker for small stakes, and enjoyed chess. Never robust, he drank martinis and smoked to excess. In the late 1940's, while suffering from pleurisy, he had a third of his right lung removed. Poor health plagued his last years. With cigarette in hand, he died, officially of congestion and cyanosis of the lungs, although his distraught wife suspected suicide, at his Fire Island home, while reading an advance copy of his collection *More in Sorrow*.

[Virtually all of Gibbs's writings first appeared in the *New Yorker*, but a sampling may be found in *Bird Life at the Pole* (1931); *Bed of Neuroses* (1937); *Season in the Sun and Other Pleasures* (1946); *Season in the Sun: A Comedy* (1951); and *More in Sorrow* (1958). On his family background, see George Gibbs, *The Gibbs Family of Rhode Island and Some Related Families* (1933). On Gibbs's life, see the obituary notices in the *New York Times*, Aug. 17, 1958, *Newsweek*, Aug. 25, 1958; and *New Yorker*, Aug. 30, 1958; and Arthur Gelb, "Critic in the Spotlight," *New York Times*, Oct. 15, 1950. Other sources include Dale Kramer, *Ross and the New Yorker* (1952); James Thurber, *The Years With Ross* (1959); and Brendan Gill, *Here at the New Yorker* (1975).]

ARI HOOGENBOOM

GILLIS, JAMES MARTIN (Nov. 12, 1876–Mar. 14, 1957), political commentator, theologian, orator, and religious editor and writer, was born in Boston, Mass., the son of James Gillis, a machinist, and Catherine Roche. He attended Boston Latin School (1892–1895), then went on to schools specializing in preparation for the Roman Catholic priesthood: St. Charles College, Baltimore (1895–1896), and St. John's Seminary, Brighton, Mass. (1896–1898).

Toward the end of his theological course at St. John's Seminary, Gillis came into contact with the Paulist Fathers, a small congregation of secular priests who made the conversion of Americans their primary mission and the use of the modern media of mass communications their special technique. They also served in parishes and did other conventional pastoral work.

Gillis decided to abandon his earlier plan to become a parish priest in Boston, and entered the Paulist community in 1900. A year later he was ordained to the priesthood and, after receiving a licentiate in theology at the Catholic University of America (1903), was assigned to the faculty of St. Paul's College, the Paulist major seminary, in Washington, D.C. In 1910 and for twelve years thereafter, he preached at retreats and parish missions throughout the United States.

In 1922 Gillis was named editor of *Catholic World*, a monthly that had been established by Isaac Hecker, the founder of the Paulists. From the beginning of his editorship Gillis' vigorous writings were the outstanding feature of the magazine. He often criticized both ecclesiastical and political figures, and particularly Italian fascism, which was then viewed kindly by a number of prominent American prelates. (Benito Mussolini retaliated by having the Paulists removed from the American parish in Rome, Santa Susanna, to which they returned after World War II.)

Gillis' antifascism (which included opposition to Francisco Franco in Spain) did not lead him, as so often happened to others, into political liberalism. He was an old-fashioned patriot and diehard isolationist, with particulary acerbic views about Franklin D. Roosevelt and the New

Deal. The president's policies, he felt, would inevitably entangle the United States in European affairs and lead to involvement in another useless world war.

Gillis was an impenitent conservative. His only suggested religious reform for Roman Catholicism was that it continue to do what it was already doing, but more zealously. His influence was magnified in 1928, when he began to write a weekly column for fifty diocesan papers throughout the United States. He wrote this column, "Sursum Corda," for more than twenty years. He often appeared, from 1930 until his retirement in 1948, on "The Catholic Hour," which was heard on the National Broadcasting Company. Between speaking assignments and editorial work, Gillis managed to write a great many articles for the Catholic press and to produce a number of popular books.

Gillis, short and stocky, was known for his striking memory. He seemed to confine his powerful political gifts to the affairs of the Congregation of St. Paul, which he dominated during a period of quiet growth. Ill health forced him to retire from the editorship of *Catholic World* in 1948, but he remained a contributing editor until his death in New York City.

[Gillis' books include *False Prophets* (1925); *The Catholic Church and the Home* (1928); *The Paulists* (1932); *This Mysterious Human Nature* (1956); and *My Last Book* (1957). The only book about Gillis is J. F. Finley, *James Gillis, Paulist* (1958).]

JOHN COGLEY

GIOVANNITTI, ARTURO (Jan. 7, 1884–Dec. 31, 1959), poet and labor organizer, was born in Ripabottoni, Campobasso, Italy. He was the son of Rosanna and Massimo Giovannitti, a prosperous and liberal-minded physician. Giovannitti received an excellent education for the time, including Gymnasium and some college work, as was commensurate with his family's position.

Compassionate and idealistic, Giovannitti turned away from the secure and economically successful life that he was assured in Italy. At the age of seventeen he immigrated to the United States, seeking the freedom and equality that he felt did not exist in Italy. Reared as a Catholic, Giovannitti became interested in Protestantism in the New World, briefly studied theology at McGill University in Montreal, and worked on a railroad gang. He then studied at Columbia University and worked at various manual and clerical jobs throughout the East Coast. He also attended several seminaries. Giovannitti, however, eventually abandoned his religious calling and became more interested in socialist causes. In 1906 he became a member of the Italian Socialist Federation and thereafter devoted his efforts to organizational activities and to writing for radical newspapers and magazines. In 1911 he became editor of the syndicalist-controlled paper *Il Proletario*.

The following year the textile strike at Lawrence, Mass., brought Giovannitti to the attention of the nation. A cut in wages at the city's textile mills precipitated the strike in January 1912. Consisting largely of unskilled immigrants, the work force quickly came under the control of the Industrial Workers of the World (IWW). Led by Giovannitti and Joseph J. Ettor, a member of the IWW executive board, many Italian workers participated in the strike. During a fight between police and strikers on January 29, Anna Lo Pezzi, a young striker, was shot and killed. Giovannitti and Ettor were arrested and in September stood trial in Salem, Mass., on the charge of being accessories to murder by inciting to riot. After nearly two months of testimony, they were acquitted.

During his long stay in prison before and during the trial, Giovannitti wrote his most powerful and acclaimed poems, which were published as *Arrows in the Gale* (1914). "The Walker" was inspired by the continual pacing of a fellow prisoner in a cell directly above his own. Written in English in an irregular unrhymed verse, it became his best-known work. Louis Kreymborg described this poem as "the most impassioned American tract [written] against the prison system" and compared it favorably with Oscar Wilde's *Ballad of Reading Gaol*, concluding that Giovannitti's writing was "simpler, more realistic, more potent." Louis Untermeyer judged "The Walker" to be "one of the most remarkable things our literature can boast." Although rated highly by contemporaries, Giovannitti's poetry is now largely forgotten or ignored—an undeserved fate, for many of the writings are moving social documents.

In 1912 Giovannitti met Carrie Zaikaner, a Russian Jew. They lived together until 1939, and had two children.

Because he disliked William Dudley Haywood's leadership of the IWW, Giovannitti left the organization in 1916 and subsequently organized for the International Ladies' Garment Workers' Union (ILGWU). He then became secretary of the Italian Chamber of Labor and then the Italian Labor Education Bureau, a post he held until 1940. In 1923 Giovannitti founded the Anti-Fascist Alliance of North America. During the 1920's and 1930's he was a popular speaker at labor rallies, where he addressed both Italian and English speaking crowds with what the *New York Times* called "flowery fluency." He also wrote (in Italian, English, and French) a profusion of poems, plays, short stories, and articles dealing with labor and social questions. A collection of his Italian poems, *Quando Canta Il Gallo (When the Cock Crows)*, appeared in 1957. He was editing his English poems for publication at the time of his death; they were published posthumously as *The Collected Poems of Arturo Giovannitti* (1962). Giovannitti died in the Bronx, N.Y. His funeral service was held in the auditorium of the Amalgamated Clothing Workers of America headquarters in New York City.

[The following sources discuss Giovannitti's life and work and are of value: *Report on the Strike of Textile Workers at Lawrence, Mass.*, 62nd Cong., 2nd S. Doc. 870 (1912); Olga Peragallo, *Italian-American Authors and Their Contribution to American Literature* (1949), 124–128; the *New York Times* obituary, Jan. 1, 1960; and Donald B. Cole, *Immigrant City: Lawrence, Massachusetts, 1845–1921* (1963), in which the Lawrence strike is examined.]

HUMBERT S. NELLI

GLASSFORD, PELHAM DAVIS (Aug. 8, 1883–Aug. 9, 1959), army officer and police official, was born in Las Vegas, N.M., the son of William Alexander Glassford, an army officer, and of Allie Davis. Raised mainly in Denver, Colo., he was graduated from West Point in 1904, ranking eighteenth in a class of 124. (He led the corps in Spanish and drawing.) A field artillery officer who served three years as an instructor at West Point, he was a captain by the time the United States entered World War 1. Sent to France in one of the first contingents of the American Expeditionary Force (AEF), Glassford was on the staff of several artillery schools until July 1918, when he assumed command of the 103rd Field Artillery. On Oct. 1, 1918, he became commanding general of the 51st Field Artillery Brigade, the youngest general officer in the entire AEF. A participant in the Marne defensive and the St.-Mihiel salient, he was slightly wounded by enemy shellfire. He was awarded the Distinguished Service Medal and a Silver Star.

The war over, Glassford reverted to his permanent rank of major and received a series of staff appointments: he served at the General Service Schools, Fort Leavenworth, Kans.; attended and taught at the Army War College, Washington, D.C.; and commanded the 1st Field Artillery for a little over a year. He returned to Washington in October 1928. From then until his voluntary retirement in July 1931, Glassford held staff positions culminating in a tour as chief of Mobilization Branch, G-3, War Department General Staff. At the time of his separation from the army, he and his wife, Cora Carleton, whom he had married in 1906, were in the process of being divorced. They had four children. In 1934 he married his secretary, Lucille K. Painter.

In November 1931, Glassford was appointed police chief of Washington, D.C. (The precise title was major and superintendent of police.) Although the appointment of an outsider was resented by senior police officials and liberals were troubled by his military background, Glassford quickly captured the imagination of press and public by appearing almost everywhere on an oversized blue motorcycle. However, he soon faced serious problems. In December 1931, as the Great Depression deepened, a Communist party–organized hunger march, several thousand strong, came to the capital for the opening of Congress. Although similar demonstrations elsewhere were treated brutally by police, Glassford insisted publicly, to the delight of liberals, that since the Communist party was legal and on the ballot, its lawful activities should not be interfered with.

At the end of May 1932, thousands of veterans of World War 1 began to descend on Washington as a "petition in boots" to pressure Congress to approve advance payment of a "bonus" (technically "adjusted service compensation") that had been voted in 1924 but was not payable until 1945. These "bonus marchers" insisted that they would stay in the nation's capital until the bonus was paid, and began what became a two-month sit-in. The only official in the District of Columbia who was willing and able to deal with them was Glassford. He tried to discourage them, yet insisted that they had a right to stay. He urged them to go home, but organized public donations for their succor. He hoped, eventually, that all but a few diehards would leave. Although Glassford's Fabian tactics seemed to be working—by the last week of July, the number of bonus marchers had shrunk to less than half of June's 20,000 peak—the administration of Herbert Hoover was determined to force the veterans out of the nation's capital and off the front pages, where they were a distinct embarrassment in an election year.

Glassford reluctantly complied with orders to evict the veterans from selected national property in the Federal Triangle area of downtown Washington. Despite his desire to avoid bloodshed and his personal supervision, violence erupted and a policeman shot and killed two veterans. The federal administration, against Glassford's advice, then called on the army. Under the personal direction of Chief of Staff Douglas MacArthur, infantry, cavalry, and tanks dispersed the marchers and their families, and expelled them without serious casualties. Almost three months later, on October 20, the district commissioners asked for and received Glassford's resignation. He then attacked Hoover in a preelection series of articles in the Hearst newspapers and in political addresses, describing how the army of Herbert Hoover "drove from the National Capital . . . the disarmed, disavowed and destitute army of Woodrow Wilson."

Glassford was an unsuccessful federal conciliator in an agricultural labor dispute in the Imperial Valley of California in 1934; and in 1936 he served briefly—and spectacularly—as police chief of Phoenix, Ariz., where he demoted his predecessor to patrolman and advocated legalized prostitution. That same year he ran unsuccessfully for Congress from Arizona as an "anti-New Deal Democrat." In February 1942 he was recalled to active duty and served as director of the internal security division, office of the provost marshal general, until Dec. 25, 1943, when he retired. He still wore only the single star he had won in France.

Glassford spent the rest of his life in Laguna Beach, Calif., where he painted, became the unsalaried president of the Chamber of Commerce, and participated in the United World Federalist movement. In 1948 he organized a MacArthur for President club.

[The Glassford Papers are in the research library, University of California, Los Angeles. His public account of the bonus march appeared serially as "General Glassford's Own Story" in most Hearst newspapers, Oct. 30–Nov. 6, 1932. The most detailed analyses are in Irving Bernstein, *The Lean Years* (1960); and Roger Daniels, *The Bonus March: An Episode of the Great Depression* (1971).]

ROGER DANIELS

GODDARD, HENRY HERBERT (Aug. 14, 1866–June 19, 1957), psychologist, was born in Vassalboro, Me., the son of Henry Clay Goddard and Sarah Winslow. His father, a modestly prosperous farmer, died in 1875, but financial assistance from the Society of Friends supplemented Sarah Goddard's earnings as a traveling minister and allowed Goddard to attend the Moses Brown School, Providence, R.I., and Haverford College, where he received the B.A. in 1887. After a year as an instructor in Latin, botany, and mathematics at the University of Southern California, he returned to Haverford for the M.A. (1889). He married Emma Florence Robbins on Aug. 7, 1889. They had no children. Until 1896 he was a secondary school principal; then he entered Clark University as a fellow in psychology, studying with G. Stanley Hall. He received the Ph.D. in 1899.

Goddard became professor of psychology at Pennsylvania State Normal School, West Chester, Pa., in 1899. While there he served as a psychological consultant to Edward R. Johnstone, superintendent of the New Jersey Training School for Feeble-Minded Boys and Girls, Vineland, N.J. In 1906 Johnstone offered Goddard the post of psychologist and director of research. He accepted, and he established the first department of research in any American institution of that type.

Goddard spent the next twelve years at Vineland. While on a trip to Europe in 1908, he was introduced to the work of the French psychologists Alfred Binet and Theodore Simon. Goddard was the first American to translate and publicize their intelligence tests, but he was skeptical of their ability to actually classify intelligence. Only after he had tested four hundred Vineland residents and cross-checked the results with the traditional criteria (observation, anthropometric measurements, and psychomotor and memory tests) was he convinced that the Binet test was a powerful tool for psychological analysis. Later he proposed a tripartite division (idiots, imbeciles, morons) of mental defect based on mental ages. He coined the word "moron" from the Greek for "slow" or "sluggish." His terminology was adopted by the American Association for the Study of the Feeble-Minded in 1910.

In 1911, after testing 2,000 public school children with the Binet method, Goddard claimed that the tests did not measure conscious learning but actually gauged basic mental processes. This point has been in constant dispute among psychologists and educators. Goddard next investigated the New York City public schools and concluded that 2 percent of the students were retarded enough to require special education. He later expanded his views in *School Training of Defective Children* (1915).

Goddard pursued his ideas with great zeal and determination. Out of his investigation of the ancestry of a Vineland student, Deborah Kallikak (a pseudonym coined from the Greek meaning "good and bad"), came Goddard's best-known work, *The Kallikak Family: A Study in the Heredity of Feeble-mindedness* (1912). Goddard engaged Elizabeth S. Kite as a fieldworker, and together they traced the family to Martin Kallikak, Sr., who had fathered two sons, one by a promiscuous tavern maid and the other by his wife. Goddard found 496 descendants of the legitimate union, all normal, while the 480 descendants of Deborah's great-grandfather, Martin Kallikak, Jr., presented an almost unbroken line of degeneracy. There was a mutual reinforcement between Goddard's work and the heredity studies of the eugenicist Charles B. Davenport, with whom Goddard maintained an active correspondence.

In *Feeble-mindedness: Its Causes and Consequences* (1914), Goddard examined the heredity of 300 Vineland residents and seemingly confirmed the belief that retardation was subject to hereditary transmission according to the Mendelian laws of inheritance. Much of this study has been criticized for poor research methods, but Goddard believed that mental defects were hereditary and that custodial segregation or eugenic sterilization was necessary to halt their perpetuation. He pressed this point in lectures, articles, and books, such as *The Criminal Imbecile* (1915).

In 1917 Goddard served on the committee that devised the army Alpha and Beta tests of intelligence administered to recruits in World War 1. In 1918 he left Vineland to become director of the Ohio State Bureau of Juvenile Research. While in that post he published *The Psychology of the Normal and Subnormal* (1919), *Human Efficiency and Levels of Intelligence* (1920), and *Juvenile*

Delinquency (1921). After moving to Ohio State University as professor of abnormal and clinical psychology in 1922, he wrote *School Training of Gifted Children* (1927) and *Two Souls in One Body?* (1927). He maintained a warm and friendly relationship with his students until his retirement in 1938. His last book, *How to Raise Children in the Atomic Age*, appeared in 1948. After his retirement he moved to Santa Barbara, Calif., where he died.

[The principal collection of Goddard papers is in the Archives of the History of Psychology, University of Akron. The Charles B. Davenport Papers at the American Philosophical Society Library, Philadelphia, Pa., have Goddard's correspondence with Davenport from 1909 to 1920. A guide to Goddard's articles is in Edgar A. Doll, ed., *Twenty-fifth Anniversary: Vineland Laboratory, 1906–1931* (1932). Much of Goddard's work ultimately appeared in the *Training School Bulletin*, published at Vineland, and in the *Journal of Psycho-Asthenics*. Obituaries appeared in the *New York Times*, June 22, 1957; *Newsweek*, July 1, 1957; and *American Journal of Psychology*, Dec. 1957.]

PETER L. TYOR

GOLDMAN, EDWIN FRANKO (Jan. 1, 1878–Feb. 21, 1956), bandmaster and composer, was born in Louisville, Ky., the son of David Henry Goldman, a lawyer and amateur musician, and his first cousin Selma Franko. The Franko (originally Holländer) family had emigrated from Germany and was known for its musicians— Goldman's mother and her four brothers and sisters, child prodigies on the piano and violin, toured professionally in 1869 and the early 1870's.

After the death of Goldman's father in 1887, his mother moved the family to New York City, the home of her parents, where she gave violin and piano lessons. For seven years Goldman lived at the Hebrew Orphan Asylum, a boys' home run by a family friend. He had his first musical instruction from George Wiegand and Alfred Remy, and played the cornet in the asylum's band. His mother gave him piano lessons for three years. He attended the National Conservatory of Music on a scholarship (1892–1893) while Antonín Dvořák was director. Goldman studied the cornet with Carl Sohst and was in the Conservatory orchestra class conducted by Dvořák. He also received free lessons from the pioneer cornet soloist Jules Levy.

In 1893 Goldman was hired as librarian, performer, and general assistant in the orchestra of his uncle Nahan Franko. Working under the name Edwin G. Franko, he learned the life of the professional orchestra musician, playing in theaters and hotels, and with touring opera companies. He became experienced as a business manager and by 1897 was hiring personnel for Franko's orchestra and handling the payroll. (A decade later he conducted his own agency as musical contractor.) Starting at the age of twenty-three, he worked for eight seasons (1901–1908) as cornetist in the orchestra of the Metropolitan Opera House, where Nahan Franko was concertmaster (later conductor). He used his own name professionally from this time on. On Oct. 8, 1908, he married Adelaide Maibrun. They had two children.

From 1909 until 1919 Goldman worked for the music publisher Carl Fischer as editor and writer. He gained an excellent reputation as an educator and attracted a large number of private students in cornet and trumpet. Fischer eventually became Goldman's publisher; of his six books and technical studies, the influential *Foundation to Cornet Playing* (1914; revised 1936) is the most notable.

In 1911 Goldman formed The New York Military Band, with himself as conductor, for the purpose of giving outdoor concerts. At this time municipal band music in New York City was at a low ebb, creating opportunities for a musician of Goldman's abilities and enterprise. The New York Military Band (the name was changed to the Goldman Band in 1922) became a superior and uniquely durable concert organization. The band appeared irregularly until 1918, when it gave its first full season of about thirty summer concerts at Columbia University. The series became annual events and through 1922 were held on the Columbia campus. Beginning in 1923, the concerts were given primarily in Central Park and Prospect Park, Brooklyn.

The most important factor in the survival of the band was the financial support of Daniel and Murry Guggenheim. The concerts were highly successful with critics and the public (attendance by 10,000 to 15,000 persons at a performance was not unusual), but although Goldman was praised as "a combination of artist and businessman," the public donations he had to solicit barely financed each season. In 1924 the Guggenheim family (later the Daniel and Florence Guggenheim Foundation) assumed support of the series. Their subsidy perpetuated the organization long after the demise of the famous bands of Sousa and Arthur Pryor, which were dependent on touring for support.

Goldman's fame resulted from his close association with radio from the earliest days of the medium. On Nov. 13, 1926, the band was heard on the first NBC network program; New York radio had already carried its concerts for three years. In addition to regular studio programs, all the summer concerts were also broadcast.

Goldman composed 104 marches for band and fifty other light vocal and instrumental pieces. His march *On the Mall* (1923), written for the opening of the Elkan Naumburg bandstand in Central Park, was a great popular favorite and became a standard with bands in the United States and abroad. His concern for the improvement of American bands and band music led him to form the American Bandmasters Association in 1929. The aims of the organization were raising artistic standards of bands, promoting a universal band instrumentation, and enlarging the repertory.

Goldman brought to band work the knowledge and techniques of a classical training and the discipline of an experienced orchestra musician. His band was noted for its shading, flexibility, and precision. His ideas about instrumentation, and even the seating arrangement of the band, touched school bands throughout the United States. He called his work a "high mission" for the purpose of expressing "the best forms of music in the finest and most artistic manner . . . to stimulate the people to an increased desire and appreciation for this music." He accomplished this by altering the traditional band concert of marches and dances to include new works composed especially for concert band and transcriptions of classical orchestra music.

His promotion and performance of new music during his long career (he conducted until 1955) was responsible for the emergence of the modern repertory of the concert band. Starting in 1949, he personally commissioned a series of new band compositions by Virgil Thomson, Walter Piston, Vincent Persichetti, and other prominent American composers. It was his final contribution to dignifying the band as a medium for creative expression.

[Scrapbooks documenting Goldman's career, programs, correspondence, and a copy of his unpublished autobiography, "Facing the Music," are at the American Bandmasters Association Research Center, McKeldin Library, University of Maryland (College

Park). Goldman's writings include *Band Betterment* (1934) and many articles in *Metronome* (1908–1919) and *Etude* (1933–1948). On his life, see Kirby Reid Jolly, *Edwin Franko Goldman and the Goldman Band* (Ph.D. diss., New York University, 1971). On his career and the history of American bands, see Richard Franko Goldman, *The Concert Band* (1946) and *The Wind Band: Its Literature and Technique* (1961); and Paul Yoder, "The Early History of the American Bandmasters Association," *Journal of Band Research*, Autumn 1964.]

RICHARD JACKSON

GRACE, EUGENE GIFFORD (Aug. 27, 1876–July 25, 1960), industrialist, was born in Goshen, N.J., the son of John Wesley Grace, a sailor and grocery store operator, and Rebecca Morris. After attending Goshen public schools, Grace was sent to the Pennington Academy in New Jersey to prepare for college. In 1895 he entered Lehigh University in Bethlehem, Pa., where he won a prize in mathematics and played shortstop on the varsity baseball team, of which he was captain in 1898. He ranked first in his class in 1899, graduating with honors in electrical engineering. As class valedictorian he spoke on "The Future of Electricity," stressing its labor-saving applications to industry. He then went to work at the nearby Bethlehem Steel Company, after having turned down an offer to become a professional baseball player.

His first job was operating an electric crane. In 1902, after suggesting ways to eliminate the waste and bottlenecks in the flow of raw materials he had observed within the Bethlehem yards, Grace was promoted to supervise and overhaul yard traffic. Shortly thereafter he married Marion Brown, the daughter of a local lumberyard owner. They had three children.

In 1904 Grace met Bethlehem's new owner, Charles M. Schwab, Andrew Carnegie's protégé, who had recently resigned as president of United States Steel. Schwab was impressed by Grace's quick mind and his intimate knowledge of all aspects of Bethlehem's facilities. In January 1906 Schwab sent him to Cuba to reorganize the Juragua iron mines, which were Bethlehem's primary source of ore. Grace greatly improved production by mechanizing almost every operation of the mines. Two senior Bethlehem officials wanted to station Grace in Cuba permanently, but Schwab overruled them. He wanted a man of Grace's organizational talent closer at hand.

Before Schwab's ownership Bethlehem was heavily dependent upon military orders (armor plate for the U.S. Navy and gun forgings for the U.S. Army), which had begun to decline in volume. Schwab began to diversify into products for the civilian market. His most expensive gamble was the decision to produce a revolutionary type of structural beam, which could be rolled as a long section instead of being riveted together as conventional beams then were. He chose Grace to construct the new beam mill, and when Grace completed the mill and made it operational, Schwab promoted him to chief executive officer of Bethlehem Steel, with the title of general manager. In 1913, five years later, Grace was named president of Bethlehem and Schwab became chairman of the board.

As president, Grace had full authority over production. (Schwab concentrated on broadening the market for Bethlehem's products in the United States and abroad.) Both men wanted to make Bethlehem Steel into a fully integrated producer: they acquired new ore mines and subsidiaries; they enlarged Bethlehem's shipbuilding and repair facilities, which, during periods of economic depression, produced nearly half of Bethlehem's profits; and they continued an aggressive program of expansion, buying strategically located facilities to strengthen Bethlehem's competitive position. Three major acquisitions—Pennsylvania Steel Company in 1916 and Midvale Steel and Lackawanna Steel in 1922—gave Bethlehem over 15 percent of the nation's capacity. However, their attempts to merge with Youngstown Sheet and Tube Company, in order to challenge United States Steel's dominance of the Chicago steel market, were repeatedly thwarted.

Schwab and Grace agreed that the best way to generate additional profits was to reduce production costs and that a giant firm could only be successful if its workers and managers had a direct share in its profits. They adopted a system of measuring each man's performance and awarding bonuses accordingly. Grace was a prime beneficiary of the bonus system: until the 1930's his salary never exceeded $12,000, but his bonuses were huge, averaging $814,000 a year between 1918 and 1930 and $1.6 million in 1929 alone.

Although Grace was not an innovator in the steel business like Carnegie or Schwab, he possessed an undeniable brilliance as an administrator. He combined an encyclopedic mastery of steelmaking with a relentless determination to cut costs and expand production. He drove his subordinates hard but earned their respect because he drove himself just as hard. While Schwab relied upon coaxing and gentle persuasion to achieve his goals, Grace was always ill at ease with such methods. A shy man with a quick temper, he was accustomed to command and was impatient for results. "Always more production" was his watchword.

In 1946 Grace became chairman of the Bethlehem Steel Corporation. He held the reins of power tightly until 1957, when a stroke forced his retirement. When he died in Bethlehem, Pa., Bethlehem Steel was the nation's second largest steelmaker and its largest shipbuilder.

[The sources for Grace's life and career are meager, in large measure because of lack of interest in history and reminiscing. Clipping files on Grace, some of his speeches, and some fragmentary reminiscences by and about Grace can be found in the Schwab Memorial Library, Bethlehem Steel Corporation, Bethlehem, Pa. Robert Hessen, *Steel Titan* (1975), traces Bethlehem Steel from its origins to 1939. Major articles on Grace include those by Noel F. Busch, *Life*, Jan. 26, 1942; B. C. Forbes, *American Magazine*, July 1920; Floyd W. Parsons, *Saturday Evening Post*, Aug. 30, 1919; Jack R. Ryan, *New York Times*, Aug. 26, 1956; and Homer H. Shannon, *Forbes*, Nov. 1, 1948. See also the obituary in the *New York Times*, July 26, 1960; and Alfred D. Keator, ed., *Encyclopedia of Pennsylvania Biography*, XXXI (1963). "Bethlehem Ship," *Fortune*, Sept. 1937, and "Bethlehem Steel," *Fortune*, Apr. 1941, should be supplemented by William T. Hogan, *An Economic History of the Iron and Steel Industry in the United States*, 5 vols. (1971).]

ROBERT HESSEN

GRADY, HENRY FRANCIS (Feb. 12, 1882–Sept. 14, 1957), diplomat, educator, and businessman, was born in San Francisco, Calif., the son of John Henry Grady and Ellen Genevieve Rourke. He went east for his undergraduate education, receiving a B.A. from St. Mary's University in Baltimore in 1907. He subsequently did graduate work at Catholic University (1907–1908) and the University of California (1915–1917). He later received a doctorate in international finance from Columbia University (1927). On Oct. 18, 1917, he married Lucretia del Valle, the daughter of a prominent Los Angeles attorney. They had four children.

Grady began early to combine three careers in one. He was teaching economics at Columbia when the United States entered World War I, and in 1918 he moved to Washington to work in the Bureau of Planning and Statistics of the U.S. Shipping Board. After the armistice he was sent to Europe as the first American trade commissioner to report on postwar economic conditions, and in late 1919 he assumed the post of commercial attaché at the London embassy. Six months later he resigned to resume his doctoral research on British wartime finances. Early in 1921 he was back in both the government, this time as acting chief of research in the U.S. Bureau of Foreign and Domestic Commerce, and in academia, lecturing at the Foreign Service School of Georgetown University. For a while Grady seemed to settle on teaching, and in the fall of 1921 he returned to California to teach at Berkeley, where in 1928 he became professor of international trade and dean of the College of Commerce. He remained at Berkeley until 1937.

Grady's energies could not be confined to the classroom. He became involved in numerous civic enterprises in the San Francisco area, and he developed a reputation for getting things done. He also became a spokesman for improved trade relations with the Far East, a viewpoint he developed in a number of articles and speeches. He took a leave of absence from the University of California in 1934 to serve as chief of the State Department Trade Agreements Division, and he was the main figure in the drafting of the act that allowed the United States to enter into reciprocal trade agreements. In 1937 Grady was named vice-chairman of the United States Tariff Commission. In August 1939 he was appointed assistant secretary of state for general economic matters and trade agreements.

The new assistant secretary, said *Fortune* several months later, "lacks the evangelical fervor of his predecessor; however, that lack is offset by his extraordinary technical knowledge and his ability to get along with people." Grady stayed in that office until January 1941, when he resigned to assume the presidency of the American President Line. He also made an extensive trip throughout the Far East as President Franklin D. Roosevelt's personal representative to determine the availability of strategic defense materials and the means for getting them to the Allies. Although Grady headed the shipping line until April 1947, he took on one special assignment after another, constantly traveling, and was known as a man "who thrived on living out of a suitcase."

He served as chairman of the American

Technical Mission to India in March 1942, vice-president of the economic section of the Allied Control Commission in Italy in 1943 and 1944, and chairman of the Federal Reserve Bank of San Francisco from 1942 to 1947. By 1945 Grady had become the man to call on to handle difficult assignments. In October of that year President Harry S. Truman named him to head the American Section of the Allied Mission for Observing the Greek Elections. With the rank of ambassador, he went to Greece to supervise the 1,400 Americans, Britons, and Frenchmen who composed the inspection teams for the March 1946 elections. He did an outstanding job in a sensitive role, winning plaudits for his own conduct as well as friends for the United States.

President Truman next sent Grady to London as the American representative for the Committee on Palestine and Related Problems. No issue vexed Anglo-American relations as did the Zionist demand for a Jewish homeland. For once Grady allowed the situation and his peers in the State Department to get the better of him. Despite earlier reports supporting an independent Jewish Palestine, both British and American career officials opposed the idea, and the so-called Morrison-Grady plan was obviously designed to keep Palestine firmly under British control. So furious were Zionist supporters when they heard of its details that Truman disavowed the plan before it could even be made public.

In April 1947 Grady became the first American ambassador to India. A year later he returned to Greece, where he served as ambassador for two critical years, during which the Communist guerrillas were suppressed and economic life was restored to the country. Then in 1950 he went to another trouble spot, Iran, where State Department officials hoped he would be able to repeat his success in Greece. But the large amounts of foreign aid that Grady had utilized so effectively in Greece were denied him in Iran. At one point he irately cabled the State Department: "Where are the chips you promised me for this poker game?" Grady also differed with Washington's views on how to handle the anti-British, anticolonialist sentiment then rampant in Iran. In September 1951 he sent in his resignation and retired from diplomatic service.

In his remaining years, Grady led a quieter but still active life. He was a foreign policy adviser to Adlai Stevenson and headed a group working for the recall of Senator Joseph McCarthy. In the mid-1950's he spoke and worked for a freer American trade policy and for easing economic restrictions on trade with Communist nations. He died while on a cruise to the Far East on board the *President Wilson*.

[Grady's papers are at the Harry S. Truman Library, Independence, Mo. Numerous reminiscences in the Oral History Collection, Columbia University, notably one by Goldthwaite H. Dorr, contain material on Grady. In addition to articles in business, economic, and trade journals, see Grady's *British War Finance, 1914–1919* (Ph.D. diss., Columbia University, 1927); *The Port of San Francisco* (1934), written with Robert M. Carr; "The Present Need for a Sane Commercial Policy," *Vital Speeches*, Jan. 15, 1940; "Reciprocal Agreements for Trade Expansion," *Annals of the American Academy*, Sept. 1940; and the obituary notice, *New York Times*, Sept. 15, 1957.]

MELVIN I. UROFSKY

GRAHAM, EVARTS AMBROSE (Mar. 19, 1883–Mar. 4, 1957), surgeon and medical educator, was born in Chicago, Ill., the son of David Wilson Graham, a surgeon and a charter member of the Presbyterian Hospital, and Ida Anspach Barned. Following education in public schools and the Lewis Institute of Chicago, Graham attended Princeton from 1900 to 1904, and was awarded the B.A. in the latter year. Upon graduation he returned to Chicago, took a year of preclinical training at the University of Chicago, and entered the affiliated Rush Medical College, from which he received the M.D. in 1907.

Over the protestations of Arthur Dean Bevan, his chief at the Presbyterian Hospital during his internship, Graham withdrew from surgery and from 1908 to 1914 conducted research in pathology and chemistry. While working at the Otho S. A. Sprague Memorial Institute for Medical Research, he met Rollin T. Woodyatt, who subsequently had an important influence on his career. Woodyatt had been a pupil of Friedrich Müller in Munich, and had returned to Chicago a confirmed disciple of scientific medicine.

In 1915 Graham began the private practice of surgery in Mason City, Iowa, where he gained experience in major operative technique and was exposed to the practice of fee-splitting, in which, unknown to the patient, the referring physician received a rebate from the surgeon. He began a campaign against the practice as unethical, and consequently found himself alienated from many of his professional associates. In later years he fought fee-splitting, "ghost" surgery, and similar practices on a national level.

On Jan. 29, 1916, Graham married Helen Tredway, a graduate student in chemistry at the University of Chicago, who subsequently achieved a distinguished career as a pharmacologist. They had two sons. The following year he entered military service and rose to the rank of captain in the United States Army Medical Corps. His major work during World War I was with the Empyema Commission in 1918–1919. Empyema was frequently a complicating factor in epidemics of influenza in military training camps. The commission's findings resulted in the substitution of needle aspiration and closed-tube drainage for rib resection and open drainage, procedures that significantly lowered the mortality and morbidity rates. The principles elaborated by Graham and his colleagues also laid the foundation for the future development of thoracic surgery. In 1919 he was appointed professor and chairman of the department of surgery at the Washington University School of Medicine, St. Louis. As the first full-time salaried professor of surgery at that institution, he proceeded to develop one of the major teaching programs in general and thoracic surgery in the United States. He held this post until his retirement in 1951.

Graham was the first surgeon to remove an entire lung successfully for carcinoma. This achievement (1933), together with his studies on the Empyema Commission and his development of the technique of cholecystography with Warren H. Cole and Glover H. Copher (1924), were the major sources of his recognition. Less well-known are his contributions as an unyielding opponent of surgical mediocrity. In the early 1930's, Graham led a group of university surgeons in criticizing the admisssion requirements and internal governance of the American College of Surgeons, which they felt was not fulfilling its potential for the improvement of surgical practice. He was the driving force responsible for the founding, in 1937, of the American Board of Surgery, an independent examining body for the certification of surgeons.

Graham occupied positions of authority on the American Board of Surgery, the American College of Surgeons, the American Surgical Association, and the International Society of Surgery. In each organization he used the position to demand excellence in surgical training and practice. Forceful and outspoken, he never minced words or sidestepped an issue if he felt action was needed. He battled hard for principles, including the right of all physicians—regardless of race, religion, or ethnic background—to acquire the best training, appropriate certification, and membership in national medical organizations.

Graham's strengths as a teacher, organizer, and forceful advocate overshadowed his contributions as an operating surgeon. He became the elder statesman of his profession and was consulted on almost every major issue in surgery. He was constantly involved with governmental committees, national boards, and commissions; in 1941 he was the third surgeon to be elected to the National Academy of Sciences, being preceded by William S. Halsted and Harvey Cushing. Graham was the second American surgeon to be awarded the Lister Medal of the Royal College of Surgeons.

From 1906 until his death, Graham was a frequent contributor to the literature of general and thoracic surgery. Among his important monographs are *Some Fundamental Considerations in the Treatment of Empyema Thoracis* (1925) and *Diseases of the Gall-Bladder and Bile Ducts* (1928), written with J. J. Singer and H. C. Ballon. He was editor of the *Journal of Thoracic Surgery* from 1931 to 1957 and served on the editorial boards of *Archives of Surgery* and *Annals of Surgery*. While editor of the *Year Book of General Surgery* from 1926 to 1957, he left a permanent record of both his broad surgical knowledge and his outspoken personality in the pithy comments that followed the abstracts.

In his later years Graham devoted much time to studying the relationship between smoking and carcinoma of the lung. Once a heavy smoker, he modified his habit when he was well along in his studies. Ironically, he succumbed to the disease for which he was the first to operate successfully. Graham died in St. Louis, Mo.

[The Evarts A. Graham Papers are in the Washington University School of Medicine Library, St. Louis. A microfilm copy of this collection is in the History of Medicine Division, National Library of Medicine, Bethesda, Md. A complete curriculum vitae and list of publications are in the Evarts Ambrose Graham memorial volume published by the Washington University School of Medicine (1957?). Graham's autobiographical essay, "A Brief Account of the Surgery of a Half Century Ago and Some Personal Reminiscences," is in *Medical Clinics of North America*, XLI (1957). His early life and career are critically examined by E. D. Churchill, in "Evarts Graham: Early Years and the Hegira," *Annals of Surgery*,

(1952); and Graham's struggle to improve surgical standards and his role in the founding of the American Board of Surgery are described by P. D. Olch, in "Evarts A. Graham, the American College of Surgeons, and the American Board of Surgery," *Journal of the History of Medicine and Allied Sciences*, 27 (1972). A portrait of Graham appears with an obituary in *Transactions of the American Surgical Association*, 75 (1957).]

PETER D. OLCH

GRAY, GILDA (Oct. 24, 1899–Dec. 22, 1959), dancer and entertainer, was born Marianna Michalska in Cracow, Poland, the daughter of Maximilian and Wanda Michalski. The family immigrated to Bayonne, N.J., around 1907 but soon moved to Cudahy, Wis., a suburb of Milwaukee. After attending a parochial school where her classmates included another future actress, Lenore Ulric, she married John Gorecki, a bartender in his father's saloon, on Oct. 16, 1912. They had one son.

Gray's theatrical career began the following year in a local bar, where as Mary Gray she entertained patrons by singing popular ballads for eight dollars a week. Shortly afterward she left her husband and began performing at the Arsonia Bar in Chicago, where she had her first success. Stridently singing "Beale Street Blues," her face a total blank, she shook her body seductively from her shoulders to her hips. When asked what she was doing, she is said to have explained, "I said I was shaking my chemise—only I pronounced it shimmy."

After being spotted by a talent scout, Gray went to New York. Sophie Tucker described her as a tough blonde, agile as a snake. Under a new name, Gilda Gray, suggested by Tucker, she scored an instant success at Reisenweber's Cafe. Her subsequent appearance in the *Shubert Gaieties of 1919* made her a national sensation.

Though Gray claimed to have been the first to popularize the shimmy, others, including Mae West, have disputed this. Her accounts of the birth of the shimmy, though they made good copy, have also been challenged. Contrary to her notion that it originated in India and the South Seas, dance historians have variously traced it to the *shika* of Nigeria, the shake, and the shim-me-sha-wabble, danced by Ethel Waters as early as 1917.

In the public's mind, however, Gilda Gray was the undisputed "Queen of Shimmy," the girl who launched a thousand hips. Her appearance in the *Ziegfeld Follies of 1922* consolidated her claim. From then on, she appeared almost exclusively in supper clubs and vaudeville under the management of nightclub owner Gil Boag, whom she married in 1924. In the same year she appeared at his Rendezvous Room and capitalized on the recent discovery of King Tutankhamen's tomb by making her entrance lying in a coffin. Casting aside her silver funerary wrappings, she writhed and shimmied while Rudy Vallee sang.

Gray's career in movies was similarly tailored to her specialized talents. In *A Virtuous Vamp* (1919) she did the shimmy; and two of her films, *Aloma of the South Seas* (1926) and *The Devil Dancer* (1927), were inspired by the vogue for romance in exotic settings and gave her the opportunity for quasi-ethnic dances. Two others, *Cabaret* (1927) and *Piccadilly* (made in England in 1919), dramatized the nightclub life she knew so well. They were well received and the critics were on the whole generous, particularly with regard to her performance in *Piccadilly*, in which she revealed unsuspected talent as an actress.

From 1919 to 1929 Gray enjoyed extraordinary success. She lived extravagantly, appearing at the Palace Theater in New York for a reputed salary of $2,500 a week. In 1929, however, she was ruined in the stock market crash. She divorced Boag, and her decline began. She continued to tour in vaudeville, but dismayed audiences by singing rather than dancing. In 1933 Gray married Hector de Briceno, a Venezuelan diplomat eight years her junior; but this marriage also ended in divorce. She returned to Hollywood for a cameo role in the Nelson Eddy–Jeanette Macdonald *Rose Marie* (1936) and played herself in *The Great Ziegfeld* (1936), but her performance was cut from the final print. Subsequently Gray traveled to Mexico to film ethnic dances, hoping to put together a lecture-demonstration. She made a similar trip to Africa in 1939. Stopping in her native Poland on the way home, she barely escaped the invading Nazi armies.

In 1941 Gray declared bankruptcy. An appearance at Billy Rose's Diamond Horseshoe in a nostalgic revue in which she shimmied to "St. Louis Blues" failed to return her to public favor. In addition to her financial problems, poor health plagued her; and for a time she retired to a small ranch in Larkspur, Colo. She briefly emerged when she brought suit against the producers of *Gilda* (1946), claiming that the film was partly based on her career. The suit was settled out of court. In 1952 she was engaged as a "sex consultant" to young starlets. Her last attempt at a comeback (1955) failed dismally.

Gray died in Hollywood. Her funeral expenses were paid by the Motion Picture Relief Fund. Gray left an unfinished autobiography, *Glamor Be Damned*. Despite her limited talents, she helped set the style of the Roaring Twenties and her career epitomized the spirit of that raucous era.

[See William F. Pillich, *Social Dance* (1967); Marshall and Jean Stearns, *Jazz Dance* (1968); Sophie Tucker, *Some of These Days* (1945); and clippings in Lincoln Center Dance and Theatre Collections.]

WILLIAM W. APPLETON

GRAY, WILLIAM SCOTT, JR. (June 5, 1885–Sept. 8, 1960), teacher, specialist in reading development and testing, and university administrator, was born in Coatsburg, Ill., the son of William Scott Gray, a schoolteacher and one-term state senator, and Annie Gilliland. Following graduation from Camp Point High School in 1904, Gray taught in a rural school in Adams County, Ill. From 1905 to 1908 he served as principal and teacher in the elementary school at Fowler, Ill. He studied at Illinois State Normal University from 1908 to 1910. In the latter year he became principal of the training school of that institution, a post he held until 1912. He then entered the University of Chicago, which awarded him a B.S. in 1913. The following year, after receiving an M.A. at Teachers College, Columbia University, he returned to Chicago to pursue further graduate study. Also in 1914 he was appointed assistant in education at the University of Chicago, and in 1915 he was made instructor. After receiving the Ph.D. in 1916, Gray was promoted to assistant professor and named dean of the College of Education, a post he held from 1917 to 1931. He became associate professor in 1918 and professor in 1922. On Sept. 14, 1921, Gray married Beatrice Warner Jardine; they had two children. He retired in 1950.

Gray stands as the dominant educator in the field of reading. He was a pioneer innovator and developer of such measurements of reading skills and teaching effectiveness as the Gray Standardized Oral Reading Paragraphs and the Gray Silent Reading Test. He was also an early exponent of the "sight method" of reading instruction. Between 1909 and 1950 he published more than 400 reports, essays, articles, and books. He continued writing after his retirement, producing some 100 more published pieces. As senior editor of the reading publications division of Scott, Foresman, book publishers, he was the creator of the "Dick and Jane" elementary reading books. They were the basis of reading instruction for students in the United States and Canada for almost half a century. Through his work with UNESCO he aided reading education worldwide.

Gray's writing career began with the essay "Society and the Delinquent" (1909), which was the subject of an oratorical contest he won at Illinois State Normal School. In 1911 and 1912 he published a dozen articles on the study of geography in *School Century*. His doctoral dissertation, *Studies of Elementary School Reading Through Standardized Tests* (1917), was one part of the Educational Monographs series. He contributed nineteen volumes to this series, one of which, *Summary of Scientific Investigations in Reading* (1925), brought together 500 investigations in reading and their results. He continued his summary analysis of research work with articles in the *Elementary School Journal* (1925–1932), the *Journal of Educational Research* (1932–1957), and the *Review of Educational Research* (1937–1940).

Gray inspired and promoted the establishment of national conferences on reading at the University of Chicago, making it the center of research and organization in reading. As compiler, organizer, and editor of proceedings of these conferences, he encouraged colleges and universities throughout the country to model programs after those at the University of Chicago.

Gray's *Remedial Cases in Reading* (1921) called attention to the many types of reading problems among children and demonstrated methods for solving them. His monograph *The Reading Interests and Habits of Adults*, written with Ruth Monroe (1929), isolated the kinds of books read by a cross section of adults. It was followed by a *Manual for Teachers of Adult Illiterates* (1930), sponsored by the Office of Education of the Department of Interior as a part of a national drive to reduce adult illiteracy. His later work included *Reading in General Education* (1940) and *On Their Own in Reading* (1948), an exposition of the effects of reading techniques on students. Two final monographs, *The Teaching of Reading and Writing* (1956) and *Maturity in Reading* (1956), written with Bernice Rogers, brought together his research interests.

Gray was a man of simple tastes, a devoted teacher who was revered by his students. He died in Wolf, Wyo. In 1960 the William S. Gray Research Professorship in Reading was established by Lawrence A. Kimpton, who was then chancellor of the University of Chicago.

[Gray's papers are at the University of Chicago. An assessment of his career and impact on reading education is found in Walter J. Moore, "William Scott Gray," in *Pioneers in Reading*, I, *Elementary English* (1957). A short personal article with photograph can be obtained from the office of the president of the University of Chicago. Obituaries are in the *New York Times* and *Chicago American*, Sept. 9, 1960. A new edition of *Record of the Family of Isaac and Sarah Hawkins Gray* (1955) completed the work of Gray's sister, Lilian; it includes photographs and other illustrations.]

JACK J. CARDOSO

GREENE, CHARLES SUMNER. *See* Supplement Five.

GREENE, JEROME DAVIS (Oct. 12, 1874–Mar. 29, 1959), university officer, international banker, and foundation executive, was born at Yokohama, Japan, the son of the Reverend Daniel Crosby Greene and Mary Jane Forbes. Until he was thirteen, he lived chiefly in Japan, where his parents were Congregational missionaries.

After a year's furlough in Europe (1887–1888), the family lived in Auburndale, Mass., and Greene attended Newton (Mass.) High School. Within a year his parents returned to Japan, and thereafter he saw them infrequently. He won a $250 freshman scholarship to Harvard and from then on paid all his academic and living expenses by newspaper reporting, proofreading, and summer "tutoring." As an undergraduate Greene worked on the *Harvard Crimson*, serving as managing editor and president in 1895–1896. In the second half of his senior year he accepted a fifteen-month post as tutor and companion to a Harvard undergraduate. Most of the time was spent in Switzerland, where Greene enrolled for a semester in the faculty of law at the University of Geneva. In the fall of 1897 he entered the Harvard Law School and a year later, while continuing his newspaper reporting, became editor of a new alumni weekly, the *Harvard Bulletin*. During his tenure (1898–1899, 1900–1901), he transformed it from an athletic journal into a general medium of Harvard news.

This activity led Greene to abandon his law studies, and in 1899 he joined the staff of the University Press of Cambridge, which he served as New York salesman, printing plant superintendent, and assistant to the general manager. On Apr. 28, 1900, he married May Tevis; they had one son. In the summer of 1901, Greene became secretary to Harvard President Charles W. Eliot. In 1905 he was elected secretary to the Harvard Corporation (the president and fellows of Harvard College), member of the faculty, and member of the reorganized admissions committee. He was instrumental in establishing the first alumni directory and the official *University Gazette*.

Eliot retired in 1909, and for a year Greene (who was commonly said to have been Eliot's personal choice for the presidency) continued as secretary to the Harvard Corporation. However, the new president, A. Lawrence Lowell, seemed unprepared to give him the wide responsibilities he had enjoyed under Eliot. Greene nevertheless recognized Lowell's great capacities, and the parting a year later was entirely amicable.

Greene then became general manager of the Rockefeller Institute for Medical Research in New York City. This led in 1912 to five years of close association with John D. Rockefeller, Jr., first as an adviser on business and philanthropic matters and representative of Rockefeller interests on the boards of two railroads and several industrial corporations, and in 1913, after its incorporation under New York law, as secretary and executive officer of the new Rockefeller Foundation. Greene was particularly interested in the International Health Division of the foundation, which sponsored work on the control of hookworm, malaria, and yellow fever. He enthusiastically supported John D. Rockefeller, Jr.'s, successful effort to break the taboo against public discussion of venereal disease control and in 1916 became one of the organizers, treasurer, and executive committeeman of the American Social Hygiene Association.

With the outbreak of World War I, Greene took charge of the war relief activities of the Rockefeller Foundation and, at the request of Herbert Hoover, supervised arrangements for the shipment of the first relief supplies to Belgium and organized the commissions sent to Europe under Rockefeller sponsorship to recommend and inspect relief activity. He resigned his Rockefeller connections in 1917, but continued as a trustee of the Rockefeller Institute (later Rockefeller University) until 1932. In 1928 he renewed his tie with the Rockefeller Foundation and the General Education Board, serving as a trustee until he reached retirement age in 1939.

Under the influence of Frederick A. Cleveland, head of the New York Bureau of Municipal Research, Greene helped establish the Institute for Government Research (1916), a Washington-based group dedicated to public efficiency and economy at the national level. Eventually it took the name of one of its most generous benefactors and leading trustees, Robert S. Brookings. Greene remained a trustee and member of the executive committee until 1945.

In 1917 Greene was appointed executive secretary of the American Shipping Mission, representing the United States on the Allied Maritime Transport Council in London. The council virtually controlled the allocation of Allied shipping resources. After the war he attended the Versailles conference, where he served as one of the four joint reparation secretaries.

Elected a partner of the banking house of Lee Higginson and Co. in 1918, Greene returned to New York in May 1919. For the next thirteen years he handled loan negotiations (particularly in the public utility field) in England, South America, and Japan. He brought to his work "the strength of an unusually agreeable personality, wide experience of men and imperturbable good sense." Greene continued to devote more than half his time to public service projects, one of which was the Institute of Pacific Relations. He was chairman of the American Council of the institute from 1929 to 1932; and after the Japanese takeover in Manchuria in September 1931, he spoke and wrote frequently on the Asian situation.

In 1932 Greene suddenly faced nearly total ruin with the failure of Lee Higginson, which was precipitated by the collapse of the financial empire of Ivar Kreuger, the Swedish "match king" who left the firm holding some $8 million of his debentures based on fraudulent credit. Although he had had little to do with Kreuger, Greene was chosen to announce to the public, on June 14, 1932, the plan to liquidate the banking partnership and create a new firm, capitalized by outside sources. Needing to make a fresh start, he accepted the Wilson professorship of international politics at the University College of Wales, Aberystwyth, which provided opportunities for public discussion of international issues, particularly those concerning the tense situation in the Far East.

Greene felt most comfortable in an academic setting. One of his principal interests remained Harvard University, which he served as overseer in 1911–1913, 1917–1923, and 1944–1950. During the early 1920's, he had opposed with characteristic forthrightness President Lowell's statements and actions regarding the proportion of Jewish students and the status of black students in Harvard College.

In 1934 Greene returned to Cambridge as secretary to the Harvard Corporation and director of the Harvard tercentenary. This great academic festival, which he spent two years planning, admirably saluted both Harvard's accomplishments and the achievement of American higher education. President Franklin D. Roosevelt attended and spoke, and seventy-one scholars received honorary degrees and participated in a series of major conferences. Greene continued his career at Harvard as secretary to the two governing boards until his retirement in 1943.

After the death of his first wife in 1941, Greene married Dorothea Rebecca Dusser de Barenne on Aug. 20, 1942; they had one son. Physically strong to the end of his life, erect and confident in bearing, precise in manner, meticulous in matters of detail, Greene appeared to some a bit of an autocrat, somewhat rigid in questions of propriety, a high-minded and urbane gentleman of the old school. His colleagues at Harvard, however, greatly valued "his clarity, candor, imagination, and fine sense of decorum." His calm determination, carefully considered opinions, and broad viewpoint made him an outstanding example of the disinterested, prudent trustee.

[The Jerome Greene Papers are in the Harvard University Archives. Greene also left an autobiographical typescript, "Recollections of a Varied Life," major portions of which appeared as *Years with President Eliot (ca.* 1960); and *Reminiscences* (1964). For the family background, see Evarts B. Greene, *A New Englander in Japan: Daniel Crosby Greene* (1927). For a short account of Lee Higginson and Co., see Barrett Wendell, *History of Lee Higginson and Company 1848–1918* (1921). *The Tercentenary of Harvard College, Chronicle of the Tercentenary Year 1935–1936* contains Greene's narrative and the major documents bearing on the celebration.]

WILLIAM BENTINCK-SMITH

GREENSLET, FERRIS (June 30, 1875–Nov. 19, 1959), editor, publisher, biographer, and sportsman, was born in Glens Falls, N.Y. He was the son of George Bernard Greenslet, a merchant, and Josephine Ferris. He grew up in the genteel surroundings so typical of the Victorian middle class. He was introduced early to the two greatest loves of his life, books and fishing.

Greenslet graduated Phi Beta Kappa from Wesleyan University in 1897. He went on to Columbia University, earned the M.S. in 1898 and the Ph.D. in 1900. His dissertation, *Joseph Glanvill—A Study in English Thought and Letters of the Seventeenth Century,* was published the same year. In 1901, with "no warning, intention or spiritual preparation," "FG," as he was affectionately known, moved to Boston, working first in the Boston Public Library as a researcher and then for the *Boston Advertiser* before becoming associate editor of *The Atlantic Monthly* in 1902. Greenslet married Ella S. Hulst of Cambridge on April 25, 1905. They had two children.

In 1907, when the post of literary editor of Houghton Mifflin publishing company opened up, he accepted, beginning an association that would last fifty-two years.

Before becoming an editor, Greenslet established himself as a superb scholar with *The Quest of the Holy Grail* (1902), and as a biographer with *Walter Pater* (1903), *The Life of James Russell Lowell* (1905), and *The Life of Thomas Bailey Aldrich* (1908). His skills remained sharp enough even after thirty-five years as literary editor to write *The Lowells and Their Seven Worlds* (1946). Three years later he collaborated with Charles P. Curtis, Jr., on an anthology, *The Practical Cogitator.* But his most fascinating work is his spicy and impressionistic collection of reminiscences, *Under the Bridge* (1943). One reviewer observed that *Under the Bridge* revealed "the working of an unprejudiced, mature mind," lamenting only "that the multiplicity of its author's memories too often reduces to a page what might in other books have filled a chapter."

Many of those memories showed Greenslet to be proudest of his angling prowess, and that his visits to London received more notice in the *Fishing Gazette* than in the *Bookseller.* No year passed between 1910 and 1955 without several of his articles about fishing, particularly salmon and trout fishing, appearing in fishermen's magazines throughout the world.

Semiretirement after 1942 provided Greenslet with time to clear the name of an ancestor, Ann Pudector Greenslet, hanged as a witch at Salem in 1692. Even the 1957 pardon of all Salem witches

did not satisfy him, as Greenslet pointedly proclaimed in a newspaper interview.

As the years passed Greenslet added additional duties to his position as literary editor at Houghton Mifflin. He became a director in 1910, a member of the executive committee in 1918, general manager of the trade department in 1933, and a vice-president in 1936. Highly esteemed for his work, he turned down numerous offers to work in other publishing houses and to edit the *Dictionary of American Biography* in order to remain in a Boston that he had come to love. In 1959 *Publishers Weekly* put Greenslet's career into perspective. Crediting him with being a literary man who also possessed a healthy respect for budgets and profits, the editors called him an extraordinary individual, his most impressive quality being an ability to talk knowledgeably with sales managers, production chiefs, and advertising and publicity directors, as well as with authors.

Greenslet's talent for making money for Houghton Mifflin while upholding high standards helped make the Boston house one of the most important in the nation. He discovered Laura Krey as well as Stuart Cloete, and turned Willa Cather into an important author. He pursued Henry Adams for ten years before convincing Adams to give him the manuscript for *The Education of Henry Adams.* Six publishers rejected Henry Sydnor Harrison's *Queed,* but Greenslet took a chance. The sales of the novel totaled $225,000—a tribute to Greenslet's perspicacity. Greenslet once observed that "when we are young, we read with excitement and wonder, to find out and forecast. Later for pleasure and participation, sometimes for mere recollection and change. In the third stage, we read for memory and recognition."

Greenslet was a learned man who did not tolerate the pretentious, pompous, or pedantic in authors. A warm writer with a felicitous style and a master of repartee, he appreciated the well-fashioned phrase and the carefully chosen word. "The more the marble wastes, the more the statue grows," he explained. Yet another point of editorial insistence can be summed up in the question, "Does it bleed if you prick it?" He looked for sensitivity and passion plus a recognition of the human condition.

Greenslet was the epitome of the "gentleman and scholar." *Under the Bridge* reveals the author to be a reasonable and likable man. Perhaps ultimately this explains his success, for he was influential in the careers and lives of most of the New England authors—he personally knew 192 of the 230 mentioned by Van Wyck Brooks in *New England: Indian Summer.* He died in Cambridge.

[On Greenslet's life and work, see Dale Warren, "The Editor Who Outwhistled Shaw," *Saturday Review*, Apr. 9, 1960.

See also obituaries in the *New York Herald Tribune,* Nov. 20, 1959; *New York Times,* Nov. 20, 1959; *Publishers Weekly,* Nov. 30, 1959; and *Wilson Library Bulletin,* January 1960.]

WILLIAM E. STEIRER, JR.

GREGG, ALAN (July 11, 1890–June 19, 1957), foundation officer and medical educator, was born in Colorado Springs, Colo., the son of James Barlett Gregg, a Congregational minister, and Mary Needham. In 1907 he enrolled in Harvard College, where he was elected president of the Signet Society and the *Lampoon.* Perhaps the most portentous event of his college days, however, was hearing Sigmund Freud, Carl Jung, and Sandor Ferenczi lecture in 1909. Gregg developed an interest in psychiatry that he pursued throughout his career.

After graduating from Harvard in 1911, Gregg traveled extensively in Europe, then entered Harvard Medical School in 1912 and received the M.D. in 1916. Following an internship at the Massachusetts General Hospital, he joined the Harvard Medical Unit serving in France in 1917.

When he returned to the United States in 1919, Gregg had decided upon a career in public health. Wickliffe Rose, director of the International Health Board of the Rockefeller Foundation, promptly hired him to work on malaria and hookworm in Brazil. Gregg impressed his superiors during the three years that he worked in Brazil, and in 1922 he was named associate director of the Division of Medical Education of the Rockefeller Foundation in New York.

Despite this impressive title, Gregg's service for the next two years amounted to an apprenticeship. He spent most of his time reading applications for new programs in medical schools and writing declinations. This assignment was vital to his training, for by explaining to applicants why their proposals had to be turned down, he learned a great deal about what needed to be done to improve medical education. Trips to Panama and Colombia to survey opportunities for making grants to medical schools added depth to his

training. It was during this period, in 1923, that Gregg married Eleanor Agnes Barrows; they had four children.

Gregg's career as a foundation officer really began in 1924, when he was sent to Europe to head the Paris office of the Rockefeller Foundation. For the next seven years, Gregg steeped himself in European medical education, visiting scores of institutions. These visits yielded firsthand information that proved of great help when he evaluated proposals and made policy recommendations for grants. Gregg learned the strengths and weaknesses of the European systems; and, above all, his years in Europe convinced him that a "one world" approach to medical research and medical education should prevail.

In 1931 Gregg became director of the newly reorganized division of medical sciences of the Rockefeller Foundation in New York City, a position he held for the next two decades. Priorities within the foundation were uncertain, and he immediately established himself as an effective spokesman for medical interests. Gregg consistently won a handsome share of the foundation's budget for his division. Moreover, he recruited distinguished officers for his staff and made effective use of their services.

Gregg came to realize quite early in his relationship with the trustees of the foundation that the professional staff would have to serve as a conduit between the applicants, all of whom were highly specialized experts, and the trustees, most of whom were laymen. His presentations to the trustees were models of clarity and precision, cutting through the technical and the extraneous in order to reach the important features of the proposals. And while he sought to anticipate and circumvent disagreements, he did not shrink from differences when they arose, defending staff recommendations vigorously and with great eloquence.

Perhaps the best example of Gregg's courage under fire was his support of projects that were too controversial to secure funding elsewhere. For more than a decade he defended grants for Alfred Kinsey's pioneering work on human sexual behavior against critics within and outside the foundation. In this particular case, as in numerous others, the division of medical sciences of the Rockefeller Foundation was a forward-looking institution.

Unabashed elitism was the essence of Gregg's approach to philanthropy. He thought that his task was to identify the best minds and to create optimal environments in which they could work.

To accomplish these goals, he advocated the establishment of a small number of research institutes in specific fields, with endowments large enough to support long-range projects. No issue generated more friction with the trustees, most of whom favored disbursing funds more broadly through small, short-term grants to numerous investigators. It was a credit to his powers of persuasion that Gregg secured approval for a few major centers, such as the Montreal Neurological Institute, and for a number of endowed chairs in crucial areas of research at outstanding medical schools.

In 1951 Gregg became vice-president of the Rockefeller Foundation. This appointment relieved him of administrative duties and made possible more consulting, lecturing, and writing. In 1954 he retired. His final years were devoted to the role of medical statesman, a duty that he discharged with dignity and charm. He died at Big Sur, Calif.

Gregg was the exemplar of a new breed of professional to which the twentieth century gave rise—the foundation officer. He insisted that philanthropic programs be conducted like scientific experiments: with careful planning, with the courage to take risks, with continuing evaluations that would follow the evidence wherever it led, and with the provision to terminate the experiment. Because he had a view of medicine that few could equal, he usually recognized which investigators were pursuing truly original and important work. He was no less perspicacious with regard to the potential of new disciplines. Throughout his career Gregg did everything within his power to promote the development of psychiatry through grants to such allied fields as neurophysiology, neurology, and psychology.

[Wilder Penfield, *The Difficult Art of Giving: The Epic of Alan Gregg* (1967), is the only biographical study. It contains a reasonably complete bibliography of Gregg's many articles and books. Gregg's official papers are in the Rockefeller Foundation Archives. A partially complete oral history of Gregg, done by Saul Benison, is on file at the Oral History Research Office of Columbia University. Gregg gave a memoir to the Columbia University Oral History Collection (1956). His work for the Rockefeller Foundation is discussed in memoirs by Flora Rhind and by John B. Grant, both in the same collection. For an obituary see the *New York Times*, June 21, 1957.]

JAMES H. JONES

GRISCOM, LLOYD CARPENTER (Nov. 4, 1872–Feb. 8, 1959), diplomat, lawyer, and newspaper publisher, was born at Riverton, N.J., the son of Clement Acton Griscom, cofounder and president of the Red Star Line, and Frances Canby Biddle. He grew up among the social elite of Philadelphia; but the luxury of wealth was tempered by the family's Quaker heritage and, for him, by the austere regimens of the private schools he attended in Switzerland, Paris, and Philadelphia.

After receiving the B.Phil. in 1891 from the University of Pennsylvania, Griscom entered the university law school but left in 1893 because of poor health. He soon secured appointment as unpaid private secretary to Thomas F. Bayard, newly appointed United States ambassador to Great Britain. During the next year Griscom had his first experience of the diplomatic world and began a lifelong acquaintance with the British aristocracy. After returning home in September 1894, he resumed his law studies at the New York Law School. Griscom's legal education was again interrupted from January to April 1895, when he accompanied the noted writer Richard Harding Davis on a journey later described in Davis' *Three Gringos in Venezuela and Central America* (1896). He then completed his studies and was admitted to the New York bar in 1896.

After a brief term in 1897 as deputy assistant district attorney of New York City, his health again declined and Griscom moved to Arizona to recover. He left there to enlist for service in the Spanish-American War, and was commissioned a captain in the Army Quartermaster Corps in May 1898. Made aide-de-camp to Major General James F. Wade, Griscom spent the war months in an army camp in Georgia. In September 1898 he accompanied General Wade to Cuba, where Wade headed the United States commission that arranged the evacuation of the Spanish forces from the island. He returned home and was discharged in January 1899.

Determined to return to diplomatic service, Griscom used his father's influence to secure appointment as secretary of the United States legation at Constantinople. He became chargé d'affaires in December 1899, when Minister Oscar Straus returned home on leave. Straus did not resume his post; and for the next fifteen months Griscom, not yet thirty years old, conducted a vigorous campaign to persuade the Turkish government to pay $90,000 to United States citizens as settlement of claims arising from the Armenian massacres of 1894. Using the visit of an American battleship to imply the threat of force, he finally collected the money. This established his reputation with Secretary of State John Hay, and he was made minister to Persia. On his way there, Griscom stopped in England to marry Elizabeth Duer Bronson, whom he had met in Constantinople. They had two sons.

After a fashionable London wedding on Nov. 2, 1901, the couple journeyed to their new post, where they spent the following year. Late in 1902 Griscom achieved senior diplomatic status with his appointment as minister to Japan, where he served during the Russo-Japanese War of 1904–1905. Although the post was a responsible one, most of the diplomatic activity that led to the peace conference at Portsmouth, N.H., occurred in Washington and St. Petersburg, the Japanese having desired the conference from the start. Furthermore, Griscom found himself handicapped by his extreme youth in a land where age and status were closely associated. Nevertheless, he was regarded by President Theodore Roosevelt as having performed creditably; and in 1906 he became United States ambassador to Brazil. His main duty there was to prepare for the visit of Secretary of State Elihu Root to the Pan-American Conference at Rio de Janeiro. At the end of the year Griscom was named to his last and highest post, that of United States ambassador to Italy. He served in Rome from 1907 to 1909, and took a leading part in organizing relief work after the great Messina earthquake of Dec. 27, 1908.

The advent of the William Howard Taft administration in 1909 ended Griscom's diplomatic career. The policy of promotion for merit and retention of able men in the diplomatic service, put into practice by John Hay and Theodore Roosevelt, was counter to the political patronage tradition; and Taft's term saw a revival of the older practices. Griscom had thus been one of a small body of American diplomats who for a time had enjoyed something like career status, his youthfulness and meteoric rise making him perhaps the most striking example of them all.

Returning to New York to practice law, Griscom was briefly involved in politics. He served as president of the New York County Republican Committee in 1910–1911, resigning after an unsuccessful attempt to harmonize the Taft and Roosevelt wings of the party. Upon United States entry into World War I in 1917, he joined the army as a major in the Adjutant General's Corps and served in France with the Seventy-seventh Division (1918). In France, General John J. Pershing, who had been military attaché at Tokyo when Griscom was there, detached Griscom to serve in London as his personal liaison with the British War Office. In this obscure but important post, Griscom brought his diplomatic skills to bear on behind-the-scenes frictions among the Allies. He was promoted to lieutenant colonel; and after the armistice he received the Distinguished Service Medal, and King George V made him a knight commander of St. Michael and St. George.

After the war Griscom was president of the Huntover Press, which published daily and weekly newspapers on Long Island. In 1929 he married Audrey Margaret Crosse (his first wife had died in 1914); they had no children. In later life he was coauthor of a drama, *Tenth Avenue*, which was made into a motion picture, and wrote a volume of memoirs entitled *Diplomatically Speaking*. He died at Thomasville, Ga.

Griscom was intelligent, energetic, and a good organizer. An amateur linguist, he learned nine languages and wrote English prose with wit and facility. Although he mixed well with all sorts of people, he was always an aristocrat in manner and outlook, and his career owed much to his privileged beginnings.

[Lloyd C. Griscom, *Diplomatically Speaking* (1940), is a lively account of the subject's youth and public life. Richard Harding Davis, *Three Gringos in Venezuela and Central America* (1903), contains information on the Caribbean journey of 1895. An obituary is in the *New York Times*, Feb. 9, 1959; and references are in E. E. Morison, ed., *The Letters of Theodore Roosevelt*, 8 vols. (1951–1954). The Oral History Collection of Columbia University has a memoir by Griscom recorded in 1951.]

DAVID F. HEALY

GRISCOM, LUDLOW (June 17, 1890–May 28, 1959), ornithologist, was born in New York City, the son of Clement Acton Griscom and Genevieve Sprigg Ludlow. His socially prominent parents were in comfortable circumstances, and the boy received instruction from private tutors until he entered the Symes School at the age of eleven. His parents frequently took him to Europe, and these experiences stimulated his interest in languages. His linguistic ability was unusual; he ultimately spoke five languages fluently, was able to read ten others with ease, and could translate another dozen and a half with the assistance of dictionaries and other aids.

Griscom's parents understandably felt that he was destined for the foreign service. He completed his preparatory studies at age fifteen, and passed the entrance examinations for Harvard. Since he was too young to enter college, he remained at home for two years, studying music (principally piano) and languages. His proficiency at the keyboard was such that he considered becoming a concert pianist, but a growing fascination with birds, begun in early childhood, prompted him to reconsider. In the fall of 1907, Griscom entered Columbia University as a prelaw student, but by the time of his graduation in 1912 he had determined on a career in ornithology.

He began graduate work in ornithology at Cornell in the fall of 1912, studying under Arthur A. Allen. Griscom spent several summers teaching ornithology at the University of West Virginia, having declined his father's offer of financial assistance. In 1915 he received the M.S. and remained at Cornell as an instructor in biology for a year, then worked at the American Museum of Natural History in New York City. Since no opening was available in the Ornithology Department, Griscom briefly held a position in the Department of Fishes. He entered the Department of Ornithology as an assistant under Frank M. Chapman early in 1917. His duties were interrupted by service as a second lieutenant in Army Intelligence from 1917 to 1919. During part of 1918, Griscom was a delegate to the Second Interallied Propaganda Conference in London.

Griscom was made assistant curator of ornithology at the American Museum in 1921. His *Birds of the New York City Region* (1923) became the standard text on the subject. While a member of the museum staff, Griscom participated in expeditions to Nicaragua (1917), Panama (1924, 1927), and Yucatán (1926). In addition to his expertise in ornithology, he was also an accomplished botanist, and was credited with discovering and naming a number of new species. In 1923 he accompanied the Gray Herbarium expedition to the Gaspé Peninsula as a volunteer botanical assistant, and in 1925 served in the same capacity on a similar expedition to Newfoundland. Griscom met Edith Sumner Sloan, a nurse working at one of the Grenfell missions, during the latter trip. They were married Sept. 14, 1926, and had three children. Their honeymoon in

Panama was shared in part with Griscom's colleague Maunsell Crosby, since both men were interested in frigate birds, which are resident there.

Relations between Griscom and Frank Chapman were not cordial, and Griscom therefore accepted an appointment as research curator in zoology at the Museum of Comparative Zoology at Harvard in 1927. In 1930 he directed a Harvard-sponsored expedition to Guatemala. Griscom's work in Central America resulted in monographs on the birds of Guatemala (1932) and Panama (1935). A study of the ornithology of Nicaragua remained unpublished at the time of his death. The major work to come out of his travels to the region was *Distributional Check List of the Birds of Mexico* (1940, 1957).

Griscom's other books include *Monographic Study of the Red Crossbill* (1937), *Modern Bird Study* (1945), *Birds of Nantucket* (1948), *Birds of the Concord Region* (1949), *Birds of Massachusetts* (1955), and *Birds of Martha's Vineyard* (1959), written with Guy Emerson.

Griscom was unusual among museum ornithologists in that he was a tireless and enthusiastic fieldworker. He pioneered in developing techniques of field identification, some of which were later used with great success by Roger Tory Peterson in his field guide series. Griscom had unusually acute sight and hearing, and could readily identify birds by their shape, color pattern, and song. He was greatly interested in local faunistics, and was commonly regarded as the best field identifier of birds in the northeastern states. Difficult problems of identification were generally referred to him by others. Griscom irked some colleagues because, as one of them put it, he had an opinion about everything and he was invariably right. He expressed himself strongly and was very positive in his views. As he grew older, he cultivated the idea that he was a character, and he could be brusque to the point of discourtesy.

In the last decade of his life Griscom suffered from Buerger's disease, a circulatory disorder. He suffered strokes in 1949 and in 1956. As his condition worsened, he had difficulty speaking, had trouble walking and writing, and could not hold a pair of binoculars. He could still identify birds with ease, though, and found friends to drive him into the field, failing which a hired driver and nurse would accompany him. In 1958, although he was forced to spend most of his time in a wheelchair, Griscom and his wife traveled from southern and western Africa to Morocco, locating hundreds of bird species that he had not previously seen. He died in Cambridge, Mass.

[An additional work by Griscom is "Historical Developments of Sight Recognition," *Proceedings of the Linnaean Society of New York*, March 1954. A major source of information is Roger Tory Peterson, "In Memoriam: Ludlow Griscom," *Auk*, October 1965. Additional information was supplied by Eugene Eisenmann of the Department of Ornithology, American Museum of Natural History.]

KEIR B. STERLING

GROSZ, GEORGE (July 26, 1893–July 6, 1959), painter and caricaturist, was born in Berlin, Germany, the son of Carl Grosz and Marie Schultze. In 1902 Grosz attended the Oberrealschule in Stolp, Pomerania, and studied art briefly with an interior decorator named Grot. He also copied the spirited *Max und Moritz* illustrations of Wilhelm Busch and filled a notebook with his own drawings of knights and castles, American Indians, and frontiersmen (he had read James Fenimore Cooper).

After expulsion from school for attacking a teacher who had struck him, Grosz decided to become a painter. In 1909 he entered the Royal Saxon Academy of the Fine Arts in Dresden. There he studied under conservative artists, including Richard Müller, a picturesque academician who attacked all modern art as "smears of offal" and insisted on rigorous draftsmanship. Outside class, however, Grosz discovered the expressionist paintings of Edvard Munch, whose somber mood appealed to him. He also began to draw cartoons in *Linienstil* ("line style"), a mannered outgrowth of the earlier *Jugendstil* ("youth style") or art nouveau then popular in magazines like *Simplizissimus*. He began selling these works in 1910.

Grosz graduated from Dresden in 1911, then continued his studies at the Royal Arts and Crafts School in Berlin, to which he had won a scholarship. His teacher, Emil Orlik, urged him to forget style and train himself in the rapid sketching of city scenes. He also began to experiment with oil painting, an area in which he was largely self-taught, since neither at Dresden nor at Berlin was he permitted to work in oil.

After a brief trip to Paris in the spring of 1913, which had little influence on his art, Grosz returned to Berlin to work independently. At the German Autumn Salon of that year (modeled on the French Salon d'Automne) the work of the futurists was heavily represented, and had an immediate effect on him. He began to paint angular, semicubist pictures with ray lines of movement, in which different aspects of a scene were depicted simultaneously. His mature style was just beginning to emerge when World War I broke out.

In 1914 Grosz enlisted in the infantry, and was appalled by his experience; the shaved head, the ill-fitting uniform, and the insolent officers filled him with rage. The bitter drawings that followed were not strictly antiwar; they were antiarmy or were aimed at the civilian effects of war—the profiteering, prostitution, and general collapse of moral standards. Grosz began these drawings in 1916, when illness won him a discharge from the army. His drawings became even more savage when he was conscripted in 1917. He had a nervous breakdown and was discharged in 1918. Among the acid cartoons that established him, almost overnight, as one of the great caricaturists of his time was one of a doctor inspecting a skeleton and pronouncing it "K V" (*Kriegs Verwendungsfähig*, "fit for military service"). In other drawings Grosz attacked the church for its "Gott mit Uns" attitude toward the war; his cartoon of Christ crucified in a gas mask shocked agnostics. During the inflation of the 1920's profiteers were a favorite target; often he portrayed their greed and lust in contrast with legless veterans begging alms on the street.

Grosz was also a member of the German Dada movement, which held a nihilistic concept of human beings as unthinking machines. He was an editor of the Dada magazine, *Every Man His Own Football*; designed Dada theater sets; and walked Berlin in a death's-head, carrying a calling card with an eye printed on one side and the legend "How do you think tomorrow?" on the other.

Grosz's fame spread with the publication of his satirical drawings: *The Face of the Ruling Classes* (1919), *Ecce Homo* (1922), *Mirror of the Bourgeoisie* (1924), and *Love Above All* (1931). They also brought him into conflict with the state; he was tried and fined twice, in 1920 for attacking the *Reichswehr* and in 1923 for "corrupting the inborn sense of shame and virtue innate in the German people." On May 26, 1920, he married Eva Louise Peter; they had two sons. A third brush with the law, for blasphemy and sacrilege, resulted in a conviction (1928) that was reversed by the State Court of Berlin (1929), the judge holding that the artist had "made himself the spokesman of millions who disavow war" by showing "how the Christian Church had served an unseemly cause which it should not have supported."

In 1931 Grosz had his first one-man exhibition in the United States at the Weyhe Gallery in New York. The next summer he taught a class at the Art Students League in New York. Returning to Germany that fall, he sensed the threat of Nazism and in January 1933 brought his wife to Bayside, N.Y., and took out his first citizenship papers. The children joined them later that year. It was none too soon. Grosz was branded Cultural Bolshevik Number 1 by the Nazis, his work was included in the "degenerate art" exhibition in Munich (1937), and in 1938 he was deprived of German citizenship. On November 29 of that year he became an American citizen.

In America, Grosz supported himself for many years by teaching. With Maurice Sterne he founded a small art school in 1933; and when Sterne withdrew the next year, he continued as its director and only instructor until 1937. He also taught at the Art Students League in the academic years 1933–1936, 1940–1942, 1943–1944, 1950–1953, and in the summer sessions of 1932, 1933, 1949, and 1950. In 1941–1942 he taught at the School of Fine Arts, Columbia University.

From the moment Grosz came to New York he began to fill his sketchbooks with faces, bits of architecture, ash cans, street signs, and a range of people from dowagers to burlesque queens. He explored the Bowery, the waterfront, and the theater section. He found some of his richest material in Central Park. In 1933–1936 he used these sketches as the basis for a series of watercolors representing his impressions of the city. While they are technically close to his German watercolors, their spirit is quite different; they reflect his admiration of New York, and even the satirical ones are mild compared with the ferocity of his Berlin works. Nor are his drawings of the time much sharper. Alexander King commissioned him to do cartoons for *Americana*, a short-lived magazine published erratically in 1932–1933, and told him to "scratch their eyes out, George." But "for me," Grosz wrote in his autobiography, "something of that spirit had died."

Grosz spent the summer of 1936 on Cape Cod and returned there nearly every summer for the next ten years. He also began to paint again in oil. The result was a series of landscapes and nudes (the latter often painted on the dunes) quite unlike anything he had done before. In Germany his early oils had been strongly futurist in character and had been followed, in the late 1920's, by a few

painstakingly realistic canvases related to the work of Otto Dix and the *Neue Sachlichkeit* ("new objectivity") movement. Now, however, a new side of Grosz appeared—romantic, even sentimental—a side that reacted against modernism and was drawn toward the storytelling pictures he had admired as a child. "How I would have loved," he wrote in his autobiography, "to be able to control the sweet, the dainty, the normal and the beautiful." The pictures, apparently an aberration (not a happy one) in a career devoted principally to the dark side of life, are witness to the complexity and contradictions in Grosz's nature.

After 1936, Grosz turned away from summer idylls. In the next ten years he painted a series of powerful oils that were apocalyptic visions of destruction and death: *A Piece of My World, I* and *II, The Survivor, I Was Always Present, Peace,II,* and *The Pit.* These were followed by the even more gruesome watercolors of the Stickmen series. In 1943 Grosz had painted an oil, *The Ambassador of Goodwill* (Metropolitan Museum of Art), in which two emaciated and fanatical soldiers threaten a fat one in a war-torn landscape. The thin soldiers seem to have been the genesis, at least in part, of the Stickmen—a race of insane zealots who lived in a land of mud and ruins, had their own gray flag, crucified hams, and attacked humans with an improvised arsenal of iron hooks and spears. In the watercolors depicting their antlike frenzies (1947–1948), Grosz created a powerful image of despair; perhaps the best is *Waving the Flag* (Whitney Museum of American Art).

A few oils of 1948–1950 continued the same mood, including *The Painter of the Hole, I* and *II,* and *The Gray Man Dances.* But as the war receded, Grosz turned back to pleasanter subjects that lacked the compelling quality of the war pictures. He did not again find a theme that evoked his full creative powers.

The peak of Grosz's American reputation was reached in 1954, when the Whitney Museum of American Art gave him a large retrospective exhibition. In May 1959 he was awarded the gold medal of the American Academy of Arts and Letters. That spring he returned to Berlin, where he died.

[A principal source of information is *A Little Yes and a Big No: The Autobiography of George Grosz* (1946). A biographical and critical study that includes an extensive bibliography of English-language publications on Grosz is John I. H. Baur, *George Grosz* (1954). A bibliography of foreign-language sources, compiled by Grosz, is in an exhibition catalog issued by Associated American Artists Gallery, *A Piece of My World in a World without Peace* (1946). Beth Irwin Lewis, *George Grosz, Art and Politics in the Weimar Republic* (1971), includes many German drawings. Herbert Bittner, ed., *George Grosz* (1960), illustrates 114 works and has an extensive bibliography.

In New York, Grosz is well represented in the Museum of Modern Art, the Metropolitan Museum of Art, and the Whitney Museum of American Art. Major American works by Grosz are also in the Wichita Art Museum; the Newark Museum; the Museum of Cranbrook Academy of Art; the Memorial Art Gallery, Rochester; and Arizona State College, Tempe. The George Grosz estate in Princeton, N.J., has a large collection of the artist's works and material pertaining to him.]

JOHN I. H. BAUR

GUEST, EDGAR ALBERT (Aug. 20, 1881–Aug. 5, 1959), writer of popular verse and newspaper columnist, was born in Birmingham, England, the son of Edwin Guest and Julia Wayne. After his father's copper brokerage venture failed in the hard times of the late 1880's, he immigrated to the United States. Settling in Detroit, he became an accountant for a brewery; then, in 1891, he brought over his wife and children.

Edwin Guest lost his job in the financial panic of 1893, with the result that his eleven-year-old son, "Little Eddie," was obliged to hunt out odd jobs after school. He ran errands and worked evenings at soda fountains until 1895, when he was hired as an office boy in the bookkeeping department of the *Detroit Free Press*. It was the start of an affiliation that lasted almost sixty-five years.

Left fatherless at seventeen, Guest was unable to finish high school. When a cub reporter's job opened at the newspaper, he moved to the news department. A temporary assignment on the exchange desk—where filler verse and feature items were clipped for reprinting—led him to volunteer a few lines of his own verse to the Sunday editor, Arthur Mosely, who printed them on Dec. 11, 1898. Other verses of a light, topical nature followed, and soon Guest's rhymes were appearing regularly in a weekly column called "Chaff" and later in "Blue Monday Chat." He took a turn on the police beat and then settled down to producing his own daily column of homespun verse and witty observations, "Edgar A. Guest's Breakfast Table Chat."

This feature became popular with readers, many of whom preserved the verses in scrapbooks and urged the editor to publish them in book form. Guest's brother Harry, a printer, brought out an 800-copy edition of *Home Rhymes* in 1909. Two years later *Just Glad Things* was similarly produced in a printing of 1,500 copies. Detroit Rotarians then became promoters of the short, genial, warmhearted bard of family and fireside. Entitled *Breakfast Table Chat* (1914), the Rotarian collection sold out so quickly that publishers and syndicates took notice. Beginning in 1916, Guest arranged with the Chicago firm of Reilly and Britton to publish his books. Guest's verses were soon blossoming in newspapers throughout the country, and a new collection came out every year or so.

Guest's subjects were the simple things of everyday life—relatives, friends, neighbors, the pleasures of childhood, the role of parents, the delights of nature, basic virtues, love of country, grief, and joy. First lines from some of the most widely quoted verses included:

It takes a heap o' livin' in a house to make it home . . .
Somebody said it couldn't be done . . .
My religion's lovin' God who made us one and all . . .
I like the olden way the best . . .
Success is being friendly when another needs a friend . . .
It never comes to Christmas but I think about the times . . .
The rich may pay for orchids but, oh, the apple trees . . .
What can I do for my country—I that have little of skill? . . .
Sittin' on the porch at night when all the tasks are done . . .
I'd rather be a failure than a man who's never tried . . .
A boy and his dog make a glorious pair . . .

On June 28, 1906, Guest married Nellie Crossman, and their domestic life—they had three children—provided the ideas for hundreds of Guest's verses. When *A Heap o' Livin'* (1916) sold 50,000 copies, it became amply evident that here was a phenomenon in the verse publishing field. Subsequent titles were *Just Folks* (1917), *Over Here* (1918), *Path to Home* (1919), *When Day Is Done* (1921), *All That Matters* (1922), *The Passing Throng* (1923), *Rhymes of Childhood*

(1924), *The Light of Faith* (1926), *Harbor Lights of Home* (1928), *The Friendly Way* (1931), *Life's Highway* (1933), *All in a Lifetime* (1938), *Today and Tomorrow* (1942), and *Living the Years* (1949). During World War I, Guest's verses cheered the doughboys on their way overseas while also giving special encouragement to the home front. Thousands of copies of *Over Here*, bound in khaki, were sent to France for distribution through military channels

Poetry critics did not exult. Dorothy Parker summarized their disdain with singular bluntness:

I'd rather flunk my Wassermann test
Than read a poem by Edgar Guest.

The increasingly popular versifier was unperturbed. As his stanzas were printed daily in more than 100 newspapers and a veritable procession of books appeared, his annual income soared above $130,000.

Meanwhile, Guest contributed to the development of the newer modes of communication. In the 1930's he was host of two radio programs, "It Can Be Done" and "Welcome Valley," and in 1951 he appeared on "A Guest in Your Home" on television. He also made phonograph recordings of his poems. In 1935 he went to Hollywood at the invitation of Universal Pictures. But he disliked the prepared scripts and a $3,500-a-week contract did not hold him beyond several months. Once a Swedenborgian, he joined the Episcopal Church after his marriage. He was a thirty-third-degree Mason and also served the American Press Humorists Association as president. When he died in Detroit, the city's flags were hung at half staff by order of the mayor.

Guest had never presumed to call himself a poet; by his own description he was "a newspaper man who wrote verses." The statistic that he had typed off more than 12,000 supported him in more ways than one.

[Guest's manuscripts, papers, and correspondence are in the Michigan Historical Collection at the University of Michigan and the Burton Historical Collection at the Detroit Public Library. On his life and work, see Edgar A. Guest, *Between You and Me* (1938); L. Cline, "Eddie Guest: Just Dad," *American Mercury*, Nov. 1925; B. Casseres, "Complete American," *ibid.*, Feb. 1927; J. Bakeless, "Laureate of the Obvious," *Outlook*, Aug. 6, 1930; *Rotarian*, June 1934, Sept. 1940, and Mar. 1946; *Time*, Sept. 9, 1935, and "A Heap O'Rhymin'," Mar. 19, 1951; *American Home*, Aug. 1935; J. P. McEvoy, "Sunny Boy," *Saturday Evening Post*, Apr. 30, 1938; *Saturday Review of Literature*, Mar. 4, 1939; M. W. Bingary, "Eddie Guest Himself," *Rotarian*, Sept. 1940; N. W. Kutner, "If You Were Mrs. Edgar Guest," *Good Housekeeping*, Aug. 1944; R. C. Hedke, "Poet Laureate of the Home," *Rotarian*, Mar. 1950; "Ever-Steady Eddie," *Newsweek*, Aug. 22, 1955; Royce Howes, "From Humble Start to Fame," *Detroit Free Press*, Aug. 6, 1959; "Into God's Slumber Grove," *Time*, Aug. 17, 1959; "10 Million Liked Him," *Newsweek*, Aug. 17, 1959, and E. A. Guest, Jr., *Detroit Magazine*, Aug. 21, 1966. An oil portrait of Guest by John S. Coppin is in the Detroit Community Arts Building.]

IRVING DILLIARD

GUFFEY, JOSEPH F. (Dec. 29, 1870–Mar. 6, 1959), U.S. senator, was born in Westmoreland County, Pa., the son of John Guffey, a farmer, and Barbaretta Hough. Guffey's uncles, James M. and Wesley Guffey, were prosperous oil speculators and influential in the Democratic party. A sister, Emma Guffey Miller, was a member of the Democratic National Committee in the 1920's and 1930's. Politics and his various enterprises occupied Guffey's life; he never married. He attended Princeton University for two years (1890–1892), and, while there, became a lifelong admirer of Woodrow Wilson.

Self-conscious as a public speaker, Guffey spent most of his political life in back rooms, where loyalty and connections advance careers. His first political assignment was as clerk of the Democratic City Committee of Pittsburgh, and at the age of twenty-four he became superintendent of city delivery in the Pittsburgh post office, both jobs being a tribute to an uncle's political influence. In 1899, through Judge James Hay Reed, a Republican family friend, Guffey joined the Philadelphia Company, a utilities' holding company, where he became general manager in 1901. (Thirty-five years later he defeated Reed's son in a senatorial election and then voted for a bill outlawing holding companies.) As a sideline Guffey invested in coal and oil leases, amassing enough wealth to strike out on his own in 1908. He concurrently broadened his Pennsylvania Democratic contacts, teaming with A. Mitchell Palmer and Vance McCormick to put together a slate of delegates supporting Woodrow Wilson at the Democratic Convention. His allies moved to Washington during the Wilson administration and left Guffey as chairman of the Pennsylvania Democratic State Committee. During World War I he worked for the petroleum service division of the War Industries Board before becoming sales director of the Alien Property Custodian's Office. Through a technicality in the law, he was able to pocket the interest on alien property seized during the war. In 1922 he was indicted for misuse of government funds, but the charges were dropped in 1930 after Guffey repaid more than $400,000 to the government.

The indictment hit Guffey at a low point in his business fortunes. His Guffey-Gillespie Oil Corporation and its subsidiary, the Atlantic Gulf Company, speculating in oil leases in the southwestern United States, Mexico, and Colombia, went bankrupt in 1921 and Guffey lost a considerable fortune. Yet within a few years, using funds borrowed from his sisters, he was again on his way to becoming a wealthy man through investments in East Texas oil fields. At the same time he built political alliances within the Pennsylvania and national Democratic parties, both of which, having come upon hard times, needed Guffey's organizational and fund-raising skills. He became an early Roosevelt-for-President booster and the state's most prominent Democrat in the early 1930's, although he failed to "deliver" Pennsylvania to Franklin D. Roosevelt in 1932.

But the New Deal's patronage power and the restlessness of union and black voters loomed as potential sources of victory. Guffey swiftly established himself as the principal conduit for federal patronage in Pennsylvania. One job, assistant to the attorney general, went to Robert L. Vann, editor-publisher of the *Pittsburgh Courier*, the most widely read black newspaper in the state. It was Vann who in 1932 had told his fellow blacks to turn Lincoln's picture to the wall, that their debts to the Republicans had been paid in full, and who persuaded Guffey that blacks would vote Democratic if the party demonstrated its concern. At Guffey's insistence the Democratic National Committee set up a special division for blacks. In 1934, with the help of steelworker and mineworker votes, Guffey became the first Democrat to be elected to the Senate from Pennsylvania since 1881.

At a time when liberalism was synonymous with New Deal idealism, Guffey stood out as a liberal who preached and practiced a tough brand of organization and patronage politics. Government jobs, he believed, were for loyal workers; civil service simply "develops inefficiency, protects incompetence, and promotes extravagance." Known as the "boss" of Pennsylvania's Democrats, Guffey insisted: "Ours isn't a machine; it's an organization for service." He was an un-swerving New Deal supporter, a friend of organized labor, and a staunch advocate of civil rights for blacks. He courted the South's hostility with his outspoken opposition to poll taxes and support of federal antilynching legislation. One major law bore his name, the Guffey-Vinson Act of 1937, which followed NRA price-fixing in the bituminous coal industry to the benefit of producers and workers; it also set a price-fixing precedent useful for the oil industry, which suffered from overproduction following the boom in East Texas fields where Guffey had speculated so successfully.

Guffey was one of the first to suggest that Roosevelt seek a third term (having Roosevelt on the ticket would help his own reelection campaign in 1940). The Pennsylvania Democratic party had been rent with factionalism as some of the businessmen Guffey had converted from Republicanism with the lure of WPA contracts sought to displace him. As New Deal liberalism declined, Guffey's commitment seemed to intensify. The Congress of Industrial Organizations considered his Senate voting record "100 per cent right." At the 1944 Democratic Convention, Guffey led the losing fight to retain Henry Wallace as the party's vice-presidential nominee. His political eclipse probably was foreshadowed by his unremitting support of Wallace in a time of increasing anti-New Deal feeling. Ironically, although known as a political boss, Guffey could not deliver the Pennsylvania delegation or the industrial-state Democratic bosses, who flocked to the candidacy of Senator Harry S. Truman of Missouri. Ever loyal to Roosevelt, Guffey campaigned vigorously for the ticket in 1944. But, when Roosevelt nominated six conservatives for State Department positions that December, Guffey unsuccessfully opposed their nominations. Younger Democrats eroded Guffey's base of support in Pennsylvania while, on the national scene, Truman privately labeled him a synthetic liberal. In 1946 Guffey lost a third-term bid by more than 600,000 votes. He retired in Washington, where he died.

[Guffey's papers are in the Washington and Jefferson College Library, Washington, Pa. His autobiography, *Seventy Years on the Red-Fire Wagon*, was privately printed in 1952. His only other book is a campaign tract, *Roosevelt Again!* (1940). Useful biographical information can be found in Charles Eugene Halt, "Joseph F. Guffey, New Deal Politician From Pennsylvania" (D.S.S. diss., Syracuse University, 1965);

and Joseph Alsop and Robert Kintner, "The Guffey," *Saturday Evening Post*, Mar. 26 and Apr. 16, 1938. For insights on Guffey as a New Deal politician, see *The Secret Diary of Harold L. Ickes*, 3 vols. (1954); J. David Stern, *Memoirs of a Maverick Publisher* (1962); Alfred B. Rollins, Jr., *Roosevelt and Howe* (1962); Richard Keller, "Pennsylvania's Little New Deal" (Ph.D. diss., Columbia University, 1962); Andrew Buni, *Robert L. Vann of the Pittsburgh Courier* (1974); Bruce M. Stave, *The New Deal and the Last Hurrah: Pittsburgh Machine Politics* (1970); and Ellis W. Hawley, *The New Deal and the Problem of Monopoly* (1966). On Guffey and World War II politics, see Allen Drury, *A Senate Journal 1943–1945* (1963); and John Morton Blum, ed., *The Price of Vision: The Diary of Henry A. Wallace 1942–1946* (1973). Also see Ray Sprigle, "Lord Guffey of Pennsylvania," *American Mercury*, Nov. 1936. The memoir of Henry A. Wallace in the Oral History Collection, Columbia University, includes substantial material on Guffey.]

JORDAN A. SCHWARZ

GUTHRIE, EDWIN RAY, JR. (Jan. 9, 1886–Apr. 23, 1959), psychologist, was born in Lincoln, Nebr., the son of Edwin Ray Guthrie, a store owner, and Harriet Louise Pickett. The family was of moderate means; Guthrie worked outside the home as soon as he could. While in high school he was a clerk for the railroad.

Guthrie showed scholastic promise early, reading Darwin's major works while in the eighth grade. His high school graduation thesis took the position that both science and religion, being dependent on words, and words being symbols dependent for their meanings on the experience of their users and auditors, could not express "Absolute Truth." Guthrie's later support of John Dewey's humanism and views on the nature of truth might be seen as related to Guthrie's early acceptance of that conclusion.

Psychology was still taught in the philosophy department when Guthrie entered the University of Nebraska in 1903. As an undergraduate he had several courses in philosophy but only one in general psychology. He graduated Phi Beta Kappa in 1907 with a degree in mathematics. He received the master's degree in philosophy at Nebraska in 1910 after taking graduate courses in psychology under Harry Kirke Wolfe, whose views on the philosophy of science were of great interest to Guthrie.

The "most stirring event" of Guthrie's academic life was hearing a paper, "Mind as an Observable Object" (published in 1911), by the philosopher E. A. Singer, whose interests extended into psychology. The paper was delivered at a meeting of the American Philosophical Association in 1910, the year Guthrie entered the University of Pennsylvania as a Harrison Fellow. Singer's contention that a relatively objective method could be applied to the scientific treatment of mind revived Guthrie's interest in psychology, which was waning as the result of an excursion into the field of psychophysics. Guthrie credited Singer with the first systematic statement that mind could be described in terms of behavior. His doctorate, in symbolic logic, was completed under Singer's supervision in 1912.

After two years of teaching mathematics at Boys Central High School in Philadelphia, Guthrie assumed his first academic position in the department of philosophy at the University of Washington. His early papers reflected his philosophical interest: "Formal Logic and Logical Form" (1914), "Russell's Theory of Types" (1915), and "The Field of Logic (1916). In 1919 he moved to the psychology department, directed by Stevenson Smith, with whom he collaborated on an elementary text, *Chapters in General Psychology* (revised as *General Psychology in Terms of Behavior* [1921]). This work established the authors as important proponents of a unified theory of learning.

A brief career as a second lieutenant in an infantry and an artillery officers' training school in 1918 served to turn Guthrie's attention away from books. In 1920, when Guthrie was an assistant professor at the University of Washington, he married Helen MacDonald of Berkeley, Calif. They had one son.

Guthrie was promoted to associate professor in 1926, and to full professor in 1928. He was dean of the graduate school from 1945 until 1951. From 1947 to 1951 he also served as executive officer in charge of academic personnel. As emeritus dean and emeritus professor he participated in teaching and other academic affairs until his final retirement in 1956.

Guthrie held strong beliefs concerning the nature of human communication and language, the nature of facts and explanation, and the nature of scientific truth—views that undoubtedly influenced his excursions into learning theory. His prejudice was clearly in favor of a behavioristic approach to the problems of psychology. He believed that the restriction of psychology to objectively observable behavior was necessary for its establishment as a science, and the phenomena of inner experience were to be neglected except as they could be translated into action. Guthrie stressed stimuli and movements in combination. The main characteristics of learning, according to him, were to be understood as instances of a very simple and very familiar principle: association by contiguity in time. His position is frequently referred to as one-trial learning, the idea that a single pairing of stimulus and response is at the basis of learning. Associations are established by contiguity in time. There is only one type of learning, and the same principle applies in all instances.

The modification of behavior generally requires repeated pairings of stimulus and response before one can predict when the response will occur in the presence of the cue. Reinforcers were effective because they changed the stimulus situation, thereby preserving the connection between the original stimulus situation and the response. Guthrie's position was supported by one major study conducted with George Plant Horton, the classic "cats in the puzzle box" series of experiments. The purpose of the study was to test Guthrie's prediction that what is learned tends to be a stereotyped movement, usually the one that obtains the first release from the box. The conclusion was that the stereotyped movement pattern of escape was initiated by the specific pattern of stimuli encountered. Other than this study, there was little support for Guthrie's position; he was accused of not being precise enough in his definitions of stimulus, response, and movement.

Guthrie was neither an experimentalist nor a formal theorist, and he was well aware of his failure to lay down specifications for the data of learning that were sufficiently precise to meet the requirements of laboratory experiments. He saw no need to become involved with detailed specificity of stimulus and response. Much of the appeal of his theory resulted from its not being committed to any particular unit of response. According to Guthrie, there are some phenomena of learning that can be understood only by taking specificity of response into account. At the molecular level it is the activity of effectors that is predicted from associative learning principles. On the other hand, there are cases in which a very molar response may properly be described according to its outcome rather than in terms of the effectors involved, and can be dealt with as a response unit in associative terms.

A number of ideas that have played important roles in the development of statistical learning theory bear signs of Guthrie's influence. These include the stimulus-response contiguity principle and the conception of gradual learning as the outcome of all-or-none laws operating on many components of a situation.

Guthrie was witty and warmhearted, and had a clear and charming style of exposition. Although his position was referred to as informal and intuitive, he maintained his status as a leading learning theorist primarily through the simplicity of his approach. Guthrie's contributions to other areas of learning included the translation, with his wife, of Pierre Janet's *Principles of Psychotherapy* (1924). In 1945 he served as president of the American Psychological Association.

Guthrie tended to focus his attention on the practical applications of theory but admitted that his chief interest was in undergraduate teaching, which may have accounted for his strong bent toward simplification. In 1958 Guthrie was awarded the gold medal of the American Psychological Association "for his distinguished contribution to psychology, as a theorist of the science of learning and a practitioner of the art of teaching." He died in Seattle.

[Guthrie's papers and correspondence from 1921 to 1958 are in the University of Washington Record Center. Other papers are in the manuscript collection. Additional works by Guthrie are *The Paradoxes of Mr. Russell* (1915); *General Psychology in Terms of Behavior* (1921), with S. Smith; "Exhibitionism," *Journal of Abnormal and Social Psychology*, 1922, with S. Smith; "Purpose and Mechanism in Psychology," *Journal of Philosophy*, 1924; "The Fusion of Nonmusical Intervals," *American Journal of Psychology*, 1928, with H. Morrill; "On the Nature of Psychological Explanations," *Psychological Review*, 1933; "Association as a Function of Time Interval," *ibid.*; "Discussion: Pavlov's Theory of Conditioning," *ibid.*, 1934; *"Reward and Punishment,"* ibid.; *The Psychology of Learning* (1935); "Tolman on Associative Learning," *Psychological Review*, 1937; "A Comparative Study of Involuntary and Voluntary Conditioned Responses," *Journal of General Psychology*, 1937, with G. Yacorzinski; "The Effect of Outcome on Learning," *Psychological Review*, 1939; "Association and the Law of Effect," *ibid.*, 1940; "Psychology of War Time," *Marriage and Family Living*, 1943; *Cats in a Puzzle Box* (1946), with G. P. Horton; "Pierre Janet: 1859–1947," *Psychological Review*, 1948; *Psychology* (1949), with A. I. Edwards; *Educational Psychology* (1950), with F. F. Powers; and "The Status of Systematic Psychology," *American Psychologist*, 1950.

For biographical information, see S. Koch, ed.,

Psychology, II (1959); the obituary in the *Seattle Times*, Apr. 24, 1959; and Fred D. Sheffield, "Edwin R. Guthrie 1886–1959," *Journal of Psychology*, 1959.]

BARBARA ROSS

GUZIK, JACK (1886/1888–Feb. 21, 1956), criminal entrepreneur and perhaps the most important figure of the Chicago underworld in the twentieth century, was probably born in Russia, the son of Max Guzik. He was raised in Chicago and became a citizen through the naturalization of his father in November 1898.

During the early years, newspapers and books spelled Guzik's last name many ways—Cusack, Cusick, Gusick—but eventually Guzik became the spelling used by newspapers and by Guzik himself. With regard to a first name, Guzik once told a reporter he did not know his real name but "everybody calls me Jack." Most writers have assumed, not unreasonably, that his original name was Jacob, and his nickname is generally given incorrectly as Jake. Finally, writers refer to both Jack and his brother Harry as "Greasy Thumb" Guzik, and there are many anecdotes explaining how one or the other earned that nickname. So far as can be determined, neither was called Greasy Thumb, and the name is probably a journalist's creation to spice up a news story.

In the decade preceding World War I, Guzik, like his brother Harry, emerged as a vice operator in Chicago's South Side red-light district. Harry was the better-known because of highly publicized convictions for white slavery in 1907 (and again in 1921). With the closing of the red-light district in 1914, the brothers moved their activities to the suburbs. Jack's early years were important for the contacts he made. These included "Bathhouse" John Coughlin, First Ward alderman, and his political associate, Michael ("Hinky Dink") Kenna, who between them protected gambling and vice in downtown Chicago from the 1890's through the 1930's. More important was John Torrio, who, as manager of James ("Big Jim") Colosimo's vice and entertainment activities in Chicago and its suburbs, was a rising underworld figure. Indeed, according to one account, Torrio financed Guzik's purchase of a Chicago brewery about 1919, thus launching him in the liquor business even before prohibition.

With the coming of national prohibition in January 1920 and the convenient assassination of Colosimo that May, Torrio was free to devote his considerable managerial skills to bootlegging. His most important aides were Guzik and a young man, recently arrived from Brooklyn, named Al Capone. In addition to interests in suburban vice resorts and growing participation in gambling, their rapidly expanding enterprises involved ownership of breweries, arrangements with importers in port cities such as Detroit and New York, and distribution of liquor to speakeasies in the downtown Loop and suburbs. At first Torrio was generally able to keep peace with other bootleggers, to the mutual profit of all. But from the beginning, Torrio's organization had a reputation for violence.

Several events soon altered the context of Chicago bootlegging. William E. Dever, elected mayor in 1923, ordered enforcement of the prohibition laws. In May 1924, Torrio was arrested while overseeing removal of beer from the Sieben brewery. Concurrently, open warfare broke out among bootleggers, especially between Torrio's associates and the North Side gang led initially by Dion O'Banion. In January 1925, Torrio pleaded guilty in federal court to charges arising from his arrest and received a nine-month sentence. On January 24, while riding with his wife in Guzik's limousine, Torrio was shot. He was hospitalized, then served his sentence, and afterward prudently left Chicago. With Torrio's departure, senior partners in the organization, sharing the profits of all enterprises, were Al Capone, his brother Ralph, Frank Nitti, and Jack Guzik. Guzik, the only Jew and some twelve years older than Capone, was respected for his business sense and was especially close to Capone, who was more violent and publicity-prone.

Building on earlier investments and on the political influence gained when Capone-led gunmen controlled the polling booths in April 1924, the senior partners turned Cicero, a Chicago suburb, into a regional gambling center. Guzik and the Capones spent much of their time there on business and pleasure. In 1927 they financed the Hawthorne Kennel Club in Cicero to provide the finest dog racing in the Chicago area. This was the beginning of investments in dog racing that soon extended into Florida and other states. In the Loop, where the group had firm political connections through Coughlin and Kenna, they not only dominated bootlegging but also, by 1930, coordinated gambling. Guzik, working with Hymie Levin, took special responsibility for Loop gambling. The success of the group in gang wars allowed its members to expand their bootlegging activities. After elimination of the beleaguered North Side gang in the notorious St. Valentine's Day Massacre of Feb. 14, 1929, the Capone mob tapped the economic opportunities in the growing entertainment district on Near North Side. Because Capone spent much of his time in Florida from 1927 on, and part of 1929–1930 in Philadelphia jails, Guzik often exercised day-to-day supervision for the senior partners.

Guzik's relatives shared the wealth. His brother Harry managed a number of syndicate vice activities. Another brother, Sam, operated slot machines in the western suburbs of Chicago. Louis Lipschultz, brother of Jack's wife, was in charge of bootlegging in Cicero and nearby suburbs. Finally, after the marriage of Guzik's daughter, Jeanette, in 1929—a social event attended by aldermen, policemen, and gunmen—his son-in-law became a business associate. His son Charles, born in 1909, and a younger adopted son apparently did not become active in Jack's businesses.

The worldwide notoriety of the Capone gang triggered investigations by the Internal Revenue Service (IRS) that, from 1929 to 1931, resulted in prison terms for the four senior partners, as well as Sam Guzik and Louis Lipschultz. In November 1930, Jack Guzik was found guilty of evading taxes of $229,000 on an income of $650,000 for 1927–1929 and was sentenced to five years and a fine of $17,500. When the appeal failed, he served from Apr. 7, 1932, until Dec. 14, 1935. Upon release he still faced civil tax liabilities, which the government in 1939 set at $628,787. After protracted negotiations he settled for $100,000 in 1942.

When Guzik left prison, prohibition had ended. Al Capone, still incarcerated, was later released, suffering from syphilis of the brain. But the enterprises they had put together in gambling, prostitution, nightclubs, labor racketeering, and numerous legal businesses were still expanding. Guzik and Nitti remained as senior figures until Nitti's suicide in 1943; then Guzik and Tony Accardo became major coordinators. So close was their partnership that they often filed joint tax returns.

Guzik, along with Hymie Levin, resumed responsibility for Loop gambling. For the remainder of his life, he maintained offices in the Loop, coordinated politics in the First Ward, and oversaw the lucrative gambling of downtown Chicago. He also had interests in casinos and

handbooks throughout the Chicago area. By the 1940's, Guzik and Accardo controlled the local company that, on contract with Continental Press (the national race wire), distributed racing and sports news to bookmakers. After 1947 they further expanded their Chicago gambling interests by systematically muscling in on the city's black- and Italian-run policy syndicates. By the 1940's, if not earlier, Guzik was the most important figure in Chicago-area gambling.

In the early 1940's, Guzik, Accardo, and their Chicago associates became interested in Continental Press. When James Ragen, chief owner and manager, refused them a partnership, they established a rival Trans-American Publishing and News Service. They called on underworld acquaintances throughout the country to set up regional distribution companies for Trans-American; and they used their own control in Chicago to give Trans-American a local near-monopoly in distributing sports news to gamblers. On June 24, 1946, Ragen was shot, and died following hospitalization. Within a year Guzik and friends reached an accommodation with Ragen's successors, leading to the dissolution of Trans-American and its merger with Continental. Three gunmen associated with Guzik were indicted for Ragen's murder, but were freed after witnesses died, recanted, or fled. In addition, a Chicago detective who pursued the case too vigorously was dismissed from the force and subsequently was killed—just before he was scheduled to talk with an investigator from the U.S. Senate Special Committee to Investigate Crime in Interstate Commerce, chaired by Estes Kefauver. In his own appearance before the Kefauver Committee in March 1951, after dodging a subpoena for months, Guzik gave only his name and claimed his Fifth Amendment right to silence.

In addition to his Chicago interests and the race wire, Guzik was an investor on a national scale in a variety of enterprises. In 1926 he purchased Miami real estate; and he and his family became frequent visitors to Florida. Over the years he invested in dog tracks and race tracks in the state, as well as casinos in the Miami area. In 1949 Guzik and Accardo muscled in on the "S & H Syndicate," which controlled Miami-area bookmaking. This investment did not turn out well, however. Guzik was also among those who transformed Las Vegas into a national gambling center after World War II.

Because the IRS showed continued interest in

Guzik's finances, his investments were often hidden; and it is impossible to trace the full range of his influence. Despite his local and even national importance as a coordinator of illegal enterprises, he seldom gained the notoriety of his more flamboyant colleagues. Barely five feet tall, and sometimes known to friends as "The Little Fellow," he resembled a fat penguin more than a criminal leader. He died in Chicago.

[The best sources on Guzik's life are the files of the Chicago Crime Commission, including nos. 65 and 65–100. The extensive Capone IRS file (SI 7085-F) has important materials, including a record of a long interview with Guzik in envelope 25 and copies of Guzik's bank accounts of the 1920's in envelope 80. The Guzik-Accardo IRS file (42739-FR) contains investigative reports on Guzik extending into the 1950's. The central files of the Department of Justice, in the National Archives, Washington, D.C., contain the prosecution file (no. 5-23-283) for Guzik's trial and appeal for income tax evasion. In negotiations concerning his civil tax liability, Guzik employed attorney Arthur W. Mitchell, whose correspondence with his client and with the IRS is in the Mitchell Papers, Chicago Historical Society. Many journalistic histories of Chicago and national crime mention Guzik's career: Jack McPhaul, *Johnny Torrio: First of the Gang Lords* (1971); John Kobler, *Capone: The Life and World of Al Capone* (1971); Ovid Demaris, *Captive City* (1968); and Estes Kefauver, *Crime in America* (1951), chapters 3, 4, 7.]

MARK H. HALLER

HAGUE, FRANK (Jan. 17, 1876–Jan. 1, 1956), political boss, was born in Jersey City, N.J., the son of John Hague and Margaret Fagen, both Irish immigrants. His father was a blacksmith and, later, a bank guard. Hague had little formal education, leaving public school when he was fourteen and in the sixth grade. During the next decade he managed a prizefighter, worked as a blacksmith's helper, and held various other jobs.

Downtown Jersey City was a Democratic stronghold dominated by Irish politicians. Hague began his public career there in April 1899, running successfully for the post of Second Ward constable. He then moved up the political ladder, maneuvering among warring Democratic factions. On Apr. 15, 1903, he married Jennie W. Warner; they had two children and adopted a third.

Hague's big political break came in 1913, when Jersey City adopted the commission form of government following a campaign led by the city's Progressive Republican newspaper, the *Jersey Journal*. He donned the mantle of civic reformer and, in a wide-open race among ninety-one candidates, obtained one of the five commission seats. During his first term Hague added to his reform image by conducting a well-publicized drive to root out police corruption. He also gained the backing of three other commissioners, including A. Harry Moore, leaving Republican Mayor Mark Fagan isolated and relatively helpless. In 1917 the Hague ticket (which included Moore) swept the field and Hague became mayor of Jersey City. This pattern was repeated in 1921 and 1925. The only major challenge to his local hegemony came in 1929, from a coalition of Republicans and dissident Democrats supported by the *Jersey Journal*. Despite sensational charges of corruption, developed by a state investigating committee, the Hague ticket won again.

Jersey City, the state's second most populous urban center, customarily played a strong role in Hudson County and New Jersey politics. Hague secured control of the county Democratic party apparatus, most county offices, and the Hudson County state legislature delegation by the end of 1917. In 1919, with a phalanx of county votes behind him, Hague obtained the governorship for a local banker, E. I. Edwards. In 1922 he moved Edwards into the U.S. Senate and won the governor's office for George Silzer, and the post of Democratic national committeeman for himself. In 1924 he became a national Democratic vice-chairman.

Hague dominated the Hudson County and New Jersey Democratic party, and was an influential figure in national party circles until the late 1940's. He supported Alfred E. Smith at the national conventions of 1924, 1928, and 1932, but then abandoned Smith to become Franklin D. Roosevelt's New Jersey bulwark. Hague's chief claim to fame in the state was his success in its gubernatorial elections. In 1925, 1931, and 1937 he won with A. Harry Moore; in 1940, with Charles Edison. State power gave Hague access to the judiciary and the prosecutor's office, and enabled him to withstand numerous investigations into his political practices. The only major case he lost was in the federal courts (*Hague* v. *C.I.O.*, 1939), where a local ordinance restricting freedom of speech and assembly was overturned.

The base of Hague's power was the Jersey City Democratic party, which was unified, reorganized, and made into a model political machine. Year-round nursing of the city's thirteen wards, plus maximum effort in each primary and general election, were the organization's operating principles. Hague also believed that the citizens should be given city services of high quality. His police and fire departments acquired enviable reputations; and in the 1930's he constructed a magnificent medical center, largely with federal funds. A tall, dour, menacing-appearing figure, Hague ran party and government with a heavy, ruthless hand. His softer side showed in his concern for youth, which led in 1937 to his notorious "I am the law" statement. Where the welfare of the city's children was concerned, he claimed that he made the ultimate decisions, that he was the law.

Although in the long run the New Deal undermined the service-for-votes style employed by the Hague machine, its short-range impact was supportive. Relief and public works programs were channeled through the organization, while Roosevelt strengthened the appeal of the Democratic party to Jersey City voters. Hague's local power reached its apex in 1937. He received 110,743 votes in the commission elections that May, compared with 6,798 for his principal opponent. The slide downhill began in 1941, when Governor Edison broke with Hague and initiated a drive for judicial and constitutional reform in New Jersey. Republican gubernatorial victories in 1943 and 1946 broke the web of state influence that had long buttressed his regime. Hague's inattention to the organizational needs of an aging party machine hurt him, as did his refusal to give adequate political recognition to Jersey City's Italian and Polish leaders. His 1945 ticket stayed with the old formula: four Irish Catholics and one Anglo-Saxon Protestant. Lulled by another easy victory that year, Hague continued to enjoy the spoils of office and the game of national politics, allowing his power base to atrophy.

In 1947 Hague resigned as mayor and turned the office over to a nephew, Frank Hague Eggers. This nepotism produced intraparty dissension. John V. Kenny, Hague's Second Ward leader, led a coalition of Democrats, Republicans, war veterans, and ethnic leaders to victory in the 1949 commission elections. When the Republicans again captured the governor's office that autumn, Hague resigned as county party leader. In 1952 he retired as Democratic national committeeman and national vice-chairman.

Hague attempted a comeback in 1953, supporting Elmer Wene in the gubernatorial primary and an Eggers-led slate in the Jersey City elections. Wene lost the nomination to Robert Meyner. Although Eggers won a city commission seat, Kenny retained control of the majority. These failures, followed by Eggers' death in July 1954, ended Hague's long political career. He died in New York City.

[See Richard Connors, *A Cycle of Power* (1971); George Creel, "The Complete Boss," *Colliers*, Oct. 10, 1936; John Davies, "Frank Hague: Last of the Bosses," *Newark Evening News*, July 17–Sept. 2, 1949; Thomas Fleming, "I Am the Law," *American Heritage*, June 1969; Mark Foster, "Frank Hague of Jersey: The Boss as Reformer," *New Jersey History*, Summer 1968; Martin Gately, " '49–The Wildest Election," *Jersey Journal*, Apr. 14–May 12, 1969; Dayton McKean, *The Boss: The Hague Machine in Action* (1940); and George Rapport, *The Statesman and the Boss* (1961). A number of memoirs in the Oral History Collection at Columbia University touch on various aspects of Hague's career.]

RICHARD J. CONNORS

HALSEY, WILLIAM FREDERICK, JR. (Oct. 30, 1882–Aug. 16, 1959), naval leader, was born in Elizabeth, N.J., the son of William Frederick Halsey, a naval officer, and of Anne Masters Brewster. He attended schools in California, Pennsylvania, and Maryland, then had one year at the University of Virginia (1899–1900) while he sought a presidential appointment "at large" to the Naval Academy. Halsey entered the academy in 1900. He had a mediocre academic record, played football on a losing academy team, and graduated in the bottom third of his class in February 1904.

Halsey's early career was routine. He served aboard the new battleship *Missouri* (1904–1905) and the former Spanish gunboat *Don Juan de Austria* (1905–1907) in the Caribbean, during which time (February 1906) he received his commission as ensign. Joining the battleship *Kansas* upon her commissioning in April 1907, Halsey participated in the global cruise of the "Great White Fleet" sent by President Theodore Roosevelt. Upon its return early in 1909, he was promoted concurrently to lieutenant (junior and senior grade). Immediately thereafter he began a twenty-three-year career in torpedo warfare and escort duties by taking command of the torpedo boat *Dupont* for her first six months in commission. On Dec. 1, 1909, Halsey married Frances Cooke Grandy; they had two children.

After several months helping to outfit the destroyer *Lamson*, Halsey spent two years (1910–

1912) in charge of training at Norfolk, Va., aboard the receiving ship *Franklin*. Command of the reserve destroyer *Flusser* (August 1912) and the First Group, Torpedo Flotilla, Atlantic Fleet (February 1913) preceded a two-year tour of duty in command of the destroyer *Jarvis* (September 1913–July 1915), which included participation in the Mexican intervention. Halsey spent the ensuing two years on the staff of the executive (discipline) department at the Naval Academy, during which time (August 1916) he was promoted to lieutenant commander.

Halsey's World War I service centered on antisubmarine escort duty out of Queenstown, Ireland, first for several weeks in 1918 aboard the destroyer *Duncan*, at which time he received promotion to the temporary rank of commander. He commanded the destroyers *Benham* from February to May and the *Shaw* until August 1918, but never sighted any enemy submarines. Promoted to the permanent rank of commander in 1921, Halsey held several postwar destroyer commands: the *Yarnall* (1918–1920), the *Chauncey* and the *John Francis Burnes* (1920), the *Wickes* (1920–1921), the *Dale* (1924–1925), and the *Osborne* (1925). His shore duty included the Office of Naval Intelligence (1921–1922) and naval attaché in Germany (1922–1924) and, concurrently, Norway, Denmark, and Sweden (1923–1924). Returning briefly to battleships, he served one year as executive officer of the *Wyoming*. In February 1927 he was promoted to captain.

Assigned to the Naval Academy as commanding officer of the station ship *Reina Mercedes*, Halsey immediately came under the spell of naval aviation, for the local unit was based on board his ship. After failing the eye examination necessary for flight training, he returned to sea as commander of Destroyer Squadron Fourteen, Scouting Fleet (1930–1932), and went on to the Naval War College (1932–1933) and Army War College (1933–1934) as a student. He reported to Pensacola, Fla., in July 1934 for training as a naval aviation observer but somehow managed to obtain instruction meant for a full-fledged pilot, and in May 1935 received the designation of naval aviator—at age fifty-two. Halsey commanded the aircraft carrier *Saratoga* from mid-1935 until mid-1937, and the naval air station at Pensacola from 1937 to 1938. Promotion to rear admiral came on Mar. 1, 1938. After commanding Carrier Division Two from June

1938 on board the *Enterprise* and then the *Yorktown*, in 1939 he returned to the *Saratoga* as commander of Carrier Division One.

Until World War II, Halsey, although a very good officer, was generally unknown to the public. But with the deterioration of the balance of power in the Pacific and the rise of Japan, Halsey's promotion to vice admiral and appointment as commander of Aircraft Battle Force (with additional duty as commander of Carrier Division Two) in June 1940 made him senior carrier admiral in the Pacific. On board the *Enterprise* throughout 1941, he placed his command on a war footing while it delivered aircraft from Hawaii to Wake Island in December. In his absence the Japanese carrier fleet attacked Pearl Harbor, leaving Halsey's carriers the only unscathed element of the Pacific Fleet. By then he had begun to develop a reputation as an aggressive fighter; his routine impending change of assignment was therefore canceled, and in February 1942 he led his two-carrier task force on raids against the Japanese-held Marshall, Gilbert, Wake, and Marcus islands. The psychological boost to public morale of this small offensive action immediately projected Halsey into the public eye, where he remained throughout the war.

Never a "spit-and-polish" officer, Halsey was popular with his men for his devil-may-care readiness to fight. He projected a physical image of "red-faced ruggedness and bulldog build." His heavy jaw seemed to pull him forward, and his blue eyes peered from below thick eyebrows. He had looked like an old sea dog since Naval Academy days, and by 1942, Halsey's appearance "gave an impression of boldness, aggressiveness, dash, dynamism and toughness. . . ." Knowing the value of fleet morale and public confidence, he did nothing to discourage this image.

In April 1942, Halsey became commander of carriers, Pacific Fleet, and, with the carriers *Hornet* and *Enterprise*, launched the U.S. Army bombers of James Doolittle in their raid on Tokyo. Public credit eluded Halsey, however, because of the extreme secrecy surrounding the bombers' "base." Late in May an acute form of dermatitis forced Halsey into the hospital, whereupon he relinquished his command and personal staff to R. A. Spruance, who led both to victory in the battle of Midway.

When the American foothold established at Guadalcanal in August 1942 became tenuous, Halsey was placed in charge of operations there as commander of the South Pacific Force on October 24. His forces won the key naval battles of Santa Cruz (October 25–26) and Guadalcanal (November 13–15), and cleared the island of organized Japanese resistance by February 1943. In recognition of these successes, Halsey was promoted to full admiral on Nov. 18, 1942. Much of his fame arose from his leadership of the Guadalcanal campaign.

As South Pacific theater commander, Halsey directed the Solomon Islands offensive throughout 1943 and early 1944. His forces captured the islands of New Georgia, Vella Lavella, and Bougainville, bypassing lesser islands. They ringed, and thus neutralized, the Japanese fleet and air base at Rabaul in the Bismarck Archipelago. With the South Pacific secured, Halsey was designated commander of the Third Fleet on June 16, 1944. In an ingenious two-platoon command arrangement, the Pacific Fleet, ground forces, and air forces would attack Japan's inner defenses continuously, with Halsey and Spruance rotating between major campaigns so that one could plan while the other fought. In fact, however, whenever Halsey commanded (the Philippines campaign and final blockade of Japan's home islands), he acted not as a fleet commander of battle, amphibious, and logistical forces but only as tactical commander of the Fast Carrier Task Force in strategic support of the U.S. Army's landings under General Douglas MacArthur. Also, he was under the operational control not of MacArthur but of Admiral Chester W. Nimitz in Hawaii, a clear violation of unity of command that had grave consequences.

After returning to sea aboard his flagship, the battleship *New Jersey*, in late August 1944, Halsey covered the Third Fleet landings in the Palau Islands in September and began attacking the Philippines in preparation for assaults there, only to discover that Japanese defenses were severely weakened. He recommended to the Joint Chiefs of Staff that the landing date for Leyte Island be advanced two months, to October 20, a suggestion that was immediately approved. Soon after MacArthur's assault on that date, with Third Fleet carriers providing strategic cover, the Japanese fleet sortied to begin the battle for Leyte Gulf. Utilizing their knowledge of Halsey's reputation as an aggressive fighter, the Japanese commanders lured Halsey away from the landing beaches with a decoy force of virtually planeless carriers as bait while they sent two battleship forces to attack the amphibious shipping.

The battle unfolded on the afternoon of October 24 as Halsey's planes sank the super-battleship *Musashi* in the Sibuyan Sea and temporarily turned back the "Center Force" of Japanese battleships. Halsey immediately took the Third Fleet north during the night, to attack the decoy "Northern Force" on the morning of October 25 off Cape Engaño, Luzon. His planes sank all four Japanese carriers. Meanwhile, during the night the "Southern Force" of Japanese battleships had been decimated by the American battleships covering the beach at Surigao Strait, but the "Center Force" had turned around to penetrate San Bernardino Strait and attack MacArthur's shipping off Leyte and Samar shortly after dawn. The divided command system and imperfect communications between Halsey and MacArthur led to the failure to maintain a watch over San Bernardino Strait, and now Nimitz ordered Halsey to disengage the remnants of the "Northern Force" and try to cut off the retreat of the "Center Force" at the strait. Halsey reluctantly complied, but the latter force made good its escape during the night.

Controversy over Leyte has continued, with Halsey and his chief of staff, Admiral R. B. Carney, steadfastly defending their actions (as have the historians C. Vann Woodward and Stanley L. Falk). Others (Samuel Eliot Morison and Clark G. Reynolds) have argued that Halsey's aggressiveness had finally worked against him. Unfortunately, more controversy developed when Halsey, in his zeal to continue in support of MacArthur's operations, took the Third Fleet into a disastrous typhoon (December 17–18) that resulted in the loss of three destroyers and almost 800 men. Historians have both excused Halsey on the basis of faulty fleet meteorological intelligence and criticized him for poor judgment and administrative practices. After covering amphibious operations in the northern Philippines, he relinquished command to Spruance on Jan. 26, 1945. Returning with his flag on the battleship *Missouri* on May 27, Halsey directed the Third Fleet in the final days of the Okinawa campaign, then took his ships into another damaging typhoon (June 4–5), primary responsibility for which was placed squarely on him. During the July–August 1945 operations blockading the Japanese homeland, Halsey's planes sank several heavy Japanese fleet units at anchor and attacked targets on land. The Japanese surrender occurred officially on Halsey's flagship in Tokyo Bay on Sept. 2, 1945.

Halsey's difficulties as Third Fleet commander

from Leyte to the end of the war have been explained on the basis that he "was not a Fleet commander in the same sense as Spruance, employing amphibious forces and escort carriers as well as battle forces; he was in fact the fast carrier task force commander. . . ." He also was prone to ad hoc rather than detailed planning, apt to use sloppy techniques, and often guilty of sending vague dispatches. These traits were acceptable in 1942, when the goal was to win Guadalcanal or to raid enemy island outposts. By late 1944, however, inefficiency was intolerable. The strain of his long service was also a factor.

Nevertheless, in World War II there probably was no naval commander as well known, liked, and respected. He was one of those rare individuals who could create in his subordinates a fierce loyalty. Halsey was promoted to fleet admiral in December 1945. Following a year of public appearances, he requested and was granted retirement early in 1947. He died at Fishers Island, N.Y.

[In addition to the Navy Department's official outline biographical sketch (1963) and the obituary in the *New York Times*, Aug. 17, 1959, full accounts of Halsey's life are Benis M. Frank, *Halsey* (1974); and the autobiography written with J. Bryan, III, *Admiral Halsey's Story* (1947). For World War II, see Samuel Eliot Morison, *History of United States Naval Operations in World War II*, vols. V (1949), VI (1950), XII (1958), XIII (1959), and XIV (1960), and *The Two Ocean War* (1963); and Clark G. Reynolds, *The Fast Carriers: The Forging of an Air Navy* (1968). For Leyte Gulf, see especially C. Vann Woodward, *The Battle for Leyte Gulf* (1947); Hanson Baldwin, "The Battle for Leyte Gulf," *Sea Fights and Shipwrecks* (1955); and Stanley L. Falk, *Decision at Leyte* (1966). The Naval Oral History Project at Columbia University has a number of memoirs dealing with Halsey and his role in World War II. See especially those of Thomas C. Kinkaid and Robert B. Carney.]

CLARK G. REYNOLDS

HAMILTON, MAXWELL McGAUGHEY (Dec. 20, 1896–Nov. 12, 1957), diplomat, was born in Tahlequah, Okla., the son of Wallace Maxwell Hamilton, a clergyman, and May Calvin Dobson. He graduated from Sioux City, Iowa, High School; attended Washington and Jefferson College for one year; and then transferred to Princeton University, where he received the B. Litt. degree in 1918. He served in the United States Army in 1918 and taught at the Jacob

Tome Institute, Port Deposit, Md., from 1919 to 1920.

Hamilton entered the United States Foreign Service on May 20, 1920, as a Chinese language officer, beginning as a student interpreter at the legation in Peking. In October 1922 he was transferred to the consulate at Canton, where he was given the rank of vice-consul and junior interpreter. At Canton he advanced to senior interpreter in 1923 and to consul in 1924. On Dec. 20, 1924, he married Julia Fisher. They had one child. The following year Hamilton was assigned to Shanghai as an assessor in the Mixed Court, a position that he held until July 1927, when he was transferred to duty in Washington, D.C.

During the next sixteen years Hamilton, as a staff member, assistant chief (1931–1937), and chief (1937–1943) of the Division of Far Eastern Affairs, was among the principal policymakers in the development of the American response to the deteriorating international system in East Asia. Stanley Hornbeck, who was appointed chief of the division of Far Eastern Affairs in 1928, promoted Hamilton to the newly created office of assistant chief in 1931. From the time of the Manchurian incident in 1931–1932 to the Japanese attack on Pearl Harbor, Hornbeck, Hamilton, and other members of the division sought to define American interests, objectives, and capabilities in the Pacific. Hamilton often took positions regarding Japanese expansion that were more restrained and conciliatory than those advanced by Hornbeck. For instance, in responding to the Amō press statement of 1934, in which the Japanese government asserted responsibilities in the Pacific modeled on those claimed by the United States in Latin America, Hamilton urged American inaction on the grounds that resistance to Japan necessitated force and determination, both of which had been lacking at the time of the Manchurian incident.

While disinclined to challenge the Japanese, Hamilton was not sanguine about the prospects for Japanese moderation. He declined to accept the arguments advanced, principally by the ambassador in Tokyo, Joseph Grew, that mature, liberal leadership was gaining strength in Japan. When, in late 1936, President Franklin D. Roosevelt proposed a plan for the "neutralization" of the Pacific Islands as a means of reducing international tensions, Hamilton drafted the State Department response. In a sixteen-page memorandum he argued strongly against the plan on the grounds that conditions in the region were too unstable and that Japan could not be trusted to keep treaty pledges. An irritated Roosevelt criticized this "argument of defeatism."

In August 1937, Hamilton was appointed chief of the Division of Far Eastern Affairs, but Hornbeck became political adviser to Secretary of State Cordell Hull and continued to exert the predominant influence on East Asian policy. In developing an American position for the Brussels Conference of November 1937 within the context of Roosevelt's "quarantine" speech, Hornbeck outlined the State Department position and Hamilton prepared a lengthy supporting statement. By 1940–1941 differences between Hamilton and Hornbeck over Asian policy, long ignored as a consequence of Hamilton's deference to his superior, surfaced within the context of the continuing high-level debate over the extent to which the United States should utilize economic sanctions to discourage Japanese expansion. Hamilton led the moderate element in the State Department, which sought to avoid a showdown with Japan; he took a strong stand in July 1940 against imposing an oil embargo, arguing that it would only encourage Japanese expansion into Southeast Asia. During the crisis in Japanese-American relations in the fall of 1941, Hamilton remained an advocate of compromise and endorsed initiatives directed toward reaching an agreement with Japan.

Following the attack on Pearl Harbor and the Japanese conquest of Southeast Asia, the Division of Far Eastern Affairs focused on Sino-American relations and planning for postwar Asia. Hamilton urged increased military support for the Chinese government. In anticipation of important postwar problems in China, he also pressed for American cultivation of Communist-Kuomintang collaboration within a liberalized government and for Soviet-American agreement on mutual noninterference in Chinese affairs. Looking toward the future of European imperialism in Southeast Asia, Hamilton maintained that since the United States was destined to become the predominant Pacific power, it should insist upon early liberalization of colonial policies as a means of undercutting Japanese propaganda and of upholding the principles of the Atlantic Charter.

In June 1943, Hamilton was assigned to the position of minister-counselor of the embassy in Moscow. For the remainder of his career he held a number of positions for rather brief periods and exerted little influence on policy. The position at Moscow was largely administrative and lasted only until September 1944, when he returned to the Department of State as a special assistant to the secretary of state. Three months later he became United States representative at Helsinki, and in September 1945 he was designated minister to Finland. Hamilton returned to the Department of State in January 1948 to help work on the plans for a Japanese peace treaty. In November 1949 he became United States representative on the Far Eastern Commission, holding the rank of ambassador and serving as commission chairman. The commission, composed of representatives of eleven nations, was the policymaking body for occupied Japan, but in practice the important decisions on occupation were made by diplomatic and military officials in Washington.

Hamilton retired in 1952 and spent the rest of his life in Palo Alto, Calif., where he died. He taught at Mills College in Oakland, Calif., during 1956–1957.

[The Hamilton papers are at the Hoover Institution on War, Revolution and Peace, Stanford University. Other manuscript collections with materials on Hamilton include the papers of Stanley Hornbeck at the Hoover Institution, Nelson Johnson at the Library of Congress, and John V. A. MacMurray at Princeton University.

Edward M. Bennett, "Joseph C. Grew: The Diplomacy of Pacification," in Richard Dean Burns and Edward M. Bennett, eds., *Diplomats in Crisis* (1974), is valuable for understanding the Hornbeck-Hamilton relationship. Dorothy Borg, *The United States and the Far Eastern Crisis 1933–1938* (1964), examines American policy and its formulation. Richard Dean Burns, "Stanley K. Hornbeck: The Diplomacy of the Open Door," in Richard Dean Burns and Edward M. Bennett, eds., *Diplomats in Crisis* (1974), is valuable for understanding the Hornbeck-Hamilton relationship. Norman Graebner, "Hoover, Roosevelt, and the Japanese," in Dorothy Borg and Shumpei Okamoto, eds., *Pearl Harbor as History* (1973), aids understanding of White House–State Department relations. There is an obituary in the *New York Times*, Nov. 13, 1957. James C. Thomson, Jr., "The Role of the Department of State," in Dorothy Borg and Shumpei Okamoto, eds., *Pearl Harbor as History* (1973), analyzes the making of East Asian policy and Hamilton's role in it. U.S. Department of State, *Foreign Relations of the United States*, especially the volumes covering his years as chief of the Division of Far Eastern Affairs, is the best source for tracing Hamilton's positions on foreign policy.]

GARY R. HESS

HAMILTON, WALTON HALE (Oct. 30, 1881–Oct. 27, 1958), economist and jurist, was born at Hiwassee College, Tenn., the son of Hale Snow Hamilton, a minister, and Bettie Dixon Hudgings. He grew up in an atmosphere of small-town southern fundamentalism against the "eternal verities" of which much of the rest of his life was a continuing revolt. He received preparatory schooling at the Webb School in Bellbuckle, Tenn. (1898–1901), attended Vanderbilt University (1901–1903), and received the B.A. from the University of Texas (1907). Hamilton's main interest was in history, which he taught in preparatory schools until 1909; he also was an instructor in medieval history at the University of Texas (1909–1910). In 1909 he married Lucile Elizabeth Rhodes; they had three children.

Hamilton was almost thirty when his interest shifted to economics. He taught economics at the University of Michigan (1910–1913), which awarded him the doctorate in 1913. It was a field in which he remained—to the extent that his restless mind could fix on any field—for roughly the next two decades.

After a year of teaching economics at the University of Chicago (1914–1915), Hamilton became professor of economics at Amherst College, where his heterodox views on economics and the heterodox views of President Alexander Meiklejohn on education accorded well. He remained at Amherst until 1923, making a reputation as one of the younger institutional economists who broke with the dominant neoclassical school of Alfred Marshall and John Bates Clark. He was quoted as saying that he had mastered the techniques of marginal utility and supply-and-demand economics so as to be able to reject them.

When the Robert Brookings Graduate School of Economics and Government was founded at Washington, D.C., in 1923, Hamilton was appointed professor of economics. He became the effective intellectual head of its small faculty. The school broke new ground in graduate education, joining economics, politics, law, and intellectual history; moving away from the formalisms of the traditional system inherited from Germany; and stressing informal dialogue between students and faculty in a residential setting. Hamilton had no intellectual system of his own. He was most deeply influenced by the iconoclasm of Thorstein Veblen, by the British Fabian socialists and guild socialists (Graham Wallas, Richard H. Tawney, G. D. H. Cole, and J. L. Hammond), by the

political pluralism of Harold J. Laski, by Frederic W. Maitland's work in English legal history, and by the constitutional theory and practice of Oliver Wendell Holmes, Jr., and Louis Brandeis. For students it was a heady brew, but for fellow professional economists it was too heretical and too formless. Largely under pressure from Harold G. Moulton, head of the Brookings Institution, support was withdrawn and the school was dissolved in 1928.

Hamilton then accepted a post at Yale Law School, where he taught the relations between law and economics until 1948. From 1945 until his death he was a member of the Washington law firm of Arnold, Porter, and Fortas. Hamilton was a rare instance of a law professor and legal practitioner who never attended law school or received a law degree. On July 20, 1937, after divorcing his first wife, he married Irene Till, who had been his research assistant; they had three children. Together they worked on a number of studies, especially on the costs of medical care and on the milk industry.

It was also in the 1930's that Hamilton became involved with government service. He received considerable publicity when he became a member of the NRA Advisory Board, reporting directly to President Franklin D. Roosevelt and with special concern for the consumer (1934–1935), but resigned before he could achieve much. He was happier as a special assistant to the attorney general (1938–1945), a position in which he could work with a former Yale Law School colleague, Thurman Arnold, who was in charge of antitrust enforcement. Hamilton returned for a time to Yale Law School, then concentrated on his legal work in Washington, which was largely advisory and dealt with constitutional, labor, and patent law.

Viewing his career as a whole, one must conclude that Hamilton scattered his energies, developed no theory, founded neither school nor doctrine. He had few disciples. Nevertheless, he left his mark on economic-legal research and thinking. His central approach was institutional, in the sense that he looked for the fault lines between the movement of technology and economic circumstance and the response shown by the political and legal organization of economic activity, as well as the response in doctrines and thought. Skeptical of all packaged solutions, Hamilton was a particularist who believed that every industry and situation required its own specific approach. He left his deepest mark in the area he called "the government of industry." Neither a statist nor a free-market believer, he moved always toward a "way of order" in which all the parties concerned—managers, investors, labor, consumers, the people—would play a role, have a voice in control, and benefit from the results.

Hamilton was tall and gangling. Never an eloquent lecturer but an exciting teacher, he delighted his students (who called him "Hammy") with his informality, wit, and irreverence for every establishment, including those of teaching and the law. In his last years he was partially blind but continued his legal work and writing. He died in Washington, D.C.

[Hamilton wrote two books on the coal industry, both with Helen R. Wright: *The Case of Bituminous Coal* (1925) and *A Way of Order for Bituminous Coal* (1928). *The Power to Govern* (1937), written with Douglas Adair, was a plea for finding adequate institutional means to make social controls effective. Three related studies dealt with the central problem of the competitive system: *The Pattern of Competition* (1940); *Antitrust in Action* (1940), written with Irene Till; and *Patents and Free Enterprise* (1941). Hamilton's thought is best summed up in *The Government of Industry*, University of Michigan Lectures.

Some memoirs in the Columbia University Oral History Collection contain material on Hamilton.]
MAX LERNER

HAMLIN, TALBOT FAULKNER (June 16, 1889–Oct. 7, 1956), architect, teacher, and librarian, was born in New York City, the son of Alfred Dwight Foster Hamlin, architectural historian and teacher, and of Minnie Florence Marston. His granduncle was Vice-President Hannibal Hamlin. He received the B.A. from Amherst College (1910) and the B.Arch. from the Columbia School of Architecture (1914). Hamlin began his professional career as a draftsman with the architectural firm of Murphy and Dana, of which he became a partner in 1920; and from 1920 to 1923 he was a partner in Murphy, McGill and Hamlin. Ginling College in Nanking, China, was one of the firm's most prominent buildings. From 1930 to 1934 Hamlin practiced alone. The major designs of those years were the dormitory and science buildings of the College of New Rochelle, N.Y., which expressed the prevailing eclecticism. On Sept. 11, 1916, Hamlin married Hilda B. Edwards; they had three sons. The marriage ended in divorce; and on Nov.

17, 1926, he married Sarah H. J. Simpson. They had no children. After being widowed in 1930, he married Jessica V. Walters on June 10, 1931; they had no children.

In 1916 Hamlin became an instructor of history and theory of architecture at Columbia. In addition to his practice and his teaching, during this period he started his career as an architectural writer. His first book was *The Enjoyment of Architecture* (1916), a pioneering attempt to convey an appreciation of the field to the layman; he later revised the work as *Architecture, an Art for All Men* (1947). *The American Spirit in Architecture* (1926) was a masterly pictorial survey. Hamlin was also a prolific critic and contributor to architectural journals. He strove to interpret the rising modern movement within the historic context.

In 1934 Hamlin was appointed librarian of the Avery Architectural Library at Columbia. Although he had no previous library training, he brought great scholarship to his job; and the rise of Avery to outstanding rank among architectural libraries can be credited to him. He initiated the Avery Index to Architectural Periodicals and organized a noteworthy collection of architectural drawings. As librarian, teacher, and writer he exerted a widespread influence while continuing to be a highly productive scholar. He wrote *Some European Architectural Libraries* (1939); *Architecture Through the Ages* (1940; rev. eds.: 1944, 1953), an architectural history of all-encompassing scope; and *Greek Revival Architecture in America* (1944), which has remained the basic book on the subject. In 1945 Hamlin resigned as Avery librarian to devote himself to his most ambitious project, the editorship of the four-volume *Forms and Functions of Twentieth Century Architecture* (1952). The first two volumes—on the elements of building and the principles of composition—were written by Hamlin.

In 1947 Hamlin became professor of architecture at Columbia. His last work was *Benjamin Henry Latrobe* (1955), a biography of America's first major professional architect, for which he received a Pulitzer Prize. He retired in 1954.

Hamlin was a man of wide intellectual and artistic interests, gentle in personality, and indefatigable in his pursuits. He was an accomplished watercolorist. Among his favorite activities was sailing; one of his cruises is described in *We Took to Cruising* (1951), written with Jessica Hamlin. He spent much of his last year on his yacht *Aquarelle,* on which he became ill while en route from Maine to Florida. He died in Beaufort, S.C.

[Obituaries are in the *New York Times,* Oct. 8, 1956; and *AIA Journal,* Jan. 1957. A list of his writings is in the catalog of the Avery Architectural Library and the Avery Index to Architectural Periodicals.]
ADOLF K. PLACZEK

HAMMERSTEIN, OSCAR, II (July 12, 1895–Aug. 23, 1960), librettist and lyricist, was born in New York City, the son of William Hammerstein, manager of the Victoria, the leading vaudeville house in New York City, and of Alice Nimmo. His grandfather, Oscar Hammerstein, became famous in New York as an opera impresario and builder of theaters; an uncle, Arthur Hammerstein, was a Broadway producer.

Hammerstein originally intended to be a lawyer. Between 1904 and 1912 he attended the Hamilton Institute, a semimilitary academy in New York. At Columbia College, which he entered in 1912, he had his first experience on the stage by performing and writing for Varsity Shows. While attending Columbia Law School he worked as a process server. When his employer refused him a raise in salary, Hammerstein left both his job and legal studies.

In 1917 Hammerstein entered the professional theater by becoming an assistant stage manager of *You're in Love,* a Rudolf Friml–Otto Harbach musical produced by Arthur Hammerstein in 1917. During that summer he married Myra Finn, a distant relative of Richard Rodgers. They had two children and subsequently were divorced. On May 14, 1929, Hammerstein married Dorothy Blanchard of Melbourne, Australia; their son, James, carried on the theatrical traditions of the family by becoming a producer and director.

In 1918 Hammerstein was the stage manager for *Sometime.* While employed backstage he had his first lyric interpolated into a Broadway show and completed a four-act play that opened and closed outside New York. The first musical comedy for which he provided book and lyrics was *Always You* (1920), which had a short run. A year later he collaborated with Otto Harbach and Frank Mandel in writing book and lyrics for *Tickle Me,* which ran on Broadway for more than 200 performances and had a seven-month tour. This was Hammerstein's first success, though still a modest one. The next four productions in which

he was involved were failures; but *Wildflower* (1923) began a pattern of success that continued for the next few years with Rudolf Friml's *Rose Marie* (1924), Jerome Kern's *Sunny* (1925), and Sigmund Romberg's *The Desert Song* (1926), all three among the most substantial box-office successes of the decade.

Until 1927 Hammerstein was content to work within the accepted stereotypes of the Broadway musical comedy and operetta; he readily conformed to their clichés. Within such formats he was hardly more than a skillful craftsman, as both librettist and lyricist. But with Jerome Kern's *Show Boat* (1927) he opened new vistas both for himself and for the American musical theater. Stimulated by the Edna Ferber novel of the same name, which he was adapting for Kern, Hammerstein conceived with his composer-collaborator a new type of musical production that was unconventional in its treatment of American backgrounds, characters, social problems, and local color. Discarding the paraphernalia and ritual that had so long burdened the American musical theater (the line of chorus girls, synthetic humor and dances, big production numbers, contrived songs), Hammerstein and Kern realized in *Show Boat* a folk play with music in which all the elements of musical theater were subservient to the aesthetic and dramatic demands of the play, and in which the songs, humor, and stage play were basic to the text. In his dialogue, characterizations, and lyrics, Hammerstein revealed a deep, rich strain in his writing, bringing to it simplicity, freshness, and often a touch of eloquence.

After *Show Boat,* Hammerstein continued to enjoy success on Broadway, both in operetta—as with Sigmund Romberg's *The New Moon* (1928)—and in the musical play—as with Kern's *Music in the Air* (1932). He was also thriving in Hollywood, where in 1935 he wrote the words for one of Romberg's most famous waltzes, "When I Grow Too Old to Dream," introduced in *The Night Is Young* (1935), and those for Kern's "The Last Time I Saw Paris" in 1941, which received the Academy Award after its interpolation in *Lady Be Good* (1941).

Hammerstein's collaboration with Richard Rodgers was launched in 1943 with the sensational musical folk play, *Oklahoma!* It began the richest phase of his career in the theater, both creatively and financially, as well as an unparalleled epoch in the American musical theater. He and Rodgers, determined to extend the horizons of musical-play writing by seeking unusual subjects and treating them with fresh and often unorthodox approaches, created a new stage art form in which all elements of the theater were integrated. Their *Carousel* (1945), *South Pacific* (1949), and *The King and I* (1951) became classics in which the musical play was finally crystallized. Though other of their successful musical productions leaned more toward formal musical comedy than the musical play, they nevertheless revealed originality of material and new attitudes toward the stage. These productions included *Me and Juliet* (1953), *Pipe Dream* (1955), *Flower Drum Song* (1958), and *The Sound of Music* (1959), the last of which, in its motion-picture adaptation, became one of the industry's most profitable box office attractions.

Rodgers and Hammerstein provided the score for the motion picture *State Fair* (1945); one of the songs, "It Might as Well Be Spring," received the Academy Award. For television they wrote *Cinderella* (1957).

Hammerstein's lyrics, set to the music of Richard Rodgers, brought him to the front rank of his profession. Using the simplest possible vocabulary, with phrases from everyday speech and with partiality for dialect and colloquialisms, Hammerstein managed to bring to his writing not only warmth, charm, and a broad humanity but also many flashes of poetic beauty. He often drew his imagery from subjects within the play, and he avoided unusual techniques or sophisticated versification. His verses were so simple and direct that at times they almost appeared threadbare, but they possessed the lyric quality of true poetry.

Within the musical-play context, Hammerstein was responsible for one other significant production, this without the help of Rodgers. It was *Carmen Jones* (1943), a musical-play modernization of Bizet's opera *Carmen* with an American black setting during World War II. What was particularly novel about *Carmen Jones*, above and beyond its all-black cast, was the fact that Bizet's music was used, with almost no changes, but with new lyrics.

The Sound of Music was Hammerstein's farewell to the theater. He died at Doylestown, Pa., a little less than one year after the show had opened on Broadway. In London and New York, during the week of Hammerstein's death, the lights of every theater were dimmed for several moments each night to mourn his passing.

[See Hugh Fordin, *Getting to Know Him: A Biography of Oscar Hammerstein* (1977); Stanley Green,

The Rodgers and Hammerstein Story (1963); Richard Rodgers, *Musical Stages* (1975); Deems Taylor, *Some Enchanted Evenings* (1953). The Oral History Collection at Columbia University has a memoir done by Hammerstein in 1959 and a longer one by Richard Rodgers that contains much on Hammerstein.]

DAVID EWEN

HANDY, WILLIAM CHRISTOPHER (Nov. 16, 1873–Mar. 28, 1958), songwriter, cornetist, bandmaster, and music publisher, was born in Florence, Ala., the son of Charles Bernard Handy, a Methodist minister and former slave, and of Elizabeth Brewer, also a former slave. His father rejected a guitar that his son had purchased with his savings as "one of the devil's playthings"; church taboos likewise stopped his mother from playing the instrument. Nevertheless, Handy learned the rudiments of music at his father's expense by studying sacred music on an old Estey organ.

While he was still in school, Handy learned how to play the cornet by stopping daily at a barbershop where a white bandmaster was teaching a stranded circus band the fingering of instruments. Studying the charts by peering through the window, he practiced on his school desk until he was able secretly to acquire a cornet for $1.75, payable in installments. By the time his father discovered that he was playing in the Florence band, his musical interest could not be checked either by his father's opposition or a schoolteacher's hickory stick.

When he was fifteen, Handy joined a traveling minstrel show that quickly failed. Returning home, he completed his education at the all-black Agricultural and Mechanical College in Huntsville, Ala. Although he passed the teacher's examination in Birmingham in 1892, he declined a teaching position and instead took a better-paying job as a molder's helper at the Howard and Harrison Pipe Works in Bessemer, Ala. There he organized and taught his first brass band. Attracted by the World's Fair, he went to Chicago, only to discover that the fair had been postponed for a year. He thereupon traveled to St. Louis, where his inability to find employment forced him to sleep on the streets and the levees of the Mississippi River. The melancholy songs he heard roustabouts singing struck a responsive chord and, together with his own deprivations, left an imprint on his most famous song, "St. Louis Blues."

A stint as a bandmaster in Henderson, Ky., led to a four-year position (1896–1900) as bandmaster of Mahara's Minstrels, a famous troupe of the day. On July 19, 1898, he married his childhood sweetheart, Elizabeth V. Prince; they had six children. In 1900 he returned to teaching, working for two years as a music instructor at his alma mater. A return engagement with Mahara's Minstrels in 1903 took Handy to Clarksdale, Miss., a fountainhead of Delta blues, where he directed the Knights of Pythias Band and became acquainted with the rural songs of pioneer bluesman Charley Patton.

In 1905 Handy moved to Memphis, Tenn., where he had been instructing the local Knights of Pythias Band as well as the Clarksdale Band. Organizing Handy's Band around some of the musicians in the Pythias Band, he embarked on a career of composing and arranging that brought him worldwide recognition. His achievement was to give national currency to blues and spirituals by creating popular melodies and making guitar-accompanied vocal music available for band performance. In his words, he gave "African ideas a new American dress."

Handy's first published song, "In the Cotton Fields of Dixie," appeared in 1907. The words were by Harry Pace, who later became his partner in a music publishing business. In 1909, during the mayoralty campaign in Memphis, he wrote "Mister Crump" in support of the local boss. It became his first important song when it was published in 1912 as "Memphis Blues." In 1913 he organized Pace and Handy, the firm over whose imprint "St. Louis Blues" appeared in 1914. Though a number of blues had appeared in print earlier, "St. Louis Blues" captured public fancy and launched the blues as a vital new form and sound in American popular music. Its structure, more elaborate than traditional blues, contained an exotic habanera rhythm derived from Cuban music.

In 1915 Handy wrote "Hail to the Spirit of Freedom," a march, and the next year, "Aframerican Hymn," for military band and mixed chorus. These compositions anticipated such later ambitious works as a musical setting for Lincoln's Gettysburg Address and Blue Destiny, a symphony in four movements based on his most popular blues: "St. Louis Blues," "Beale Street Blues," "Memphis Blues," and "Harlem Blues." After the appearance of "Beale Street Blues" in 1917, there was such a demand for Handy's songs that he took the audacious step of moving to New York City. He found, however, that he could not rent an office in the Gaiety Theatre Building on Broadway. "The beast of racial prejudice," as he later said, reared its head in other ways, but did not prevent Pace and Handy from acquiring its own building at 232 West 46th Street.

After World War I, Handy temporarily lost his eyesight. A precipitous drop in the sale of sheet music and the income from record royalties brought bad times to Pace and Handy, a situation that intensified when Harry Pace, who had joined him in New York, embarked on a solo recording venture. Instead of declaring bankruptcy, Handy renamed the firm Handy Bros. It continues to flourish as W. C. Handy Music Co., administered by his son and daughter. In 1926 Handy compiled Blues: An Anthology, a watershed work that figured in the Harlem Arts Renaissance, the vogue for blues in Tin Pan Alley, and the rise of the "torch song," a derivative white form of Negro blues concerned with rejected love.

In 1931 a park and a square were named after Handy in Memphis, and in 1947, a theater. His name has also been given to a school in Florence and to a public swimming pool in Henderson, Ky.

During his career Handy wrote or refurbished more than 100 sacred songs. In 1938 alone, he produced and published nineteen spirituals. His first wife died in 1937, an event he recalled with some bitterness in his autobiography, Father of the Blues (1941), because she was "kept outside of a democratic Manhattan hospital in an ambulance for one hour" while a phone girl explained that they "don't take colored people in private rooms." He also wrote in that work on black music and black life: "All of our music is derived from suffering. During slavery the suffering was a result of the lash and cruel separation of families and loved ones. Today we suffer as a consequence of the past, through man's inhumanity to man. Then as now our music is our consolation."

In 1943 a skull fracture suffered in a fall from a subway platform left Handy totally blind, but he remained active in his publishing business and continued composing through dictation. On Jan. 1, 1954, he married Irma Louise Logan. The premiere of St. Louis Blues, a Paramount film based on his life, was held in St. Louis ten days after his death in New York City. His funeral in New York City was attended by Mayor Robert Wagner and notables in the arts. It was witnessed by more than 150,000 persons who lined the streets through which the cortege moved.

[Obituaries are in the New York Times, Mar. 29, 1958; and Newsweek, Apr. 7 and 14, 1958. Also see L. Neal, "The Ethos of the Blues," Black Scholar, 3 (1972), 42–48. His autobiography is Father of the Blues (1941).]

ARNOLD SHAW

HARDY, OLIVER NORVELL (Jan. 18, 1892–Aug. 7, 1957), film comedian, was born in Harlem, Ga., the son of Oliver Hardy, a lawyer, and Emily Norvell. After his father's death the family moved to Madison, Ga., where for a time his mother managed a hotel. Hardy, having proved himself a talented boy soprano, was occasionally permitted to join touring theatrical companies. Intermittently he was educated at Georgia Military College, the Atlanta Conservatory of Music, and the University of Georgia. For a time he considered becoming a lawyer; but when his mother moved to Milledgeville, Ga., in 1910, he abandoned this notion and opened a movie theater there instead.

Three years later, deciding that it was as easy to perform in movies as to show them, Hardy began work in Jacksonville, Fla., for Lubin Motion Pictures at five dollars a day, playing the "heavy" in comedy shorts, a role for which he was physically well equipped. Rejected as overweight for service in World War I, he was briefly employed by Pathé Films in Ithaca, N.Y., returned to Jacksonville, then moved to California. For a time he free-lanced; and in the two-reeler *Lucky Dog* (1917) he appeared for the first time with Stan Laurel, the star of the picture. Cast as a holdup-man, Babe Hardy, as he was then called, stuck a gun in Laurel's ribs as a title card flashed on the screen: "Put 'em both up, insect, before I comb your hair with lead." It was the first of their many confrontations, but almost ten years elapsed before they again appeared together.

Hardy continued to perform in one- and two-reelers, chiefly for Vitagraph, until he was signed by Hal Roach in 1926. In 1927 he and Laurel, also under contract to Roach, were billed together for the first time. They complemented each other perfectly—Stan, thin, morose, and weepy-eyed, and Ollie, elephantine, bossy, and self-important. Like two overgrown children with delusions of adequacy, they bumbled their way through a succession of two-reelers, plunging from "one fine mess" into another. In Roach they found the ideal producer. He did not interfere, allowing them to work within a loose comic framework that gave full play to the creative imagination of Laurel. By then Hardy had developed into a fine performer, capable of expressing every shade of emotion by raising an eyebrow, lifting a pinkie, or twiddling his tie. Of the 105 pictures credited to them, the best are unquestionably those made during their early years with Roach.

The team survived the period of transition from silent films to sound without difficulty. In 1931 their first full-length feature, *Pardon Us*, opened a new chapter in their careers although, like Charlie Chaplin and Buster Keaton, they found themselves not entirely at ease in more structured scripts and under firmer directorial control. Despite the increasing popularity of animated cartoons, they continued to make two-reelers. Their public remained immense, as evidenced by their triumphal tour through England and France in 1932.

Soon afterward, however, Hardy's career took a downward turn. In 1921 he had married Myrtle Lee; they were divorced in 1937. Three years later he married Virginia Lucille Jones, a script girl twenty-two years his junior. Also in 1940 his association with Hal Roach came to an end. He and Laurel made plans to produce films independently, but these projects failed to materialize. Instead, they appeared in eight undistinguished films for MGM and Twentieth-Century Fox. Perhaps they found their greatest satisfaction during these years in the 500 performances they gave for servicemen during World War II. In 1947 they continued to make stage appearances, touring Great Britain and the Continent in a pantomime act. Four years later they completed their last film, *Atoll K*, a failure.

In 1954, Hardy and Laurel undertook another European tour, from which they returned to find their talents again in demand as a result of the success of their films on television. A projected film series came to nothing, however, for in September 1956 Hardy suffered a paralytic stroke. Bedridden and incapacitated for almost a year, he died in North Hollywood, Calif.

While few would rank Laurel and Hardy with Keaton or Chaplin, a number of their short films belong among the classics of the screen. These comedies often sprang from a single incident. An insult or a misunderstanding provoked retaliation; tempers flared, and the action escalated with inexorable logic to a comic catastrophe. Of the epic pie-slinging finale in *The Battle of the Century* (1927) James Agee wrote: "Every pie made its special kind of point." The scene in *Big Business* (1929) in which they coolly demolished a house is equally famous, as is the almost surrealist sequence in *Swiss Miss* (1938) in which Stan and Ollie, struggling with a piano on a suspension bridge, suddenly confronted a gorilla.

"My life wasn't very exciting," Hardy once observed. "I didn't do very much outside of doing a lot of gags before a camera and playing golf the rest of the time." In all justice, one should add that he also gave pleasure to millions.

[See Charles Barr, *Laurel and Hardy* (1968); William K. Everson, *Films of Laurel and Hardy* (1967); John McCabe, *Mr. Laurel and Mr. Hardy* (1961); and Gerald Mast, *The Comic Mind* (1973). There are also clippings in the Lincoln Center Theatre Collection.]
WILLIAM W. APPLETON

HARING, CLARENCE (Feb. 9, 1885–Sept. 4, 1960), historian of Latin America, was born in Philadelphia, the son of Henry Getman Haring and Amalia Stoneback. After graduation from Central High School in Philadelphia, he entered Harvard, where he studied under Roger Merriman. Haring graduated *summa cum laude* in 1907. He was then a Rhodes scholar at New College, Oxford, where he earned the B.Litt. He worked under C. H. Firth, historian of seventeenth-century England, who probably shaped Haring's first publication, *The Buccaneers in the West Indies in the XVII Century* (1910).

As Austin teaching fellow at Harvard (1910–1911), Haring offered courses on Latin American history. He then spent 1911–1912 in Europe, briefly at the University of Berlin and mostly at Seville, gathering data for his doctoral dissertation. This work earned the Wells Prize at Harvard (1916) and was published as *Trade and Navigation Between Spain and the Indies in the Time of the Hapsburgs* (1918).

Haring married Helen Garnsey in 1913; they had two sons. He taught at Bryn Mawr (1912–1915), Clark University and Harvard (1915–1916), then Yale (1916–1923). In 1923 he accepted the Bliss chair in Latin American history and economics at Harvard, a post he held until his retirement in 1953. Between 1933 and 1948 Haring was master of Dunster House at Harvard, which, as an "old Oxonian," he found "a most congenial assignment."

In the 1930's Haring served as chairman of the Committee on Latin American Studies of the American Council of Learned Societies (ACLS) and of the subsequent joint committee of the ACLS and the Social Science Research Council. He also helped organize the short-lived Bureau of Economic Research at Harvard that produced *The Economic Literature of Latin America: A Tentative Bibliography* (1935–1936); and played a major role on the advisory board of the *Handbook of Latin American Studies* (1936–), the major research tool in the field.

Haring was drawn to the colonial history of Spanish America through his analysis of how English and French policy manipulated the buccaneers to attack the Spanish transatlantic commercial system at its Caribbean terminus in the late seventeenth century. For this work he relied primarily upon English and French sources. *Trade and Navigation* examines the Spanish commercial system from within, both as an aspect of colonial policy and because the system "made possible the creation of . . . Spanish American civilization." The study utilized an impressive body of Spanish printed and manuscript sources, especially the collections of the Archivo General de Indias in Seville. It covers the organizational elements of the Spanish colonial trade system, for Haring focused upon the structures of colonial monopoly rather than upon the volume and composition of trade flows, although he did include a chapter on Spanish gold and silver imports from America along with observations about their long-term effects. One indication of the quality of his scholarship is that only Pierre and Huguette Chaunu's *Seville et l'Atlantique* (1955–1959) has added substantially to his institutional approach.

Haring found the Spanish trade monopoly (or, as the French put it, *l'exclusif*) no more exclusive than that of the contemporaneous systems of England, France, or Holland. He concluded—in a vein reminiscent of modern structuralist historians—that the Spanish system was "peculiarly disastrous" because Spain was "industrially bankrupt," a premise made explicit in his earlier *Buccaneers*. On the other hand, his explanation also incorporated an element of national temperament, in that he quoted Ehrenberg's *Zeitalter der Fugger* (1896) to the effect that precious metals imported by Spain served "to feed an impractical vanity."

In the three decades after publication of *Trade and Navigation*, Haring's professional interest changed to what he termed "present politics." The move was reflected in a book and several articles on South America in the 1920's and 1930's in which Haring tried to explain contemporary political turbulence in terms of social structure, economic fluctuations, and political traditions. He rejected then-current simplistic explanations based on the "supposed instability of the Latin temperament." Yet Haring did not abandon the early focus. His "Genesis of Royal Government in the Indies" (1927) reveals that he still cultivated his interests in the early Spanish colonial period although they were shifting from economic to institutional history. This new focus was sketched in lectures delivered at the University of Seville in 1934 and was given final form in *The Spanish Empire in America* (1947). Topically presented and lucidly written, *The Spanish Empire* is primarily concerned with colonial political structures, from the Council of the Indies in Spain to such aspects of the viceroyalties in America as their territorial bases, administration, and treasury operations. These topics are supplemented by sections on ecclesiastical organization, education, and fine arts. There is a brief but perceptive chapter on the eighteenth century, "The Last Phase." As an early synthesis of Spanish colonial structures in America, *The Spanish Empire* displays thematic balance, bibliographical control, and insight. Its only peer in its genre is Charles Gibson's *Spain in America* (1966).

Assessing the influence of a distinguished historian on his field is never easy. Haring had few graduate students. Always the "cultivated moderate liberal gentleman," as his contemporary Arthur Whitaker phrased it, he understated his scholarly interests when he wrote that his "few books published . . . have not seriously deflected the course of historical scholarship." Yet his major publications worked high-grade ores. *The Buccaneers* cultivated a popular genre but focused upon a moment of extraordinary change in northwestern Europe at the end of the seventeenth century. Similarly, *Trade and Navigation*—still a classic treatment—probed the relationship between imperialism and economic growth or stagnation, a theme that once attracted Roscher and still intrigues economic historians. In his choice of subjects for investigation, careful scholarship, and logic and felicity in exposition, Haring set high standards for the field of Latin American history. He died in Cambridge, Mass.

[Obituaries and bibliographies are in the *New York Times*, Sept. 5, 1960; *American Historical Review*, Jan. 1961; *Americas*, Jan. 1961; *Hispanic American Historical Review*, Aug. 1961. The following are available in the Harvard University Archives: Class of 1907, *15th*, *25th*, and *50th Anniversary Reports*; S.-Y. Mak, "Biography of Professor Haring" (1969); and an obituary prepared by Haring's colleagues S. B. Fay, A. M. Schlesinger, D. McCord, and Crane Brinton, Harvard University, Faculty of Arts and Sciences, *Minutes*, Jan. 10, 1961.]

STANLEY J. STEIN

HARLOW, RALPH VOLNEY (May 4, 1884–Oct. 3, 1956), historian and educator, was born in Claremont, N.H., the son of Alvin Braley Harlow and Hattie Grout. His father was in the laundry business in Southbridge, Mass., to which the family moved when Harlow was very young. He attended local schools and prepared for Yale at Mount Hermon. Before entering college he worked briefly in a mill office.

Harlow graduated from Yale College in 1909. The next year was spent teaching at a private boys' school in Plainfield, N.J., where, as he put it, he was in "nominal charge of a roomful of active little fiends, with somewhat more than their due share of original sin." He returned to Yale to take the M.A. in 1911 and the Ph.D. in 1913. From 1913 to 1920 he was a member of the faculty at Simmons College in Boston; from 1920 to 1926 he taught at Boston University and lectured at Clark University; and in 1926 he was appointed associate professor at Yale. Three years later Harlow left Yale to join the faculty at Syracuse University as professor and chairman of the department of history. He remained at Syracuse for the rest of his career, retiring in 1948. In 1921 Harlow married Judith Moss; they had three daughters.

Harlow's approach to the study and writing of history was a commendable mixture of old and new ideas. His authorship of textbooks for both high school and college use in an era when the textbook carried a quasi-sovereign authority attests to the importance he attached to a systematic development of historical facts. Both *The Growth of the United States* and *The Story of America* (1937) went through six editions. His most important text, *The United States From Wilderness to World Power* (1949), had three editions. These books were conventional efforts by a working historian to offer an overview of American life without special pleading. In the preface to *The United States From Wilderness to World Power*, Harlow wrote: "I have never been able to find any factors or forces in history except those which have been created by human beings. Human behavior falls into recognizable patterns, patterns which are persistent but at the same time continuously subject to change. History is the study of these patterns." He continued: "It is easy to talk about cause and effect—about which we know considerably less than we like to admit—and about trends, as though words and terms in themselves constitute explanations." Harlow concluded: "I have never been able to see any justification at all for any purely mechanistic interpretations of history, such as economic determinism or any other determinism." All of which appeared to make Harlow a very conservative student of the past.

Harlow was aware of certain provocative dimensions of historical inquiry. In 1923 he wrote a biography of Samuel Adams in which he sought to apply some of the techniques of modern psychology in an effort to understand Adams the revolutionary. Reflecting the influences of Lytton Strachey in England and Gamaliel Bradford in the United States, he became fascinated with the possibility of revealing the inner man. Taking another tack, Harlow argued that history as politics could no longer satisfy as the unique rationale for the American past. More and more, he stated, "History is beginning to turn to business leaders because business and the commercial field are the main interests of the country—and historians deal with main interests." Emphasis on modern psychology and on the leaders of the business world combined to make Harlow an advocate of the "great man" theory of history. Such an interpretation is consonant with his opinion that history is created by human beings. Appropriately, his reputation as a research historian rests upon two biographies: *Samuel Adams, Promoter of the American Revolution* (1923) and *Gerrit Smith, Philanthropist and Reformer* (1939). Harlow also wrote *History of Legislative Methods* (1917) and a number of articles.

Harlow's biography of Adams was a daring enterprise, but not a really successful one. His stated purpose was to show the man at work and to make clear as far as possible why he followed his particular course of action. Using the vocabulary of psychology, Harlow found Adams to be the victim of an inferiority complex. He contended that Adams' revolutionary activity was the product of his emotions and that his behavior in politics was therefore irrational. The weakness of the book lies largely in its absence of the data psychologists require in order to construct meaningful analysis. There is no treatment of Adams' childhood and youth, no description of his relationships with his parents, his family, or his friends. Also absent are his sex experiences and his dreams. There is some merit in the criticism that, having postulated the inferiority complex, Harlow distorted Adams' career in order to fit it into the pattern dictated by the supposed neurosis. Reaction to the Adams biography was strong and negative. The Boston Public Library placed the

book in its "special collections," which, the author observed with characteristic good humor, was popularly known as "the Inferno."

In contrast, Harlow's treatment of Gerrit Smith, the nineteenth-century New York State businessman and abolitionist, was widely acclaimed as fine biography. Until Harlow's book, Smith was a forgotten giant among the reformers of his time. Over the years it has proven to be the definitive statement on its subject. While this study exhibited no overt reliance on psychological methodology, it was nevertheless a penetrating character analysis that demonstrated both Harlow's earlier penchant for psychological analysis and his professional maturity. He looked into Smith's family relationships and early training, as well as the man's business and personal behavior. From these solid foundations the multifaceted reform interests of Gerrit Smith were viewed as a natural outgrowth of his heritage.

Harlow exerted considerable influence on a generation of students who used his texts. He also proved himself to be a competent research historian. His writings, along with his work as an educational administrator at Syracuse, formed a well-rounded professional career. He died at Westbrook, Conn.

[On Harlow's experiments with psychoanalytical history, see John A. Garraty, "Preserved Smith, Ralph Volney Harlow, and Psychology," *Journal of the History of Ideas,* June 1954. The most complete source of information and insight is the histories of the class of 1909, Yale College, for the years 1909, 1915, 1925, 1949. There are good likenesses of Harlow in the *Syracuse Herald Journal,* Sept. 17, 1929, and Oct. 4, 1956, and in the *Syracuse Herald-American,* Mar. 8, 1948. Obituaries appear in the Oct. 4, 1956, issues of the *Syracuse Herald Journal,* the *New York Herald Tribune,* and the *New York Times.*]

DAVID H. BURTON

HARRISON, FRANCIS BURTON (Dec. 18, 1873–Nov. 21, 1957), congressman and colonial administrator, was born in New York City, the son of Burton Norvell Harrison and Constance Cary. His father, who had served as private secretary to Confederate President Jefferson Davis, became a successful lawyer in New York after the Civil War. His mother was a well-known novelist and writer. Reared in an atmosphere of wealth and culture, Harrison possessed all the advantages bestowed upon a member of the social elite. Prepared for college in several private schools, he graduated from Yale in 1895 and from the New York Law School two years later. After admission to the bar in 1898, he taught evening classes at the latter institution but never practiced law. Harrison enlisted as a private in the New York Volunteer Cavalry at the outbreak of the Spanish-American War, and rose to the rank of captain. On June 7, 1900, he married Mary Crocker, heiress to a California banking and railroad fortune; they had two daughters.

Although Harrison served for a time as vice-president of the McVickar Realty Trust Company, his primary interest was politics. A Democrat, he early identified with the Tammany Hall organization and, with its support, in 1902 secured election to Congress from New York's Thirteenth District. Two years later he ran unsuccessfully for lieutenant governor of New York. On Jan. 16, 1907, a little more than a year after the death of his wife in an automobile accident, he married Mabel Judson Cox; they had three children. Shortly after his second marriage he resumed his seat in Congress, having been elected from New York's Sixteenth District in 1906. A "well-born Tammany Democrat" whose style was more that of "a Virginia gentleman" than a ward politician, he was reelected in 1908, 1910, and 1912.

In Congress, Harrison served on several influential committees and became particularly identified with lower tariffs and drug control. He played a conspicuous role in the passage of the Underwood Tariff Act of 1913, especially the section that placed wool on the free list. In 1914, after several earlier efforts to enact a drug control measure had failed, Congress approved the Harrison Narcotics Act, the basic federal law regulating drug transactions in the United States. In foreign affairs Harrison acquired a reputation as a "consistent anti-imperialist" who regularly criticized official policies regarding Puerto Rico, Panama, and the Philippines.

When Woodrow Wilson assumed the presidency in 1913, he appointed Harrison governor-general of the Philippine Islands. Harrison arrived in Manila in October 1913, intent upon inaugurating "a new era" that would hasten Philippine independence. Although he did not believe that Filipinos were ready for complete independence, he was convinced that they could quickly prepare for it if relieved of the strictures imposed by his predecessors.

Throughout his seven and a half years as governor-general, Harrison pursued policies designed to bring about the rapid "filipinization" of the government and economy of the islands. He relied upon members of the elected Assembly rather than American insular officials for advice; appointed enough Filipinos to the Philippine Commission, the principal governing body of the islands, to give them a majority; and filled lower-echelon government offices with islanders. After the passage of the Jones Act in 1916, which provided for an elected Filipino Senate, Harrison surrendered much of his authority to the new Philippine legislature. Suspicious of foreign investment but convinced that economic development was a prerequisite for political independence, he encouraged the establishment of a state-owned railroad, the Philippine National Bank, port facilities, and various projects aimed at achieving a self-sustaining economy, a goal made difficult by the oppositon of certain American interests and by the vagaries of Filipino partisan politics. Although his administration suffered serious economic and social setbacks after World War I, Filipinos had acquired a large measure of autonomy by the end of Harrison's tenure as governor-general in 1921.

Two years before his departure from Manila, Harrison divorced his second wife and married Salena Elizabeth Wrentmore, the daughter of an American professor teaching in the Philippines, on May 15, 1919. They had three children. Rather than return to the United States, where the "Philippine Question" was a topic of heated debate in 1921, Harrison settled at Teaninich Alness, Scotland, and pursued the life of a country squire. He visited the United States long enough to complete the apologia of his administration in the Philippines, entitled *The Cornerstone of Philippine Independence* (1922); but most of the decade and a half after 1921 was spent either at his estate in Scotland or at Mediterranean resorts. During these years he wrote several books and articles related to the history of his family. After he was divorced from his third wife, Harrison married her sister, Margaret Wrentmore, on Apr. 8, 1927; they had one son. This marriage also ended in divorce; and he subsequently married Doria Lee, an Englishwoman, in Alexandria, Egypt, on Nov. 19, 1934; they had one daughter.

Throughout his residence in Europe, Harrison maintained a regular correspondence with Filipino leaders. He returned to the islands for two years in 1935 at the request of his old friend, President Manuel Quezon. He held the post of "presidential adviser" concerned chiefly with the reorganization of the government. In 1936 he was made a citizen of the Philippines by special act of the legislature. During World War II, after Harrison had moved to Charlottesville, Va., he resumed his post as adviser to Quezon's government, then in exile in Washington. After the war he returned to the Philippines as U.S. commissioner of civil claims from February 1946 to November 1947, and thereafter served as special adviser to the first three presidents of the Philippine Republic.

After his fifth marriage ended in divorce, Harrison married Maria Teresa Larrucea on Mar. 5, 1949, and became a Roman Catholic. They had no children. Late in 1950 the Harrisons went to the Philippines with the intention of residing there permanently. After a few months, however, they moved to Spain, where they remained for the next six years. Harrison died in Flemington, N.J., shortly after his return to the United States. He was given a state funeral in Manila and was buried there.

[The most important sources on Harrison's career are the Francis B. Harrison Papers within the Harrison Family Collection in the Library of Congress; "About It and About," the unpublished memoirs of Francis B. Harrison, Manuscripts Department, University of Virginia Library, Charlottesville; Michael P. Onorato, ed., *Origins of the Philippine Republic: Extracts From the Diaries and Records of Francis Burton Harrison*, Data Paper no. 95, Southeast Asia Program, Cornell University (1974); Napoleon J. Casambre, "Francis Burton Harrison: His Administration in the Philippines, 1913–1921" (Ph.D. diss., Stanford University, 1968); Michael P. Onorato, "Governor General Francis Burton Harrison and His Administration in the Philippines: A Re-Appraisal," *Philippine Studies*, 18 (1970); and Peter W. Stanley, *A Nation in the Making: The Philippines and the United States, 1899–1921*.

Also see the following works by Harrison: *Avis sonis focisque: The Harrisons of Skimino* (1910); *The Burton Chronicles of Virginia* (1933); *Archibald Cary of Carrybrook, Virginia* (1942); and *A Selection of Letters of Fairfax Harrison* (1944).]

WILLARD B. GATEWOOD, JR.

HARRISON, ROSS GRANVILLE (Jan. 13, 1870–Sept. 30, 1959), biologist, was born in Germantown, Pa., the only son of Samuel Harrison, a native of Philadelphia, and Catherine Diggs. Usually reserved about his family, Harrison enjoyed telling of his father's professional life as a mechanical engineer. After an apprenticeship as pattern maker, his father spent ten years (1844–1854) in Russia with the American engineers Andrew Eastwick, Joseph Harrison (no relation), and Thomas Winans. There they equipped and ran the first railroad between St. Petersburg and Moscow under a contract awarded by the czar to George Washington Whistler, father of James McNeill Whistler. From his father Harrison acquired a fine collection of Whistler etchings and his lifelong interest in railroads.

Harrison's early boyhood was spent in Germantown, where his interest in the natural environment was fostered in his first school. After the death of his mother, he lived with his mother's brother, John Diggs, in Baltimore, Md. He was educated in public and private schools. He then took the chemical-biological course at the Johns Hopkins University and received the B.A. degree in 1889.

Harrison had intended to study medicine, but the fascinating lectures of William K. Brooks in his third year of undergraduate study turned his interest to biological science and the study of animal form. The training at Johns Hopkins provided a point of view in advance of its time. He started his graduate studies at Hopkins in 1889; his principal teachers were Brooks, H. N. Martin, and W. H. Howell. In 1890 he had a summer job at Woods Hole, Mass., with the U.S. Fish Commission to investigate oyster development and in 1892 was a member of the Johns Hopkins expedition to Jamaica.

In 1892 Harrison transferred to the University of Bonn, where the influence and friendship of Moritz Nussbaum were of paramount importance in his life. Nussbaum suggested his doctoral dissertation, the study of the median and paired fins of the salmon. A paper on the dermal bones of the fins was followed by a more exhaustive study of all of the fins with their segmental muscle buds and nerve plexuses, and the publication of four more papers. His dissertation was finished after his return to Johns Hopkins, where he received the Ph.D. degree in 1894. On return visits to the University of Bonn as a medical student in 1895, 1898, and 1899, Harrison worked on the histogenesis of the peripheral nerves of the salmon, and was awarded the M.D. degree in 1899.

Harrison resigned a fellowship at Johns Hopkins in 1894 in order to substitute for T. H. Morgan as lecturer on morphology at Bryn Mawr College. On Jan. 9, 1896, he married Ida Lange. They had five children. In 1896 he was appointed instructor in anatomy at the Johns Hopkins Medical School under Franklin P. Mall. He became associate in anatomy (1897-1899) and then associate professor of anatomy (1899-1907). He taught anatomy, histology, and neurology and conducted research in embryology and neurology.

His research in embryology was stimulated by Gustav Born's experiments in which he united parts of amphibian embryos (1894-1897). Harrison adapted the technique for study of many different development problems, such as the growth and differentiation of the tail, muscle-nerve relationships, and the lateral line system of sense organs (1897-1903). He performed a series of experiments in which the head region of one species of frog embryo was grafted to the body of another species with different pigmentation. In these experiments it was possible to observe the shifting of the epidermis and the course of the lateral line sense organs from the head primordium to the tip of the tail. One chimeric frog metamorphosed.

Harrison's early studies of the developing nervous system were continued in an extensive series of transplantation experiments (1900-1910). They were designed to investigate three theories of nerve fiber formation: the neurone concept of nerve fiber outgrowth; derivation from peripheral preexisting and actively functioning protoplasmic bridges; and origin from nerve sheath cells. He proved first that cells in the nerve centers are responsible for the formation of the nerve fibers and that the sheath cells are not essential by removing their source, the neural crest. He then devised the first experiment of explanting small pieces of frog medullary cord in clotted lymph outside the body with the use of the hanging drop method, which permitted direct observation of the outgrowing amoeboid nerve fiber from a single nerve cell. Another set of experiments demonstrated that outgrowing nerves require solid support. Harrison continued his tissue culture experiments at Yale after he was appointed the first Bronson professor of comparative anatomy and head of the department (1907). Tissue culture has been adapted for wide use and has retained its importance in both biological and medical research laboratories.

Between 1910 and 1913, Harrison planned and supervised the construction of the Osborn Memorial Laboratories. In 1913 he initiated a series of transplantation experiments to study the localization and induction of the amphibian forelimb and demarcated its mesodermal site of origin. In subsequent years he investigated intrinsic factors in the growth of the forelimb, ear,

eye, gills, balancer, and other organs. Parts of embryos of different species with varying growth rates were combined by grafting into normal organisms. A quantitative analysis of the heteroplastic limb experiments revealed that the form, growth rate, and ultimate size are fixed mainly in the limb mesoderm. Harrison's study of the factors that influence development and symmetry of the inner ear, an ectodermal organ, equaled the limb experiments in number and importance. The constituents of composite organs such as the eye and gills were interchanged heteroplastically in order to study ultimate size and regulation in the developing organism. A wide range of developmental problems provided doctoral dissertations for Harrison's students; his influence was reflected in their future achievements.

Harrison's pervading interest in organic symmetry and asymmetry is apparent in experiments that preceded and accompanied the early localization experiments. Although many investigators supported the crystal analogy in respect to organization of living protoplasm, Harrison was the first to give concrete evidence of the relation of visible structure to molecular configuration. He used the paired organs, the amphibian limb and ear, which are in two forms, rights and lefts, and are the mirror image of each other. In early stages the cells composing these organs are essentially alike, in that any part of the rudiment can give rise to any part of the organ. Harrison transplanted the limb rudiment or ear placode in different orientations to the same or opposite side of the body at different stages of development. He found that at a given time in their development, certain elements of the protoplasm give evidence of definite orientation that they did not have before; that is, the various embryonic axes (anteroposterior, dorsoventral, and mediolateral) became polarized at different times in sequential order. Results of the experiments with forelimb and ear were similar. When the anteroposterior axis is reversed in grafting, a right limb or ear rudiment may be made to develop into a left limb or ear; when the anteroposterior axis is not reversed, a right rudiment develops into a right limb or ear, wherever placed. Harrison attributed the results to changes of a crystalline nature in the ultrastructure of the protoplasm. With W. T. Astbury and K. M. Rudall of the University of Leeds, England, an attempt was made to demonstrate this with X-ray diffraction (1940). Although the results were negative, dissatisfaction was felt with the preparation of the tissues and not with the hypothesis of oriented (crystalline) structure.

Harrison

Harrison was managing editor of the *Journal of Experimental Zoology* (1904–1946) after its founding in 1903. Administrative duties that started with his appointment as head of the zoology department continued during his tenure of the Sterling professorship of biology (1927–1938) at Yale. After retirement in 1938, he was appointed chairman of the National Research Council, where his concern was mainly with scientific aspects of defense during World War II. He served as trustee, adviser, and in various major posts at the Marine Biological Laboratory, Woods Hole, Mass., the Bermuda Biological Station, and the Rockefeller Institute for Medical Research. He died in New Haven, Conn.

Harrison was a reserved, quiet person with a great sense of responsibility and high standards in his dealings with people and in his scientific work. His warmth was apparent in his great kindness and capacity for friendship with colleagues, students, and others with whom he was associated.

He published eighty-three papers, some of them lectures that were general in scope, but no books. His Silliman lectures (Yale, 1949) were published posthumously. He was a member of the National Academy of Sciences (1913); the American Philosophical Society (1913); the Accademia Nazionale dei Lincei (1929), which awarded its Antonio Feltrinelli International Prize to him in 1956; the Royal Society (1940); and the Académie des Sciences, Institut de France (1946). The fundamental and advanced nature of Harrison's scientific discoveries affirm that he was the leading experimental embryologist of his generation and a pioneer investigator of still unsolved problems of molecular biology.

[Harrison's papers, containing his correspondence, complete records of his experiments, administrative records, manuscripts, and numerous photographs, are in the Archives of the Yale University Library. Ross Granville Harrison, *Organization and Development of the Embryo*, his Silliman lectures, edited by Sally Wilens (1969), includes a complete bibliography of his published papers and a list of memorial tributes. Selected memoirs are M. Abercrombie, "Ross Granville Harrison 1870–1959," *Biographical Memoirs of Fellows of the Royal Society*, 7 (1961); A. M. Dalcq, "Notice biographique sur M. le Professeur R. G. Harrison," *Bulletin de l'Académie r. de médecine de Belgique*, 6th ser., 24 (1959); P.–P. Grassé, "Notice nécrologique sur Ross Granville Harrison," *Comptes rendus hebdomadaires des séances de l'Académie des sciences*, 250 (1960); J. S. Nicholas, "Ross Granville Harrison (1870–1959)," *Yearbook American Philosophical Society*, 1961; and "Ross Granville Harrison 1870–1959," *Biographical Memoirs. National Academy of Sciences*, 35 (1961); P. Pasquini, "Ross Granville Harrison," *Acta embryologiae et morphologiae experimentalis*, 3 (1960). See also Victor C. Twitty, *Of Scientists and Salamanders* (1966); and C. Heygaud, *On the Edge of Evening* (1946). Newspaper obituaries are in the *New York Times*, Oct. 1, 1959; *New York Herald Tribune*, Oct. 1, 1959; *New Haven Courier*, Oct. 1, 1959; and *New Haven Register*, Oct. 4, 1959.]

SALLY WILENS

HAUPT, ALMA CECELIA (Mar. 19, 1893–Mar. 15, 1956), authority on public health nursing, was born in St. Paul, Minn., the daughter of Charles Edgar Haupt, an Episcopal minister, and Alexandra Dougan. Her grandfather, Brigadier General Herman Haupt, was a civil engineer who had been in charge of military railroads for the Army of the Potomac during the Civil War. After receiving the B.A. from the University of Minnesota in 1915, Haupt entered the university's School of Nursing, later completing her training at Johns Hopkins Hospital. Her career in public health nursing began in 1919 with the Visiting Nurse Association of Minneapolis, of which she became general superintendent in 1922.

In 1924 Haupt was invited by the Commonwealth Fund to become associate director of its child health program in Vienna. She served with such distinction that she was awarded the Gold Cross of Austria. In 1927 she was named associate director of the fund's Division of Rural Hospitals; two years later she accepted a similar position with the National Organization for Public Health Nursing. Having attained national recognition through her writings and organizational activities, Haupt became director of the Nursing Bureau of the Metropolitan Life Insurance Company, a pioneer in home nursing care, in October 1935. Under her seventeen-year administration this service became a model of its type for community and state agencies.

Haupt played an important role in the effort to provide adequate nursing care during World War II. In 1941 she was granted a leave of absence to serve as nursing consultant and executive secretary of the nursing subcommittee of the Office of Defense Health and Welfare Services, in Washington, D.C. In this dual capacity she helped to coordinate the war-nursing activities of twelve government agencies, including the Nursing Advisory Committee of the Procurement and Assignment Service of the War Manpower Commission, the American Red Cross, and the National Nursing Council for War Service. She returned to New York City in 1943 but remained a consulting member of these national committees until the end of the war.

In June 1949 Haupt visited Great Britain with Alice Girard, superintendent of nurses, Canadian head office of the Metropolitan Life Insurance Company, to study the British national health service. A month later in Stockholm, at the annual meeting of the International Council of Nurses, they gave an address containing their observations on the practical aspects of home health care in America that was published in *Public Health Nursing* (1949).

In 1950 and 1951 Haupt taught administration in public health nursing at New York University. In 1953 she published the most important of her numerous articles, "Forty Years of Teamwork in Public Health Nursing," in the *American Journal of Nursing*.

Haupt never married. Her life was dominated by devotion to the care of the needy and the determination that in the future her profession should play a more dynamic part in the health care of the general public. An efficient, authoritative administrator, she was described by fellow workers as large in stature, extraordinarily warm, generous, imaginative, and innovative. She loved to entertain her friends, who came from all parts of the world. By exerting authority with diplomacy, she helped to unify and coordinate the resources of nursing organizations. Haupt believed firmly in continuing education for graduate nurses long before this idea became popular, and the status that the profession now enjoys may be attributed in considerable degree to her insistence on self-betterment. She died in San Francisco, Calif.

[Obituaries, with photographs, are in the *New York Times*, Mar. 17, 1956; *Nursing Outlook*, Apr. 1956; and *American Journal of Nursing*, May 1956. Information is also available in the record files in the library of the Metropolitan Life Insurance Company, New York City.]

MORRIS H. SAFFRON

HAYNES, GEORGE EDMUND (May 11, 1880–Jan. 8, 1960), sociologist, race relations expert, and Urban League founder, was born at Pine Bluff, Ark., the son of Louis Haynes and Mattie Sloan. His father, an unskilled laborer, was often unemployed; his mother supported the family by domestic service. Haynes attended high schools connected with Alabama Agricultural and Mechanical College at Normal (1895–1896) and Fisk University (1896–1899). He received the B.A. from Fisk in 1903, working to pay his way and support his family. He earned the M.A. in sociology from Yale in 1904, then entered Yale Divinity School on a scholarship. He dropped out early in 1905 to help finance his sister's education.

In 1905 Haynes became coordinator of YMCA work on black college campuses. He studied at the University of Chicago in the summers of 1906 and 1907. In 1908 he resigned his job to enter Columbia University, where he majored in sociology, with cognate studies in social work at the New York School of Philanthropy (later the New York School of Social Work). Haynes was the first black graduate of the social work school (1910). He expanded the study he did there into a dissertation, for which he became the first black to receive a doctorate from Columbia (1912). His dissertation, *The Negro at Work in New York City* (1912), stressed that blacks were becoming increasingly urbanized and urged greater attention to urban blacks.

While at Columbia, Haynes worked for the Committee for Improving the Industrial Condition of Negroes, finding jobs for blacks taking vocational classes. Some of the leaders of the committee were also active in the National League for the Protection of Colored Women. Both groups were composed predominantly of upper-class whites and intellectuals working on black problems. Haynes wanted blacks trained to work as equals with whites in resolving racial problems. Accordingly, he and philanthropist Ruth Standish Baldwin set up the Committee on Urban Conditions Among Negroes on May 19, 1910. The three groups consolidated into the National League on Urban Conditions Among Negroes on Oct. 16, 1911. The National Urban League dates its founding from the Committee on Urban Conditions and considers Haynes its founder. Haynes was less militant than W. E. B. Du Bois, but more aggressive than Booker T. Washington. On balance, Urban League tactics—persuasion, self-improvement, negotiation—were more like Washington's accommodationist program than like the militancy of Du Bois' NAACP.

Haynes was the first executive secretary of the

Urban League until 1917, when he lost control of the organization. While developing the Committee on Urban Conditions, he moved to Nashville, where he set up the sociology department at Fisk in the fall of 1910. On Dec. 14, 1910, he married Elizabeth Ross, a sociologist; they had one son. Haynes tried to supervise the work of the committee from Nashville, returning to New York every six weeks. But Eugene Kinckle Jones—hired by Haynes in April 1911 as assistant secretary—gradually won over the staff and board. Haynes, who had fought his way up from poverty, was brusque and argumentative; Jones, who was the son of college professors, was tactful and conciliatory. Haynes stressed the league's mission to train black leaders and social workers, while Jones emphasized its social service role. Jones became co-executive with Haynes in 1916 and was made the full-time executive secretary in 1917, with Haynes reduced to educational secretary.

From 1918 to 1921 Haynes served in the U.S. Department of Labor as director of Negro economics and as commissioner of reconciliation. His job was to reduce friction resulting from blacks migrating north to wartime factory jobs. He surveyed migration to Detroit, publishing the results as *Negro Newcomers in Detroit,* . . . (1918). In 1922 Haynes became the first executive secretary of the Commission on the Church and Race Relations (after 1932 the Department of Race Relations) of the Federal (now National) Council of Churches, a post he held until his retirement in 1946. The Race Relations Department sponsored interracial conferences, committees, and clinics. His third book, *The Trend of the Races* (1922), hailed black accomplishments and delineated the duty of the church in racial matters. Haynes founded Race Relations Sunday in 1923 and Interracial Brotherhood Month in 1940.

Haynes administered Harmon Foundation awards to black achievers (1926–1931), formed the American Scottsboro Committee to save black youths condemned unjustly (1934), chaired the Joint Committee on National Recovery (1933–1935) to ensure blacks a fair share of New Deal programs, clashed with Du Bois over the latter's advocacy of separatism (1934), and joined A. Philip Randolph to forestall temporarily Communist takeover of the National Negro Congress (1937–1940). Haynes served on the commission that recommended a state university system for New York and on the initial board of

trustees of that system (1948–1954). He toured Africa for the YMCA in 1930 and 1947, and recorded his impressions in *Africa, Continent of the Future* (1950). From 1950 to 1959 he taught courses at City College of New York on interracial adjustments, black history, and Africa in world affairs. His first wife died in 1953, and he married Olyve Jeter, his secretary from 1922 to 1946, on Apr. 12, 1955. He died in New York City.

[Haynes's personal papers are in the home of his widow in Mount Vernon, N.Y., and in the Special Collections Division of the Erastus Milo Cravath Library of Fisk University. The records of the Department of Race Relations are in the archives of the National Council of Churches, New York City. An additional book by Haynes is *The Clinical Approach to Race Relations* (1946). His articles include "Conditions Among Negroes in the Cities," *Annals of the American Academy of Political and Social Science,* Sept. 1913; "Negroes Move North," *Survey,* May 4, 1918; "Negro Migration—Its Effect on Family and Community Life in the North," *Proceedings of the National Conference of Social Work* (1924); "The Negro's Economic Security," *Christian Century,* June 5, 1935; "Changing Racial Attitudes and Customs," *Phylon,* 1st quarter 1941. The most complete biography of Haynes is Daniel Perlman, "Stirring the White Conscience" (Ph.D. diss., New York University, 1972). Also see Nancy J. Weiss, *The National Urban League, 1910–1940* (1974), esp. pp. 30–34, 40–45, 74–77, 129–135; *Negro History Bulletin,* Oct. 1959; and the obituary in the *New York Times,* Jan. 10, 1960.]

EDGAR A. TOPPIN

HELBURN, THERESA (Jan. 12, 1887–Aug. 18, 1959), playwright, producer, and director of New York City's Theatre Guild, was born in New York City, the daughter of Julius Helburn and Hannah Peyser. Her father, a leather merchant, spent the workweek in Boston while the rest of the family lived in New York City with Hannah Helburn's parents. By Helburn's own account, two influences were key in her development: the example of her mother, whose activities ranged from encouraging aspiring painters to establishing an experimental elementary school, and her position as the youngest child in the family, which led her to try to excel the achievements of her older brother and cousins.

Helburn attended private schools in New York and Boston, and in 1908 graduated from Bryn Mawr College, where she produced the class play each year. After graduating, however, she suffered a nervous collapse. This emotional pattern of frenetic activity followed by exhaustion apparently was characteristic; it might be termed a "manic-depressive" syndrome. However, it neither interfered with her enormous productivity over the years nor was it especially noticed by her associates, who have described her as stable, energetic, powerful, and charming.

Helburn recuperated from her illness at a Massachusetts farm that her mother and brother purchased for her. There she began to write. Subsequently she enrolled at Radcliffe as a graduate student and at Harvard University took George Pierce Baker's "English 47," a theater course later renowned because of its illustrious graduates, one of whom was Eugene O'Neill. In 1910 Helburn returned to New York City. For the next four years she supported herself in various occupations. She published poetry in *Century, Harper's, New Republic,* and a number of poetry journals. She taught drama at Miss Merrill's Finishing School in Mamaroneck, N.Y. (where Katherine Cornell was one of her students). She served as governess for the Herter family in New York and Paris, where, in 1913–1914, she was exposed to avant-garde art.

With the outbreak of World War I, Helburn returned to New York City. In the next few years two of her plays were produced unsuccessfully on Broadway; one of them, *Enter the Hero,* subsequently became very popular with amateur theater groups. For a time she served as drama critic for the *Nation.* In 1920 Helburn married John Baker Opdycke, a teacher and writer of books on prose style and advertising; they had no children. Helburn continued to use her maiden name professionally.

In 1919 Helburn had become a play reader for the newly formed Theatre Guild, the creation of young Greenwich Village and uptown artists and intellectuals, many of whom had been associated with the prewar Washington Square Players and who, in rebellion against the commercialism of the Broadway theater, were determined to produce only plays of artistic merit. In 1920, with the group's administration in disarray, Helburn became its temporary executive secretary. She expected to hold this position for only a few weeks, but as executive director she occupied it for nearly forty years. With Lawrence Langner, a patent lawyer and one of the Guild's founders, she almost literally held the organization together.

The Theatre Guild was dependent on subscription audiences; eventually a season of repertory productions was expected each year;

and, at the time, a woman theatrical producer was a rarity. Yet the success of the Theatre Guild, particularly in acquainting the American public with the best recent American and European plays, was extraordinary. In the early years Helburn was criticized for producing too many European and too few American dramas; in the 1930's the charge was that commercialism rather than aestheticism dictated the choice of plays. Yet under her leadership the Theatre Guild premiered most of George Bernard Shaw's works of the 1920's and 1930's, and it regularly produced plays by Maxwell Anderson and Eugene O'Neill. Before the Great Depression and sound movies substantially reduced the number of theatergoers, the Theatre Guild had attracted subscription audiences in Baltimore, Cleveland, New York, Pittsburgh, and Philadelphia.

In addition to her executive duties at the Theatre Guild, Helburn is generally given credit for pairing Alfred Lunt and Lynn Fontanne on the stage, for having founded the innovative (though short-lived) Theatre Guild School, for encouraging young playwrights through the Bureau of New Plays and the Dramatic Workshop of the New School for Social Research, and for being the creative force behind the production of the 1943 musical *Oklahoma!*, which turned the American musical theater in a new direction through its combination of drama, music, and dance. *Oklahoma!* also assured the financial future of the near-bankrupt Theatre Guild.

Helburn, who remained active in the Theatre Guild until 1958, died at Norwalk, Conn. She was not a feminist but, as Marya Mannes characterized her, "lived feminism."

[Helburn's autobiography, *A Wayward Quest* (1960), is the major source for her life. Material can also be found in Walter Prichard Eaton, *The Theatre Guild: The First Ten Years* (1929); Lawrence Langner, *The Magic Curtain* (1951); Marya Mannes, "Profiles: The Power Behind the Throne," *New Yorker,* Dec. 6, 1930; and Roy S. Waldau, *Vintage Years of the Theatre Guild 1928–1939* (1972). Most of Helburn's papers, as well as those of the Theatre Guild, are at the Theatre Guild Archive, Collection of American Literature, Beinecke Library, Yale University. The Lincoln Center Library and Museum of the Performing Arts of the New York Public Library contains some letters, clippings, and photographs. A few Helburn letters are in the George Pierce Baker and Katharine Sergava Sznycer papers at the Harvard Theatre Collection.]

LOIS W. BANNER

HELD, JOHN, JR. (Jan. 10, 1889–Mar. 2, 1958), cartoonist, illustrator, writer, and artist, was born in Salt Lake City, Utah, the son of John Held, an engraver, bandleader, and cornetist, and of Annie Evans, who gained notoriety as Salt Lake City's first "Bloomer girl." His father taught him how to engrave and make woodcuts. Held began to draw at an early age: he sold his first cartoon to the old *Life* magazine in 1904 and was employed as sports cartoonist for the *Salt Lake City Tribune* a year later. He was largely self-taught except for some art instruction from sculptor Mahonri Young, a grandson of Brigham Young.

In 1910 Held married Myrtle Jennings, the society editor of the *Tribune.* Two years later he left for New York City where he designed display cards for the Collier Street Railway Advertising Company and produced advertisements for Wanamaker's department store. Most of his drawings were made in pen and ink; but he also made linoleum block prints, having used that medium as early as 1905. His early work was free and sketchy, in the manner of the day. By 1915 Held had restricted himself to line, which he used in a mannered and sophisticated fashion, the forms stylized and reduced to simple motifs. For instance, the eyes, nose, and mouth are little more than dots. The drawings were usually heightened and embellished with simple washes of tone. The theme of his works was lighthearted commentary on contemporary manners. During World War I, Held was a cartographer and artist for U.S. Naval Intelligence. He was sent to Central America to keep track of German submarine activities, and there he had sufficient time to develop his drawing style as well as study Mayan art.

After the war Held began to make the drawings that brought him fame. Carl J. Weinhardt describes Held's favorite subject as ". . . the Flapper, alias Betty Co-ed, escorted by Joe College in a coonskin coat to Midwestern U's big game, there to drink moon through straws from a hip flask, and thereafter to wrestle on the Zeke house porch while couples just like them danced to 'Fascinatin' Rhythm' inside." Held found a ready market for his commentary on "flaming youth" in the *New Yorker, Judge, Life, Smart Set, Liberty, Vanity Fair, College Humor,* and *Harper's Bazaar.* His flapper also was featured in a syndicated cartoon, "Margy." His figures were so characteristically stylized as to be recognized at once. His typical young man had a spherical head, brilliantined patent-leather hair, dots for eyes, a small checklike wedge of a nose, a stick of a neck, and enormous feet and hands. He dressed elegantly. Held's characteristic young lady was given kinder treatment. She usually had a "boyish bob," a turned-up nose, and often a winsome, if vacant, expression. She was very thin and long-legged, sported perilously high heels, and, like her beau, was very conscious of dress.

Held is often compared with F. Scott Fitzgerald, but he had none of Fitzgerald's tragic overtones and melancholy. He did, however, illustrate Fitzgerald's *Tales of the Jazz Age* and a number of other books. For Harold Ross, the editor of the *New Yorker,* Held did a series of drawings on the foibles of the Gay Nineties, and another of satirical maps, such as the United States as it exists in the mind of a proper Bostonian or Manhattan as it is known to a bon vivant. He also made water colors that Weinhardt claims "must have influenced Disney"; landscapes and wash drawings of animals and figures; and several bronzes, mostly of horses. These he did largely for his own satisfaction and in a style that was more conventional than his commercial products. "Serious art," he told a reporter, "is my vice."

Held was a colorful man. Like the characters he made famous, he dressed well. He was tall, dark, handsome—and lavishly tattooed with anchors, roses, girls, and eagles. He liked to tap-dance, and he raised saddle horses on his Connecticut farm. In 1918 he married Ada "Johnny" Johnson. In 1926 he was a Democratic candidate for Congress in Connecticut but failed to campaign and, much to his relief, lost. The following year he adopted three children. He suffered a nervous breakdown in 1931, was divorced, and as a result of the Great Depression, lost a great deal of money, some of it to Ivar Kreuger, the Swedish match king. Held continued to write and draw, turning out *The Saga of Frankie and Johnny* (1930), *Grim Youth* (1930), *The Flesh Is Weak* (1931), *Women Are Necessary* (1931), *The Works of John Held, Jr.* (1932), *A Bowl of Cherries* (1933), and *Crosstown* (1934). He married Gladys Moore on Nov. 11, 1931; they had one child but were divorced in 1942. On Jan. 16, 1942, he married Margaret Schuyler Janes; they had no children. Held designed the sets for a comedy revue, *Hellzapoppin,* in 1937; two years later he exhibited his bronzes at the Bland Gallery in New York City. In 1940 he was artist-in-residence at Harvard in February and then at the University of Georgia in September. During World War II he was a civilian employee of the Army Signal Corps, working on radar apparatus.

Held's Jazz Age cuties disappeared from the

American scene during the Great Depression, but in the 1950's they enjoyed a revival. His art has continued to grow in esteem, with major exhibitions in Indianapolis (1967) and at the Rhode Island School of Design (1968), and a touring show set up by the Smithsonian Institution (1969–1972). He had a one-man show at the Graham Gallery in New York City (1976).

In 1943 Held purchased a small farm in Belmar, N.J. In 1956 he suffered a mild stroke that slowed the pace of his work, but he completed a series of drawings on the flapper theme before his death in Belmar, N.J.

[*The Most of John Held, Jr.* (1972) has a foreword by Marc Connelly and an introduction by Carl J. Weinhardt (1972).]

ROBERT REIFF

HERBERT, FREDERICK HUGH (May 29, 1897–May 17, 1958), dramatist, screenwriter, and novelist, was born in Vienna, Austria, the son of Lionel Frederick Herbert, a stockbroker, and Paula Knepler. Shortly after Hugh's birth the family moved to London. He was educated at Gresham Public School in Holt, Norfolk, England, and in 1913 entered the London School of Mines to study engineering. The war interrupted his plans, however, and he joined the Officers Training Corps in 1914 and earned the rank of lieutenant. During the war he served with the Royal Garrison Artillery in London and Jamaica.

Following the war Herbert became a copy boy in the advertising section of Selfridge's department store in London. In a short time he was producing poems and stories at a remarkable rate. Herbert immigrated to the United States in 1920 to join his father, who had spent the war years in New York, and soon his short stories and essays were appearing in *Smart Set* and *Saturday Evening Post*. He also began writing movie dialogues and scenarios at Paramount's Long Island studios.

Although his ambition was to write for the theater, Herbert was tempted by a lucrative Hollywood contract and moved to the West Coast, where he ,wrote original screenplays and adapted stories for numerous films, including *Adam and Evil* (1927), *Beau Broadway* (1928), *Air Circus* (1928), *Lights of New York* (1928), and *Baby Cyclone* (1928). With the advent of sound he discovered that his gift for facile dialogue and "boy gets girl" plotting was in great demand.

He adapted *Murder on the Roof* and wrote *Vengeance* for Columbia in 1930 while directing the sound sequences for *Danger Lights* and writing the screenplay for S. N. Behrman's *The Second Man* at RKO. Equally at home in melodrama and comedy, Herbert's film credits eventually surpassed fifty. He is best remembered for *Margie* (1946), *Home Sweet Homicide* (1946), *Sitting Pretty* (1948), *Scudda Hoo! Scudda Hay!* (1948), *Our Very Own* (1949), and the controversial *Moon Is Blue* (1953).

On Sept. 19, 1927, Herbert married Arline Appleby. They had two daughters. Herbert credited his daughters with inspiring one of his most popular plays, *Kiss and Tell* (1943), in which the teenage Corliss Archer was introduced to American theater audiences. He later claimed that both girls wanted to play Corliss when the comedy became a radio series. He and Arline Herbert were divorced in 1937; and on May 14, 1938, he married Mary A. Lankey of Los Angeles.

His first play for the Broadway stage, *Quiet Please* (1940), was a failure; but *Kiss and Tell* ran for an impressive 962 performances, and Herbert added radio writing to his list of credits. The courtship of Corliss Archer and Dexter Franklin became the basis for "Meet Corliss Archer," which debuted on CBS in 1943. Herbert wrote for the series until 1955, and his skill at capturing the pangs of adolescence as well as the solid virtues of middle-class America made the program one of the most popular radio comedies of the period.

Herbert's skill as a playwright, however, was not limited to the teen set. In 1951 he shocked many theatergoers with his witty and controversial comedy *The Moon Is Blue*. The play, probably his best known, nearly duplicated the success of *Kiss and Tell* by running for 924 performances. In *The Moon Is Blue*, Herbert explored the relationship between a delightfully outspoken young woman and an engaged architect as they discussed sex in a frank and frequently funny manner. But when Herbert and Otto Preminger filmed *The Moon Is Blue* in 1953, shock became outrage. Angered by the use of such words as "virgin," "mistress," and "seduction," the Legion of Decency condemned the film and the Hollywood Production Code Administration refused to grant it a seal of approval. United Artists responded by releasing *The Moon Is Blue* without a seal, and in the resulting box office scramble it grossed over $6 million. The impact on filmmaking was enormous. The film paved the way for a reappraisal of the production code and for the eventual acceptance of such controversial films as *Lolita* and *Baby Doll.*

With the success of *The Moon Is Blue* Herbert was guaranteed the capital and freedom to produce his own fims. He also wrote a novel, *I'd Rather Be Kissed* (1954), but like his earlier efforts—*There You Are* (1925), *A Lover Would Be Nice* (1935), and *The Revolt of Henry* (1939)—the book did not sell well; and Herbert's belief that novels were only a diversion from his real love, the theater, was underscored further.

Herbert's last plays, *A Girl Can Tell* (1953) and an adaptation of *Best House in Naples* (1956), were not successful. But as was his custom, he shrugged them off and continued to work. He was proud of the fact that he could write anywhere and could deliver under pressure. He was also a modest and generous man who could not refuse a favor or the call to "doctor" a shaky script. His literary pace was exhausting. Herbert was striken with lung cancer in 1958. He died in Los Angeles, Calif., shortly after the release of *This Happy Feeling,* a film comedy based on one of his earlier stage hits, *For Love or Money* (1947). Although born in Vienna and educated in London, Herbert created some of the most typically American characters in popular entertainment.

[The Herbert papers and manuscripts have been preserved at the University of Wyoming Library in Laramie. Biographical sketches are in Stanley Kunitz, ed., *Twentieth-Century Authors* (1955); and the *New York Times* obituary, May 18, 1958. An excellent account of the radio comedy "Meet Corliss Archer" appears in John Dunning, *Tune in Yesterday* (1976); and a brief description of the impact of *The Moon Is Blue* is in Leslie Halliwell, *The Filmgoer's Companion,* 4th ed. (1974).]

BARRY B. WITHAM

HEYE, GEORGE GUSTAV (Sept. 16, 1874–Jan. 20, 1957), museum founder and director, and philanthropist, was born in New York City, the son of Carl Gustav Heye (pronounced "high"), a German immigrant who built a pipeline and oil refinery in Oil City, Pa., and Marie Antoinette Lawrence. When John D. Rockefeller bought his business, the elder Heye became head of the export branch of Standard Oil, amassing a fortune.

Heye attended the Berkeley School in New York City and graduated with a degree in electrical engineering from the Columbia University School of Mines in 1896. He worked briefly as an engineer in a variety of jobs across the country. In 1901 he joined with others to form the banking firm of Battles, Heye, and Harrison but remained active in the firm only until 1909. He severed all connections in 1914.

While working as a mining engineer in Arizona in 1897, Heye had encountered a Navajo dressed in a buckskin shirt. He acquired the shirt off the man's back. This item was the beginning of a collection numbering nearly four million pieces, the largest assembly of American Indian artifacts in the world. For most parts of the western hemisphere, the collection is the finest, surpassed only by specialists such as the National Museum of Anthropology in Mexico City. Heye, who amassed these materials with no formal training in anthropology, was personally familiar with virtually every item.

The collection had grown to such size by 1903 that two New York ethnologists, George Hubbard Pepper and Marshall Howard Saville, encouraged Heye to acquire several hundred pre-Columbian pots discovered in New Mexico. His mother continued to add to the collection. Heye married Blanche Agnes Williams in January 1904; they had two children. In the next two years items were acquired on expeditions to Mexico and Ecuador financed by the Heyes. It was the start of a twenty-five-year period of funding expeditions and collections of Indian artifacts from the entire western hemisphere.

In 1908 Heye bought a separate building at 10 East 33rd Street, New York City, for the growing collection. It became known as the Heye Museum, though it was not open to the public. Heye devoted most of his energy to acquiring artifacts, and personally headed an expedition to Panama in 1912. Upon his return he discovered his wife had left him; they were divorced in 1913. Heye continued to excavate and to finance further expeditions, finding more storage room in the University Museum at the University of Pennsylvania.

When his mother died in 1915, Heye inherited the family estate and accelerated his collecting. He had half a million items and a pressing need for space. He and a friend, Archer Huntington, purchased a site and erected a building at 155th Street and Broadway. The Museum of the American Indian, Heye Foundation, was born. Heye donated his collection in 1916, with the stipulation that he was to be director, a position he retained until 1956. He also appointed the trustees.

In 1915 Heye married Thea Page, who shared

his enthusiasm for collecting and joined him on many expeditions. They were particularly interested and involved in the excavation of Hawikuh Pueblo, N.M., between 1916 and 1923. The Heye Foundation during this period employed archaeologists and ethnologists for expeditions to Ecuador, much of the Caribbean, Guatemala, Honduras, Costa Rica, and North America.

The museum and foundation prospered in the 1920's as friends of Heye left million-dollar bequests. A library was added, and a center for research and study opened in the Bronx in 1926. The public was first admitted to the museum in 1922 but was not particularly encouraged to visit; the display area was cramped and dimly lighted. Heye considered the rapidly growing collection as essentially his own, and had little interest in displaying it to others.

In 1929 Heye went to Europe to acquire Indian items from collections there. After the Wall Street crash the Heye Foundation ceased to employ professional anthropologists and to finance further expeditions. Although Heye salvaged a considerable portion of his wealth, his collecting was limited. His son was killed in an auto accident in 1932, and his wife died three years later. In June 1936 he married Jessica Pebbles Standing. Although his wife did not share his interest in Indians, Heye spent more time in the museum, cataloging and remaining personally interested in each item. They were divorced in 1940.

Heye's avidity in collecting makes the Museum of the American Indian the best place in the world for the study of North American Indian material culture. His collections range over time and include average and even poorly made items as well as the best. This range allows anthropologists to study stylistic changes and make judgments about artistic abilities. Although Heye often clashed with professionals, they were dependent upon his collection and compromises were made. The professionals criticized his inadequate cataloging and could barely tolerate his disdain for potsherds, but they recognized his uncanny knowledge of what to collect.

Heye's contribution to anthropology and Indian history is virtually immeasurable. The Museum of the American Indian is a remarkable monument, although he seemed to have no interest in a personal monument. Indeed, no one is certain what motivated the collection. Heye suffered a series of strokes beginning in 1955 and died in New York City.

[An obituary is S. K. Lothrop, *American Antiquity*, July 1957. Biographies are Kevin Wallace, *New Yorker*, Nov. 19, 1960; John Alden Mason, Leaflet no. 6, Museum of the American Indian, Heye Foundation, 1958. Also see U. Vincent Wilcox, *American Indian Art*, Spring 1978.]

ERNEST SCHUSKY

HILL, EDWIN CONGER (Apr. 23, 1884– Feb. 12, 1957), radio commentator and journalist, was born in Aurora, Ind., the son of Harvey Boone Hill and Mary Conger. He attended local public schools and was graduated from Indiana University in 1901.

In a literature course at Indiana, Hill was excited at reading news essays from the *New York Sun*, assigned as models of English composition. Impressed by the effectiveness of clear, terse prose, he determined to make journalism his career. He did postgraduate work at Butler College in Indianapolis and in 1901 held his first newspaper post, as a cub reporter on the *Indianapolis Sentinel*. He soon moved to the *Indianapolis Journal* at $15 a week. He also worked for a short period on the *Indianapolis Press* and served as correspondent for newspapers in Fort Wayne, Ind., and Cincinnati, Ohio. His first major assignment was to report on the funeral of former President Benjamin Harrison. Another important early job was Hill's interview with the Indiana poet James Whitcomb Riley, which he later described as "a memory like old lavender."

Although still reporting a capital city's news, Hill had his eye on New York City. With $100 in his pocket he applied, in 1904, at the office of the *New York Sun*, which at the time was the goal of countless aspiring journalists. Managing editor Chester S. Lord hired him as a space writer, but he did so well that he was soon made a regular reporter. When the empty Proctor Theater was damaged by fire, Hill wrote an imaginative account of the tragedy that might have happened if the auditorium had been filled with spectators. This original approach so pleased the *Sun* editors that they placed his story on the front page.

Hill quickly became one of the busiest of New York's news gatherers. Over the next few years he covered everything from human interest drama on the city streets to the exposure and prosecution of Tammany corruptionists. He was an eyewitness to the shooting of Stanford White by Harry K. Thaw. Hill developed an intense interest in politics—especially national nominating conventions and elections. In the process he became a friend of Theodore Roosevelt, who referred to him as a member of his "unofficial Cabinet." He traveled with the president and wrote many columns about his whirlwind exploits. Hill won the esteem of Warren G. Harding, who as president paid him written tribute, and of Franklin D. Roosevelt, whom he zealously promoted prior to his election as governor of New York.

Hill married Jane Gail, a motion picture actress, on July 29, 1922. He left the *Sun* in 1923 to direct the Fox Film Corporation newsreels. He later joined the Fox studio as a scenario editor (1925–1926). But although he made a substantial contribution to the scope and quality of moving picture news, he returned to the *Sun* in 1927.

After five years at the *Sun*, Hill ventured into the new field of radio journalism with a program on news events. This assignment left him time to write a national syndicated column. His work was published by such diverse organizations as the *Literary Digest* and the Hearst chain. The name Edwin C. Hill was soon known from coast to coast. His deep, rich voice was ideal for radio, and Hill used it to transport his listeners to the scene he was describing. During his radio career he worked for the Columbia Broadcasting System, the National Broadcasting Company, and the American Broadcasting Company. His popular programs included "Your News Parade" and "The Human Side of the News." Hill's audience reached five million, phenomenal for the time. The notables that he interviewed in one medium or another in the 1920's and 1930's included Lloyd George, Ramsay MacDonald, Benito Mussolini, Alfred E. Smith, and Emma Goldman.

Tall and handsome, Hill dressed fastidiously and customarily carried a walking stick. He was a Republican and an Episcopalian. His first book, *The Iron Horse* (1925), was a novel about the conquest of the American continent by the railroad builders. *The American Scene* (1933) and the *Human Side of the News* (1934) stemmed from his broadcasting experience. Busy as he was, he found time for golf, horseback riding, and his favorite sport, fly-fishing.

Although he was a devoted New Yorker, Hill spent the winters of his later years in St. Petersburg, Fla., where he died. While his career was grounded in print journalism, Hill actively participated in the early days of electronic news broadcasting. Thus he was in a position to show that these journalistic competitors had much in common, in spite of their differences. After his death many radio stations continued to broadcast his popular, taped descriptions of the "old-fashioned" Thanksgiving and Christmas holidays as they were celebrated during his Hoosier boyhood.

[The obituary in the *New York Times*, Feb. 13, 1957, with portrait, is particularly detailed. See also short obituaries in *Newsweek*, Feb. 25, 1957; *Time*, Feb. 25, 1957; and *Variety Radio Directory* (1940). NBC, CBS, ABC, and King Features issued extensive biographical releases and portraits.]

IRVING DILLIARD

HINES, DUNCAN (Mar. 26, 1880–Mar. 15, 1959), restaurant critic, was born in Bowling Green, Ky., the son of Edward Ludlow Hines, a lawyer and local politician, and Cornelia Duncan, who died when he was four years old. He was reared by a grandmother and educated in the local public schools. He attended Bowling Green Business College for two years but did not obtain a degree. In 1898, suffering from an asthmatic condition, he moved to Albuquerque, N.M., where he became a traffic clerk for the Wells Fargo Express Co. In 1905, after a two-year stint as salesman for the Green Copper Co., of Cananea, Mexico, he married Florence Chaffin and settled in Chicago. The marriage was childless. Joining a local advertising and printing firm, he worked for the next thirty-three years on a commission basis marketing "creative printing ideas" to industrial firms throughout the country.

Not until he was well into his fifties did Duncan Hines begin the career that would make his name a household word. From boyhood he had appreciated good food well served, and in his years on the road he made a hobby of seeking out locally notable eateries. Gradually, friends began to ask his advice; and in 1935, in lieu of Christmas cards, he sent friends and business acquaintances an annotated list of some 160 restaurants that he had found exceptionally good. The following year he published *Adventures in Good Eating* in paperback and offered it for sale at one dollar. The book did well from the first, and after 1938, when it began to receive national radio and magazine publicity, sales increased dramatically. Leaving his old position that year to devote himself full-time to his new enterprise, Hines added two further titles, *Lodging for a Night* (1938) and *Adventures in Good Cooking* (1939). He regularly updated the restaurant guide and personally supervised the printing and marketing of all his books. On Dec. 9, 1939, following the death of his first wife, he married Emelie Elizabeth Daniels.

Hines then returned to his native Bowling Green, where he built a capacious home and headquarters for his growing business, which now included the sale of hickory-smoked hams under his own name. In 1943 he established the Duncan Hines Foundation to provide scholarships to graduate students in hotel and restaurant management at Cornell and Michigan State universities. By the late 1940's eleven salesmen were on the road promoting Hines's books, the cumulative sale of which he estimated in 1948 at $2 million. Although he still traveled widely to keep his evaluations current, he was assisted by a corps of some 400 part-time volunteers, including such peripatetic celebrities as Mary Margaret McBride and Lawrence Tibbett. The touring public, too, volunteered comments and criticisms at the rate of some 50,000 letters a year.

The transformation of these enterprises from an essentially one-man operation into a complex corporate undertaking was the work of Roy H. Park, a young businessman from Ithaca, N.Y., who in 1949 joined with Hines to form Hines-Park Foods, Inc. The company licensed manufacturers to use the name Duncan Hines on a variety of food products, of which the cake mixes manufactured by Omaha's Consolidated Mills proved to be the most popular.

In 1953 Hines and Park set up another company, the Duncan Hines Institute, Inc., which took over the publication and marketing of the guidebooks, which now included *Duncan Hines' Vacation Guide* (1948). Park served as president and sole owner of both these Ithaca-based companies until their acquisition by the Procter and Gamble Company of Cincinnati in 1956.

Apart from periodic revisions of the restaurant directory, Hines's involvement with the various companies bearing his name was, after 1949, largely that of a figurehead. He owned no stock in either but was remunerated on a fee and royalty basis. He still traveled incessantly and dined out frequently, however, savoring his role as a celebrity. His second marriage ended in divorce, and in his later years he was joined in his travels by his third wife, Clara Wright Nahm, a Lexington, Ky., widow whom he married on Mar. 22, 1946.

A bluff and gregarious man with a keen sense of humor, Hines freely dispensed opinions to reporters, writers, and radio food commentators. Most American restaurants, he told the *Saturday Review*, "cook beef gray as a battleship and almost as tough." In another often repeated culinary judgment, he suggested that vegetables were usually so overcooked in the United States that it would be more nutritious to throw them out and drink the juice. He praised America's regional cuisines and deplored the encroaching standardization of restaurants. He was sometimes portrayed as a sophisticated gourmet and cosmopolite, but the image he cultivated was that of an average tourist simply seeking a good, honest meal.

Cleanliness and the appetizing preparation of simple fare won higher marks in *Adventures in Good Eating* than attempts at sophistication or haute cuisine. ("Service is plain but, oh, such pie!" runs a typical entry.) For all his reservations about American cooking, he patriotically insisted that it was the best in the world—an opinion to which he clung even after his first and only trip to Europe in 1954. He died in Bowling Green.

At a time when the automobile had freed Americans to indulge their wanderlust, but before franchised restaurants and national motel chains had emerged to assure a predictable standard of quality and service, Hines played a useful role by providing a measure of consumer protection to the traveler in unfamiliar regions, and by giving restaurants and inns a strong incentive to upgrade the quality of their service. He never accepted advertising in his guidebooks, and his reputation for integrity was an important factor in his success. *Adventures in Good Eating* and the other guidebooks did not long survive their originator, however, and it was as a trademark on cake mixes, muffin mixes, and a line of stainless steel cookware that the name Duncan Hines continued to be known a generation after his death.

[See "From Hobby to Publishing," *Publishers Weekly*, Aug. 6, 1938; M. MacKaye, "Where Shall We Stop for Dinner?", *Saturday Evening Post*, Dec. 3, 1938; H. Sutton, "Wayfarer's Guardian Angel," *Saturday Review of Literature*, Nov. 27, 1948; "Best," *New Yorker*, Apr. 1954; and "Hines Abroad," *ibid.*, July 24, 1954. Biographical material and clippings are at the Kentucky Library and Museum, Western Kentucky University, Bowling Green. *Duncan Hines' Food Odyssey* (1955), with foreword by Roy H. Park, is also useful.]

PAUL S. BOYER

HINES, FRANK THOMAS (Apr. 11, 1879–Apr. 3, 1960), army officer and government official, was born in Salt Lake City, Utah, the son of Frank L. Hines, a mine superintendent, and Martha Hollingsworth. He studied civil engineering at the Agricultural College of Utah in 1897–1898. When the Spanish-American War broke out in April 1898, he enlisted as a private in the Utah Light Artillery. Shortly afterward Hines was promoted to sergeant, and in August 1898 he took part in the capture of Manila. During the ensuing war against the Philippine insurgents he saw action in numerous engagements, and in March 1899 was elevated to second lieutenant in the Utah National Guard. Hines was mustered out of the service in the summer of 1899. He returned to Utah and worked with his father. On Oct. 4, 1900, he married Nellie May Vier; they had two children.

Hines had come to like military life, and when the Regular Army was expanded in 1901 he was appointed second lieutenant. He spent the next ten years with the Coast Artillery, rising to the rank of captain in 1908. From 1911 to 1914 he was assigned to the office of the quartermaster general. While on furlough in Greece in the summer of 1914, he was put in charge of the embarkation of American citizens en route home. Hines returned from Europe that fall and, after brief service in San Francisco, was a member of the Coast Artillery Board.

In August 1917, Hines was assigned to the War Department general staff as assistant chief of the Embarkation Service, and the following January was named chief of that service. Successive promotions to brigadier general in the National Army quickly followed. As chief of the Embarkation Service, Hines developed the organization responsible for transporting American troops and represented the War Department in adjustment of transport matters with the Allies. For this work he was awarded the Distinguished Service Medal by the Army and the Navy. In April 1919, Hines was appointed chief of the Army Transportation Service, and in January 1920 he was promoted to brigadier general in the Regular Army. In August 1920 he resigned his commission to become director of operations for the Baltic Steamship Corporation.

Hines's career in the private sector was short-lived, for in 1923, at the request of President Warren G. Harding, he took over the scandal-ridden Veterans Bureau. By cutting red tape, eliminating unnecessary expenses, and bringing good managers into its operation, he turned the Veterans Bureau—and after 1930 its successor, the Veterans Administration (VA)—into an efficient and tightly run agency. He opposed bonuses for World War I veterans and emphasized economy in veterans' programs by holding inviolable the principle that benefits should be closely related to the sacrifice incurred in service. During the presidency of Franklin D. Roosevelt, Hines opposed many of the New Deal programs. Yet Roosevelt retained him as VA director, for Hines was a master bureaucrat, adept at cultivating the support of influential congressional leaders and maintaining good relations with veterans' organizations. In February 1944, Roosevelt gave him the additional job of director of the newly formed Retraining and Reemployment Administration (RRA). In this position Hines was responsible for developing and coordinating policies affecting military demobilization, war workers' and veterans' job placement, physical and occupational therapy, resumption of education, and vocational training.

As the end of World War II approached, Hines increasingly came under fire. Charges abounded that his zealous guarding of the public purse strings had led to an inadequate VA hospital program, and President Harry S. Truman felt that he was too conservative to bring the dynamism to the RRA that New Dealers desired. In the summer of 1945, Truman removed Hines from both agencies and appointed him ambassador to Panama.

Hines's tenure as ambassador to Panama was dominated by negotiations for continued American use of sites in the Republic of Panama for defense of the Panama Canal. He negotiated an agreement, but in December 1947 the National Assembly of Panama rejected it. The rejection was largely a result of an upsurge in Panamanian nationalism, although Hines's critics charged that his "cavalier" negotiating methods, particularly his brusque, authoritarian manner, were a contributing factor. Hines resigned his ambassadorship in February 1948 and retired to private life. He died in Washington, D.C.

A dark, trim, balding man, Hines was quiet-spoken, undemonstrative, austere, hard-working, and scrupulously honest. He was widely respected as an informed, nonpartisan, and trustworthy administrator.

[Hines's most important published writing is *The Service of the Coast Artillery* (1910), written with

Franklin W. Ward. Additional biographical data are available at Utah State University and the National Archives. On Hines's early Army service see Charles R. Mabey, *The Utah Batteries* (1900); and A. Prentiss, ed., *The History of the Utah Volunteers in the Spanish-American War and the Philippine Islands* (1900). His work as chief of the Embarkation Service is in *War Department Annual Reports, 1919;* and House of Representatives, Select Committee on Expenditures in the War Department. *Hearings on War Expenditures,* 66th Cong., 1st and 2d sess. (1921). On his work as VA director, see William Pyrle Dillingham, *Federal Aid to Veterans, 1917–1941* (1952); Donald J. Lisio, *The President and Protest* (1974); Davis R. B. Ross, *Preparing for Ulysses* (1969). Hines's ambassadorship to Panama is discussed in Lawrence O. Ealy, *The Republic of Panama in World Affairs, 1903–1950* (1951); and Sheldon B. Liss, *The Canal* (1967). An obituary is in *New York Times*, Apr. 5, 1960.]

JOHN KENNEDY OHL

HINES, JAMES J. (Dec. 18, 1876–Mar. 26, 1957), politician, was born in New York City on the Lower East Side, the son of James F. Hines, a blacksmith, and Mary Hines. The family was poor, Irish Catholic, and fiercely loyal to the Democratic party of Tammany Hall. Hines's paternal grandfather had captained an election district for Tammany Hall Boss William Marcy Tweed, as had his father for Boss Richard Croker.

In 1884 the Hines family moved to the Upper West Side of Manhattan. Hines's father was rewarded for his service to Croker with lucrative contracts for shoeing police and fire department horses. The spoils of politics had brought prosperity. At the age of fourteen Jimmy left eighth grade to work in the business. When his father died four years later, he inherited both the shop and the election district. Politics, not horseshoeing, soon became his life's work. Personally, attentively, he ministered to the needs of the voters in his district.

Hines's charm and handsome appearance helped his career. He was five feet, eleven inches tall, but seemed taller, with broad shoulders, a jutting jaw, and cold blue eyes. He drank and smoked infrequently. In 1904 he married Geneva E. Cox; they had three sons.

In 1907 Hines was elected alderman. Three years later he failed to win the leadership of the Eleventh Assembly District in a fraud-ridden election. He lost again in 1911 but won in 1912 after the state legislature prescribed a nonpartisan count of primary results. His growing power was

soon acknowledged by Tammany leader Charles F. Murphy.

As his political capital rose, Hines sought to improve his financial position. In 1912, foreseeing the end of horsedrawn vehicles, he sold his shop and went into the trucking business. He used his influence to procure city contracts for snow and rubbish removal. In 1913 he became chief clerk of the Board of Aldermen at $5,000 per year. Five years later he, a friend (Louis Hartog), and Boss Murphy became partners in a deal to sell glucose to the British government for use in beer brewing. When Murphy withdrew from the deal, Hartog sued Murphy. Hines testified in Hartog's behalf and although the case was settled out of court, a residue of bitterness remained between Hines and Tammany's boss.

Murphy vengefully determined to purge his former partner from power. While Hines was serving as a lieutenant in the Motor Transport Corps during World War I, Murphy established a rival organization in his district. When Hines returned in 1920, he denounced Murphy and in the next primary election defeated the new organization in forty-three of the forty-five election districts within the Eleventh Assembly District. In 1921 Hines just barely failed to win the borough presidency of Manhattan from a Murphy supporter, but his courage in challenging Boss Murphy's ironfisted rule earned the admiration of many Tammany men across the city.

Over the next ten years Hines consolidated his political influence and grew rich. From his office at the Monongahela Democratic Club, he distributed turkeys at holidays, bailed out errant youngsters, found jobs for the unemployed, and helped to solve the complexities of municipal red tape for businessmen. He served constituents efficiently, if not always legally, never permitting regulations to stand in the way of a friend obtaining a needed license, permit, or municipal contract. He was paid well for his services, although the extent of his wealth remained a mystery. Hines kept no bank account. Transactions were made in cash, and his wife handled the financial affairs. She kept a brokerage account and was known to make bank deposits of cash from unidentified sources. There was also an insurance company partnership with Hines's brother Philip and an office furniture company that prospered on city contracts.

Hines lived stylishly and gambled heavily. He was often at the racetrack, accompanied by gangsters such as Charles ("Lucky") Luciano,

Frank Costello, and Arthur Flegenheimer, alias Dutch Schultz. He charmed his constituents with his flamboyant life-style. For twenty-six years he donned a party hat and hosted an ice cream and cake party for 25,000 city youngsters at what was called his June Walk in Central Park.

Hines supported New York's Democratic Governor Alfred E. Smith until 1926, when he became disenchanted with Smith's efforts to improve Tammany's public image at the expense of local leaders' money and patronage. In 1932 Hines broke with Smith and Tammany to endorse Franklin D. Roosevelt's presidential nomination. When Roosevelt was elected, Hines was rewarded with the control of all federal patronage in Manhattan.

Throughout the 1930's, unproven accusations were leveled against Hines for protecting his underworld friends from prosecution. He responded with casual denials or silence until 1938, when three former members of the Schultz mob gave information to an ambitious, aggressive young Republican district attorney, Thomas E. Dewey. In September 1938 a New York grand jury indicted Hines for conspiring to protect Schultz's policy racket. The hearing ended in a mistrial, but on Feb. 25, 1939, after a new trial, Hines was convicted on a thirteen-count indictment for selling protection to Schultz. He was sentenced to four to eight years in prison.

The man who had been Tammany Hall's most powerful single leader served three years and ten months in prison and twice was denied parole before he was released by the parole board on Sept. 12, 1944. The terms of the parole forbade him from engaging in any political activity.

Hines quietly spent the remaining years of his life in the family's Long Island home, far from the political power he had once relished. He died in Long Beach, N.Y.

Reformers and Republican opponents recalled Hines as a blight on honest urban government. Thousands of ordinary citizens, however, remembered him fondly for his favors, generosity, and for the June Walks.

[There has been no published study of Hines's life or career. The most useful contemporary sources are a three-part profile in *New Yorker*, July 25, Aug. 1, 8, 1936; and the *New York Times*, Feb. 26, 1939. See also obituaries in the *New York Times*, Mar. 26, 1957; *Time*, Apr. 8, 1957; *Newsweek*, Apr. 8, 1957. Numerous memoirs in the Oral History Collection of Columbia University refer to Hines, notably that of

Supreme Court Justice Ferdinand Pecora, who presided at Hines's first trial.]

ALAN M. KRAUT

HOERR, NORMAND LOUIS (May 3, 1902–Dec. 14, 1958), histologist, neuroanatomist, medical teacher, and educator, was born in Peoria, Ill., the son of Christian J. Hoerr and Lydia Dallinger. He attended Bradley University in Peoria (1919–1921), then transferred to Johns Hopkins University, where he completed work for the B.A. in 1923. After working as a chemist at DuPont for a year, he entered the University of Chicago graduate school. Hoerr married Virginia Collier Gale on Sept. 10, 1927. The University of Chicago awarded him the Ph.D. in anatomy in 1929 and the M.D. degree in 1931.

Hoerr's professional life encompassed two major phases: at the University of Chicago, research, research training, and medical teaching occupied his attention; and at Western Reserve University School of Medicine, he was head of the department of anatomy and played a major role in one of the most far-reaching experiments in medical education. At Chicago, following a common custom, he was appointed assistant in anatomy in 1925, and instructor in anatomy in 1926, while still a graduate student. He became assistant professor of anatomy in 1933 and retained that rank until 1939, when he accepted the chair of anatomy at Western Reserve University.

During his years at Chicago, Hoerr was greatly influenced by the histologists Robert Russell Bensley and George William Bartelmez. Bensley and Hoerr ushered in the modern era of organelle chemistry with the publication of "The Preparation and Properties of Mitochondria from Guinea-Pig Liver" (1934). At this time, although the significance of mitochondria was appreciated by the cytologist, most biochemists and physiologists did not include the word in their vocabulary. When Bensley and Hoerr separated mitochondria from the liver cell, biochemists were preoccupied with the extraction and purification of the enzymes of the cell. It was not until much later that biochemists as a group began to appreciate the importance of localizing specific enzymes and biochemical functions within morphologic constituents of the cell.

In 1942, on the occasion of Bensley's seventy-fifth birthday, Hoerr organized a symposium entitled "Frontiers in Cytochemistry" and edited the proceedings, which were published in 1943.

The book, which has become a classic in the field, introduced the word "cytochemistry."

The original cell fractionation procedure described by Bensley and Hoerr in 1934 has been modified and improved, but the basic principle of separating the mitochondria from other cell constituents by means of differential centrifugation remains unchanged. The subsequent localization of biochemical functions of the component organelles of the cell, made possible by their classical studies, foreshadowed the great advance made in cytochemistry since the mid-1960's.

During most of Hoerr's tenure at Chicago, the neuroanatomy course was directed by Bartelmez, with the assistance of Hoerr and of younger associates. Hoerr was the students' favorite because of the clarity of his presentation and his devotion to them as individuals. In an anatomy faculty second to none in the country, he stood out as the most successful teacher. Hoerr's association with Bartelmez in the neuroanatomy course provided the stimulus for joint research and resulted in the publication of a definitive paper on the structure of the synapse, "The Vestibular Club Endings in *Ameiurus*" (1933). This paper, based on the ultimate capability of the light microscope, remained a landmark in studies of the junctions between nerve cells until 1954, when electron microscopy confirmed and extended the results obtained by Bartelmez and Hoerr.

Hoerr's other research included a histochemical study of hydrochloric acid secretion that used the freeze-drying technique, a cytological study of the adrenal cortex, a neuroanatomical study of the hindbrain of the opossum, a histophysiological study of the circulation of the spleen, an X-ray study of human skeletal development, and an anatomical study of the lymphatic drainage of the paranasal sinuses. Each of these investigations was an important contribution; collectively they illustrate the diversity of his interests.

As secretary-treasurer of the American Association of Anatomists, a post he held in 1946–1956, Hoerr served as adviser, colleague, and friend to other anatomists. In 1958 he was named president-elect of the association, but he died before taking office as president.

Hoerr's appointment as Henry Wilson Payne professor of anatomy, and head of the department, at Western Reserve University came at a germinal time in the history of that institution. The retirement of most of a generation of department heads in the medical school, and the appointment of Joseph Wearn as dean, led to the inception of the Western Reserve curriculum, in which medical students are presented with sequences based on multidisciplinary aspects of the major organ systems, rather than the coventional discipline-by-discipline approach. Hoerr was an unsung hero of this experiment, which seemed to him, as a medically qualified biologist, to strengthen the multidisciplinary approach to medical teaching that he had practiced. Although "integrated curriculum" did not win acceptance in other medical schools, and later was modified at Western Reserve, it stimulated thinking about the deficiencies and needs of medical teaching programs.

Hoerr served as associate editor of *Anatomical Record* (1948–1958), and as coeditor of the *New Gould Medical Dictionary* carried that publication through two editions (1949, 1956). He was also a founder and president of the Cleveland Chamber Music Society, which he helped mold into one of the finest and most active chamber music groups in the country. He died in Cleveland.

[Hoerr's publications include "The Cells of the Suprarenal Cortex in the Guinea Pig; Their Reaction to Injury and Their Replacement," *American Journal of Anatomy* (1931), 139–197; "The Hindbrain of the Opossum *Didelphis virginiana*," *Journal of Comparative Neurology* (1932), 277–355, written with Voris; "The Vestibular Club Endings in *Ameiurus*. Further Evidence on the Morphology of the Synapse," *ibid.* (1933), 401–428, written with G. W. Bartelmez; "Studies on Cell Structure by the Freezing-Drying Method. V. The Chemical Basis of the Organization of the Cell" and "VI. The Preparation and Properties of Mitochondria From Guinea-Pig Liver," *Anatomical Record* (1934), 251–266 and 449–455, written with R. R. Bensley; "Cytological Studies by the Altmann-Gersh Freezing-Drying Method. I. Recent Advances in the Technique" and "II. The Mechanism of Secretion of Hydrochloric Acid in the Gastric Mucosa," *Anatomical Record* (1936), 293–317 and 417–435, part II with introduction by Bensley; "III. The Preexistence of Neurofibrillae and Their Disposition in the Nerve Fiber" and "IV. The Structure of the Myelin Sheath of Nerve Fibers," *Anatomical Record* (1936), 81–90 and 91–95; and "Histological Studies on Lipins. I. On Osmic Acid as a Microchemical Reagent With Special Reference to Lipins" and "II. A Cytological Analysis of the Liposomes in the Adrenal Cortex of the Guinea Pig," *Anatomical Record* (1936), 149–171 and 317–342.]

DAVID BODIAN

HOFMANN, JOSEF CASIMIR (Jan. 20, 1876–Feb. 16, 1957), pianist and composer, was born in Podgorze, near Cracow, Poland, the son of Casimir Hofmann, a prosperous conductor and gifted pianist, and Matylda Wysocka, an opera singer. He was privately tutored and received his early musical instruction from his parents, beginning the study of the piano and composition at the age of four. He gave his first public recital when he was five, and concertized throughout Europe from 1884 to 1887. His prodigious gifts were praised by the most eminent musicians, including Franz Liszt and Camille Saint-Saëns, who called him "perfect." Anton Rubinstein heard the eleven-year-old boy's first appearance as soloist with orchestra, in Beethoven's Piano Concerto No. 1, which he played in Berlin with the Philharmonia Orchestra conducted by Hans von Bülow.

Hofmann's first American tour began on Nov. 29, 1887, with a recital at the Metropolitan Opera House in New York City. A long series of concerts was planned, but the tour was interrupted by the Society for the Prevention of Cruelty to Children, which charged that the child was being exploited and his health impaired. The American banker Alfred Corning Clark gave Hofmann $50,000 on the condition that he withdraw from concertizing and study uninterruptedly until the age of eighteen.

The family returned to Europe and settled in Berlin, where Hofmann studied composition with Heinrich Urban and the piano with Moritz Moszkowski. From 1892 to 1894 he was the only pupil of Rubinstein, whom he venerated above all other pianists. Ironically, Hofmann gave his first adult recital, in Cheltenham, England, on Nov. 20, 1894–the day of Rubinstein's death. From 1898 through 1907 he made solo tours of the United States and played chamber music with the violinist Fritz Kreisler, among others. Around 1900 he settled in the United States. Because of the enormous number of Hofmann's appearances in America, and less favorable reviews than he had received in Europe, success came more slowly. His concerts and appearances at private soirées for the very rich were aided by his marriage in October 1905 to Marie Clarisse Eustis, a New Orleans society belle. They had one daughter.

Critics lavished praise on Hofmann's staggering technical gifts and enormous sonority, as well as on his musical insights. The physical feats seemed all the more impressive because he was quite short and delicate of feature. Yet an interviewer for the *Philadelphia Enquirer* wrote in 1898 that when he touched the pianist's arms, "... muscles bulged forth as though they contemplated bursting. Steel couldn't feel any harder." Hofmann had few mannerisms while performing, and his repertoire was huge. Although a poor sight reader, he could memorize by ear with almost immediate retention. He dazzled his musical friends by learning, after three casual hearings, Leopold Godowsky's immensely difficult "Kunstlerleben" and played it faultlessly without ever seeing the music. His playing was often compared with that of Sergei Rachmaninoff, whom contemporaries considered Hofmann's only peer.

Between 1907 and 1917, Hofmann wrote a column for the *Ladies' Home Journal* in which he answered queries from amateur pianists. In Cincinnati, on Nov. 24, 1916, he premiered a piece for piano and orchestra entitled "Chromaticon" and attributed to Michel Dvorsky, "a mysterious young French composer." After repeated denials Hofmann admitted four years later that he and Dvorsky were one (*dvorsky* is the Russian equivalent of Hofmann). Under that pseudonym he produced several concerti and a symphony, but his later compositions were published under his own name. While exploiting the strongest points of Hofmann's piano style, these works are of little musical moment and were performed mainly by Hofmann and his students. They are no longer in the concert repertoire.

Hofmann contracted in 1918 to record 100 pieces over a fifteen-year period for the Aeolian Company. In the late 1920's he said that he would not continue to record, since he did not wish to be represented by small works and feared that recordings would hurt his box-office grosses. Although he made twenty-nine commercial recordings from 1903 through 1925, most have been lost, except for two long-playing reissues.

In 1924 the newly founded Curtis Institute in Philadelphia appointed Hofmann director of piano and, in 1926, general director and dean. (On November 6 of that year he became an American citizen.) He held these posts until September 1938, teaching a generation of gifted pianists that included Abram Chasins, Shura Cherkassky, and Nadia Reisenberg. The Hofmanns were divorced in 1925, and the following year Josef announced that he had secretly married

Betty Short, a piano student some thirty years his junior. They had three sons. On Nov. 28, 1937, Hofmann returned to the Metropolitan Opera House, the site of his American debut, in his golden jubilee concert. A phonograph recording of that concert exists because Mrs. Hofmann had a friend record it on home equipment.

In 1939 Hofmann moved to Los Angeles, Calif. He gradually withdrew from the concert stage to devote himself to perfecting his inventions. He had a lifelong fascination with mechanical devices and held more than sixty patents on such diverse items as shock absorbers, an electronic piano, air springs, and precision-tool shop instruments. He played in public only sporadically, and gave his last New York City recital on Jan. 19, 1946. He became increasingly reclusive until his death in Los Angeles. Commenting editorially, the *New York Times* said: "Something has gone out of the world of music with the death of Josef Hofmann. He was a symbol, a landmark—almost an institution. It is hard to imagine the piano in our time without him."

[Hofmann published *Piano Playing* (1905); and *Piano Questions Answered* (1909), compiled from his column in the *Ladies' Home Journal*. On his life and career see Henry C. Labee, *Famous Pianists of Today and Yesterday* (1901); Abram Chasins, *Speaking of Pianists* (1957); Harold C. Schonberg, *The Great Pianists* (1963); and Nell S. Graydon and Margaret D. Sizemore, *The Amazing Marriage of Marie Eustis and Josef Hofmann* (1965).]

SAUL BRAVERMAN

HOGAN, JOHN VINCENT LAWLESS (Feb. 14, 1890–Dec. 29, 1960), electrical engineer and inventor, was born in Philadelphia, Pa., the son of John Lawless Hogan and Louise Eleanor Shimer. While still a boy he became interested in wireless telegraphy and built his own station in 1902. Four years later he became chief laboratory assistant to Lee De Forest, the radio pioneer who invented the triode electronic amplifier. Hogan, who, according to De Forest, already possessed a "rich bass voice suitable for broadcasting," participated in one of the earliest radiotelephone experiments at De Forest's laboratory and assisted De Forest during the first public demonstration of the audio (triode) detector at the Brooklyn Institute of Arts and Sciences in March 1907. Hogan's father helped finance the De Forest Radio Telephone company, evidently in the hope that the experience would

help prepare his son for the Sheffield Scientific School at Yale (from which De Forest had received a Ph.D. in 1899).

Hogan studied electrical physics and mathematics at Yale in 1908–1910. He was permitted to investigate the sensitivity of crystal detectors of wireless waves by using the facilities of the graduate physics laboratory. Hogan's first published paper, "Inductance Coils Used in Wireless Telegraphy," appeared in *Electrical World* (1909). His research led to his first patent, on a crystal detector, issued in 1910. He published an analysis of wireless detectors in *Electrical World* in 1911.

Hogan's most important invention, single-dial tuning of radio receivers, was patented in 1912 (patent no. 1,014,002), after he had joined the National Electric Signaling Co., a pioneer American wireless firm founded by Reginald Fessenden. He remained with the company and its successor, International Radio Telegraph Co., until 1921. Hogan participated in the acceptance tests of a powerful transmitter built for the U.S. Navy by National Electric Signaling and installed at Arlington, Va. In a paper published in 1913, he gave the quantitative results of reception from Arlington aboard the U.S.S. *Salem* and stated that at night communication had been possible as far as Gibraltar.

In 1912 Hogan, Robert H. Marriott, and Alfred N. Goldsmith founded the Institute of Radio Engineers. Hogan had earlier been a member of the Society of Wireless Telegraph Engineers (popularly known as the "Swatties"), which had merged with the Wireless Institute to form the Institute of Radio Engineers. He was vice-president of the latter during 1916–1919 (the only man to serve in that capacity for more than one year) and was president in 1920.

During World War I, Hogan was a frequent contributor to *Electrical World* and the *Proceedings of the Institute of Radio Engineers.* He visited the German transmitting stations at Sayville, N.Y., and Tuckerton, N.J., in 1914 and reported that the operators had been able to communicate by radio directly with Germany after their transatlantic cable was cut by the British. In the same year Hogan reported on experiments with radio communication to moving trains, Guglielmo Marconi's station at New Brunswick, N.J., and French experiments using the Eiffel Tower as an antenna. In an IRE paper published in 1916, he discussed the necessary specifications for a radio system that would be as reliable as a wire telegraph system. During the war he designed military radio apparatus.

In 1917 Hogan married Edith McLennan Schrader; they had one son. In 1921 he opened a consulting engineering practice, his clients including the Westinghouse Electric Company, Atwater Kent, and commercial radio stations. Hogan was especially interested in the problem of channel allocation and interference among stations. His suggestions for coping with the problem were included in an IRE paper published in 1929.

In 1928 Hogan turned his attention to new forms of communication, including television and facsimile. He used his own experimental broadcasting station, W2XR, to test his inventions, a number of which led to patents. He was attracted by the high-fidelity potential of frequency modulation and in 1936 converted his experimental station to WQXR, the pioneer high-fidelity station in New York City. This station, later sold to the *New York Times*, became known for its quality programming, especially of classical music.

During World War II, Hogan was a special assistant to Vannevar Bush, director of the Office of Scientific Research and Development, with responsibility for the development of radar and proximity fuses. After 1945 he resumed his consulting work and also his research on facsimile transmission systems. Hogan died in Forest Hills, N.Y.

[Manuscript sources include some of Hogan's letters, in the Espenschied Papers at the National Museum of History and Technology, Washington, D.C. Hogan's publications include "Inductance Coils Used in Wireless Telegraphy," *Electrical World*, 53 (1909); "The Wireless Telephone: A Discussion of Its Present Status and Probable Lines of Future Development," *Electrical World*, 55 (1910); "Developments of the Heterodyne Receiver," *Proceedings of the Institute of Radio Engineers*, 3 (1915); "Physical Aspects of Radio Telegraphy," *ibid.*, 4 (1916); *Outline of Radio* (1923); "A Study of Heterodyne Interference," *Proceedings of the Institute of Radio Engineers*, 17 (1929); and "The Early Days of Television," *Journal of the Society of Motion Picture and Television Engineers*, 63 (1954). Articles on Hogan include "John Vincent Lawless Hogan," in Orrin E. Dunlap, Jr., *Radio's 100 Men of Science* (1944); *Who's Who in Engineering*, 1932–1933; obituary in *Electrical Engineering*, 80 (1961); and obituary in the *New York Times*, Dec. 30, 1960.]

JAMES E. BRITTAIN

HOLIDAY, BILLIE (Apr. 7, 1915–July 17, 1959), jazz singer, was born Eleanora Fagan Holiday in Baltimore, Md. According to her autobiography, *Lady Sings the Blues*, she was three when her sixteen-year-old mother, Sadie Fagan, married her nineteen-year-old father, Clarence Holiday, a guitar player. A short time later he moved to New York City, obtained a divorce, and remarried after joining Fletcher Henderson's dance orchestra. Sadie Fagan, too, married again but was soon widowed and worked as a domestic to support her daughter. Higher wages in the North induced her to leave the child with a cousin.

Childhood proved a traumatic experience for Billie Holiday. She scrubbed doorsteps for nickels when she was six and later ran errands for a whorehouse, where she was able to listen to records by her idols, Louis Armstrong and Bessie Smith. Having accumulated a few hundred dollars, her mother returned to Baltimore to invest in a rooming house and resume care of her daughter. When the ten-year-old was raped by a transient boarder, her mother assigned custody of the child to a Catholic institution. In 1928 she regained jurisdiction after her daughter had completed the fifth grade. Hoping that conditions in the North would prove better, Sadie Fagan took her to New York City. When Holiday was fifteen she was charged with prostitution and sent for four months to Welfare Island. Upon her release, finding her mother ill, she began a desperate search for work.

"I walked down 7th Ave., from 139th to 133rd, visiting every after-hours spot, every restaurant and cafe, trying to find a job," she recalled. "The boss at Gerry's Log Cabin said, 'Girl, can you sing?' '*Sure*, I can sing,' I said. For I'd been singing all my life, only enjoying it too much to suppose I'd ever make money at it." Overnight she was transformed into what Frank Sinatra would later call "unquestionably the most important influence on American popular singing in the last twenty years."

Holiday enchanted artists like alto saxophonist Benny Carter, vibraharpist Kenneth ("Red") Norvo, and clarinetist Benny Goodman, who invited her to join a studio band recruited for a record session. Although she later deprecated her performance there, her renditions of "Riffin' the Scotch" and "Your Mother's Son-in-Law" conclusively established her as a great jazz singer. In 1933 John Hammond, subsequently a Columbia recording executive, instigated on her behalf a recording series for Brunswick, under pianist Teddy Wilson's name.

But Holiday was not cut out for the exigencies of her profession. Her candid life story reveals her extreme vulnerability. Quick-tempered, proud, and bitter about racial discrimination, she experienced difficulty with bookings when agents decided that she was tempermental and obstructive. But successful records continued to enhance her reputation. A short engagement with Count Basie and his orchestra in 1937 was a memorable point in her career, providing a setting ideally suited to her talents. Besides the superb rhythm section, Basie's band included Buck Clayton on trumpet and, on tenor saxophone, the legendary Lester ("Pres") Young, who dubbed her "Lady Day." Yet ultimately she proved unwilling or unable to submit to commerical disciplines, and the relationship was terminated.

That she occasionally met with indifference from the general public was attributed by critic Henry Pleasants not to the fact that she did not sing popular material in a popular vein, but to the fact that she could not. "I have to change a tune to my own way of doing . . . like playing a horn," she explained. Where Holiday could be likened to Bessie Smith, and what set her apart from her contemporaries, was her ability to improvise. Exciting variances in intonation, expressive of the indefinable in jazz, triumphed over her limited range; while tones of a singularly abrasive quality were contrasted with nuances of the utmost delicacy. But, again like Bessie Smith, superb rhythmic authority was her greatest asset. As her popularity increased, she became an outstanding attraction in New York City, returning again and again in the 1930's to clubs like the Onyx, the Famous Door, and Café Society Downtown, and to their counterparts in other cities. In 1947 Hollywood offered her a role—as a maid—in the film *New Orleans*.

Holiday's choice of male companions was poor; when she married James N. Monroe, in Elkland, Md., on Aug. 25, 1941, her mother was distressed. Monroe confessed after a time to opium addiction, and in May 1947 Holiday herself was arrested for possession and use of drugs. Notoriety from the arrest sparked a morbid interest in her career and brought her the widespread recognition that had formerly been denied her. Hopeful of a cure, she pleaded guilty and was sentenced to a year and a day in a federal reformatory at Alderson, W. Va. "But there isn't a soul on earth," she declared, "who can say their

fight with dope is over until they are dead." Her release, after nine months, marked the occasion of a triumphal Carnegie Hall concert. "Billie's not a woman, she's a habit," remarked one of her fans.

But the conviction had deprived her of a cabaret performer's license, and she was forced to tour extensively. Her mother's death in 1945 had affected her deeply, and by 1949 her marriage to Monroe had been dissolved. Lena Horne remembered that at this time "her animals were her only trusted friends." She took comfort in the fidelity of her boxer and a tiny chihuahua that was her constant companion. In California she was again victimized by a scandal and a dubious narcotics charge but was later acquitted. The outlook brightened in the early 1950's, when she fell in love with Louis McKay. Their marriage was not formalized until 1956, but McKay accompanied her on a long-delayed tour of Europe, where she was rapturously received.

But performance levels in America fell as her health deteriorated. Nevertheless, she remained a big attraction in concert halls and theaters from coast to coast. Work eventually became an ordeal too exacting to be supported, and McKay left her. Weak and emaciated, she was scarcely able to mount the stage for her last engagement, at the Phoenix Theater in New York City, on May 25, 1959. Three days later, suffering from cardiac and kidney arrest, she lapsed into a coma. The bittersweet legend that she bequeathed inspired a film, compounded of half-truths, entitled *Lady Sings the Blues* (1972). She died in New York City.

[*Lady Sings the Blues* (1956), Holiday's autobiography, is the main source. John Chilton, *Billie's Blues* (1975), contains a discography and selected bibliographies of book, magazine, and newspaper references. See also John Chilton, *Who's Who of Jazz* (1970); Stanley Dance, *The World of Swing* (1974); Leonard Feather, *From Satchmo to Miles* (1972); and Nat Shapiro and Nat Hentoff, *Hear Me Talkin' to Ya* (1955).]

HELEN OAKLEY DANCE

HOLLY, CHARLES HARDIN ("BUDDY") (Sept. 7, 1936–Feb. 3, 1959), musician, was born in Lubbock, Tex., the son of Lawrence Odell Holley, a tailor, and Ella Pauline Drake. On his first record contract Holly's name was misspelled without the *e*, and he left it that way. He began to play the piano at the age of eleven but was soon concentrating solely on the guitar. With a high school friend, Bob Montgomery, he formed a country and western duo, which was heard on Lubbock radio during Holly's junior year. By the time Holly was fifteen, "Buddy and Bob" were in demand for local club work. Holly also worked part-time as a draftsman and printer.

In 1954 Holly and Montgomery recorded eight songs in a typical country vein, almost all of them written and sung by Montgomery. Nothing came of this effort (the recording was not released until after Holly's death), and they returned to the Lubbock area. Late the next year "Buddy and Bob," by then one of the leading acts in the area, were selected to open a traveling show featuring Bill Haley. They were seen by Eddie Crandall, a Nashville talent agent, who then had the act prepare a demonstration recording that he gave to Jim Denny, another talent agent, to peddle to record companies. Soon after, Decca Records invited Holly to Nashville to record for them. Montgomery was not invited, and the act was dissolved.

In January 1956 Holly went to Nashville, where Denny produced and provided studio musicians. The songs recorded were in the rockabilly style made popular by Elvis Presley. A single, "Love Me," was released, backed by "Blue Days, Black Nights." It failed to sell. Holly returned to Nashville in June and November—the first time with his own backup group, the Three Tunes—with similar results. At this time he began writing more of his own material. None of his recordings was particularly outstanding, however, and his relationship with Decca was served.

Late in 1956 Holly assembled the Crickets, consisting of guitarist Niki Sullivan, bassist Joe Mauldin, and drummer Jerry Allison. He took this group to Norman Petty's recording studio in Clovis, N.M., where he and Petty soon decided to work together; Petty's production and management proved the difference for Holly.

The first step was to get a recording contract, and Petty made an unusual move. He negotiated a contract with Brunswick Records for the Crickets and another contract with Coral Records for "Buddy Holly, with instrumental accompaniment." The main personnel were the same on both labels, but the styles differed slightly. The Crickets were a typical group with lead vocals and supporting harmonies, a lineup that Presley was then successfully exploiting. The Buddy Holly records were more advanced, in that his voice was double-tracked and a greater variety of instruments was used. This division was rather

loose, and Holly proved successful on both labels.

Under Petty's guidance Holly began to develop a distinctive style. While clearly rooted in the country and western tradition, his vocal inflections and mannerisms were unusual and began to draw attention. The first Buddy Holly record, "Words of Love," released in June 1957, did not sell well; but the first Crickets record, "That'll Be the Day," released around the same time, sold well over a million copies, reaching the number one position in the United States and staying on the best-selling charts for twenty-one weeks. A rock and roll classic, "That'll Be the Day," recorded at the Nashville sessions, was completely redone. In 1958 Holly had big hits with "Peggy Sue" and "Rave On," and a smaller hit with "Early in the Morning," under his own name. With the Crickets, "Oh Boy," "Maybe Baby," and "It's So Easy" were successful. The band made several television appearances and coast-to-coast tours, and toured Australia in February and England in March 1958.

On Aug. 15, 1958, Holly married Maria Elena Santiago; they had no children. His single "Heartbeat," released late that year, failed to sell well; and it appeared that he had peaked. He amicably ended his association with the Crickets and made his next recordings in New York with Dick Jacobs' Orchestra and Chorus, assembling a new backup band for live appearances. One of the first major rock stars to use strings, Holly seemed to be moving toward a stance as a nightclub entertainer. Rock and roll elements predominated in some of the later songs, such as "Peggy Sue Got Married," however, and it is unclear in what direction his music was evolving.

In 1959 Holly joined "The Biggest Show of Stars for 1959," a touring group. After a performance in Clear Lake, Iowa, he chartered a plane, along with rock stars Ritchie Valens and J. P. ("Big Bopper") Richardson, to the next stop in Fargo, N.D. Early in the morning of Feb. 3, the plane crashed outside Mason City, Iowa, and all were killed.

Holly was a major figure in the first flowering of rock and roll, in the years 1956–1958. What his music shared with the other leading artists of the period—most notably Elvis Presley, Chuck Berry, Little Richard, and Jerry Lee Lewis—was that it was full of energy. When Holly died, and when these other artists subsequently left rock and roll for various reasons, the music went into doldrums that lasted until the appearance of the similarly energetic Beatles in 1963.

Holly's trademarks were the cheerful, rolling "Tex-Mex" sound of his native area and his use of varying vocal inflections in a single song, in particular a "hiccuping" effect, so that "Sue" became "Sue-a-oo." Other distinctive features of his music included an optimistic tone in the singing—even when the subject matter was sad—and songs that sounded countryish yet emphasized drumming, unlike traditional country music.

Holly's importance, however, was not just in his music but in his total image and in the impact that it had on his listeners and on future musicians. His ordinary appearance—he wore unattractive, thick black-rimmed glasses—combined with his thin young voice to give his music an anyone-can-do-it feeling that was of great importance in the early years of rock and roll. His tragic death at the age of twenty-two helped create a mystique about him. Holly's influence can be heard in the music of Bobby Vee and Tommy Roe. More popular in England than America after his death, he was revered as a major influence by English rock and roll musicians. His two genuine rock and roll classics, "That'll Be the Day" and "Peggy Sue," rendered him one of the new music's first legends.

[The best book on Holly is John Goldrosen, *Buddy Holly: His Life and Music* (1975). For an analysis of his music, see Dave Laing, *Buddy Holly* (1971). See also Mike Jahn, *Rock: From Elvis Presley to the Rolling Stones* (1973); Norm N. Nite, *Rock On* (1974); Lilian Roxon, *Rock Encyclopedia* (1969), with discography; and Irwin Stambler, *The Encyclopedia of Pop, Rock and Soul* (1974).]

RAND HOFFMAN

HOLMES, ELIAS BURTON (Jan. 8, 1870–July 22, 1958), travel lecturer known professionally as Burton Holmes, was born in Chicago, Ill., the son of Ira Holmes and Virginia Burton. His father, a banker and broker, was the son of Elias Holmes, a New York Whig congressman of the antebellum period. His maternal grandfather, Stiles Burton, was a wealthy builder and an importer of French wines and gourmet foods. In keeping with his privileged background, Holmes attended private schools and first traveled to Europe at sixteen. After his second European trip, when he was twenty, he presented a stereopticon show, "Through Europe With a Camera, for which he had written the accompanying narrative, to raise funds for the Chicago Camera Club, of which he was secretary.

Two events turned an avocation into a career, and transformed a dilettante into a hard-working professional. The first was the Panic of 1893, which involved Ira Holmes in financial difficulties and confronted his son with the necessity of earning a livelihood. Presenting another stereopticon lecture to an audience drawn mainly from Chicago's upper class (and based on photographs taken on an 1892 tour of Japan), Burton Holmes cleared a surprising $700. The second decisive event was the retirement, in 1897, of John L. Stoddard, a popular travel lecturer of the day, whom Holmes had met at Oberammergau, Germany, in 1890. With Stoddard's endorsement he and two associates formed Burton Holmes Lectures, Inc., and in the 1897–1898 season he filled Stoddard's engagements in Chicago and at Augustin Daly's theater in New York City. Other engagements followed, and gradually Burton Holmes Travelogues (he coined the term in 1904) became an established part of the cultural and entertainment life of America's larger cities.

In 1897 Holmes introduced motion-picture segments into his program ("Neapolitans Eating Spaghetti" was his first offering), and eventually he abandoned slides altogether in favor of beautifully photographed color films complete with sound effects and musical backgrounds. The trademark of his travelogues, however, and the key to their popularity, was the engaging and sprightly narrative delivered in a crisp and cultivated voice by Holmes, dapper in goatee and formal attire. Where Stoddard's lectures had been didactic, in the older lyceum tradition, Holmes frankly sought to entertain. He had early training as a magician, and took pride in his ability to create the illusion among his audiences that they were actually experiencing "The Magic of Mexico" or "The Glories and Frivolities of Paris," and not simply attending an "illustrated lecture."

The success of the travelogues gave rise to related ventures. *Burton Holmes Lectures*, a multivolume, illustrated set of travel books, appeared in 1901; and in successive editions many thousands were sold. From 1907 to 1912 Holmes regularly contributed travel articles to the *Ladies' Home Journal*. In 1915–1921 he prepared a weekly travel short for distribution by Famous Pictures–Lasky Co., and he was subsequently involved in other film projects, including the preparation and narration of educational films. The travelogues always remained central, however; for more than five decades Holmes pursued a demanding schedule during the winter tour season, often appearing six evenings a week in as many cities. Among his regular engagements were Carnegie Hall in New York, Symphony Hall in Boston, and Orchestra Hall in Chicago. By his retirement in 1951, he had delivered more than 8,000 lectures and had amassed a considerable fortune. Holmes spent summers abroad, making movies and gathering material for new lectures.

On Mar. 21, 1914, Holmes married Margaret Elise Oliver, of a Baltimore manufacturing family, who thereafter accompanied him on his tours; they had no children. When not on the road, the couple resided in New York City or in Hollywood, Calif., where he died.

Burton Holmes's unusual but highly successful career spanned the years from the Spanish-American War to the Cold War—an era when Americans were becoming increasingly curious and apprehensive about foreign lands and foreign peoples, and yet when the actual experience of world travel was confined to a comparative handful. His travelogues helped satisfy the curiosity and allay the apprehension. Concentrating on scenery and architecture, he limited his portrayal of foreign cultures to the quaint and the picturesque. A conservative by breeding and outlook, he generally omitted from his presentations any hint of social conflict, economic exploitation, or human suffering. Indeed, through a long career he seems to have retained the zest and something of the naiveté of the beginning traveler. "I'm a Cook's tourist," he acknowledged disarmingly, "reporting how pleasant it is in such and such a place." Through decades of war, revolution, and upheaval, Burton Holmes Travelogues offered a world that was unfailingly tranquil and beautiful.

[In addition to the various editions of the multivolume *Burton Holmes Lectures* (later titled *Burton Holmes Travelogues*), his books included *The Traveller's Russia* (1934) and his autobiography, *The World Is Mine* (1953). Journalistic sketches are in *National Geographic Magazine,* May 1907; *American Magazine,* Oct. 1920, with a good photograph of Holmes in his prime; *New Yorker,* Feb. 6, 1943; and *Saturday Evening Post,* May 10, 1947. An obituary is in the *New York Times,* July 23, 1958.]

PAUL S. BOYER

HOPPE, WILLIAM FREDERICK ("WILLIE") (Oct. 11, 1887–Feb. 1, 1959), billiard player, was born in Cornwall on the Hudson, N.Y., the son of Frank Hoppe, a ho-

telkeeper, and Frances Hoffman. When Hoppe was seven, he and his older brother Frank began playing pool and billiards in their father's Commercial Hotel. Under the tutelage of their father, a good amateur player, both boys eventually were able to defeat any challenger who appeared at the hotel. Hoppe began practicing up to eight hours a day, and because of his size he often had to sit on the table or stand on a box. In 1895, at the suggestion of customers, Frank Hoppe took his sons to New York City for a two-week exhibition at Maurice Daly's Billiard Academy. Daly was sufficiently impressed to suggest that the youngsters receive further training, which they promptly accepted. The following year Frank Hoppe sold his hotel, and he and his wife accompanied their two sons on an exhibition tour of pool halls and billiard academies throughout the United States. Hoppe left school permanently at the age of nine. They toured until 1899, while Hoppe's three sisters lived with relatives. His brother Frank eventually withdrew from the exhibition circuit to return home with his mother. Already hailed as a lad of brilliant talent, Hoppe began to devote more time to billiards under the able coaching of his father.

Hoppe's first major victory over a nationally known opponent came when he was twelve. He defeated Al Taylor 300 to 207 at the American Billiard Academy in Chicago and immediately acquired a reputation. The following year he ran off 2,000 points in straight billiards and won his first professional tournament without losing a match. Hoppe's father suggested that he devote all of his time to balkline billiards, since most of the professional money was earned through these tournaments. In 1901, Hoppe and his father traveled to Paris, where balkline was the popular game. He defeated most of the second-rank professionals in France while acquiring a basic schooling in the new style of play. Two years later, Hoppe returned to Paris and won the 18.2 balkline Young Masters championship. Throughout the summers of 1904 and 1905, Hoppe toured the United States with Jacob Schaefer, Sr., one of the most renowned billiardists of the era. During the winters he and Schaefer played exhibition matches at the Olympia Billiard Academy in Paris for $600 a month plus expenses. After two years of coaching by Schaefer, Hoppe could defeat his mentor regularly and was ready for world competition.

On Jan. 15, 1906, the so-called Boy Wonder won his first 18.1 balkline world championship by defeating the fifty-nine-year-old Maurice Vignaux of France 500 to 323. Only eighteen, Hoppe set a world record average of 20.83, took all gate receipts plus a $1,000 side bet, and made the front page of most major newspapers. Three months later, at New York's Grand Central Palace, Hoppe defeated the United States great George Slosson 500–391. In May, Hoppe defeated an impressive all-star cast of billiardists in 18.2 balkline. In so doing, he ran 307 consecutive points in one inning for another world record.

Hoppe retained the world championship of 18.1 balkline in 1907, 1909–1911, and 1914–1927. He held the world title in 18.2 balkline in 1907, 1910–1920, 1923–1924, and 1927. In 1914 Hoppe won the world championship in the only 14.1 balkline competition ever held. In so doing, he established records for a high run of 303, high single average of 40, and high grand average of 25.75.

In 1910 Hoppe married Alice Walsh; they had two children. The following year President William Howard Taft invited Hoppe to exhibit his skills at the White House; the entire Cabinet was assembled for the occasion. By 1920 Hoppe was making an annual salary of more than $25,000. He worked for the Brunswick-Balke-Collender Co. in Cincinnati for an additional $7,500 a year, demonstrating their billiard equipment and creating an interest in the sport. In 1924 he divorced his first wife and married Dorothy Dowsey, a dancer in Broadway shows. The following year Hoppe wrote *Thirty Years of Billiards*, edited by Thomas E. Crozier, and then in 1926 his marriage ended in divorce.

Hoppe became so involved with billiards that everything else became secondary. He insured his hands for $100,000 and seldom drove a car or played golf because the activities tightened his wrists. He never smoked or drank, and he protected his eyes by doing very little reading. Hoppe worked diligently to be a superb athlete. He followed a careful diet, did calisthenics, and practiced four to eight hours a day throughout his career. Hoppe possessed the dedication necessary to master a sport like billiards, which demands great nerve, patience, strategy, and delicacy of touch.

Balkline billiards fell into disrepute by the early 1930's because it was so monopolized by Hoppe, Schaefer, Jr., and Welker Cochran. Hoppe then turned his attention to the three-cushion game. It took him a few years to adjust to the new game and he met with little success in his initial attempts to win the world title. He set some records in the three-cushion game for high runs and won a special cushion caroms title in 1933, thus establishing four world records. In 1936 he defeated the reigning world champion, Welker Cochran, but he lost the three-cushion world title the following three years. Hoppe won a special 71.2 balkline title in 1938, thereby setting three new world records. In 1940, he regained the three-cushion world title. While serving as general director and instructor at the Metropolitan Billiards Club in New York City, he held the three-cushion title from 1941 to 1944, and from 1947 to 1952. Despite a bad case of pneumonia, Hoppe played in the 1941 three-cushion championship; for this he won the Most Courageous Athlete of the Year award from the Philadelphia Sportswriters' Association. He wrote *Billiards as It Should Be Played* in the same year. He won the National Billiard Association's sportsmanship award in 1946 and traveled extensively, putting on exhibitions and speaking before college students and military personnel.

Hoppe's suave manner, flawless grooming, impeccable character, and personal habits, defied the stereotype of the gambling, drinking, and smoking pool shark. He was not a typical billiardist since he utilized a peculiar sidearm stroke and never used the diamond-shaped markers around the table to calculate the angles for his shots. Hoppe proved that consistent practice, not style, was the most important ingredient for success.

Whereas most athletes are considered old and finished at thirty, Hoppe was still a world champion at sixty-five. He retired from competition in 1952 but continued playing exhibitions throughout the United States until 1957. Hoppe won a total of fifty-one world billiard titles and estimated that he had spent more than 100,000 hours and walked some 26,000 miles while playing. Hoppe died in Miami, Fla.

[For more information on Hoppe, see Merle Crowell, "The Most Wonderful Billiard Player in the World," *American Magazine,* June 1920; Sidney M. Shalett, "Old Master of the Cue," *New York Times Magazine*, May 19, 1940; Robert L. Taylor, "Profiles: A Powerful Cue," *New Yorker*, Nov. 16, 1940; John Lardner, "The Perpetual Wizard," *Newsweek*, Feb. 24, 1941; Grantland Rice, "Constant Champion," *Collier's*, Jan. 16, 1943; Carl B. Wall, "Grand Old Master of the Cue," *Reader's Digest*, Feb. 1951; "The Master Retires," *Times*, Oct. 27, 1952; and "Cue Master," *Newsweek*, Apr. 20, 1953. Hoppe's records are available in his article "How to Play Three-Cushion Billiards," *Popular Mechanics*, Nov. 1946; and Frank G. Menke, *The New Encyclopedia of Sports* (1947). Also see the obituary in the *New York Times*, Feb. 2, 1959.]

JACK W. BERRYMAN

HOPPER, EDNA WALLACE (Jan. 17, 1864?–Dec. 14, 1959), entertainer, was born in San Francisco, Calif. Because she prided herself on her perpetual youth, she never revealed her age, maintaining that the records of her birth were destroyed in the San Francisco earthquake. Little is known about her early life or education; it is recorded that she attended the Van Ness Seminary in San Francisco.

Less than five feet tall and never weighing more than eighty-five pounds, Hopper first appeared in New York City on Aug. 17, 1891, in a featured role in *The Club Friend*, a musical comedy. Captivated by her charm and zest, the prominent theatrical manager Charles Frohman hired her for his stock company. After she had appeared in three of his productions, he persuaded his friend David Belasco, the foremost writer-producer of the day, to write a comedy for her; and on Jan. 25, 1893, Edna Wallace opened Belasco's ornate Empire Theater with *The Girl I Left Behind Me*. A great critical and popular success, she went on to appear in a series of popular musical entertainments and extravaganzas, including *El Capitan, Dr. Syntax, The Silver Slipper, Jumping Jupiter, Girl o' Mine, Chums, Men and Women, Yankee Doodle Dandy,* and *Chris and the Wonderful Lamp.* For almost twenty years she delighted New York theatergoers with her energetic, good-natured characterizations, her impish sense of humor, and her dainty beauty. Playing an assortment of enterprising, high-spirited characters and several times assuming the roles of boys, Hopper never ventured out of the popular mold. She made her career in plays that were meant only to entertain and seemed entirely pleased to confine her talents to purely escapist and ephemeral popular theater.

Throughout the 1890's and into the first decade of the century, she was the toast of the town, courted by dukes and millionaires, applauded by the press and an adoring public. Every play in which she appeared was a hit. Her most popular was *Floradora*, which opened on Nov. 10, 1900; the show is a landmark because it introduced the chorus line to the Broadway stage. Since she played Lady Holyrood, she was not part of the legendary Floradora Sextette, the original members of which all married millionaires. The life stories of the Floradora girls created the enduring myth of the gold-digging chorine.

Hopper was wooed by most of the prominent playboys of the period. One, the noted comedian DeWolf Hopper, married her on Jan. 28, 1893. Although they were divorced in 1898, she retained her husband's name for the rest of her life. On Nov. 25, 1908, she married Albert O. Brown, a stockbroker and later, a theatrical manager. They separated in 1913 but were reunited briefly in 1927. She had no children from either marriage.

Hopper made sporadic appearances in the usual "girl and music" shows until 1920, when she starred in a play that quickly closed. While realizing that her career as a Broadway star was over, she was not ready to abandon performing. Throughout the 1920's she went on a series of vaudeville tours to publicize a cosmetics firm bearing her name. The cosmetics were made from formulas created by her mother. Shrewdly promoted, her widely popular tours featured advertisements such as "Special Matinee for Women Only" and "See Her in Bed-Bath-Exercise, in a Most Elaborate Production Including $5,000 Bath Furnishings."

It was at this time that Hopper began to cultivate the image of eternal youth, gleefully billing herself as the "Eternal Flapper." In 1927 she underwent what she called a process of "rejuvenation." It was the first of her three face-lifts. She had the operation filmed and announced to the press that her physicians had pronounced her as "mentally and physically but fifteen years old." She then embarked on an eight-year tour of film houses where she taught women "how to remain young and beautiful, or how to regain youth and become beautiful." As part of her act, to impress her audiences with her youthful zest, she did acrobatic dancing.

Hopper had lost her fortune in 1919, and in the mid-1930's she lost most of her money again through stock market speculation. But once more she proved resilient and resourceful. This time she turned to Wall Street rather than the stage; in 1938 she decided to make investing in the stock market her third career and remained with it until her death. She was such a shrewd and steady customer at the brokerage house of L. F. Rothschild that the firm invited her to make her offices with them. For the last nineteen years of her life, she conducted daily transactions at a desk in the firm's boardroom. By 1953 she had quadrupled her capital.

Going to work every morning by subway, the ninety-year-old former entertainer dressed flamboyantly, retaining the fondness that she had developed at the turn of the century for girlish hats, high heels, and frills.

Hopper returned to the stage for a sentimental appearance in June 1953, when the Empire Theater was to be demolished. She skipped on stage in the same role that Belasco had created for her sixty years before, in *The Girl I Left Behind Me,* stunning the audience by her apparent defiance of time. "My secret?" she once said, when asked how she preserved her youthful energy. "It's leading a normal, full life. I keep busy. I take exercise. I've never smoked. I never drink. I eat sensible things, lots of proteins and no fats. I go to bed early during the week, not later than 9:30, and I get up at 6:30. Weekends, I entertain or am entertained." She died in New York City.

[*Who's Who in the Theatre,* 7th ed. (1933), is a useful source. See also interviews in the *New York Sun,* Feb. 28, 1948; *New York Times,* Apr. 19, 1953; and *Life,* June 8, 1953; and the obituary notice, *New York Times,* Dec. 15, 1959. There is a collection of photographs and reviews at the Library of the Performing Arts, Lincoln Center, New York City.]

FOSTER HIRSCH

HOWE, MARK ANTONY DE WOLFE (Aug. 23, 1864–Dec. 6, 1960), editor and biographer, was born in Bristol, R.I., the son of the Right Reverend Mark Antony De Wolfe Howe, Episcopal bishop of central Pennsylvania, who had eighteen children by three wives, and of Eliza Whitney. Howe grew up in Pennsylvania, where he attended Selwyn Hall, in Reading. After graduating in 1886 from Lehigh University, he did graduate work in English at Harvard, where he received a second B.A. with the class of 1887, and an M.A. in 1888.

Howe settled in Boston, where he became associate editor of the *Youth's Companion;* in 1893 he joined Houghton Mifflin as associate editor of the *Atlantic Monthly.* He came to know such older literary figures as Annie Adams Fields and Julia Ward Howe, and was the friend of such diverse contemporaries as Charles Townsend Copeland, Robert A. Woods, and Louis D. Brandeis. Howe's first book of verses, *Rari nantes* (1892), was published by the Merrymount Press in Boston.

In 1895, when Howe's eyesight began to fail, he returned to Bristol, R.I., where for nearly five years he farmed the family property. After a protracted courtship he married Fanny Huntington Quincy on Sept. 21, 1899. They had three children: Quincy, journalist and radio commentator; Helen Huntington (Mrs. Alfred Reginald Allen), monologist and writer; and Mark De Wolfe, Harvard law professor and legal historian.

When Howe's sight improved in 1899, he returned to Boston. His post at the *Atlantic* having been filled, he returned to the *Youth's Companion* until 1913. He edited the *Harvard Alumni Bulletin* from 1913 to 1919 and the *Harvard Graduates' Magazine* in 1917–1919. Thereafter he spent a decade as editor of the books published by the *Atlantic Monthly.*

Howe fully agreed with Dr. Johnson's dictum "Sir, the biographical part of literature is what I love most." While still farming at Bristol, he wrote a series of short biographical sketches for the *Bookman* that were reprinted in 1898 as *American Bookmen.* He persuaded the Boston publishing house of Small, Maynard and Company to undertake, under his editorship, a series entitled Beacon Biographies, little books of about twenty thousand words each. Thirty-one volumes were eventually published. For this series he wrote *Phillips Brooks* (1899).

Howe dreamed of a twenty-volume American counterpart of the *Dictionary of National Biography,* but was dashed when he could get no encouragement from publishers for the proposal. When, two decades later, the American Council of Learned Societies undertook the *Dictionary of American Biography,* he became a willing contributor.

Despite the demands of his editorial work, Howe wrote many full-length biographies, including those of George Bancroft (1908), George von L. Meyer (1919), Annie Adams Fields (1923), Barrett Wendell (1924), James Ford Rhodes (1929), Moorfield Storey (1932), John Jay Chapman (1937), and Oliver Wendell Holmes (1939). A brief autobiography, *A Venture in Remembrance,* appeared in 1941. Howe also edited letters of General W. T. Sherman (1909), Charles Eliot Norton (with Sara Norton; 1913), James Russell Lowell (1932), ladies of the Quincy family (*The Articulate Sisters;* 1946), and Francis James Child and James Russell Lowell (*The Scholar-Friends;* 1952, with G. W. Cottrell, Jr.). In 1920–1924 he edited five volumes of

Memoirs of the Harvard Dead in the War Against Germany, for which he personally wrote 234 sketches.

In 1903 Howe published *Boston, the Place and the People*. He wrote the history of many local institutions—Boston Common (1910), the Boston Symphony Orchestra (1914), the Massachusetts Humane Society (1918), the *Atlantic Monthly* (1919), the Tavern Club (1934)—as well as a book on his native Bristol (1930). When past eighty he collaborated with the photographer Samuel Chamberlain on *Boston Landmarks* (1946) and *Who Lived Here?* (1952). He published eight volumes of verse.

Howe was vice-president of the Atlantic Monthly Company from 1911 to 1929. After he retired from that post, he spent two years in Washington as consultant on biography at the Library of Congress. In 1932 he was a visiting scholar at the Huntington Library in San Marino, Calif.

For a Rhode Islander who had grown up in Pennsylvania, Howe had become a very complete Bostonian. He was a vestryman of Trinity Church; he became a trustee of the Boston Athenaeum in 1906 and of the Boston Symphony Orchestra in 1918; and he was an overseer of Harvard in 1925–1931 and 1933–1939.

Howe called himself an "unrepentant liberal." In 1933, when Charles Knowles Bolton retired as librarian of the Boston Athenaeum, the obvious candidate for his successor was Elinor Gregory. To solve the problem of appointing a woman, Howe agreed to assume nominal responsibility for the library by accepting the new post of director, with Gregory as librarian. In 1937 he quietly resigned the superfluous post and returned to his place among the trustees.

Through his seventies and eighties Howe lived in an apartment on Louisburg Square and spent much time at the Athenaeum, Symphony Hall, Trinity Church, the Tavern Club, the Club of Odd Volumes, and Harvard. In the summer he went to Bristol. The unquestioned dean of Boston letters, Howe died at Cambridge.

[Howe's papers are in the Houghton Library, Harvard University. Helen Howe, *The Gentle Americans, Biography of a Breed* (1965), includes a checklist of Howe's books. See also Arthur Stanwood Pier, Massachusetts Historical Society, *Proceedings, 1957–1960*.]

WALTER MUIR WHITEHILL

HUDSON, MANLEY OTTMER (May 19, 1886–Apr. 13, 1960), professor of international law and judge of the Permanent Court of International Justice, was born at St. Peters, Mo., the son of David Ottmer Hudson, a physician, and Emma Bibb. After attending William Jewell College in Liberty, Mo., where he received the B.A. in 1906 and the M.A. in 1907, he graduated from the Harvard Law School in 1910. From 1910 to 1918 he served on the law faculty of the University of Missouri and became an expert on real property law and conveyancing. During these years he also completed the requirements for the S.J.D. degree at Harvard, which he received in 1917.

In 1918–1919 Hudson served in Paris with the international law division of the American Commission to Negotiate Peace, under the aegis of David Hunter Miller. This experience and a subsequent brief term in the secretariat of the League of Nations confirmed the interest in international law that thenceforth dominated his career. Hudson was appointed an assistant professor at the Harvard Law School in 1919 and Bemis professor of international law in 1923. On Dec. 7, 1930, he married Janet Norton Aldrich; they had two sons.

At Harvard, Hudson immediately took up the study of what was to become his specialty—international adjudication, particularly the then new Permanent Court of International Justice. Numerous publications, including an annual review of that court that appeared in the *American Journal of International Law* for thirty-seven years (1923–1959), brought him worldwide recognition. His treatise *The Permanent Court of International Justice* (1934; revised edition, 1943) was the standard work on the subject: lucid in style, precise in analysis, and unparalleled in its documentation. Hudson also edited four volumes of *World Court Reports* (1934–1943), an elaborately annotated collection of the court's jurisprudence. These and other pioneering works greatly enlarged public understanding of the court's nature and functions, and generally illuminated the settlement of international disputes.

In this period Hudson was also engaged in the serial compilation, under the suggestive title *International Legislation* (9 volumes, 1931–1950), of the texts of 670 multilateral treaties of general interest signed between 1919 and 1945. This undertaking, inspired by his conviction that such treaties offered the most important and promising means for developing international law, was designed to make such materials more readily available to lawyers and scholars. Like the *World Court Reports*, the series reflected Hudson's belief that accurate information on the contemporary practice of states and international tribunals was essential to a correct understanding of the role (and limitations) of international law.

Parallel with this enterprise was Hudson's organization and direction of the Harvard Research in International Law (1927-1939), a cooperative project to set forth the law on selected topics in a format similar to the restatements of domestic law by the American Law Institute. Originally planned to aid the work of the 1930 League of Nations conference on the codification of international law (at which Hudson was an adviser to the U.S. delegation), the Harvard Research in International Law produced thirteen model conventions, complete with detailed commentary, on subjects including nationality, state responsibility, aggression, and the law of treaties. The collective learning and careful workmanship that went into these texts gave them an international influence traceable in all later codification efforts.

On Oct. 8, 1936, Hudson was elected to succeed Frank B. Kellogg as a judge of the Permanent Court. He participated in the court's work until its judicial activities were suspended in 1940, writing separate opinions in six of the ten cases before it in that period. Among these, perhaps the most notable was his concurring opinion in the case between Belgium and the Netherlands regarding diversion of water from the river Meuse (PCIJ Reports, Series A/B, no. 70, pp. 73-80 [1937]), in which he expounded on the role of equity in international law. Also characteristic of Hudson's judicial thinking was his separate opinion in the case between France and Greece concerning lighthouses in Crete and Samos (Series A/B, no. 71, pp. 117-130 [1937]), which illustrated his insistence that abstract juristic concepts (in this case, sovereignty) must not be applied so rigidly as to reach results discordant with the observed facts of a situation.

Between 1940 and 1945, Hudson devoted much time to plans for the postwar reconstruction of international judicial machinery. Both as a scholar and as representative of the Permanent Court, he took a leading part in discussions prior to the 1945 United Nations conference in San Francisco, and at that conference helped to draft the Statute of the International Court of Justice.

This goal achieved, Hudson joined the other members of the old court in a collective resignation, effective Jan. 30, 1946.

Hudson was a member (1948-1953) and first chairman of the United Nations International Law Commission, contributing much to setting its course and to its early substantive work on codification. From 1953 on, ill health restricted his activities; but he persevered in his writing and consulting work at his home in Cambridge almost until his death there.

Hudson's approach to international law was essentially practical and pragmatic. Unlike such contemporaries as Hersch Lauterpacht and Hans Kelsen, he was not much concerned with the deeps of legal philosophy. Yet he was far more than an able compiler. His concern was with the advancement of an international law that would be workable and effective in a real and imperfect world. This down-to-earth attitude permeated all his work. Energetic, brusque, demanding, Hudson set high standards for students and colleagues alike—at first to their discomfort, later to their enduring regard. His contributions as teacher, scholar, and judge are commemorated in the Manley O. Hudson gold medal, the highest award of the American Society of International Law, of which he himself was the first recipient in 1956.

[See *Proceedings of the American Society of International Law*, 1960; P. C. Jessup, *American Journal of International Law*, July 1960; *Harvard Law Review*, Dec. 1960; *Harvard Law School Bulletin*, Oct. 1954 and June 1960; and J. T. Kenny, "The Contribution of Manley O. Hudson to Modern International Law and Organization" (Ph.D. diss., University of Denver, 1976), which contains a bibliography of some 450 writings by Hudson on international law.]

RICHARD YOUNG

HUGHES, RUPERT (Jan. 31, 1872–Sept. 9, 1956), writer, was born in Lancaster, Mo., the son of Felix Turner Hughes, a lawyer and railroad president, and of Jean Amelia Summerlin, who, Hughes recollected, "brought us all up with artistic ideals and passions." He added, "My mother instilled the ambitions, and my father found the funds." His older brother, Howard Robard, inventor of the Hughes conical bit that revolutionized rotary drilling, was the father of Howard Hughes, the reclusive billionaire. Rupert Hughes's novel *The Old Nest* (1912), based on his family, was adapted as a motion picture in 1921 and grossed nearly a million dollars.

Hughes received his secondary education at Western Reserve Academy, then the B.A. from Adelbert College (now Case–Western Reserve University) in 1892 and the M.A. in 1894. On Dec. 12, 1893, he married Agnes Wheeler Hedge; they had no children. At this time his father put up $2,500 so that he could produce a comic opera that lasted a single night.

Intending to become a professor of English literature, Hughes earned the M.A. at Yale in 1899. But his interests in writing, music, and the theater drew him to New York City, where he established himself in the publishing world. While working as assistant editor of *Godey's, Current Literature*, and *Criterion*, he contributed short stories, articles, verse, and criticism to *Scribner's, Century, Cosmopolitan*, and other periodicals. Serials published in *St. Nicholas* appeared as his first book, *The Lakerim Athletic Club* (1898).

In May 1901 Hughes began editoral work in London with *The Historian's History of the World*, a multivolume project that took him to the British Museum, the Bibliothèque Nationale, and numerous American scholarly libraries. He dated his own research on George Washington from this period.

Upon his return to New York in November 1902, Hughes embarked upon a career as editor and author. Until 1905 he worked for the Encyclopaedia Britannica Company, meanwhile publishing on his own. He had brought out a book of verse, *Gyges Ring*, in 1901; a number of his poems are listed in *Granger's Index to Poetry*. His *Music Lovers' Encyclopedia* (1903), which went through many editions, was revised in 1950 by Deems Taylor and Russell Kerr and was reprinted in 1971.

While he was in London, Hughes saw his play *The Wooden Wedding* produced in 1902; in the next twenty years he wrote more than a dozen plays. *Alexander the Great* toured the United States in 1903–1904; and *The Transformation* (revived as *Two Women*) and *The Bridge* (revived as *The Man Between)* toured in 1910–1912. His most successful stage effort was the farce *Excuse Me,* a comedy set in two railroad cars traveling from Chicago to San Francisco, which was produced in New York in 1911, in Australia in 1913, and in London in 1915; two companies toured the United States in 1912–1914.

Hughes maintained a lifelong interest in the National Guard, rising from private to captain in the Seventh Regiment, New York National Guard, between 1897 and 1908. The preparedness movement of 1915 engaged his attention as publicist and citizen soldier. His articles in *Collier's* in 1916 stated the case for the National Guard and told of his own brief participation as a captain in the Sixty-ninth Regular Infantry of the New York National Guard in the Mexican border campaign led by General John J. Pershing. His increasing deafness prevented overseas service, and during the war he was a censor in military intelligence in Washington, rising to the rank of major.

While he was bringing out plays, Hughes also was producing fiction. His stories found purchasers in the new motion picture industry. Mary Pickford played in *Johanna Enlists*, based on a story he wrote in 1916; and Douglas Fairbanks made his stage debut in *All for a Girl,* a play that Hughes wrote. Hughes began turning many of his short stories and novels into film scripts. In 1919, when Samuel Goldwyn and Rex Beach organized Eminent Authors Pictures to exploit the talents of well-known American novelists and film writers, Hughes, with Gertrude Atherton and Mary Roberts Rinehart, was publicized throughout the country. He alone of the group produced a successful script, *The Old Nest.*

Money in large amounts was coming his way; Walter Wanger paid him $75,000 for movie righs to a novel. Before long Hughes was traveling from his farm near Bedford Hills, N.Y., to Hollywood to supervise scenario changes. Short visits became longer ones; by 1923 he was living in Hollywood, where he built a mansion inspired by illustrations in *The Arabian Nights.* Throughout the 1920's and 1930's he wrote and directed films. *The Patent Leather Kid,* based on one of his short stories, won an Oscar nomination in 1927.

Hughes's three marriages all ended tragically. In November 1903 he was divorced from his first wife after a dramatic trial in which he named ten corespondents. In 1908 he married Alelaide Manola Mould, a widow with two children. She had had a stage career that included the leading role in Hughes's play *All for a Girl.* She collaborated with Hughes on two motion picture scenarios and other works, and wrote poetry. In ill health in 1923, she committed suicide while on a round-the-world cruise taken to help her convalesce. Hughes edited a collection of her poems, *The Poems of Adelaide Manola* (1924).

On Dec. 31, 1924, Hughes married the writer Elizabeth Patterson Dial, who was thirty-one years his junior. An intense woman with loftier literary goals for herself than she could attain, she committed suicide in 1945.

After his second wife's death, Hughes entered an iconoclastic phase. Previously a writer of farce and light fiction, he now shocked religious conservatives with an indictment of religion, and superpatriots with his candid biography of George Washington. In an agnostic article in *Cosmopolitan* (1924), he explained why he had stopped going to church: "What is preached in the churches is mainly untrue, or unimportant, or tiresome, or hostile to genuine progress and in general not worth while."

Hughes's enduring reputation rests upon his three-volume life of George Washington (1926–1930). Readers were unprepared for the realistic figure presented in fresh detail. "One does not get a sense of balance [in Washington biographies] until the work of Rupert Hughes," Morton Borden asserted of this landmark in Washington historiography.

Hughes exploited John C. Fitzpatrick's unexpurgated edition of Washington's diaries (1925), the papers of Sir Henry Clinton, and other original sources. The depth of research surprised scholars accustomed to regard Hughes as a facile writer for popular magazines; the candor of his portrait of Washington provoked the ire of professional patriots. With the appearance of the third volume, the historian Henry Steele Commager observed, "This work, which at first aroused mainly . . . the supercilious wonder of some professional historians, has now justly earned the encomiums of all students of history . . . ." The Anglophobe mayor of Chicago, "Big Bill" Thompson, branded Hughes "a cheap skate looking for publicity," prompting Hughes to write "Plea for Frankness in Writing History."

Hughes showed that Washington was capable of profanity. His insistence that Washington was in love with Sally Fairfax, the wife of a friend, occasioned a spirited exchange in *American Historical Review* (1934) between Hughes and another Washington authority, N. W. Stephenson, who repudiated "the Sally Fairfax myth." Later biographers, including Douglas S. Freeman and James T. Flexner, have sustained Hughes in this dispute. Freeman, furthermore, in his account of the battle of Brandywine made full and grateful use of Hughes's research.

His success in humanizing Washington, his thoroughness in research, and his fairness to Washington's opponents (including General Thomas Conway, who reputedly plotted to oust Washington as commander in chief) earned Hughes the respect of many academic historians and laymen. For his part, looking back over the buffeting he had received for his biography of the great folk hero, Hughes acknowledged, in *Pacific Historical Review* (1933), "Countless pitfalls pockmark the field of biography. . . I think I have fallen into most of them."

While he was working on his life of Washington, Hughes continued to write light fiction and motion picture scripts. In 1940 he brought out *Attorney for the People*, an admiring biography of the future Republican presidential candidate Thomas E. Dewey. At the outbreak of World War II, Hughes helped to form the California State Guard (1940), and as a colonel he commanded the Second Regiment from 1941 to 1943. During the last years of the war he had a weekly radio program on the National Broadcasting Company network. He was among the outspoken critics of Communism and Communist sympathizers in Hollywood in the 1930's and 1940's. He died in Los Angeles.

[Hughes manuscripts are scattered, and apparently there is no general collection; see *National Union Catalog of Manuscript Collections*, index, 1959–1962. Hughes's articles include "My Father," *American* magazine, Aug. 1924; "My Mother," *American* magazine, Sept. 1924; three articles on the National Guard, *Collier's*, May 20, Aug. 26, and Nov. 11, 1916; *Why I Quit Going to Church* (1925); and "Early Days in the Movies," *Saturday Evening Post*, Apr. 6, and 13, 1935. *New York Times*, Sept. 10, 1956, contains an obituary with portrait; the issues of Dec. 15, 16, 17, and 20, 1923, have details on the death of Adelaide Mould; the issue of Dec. 15, 1923, has an account of the divorce from Agnes Hedge; that of Mar. 24, 1945, covers the suicide and contains an obituary of Elizabeth Patterson. Also see "Rupert Hughes Indicts Religion," *Current Opinion*, Dec. 1924.]

James A. Rawley

HULL, JOSEPHINE (Jan. 3, 1886[?]–Mar. 12, 1957), actress, was born Mary Josephine Sherwood in Newtonville, Mass., the daughter of William Henry Sherwood, a businessman, and Mary Tewksbury. In *Dear Josephine*, W. G. B. Carson notes that the actress never divulged the exact year of her birth. When her subsequent fame inspired speculation, she "arbitrarily picked 1886—the year of her father's death—for publicity purposes." Growing up in Newtonville, she was educated in the local schools. She also studied piano, composition, and singing. Her mother intended her to be a singer, but, as Josephine later recalled, "Almost ever since I can remember, I was stage-struck down to my toes."

In 1895 Sherwood enrolled at Radcliffe College, where she participated prominently in school theater productions. Upon graduation in 1899, she enrolled at the New England Conservatory of Music; the following year she began studying for the stage under the much-respected actress Catherine ("Kate") Reignolds. In 1902 she made her professional debut in a walk-on role with the Castle Square Theater Dramatic Company in Boston. After brief experience with the Castle Square troupe, she played numerous road engagements, touring for a time with the companies of George Ober and Wilton Lackaye.

Sherwood all but retired from the stage when she married Shelley Vaughn Hull, a gifted young actor, in 1910. All her ambitions now centered on him rather than herself, and she resolutely kept in the background. Shelley Hull was appearing in a war play, *Under Orders*, when he contracted influenza and died in 1919.

In 1921 Hull began directing and acting with Jessie Bonstelle's stock company in Detroit. She later recalled some "excellent advice" given her by Bonstelle: "You are too good an actress not to act. Start now as a character woman while you're young—you'll be very wise." Hull moved to New York late in 1922. The following year she directed the Equity Player's production of *Roger Bloomer* and appeared in *Neighbors*. Now using her husband's name professionally, she was seen in 1924 as the hero's mother in *Fata Morgana*. In 1925 she appeared in *Craig's Wife*, which won a Pulitzer Prize. Ten years were to pass before she would find herself in another Broadway hit. During this period, she appeared in such plays as *Daisy Mayme* (1926), *The Wild Man of Borneo* (1927), *March Hares* (1928), *Before You're Twenty-five* (1929), *Those We Love* (1930), *After Tomorrow* (1931), *A Thousand Summers* (1932), *An American Dream* (1933), *By Your Leave* (1934), and *Seven Keys to Baldpate* (1935). Most of these engagements were professional disappointments. Though she appeared in an extraordinary number of short-lived plays, she consistently received favorable reviews for her performances. In the late 1920's and early 1930's, Hull also traveled in Europe, did some radio work, and appeared in the film version of *After Tomorrow* (1932).

She next scored a memorable success as Pen-elope, the nitwit author-sculptor of the zany Sycamore family, in *You Can't Take It With You* (1936), a Pulitzer Prize-winning play by Moss Hart and George S. Kaufman that ran for two years on Broadway. Then, in January 1941, she opened with Jean Adair and Boris Karloff in Joseph Kesselring's comedy *Arsenic and Old Lace*. The play ran for 1,444 performances in New York alone. She played Abby Brewster, one of a pair of elderly sisters who administered poison in elderberry wine to lonely boarders. Her role in this play established Hull among Broadway's immortals; as Carson notes, had she "never played another part, she would have been secure in the possession of her niche." She also played Abby in Frank Capra's film version of *Arsenic and Old Lace* (1944). Hull's comic genius was brought into even greater prominence in late 1944, when she appeared as the bewildered sister of a man who conversed with a giant invisible rabbit in Mary Chase's *Harvey*, which won a Pulitzer Prize and ran for four years on Broadway. Playing opposite James Stewart in the film version of *Harvey*, she won an Academy Award as best supporting actress for 1950.

During the early 1950's, Hull appeared in another movie, *The Lady From Texas* (1951), and in such plays as *The Golden State* (1950) and *The Solid Gold Cadillac* (1953). Her appearance in *The Solid Gold Cadillac*, a hit by George S. Kaufman and Howard Teichmann, marked her last appearance on Broadway. The first of a series of strokes forced her to retire from the stage in 1954. Though she did manage to make several television appearances, her health continued to decline. She died in New York City.

Josephine Hull had a distinctive gift for comedy, creating memorable impressions with fleeting grimaces and gestures. Of comedy in general, she once observed, "It is made up of detail; you have to have an eye for the comic—in others and in yourself, too. Some of my best bits of comedy have grown out of blunders I have made myself." Her sole theory of comedy involved finding "the drama underneath and let[ting] it come to the surface at the right moments" (Gresham).

[See William Lindsay Gresham, "Comedienne From Radcliffe," *Theatre Arts*, June 1945; *New York Herald Tribune*, May 20, 1946; *New York World-Telegram*, Dec. 6, 1952; Daniel Blum, *Great Stars of the American Stage* (1952); "Josephine the Great," *Life*, Nov. 23, 1953; "Josephine Bedlam

Hull," *New Yorker*, Nov. 28, 1953; "Solid Josephine Hull," *Theatre Arts*, Feb. 1955; the obituary in the *New York Times*, Mar. 13, 1957; and William G. B. Carson, *Dear Josephine: The Theatrical Career of Josephine Hull* (1963).]

L. MOODY SIMMS, JR.

HUMPHREY, DORIS (Oct. 17, 1895–Dec. 29, 1958), dancer and choreographer, was born in Oak Park, Ill., the daughter of Horace Buckingham Humphrey, a compositor and hotel manager, and Julia Ellen Wells. She began to study folk and gymnastic dance at the age of eight and ten years later opened her own school in Oak Park. In 1913 she made her first professional appearance under the auspices of the Sante Fe Railroad, touring railwaymen's clubs throughout the Midwest, accompanied by her mother.

At the suggestion of Mary Wood Hinman, her first dance teacher, Humphrey traveled to Los Angeles in 1917 to study at the Denishawn School, newly founded by Ruth St. Denis and Ted Shawn. The experience gained there was instrumental in Humphrey's decision to become a professional dancer. She began to dance in company productions in 1918, and for the next ten years danced regularly in Denishawn vaudeville and concert tours, including a long tour of the Far East (1925–1926).

A turning point in Humphrey's career followed the company's return from this tour. It stemmed from the weariness induced by a cross-country engagement that brought the company to New York City in a series of one-night stands. Plans were announced for a Greater Denishawn School, to be established in New York. But Humphrey had become increasingly dissatisfied with what she considered "decorative" exotic dance and was unwilling to become a cog in the Greater Denishawn superstructure. Accordingly, when the company was engaged for a tour with the Ziegfeld Follies in 1927, she, together with fellow Denishawn dancers Charles Weidman and Pauline Lawrence, elected to remain in New York to supervise the school. While the company was away, Humphrey presented several concerts of her own work, which differed radically from Denishawn dance in its stark abstraction. Shawn himself voiced the most vigorous opposition to it. Unwilling to subordinate private expression to the Denishawn company, Humphrey, Weidman, and Lawrence left in the autumn of 1928 to establish their own studio and ensemble.

Humphrey's independence was hampered by financial difficulties resulting from the stock market crash the following year and the ensuing economic depression. Teaching, with its substantial demands, became a necessity in order to support her creative activity. Nevertheless, she choreographed such important works as *Water Study* (1928) and *Life of the Bee* (1929), which reflected her strongly analytical approach to movement. At this time she began to formulate a distinctive approach to dance technique, based on the disequilibrium attendant upon moving from a state of repose and the effort required to reestablish balance. Humphrey characterized it by the term "fall and recovery."

With codirector Charles Weidman, Humphrey participated in the first series of cooperative programs—with Martha Graham and Helen Tamiris, among others—presented by the Dance Repertory Theater in 1930. Also that year Humphrey was choreographer for the Broadway production of *Lysistrata* and for the Metropolitan Opera's production of Schönberg's *Die glückliche Hand*. She and Weidman danced with several symphony orchestras, and that summer the Philadelphia Orchestra presented the premiere of her *La Valse* at Robin Hood Dell. *Two Ecstatic Themes* (1931) was a manifesto of her creative style with its emphasis on heightened and theatricalized natural movement. For the next several years she demonstrated her interest in the formal aspects of dance construction in a series of works that included *The Pleasures of Counterpoint* (1932), *Suite in F* (1933), and *The Pleasures of Counterpoint No. 2 and No. 3* (1934). On June 10, 1932, she married Charles Francis Woodford. They had one son. When the Bennington College School of the Dance was established in 1934, Humphrey became a member of the faculty. The summer program became a focal point of modern dance through the 1930's, and many of her major works were presented during the concluding festival week.

By 1936 Humphrey had completed her trilogy *New Dance*, comprising *New Dance*, *Theater Piece*, and *With My Red Fires*. In the last she created a masterly character role for herself as the dominating matriarch who rules the destinies of a young couple with cruel malevolence. Her powers were at flood tide, as she began to explore the themes of conflict and resolution that were to dominate her later work. With Martha Graham, Humphrey represented the emerging American modern dance—in the eyes of observers they were considered to be "fire and ice"—Graham's passionate intensity contrasting with Humphrey's analytical sense. The characterization was not entirely fair to either and, in Humphrey's case, did not take into account the broad humanistic approach that she brought to her work. By 1940 the Humphrey-Weidman Company had made two transcontinental tours and was able to establish a permanent studio and performance space in New York City. While touring that year, Humphrey sustained a hip injury in a fall that eventually led to her retirement as a performer in 1945.

In 1946 Humphrey became artistic adviser to José Limón's newly formed company, a position she held until her death. The company became her major artistic outlet and presented the first performances of *Lament for Ignacio Sánchez Mejías* (1946), *Day on Earth* (1947), *Night Spell* (1951), and *Ritmo Jondo* (1953). The Bennington College Summer School of the Dance had been suspended during World War II; it was succeeded, in 1948, by the American Dance Festival at Connecticut College. Humphrey taught there regularly while choreographing for the Limón company during its summer residence. In the fall of 1951 she joined the staff of the newly formed dance department of the Juilliard School of Music in New York City.

During these years a painful arthritic condition had forced Humphrey to use crutches, but she continued to teach and to choreograph. Hospitalized in 1955, she resumed work after her release and accompanied the Limón company on a European tour in 1957. For several years she had been making notes for a book on choreographic method, and in 1958 she devoted all of her energy to completing it. The result, *The Art of Making Dances* (1959), was published posthumously and became a standard text. Her creative legacy is to be found in her technique of "fall and recovery" and in her humanistic social concern for humanity's struggle in an imperfect world. She died in New York City.

[*New Dance* (1966), Humphrey's autobiography, covers her life to 1928. Edited and completed by Selma Jeane Cohen, it was published as *Doris Humphrey: An Artist First* (1972). See also the obituary notices, *New York Times*, Dec. 30, 1958; *Dance*, Feb. 1959; and *Dance News*, Feb. 1959. Andrew Mark Wentink, "The Doris Humphrey Collection. An Introduction and Guide," *Bulletin of the New York Public Library*, Autumn 1973, contains substantial illustrative material and a précis of the collection.]

DON MCDONAGH

HURSTON, ZORA NEALE (Jan. 3, 1901 [?] –Jan. 28, 1960), novelist, anthropologist, and folklorist, was born in the all-black town of Eatonville, Fla., the daughter of John Hurston, a tenant farmer, carpenter, and itinerant Baptist preacher, and of Lucy Ann Potts. Her father, she believed, resented her spirit and independence; her mother encouraged her daughter's ambitions, but died when Hurston was thirteen. Her father remarried; and she was "passed about like a bad penny" until, at the age of fifteen, she became lady's maid to a member of a Gilbert and Sullivan troupe. She toured with the company for eighteen months before enrolling, in September 1917, at Morgan Academy in Baltimore, Md.

In September 1918, Hurston entered Howard University in Washington, D. C., as a student in the Preparatory School. A year later she enrolled in the College Division, where, with the encouragement of faculty member Alain Locke, she began to write and joined the staff of the undergraduate literary magazine, *Stylus*. Intermittently dropping out of school to work, she was still a sophomore five years after matriculation. In January 1925, Hurston moved to New York City in hopes of pursuing a writing career. That year her short story "Spunk" won second prize in a contest sponsored by *Opportunity*, a black journal; the resulting contacts both introduced her to the New York literary world and won her a scholarship to Barnard College in New York City. She enrolled in September 1925 and received the B.A. in 1928.

On May 19, 1927, Hurston married Herbert Sheen, once her fellow student at Howard. They separated within months and were divorced in 1931.

In February 1927, while still an undergraduate at Barnard, Hurston received a research fellowship from the Association for the Study of Negro Life and History for a six-month study of Afro-American folklore in the South. This was supplemented, in December of the same year, by a two-year grant, eventually extended until September 1932, from Mrs. Rufus Osgood Mason, a wealthy patron of Afro-American arts.

The anthropological research, together with the reimmersion in the atmosphere of her childhood home of Eatonville, led to Hurston's first novel, *Jonah's Gourd Vine* (1934), and her first collection of folklore, *Mules and Men* (1935). *Jonah's Gourd Vine* was a fictional retelling of the relationship between her father and mother. The interest of the book is due less to plot and characterization than to the rendition of Eatonville (here called Sanford) and the language and mores of its people.

Mules and Men, still considered a landmark in the study of black American folklore, had much the same Florida locale, although a concluding section on voodoo was set in New Orleans. It recorded the folkways and songs of the rural South, but kept the personality of Hurston at the fore: how she gained the confidence of her subjects and her own participation in parties, "jook" brawls, and fishing expeditions.

Between 1932 and 1936, Hurston was involved intermittently with teaching and with writing and theatrical productions. An abortive collaboration on a play, *Mule Bone*, with an old friend, the poet Langston Hughes, led to a bitter quarrel and a permanent break between the two. The play was never produced.

A Guggenheim fellowship (1936–1938) made it possible for Hurston to study in Jamaica and Haiti. There she acquired material for *Tell My Horse* (1938), a combined travelogue and study of Caribbean voodoo and magic, and wrote her greatest novel, *Their Eyes Were Watching God* (1937).

In *Their Eyes Were Watching God*, Hurston returned to Eatonville and southern Florida. With a control of characterization, plot, and philosophy lacking in her earlier fiction, she explored a woman's search for fulfillment, examining and striking down the accepted standards of security, wealth, and convention. The book was as rich in its language as in its characters, and apparently extraneous events (the "pensioning" of an ancient mule, for instance) merged the skills of folklorist and novelist.

On June 27, 1939, Hurston married Albert Price III, who was fifteen years her junior. This marriage also was short-lived, and Hurston filed for divorce in February 1940. Her last two novels, *Moses, Man of the Mountain* (1939) and *Seraph on the Suwanee* (1948), were well received, but failed to attract many readers.

Moses, Man of the Mountain, which has received increasingly favorable attention in recent years, was a tour de force: Exodus told in the idiom of black Americans. It was also an attempt to deal seriously with the question of racial leadership. *Seraph of the Suwanee*, although set in Florida, dealt unconvincingly with the lives of whites rather than those of blacks.

In 1942, Hurston published her autobiography, *Dust Tracks on a Road*, a lively if sometimes unreliable account, perhaps most notable for

character sketches of the anthropologist Franz Boas; the novelist Fannie Hurst, for whom she had once worked; and the singer Ethel Waters, as well as for Hurston's proclaimed indifference to American racial conflicts.

Always independent, Hurston had earlier quarreled bitterly with her mentor Alain Locke and her friend Langston Hughes, and had existed restlessly under the patronage of Mrs. Mason. In the latter part of her life, she developed an increasing political conservatism that drew her apart from the major social and literary developments of her time. She claimed to detest "race books" in general and those of Richard Wright in particular. As the civil rights movement developed in the 1950's, Hurston remained intransigent, opposed to what she called the "tragedy of color" school. From this perspective she criticized school integration, wrote articles suggesting that black votes in the South were sold or misused, and campaigned for right-wing Republican candidates.

As she aged, Hurston moved from job to job, teaching, writing, even working as a domestic. Early in 1959 she suffered a stroke, and in October of that year she entered the St. Lucie County Welfare Home in Fort Pierce, Fla., where she died. Funeral expenses were paid by contributions from friends and neighbors. There was not enough money for a headstone, and the exact site of her grave has been lost.

Hurston was part of the Harlem Renaissance of the 1920's and 1930's. Her contribution to Afro-American literature was to incorporate into it an image of the rural black American leading an independent and dignified existence outside the framework of white neighbors and oppressors. Her fiction was drawn not only from childhood memories but also from professional anthropological research, and her published folklore material underscored the sensitivity and complexity of Afro-American social systems. She believed that black Americans possessed a unique and valuable culture, and her work at its best was dedicated to preserving and celebrating that culture.

[The major study of Hurston's life and work is Robert E. Hemenway, *Zora Neale Hurston* (1977). An obituary is in the *New York Times*, Feb. 5, 1960. See also Alan Lomax, "Zora Neale Hurston—A Life of Negro Folklore," *Sing Out!*, Oct.–Nov. 1960; Alice Walker, "In Search of Zora Neale Hurston," *Ms.*, Mar. 1975; and S. Jay Walker, "Zora Neale Hurston's

Their Eyes Were Watching God: Black Novel of Sexism," Modern Fiction Studies, Winter 1974–1975.]

S. JAY WALKER

HUTCHINSON, PAUL (Aug. 10, 1890–Apr. 15, 1956), editor and writer on religious subjects, was born in Madison, N.J., the son of the Reverend Charles Xerxes Hutchinson and Annie Mixsell Petrie. He received his secondary education at Centenary Collegiate Institute at Hackettstown, N.J., and the Ph.B. at Lafayette College, from which he was graduated in 1911. Having decided to follow his father in the ministry, he entered Garrett Biblical Institute at Evanston, Ill. Upon graduation he married Agnes Mitchell on June 24, 1915; they had four children.

Although Hutchinson relished the grass-roots ministry of a Congregational pastorate in rural Iowa, he believed that the aspect of church work meant for him was religious journalism. He therefore accepted the post of assistant editor of the *Epworth Herald*, the publication of the Epworth League of the Methodist Episcopal Church. After helping to enliven the *Epworth Herald* for two years (1914–1916), Hutchinson became editor of the *China Christian Advocate*, published in Shanghai. For the next five years (1916–1921) the Far East was his parish. Besides carrying out his editorial duties he traveled in China and nearby countries. He organized and developed the Epworth League in China and served as its secretary. Hutchinson was also chairman of the China Christian Literature Council. In his fifth year in the Orient he was executive secretary of the China Centenary Movement of the Methodist Church.

Hutchinson contracted amoebic dysentery and returned home in 1921. He expected to go back to China, but the Methodist Board of Foreign Missions prevailed on him to remain in the United States. From 1922 to 1924 he worked in the publicity department of the Methodist Church headquarters in Chicago. In the latter year he submitted a manuscript to *Christian Century*, and was hired as managing editor of the nondenominational weekly. In the absences of the editor and founder, Charles Clayton Morrison, editorial responsibilities rested on Hutchinson. When Morrison retired in 1947, Hutchinson became editor. An early testimonial characterized his views. The church, he said, "has had its hours of conformity, of regularity, of walking in well-marked roads. But these have not been the high

hours. Whenever the moment comes when the church is ready to break the trammels of convention, to forsake the trodden paths, to mount again some new circuit through some new wilderness, or along some new border, then it comes aflame once more." This outlook led him to seek out and encourage the application of Christian principles to the social and economic scene.

Along with his editorial duties, which included the recruiting of clergymen of diverse faiths as correspondents and commentators, Hutchinson was seldom without a major research or writing project of his own. Out of his experience in the Orient came *Guide to the Mission Stations in Eastern China* (1919), *The Next Step* (1921), *The Spread of Christianity* (1922), *China's Real Revolution* (1924), and *What and Why in China* (1927). He was a major writer and editorial assistant in the production of *The World Service of the Methodist Church* (1923). With Halford E. Luccock he brought out *The Story of Methodism* (1926). His other books included *World Revolution and Religion* (1931), *Storm Over Asia* (1932), *The Ordeal of Western Religion* (1933), *From Victory to Peace* (1943), and *The New Leviathan* (1946). In *Men Who Made the Churches* (1930) he summarized the contributions of the founders of Protestantism. His nondenominational treatment of religion made him a leader in the ecumenical movement. To assess the effects of World War II, in 1946 *Life* commissioned Hutchinson to make a global tour to report on the state of Christianity. The first article, "Does Europe Face a Holy War?", appeared in *Life* on Sept. 23, 1946.

To write spot reports for the *Christian Century*, he went around the world by way of India and China. His findings led to his summary conclusion that Christianity was the main force to oppose Communism. Hutchinson preached from time to time, and the announcement of his name as the preacher assured a full church.

Chiefly because of his health, he retired from the editorship of *Christian Century* in January 1956. After a winter sojourn in Florida and delivering a series of lectures in New Orleans, he became ill on a drive west and died in Beaumont, Tex.

Calling Hutchinson a "born journalist," Morrison wrote in the *Christian Century*: "There was a mild but wholesome skepticism in his mentality that made him look below the surface for hidden motivations. His perceptive mind was quick to detect both unconscious and deliberate intentions behind unctuous phrases. He hated cant. His composition was an evidence of a tidy and honest mind. His manuscript came from the typewriter so clean that he rarely needed to change a single word. It was an exact mirror of his mind."

[Appraisals by associates are in the *Christian Century*, Apr. 25, 1956. See also Harold E. Fey, "Seventy Years of the *Century*," *Christian Century*, Oct. 11, 1978; and the *New York Times* obituary, Apr. 16, 1956.]

IRVING DILLIARD

JACKLING, DANIEL COWAN (Aug. 14, 1869–Mar. 13, 1956), mining engineer, metallurgist, and industrialist, was born near Appleton, Mo., the son of Daniel Jackling, a tugboat operator and trader, and Lydia Jane Dunn. His father died when Jackling was only a few months old; his mother, when he was not quite two. He was reared by his mother's sister, Abigail Dunn, who later married a Baptist minister, John T. Cowan. Danny Cowan, as he was called, grew up in a large family. While attending local schools he did farm work and other labor, and saved enough to put himself through two years of college. He enrolled at the state normal school in Warrensburg, Mo., and resumed the name of Jackling, taking Cowan as his middle name.

Working part-time at Warrensburg, Jackling managed to save enough during his freshman year to transfer to the Missouri School of Mines at Rolla. He was a brilliant student, and during his second and third years served as a special assistant to the professor of chemistry and metallurgy. A few months after Jackling received the B.S. and a degree in metallurgical engineering in 1892, the professor died. Jackling was appointed assistant professor and was placed in charge of the department of chemistry and metallurgy.

In 1893, Jackling worked for a few months at the Kansas City Consolidated Smelting and Refining Company's plant at Argentine, Kans., then moved to Cripple Creek, Colo. His work there as a chemist and metallurgist induced Joseph R. De Lamar, in 1896, to invite Jackling to take charge of the construction and operation of a gold recovery mill in Mercur, Utah. This involved a revolutionary gold metallurgy, mill construction, and application of high-potential electricity. Jackling's work there during the next three years established him as a brilliant metallurgist and able administrator before he was thirty.

In 1898, De Lamar asked Jackling and an associate, Robert C. Gemmell, to study the ore potential of properties at Bingham Canyon, Utah. Here lay a mountain of porphyry copper of such low grade (estimated to be less than 2 percent) that it would not pay to work it under contemporary technology. Jackling's report (September 1899) suggested a means of working the mine by opencut, mass-production procedures, and treating the low-grade porphyry ores by a similar mass-production process. Such a procedure had never been considered, and its later successful application made the report an international classic. Nevertheless, De Lamar was unwilling to pay the price upon which the owner of the property insisted, in addition to the heavy initial investment required before the copper could be reclaimed economically. De Lamar regarded the undertaking as "too precarious." Jackling left Mercur for the state of Washington, where he built a plant employing the cyanide process to recover gold for Canadian capitalists.

In 1901, Jackling moved to Colorado Springs, where he became associated with Charles M. MacNeill and Spencer and Richard Penrose, owners of a controlling interest in the United States Reducation and Refining Company, which operated two mills near Colorado Springs. As consulting engineer for the firm, Jackling was given the job of rebuilding and managing a zinc-pigment plant at Canon City, Colo. But he could not forget the Bingham properties; and he succeeded in inducing MacNeill and the Penroses to buy the property, and with them organized the Utah Copper Company to develop it in 1903. He became vice-president and general manager of Utah Copper, and later president, and retained the last post until his retirement in 1942.

The Bingham operation was unprecedented —copper that yielded only twenty-five pounds per ton was successfully exploited. This success led to the development of other porphyry properties in the West. Jackling assisted in the development and operation of similar properties in Nevada under the Nevada Consolidated Copper Company, in Montana under the Butte and Superior Mining Company, in Arizona under the Ray Consolidated Copper Company, and in New Mexico under the Chino Copper Company. He served as either president or managing director of each of these companies. In order to make the properties accessible, railroads were constructed; Jackling was general manager of the Ray and Gila Valley Railroad Company in Arizona, the Bingham and Garfield Railway

Company in Utah, and the Nevada Northern Railway Company. He was a director and chairman of the operating committee, and later president, of Kennecott Copper. In addition he was president of the Mesabi Iron Company and vice-president of the Alaska Gold Mines Company, president of the Utah Power and Light Company, and a director of Sinclair Consolidated Oil Company, Chase National Bank of New York, and a number of banks in Utah.

The revolutionary methods that Jackling introduced led to the development of porphyry copper deposits in Russia, Chile, and Africa. His enterprises in the West furnished approximately one-third of the copper produced in the United States during both world wars, as well as much gold, molybdenite, and silver.

Shortly after moving to San Francisco, Jackling married Virginia Jolliffe in April 1915; they had no children. He was a staunch Republican and a strong antiunion man; his adamant and forceful stand postponed the unionization of plants under his direction until the 1930's. Appointed honorary colonel of the Utah National Guard in 1909, Jackling used that title for the rest of his life. He died at Woodside, Calif.

Jackling was appointed director of American explosives plants from 1917 to 1919. During this period a large plant was built at Nitro, near Charleston, W.Va., that produced more than one-hundred-thousand pounds of explosives per day. He was awarded the Distinguished Service Medal in 1919. In gratitude for his services to the state of Utah, the Sons of Utah Pioneers erected a life-size statue of Jackling in the rotunda of the state capitol in Salt Lake City.

[The bulk of the Jackling papers are in the Stanford Collection, Stanford University, although there are some in Special Collections, Brigham Young University, Provo, Utah; Mormon Church Archives, Salt Lake City; and Utah State Historical Society, Salt Lake City. There are brief biographies in Wain Sutton, ed., *Utah* (1949), II, 875–877; and Noble Warrum, *History of Utah Since Statehood* (1919), III, 5–6. Biographical articles are in the *Deseret News* (Salt Lake City), Aug. 11, 1954, and July 6, 1955; and in *Deseret News* and *Salt Lake Tribune*, Mar. 14 and 15, 1956. See also Leonard J. Arrington and Gary B. Hansen, *"The Richest Hole on Earth"* (1963); and Sons of Utah Pioneers, *Presentation and Unveiling of the Statue of Daniel Cowan Jackling* (1954).]

LEONARD J. ARRINGTON

JACKSON, CHEVALIER (Nov. 4, 1865– Aug. 16, 1958), physician, was born in Pittsburgh, Pa., the son of William Stanford Jackson, a stock raiser and veterinarian, and Katherine Ann Morage. Jackson's early life changed abruptly when financial reverses forced the family to move to nearby Idlewood (part of Crafton, Pa.). The mundane ways of that working-class community appalled the sensitive lad. Since arduous work was the order of the day and education was secondary, many of Jackson's classmates were much older. Jealous of the studious lad, they abused and bullied him. He suffered in self-imposed silence, never complaining to his parents or teachers. Undoubtedly these experiences had much to do with his later social aloofness and deep compassion for children. When the financially pressed father turned their home in 1874 into a summer hotel, he served as handyman, maintaining the plumbing and heating systems.

Money earned by decorating glass and pottery enabled Jackson to attend the University of Western Pennsylvania (the University of Pittsburgh) from 1878 to 1882 as a day student. He then apprenticed himself to a local physician, Gilmore Foster. By continuing to paint china at night, he earned enough money to enroll at Jefferson Medical College in Philadelphia in 1884. During summer vacations he sold medical books and served as a cook on a fishing schooner.

After graduating in 1886, Jackson went to England to pursue his interest in laryngology under the world-renowned authority Morell Mackenzie. In 1887 he opened an office limited to the practice of laryngology in downtown Pittsburgh. His patients were mostly indigent and his income was limited; he was unable to satisfy the family creditors when his father died in 1889.

In 1890 Jackson devised an instrument through which he successfully removed a dental plate that a man had swallowed. News of this and other achievements brought him in contact with similar problems causing obstruction of the esophagus. The most distressing was stricture in children due to swallowing lye. He continued to campaign to have lye bottles labeled as poison. Congress passed the Federal Caustic Labeling Act in 1927, the culmination of almost three decades of unrelenting lobbying.

On July 9, 1899, Jackson married Alice Bennett White. They had one child. In that year he also developed a bronchoscope that could be passed through the larynx to visualize the bronchi.

He became chief of laryngology at the Western Pennsylvania Medical College in 1900.

In 1902 Jackson adapted Max Einhorn's suggestion of placing a light carrier at the far end of the scopes used in bronchoscopy and esophagoscopy and rendered these procedures relatively safe. He and a friend, Andrew Lascher, a machinist, built the instruments in Lascher's shop in Pittsburgh. He was further aided in much of his investigative and clinical work by Dr. Ellen Patterson, his assistant at the Western Pennsylvania Hospital in Pittsburgh.

In 1911 Jackson was stricken with pulmonary tuberculosis. During a two-year convalescence he wrote one of his most important texts, *Peroral Endoscopy and Laryngeal Surgery* (1915).

In 1916, unable to develop a bronchoscopy clinic in Pittsburgh, Jackson accepted an offer from Jefferson Medical College to head a department of laryngology. Appointments followed at the Graduate School of Medicine, University of Pennsylvania, and the Women's College of Pennsylvania. With his appointment to the Temple University faculty in 1930, Jackson became the only man ever to hold simultaneous appointments at all five Philadelphia schools. He administered and attended clinics at all institutions without remuneration. From 1935 to 1941 he was president of the Women's College of Pennsylvania. An early advocate of equal rights, he forever championed the role of women in medicine.

Jackson later relinquished all these appointments except his chair at Temple University. When he retired there in 1938, his son, Chevalier Lawrence Jackson, succeeded him. A popular lecturer, Jackson spoke without notes and enchanted audiences by his ambidextrous drawing on blackboards with pastel crayons. During his career he wrote 250 papers, twelve textbooks, chapters in many other books, and an autobiography (1938). He was also not without eccentricities. He protected his hands by wearing silk gloves, even in summer; turned doorknobs by placing a hand in a coat pocket; and preferred the Oriental bow to shaking hands. He died in Philadelphia.

[Many of Jackson's papers and memorabilia are at the National Library of Medicine, History of Medicine Division, Bethesda, Md.; Library and Museum of the College of Physicians of Philadelphia; and Library of the School of Medicine, Temple University. Other sources include *The Life of Chevalier Jackson* (1938), his autobiography; and his curriculum vitae at the library of the College of Physicians of Philadelphia. See also L. H. Clerf, "Memoirs of Chevalier Jackson," *Transactions and Studies of the College of Physicians of Philadelphia*, 27 (1959–1960); J. J. O'Keefe, "The Development of Bronchoscopy at Jefferson," *ibid.*, 32 (1965); S. L. Shapiro, "Chevalier Jackson: A Notable Centenary," *Eye, Ear, Nose and Throat Monthly*, 128 (1965); and L. H. Clerf, "Chevalier Jackson," *Archives of Otolaryngology*, 83 (1965).]

HARRY L. WECHSLER

JANIS, ELSIE (Mar. 16, 1889–Feb. 26, 1956), entertainer and writer, was born Elsie Jane Bierbower in Columbus, Ohio, the daughter of John Eleazer Bierbower and Jane Elizabeth Cockrell. Urged on by her mother, "Little Elsie," as she was called, began entertaining friends of the family at the age of four with recitations and imitations. She made her professional debut in Columbus on Dec. 24, 1897, as Cain in *The Charity Ball*. The following year she appeared with the local stock company in *Little Lord Fauntleroy, East Lynne*, and *The Gallery Slave*. Janis was educated privately, chiefly by her mother—the archetypal stage mother—who devoted the rest of her life to her daughter's career. "The Siamese twins were estranged as compared to my mother and myself," Janis later remarked. Under her mother's guidance she appeared at the Casino Theater Roof Garden in New York City in 1900, but even Jenny Bierbower was no match for the protective Gerry Society, which carefully restricted child performers in New York. For the next three years Little Elsie toured in vaudeville with her program of impersonations. Adopting the stage name of Elsie Janis (derived from her middle name), she next appeared in the road companies of two successful musicals, *The Belle of New York* and *The Fortune Teller*. She returned to New York in *When We Were Forty-One* (1905), her first real success. Her talents as a mimic, singer, and dancer won her the leading role in the musical comedy *The Vanderbilt Cup* (1906). Its success led to other starring roles in *The Fair Co-ed* (1909), *The Slim Princess* (1911), and the melodrama *A Star for a Night* (1911), written by herself, all produced by Charles B. Dillingham, her manager for many years.

A London engagement in *The Passing Show of 1914* opened a new phase in her career. The versatile, dark-haired girl with the flashing smile and boundless energy captivated British theatergoers. Inevitably, Hollywood made her an offer.

Under contract as a performer and scenario writer, in 1914–1915 she appeared in four undistinguished films, *The Caprices of Kitty, Betty in Search of a Thrill, Nearly a Lady,* and *'Twas Ever Thus.* Her talents were obviously more suited to the stage, and she returned to London for the 1915 edition of *The Passing Show.* Subsequently she appeared in New York in *Miss Information* (1915), playing no less than six characters, and soon after embarked on a lengthy vaudeville tour.

When the United States declared war on Germany in 1917, she devoted all her energy to the war effort. Passionately patriotic, she made more than 600 appearances in camp shows on the Western Front, earning the title Sweetheart of the A.E.F. She was made honorary commanding officer of the Ninety-fourth Flying Squadron. By then an international celebrity, she again conquered London in her revue *Hullo, America!* (1918).

At the conclusion of the war she returned to New York in *Elsie Janis and Her Gang* (1919), the first of a series of entertainments based on her wartime experiences. Supported by a cast largely recruited from ex-servicemen, she contributed much of the material and dominated the performance. She sang, she danced, and her imitations were, as always, wickedly accurate. Unlike most mimics, she gave impressions of various celebrities as they might appear doing somewhat unlikely things—Ethel Barrymore, for example, singing "Yes, We Have No Bananas." London subsequently enjoyed this entertainment, and even Paris succumbed to *La Revue d'Elsie Janis* (1921), which daringly included her impression of "Swanee" as it might have been sung by Sarah Bernhardt.

Through much of the 1920's she continued to appear in her own revues. Janis also contributed light pieces to the *Saturday Evening Post* and *Liberty,* and even attempted a comic strip. Her energy was seemingly inexhaustible. An established headliner in vaudeville, she periodically toured the country from coast to coast. In 1927, making a rare appearance in a more conventional musical show, she played the lead in a West Coast production of the Gershwins' *Oh, Kay!*

But as memories of World War I began to fade, her popularity declined. From 1930 on she spent most of her time in Beverly Hills and served as a writer and production superviser on three early talkies: *Paramount on Parade, Close Harmony,* and *Madam Satan.* On Dec. 31, 1931, one year after the death of her mother, she married Gilbert

Wilson, a would-be actor sixteen years her junior. They had no children.. With the onset of the Great Depression, her troubles began. She lost much of her fortune in a Beverly Hills bank failure. In 1935 she was seriously injured in an auto accident, and subsequent heavy expenses forced her to auction off her historic Tarrytown estate, Philipse Manor. She and her husband drifted apart, and an attempt at a comeback in vaudeville in 1939 failed to revive public interest. Her final professional appearance was in a film, *Women in War* (1940). She spent her last years in retirement in Hollywood, where she died.

Seasoned professionals such as Maurice Chevalier, who appeared with her in London, praised her as a perfectionist and tireless worker. A woman of multiple talents, she had much in common with her contemporary, George M. Cohan. She too was a writer, composer, and performer, epitomizing the patriotic, optimistic spirit of the United States from the beginning of the twentieth century to the Great Depression. And like him she faded from view as times changed. Nonetheless, she was a remarkable entertainer. To paraphrase Charles Lamb's famous tribute to Robert Ellison, an earlier performer, "Wherever she was, there was theater."

[Janis wrote *Love Letters of an Actress* (1913); *The Big Show* (1919), dealing with her six months with the A.E.F.; *If I Know What I Mean* (1925); and *So Far, So Good!* (1932), an autobiography. On her life and career, see Maurice Chevalier, *The Man in the Straw Hat* (1949); and Eva Le Gallienne, *At 33* (1934).]

WILLIAM M. APPLETON

JOHNSON, ALBERT (Mar. 5, 1869–Jan. 17, 1957), newspaper editor and politician, was born in Springfield, Ill., the son of Charles W. Johnson, a lawyer, and Anna E. Ogden. When he was an infant, the family moved to Hiawatha, Kans., a frontier community. He attended elementary and high schools in Atchison and Hiawatha, and learned the printer's trade on the side.

Johnson became a reporter for the *Saint Joseph* (Mo.) *Herald* in 1888 but soon went to work for the *Saint Louis Globe-Democrat.* In 1892 or 1893 he joined the *Washington D.C.) Morning Post.* From 1896 to 1897 he was managing editor of the *New Haven* (Conn.) *Register,* then returned to the *Washington Morning Post* in 1898 as news editor. In that year S. Albert Perkins, the Republican National committeeman from the state of Washington, selected Johnson to edit his *Tacoma News*, a conservative Republican organ. Also in 1898, Johnson became convinced that Japanese immigration should be prohibited when he viewed hordes of laborers from that nation being shipped into Washington, not only taking the jobs of young Americans who were fighting in the Philippines against insurgents but threatening to degrade the democratic values and civilization of the United States. On Aug. 16, 1904, Johnson married Jennie S. Smith; they had one child.

In 1907, Johnson became night editor of the *Seattle Morning Times*, and when it ceased publication after eight months, he was employed on the *Seattle Sunday Times*.

In 1909, Johnson moved to Hoquiam, a lumber center on the southeast coast of Washington, and purchased the *Grays Harbor Washingtonian*, which he edited and published until 1934. His local political prominence was assured in 1912 when he led a citizens' movement that broke up an Industrial Workers of the World (IWW) strike that had paralyzed the lumber industry. Johnson ran for Congress in that year as a Republican, crusading against radicalism and favoring immigration restriction. He defeated the incumbent, a Republican who ran as a Progressive.

In 1913, Johnson began a twenty-year tenure in the House of Representatives from the Third District of Washington. He served as a captain in the Chemical Warfare Service of the United States Army in 1918. The following year he became chairman of the House Committee on Immigration and Naturalization, on which he had served since 1913. Taking the post at a time of strong interest in immigration restriction, Johnson proved to be an unusually energetic and vehement racist and nativist, and he provided the chief congressional leadership for the restrictionist movement in the 1920's.

Anticipation of a new wave of immigrants from southern and eastern Europe in 1920 encouraged restrictionists to attempt severe limitations on immigration. Johnson introduced a bill to suspend immigration for two years while Congress worked out a permanent policy. Senator William P. Dillingham of Vermont got a bill through the Senate that would limit European immigrants to 5 percent per year of the number of each nationality already present according to the 1910 census. Johnson adopted this plan, reducing the quotas to 3 percent, and in this form the bill became law. President Woodrow Wilson vetoed

it; but it was reintroduced in Congress, passed a second time, and signed by President Warren Harding in 1921. Johnson's committee then proceeded to public hearings on a permanent law, taking a great deal of testimony. Especially influential were leaders of the eugenics movement, to whose claims for restriction Johnson had been so attentive that in 1923 he was elected president of the Eugenics Research Institute.

Although public opinion was ambivalent, alternating between a desire for cheap immigrant labor and a nativist demand to keep America free from undesirable aliens, Johnson never wavered in his drive for restriction of Europeans and exclusion of Japanese. He adopted the "national origins" plan advanced by Senator David A. Reed of Pennsylvania, a device to apportion quotas directly, according to the percentage of the total population of the nation represented by each national stock. Johnson and his supporters justified the plan on the ground that it faithfully represented the existing American society, but others regarded it as a rationalization for the fears of the nativists. The measure, known as the Johnson-Reed Act, became law on May 26, 1924. It completed exclusion of all Orientals when it excluded the Japanese. In the process it abrogated the Gentlemen's Agreement of 1907, whereby the Japanese government had voluntarily withheld passports from Japanese laborers intending to migrate to the United States, a device that the dogmatic Johnson had never found satisfactory. Until 1927 quotas of 2 percent of the foreign-born of each nation who were already present and had immigrated legally calculated on the 1890 census might be admitted each year. After 1927 the total quota for immigration was 150,000 per year, prorated according to the national origins of the population in 1920. Canadian and Latin American immigration was not restricted. The law went into full effect in 1929, terminating the traditional open door policy of the nation.

Johnson was swept out of office in the Democratic landslide of 1932. He retired from publishing the *Grays Harbor Washingtonian* in 1934, but from 1937 to 1939 was a special writer for the *Wenatchee* (Wash.) *Daily World*. He died in a veterans' hospital at American Lake, near Tacoma, Wash.

[For collections that contain some of Johnson's papers, see *National Union Catalog of Manuscript Sources, 1970* (1971). Johnson wrote voluminous reminiscences of his early career that appeared weekly, with a few gaps, in the *Grays Harbor Washingtonian*, Jan. 7–Sept. 9, 1934. The most important source on his work as a congressman is John Higham, *Strangers in the Land* (1955). A sympathetic biographical sketch is Alfred J. Hillier, "Albert Johnson, Congressman," *Pacific Northwest Quarterly*, July 1945. See also "Who's Who—and Why," *Saturday Evening Post*, May 19, 1923.]

GEORGE A. FRYKMAN

JOHNSON, CHARLES SPURGEON (July 24, 1893–Oct. 27, 1956), sociologist and educator, was born in Bristol, Va., the son of the Reverend Charles Henry Johnson, a Baptist minister, and Winifred Branch. There was no high school for blacks in Bristol, so Johnson was sent to Richmond, where he also graduated from Virginia Union University, with honors, in 1916. In Richmond, as a part-time social worker, he observed firsthand the terrible social conditions under which blacks had to live. Determined to learn more in the urban-industrial setting, he moved to Chicago, where he completed a Ph.B. at the University of Chicago in 1918 and began a lifelong association with Robert E. Park, a founder of the "Chicago school" of sociology. Park insisted that his students supplement their textbook knowledge with direct, participant observation in the living urban laboratory. Throughout his career Johnson applied Park's precepts to race relations.

After a year of combat service in France, Johnson returned to Chicago in 1919, virtually on the eve of one of the worst race riots up to that time in American history, which left twenty-five blacks and fifteen whites dead and hundreds wounded. Appointed secretary and research director of the Chicago commission of investigation in 1920, Johnson produced a massive report, *The Negro in Chicago* (1922), a landmark study that demonstrated that the riots were the surface manifestation of the deep problems of job and housing discrimination.

Also in 1922, Johnson became national research director for the new Urban League in New York. On Nov. 6, 1920, he married Marie Antoinette Burgette; they had four children. At the Urban League, Johnson founded and edited *Opportunity*, a journal of black life dedicated to the improvement of social conditions and to furthering black creativity in literature and art.

In the 1920's, Harlem, for all its problems, pulsed with life; and Johnson, aided by his assistant editor, the poet Countee Cullen, effectively assumed the task of bringing talented young black writers and artists to the attention of white writers and publishers in New York. The "entrepreneur of the Harlem Renaissance" opened the pages of *Opportunity* to Langston Hughes, Zora Neale Hurston, James Weldon Johnson, Claude McKay, the artist Aaron Douglas, and many others. The "New Negro" movement inevitably faded in the grim days of the Great Depression, but it had a lasting impact on black creative expression.

Through these years Johnson never ceased to think about the South, his own roots there, and the great need to document the socioeconomic and racial system in the region. In 1928 he became professor of sociology and director of the social sciences department at Fisk University.

The next eighteen years established Johnson's national reputation. With limited resources and in the face of a hostile structure of racial segregation that made a black university in the South seem like a city under siege, Johnson went to work. As research director for both the Julius Rosenwald Fund and the American Missionary Association, he traveled constantly between Chicago, New York, and Nashville, raising funds for field studies. He succeeded in making Fisk a center of southern social science research second only to that at the University of North Carolina at Chapel Hill, carrying out the projects and training students on an interracial basis. He wrote a dozen books and more than sixty articles. The most important of his books—*Shadow of the Plantation* (1934), *Growing up in the Black Belt* (1941), and *Patterns of Negro Segregation* (1943)—are valuable for their forceful analysis of white exploitation of blacks and the resilience of the black community in adapting to it. They were also a distinctive contribution to methodology, combining survey data with folk ethnography and individual personality profiles. Johnson's lesser works, such as *The Negro in American Civilization* (1930) and *Race Relations* (1934; written with W. D. Weatherford, a white collaborator), were sometimes criticized as too cautious in accommodating to the white power structure. But Johnson never concealed his anger at segregation; rather, he wanted sociological analysis itself to stand as the irrefutable indictment of racism.

Johnson served on national commissions dealing with such issues as housing and rural farm tenancy. He investigated forced labor in Liberia for the League of Nations, was a member of the first American delegation to UNESCO at Paris in 1946, and served on President Harry S. Truman's commission for the reorganization of education in postwar Japan. Moreover, the annual Race Relations Institutes that he developed brought a steady stream of foreign scholars and political leaders to the Fisk campus. When he was named president of Fisk in 1946—the first black to be appointed—Johnson remained the entrepreneur, pressing for reform of and research on southern race relations. But the task of maintaining the national importance of Fisk did not leave enough time for effective day-to-day administration.

In 1956, two years after the Supreme Court decision declaring racial segregation in the public schools unconstitutional (*Brown* v. *Board of Education of Topeka*), Johnson, in the *New York Times Magazine*, realistically described the massive resistance to change in the South. With continued faith in democracy he also wrote of the prospects for further changes, inevitably in the direction of liberation for black Americans. He died at Louisville, Ky.

As a "founding father" of race relations research, a national leader in education and in intergroup relations, and as president of Fisk University, one of the most important black universities in the country, Johnson was passionately devoted to the cause of equality of opportunity and full freedom for blacks. At the same time, as a black man and social scientist, he chose to work toward that end primarily through rigorous research that could demonstrate objectively the appalling human cost of racial segregation and discrimination. In his prolific writing and in his role as adviser to public agencies and private foundations, he pursued the two goals of reform and research calmly and consistently. In these terms he is often linked with two other black social science contemporaries, W. E. B. DuBois and E. Franklin Frazier, though DuBois combined the roles into a more militant strategy against racism than either Johnson or Frazier were prepared to undertake, given their priorities for scholarship.

[The complete collection of Johnson's papers is in the Special Collections Department, Fisk University Library, Nashville, Tenn., which also holds Johnson's collected speeches and taped interviews with many of Johnson's associates and students. Related materials are in the Armistad Research Center, Dillard University, New Orleans, and in the libraries of Howard University and the University of North Carolina. For a complete bibliography, see George L. Gardner, *A*

Bibliography of Charles S. Johnson's Published Writings (1960), published by the Fisk University Library.

Additional works by Johnson are *The Negro College Graduate* (1938); *Into the Mainstream* (1947); and *Education and the Cultural Crisis* (1951). The most comprehensive study of Johnson to date is Patrick J. Gilpin, "Charles S. Johnson" (Ph.D. diss., Vanderbilt University, 1973). Also see Ernest W. Burgess, "Charles S. Johnson: Social Scientist, Editor and Educational Statesman," *Phylon,* 1956; Edward R. Embree, "Charles S. Johnson, Scholar and Gentleman," in his *Thirteen Against the Odds* (1944); Lewis W. Jones, "The Sociology of Charles S. Johnson," draft notes, undated, Fisk University Library; Preston Valien, "Sociology Contributions of Charles S. Johnson," *Sociological and Social Research,* Mar.–Apr. 1958. The most recent interpretations are Richard Robbins, "Shadow of Macon County," *Journal of Social and Behavioral Sciences, Fall-Winter* 1971–1972; and "Charles S. Johnson," in James Blackwell and Morris Janowitz, eds., *Black Sociologist* (1974).]

RICHARD ROBBINS

JOHNSON, EDWARD (Aug. 22, 1878–Apr. 20, 1959), operatic tenor and general manager of the Metropolitan Opera, was born in Guelph, Ont., Canada, the son of James Evans Johnson, a grain merchant, and Margaret O'Connel. Johnson's father, an amateur clarinetist in the local band, encouraged his interest in music, and Eddie (as he was called throughout his life) became proficient on the flute and piano. But singing was his real interest, and at the age of five he first appeared before an audience, singing "Throw Out the Lifeline" at a Guelph Sunday school.

Johnson attended local schools and then studied law at the University of Western Ontario, but before taking any examinations he left Canada to study singing in New York. His good looks, beautiful manly tenor, and engaging personality ensured his success. He seems not to have struggled inordinately. A soloist's job at the Brick Church on Fifth Avenue enabled him to pursue his studies, and he was soon a sought-after performer. In one season, he appeared in forty-eight cities and towns in the United States in song recitals, concert versions of operas, and oratorios. His first professional engagement in New York was in Elgar's *The Apostles,* with the Oratorio Society. Johnson appeared in English-language performances of *Aida, Faust, Carmen, Cavalleria Rusticana, The Damnation of Faust, The Flying Dutchman,* and *Il Trovatore.*

In late 1907, Johnson was persuaded by a friend, the bass Herbert Witherspoon, to audition for the role of Lieutenant Niki in Oscar Strauss's operetta *A Waltz Dream,* which was being prepared for a Broadway opening. The role's seven high B naturals required an operatic voice. Johnson was reluctant to accept the part, but as *Musical America* reported at the time, "he received an offer too tempting to refuse." The weekly salary was $500, and he was excused from the two matinees (an understudy was to be paid $200 for those performances). Johnson hired himself as his own understudy and thus received $700, the highest salary paid a tenor on Broadway. This business acumen was to characterize his entire career.

A Waltz Dream opened in January 1908 and was hugely successful. Johnson immediately became a great favorite with the public. The show ran for four months, and besides the music was noted for a forty-five-second kiss between Johnson and his leading lady, Sophie Brandt. Newspapers breathlessly reported that some members of the audience timed the kiss with stopwatches at every performance.

Rejecting a career in operetta, Johnson left the United States in the summer of 1908 to study opera in Europe. He had auditioned for, and impressed, Enrico Caruso, who recommended Johnson to Vincenzo Lombardi, the great tenor's own teacher. By 1911, Johnson was ready. Under the name Edoardo di Giovanni, Edward Johnson made his debut in *Andrea Chenier* at Padua. Within two years, he was singing at La Scala, Milan, and was being called Italy's leading dramatic tenor. His repertoire ranged from Tristan to Rinuccio in *Gianni Schicchi.* He was the first Parsifal in Italy.

In 1919, Johnson's wife, the Countess Beatrice d'Arneiro, whom he had married in Paris on Aug. 2, 1909, died. With his ten-year-old daughter, Fiorenza, he returned to America, where on Nov. 30, 1919, Johnson made his debut with the Chicago Opera—under the name Edward Johnson. As Loris, in Giordano's *Fedora,* he stopped the show with the famous, albeit brief, romanza and was obliged to repeat the aria before the opera could continue. Johnson appeared regularly at Chicago until 1922, when he joined the Metropolitan Opera.

Johnson's debut at the Metropolitan, as Avito in *L'Amore dei Tre Re,* was a resounding success, and for the next thirteen years he was a favorite tenor at that house. For many operagoers there

was no other Pelléas, Rodolpho, or Romeo, especially when he sang opposite Lucrezia Bori. Johnson and Bori became a major box office attraction, and this close professional relationship extended into their personal lives as well.

Johnson sang twenty-three roles with the Metropolitan in 208 performances, including the lead in the world premieres of *Peter Ibbetson, The King's Henchman,* and *Merry Mount.* In his first season, he appeared in ten different operas in less than three months. His matinee idol appearance, superior acting ability, and great musical intelligence—combined with a uniquely beautiful voice—enthralled his audiences. His appearance in the first Metropolitan performance of *Pélleas et Mélisande* on Mar. 21, 1925, was the first of thirty-two times he would sing the part with the Metropolitan Opera. He and Bori became the very personification of the two lovers for Met audiences.

Johnson's voice remained unimpaired throughout his twenty-five-year career. As W. J. Henderson wrote of the 1933 revival of *Roméo et Juliette,* "His vocal powers were at their zenith." A fellow critic reported of the same performance that the house was "held spellbound by the beauty of acting and glory of voice." Of Bori, Henderson remarked in the same review that her Juliette was perhaps the greatest achievement of her career.

Johnson was also a popular speaker and writer, and his talks and articles reveal a man of intellect and good sense—with an unfailing sense of humor. He was generally conceded to be the most popular man at the Metropolitan. Johnson received several honorary degrees, and in 1928 he gave $25,000 to further musical education in his Canadian birthplace, Guelph.

While still at the peak of his performing career, at the age of forty-seven, Johnson entered a new career. Giulio Gatti-Casazza had retired as general manager of the Metropolitan Opera and his successor, Herbert Witherspoon, Johnson's old friend, died before assuming the position. Johnson was prevailed upon by the board of directors to become general manager.

With the nation in the midst of the Great Depression, and the Metropolitan Opera fighting to survive, Johnson accepted the challenge. Opening night, Dec. 16, 1935, was one of the most glittering in Metropolitan history. He had obviously decided to "put out more flags," and the performance on stage reflected the glamour of the opening-night audience. The opera was *La Traviata* and starred Bori, Richard Crooks, and

Lawrence Tibbett. The new regime had served notice that the show would go on.

As general manager, Johnson saw the broadcasts of the Metropolitan Opera become a national institution, initiated the Metropolitan Opera Auditions of the Air, aided the founding of the Metropolitan Opera Guild, under Mrs. August Belmont, and raised the money for the Metropolitan Opera Association to buy the Metropolitan Opera House from the stockholders. But perhaps his greatest achievement was the encouragement and employment of American singers. After Johnson, it would no longer be necessary for an American artist to become an Edoardo di Giovanni to have a career. Among his discoveries were Richard Tucker, Jan Peerce, Risë Stevens, Helen Traubel, Eleanor Steber, Robert Merrill, Leonard Warren, Dorothy Kirsten, Regina Resnik, Blanche Thebom, and Jerome Hines. European singers continued to be mainstays of the house, and Johnson introduced such legendary figures as Zinka Milanov, Jussi Bjoerling, Licia Albanese, and Ljuba Welitsch; and it was under his aegis that Kirsten Flagstad and Lauritz Melchior came to represent Wagnerian opera for millions of Americans.

Johnson produced seventy-two operas in all and must be credited with making *Don Giovanni* and *The Marriage of Figaro* popular. He also successfully revived *Falstaff* and *Otello* and hired Bruno Walter, Sir Thomas Beecham, George Szell, Fritz Busch, and Fritz Reiner to conduct at the Met. His belief that opera should be accessible to everyone was realized on the tours and the radio broadcasts. Seven of his fifteen seasons ended in the black.

After his retirement in 1950, the entire company honored him at a gala benefit (produced by Bori) in the Opera House. He then returned to the town where he was born. He stayed in music, however, as chairman of the board of the Royal Conservatory of Music at the University of Toronto. He died in Guelph, while attending a ballet performance.

By all accounts, Edward Johnson was an extremely likeable and talented man who succeeded both as a performer and administrator. As he put it on taking over the post of general manager: "My policy may be expressed in a little twist of the Golden Rule: I am doing unto others as I have wished for a long time to be done by." His good manners and lack of pretension endeared him to colleagues and employees. It was a source of delight to him that the doorman at the Met-

ropolitan was also named Edward Johnson. He continued to live in a three-room walkup apartment on Madison Avenue and disdained a car and driver, preferring to walk to work. As Francis Robinson observed at a 1960 memorial tribute, "There was not one of us who wouldn't have gone out and died for him."

[The standard biography is Ruby Mercer, *The Tenor of His Time* (1976). *Musical America* covered Johnson's career from its inception, and there is considerable material at the Lincoln Center Library for the Performing Arts, New York City. The *New Yorker* profile, Dec. 14, 1935, and a *New York Times Magazine* interview, June 9, 1935, are both helpful in assessing the man and his career. See also Eleanor R. Belmont, "Edward Johnson," *Opera News,* Oct. 31, 1959. Robert J. Wayner, ed., *What Did They Sing at the Met?* (1971), lists all of Johnson's roles with that company.]

MARSHALL DE BRUHL

JONES, JESSE HOLMAN (Apr. 5, 1874– June 1, 1956), lumber magnate, banker, and public official, was born in Robertson County, Tenn., the son of William Hasque Jones, a tobacco farmer, and Anne Holman. He received his education in the public schools of Robertson County.

Jones first worked on his father's plantation, but after the family moved to Houston, Tex., he began working as a clerk in his uncle's lumber business. Through his shrewd handling of money and management, Jones was general manager of the firm by 1898. Not satisfied with working for someone else, he organized the South Texas Lumber Company four years later. His experience in the lumber business led to a combination of real estate, construction, and banking ventures—all centered in Houston. His firm erected numerous office buildings, and his real estate dealings soon made him a millionaire. After the financial panic of 1907, Jones quickly moved to fill the void left by the failure of many of his competitors. He became associated with a number of Houston banking institutions, and in 1909 organized the Texas Trust Company.

Although Jones never lost either his personal or his financial interest in Houston, his banking interests soon brought him into contact with the financial leaders of New York City and the eastern political establishment. Through his contributions to the political coffers of New Jersey

Governor Woodrow Wilson, Jones became a significant force within the Democratic party after Wilson's election as president in 1912. Content to be a back-room politician, and preoccupied with Houston civic affairs as well as his real estate and banking interests, Jones's only public exposure during the eight years of the Wilson administration came with a brief service as director of general military relief for the American Red Cross in 1917–1918. On Dec. 15, 1920, he married Mary Gibbs; they had no children.

During the Republican administrations of the 1920's, a difficult period for the Democratic party, Jones was instrumental in preventing the financial collapse of the party. In keeping with his commitment to Houston, he arranged for the Democratic National Convention of 1928 to meet in that city. But it was Republican President Herbert Hoover who brought Jones into public life. In 1932, in an unsuccessful attempt to gain support from conservative southern Democrats, Hoover appointed Jones as director of the Reconstruction Finance Corporation (RFC).

The RFC, designed to provide loans to depression-stricken businesses, became something quite different under President Franklin D. Roosevelt, who appointed Jones its chairman in 1933. Jones turned the RFC into the largest bank in the nation by forcing banks and many major corporations to accept his terms in order to obtain the funds they so desperately needed. He firmly opposed government ownership of banks; but he just as firmly opposed the domination of the banking industry by New York City firms, and he worked to broaden the role of banks outside the eastern seaboard.

Jones's success as chairman of the RFC and his long-time role as a Democratic party financier were appreciated by Roosevelt. He was made a member of the National Emergency Council (1933–1939) and was appointed chairman of the executive committee of the Export-Import Bank of Washington in 1936.

Jones's experience in the Roosevelt administration whetted his political ambitions. He hoped to be the Democratic vice-presidential candidate in 1940, but Roosevelt's decision to seek a third term ended that hope and placed Jones at odds with the president. Jones also, at least temporarily, supported the anti-interventionist movement in foreign policy, an attitude that further removed him from Roosevelt's favor. Nevertheless, in keeping with his conscious and persistent at-tempts to create a broad national coalition as the basis of the Democratic party, Roosevelt in 1939 appointed Jones administrator of the Federal Loan Agency, a supervisory organization that controlled the activities of the Federal Housing Administration and the Export-Import Bank. Since Jones retained overall supervision of the RFC, he became enormously powerful.

Roosevelt appointed Jones secretary of commerce in 1940. Always the cautious politician, the president hoped to avoid making more enemies within his party as he sought an unprecedented third term in office. Jones's economic policies were at variance with those of most other members of Roosevelt's cabinet; but the president frequently stated his belief in a competitive bureaucracy, and Jones provided a viewpoint held by large numbers of conservative Democrats. During World War II he served on a number of boards, including the Supply Priorities and Allocations Board (1941–1942); the Economic Defense Board (1941–1945), which was later the Board of Economic Warfare; the War Production Board (1942–1945); and the Economic Stabilization Board (1942–1945).

Private disputes were acceptable to Roosevelt, but public ones were not. When Jones and Vice-President Henry A. Wallace feuded angrily over Jones's alleged malfeasance in permitting profiteering in the importing of strategic raw materials during the war, Roosevelt replaced Jones with Wallace (1945). Jones returned to his home city and spent the remainder of his life publishing the *Houston Chronicle*. Until his death in Houston he continued his almost unbroken succession of successful investments and business ventures, and became a major contributor to various philanthropic causes in the Houston area.

Jones was a self-made man and an indefatigable worker. A shrewd and effective administrator, he possessed concepts of civic duty and patriotism that never conflicted with his business ethics; all were firmly based on the work ethic and profit motive. His firm loyalty to personal friends and his conservative philosophy probably cost him the nomination for the vice-presidency in 1940. With his separation of private and public ethics, he epitomized the American image of the business community.

[Jones left no significant body of personal papers. His personal views of the New Deal are found in his *Fifty Billion Dollars* (1951). The best biography is an uncritical but accurate account by Bascom N. Timmons, *Jesse H. Jones* (1956). Some valuable information can be gleaned from various collections at the Franklin D. Roosevelt Library in Hyde Park, N.Y. Extensive references also appear in the Oral History Collection of Columbia University, particularly in memoirs by Frances Perkins, Henry A. Wallace, and Claude Wickard.]

WARREN F. KIMBALL

JOY, CHARLES TURNER (Feb. 17, 1895–June 6, 1956), naval officer, was born in St. Louis, Mo., the son of Duncan Joy, a prosperous cotton broker, and Lucy Barlow Turner. Joy was educated at private secondary schools prior to entering the U.S. Naval Academy in 1912. He was graduated and commissioned ensign in 1916.

Joy first served in the battleship *Pennsylvania*, which became the flagship of the Atlantic Fleet and late in 1918 escorted the ship carrying President Woodrow Wilson to the Paris Peace Conference. In 1921 he was selected for the navy's elite postgraduate program in ordnance engineering. He continued that course for the next two years at various places, including the University of Michigan, from which he received the M.S. in 1922. During 1923–1925, as a lieutenant, he had his first duty in the Far East, serving on the staff of the commander of the Yangtze Patrol. On Oct. 16, 1924, Joy married Martha Ann Chess; they had three children.

Over the next seventeen years Joy served at sea as the executive officer of destroyer *Pope* and assistant gunnery officer in battleship *California*, and on the staff of the commander of destroyers, Battle Force. His first command was of the destroyer *Litchfield* in 1933–1935. These tours alternated with shore billets in his ordnance specialty, including assignments in the aviation ordnance section of the Bureau of Ordnance, the Naval Mine Depot at Yorktown, Va., and the ordnance and gunnery department at the Naval Academy.

In 1941–1942, Joy served in the Pacific on board the cruiser *Indianapolis* and later the carrier *Lexington* as operations officer for the commander of the Scouting Force. Despite the alleged battleship orientation of the gunnery specialists, Joy was decorated early in the war for planning successful carrier task force engagements with Japanese forces near Rabaul and New Guinea. Later in 1942 he took command of the cruiser *Louisville*, which subsequently saw combat in the Solomons and Aleutians campaigns.

From August 1943 to April 1944, Joy headed the Pacific Plans Division in the Washington headquarters of the Navy. At the end of that tour he was promoted to rear admiral and returned to the combat zone as commander of Cruiser Division 6. During the next year Joy participated in virtually all of the major operations marking the American advance across the Pacific, including the Marianas campaign, the recapture of the Philippines, the seizure of Iwo Jima and Okinawa, and fast carrier task force raids against other Japanese positions. His forces were noted for their effective shore bombardment and antiaircraft gunnery.

Near the end of World War II, Joy commanded Amphibious Group 2, which was preparing for the invasion of Japan. Detached in September 1945, he proceeded to China, where for the next eight months he commanded Task Force 73 and later Task Force 74 operating in the Yangtze River and from Hong Kong. These units cleared mines, transported Chinese troops reoccupying Japanese positions, and undertook other postwar operations. From 1946 to 1949, Joy resumed his ordnance specialty as commander of the Naval Proving Ground, Dahlgren, Va., which tested and assisted in the development of new naval ordnance.

In August 1949, Joy was promoted to vice admiral and appointed commander of the U.S. Naval Force, Far East, with headquarters in Tokyo. Upon the outbreak of the Korean War in June 1950, he became the Allied naval commander for that conflict. His ships landed Allied troops in the war zone and supported them with supplies, gunfire, and carrier air strikes; blockaded North Korea; undertook mine-sweeping; and patrolled the Taiwan Straits to prevent hostile action between mainland China and Taiwan. Joy was a key leader in the highly successful Inchon landing of September 1950. By November 1950 he commanded 400 Allied and American ships.

For ten months after July 1951, Joy additionally served as the senior United Nations delegate at the Korean Armistice Conference held at Kaesong and, later, Panmunjom. For his role in these almost daily negotiations, Joy received worldwide notice for his calm, tenacious, but fruitless efforts to achieve a cease-fire agreement. He asked to be relieved of his assignment in May 1952. Following the Korean armistice of 1953, he wrote *How Communists Negotiate* (1955). Joy concluded that only the "imminent threat of application of our military power" would compel Communist governments throughout the world to "negotiate seriously." He wrote that the "greatest single influence on the Korean armistice negotiations was the failure of the United States to take punitive action" against China following its entry into the conflict. Because of the failure of American will to seek military victory, Joy believed that the 1953 armistice represented a triumph for mainland China.

Joy served as superintendent of the Naval Academy from 1952 to 1954, then retired with the rank of admiral. He died in San Diego, Calif.

The career of this reserved, modest, and thoroughly competent naval officer was notable for its versatility. He was a highly effective operational commander and planner who displayed flexibility in integrating new air and amphibious tactics into the fleet. He made significant contributions as an ordnance specialist. Finally, in his role as negotiator and through his writings on the relationship of force and diplomacy, Joy was an important figure in the history of American foreign relations in the period after World War II.

[The Navy biographical file and collection of Joy's papers, relating especially to the armistice talks, are in the Operational Archives of the Naval History Division, Washington, D.C. Joy's diaries from the period of the armistice talks are at the Hoover Institution, Stanford, Calif. These documents have been edited by Allan E. Goodman as *Negotiating While Fighting* (1978). See also Samuel Eliot Morison, *History of the United States Naval Operations in World War II*, 15 vols. (1947–1962); Malcolm W. Cagle and Frank A. Manson, *The Sea War in Korea* (1957); and James A. Field, Jr., *History of United States Naval Operations, Korea* (1962).]

DEAN C. ALLARD

KAEMPFFERT, WALDEMAR BERNHARD (Sept. 23, 1877–Nov. 27, 1956), science editor and author, was born in New York City, the son of Bernhard and Juliette Kaempffert. After receiving a B.S. from the College of the City of New York in 1897, he continued part-time studies at New York University and in 1904 received the LL.B. Although he subsequently was admitted to the bar and intended to become a patent attorney, he never practiced. While studying law, Kaempffert was also an assistant editor at *Scientific American*, a periodical that discussed science for a general audience. On Jan. 7, 1911, he married Carolyn Lydia Yeaton; they had no children. Later that year he was promoted to managing editor. In 1915 Kaempffert was named editor of *Popular Science Monthly*, which became more pictorial and accessible under his guidance. In 1920 he left editorial work and for seven years was associated with the New York City engineering firm of Logan, Lord, and Thomas.

Kaempffert continued the prodigious freelance output that he had begun while at *Scientific American*. His earliest article for a general magazine had been an account of a visit to Thomas Edison's home for *Woman's Home Companion* of February 1904. Over the next fifty years he wrote well in excess of two hundred articles for general magazines, as well as numerous books and pamphlets, on subjects ranging from questions of public importance, such as cancer research or nuclear energy, to topics of speculation, such as the nature of the Star of Bethlehem. The books that he wrote and edited praised the achievements of inventors or advances in technology; he was not only a skilled popularizer but also an advocate of science and of scientists' importance in society.

Kaempffert returned to journalism in 1927, when he was hired as science editor by Adolph S. Ochs, publisher of the *New York Times*, and was appointed to the *Times* editorial board. He was perhaps the first such specialist in such a position on any major newspaper. As science editor—a post he held, with one interruption, until his death—Kaempffert wrote editorials and columns, covered meetings and other major scientific events, and contributed articles to the Sunday *Times Magazine*. The interruption occurred in 1928, when he was named the first director of the Museum of Science and Industry in Chicago. Kaempffert set out to create exhibits that would convince visitors that scientists did more to "transfrom the . . . earth and mold institutions than Alexander the Great, Julius Caesar, and Napoleon. . . ." Pursuing this goal, he increased expenditures for research, the museum library, and staff. In 1931 he resigned from the museum. Many of his policies were later abandoned in favor of spectacular displays.

Back at the *Times*, Kaempffert became a fixture of the editorial staff. Monocled and elegantly dressed, he was sometimes addressed affectionately as "Count." A leader in the developing journalistic specialty of science writing, he was a charter member of the National Association of Science Writers, founded in 1934, and served as its president in 1937. Of science journalism, he wrote in 1935: "It is the business of the journalist to present the discoveries of the laboratory so that many will understand. . . . We have passed the stage when gaping wonder can pass for popularization. The facts, simply, humanly and interestingly presented, are what the public wants." Yet his own work was not always free of appeal to sensation or shallowness. It was said of Kaempffert's reader that "the depths of his mind remain untouched by the importunate knocking of ideas." Kaempffert would have responded to this charge, as he sometimes did, that it was sufficient for the lay reader to accept the principal scientific concepts; he did not necessarily have to understand them.

Although not a controversialist by nature, Kaempffert nonetheless created controversy on occasion. He called for organization of cancer research along the lines of laboratories in major industries. In World War II he criticized the American Medical Association for its handling of physicians' assignments to the armed forces. During the Korean War he joined in rejecting Communist claims that germ warfare had been practiced against North Korea.

But through most of his career Kaempffert confined himself to the role of translator, spokesman, and friend of the growing scientific community. His last notable book was *Explorations in Science* (1953). His earlier works included *History of Astronomy* (1910), *The New Art of Flying* (1911), *The ABC of Radio* (1922), *Invention and Society* (1930), and *Science Today and Tomorrow* (1939). He also edited *Collier's Wonder Book* (1920), *The Boys' Story of Invention* (1924), *A Popular History of American Invention* (1924), and *Modern Wonder Workers* (1931). In 1954 he was awarded the Kalinga Prize for his science writing. Kaempffert never retired and continued to work until felled by a stroke. He died in New York City. A *Times* editorial commented on his career: "If Waldemar B. Kaempffert did not create the profession of science writer, he certainly, over the last half century, invested it with new standards of ethics, scholarship, dignity and usefulness."

[The *New York Times* maintains a modest file of clippings about Kaempffert. The *New York Times* obituary, Nov. 28, 1956, is extensive. See also the *Times* editorial of Nov. 29, 1956; and an article by William D. Ogdon in *Times Talk*, the house organ, Dec. 1956. Scattered additional material appears in Meyer Berger, *The Story of the New York Times* (1951); and Frank Luther Mott, *A History of American Magazines*, vols. II–V (1938–1968).]

JAMES BOYLAN

KELLEY, EDITH SUMMERS (Apr. 28, 1884–June 9, 1956), author, was born in Toronto, Canada, the daughter of George Summerss and Isabella Johnstone, Scottish immigrants. Her father owned a shingle mill. At the age of thirteen, she sold her first manuscript to a local newspaper; by her own admission this was the greatest literary thrill of her life. She attended the University of Toronto on scholarship, winning honors in language study, and was graduated in 1903.

Summers then moved to New York, where she worked on Funk and Wagnall's *Standard Dictionary*. From doing much close work, she incurred eyestrain which plagued her for the rest of her life. She also did free-lance writing. In 1906–1907 she became Upton Sinclair's secretary, working for him at Princeton and, later, at Helicon Hall, in Englewood, N.J. (Helicon Hall, an experiment in cooperative group living, was founded by Sinclair in 1906. Summers was exposed there to radical opinions that were to influence her novels, especially *The Devil's Hand*) Sinclair described Summers as a "golden-haired and shrewdly observant young person whose gentle voice and unassuming ways gave us no idea of her talent."

For a few weeks Sinclair Lewis lived in the colony. He fell in love with Summers, and they became engaged. In the spring of 1907, Lewis suggested that they marry the following September, but for some reason the engagement was broken. At Summers' request he burned all of her letters to him. In January 1908 she married Allan Updegraff, another resident of Helicon Hall. They had two children. Shortly after their marriage Updegraff lost his editorial position with *Transatlantic Tales* and the couple lived on Summers' salary as a teacher. They separated about 1915. Thereafter, Summers moved to Greenwich Village. She wrote short stories to support her children—"stuff that I am not proud of, frothy and inconsequential." There she met C. Frederick Kelley, an artist. Although never formally married, she used his surname. They lived together for some forty years. They had one son.

The Kelleys wandered all over the United States, searching for an answer to their financial problems. From 1914 to 1916 they tried tobacco farming in Kentucky. From this experience Kelley amassed the background for her magnum opus, *Weeds*. From 1916 to 1920 they ran a boardinghouse in Stillwater, N.J.

In 1920 the family moved to a sixty-acre alfalfa farm in the Imperial Valley of California, close to the Mexican border. Their stay was "long enough to get us cleaned out of everything we had," Kelley recalled. Material for her second book, *The Devil's Hand,* was gathered during this period. The next stop was a northern section of San Diego, on a chicken ranch. There, under the most adverse conditions, Kelley wrote *Weeds,* which was published in 1923. In spite of generally favorable reviews, the novel was a commercial failure. After having offered to edit the book, Sinclair Lewis promoted it vigorously. Nothing saved it from oblivion during Kelley's lifetime.

Weeds portrays the life of a Kentucky farming couple during the early twentieth century. The main character is Judith Blackford, a simple, untutored, high-spirited and beautiful girl, innately superior to her wretched lot, who eventually succumbs to the monstrous brutality of farm life. The story is forceful and realistic, as well as naturalistic. *Weeds* is a minor masterpiece of twentieth-century fiction. As early as 1925, Kelley had completed nine chapters of *The Devil's Hand,* but it was not published during her lifetime.

During the Great Depression the family suffered greatly. In 1937 Kelley worked for a time as a charwoman. In 1946 she moved to Los Gatos, Calif., where she died, ten years later, almost unknown.

In 1972, through the efforts of Matthew J. Bruccoli, the Southern Illinois University Press republished *Weeds* as part of its Lost American Fiction series. Using a manuscript obtained from Kelley's son Patrick, Bruccoli published *The Devil's Hand* in 1974. It proved to be a readable tale about agricultural hardship in the Imperial Valley during the early twentieth century. Although Kelley's social criticism is dated, the book offers a compassionate picture of an emotionally strained partnership of two independent, "new-type" women, Rhoda Malone and Kate Baxter. The main character is Rhoda, a Philadelphia office worker, who evolves into a hardy farmer with a deep feeling of sympathy for the valley underdogs—the Hindus, Mexicans, and Chinese. She has to choose between an unrewarding unmarried life as a farmer and a comfortable, safe marriage to a member of the Establishment. She opts for the latter.

As a result of the publication of *The Devil's Hand* and the reprinting of *Weeds,* Kelley's literary reputation is on the rise.

[There is no definitive biography of Kelley. Chief published sources of information about her are Matthew J. Bruccoli's introduction to *Weeds* and his afterword to *The Devil's Hand,* and in Patrick Kelley's postscript to *The Devil's Hand.* Comments on her life and work are in Mark Schorer, *Sinclair Lewis* (1961). Reviews of her novel *Weeds* are in *Book Review Digest* for 1923, pp. 276–277; *Independent,* Dec. 8, 1923; *Nation,* Jan. 16, 1924; *Ms.,* Apr. 1974; *Choice,* Feb. 1975; *Nation,* May 3, 1975; and *Signs,* Winter 1975.]

THEODORE L. MAYHEW

KELLOGG, PAUL UNDERWOOD (Sept. 30, 1879–Nov. 1, 1958), editor and social reformer, was born in Kalamazoo, Mich., the son of Frank Israel Kellogg, who was in the lumber business, and Mary Foster Underwood. When the family business failed in the early 1890's, his father departed for Texas, leaving his wife to care for two young boys. Kellogg attended Kalamazoo High School, where, with his older brother, Arthur, he edited the school newspaper. After graduating in 1897, he became a reporter for, and 1898 city editor of, the *Kalamazoo Daily Telegraph.*

Ambitious to make his mark, Kellogg went to New York City in the summer of 1901 and enrolled as a special student at Columbia University, full-time during the academic year 1901–1902 and part-time for several years thereafter. In 1902, while he was studying at the Summer School in Philanthropic Work, sponsored by the New York Charity Organization Society, his abilities were recognized and he was offered a position as assistant editor of *Charities.* With his brother, who joined the staff in 1903, Kellogg broadened the focus of the journal from a parochial concern with the delivery of charitable services to include the critical discussion of pressing social issues. *Charities* further enlarged its scope and its circulation when, in 1905, it merged with *Commons,* the official organ of the settlement house movement. Kellogg became managing editor.

In 1907 Kellogg headed the first major in-depth social survey of any American urban community. This research project enlisted the efforts of a team of scholars and community leaders, and led over the next several years to the gathering of a mass of data on every aspect of life and labor in the modern industrial complex of Pittsburgh. The results were published in a series of articles and then in six large volumes, *Pittsburgh Survey* (1910–1914). They set a model for sociological investigation, stimulated national movements for housing reform and for workmen's compensation, and provided ammunition in the prolonged war to eliminate the twelve-hour day in the steel industry.

His national reputation enhanced by his direction of the *Pittsburgh Survey*, Kellogg returned in 1909 to his editorial position on *Charities and the Commons*, now renamed *Survey*. In 1912 he assumed command as editor in chief, his brother Arthur serving as managing editor. For the next forty years *Survey* was the leading journal for the emerging profession of social work and a significant force in social reform.

Moved by the faith that an elite of professional persons and community leaders, if well informed, could move the nation along the paths of welfare and progress, *Survey* dedicated itself to sound reporting of social facts and to the elaboration of policies and programs designed to ameliorate social evils and reconstruct a more just America. The agenda of concern included many major causes: public housing, parks and playgrounds, urban renewal, government regulation of industrial conditions (maximum hours, minimum wages, the protection of women workers, the prohibition of child labor), social insurance (workmen's compensation, unemployment insurance, old age pensions, aid to dependent children), the conservation of natural and human resources, the rights of women and ethnic and racial minorities, civil liberties, the right of labor to organize and bargain collectively, regional planning, rural electrification, public health, and world peace. During the Great Depression, *Survey* was a voice for federal work relief programs and for all the diverse welfare policies of the New Deal. Kellogg himself served on the advisory committee that helped to shape the Social Security Act of 1935. Over the years *Survey* also continued to publish specialized articles designed to improve the level of social services, to make them both more efficient and more humane. Under Kellogg's editorship experts were solicited to set forth new techniques in penology, treatment of juvenile delinquency, mental health and retardation, adult education, casework, settlement work, community organization, and social work education.

Although a brilliant, inspired, and skilled editor, Kellogg was never an efficient administrator. After the death of his brother in 1934, he was unable to find another manager as skilled and reliable. Slow to delegate authority and unwilling to train a successor, Kellogg squandered his de-

clining energies in trying to meet every responsibility. By the end of the 1940's he was in ill health, and *Survey* was in acute financial troubles. The journal ceased publication in 1952.

Although the editing of *Survey* consumed most of Kellogg's energies, he found time for other activities. He was opposed to the entrance of the United States into World War I, but accepted the fact of its belligerent role after April 1917 and worked with others for an official declaration of idealistic war goals. He played a major part in the creation, in 1918, of the organization that became the Foreign Policy Association and of the American Civil Liberties Union, and served on their national boards for many years. He also participated in the defense of Nicola Sacco and Bartolomeo Vanzetti. Kellogg did field surveys in Belgium, France, and Italy for the American Red Cross in 1917–1918. As a leading member of the American Friends of Spanish Democracy in the mid-1930's, he joined others in seeking a lifting of the arms embargo against the Spanish Republic. In recognition of his lifelong efforts in welfare, he was appointed president of the National Conference of Social Work in 1939.

On Oct. 5, 1909, Kellogg married Marion Pearce Sherwood, a Kalamazoo acquaintance; they had two children. They were divorced in 1934, and on Feb. 26, 1935, he married Helen Hall, director of the Henry Street Settlement in New York. Kellogg died in New York City.

Like the settlement workers to whom, of all social servants, he felt the closest, Kellogg hoped to find ways to reconcile classes, religions, and peoples, to resolve divisions and antagonisms so that social harmony would prevail. He was impatient with exploitation and injustice but patient in the face of evil because he believed in the ultimate beneficence of history. From that progressive faith he never wavered.

[A great body of primary documentation is in the Survey Associates Papers and in the Paul U. Kellogg Papers at the University of Minnesota. Detailed descriptions of these two collections are in *Descriptive Inventories of Collections in the Social Welfare History Archives Center* (1970). In addition to many editorials, articles, speeches, and pamphlets, Kellogg published *British Labor and the War* (1919), written with Arthur Gleason. Also see Clarke A. Chambers, *Paul U. Kellogg and the "Survey"* (1971).]

CLARKE A. CHAMBERS

KELLY, JOHN BRENDAN (Oct. 4, 1889–June 20, 1960), building contractor,

Olympic rowing champion, and Democratic party leader, was born in Philadelphia, Pa., the son of Irish immigrant parents, John Henry Kelly, a laborer in a woolen mill, and Mary Ann Costello. John, the youngest son, was the only one of their ten children to go beyond the eighth grade. The family was dominated and inspired by the self-educated mother, who urged her sons to excel. All five achieved success. For example, Walter was a well-known actor and George was a Pulitzer Prize-winning playwright.

After laboring briefly with his father in the woolen mill, Kelly in 1902 joined his older brother Patrick's thriving construction firm. Five years later a rift developed, and he left to apprentice himself as a bricklayer. In 1909 he took up rowing with clubs on the Schuylkill River course. Kelly began rowing in a four-oar gig and quickly moved into single sculls and double sculls competition. In his first year he won the first of his 126 sculling victories, a total unmatched by an American rower. In 1913 he won nine races, including the senior doubles, senior four-oar shells, senior paired, and senior singles. His victory in the American Henley singles at Boston that year established him as the leading American rower.

Kelly also boxed, swam, and played football and basketball. During his service with the American Expeditionary Force in France in 1918, his athletic prowess led to his transfer into the Special Services unit and to his rapid advancement in rank from private to lieutenant. While overseas he fought and defeated twelve heavyweight opponents. Only a broken ankle prevented him from fighting Gene Tunney, then a marine, in what might have been a turning point in his athletic career.

In 1919 Kelly borrowed $7,000 from his brother Walter and, with his brother Charles and Jess Otley, established John B. Kelly Inc., a building construction firm that was to make him a millionaire. He also resumed rowing and in 1919 and 1920 was national single sculls champion. At the 1920 Olympics in Antwerp, Kelly won the singles and (with his cousin Paul V. Costello) the doubles in the same day, a feat unmatched in Olympic rowing. His singles victory over the British Diamond Sculls champion was particularly satisfying, for he had been barred from competing in the British Henley Royal Regatta that year because officials ruled that he was no "gentleman."

Kelly's 1920 Olympic victories linked him with Jack Dempsey, Babe Ruth, and Jim Thorpe as the brightest stars in the American athletic galaxy of the 1920's. At the Paris Olympics in 1924, Kelly and Costello again won the doubles. On Jan. 30, 1924, Kelly married Margaret Majer, a magazine cover girl and teacher of physical education at the University of Pennsylvania. They had four children, one of whom, Grace, became an Academy Award–winning film star and, as Princess Grace of Monaco, an international celebrity. Their son, John B., Jr., twice won the Diamond Sculls at Henley and participated in four Olympic rowing competitions.

Although a millionaire and a nationally acclaimed sports celebrity, Kelly was denied listing in the Philadelphia *Social Register*. The family nevertheless became socially prominent. As a gentleman-sportsman Kelly patronized rowing competitions, track-and-field events, horse racing, and Davis Cup tennis. From 1934 to 1941 he served as Democratic party chairman in Philadelphia. In 1935, in a campaign marked by slurs on his Irish-Catholic background, Kelly was defeated for mayor. The following year he lost his bid for the nomination for the U.S. Senate. Nevertheless, he was a powerful figure in the Democratic party in Philadelphia. In 1940, at the Democratic National Convention held in that city, Kelly introduced Franklin D. Roosevelt as the third-term presidential candidate. His increasing conservatism and his support of Senator Joseph McCarthy in the 1950's ended his power in Democratic circles. In 1945 Kelly established the John B. Kelly Award, given annually to the person who has done the most to promote athletics among young people.

Kelly died in Philadelphia. His will, which was widely acclaimed for its informality, wit, and candor, bequeathed an estate valued at $1.1 million to his immediate family. He left nothing to his sons-in-law, saying that they should provide for themselves. He died, he said, "unafraid and, if you must know, a little curious."

[No biography of Kelly exists at present, but the social science and history department of the Free Public Library of Philadelphia maintains an exhaustive, chronologically arranged clipping file on the Kelly family. Arthur H. Lewis, *Those Philadelphia Kellys* (1977), deals extensively with Kelly's life, albeit in sensationalized and often inaccurate fashion. Gwen Robyns, *Princess Grace* (1976), touches on the father. Foster Hirsch, *George Kelly* (1975), offers a fuller and more accurate picture of the Kelly family. Also useful is Walter Kelly, *Of Me I Sing* (1953). For Kelly's rowing exploits see Louis Heiland, *The Schuylkill Navy* (1938), and Richard Schaap, *An Illustrated History of the Olympics* (1963). An excellent background source is E. Digby Baltzell, *The Philadelphia Gentlemen* (1971). Obituaries are in *New York Times* and *Philadelphia Inquirer*, June 21, 1960.]

DAVID Q. VOIGT

KETTERING, CHARLES FRANKLIN (Aug. 29, 1876–Nov. 25, 1958), inventor and engineer, was born near Loudonville, Ohio, the son of Jacob Kettering and Martha Hunter. "All we knew about the Ketterings and the Hunters," he said later, "was that they all had to work hard for a living." His father was a carpenter as well as a farmer, and the boy was familiar with tools and machines as well as farm work.

Kettering attended rural schools and Loudonville High School. Next he taught for three years in country schools and in 1896 attended a summer session at the College of Wooster. In 1898 he entered Ohio State University to study engineering, but dropped out during his second year because of eye trouble. He then spent two years working for a telephone company on construction and installation crews. With a new interest in electrical machinery, he returned to Ohio State and took a degree in electrical engineering in 1904, at the age of twenty-eight. For the next five years Kettering worked for the National Cash Register Company (NCR) in Dayton. On Aug. 1, 1905, he married Olive Williams; they made their home in Dayton and had one son.

In those years NCR, under the eccentric martinet John H. Patterson, was a source of ideas and leaders for American business. It was also Kettering's graduate school. He worked on electrical projects, notably the electrification of the cash register, which required a new kind of small motor that could handle sudden overloads. On the side he also worked on projects of his own, often with other enthusiasts from NCR. His first independent success was a battery-powered electric ignition system for automobiles, which was adopted by Cadillac in 1910 and spread quickly through the industry. The following year, drawing on his experience with small motors, he designed the first practical electric starter for automobiles. This was Kettering's first great achievement: by making the gasoline engine easy to start, he gave it a decisive advantage over steam and electric power for road vehicles, and estab-

lished the central position of the internal-combustion engine in twentieth-century transportation.

In 1909 Kettering left NCR and devoted himself full-time to his own enterprises, incorporated under various names, the most important of which was Dayton Engineering Laboratories Company (Delco). Kettering always wanted to concentrate on research, but in the early years he was sometimes forced into manufacturing in order to provide the expert control necessary for the successful production of new electrical systems. Delco grew rapidly and was very profitable. In 1916 it was taken over by United Motors, which was absorbed by General Motors in 1918, with Kettering continuing as general manager. This enterprise evolved into the central research and development organ for General Motors (GM), now known as General Motors Research Laboratories. Kettering became vice-president of General Motors and head of the laboratories.

Both the ignition system and the starter were early Delco projects. Another was a small electric plant for American farms. The problems of the one-cylinder engine for this system turned Kettering's attention to the internal-combustion engine and its fuel, which remained a central preoccupation for the rest of his life. As early as 1916 he encountered a mysterious and destructive form of combustion in engines known as knock or detonation, which limits the power of a gasoline engine. He recognized it as a key obstacle and began a long study of combustion, engines, and fuels in an effort to understand it.

In 1917 Kettering turned to more urgent military problems, especially the development of engines and fuels for aircraft. (Dayton was a center of interest in aeronautics—the Wright brothers lived there, and McCook Field, where much early experimental work was done, was nearby.) Kettering's laboratories designed an early form of guided missile, too late for use in the war, and also made the first synthetic high-test gasoline.

After the war Kettering and his assistants, Thomas Midgley, Jr., and T. A. Boyd, resumed their search for ways of avoiding knock, so that the compression of an engine could be raised and its power increased. They concentrated on the fuel side of the problem and, in particular, began looking for a chemical substance that could be added to gasoline to prevent knock. This search resulted in the discovery, in 1921, of the remarkable knock-suppressing property of tetraethyl lead. The Ethyl Gasoline Corporation was formed to exploit this invention, with Kettering as first president.

This was only the most memorable episode in the long story of progress in engine-fuel technology, which over the next thirty years doubled and then tripled the power per pound of engine. Much of the work—in petroleum technology, in the study of combustion, and in engine design —was done at GM. In addition, Kettering's laboratories worked on many practical problems for the various GM divisions and made many contributions to American industry, such as a durable, fast-drying automobile paint and Freon, a safe refrigerant, both now universally used. In later years the most important single product of the GM laboratories was the diesel locomotive, which revolutionized railroad power in the 1950's. Kettering had begun work in the late 1920's on a light, fast diesel that could be used for heavy road vehicles and light ships, as well as for locomotives. The development period was unusually long and difficult. Success came with the accumulation of many incremental improvements resulting from the joint efforts of many scientists and engineers from GM and many other firms. The key problem was how to get the right amount of fuel into the cylinder against high pressure at exactly the right time. Kettering's chief contribution was an improved unit injector, which gave each cylinder its own, very precisely controlled injection system.

Kettering's weak eyes gave him a stooping posture and made him more of a talker than a reader. He was a large, genial man and a natural storyteller, in great demand as a speaker at academic and professional ceremonies. He spoke loosely and spontaneously, in parables, preaching the traditional American virtues of individual enterprise and faith in technological progress. One year he gave talks during the intermissions of the radio broadcasts of the NBC Symphony concerts. He told anecdotes about inventors, using the rhetoric of heroic invention, celebrating practical experience and Yankee ingenuity, and sometimes speaking scornfully of book learning, in the tradition of Edison and Ford. Kettering's self-starter may seem like an old-fashioned, one-man invention, but the great achievements of his later years were actually the product of a large organization of well-trained scientists and engineers using the most sophisticated methods.

Kettering used the great wealth he accumulated to support many causes and projects.

He was interested in the work-study program of Antioch College, and in a number of medical fields such as homeopathy and fever therapy. Later, with his friend Alfred P. Sloan, Jr., he endowed the Sloan-Kettering Institute for Cancer Research. In science he had a lifelong interest in the mysteries of magnetism and photosynthesis. In 1947 Kettering retired as leader of the GM Research Laboratories, but remained a spokesman for American industry and technological progress. He died in Dayton.

[The Kettering Archives in the library of GM Research Laboratories in Warren, Mich., contain books and articles by and about Kettering; manuscripts (some by Kettering); copies of his 185 patents; and eighty transcripts of oral-history interviews with his associates. His radio talks were published as *Short Stories of Science and Invention* (1945). Thomas A. Boyd edited a selection of his speeches in *Prophet of Progress* (1961). An obituary is in *New York Times*, Nov. 26, 1958; a sketch by Zay Jeffries is in *Biographical Memoirs, National Academy of Sciences*, 1960, with incomplete and inaccurate list of publications. Thomas A. Boyd, *Professional Amateur* (1957), is the best biography, undocumented but sound. Additional biographical work by Boyd, with more detail and full documentation, is in the Kettering Archives. For Kettering's technical contributions, see engineering journals to which Kettering and his men (Boyd, Midgley, Lloyd Withrow, Gerald M. Rassweiler, Wheeler G. Lovell, and John M. Campbell) contributed. See especially Thomas A. Boyd, "Pathfinding in Fuels and Engines," *Quarterly Transactions of the Society of Automotive Engineers*, 1950.]

LYNWOOD BRYANT

KHARASCH, MORRIS SELIG (Aug. 24, 1895–Oct. 9, 1957), organic chemist and pioneer in the study of free radical chemistry, was born in Kremenets, the Ukraine, the son of Selig Kharasch, a tobacco grower and merchant, and Louise Kneller. In 1907, he and a younger brother traveled to Chicago, where two older brothers had settled. Their parents joined them in 1914.

Kharasch was a brilliant student, facile in languages and fascinated by science. He attended the University of Chicago, received a B.S. in 1917, and began graduate study in chemistry. Although he was working part of that time for the Chemical Warfare Service, he completed the Ph.D. in 1919, working under Jean Piccard on organic compounds of mercury. For the next three years he held a National Research Council fellowship in organic chemistry at the University of Chicago.

In 1922 he went to the University of Maryland, where he taught for six years. In 1923 he married Ethel May Nelson; they had two children.

While at Maryland, Kharasch conducted further research on organic mercurials. Merthiolate, which he patented in 1928, was one result. In the fall of 1928 he returned to the University of Chicago as associate professor. He became professor in 1930 and remained at Chicago for the rest of his life.

Kharasch soon launched a research program that contributed in a major way to the development of free-radical chemistry, the understanding and utilization of free-radical chain reactions, the fuller understanding of polymerization, the development of petrochemistry and the plastics industry, and the general advance of organic chemistry, especially in the United States. For nearly thirty years the progress of his career and the development of free-radical chemistry were much the same.

Although Moses Gomberg, at the University of Michigan, had prepared the first free (that is, uncombined) chemical radical in 1900, most chemists did not believe that radicals could exist independently; and when Friedrich Paneth demonstrated conclusively in 1929 that this was possible, little was still known about these inherently active substances.

In 1929, Kharasch assigned a graduate student, Frank Mayo, to study addition reactions of hydrogen bromide. The results of these experiments varied, and not until 1936 were Kharasch and Mayo satisfied that they understood why. Old reagents were affected by oxygen from the air; the presence of a peroxide led to the formation of a free radical, which in turn gave rise to a free-radical chain reaction and the production of a compound that would not be formed in "normal addition." Their paper explaining the "peroxide effect" was published in 1937. In the same year, in England, D. H. Hey and William A. Waters presented the concept of free radicals as reactive intermediates in organic chemistry. Free radical chemistry is often said to have been born with the publication of these two papers. Reactions that had never been fully understood could now be comprehended, and hundreds of new reactions, processes, and substances could be developed.

Kharasch and his associates were already striding ahead in this new field, aided by various circumstances, some of his doing and some not. His own productivity, attested by dozens of patents on new compounds and processes, helped him obtain support for his investigations. His impressive record resulted not only from his diligence and insight but also from his development and leadership of a large group of graduate students and research associates. This too was one of his major accomplishments, reflecting both his scientific and administrative abilities.

Simultaneously, World War II hampered scientific activity in Europe and tended to shift research on current problems to the United States. The shortage of rubber was a pertinent example. Polymer chemistry was one area that was greatly illuminated by the new concepts of free-radical chain reactions, and from 1942 on, Kharasch participated in the government's synthetic rubber program. After the war emphasis in this field shifted to the production of vinyls, epoxies, and other plastics. In a period when the creation of chemicals from petroleum was becoming a major industry comparable with the earlier development of coal-tar derivatives, Kharasch's work on the initiation and control of reactions had continued application.

The significance of Kharasch's work was thus, most fundamentally, that in clarifying one of the basic types of chemical reactions, he aided the advance of the science along broad fronts. At the same time his theoretical conclusions came from specific investigations that often had direct practical results. He developed a commercial method for the preparation of the anesthetic cyclopropane. In 1935 he received a gold medal from the American Medical Association for the isolation of ergotocin (ergonovine), the active principle in rye fungus, which is useful in checking hemorrhaging. He was elected to the National Academy of Sciences in 1946 and the following year received the Presidential Merit Award for his contributions to the synthetic rubber industry. He developed fungicides and germicides applicable to cotton and grain seeds, and received awards in 1948 and 1952 for his services to American agriculture. In 1956 the University of Chicago honored him by creating the Institute of Organic Chemistry under his direction, but this was scarcely under way at the time of his death.

Kharasch's bibliography includes more than 200 items. He also contributed to the literature of his profession by helping to develop journals. More than any other person, he was responsible for the founding (and perhaps the early financial stability) of the *Journal of Organic Chemistry*.

When *Tetrahedron*, a European journal in this field, was started, he became its first American editor.

Kharasch, a short man, was quick, articulate, and intense, and had great charm. His humor was famous; his conversation, class lectures, and even professional papers were enlivened with anecdotes and witticisms. He had rigorous professional standards and would not accept slipshod work, but in personal relationships he was generous, loyal, and sympathetic. Relatives and students benefited, sometimes unknowingly, from philanthropies that his shrewd investments made possible. In some cases he is believed to have funded jobs for his former students and other chemists.

Kharasch loved wrestling with a chemistry problem and quickly grew restless away from the laboratory. Vacations were apt to be terminated early so that he could get back to work. He enjoyed bridge and poker, and chess and billiards, games that provided problems as well as competition and companionship. He played, as he worked in the laboratory, with zest and flair, willing to try something new, not satisfied to limit himself to tried and tested procedures.

Kharasch died in Copenhagen. He left much work unfinished, but his influence was permanent. He had made free radicals a standard part of the thinking of organic chemists and had almost explosively expanded their comprehension of their science.

[The two most useful sources are William A. Waters, ed., *Vistas in Free-Radical Chemistry* (1959); and Frank Westheimer, "Morris Selig Kharasch," *Biographical Memoirs. National Academy of Sciences*, 34 (1960). Both sources provide a bibliography of his writings.]

MAURICE M. VANCE

KILGORE, HARLEY MARTIN (Jan. 11, 1893–Feb. 28, 1956), U.S. senator, was born in Brown, W.Va., the son of Quimby Hugh Kilgore, an oil well driller and contractor, and Laura Jo Martin. When he was a child, the family moved to Mannington, where he graduated from high school. After considering a medical career, Kilgore took the LL.B. in 1914 from West Virginia University, and was admitted to the bar in the same year. When only twenty-one, he unsuccessfully ran for circuit clerk of Monongalia County. In 1914–1915, he taught school in Hancock County. After moving to Beckley in 1915, Kilgore organized the first high school in Raleigh County and served as its principal. Also in 1915, he began to practice law.

Kilgore enlisted in the army in May 1917, receiving a commission as second lieutenant. After three years of service, he left active duty with the rank of captain. He then helped to organize a National Guard regiment with the understanding that it would not be used to break strikes. In 1921 he joined the Guard, rising to the rank of colonel. From 1922 to 1932 he commanded the Second Battalion, 150th Infantry, and served in the judge advocate general's department until 1953. On May 10, 1921, Kilgore married Lois Elaine Lilly; they had two children.

During the 1920's, Kilgore and others reorganized the Democratic party in West Virginia. In 1928 they carried Raleigh County, and in 1932 and 1938 Kilgore was elected judge of the county criminal court. More interested in rehabilitation than in punishment, Kilgore manifested much concern for juvenile offenders, working diligently to reform the state juvenile system.

A split in the West Virginia Democratic party in 1940 between the statehouse clique led by former Governor Guy Kump and the "federal" faction led by Senator Matthew Neely pulled Kilgore off the bench and thrust him into the United States Senate in 1941, with the backing of the prolabor and pro–New Deal "federal" wing. When Neely resigned to become governor in January 1941, Kilgore became the senior senator and soon took his place as a liberal supporter of New Deal policies. During World War II he rose to national prominence. His conversations with Senator Harry S. Truman contributed to the establishment of the special committee to investigate the National Defense Program, to which Kilgore was appointed in 1941. A severe critic of military waste, he chaired many important investigations, the most important being the Canol investigation, which involved inefficient attempts by the army to obtain oil from Alaska. In 1946 he became chairman of the committee.

Of more importance, Kilgore chaired the Special Subcommittee on War Mobilization of the Senate Committee on Military Affairs, the investigations of which revealed weaknesses in the mobilization effort. His proposal to create the Office of War Mobilization put pressure on Roosevelt, and he did so in 1943. The investigations into scientific mobilization led Kilgore to sponsor a bill for the establishment of the National

Science Foundation, for which he fought until its passage in 1950. In addition, his subcommittee exposed the harmful influence of international cartels on the war effort, thus helping to influence government policy and public opinion.

With the end of the war in sight, Kilgore led Senate liberals in proposing a reconversion program that included national planning and a system of unemployment compensation. Even though his bill was not adopted in full, he did move the conservative opposition to the left in 1945. Kilgore also fought against the labor draft, which would have used the selective service system to force workers into jobs designated by the government; and he played a major role in defeating the legislation that embodied the draft concept. His growing national prominence caused him to be mentioned as a vice-presidential possibility in 1944 and in 1948. He also was approached about the position of secretary of labor in 1945, but he preferred to remain in the Senate.

In 1946, Kilgore won a disputed election, despite opposition from the United Mine Workers leadership. In his second term he was a loyal supporter of President Harry Truman. In foreign policy he favored a strong defense posture, aid to Greece and Turkey, the North Atlantic Treaty Organization, the Point Four Program, and the Marshall Plan. In domestic matters he participated in the unsuccessful filibuster against the Taft-Hartley Act in 1947. He also backed federal aid to education, increases in the minimum wage and social security, labor legislation, a federal program to combat adult illiteracy, and rural electrification. In 1950, Kilgore drafted the liberalized Displaced Persons Act and the Youth Corrections Act, which gave judges the option of providing rehabilitation programs for young offenders.

In 1952, despite attempts to link him to Communism, Kilgore soundly defeated his opponent, thus becoming the first senator from West Virginia to win three successive terms. In his third term he stood against McCarthyism, and conducted investigations of monopolies as chairman of the Antitrust and Monopoly Subcommittee of the Judiciary Committee. In 1954 he struggled from his sickbed to cast the deciding vote against the Bricker Amendment, which would have limited the scope of international treaties and the treaty-making power of the president. The following year he became chairman of the Judiciary Committee and was a ranking member of the Appropriations Committee.

Round-faced, with thinning gray hair, Kilgore looked like the typical judge. He was deaf in one ear as the result of an automobile accident in 1927. Amiable and approachable, he was well-liked by colleagues and constituents. An omnivorous reader of history, he wrote his speeches to appeal to the intellect rather than the emotions. He died in Bethesda, Md.

[Kilgore's papers are in the Franklin D. Roosevelt Library, Hyde Park, N.Y., and at West Virginia University, Morgantown, W. Va. The account of the memorial services for Kilgore, *Congressional Record*, 84th Cong., 2d sess., 1956, contains much anecdotal material. *The Congressional Record*, 77–84 Cong., contains much material on Kilgore's legislative activities, Robert Franklin Maddox, "Senator Harley M. Kilgore and World War II" (Ph.D. diss., University of Kentucky, 1974), is an in-depth examination of Kilgore's work during World War II.]

ROBERT FRANKLIN MADDOX

KILPATRICK, JOHN REED (June 15, 1889–May 7, 1960), sports executive, was born in New York City, the son of Frank James Kilpatrick, a wealthy realtor, and Manie Patterson. His father was a founder of the New York Athletic Club, a trotting horse driver of renown, and the winner in 1879 of the All-Round Championship of America, a test of athletic versatility similar to the decathlon. When Kilpatrick was one year old, the family moved to Bridgeport, Ala., where his father headed a syndicate that sought to transform Bridgeport into an industrial center. The effort was abandoned as a failure after nine years and the family returned to New York City, where Kilpatrick completed his primary education.

His father had planned to send Kilpatrick to Harvard, but he preferred Yale because it had the best football team in the country. Learning that many Yale football players had prepped at Phillips Andover Academy, he persuaded his father to enroll him there in the fall of 1903. At Andover, Kilpatrick played varsity football, won the heavyweight boxing championship in his senior year, and was a track-and-field star, excelling at sprints, broad and high jumps, low and high hurdles, the hammer throw, and the shot put. Later he claimed that he and classmate Upton Favorite had invented the spiral forward pass in 1906—a claim not generally accepted by football historians.

Kilpatrick entered Yale in 1907, and if he did

not invent the overarm forward pass, he certainly made it famous. Playing left end, he was named to the All-America team in 1909 and in 1910. Many consider him the best left end ever to play the game. Damon Runyon wrote of him: "No one ever left behind him a more glittering reputation." In 1955 he was elected to the Hall of Fame of the National Football Foundation.

Kilpatrick received the B.A. in 1911 and, although not an outstanding scholar, was elected to Phi Beta Kappa—in 1911 Yale broadened its Phi Beta Kappa admissions requirements to include any senior who received straight A's, and on a lark he decided to make Phi Beta Kappa much as one would make an athletic team. After turning down a number of college football coaching jobs, Kilpatrick joined the New York City construction firm of Thompson-Starrett as a supervisor.

In 1912 Kilpatrick became a member of the elite Squadron A of the New York National Guard, a cavalry unit that attracted sons of the socially prominent families in the city. He had attained the rank of sergeant when his unit was federalized in June 1916, during the Mexican border campaign, and was sent to the southernmost corner of Texas. The unit saw no action. Shortly after his return to New York, the United States entered World War I. Anxious to reach Europe, Kilpatrick transferred to the Quartermaster Corps in the belief that it had a higher shipping priority than the cavalry and would enable him to get to the war zone more quickly. He was promptly promoted to major but was assigned to Washington, D.C. He reached France in January 1918, and as headquarters regulating officer he supervised rail transport of men and supplies to the front lines. By the end of the year he had been promoted to lieutenant colonel and was chief regulating officer for the Allied Expeditionary Force. In April 1919 he became a full colonel.

In March 1919, Kilpatrick followed a friend's suggestion that while in Paris he look up Stephanie d'Hengster Raymond. Married on Oct. 25, 1919, they had one daughter.

Upon returning to America, Kilpatrick spent four years with the International Coal Products Corporation in an unsuccessful effort to distill liquid fuel from bituminous coal. In 1923 he joined the construction firm of George A. Fuller as a vice-president. He stayed with the company for ten years, supervising such major construction projects as the New York County Courthouse and the New York Times Building. In 1927 he was elected to the board of directors of Madison Square Garden.

The Great Depression had a devastating impact on Madison Square Garden, a corporation specializing in the promotion of sports events. By the early 1930's it was deeply in debt, and the board of directors named a three-man committee consisting of Kilpatrick; Dewees Dilworth, a broker; and William M. Greve, president of New York Investors, to study the administration of the corporation and recommend a replacement for its president, William F. Carey.

Kilpatrick, named Carey's successor, assumed office on July 1, 1933. John S. Hammond, who had been the general manager of Madison Square Garden under the legendary "Tex" Rickard (Carey's predecessor), wanted the presidency for himself. By May 1934 he had purchased enough stock to force his election as chairman of the board of directors, and he expected Kilpatrick to resign as president. But other board members, among them Greve, Walter P. Chrysler, and Bernard F. Gimbel, threatened to leave if Kilpatrick resigned. This forced an agreement that Kilpatrick and Hammond would run Madison Square Garden together—an agreement that soon collapsed, leading to a bruising proxy fight. Hammond's bid for control was turned back, and thereafter Kilpatrick's control was never challenged.

Except for the period 1942–1945, when, as a brigadier general, he commanded the port of embarkation at Hampton Roads, Va., Kilpatrick served as president of Madison Square Garden until 1955, when he became chairman of the board of directors. As president he restored prosperity by adding such events as rodeos, horse shows, concerts, track meets, and the Harvest Moon Ball to the traditional athletic fare of boxing, basketball, and hockey at Madison Square Garden. In his later years Kilpatrick devoted much time to civic and political causes. In 1956 he was national chairman of Citizens for Eisenhower and Nixon, and he served as chairman of the New York City Committee of the American Cancer Society from 1951 to 1960. He died in New York City.

[For a biographical sketch, see E. J. Kahn, Jr., "For God, Country, Yale, and Garden," *New Yorker*, Jan. 28, 1956. Obituaries are in the *New York Times*, May 8 and 11, 1960; *Newsweek*, May 16, 1960; and *Time*, May 16, 1960.]

GERALD KURLAND

KING, ERNEST JOSEPH (Nov. 23, 1878–June 25, 1956), naval officer, was born in Lorain, Ohio. His father, James Clydesdale King, was born in Scotland and had been brought to Ohio as a child. He sailed in Great Lakes schooners and worked at bridgebuilding before becoming foreman in a Lorain railroad repair shop. King's mother, Elizabeth Keam, was born in England and her family had immigrated to Ohio in 1870. When King was in high school, his mother fell ill and moved to Cleveland to be cared for by a sister. He and his father stayed in Lorain. The solitary, emotionally cold years spent with his father, a man of upright and inflexible character, shaped his future. He became a single-minded hard worker with a consuming desire to get on in the world.

In 1897 King obtained an appointment to the U.S. Naval Academy, from which he graduated in 1901, standing fourth in a class of sixty-seven. After being commissioned ensign in 1903, he served in the Asiatic Fleet and saw the Russo-Japanese War from the sidelines. On Oct. 10, 1905, he married Martha Rankin Egerton; they had seven children.

After service at sea on the battleship *Alabama*, King was promoted in 1906 to lieutenant. He spent three years teaching at the Naval Academy, where he became interested in military and naval history, and wrote an essay that won the 1909 gold medal of the Naval Institute. Four years of staff and engineering duty at sea followed, after which he returned to Annapolis as executive officer of the Engineering Experiment Station. He was promoted to lieutenant commander in 1913.

During the bombardment and occupation of Vera Cruz in 1914, King had his first command, the destroyer *Terry*. Later that year he became commanding officer of the destroyer *Cassin* and, in June 1915, commander of the Sixth Division of the Destroyer Flotilla. In December 1915 he joined the staff of Vice Admiral Henry T. Mayo, commander of the Battleship Force of the Atlantic Fleet, with whom he served until April 1919. By accompanying Mayo, whom he greatly admired, on inspection trips to Europe, King saw World War I at close range and came to know many of its naval and military leaders. He was promoted to commander in 1917 and to temporary captain in 1918.

In May 1919 King reopened the Naval Postgraduate School at Annapolis, which had been closed during the war; there he developed ideas about the improvement of naval education. He

was constantly striving to broaden and perfect his professional competence. Having had only a casual acquaintance with submarines, in July 1922 he went to the submarine base at New London, Conn., where he spent four months as a student at the Submarine School.

Upon completion of this course, King assumed command of Submarine Division 11; and in September 1923 took command of the submarine base at New London, where he spent the next three years. When the submarine *S-51* was sunk in a collision off Block Island on Sept. 25, 1925, King was put in charge of the salvage force. After nine months of labor, *S-51* was successfully raised. King received the Distinguished Service Medal for his part in the work.

King next turned to the air, becoming commanding officer of the aircraft tender *Wright* in September 1926. The following January he entered the Naval Air School at Pensacola, Fla. At the age of forty-eight, he qualified as a naval aviator in five months rather than the usual ten. He returned to the *Wright*, but on Dec. 17, 1927, was called to take command of a salvage force to raise the submarine *S-4*, which had been rammed and sunk off Provincetown, Mass. On completing this duty in March 1928, for which he was awarded a second Distinguished Service Medal, King was appointed commander of aircraft squadrons in the Atlantic. He next served as assistant chief of the Bureau of Aeronautics and as commander of the air base at Hampton Roads, Va., before taking command of the aircraft carrier *Lexington* on June 20, 1930. After two years in this highly congenial duty, King enrolled in the senior course of the Naval War College at Newport, R.I.

Having been promoted to rear admiral, King became chief of the Bureau of Aeronautics on May 3, 1933, holding the post for three years. During 1936–1937 he commanded patrol planes in the Pacific and the Caribbean. In January 1938 he became commander of the Aircraft Battle Force with temporary rank of vice admiral. By unremitting diligence he had mastered all aspects of his profession, yet it seemed unlikely that he would have an opportunity to put his experience into practice. When, on the retirement of Admiral William D. Leahy, Admiral Harold R. Stark was appointed chief of naval operations in 1939, King's road to the summit seemed forever blocked, for the term of office was four years and King would reach the statutory retirement age in three and a half.

When King hauled down his flag in the Aircraft Battle Force on June 15, 1939, reverting to his permanent rank of rear admiral, he felt that his sea duty was over. He was ordered to the General Board, a dignified body on which he would probably remain until retirement. But in the spring of 1940, Secretary of the Navy Charles Edison, about to pay his first visit to the fleet at Pearl Harbor, asked King to accompany him. Edison was impressed by King's character and the breadth of his experience. Later in the year King joined Edison's successor, Frank Knox, on a visit to Caribbean bases. Then, with pressure mounting in the Atlantic, there arose an opportunity for King to go back to sea, which he enthusiastically embraced.

When King became commander of the Patrol Force on Dec. 17, 1940, and broke his flag on the battleship *Texas* at Norfolk, he assumed a major role in an undeclared war. On Jan. 22, 1941, he was designated commander in chief, Atlantic Fleet, with the rank of admiral. In August 1941, King transported President Franklin D. Roosevelt in the cruiser *Augusta* to Newfoundland for the Atlantic Charter conference with Winston Churchill.

After the bombing of Pearl Harbor, a "new deal" in naval command became imperative. President Roosevelt and Secretary of the Navy Knox determined that King should be made commander in chief of the United States Fleet (abbreviated to COMINCH rather than the traditional CINCUS, which now seemed to have undesirable connotations). King was appointed on Dec. 20, 1941, and immediately began setting up his new command. In doing so he brought ashore the concept of a fleet staff, applying many of the principles he had evolved in the Atlantic and employing some of the personnel who had aided him in their application.

Although King was obliged to create COMINCH headquarters practically from nothing, he assumed command on Dec. 30, 1941, and sent a dispatch to Admiral Chester Nimitz at Pearl Harbor, summarizing his tasks as covering and holding the Hawaii-Midway line and maintaining communications between the West Coast and Australia. While planning the best disposition of available forces in the Pacific, King was simultaneously involved in discussions of allied strategy in Europe, for on Dec. 22, 1941, Churchill and the British chiefs of staff arrived in Washington to confer with Roosevelt on the conduct of the war. King; Admiral Harold R. Stark, chief of naval operations; General George

C. Marshall, chief of staff of the army; and Lieutenant General H. H. Arnold, deputy chief of staff for the army air corps were among the officers who met with their British counterparts during the Arcadia Conference, which lasted until Jan. 14, 1942. From this meeting evolved the creation of the combined chiefs of staff, the heads of the United States and British military and naval forces, who met formally for the first time in Washington on Jan. 23, 1942. To prepare for future meetings, the United States representatives had to confer among themselves to be sure of agreement in dealing with the British. The joint chiefs of staff, as the American group was called, initially consisting of admirals Stark and King and generals Marshall and Arnold, first met on February 9. They had the duty of coordinating the military efforts of the army and the navy, in which capacity they reported directly to the president, and of advising him on the strategic conduct of the war.

President Roosevelt's Executive Order 8984 of Dec. 18, 1941, which gave the new COMINCH supreme command of the operating forces, did not specifically establish the relationship between the new command and the chief of naval operations (CNO), who had responsibility for the logistic and other needs of the operating forces. From time to time King asked that a clearer relationship be established, indicating that as COMINCH he was perfectly willing to be under CNO, and in fact thought that the logical arrangement. The president stated that he and Secretary Knox would take care of the situation. They did so in a way that King neither sought nor anticipated, by determining in March 1942 to send Stark to London as commander of American naval forces in Europe. By Executive Order 9096 of Mar. 12, 1942, the duties of Stark's office were added to those of King, who henceforth, as COMINCH-CNO, became "the principal naval adviser and executive to the Secretary of the Navy on the conduct of the Naval Establishment." King relieved Stark on March 26 and assumed duty as chief of naval operations, while Vice Admiral F. J. Horne (Stark's principal assistant) became vice chief of naval operations. Throughout the war the organizations of COMINCH and CNO were maintained separately and distinctly, the two activities being united in the person of King.

With Stark's departure for London in March 1942, the joint chiefs of staff membership was reduced to King, Marshall, and Arnold. In July 1942, William D. Leahy was added and, because of his seniority, acted as chairman. There were no changes in membership during the rest of the war.

King participated in the conferences held at Washington in 1942; at Casablanca, Washington, Quebec, Cairo, and Teheran in 1943; and at Malta, Yalta, and Potsdam in 1945. At the Arcadia Conference it was affirmed that Germany was still the primary enemy and its defeat the key to victory, and that once Germany was defeated, the collapse of Italy and the defeat of Japan must follow. This was the genesis of one of King's greatest difficulties: to obtain enough resources for the Pacific war, in order to keep pressure on the Japanese. When areas of strategic responsibility were divided among the Allies in the spring of 1942, the Pacific was assigned to the United States. The Pacific Ocean Area was under the command of Nimitz at Pearl Harbor and the Southwest Pacific Area under General Douglas MacArthur.

During the war two-thirds of King's time was devoted to joint and combined chiefs business. He took part in the discussions of international strategy and of interservice cooperation that were to govern the actions of the naval forces he commanded. Although he agreed completely with the American-British grand strategy, King constantly and strenuously urged the more rapid prosecution of the war against Germany so that he might obtain more adequate forces in the Pacific. Indeed his vigorous advocacy led Churchill to call the Pacific "King's pet ocean."

King was able to command the greatest fleet in the history of the world in one-third of his time because he could delegate authority. COMINCH headquarters in Washington preserved a seagoing character. It remained small. There were no civilians. Senior officers who had been successful in combat were brought in for a year or two. Experienced chief petty officers, many of whom were later commissioned, junior Reserve officers, and later Waves remained for longer periods and formed a dependable crew. The fleet point of view was constantly maintained by the constant flow of officers with active combat experience. King lived on his flagship, the yacht *Dauntless*, at the Washington Navy Yard, so that he and senior members of his staff might work at any hour of the night in secure surroundings with full communications facilities.

In February 1942, King told Secretary Knox, "We are faced with the continuation and maintenance of what is technically called 'the defensive-offensive,' in order that we may get ready

for 'the offensive-defensive' in 1943." He paraphrased the "defensive-offensive" as "hold what you've got and hit them when you can, the hitting to be done not only by seizing opportunities but by making them." The following month King summarized for the president the lines of military endeavor in the Pacific as "Hold Hawaii. Support Australasia. Drive northwestward from New Hebrides." The battle of Midway threw the Japanese off balance for the first time; King saw to it that they did not regain their equilibrium. The landings in the Solomon Islands on Aug. 7, 1942, a calculated risk that barely escaped disaster, were both an early beginning of the "offensive-defensive" and the turning point of the war. In the autumn of 1943, when divisions of new carriers had joined the Pacific Fleet, the great central Pacific offensive began. Japan was defeated in less than two years.

In late October 1942, when it was still touch-and-go in the Solomons, King wrote to Roosevelt, reminding him that he would attain the age of sixty-four—the statutory retirement age—on Nov. 23, 1942. King's letter was returned with the hand written endorsement: "So what, old top? I may even send you a Birthday present! FDR." When five-star ranks were authorized by Congress in December 1944, King was promoted to fleet admiral.

After V-J Day, King persuaded President Harry S. Truman to sign an executive order abolishing the duties of COMINCH and assigning new duties to the chief of naval operations. On Oct. 10, 1945, King signed the order making this effective, and moved down one step to the traditional CNO office. On Dec. 15, 1945, he was relieved by Nimitz, wartime commander in chief of the Pacific Fleet. King's naval career was over, but since fleet admirals are not subject to retirement, he remained technically on active duty for the rest of his life.

Congress voted King a gold medal "on behalf of a grateful nation." It showed Neptune driving a team of three horses, one winged, with the inscription "Neque Glauci Regno nec Neptuni nec Ipsius Iovis Tonantis Intemerato," in graceful reference to his "triple threat" as submariner, destroyerman, and aviator.

King's memoirs, published in 1952 as *Fleet Admiral King, A Naval Record*, were written with Walter Muir Whitehill. In August 1947, King suffered a brain hemorrhage that for a time deprived him of speech and caused him to take up residence at the Bethesda Naval Medical Center.

By sheer determination he taught himself to speak again and resumed a measured and limited life. But he continued to live at Bethesda, going in summers to the U.S. Naval Hospital, Portsmouth, N.H., where he died.

King was as uncompromising as the Washington Monument, and to those who did not know him he seemed about as genial. He worked hard, with few diversions beyond reading military history. He was wrongly accused of being anti-British, largely because it must have been trying for some of his Royal Navy colleagues to understand a Scot's wearing a "foreign" device on his cap, yet having the superiority in ships that had once been theirs. Although naturally courteous, he had few niceties of polite address.

King's mind was of Olympian simplicity. He concentrated on broad principles, and was totally uninterested in the smaller details of problems or personalities. His deputy, Richard S. Edwards, once remarked that in conferences King would "encourage free and uninhibited debate until he had absorbed all points of view. He would then come forth with a clear-cut scheme, usually so obviously applicable as to cause all concerned to wonder why they had not thought of it themselves." This, joined to his intuitive power of divining the heart of the enemy, led Samuel Eliot Morison to assess King not only as "the Navy's principal architect of victory," but also as "undoubtedly the best naval strategist and organizer in our history."

[King's official files as COMINCH are in the Division of Naval History, Navy Department; his personal papers are in the Naval Historical Foundation collection in the Library of Congress. Walter Muir Whitehill, *Analecta Biographica: A Handful of New England Portraits* (1969), ch. 13, is an appreciation of King written after his death. Many oral history memoirs in the Naval Project of the Oral History collection in the Library of Congress deal with King, that of Admiral Donald Duncan being the most extensive. Samuel Eliot Morison's appraisal is in *The Two-Ocean War* (1963), pp. 579–580.]

WALTER MUIR WHITEHILL

KINGSLEY, ELIZABETH SEELMAN (Oct. 9, 1871–June 7, 1957), puzzlemaker, was born Hannah Elizabeth Seelman in Brooklyn, N.Y., the daughter of Maurice Seelman and Elizabeth Paris. Little is known of her family background or of her early years. At a young age she displayed an aptitude for solving scrambled-

word puzzles in children's magazines. After graduation from Girls High School in Brooklyn, she attended Wellesley College, where she earned a B.A. in English literature in 1898. Returning to Brooklyn, she taught English at Girls High School from 1900 to 1914. In 1905 she received the M.A. from New York University.

She married Clarence Darwin Kingsley, a teacher, in 1914; they had no children. Shortly after their marriage they moved to Boston, where Clarence Kingsley became an assistant superintendent of education. While living in Massachusetts, Elizabeth Kingsley worked for the Boston publishing house of Houghton Mifflin and served as a faculty member of the Babson Institute at Wellesley Hills. She and her husband were among the founders of the Boston Ethical Culture Society; they had earlier been among the founding members of the Brooklyn Ethical Culture Society.

After the death of her husband in 1926, Kingsley returned to Brooklyn, where she held secretarial and clerical jobs for the next eight years. Not long after her return to Brooklyn, she was introduced to the crossword puzzle, which was then at the height of its popularity, by a niece. After completing the puzzle, Kingsley remarked, "How futile. It's fun, but what's the good?" Although she was not caught up in the crossword puzzle craze, an idea had been planted that would germinate years later.

In the early 1930's Kingsley, who remained active in Wellesley alumnae affairs throughout her life, attended a class reunion and was appalled to find the undergraduates reading James Joyce and Gertrude Stein in preference to the more traditional masters of English and American literature. To counter this trend, she conceived the idea of creating a puzzle with a goal, one that, she said, "stimulated the imagination and heightened an appreciation by reviewing classical English and American poet and prose masters."

The result was the invention of the Double-Crostic, considered by many to be the highest achievement of the crossword puzzle form. The Double-Crostic is part crossword puzzle, part acrostic, and part anagram. The reader begins by figuring out word definitions that are to be written out over numbered dashes—there is a numbered dash for each letter of the defined word. The letters of the defined words are then transferred to the corresponding numbered squares in a pattern resembling the crossword puzzle. If all the words in the puzzle are correctly defined by the reader, the crossword puzzle pattern will give a quotation from an author's work. The first letter of each properly defined word forms an acrostic giving the author's name and the title of the work from which the quotation was taken.

Within six months Kingsley had constructed 100 Double-Crostics. Early in 1934, at the suggestion of a friend, she submitted a portfolio of her puzzles to Amy Loveman of the *Saturday Review*. Four days later the magazine contracted with her for a series of Double-Crostics. The first puzzle appeared in the issue for Mar. 31, 1934, and the Double-Crostic quickly became one of the most popular weekly features in the magazine. Besides appearing each week in the *Saturday Review*, Kingsley's Double-Crostics were run every second week in the *New York Times* magazine, and beginning in 1934 two volumes of Double-Crostics were published each year in paperback by Simon and Schuster.

The popularity of the Double-Crostic permitted Kingsley to give up other work and to devote herself to producing puzzles. She began by selecting a quotation. This was broken down into its component letters, which were put on standard anagram blocks and placed in a box compartmentalized for each letter of the alphabet. Selecting the first letters of her acrostic, she would arrange them in a column. Then she would use the remaining letters to form the words to be guessed by the reader. It was estimated that Kingsley used more than 50,000 words for her definitions, but the only references she consulted were the *Oxford Companion to English Literature*, the *Oxford Companion to American Literature*, Shakespeare, Charles Gayley's *Classic Myths*, a Bible with concordance, Webster's *New International Dictionary*, and dictionaries of synonyms and of American slang.

After illness forced Kingsley to give up her column in 1951, her longtime associate, Doris Nash Wortman, then took over construction of the puzzles. Kingsley died in New York City.

[Obituaries appeared in *Newsweek*, June 17, 1957; *New York Times*, June 8, 1957; *Publishers Weekly*, July 8, 1957; and *Saturday Review*, June 29, 1957.]

GERALD KURLAND

KINSEY, ALFRED CHARLES (June 23, 1894–Aug. 25, 1956), zoologist, entomologist, and author of landmark studies of human sexual behavior, was born in Hoboken, N.J., the son of Alfred Seguine Kinsey, an instructor in mechanical arts at the Stevens Institute of Technology, and Sarah Ann Charles. When he was ten, his family moved to nearby South Orange, where he graduated from Columbia High School. His father was determined that Alfred should study mechanical engineering, a field toward which he had no inclination. After two unsuccessful years at Stevens he rebelled and turned to his own first choice, biology. His interest in plants, animals, and outdoor life had been awakened by an enthusiastic biology teacher, Natalie Roeth, and was fostered by Boy Scout work and summer camp experiences. Twenty years later he wrote to her, "I shall always consider that you did more than anyone else at the very crucial age to turn me to science."

Kinsey entered Bowdoin College in 1914 as a junior and graduated with the B.S. two years later. At the Bussey Institution of Harvard University he specialized in entomology, centering his interest on the gall wasp. A Sheldon traveling fellowship enabled him to undertake a year of independent field study (1919–1920), which he spent largely in the South and West, camping alone and covering 18,000 miles, 2,500 of them on foot. Kinsey collected more than 300,000 gall wasp specimens, which he sent back to the Harvard laboratories. His unequaled collection of gall wasps was later housed in the American Museum of Natural History in New York.

After receiving the Sc.D., Kinsey joined the faculty of Indiana University in the fall of 1920 as assistant professor of zoology. On June 3, 1921, he married Clara Bracken McMillen, a graduating senior. They had four children. Kinsey spent his entire professional career at Indiana, the first half as teacher and research scholar in entomology and zoology. He was by all accounts an excellent teacher and a dynamic lecturer who thoroughly enjoyed both roles. His interest in the development of teaching methods led him to write a widely used high school text, *An Introduction to Biology* (1926), which offered a fresh and practical approach to field and laboratory work.

Appointed associate professor in 1922 and professor in 1929, Kinsey continued his fieldwork and research and published a number of articles on gall wasps. Two pioneering trips to the more rugged areas of Mexico and Central America during the 1930's extended his observations and broadened his collection. His entomological work culminated in *The Gall Wasp Genus Cynips* (1930) and *The Origin of Higher Categories in*

Cynips (1936), which, together with his many scholarly papers, earned him an international reputation. Based on painstaking study and classification of more than a million specimens, they were not only definitive works on the taxonomy of the gall wasp but also important contributions to genetic and evolutionary theories.

In 1938 Kinsey's attention was drawn to the scientific study of human sexual behavior; a marriage course, newly instituted by petition of the students, was the starting point. In preparing the three lectures he was to give as his share of the course, he realized the scarcity of sound scientific information on the subject. To provide more adequate answers to questions raised in conferences, he began to question students about their own opinions and experiences. His inquiries were gradually extended to a wider circle of students and to colleagues. For a year Kinsey kept his investigations in this new field quiet and traveled on weekends, at his own expense, to nearby communities to broaden the base of his sample. A standard interview format was developed and memorized, and the answers were recorded in a special code. The questions covered a wide range of topics and were far more comprehensive than those used in any earlier studies. Elaborate precautions were taken to protect the identities of those interviewed. The complete confidentiality of the sex history, combined with Kinsey's earnestness and evident belief in the far-reaching significance of such research, aided him in obtaining the cooperation of his subjects.

Early in his interviewing, Kinsey realized that sexual behavior and attitudes varied widely according to socioeconomic status, and that the data from his student sample were not typical of the general population. This awareness led him to extend his off-campus interviews to such centers as Gary, Chicago, St. Louis, and Philadelphia and to record histories from inmates in the Indiana state prisons. When it became known that Kinsey was gathering firsthand data on sexual behavior in this manner, there was a substantial amount of criticism, chiefly from the more conservative faculty members. Some of his friends tried to dissuade him from his course. But the university administration, especially President Herman B Wells, strongly supported him, believing the principle of academic freedom was involved.

Kinsey received his first outside financial help ($1,600) in 1941, from the National Research Council on the recommendation of its Committee for Research on Problems of Sex. The funds were provided by the medical division of the Rockefeller Foundation. The grant was subsequently increased to $35,000 by 1946. These funds allowed Kinsey to employ research assistants and to expand greatly the geographical scope of his work. The Institute for Sex Research, an Indiana nonprofit corporation formed in 1947, held ownership of the files of sex history interviews, the collections and archives, and the library holdings. Royalties from publications were also to accrue to the institute, which was directed by research associates Clyde E. Martin, Wardell B. Pomeroy, and Paul H. Gebhard, in addition to Kinsey. All of them had been trained by Kinsey as interviewers, using the format he had developed. By this time Kinsey's entomological research and classroom teaching had been largely left behind, certainly with some regret. He and his staff were devoting their full energies to tabulating and preparing for publication the extensive data they had amassed.

The institute's first book, jointly authored by Kinsey, Pomeroy, and Martin, appeared early in 1948. Largely unheralded, *Sexual Behavior in the Human Male* was on the best-seller list three weeks after publication and remained there for six months. By mid-March 100,000 copies had been sold, foreign editions had been contracted for, and Kinsey's name had become a byword. The quantification of many types of sexual activity based on a sample of 5,300 males was the book's greatest contribution. The most significant finding was that sexual patterns and attitudes differed to a marked degree among males of varying social and economic levels.

While the reception of the book was generally favorable, some critics challenged the validity of the findings, arguing that Kinsey's sampling had been faulty and that he had made too broad a projection from his data to a larger population. In general, however, the work was hailed as a pioneering contribution.

Kinsey and his co-workers turned immediately to intense work on the next volume, based chiefly on the data gathered in interviews with 5,940 female subjects. The criticisms leveled at the book on males were carefully weighed, and a concerted effort was made to take them into consideration. *Sexual Behavior in the Human Female* (1953) was much sounder than its predecessor. Nevertheless, perhaps because its publication was accompanied by a surfeit of largely unsought publicity, criticism was much more severe—much to Kinsey's dismay and surprise. Findings in this volume again broke new ground. The greater range of women's biological sexual capacities, their ability to respond to sexual stimulation virtually as rapidly as males, and their low incidence of frigidity were all new insights.

The exceptionally bitter attack on Kinsey and on the book came from many sides. New York congressman Louis B. Heller proposed that the post office ban the reports from the mails. The U.S. Bureau of Customs continued to confiscate shipments of erotic books and art objects sent to the institute from abroad because they considered them to be obscene. At hearings of a special committee of the House of Representatives, the Rockefeller Foundation was interrogated as to its support of Kinsey's research program, following testimony that branded his findings as unscientific and un-American.

In 1954 the Rockefeller Foundation terminated its support of Kinsey's research and for the next two years he tried in vain to find a sponsor. A token grant from the National Research Council provided the only outside support, although Indiana University continued to underwrite its share of overhead expenses and to pay Kinsey's salary. The accumulated royalties were sufficient to fund the institute for a year or two, but it was unrealistic to hope to bring out new books fast enough to finance the continuation of the research at previous levels.

Kinsey had pushed himself hard, setting a whirlwind pace of interviewing, traveling, lecturing, and writing; and his health gradually deteriorated under the strain. To this was added the burden of the uncertain future of the institute.

His first trip to Europe, in the fall of 1955, planned as a vacation with his wife, turned instead into an exhausting lecture tour. Indignantly refusing to follow the schedule of rest prescribed by his doctor, he explained, "I'd rather be dead than not put in a full day's work." In August 1956, he was hospitalized with pneumonia. He died shortly afterward in Bloomington, Ind.

While Kinsey's work was gradually given wide recognition and finally accepted as having established a benchmark against which later investigations could be measured, it is doubtful if it was a major influence in the liberalization of sex attitudes in the two decades following his death. There were so many other powerful social and historical forces at work during those years that it is unlikely that Kinsey's findings played the chief role in these shifts. They undoubtedly had an influence, however, especially in opening the way to further sex research.

[The principal source is Cornelia V. Christenson, *Kinsey: A Biography* (1971); Wardell B. Pomeroy, *Dr. Kinsey and the Institute for Sex Research* (1972), a more personalized and popularly written account, includes material on the post-Kinsey years. On Kinsey's findings, see Donald P. Geddes, ed., *An Analysis of the Kinsey Reports* (1954); and Jerome Himelhoch and Sylvia F. Falva, eds., *Sexual Behavior in American Society* (1955).]

CORNELIA V. CHRISTENSON

KIRK, NORMAN THOMAS (Jan. 3, 1888–Aug. 13, 1960), surgeon, was born in Rising Sun, Md., the son of Thomas Kirk and Anna Brown. He graduated from Jacob Tome Institute, Port Deposit, Md., in 1906 and received the M.D. from the University of Maryland in 1910. He added to his medical knowledge by working for a druggist during vacations from medical school. From 1910 to 1912 Kirk served as clinical assistant at the U.S. Soldiers' Home Hospital, Washington, D.C. In 1912 he enlisted in the army and was commissioned first lieutenant. The following year he graduated from the Army Medical School and was stationed at Texas City, Tex. During 1914 he was at Field Hospital 3 in Vera Cruz, Mexico, as part of the punitive expedition against the forces of President Victoriano Huerta of Mexico.

In 1915–1916 Kirk served at Fort Grant and Fort Sherman in the Panama Canal Zone. In 1917, after a brief stay at the Base Hospital in Brownsville, Tex., he was assigned to Camp Greenleaf, Ga. On Sept. 21, 1917, he married Anne Duryea, a nurse in training in Brownsville; they had two children. In 1919 Kirk was ordered to Walter Reed Hospital, Washington, D.C. That same year he switched from general surgery to specialization in bone and joint surgery. While at Walter Reed he was credited with treating at least one-third of all American major amputation cases resulting from World War I. In 1924, Kirk published *Amputations: Operative Technique*, which became a standard text. (During his career he published thirty-two articles on various aspects of surgery and military medicine.)

In 1925 Kirk studied briefly at Johns Hopkins University Hospital and Massachusetts General Hospital. From 1925 to 1928 he was assigned to the orthopedic section of the Station Hospital at Fort Sam Houston, as assistant chief of surgical service. During the next two years Kirk was in the Philippine Islands, as chief of surgical service at Sternberg General Hospital in Manila. In

1930–1931 he was back in the United States as head of the orthopedic section at Walter Reed Hospital. In December 1931, after a three-month advanced course at the Medical Field Service School, Carlisle Barracks, Pa., he returned to Walter Reed. From 1934 to 1936, Kirk was again in the Philippines, first at Fort Mills and then at Sternberg General Hospital. Next (1936–1940) he was chief of the surgical service at Letterman General Hospital in San Francisco. In January 1941, by then a general, Kirk returned to Walter Reed as head of the surgical service.

In June 1942, Kirk was sent to Battle Creek, Mich., to convert the Kellogg Sanatorium into a specialized treatment center for amputations, neurosurgery, deep X-ray therapy, and neurology. The sanatorium, renamed Percy Jones Hospital, was expanded (with nearby Camp Custer) from 1,750 patients to a maximum patient load of 12,000. For his work as commanding officer at Percy Jones, Kirk was awarded the Legion of Merit.

After a brief stint at the Pentagon in the spring of 1943, Kirk was appointed surgeon general of the Army and was promoted to major general. His leadership was credited by Gen. Brehon Somerville with the reduction of the fatality rate among wounded American soldiers to half the figure for World War I. Kirk was particularly praised for the use of well-equipped hospital ships and planes that quickly transported the wounded to safely situated hospitals. His other noteworthy accomplishments included preventive medicine measures that made smallpox, typhoid fever, other communicable diseases, and tetanus very rare in the army. Of particular importance was the development of rehabilitative convalescent programs in army hospitals that measurably reduced the period of hospitalization. Moreover, the development of blood plasma and whole blood programs saved many lives.

During the war Kirk made three overseas inspections with the secretary of war. He also accompanied President Harry Truman to Potsdam. For his service during the war, Kirk received the Distinguished Service Medal, the Cross of the Legion of Honor from France, and the Order of the Crown from Italy.

Kirk retired as surgeon general on July 31, 1947. He divided his remaining years between Montauk, N.Y., and Melbourne Beach, Fla., indulging his avid interest in fishing. He died in Washington, D. C.

Kirk was a governor of the American College of Surgeons and a diplomate of the American Board of Surgery. The army hospital at Aberdeen Proving Ground, Md., bears his name.

[A collection of Kirk's speeches and articles is in the Military History Research Collection, Carlisle Barracks, Pa. Roderick M. Engert, "A Concise Biography of Major General Norman Thomas Kirk" (1964), and "Dedication of Kirk Army Hospital," an address by Maj. Gen. Achilles L. Tynes (1963), are available on request from Dept. of Army, Center of Military History, Medical History Division, Fort Dietrick, Md. 21701. See also *Newsweek*, July 10 and 17, 1944; *New York Times*, Aug. 14, 1960; *Washington Star*, Aug. 14, 1960; and *Medical Annals of the District of Columbia*, Oct. 1960.]

WILLIAM H. WILLIAMS

KIRKWOOD, JOHN GAMBLE (May 30, 1907–Aug. 9, 1959), physical chemist, was born in Gotebo, Okla., the son of John Millard Kirkwood and Lillian Gamble. The family moved to Wichita, Kans., two years after his birth, and he was educated in the local public schools. He entered California Institute of Technology in 1923 without taking the senior year of high school work, then transferred to the University of Chicago, from which he received the B.S. in 1926. Kirkwood took his Ph.D. at the Massachusetts Institute of Technology in 1929, on the basis of research done under the direction of Frederick G. Keyes. During the next five years he held research fellowships that enabled him to work with Keyes at MIT, John C. Slater at Harvard, Peter Debye in Leipzig, and Arnold Sommerfeld in Munich.

In 1934 Kirkwood joined the chemistry faculty at Cornell University; in 1937 he moved to an associate professorship at the University of Chicago. He returned to Cornell as Todd professor of chemistry in 1938. Kirkwood was appointed A. A. Noyes professor at California Institute of Technology in 1947, and in 1951 moved to his final position as Sterling professor of chemistry and head of the department at Yale University. On Sept. 5, 1930, he married Lillian Gladys Danielson; they had one son and were divorced in 1952. He married Platonia Kaldes on Mar. 11, 1958.

Kirkwood combined enthusiasm for life with intellectual brilliance. His hard-driving personality enabled him to accomplish much in theoretical physical chemistry during a relatively short lifetime. His interest in chemistry was entirely theoretical but far-ranging, including the nature of intermolecular forces, theory of solutions, theory of liquids, nature of proteins and other macromolecules, transport processes, quantum statistics, and the nature of shock waves.

Kirkwood's early study of dielectric constants (a measure of the ability of a dielectric material to store electrical potential energy under the influence of an electric field) was directed toward the experimental measurement of the influence of temperature and density of gases. Extensive work on carbon dioxide and ammonia led to the theoretical explanation of the constitution of gases that utilized the statistical theory of intermolecular forces. These studies were followed by a series of papers (1939) dealing with dielectric characteristics of polar liquids. This led to clarification of solution theory by introducing models for understanding short-range molecular interactions such as those found in liquids with hydrogen bonding. His work on dielectric properties was also useful for understanding electrical characteristics of polymer solutions.

Kirkwood's interest in proteins began when he took a course from George Scatchard at MIT. Two years later he and Scatchard published a paper dealing with the electrical charges on protein, the first of forty-four works dealing with protein chemistry. In his early years Kirkwood was particularly interested in the distribution of electrical charges on protein molecules. Since proteins and their building blocks, amino acids, contain both acidic (carboxyl, $-COOH$) and basic (amino, $-NH_2$) groups, these molecules undergo ionization resulting in the formation of zwitterions with positively and negatively charged residues on nearby portions of the molecule. Kirkwood sought, in a series of papers, to develop the theoretical implications of the behavior of such charged particles.

He soon became interested in the separation of proteins by electrophoresis, a technique that causes charged particles such as proteins to migrate in an electrical field. He treated the technique, which had been developed by colloid chemists in Sweden, in a theoretical manner that led to new understanding and improvements in the methodology. In this connection he studied the role of convection (movement of molecules in the presence of temperature variations) in electrophoretic separations.

Kirkwood's interest in proteins led naturally to an interest in macromolecules in general. From 1940 he made extensive studies of the viscosity and the elasticity of macromolecules in solution, paying particular attention to the influence of the shape of such molecules on their migration in fluids under various external factors.

During World War II, Kirkwood became involved in the theoretical study of explosions in connection with his post as a consultant to experimental groups working on government-sponsored problems. He gave attention to the theories of shock and of detonation waves in air and in water. For this work, published in ten papers after the war, he received the Meritorious Civilian Service Award from the navy (1945) and the Presidential Certificate of Appreciation (1947).

In all of Kirkwood's work there is a consistent pattern of interest in the nature of intermolecular forces as affected by such internal factors as molecular shapes, distribution of electrical charges, and location of reactive centers, and such external factors as temperature, pressure, and electrical environment. A talented mathematician, he was inclined to apply unique approaches to chemical problems and never hesitated to use quantum and statistical mechanics. Of his 160 scientific papers, many were published alone, a few with academic peers, and a sizable number with students. He died in New Haven, Conn.

[Kirkwood's published papers have been issued in a bound eight-volume set, *John Gamble Kirkwood Collected Works,* under the general editorship of Irwin Oppenheim (1965–1968): *Dielectrics–Intermolecular Forces–Optical Rotation,* R. H. Cole, ed. (1965); *Quantum Statistics and Cooperative Phenomena,* F. H. Stillinger, Jr., ed. (1965); *Macromolecules,* P. L. Auer, ed. (1967); *Proteins,* G. Scatchard, ed. (1967); *Shock and Detonation Waves,* W. W. Wood, ed. (1967); *Selected Topics in Statistical Mechanics,* R. W. Zwanzig, ed. (1967); *Theory of Liquids,* B. J. Adler, ed. (1968); *Theory of Solutions,* Z. W. Salsburg, ed. (1968). See also the obituary by George Scatchard, *Journal of Chemical Physics,* 1960, which contains papers related to Kirkwood's interests; and a short sketch by John Ross, in *Dictionary of Scientific Biography,* VII.]

AARON J. IHDE

KLEIN, CHARLES HERBERT ("CHUCK") (Oct. 7, 1904–Mar. 28, 1956), baseball outfielder, was born on a farm near Southport, Ind., the son of Frank Klein and Margaret Vacker. His father, a farmer, had been a deputy sheriff and held other minor political jobs in Indianapolis. Klein was a star athlete at Southport High School. After graduation in 1923, he went to work at a local steel mill.

Klein played semiprofessional baseball on weekends. In the summer of 1927 he was spotted by a prohibition agent, who recommended him to the Evansville club of the 3-I League. Klein performed well in his tryout, and was given a contract; but his season ended abruptly after fourteen games when he sprained his ankle. He was sold in 1928 for $200 to Fort Wayne of the Central League, where he batted .331 with twenty-six home runs. He was purchased for $7,500 on July 30 by the Philadelphia Phillies of the National League. Klein performed brilliantly, averaging .360 in sixty-four games.

During 1929, his first full year in the majors, Klein hit .356. He took advantage of the short 280-foot right-field fence in his home park, Baker Bowl, to establish a new league record for home runs (43). A year later he hit .386, third highest in the National League, and led in total bases (445), extra-base hits (107), runs (158), and doubles (59), the last three new league records. He was also second in home runs (43), hits (250), runs batted in (RBI; 170), and slugging (.687). This was the height of the lively ball era, and the entire team averaged .315, second highest in the National League. Yet the Phillies still came in last, with 102 losses, because of poor fielding and pitching.

Klein's average fell to .337 in 1931, when a less lively ball was used, but he led the league in home runs (31), runs (121), RBI (121), slugging (.584), and total bases (347). The next season he hit .348 third highest in the National League; he also led in runs (152), hits (226), slugging (.646), total bases (420), stolen bases (20), and tied Mel Ott in home runs (38). Klein reached his peak in 1933, winning the triple crown by batting .368 with 28 home runs and 120 RBI. He also led in slugging (.602), total bases (365), doubles (44), and hits (223). Despite his brilliant performance, the club came in seventh.

Desperately in need of cash and believing they could not do much worse without him, the Phillies sold Klein to the Chicago Cubs for $65,000 and three players. The Cubs expected that Klein would lead them to a pennant in 1934, but he was never the same after leaving the friendly confines of Baker Bowl. A chronic charley horse kept him on the bench for weeks, and he appeared in only 115 games, batting .301 with 20 home runs. In 1935 Klein's batting average dropped to .293; he was benched for most of September, and contributed very little to the Cubs' thrilling twenty-one-game winning streak that brought them

the pennant. He appeared in five games during the World Series, won by the Detroit Tigers, four games to two, starting the final two games. Klein had four hits, including a home run, in twelve plate appearances.

Klein's performance greatly disappointed the Cubs. Some sportswriters felt that the pressure of playing for a contender might have been too great for him. Others argued that he was finally forced to see first-rate pitching every day, which had not been the case with the Phillies. Klein was traded back to Philadelphia early in the 1936 season along with a pitcher and $50,000 for three men, primarily hurler Curt Davis, who was needed to bolster up a depleted Cubs pitching staff. Klein batted .306 that year, with 25 home runs and 308 total bases. On July 10 he hit four home runs in a ten-inning game, the first time that feat had been accomplished in the National League since the 1890's.

Klein's last good year was 1937, when he batted .325. He was unconditionally released by the Phillies in June 1939 and signed with the Pittsburgh Pirates, who released him at the end of the season. He rejoined the Phillies in 1940, mainly as a pinch hitter, until he retired as a player in 1944. He coached from 1942 to 1945, and scouted in 1946. Klein operated a tavern after leaving baseball. A heavy drinker, he was stricken in 1948 with a disease of the nervous system, and was a semi-invalid for the rest of his life. In 1956 he was divorced from Mary Torpey, whom he had married in 1936; they had no children. He died at Indianapolis.

Chuck Klein played seventeen years in the majors, appearing in 1,753 games, batting .320 with 2,076 hits and 300 home runs. He was a strong man, six feet tall and weighing 185 pounds, and used a heavy thirty-eight-ounce bat. He made his mark as a batting star. Several of his accomplishments in 1930 rank high as all-time single season records: extra-base hits (third), total bases (fourth), and hits (fifth). Klein was not well regarded as a fielder, leading the National League in errors in 1936 and tying for the lead in 1932; but he did have a very strong arm, and led in assists three times, including the major league record of forty-four, which he set in 1930. Klein was twice named Most Valuable Player by *Sporting News* (1931 and 1932), and was a starter in the first All-Star game in 1933. In his time he was one of the highest-paid players in the majors, earning $23,000 in 1934, the top salary in the National League.

[There is a file of newspaper articles about Klein at the Baseball Hall of Fame Library, Cooperstown, N.Y. Klein is dealt with in Warren Brown, *The Chicago Cubs* (1946). Frederick G. Lieb and Stan Baumgartner, *The Philadelphia Phillies* (1953), has a photograph, as does *A Baseball Century* (1976), p. 149. A series on Klein appeared in the *Chicago Tribune*, Nov. 23–25, 1933. Klein's statistics can be found in *The Baseball Encyclopedia* (1969). Obituaries are in *Philadelphia Inquirer* and *New York Times*, Mar. 29, 1958; and *Sporting News*, Apr. 9, 1958.]

STEVEN A. RIESS

KNOX, DUDLEY WRIGHT (June 21, 1877–June 11, 1960), naval officer, historian, and publicist, was born in Walla Walla, Wash., the son of Thomas Taylor Knox, an army officer, and Cornelia Manigault Grayson. He attended high school in Washington, D.C., graduated from the United States Naval Academy in June 1896, and was assigned to the battleship *Massachusetts*. During the Spanish-American War he served on the U.S.S. *Maple* on blockade duty in Cuban waters. He subsequently served in the Philippines during the insurrection and, while still an ensign, commanded two small gunboats, the U.S.S. *Albay* and the U.S.S. *Iris*. Knox was among the first American officers to command destroyers, a type of warship developed around the turn of the century. After commanding three destroyers he served as ordnance officer on the battleship *Nebraska* during the round-the-world voyage of the battle fleet from 1907 to 1909. On May 18, 1908, Knox married Lily Hazard McCalla, the daughter of Rear Admiral Bowman H. McCalla. They had one child.

In 1912, having attained the rank of lieutenant commander, Knox was assigned to the Naval War College at Newport, R.I. At the war college, which was then in one of its most important and creative periods, he became closely acquainted with such future leaders of the navy as Royal E. Ingersol, William V. Pratt, and William S. Sims. In 1913, when Sims was appointed to command the Atlantic Torpedo Flotilla, Knox went along as his staff aide. Applying the concepts and methods of the Naval War College, Sims, Knox, and Pratt (who served as Sim's chief of staff) transformed the destroyers of the Atlantic Fleet from a sort of low-grade scouting force into a formidable offensive weapon. With his extensive destroyer experience and war college background, Knox played a leading role in developing a "doctrine,"

or set of standard operating procedures agreed upon and understood by all, for the flotilla.

When the United States entered World War I in April 1917, Knox was serving as commandant of Guantanamo Bay Naval Station in Cuba. In November he was ordered to London to join the staff of Admiral Sims, commander of all American naval forces in European waters. Although temperamentally very different from Sims, he worked closely and loyally with his chief. For his services in the war he was awarded the Navy Cross and decorated by the Allied governments.

In March 1919 Knox was assigned to the staff of the Naval War College. One year later he returned to sea as commander of the cruiser *Brooklyn* and subsequently of the cruiser *Charleston*, flagship of the destroyer force, Pacific Fleet. But by this time his health, never very robust, had badly deteriorated, and he suffered from poor hearing. In October 1921 he was transferred to the retired list.

Although he was ostensibly "retired" the most important phase of Knox's career was only beginning. Appointed officer in charge of the Office of Naval Records and Library in 1921, he transformed this establishment, in the course of the next two decades, into one of the most important agencies in the United States for the study and preservation of naval history. When Knox assumed command of the office, its vast collections of records, including large numbers of those from the recent war, were in an unorganized, almost chaotic state. With a tiny staff, he established a modern archival system and managed to collect and classify most of the important records relating to the navy's activities in World War I. At the suggestion, and with the support, of President Franklin D. Roosevelt, the office undertook the collection, editing, and publication of records relating to the activities of the navy in the early days of the Republic. Between 1934 and 1941 seven volumes of documents relating to the quasi-war with France were published, followed by seven more relating to the Barbary wars.

Knox also took a lively interest in the naval questions of his day. From his vantage point in the Office of Naval Records he watched the events of the 1920's and 1930's with grave uneasiness. He perceived his beloved service assailed, on the one hand, by the advocates of disarmament and, on the other, by the enthusiasts of air power. As naval editor of the *Army-Navy Journal*, naval correspondent for the *Baltimore Sun* and the *New York Herald*, and frequent contributor to other periodicals, he tirelessly inveighed against the perils of disarmament and the extravagant claims of the air power advocates.

Addressing the Foreign Policy Association of New York in 1927, Knox said that arms limitation was desirable as "the best middle ground between no armaments and armaments so swollen as to be provocative of aggression." But he adamantly opposed the arms limitation agreements reached by the great powers at Washington in 1922. His book, *The Eclipse of American Seapower* (1922), has been described as "the classic statement" of the navy's arguments against the Washington treaties. Knox believed that the navy must "learn to use the press in its own interests and in the broader interests of the country to present the American side of important issues" (Knox Papers).

Like all of his work, Knox's *History of the United States Navy* (1936) was designed to show the importance of the navy and was therefore, at least in part, a public relations project. The book was nevertheless a milestone. Knox was the first naval historian to go beyond heroic deeds and battles and to demonstrate, in the words of one reviewer, "the interdependence of the navy with every national activity." Although in some respects out of date, it remains a standard work.

Knox was a friendly man who tried never to allow the controversies in which he was involved to degenerate into personal feuds. His papers bear witness to his many acts of personal kindness. Whether it was a seaman AWOL, a widow applying for workmen's compensation, a third-class civil service printer laid off for lack of work, or a former shipmate, Knox was never too busy to take up their causes, sometimes at considerable personal expense.

Knox remained on active duty at the Office of Naval Records through the end of World War II, finally retiring in June 1946. He died at Bethesda (Md.) Naval Hospital.

[The Knox Papers are at the Library of Congress. His journal as commander of the gunboat *Albay* is preserved in the National Archives (Record Group 45, entry 392). A number of Knox's lectures and papers from the Naval War College are in the Naval Historical Collection of the college. Among the best guides to Knox's ideas are his more than thirty articles written for the *Naval Institute Proceedings* between 1913 and 1948. See also his other books, *The Naval Genius of George Washington* (1952); and *Naval Sketches of the War in California* (1939).]

RONALD SPECTOR

KOHLBERG, ALFRED (Jan. 27, 1887–Apr. 7, 1960), importer, publisher, and political organizer, was born in San Francisco, Calif., the son of Manfred Kohlberg, a dry-goods merchant, and Marianne Wurtenberg. His four grandparents, German Jews, immigrated to the United States before the American Civil War. Kohlberg attended Turk Street School, Hamilton Grammar School, and Lowell High School, where he made the track team and acquired two lifelong interests—printing and writing. In 1904 he entered the University of California at Berkeley, working part-time as a reporter for Oakland newspapers and the *Daily Californian*, but his college education ended abruptly during the great San Francisco earthquake and fire of April 1906, in which his father's shop was destroyed. Kohlberg took charge of an emergency printing plant; this first business venture lasted two years. In 1908 he sold the shop and began selling fancy dry goods for his father. He traveled extensively in California and added Dallas, Tex., to his territory in 1910 after meeting a Texan, Selma Bachrach, whom he married on July 26, 1911. They had one son.

Kohlberg made the first of many trips to the Orient in 1916. By then he had become a western states representative, dealing in silks and laces, for a number of New York firms. Handkerchiefs eventually became his chief product. Made of Irish linen purchased in Belfast and shipped to China, they were embroidered by Chinese women from designs created in the United States. Kohlberg's wife died in 1919, and two years later he married a former employee, Charlotte Albrecht. They had four children and were divorced in 1932. The following year he married Jane Myers Rossen.

Until the Sino-Japanese war, Kohlberg remained an obscure, if well-traveled, businessman whose enterprises took him to Japan, Iran, France, Switzerland, and the United Kingdom, as well as to China. At first Kohlberg accepted Japan's reasons for its Manchurian occupation, but he later reacted strongly to Japanese aggression, taking an active role in the American Bureau for Medical Aid to China (ABMAC), a member of United China Relief.

A licensed pilot, Kohlberg volunteered in 1940 to fly for the Royal Canadian Air Force. Rejected because of his age, he offered his services as a suicide pilot before settling, in 1942, for flying briefly with the Civil Air Patrol on antisubmarine missions over the Gulf of Mexico. During a trip to

China in 1943, Kohlberg decided that charges of graft and corruption in the Chinese army medical services were either untrue or exaggerated. He wanted those responsible for the reports recalled, and when they were not, he resigned from ABMAC at the end of 1943.

In 1944 Kohlberg began to believe "that the lies about the Chinese Government and Army were Communist propaganda; and that the main source for spreading them in this country was the Institute of Pacific Relations" ("Kohlberg Affidavit"). His vendetta against the Institute of Pacific Relations (IPR), a research organization formed in 1925 to foster American understanding of Asia, launched a lifelong crusade against communism in general and Chinese communism in particular. Frequenting the New York Public Library several blocks from his Manhattan office, he read articles on the Chinese military and political situation in some IPR publications and compared them to articles from two Communist publications. Then he put together an eighty-eight-page document of clippings and comments and, in an "open letter" (which later became a Kohlberg trademark), called on IPR trustees in November 1944 to "fire all the Reds, because the truth is not in them." An IPR committee rejected the charges, but Kohlberg demanded an impartial investigation, sued to obtain the group's mailing lists, and publicized his case widely to fellow members before finally losing a proxy fight in 1947 (1,163 votes to 63) and resigning.

In 1946 he helped organize the American China Policy Association, which steadfastly supported the Nationalist regime of Chiang Kai-shek. He served first as vice-president and later as chairman of the board. Also in 1946 he started *Plain Talk*, a journal that merged with *The Freeman* in 1950. He also contributed to the founding of *Counterattack*, a newsletter of "facts to combat Communism." In 1948 he helped initiate the American Jewish League Against Communism and in 1950 joined the Joint Committee Against Communism, a group that spurred the blacklisting of radio and television people in the 1950's. Kohlberg's charges against the IPR resurfaced early in 1950 with Senator Joseph R. McCarthy's sensational accusations of espionage and Communist subversion in government. Although McCarthy apparently did not consult him prior to publication of the charges, Kohlberg soon furnished McCarthy with his own IPR materials, which then received national publicity during two consecutive Senate investigations.

Jane Myers Kohlberg died in 1951, and in June 1952 Kohlberg married Ida Jolles, a widow whom he had met in China in 1941. Kohlberg was now at the peak of his reputation as "the China Lobby man." He supported Senator Robert A. Taft of Ohio for the Republican presidential nomination that year. He disliked the Eisenhower administration's foreign policy and in 1955, with others, formed the Council Against Communist Aggression, which called on the government to "exterminate the Communist conspiracy in the United States," "withdraw recognition from the Soviet Union and its satellites," "employ all measures to sap the economic strength of the Communist World," and return American policies to those of George Washington, the Monroe Doctrine, and the Open Door.

In 1956 he got into a controversy with the Treasury Department, which denied him a permit to import more than 600,000 Chinese handkerchiefs suspected, ironically, of being made in the People's Republic of China and not, as Kohlberg had insisted, in Hong Kong. Heart attacks in 1954 and 1955 somewhat curtailed his organizational activities, but Kohlberg kept up a prodigious correspondence, bombarding heads of state, government officials, celebrities, and newspaper editors with long and importunate letters about international affairs. He contributed occasional articles on communism to *New Leader* and the pro-Nationalist *China Monthly*. He circulated a 1959 exchange with Egypt's President Gamal Abdel Nassar to members of the Eighty-sixth Congress. One of his last letters, dated Feb. 29, 1960, implored Secretary of State Christian Herter to deny a magazine report that Herter and others had encouraged Eisenhower to get Chiang Kai-shek to resign in order to make Formosa a United Nations protectorate and admit the People's Republic of China to the United Nations. Six weeks later Kohlberg died in New York City.

As a friend observed, Kohlberg saw things in black and white. He argued politics in high-sounding principles, without bitterness, in a courteous though blunt manner. He was simplistic but subtly sarcastic and dryly humorous. A political gadfly, he seemed to enjoy his notoriety as "the China Lobby man." "His basic aim was to show the evil of Communism and the threat it posed to free men everywhere," wrote his biographer Joseph Keeley. "Once he became aware of this evil his sole aim in life was its destruction," a judgment that encapsulates this indefatigable cold-warrior. Kohlberg left a large bequest to the American Bureau for Medical Aid to China that made possible the Alfred Kohlberg Memorial Research Laboratory on Taiwan, dedicated in 1963.

[Kohlberg's papers are at the Hoover Institution Archives, Stanford University, but will not be available for research until after May 1, 1991. An unpublished autobiography, "To My Grandchildren," has been used by Joseph Keeley in *The China Lobby Man* (1969), and John N. Thomas, *The Institute of Pacific Relations: Asian Scholars and American Politics* (1974), contains a chapter on Kohlberg. The "Kohlberg Affidavit," an important source of autobiographical material, is found in U.S. Senate, Judiciary Subcommittee, Hearings, *Insitute of Pacific Relations,* 82nd Congress, 2d session, pt. 14, pp. 4934–4944.

Ross Y. Koen, *The China Lobby in American Politics* (1960; repr. 1974), is useful; and Stanley D. Bachrack, *The Committee of One Million: "China Lobby" Politics, 1953–1971* (1976), adds what is known about Kohlberg's minor ties to this post–Korean War "China Lobby" group. A sensational two-part series on the "China Lobby" in *The Reporter,* Apr. 15 and 29, 1952, should be read discerningly. See also *American Legion,* July 1952; the obituary in the *New York Times,* Apr. 8, 1960; and "An Affectionate Farewell to Alfred Kohlberg," *National Review,* Apr. 23, 1960.]

STANLEY D. BACHRACK

KORNGOLD, ERICH WOLFGANG (May 29, 1897–Nov. 29, 1957), composer, was born in Brünn, Austria (now Brno, Czechoslovakia), the son of Julius Korngold, a music critic, and Josefine Witrofsky. In 1901 the family moved to Vienna. Korngold received his earliest musical training from his father and began to compose at the age of nine. A year later he played one of his piano pieces for Gustav Mahler, who (according to Alma Mahler) listened attentively. "A genius!" he exclaimed, suggesting the Austrian composer Alexander von Zemlinsky as a teacher. Korngold subsequently studied with Robert Fuchs, Hermann Grädener, and Karl Weigl.

Korngold attracted serious attention with the publication of a piano trio written when he was thirteen. So astonishing was the work's craftsmanship that rumors spread attributing it to Richard Strauss or another well-known composer. Facetiously dubbed "L'affaire Korngold," the controversy was given further impetus with the production of Korngold's pantomime *Der*

Schneemann at the Vienna Opera on Oct. 4, 1910. The following year Arthur Nikisch, director of the Gewandhaus Concerts in Leipzig, commissioned Korngold to write an orchestral overture.

By then, the Korngold legend, commingling fantasy and fact, had become a sensation. Ernest Newman, an otherwise sober-minded critic, equated Korngold with Mozart—a comparison helped by the fact that Korngold's father had named him Wolfgang after Mozart. "Why does Mozart spontaneously lisp music in the simple idiom of his own day," Newman asked rhetorically, "while Korngold lisps in the complex idiom of his?" Newman described Korngold's music as "the spontaneous product of a most subtly organized brain that embraces practically all we know and feel today in the way of harmonic relation." The German critic Paul Bekker went one step further, suggesting that Korngold anticipated the music of the future, and the American critic Philip Hale wondered, "If Master Korngold could make such a noise at fourteen, what will he not do when he is twenty-eight?"

These judgments are perplexing; Korngold's pieces written in adolescence seem no more remarkable than the works of any gifted thirteen-year-old. Neither a Mozart nor a modernistic noisemaker, he never deviated from the basic principles of tonality throughout his career. Nevertheless, Korngold's success was impressive. He was barely eighteen when his two one-act operas, *Der Ring des Polykrates* and *Violanta*, were produced in Munich under the direction of Bruno Walter; Korngold himself conducted them at the Vienna Opera the following year. By 1920 he had filled several engagements at the Hamburg City Theater and had appeared as a pianist in programs of his own works.

On Dec. 4, 1920, Korngold's opera *Die tote Stadt* was produced simultaneously in Hamburg and Cologne; a Vienna performance followed shortly afterward, with the soprano Maria Jeritza in the leading role. The libretto, based on Georges Rodenbach's novel *Bruges-la-Morte*, was written by the composer's father, under the pseudonym Paul Schott. The enormously successful opera was performed throughout Europe and was produced at the Metropolitan Opera House in New York City on Nov. 19, 1921, again with Jeritza in the leading role. (*Die tote Stadt* was revived by the New York City Opera in 1975, in a spectacular production in which the techniques of film montage were used with great effect. The production was praised for its originality, but the score was almost unanimously condemned as stylistically derivative and dramatically weak.)

On Apr. 30, 1924, Korngold married Luise von Sonnenthal. They had two children. His next opera, *Das Wunder der Heliane* (1928), was produced in Hamburg and Vienna with almost excessive lavishness but little success. Two years later he became professor at the Wiener Staatsakademie für Musik.

In 1934 Korngold interrupted work on a new opera to follow the director Max Reinhardt to Hollywood as musical arranger for Reinhardt's film version of *A Midsummer Night's Dream.* Hired by Warner Brothers to compose music for the film *Give Us This Night* (1936), Korngold soon became one of the most successful Hollywood composers. His romantic flair suited the medium perfectly. Not satisfied merely with writing background music, he organized his scores in the manner of symphonic suites. The superiority of his craft was unmistakable, and the suites that he arranged from his film scores became independently popular through numerous recordings. His scores for *Anthony Adverse* (1936) and *The Adventures of Robin Hood* (1938) received Academy Awards. His other credits included *The Prince and the Pauper* (1937), *Another Dawn* (1937), *Juarez* (1939), *The Private Lives of Elizabeth and Essex* (1939), *The Sea Hawk* (1940), *The Sea Wolf* (1941), *King's Row* (1942), *The Constant Nymph* (1943), *Between Two Worlds* (1944), *Of Human Bondage* (1946), *Deception* (1946), and *Escape Me Never* (1947). His last opera, *Die Kathrin,* was given its premiere in October 1939 in Stockholm after its first performance in Vienna, scheduled for the spring of 1938, had been canceled by the invading Nazis.

Korngold became an American citizen in February 1943. On Feb. 15, 1947, his Violin Concerto in D Major, commissioned by Jascha Heifetz, was first performed, in St. Louis. Once hailed as the twentieth-century Mozart, Korngold had lived to see the popularity of his music succumb to the vicissitudes of time and taste. "In this Concerto," Irving Kolodin worte in the *Saturday Review of Literature,* "there was more corn than gold." He died in Hollywood, Calif.

[On Korngold's life and work, see Rudolf S. Hoffmann, *Erich Wolfgang Korngold* (1922), in German; Julius Korngold's brief monograph, published in English as *Child Prodigy* (1942); Irwin Sonenfield, "Korngold's *Die tote Stadt,*" *Musician,* Nov. 1948; Royal S. Brown, "The Korngold Era," *High Fidelity,* Feb. 1973; Ann M. Lingg, "Master of Melody," *Opera*

News, Apr. 5, 1975; and Andrew Porter, "A Tale of Two Cities," *New Yorker,* Apr. 14, 1975.]
                                          NICOLAS SLONIMSKY

KROEBER, ALFRED LOUIS (June 11, 1876–Oct. 5, 1960), anthropologist, was born in Hoboken, N.J., the son of Florence Martin Kroeber, a prosperous importer, and Johanna Muller, both of whom had been born in Germany. The family soon moved to New York City and became part of a cultivated, Jewish upper-middle-class set, complete with servants, private tutors and schools, and a German-derived, liberal bourgeois culture. Great emphasis was placed on aesthetic, intellectual, and professional attainment, and there was a strong respect for learning.

Kroeber was educated by Hans Bamberger, a private tutor, before attending the Ethical Culture School, Sach's Collegiate Institute, and the Gunnery, a private boarding school in Connecticut. He entered Columbia College in 1892, receiving the B.A. in 1896, the M.A. in English in 1897, and the Ph.D. in anthropology (under Franz Boas) in 1901. He married Henrietta Rothschild in 1906; she died in 1913. On Mar. 26, 1926, he married Theodora Kracaw Brown, a graduate student of anthropology. They had two children.

Kroeber was shy and reserved as a young man. He developed an enduring interest in natural history and facility in four languages. These early enthusiasms, supported by hard work and single-minded purposefulness, maintained Kroeber's consistently successful intellectual and entrepreneurial trajectory. In 1917 undiagnosed Ménière's disease attracted him to psychoanalysis. His brief experience as an analyst temporarily deflected him from anthropology to the private prictice of psychoanalysis (1918–1923).

Kroeber began work in anthropology out of curiosity about Boas' American Indian language seminar in 1896. The work with Eskimo and Chinook native speakers captivated him and led to work with Eskimo language and culture, and to publish material on Eskimo folklore and ethnology. After more courses in anthropology, a three-month field trip to study the Arapaho, Ute, Shoshone, and Bannock, he was committed to a major in anthropology with a minor in psychology. His doctoral dissertation, "Decorative Symbolism of the Arapaho," reflects his earliest intellectual interests as well as the milieu of his youth. In it were fused a taste for "culture," a humanistic orientation, an aesthetic sensibility, the natural-history approach to a "collection," and the charm of an exotic grammar contained within yet another symbolic language.

Kroeber's professional career began at the University of California at Berkeley in 1901. The first member of the anthropology department, he remained there until his retirement in 1946. Phoebe A. Hearst, a university regent, provided the support, patronage, and motive for the establishment of a museum and department of anthropology in 1901. They were the material basis for Kroeber's professional career and the foundation on which he built the department. Through his staffing and research policies, he directed an anthropological empire covering the western half of the United States.

Often regarded as the dean of American anthropology and as Boas' successor, Kroeber long dominated the discipline that Boas had virtually created in its American version. Although he was outstanding for his intellectual breadth, the large number of his personal students, the magnitude of his scholarly research and publications, and his dominance (after Boas) of a vast portion of the field, he is nevertheless a very difficult figure to assess. He led one of the most important departments and museums of anthropology; and at a time when the discipline was still in its formative stage, with few centers and few competitors of his stature, he was able to direct its concerns, research interests, theoretical orientation, relations with adjacent disciplines, professional training, fieldwork, financial allocations for research, and even the staffing of many important academic and museum positions. His preferences, and decisions, his textbooks, and his research were very influential throughout his professional life and for a time afterward. He possessed distinguished intelligence, personal charm, and powerful character; and his public career was a record of success and honors.

Yet Kroeber was almost a paradox as an anthropologist, standing outside the discipline and quite self-consciously directing it, as might a philosopher and epistemologist not fully immersed in the concerns of anthropology. It is hard to isolate in his work any lasting theoretical contribution to any subdiscipline or even to the general subject matter of anthropology. It is also difficult to point to any general or narrow work that is as intellectually successful as that of such contemporary colleagues as Boas, Robert Lowie, Bronislaw Malinowski, or Edward Sapir. In fact,

it is hard to discover any enduring intellectual achievement, especially in comparison with others then working in sociocultural, linguistic, or archaeological areas.

Kroeber had strong roots in cultural history, literary analysis, and psychoanalysis. He nearly came to operate in these other areas as a professional. These three interests and a statistical orientation, coupled with repeated avowals that anthropology was neither a social science nor a behavioral science nor a science at all, led in a few characteristic directions that are reiterated throughout his more than 700 publications.

Kroeber's major contributions include *Anthropology* (1923), for many years the only available text; the influential *Handbook of the Indians of California* (1925), based on many but very brief fieldwork contacts at a time when increasingly accurate data were still easily collectable; *Cultural and Natural Areas of Native North America* (1939); *Configurations of Culture Growth* (1944); *The Nature of Culture* (1952); and *Style and Civilizations* (1957).

[See Carl L. Alsberg, "Alfred L. Kroeber," in *Essays in Anthropology Presented to A. L. Kroeber* (1936); Dell Hymes, "Alfred Louis Kroeber," *Language*, Jan.–Mar. 1961; Robert F. Heizer, "Alfred Louis Kroeber: 1876–1960," *Man*, June 1961; Ann J. Gibson and J. H. Rowe, "A Bibliography of the Publications of Alfred Louis Kroeber," *American Anthropologist*, Oct. 1961; Julian H. Steward, "Alfred Louis Kroeber 1876–1960," *American Anthropologist*, Oct. 1961; John H. Rowe, "Alfred Louis Kroeber: 1876–1960," *American Antiquity*, Jan. 1962; Ralph L. Beals, "Kroeber, Alfred L.," in *International Encyclopedia of the Social Sciences*, VIII (1968); Theodora Kroeber, *Alfred Kroeber* (1970); and Julian H. Steward, *Alfred Kroeber* (1973).]

HARVEY PITKIN

KYNE, PETER BERNARD (Oct. 12, 1880–Nov. 25, 1957), author, was born in San Francisco, Calif., the son of John Kyne, a farmer and cattle dealer, and Mary Cresham. With the exception of a six-month course at a business college, he received all of his formal education in a one-room country school. He left school at fifteen to work on his father's farm. A year later he took a job as a store clerk in a nearby town. He left this job, which paid $7 a week, for one in a lumber and shipping firm that paid $30 a month. Finding that he liked working as a salesman, he later became a lumber broker.

At the outbreak of the Spanish-American War, Kyne, although not yet eighteen, enlisted in the army. He was assigned to the Fourteenth Infantry and saw action in the Philippines, fighting insurrectionists commanded by Emilio Aguinaldo. This experience and his service in World War I as a captain in the 144th Field Artillery provided material for his war stories.

Kyne was married on Feb. 2, 1910, to Helene Catherine Johnston; they had no children. His first significant publication came in the year of his marriage, when "A Little Matter of Salvage," a story written while he was out of a job and ill with pneumonia, was accepted by the *Saturday Evening Post*. It was the first of more than sixty stories to be published by the *Post*. He then wrote several sea and western stories for *Sunset* magazine and, in 1913, the first of his twenty-five novels, *Three Godfathers*, was published. A dozen of his novels sold well over 100,000 copies each. They included *The Valley of the Giants* (1918), a tale of the California timber region, which was made into a motion picture starring Wallace Reid; *Pride of Palomar* (1921), a story of romance and adventure stressing the "menace" of Japanese immigrants in California; and *Enchanted Hill* (1924), which portrayed life on a ranch in New Mexico.

In 1916, Kyne published *Cappy Ricks*, a collection of stories about a shrewd, waspish, but kindhearted old sea captain who owned a coastal shipping line and a lumber company. Kyne, who had worked around 1905 for a time as a reporter on the *San Francisco Morning Call*, knew the waterfront well. Cappy Ricks, with his mutton-chop whiskers and black string tie, was one of the few complex fictional characters Kyne created. He eventually joined the group of popular characters that included Clarence Budington Kelland's Scattergood Baines and William Hazlett Upson's Alexander Botts. Cappy Ricks, whose favorite pastime was beating his son-in-law, Matt Peaslee, in business deals, was modeled, to a large extent, on Captain Robert Dollar, a chin-whiskered Scotsman who founded the Dollar Steamship Lines and owned extensive western lumber interests. Ricks and his adventures were the subject of two novels, more than fifty short stories, and an unsuccessful play.

Kyne tended to create characters that are radical or national stereotypes based upon the theory, as Carl Bode put it, that "what is pure-bred and Aryan is good and what is hybrid or pigmented is bad." Kyne expressed this racist theory explicitly in *Never the Twain Shall Meet* (1923). For the most part he wrote about people he knew and understood: lumbermen, miners, ranchers, seamen, and businessmen, the last of whom he especially admired. *The Go-Getter* (1922), a tale of a canny businessman, was widely used by commercial organizations as a gospel of successful selling.

Kyne's aim was to reach the largest possible audience, and he was shrewd in tailoring his writing to popular taste. "When an editor buys a story from me for a good price," Kyne wrote, "he expects it to help his circulation. If I sell him a product which is not a good story or a serial with not as much pull as I can give it, I'm not an honest business man."

Kyne had no literary pretensions, and his work was largely ignored by critics. Yet he sometimes wrote with a freshness and sincerity that made one forget the banality of his theme. He also wrote with great speed. ("At times I have written over 13,000 words in twelve hours.") The large income from his writing and from motion pictures was invested heavily (and often unprofitably) in a number of business ventures, including gold mines, oil wells, cattle ranches, and race horses.

In the early 1930's, Kyne's health began to fail. Changes in reading tastes and financial problems in the publishing business also caused difficulties for him. In 1939 a $30,000 judgment was rendered against him for failure to pay income tax. His 1940 novel *Dude Woman* did not sell well, and two novels written in his last years were never published. An occasional short story or magazine article appeared in the late 1940's. Although Kyne traveled widely, he maintained his home in San Francisco, where he died. "I dwell there," he once said, "for much the same reason a cat eats liver. I love it."

[A collection of Kyne's papers, including more than 3,000 letters and more than 100 manuscripts, is deposited at the University of Oregon Library, Eugene. His short works include "From Lumber to 'Literature,' " *America*, Sept. 1917; "I Used to Be a Business Man," *America*, June 1933; and "Turning Point," *America*, Dec. 1948. A bibliography is in *Two San Francisco Writers*, University of Oregon Library Occasional Paper no. 6 (1974). See also C. C. Baldwin, *The Men Who Make Our Novels* (1924); Carl Bode, "Cappy Ricks and the Monk in the Garden," *PMLA*, Mar. 1949; and Arnold Patrick, "Getting Into Six Figures," *Bookman*, Mar. 1925. Obituaries are in the *New York Times* and *San Francisco Examiner*, Nov. 26, 1957.]

WILLIAM McCANN

LA FARGE, CHRISTOPHER GRANT (Dec. 10, 1897–Jan. 5, 1956), novelist, poet, and architect, was born in New York City, the son of the architect C. Grant La Farge and Florence Bayard Lockwood. His grandfather was the painter and glass designer John La Farge, and his younger brother Oliver was the novelist and student of American Indians. Christopher grew up on the family farm near Saunderstown, R.I. Secure in its New England tradition, it was a remarkably energetic and stimulating family. Christopher attended St. Bernard's School in New York and Groton (Mass.) School and entered Harvard in 1915. His studies were mainly literary and architectural. He helped edit the *Advocate* and *Monthly* and wrote for amateur theatricals. He took reserve officer's training at Plattsburg, N.Y., in 1916 and again in 1918, when he was commissioned second lieutenant. After four months he was discharged (December 1918). He graduated from Harvard with the B.A. in 1920 and took a B.S. from the School of Architecture at the University of Pennsylvania in 1923. In June of that year he married Louisa Ruth Hoar, daughter of Congressman Rockwood Hoar of Massachusetts. They had two children.

La Farge began his career as a designer with the noted New York City firm of McKim, Mead, and White, where he remained from 1924 to 1931. He became a skillful watercolorist, exhibiting his work in New York at the Ferargil Gallery in 1930 and the Wildenstein Gallery in 1931. After his younger brother Oliver became famous for his studies of the Navajo Indians and his novel *Laughing Boy* (1929), Christopher and his father helped to conceive and set up exhibits at the Exposition of Indian Tribal Arts at the Brooklyn Museum in 1931. That same year he joined his father at La Farge, Warren, and Clark, but the Great Depression soon deprived the firm (now La Farge and Son) of business, and his career as an architect was over.

He decided to become a writer. In 1932 he packed up his family and went to Kent, England, where he began *Hoxie Sells His Acres* (1934), a novel in verse about a man who upsets his community by planning to cut up his Rhode Island farmland and sell it to summer people for building lots. La Farge explained that his purpose was to "make this a comprehensible form as interesting as the novel in prose and more moving." He was quickly recognized as an adept chronicler of his region. He took up residences again in Saunderstown and New York in 1934 and began

contributing stories and poems to such magazines as the *American, Harper's,* and the *Saturday Review of Literature.* His second novel in verse, *Each to the Other* (1939), concerned the marital problems of a father and son. Reviewer William Rose Benét, a friend, observed that "he wrote it out of the compulsion of his own life. . . . In the fundamentals, it is his own story." It was awarded the Benson Silver medal by the Royal Society of Literature, London. In 1940 he issued a volume of verse, *Poems and Portraits,* which reviewers found slight. A group of stories about one family published serially in the *New Yorker* became *The Wilsons* (1941). His first work of conventional prose fiction, it was described as a "wicked and graceful . . . study of American snobbism."

During World War II, La Farge was active on the War Writers' Board. In 1943 *Harper's* magazine sent him to the South Pacific as a war correspondent. "His intention," wrote *Newsweek,* "was to report the war not with named and dated facts, but deliberately in the form of fiction." The ten stories of this series became *East by Southwest* (1944). His play, *Mesa Verde* (1945), was conceived and written as an opera libretto. In it La Farge faithfully reproduces Navajo speech and customs, acknowledging a debt "to my brother Oliver, who first in American literature succeeded in writing of the Indian as a human being instead of an inaccurate symbol." La Farge's wife died in 1945, and on Sept. 2, 1946, he married Violet Amory Loomis, daughter of Boston stockbroker John Austin Amory. They had one son.

La Farge's most successful work was *The Sudden Guest* (1946), another novel in verse. A Book-of-the-Month-Club selection, it sold more than half a million copies. It concerned another Rhode Island landowner, a selfish old woman who recalled the hurricane of 1938 during a similar one in 1944. The "sudden guest" of the title, borrowed from a line in Pushkin, is her awakened conscience. La Farge published seventeen of his best short stories, with prefatory comments, in *All Sorts and Kinds* (1949). His last verse novel, *Beauty for Ashes* (1953), dramatized the effect of a beautiful nineteen-year-old girl on the lives of three men in rural Rhode Island: an architect, a novelist, and a young navy veteran down from Harvard. It was more successful as a narrative than a poem. One reviewer pointed out that its male characters "were but different ages and aspects of the same personality." That personality was essentially the author's own.

La Farge's work was always autobiographical, but that was not a flaw. Widely admired for his careful craftsmanship and convincing dialogue, frequently criticized for conventionality and lack of a dramatic creative energy, La Farge remains a valuable and interesting writer. He was a subtle analyst of the mores of his Rhode Island world, and from first to last his moral theme remained the responsibility of the single individual to his community. He died in Providence.

[Unreprinted articles, poems, and stories published in England, in little magazines, and in alumni journals are collected in the Harvard University Library. Significant manuscripts and letters are held by the American Academy and Institute of Arts and Letters, New York Public Library, University of Buffalo, University of Chicago, and Yale University. For the family history, see Oliver La Farge's reminiscences, *Raw Material* (1945). More information may be found in the obituary in the *New York Times*, Jan. 6, 1956. For brief criticism and interpretation, see *Saturday Review of Literature*, Sept. 13, 1941; John Peale Bishop, *Collected Essays* (1948); *Newsweek*, July 24, 1944; and *New York Herald Tribune Book Review*, Oct. 11, 1953.]

DEAN FLOWER

LAJOIE, NAPOLEON ("LARRY") (Sept. 5, 1875–Feb. 7, 1959), baseball player, was born in Woonsocket, R.I., the son of Jean Baptist Lajoie and Celina Guertin. The Lajoies were French-Canadians who had come to the United States from St. Hyacinthe, Quebec, in October 1865. A carpenter and wood finisher by trade, Lajoie also raised and traded horses. After completing the ninth grade at the Globe Public School in Woonsocket, Napoleon Lajoie worked as a hack driver and played baseball as a catcher for the local amateur club. In 1895, Woonsocket played an exhibition game against a professional team led by Fred Woodcock, a former pitcher for the St. Louis Browns. Lajoie hit safely every time he came to bat, with two of his hits being home runs, a rare feat in baseball's "dead ball" era. On Woodcock's recommendation, Lajoie was signed for $100 a month by Fall River of the New England League. The right-hand-hitting Lajoie combined power at the bat with speed and agility in the field. Batting .429 in his first year in professional baseball, he led Fall River to the New England League championship in 1896. He was sold to the Philadelphia Phillies, along with outfielder Phil Geier, for $1,500 in August 1896. Joining the Phillies on August 12, Lajoie played the last thirty-nine games of the major league season at first base. The next year, he played first base, third base, and the outfield for the Phillies. George Tweedy Stallings made Lajoie a second baseman in 1898 in order to take full advantage of his fielding prowess. By all accounts, Lajoie was perhaps baseball's finest fielding second baseman. "What a ballplayer that man was!" Tommy Leach of the Pittsburgh Pirates recalled. "Every play he made was executed so gracefully that it looked like it was the easiest thing in the world." A hard hitter, Lajoie made stinging line drives that were the terror of opposing fielders.

In 1901, Lajoie jumped the Phillies and signed on with Connie Mack's American League Philadelphia Athletics at a salary of $4,000 per year. It was $1,600 more than his National League salary and made him one of the highest-paid baseball players of his era. Lajoie established himself as the premier star of the new league by leading it in batting with a .426 average (becoming one of only eight men in baseball history to hit .400 for a season), in runs batted in (125), and in home runs (14). The Phillies obtained a court injunction forbidding Lajoie to play in Pennsylvania for any team other than the Phillies. The Athletics promptly traded him to the Cleveland Blues in 1902, where he was given a four-year contract at $7,500 per year. As a result of that trade, Lajoie was cited for contempt of court but was subsequently purged of contempt when the National and American Leagues agreed to mutual recognition in 1903. With Cleveland, Lajoie led the American League in batting in 1902 (.378), 1903 (.344), and 1904 (.376). After the 1904 season, Lajoie was named manager of the Cleveland club, which changed its team name to the Naps in his honor. He missed more than half of the 1905 season when he suffered blood poisoning as the result of a spike wound.

Napoleon Lajoie was married on Sept. 5, 1907. They had no children. Myrtle Lajoie (maiden name unknown) died in 1954.

Lajoie, who enjoyed the sport and economic rewards of baseball, once declared, "I can make $10,000 a year playing baseball, while I couldn't make more than fifty cents a day at anything else." He did not enjoy managing, however, finishing no higher than second in the league standings (1908). After the 1909 season, he gave up managerial responsibilities, feeling that its burdens detracted from his effectiveness as a player.

The most dramatic year of Lajoie's career was 1910, when he battled Ty Cobb for the American

League batting championship down to the final day of the season and became the center of a baseball scandal. The Naps were closing out their season with a doubleheader in St. Louis against the Browns. Cobb was disliked by opposing players, who felt that he deliberately tried to spike them while running the bases. Lajoie, on the other hand, always talking and joking with opposing players, was one of the most popular men in the game. Browns' manager Jack O'Connor ordered his rookie third baseman, John ("Red") Corriden, to play deep on Lajoie, ostensibly as protection against his hard line drives down the third-base line. Lajoie got eight hits in the doubleheader, six of them bunt singles down the third-base line. It was obvious that the Browns were helping Lajoie in his battle with Cobb. An investigation by American League President Ban Johnson absolved Lajoie and Corriden of wrongdoing, but O'Connor and Browns coach Harry Howell were banished from baseball. It was to no avail, though. Lajoie finished the year with a batting average of .3841 to Cobb's .3848.

Toward the end of his career, Lajoie was traded back to the Philadelphia Athletics (1915). After two mediocre years with the team, he retired as an active player at the close of the 1916 season. In 1917, he managed Toronto, leading the team to the International League championship. The next year, he managed Indianapolis of the American Association before quitting baseball for good and going into business.

Lajoie was elected one of the nine charter members of the Baseball Hall of Fame in 1937. His commemorative tablet is the only one in the Hall of Fame to bear the inscription "most graceful." He must rank as one of the best players of baseball's first century. His total of 3,242 career base hits was exceeded by only five other players, his 657 career doubles places him fourth on the all-time list, and his .338 career batting average was equaled or bettered by only sixteen others. He died at Daytona Beach, Fla.

[See John U. Ayotte, "Napoleon Lajoie, New England's Greatest Ball Player," *Yankee,* Apr. 1969; Bob Broeg, *Super Stars of Baseball* (1971); and Lawrence S. Ritter, *The Glory of Their Times* (1966). For Lajoie's career statistics, see *The Baseball Encyclopedia* (1969). Some genealogical information is available at the Library, National Baseball Hall of Fame and Museum, Cooperstown, N.Y. There are obituary notices in the *New York Times* and *St. Louis Post-Dispatch,* Feb. 8, 1959.]

GERALD KURLAND

LANDOWSKA, WANDA ALEKSANDRA (July 5, 1879–Aug. 16, 1959), harpsichordist, pianist, composer, musicologist, writer, and teacher, was born in Warsaw, Poland, the daughter of Marian Landowski, a lawyer, and Ewa Lautenberg, a linguist. The Landowskis were of Jewish ancestry but had converted to Roman Catholicism. Landowska showed pronounced musical gifts at an early age and gave her first public recital, at the piano, at the age of four. She studied under Jan Kleczynski and with the renowned Chopin interpreter Aleksander Michalowski at the Warsaw Conservatory, from which she graduated in 1896. Although her studies included the nineteenth-century repertoire, her inclination was toward the music of Bach, Mozart, Haydn, and Rameau. Astonished at hearing her play Bach so well, the conductor Arthur Nikish nicknamed her "Bacchante." In 1896 she went to Berlin to study composition with Heinrich Urban. Four years later she eloped to Paris with Henri Lew, a Polish journalist, actor, ethnographer, and specialist in Hebrew folklore.

Consumed by her love for early keyboard music, Landowska decided to devote herself to its authentic performance and to reviving the harpsichord, a precursor of the piano that had fallen into disuse. Assisted by her husband, she visited libraries and museums, studying documents and musical instruments. She also met the founders of the Schola Cantorum, Vincent d'Indy, Charles Bordes, and Alexandre Guilmant, as well as musicologists involved in the revival of early music. Performing at first on a small, inadequate reconstruction of a small Pleyel harpsichord, she introduced such music as part of her first piano recital in Paris in 1903. She subsequently commissioned the piano firm of Pleyel to build a harpsichord suitable for playing not only early sixteenth-century music, but also all keyboard music written before the nineteenth century, especially the works of Bach. The plan was devised after Landowska and the chief engineer of Pleyel had carefully studied keyboard instruments preserved in European museums. The first two-manual, concert-size Pleyel harpsichord was completed in 1912. It had four sets of strings (two eight-foot, one four-foot, and one sixteen-foot register) as well as a coupler, a lute stop, and a second row of jacks for the upper keyboard. Landowska introduced it at a Bach festival in Breslau later that year.

While the instrument was being built, Landowska devoted much effort to promoting the results of her research on the interpretation of early keyboard music, the performing tradition of which had been distorted or obliterated by romantic pianism. She wrote about the historical fluctuations of styles, the realization of ornaments, the rhythmic particularities of baroque music, the special technique required to play the plucked-string harpsichord, and the manner of applying registration. In 1905 she published "Sur l'interprétation des oeuvres de clavecin de J. S. Bach." Other articles followed and, in 1909, she wrote *La musique ancienne*, in collaboration with her husband.

In 1913 a harpsichord class was created for Landowska at the Hochschule für Musik in Berlin. When World War I began, she and her husband were detained in Germany; in April 1919, Lew was killed in a car accident. Alone and deprived of most of her possessions, Landowska went to Switzerland, where she participated in a performance of Bach's *St. Matthew's Passion*, accompanying recitatives and arias at the harpsichord; it was the first time the harpsichord was used in performances of the Passion since Bach's death. She also gave master classes in Basel and Barcelona before returning to Paris. She then resumed her concert tours and taught privately and at the École Normale de Musique. In 1923, at the invitation of Leopold Stokowski, Landowska came to the United States for the first of several seasons of concert tours, bringing with her four large Pleyel harpsichords. That year she made her first recordings for the Victor Company.

In 1925 Landowska bought a house in St.-Leu-la-Forêt, twelve miles north of Paris, and had a small concert hall built. There she founded the École de Musique Ancienne and in July 1927 inaugurated a series of summer concerts, as soloist and with her students. The performances were attended by musicians, artists, and writers in ever-increasing numbers. In May 1933 she gave this century's first integral performance of Bach's Goldberg Variations on the harpsichord. Other programs were devoted to the music of Couperin, Rameau, Handel, Scarlatti, Mozart, Haydn, and other baroque composers.

Inspired by Landowska's revival of the harpsichord, composers began writing for it. In 1923 Manuel de Falla introduced it in his *Retablo* and soon after composed a concerto for harpsichord and five instruments (1926), dedicated to Landowska. Francis Poulenc attended the premiere and in 1929 dedicated his *Concert Champêtre* for harpsichord and orchestra to her.

Landowska collected an important library that included manuscripts and rare first editions as well as a number of early instruments. But with the German invasion of France in June 1940 she had to abandon her home and school, which were ransacked by the Nazis. She took refuge in Banyuls-sur-Mer. In October 1941 she gave a few concerts in Switzerland, and the following month she sailed for the United States, bringing with her a Pleyel harpsichord secured through a loan from a former student.

On Feb. 21, 1942, Landowska performed the Goldberg Variations in New York City's Town Hall to a tremendous ovation and unprecedented rave reviews. After settling in New York City, she resumed her teaching, recorded for RCA Victor, and concertized. In 1947 she moved to Lakeville, Conn., a country setting that she loved, and at the age of seventy-five completed there the recording of Bach's entire *Well-Tempered Clavier*. This significant achievement was selected in 1977 by the National Academy of Recording Arts and Sciences for its hall of fame as "a work of lasting qualitative and historical significance." Despite her dedication to the harpsichord, Landowska never ceased playing the piano, giving special attention to the manner of transferring to the modern instrument the tonal qualities of the fortepiano of Mozart and Haydn's time.

The manuscripts of most of her own compositions have been lost, but her cadenzas for several Mozart, Haydn, and Handel concertos have been published. In 1953 NBC television taped an interview with her as part of its "Wisdom" series. She died in Lakeville, Conn. Her house, preserved as the Landowska Center, contains her instruments, library, papers, and memorabilia and is also a school at which her teachings are perpetuated.

Only five feet tall, Landowska was a regal stage presence. Her abundant black hair, deep brown eyes, and Hebraic profile were striking. She had a warm, generous, and witty personality and a genuine simplicity. Her artistic convictions, forcefully expressed, have stirred many controversies; yet no one can deny her seminal role in the revival of the harpsichord and its literature, or challenge the technical mastery, authority, and beauty of her interpretations.

[Landowska's *Musique ancienne* (1909) was translated as *Music of the Past* (1924). On her life and work, see Roland Gelatt, *Music Makers* (1953); James Nelson, ed., *Wisdom* (1958); Denise Restout, "Mamusia. Vignettes of Wanda Landowska," *High Fidelity*, Oct. 1960; and Denise Restout, ed., *Landowska on Music* (1964), the primary source, which includes a complete bibliography of her writings. A complete bibliography is in preparation.]

DENISE RESTOUT

LANE, ARTHUR BLISS (June 16, 1894–Aug. 12, 1956), diplomat and author, was born in Bay Ridge, N.Y., the son of James Warren Lane and Eva Metcalf Bliss. The family was quite wealthy, and James Lane controlled a large cotton factor business as well as the machine and armaments factories founded by his wife's father, Eliphalet Williams Bliss. Young Lane was educated at private schools in New York and France and at Yale University, where he received the B.A. in 1916. He immediately accepted an invitation to become secretary to the American ambassador to Italy, Thomas Nelson Page. This was an unpaid appointment, but Lane's private means stood him in good stead. While in Rome he met Cornelia Thayer Baldwin, the daughter of an American physician living in Italy, and they were married in Florence on June 19, 1918. They had one daughter, Margaret Bliss, who died in 1947.

Lane's natural abilities and personal charm soon set him on a steady rise through foreign service ranks. In 1919 he was transferred to the American legation in Warsaw as second secretary, and met Paderewski and other political leaders. He moved to the London embassy in 1920, and the following year served as secretary to the American delegation to the Supreme Allied Council in Paris. After an assignment in Bern, he returned to the United States as assistant to Undersecretary of State Joseph C. Grew.

After this apprenticeship, Lane entered on the first stage of his major diplomatic career, duty in Latin America. In 1924, he was assigned as first secretary of the American embassy in Mexico City, considered a key post in the Western Hemisphere. He returned to Washington to head the Division of Mexican Affairs in 1926 and then was reassigned to Mexico City, this time as counselor of the embassy and chargé d'affaires. Because of his extensive knowledge of Latin America, Lane was chosen to head the American mission to Nicaragua in 1933. At age thirty-nine he was the youngest career minister in the history of the American diplomatic service.

Lane's tenure in Managua was a difficult one, and for the first time he found himself torn between what he saw as his duty to follow State Department directives and his own beliefs. The United States, under the Good Neighbor policy of Franklin Roosevelt and Cordell Hull, was disengaging itself from involvement in the internal affairs of Latin-American countries, a policy with which Lane concurred. Unfortunately, in Nicaragua the democratic government created by the United States proved too weak to stand by itself, and it gave way to the military regime headed by the Somoza family. Lane opposed Somoza, but he acquiesced when Washington made clear that it would accept the new government and not intervene in internal Nicaraguan affairs.

By 1936 Lane felt he had outlived his usefulness in Nicaragua and welcomed reassignment to his other major area of experience, eastern Europe. He served for a year as envoy to Estonia, Latvia, and Lithuania and then as minister to Yugoslavia from 1937 to 1941. During the first part of his Yugoslavian tour, Lane again felt frustrated by State Department directives ordering him to go along with the corrupt regime of the regent, Prince Paul, who was slowly aligning the country with the Axis, because of Paul's supposedly neutral position. Finally, when war broke out in Europe, Lane was allowed to act and backed King Peter in his successful overthrow of the regent. When the Germans invaded Yugoslavia in early 1941, Lane became de facto dean of the Belgrade diplomatic corps and oversaw the complex job of evacuating American and other neutral civilians from the war-ravaged country. He was hampered in much of this work by the State Department's insistence on itemized expense statements and prior clearance for emergency expenditures; in frustration, Lane frequently paid for these items out of his own pocket.

After returning to the United States, Lane toured the country speaking about his experiences in Europe and warning about the dangers of fascism. Although his supervisors in the State Department had approved his speaking and writing engagements, they soon found his candor somewhat embarrassing. Offered a relatively minor mission in Costa Rica, Lane, despite his reluctance to go there, decided to be a good soldier and accept the assignment. In 1942, he became ambassador to Colombia, a more important posting but still far from the major activity of the European war.

Lane's last and most frustrating diplomatic task was in Poland. In September 1944, President Roosevelt nominated Lane as ambassador to the

Polish government-in-exile. By the time Lane finished a six-month briefing in Washington on Polish affairs, Warsaw had been liberated, and the coalition government created at the Yalta Conference was in power. In July 1945, Lane was named American ambassador to this new Polish government, with a specific charge to register Soviet and Polish compliance with the agreement calling for free elections.

Instead of compliance, Lane found massive communist fraud and terrorism, and his reports formed the basis for American protests to the Russians. When the United States did not back its diplomatic notes with more forceful action, Lane asked to be recalled and resigned from the Foreign Service after more than three decades of service.

In the last years of his life, Lane became a leading member of the anticommunist movement. He published *I Saw Poland Betrayed* (1948) and wrote and spoke widely on the communist threat. He joined numerous anticommunist groups and in 1952 wrote the Republican party plank calling for the liberation of the peoples of eastern Europe from communist domination. That same year he campaigned for Senator Joseph R. McCarthy, lauding him for pointing out "treason and subversion in government." An opponent of containment, he grew increasingly bitter about American foreign policy in his last years. He died in New York City.

[The Lane Papers are in Yale University Library. On Lane, see Vladimir Petrov, *A Study in Diplomacy* (1971); and *Vital Speeches*, June 15, 1947.]
MELVIN I. UROFSKY

LANGER, WILLIAM (Sept. 30, 1886–Nov. 8, 1959), senator from North Dakota, was born on a farm near Everest, N. Dak., the son of Frank J. Langer, a prosperous homesteader, and Mary Weber. Langer's father increased his landholdings and became director of the local bank and insurance company. After attending rural schools, Langer completed work at the University of North Dakota Law School in 1906. Unable to practice law in his native state until he was twenty-one years of age, Langer entered Columbia University in New York City as a freshman. He received his B.A. in 1910, being valedictorian and president of his class.

Langer returned to North Dakota only after a harrowing experience in Mexico, where he was captured and almost killed by revolutionaries while inspecting landholdings in which he had speculated—and lost—some $30,000 borrowed from his father. Settling in Mandan, he was soon appointed assistant state's attorney for Morton County. He made a statewide reputation suing the Northern Pacific Railroad and other major corporations for back taxes. After being elected state's attorney for the county in 1914, he won the support of temperance organizations for his prosecution of prominent businessmen and others as violators of state vice and prohibition laws. In 1916, with the endorsement of the newly organized Nonpartisan League, a neo-Populist political faction, he was elected attorney general on the Republican ticket. He enforced prohibition and blue laws throughout North Dakota, at one point taking a town telephone exchange at gunpoint to prevent violators from being warned of an impending raid. But Langer soon quarreled with the Nonpartisan League leadership. He ran against the league's candidate in the Republican gubernatorial primary in 1920 but was defeated. Langer then returned to an increasingly lucrative private law practice. He had married Lydia Cady, the daughter of a prominent New York architect, whom he met while a student at Columbia University, on Feb. 26, 1918. They had four daughters.

Langer ran for office only once in the 1920's, a losing effort to regain the office of attorney general in 1928. But he was politically active, working for Senator Robert M. La Follette's third-party presidential ticket in 1924.

In 1932 Langer rejoined the Nonpartisan League as attorney and campaign manager. Endorsed by the league in 1933, he secured the Republican nomination for governor. He swept to victory in a campaign against the grain-trade monopoly without once mentioning President Herbert Hoover. In office Langer ignored league leaders, attacked President Franklin D. Roosevelt's agricultural program, and declared an embargo on North Dakota wheat in an effort to push up prices. The state's durum wheat farmers supported the embargo and his moratorium on the foreclosure of farm mortgages.

Langer's political strength was therefore growing when he was indicted by a federal grand jury in May 1934. The charge was soliciting funds from federal employees for personal and political gain; Langer had allegedly coerced government workers to purchase subscriptions to a Nonpartisan League newspaper. He was found guilty and removed from office. He appealed the verdict, and after a second trial ended in a hung jury, he was found not guilty in a third trial. By now the Nonpartisan League was split into pro- and anti-Langer factions. But he had enough support to win the race for governor in 1937.

His second term in the statehouse was marked by intensive efforts to win election to the U.S. Senate. In 1938 he unsuccessfully challenged incumbent Senator Gerald Nye both in the Republican primary and as an independent in the general election. In 1939 he challenged the other Republican senator, Lynn Frazier. With the support of a faction of the Nonpartisan League he won the Republican nomination and in 1940 triumphed in a close election.

In an unprecedented action Langer's political enemies in North Dakota petitioned the Senate Committee on Elections and Privileges, charging that he was guilty of vote fraud, corruption, income-tax evasion, soliciting false endorsements, and making an illicit deal with the Northern Pacific Railroad by lowering its assessment in return for the purchase of worthless land stock. An extensive senatorial investigation filled four thousand pages of congressional reports. The committee majority found a pattern of "continuous, contemptuous and shameful disregard for public duty." The minority insisted that the evidence was hearsay and inconclusive. After an extensive Senate debate, the committee was overruled 52 to 30, and Langer retained his seat.

Langer never again faced a serious challenge to his position; he was reelected overwhelmingly in 1946 and carried every county in the state in his 1952 race. In 1958, too ill to return home to campaign, he sent only a television clip to local stations but again carried every county.

Langer's popularity as a senator can be attributed to his hard work for constituents—"Write to Bill Langer" was a campaign theme—and to his effective advocacy of agrarian and North Dakota interests in Washington. He was a strong supporter of liberal legislation throughout the war and postwar period, endorsing a higher minimum wage, extending Social Security benefits, federal aid to education, rigid price supports for agricultural products, and a wide variety of social welfare initiatives. He championed higher pensions for older Americans and increased pay for postal workers and servicemen. Responding to the charge that he was "unpredictable," he told a reporter in 1954, "I'm the most predictable damn fellow in the Senate; I'm always on the side of the underdog." Indeed,

the rangy, rumpled, hard-working senator enjoyed confronting his enemies. His speeches were filled with derogatory images: "monsters," "cringing mongrel servants of the plutocrats," "pirates," and "bandits" opposed his programs and his candidacy.

But if Langer won support at home for his domestic programs, he gained national attention because of his fervent isolationism. In 1941 he opposed lend-lease to Great Britain. After the war he strenuously attacked the Marshall Plan, the Truman Doctrine, and other mutual aid programs as "giveaways" of dollars that were needed for social programs in the United States. He lamented the loss of congressional influence in foreign affairs and assailed presidents Roosevelt, Harry S. Truman, and Dwight D. Eisenhower for centralizing foreign policy-making in the White House. He was an early supporter of the Bricker amendment, which sought to subject executive agreements to congressional ratification. Langer voted against joining the United Nations, insisting that it was unrealistic, a "tissue paper shield" against the international problems of the future. He claimed that moneyed interests dictated promotions and influenced policy in the State Department. He reserved special animus for Great Britain. On Dec. 31, 1951, he sent a telegram to the Old North Church in Boston asking that lanterns be lit to warn of the visit of Winston Churchill, who represented, he said, as much of a threat to America as the Redcoats had in Paul Revere's day. For midwestern Populists like Langer who had long feared international bankers, Anglophobia was a natural posture. One of his lectures was entitled "England: Enemy of Liberty."

Langer's isolationism was influenced perhaps by the German-American constituency he represented; he accused Roosevelt and Churchill of betraying both the Atlantic Charter and President Woodrow Wilson's earlier dream of a peace without victory when they insisted on a doctrine of harsh unconditional surrender against Germany. But it was more than ethnic isolationism that informed his approach. He was from an insular, agricultural community that had not fully shared in the affluence that the war and postwar years brought to most of the nation. His American Recovery Program would distribute money to needy Americans and not to Europeans, potential competitors, and undependable allies. He was not an advocate of military spending and consistently called for negotiated disarmament with the Soviet

Union. He was not a virulent anti-Communist and not an "Asia First" isolationist. He opposed both the North Atlantic Treaty Organization and the Southeast Asia Treaty Organization as paper pacts that might provoke the Soviet Union while offering little protection. His was an older isolationist ideology, rooted in the hostility felt by liberal spokesmen of less privileged groups for international involvements of any kind. He always insisted that he was for the underdog; he cheered Indian efforts to win independence from Britain and supported the creation of a Jewish homeland in Palestine. In foreign policy as in domestic affairs, he was an irrepressible and unforgettable maverick who could not be dismissed easily. He had achieved considerable senatorial seniority (serving as chairman of the Senate Judiciary Committee in 1953–1954) by the time he died in Washington, D.C.

[See the William Langer Papers, Orin G. Libby Historical Manuscripts Collection, Chester Fritz Library, University of North Dakota, Grand Forks. Also useful are two other manuscript collections at the University of North Dakota: the William Lemke Papers and the correspondence of Ole H. Olson for 1934–1935. Langer wrote a short history, *The Nonpartisan League: Its Birth, Activities and Leaders* (1920). A number of senatorial colleagues discussed his career in *William Langer: Late a Senator From North Dakota, Memorial Addresses Delivered in Congress* (1960). The best scholarly study is Glenn H. Smith, "Senator William Langer: A Study in Isolationism" (Ph.D. diss., University of Iowa, 1968). Two other unpublished works are useful: Gary L. Hjalmervik, "William Langer's First Administration (1932–1934)" (master's thesis, University of North Dakota, 1966), and Robert M. Horne, "The Controversy Over the Seating of Senator William Langer: 1940–1942" (master's thesis, University of North Dakota, 1964). A lively contemporary account of Langer is presented in Beverly Smith, "The Most Baffling Man in the Senate," *Saturday Evening Post*. Two studies by Robert Poole Wilkins that present useful background material for assessing Langer's role in the Senate are "The Nonpartisan League and Upper Midwest Isolationism," *Agricultural History*, Apr. 1965; and "The Non-Ethnic Roots of North Dakota Isolationism," *Nebraska History*, Sept. 1963.]

DAVID H. BENNETT

LANGFORD, SAMUEL (Mar. 4, 1883–Jan. 12, 1956), boxer, was born on a farm in Weymouth Falls, Nova Scotia, the third son of Robert Langford, a river driver, and Priscilla Robart. His parents were Canadian citizens.

Langford never attended school, and he ran away on a lumber schooner to Boston in 1899. After working as a stevedore and drifting around, he became a janitor at Joe Woodman's Lenox Athletic Club, a Boston boxing gymnasium. He went from janitor to sparring partner, to amateur boxer, and finally made his successful professional debut against Jack McVickar in January 1902. He quickly proved his extraordinary talent by defeating lightweight champion Joe Gans in an "overweight for the class" bout in 1903. The victory over Gans and a hard-fought draw with world welterweight champion Joe Walcott in a nontitle fight in 1904 established Langford as a prime contender. Indeed, his rise to prominence was so spectacular that he frightened off many potential adversaries and often was forced to fight opponents much heavier than himself. He was married to Martha Burell Langford on Dec. 7, 1904. They had one daughter.

Langford's best-known fight was a fifteen-round decision he lost to future heavyweight champion Jack Johnson at Chelsea, Mass., in 1906. Langford, who was badly outweighed, was soundly defeated, but his astute manager, Joe Woodman, spread the story that Langford had knocked Johnson down and been robbed of the decision. When the genial Langford became a ring favorite in England, this false account received wide currency and was frequently published. Johnson never did give Langford a rematch despite much public clamor for the match after Johnson became champion. Langford remained bitter toward Johnson throughout his life, claiming ironically that Johnson, who was also black, had "drawn the color line on him."

Langford made several appearances in England between 1907 and 1913, including a victory over the English heavyweight champion Ian Haig. His best-known English fight was with Bill Lang, which was one of the first occasions in which a fight was a "society affair," attended by both men and women. In an effort to get matches, Langford fought in England, France, Australia, New Zealand, Canada, Mexico, Panama, and Argentina. He would fight his way across the United States, stopping in any town in which he could arrange a bout. To get a match he was often forced to "carry" an opponent, and frequently he bet his share of the gate on himself.

Among the most memorable of Langford's many fights was a series of epic battles with Joe Jeannette, Harry Wills, and Sam McVey, other topflight black heavyweights of the time. At the turn of the century talented black fighters had great difficulty in obtaining matches with white opponents and consequently fought one another frequently. Of these black fighters, Langford was the smallest in size and greatest in ability.

Langford remained a top-rated heavyweight until 1917, when he sustained eye damage in a fight with Fred Fulton. Despite several operations and a rapid decline in his prowess, he continued fighting until 1928. His last major triumph was a victory in 1923 over the Spanish heavyweight champion Andre Balsas in Mexico. It is said that he was virtually blind at this time. Joe Woodman, his lifelong manager and friend, quit in 1919 after unsuccessfully pleading with Langford to retire. (Woodman took the standard 25 percent manager's fee but never had a contract with Langford.)

After a futile attempt to run a Boston gymnasium, Langford moved to New York City. As his eyesight continued to fail, he became dependent upon friends and relatives for subsistence. A baseball game for his benefit was held in Yankee Stadium in 1935, and New York Mayor Fiorello La Guardia, hearing of his condition, obtained a position for him on the New York City Hall custodial staff in 1937. By 1942 he was completely blind. In 1944 Al Laney, sportswriter for the *New York Herald Tribune,* discovered him poverty-stricken in Harlem and wrote a moving article about his plight that was given national circulation. This resulted in the creation of a Sam Langford Fund. In 1947 he returned to Boston, where he lived with his daughter, who eventually became his legal guardian. He died in a Cambridge nursing home ten weeks after he was voted into the Boxing Hall of Fame Old Timers Division. His official ring record lists 252 bouts, but he fought well over 600. His ring nickname was the "Boston Tarbaby."

Langford was forced for economic reasons to fight far too often and far too long, with obvious consequences to his health. This sad finale to an outstanding career was not atypical for talented ring sluggers of the early twentieth century. In particular, the great black athletes of this period suffered from racial prejudice during their careers and from a lack of other skills to aid them after retirement. Langford is remembered by boxing writers as "the greatest fighter who never fought for the championship" and, pound for pound, may have been the greatest fighter who ever lived.

[The most valuable account of Langford's career is Nat Fleischer, *Fighting Furies* (1939). A more comprehensive, though occasionally erroneous, treatment of Langford's life may be found in *Ebony,* Apr. 1956. Alexander Young's article in the *Nova Scotia Historical Quarterly,* Sept. 1974, discusses Langford's career and early history in the larger context of the role of the black athlete in Canada.]

WILLIAM DONN ROGOSIN

LANGMUIR, IRVING (Jan. 31, 1881–Aug. 16, 1957), chemist and physicist, was born in Brooklyn, N.Y., the son of Charles Langmuir and Sadie Comings. The elder Langmuir was a traveling insurance man and his mother often accompanied him, leaving Irving and his three brothers, together and separately, with aunts, uncles, and cousins.

Langmuir's interest in science was already evident by the time the family moved to Elmsford, N.Y., when he was four. It stemmed partly from his energetic curiosity and partly from the interest and encouragement of his two older brothers. His parents had no explicit scientific interests, but they conscientiously instilled in their children habits valuable to a future scientist: keeping detailed daily records, financial and personal; making careful observations of the surrounding world and putting them down on paper, often in the form of long letters to other members of the family; analyzing and discussing ideas critically rather than accepting "authority." Of great importance was the belated recognition, when Irving was eleven, that he had extremely poor eyesight. His first pair of spectacles opened up a new universe. He was amazed, for instance, to discover that the blurred greenery on trees was made up of thousands of individual leaves, each with its own distinct shape and structure. Thereafter he never tired of examining the myriad tiny details of the natural world, a penchant that later helped him turn his vigorous outdoor activities (hiking, bicycling, mountain climbing, skiing, skating, skate-sailing, flying) to scientific advantage.

In 1887 the family moved back to Brooklyn, where Langmuir attended public schools until 1892. From 1892 to 1895, his father was in Paris as director of European agencies for the New York Life Insurance Company, and Irving attended boarding schools in the Paris suburbs. He was extremely unhappy because of the rote learning, strict discipline, and poor physical facilities. In the academic year 1895–1896 he was sent to the newly established Chestnut Hill Academy in Philadelphia, where, under the guidance of Frederick Reed, his intellectual, scientific, and outdoor interests were all permitted to flower. In 1896 he entered Pratt Institute's Manual Training High School in Brooklyn, where he earned his diploma in 1899, not long after the untimely death of his father (from pneumonia caught while traveling by sea). Upon graduation from Pratt, he attended Columbia University's School of Mines, receiving the B.S. in metallurgical engineering in 1903.

Langmuir did graduate work at Göttingen, Germany, where his major professor was Walther Nernst. (He was dissatisfied with Nernst, feeling he spared too little time for his students, but his debt to Nernst was great.) Nernst was as much a physicist as a chemist, a combination that appealed to Langmuir. Although interested in theory and basic research, Langmuir also had an eye to practical applications. Here, too, Nernst served as a model. He was not only a superb theoretician and researcher but also an inventor of some note. In fact, the dissertation study that he arbitrarily assigned Langmuir was on his own electric lamp, the Nernst glower. This was a routine piece of research that someone else might have considered pure drudgery, a painstakingly detailed set of manipulations, observations, calculations, and analyses to determine what happened to various gases produced in the presence of a hot platinum filament. But the project fascinated Langmuir, combining as it did aspects of both physics and chemistry, and theoretical as well as practical considerations; and it laid the groundwork for many of his later interests. He received his Ph.D. in 1906, and almost immediately accepted a teaching position at the Stevens Institute of Technology in Hoboken, N.J.

Langmuir's years at Stevens (1906–1909) produced more frustration than satisfaction. He carried a heavy teaching load and worked long hours with little assistance. He felt underappreciated and underpaid, and was able to squeeze in a little time for research only in his last year there. In 1909, he took a summer job at the General Electric Research Laboratory in Schenectady, N.Y., where he was astonished at the freedom allowed the scientists compared with his full-time bondage in the supposedly academic atmosphere at Stevens. Fortunately, Willis R. Whitney, director of the General Electric laboratory, recognized Langmuir's potential and offered him a permanent position with the promise that he would be free to pursue any line of research that pleased him. Langmuir accepted and remained happily at General Electric for the

rest of his working life. Except in wartime, he was never given a specific mission but merely told to "have fun." He did, and the commercial payoff for the company was, and continues to be, enormous. He was made associate director of the lab in 1929. After he retired in 1950, he remained as a consultant.

On Apr. 27, 1912, Langmuir married Marion Mersereau of New York City, whom he had met at a church social. They had no children of their own, but adopted two.

Langmuir was briefly attracted to socialism during his early years in Schenectady, but he voted the straight Republican ticket most of his life. He ran unsuccessfully for the city council in 1935, his only venture into politics; after World War II, however, he lobbied for the international control of atomic energy.

Throughout Langmuir's scientific career, he carried on a diversity of research programs simultaneously. His interests were interrelated and often overlapped; and some ran as continuing or recurrent themes through his life.

Scientists traditionally make their creative contributions in their twenties or thirties; but Langmuir's output remained steady and of high quality into his seventies. It was for work begun late in life—his controversial attempts to modify the weather through such techniques as cloud seeding—that he gained his most widespread celebrity.

At General Electric, Langmuir started out with essentially the same simple apparatus that he had used with Nernst at Göttingen, the electric lamp with its incandescent metal filaments. A light bulb provided a well-defined space that could serve either as a vacuum or as a container for precisely measured quantities of any gas that he cared to study under varying temperatures and pressures. It sufficed to launch him on a multiple branching series of experiments, discoveries, theories, and inventions.

He was the first to discover hydrogen in its atomic form (locked into the inside surface lattices of the lamp, driven there by the searing heat of the tungsten filament). He offered the first clear elucidation of thermionic emission (the flow of electrically charged particles from the hot metals) and space charge (the cloud of charged particles between two electrodes). He was among the first to experiment with, and theorize about, those swarming aggregations of ionized gases now known as plasmas, which possess electrical and magnetic properties so unusual as to be called a "fourth state of matter." Langmuir coined the name "plasma," introduced the concept of electron temperature, and invented a device (the Langmuir probe) for studying it. These early investigations opened the way for important studies in electron physics and astrophysics, and inaugurated the new discipline of magnetohydrodynamics (MHD), crucial in a spectrum of developmental studies ranging from plasma-jet engines to controlled thermonuclear fusion. Langmuir also invented the mercury-condensation vacuum pump, the atomic-hydrogen welding torch, the thoriated tungsten filament, the gas-filled incandescent lamp (hundreds of millions are still bought every year), and a whole family of high-vacuum radio tubes.

During World War I he gave his major attention to the development of submarine-detection devices. His wartime studies in binaural sound led to a series of projects years later with conductor Leopold Stokowski to improve the quality of sound recordings. For a brief period immediately after the war (1919–1921), Langmuir turned his attention to atomic theory. Elaborating on the earlier ideas of G. N. Lewis, he put forth the "octet" theory of atomic structure, which explained a multitude of physical and chemical characteristics of atoms better than any prior model. Some still consider this his crowning intellectual achievement. Its success was short-lived because it failed to account for some of the atom's dynamic, quantum-mechanical aspects.

Meanwhile, Langmuir had resumed his prewar interests, including a fascination with surface chemistry, which he turned into a full-fledged scientific discipline. He was interested not only in the "tops" of things but in all the interfaces where boundaries come together, whether in solids, liquids, or gases. He clarified for the first time the true nature of surface adsorption (using as a tool a method soon known as the Langmuir isotherm) and discovered the existence of monolayers (surface films a single atom or molecule in thickness, with peculiar two-dimensional qualities). It was mainly for these studies that he was awarded the Nobel Prize in chemistry in 1932.

Langmuir enjoyed outdoor activities. He once walked fifty-two miles in a single day, and he climbed the Matterhorn after forty with virtually no preliminary conditioning. From his earliest years in Schenectady he explored the Adirondacks, especially with a rugged friend named John Apperson, with whom he joined forces to preserve the wilderness areas from outside encroachments. Between 1925 and 1930 the Langmuirs bought property at Lake George, where they spent much of their free time over the years. Langmuir made thousands of measurements over these years, studying the "energy budget" of Lake George, just for his own amusement.

Langmuir's interest in weather led to experiments, indoor and outdoor, especially with Vincent J. Schaefer, who was first his assistant, then his full collaborator. During World War II, Langmuir and Schaefer worked on developing generators for laying down protective smoke screens and methods for deicing aircraft wings. This wartime work led to controversial postwar experiments in seeding clouds for purposes of "artificial rainmaking," attempting to change the course of hurricanes (in projects carried out by the Air Force), and inducing large-scale weather periodicities throughout the eastern United States.

Langmuir traveled all over the world during his later years, usually accompanied by his wife, and he was probably more honored abroad than at home. Although he collaborated with, and contributed to the work of, researchers in many nations, his own major work was carried out with small teams of researchers at General Electric. His success encouraged other corporations, as well as governments, to invest large sums of money in basic, undirected scientific research. This was perhaps his greatest contribution.

Langmuir underwent an operation for cancer of the large intestine in 1939, but he remained active until his death eighteen years later in Woods Hole, Mass.

[See *The Collected Works of Irving Langmuir*, C. Guy Suits, 12 vols. (1962); and his *Phenomena, Atoms and Molecules* (1950). The Langmuir Papers are in the Library of Congress. The only existing book-length biography is Albert Rosenfeld, *The Quintessence of Irving Langmuir*, originally included in vol. XII of the *Collected Works* but since published separately as *Men of Physics: Irving Langmuir* (1966).]

ALBERT ROSENFELD

LARDNER, JOHN ABBOTT (May 4, 1912–Mar. 24, 1960), journalist, was born in Chicago, Ill., the son of the writer Ringgold (Ring) Wilmer Lardner and Ellis Abbott. Both parents came from prosperous small-town Middle West families. When John was four, the Lardners moved to Greenwich, Conn., and soon thereafter to Great Neck, Long Island. John attended private school in Great Neck and then Phillips Academy at Andover, Mass. While still a boy, he had demonstrated the interest in sports and the wit that would mark his later writing. A family friend and neighbor, the columnist Franklin P. Adams, published in his column the ten-year-old's first printed work, which was, typically, about sports:

> Babe Ruth and old Jack Dempsey,
> Both sultans of the swat;
> One hits where other people are,
> The other where they're not.

Ironically, thirty-eight years later, John Lardner suffered a fatal heart attack while writing an appreciation of Adams, who had died the day before.

Although he had already decided on a career in journalism, Lardner acceded to the urging of his parents and entered Harvard College in 1929. He remained only a year before leaving for Paris, where he studied briefly at the Sorbonne and then spent a few months working on the European edition of the *New York Herald Tribune*. When he returned to New York in 1931, he found a job as a reporter with the *Herald Tribune*. For the next two-and-a-half years he wrote general news stories for the city desk and reviewed books on sports for the Sunday book section. Lardner left the *Herald Tribune* to concentrate on sports by writing a syndicated column for the North American Newspaper Alliance (NANA), a position he held until 1948.

On Sept. 14, 1938, Lardner married Hazel Cannan Hairston, a reporter. To support his family, which eventually included three children, he began writing sports articles for magazines. In 1939 he took on a column for *Newsweek* called "Sport Week." But when World War II broke out in Europe, Lardner requested a foreign assignment. Two months after Pearl Harbor, *Newsweek* sent him overseas as a war correspondent; his column, "Lardner Goes to the Wars," appeared throughout the war datelined Australia, the South Pacific, North Africa, Italy, and finally Iwo Jima and Okinawa. At the same time he also wrote stories for newspapers syndicated by NANA and longer magazine articles for the *Saturday Evening Post* and the *New Yorker*, which were published in book form as *Southwest Passage: The Yanks in the Pacific* (1943). The Lardner sons seemed to share a family characteristic of bravery. A fellow journalist described the

nearsighted Lardner as a man "who walked toward the bomb flashes in order to see better." Two of his brothers were less lucky: James died fighting for the Loyalists in the Spanish civil war, and David was killed during World War II while working as a war correspondent for the *New Yorker*.

After World War II Lardner's work was much in demand, and in 1948 he dropped his syndicated sports column and began writing exclusively for magazines. Although sports remained a special love, his interests were diverse. Lardner's articles ranged from the war, to an analysis of the Lindbergh legend, to a history of drinking in America, on which he was working when he died. His material was published by twenty magazines during the postwar years, and it also appeared in three collected sets of essays: *It Beats Working* (1947), *White Hopes and Other Tigers* (1951), and *Strong Cigars and Lovely Women* (1951). In 1952 Lardner initiated a feature page in *Look* called "John Lardner's New York," which gave him the scope to write on varied subjects, although most of the articles discussed the theater. A bout with tuberculosis forced him to drop this new venture by the end of the year. At that point Lardner changed his *Newsweek* column from "Sport Week" to "Lardner's Week," thus enabling him to extend the range of his interests. In 1958, when he began to fear a loss of mobility due to an advancing case of multiple sclerosis, he decided to concentrate on television criticism in a new *New Yorker* column called "The Air."

By the late 1950's Lardner had achieved a considerable reputation. His peers considered him a fastidious writer with a sophisticated sense of humor. His prose was "sinewy and spare. . . and moved in lean brisk tempos" yet left "a curious impression of belonging to a richly romantic past." One journalist observed that Lardner had a great deal of "that fine, old-fashioned quality called taste." Roger Kahn, eulogizing him in a posthumous collection of his essays, observed that although Lardner was a matchless sportswriter, his craft was not sportswriting or profile-writing or column-writing but "purely writing: writing the English sentence, fusing sound and meaning, matching the precision of the word with the rhythm of the phrase. It is a pursuit which is unfailingly demanding, and Lardner met it with unfailing mastery."

Although his three brothers all became writers or journalists, Lardner most resembled his father in character and interests. He had the same quiet, deadpan humor; the same love of sports, poker, and good fellowship; and the same dignity, reserve, and literary standards. Like his father, Lardner was a craftsman and an individualist. And like his father, he died young as he had predicted, in New York City.

The editors of *Newsweek* recalled that "he had liked Shakespeare for his genius and Jane Austen for her style and sports for their excitement and good Scotch for the camaraderie that comes after a drink or two. He disliked anecdotes and pomposity and shouting, and, most of all, he disliked bad writing."

[See Roger Kahn, ed., *The World of John Lardner* (1961), an anthology of his writings; and Ring Lardner, Jr., *The Lardners: My Family Remembered* (1976). There are obituary notices in the *New York Times*, Mar. 25, 1960; *Newsweek*, Apr. 4, 1960; and *New York Herald Tribune Book Review*, Aug. 6, 1961.]
SYDNEY WEINBERG

LASHLEY, KARL SPENCER (June 7, 1890–Aug. 7, 1958), physiological and theoretical psychologist, was born in Davis, W.Va., the only child of Charles Gilpin Lashley and Margaret Blanche Spencer. His father, whose family included several generations of shopkeepers in West Virginia and Maryland, occupied minor political offices from time to time but mainly continued in the family business. His mother, also from a comfortable middle-class background, had substantial literary and artistic talents and interests. For most of his formal education Lashley attended Davis public schools, graduating from the then unaccredited high school at the age of fourteen.

He took a B.A. at the University of West Virginia in 1910. Although he started college as a Latin major, he soon changed to biology. An M.S. in bacteriology at the University of Pittsburgh in 1911 was followed by a Ph.D. in zoology at the Johns Hopkins University in 1914. At Johns Hopkins University his major professor was H. S. Jennings, a zoologist concerned with animal behavior. For his minor subject, Lashley studied psychology under John B. Watson and Adolf Meyer, two leaders of the movement that transformed American psychology from a subject based on introspection, speculation, and often metaphysics to an empirical science, which Watson dubbed "behaviorism" in 1913. It was in the shaping of this new psychology that Lashley was to make his most lasting contributions.

For three years after receiving his doctorate, Lashley held research fellowships at Johns Hopkins, providing him with the freedom to complete the transition from biologist to psychologist. Lashley's first regular academic appointment, in 1917, was as instructor in psychology at the University of Minnesota. Advancing rapidly through the academic ranks, Lashley was a professor when he left Minnesota in 1926 for the Institute for Juvenile Research in Chicago. Professorial appointments at the University of Chicago and later at Harvard University preceded his final academic post as research professor of neuropsychology at Harvard and, concurrently, director of the Yerkes Laboratories of Primate Biology in Orange Park, Fla. Lashley's honorary degrees, memberships in learned societies, high offices in professional organizations, and honorific lectureships are too numerous to list.

Lashley married Edith Ann Baker in 1918. Their one child, a son, died in infancy. Mrs. Lashley died in 1948, and in 1957 Lashley married Claire Imrédy Schiller, the widow of the distinguished Hungarian psychologist Paul Schiller. The second marriage was short-lived; Lashley died on a vacation trip to Poitiers, France, the following year.

Lashley's scientific contributions have been absorbed into the body of psychological knowledge; few are recalled as specific discoveries or laws. As a sophomore studying comparative anatomy, he resolved to trace all the nerve connections that he saw in microscopic sections of a frog's brain so as to "know how the frog worked." The project was, of course, doomed, not only because microscopic sections fail to show many neural elements, but also—and more significantly—because the nervous system does not function connectionistically, like a miniaturized telephone switchboard, as he and many scientists of the day believed. As Lashley matured into the leading physiological psychologist of his time, his experiments on rats and other vertebrates demonstrated that behavior was not mediated by sharply localized bits of nerve tissue. Instead the brain showed itself to be a vastly complex, continuously active organ that somehow acts as a whole while still preserving some degree of anatomical localization.

The early behaviorists liked to characterize action as a chain of reflexes, with each tiny link stimulating the next, equally tiny link. They denied any overriding organizational principle guiding action as a whole. But Lashley showed, by research and by rational argument based on his findings, that behavior is inescapably organized. Neither simple animal behavior nor the more complex human variety could often be explained away as mere chain reflex. Lashley proposed a hierarchical organization for action and for the nervous system that governs it. The actual movement of an organism is the outcome of nested levels of functioning, each with its own rules and purposes. Modern psychology has found Lashley's hierarchical conception of behavior the natural framework within which to make sense of its subject.

For the early behaviorists, motivation could be reduced to a few energizing influences, epitomized by hunger, thirst, sex, and the avoidance of pain. From a handful of inborn drives, according to the behaviorist theory, the environment molds the endless variety of goals and preferences found in animals and people. Lashley disliked that environmentalistic doctrine because it clashed with his Darwinian outlook. He believed that psychology should seek diversity, not uniformity, in the inherited drives guiding behavior, comparable to the diversity of animal forms. The rise of ethology in the 1970's showed that Lashley's lesson in motivation had at last been learned by American psychologists.

Lashley was behaviorism's great dissenter because he resisted its optimism and because he proved how naive it was. His problems—the organization of behavior and of the nervous system, and the role of inheritance in psychological processes—are still the major problems of objective psychology.

[On Lashley's life and work, see Frank A. Beach, *Biographical Memoirs of the National Academy of Sciences*, 35 (1961); and Donald O. Hebb, *American Journal of Psychology*, 72 (1959). Lashley's only book was *Brain Mechanisms and Intelligence* (1929); his work appeared mainly as experimental and theoretical articles in scholarly journals and symposia. Some of his most important papers are collected in *The Neuropsychology of Lashley* (1960), F. A. Beach, D. O. Hebb, C. T. Morgan, and H. W. Nissen, eds.]

R. J. Herrnstein

LASKY, JESSE LOUIS (Sept. 13, 1880– Jan. 13, 1958), motion picture industry executive, was born in San Francisco, Calif., the son of Isaac Lasky and Sarah Platt. Although Jewish like many of the American film industry's pioneers, Jesse Lasky was unusual in being a native Californian whose roots went back to the Gold Rush. In 1888 he moved with his family to San Jose, where he attended school. He never graduated from high school. Isaac Lasky's deteriorating health resulted in the failure of his once-flourishing shoe store, and while Jesse was still a teenager, the family moved back to San Francisco.

The young Lasky's main interest was in playing the cornet. By the time he was sixteen he was good enough to substitute in a professional band, and within two years he had a union card. When he was nineteen, his father died, leaving only a tiny estate. Lasky worked at various jobs, was unsuccessful in supporting himself and his family, and early in 1900 took part in the Alaska Gold Rush. A failure as a prospector, he earned his subsistence as well as steerage passage back to San Francisco in the fall as a cornetist. Throughout his life the imaginative and hardworking Lasky proved able to deal with adversity.

In 1901 he went to Hawaii, where he eventually played with the Royal Hawaiian Band. He returned again to California and toured the country as a vaudeville "bugle act" with his younger sister, Blanche, who had also learned to play the cornet. In 1903 he became business manager of the well-known magician Hermann the Great, with whom he and Blanche had toured. Soon Lasky gave up performing. Aided by Blanche, he managed various performers and presented vaudeville acts and musical comedies.

Lasky had become an established and commercially successful manager and producer by December 1909, when he married Bessie Ginzberg. They had three children.

On talent-scouting trips to Europe, Lasky became convinced that the time was ripe for an American Folies Bergère. In 1911, with a partner, he opened such a cabaret-style operation in New York City. Although an artistic success, it was a commercial failure, and Lasky lost all of the more than $100,000 that he had invested. Starting over again, he resumed his vaudeville and production activities. In 1912 he engaged Cecil B. De Mille to write and stage an operetta. De Mille became a fast friend and one of Lasky's partners the following year when they became involved with motion pictures.

The fledgling movie industry was in disarray in 1913: the attempt of the Motion Picture Patents Company to control American filmmaking had clearly failed, and movies were becoming longer as the feature film gained favor over the traditional one- and two-reelers of twelve to twenty-five minutes. That summer, according to Lasky's autobiography, Samuel Goldfish (the extraordinarily successful glove salesman who had married Blanche and who later gained prominence as Goldwyn) finally succeeded in convincing him to participate in making movies, notwithstanding Lasky's renewed, if moderate, success as a manager and producer.

The Jesse L. Lasky Feature Play Company, with Lasky as president, Goldfish as general manager, and De Mille as director general, began shooting its first film on Dec. 29, 1913. *The Squaw Man*, based on a popular stage drama of the day, was the first feature filmed in Hollywood; until then only shorts and serials had been shot there. The film, released in March 1914, was a smash hit; and the Lasky Company, under its namesake's astute guidance, went from one success to another. Lasky concentrated on acquiring proven stage properties and performers. Among his more noteworthy ventures was the purchase of rights to ten David Belasco theatrical productions (nine of which became successful movies) and the presentation of *Carmen*, one of the company's biggest money-makers.

In mid-1916 the Lasky Company merged, on favorable terms, with its main competitor, Adolph Zukor's somewhat more successful Famous Players Company. The resulting corporation, which became known as Paramount (the name of its distribution arm), dominated the film industry during the 1920's, in large part because of Zukor's astute management. But if subordinate to Zukor, Lasky was still a most important executive and until 1932 was first vice-president in charge of production.

And the corporation benefited enormously from his vigorous imagination, willingness to gamble on unknowns, and intelligent close attention to production details. Between 1916 and 1932 Lasky supervised the production of nearly 1,000 films, among them *The Covered Wagon* (1923), the first Western epic, and *Beau Geste* (1926), the first and probably the best filming of the P. C. Wren novel. Lasky developed the careers of such disparate performers as Maurice Chevalier, Gary Cooper, Pola Negri, and Gloria Swanson. He had his fair share of flops, but his career during those years was, in Alva Johnston's words, "a success story in the old tradition."

In 1932 Paramount, as a consequence of the Great Depression, went into receivership, and Lasky was forced to resign. Meanwhile the economic hard times had ruined his investments, and he lost another fortune, estimated at more than $10 million. (Lasky had a penchant for lavish living: in 1932 when he seemed to have been wiped out financially a friend remarked, "I hear the Laskys are cutting down. They have only two butlers now.")

For the next twenty years Lasky worked with mixed success as an independent producer (releasing through various studios) and at different film companies as an employed producer. Among his noteworthy independent productions were *Zoo in Budapest* (1933), *Berkeley Square* (1933), and *Without Reservations* (1946). His most important studio film was Warner Brothers' *Sergeant York* (1941). Lasky's last film venture came at Metro-Goldwyn-Mayer in 1951 as associate producer of *The Great Caruso*, a project of long standing. At the time of his death, Lasky was preparing a movie about American brass bands. He died in Beverly Hills, Calif., while promoting his autobiography.

Lasky was optimistic, pragmatic, and energetic. Although not an artist as such, for nearly two decades he determined the production qualities of Hollywood's dominant studio and, because of his understanding of mass taste, contributed greatly to Hollywood's dominance of world film production.

[Lasky's autobiography, written with Don Weldon, *I Blow My Own Horn* (1957), must be used with care; as must Bessie Mona Lasky, *Candle in the Sun* (1957), which gives an interesting picture of the Lasky domestic life. See also Alva Johnston, "Profiles: A Bugler's Progress," *New Yorker*, July 10, 1937; and obituaries in the *New York Times* and *New York Herald Tribune*, Jan. 14, 1958, and in *Variety*, Jan. 15, 1958. For Lasky's film career prior to 1931, see Benjamin B. Hampton, *History of the American Film Industry From Its Beginnings to 1931* (1931; repr. 1970).]

DANIEL J. LEAB

LAWRENCE, ERNEST ORLANDO (Aug. 8, 1901–Aug. 27, 1958), physicist, was born in Canton, S.Dak., the son of Carl Gustav Lawrence and Gunda Jacobson, both children of Norwegian Lutheran immigrants. His father taught Latin and history at the Lutheran Augustana Academy. Lawrence's early upbringing had a profound and lasting influence on his life in establishing his uncompromising integrity, disdain of petty gossip and profanity, deep loyalty to his friends, and complete dedication to his work.

After attending Canton and Pierre public schools, Lawrence entered St. Olaf College in Northfield, Minn., in 1918. The following year he transferred to the University of South Dakota in Vermillion, where he was most influenced by Lewis Akeley, dean of the College of Electrical Engineering, who transformed his interest in a medical career into one in physics. He received his bachelor's degree in the latter subject with high honors in 1922.

Lawrence then entered the University of Minnesota graduate school primarily because of the strong recommendation given Minnesota's physics department, which included John T. Tate and W. F. G. Swann, by Merle Tuve. Lawrence's closest childhood friend, Tuve had already embarked upon his own graduate career in physics there. He had personal knowledge of Lawrence's abilities through their early tinkering with radio in Canton, and he now was instrumental in securing a teaching assistantship for Lawrence at Minnesota.

Lawrence completed his master's degree under Swann in only one year, with a thesis on the charging effect produced by rotating a prolate iron spheroid in a uniform magnetic field. When Swann left Minnesota, going first to the University of Chicago and then to Yale University, Lawrence followed him as a graduate student to both institutions. He received his Ph.D. at Yale in 1925 with a thesis on the photoelectric effect in potassium vapor. Lawrence's master's and doctoral theses left no doubt of his outstanding abilities as an experimentalist, and both were published in the *Philosophical Magazine*.

Lawrence remained at Yale for three more years, first as a fellow of the National Research Council (1925–1927), then as assistant professor (1927–1928), continuing his researches on the photoelectric effect; making the most precise determination of the ionization potential of mercury to date; and, with Jesse W. Beams, setting a precise upper limit on the time lag involved in the emission of photoelectrons. Against the advice of many of his friends, he then decided to accept an associate professorship at the University of California at Berkeley, at the time little known. Two years later, with the strong support of G. N. Lewis of the chemistry department, Lawrence became the youngest full professor on the Berkeley faculty. He remained at Berkeley, apart from leaves and travels, for the rest of his life. On May 14, 1932, he married Mary ("Molly") Kimberly Blumer, daughter of the dean emeritus of the Yale Medical School. They had six children.

Lawrence conceived his most famous invention, the cyclotron, in early 1929, shortly after going to Berkeley. Skimming the foreign scientific periodicals one evening in the library, he chanced upon an article in German by the Norwegian engineer Rolf Wideröe. Unable to read the article with facility but quickly taking in its illustrations and equations, Lawrence saw that Wideröe (and the Swedish physicist Gustaf A. Ising before him) was proposing a linear acceleration scheme for charged particles. Lawrence immediately realized that to achieve particle energies on the order of a few MeV (million electron volts), which were required for nuclear experiments, Wideröe's accelerator would have to be too long to be practical. It suddenly struck him, however, that he could convert the particle's linear trajectory into a circular one by superimposing a magnetic field at right angles to the particle's path.

He immediately proved that a particle's frequency of revolution depends only upon the strength of the magnetic field and the charge–mass ratio of the particle, not upon the radius of its orbit. Hence, by placing two flat, hollow, semicircular chambers ("Dees") back to back in a vacuum chamber with a small gap between them, and applying an alternating voltage to ensure that when one Dee was positively charged the other would be negatively charged, the circling particles would receive an accelerating "kick" each time they crossed the gap between the Dees. Moreover, each half circle of the particle's orbit would be larger than the preceding one; and since, as Lawrence easily proved, the particle's kinetic energy increases as the square of its orbital radius, they could possess potentially large energies if injected into the chamber at its center and extracted at some point on its perimeter. This was the basic principle of the cyclotron, which Lawrence and his student Niels F. Edlefsen first reported in the fall of 1930.

In early 1931, M. Stanley Livingston, in connection with his doctoral thesis supervised by Lawrence, demonstrated the cyclotron resonance principle using a four-inch model; later in the year Livingston constructed a ten-inch model that was producing 1.2-MeV protons by early 1932.

Thus began an era of cyclotron construction by Lawrence and his co-workers at Berkeley that saw the birth of "big science" in the United States and inaugurated the modern group approach to research in physics. Lawrence had tremendous stamina and drive. He made enormous demands on himself, his students, and his colleagues—100-hour workweeks were common. He was certain that he was doing what was best for American science. He obtained the necessary funds and oversaw the construction of cyclotrons of ever-increasing size at Berkeley in the 1930's. A 27-inch model, the magnetic pole faces of which were later expanded to 37 inches, was yielding 8-MeV deuterons and high beam intensities by 1937; a 60-inch cyclotron was in operation by 1939; and a 184-inch model, funded by the Rockefeller Foundation, was authorized in 1940, although its completion had to await the end of World War II.

Throughout the 1930's Lawrence gave freely of his time and advice to other physicists throughout the world in their own cyclotron construction efforts. His work brought him widespread recognition and fame: he was elected to the National Academy of Sciences in 1934 and was awarded the Nobel Prize in physics in 1939.

All the key discoveries in nuclear physics in the 1930's—the neutron (1932), the disintegration of lithium by protons (1932), induced radioactivity by alpha particles and neutrons (1934)—were confirmed and exploited at Berkeley, and a vast amount of entirely new information was obtained by the Berkeley group. Many nuclei were studied extensively by proton and deuteron bombardment, and radioisotopes and neutrons produced in intermediate reactions were used in the treatment of cancer and for the medical research programs of his brother John and others at Berkeley. Surely the most dramatic event in the lives of the two brothers occurred in 1937, when the Sloan-Lawrence X-ray machine, which Lawrence and his co-workers had installed in the San Francisco Hospital, was used to treat and save the life of their mother, who had an inoperable tumor.

During World War II, Lawrence became one of the select group of scientists in America with responsibility for developing a nuclear weapon. The key problem initially was to find a technique for separating the fissionable isotope of uranium, uranium 235, from its much more abundant companion, uranium 238, on a scale large enough to assemble a critical mass for a bomb. Alfred O. Nier at Minnesota had first separated these isotopes with mass spectroscopic techniques. From mid-1941 to mid-1945 Lawrence and his co-workers at Berkeley worked continuously to perfect this electromagnetic separation method. The 184-inch cyclotron magnet was employed in a prototypical mass spectrometer that later served as a model for hundreds of similar ones at Oak Ridge, Tenn., and ultimately produced most of the uranium 235 used in the Hiroshima bomb.

By early 1945, however, the enormous technical problems associated with another isotope separation technique, the gaseous diffusion technique, had been solved. This method rendered the electromagnetic technique obsolete. Meanwhile, the discovery of plutonium and its fissionable properties at Berkeley had spawned an entirely independent project at Hanford, Wash., to produce plutonium 239, the fissionable isotope of plutonium. The ultimate success of this project, too, owed a great deal to Lawrence's scientific and organizational genius. He also made important contributions to the wartime radar and antisubmarine programs. After the war the 184-inch cyclotron (which was redesigned as a synchrocyclotron following Edwin M. McMillan's discovery of "phase stability") was completed. By late 1946 it was yielding 180-MeV deuterons and was being used in a host of new experiments made possible by its greatly increased energy.

In 1948 William Brobeck convinced Lawrence that a proton synchrotron operating in the billion-electron-volt range (hence the name "bevatron") could be constructed. Lawrence once again sought the necessary funds to bring this project to completion several years later. Other accelerator projects were also undertaken at Berkeley, and together they made possible research of fundamental significance for particle physics and led to a galaxy of Nobel Prize winners at Berkeley; Luis W. Alvarez, Owen Chamberlin, McMillan, Glenn T. Seaborg, Emilio G. Segré. In 1952 Lawrence offered to use the laboratory's Livermore site as a second site as a second weapons laboratory (the first being Los Alamos) for the United States. His unflinching support of the thermonuclear bomb project in the United States was one of the factors contributing to his final break with his former colleague J. Robert Oppenheimer.

The excessive demands in time and energy that Lawrence placed upon himself ultimately undermined his health. He developed an intestinal ulcer. While representing the United States at the International Conference on Scientific Detection of Nuclear Explosions in Geneva, he became critically ill and was rushed back to the United States for surgery. He died without regaining consciousness in Palo Alto, Calif.

In addition to the Nobel Prize, Lawrence received the Medal of Merit in 1946 and the Fermi Award in 1957. The Berkeley laboratory that he directed is now called the Lawrence Radiation Laboratory; the transuranic element of atomic number 103 was named lawrencium in his honor after its discovery at Berkeley in 1961; and the Lawrence Hall of Science was endowed after his death to enable teachers to come to Berkeley to learn the most modern methods of teaching science.

[Lawrence's scientific and personal papers are at the Bancroft Library at Berkeley. The principal biographical sources are Luis W. Alvarez' obituary, *Biographical Memoirs. National Academy of Sciences*, 41 (1970); Herbert Childs, *An American Genius* (1968); and Nuel Pharr Davis, *Lawrence and Oppenheimer* (1968). Lawrence discussed his invention of the cyclotron in his Nobel lecture, reprinted in *Nobel Lectures in Physics*, II (1965). See also M. Stanley Livingston's article in *Physics Today* (1959); *The Development of High-Energy Accelerators* (1966), of which he was editor; and *Particle Accelerators* (1969); and M. L. Oliphant's two-part article in *Physics Today* (1966). On Lawrence's contributions to the Manhattan Project, see R. G. Hewlett and O. E. Anderson, Jr., *The New World 1939–1946* (1962).]

ROGER H. STUEWER

LAWSON, ROBERT RIPLEY (Oct. 4, 1892–May 26, 1957), illustrator and author of children's books, was born in New York City, the son of William Bethel Lawson and Elma Cecilia Bowman. He first became interested in drawing while in high school. After graduating from Montclair (N.J.) High School in 1911, he attended the New York School of Fine and Applied Arts until 1913, studying under Rae Sloan Bredin and Howard Giles. From 1914 to 1917 he did magazine illustrations, stage settings, and commercial art work in Greenwich Village. One of Lawson's first illustrating jobs was done for the *Designer* for Carl Sandburg's *Rootabaga Stories* (1922). He served in France during World War I in the Camouflage Section, Fortieth Engineers. On Sept. 6, 1922, he married the illustrator and author Marie Abrams.

During the 1920's Lawson did commercial work and magazine illustration. In 1930 he took up etching and illustrated his first book, *The Wee*

Men of Ballywooden, by Arthur Mason. In 1931 he won the John Taylor Arms Prize of the Society of American Etchers. He soon gave up commercial work and concentrated entirely on book illustrating. During the 1930's he illustrated Ella Young's *The Unicorn with Silver Shoes* (1932), Margery Bianco's *Hurdy-Gurdy Man* (1933), Elizabeth Jane Coatsworth's *The Golden Horseshoe* (1935), Walter Russell Bowie's *The Story of Jesus for Young People* (1937), Ruth A. Barnes' *I Hear America Singing* (1937), Mark Twain's *The Prince and the Pauper* Richard and Florence Atwater's *Mr. Popper's Penguins* (1938), and an edition of John Bunyan's *Pilgrim's Progress* (1939) abridged by Mary Godolphin.

Lawson's most notable accomplishment during the 1930's was illustrating Munro Leaf's *Story of Ferdinand* (1936). Leaf later recounted that he used the story of the gentle bull that would not fight in a Spanish bullring in order to give Lawson "an animal to draw that was not a cat, a mouse, a dog or a horse—something different in children's books." The book was variously attacked as Communist propaganda, an argument for pacifism, and a glorification of fascist militarism. The controversy surrounding *Ferdinand* was partially responsible for its immediate popularity, and it was made into an animated cartoon by Walt Disney in 1938. Leaf and Lawson collaborated again in 1938 in *Wee Gillis*.

Lawson's work with Leaf lead him into writing and illustrating his own books. His *Ben and Me* (1939) was the story of Benjamin Franklin's life seen through the eyes of his closest friend, adviser, and constant companion, a mouse named Amos. In 1941 Lawson was awarded the Caldecott Medal of the American Library Association for the most distinguished American picture book for children for *They Were Strong and Good* (1940), the story of Lawson's parents and grandparents. He won the Newberry Medal of the American Library Association in 1945 for the most distinguished contribution to American literature for children for *Rabbit Hill* (1944). The book relates the adventures of Father and Mother Rabbit, their high-leaping son Little George, the aged Uncle Analdas, Willie Fieldmouse, and Porkey the Woodchuck. *The Tough Winter* (1954) was a sequel to *Rabbit Hill*.

Among Lawson's other books are *I Discover Columbus* (1941), *Mr. Twig's Mistake* (1947), *Robbut* (1948), *Fabulous Flight* (1949), *Dick Whittington and His Cat* (1949), *McWhinney's*

Jaunt (1951), *Edward, Hoppy and Joe* (1952), *Mr. Revere and I* (1953), *Captain Kidd's Cat* (1956), *Watchwords of Liberty* (1957), and *The Great Wheel* (1957).

Critics of Lawson's illustrations have characterized them as old-fashioned because of their clarity of expression and exquisite detail. Although an illustrator of children's books, Lawson did not consciously draw for children. "I have never, as far as I can remember, given one moment's thought as to whether any drawing that I was doing was for adults or children. I have never changed one conception or line or detail to suit the supposed age of the readers," he said in the *Horn Book* of November 1940.

Humor was another characteristic of Lawson's illustrations and writings. *Mr. Revere and I*, for example, is the story of Paul Revere's horse. This British-born, cultured horse at first loathed the "American peasants," but later became an ardent patriot and carried Revere on his famous ride despite the silversmith's atrocious horsemanship. Even Lawson's illustrations for the juvenile edition of *Pilgrim's Progress* were funny. Lawson justified their levity by arguing in the book's introduction that "if a certain element of caricature or humor appears, seemingly out of place in a book so . . . religious, I can only say that it is there because I think John Bunyan would have wanted it that way."

[Lawson recounted his family background in *They Were Strong and Good* (1940). Brief biographies are in May Hill Arbuthnot, *Children and Books* (1947); and Ruth Hill Viguers et al., *Illustrators of Children's Books, 1946–1956* (1959). Helen Dean Fish discusses Lawson in the *Horn Book*, Jan.–Feb. 1940. Other sources include Bertha E. Mahony et al., *Illustrators of Children's Books, 1744–1945* (1947); Cornelia Meigs et al., *A Critical History of Children's Literature* (1953); Lawson's obituary notice, *New York Times*, May 28, 1957; and Munro Leaf's obituary notice, *New York Times*, Dec. 22, 1976.]

EDWARD S. SHAPIRO

LEAHY, WILLIAM DANIEL (May 6, 1875–July 20, 1959), naval officer, was born in Hampton, Iowa, to Michael Arthur Leahy and Rose Hamilton. A prosperous attorney and Populist legislator, Michael in 1882 took the family back to his native Wisconsin, where William grew up. In 1893 William was appointed to the U.S. Naval Academy and graduated thirty-fifth of the forty-seven members of the class of 1897.

Leahy's first billet inaugurated a long association with gunnery and a career of combat assignments. Aboard the *Oregon* he made the famous cruise in 1898 from Seattle around Cape Horn to the Caribbean in time to join in the sinking of the Spanish fleet off Santiago, Cuba. Assigned shortly thereafter to Asian waters, he saw action in the Boxer Rebellion and in the suppression of the Philippine Insurrection. At the close of hostilities Leahy returned to the United States and in early 1904 married Louise Tennent Harrington; their only child, William Harrington Leahy, was born later that year. Service aboard cruisers and battleships followed, as did a term as an instructor at the naval academy and assignment with American forces intervening in the 1912 Nicaraguan civil war.

The opening of World War I found Leahy commanding the navy secretary's dispatch boat *Dolphin*, and during this duty he struck up his lifelong friendship with Assistant Secretary of the Navy Franklin D. Roosevelt. In 1918 Leahy won the Navy Cross for service as captain of the converted German liner *Princess Matoika*, which transported troops to France. Postwar commands included the cruiser *St. Louis* and the *New Mexico*, plus several gunnery billets.

A fine captain and shrewd bureaucratic politician, Leahy won flag rank and nomination as chief of the Bureau of Ordnance in 1927. He improved antiaircraft guns, demanded more realistic target practice, and championed battleships over the claims of naval aviators. After additional duty at sea, Leahy returned to Washington as chief of the powerful Bureau of Navigation in 1933. As head of the navy's personnel office, he assigned conservative admirals, members of the "Gun Club" clique, to most key fleet billets and resisted an attempt to curtail the independence of the bureaus.

After brief commands of battleships and the battle force, Leahy was appointed chief of naval operations in 1937. He solidified the authority of his office over the fleet; persuaded Congress to adopt a 20 percent increment in tonnage; fathered the Hepburn report on base construction; and presided over a major reappraisal of strategic planning to deal with a possible two-ocean war. Leahy's keen sense of the possible permitted these accomplishments in an isolationist era.

Forced by age to retire in 1939, Leahy was nominated governor of Puerto Rico, where he demonstrated competence and impartiality in handling volatile elections. Roosevelt consulted Leahy frequently on military policy, and after Admiral J. O. Richardson opposed the president's decision to base the United States Fleet at Pearl Harbor, Leahy recommended his protégé's relief as fleet commander.

In 1941 Leahy embarked upon his most controversial duty as Roosevelt's ambassador to Vichy France, with orders to try to prevent the transfer of the French fleet to Germany and to minimize French collaboration with Hitler. He succeeded in the former task but was helpless to relieve German pressure on the French and thus became the target of critics of American dealings with Vichy. With his influence at its nadir in the spring of 1942, Leahy was recalled; but his departure was delayed by his wife's unexpected death.

In July 1942 Leahy became chief of staff to the president and chairman of the Joint Chiefs of Staff. He chose the role of moderator over that of advocate and served as spokesman in the White House for the military view. He restrained military influence over civilian affairs but discouraged civilian control over strategy, operations, and often foreign policy. Leahy favored an early cross-Channel invasion of France and other operations in 1942–1943 to aid the Soviets but at the same time urged greater emphasis on the war against Japan. He discouraged support for Charles de Gaulle and the Free French and distrusted Roosevelt's policy of concessions to the Soviet Union. A realist and articulate nationalist, Leahy scoffed at universalist plans to ease postwar tensions.

After Roosevelt's death, Leahy was retained by President Truman. Skeptical of the feasibility of the atomic bomb, he opposed its use, according to his own account. He persuaded the new chief executive to curtail lend-lease to Russia shortly after V-E Day; castigated Secretary of State James Byrnes in 1946 for his policy of accommodation with the Soviets; and usually pressed for a strong anti-Communist stance. Throughout his tenure Leahy championed aid to the Nationalist Chinese and opposed Truman's decision to embargo weapons during 1947. Less influential with Truman than with Roosevelt, Leahy failed to prevent service unification and increasing centralization within the Navy Department but did persuade Truman to appoint Admiral Louis Emil Denfeld over several aviators as Chief of Naval Operations in 1947.

Discouraged by demobilization, reduced military appropriations, and the discontinuity of American foreign policy, Leahy retired in March 1949. To defend the wartime Democratic administration, Truman persuaded Leahy to publish his diary in amended form in 1950 under the title *I Was There.* In retirement Leahy retained an interest in public affairs, but his influence on policy had ended. He died in 1959, survived by his son, who had achieved flag rank in the navy.

Although Leahy probably saw as much combat as any naval officer of this century, he never led significant forces in battle. As the ranking American officer of World War II, he became the first fleet admiral in 1944, a tribute both to his sagacity as a presidential adviser and skill as a bureaucratic leader. Contemporaries often accused him of enjoying power too much, but from his diary and letters Leahy emerges as a deeply moral man committed to a code of chivalry in war that civilized men had long before forsaken.

[No biography of Leahy has been written; his achievements are seldom mentioned in standard accounts of his era; and no published assessment of his influence on naval policy or grand strategy is available. The best manuscript sources are Leahy Diary and MSS, Library of Congress; Leahy MSS, Wisconsin Historical Society; Records of the Chief of Naval Operations, National Archives; Records of the War Plans Division, Naval Historical Division; Records of the Joint Chiefs of Staff, National Archives; Roosevelt MSS, Hyde Park, N.Y.; William Standley MSS, University of Southern California; Charles M. Cooke MSS, Hoover Institute, Palo Alto, Calif.; and James Forrestal MSS, Princeton, N. J. See also H. H. Arnold, *Global Mission* (1948); Herbert Feis, *Churchill, Roosevelt, and Stalin* (1956); Frank Gervasi, "Watchdog in the White House," *Collier's,* Oct. 9, 1948; Harold Ickes, *Secret Diary,* vol. III (1955); E. J. King and W. M. Whitehill, *Fleet Admiral King* (1952); William Langer, *Our Vichy Gamble* (1947); John Major, "William D. Leahy," in Robert William Love, Jr., ed., *The Chiefs of Naval Operations* (to be published in 1980). Forrest Pogue, *George Marshall,* vol. III (1973); and Thaddeus Tujela, *Statesmen and Admirals* (1965). A number of reminiscences in the Oral History Collection of Columbia University and in the U.S. Naval Institute Collection have material on Leahy.]

ROBERT WILLIAM LOVE, JR.
WINSTON B. LEWIS

LEE, JOHN CLIFFORD HODGES (Aug. 1, 1887–Aug. 30, 1958), army officer, was born in

Junction City, Kans., the son of Charles Fenlon Lee and John Clifford Hodges. Lee was named for his mother, John Clifford Hodges, who had been named for her father, a captain in the Confederate army. Lee graduated from the U.S. Military Academy at West Point and was commissioned a second lieutenant in the Army Corps of Engineers on June 11, 1909. His early assignments were typical for a young engineer officer, including attendance at the Army Engineer School in Washington, D.C., and duty in the Panama Canal Zone, Guam, and the Philippine Islands and on the Ohio River. Service in World War I included attendance at the Army General Staff College at Langres, France, and assignment as G-2 (intelligence) with the Eighty-second Division and as G-3 (operations) and then chief of staff of the Eighty-ninth Division. In the latter capacity he had a prominent role in planning the St. Mihiel and Argonne-Meuse offensives, which earned him the Distinguished Service Medal. Major assignments between the two world wars included service in the Office of the Chief of Engineers, as G-2 of the Philippine Department; as district engineer in charge of navigational improvements and flood control work on the Mississippi River; as district engineer at Washington, D.C., and Philadelphia, Pa.; and as division engineer, North Pacific Division, at Portland, Ore. In October 1940 he assumed command of the San Francisco Port of Embarkation and a year later was given command of the Second Infantry Division at Fort Sam Houston.

Lee's role in World War II was in the field of logistics rather than as commander of major tactical units. On May 24, 1942, he arrived in the United Kingdom to take command of the Services of Supply of the newly activated European Theater of Operations. For the next two years he presided over the unprecedented buildup of American forces and their munitions in preparation for the cross-channel assault and, following the invasion of Normandy in June 1944, over the organization of the Communications Zone (successor to the Services of Supply) on the Continent. At the theater's peak strength early in 1945 this involved the support of more than 3 million men, with the attendant problems of housing, transportation, the reconstruction of ports, roads, airfields, depots, and railways. The support of such a force was inevitably accompanied by difficulties because of the unpredictability of the course of tactical operations, and much of the dissatisfaction over supply inevitably

focused on the commander of the Communications Zone.

Lee was a controversial figure and the target of much criticism. He was a spit-and-polish soldier, heavy on outward form and ceremony, somewhat forbidding in manner and appearance, and sometimes tactless in exercising authority that he regarded as coming within the province of his command. He wore his uniform with great pride and expected every soldier to measure up to his own concept of soldierly qualities. Few of his subordinates knew him well or understood his rigid sense of discipline, and many regarded him as pompous and a martinet. Those who were close to him insisted he was a kindly, modest, and extremely religious man, but this seemed to be contradicted by the ostentatious living arrangements of his staff and by his use of a special train for his endless inspection trips in the United Kingdom. The attitude toward him and his command was undoubtedly reinforced by the traditional suspicions that the combat elements held for rear-area troops. The major field commands never were convinced that Lee's staff treated their requests with the proper urgency, and they objected to the command arrangements under which Lee for a long time was designated deputy theater commander (under Eisenhower) as well as commanding general, Services of Supply. General Eisenhower deprived Lee of the title of deputy at the time of the landings in France, but this did not end the distrust between the field and service forces. Lee no longer wore two hats, but his staff did, for it doubled as the Communications Zone and theater staff. The thought that the Communications Zone, a command coequal with the army groups, was passing on the validity of their requests was unacceptable to them.

In the general liquidation of the wartime commands after V-E Day (May 8, 1945), the Communications Zone was dissolved, and Lee served temporarily as commander of the successor command, Theater Service Forces, European Theater. On Jan. 3, 1946, he was named commanding general of the Mediterranean Theater of Operations and deputy supreme commander of Allied Forces, Mediterranean. This put him in command of thousands of men anxious to return to the United States. The deteriorating morale of his command made him the target of a critical press, which charged that he and his staff were living in luxury while enlisted men were ill fed, ill housed, and badly treated. An investigation by the inspector general of the army cleared Lee; and General Eisenhower, now chief of staff of the army, who had once considered relieving Lee, defended him and praised him warmly.

Lee married Sarah Ann Row on Sept. 24, 1917; they had one son. After Sarah's death, Lee wed Eve B. Ellison on Sept. 19, 1945. Lee retired on Dec. 31, 1947, and thereafter made his home in York, Pa. There he became vice-president for the Brotherhood of St. Andrew, an international lay organization of Protestant Episcopal men and boys, and worked with the armed forces division of that organization until his death in York, Pa.

[Information was provided by Department of the Army Resumé of Service, Office of the Chief of Information, U.S. Army. See Roland G. Ruppenthal, *Logistical Support of the Armies: European Theater of Operations,* 2 vols. (1953–1959); and obituaries in the *New York Times,* Aug. 31, 1958; *Gazette and Daily York* (Pa.), Sept. 2, 1958; and *York Dispatch,* Oct. 9, 1952.]

ROLAND G. RUPPENTHAL

LEFFINGWELL, RUSSELL CORNELL (Sept. 10, 1878–Oct. 2, 1960), lawyer, banker, and government official, was born in New York City, the son of Charles Russell Leffingwell and Mary Elizabeth Cornell. The paternal family had, since the seventeenth century, played a leading part in the development of Connecticut, but Charles Leffingwell was an executive in the New York iron business owned by his wife's family. Russell Leffingwell attended the Yonkers (N.Y.) Military Academy, graduated from the Halsey School in New York City, and received a B.A. from Yale University in 1899. At Columbia Law School he became the first editor in chief of the law review and was awarded an LL.B. in 1902.

Leffingwell began his career as a law clerk with Guthrie, Cravath and Henderson, a distinguished Wall Street firm; he was made a partner in January 1907. During the next decade he won growing renown as a specialist in corporate finance. On Jan. 27, 1906, he married Lucy Hewitt; they had one daughter.

A strong patriot, Leffingwell took part in the Plattsburgh Reserve Officers Training Camp in 1916. When the United States declared war the next spring, he responded to an appeal from Secretary of the Treasury William McAdoo, a long-time friend, and joined the Treasury as a dollar-a-year man. Originally special counsel

in charge of floating the first Liberty Loan, Leffingwell became assistant secretary of the Treasury for fiscal affairs when Congress created the post for him in October 1917. Serving in that capacity under both McAdoo and his successor, Carter Glass, he figured as the the real architect of American wartime financial policies. He developed the Liberty Loan organization, supervised the vast bond issues, and negotiated loans to the European allies. In 1919, Colonel Edward M. House wanted him named chief financial adviser on the American Commission to Negotiate Peace, but Secretary Glass could not spare him. Nonetheless, Leffingwell helped to determine American strategy in Paris through daily cables to financial advisers Norman Davis and Thomas Lamont. Owing largely to his prudent management, the United States emerged from the war with less inflation and a sounder debt structure than any other belligerent.

Although Leffingwell was not a partisan Democrat, his promotion to Treasury secretary was widely expected when Glass resigned in November 1919. Glass and McAdoo recommended him strongly. The White House Press Office intimated that the appointment was pending. Congressional leaders expressed enthusiasm. But, for reasons that remain obscure, a two-month delay ensued; an edict then came from President Woodrow Wilson's sickroom naming David Houston instead. Leffingwell stayed on until May 1920, in order to provide for an orderly transition. Thereafter he returned to his law firm, which was renamed Cravath, Henderson, Leffingwell and de Gersdorff.

In July 1923, Leffingwell joined J. P. Morgan and Company, the foremost investment banking institution in the United States. Although nominally one of fourteen senior partners, he quickly established himself as one of three guiding spirits in the firm, along with Thomas Lamont and J. P. Morgan, Jr. Morgan set general policy; Lamont handled outside negotiations; and Leffingwell bore primary responsibility for financial analysis of pending issues. During the 1920's Morgan and Company floated more than $2 billion in loans to foreign governments and did much to aid European reconstruction; in the troubled 1930's it sought to mitigate the effects of the depression and to promote currency stability. Leffingwell became vice-chairman of the Morgan executive committee when the firm incorporated in March 1940 in order to do trust business. He was made chairman of the executive committee in

1943 and chairman of the board in 1948. He stepped down to vice-chairman in November 1950, making way for a younger man. Although he retired formally in November 1955, he remained a director of Morgan and Company and of its successor, the Morgan Guaranty Trust Company, until his death.

Leffingwell helped found the Council on Foreign Relations and for many years served as chairman of its board. He was also board chairman of the Carnegie Corporation and a patron of the Yale University Library. On Wall Street, Leffingwell was considered a business intellectual who gained his points by persuasion, not by table-pounding. He was credited with having the keenest analytic mind among the Morgan partners, and in his work demonstrated unfailing rigor and a disdain for cant or loose thinking. He was highly cultured and possessed a command of English prose style unusual among the financial elite.

A trim six-footer with a prominent nose, a shock of white hair, and a piercing gaze, Leffingwell cut an imposing figure. Those who did not know him well thought him courtly but slightly forbidding. In private, though, he exhibited considerable charm and a notable talent for friendship; he encouraged younger men and in turn inspired loyalty and admiration.

Between 1920 and 1950, Leffingwell produced a stream of popular articles that projected his influence beyond the confines of the financial community. In the 1920's he favored "balanced budgets and honest money," and championed the interests of what his Yale mentor, William Graham Sumner, had called "the Forgotten Man": the producer and taxpayer. But he also advocated the reduction of tariff barriers, a liberal immigration policy, generous treatment of European war debtors, and prudent disarmament. When the depression struck, he modified his belief in classical economics and proclaimed, "A government cannot balance its budget by increasing the tax rate to be imposed upon declining incomes."

In 1933, President Franklin D. Roosevelt vetoed the proposed appointment of Leffingwell as undersecretary of the Treasury on the ground that politically "We simply cannot tie up with 23 [Wall Street]." Nevertheless, Leffingwell helped to rally business support for the New Deal and backed monetary reflation and suspension of gold payments. He was one of the few Wall Street leaders to support Roosevelt's reelection campaign in 1936. By 1940, though, Leffingwell had become skeptical of the ability of the government to "fine-tune" the economy, and warned that countercyclical fiscal-policy theories ignored the political tendency to perpetuate make-work spending. He criticized the "extreme cheap-money policy" of the Treasury during World War II and correctly predicted a postwar inflation when almost everyone else feared another depression. Over a generation few observers described so lucidly the vicissitudes of monetary policy and the structural problems of the American economy. Leffingwell died in New York City.

[Leffingwell's letterbooks dealing with his tenure at the Treasury are in the Library of Congress. His individual case file and "assistant secretary" file are in record group 56, general records of the Treasury, at the National Archives; also see the country files in record group 39, Bureau of Accounts. Substantial Leffingwell correspondence is in the Thomas Lamont Papers, Harvard Business School; Dwight W. Morrow Papers, Amherst College Library; William G. McAdoo and Norman Davis Papers, Library of Congress; Carter Glass Papers, University of Virginia Library; and Franklin D. Roosevelt Papers, Roosevelt Library, Hyde Park, N.Y. His business papers for the period after 1923 are at J. P. Morgan and Company; personal correspondence for that era is in family hands. The Yale University Library (Manuscripts and Archives) has Leffingwell's scrapbook of Yale memorabilia and his album of family photographs. Family genealogy is traced in Albert Tracy Leffingwell and Charles Wesley Leffingwell. *The Leffingwell Record, 1637–1897* (1897).

Biographical sketches appear in *New York Times,* July 8, 1923; *Business Week,* Feb. 21, 1948; and the *New York Times* (obituary), Oct. 3, 1960.

Studies treating facets of Leffingwell's career include Vincent Carosso, *Investment Banking in America* (1970); Frank Freidel, *Franklin D. Roosevelt: Launching the New Deal* (1973); Charles Gilbert, *American Financing of World War I* (1970); Stephen A. Schuker, *The End of French Predominance in Europe* (1976); John Brooks, *Once in Golconda* (1969). Leffingwell's major writings include "Treasury Methods of Financing the War in Reference to Inflation," *Proceedings of the Academy of Political Science,* June 1920; "The Soldier and His Bonus," *Saturday Evening Post,* May 15, 1920; "The Discount Policy of the Federal Reserve Banks," *American Economic Review,* Mar. 1921; "Retrenchment in National Expenditure," *Proceedings of the Academy of Political Science,* July 1921; "An Analysis of the International War Debt Situation," *The Annals,* July 1922; "America's Interest in Europe," *Foreign Policy Association Pamphlet No. 14,* July 1922; "The War

Debts," *Yale Review*, Oct. 1922; "The Post-War Years," in *Hearings before the Committee on Banking and Currency*, U.S. Sen., 72nd Cong., 1st Sess., *Stock Exchange Practices*, Pt. 2, Exhibit 53 (1933); "The Gold Problem and Currency Revaluation," *Proceedings of the Academy of Political Science*, Apr. 1934; testimony on war finance in *Hearings before Special Committee Investigating the Munitions Industry*, U.S. Sen., 74th Cong., 2nd Sess., Pt. 32 (1936); "Notes for T.N.E.C.," *Wall Street Journal*, Jan. 19, 1940; "Managing Our Economy," *Yale Review*, summer 1945; "How to Control Inflation," *Fortune*, Oct. 1948; "Devaluation and European Recovery," *Foreign Affairs*, Jan. 1950; "Our Fiscal and Banking Policy," *Barron's*, Nov. 13, 1950.]

STEPHEN A. SCHUKER

LEISERSON, WILLIAM MORRIS (Apr. 15, 1883–Feb. 12, 1957), labor economist and mediator, was born in Revel (now Tallin), Estonia, the son of Mendel Leiserson and Sarah Snyder, Russian Jews active in anticzarist movements. After the disappearance of her husband, Sarah Leiserson took her children to New York City in 1890. Leiserson left school at age fourteen to work in a shirtwaist factory but attended night classes and political discussions at the Cooper Union and the University Settlement. In 1904 he entered the University of Wisconsin. There his youthful socialism was tempered by the growth of a close professional and personal relationship with Professor John R. Commons, whose empirical and progressive intellectual tradition Leiserson would follow throughout his academic and public career. He spent much of his junior year with Commons, as a staff member of the Pittsburgh Social Survey; and after graduation with the B.A. in 1908, he helped to edit two volumes in Commons' *Documentary History of American Labor*.

While a graduate student in economics at Columbia University, Leiserson worked as an investigator for the New York Commission on Unemployment and Workmen's Compensation. His 1911 report to the commission, which served as the basis for his doctoral dissertation, recommended the establishment of public employment offices. He regarded such bureaus as a means of reducing frictional unemployment and assimilating recent immigrants, not as a form of state aid to those unfit for regular employment.

Although his proposals, which were much influenced by the ideas of the English reformer William H. Beveridge, were not then adopted in New York, Leiserson was able to put some of them into effect in Wisconsin when Commons secured his appointment as deputy industrial commissioner of the state in 1911. He set up a model network of public employment offices and also helped to found the National Association of Public and Private Employment Agencies. His advocacy of unemployment insurance, begun in 1913, was predicated upon an assumption that unemployment was an "unavoidable risk" of modern industrial life, to be ensured against by state action, but not eliminated or even substantially reduced. Leiserson continued his investigation of the employment market for the U.S. Commission on Industrial Relations in 1914 and 1915, then accepted a professorship in economics and politics at Toledo University.

On June 22, 1912, Leiserson married Emily Nash Bodman; they had seven children.

Although Leiserson was a popular teacher and a productive scholar at Toledo and at Antioch College, where he taught from 1925 to 1933, he happily devoted the bulk of his career to public administration and the arbitration or mediation of labor disputes. During World War I he took administrative posts, first in Ohio and then in Washington, D.C., to help organize an emergency system of public employment offices. While in the capital Leiserson worked frequently with Sidney Hillman, president of the Amalgamated Clothing Workers, who asked him in 1919 to serve as arbitrator on the new Labor Adjustment Board of the union. For the next seven years Leiserson worked in Rochester, N.Y., and other centers of clothing manufacture to help institutionalize collective bargaining in the industry. In numerous articles and speeches he argued that strong unions and routine labor relations served to increase productivity and worker income, to bulwark social stability, and to counter the growth of left-wing ideology among American workers.

Leiserson achieved his greatest influence as a formulator and administrator of social legislation during the Great Depression. As chairman of the Ohio Commission on Unemployment Insurance in 1931 and 1932, he did much to advance the idea that unemployment benefits should be financed by pooled employer contributions administered by the state. Called to Washington in the early days of the New Deal, he helped draft National Recovery Administration (NRA) labor codes and served as secretary of the short-lived National Labor Board. Although he enjoyed the excitement of the New Deal, he disliked the improvised, often contradictory character of NRA labor policy. Hence he welcomed the opportunity in mid-1934 to chair the new, autonomous National Mediation Board, empowered to hold representation elections among railroad employees and to mediate labor disputes. A tough but supple and inventive mediator, he won the confidence of the railway brotherhoods and the American Federation of Labor (AFL), presiding over the elimination of company unionism while respecting traditional craft and class jurisdictions among the unions.

In 1939, Secretary of Labor Frances Perkins secured Leiserson's appointment to the National Labor Relations Board (NLRB). At the time the NLRB was under sharp attack by conservatives and by the leadership of the AFL, which thought the board favored the Congress of Industrial Organizations (CIO). Fearful that these forces might amend the Wagner Act, Perkins and President Franklin D. Roosevelt expected Leiserson to alter NLRB policy and personnel so as to conciliate the AFL and defuse demands for a major change in New Deal labor law.

Once on the board Leiserson called for the dismissal of the powerful NLRB secretary, Nathan Witt, and a thorough reorganization of the large field division of the board controlled by the office of the secretary. He accused Witt and those loyal to him of incompetence, excessive legalism, left-wing politics, and a pronounced bias toward the CIO, but his controversial efforts to reorganize the NLRB were frustrated for more than a year because he was usually outvoted on the three-man board. In November 1940, Roosevelt appointed Harry A. Millis, a friend and early student of Commons', chairman of the NLRB. The Leiserson-Millis majority forced Witt and many of his staff to resign. On the crucial issue of unit jurisdiction, they stressed the importance of stability and respect for the history of the collective bargaining relationship; hence, they tended to defend the claims of an older craft unit against those of a newer factorywide union. Where industrial unions were found to be appropriate, the new majority reversed an earlier board policy ordering multiplant units and instead mandated elections on a plant-by-plant basis. They also narrowed somewhat the employer duty to bargain and allowed replacements to vote in representation elections following a strike over chiefly economic issues.

Leiserson remained on the NLRB until 1943,

but his commitment to traditional collective bargaining and minimal governmental interference in the process soured him on the wartime labor policy. He criticized the National War Labor Board for undermining free bargaining and union independence, and in May 1944 resigned in protest from the National Railway Labor Panel. He did so because the Roosevelt administration, inconsistent in its wage guideline policy, had rejected as inflationary a settlement that Leiserson had helped to mediate. During the next three years he was a visiting professor at Johns Hopkins, where he began a critical study of internal union life, *American Trade Union Democracy* (1959). Leiserson died in Washington, D.C.

[Leiserson's papers are on deposit at the State Historical Society of Wisconsin, at Madison. His New Deal career can also be followed in the files of the National Mediation Board and the NLRB, in the National Archives. See also J. Michael Eisner, *William Morris Leiserson* (1967); Daniel Nelson, *Unemployment Insurance* (1969); and James A. Gross, *The Making of the National Labor Relations Board*, vol. II (forthcoming). A number of memoirs in the Columbia University Oral History Collection mention Leiserson, especially that of Thomas Emerson. A short obituary appeared in the *New York Times*, Feb. 13, 1957.]

NELSON LICHTENSTEIN

LENZ, SIDNEY SAMUEL (July 12, 1873–Apr. 12, 1960), authority on contract bridge, was born in a suburb of Chicago, the son of John J. and Joanna L. Lenz. The family moved to New York City in 1888. Sometime before his twenty-first birthday, Lenz returned to the Midwest. A combination of enterprise and good luck made him immediately successful in business, and he soon became owner of a lumber mill and paper-box factory in Wisconsin. At the age of thirty-one he announced his retirement, intending to devote the rest of his life to his athletic and intellectual interests.

Lenz first turned his attention to sports: table tennis, golf, and especially bowling. In 1909 he bowled an average of 240 over twenty consecutive games, a record of long standing. At about the same time he became fascinated by whist, and barely a year later was a member of the team that won the Hamilton Trophy, representing the most important championship of the American Whist League.

The transition to auction bridge, when it became popular in the second decade of the century, posed few difficulties for a player of Lenz's talent; and in 1924 he led a team from the Knickerbocker Whist Club of New York to victory in the first "All America" trophy competition, sponsored by the American Whist League. This team maintained its reputation as the best in the country throughout the period when auction bridge was popular. Lenz's greatest successes, however, came in pairs events, of which he won a great many during his career, including the American Whist League Open Pairs and Men's Pairs in whist four times each, and its Auction Open Pairs Twice.

Nevertheless, Lenz's popular fame stemmed less from his triumphs at the table than from his writings. From the early 1920's on, he published a large number of articles in bridge magazines and general periodicals, including instructional pieces, humorous essays, verse parodies, and fiction, with and without bridge themes. He was the first bridge columnist of the *New York Times*, beginning in 1923. He also wrote for the humor magazine *Judge*, of which he was part owner. His most important book, *Lenz on Bridge* (1926), was an immediate success as much for the informality of its tone as for its clarity of exposition and technical excellence.

Lenz's writings on bridge earned him a large income. He refused to play cards for money, explaining that his ability at sleight of hand would cast suspicion on his victories. (He was widely regarded as the best amateur magician in the United States, and was the first nonprofessional elected an honorary member of the American Society of Magicians.)

By the time contract bridge began its rise to popularity in the late 1920's, Lenz was firmly established as one of the foremost experts at all forms of the game. This circumstance brought him to the front rank of the battle against the growing empire of Ely Culbertson, whose attempt to dominate the new game was viewed with mounting consternation by other professionals. Some of them, including Lenz, formed Bridge Headquarters and promulgated a system of bidding, in which Lenz's ideas were prominent, in opposition to the one recommended by Culbertson. When Culbertson and his wife challenged the combined forces of Bridge Headquarters to a match, ostensibly to test their competing systems but actually for effective control of the American bridge market, Lenz, in partnership with the young New York expert Oswald Jacoby,

was selected to represent the Headquarters side.

The match, often called the Bridge Battle of the Century, began on Dec. 7, 1931, at the Hotel Chatham in New York. This encounter, lasting more than 150 rubbers, attracted strong public attention. According to one account, "The quondam parlor game of bridge was converted on that night to the status of a national spectacle, comparable to the gridiron, World Series baseball games, or a national political convention." The match was won on Jan. 8, 1932, by the Culbertsons, with a margin of 8,970 points. Lenz had opposed them throughout, with a second partner, Commander Winfield Liggett, after a dispute over a bid had caused Jacoby to withdraw.

Although Lenz continued to appear in bridge competitions for a few years afterward (winning the 1932 Eastern States Open Pairs, for example), the result of the match, and the acrimony attending it, diminished his taste for play. He remained a revered member of the bridge community, in his later years often acting as an honorary referee at major matches. He continued to play privately until his death. He also retained an interest in magic, practicing sleight of hand for an hour a day until his last illness. Lenz, who never married, died in New York City.

[Lenz's less important books are *How's Your Bridge;* (1929), written with Robert Rendel; *My System of Contract Bidding* (1930); and *1-2-3. Sidney S. Lenz's Book on the Official System of Contract Bidding* (1931). Biographical material is scanty. The obituary notice, *New York Times,* Apr. 13, 1960, provides some information; and there is a useful article by Albert Morehead in Richard L. Frey, ed., *Encyclopedia of Bridge* (1964).]

DAVID I. DANIELS

LITCHFIELD, PAUL WEEKS (July 26, 1875–Mar. 18, 1959), rubber manufacturer, was born in Boston, Mass., the son of Charles Manfred Litchfield, a commercial photographer, and Julia Winter. Litchfield attended English High School and graduated from the Massachusetts Institute of Technology in 1896. After a stopgap job, he took a position at $9 a week with a manufacturer of bicycle tires. He designed tires for New York City's Fifth Avenue buses, which attracted the attention of Frank Seiberling of Goodyear. In July 1900 Litchfield was hired by Goodyear as "production superintendent, chemist, engineer, employment manager and company doctor," at $2,500 a year. His background in chemical engineering was useful in an industry that was moving toward the scientific manipulation of a complex raw material in the revolutionary age of transportation and synthetics.

Litchfield joined a company of 176 employees; when he became president of Goodyear in 1926, it was the largest in the industry. Facing patent strangulation problems in 1900, Litchfield responded with the tire of the future: the straightside. With the sense of the importance of time, which he always emphasized, he struck fast to reap the rewards. In 1908 he set up the company's research and development department. He added the wire bead for holding the tire on the rim better, invented the nonskid tire, and introduced a superior cord tire. In 1916 Goodyear pioneered in pneumatic tires for trucks, which, by extending the speed and range of trucks, sparked a revolution in freight transportation. In the 1930's, Goodyear led rubber's expansion into tires for farm machinery. Litchfield also expanded his product line by adding belting and other rubber mechanical goods. Vertical integration of the processes began with a textile mill to provide the fabrics used in rubber products, coal mines for power, and in 1916 an Arizona cotton plantation and rubber plantations in Sumatra. A Canadian facility in 1910 was its first foreign factory.

Litchfield again anticipated the future by branching into air transportation, building the first practical airplane tire in 1910. His interest led to the famous Goodyear blimps and two large navy airships. In 1939 he incorporated the Goodyear Aircraft Corporation to make airplane parts. This expanded into a contract for Corsair fighters that made Goodyear one of the ten largest producers of aircraft during World War II. Goodyear also operated synthetic-rubber plants for the government, having built its first synthetic tire in 1937. After the war Litchfield continued diversification with plastics, electronics, and atomic energy.

From the first Litchfield had emphasized management training, and he was confident that his "team" could make any product it set out to. In 1913 he created the "Flying Squadron," a team of workers trained to be able to fill in anywhere and to take on special projects. The training was soon extended to include executives. Litchfield saw the value of high wages, both in improving efficiency and in stimulating consumption. In 1910 he established a labor department and in 1912 a

newspaper, hospital, restaurant, and employees residential community. Shortly after Henry Ford, he established the eight-hour day and, during the Great Depression, the six-hour day. He organized an association for the purchase of sickness and accident insurance, a pension plan, and Americanization classes. In 1915 he established the Service Pin Association for employees with five or more years of service, and personally contributed $100,000 to a fund for them to manage and profit from. In 1919, in order to allow workers participation in decisions affecting their rights, he established the Goodyear Industrial Assembly. By the mid-1930's paternalism was out of date. Litchfield had early established an efficiency department; now men complained of the speedup. In 1937 sitdown strikes came to Goodyear, and union recognition followed.

A pioneer in mass distribution, Litchfield in 1926 signed the first contract for tire distribution with a mass merchandiser, Sears-Roebuck, revolutionizing the marketing of tires.

His most difficult experience was the near bankruptcy of the company in 1920–1921. Inventory losses in rubber and cotton forced Seiberling out, and banker control was established. After five years Litchfield managed to return control of the company to its stockholders, although banks retained large interests. Litchfield became chairman of the board in 1930 and retained the position until 1958.

Litchfield married Florence Pennington Brinton on June 23, 1904. They had two daughters. He created the first Boy Scout Air Troop and served on the national board of the Boy Scouts. After contract with Future Farmers of America, he established a program that enabled young men to be trained in farming and eventually to own their own farms. His unusually articulate writings, as well as his vision, were strongly grounded in the study of history. They include *Autumn Leaves* (1945), a distillation of his business philosophy for the young, and *Industrial Voyage* (1954), an autobiography. Litchfield died in Phoenix, Ariz.

[The most useful material comes from Litchfield's cited books and his *Industrial Republic* (1946). The most useful articles about Litchfield are in the following: *Business Week*, July 29, 1950, and Nov. 20, 1954; *Coronet*, Oct. 1954; *Fortune*, Nov. 1939; *Newsweek*, Apr. 16, 1956; *New York Times*, Aug. 21, 1949, III, 3:2; and *Rubber Age*, July 1950 and Apr. 1959. His obituary appears in the *New York Times*, Mar. 19, 1959.]

NANCY P. NORTON

LITTLEDALE, CLARA SAVAGE (Jan. 31, 1891–Jan. 9, 1956), journalist and editor, was born in Belfast, Me., the daughter of John Arthur Savage and Emma Morrison. Her father was a Methodist minister who developed doctrinal differences with his church and later was ordained in the Unitarian ministry. When Clara Savage was a year old the family moved to Medfield, Mass., where she spent her childhood and attended high school. Upon her father's retirement, the family moved to Plainfield, N.J., where she finished high school.

Influenced by Charles A. Selden, a New York newspaperman, foreign correspondent, and husband of an older sister, she began to think of a career in journalism. She enrolled at Smith College, where she became a member of the press board. While at college she sold short feature articles to the *New York Times* and other newspapers.

After graduating from Smith in 1913, Savage got a job on Oswald Garrison Villard's *New York Evening Post*, which had never before employed a woman reporter in its city room. After moving up to woman's page editor, Savage became interested in the woman suffrage movement and resigned in 1914 to become press chairman of the National American Woman Suffrage Association. On one occasion she paraded down Fifth Avenue in New York City, carrying a sign reading, "Insane and Idiots Can Vote, Why Can't I?" Finding, however, that she did not care for publicity work, Savage joined *Good Housekeeping* magazine in 1915 as associate editor and persuaded the editor in chief to send her to Washington to report each month upon political developments at the capital as seen from the woman's angle.

In June 1918 the magazine sent Savage to Europe on a six-month assignment to write on aspects of the American participation in World War I. She found so much that she wished to see and record that she asked the editor to extend her stay for another six months. When he refused, she replied with a three-word cable: "Resigning and remaining." She continued to travel and write as a free-lancer based in Paris until the fall of 1919. After returning to the United States, Savage demonstrated her versatility by contributing articles and stories to a wide range of general and specialized magazines. On Dec. 20, 1920, she married Harold Aylmer Littledale, a newspaper colleague whom she had met while working for the *New York Evening Post*. They were divorced in 1945.

Following several years of domesticity, during which she had a daughter, Littledale was persuaded by the publisher George J. Hecht to return to the magazine field. In July 1926 she became managing editor of a new venture that Hecht was launching, *Children, the Magazine for Parents*. A monthly publication devoted editorially to pre-natal and infant care, it advised on the problems of adolescence, on books, movies, and the comics, and on the whole range of parent-child relationships. It was sponsored by prominent consultants, educators, clinicians, agencies of the federal government, and child-welfare organizations. In 1928 Littledale took a six-month leave of absence in connection with the birth of a second child. The following year *Children* evolved into *Parents' Magazine* with Littledale's name on the masthead as chief editor. It remained there until her death.

Under Littledale's guidance, *Parents' Magazine* became a far-reaching influence. It was used as a text in college and university classes and by thousands of child-study and parent-teacher associations. It was widely quoted in periodicals, in books, and on the air. At the time of Littledale's death *Parents' Magazine* was the most widely read publication in its field, with a circulation of 1,675,000.

As editor and regular contributor to the magazine and in her frequent radio, television, and platform appearances, Littledale sought to translate technical scientific studies on family health and nutrition, child training, vocational guidance, and experimental work in the field of education into practical, understandable articles. *Parents' Magazine* supported legislation prohibiting the exploitation of child labor; advocated better school health facilities, more child care centers, expanded nursery- and play-school programs, and increased federal aid to education; and rallied support for the United Nations International Children's Emergency Fund (UNICEF). Littledale was coauthor of *Parents' Magazine Book of Baby Care* (1952) and edited a number of condensations of standard literary works.

Common sense was the hallmark of Littledale's advice to parents. To a mother who called her in great distress, asking what to do when her son refused to eat breakfast, the editor replied solemnly, "Try him on lunch." Littledale's gentle manner, light touch, and sense of humor masked, but only slightly, her essential character as a compassionate, articulate, and determined crusader for child-welfare causes.

[Genealogical data and biographical and autobiographical material are in the Clara Savage Littledale Collection of the Schlesinger Library, Radcliffe College; and in the archives of the Alumnae Association of Smith College. See also the obituary notices in the *New York Herald Tribune* and *New York Times*, Jan. 10, 1956.]

GERALD CARSON

LIVINGSTONE, BELLE (Jan. 20, 1875?–Feb. 7, 1957), adventuress, was born in Kansas. Abandoned as an infant by her father, allegedly a mining prospector on his way west, she was found under a sunflower and was adopted by John Ramsey Graham, editor and co-owner of the *Emporia News*, and his wife, Annie M. Likly, who named her Isabelle Graham. In 1892 Graham sold his interest in another Emporia paper, the *Gazette* (which he had founded), and moved the family to Chicago. Livingstone attended the Academy of the Immaculate Conception in Oldenburg, Ind. (1891–1893), before her burgeoning interest in the theater led her to join the chorus of the second road company of *Wang*. When her parents refused to let her live away from home unmarried, she asked the first well-dressed man she met to marry her. After the ceremony, in Saginaw, Mich., they parted. To avoid further family scandal, she took the name Livingstone, in honor of the British missionary explorer David Livingstone. She subsequently appeared in an Atlantic City summer production of the opera *Falka*.

The details of Livingstone's theatrical career, as well as of her life, are a curious blend of press agentry, inspired fantasy, and self-created legend, diligently disseminated in three autobiographies. In these sources, her memory starred her as the Leader of the Drum Corps in the Broadway production of *The Milk White Flag*. Surviving programs record only her one-week appearance, in February 1897, in a Boston revival—last in the line. Nor can confirmation be found for her claim that she "led the beauty march" in *Jack and the Beanstalk* in 1896.

The death of her absentee husband, Richard John Wherry, a paint salesman, and a $150,000 legacy from his estate enabled Livingstone to broaden her horizons, and she sailed for Europe in the summer of 1897. She soon established herself in London as a leading demimondaine, allegedly becoming an intimate of Prince Hussein, James Gordon Bennett, King Leopold II of Belgium, Lord Kitchener, the Prince of Wales, and Harry K. Thaw, in addition to luminaries of the stage and of bohemian society. Her fortune hunting led to a brief and unsuccessful foray to Cairo in 1901 to speculate in a turquoise mine. Capitalizing on her attractiveness and the novelty of her Kansas forthrightness, Livingstone lived in the lap of luxury until 1902. In that year luxury stood up. She discovered that she had been swindled in a stock certificate forgery and that her extensive investments in the Great Fingalls mine in Australia were worthless. On a whim, she bet her friends £5,000 that she could travel around the world on a £5 bill—and her wits.

Funded by friends along the way, Livingstone headed for the Far East. In March 1903, while in Yokohama, she married Count Florentino Ghiberti Laltazzi, whom she had met on the trip. Laltazzi died of pneumonia in St. Petersburg while en route to rejoin her in Paris; and their marriage, performed by a missionary priest, was subsequently declared invalid.

Broke again, and the widowed mother of a daughter, Livingstone sold her possessions and subsisted on handouts and loans from friends. To support herself she published her first volume of memoirs in 1906 and embarked for Monte Carlo to recoup her fortune at the gaming tables. After marrying an American millionaire, Edward Keene Mohler, on Mar. 21, 1906, she moved to Paris. They had one son. But tiring of her new life, which she found "too tame," she divorced Mohler in 1911.

Now notorious for being a "dangerous woman," Livingstone married Walter James Hutchins, an American engineer, on Sept. 3, 1912. After World War I, she attended the University of Paris, before fortune again frowned on her. Hutchins, having learned that she had spent all his money, left her. Destitute again, Livingstone returned to Monte Carlo, where she lost what little money she had realized from the sale of her possessions. She struggled to regain her past glory in London, fawning and pawning as she went. A series of memoirs for *Cosmopolitan* (1925) brightened things somewhat. Two years later, her patriotic feelings aroused, she was invited to return to the United States and write about her native country, which she had not seen for thirty years.

Finding America dull, and Prohibition hardly to her taste, Livingstone announced plans to open a salon "modeled on those of Mme. Récamier and Mme. de Staël," where luminaries would gather to bandy trifles destined for immortality. The result was One Man House, a short-lived speakeasy on New York City's East 52nd Street. Despite its $200 membership fee, the "salon" went broke the following year. Undaunted, Livingstone opened The Silver Room, a Park Avenue after-hours rendezvous, in the fall of 1929. But her cultural ambitions were not without their detractors, and the following April she was arrested for the third time in as many months following a raid by federal agents. Arraigned in "bootleggers' row" the next day, she denied having violated the Volstead Act. "I merely did as any hostess did," she explained. "I offered them a glass of champagne." The confiscated liquor, she maintained, was owned by her clients.

Following the demise of The Silver Room, Livingstone moved to East 58th Street with her third venture, The Country Club. Guests who attended its opening, on Oct. 29, 1930, entered a reconverted townhouse strikingly decorated in red and black with an ornamental motif of champagne magnums. In keeping with that year's fad, a miniature golf course was implanted on the fourth floor, together with Ping-Pong tables. The second and third floors offered a bar and jazz orchestra.

On Dec. 4, 1930, shortly before midnight, tuxedoed government agents entered the premises and, seizing a megaphone, ordered the 400 assembled patrons to leave. As the raid started, Livingstone recalled, "I saw agents all around. Someone shouted 'Fore!' 'Hell, no,' I replied, 'there are twenty of 'em!' " Fifty bottles of bootleg liquor, as well as Livingstone, were seized. Livingstone again denied that she was the owner or had any proprietary interest and was released on bail the following day.

Another raid six weeks later had more serious consequences. Livingstone was in her top-floor apartment when a lookout signaled by bell that her patrons were scrambling for the door. Hastily donning a cloak over flaming red pajamas, she fled through the roof trapdoor reserved for such contingencies, dashed across to the neighboring brownstone, and raced downstairs to a waiting cab, where she was greeted by federal agents. "I could have escaped," she told reporters at her arraignment, "but like Lot's wife, I looked back and that's all there is to it." She pleaded not guilty to the charge of criminal contempt (violating a temporary personal dry-law injunction pending the outcome of her two previous proceedings). Describing the exercise as "a good way to keep from getting old," she claimed to be guilty "only

of good taste in being hostess in this club and not in another."

But Livingstone's elan diminished as her trial got under way. She insisted—as reporters devoured her testimony—that she had been hired only to supervise the decor, adding that her years of study at Cambridge and at the Sorbonne had made her eminently qualified for the job. When asked to name the owners, she demurred. "If I did," she testified, "I'd be shot as soon as I walked out of here." A lenient judge handed down the minimum, thirty-day sentence, taking into consideration her age, which she gave as sixty-five. Livingstone tearfully called herself a "fall guy" and avowed that "just a lot of lunatics" obeyed the Prohibition act. Ever adamant in her denial, she confessed that she was using the speakeasy only for material for her book, to be entitled *With Livingstone Through Darkest America*.

Released from Harlem Prison in March 1931, Livingstone was whisked to The Country Club in Texas Guinan's armored limousine and feted at a "coming-out party." Jokingly praising the prison food, she was asked by a reporter if she thought that her morals had been impaired by her contact with prisoners. "No," she replied, "in my opinion they have been improved." Two months later The Country Club was padlocked, and after pleading guilty to dry-law charges Livingstone was fined $100.

Expecting to profit from Nevada's relaxed divorce and gambling laws, Livingstone announced her plans for another "salon," in Reno, "the one spot in America that is not infested with Puritans." After filing for bankruptcy and claiming $33,000 of debt, she left New York. Two months later, over the protests of ranchers owning adjacent property, she was granted a gambling license. In October her club was raided. Another attempt, at East Hampton, N.Y., in the summer of 1933, proved equally unsuccessful.

To a nation burdened by deepening economic depression and massive unemployment, Livingstone's free-spirited antics and lighthearted defiance of authority provided a bright light of escapism. But with the repeal of Prohibition and worsening conditions, her luster dimmed. In December 1934 she opened her last nightclub, the Reno, in Texas Guinan's former New York City headquarters on West 54th Street. Ten days later it closed. The following summer she was denied a liquor license for a nightclub in Falmouth, Mass. No longer a headline-maker, she sank into obscurity, surfacing briefly in March 1939, when her top-floor apartment caught fire. In an encore of her pajama performance, she escaped by running across the roof.

By 1949, when she was hospitalized for a heart attack, she was all but forgotten except by policemen, reporters, night workers, and habitués of East Side watering spots. After a second heart attack in 1955, she was confined to a nursing home in the Bronx, where she died. Her epitaph was to have read: "The Only Stone I Left Unturned."

[Livingstone's life is thoroughly—if not always accurately—documented in her writings: *Letters of a Bohemian* (1906); "The Story of My Life (They Called Me the Most Dangerous Woman in Europe)," *Cosmopolitan,* June–Sept. 1925, reprinted as *Belle of Bohemia* (1927); and the posthumously published *Belle Out of Order* (1959), which should be read in conjunction with Patrick Dennis' satiric *Little Me* (1961). Her battles with Prohibition are chronicled in the *New York Times,* 1930–1931. Livingstone threatened to sue over a brief article in *Vanity Fair,* May 1931, p. 44. Laura M. French, *History of Emporia and Lyon County* (1929), pp. 223–225, is useful on John Graham's journalistic background.]

JOEL HONIG

LOCKHEED, MALCOLM (1887?–Aug. 13, 1958), aircraft manufacturer and inventor, was born Malcolm Loughead in Niles, Calif., the son of John Loughead and Flora Haines. A self-taught mechanic who left school early, he worked in garages in San Francisco with his brother Allan Haines Lockheed. Allan persuaded Malcolm to help him build an airplane, the Model G, so named so that people would not think it was their first. On June 15, 1913, the aircraft made its first flight, over San Francisco Bay. Malcolm ran the ground side, and Allen flew. Soon they were taking passengers up at $5 a ride.

For the next two years the brothers worked as mechanics and sporadically prospected for gold. Malcolm then served briefly as "chief engineer" of the Carranzista air force in Mexico in 1914. When World War I broke out in August 1914, he was on his way with a Curtiss biplane to Hong Kong to establish a sales and service agency. But off the China coast a British warship stopped the freighter and confiscated the Curtiss as contraband. Lockheed returned to the Bay area, where he and Allan found a wealthy Alaskan backer for their Model G. They obtained the flying concession at the Panama-Pacific Exposi-

tion and grossed $6,000 in fifty flying days with a charge of $10 for a ten-minute ride. When the exposition closed, the family moved back to Santa Barbara, where they had once lived, with the Model G being shipped down in crates.

In 1916 the brothers founded the Loughead Aircraft Manufacturing Company with Malcolm as secretary and treasurer and Berton R. Rodman of Santa Barbara as president. (A successor company that emerged in 1934 was the forerunner of the Lockheed Aircraft Company.) John K. Northrop, a new addition, was at once put to work on the stressing of the wings of the F-1, a twin-engine flying-boat of seventy-four-foot span that could carry ten persons. In early 1917, with America's entry into the war imminent, the Lockheeds offered to make their services available to the government. In April 1918 the navy asked that the F-1 be flown to North Island, San Diego, where it was tested, but it was rejected because the navy wished to standardize on the Curtiss HS2L. The Lockheeds were given a contract to build two variations, on which they lost $4,000 or more. In August 1918 they decided that the F-1 should be converted to a landplane and demonstrated in Washington. Unfortunately it crashed at Tacna, Ariz., because of engine failure. In the meantime the Lockheeds had developed and patented a molded plywood system first used in the S-1 biplane of 1918, which did not sell.

Lockheed left the company in 1919, and it was dissolved in 1921. In 1918 he had designed and patented (no. 1,288,944) the Lockheed four-wheel hydraulic automobile braking system, which had been conceived in 1904; it was sold to Chrysler in 1922 for a million dollars. Many details of his later life are obscure, and after 1925 he became a recluse of whom almost no trace exists. He died in Mokelumne Hill, Calif.

[The best source is *Of Men and Stars* (1957), an informal history of Lockheed Aircraft issued by the corporation. See also the *New York Times* obituary notice, Aug. 14, 1958.]

ROBIN HIGHAM

LOEB, LEO (Sept. 21, 1869–Dec. 28, 1959), pathologist and experimental biologist, was born in Mayen, near Koblenz, Germany, the son of Benedict Loeb, a prosperous businessman, and Barbara Isay. His older brother, Jacques, became a celebrated physiologist. Their mother died when Loeb was three years old; their father, three years later. Loeb lived with his maternal grand-father at Trier until he was ten, and then with a maternal uncle who was a professor of medieval German history at the University of Berlin. In that city he attended the Askendische Gymnasium. Because of ill health in adolescence, presumably of a tubercular nature, he spent several years in health resorts while continuing his schooling. He graduated from a gymnasium at Heidelberg and began his university studies at Freiburg im Breisgau, where he attended the lectures of August Weismann, then continued at Basel, where he studied under Gustav von Bunge and Johann Friedrich Miescher.

In 1890, having decided to study medicine but unhappy about rising German nationalism and militarism, Loeb went to Zurich for preclinical studies, and in 1892 to the University of Edinburgh and to London Hospital for clinical work. In 1895 he returned to Zurich, where he passed the state examination admitting him to medical practice, but remained at the university to complete his dissertation for the M.D., which he received in 1897. With Hugo Ribbert, a pathologist and experimental scientist, Loeb did his thesis work on the results of skin transplantation experiments on guinea pigs. This work raised many fundamental biological questions relating to the growth and degeneration of epithelium, resistance to transplants, and tumors and malignancy.

In 1892 and 1894, Loeb had visited his brother Jacques at the Woods Hole Marine Biological Laboratory in Massachusetts. Attracted by democratic American ways and the opportunities offered for biological research, he immigrated to Chicago. There for a short time he practiced medicine while teaching at Rush Medical College and carrying out research privately in a rented room behind a drugstore. This interlude was followed by a few months at the Johns Hopkins University Medical School, in W. H. Welch's laboratory. Loeb held a research fellowship at McGill University with John George Adami (1902–1903), and then was assistant professor of experimental pathology at the University of Pennsylvania from 1904 to 1910. In the latter year he settled in St. Louis, where he became director of the pathological laboratory at Barnard Skin and Cancer Hospital, then (1915–1924) professor of comparative pathology at Washington University, and finally professor and head of the department of pathology (1924–1937). On Jan. 3, 1922, Loeb married Georgianna Sands, a physician. They had no children. After retiring

in 1937, he continued to work as research professor until 1941, and to write until his death, in St. Louis.

Loeb published more than 400 research papers. This prodigious list resulted in part from his tendencies to publish brief reports rather than comprehensive monographs and to republish work in English or German. His scientific career was one of pioneering research often marked by valuable discoveries that were not always carried through to perfected results. Loeb was one of the earliest experimenters to make successful serial transfers of tumors from animal to animal. Observing in transplants the growth of tongues of epithelial cells into blood clots, he repeated the experiment deliberately and produced the first recorded growth of cells of higher animals outside the body, a little-noticed preamble to the work of Ross Harrison and Alexis Carrel.

In 1903–1910, with A. E. C. Lathrop, Loeb demonstrated hereditary factors in the development of cancer, especially in the mammary glands of white mice. In 1907 he discovered by experiment on guinea pigs that the corpora lutea, appearing in the ovary in each reproductive cycle, act upon the uterus in such a way that if its lining is lightly scratched by the experimenter, placentalike tumors develop at the sites of injury, imitating placenta formation by the stimulus of implanting embryos. This was one of the first clues to the endocrine function of the corpus luteum. His continuing study of the reproductive cycle of the female guinea pig and his clear account of the relation of the ovarian cycle to uterine changes were very helpful to workers with other animals in their efforts to understand the physiology of the female reproductive cycle.

Beginning about 1930, Loeb pioneered in another field of endocrinology, making valuable contributions with several collaborators regarding the action of the pituitary gland upon the thyroid and the ovary. He published *The Venom of Heloderma* (1913), *Edema* (1924), and *The Biological Basis of Individuality* (1945), in which he applied his wide knowledge of animal organs and tissues to the problem of individual differences in structure and behavior in man and the higher animals.

Loeb was rather frail but resilient and had a retiring disposition. His lectures to medical students were notably clear and stimulating. To his numerous research associates he was generous with both assistance and credit for collaboration. His reputation was overshadowed by that of his famous brother. If he perhaps diffused his research interests too widely, if he sometimes followed unprofitable leads and failed to pursue promising ones, his incessant curiosity and often brilliant experimentation nevertheless make him one of the founders of experimental pathology and of modern cancer research in America.

[Loeb's "Autobiographical Notes" are in *Perspectives in Medicine and Biology*, Autumn 1958; a complete bibliography to 1949, with introduction by Philip A. Shaffer, is in *Archives of Pathology*, Dec. 1950. On his life and work see Ernest W. Goodpasture, "Leo Loeb," *Biographical Memoirs. National Academy of Sciences*, 1961, with full bibliography and portrait; and W. Stanley Hartroft's obituary notice, *Archives of Pathology*, Aug. 1960.]

GEORGE W. CORNER

LONG, BRECKINRIDGE (May 16, 1881–Sept. 26, 1958), diplomat, was born in St. Louis, Mo., the son of William Strudwick Long and Margaret Miller Breckinridge. He studied with private tutors and attended a local public high school. In the fall of 1899, following a Breckinridge family tradition, he entered Princeton University, graduating in 1904. He studied law at Washington University in St. Louis (1905–1906) and was admitted to the Missouri bar in 1906.

Long's law office records reveal that his was a small criminal and civil practice and that he had considerable difficulty in obtaining clients and collecting fees. In his spare time Long completed a master's thesis, "The Impossibility of India's Revolt from England" (Princeton, 1909). As a hobby he compiled material for a study of American colonial governments, a subject in which he first became interested as a student in Woodrow Wilson's constitutional law course. In this study, published in 1925 as *The Genesis of the Constitution of the United States,* Long argued that the Constitution drew extensively from colonial precedents and was not a "result of a stroke of genius on the part of the framers."

On June 1, 1912, Long married Christine Graham, the wealthy and socially prominent granddaughter of Francis Preston Blair, Democratic nominee for vice-president in 1868. With the necessity of building up his law practice no longer compelling, politics became his principal interest. In 1913, through his wife's political connections, Senator William Stone and Representative Champ Clark, both Missourians, urged

Long's appointment as third assistant secretary of state. But Secretary of State William Jennings Bryan objected, and the appointment was not forthcoming.

Undaunted, Long worked zealously in Missouri politics. He contributed more than $30,000 to the Democratic National Committee during the 1916 campaign and also lent the committee $100,000. The reward came shortly thereafter. On Jan. 29, 1917, Long was sworn in as third assistant secretary of state.

"During my first weeks in the Department I had a perfectly terrible time," recorded Long. "I worked from nine in the morning until midnight, or later, almost every night. . . . The supervision of the Bureau of Accounts and the entire financial end of the Department was entrusted to me. Then, I had all the ceremonial work. . . . The Far East was put under my supervision, including our relations with China and Japan, Siam, the South Sea Islands, Siberia, Australia and India. . . . I was the disbursing officer of the Department and had to sign all the warrants."

The Far East responsibilities almost overwhelmed Long. "Mr. [Edward T.] Williams who probably knows more about China than most any other man alive, was the Chief of the Far Eastern Bureau [1914–1918]. He would come down almost every day and we would talk about the Far East. . . . There were more complications internal and external than I had ever imagined and more than anybody had any right to believe. . . . Japan was easier, and Siam—poor, little Siam—was not at all hard. With India, Siberia, and Australia I had to do only with political problems which arose there or which arose in Europe and affected those countries" (Long diary).

Within three months of Long's appointment, the nation shifted from neutrality to armed neutrality and then to belligerency against Germany. New assignments were thrust upon the already burdened assistant secretary. One of the most time-consuming but interesting of these involved preparations for the many Allied missions—military, naval, parliamentary, financial, shipping—that now streamed into Washington. Long met each with proper protocol and arranged for housing, servants, food, flags, military guards, receptions, and a thousand other details. "I went through the performance so many times I could do it in my sleep."

During his service in the State Department, Long, motivated by a strong desire for higher political office, did his best to have Missourians placed on the federal payroll. He spoke to, wrote to, and entertained numerous government officials, securing all sorts of varied favors for his local backers. In addition, Long zealously worked for the Democratic National Committee, and his generous contributions placed him in that inner circle of politicians who mapped party strategy. Missouri was to choose a senator in 1920, and almost a full year before Long's family, friends, and fortune were at work to secure him the Democratic nomination. Long resigned from the State Department in June 1920 and immersed himself in state politics.

The Missouri political scene, however, was far from tranquil. The League of Nations controversy became the principal issue both in the primary and in the ensuing election. As an enthusiastic supporter of Wilson's internationalist policies, Long had participated in an intraparty fight that caused Senator James Reed, a bitter foe of the League, to be rejected as a delegate to the 1920 Democratic national convention. Although Long soundly defeated Reed's choice for the Senate in the August primary, the state Democratic party was shattered. Reed refused to support either Long or the national ticket, denouncing Wilson's foreign policy as a treacherous betrayal of the United States. Long, nevertheless, campaigned throughout the state on a platform that endorsed the League without any reservations. But Long's opponent, the incumbent Selden P. Spencer, won with a plurality of more than 120,000 votes.

Long then returned to his law practice, but political office still remained his goal. He maintained close contact with state and national Democratic leaders; and in 1922, when James Reed ran for reelection, he decided to oppose the senior senator.

The bitter primary campaign developed into a battle between Reed and Woodrow Wilson. The former president asserted that "Missouri cannot afford to be represented by such a marplot." Reed, who had referred to Wilson in 1920 as "that long-eared animal that goes braying about the country," welcomed the challenge. In spite of the former president's support, the Reed organization, in cooperation with Tom Pendergast, the acknowledged political boss of Kansas City, narrowly defeated Long with a majority of about 6,400 out of approximately 390,000 votes cast.

The Missouri electorate had destroyed Long's hopes for a Senate seat, and except for occasional visits to the state he now lived at Montpelier Manor, near Laurel, Md. As he wrote, "I have felt it would be the best thing for me and the party . . .

so the smoke of battle could blow away." Most of his time was occupied by breeding and racing horses, traveling, and politics. He continued to donate considerable sums to the Democratic National Committee. By the beginning of 1928 the consensus among Democrats was that Al Smith's candidacy was growing stronger every day. Long, who had opposed Smith in 1924, now considered his selection inevitable. At the convention in Houston, he fought for a strong World Court platform statement but grudgingly agreed to a compromise. After the convention Long worked at New York headquarters, "running the radio part of the campaign." But on election day of 1928 the Democratic party suffered a most humiliating defeat. The decisive verdict—Herbert Hoover received 444 electoral votes to Smith's 87—shocked Long: "There is no doubt now about how the American people feel." And in his diary he wrote: "Badly beaten—disgusted."

The 1930 election returns reduced the Republican majority in the House of Representatives from 103 to 2, and in the Senate the Republican administration barely retained organizational control. The Great Depression convinced Long that a strong leader was needed to prevent another convention split and to ensure a 1932 Democratic victory. After the 1930 elections he felt sure that this strong leader had emerged in the person of Franklin D. Roosevelt. In the preconvention wrangle for delegates, Long made a sizable contribution to Roosevelt's campaign chest. During the convention Long served as a Roosevelt floor manager. Because of this position and his financial contributions during the previous two decades, after Roosevelt's victory Long at last was rewarded with the high political office that he had coveted for so many years: Roosevelt appointed him ambassador extraordinary and minister plenipotentiary to Italy.

Long's first months in Italy were a glorious and exciting adventure. Finding the embassy quarters too "dingy," he leased the magnificent Villa Taverna. The ambassador's first reports and letters lauded Mussolini and fascism. Long wrote to Roosevelt (June 27, 1933), "Mussolini is an astounding character and the effects of his organized activities are apparent throughout all Italy. . . . Italy today is the most interesting experiment in government to come above the horizon since the formulation of our Constitution 150 years ago. . . .

"The Fascisti in their black shirts are apparent in every community. They are dapper and well dressed and stand up straight and lend an atmosphere of individuality and importance to their surroundings. . . . The trains are punctual, well-equipped, and fast."

Throughout 1933 Long's diplomatic reports stressed the political novelty of the corporate state, drawing parallels to the New Deal and especially to the National Recovery Administration. He praised the emerging imperialist policy of Mussolini. By 1933 Albania had come almost completely under Italian protection. "I think that we are entirely justified in playing the game with Italy in Albania," Long advised Roosevelt in July 1933. Nineteen months later, however, he counseled the president to equip "your diplomatic and consular officers in Europe with gas masks. . . . I am satisfied [Mussolini] is looking forward to the certainty of war and is preparing." And a few months later he was describing the regime as "deliberate, determined, obdurate, ruthless, and vicious."

This change in attitude ended Long's apprenticeship. His dispatches became more perceptive, his observations more acute. He spent hours reading and evaluating advisory papers. The realization of the importance of his position at the center of a country bent toward war transformed the millionaire politician into a sober diplomat. He made amazingly accurate reports, even predicting seven months in advance the week that Mussolini would invade Ethiopia. His intelligence information in the early part of 1935 contained excellent analyses of the types and amounts of war materials produced throughout Italy.

Roosevelt repeatedly chided Long for his pessimistic views, to which the ambassador responded, "You think I am a pessimist. As a matter of fact I am a realist. I see the situation in Europe as it exists. They are all prepared for war, and they have got to have it. A new order is in the making, and the results of it cannot yet be foreseen."

On Oct. 3, 1935, Italy launched the long-expected attack on Ethiopia. The League of Nations Council declared Italy to be the aggressor, and the Assembly voted to impose economic sanctions. President Roosevelt had already invoked neutrality legislation, and in a proclamation he enumerated the items on which trade was restricted, mainly arms and munitions.

It was soon apparent, however, that the League did not intend to impose oil sanctions against Italy. But Long, who had now developed an unshakable conviction that war in Europe was inevitable, advised that an Ethiopian solution remained completely in the hands of European diplomats and that the United States should keep out of the conflict. Cautioning against a unilateral oil blockade, he warned Roosevelt that such sanctions "may be neutral from the American point of view, but it is not consonant with the status of neutrality as fixed in the principles of international law." Roosevelt followed Long's advice, especially after it became clear that the League would not support strong collective action against Italy.

Beginning in 1934, severe stomach ulcers caused Long great pain. However, he continued to work at his post until the spring of 1936, when he had to resign and return to the United States for an operation. James Watts argues that Long's resignation was caused by a smoldering feud between the ambassador and the State Department and that illness was a secondary reason. Long, for example, presented his own sweeping scheme for ending the Ethiopian conflict to Mussolini without consulting Secretary of State Cordell Hull, for which Long was reprimanded.

For the next three years, Long remained in semiretirement, but on the outbreak of World War II, Roosevelt asked Long to serve as special assistant secretary of state to handle emergency war matters; in January 1940 he succeeded George Messersmith in that position. When the United States entered the war, he served on several special committees to explore postwar settlements.

Of the twenty-three State Department divisions under his supervision, the Visa Section placed Long in a position where his decisions were crucial on refugee rescue matters. Although not an anti-Semite, he somehow linked communism and international Jewry, and he had a strong dislike for both. Many supporters of a liberal refugee admissions policy were Jewish, and Long referred to them in his diary as the "radical boys" or "Frankfurter's boys," because, as Long viewed it, they were "representatives of his racial group and philosophy." Recent studies by Henry Feingold and Arthur Morse have accused Long of being insensitive to the plight of refugees. But Long was limited by the 1924 immigration law, which restricted immigration to some 150,000 aliens a year. Half of this quota was assigned to applicants from England or Ireland. The immigration law had been buttressed with an incredible mosaic of regulations, including rigid screening procedures. Furthermore, Roosevelt was ambivalent on the refugee issue, and Long believed that he was carrying out administration policy by protecting the nation against an invasion by those whom he considered radicals and foreign agents.

Long resigned from the State Department on Nov. 28, 1944. On July 28, 1945, he sat in the Senate gallery and heard the roll call on the resolution to ratify the United Nations Charter. "The faith of Woodrow Wilson has been vindicated.... This has been the motivating thought of my political life for about thirty years," he wrote. "Civilization has a better chance to survive—but the will to make it work will be a continuing necessity."

[Long's personal papers and diaries are in the Library of Congress. See also Fred L. Israel, ed., *The War Diary of Breckinridge Long* (1966); and James F. Watts, Jr., "The Public Life of Breckinridge Long, 1916–1944" (Ph.D. diss., University of Missouri, 1964). Two studies that are highly critical of Long's handling of war refugees are Henry L. Feingold, *The Politics of Rescue: The Roosevelt Administration and the Holocaust, 1938–1945* (1970); and Arthur D. Morse, *While Six Million Died* (1967).]

FRED L. ISRAEL

LONG, EARL KEMP (Aug. 26, 1895–Sept. 5, 1960), governor of Louisiana, was born in Winnfield, La., the son of Huey Pierce Long and Caledonia Tison. He had a comfortable childhood in Winnfield, playing ball or combing the nearby woods for his father's livestock. He so enjoyed the carefree environment that, despite parental prodding, he developed a lackadaisical attitude toward education. Yet, although he never received a college degree, he learned enough law at Loyola University Law School in New Orleans to pass the state bar examination in 1926. During his early years his only serious interest was in a sales career, which he successfully pursued from 1912 to 1927 in Louisiana and nearby states. At various times he sold patent medicines, hardware items, baking powder, and shoe polish. Salesmanship contributed to his political personality, for it enabled him to see firsthand the needs of the people and to establish contacts with local courthouse leaders.

Long's older brother Huey was the central figure in his involvement in politics. The brothers were especially close, and Earl helped Huey win election to the Louisiana Public Service Commission (1918), to the office of govenor (1928), and to the U.S. Senate (1930) by raising funds, making speeches, and helping in other ways. In 1928 Long became inheritance tax attorney for

Orleans Parish, but he worked primarily with the legislature as his brother's lobbyist or negotiator, pushing administration proposals to ribbon the state with paved roads, to replace antiquated ferries with new bridges, and to distribute free textbooks to public and parochial school pupils. These measures benefited poor white farmers. For more than a quarter of a century, voters would be divided into pro-Long and anti-Long camps. In 1929, Earl helped to prevent the conviction of his brother during impeachment proceedings. Huey later commented, "You give Earl a few dollars and turn him loose on the road, and he will make more contacts and better contacts than any ten men with a barrel of money."

But initial successes blunted Earl's judgment. In 1932 he lost the race for lieutenant governor because Huey refused to endorse him, fearful that Earl would be more interested in his own political future than in Huey's. The defeat embittered him. During the next two years he fought the administration, going so far as to accuse his brother of accepting graft payments and of running one of the worst dictatorships in the world. In 1934 Huey's presidential ambitions surfaced, and the brothers patched up their differences. But the assassination of Huey in September 1935 did not thrust Earl to the forefront as his legitimate heir. Other lieutenants came to power, but after some controversy the organization endorsed Earl as its candidate for lieutenant governor. Easily elected in 1936, he began to prepare for the 1940 gubernatorial primary. He avoided factional conflict and used every opportunity to extend his own base of support. The political climate changed suddenly in June 1939, when Governor Richard W. Leche resigned amid allegations of graft and corruption, leaving the executive office to Long. In the next eleven months Long attempted to mount a gubernatorial campaign while many former state officials were being indicted for stealing public funds. Although cleared of any personal wrongdoing, he lost the election to Sam Houston Jones, a Lake Charles attorney, by less than 10,000 votes.

Long had no intention of abandoning politics after his defeat. He had lost by a narrow margin, but the voters had returned a large delegation of Long supporters to the legislature. In 1944 he tried to win the post of lieutenant governor, but was unable to overcome the lingering resentment of the 1940 scandals. In a bitterly contested gubernatorial campaign in 1948, though, he defeated former Governor Jones overwhelmingly.

As governor, Long continued and accelerated the populist and progressive traditions established by his brother. The state expanded highway construction, made medical services and facilities more accessible to the underprivileged, and greatly increased pensions to citizens over sixty years of age. In addition, he made charity beds available to the poor in private hospitals, provided bonuses for veterans, and made salaries of black teachers equal to those of white teachers. He could truthfully brag, "I've done more for the poor people of this state than any governor. The only governor who came close was my brother Huey, and he was just starting out."

But Long allowed controversies to tarnish his image. Civil service proponents objected when he backed abolition of the program in the state because, he charged, his opponents dominated its administration. State Democratic party leaders were upset after he headed off Dixiecrat attempts to deny President Harry Truman a place on the Democratic ballot. New Orleanians decried his attempts to punish their mayor, de Lesseps S. Morrison, for past attacks on the Long faction. (At Long's insistence the legislature had cut the share of tobacco tax revenues allotted to the city and had reduced the mayor's power by enlarging the size of the Commission Council.) In 1952 voters rejected his handpicked successor, Carlos Spaht, and elected Robert F. Kennon, an independent candidate.

Four years later Long won an unprecedented third term as governor. But his administration had to concentrate on segregation problems rather than economic issues. Under the leadership of Judge Leander Perez and State Senator Willie Rainach, the segregationists demanded the removal of 150,000 blacks from voter registration rolls and the prohibition of all interracial activity. Although a segregationist, Long ignored their appeals; neither he nor Huey ever found it necessary to appeal to negrophobia. As the influence of white supremacists spread, he fought them and their bills. He told one joint legislative session that if the provisions of one measure were applied honestly, "There ain't ten people looking at me who could qualify to vote."

Ultimately the political tensions generated by the racial struggle broke Long's health, and his behavior became erratic and eccentric. He was in and out of three hospitals; he dated Bourbon Street strippers; he conducted a highly publicized tour of Texas; and he left his wife, Blanche Revere, whom he had married on Aug. 7, 1932. Meanwhile, he made an unsuccessful bid for

lieutenant governor, and observers believed him politically dead. But in August 1960 he made a remarkable comeback by defeating Harold Barnett McSween, the incumbent, in the Eighth Congressional District primary election. A week later he died in Alexandria, La.

[Long's papers were destroyed after his death. The following works touch on various phases of his life: Huey P. Long, *Every Man a King* (1933); Harnett T. Kane, *Louisiana Hayride* (1941); Allan P. Sindler, *Huey Long's Louisiana* (1956); A. J. Liebling, *The Earl of Louisiana* (1961); Richard B. McCaughan, *Socks on a Rooster* (1967); and T. Harry Williams, *Huey Long* (1969).]

J. PAUL LESLIE

LOVETT, ROBERT MORSS (Dec. 25, 1870–Feb. 8, 1956), educator and editor, was born in Boston, Mass., the son of Augustus S. Lovett, who was in the insurance business, and of Elizabeth Russell. After a studious boyhood in Roxbury, Mass., Lovett entered Harvard University. He was an assistant in English while completing the B.A. (1892) and an instructor the next year. In 1893 he was appointed an instructor in rhetoric at the University of Chicago. On June 4, 1895, he married Ida Mott-Smith, whom he had met at Hull House. They had three children.

Lovett became dean of the junior college department at Chicago in 1903, and in 1909 was made professor of English. His friendship at Chicago with William Vaughn Moody resulted in their collaboration on the widely used *History of English Literature* (1902). Both authors, though, were interested in other work. Moody became absorbed in verse, and Lovett wrote two novels, *Richard Gresham* (1904) and *A Winged Victory* (1907). Sympathetic reviewers appreciated Lovett's emotionalism but noted his limited ability to portray character. His play *Cowards*, which caused some local stir for indirectly discussing contraception, was presented by the Fine Arts Theater in Chicago (1914) and was subsequently published in *Drama* (Aug. 1917).

Although Lovett early became interested in social issues, his literary standards remained conventional, as shown by his enthusiasm for Moody's verse, which he issued as *Selected Poems of William Vaughn Moody* (1931), with a long introduction. His well-regarded critique, *Edith Wharton* (1925), failed to note her indifference to social causes. He himself took no account of them in his *Preface to Fiction* (1930) or in the college texts he prepared with others. He remained in touch with liberal and radical literary thought through his long editorial association with the *New Republic* (1921–1929).

The sources of Lovett's own alleged radicalism can be traced to Christian socialism, as shown, for instance, in his quotation from John Ruskin that wealth is the result of other people's work. Lovett resided for long periods at Hull House in Chicago, sharing the views and experiences of social workers, journalists, and ethnic leaders. In 1912 he began his career as a "third-party hack" seeking charismatic leaders who would refresh the social and political scene. During the early stages of World War I he cooperated with the League to Enforce Peace but accepted American entrance into the war as necessary. In 1920 he began an association with the American Civil Liberties Union that continued throughout his life.

The death of his son at Belleau Wood in 1918 confirmed Lovett's antiwar principles. In the following years he gave time to many causes, including independence for India and Ireland, the fight against capital punishment, and the Sacco-Vanzetti Defense League. The antiwar cause led him to approve of the Bolshevik Revolution, the pacifist Oxford Pledge, and the government-sponsored Kellogg-Briand Pact. Although Lovett was later accused of being a Communist, and admitted to having worked with Communists, his basic cause was peace. His most notable presidency was of the League for Industrial Democracy (1921–1938), which the Communists disliked.

In 1935 an Illinois Senate committee investigating subversive activities at the University of Chicago recommended that Lovett be dismissed. The next year he retired. Among his interests was the future of the Virgin Islands, of which his friend Robert Herrick was government secretary. Herrick died in 1938, and Lovett was appointed to the post the following year. In 1943 the Dies committee denounced Lovett, among others, as a subversive in government who ought to be relieved of his duties. The committee pointed to his work with the American League Against War and Fascism (later "for Peace and Democracy") and to his approval of the Republican government during the Spanish Civil War as evidence of Communist associations.

Acting on Dies committee charges, the Kerr committee acquitted Lovett but recommended that he be discharged. The House of Representatives attached a rider to its Urgent Deficiency

Bill stipulating that Lovett and two others not be paid their salaries. Although President Franklin D. Roosevelt and Secretary of the Interior Harold L. Ickes both protested this action, they were unable to overcome an adamant Congress. Ickes, a former student of Lovett's at the University of Chicago, spoke with particular eloquence against what was widely recognized as a bill of attainder, forbidden by the Constitution.

In 1944 Lovett was visiting professor of English at the University of Puerto Rico, where he remained until 1946. In that year a Supreme Court decision vindicated him and authorized payment of back salary. In his "elegiac" period of life, Lovett retired to Lake Zurich, Ill. He died in Chicago.

[*All Our Years: The Autobiography of Robert Morss Lovett* (1948) offers details concerning Lovett's life and opinions and an appendix covering the landmark case involving him. Lovett's introduction to *Selected Poems of William Vaughn Moody* (1931) tells much about his own life as an academic figure and family man. For contemporary views of Lovett and his alleged radicalism, see Louis Filler, "An American Liberal," *Antioch Review*, Sept. 1948; the *New York Sun*, May 29, 1943; and the *New Republic*, Sept. 27, 1943. See also the obituary in the *New York Times*. Feb. 9, 1956.]

LOUIS FILLER

LOWIE, ROBERT HARRY (June 12, 1883–Sept. 21, 1957), ethnologist, was born in Vienna, Austria, the son of Samuel Lowie, a merchant from Budapest, and Ernestine Kuhn Lowie. The family immigrated to New York City in 1893. Lowie graduated from the New York public schools in 1897, then earned the B.A. at the College of the City of New York in 1901. He began teaching in the New York public schools, taking courses at Columbia University while considering a choice of career. Drawn strongly to anthropology and psychology, he entered the graduate school at Columbia in 1904 and received the Ph.D. in anthropology in 1908 with the dissertation "The Test-Theme in North American Mythology," which was published in *Journal of American Folklore*.

In the meantime Lowie had begun work as a volunteer for Clark Wissler at the American Museum of Natural History. Wissler sent him to survey the culture of the Shoshone Indians at Lemhi, Idaho, in 1906 and to visit a number of northern Plains tribes in 1907. He spent the last month with the Crow Indians of Montana, the ethnography of whom was to become an abiding passion. Lowie was appointed assistant in the department of anthropology of the Museum of Natural History in 1907 and spent several months in the vicinity of Lake Athabasca in Alberta in 1908. His duties on these early field studies were to purchase ethnographic specimens, collect anthropometric data on adult men, record folktales in transcript and translation, and investigate social structure—a difficult mix of unrelated objectives. It led him, though, into the grand problems of the social organization of the Crow Indians and thus into the virtually boundless universe of human social orders. Lowie's first contact with the Crow threw him into the center of an academic conflict between social evolutionism and the antievolutionary backlash that was centered at Columbia but had become a prevailing movement of his age. This conflict was to mold the rest of his professional life.

Lowie's youthful scientific materialism and anticlericalism had been greatly tempered by experience. His field contacts with Indians and whites of many faiths had taught him a true tolerance in which he showed equal respect, intellectual and otherwise, for all. The sciences at Columbia had trained him to the post-Darwinian reaction, in which only limited and highly qualified concepts that could be fully elaborated by firsthand data were considered respectable. The relentless attack upon cultural evolution, led by Franz Boas, had trained him to the ways of historical particularism, empiricism as the source of theory, a demand for the rigor in proof of the physical sciences, geographical diffusionism, and cautious reserve about conclusions. His own background (he considered himself a marginal person between German and American cultures) was related to the manner in which he frequently found himself in a border area between dogmatic stands. It was within such an area, that between Boasian doctrine and evolutionary thought, that Lowie was to concentrate his greatest efforts and find his worst dilemmas.

Crow ethnography first threw him into such a quandary. Lewis Henry Morgan, the father of American cultural evolution, had studied Crow society before 1871, noting matrilineal clans and a skewing of relationship terms resulting from classification of a man's mother's brother as ego's brother and of his children as ego's children. This pattern of kinship exists in many other parts of the world and has profound correlations in social order and behavior that are still being explored. As in many other instances, Morgan had been con-

tradicted by the antievolutionists on the ground that his data on Crow kinship were incorrect or imaginary. Lowie proved in 1907 that the system described by Morgan was indeed the Crow system, and in later fieldwork with other tribes he was to substantiate additional rejected descriptions of Morgan's. His most important publications were in some way imaginary arguments with Morgan, in which Lowie retained an antievolutionary stand but met evolutionary theory on its own ground rather than on false ones. In this he provided the major link between Boas' age and the present in the history of ideas, the transition between the reaction against Darwinism and multilinear evolution.

Lowie remained at the American Museum of Natural History until 1921, becoming assistant curator in 1909 and associate curator in 1913. He did most of his intensive Crow fieldwork and almost all of his other American field studies during this period. In 1921 he moved to Berkeley as associate professor at the University of California and remained there, devoting most of his later life to teaching, writing, editing, and study of cosmopolitan cultures. He became a full professor and chairman of the department of anthropology in 1925.

Culture and Ethnology (1917) was a series of essays on the philosophy and conduct of field research, and on the relationships of ethnographic research to world view. It was Boasian in mood but contained a long essay on terms of relationship that revealed the malaise produced by his firsthand experience with classificatory kin systems. *Primitive Society* (1920) displayed remarkable intellectual contortions in the analysis of social institutions. This book left the reader confused, especially about the nature of bilateralism in descent systems, but also gave a sense of the broad variety of human social forms. He revealed most clearly the use of tests in individual situations, rather than any sense of degrees of statistical correlation, to question the generality, and thus the validity, of relationships. The book was closely related to recent publications, especially by A. L. Kroeber and W. H. R. Rivers, who represented antagonists in a new conflict between evolutionary and antievolutionary positions, but Lowie's ponderous volume scarcely alluded to such a conflict.

Primitive Religion (1924) was a remarkable study in absolute cultural relativity, admirable in style but marked by a cold intellectualism and remoteness from religious experience that was markedly nonevolutionary. *The Origin of the*

State (1927) expanded on a theme in *Primitive Society,* that sodalities in tribal societies may carry rudiments of central power and be potential nuclei for statehoods. This book broached, in hesitant terms, the forbidden topics of social evolution. "Relationship Terms," in *Encyclopaedia Britannica* (1929), was a remarkable paper, filled with disclaimers and hesitation, in which Lowie tried to find a common ground between disputants and in which he equivocally accepted the basic tenets of Rivers' evolutionary conjectures. He was scarcely to go beyond this in print, leaving such problems obscured in his *Introduction to Cultural Anthropology* (1934), *History of Ethnological Theory* (1937), and *Social Organization* (1948).

Lowie's professional life may be divided into three overlapping stages. The first, that of museum employment and intensive fieldwork, ended after the publication of *Primitive Society* but was reflected in later ethnographic reports. The second, that of teaching and of formal social theory, graded into a third stage of more introspective thought about civilization marked by more informal communication. The transition was marked by his marriage on Aug. 23, 1933, to Luella Cole, a psychologist. They had no children. His teaching focus gradually shifted to small classes, seminars, and individual students, and his antievolutionary bias and scientism dwindled. A new term of his, "multilinear evolution," was to inspire a generation. At the same time his theoretical writings were having their effect. Despite his hedgings and conclusions, his methods of data handling and analysis were models that led to new breakthroughs. Those who knew him at this stage remember a shy and formal man of refined manners, always gentle and kindly.

Are We Civilized? (1929) examined the irrational bases of Western cultures, dealing pessimistically with the Nordic myth and National Socialism. This book marked the beginning of Lowie's ethnological examination of German culture and his increasing enjoyment of German literature. During World War II, Lowie was involved in the education of soldiers for the approaching occupation of Germany. He wrote *The German People* (1945) and, after field surveys in German-speaking Western Europe, *Toward Understanding Germany* (1954), a notable experiment in ethnography.

These books, like Lowie's papers on social theory, are little read today, whereas his numerous papers on American Indians remain essential to knowledge of Plains Indian culture. Never-

theless, his greater significance lies in general literature on the social orders, for he formed a personal and intellectual bridge of creativity between the Edwardian world and the troubled intellectualism that followed World War II. He died in San Francisco.

[Lowie's surviving papers are at the American Museum of Natural History and the Archives of the University of California Library, Berkeley. *Robert H. Lowie, Ethnologist* (1959), is an autobiographical sketch with vita and bibliography in which Lowie appears as his most severe critic. Lowie's formal obituary and bibliography is Paul Radin, *American Anthropologists,* Apr. 1958. Other obituaries are Alfred L. Kroeber, *Yearbook of the American Philosophical Society* for 1957 (1958), and *Sociologus,* 1958; and Erminie Wheeler-Voegelin, *Journal of American Folklore,* 1958. See also Alan Dundes, ed., *The Complete Bibliography of Robert H. Lowie* (1966); and Robert F. Murphy, *Robert H. Lowie* (1972).]

JOHN WITTHOFT

LUGOSI, BELA (Oct. 20, 1882–Aug. 16, 1956), actor, noted particularly for his portrayal of Count Dracula, was born Béla Ferenc Dezsö Blaskó in Lugos, Hungary (now Lugoj, Romania), the son of Paula Vojnits and István Blaskó. His father had been a baker and later also a banker; but when he died, the family fortunes were reversed and Bela left school to train as an ironworker. In his late teens he decided to become an actor and changed his last name to Lugossy (meaning "from Lugos," the ending "sy" denoting aristocracy). He acted in provincial theaters throughout Hungary and occasionally sang some minor roles in opera and musical comedies. In 1911 he modified the spelling of his name to the less pretentious Lugosi.

Lugosi's good looks and impassioned delivery made him a matinee idol. He starred as Romeo, as Armand in *The Lady of the Camellias,* and as Vronsky in *Anna Karenina.* In 1914 he joined the National Theater of Hungary in Budapest, where he won a few leading parts but generally had smaller roles. When World War I broke out, Lugosi entered the army; he was wounded, and returned to the stage in 1916. A year later he began playing romantic leads in motion pictures. Unfortunately, none of these films survives.

In March 1919, when revolution broke out in Hungary, Lugosi became a leader of the actors' union, charging that producers were unfairly exploiting players. When the revolution was suppressed that summer, he had to flee the country, his career in the National Theater ruined. He went to Vienna and Berlin, where he appeared in German films. His wife, "Baby," whom he had married in 1917, was unwilling to join him and they were divorced. Although he was quite a ladies' man and remarried four times, he always maintained that she was the love of his life.

In 1921 Lugosi left for the United States, where he toured in a small Hungarian-language troupe of which he was the star. This proved financially unrewarding, and he resumed his film career in *The Silent Command* (1923), made in New York; significantly, he played the villain. He also appeared in other films made on the east coast and received leading roles on Broadway, most notably as a romantic Parisian apache in *The Red Poppy* (1922), as a sheikh in *Arabesque* (1925), and as a villainous Greek monk in *The Devil in the Cheese* (1926).

In the summer of 1927 Lugosi was cast as the count in *Dracula*, a play imported from England. Opening in October, *Dracula* was an immediate success and Lugosi starred on Broadway for a year before touring in the role. In 1929 he resumed his motion picture career, and the following summer Universal cast him in the film version of *Dracula*. The first American sound horror film, *Dracula* (1931) proved an extraordinary success. Although he loved comedy and romantic roles, Lugosi—with his piercing eyes, thick accent, and peculiar inflections—found himself typecast as the supreme villain, a role he would never escape.

Lugosi was next selected to appear in *Frankenstein*. The script originally intended him to be the scientist, but the studio—thinking of him as a new Lon Chaney—wanted him as the monster. Spoiled by thousands of fan letters praising his role as the mysterious but attractive Count Dracula, Lugosi balked at the role and its grotesque makeup. (The relatively unknown Boris Karloff was chosen.) Lugosi then played the mad scientist, Dr. Mirakle, in *Murders in the Rue Morgue* (1932), but he had created his own Frankenstein monster; *Frankenstein* was a great success (*Murders* was not) and Karloff immediately became Hollywood's leading horror actor, eclipsing Lugosi for the rest of his life. On Jan. 31, 1933, Lugosi married his secretary, Lillian Arch; they had one son.

Lugosi's career subsequently flourished and waned with the demand for horror films. Not overly selective in choosing scripts and extravagant with money, he often took whatever roles came along—and found himself in a number of poor films and serials. In 1932 he appeared in *White Zombie*, an independent production in which he gave one of his most demonic portrayals. In 1934 he was paired with Karloff in *The Black Cat*, playing a relatively benign role, as he did in the serial *The Return of Chandu* (1935). Thereafter he almost always played a villain—or a seeming one. In *The Raven* (1935), again paired with Karloff—who as usual got top billing—he played the sadistic mad doctor so obsessed with Edgar Allan Poe that he not only re-created his torture devices but also used them. In 1936 he appeared with Karloff in *The Invisible Ray*, as a good scientist. The next two years brought a halt to horror films and Lugosi found himself unemployed; but in 1939 the genre was revived and he gave one of his best performances, as Igor in *Son of Frankenstein*. He repeated the part in *The Ghost of Frankenstein* (1942), and a year later finally played the Frankenstein monster in *Frankenstein Meets the Wolf Man*.

During World War II, Lugosi was offered one leading role in a Columbia production, *The Return of the Vampire*, but otherwise only received smaller parts. Anxious to play larger roles, he appeared in a number of low-budget films for Monogram and thus diminished his reputation. In 1945, when mad scientist films stopped being made, he again found himself out of work. During this period he became addicted to drugs, first taking morphine to assuage the pain from sciatica and later switching to Demerol and Methadone.

Lugosi returned to the stage in a 1947 summer stock production of *Dracula*, and the next year in *Arsenic and Old Lace*. In the late 1940's and early 1950's he played in a horror act booked into movie theaters to the hoots and catcalls of teenagers. The closest he came to a remake of the original *Dracula* was *Abbott and Costello Meet Frankenstein* (1948), a clever spoof of the genre in which he played Count Dracula for the last time.

Thereafter, Lugosi's film career was virtually over. After touring England in a stage version of *Dracula*, he appeared in a horror spoof, *Old Mother Riley Meets the Vampire*, and then only in third-rate, low-budget productions. In 1953 he was divorced and in April 1955, penniless, he surrendered to the authorities as a drug addict. Four months later he was released as cured. Encouraged by thousands of fan letters, he married Hope Lininger, who had written to him steadily while he was in the hospital. He vainly hoped that his new notoriety would help him to a comeback, but he had only the part of a mute in *The Black Sleep*. He died in Los Angeles, during the shooting of

Plan Nine From Outer Space. According to his wishes, he was buried in his Dracula cape. The famous vampire was interred in Holy Cross Cemetery in Hollywood, where his grave still attracts many visitors.

[Arthur Lennig, *The Count: The Life and Films of Bela "Dracula" Lugosi* (1974), is a full-length study and includes an annotated list of Lugosi's films.]

ARTHUR LENNIG

LUNDEBERG, HARRY (Mar. 25, 1901– Jan. 28, 1957), labor leader, was born in Oslo, Norway, the son of Karl Gunnar Lundeberg and Allette Koffeld. His father, a sailor turned small businessman, advocated syndicalism. His mother publicly championed women's equality and workers' rights. Lundeberg attended Norwegian public schools until the age of fourteen and then, following his family's tradition, went to sea.

For the next nineteen years Lundeberg's life centered on ship forecastles. He sailed by both wind and steam, in and out of most major world ports, and under the flags of nine nations. He joined Norwegian, British, and Australian maritime unions, a Spanish syndicalist union, and, according to some reports, the anarcho-syndicalist Industrialist Workers of the World. In 1923 Lundeberg made Seattle, Wash., his home port. He transferred his membership from the Australian Seamen's Union to the Sailor's Union of the Pacific (SUP) in 1926 and became an American citizen in 1933. By 1934, when he came ashore for full-time union work, he had the rank of boatswain, the highest-paid deckhand.

Lundeberg's experiences as a nomadic, disenfranchised sailor reinforced the syndicalist views he had acquired from his parents. Throughout his life he upheld the primacy of economic action over legislative reform, saw strikes as essential tactics for improving seamen's working conditions, and condemned the increasing tendency of political systems to limit the actions of individuals and voluntary associations. Yet as social, economic, and political conditions in the world changed, he evolved from a rank-and-file insurgent in the early 1930's to a traditional "business unionist" in the late 1930's and 1940's, to a conservative, anti-Communist Republican in the 1950's.

Lundeberg initially became prominent in labor affairs as a radical critic of the conservative American Federation of Labor (AFL) maritime unions. In 1934, when Pacific seamen ignored the

advice of SUP leaders and stopped work in sympathy with the embattled longshoremen, the Seattle sailors chose Lundeberg to head their local strike committee. After the walkout he became the sailors' port agent in Seattle and rapidly developed a power base. In April 1935 Harry Bridges of the International Longshoremen's and Warehousemen's Union (ILWU) backed his election as president of the newly formed, loosely structured Maritime Federation of the Pacific (MFP). Lundeberg used this position to undermine the entrenched SUP leadership by directing the movement to expel Paul Scharrenberg, editor of the *Seamen's Journal* and secretary of the California Federation of Labor, from the union. With the power of the incumbent officers weakened, in 1935 the rank and file elected Lundeberg secretary-treasurer, the highest post within SUP. Thereupon he resigned as head of the MFP and moved to San Francisco.

The old guard of the International Seamen's Union (ISU), with which SUP was affiliated, became alarmed at the Pacific sailors' increased militancy and expelled them from its ranks in January 1936. For the next year Lundeberg considered taking his now independent SUP into the Committee for Industrial Organization (CIO), but finally decided against this move because he feared he would have minor influence in CIO affairs compared with Harry Bridges of the ILWU and Joe Curran of the National Maritime Union. Needing allies, in October 1938 Lundeberg convinced the AFL to replace the discredited ISU with the Seafarers' International Union (SIU), a confederation of various small unions of sailors, fishermen, and warehouse and cannery workers dominated by SUP and headed by Lundeberg.

As secretary-treasurer of SUP and president of SIU, Lundeberg advocated "bread and butter unionism" and earned the nickname "Lunchbox." Through hard bargaining he raised the average seaman's wage from $67 per month in 1935 to $400 in 1953. In 1949 he won for his members a welfare program and the Sailor's Home Trust Fund, financed by the shipowners. Lundeberg most often relied on quick "job actions" to pressure the employers, but in 1936, 1946, and 1952 he initiated major strikes, the last of which lasted sixty-three days.

Although Lundeberg had worked with Harry Bridges in his early climb to power, by the late 1930's they had become bitter foes. Several times their followers engaged in brawls, Lundeberg receiving a broken jaw in one such fray. Personally, Lundeberg resented Bridges' greater prominence in the West Coast labor movement. Economically, he condemned the ILWU incursions into SUP jurisdiction (while coveting certain longshoring jobs for his sailors). Ideologically, he detested Bridges' association with Communists, his acceptance of political action, and, in later years, his cooperativeness with employers.

Throughout his union career Lundeberg closely followed the life-style of the sailors he led. A critic of "tuxedo unionism," he appeared everywhere in the standard sailors' garb of gray cap, shirtsleeves, and black dungarees. In 1949 he worked his passage to a European conference as a hand, although the union had appropriated enough money for him to travel first class. He kept his salary equivalent to the highest pay for a sailor of his rank, and lived with his wife, Ida, and three children in a modest home in the San Francisco suburb of Burlingame, where he died. He did not smoke, drink, or chew tobacco, but he did swear profusely in a thick Scandinavian accent, and played a skillful game of poker.

[Lundeberg's views can be found in *West Coast Sailor*, which he edited from 1938 to 1952. Joseph P. Goldberg, *The Maritime Story* (1958), provides the fullest treatment of Lundeberg's union activities. Irving Bernstein, *Turbulent Years* (1970), pp. 574–589, gives a good account of Lundeberg's activities in the 1930's. See also Gary M. Fink, ed., *Biographical Dictionary of American Labor Leaders* (1974); and Frank J. Taylor, "Roughneck Boss of the Sailors' Union," *Saturday Evening Post*, Apr. 18, 1953.]

WARREN R. VAN TINE

LYBRAND, WILLIAM MITCHELL (Aug. 14, 1867–Nov. 19, 1960), public accountant, was born in Philadelphia, Pa., the son of George W. Lybrand and Sarah Aldred. His father was a Methodist-Episcopal minister. Since the service of a pastor in any church was limited to three years, the family moved frequently. His maternal ancestors were businessmen, and Lybrand later noted with pride that his great-grandfather, William Connolly, was listed in an 1801 New York directory as an accountant.

Lybrand's education was limited to a series of one-room schoolhouses in various towns followed by two years at Philadelphia High School. He left school in 1884 to go to work as a clerk for a machine toolbuilding company. Lybrand later wrote that he knew "little or nothing about an accountant's work," but when he was promoted to assistant bookkeeper, he developed a keen interest in the topic of cost accounting.

There were no schools at that time where one could gain the necessary expertise to enter the field of public accounting. In 1887 Lybrand made a fortuitous decision when he joined the public accounting firm of Heins and Whelan. John Heins was respected in the field, and a person working for him met the most eminent practitioners of the day. It was not easy to work with Heins, for as Lybrand noted, he was "peppery— red pepper." But although Heins had a violent temper and demanded perfection, he was one of the best accounting teachers of the day. In 1891 Lybrand was promoted to partner. His future seemed secure, but he chose to ally himself with three assistants (T. Edward Ross, Adam Ross, and Robert Montgomery) and start the firm of Lybrand, Ross Brothers and Montgomery, which became the international public accounting firm Coopers and Lybrand.

Membership in the accounting profession was small at the turn of the century, and Lybrand's greatest contributions came through his work in professional organizations. In 1897 the Pennsylvania Association of Public Accountants was formed, and Lybrand was a charter member. The initial goal of the group was to secure state public-accounting legislation, and in a relatively short time it was successful. The association then turned its attention to providing educational opportunities for prospective accountants.

Lybrand, as treasurer (1897–1901) and president (1902–1904) of the Pennsylvania society, was instrumental in both efforts. He supported the publication of the *Public Accountant*, one of the first professional accounting journals in the United States. During his first year as president of the society, he helped design an evening program for assistants in practitioners' offices and taught "practical accounting" two evenings a week. In 1904 he was instrumental in persuading the Wharton School at the University of Pennsylvania to take over the program.

Lybrand was also one of the organizers and an officer of the Federation of Societies of Public Accountants and the American Association of Public Accountants.

In 1908 Lybrand moved to the New York City office of his firm and began to concentrate on the cost accounting area. In the same year, at the annual meeting of the AAPA, he delivered a paper, "The Accounting for Industrial Enterprises," in an attempt to generate greater interest in the cost accounting area among accountants. In 1919, believing that the needs of cost accountants were not being met by existing organizations, he helped to organize the National Association of Cost Accountants (now the National Association of Accountants) and served as its second president from 1920 to 1922.

Associates recall that Lybrand was a man of good humor, genial temperament, and absolute dedication to the accounting profession. He married Lenore Montgomery. (The date of the marriage is unknown, and there are no references to the marriage except in the personnel records at Coopers and Lybrand.) They had no children. Perhaps it is significant that some of his partners expressed surprise that he was married; they had believed he was a bachelor.

By the time Lybrand died, in Stamford, Conn., he had witnessed the attainment of professional status by public accountants, largely because he was one of those men who dedicated their lives to this achievement. His ability to organize men in cooperative efforts provided not only his firm but the accounting profession as a whole with vital leadership in the early struggle for professional recognition. In 1947 the Lybrand Awards were established to recognize the best manuscripts submitted to the National Association of Accountants. Lybrand's dedication to cost accounting is commemorated by these awards and his firm, Coopers and Lybrand, stands as a monument to his success as a public accountant.

[For an autobiographical sketch of Lybrand, see "As I Look Back Over Half A Century," *L.R.B. and M. Journal*, Jan. 1938. Edward T. Ross, *Pioneers of Public Accountancy in Pennsylvania* (1940), provides biographical sketches of some early leaders in Pennsylvania. A memorial to Lybrand by Edward T. Ross, et al., "William M. Lybrand—In Memoriam," *Lybrand Journal*, Jan. 1961, provides additional data. For a history of Coopers and Lybrand, see William Lybrand, "History of the Firm," *L.R.B. and M. Journal*, Feb., Mar., May, and Nov. 1920. Issues of the journal commemorating the twenty-fifth (1933), thirty-fifth (1933), and fiftieth (1948) anniversaries of the firm contain substantial information about Lybrand.

A comprehensive treatment of the evolution of the accounting profession can be found in John Carey's *The Rise of the Accounting Profession*, 2 vols. (1969). An earlier account of the institutional development in the profession is found in Norman Webster, *The AAPA: Its First Twenty Years* (1954). Lybrand's view of the development of the profession is found in "Development of the Accounting Profession in the United States," *Canadian Chartered Accountant*, Nov. 1924.

For a record of the early activities of the Pennsylvania society, see *Fifth Annual Banquet Proceedings*, 1905; a more comprehensive treatment is in *Record of the Twenty-Fifth Anniversary Proceedings*, 1925.]

BARBARA B. MERINO

LYDENBERG, HARRY MILLER (Nov. 18, 1874–Apr. 16, 1960), librarian, was born in Dayton, Ohio, the son of Wesley Braxton Lydenberg and Marianna Miller. His father, a Civil War veteran, died in 1879, leaving his family in genteel poverty. Lydenberg learned to work hard and live sparingly, habits that remained with him throughout his life. The boyhood jobs he took to help his mother served as apprenticeships for his lifework. His newspaper route drew him into the press room and gave him an early familiarity with printing; he later worked as a page in the Dayton Public Library. At Harvard University, which he attended from 1893 to 1896 on a Bowditch Scholarship, he worked in the library and completed four years' work in three. He graduated with the class of 1897 and received the B.A. magna cum laude.

In July 1896, Lydenberg began work as a cataloger at the Lenox Library in New York City, a privately endowed reference collection of rarities and Americana that in 1895 had merged with the Tilden Trust and the Astor Library, an endowed general reference library, to form the New York Public Library. Lydenberg was soon given charge of manuscript collections and in 1899 was made assistant to the director. In 1908 he was appointed reference librarian, or chief of the research collections; in 1928 he was named assistant director, and in 1934 director, a position he held until his retirement in 1941. On Jan. 23, 1912, he married Madeliene Rogers Day, who had been chief of periodicals at the library; they had two children.

As assistant director and director Lydenberg had librarywide responsibilities, including the extensive branch library system. His passion, though, was for the research collections, which he shaped into a world-renowned intellectual and cultural resource, second only to the Library of Congress among American libraries. His consistent, careful attention to acquisitions resulted in a comprehensive, immensely varied, but balanced collection that under his guidance grew to nearly three million items and embraced many unusual and rare materials and subjects. This quantitative achievement constituted, in a library that acquired comparatively few duplicate copies of works, a dazzling qualitative accomplishment considered unequaled in its time. In amassing such resources—among other things he made a strenuous trip through Europe, including Russia, in the fall and winter of 1923–1924—Lydenberg believed that he was creating a cumulative record of human endeavor; the universality of his collecting was an expression of his sense of responsibility to posterity and of his respect for, and understanding of, scholarship and research.

This approach, together with a commitment to serve a varied, cosmopolitan public, helped to make the New York Public Library under Lydenberg almost like a scholarly academy. Staff members were encouraged to pursue their own scholarly interests. Much of their work was published in the *New York Public Library Bulletin*, which Lydenberg developed into a great bibliographical resource.

Lydenberg was interested in the production and preservation, as well as the collection and bibliographical description, of books. He cultivated warm relations between the New York Public Library and book publishers; fostered high editorial, technical, and aesthetic standards for the publishing and printing programs of the library; and stood in the forefront of efforts to preserve deteriorating library materials. With the chief of the library printing office, he devised a laboratory to experiment with preserving books and paper; and in the 1930's, at his initiative, the National Bureau of Standards undertook research on the effects of the environment on books and other records. Lydenberg was also instrumental in convincing newspaper publishers to issue rag editions for libraries and to microfilm their files. He experimented with microfilm and was one of the first American librarians to have installed (in 1912) a Photostat machine so that readers could make copies of materials.

Lydenberg knew virtually everyone in the library and bibliographical world and was involved in almost every significant effort in the United States to improve or expand access to resources for scholars, including cooperative bibliographical enterprises, national planning for libraries, and planning for the acquisition and preservation of research resources. He was secretary-treasurer of the American Council of Learned Societies (1937–1941) and president of the American Library Association (1932–1933) and the Bibliographical Society of America

(1929–1931). He also taught library history at the Columbia University School of Library Service from 1929 to 1933 and was active in civic affairs in Scarsdale, N.Y., where he lived.

Upon his retirement Lydenberg became director-librarian of the Biblioteca Benjamin Franklin in Mexico City, which was sponsored by the American government and the American Library Association. It was a forerunner of U.S. Information Service libraries abroad. In 1943, Lydenberg returned home to direct the Board on International Relations of the American Library Association, in Washington. His work with governments, international organizations, and scholarly associations to develop programs to aid foreign libraries and ease the international flow of publications and scholarship, took him all over Latin America and laid the basis for the library and bibliographical programs later sponsored by the United Nations. In 1946 he spent six months in Western Europe as a member of the Library of Congress Purchasing Mission, assessing the publishing and library situations and acquiring publications for American research libraries. At the end of October 1946, Lydenberg retired from active library work. He died at Westerville, Ohio.

Throughout his career Lydenberg engaged in historical or bibliographical research. His publications include *History of the New York Public Library* (1923); *John Shaw Billings* (1924); a standard manual, written with John Archer, *The Care and Repair of Books* (1931); and translations from the French of two books by André Blum: *On the Origin of Paper* (1934) and *The Origins of Printing and Engraving* (1940).

Immensely respected and much honored for his many accomplishments, Lydenberg was always modest and unpretentious, characteristics that his small stature, spare build, and reserved, almost austere personality accentuated. His strength of character, keen intellect, and prodigious energy were legendary among his colleagues, as were his foresight and ability to get things done. One of the great bookmen of his day, he was an exemplar of the scholarly librarian of humanistic persuasion.

[The Lydenberg Papers, dated 1919–1960, are in the New York Public Library Manuscript Division. The library archives contain much Lydenberg material, as do various library publications and the American Library Association archives. Lydenberg supplied many details of his life in Harvard College, Class of 1897, *Fiftieth Anniversary Report* (1947). A *festschrift* in his honor is *Bookmen's Holiday* (1943); its bibliography is supplemented by David H. Stam, "A Bibliography of the Published Writings of Harry Miller Lydenberg, 1942–1960," *New York Public Library Bulletin*, June 1960. Also see Luther Evans, "The Little Man Who Isn't There," *Library Journal*, Jan. 15, 1947; Deoch Fulton, in *American Library Association Bulletin*, Apr. 1953; Karl H. Brown, in *Library Journal*, May 15, 1960; Edward G. Freehafer, in *New York Public Library Bulletin*, June 1960; Deoch Fulton, in *American Library Association Bulletin*, Summer 1960; David C. Means, in *U.S. Library of Congress. Information Bulletin*, Apr. 1960; Keyes D. Metcalf, in *College and Research Libraries*, July 1960; Phyllis Dain, *The New York Public Library* (1972); Keyes D. Metcalf, in *College and Research Libraries*, July 1976; and Phyllis Dain, "Harry M. Lydenberg and American Library Resources," *Library Quarterly*, Oct. 1977; and "Harry Miller Lydenberg," *Dictionary of American Library Biography* (1978).]

PHYLLIS DAIN

MACARTHUR, CHARLES GORDON (Nov. 5, 1895–Apr. 21, 1956), journalist, playwright, scenarist, and motion picture producer, was born in Scranton, Pa., the son of William Telfer MacArthur, an itinerant, self-ordained clergyman, and Georgiana Welstead. His father, wanting Charles to become a preacher, sent him at fourteen to the Wilson Memorial Academy, a school for training ministers and missionaries at Nyack, N. Y., but the boy had no desire to be a clergyman. After three years of austere schooling at the academy, MacArthur ran off to New York City, where he became a necktie salesman.

In 1914 MacArthur went to Chicago to work for an older brother, Telfer, who published a newspaper in Oak Park. He thereafter got a $10-a-week job with the Chicago City Press, a news-gathering agency. Showing exceptional ability as a reporter, he was soon taken on by the *Chicago Herald and Examiner*. Later, he went to the *Chicago Tribune*. During these years (1914–1922) Chicago journalism was distinguished by the presence of numerous talented newspapermen, among them Henry Justin Smith, Keith Preston, Ring Lardner, Carl Sandburg, Henry B. Sell, Ben Hecht, Floyd Dell, Harry Hansen, Vencent Starrett, Lloyd Lewis, and Burton Rascoe.

In 1916 MacArthur enlisted in the First Illinois Cavalry and went to the Mexican border with Pershing's expedition. During World War I, he was a private in the 149th Field Artillery, 42nd (Rainbow) Division, serving in a number of campaigns, including the Meuse-Argonne offensive, and with the army of occupation on the Rhine. In three years of military service he never rose above the rank of private. His book, *A Bug's Eye View of the War* (1920), revised and retitled *War Bugs* (1928), was a humorous, lusty account of the life of the common soldier. During World War II, MacArthur served as an assistant to the chief of the Chemical Warfare Service with the rank of lieutenant colonel.

At the end of World War I, MacArthur returned to Chicago and gained the distinction of being the city's first $100-a-week reporter. In 1920 he married Carol Frink, a reporter for the *Herald and Examiner*. They had no children and were divorced in 1926.

MacArthur returned to New York in 1922 and went to work for Hearst's *New York American*. He became a friend of Robert Benchley, with whom he shared an apartment for a time; Dorothy Parker; Alexander Woollcott; and other writers and wits of the Algonquin Hotel group. Edward Sheldon, an established playwright and relative of MacArthur's by marriage, suggested they collaborate on a play for Lionel Barrymore. The play did not come off, but the two continued to work together and the result was *Lulu Belle,* a melodrama about a black prostitute. It was successfully produced in 1926 at the Belasco Theatre, starring Lenore Ulric. It was the first of the three highly successful plays on which MacArthur collaborated, the others being *The Front Page* (1928), written with Ben Hecht, and *Twentieth Century* (1932), also with Hecht. All but one of MacArthur's stage plays (*Johnny on the Spot*, 1941, a financial failure) were collaborations. Besides those already mentioned, they were *Salvation* (1927), about a female evangelist, written with Sidney Howard, and, with Hecht, *Jumbo* (1935), a circus extravaganza, *Ladies and Gentlemen* (1939), and *Swan Song* (1946). *Stag at Bay,* written with Nunnally Johnson in the late 1930's, was not produced during MacArthur's lifetime.

The two most successful plays and the most highly regarded by drama critics were *The Front Page* and *Twentieth Century*. Foremost was *The Front Page,* a derisive and profane drama based on Hecht's and MacArthur's newspaper experiences in Chicago. The setting was the pressroom of the city's criminal courts building. Produced by Jed Harris, directed by George S. Kaufman, and starring Lee Tracy and Osgood Perkins, the play was a smash hit on Broadway in 1928–

1929. The play, Brooks Atkinson wrote, "bowled over the public with the excitement and sting of a callous newspaper story." Most critics have agreed that the frequently revived play, though realistic in many details, is essentially a romantic account of the newspaper world.

In New York, on Aug. 17, 1928, MacArthur married Helen Hayes, the actress. They had one daughter and an adopted son, James, who became an accomplished film and television actor.

MacArthur went to Hollywood in 1929 and in the early 1930's wrote numerous motion picture scenarios. His best-known screenplay was *The Sin of Madelon Claudet* (1931), which won an Academy Award for his wife in her film debut. Besides their stage collaborations, MacArthur and Hecht became prominent writers and producers of motion pictures, using a production studio at Astoria, Long Island. Notable among their films were *Crime Without Passion* (1934), with Claude Rains and Margo; *The Scoundrel* (1934), with Noel Coward, which won the Academy Award for the best original story of the year; and *Soak the Rich* (1936).

MacArthur, a handsome man, had great personal charm. He especially enjoyed the companionship of friends like Hecht, Gene Fowler, John Barrymore, and Charles Lederer, who shared his liking for merriment and conviviality. Alexander Woollcott, who was credited with persuading MacArthur to turn from journalism to the drama, said, "Everyone who knows him lights up when he hears his name, and starts talking about him as if he were a marvelous circus that once passed his way." But MacArthur took his craft seriously and worked at it with great dedication. He wrote during a period in the American theater when comedies featuring wit, "slickness," and highly charged dialogue came to the fore. Particularly in his work with Hecht, MacArthur contributed significantly toward a new Broadway realism. "The newshounds of *The Front Page,*" one commentator observed, "were too scruffy to be heroes, too heroic to be villains." MacArthur's foremost talent was an exceptional skill in writing graphic and apt dialogue. His perceptive ear for the way people speak, his sense of the comic, and his ability to compress subject matter remind one of his gifted contemporary Ring Lardner.

MacArthur wrote magazine and newspaper articles as well as plays and scenarios. His memorable short story "Rope" (*American Mercury,* Feb. 1937), about the frustrated courtship of a professional hangman, was reprinted in a number of anthologies. From 1948 to 1950 he was editor of the faltering magazine *Theatre Arts.* A new idea he brought to his editorship was the publication of the unabridged text of an interesting new play in each issue.

For years MacArthur had been a heavy drinker, and after his daughter died of polio at the age of nineteen, he drank even more heavily, though "his sense of guilt towards his drinking," Hecht said, "was as strong as if he were under the eyes of the deacon in the Missionary Academy." In 1932 he and Helen Hayes had purchased a handsome house at Nyack with a spacious lawn fronting on the Hudson. They spent much of their time there. The Hechts lived nearby. As he grew older, MacArthur often became restless and moody. "The minutiae of daily life were his undoing," his wife wrote. Gradually his health failed, and he faced the ravages of disease stoically and good-humoredly. During the last year of his life he worked with Anita Loos and Ludwig Bemelmans on what was to be a play for Helen Hayes. It was not completed. Nephritis and anemia at last overwhelmed him, and he died at a New York hospital.

[Arthur Dorlag and John Irvine, eds., *The Stage Works of Charles MacArthur* (1974), is a valuable collection of MacArthur's eight stage plays with scholarly introductions and informative notes. Ben Hecht, *Charlie: The Improbable Life and Times of Charles MacArthur* (1957), is a rambling volume of florid reminiscences, but the book reveals the subject's personality amusingly, explores his relationships with friends and colleagues, and portrays colorfully the background of his life and work. Other sources are Gene Fowler, *Good Night, Sweet Prince* (1944); Helen Hayes (with Lewis Funke), *A Gift of Joy* (1965); Helen Hayes (with Sandford Dody), *On Reflection* (1968), with a number of good photographs of MacArthur; Helen Hayes, "The Most Unforgettable Character I've Met," *Reader's Digest,* Sept. 1947; Ben Hecht, *A Child of the Century* (1954), and *Letters from Bohemia* (1964); George Jean Nathan, *Theatre of the Moment* (1936); Anita Loos, "To Charlie," *Theatre Arts,* June 1957; and obituaries in *Time,* Apr. 30, 1956; and *New York Times,* Apr. 22 and 24, 1956.]

WILLIAM MCCANN

McCARDELL, CLAIRE (May 24, 1905–Mar. 22, 1958), fashion designer, was born in Frederick, Md., the daughter of Adrian Leroy McCardell and Eleanor Clingan. Her father was president of the Frederick County Bank and had been a member of the state tax commission and a state senator.

McCardell's interest in fashion began as a child as she watched the family dressmaker at work, an interest she pursued by creating paper dolls from figures cut from fashion magazines. Another early interest that was to influence her fashion designs was sports; as a teenaged participant so active that she was given the nickname "Kick," she learned at firsthand what kinds of clothes were practical for active wear.

After graduating from the local high school in 1923, McCardell enrolled as a student at Hood College in Frederick. After two years there, she moved to New York City to attend the Parsons School of Design (then known as the New York School of Fine and Applied Arts).

While studying in New York, McCardell lived at the Three Arts Club, where she and the other residents often were recipients of French designer clothes passed along by the club's wealthy patrons. Impressed by the detailing and workmanship she saw in these couturier clothes she took advantage of the school's having a Paris branch and went there to study in 1927. In addition to attending classes, she took a part-time job tracing fashion drawings for a company that sold sketches of Paris designs. Back in New York, she completed her studies at Parsons in 1928, then held a series of minor jobs including painting floral designs on lamp shades, modeling fashions at B. Altman and Company, sketching in a dress shop, and working as an assistant and designer for a knit goods manufacturer.

In 1930, she was hired by Robert Turk as his assistant. Two years later, when Turk was forced to disband his house, he took her with him to Townley Frocks. A few months after the move, Turk died in a drowning accident, and McCardell was assigned to complete his designs for that season. Her success in carrying out the assignment earned her appointment as the company's designer.

At the start of her designing career, McCardell's clothes—simple, uncomplicated, designed for ease and comfort—were considered daring and were worn principally by women in the fashion avant garde; indeed some were worn only by McCardell herself. She was the first to wear the evening and daytime wool jersey separates that she found so easy to pack for her many trips abroad. It was not until 1938 that one of her designs, the free-flowing "Monastic" dress, captured the popular imagination. Not properly protected by copyright, it was copied freely by other manufacturers. Business losses caused by the piracy of this design, and production problems associated with it, prompted Townley's president, Henry Geiss, to close the business.

McCardell was then hired by Hattie Carnegie to design "Workshop Originals" under the Carnegie label. She worked there for a year and a half, but most Carnegie customers, accustomed to more formal haute couture, did not appreciate the free, unconstructed, uncluttered lines of McCardell clothes. Next, she worked briefly for a small, low-priced house before being hired again by Henry Geiss, who, with Adolph Klein and Harry Friedman, was forming a new Townley Frocks in 1940. The partners gave her considerable leeway, and in 1942 one of her designs, a wrap-and-tie housedress called the "Popover," featured first in *Harper's Bazaar,* was a huge success. More than 75,000 Popovers were sold the first season. The next year, her "Diaper" wrap-and-tie bathing suit created a sensation.

During one of her trips to Europe, McCardell met Irving Drought Harris, an architect; they were married on Mar. 10, 1943. In the 1940's McCardell came into her own as a top designer. *Vogue* called her a "designer for moderns." The prestigious department store Lord and Taylor promoted her "American look." She was among the first American designers to win name recognition, an honor previously bestowed only on French couturiers. She received the Mademoiselle Merit Award in 1943, the Coty American Fashion Critics Award in 1944, and the Neiman-Marcus Award in 1948. In 1950 she was presented the Woman's National Press Club Award by President Truman. She became a Townley partner in 1952.

Throughout her career, McCardell was an active alumna of the Parsons School, working with students as critic and consultant. In 1956 she put her feelings about fashion into words in *What Shall I Wear?* She died in New York City.

[See Jessica Daves, *Ready-Made Miracle* (1967); Imelda DeGraw, "25 Years Couturiers," in *Catalog* of the Denver Art Museum (1975); Sally Kirkland, "McCardell," in *American Fashion*, ed., Sarah Tomerlin Lee (1975); Walter Vecchio and Robert Riley, *The Fashion Makers* (1968); and obituary in the *New York Times*, Mar. 23, 1958.]

DOROTHY BRIGSTOCK SCHOENFELD

McCARTHY, DANIEL JOSEPH (June 22, 1874–Oct. 9, 1958), neurologist, neuropsychiatrist, and professor of medical jurisprudence, was born in Philadelphia, Pa., the son of Daniel McCarthy, a railroad superintendent, and Rebecca Maher.

In 1892 he graduated from Central High School in Philadelphia, then entered the medical department of the University of Pennsylvania. He received the M.D. degree in 1895. The following year he interned at the Philadelphia Hospital, "Blockley," which was the center of American neurology. He received further neurological training in 1897 under the dean of American neurologists, S. Weir Mitchell, at the Philadelphia Orthopedic Hospital and Infirmary for Nervous Diseases. McCarthy spent 1898–1899 in postgraduate studies in Paris, Vienna, Berlin, and Leipzig. He then returned to Philadelphia, where he did work at the William Pepper Laboratories in neuropathology and at the Phipps Institute in the study of tuberculosis.

By 1896, McCarthy held a certificate of proficiency in medical jurisprudence, and from 1904 to 1940 he served as professor of the subject at the University of Pennsylvania School of Medicine; from 1926 to 1932 he served as auxiliary lecturer on insanity and expert medical testimony at the University of Pennsylvania School of Law. He also was lecturer (1904—1912) and adjunct professor (1912—1918) of medical jurisprudence at the Women's Medical College of Pennsylvania.

His increasing experience with the neuropsychiatric aspects of expert medical testimony was shown in McCarthy's first book, a revision of John J. Reese's *Text-Book of Medical Jurisprudence and Toxicology* (1911), which included an entirely new chapter on commitment of the insane and an extensively reworked chapter on insanity. In the latter chapter McCarthy affirmed that the "doctrine that insanity is due to diseased physical media seems to be most consistent with sound philosophic and physiologic views. . . ." He also suggested that in "every case of true insanity . . . there are pathological changes produced in the brain, although these may . . . be too subtle and recondite to be discovered by our present means of research."

The book that did most to establish McCarthy's reputation was his *The Prisoner of War in Germany: The Care and Treatment of the Prisoner of War With a History of the Development of the Principle of Neutral Inspection and Control* (1917). McCarthy had served with the University of Pennsylvania unit of the American Ambulance Hospital, Neuilly-sur-Seine, near Paris, for about six months in the early part of World War I, and as liaison officer with the French army. Finally, in March 1916, he was appointed as special assistant to the American embassy at Berlin. In the latter role he investigated the prisoner-of-war problem, supervising both a detailed survey of all the physical conditions within the prison camps and a thorough inspection of the prisoners themselves. He also reviewed sanitary conditions, handled diplomatic aspects of the exchange of wounded men, corrected hospital abuses and reviewed judicial matter concerning courts-martial. McCarthy excelled in this unique position that allowed him to blend his knowledge of neuropsychiatric disorder and tuberculosis with his knowledge of medical jurisprudence. He returned briefly to the United States, but in late 1917 was again sent abroad by the State Department to investigate the condition of the Russian people following the Revolution. During 1918 McCarthy served as consulting neurologist and commanding officer for the American Expeditionary Force Base Hospital No. 115, Vichy, France.

Before the war McCarthy had developed a rather large private practice, holding appointments as a neurologist to the Philadelphia Hospital, the Pennsylvania State Hospital for the Insane at Norristown, St. Agnes Hospital, and the Kensington Dispensary for the Treatment of Tuberculosis. He also had served as chairman of the State Council of the Mental Hygiene Division of the Public Charities Association of Pennsylvania (1912–1915). Just after the war he founded and became director of two Philadelphia area sanitariums, Roseneathe Farm and Fairmount Farm. He married Elizabeth Allen White on June 21, 1926; they had one son.

During the 1930's and 1940's McCarthy became more interested in experimental and sociological concerns. In addition to his Philadelphia Institute for the Study and Prevention of Nervous and Mental Disorders, he organized the McCarthy-Kirby Foundation at the University of Pennsylvania, the McCarthy-Dobbs Foundation at Jefferson Medical College, and the McCarthy Research Foundation at Temple University. All of these provided financial assistance for neurological investigators, with the funds at Temple specifically supporting departments of experimental neurology and medical colloidal chemistry. Between 1933 and 1948, McCarthy was involved with the problems of juvenile delinquency, serving first as director of the Medical Division, then as director of sociological research, and finally as director of probation for the Philadelphia Municipal Court.

For many years McCarthy was a trustee of

Drexel Institute, an associate trustee of the University of Pennsylvania, and a substantial supporter of Florida Southern College. He was president of the Pathological Society of Philadelphia (1914), the American Neurological Association (1932–1933), and the Philadelphia Neurological Society (1934).

In the last years of his life, McCarthy, assisted by Kenneth M. Corrin, wrote a textbook of psychiatry, the title of which succinctly reveals his orientation: *Medical Treatment of Mental Diseases: The Toxic and Organic Basis of Psychiatry* (1955). He firmly believed that mental diseases were caused by physical disorders, and should be treated "as a matter of disordered chemical, physiologic, and pathologic processes affecting brain function"—that is, as medical and not as psychological problems. While recognizing "that emotional factors are important, constituting a part of the illness," McCarthy stated that "they represent effects of diseases, not causes." McCarthy died at Ventnor, N. J.

[There is no collection of McCarthy's papers. Biographical sketches appear in *Transactions and Studies of the College of Physicians of Philadelphia*, 1959; and Derek Denny-Brown, ed., *Centennial Anniversary Volume of the American Neurological Association* (1975).]

ROBERT CHARLES POWELL

McCARTHY, JOSEPH RAYMOND (Nov. 14, 1908–May 2, 1957), United States senator, was born in Grand Chute, Wis., the son of Timothy Thomas McCarthy, a farmer, and Bridget Tierney. He grew up on a farm located in the "Irish settlement" outside Appleton, Wis. Later the family moved to another farm near Manawa, Wis. He received a rudimentary education in a one-room country school and then worked on the family farm until early 1929, when he moved to Manawa to manage a grocery store. In the autumn of 1929 he entered Little Wolf High School in Manawa, and with the aid of the principal completed the four-year curriculum in one year. He enrolled at Marquette University in 1930, and graduated with an LL.B. in 1935. After admission to the Wisconsin bar, he practiced in Waupaca and, later, in Shawano.

In 1936, McCarthy ran unsuccessfully as a Democrat for the post of district attorney of Shawano County. Three years later he again sought election, this time as judge of the Tenth Judicial Circuit in Wisconsin, a nominally nonpartisan post for which no party declaration was required. He campaigned hard and succeeded in unseating the incumbent, a veteran of twenty-four years on the court. McCarthy's tenure as judge, like much of his later career, was riddled with controversy; at one point he was reprimanded by the Wisconsin Supreme Court for "highly improper" trial procedures. Nevertheless, he was reelected in 1945.

In July 1942, McCarthy took temporary leave from his judicial duties and was commissioned a first lieutenant in the marine corps. He served as an intelligence officer in the Pacific for more than a year before returning to the United States in July 1944. He was relieved from active duty, at his own request, on Feb. 20, 1945, and resigned his commission effective Mar. 29, 1945. McCarthy later inflated his military record by claiming that he had enlisted as a "buck private," that he had served as a tail gunner, and that he had been wounded in action.

In 1944, while still on active duty, McCarthy returned briefly to Wisconsin in order to run for the Republican nomination for the United States Senate, but was easily defeated by the incumbent, Alexander Wiley. Two years later he again sought the Republican nomination, this time challenging Robert M. La Follette, Jr., a veteran of more than twenty years in the Senate. Supported by the powerful and conservative Republican Voluntary Committee, McCarthy campaigned aggressively and won a narrow victory. In the November general election he stressed his opposition to farm price controls, national health care and New Deal "bureaucracy," and branded his Democratic opponent as "communistically inclined." He was easily elected.

In the Senate, McCarthy generally voted with the conservatives, opposing most social welfare programs though supporting, with reservations, the bipartisan foreign policies of the Truman administration. As one of the "meat shortage boys," as those Republicans elected in the resounding victory by their party in 1946 were sometimes called, he voted against price, rent, and credit controls and in favor of tax reductions. He drew sharp criticism for his close ties with real estate lobbyists, and his support for the soft drink industry campaign to decontrol sugar led reporters to dub him the "Pepsi Cola Kid." McCarthy's Senate career was principally distinguished by his sharp, frequently personal attacks on other senators and by his continual violation of Senate tradition and etiquette. By 1949 he had incurred the displeasure of powerful senators in both parties who considered him an upstart and a troublemaker.

McCarthy emerged from this undistinguished obscurity on Feb. 9, 1950, following an address in Wheeling, W. Va., in which he charged that Communists in the State Department were shaping American foreign policy. His accusations were scarcely original. Indeed, much of his speech had been lifted verbatim from earlier attacks on the Roosevelt and Truman administrations by conservative Republicans and Democrats. The timing of the address—less than three weeks after the conviction of Alger Hiss—together with McCarthy's flamboyant and exaggerated claims that he had the documentation to prove his charges, produced sensational headlines and catapulted him into sudden (and unexpected) prominence.

A congressional investigation chaired by Democratic Senator Millard Tydings of Maryland found no evidence to substantiate McCarthy's accusations, but failed to diminish his influence or notoriety. Indeed, the hearings attracted widespread publicity and served to rally support among conservatives for McCarthy's scathing attacks on the Truman administration. Although he was by no means the first or only politician to charge prominent Democrats with appeasement and disloyalty, McCarthy was undoubtedly the most daring and reckless of those who did so. The term "McCarthyism" rapidly became synonymous with the charge of Communism in government. He campaigned extensively on behalf of fellow Republicans in 1950 and in 1952, and he was widely, if inaccurately, credited with the election of more than a dozen senators and with the defeat of such Democratic opponents as Tydings and William Benton of Connecticut. McCarthy was reelected in 1952 by a large margin, although he ran far behind Dwight D. Eisenhower and other Republicans in Wisconsin.

When the Republicans organized the 83rd Congress in 1953, McCarthy became chairman of both the Senate Committee on Government Operations and its investigative arm, the Permanent Subcommittee on Investigations. He quickly launched a series of investigations ostensibly designed to document his charges of Communism in government. Although these investigations produced little evidence of wrongdoing, they stirred up enormous amounts of controversy and publicity. They also brought McCarthy into growing conflict with President Dwight D. Eisenhower, who had supported the senator in the heat of the 1952 campaign but now sought to disassociate himself and his administration from McCarthy's tactics.

McCarthy's last investigation, into alleged subversion in the army, aroused the wrath of many military leaders and contributed, indirectly, to his sudden political demise. The army, in an effort to descredit McCarthy, charged that he and the chief counsel of the committee, Roy Cohn, had sought to obtain special privileges for G. David Schine, a young committee aide who had been drafted. McCarthy responded by countercharging that the army was holding Schine "hostage" in order to halt his investigation. The hearings into these and related charges, conducted before a television audience estimated at 20 million viewers, lasted from April to June 1954 and, together with McCarthy's increasingly sharp attacks on the Eisenhower administration, served to erode support for the senator among Republican party leaders and the public at large. On June 11, 1954, Republican Senator Ralph Flanders of Vermont introduced a resolution calling for McCarthy's censure; and on Dec. 2, following lengthy hearings and debate, the Senate voted 67–22 to condemn McCarthy for behavior that was "contemptuous, contumacious, and denunciatory" and obstructive of the legislative process.

McCarthy's last years were spent in relative obscurity. He was largely ignored by the White House, by his fellow senators, and by the press. There was time now for a private life—he had married Jean Fraser Kerr, a long-time member of his staff, on Sept. 29, 1953, and in 1957 they adopted a daughter. But these years were marked by illness and heavy drinking. He died at the naval hospital in Bethesda, Md.

As a child McCarthy had been withdrawn and insecure, shunning strangers and clinging fearfully to his mother. As an adult he was loud and aggressive, submerging whatever insecurities he may still have felt in frenetic displays of energy and assertiveness. His political style was crude but, in the context of the early 1950's, startlingly effective. He had an unparalleled talent for political invective, a flair for self-dramatization, and a willingness to lie so flagrantly and consistently that one critic credited him with the invention of a new technique of propaganda: the "multiple untruth." He was extremely combative and, perhaps because of an inner sense of desperation, stubbornly unwilling to retreat. "One should play poker with him to really know him," wrote a friend. "He raises on the poor hands and always comes out the winner."

McCarthy's influence and notoriety owed less to his personality and style than to the transformation of American politics wrought by the cold war. Since 1947 the Truman administration had been emphasizing the menace of Soviet Communism in an attempt to win public support for the new diplomacy of containment. Conservative critics of the administration took an even more belligerent position, condemning the Democrats for their "softness" on Communism at home and abroad. The conservative attack on the Truman administration intensified following the victory of the Communists in China, the arrest of men and women accused of spying for the Soviet Union, and the outbreak of hostilities in Korea. By 1950 the targets of such charges included even such staunch anti-Communists as Secretary of State Dean Acheson and Secretary of Defense George C. Marshall.

McCarthy's real triumph following his Wheeling address lay in identifying himself so completely with the issues generated by this attack. Restraining him thereafter became immensely complicated. Republicans generally endorsed his assaults on the Truman administration, although with varying degrees of enthusiasm. Democrats, fearful of being labeled pro-Communist, sought to undercut his appeal by stressing their own fervent anti-Communism. McCarthy's influence declined rapidly after 1953, partly because of the moderation in international tensions produced by the Korean armistice and partly because the election of a Republican administration removed much of the partisan rationale of his attacks on the Democrats. He contributed to his own downfall by attacking the Eisenhower administration. Even in condemning him, the Senate avoided the issues on which he had built his career, choosing instead to censure him for conduct "contrary to senatorial traditions."

Although McCarthy was more the product than the cause of the second great "red scare" in America, he symbolized, more than any other person, the political extremism of the era. His legacy, and the legacy of all those who contributed to the strident politics he represented, included the erosion of civil liberties, the restriction of dissent, and a foreign policy of reflexive anti-Communism.

[McCarthy's private papers are at Marquette University but at present are unavailable to scholarly researchers. McCarthy published *America's Retreat From Victory* (1951) and *McCarthyism* (1952); the reader should not assume that he wrote either volume. There is no fully adequate biography of McCarthy, but see Richard H. Rovere, *Senator Joe McCarthy* (1959). See also Robert Griffith, *The Politics of Fear* (1970), which includes an extensive bibliographical essay and a discussion of primary sources; Athan Theoharis, *Seeds of Repression* (1971); and Richard M. Freeland, *The Truman Doctrine and the Origins of McCarthyism* (1972). On McCarthyism, see Daniel Bell, ed., *The New American Right* (1955); Michael Paul Rogin, *The Intellectuals and McCarthy* (1969); and Robert Griffith and Athan Theoharis, ed., *The Specter* (1974). Scores of memoirs in the Oral History Collection of Columbia University contain recollections of McCarthy, especially the series on the Eisenhower administration.]

ROBERT GRIFFITH

McCLURE, ROBERT ALEXIS (Mar. 4, 1897–Jan. 1, 1957), army officer and first chief of psychological warfare, was born at Mattoon, Ill., the son of George Hurlbert McClure, a railroad manager, and Harriet Julia Rudy. His father died when Robert was small. After his mother remarried, the family moved to Madison, Ind. McClure attended public school in Madison, and in 1912 he entered the Kentucky Military Institute in Lyndon, Ky., from which he graduated in 1915. The next year he left home and enlisted in the Philippine Constabulary. That same year he was commissioned a second lieutenant in the U.S. Army. On Nov. 11, 1918, he married Marjory Leitch; they had two sons.

In addition to his tour of duty in the Philippines, McClure also served in China and Japan. In 1923 he returned to the United States for further military training at the Army Infantry School (1923–1924) and the Army Cavalry School (1925–1926). He served as an instructor at the Infantry School for four years (1926–1930). His next assignment was to the Command and General Staff School (1930–1932), and later he studied at the Army War College (1935), where he remained as an instructor until 1940. He also had a tour of duty in this period as a personnel officer.

Soon after the outbreak of World War II in Europe, McClure was assigned to the American embassy in London as military attaché. His service there, beginning in 1941 and continuing into 1942, brought him the Legion of Merit. It also led to his advancement in 1942 to chief of intelligence for the American forces in the European theater of operations. As the G-2 (intelligence) officer on the staff of Lieutenant General Dwight D. Eisenhower, McClure was responsible for the security of the plans for the invasion of North Africa. This necessitated service in Africa and delicate relations with the French civil and military authorities. In Africa, McClure was in charge of military information for the press for Eisenhower and served as censor. These responsibilities brought him into frequent contact with war correspondents, for whom he generally favored as much freedom as combat plans and operations would allow.

Thus, by both training and experience, McClure was well equipped to take charge of psychological warfare when it was established as a constituent responsibility of the Supreme Headquarters Allied Expeditionary Force (SHAEF) early in 1944, before the invasion of France. At first McClure, then a brigadier general, was chief of a G-6 section which handled both public relations and psychological warfare. These responsibilities were separated in April 1944, with McClure at the head of the Psychological Warfare Division. His mission was twofold: to plan and conduct psychological warfare ventures during combat and to be ready to establish, under military authority, a new set of information control programs for the American zone in Germany after the war.

McClure supervised activities ranging from radio reports on the course of the war beamed to enemy troops and civilians to the printing and circulation of counterfeit ration stamps inside Germany. Combat psychological warfare teams accompanied field troops for broadcasting and leaflet distribution. Printed appeals were dropped during bombing raids over Germany.

After the war ended, McClure was made director of the Information Control Division in Germany. This placed him in charge of developing de-Nazified print media, theater, film, music, and other information and cultural facilities organizations. The publication of "clean" newspapers and the performances of purged theatrical companies were notable events in German cities, and McClure regularly attended the formal licensing ceremonies. His Information Control Service commands encompassed Bavaria, Württemberg-Baden, and Hesse.

To plan and execute this assignment, McClure assembled a staff of military and civilian personnel from both sides of the Atlantic. These specialists included linguists, lawyers, journalists, publishers, radio technicians and administrators,

musicians, theatrical producers, psychologists, and academicians. The Americans, some with military rank and some civilians in uniforms, represented the Office of Strategic Services and the Office of War Information; their British counterparts came from the Political Warfare Executive, the Ministry of Information, and other wartime forces. Oxford, Cambridge, and leading American universities and colleges contributed scholars. McClure also allowed some women to advance to a degree not common to other SHAEF staffs.

McClure's assignment, totally different from that of every other World War II general officer, was less than fully understood or appreciated by his superiors. He served through the entire war without a promotion to major general. He was still a brigadier general when, in 1950, he began a three-year tour of duty as chief of the Psychological Warfare Division in the Pentagon. After Eisenhower's election as president, McClure was sent in 1953 to Teheran as head of the American military mission. In 1955, while on this assignment, he was belatedly awarded the rank of major general. The following year he retired but died at Fort Huachuca, Ariz., on the way to his retirement home in Carmel, Calif. At his instruction he was buried not in a military cemetery but in the family plot at Madison, Ind.

[McClure's papers, journals, and correspondence are in his family's possession. McClure supervised the publication of the *Manual for the Control of German Information Services* (1945), which was adapted by the British and translated into French. There is an obituary in the *New York Times*, Jan. 5, 1957. See also Harry C. Butcher, *My Three Years with Eisenhower* (1946); Harold Zink, *American Military Government in Germany* (1947); Hans Speier, "The Future of Psychological Warfare," *Public Opinion Quarterly*, Spring 1948; Charles A. H. Thomson, *Overseas Information Services of the United States Government* (1948); Irving Dilliard, *The Development of a Free Press in Germany* (1949); Daniel Lerner, *Sykewar* (1949); Lucius D. Clay, *Decision in Germany* (1950); Lucian K. Truscott, Jr., *Command Missions* (1954); William E. Daugherty and Morris Janowitz, *A Psychological Warfare Casebook* (1958).]

IRVING DILLIARD

McCORMICK, LYNDE DUPUY (Aug. 12, 1895–Aug. 16, 1956), naval officer, was born in Annapolis, Md., the son of Lieutenant (later Rear Admiral) Albert Montgomery Dupuy McCormick of the Navy Medical Corps, and Edith Lynde Abbot. He studied at St. John's College,

Annapolis, for two years before accepting an appointment by President William Howard Taft to the United States Naval Academy in 1911. He graduated, second in his class, in 1915.

Assigned to the battleship *Wyoming*, which operated with the British Grand Fleet, McCormick witnessed the surrender of the German High Seas Fleet in 1918. On Oct. 2, 1920, he married Lillian Addison Sprigg Graham. They had two children, and McCormick subsequently adopted her son by her first husband. He commanded the destroyer *Kennedy* for a few months in 1921 before returning to the Naval Academy as an instructor.

Following a course of instruction at the Submarine School in New London, Conn., in 1923, McCormick served in submarines. He commanded the *R-10* at Pearl Harbor from 1924 to 1926 and the *Bass* from 1928 to 1931. Following these assignments, he had tours of sea and shore duty until the Japanese attacked Pearl Harbor on Dec. 7, 1941. At that time McCormick was assistant war plans officer on the staff of Admiral Husband E. Kimmel, commander in chief of the Pacific Fleet. After Chester W. Nimitz succeeded Kimmel, he appointed McCormick, then a captain, as his war plans officer. McCormick served in this billet in 1942, during the battles of the Coral Sea and Midway, and the Guadalcanal campaign, for which service he was awarded the Legion of Merit. As commanding officer of the battleship *South Dakota* in 1943, he saw duty in the Atlantic, in northern European waters with the British Home Fleet, and in the South Pacific. McCormick was promoted to rear admiral in 1943.

After his extensive war experience on a major staff and in command, Admiral Ernest J. King, the chief of naval operations, brought McCormick to Washington as his assistant for logistics plans. In this capacity McCormick became chairman of the Joint Logistics Committee of the Joint Chiefs of Staff and accompanied King to the Quebec Conference in 1944 and to Yalta in 1945. Later in 1945, as commander of Battleship Division 3, McCormick was a task group commander during the battle for Okinawa.

Immediately after the war McCormick served as chief of staff to the commander in chief of the Pacific Fleet and, later, he commanded battleships and cruisers of the Atlantic Fleet. Following this command he reverted to his permanent rank of rear admiral when he became commandant of the 12th Naval District, with headquarters in San Francisco. Late in 1949 President Harry S.

Truman appointed him vice chief of naval operations, the second-ranking position in the navy. He assumed his new duties in April 1950 as a vice admiral and was promoted to admiral in December of that year.

Upon the death of the chief of naval operations, Admiral Forrest P. Sherman, on July 22, 1951, McCormick became acting chief of naval operations. The following month the president appointed him commander in chief of the Atlantic Fleet. In January 1952, McCormick assumed additional duties as the first supreme allied commander, Atlantic, a major command in the North Atlantic Treaty Organization that covers the area from the Arctic to the Tropic of Cancer and from North America to the coasts of Africa and Europe. An operational rather than administrative command, it is charged with the task of keeping the sea-lanes open between the Western Hemisphere and Europe in the event of war.

McCormick served in this capacity until 1954, when he was appointed president of the Naval War College in Newport, R.I. His major contribution while there was to institute a year-long course for foreign officers that has become a permanent part of the college curriculum. He died in Newport.

[The most complete account of McCormick's wartime activities is in Samuel Eliot Morison, *History of United States Naval Operations in World War II* (1947–1962), esp. vols. VI, X, and XIV; and in Walter Karig, Earl Burton, and Stephen Freeland, *Battle Report* (1949). See also Duncan S. Ballantine, *U.S. Naval Logistics in the Second World War* (1947); and Julius A. Furer, *Administration of the Navy Department in World War II* (1959).]

B. M. SIMPSON, III

MacDONALD, BETTY (Mar. 26, 1908–Feb. 7, 1958), author, was born Anne Elizabeth Campbell Bard in Boulder, Colo., the daughter of Darsie Campbell Bard, a mining engineer, and Elsie Tholimar Sanderson. Her family moved from one mining project to another in Colorado, Mexico, Montana, and Idaho; finally, when she was nine, they settled in Seattle, Wash. She was an honor student at Roosevelt High School in Seattle and attended the University of Washington for one year, planning to major in art. Her formal education was ended in 1927, when she married Robert Eugene Heskett, an insurance salesman; they had two children. The marriage ended in divorce in 1935.

Heskett wanted to be a chicken farmer, so the couple moved to an isolated farm near Chimacum, Wash., that they had bought for $450. Living conditions were primitive, and MacDonald could arouse no enthusiasm for raising chickens. "By the end of the second spring," she wrote later, "I hated everything about the chicken but the egg." The farming experiences became, fifteen years later, the subject of her first and most widely read book, *The Egg and I* (1945). It was an exuberant account of an unconventional childhood and a crisp, light-hearted description of the endless work, odd characters, loneliness, and other rigors and infelicities of simple rural life. MacDonald was encouraged to write the book by an older sister, Mary Bard, who wrote *The Doctor Wears Three Faces* (1949).

The Egg and I, which was partially serialized in the *Atlantic Monthly*, climbed quickly to the top of the best-seller list and stayed there for months. By August 1946, less than a year after publication, sales reached a million copies; eventually the book sold more than two million copies in all editions. MacDonald was paid $100,000 by International Pictures for the rights to the motion picture, which starred Claudette Colbert and Fred Mac-Murray. A successful series of "Ma and Pa Kettle" films, based on characters in the book, came later.

After separating from her first husband in 1931, MacDonald had returned to Seattle to begin a business career. During the Great Depression she held various jobs, including secretarial work for a mining engineer, managing a chain letter office, and selling advertising. She also worked for a number of government agencies, becoming the only woman labor adjuster in the National Recovery Administration. Later, MacDonald was employed by the Treasury Department, and by the National Youth Administration as a director of publicity (1939–1942). This period of her life was chronicled in *Anybody Can Do Anything* (1950).

In 1938, MacDonald contracted tuberculosis and was confined until mid-1939 in a Seattle sanatorium. Her experiences there, which ended with her cure, were narrated with her customary gusto and irreverence in *The Plague and I* (1948). The book contained helpful and interesting information about tuberculosis and treatment of the disease at that time.

On Apr. 24, 1942, she married Donald Chauncey MacDonald, a real estate operator; they had no children. They lived on Vashon Island, Wash., in a rambling old house, with her two daughters. They were "at the mercy" of tides, ferry schedules, fog, weeds, and the strains of raising adolescent children. The period is described in her last autobiographical book, *Onions in the Stew* (1955). Like her earlier works, this is a projection of a remarkably spirited personality. After 1945, MacDonald wrote five books for children—stories about Mrs. Piggle-Wiggle, who specialized in concocting cures for bad habits.

A suit seeking $900,000 from MacDonald and her publisher was filed in a Seattle court in 1950 by nine members of a single family who contended they were humiliated by being identified as the real-life characters pictured as the Kettles in *The Egg and I*. A tenth person, seeking $75,000, claimed to be humiliated because he was portrayed in the book as Indian Crowbar. The defendants were cleared on all counts after a jury trial.

The MacDonalds bought a cattle ranch in Carmel Valley, Calif., in 1953 and moved there in 1956. Two years later MacDonald returned to Seattle for medical treatment, and died there.

[Portions of MacDonald's four books of reminiscence are brought together in chronological sequence in *Who, Me?* (1959). Obituaries are in the *New York Times* and *Seattle Times*, Feb. 8, 1958. See also *Life*, Mar. 18, 1946; *New York Times Book Review*, Dec. 5, 1948; James D. Hart, *The Popular Book* (1950); *New York Herald-Tribune Book Review*, Oct. 8, 1950; *Publishers Weekly*, Mar. 17, 1951; *Newsweek*, May 15, 1955; and Don Duncan, "Betty MacDonald's Scramble to the Top," *Seattle Times*, Mar. 11, 1973.]

WILLIAM McCANN

McELROY, ROBERT McNUTT (Dec. 28, 1872–Jan. 16, 1959), historian and publicist, was born in Perryville, Ky., the son of William Thomas McElroy, a Presbyterian minister, and Eliza Casseday. In the early 1880's the family moved to Louisville, where he was educated in the public schools. He attended Princeton University, from which he received the B.A. in 1896, the M.A. in 1897, and the Ph.D. in 1900. In the latter year McElroy married Louise Robinson Booker; they had two children. After a year of study in Europe, he returned to Princeton in 1901 as assistant professor of American history. In 1909 he published his first book, *Kentucky in the Nation's History*. That year Princeton named him Edwards professor of American history, and in 1912 he became chairman of the department of history and politics, a post he held for the next thirteen years. In 1914 he published *The Winning of the Far West*, a continuation of Theodore Roosevelt's *Winning of the West*.

At the outbreak of World War I, McElroy was forcibly detained in Germany for a month. Making no secret of his hope for British victory, he argued as early as November 1914 that the United States might eventually have to join Britain in defense of "representative government." He considered President Woodrow Wilson's early resistance to calls for preparedness unpatriotic, and in 1915 he was one of the founders of the Plattsburgh civilian training movement.

In 1916–1917, McElroy served as the first American exchange professor to China, lecturing at Tsing Hua University in Peking and elsewhere. His lectures were published as *The Representative Idea in History* (1917). Afterward he continued to work for Chinese-American understanding as managing director of the China Society of America.

Back in the United States and eager to aid the war effort, McElroy accepted an invitation to work for the National Security League (NSL), an organization founded in 1914 to press for preparedness that was now launching an intensive loyalty campaign. As the educational director of the league, McElroy frankly avowed his intention to "conduct propaganda" through an "Americanization" program designed to overcome the effects of what he termed "nullification in education"—the neglect or refusal of the diverse educational systems in the country to instill patriotism in their students or to provide the means or the desire for assimilation among immigrants. His Committee on Patriotism Through Education, composed largely of historians, issued scores of pamphlets and dispatched a virtual army of lecturers to teachers' meetings and other groups throughout the country. The league prepared a series of lessons on American war aims and sought to rid the schools of instruction in the German language, which McElroy branded as a vehicle for German propaganda and an obstacle to assimilation.

One of the league's most effective speakers, McElroy addressed 104 audiences totaling 130,000 listeners in his first year. His reliance upon shock techniques occasionally backfired, as in April 1918, when he charged a University of Wisconsin audience with pro-German sympathies. Outraged university officials defended the students' loyalty and banned further NSL speakers. The incident figured largely in a con-gressional investigation of the league (December 1918–February 1919), during which McElroy defiantly defended his conduct. After the war the organization turned to anti-Communism, and McElroy produced pamphlets characterizing Bolshevism as a bloodthirsty dictatorship.

In the fall of 1919, McElroy resumed his duties at Princeton, although he remained in touch with public affairs. In 1920 he did publicity work for Leonard Wood's campaign for the Republican presidential nomination, and later gave speeches for Warren G. Harding. He campaigned for Calvin Coolidge in 1924 and for Herbert Hoover in 1928. His scholarly interests at this time turned toward biography. At the request of Grover Cleveland's widow, McElroy wrote a life of the former president in 1923, and he honored a similar request by the family of former Vice-President Levi P. Morton in 1930. Seven years later he completed a biography of Jefferson Davis. Although these works rested on substantial research, none of them achieved sufficient critical distance from its subject. Only the Morton work remains unsuperseded.

Despite his conservatism and his record as a professional patriot, in the 1920's McElroy persistently decried isolationism and advocated "the international mind," a somewhat vague notion of a worldwide consensus emphasizing the congruence of interests among nations rather than their differences. He argued for a stronger League of Nations and for American participation in the World Court. In 1924 he wrote on world events as international editor of *Current History*. The next year he was elected Harmsworth professor of American history at Oxford, where for fourteen years his teaching focused upon the evolution of America from disparate states into a united nation as a metaphor for evolving world unity. Always an Anglophile, he criticized traditional American historical writing on the Revolution and the War of 1812 for portraying Britain as an unmitigated villain and thereby impeding Anglo-American friendship. As Sir George Watson professor at several British universities in 1926, McElroy entitled his lectures on past British-American crises *The Pathway of Peace* (1927).

In the mid-1930's, at the Institute of Public Affairs held annually at the University of Virginia, he continued to denounce the "provincial mind" and to call for international understanding and cooperation to preserve peace. McElroy retired from Oxford in 1939 and returned to Princeton. He died at Lihue, Hawaii.

[McElroy's papers (some 5,700 items) are in the Library of Congress. Published historical works include an edition of William Bourke Cockran's speeches, *In the Name of Liberty* (1925); and *The Unfortified Boundary* (1943), edited with Thomas Riggs. On World War I, see "The Prussian War Against Teuton Ideals," *Outlook*, Nov. 14, 1914; pamphlets in the NSL's Patriotism Through Education series; and several articles in *Independent*, Mar. 1918. His internationalist thinking is reflected in "The International Mind Speaks," *New York Times Magazine*, June 28, 1925; *American History as an International Study* (1926); "America's Duty in Promoting International Justice," *Current History*, Nov. 1926; and "What Is International Justice?" *ibid.*, Sept. 1935. There is no biographical study. Obituaries are in the *New York Times*, Jan. 17, 1959; and *Princeton Alumni Weekly*, Feb. 13, 1959. See also *NSL Bulletin*, 1917–1918; Winslow, Van Hise, and Birge, *Report Upon the Statements of Professor Robert McNutt McElroy . . . Relating to the University of Wisconsin* (1918); *NSL Hearings*, 65th Cong., 3rd sess. (1918–1919); and George T. Blakey, "Historians on the Homefront" (Ph.D. diss., Indiana University, 1970).]

CHARLES W. CALHOUN

McENTEE, JAMES JOSEPH (Sept. 9, 1884–Oct. 13, 1957), labor arbitrator and government administrator, was born in Jersey City, N. J., the son of James Lawrence McEntee and Mary Sullivan. After attending parochial schools, he became an apprentice machinist at the Blair Tool Works in New York City. After completing his term he remained with Blair, becoming very involved with the activities of the International Association of Machinists at the local and district levels. In 1911 he was made a full-time officer of the association. McEntee quickly gained a reputation as an effective conciliator and in 1917 was appointed by President Woodrow Wilson to the three-man New York Arbitration Board. His special areas of expertise were the munitions and maritime labor industries. It was in this latter connection that he first met Franklin Delano Roosevelt, then assistant secretary of the navy. During the 1920's he continued his work with both the Machinists' Association and the Arbitration Board and was particularly prominent in the settlement of several newspaper strikes and in railway contract negotiations.

In March 1933, President Franklin D. Roosevelt and Congress created the Civilian Conservation Corps (CCC). The first measure of the new administration to be aimed specifically at the plight of unemployed youth, its function was to employ young men on conservation work throughout the country. Simple in operation and administration, the CCC worked through four federal departments: Labor, which selected the men from relief rolls; War, which administered the camps where they lived; Agriculture and Interior, which supervised the work projects. Coordinating the activities were an advisory council of representatives of the departments and a small central office headed by a director. For the latter position, largely as a placatory gesture toward organized labor, Roosevelt chose Robert Fechner, a member of the General Executive Board of the International Association of Machinists and a vice-president of the American Federation of Labor. Fechner and McEntee had been associates since 1911; had worked closely on conciliation activities during and after World War I; and had become firm friends. At Fechner's request Roosevelt offered McEntee the post of assistant director of the CCC, which he accepted. He went to Washington in April 1933, remained as assistant director until Fechner's death in 1940, and then succeeded him as director, a position he held until abolition of the CCC in June 1942.

McEntee and Fechner quickly developed a harmonious working relationship. Indeed, Fechner was content to leave much of the business of day-to-day administration to McEntee, preferring to spend as much time as possible visiting individual camps. Less harmonious were McEntee's relationships with representatives of the cooperating federal departments. He soon became convinced that the administrative machinery of the CCC was far too loose and unwieldy. In particular, he wanted to strengthen the role of the central office at the expense of the cooperating departments and in time persuaded Fechner to accept this point of view. The administrative history of the CCC from about 1937 was, increasingly, one of tension, as Fechner and McEntee attempted, generally unsuccessfully, to effect centralization. McEntee's appointment as director in 1940 was bitterly opposed by Secretary of the Interior Harold L. Ickes for precisely this reason.

McEntee's term of office as CCC director was far from tranquil. He continued to advocate centralization and to be opposed. But, increasingly, his time was occupied with preventing abolition of the agency. With the approach of war, the Congress, spearheaded by the Joint Committee on the Reduction of Non-essential Federal

Expenditures, began to question the need for its existence in a situation that demanded general financial stringency and in which unemployment was becoming much less of a national problem, as defense industries began to boom. In response, McEntee broadened selection and work policies and stressed the importance of the CCC as an adjunct to the war effort, particularly in the areas of fire prevention and the maintenance of military reservations. Roosevelt vigorously supported his efforts, but to no avail.

Soon after termination of the CCC, McEntee returned to the Machinists' Association as vice-president of the New Jersey Council of Machinists and a delegate to the New Jersey Federation of Labor. In 1952, President Harry S. Truman appointed him to the National Production Authority, on which he served until 1954. He died in Jersey City, N.J.

[See John Salmond, The *Civilian Conservation Corps, A New Deal Case Study* (1967).]

JOHN SALMOND

McHALE, KATHRYN (July 22, 1889–Oct. 8, 1956), educator, psychologist, and administrator, was born in Logansport, Ind., the daughter of Martin McHale and Margaret Farrell. After attending public schools in Logansport, she taught there from 1910 to 1917. She then entered Columbia University, where she was awarded the B.S. in 1919, the M.A. in 1920, and the Ph.D. 1926.

After receiving the M.A., McHale became an instructor in education at Goucher College, Baltimore, Md. She was subsequently assistant professor (1922–1926), associate professor (1926–1927), and full professor (1927–1935). During the summer she taught at Columbia (1918–1926), the University of Minnesota (1928), and Carleton College (1921–1931). After 1935 she continued on the faculty of Goucher as a nonresident professor.

While at Goucher, McHale developed the McHale Vocational Interest Test for College Women. Using her studies of vocational guidance and testing, and encouraged by her colleague Agnes L. Rogers, she adapted portions of the Thorndike Intelligence Tests to form an instrument designed particularly for women. The purpose of the test, she wrote, was to "formulate a working idea to guide an objective study of vocational interests . . . the idea being, that if one

made an information test based on interests, perhaps one would arrive at something more tangible by way of a guidance tool." In 1922 she administered the first form of her test to 133 Goucher College juniors; by 1933 a revised form was being used in twenty colleges. It was also during her tenure at Goucher that McHale published her doctoral dissertation, *Comparative Psychology and Hygiene of the Overweight Child* (1926). After extensive testing of 312 children, she concluded that "over-weight children are not very different from other children" and that "it is difficult if not impossible to explain by the environmental hypothesis the relatively superior educational achievement of the over-weight group."

From 1929 to 1950, McHale served as the general director of the American Association of University Women (AAUW). During her tenure the membership of the organization grew from 31,674 to 115,402. As it increased in size, its program of adult education grew to include diverse social and economic problems and the arts, and it developed support for higher standards in education. Its work on behalf of the status of women also was expanded. As director of the AAUW, McHale worked to increase the number of fellowships for graduate study awarded to women.

Her interest in higher education led to a comprehensive study of 315 liberal arts colleges, *Current Changes and Experiments in Liberal Arts Education* (1932), which was the thirty-first yearbook of the National Society for the Study of Education. This major AAUW study, which showed the important trends in the care and direction of students, curriculum and instruction, organization and administration, set forth 128 specific changes and experiments aimed at improving liberal arts education. McHale noted that "the tendency of the college to become a progressive agency in society . . . has brought it into conflict with other social institutions and introduced problems that will require unusual wisdom and skill in their solution."

In dealing with these problems, McHale wrote or edited three books, including *Housing College Students* (1934); numerous pamphlets; and articles in journals. Her more than forty publications dealt with such varied subjects as child development, educational opportunities for women, and studies in higher education. Deeply concerned about adult education, she stated, "Every woman . . . is forced by . . . events to feel a greater responsibility for taking part in community, national, and international affairs, and for understanding economic and social forces."

McHale also encouraged women to become involved in the international aspects of education, including the Information and Research Bureau of International Education of the AAUW. She urged the formation of the United Nations as early as 1943, and was instrumental in securing the appointment of women to the San Francisco Conference in 1945. According to Delos W. Lovelace of the *New York Sun*, McHale was "a moving spirit" at the Women's Conference on Post-War Planning in 1944. Later she served on the executive committee of the U.S. National Commission for UNESCO.

As leader of the AAUW, McHale was involved in numerous national projects. She served on the Citizens' Federal Committee of the U.S. Office of Education, the Women's Interest Section of the Advisory Council of the War Department, the executive council of the American Association of Adult Education, the board of educational advisers to the National Foundation for Education in American Citizenship, and the board of the National Association of Foreign Student Advisors. In 1950, President Harry S. Truman appointed her to the Subversive Activities Control Board, on which she served until 1956. She regarded this appointment as an opportunity "to give close thought and a fair approach to a fundamental problem." The only woman on the board, she sat with the chairman as a subcommittee of two at hearings to determine whether the Communist party in the United States was under foreign domination and control. She also conducted lengthy hearings on the Veterans of the Abraham Lincoln Brigade, members of which had served with the Loyalists in the Spanish Civil War. Her report condemned the group for its left-wing activities. McHale, who never married, died in Washington, D.C.

[The primary location of materials by and about McHale is the library and archives of the American Association of University Women, Washington, D.C. Biographical articles about her are in *Woman's Journal*, Apr. 1930; *Woman's Home Companion*, Mar. 1935; *School Life*, Dec. 1947; and *AAUW Journal*, Jan. 1957. An obituary is in *New York Times*, Oct. 9, 1956.]

JACOB L. SUSSKIND

McINTIRE, ROSS (Aug. 11, 1889–Dec. 8, 1959), personal physician to President Franklin D. Roosevelt, surgeon general of the navy, and chief of the Bureau of Medicine and Surgery, was born in Salem, Oreg., the son of Charles McIntire, a building contractor, and Ada Thompson. After early schooling in Salem, McIntire entered Willamette University (now the University of Oregon) Medical School in 1907. He received the M.D. in 1912 and began private practice in his hometown.

In April 1917, two days before America declared war on Germany, McIntire was commissioned assistant surgeon with the rank of lieutenant (j.g.) in the navy medical corps. His first duty was aboard the armored cruiser *New Orleans*. At the end of the war, McIntire, now a full lieutenant, decided to stay in the navy and remained with the *New Orleans* on her postwar cruise with the Asiatic fleet and as a station ship at Vladivostok. In 1920 McIntire returned to the United States and during the next decade was stationed at naval hospitals in San Diego and Washington, D.C., served three tours of duty aboard the hospital ship *Relief*, and pursued graduate work in his medical specialties, ophthalmology and otolaryngology. He married Pauline Palmer of New York in 1923. They had no children. He returned to the Naval Hospital, Washington, in 1931 at which time he renewed a wartime friendship with Admiral Cary Grayson, President Woodrow Wilson's physician and former medical director of the navy. It was Grayson who recommended McIntire when Roosevelt asked about a personal doctor.

From 1935 to 1945, as personal physician to the president, McIntire saw more of Roosevelt than anyone except Eleanor Roosevelt. Affable and self-assured, McIntire easily joined the small circle of White House intimates who enjoyed the president's confidence. It was McIntire's habit to sit with the president in his bedroom each morning to watch him for any indication of ill health. He visited the president again at 5:30 P.M. and finally at bedtime. Although McIntire was not a specialist in rehabilitation for polio—the disease that struck Roosevelt in 1921—he became a conscientious monitor of the president's physical therapy program. McIntire was at Roosevelt's side on many trips, including the Atlantic Conference, Hawaii in 1944, Teheran, and Yalta.

Roosevelt's sudden death on Apr. 12, 1945, prompted questions about the state of the president's health during the war years and particularly at the time of the election of 1944. McIntire was widely criticized for having been overly sanguine about the chief executive's health. Some observers complained that he had been secretive and deceptive, and that because of political considerations had cynically certified a dying man as fit for a fourth term. In rebuttal McIntire said that in 1944 the president had been in excellent condition for a man his age. He never wavered in this opinion.

Years later McIntire received support from the doctor most qualified to comment on the case. In 1970 Dr. Howard Bruenn, a young navy cardiologist who had attended Roosevelt in his last year, wrote that during his final year Roosevelt was not too ill to perform the duties of the presidency. While fatigued by hypertension and reduced cardiac reserve, Bruenn said, Roosevelt was able to exercise his judgment and "to use the fruits of his unique knowledge and experience in guiding the war effort." In the end, the president was felled by a sudden cerebral hemorrhage, a medical occurrence that could not be predicted.

While McIntire was well known as Roosevelt's doctor, he received insufficient recognition for his achievements as surgeon general of the navy and chief of the Bureau of Medicine and Surgery. Roosevelt appointed him to the dual posts in 1938 with the temporary rank of rear admiral, assignments that he held in addition to his White House duty. In 1944 he was promoted to vice admiral, the first navy medical man to wear three stars. As surgeon general, McIntire supervised the tremendous wartime expansion of the navy's medical department and, by all accounts, was an outstanding administrator. He retired as surgeon general on Dec. 31, 1946.

In 1947, after leaving the navy, McIntire organized the American Red Cross blood program under which the first regional blood center was opened in Rochester, N.Y., the following year. When he resigned as national administrator of the program in 1951, he had established forty-three regional blood centers and 120 mobile units. President Harry S. Truman, on the occasion of McIntire's departure, lauded him for his energetic leadership, remarking that the admiral was "one of the large number of people who are willing to do whatever is necessary for the welfare of the country."

From 1947 to 1954 McIntire served as first chairman of the President's Committee for Employment of the Physically Handicapped. This marked the start of the nation's program to meet the employment problems faced by handicapped persons, including 250,000 disabled World War II veterans. In his quiet but forceful way he helped break down the barriers impeding qualified handicapped people seeking employment. The National Association of Manufacturers cited his leadership as "one of the outstanding achievements of the postwar period."

The final years of McIntire's life were spent as executive director of the International College of Surgeons, a worldwide association devoted to publicizing medical developments and new surgical techniques. He died in Chicago.

[Manuscript sources are the McIntire Papers in the Franklin D. Roosevelt Library and the Correspondence File, Records of the Bureau of Medicine and Surgery (Record Group 52) in the National Archives. There is no full account of McIntire's life. There is scattered biographical information in *White House Physician* (1946), McIntire's medical history of Roosevelt. See also the obituaries in the *New York Times* and *New York Herald Tribune*, Dec. 9, 1959.]

WILLIAM J. STEWART

MACK, CONNIE (Dec. 22, 1862–Feb. 8, 1956), baseball manager and club owner, was born Cornelius McGillicuddy in East Brookfield, Mass., the son of Michael McGillicuddy and Mary McKillop. His surname was informally shortened to Mack by his father, a wheelwright, laborer, and Union army veteran who was hard-pressed to support his family. Mack's education ended with grammar school, and he spent his youth working twelve-hour days in a shoe factory. At age twenty-one he was a $15-a-week factory foreman.

A skilled catcher, the lanky, six-foot four-inch Mack played baseball on Sundays with a local amateur champion team in 1883. The following year he joined the professional Meriden team of the Connecticut State League. In 1885 he was earning $200 a month playing for Hartford in the Eastern League, and at the end of that season he was acquired by Washington of the National League. With last-place Washington, Mack was rated as a fair-hitting, good-fielding catcher who was clever at handling pitchers. On Nov. 2, 1887, he married Margaret Hogan. After her death in 1892, their three sons were raised by Mack's mother. In 1910 he married Katherine Hallahan; they had five children.

In 1890, Mack joined the Brotherhood of Professional Baseball Players in battling the major-league restrictive reserve clause and salary limitation policies. He became a member of the Buffalo club of the Players' League and invested his life's savings in this losing venture. When the league collapsed that fall, he joined the Pittsburgh Pirates of the National League, remaining with that weak team for six seasons, three of them as manager.

After being dismissed as manager in 1896, Mack accepted an offer from President Byron Bancroft Johnson of the Western League to manage the Milwaukee team. During the next four years he gained valuable experience in administration and led the team to four first-division finishes. In 1901, when Johnson renamed the circuit the American League and battled the National League for recognition, Mack moved the Milwaukee team to Philadelphia. With the financial support of Benjamin F. Shibe, a sporting-goods manufacturer, Mack as manager and part owner made the Philadelphia Athletics one of the strongest franchises in the new league. Over the next half-century the Athletics won nine league championships and five World Series titles—but also a share of infamy for many last-place finishes.

In the early years of the American League's struggle for recognition, Mack's team was a bulwark, winning championships in 1902 and 1905 although losing the 1905 World Series to the New York Giants. Mack recruited a powerful young team dominated by collegiate stars like Eddie Plank, Jack Barry, Eddie Collins, and John ("Stuffy") McInnis. In 1909 the team moved into Shibe Park, a structure capable of seating 33,000. The following year, with their celebrated "$100,000 infield," the Athletics won the league pennant and the World Series, and over the next four years they added three league titles and two World Series victories. The two Series wins over the Giants established the American League on a par with the National and enhanced Mack's reputation as a tactician and developer of players.

In 1914 falling attendance and rising salary demands brought on by the bid of the interloping Federal League for major-league status hurt Mack badly. Unable to compete in an atmosphere of rising costs and fearing the inroads from World War I, he sold or released his star players, a much-criticized retrenchment policy that consigned his team to last place for seven straight seasons.

Shibe's death in 1922 enabled Mack to acquire half-ownership and to control club operations. Shibe Park was remodeled, and growing profits were used to acquire young talent, including several players purchased from Jack Dunn, a friend and owner of the strong minor-league Baltimore franchise. Mack bought pitcher Robert

("Lefty") Grove from Dunn for $100,600 in 1925. With players like Jimmy Foxx, Al Simmons, Max Bishop, George Earnshaw, and Mickey Cochrane, the Athletics challenged the Yankees, and in 1929, with one of the strongest teams in baseball history, Mack won his seventh league pennant and fourth World Series. For this achievement he received the Edward Bok Philadelphia Award for his inspiration both to youth and to the elderly. At the peak of his fame the white-haired Mack, who habitually managed in a business suit and straw hat and positioned his outfielders by waving a scorecard, was acclaimed as the elder statesman of baseball. His Athletics added two more pennants and one World Series title in 1930–1931.

Until 1933 the team remained a pennant contender. Then falling gate receipts brought on by the Great Depression prompted Mack again to sell star players to meet expenses. Although he was criticized for destroying another great team, he argued that the team payroll had been among the highest in the game and that his decision was forced by pressing creditors, falling attendance, and a state ban on Sunday baseball.

In 1937, Mack acquired full control from the Shibe heirs and became president of the Athletics. With the coming of night baseball and with the National League Phillies also using Shibe Park, the financial plight improved. But Mack's teams remained perennial losers, and his reputation, despite his election to the Baseball Hall of Fame in 1938 and national acclaim as the "Grand Old Man" of baseball, became that of the pinchpenny who tore down champion teams.

Stubbornly clinging to his management post, Mack became increasingly ineffective. For placing his sons Roy, Earle, and Connie, Jr., in key positions, he was accused of nepotism. By giving the sons half his stock, he embittered his wife. His players accused him of penury for opposing higher salaries. His sons took full control in 1950, Mack retaining the empty title of president. In 1953, Shibe Park was renamed Connie Mack Stadium, a break with tradition that Mack resisted and that portended the end of his baseball career. The following year his financially pressed sons persuaded Mack to sell the team to Arnold M. Johnson, a Chicago businessman, for $3.5 million. Mack signed from a sickbed, unaware of Johnson's decision to move the franchise to Kansas City, Mo. When the move took place in 1955, the family was shocked. Mack survived the sale by fifteen months, dying at his home in Germantown, Pa. His sixty-six years in the major leagues had shown him to be a brilliant innovator. But his triumphs were blighted by his inability to recognize his fading abilities and his failure to delegate authority to dynamic successors.

[Two autobiographies are ascribed to Mack: *My 66 Years in the Big Leagues* (1950) and *From Sandlot to Big League* (1960). The Baseball Library, Cooperstown, N.Y., has journal articles on Mack, some of his correspondence, scrapbooks, and manuscript notes of authors who wrote about him. There is no critical study. The best popular biography is Frederick G. Lieb, *Connie Mack* (1945). See also *Sporting News,* Oct. 27, 1954; Edwin Pope, *Baseball's Greatest Managers* (1960); David Q. Voigt, *American Baseball,* 2 vols. (1966–1970); and Ray Robinson, *Baseball's Most Colorful Managers* (1969).]

DAVID Q. VOIGT

McKAY, (JAMES) DOUGLAS (June 24, 1893–July 22, 1959), cabinet officer, governor, and businessman, was born in Portland, Oreg., the son of E. D. McKay, a carpenter, and Minnie A. Musgrove. Reared in modest circumstances, he worked while still a schoolboy to help support the family. A job that paid $35 a month led him to leave high school in 1911 without receiving his diploma, but later, in 1913, he was admitted to Oregon State College at Corvallis as a "sub-freshman" agriculture student. Despite the need to earn his way and his heavy involvement in campus politics, which included winning the presidency of the student body, McKay graduated with a B.S. degree in 1917. On Mar. 31, 1917, he married Mabel C. Hill; they had three children. After enlisting as an officer, McKay was wounded in the right arm and shoulder during the battle for Sedan in the Meuse-Argonne offensive, a disability that required him to abandon arduous work in agriculture for a career in business.

McKay began his Horatio Alger-like rise to commercial success as an insurance salesman. Next he worked for a Portland automobile dealer. After promotion to sales manager, he was placed in charge of the company's agency in Salem, where in 1927 he opened his own Chevrolet dealership. He subsequently expanded his enterprise and added Cadillacs to his franchise.

Entering local politics as a Republican, McKay had no difficulty winning a succession of elections. He was chosen mayor of Salem in 1932 and guided that city through fiscal troubles, an experience that, according to a contemporary journalist, made McKay "a firm advocate of

government as well as business preserving and guarding its financial foundation." Elected to the state senate in 1934 and ultimately serving four terms before and after the outbreak of World War II, he interrupted his political career briefly to enlist in the army, where he was a public relations officer with the rank of major. In 1948 he was elected governor of Oregon.

A fiscal conservative prone to condemn the unpalatable as "socialistic," McKay as governor emphasized the virtues of private enterprise and abhorred federal power, advocating the importance of state and local responsibility. Yet, although he valued the role of business and favored the development of natural resources by private investors, his position was sufficiently flexible to permit support for city-owned water projects and treatment of stream pollution. In 1950, McKay was reelected governor. Although generally identified with the conservative wing of the Republican party, he had little confidence that Senator Robert A. Taft could win the presidency in 1952. Highly impressed with General Dwight D. Eisenhower's personal qualities and outlook, McKay became one of his earliest boosters. His reward was being named secretary of the interior.

Ideologically and temperamentally McKay was an ideal choice. He was a native of the West, a political asset because of the concern for natural resources in that region. His nomination was particularly comforting to business interests eager to reverse the trend toward nationalization of hydroelectric power. Nevertheless, McKay maintained that he did not favor dismantling the Tennessee Valley Authority. He was committed to the middle-of-the-road approach in the debate between the conservationists and the developers over the role of the federal government versus the interests of private enterprise. Like President Eisenhower he advocated the "partnership" approach, in which the states, local public groups, and private enterprise would join with the federal government in building facilities.

As secretary of the interior, McKay helped to block such Democratic concepts as the Columbia Valley Authority and public development of the Hell's Canyon project. Despite the heated opposition of preservationists concerned with maintaining the beauty of natural sites, he favored building a dam at Echo Park, a project that would have created a vast reservoir at Dinosaur National Monument. He was especially embarrassed by the Al Serena scandal, in which an Alabama mining company won access to choice Oregon timberlands. The target of the preservationists, he was denounced by his political opponents as "Give-away" McKay. He resigned on Mar. 9, 1956, to contest the Senate seat held by Wayne Morse. He lost after a bitter campaign that saw him on the defensive on the conservation issue.

In many ways typical of the businessmen in the Eisenhower administration, McKay was plain-spoken, often with a tendency to "shoot from the hip." Somewhat ill-prepared for his responsibilities and forced to rely on the expertise of subordinates, he was often blamed for decisions made by others. With the difficult mission of altering the accretion of federal responsibility for the development of public power and the preservation of resources, he nevertheless resisted many attempts to reduce national park lands, a role for which he received little credit. If he was not a true friend of conservationism, neither was he quite the villain portrayed by his enemies. He died in Salem, Oreg.

[McKay's papers are at the University of Oregon, Eugene. An interview with him and a biographical sketch are in *U.S. News and World Report*, Oct. 9, 1953; his views also are in his article "Government a Partner, Not a Competitor," *Nation's Business*, Jan. 1956. Also useful are *Reporter*, May 3 and 17, 1956, and Oct. 18, 1956; Cabell Phillips, "Morse vs. McKay—Key Senate Race," *New York Times Magazine*, Oct. 14, 1956; and "McKay Gets Mired in the 'Middle' of the Road," *Fortune*, Oct. 1953. An obituary is in *New York Times*, July 23, 1959. The most thorough analysis of his career is Elmo Richardson, *Dams, Parks and Politics* (1973). See also Daniel Mahar, "Douglas McKay and the Issues of Power Development in Oregon, 1953–1956" (Ph.D. diss., University of Oregon, 1968). Other useful works are Sherman Adams, *Firsthand Report* (1961); Dwight D. Eisenhower, *Mandate for Change* (1963); Herbert S. Parmet, *Eisenhower and the American Crusades* (1972); and Ralph A. Tudor, *Notes Recorded While Under Secretary, Department of the Interior* (1964).]

HERBERT S. PARMET

MacKAYE, PERCY WALLACE (Mar. 16, 1875–Aug. 31, 1956), poet, playwright, and essayist, was born in New York City, the son of James Morrison Steele MacKaye and Mary Keith Medbery. His father, better-known as Steele MacKaye, was an actor, director, and playwright. MacKaye received much of his education at home, although for short periods he attended public schools in New York and Washington, D.C., and Lawrence Academy in Groton, Mass.

Brought up in a hectic but cultivated theatrical and literary environment where dreams of new theaters vied with schemes for raising money, he tried his hand at plays and poems as a very young man. He composed choral songs for his father's spectacle-drama about Columbus, *The World Finder*, designed to be played at Steele MacKaye's original but ill-fated colossal Spectatorium at the 1893 World's Columbian Exposition in Chicago. At his graduation from Harvard (B.A., 1897), he delivered the first student commencement address on the theme of modern drama; "The Need for Imagination in the Drama of Today."

On Oct. 8, 1898, MacKaye married Marion Homer Morse, a poet. They had three children. After travel and study abroad, the couple returned to New York City, where MacKaye taught from 1900 to 1904 at the Craigie School for Boys. When E. H. Sothern commissioned him to write *The Canterbury Pilgrims*, he was freed from teaching and took his family to live in Cornish, N.H., where he made his home for the rest of his life.

Although Sothern did not produce *Pilgrims*, he did give MacKaye his first professional production when he and Julia Marlowe appeared in MacKaye's *Jeanne d'Arc* in 1906. It was followed by some twenty-five produced plays and more than a hundred books of poetry, essays, and biography.

MacKaye championed a democratic, poetic drama for America that would be a "fresh imagining and an original utterance of modern motives which are as yet unimagined and unexpressed." His *Sappho and Phaon, a Tragedy* was produced by Harrison Grey Fiske with Bertha Kalich (1907); *Mater, an American Study in Comedy* was produced by Henry Miller (1908); and *The Scarecrow*, his most accomplished and best-known drama, was produced first by the Harvard Dramatic Club (1909) and then in New York with Frank Reicher (1911). *Anti-Matrimony, a Satirical Comedy*, starred Henrietta Crossman (1910); and a group of one-acts plays collectively called *Yankee Fantasies* (1912) was staged by groups like the newly organized Washington Square Players.

MacKaye was also becoming a kind of American poet laureate. He wrote many commemorative poems for public occasions and public figures, including Abraham Lincoln, Walt Whitman, and Thomas Edison; he also developed the masque as a unique "drama of democracy," a form of "poetry of the masses." Beginning in 1905 with the masque honoring the sculptor

Augustus Saint-Gaudens, in which more than seventy members of the Cornish, N.H., summer colony participated along with the Boston Symphony Orchestra, MacKaye spent much of his energies on this new form. He wanted to evolve a participatory drama that would be a civic rite, a theater that would serve as an "unsectarian temple."

The *Canterbury Pilgrims*, produced in a natural amphitheater overlooking the harbor in Gloucester, Mass., with music by Walter Damrosch, was staged in 1909 by 1,500 citizens of the town before President William Howard Taft and some 25,000 other spectators. MacKaye produced or projected a bird masque, a masque of labor, a civic ritual for new citizens, a masque for the Red Cross, and one for the American Bible Society. In 1914 *Saint Louis, a Civic Masque*, celebrated the one hundred fiftieth anniversary of the city. It required a cast of almost 8,000 and played to an audience of nearly a million in five nights.

MacKaye was commissioned by New York City to create a masque for the tercentenary of Shakespeare's death (1916). *Caliban by the Yellow Sands, a Community Masque of the Art of the Theatre* dramatized the transformation of Caliban, "the passionate child-curious part of us all," through the power of reason, love, and art—especially that of poetic theater. On opening night at Lewisohn Stadium, Isadora Duncan danced and John Drew led a cast of 2,500 in a production that had sets and costumes by Joseph Urban and Robert Edmond Jones. When it was repeated the following year in the Harvard Stadium, more than 5,000 people participated. Although most of these masques do not seem important works of art, the articles and addresses that MacKaye wrote advocating his vision of the role of drama in American life can still stir readers who turn to *The Playhouse and the Play* (1909), *The Civic Theatre*(1912), and *Community Drama* (1917).

In 1920, MacKaye became professor of creative literature at Miami University in Oxford, Ohio. He toured the remote regions of the Kentucky mountains during the succeeding years and wrote poems, tales, and plays that told of the people of Appalachia in their rich, archaic language. In 1927 he published *Epoch*, a biography of his father. This "grandiose portrait of an indomitable genius" was a rich source book on the theater of the late nineteenth century. In 1932 his "folk masque" *Wakefield*, performed in celebration of the two-hundredth birthday of George

Washington, was the first play commissioned, published, and produced by the federal government.

MacKaye's poetic tetralogy, *The Mystery of Hamlet*, one of his major works, was performed at the Pasadena Playhouse in 1949. It revealed again his devotion to Shakespeare by chronicling the tragic events preceding the action of *Hamlet*. Greeted as a work of "soaring imagination" written in "astonishingly vivid verse" in the "grand manner of the classics," it was also recognized as being outside the limits of popular theater in America.

In 1951 and 1952, MacKaye published two tales of his childhood memories, *Poog's Pasture* and *Poog and the Caboose-Man*. Filling a "noctary" he kept by his bed with verses, he continued writing almost until his death in Cornish, N.H.

[The major collection of papers of the MacKaye family is at Dartmouth College, Hanover, N.H. Edwin Osgood Grover, *Annals of an Era* (1932), is a biography based on the Dartmouth collection. The Harvard Theater Collection also contains important MacKaye materials. The symposium *Percy MacKaye* contains important material. See also the obituary in *New York Times*, Sept. 1, 1956; and Richard Moody, "The Playwright: Percy MacKaye," special program notes for the Kennedy Center production (1976) of *The Scarecrow*.]

HELEN KRICH CHINOY

McKELLAR, KENNETH DOUGLAS (Jan. 29, 1869–Oct. 25, 1957), U.S. senator, was born near Richmond, Ala., the son of James Daniel White McKellar, an unprosperous lawyer and investor in land, and of Caroline Howard. He earned a B.A. from the University of Alabama in 1891 and an LL.B. in 1892, in both cases at the head of his class. He also received an M.A. from Alabama in 1891.

Seeking new opportunities, "K. D.," as he was always called, paused on the way to California for a visit with his brothers in Memphis, Tenn., and decided to settle there. He entered the law firm of William H. Carroll, a Civil War veteran and leader in the state Democratic party. This association formed the basis both of McKellar's personal wealth and of his growing prominence in the affairs of Memphis. Although he never married, he maintained an active family life, establishing a home in Memphis with his mother and sisters. His favorite entertainment was western movies.

McKellar was affable, intelligent, and an exceptionally colorful orator. His quick temper and ad hominem approach to politics did him little harm in the early stages of his career, but much more later on. He served as a presidential elector in 1904, a delegate to the Democratic National Convention in 1908, and a member of the House of Representatives from 1911 to 1917. He took his seat in 1917 as the first popularly elected senator from Tennessee, under the provisions of the Seventeenth Amendment. By the time of his defeat in 1952, he had served six terms and had established a record for continuous service in the Senate.

Throughout his senatorial career McKellar cultivated a relationship with Edward Hull ("Boss") Crump of Memphis, who for a generation reigned as the leading political force in Tennessee. Although McKellar seldom differed with Crump, he never became a mere puppet. On occasion he went his own way—for instance, over prohibition, which McKellar, an abstainer from both alcohol and tobacco, endorsed even though Crump opposed it.

Within the Senate, McKellar seldom rose to statesmanship but did win a reputation for hard work and close attention to his committee assignments. An ardent Wilsonian, he inclined to internationalist views; but his real interest lay in domestic affairs. He advocated federal aid to road construction, flood control, agriculture, and air travel. He played down the race issue whenever possible. During the 1930's he provided important support for most of President Franklin D. Roosevelt's programs, but he later opposed some of the social welfare measures of the New Deal, such as the National Youth Administration. By the late 1930's, through a combination of seniority and advantageous committee assignments, McKellar had acquired significant power. As chairman of the Post Office and Post Roads Committee (1933–1946) and as acting chairman (1937) and chairman of the Appropriations Committee, he held the keys to federal patronage and expenditures.

Expertly manipulating his prerogatives, he accumulated vast influence with his colleagues and the executive branch. He tirelessly attempted to maintain congressional control over mushrooming national budgets. The "McKellar bill" of 1943, which passed the Senate but failed in the House, in effect would have required Senate confirmation of all federal appointees to positions paying more than $4,500 annually. Had it become law, it would likely have provided a check on the growth of executive power but would also have brought politics into the higher civil service.

The interests of Tennessee took McKellar's highest priority. Thousands of his constituents owed him their jobs in the federal bureaucracy, and they repaid his patronage with political support. By the 1940's he was reputed to have secured the appointments of more officeholders than any other man in Congress. He excelled at making Tennesseans aware of the benefits he had brought the state, and his huge signature was a palpable reminder on letters to constituents. Symptomatic of McKellar's perspective was his attitude toward the Tennessee Valley Authority (TVA), which he viewed not so much as an integrated venture in regional planning as a means of funneling federal appropriations into Tennessee through the construction of dams. Jealous of the designation of Senator George W. Norris of Nebraska as "father of the TVA," McKellar pointed to his own substantial role in securing, year after year, the appropriations essential to the success of the agency.

The genuineness of these contributions made it ironic that McKellar's relationship with the TVA occasioned grievous harm to his national standing. In 1941 he became involved in a vendetta with David E. Lilienthal, chairman of the TVA, which carried over to Lilienthal's reappointment to the TVA in 1946 and his confirmation in 1947 as chairman of the Atomic Energy Commission. Convinced of Lilienthal's unfitness, McKellar for weeks early in 1947 filled the newspapers with outrageous "Red-baiting" and personal denunciation. Lilienthal emerged with job intact and reputation enhanced. McKellar, on the other hand, stood exposed in unfavorable light. Exaggerated into caricature by advancing age, his lifelong traits appeared at their worst: his colorful but sometimes reckless rhetoric, his inability to separate issues from personalities, and his propensity to engage in feuds (Lilienthal was not his only bête noir). At the height of his formal power and distinction, as president pro tempore of the Senate during most of the administration of Harry S. Truman, McKellar seemed a throwback.

In 1952, against the advice of a host of friends, McKellar ran for reelection. Now eighty-three years of age, he campaigned feebly and was defeated in the primary by Albert Gore, a liberal congressman thirty-nine years his junior. McKellar returned to Memphis, and until his death worked intermittently on his memoirs, which were never published. He died at Memphis.

[McKellar's personal papers are in the Memphis-Shelby County Library. He wrote *Tennessee Senators, As Seen by One of Their Successors* (1942). The most thorough biography is Robert Dean Pope, "Senatorial Baron: The Long Political Career of Kenneth D. McKellar"(Ph.D. diss., Yale, 1975). A long obituary, several feature articles, and a photograph appeared in the *Memphis Commercial Appeal*, Oct. 26, 1957. Other useful sources include Hugh Morrow, "Tennessee Tartar," *Saturday Evening Post*, June 2, 1945; and Joseph H. Riggs, *A Calendar of Political and Occasional Speeches by Senator Kenneth D. McKellar, 1928–1940* (1962). On McKellar's alliance with Crump, see Allan A. Michie and Frank Rhyslick, *Dixie Demagogues* (1939); V. O. Key, Jr., *Southern Politics in State and Nation* (1949); and William D. Miller, *Mr. Crump of Memphis* (1964). McKellar's battles with Lilienthal may be traced in Lilienthal's *Journals*, vol. I, *The TVA Years, 1939–1945* (1964), and vol. II, *The Atomic Energy Years, 1945–1950* (1964). Among memoirs in the Oral History Collection at Columbia University with material on McKellar, that of Henry A. Wallace deserves mention.]

THOMAS K. McCRAW

McLAGLEN, VICTOR (Dec. 11, 1886–Nov. 6, 1959), actor, was born in Tunbridge Wells, England, the son of Andrew McLaglen, an Anglican clergyman, who later became bishop of Clermont, South Africa, and Lillian Burke. In his autobiography McLaglen claimed that between 1900 and 1920, when he began his film career, he had tried twenty vocations, "the only thing which ever thrilled me was boxing."

McLaglen began his schooling in the military arts by lying about his age and enlisting in the Life Guards at the age of fourteen. He was able to convince the recruiters because of his size; in fact, his stature and massive build became his most distinguishing characteristic. He grew to six feet, three inches and weighed 230 pounds; during his forty-year career he was most frequently cast as a brawling giant.

McLaglen served in the army for three years before his parents forced his release. By then, he had acquired a taste for adventure. He went to Canada, where he earned his living by boxing—he once took part in a six-round exhibition match with world heavyweight champion Jack Johnson—wrestling, prospecting for gold, and working as a railroad policeman.

McLaglen traveled to Tahiti, the Fiji Islands, Australia, India, Ceylon, and Africa. He joined a circus as a boxer and ended up as a physical training instructor for the rajah of Akola in India. He was in South Africa in 1914 when World War I began and joined the British army, securing a lieutenant's commission in the Middlesex regiment. Twice wounded, he later served in Mesopotamia and headed the British espionage system in Baghdad. In 1919 he returned to England and married Enid Mary Lamont; she died in 1942. They had two children.

McLaglen left the army for a film career. The producer I. B. Davidson saw him in a boxing match and gave him the role of a gambler who becomes a boxer in *Call of the Road* (1920), the first of his more than 115 films. In 1924 J. Stuart Blackton invited him to Hollywood to play in *The Beloved Brute*. Subsequent roles included Hank, the foreign legionnaire who fights Ronald Colman in *Beau Geste* (1926), Captain Flagg in *What Price Glory?* (1926), Marlene Dietrich's lover in *Dishonored* (1931), and a platoon sergeant lost in the Mesopotamian desert in *Lost Patrol* (1934). In 1933, McLaglen become an American citizen.

McLaglen won an Academy Award for best actor for his portrayal of Gypo Nolan in *The Informer* (1935), directed by John Ford and based on the Liam O'Flaherty novel about the Irish civil war. McLaglen's performance as the tormented Nolan, torn between greed and loyalty, was masterful, but he himself never liked the role. In 1946 he wrote that Gypo Nolan was a "weak, unintelligent and unresourceful man." McLaglen continued, "About every ice age you encounter a role you know is exactly your meat, one you'd choose for yourself without a second's hesitation. Sergeant MacChesney in *Gunga Din* was like that."

McLaglen's affection for the military and his love of companionship and a shared purpose led him in 1936 to establish a fraternal group known as the Light Horse Troop. "In time of war, we can be counted upon as a government unit," he announced. In the politically charged atmosphere of the times, however, McLaglen's group created ripples of concern and elicited fear that his group was proto-fascist.

McLaglen was among the first to demonstrate a respect and appreciation for other crafts and talents in the industry. He supported the Motion Picture and Television Fund, which takes care of the needy and ill of the motion picture and television industry. He worked and lived hard, spending money quickly. By 1945 he owed the government $250,000 in taxes, but he battled his way back from bankruptcy.

Although McLaglen was often mistaken for being merely tough, he loved the seclusion of his ranch in the San Joaquin Valley, where he raised horses and farmed. He cultivated fruit trees and at one time had 20,000 grapevines. On Nov. 20, 1943, after the death of his first wife, McLaglen married his secretary, Suzanne Brueggemann; the marriage ended in divorce in 1947. On Dec. 19, 1948, he married Margaret Pumphrey.

In 1952 McLaglen won an Academy Award nomination for best supporting actor for his role as the father in John Ford's *The Quiet Man*. He continued to work until the end of his life. "I've never stopped," he said in an interview given shortly before his death. "I've been acting thirty-seven years and there's always been at least one picture a year." His last films include *She Wore a Yellow Ribbon* (1949) and *Around the World in 80 Days* (1956). He died in Newport Beach, Calif.

[McLaglen's autobiography, *Express to Hollywood* (1934), is a breezy, fast-moving account. See also "The Role I Liked Best," *Saturday Evening Post*, Apr. 13, 1946. The best collection of clippings and press releases is at the Margaret Herrick Library of the Academy of Motion Picture Arts and Sciences Foundation, Beverly Hills, Calif. Evelyn M. Truitt, *Who Was Who on Screen*, 2nd ed. (1977), lists 177 films; see also Mel Schuster, ed., *Motion Picture Performers* (1976); *Oxford Companion to Film* (1976); and obituary notices, *Los Angeles Examiner* and *Los Angeles Times*, Nov. 8, 1959; and *Films in Review*, Jan. 1960.]

SOL LESSER

McLOUGHLIN, MAURICE EVANS (Jan. 7, 1890–Dec. 10, 1957), tennis player, was born in Carson City, Nev., the son of George McLoughlin and Harriet Louise Verrill. His father, a mason employed at the mint in Carson City, was transferred in 1898 to the Philadelphia mint as superintendent of machinery and in 1903 to the same position at San Francisco.

McLoughlin began playing tennis on the public courts of San Francisco. He was junior parks champion in 1906 and a year later won both the San Francisco and the Pacific Coast championships. After graduating from Lowell High School (1918), he entered the University of California at Berkeley, but his education was restricted and eventually terminated by his tennis career. In 1909 the Pacific Coast Tennis Association sent McLoughlin, Melville Long, and Thomas Bundy to compete in the national championships at

Newport, R.I. Until then tennis had been something of a society game, usually played by wealthy young men of the upper social class. When Long and McLoughlin were matched against each other, they played the type of tennis bred on the fast, hard courts of San Francisco, which in terms of power and excitement surpassed anything ever seen on the courts of the East. Before the five-set match was over, the gallery had stopped talking and many members were standing on chairs for a better view of the court. With his powerful serve and deadly overhead smashes, McLoughlin had introduced a new kind of tennis, and the game would never be the same. Modern tennis may be said to have been born that day at Newport.

The nineteen-year-old McLoughlin—known as "California Comet," "Red Mac" (for his red hair), or "Maury"—was sent to Australia later that year with the American Davis Cup team. In 1910 he ranked fourth among American players; by 1911 he was ranked second and played on the Davis Cup team that defeated Great Britain. In 1913, McLoughlin and Harold Hackett won the Davis Cup for the United States, and McLoughlin reached the finals at Wimbledon, where he lost the British championship to Anthony Wilding. In 1912 and 1913, McLoughlin won the American championship and was ranked first among American players. In 1912, 1913, and 1914 he and Tom Bundy won the national doubles championship.

In the Davis Cup finals of 1914 came what has been termed the greatest match in tennis history: McLoughlin versus the Australian Norman Brookes. In the first set service was unbroken for thirty games, McLoughlin eventually winning 17–15. He won the next two sets, 6–3, 6–3.

The match with Brookes was the high point of McLoughlin's career. In the U.S. national finals that year he was defeated by Richard Norris Williams II, a stunning upset that shocked the tennis world—but McLoughlin nevertheless retained number-one ranking. In 1915 he again reached the national finals, only to be defeated by William Johnston. His book *Tennis as I Play It* was published in 1915. After serving in the navy during World War I, McLoughlin returned to competitive tennis in 1919. In the quarter finals of the nationals, he was badly defeated by Williams; he never again played in national competition.

On May 28, 1918, McLoughlin married Helen Mears; they had three children. They lived for many years in Pasadena, Calif., where McLoughlin was an avid golfer. During the

1930's he was associated with horse racing, serving the Turf Club as its first secretary-treasurer. He continued his interest in tennis, often refereeing matches and participating in the organization of tournaments. In 1942 the family moved to Hermosa Beach, Calif., and McLoughlin worked for both the War Production Board and the War Assets Administration. During the last years of his life, he was employed by the North American Aviation Corporation.

Only a few months before his death came one of the great satisfactions of McLoughlin's life: election to the Tennis Hall of Fame in March 1957. He died at Hermosa Beach, Calif. McLoughlin, the sports writer Arthur Daly noted, brought the "home run ball into tennis. . . . He gave it [tennis] popularity, respectability, and the 'big games.'" Certainly the "big serve" began with McLoughlin. As the great champion Don Budge put it, "All the big hitters . . . owe their service to Maury."

[Biographical materials are on file at the Tennis Hall of Fame, Newport, R.I.; the Helms Hall of Fame, Los Angeles; and the U.S. Tennis Association, New York City. Obituaries are in the *New York Times, Los Angeles Times,* and *Los Angeles Herald-Examiner,* all of Dec. 12, 1957. See also E. B. Dewhurst, "McLoughlin the Champion," *Outing,* Nov. 1913; Herbert Reed, "McLoughlin and the Davis Cup," *Harper's Weekly,* Sept. 5, 1914; U.S. Lawn Tennis Association, *Fifty Years of Lawn Tennis in the United States* (1931); Parke Cummings, *American Tennis* (1957); Arthur Daly, *New York Times,* Dec. 17, 1957; *Newsweek,* Dec. 23, 1957; *Time,* Dec. 23, 1957; Bill Talbert, *Tennis Observed* (1967); and Max Robertson and Jack Kramer, eds., *The Encyclopedia of Tennis* (1974).]

RALPH ADAMS BROWN

McNULTY, JOHN AUGUSTINE (Nov. 1, 1895–July 29, 1956), journalist and short story writer, was born in Lawrence, Mass., the son of John McNulty, a bricklayer, and Mary Theresa Carty. Both parents came from the west of Ireland. After her husband died in 1898, McNulty's mother opened a small candy and tobacco store, and the family lived in the rooms behind. McNulty recalled the store as a neighborhood social center, and it was there he learned to relish storytelling and talk. He graduated from high school in 1912 and, after various jobs including work on the *Lawrence Tribune,* in 1913 entered Holy Cross College in Worcester, Mass.

The following year he transferred to Colby College in Waterville, Me., but left without a degree to join the army. He fought in France with the Ninth Infantry, rose to the rank of sergeant, was wounded at Fère-en-Tardenois, and spent a year in an army hospital at Lakewood, N.J.

McNulty moved to New York in 1921, studying at Columbia University by day and working for the Associated Press by night. He left the Associated Press for the *New York Post* but by 1923 was out of work because of heavy drinking and temperamental behavior. He reluctantly left New York to work for the *Ohio State Journal* in Columbus. There he met James Thurber, then a reporter for the *Columbus Dispatch,* and they became lifelong friends. Thurber introduced McNulty to Donia Williamson, whom he married in 1924. For a time his career prospered and his reputation for humorous, graceful writing soared. He became editor of the drama page of the *Columbus Citizen* and made numerous friends in show business, but his fondness for saloons led to neglect of duty. Thurber recalled one occasion on which McNulty was fired. Next day he returned to the city room and said meekly, "I guess since I was fired, there is a vacancy." He was told there was. "Then I'd like to apply for the job." He got it. When forgiveness finally ran out, McNulty moved to the *Pittsburgh Press* and thence to a job as a speech writer for Ohio Governor George White. About 1934, at the urging of Thurber, McNulty returned to New York. He was hired by the *New Yorker,* but, after about a year, felt uneasy in its atmosphere and returned to newspapers. As a rewrite man for the *New York Mirror* and later the *New York Daily News,* McNulty was known for the skill and speed with which he transformed reporters' notes into finished stories. He stopped drinking and, proud of his sobriety, became a listener and observer of saloon life. During free time at the *News* in 1941, McNulty wrote the story that launched his career in fiction, "Atheist Hit by a Truck" (*New Yorker,* Apr. 12, 1941). The editor, Harold Ross, liked the story greatly, and McNulty followed it with a dozen more. He was given a staff writer's contract with the magazine and over the next decade continued to write much of his best material about the smaller events of city life. His first collection of such pieces, *Third Avenue, New York,* was published in 1946.

In 1943, McNulty left the *News* to write scripts for the "March of Time" radio news program. Then, succumbing to a lucrative offer from Paramount Studios, he went to Hollywood in 1945.

He finished his first rewrite of a film script at city room speed, appalling his fellow writers, who threatened to lock him up if he did not slow down.

His first marriage having ended in divorce, McNulty was married on Sept. 24, 1945, to Faith Corrigan Fair, whom he had met at the *Daily News*. They had one son. Unhappy in Hollywood and unsuited to film writing, McNulty returned to New York City in 1946. He wrote a sports column for the newspaper *PM* that became a personal column called "Easy Does It." At the same time, he wrote "casuals" and "Reporter at Large" pieces for the *New Yorker*. After a heart attack in 1947, he wrote an account of his stay in Bellevue Hospital, one of his best long pieces. *A Man Gets Around*, McNulty's second collection of sketches and stories, was published in 1951; and his third book, *My Son Johnny*, in 1955. He died at his summer home in Wakefield, R.I.

The World of John McNulty, a collection of his best writing, came out in 1957 and was extensively reviewed. The reviewers especially noted his perceptive observation and his keen and accurate ear for language. Virtually everyone who knew McNulty seems to have felt his personal magnetism. Thurber wrote, "Nobody who knew McNulty . . . could ever have confused him for a moment with anybody else. His presence in a room was as special as the way he put words down on paper." Many of McNulty's stories originated in a Third Avenue saloon run by Tim Costello, whose friendship McNulty shared with Thurber and many other writers.

Never an intellectual, McNulty avoided the word "art" as embarrassing and pretentious. He loved language and regarded it with the eye of a perfectionist. He often reread H. L. Mencken's *The American Language* and greatly admired the work of E. B. White and Ring Lardner; but wit and satire simply did not interest him. He was one of the very few American storywriters of the twentieth century whose skill was balanced by an inexhaustible generosity of feeling. Gifted in many of the same ways as Ernest Hemingway, Lardner, and Dorothy Parker—all masters of the American vernacular—McNulty never fell into irony or despair, never hardened under his experience of human suffering or lost his delight in mankind.

[James Thurber's preface to *The World of John McNulty* (1957) is the only substantial essay, but further material can be found in obituaries in the *New York Times* and *New York Herald Tribune*, July 30, 1956; James Thurber, *The Years With Ross* (1959); Burton Bernstein, *Thurber* (1975); and Brendan Gill, *Here at the New Yorker* (1975). Significant reviews are in *New York Times*, Sept. 22, 1957; *Saturday Review of Literature*, Sept. 14, 1957; and *Time*, Nov. 4, 1957. McNulty's role in his favorite Third Avenue saloon is described in Joe McCarthy, "Costello's: The Wayward Saloon," *Holiday*, Oct. 1959.]

DEAN FLOWER

MAHONEY, JOHN FRIEND (Aug. 1, 1889–Feb. 23, 1957), physician and public health administrator, was born in Fond du Lac, Wis., the son of David Mahoney, a locomotive engineer, and Mary Ann Hogan. After graduating from high school in Fond du Lac in 1908, he worked for one year as a truck farmer before undertaking studies at Milwaukee University and Marquette Medical College. He received the M.D. in 1914 and began two years of intern training, first at the Milwaukee County Hospital and later at the Chicago Lying-in Hospital.

Mahoney's professional career was divided into two phases. The first consisted of thirty-two years as a commissioned officer of the U.S. Public Health Service. Mahoney was commissioned in September 1917 and, after various assignments characteristic of a junior officer, was detailed to the U.S. Foreign Service in 1925. During the ensuing four years he served as public health adviser in Haiti, Ireland, England, and Germany. He married Leah Ruth Arnold on Sept. 29, 1926; they had two children. While serving abroad Mahoney exploited the opportunity to observe the management of sexually transmitted diseases in foreign clinics and the laboratory methods used in their diagnosis. This experience enhanced his interest and skill in dealing with venereal diseases, which were a very important problem for Public Health Service medical officers, most of whose patients were seafaring men exposed to the diseases in port cities throughout the world. At that time there was no effective treatment for gonorrhea and the treatment for syphilis consisted of injections of toxic drugs administered weekly over periods of months to years.

In July 1929 Mahoney was appointed director of the Venereal Disease Research Laboratory located at the Marine Hospital (now the U.S. Public Health Service Hospital) at Stapleton, Staten Island, N.Y. During the next twenty years he was associated there with a series of young investigators working on both laboratory and clinical problems. Mahoney's scientific publications, frequently written with one or more associates, mark the progress of technology as applied to diagnosis and treatment of venereal infections. His early work was devoted to experimental infection of rabbits with the corkscrew-shaped syphilis organism, using the dark-field microscope, which enables one to see the unstained living organism. Knowledge of the mechanism and rate of penetration into tissues by the germ became the basis for more rational procedures for prophylaxis against infection. Later he turned to studies of the serologic tests for syphilis, the blood tests that for many years have been the principal aid to diagnosis after the earliest stage of the disease has passed. Although now invaluable, these tests had many deficiencies in Mahoney's time: the reagents were crude, the techniques were not standardized, the test results were inconsistent, and there was an undesirable incidence of both false positive and false negative reactions.

When Surgeon General Thomas Parran made the control of venereal diseases a major concern of the Public Health Service during his tenure from 1936 to 1948, Mahoney's laboratory played the key federal role in improving diagnostic methods. Because serologic testing was being done on a massive scale by state and local governmental laboratories, much importance was attached to minimizing the test deficiencies. Interstate evaluation surveys were conducted and information about sources of error was disseminated, which resulted in improved reagents and standardized methods. During this period he published several papers dealing with the efficacy of sulfonamide drugs in treatment of gonorrhea. When penicillin first became available during World War II, it was in very short supply and subject to allocation. After meeting the military needs for treatment of wound infections there was little available for study of novel uses. Mahoney obtained enough to demonstrate in rabbits that the drug might kill the spirochete of syphilis. This led to the allocation of a supply of penicillin to continue the rabbit studies concurrently with clinical trial in four patients with early syphilis. The success of this experiment, reported in December 1943, led to a large clinical trial by collaborating investigators that confirmed the value of the drug and quickly made it the standard treatment.

Mahoney is probably most widely known for this role in revolutionizing the treatment of syphilis. In 1946, when the first Lasker Awards were conferred by the American Public Health Association, he was one of five individuals chosen for the honor in recognition of his "outstanding leadership in the treatment of syphilis by penicillin." In succeeding years he contributed knowledge derived from long-term follow-up of treated patients. In particular, he studied the changes in serological reactions after treatment and continued to improve reagents and test methods.

In December 1949 he retired from the Public Health Service and began the second phase of his career, as director of the Bureau of Laboratories in the New York City Health Department. Four days later Mayor William O'Dwyer appointed him to the post of health commissioner, in which he served until 1953. Under his leadership the department initiated a number of important programs. Among these were a campaign to prevent lead poisoning in children, the introduction of isoniazid chemotherapy in tuberculosis clinics, and the recommendation that New York City's water be fluoridated. Upon appointment of a new commissioner in 1954, he resumed the direction of the Bureau of Laboratories, where he served until his death.

Mahoney held appointments in clinical syphilology at New York University School of Medicine and in dermatology at Columbia University School of Medicine. He was a member of the Syphilis Study Section of the National Institutes of Health and of the Committee on Research and Standards of the American Public Health Association. He served as chairman of the committee of experts on venereal disease of the World Health Organization, of the National Serology Advisory Council, and of the Committee on Standardization of Serological Tests for Syphilis of the American Public Health Association. He died in Staten Island, N.Y.

[On Mahoney and his work, see an editorial in the *American Journal of Public Health*, Dec. 1946; Ralph C. Williams, *The United States Public Health Service 1798–1950* (1951); *Quarterly Cumulative Index Medicus*, 1930–1956; a mimeograph, *Chronology of New York City Health Department*, Mar. 1966; Bess Furman, *A Profile of the United States Public Health Service, 1798–1948* (1973); and the *New York Times* obituary, Feb. 24, 1957.]

DAVID E. PRICE

MALLORY, ANNA MARGRETHE ("MOLLA") BJURSTEDT (1892–Nov. 22, 1959), tennis player, was born in Norway, the daughter of a retired army officer. She began playing tennis with her sister Valborg at an early age in Norway and in 1903 entered international competition in Sweden, England, and Germany. Excelling at the game, by 1913 Mallory had captured the Norwegian women's singles title eight times and held the doubles championship with her sister. Accordingly, Mallory was selected to represent her country in the 1912 Olympic Games at Stockholm, where she won the bronze medal.

In October 1914 Mallory visited the United States and decided to settle in New York City, where she hoped to practice her profession as a masseuse. However, upon hearing of the upcoming women's national indoor singles tennis championship to be held in New York the following March, she promptly added her name to the list of competitors. She won the tournament by defeating three-time champion Marie Wagner. Mallory went on to have a stunning first year of competition by winning the women's metropolitan championship, the Middle States championship, and both the national outdoor and national clay court singles titles. In the latter two championships Mallory defeated Hazel Hotchkiss Wightman, one of the most celebrated American players. By the end of 1915, her first year of competition, Mallory held five major women's titles and was ranked number one by the United States Lawn Tennis Association.

Mallory's fame spread rapidly, and she soon became the recognized spokesman for women's tennis. In 1916 she wrote *Tennis for Women* (with Samuel Crowther) and an article, "How I Play Championship Tennis," for the *Ladies' Home Journal.* She stressed the value of vigorous tennis for health and recommended to women the beauty of a sun-tanned complexion. Specifically, she suggested that aspiring female tennis players should hit harder, play more for the baseline, and stop relying on net play. Above all, Mallory advised her followers to hit the ball on the rise instead of as the ball was dropping. She was a master of her own advice and was peerless in her steady and accurate all-court game.

After her victories in 1915, Mallory continued to lead women's tennis for the next eleven years. In 1916 she again won the national outdoor and indoor singles tournaments and also the national outdoor doubles with Eleanora Sears and the national indoor doubles with Marie Wagner. She again was ranked the number one female player in the United States. World War I disrupted some competition in 1917, but Mallory won the Patriotic Tournament, which had been substituted

for the national outdoor singles championship; successfully defended her national outdoor doubles championship with Eleanora Sears; and teamed with Irving C. Wright to win her first national outdoor mixed doubles title. The next year Mallory again won both the national outdoor and indoor singles championships and remained the number-one ranked woman. During the war, with Mary Browne and several male players, she played exhibition matches throughout the United States and netted $85,000 for the ambulance service. In 1919 she married Franklin I. Mallory, a stockbroker. Playing under her married name, she only placed in the semifinals of the national outdoor singles championship and dropped to third place in the national rankings.

Mallory's decline was short-lived. The following year she regained her national outdoor singles title and her number-one ranking. She went on to win both the national outdoor and indoor singles championships in 1921 and 1922; and paired with the leading male player, William T. ("Big Bill") Tilden, II, captured the national outdoor mixed doubles title the following year. Mallory's defeat of France's Suzanne Lenglen, the reigning Wimbledon champion, in the national outdoor singles championship in 1921 was probably her greatest victory. After losing to Lenglen in several previous international matches, Mallory met her at Forest Hills for their first United States match. Mallory promptly won the first set 6–2, which sent the foreign star off the court coughing and weeping, and defaulting the match. In 1923 Mallory and Tilden successfully defended their doubles title and she was selected for a spot on the U.S. Wightman Cup team.

Mallory did not win the national title from 1923 through 1925, primarily as a result of the sterling play of Helen Wills, later Mrs. Helen W. Moody. With Wills out of the 1926 competition with appendicitis, Mallory defeated Elizabeth Ryan 4–6, 6–4, 9–7, to regain the national outdoor singles title and the number-one United States ranking. She was a quarter-finalist and semifinalist in 1927 and 1928 and, on account of cartilage damage in her knee, ended her active tennis competition in 1929. Overall, Mallory won seven national outdoor singles titles (eight if the 1917 title is counted), five national indoor singles titles, two national outdoor doubles titles, one national indoor doubles title, and three national outdoor mixed doubles titles. She also was named to the United States Wightman Cup team five years, was the number-one ranked woman tennis player for seven years, and from 1915 to 1927 was one of the three top-ranked United States competitors. Her seven national women's singles championships was equaled only by one other player, her rival, Helen Wills Moody.

After the death of her husband in 1934, Mallory worked as a salesgirl in a department store in New York City. Fluent in French, German, English, and the Scandinavian languages, she served as a language specialist with the United States Office of Censorship during World War II. She was elected to the National Lawn Tennis Hall of Fame in 1958. She died in Stockholm, Sweden.

More than any other female tennis player, Mallory changed women's tennis from a slow, controlled game to a very competitive, scientific, and forceful sport. She was best known by her contemporaries for her courage, sportsmanship, and intense desire to win.

[Material on Mallory's life in Norway is very difficult to find. On her early career in the United States, see "Norway's Woman Tennis Champion," *Outlook*, June 2, 1915, and "Miss Bjurstedt's Burst Into Fame," *Literary Digest*, 51, Aug. 28, 1915. Information concerning Mallory's tennis exploits throughout the remainder of her competition is included in Helen Hull Jacobs, *Gallery of Champions* (1951); the *U.S.L.T.A. Official Encyclopedia of Tennis* (1972); and "How Molla Mallory Came Back," *Literary Digest*, Sept. 25, 1926. There is valuable material at the National Lawn Tennis Hall of Fame and Museum in Newport, R.I., and the United States Tennis Association in New York City. See also the obituaries in the *New York Times*, Nov. 23, 1959; *Illustrated London News*, Dec. 5, 1959; and *Time*, Dec. 7, 1959.]

JACK W. BERRYMAN

MANNES, DAVID (Feb. 16, 1866–Apr. 25, 1959), educator, conductor, violinist, and co-founder of the Mannes College of Music, was born in New York City, the son of Henry Mannes and Natalia Wittkowsky, German-Polish immigrants. Owing to a serious accident at age five that left him frail and to his early fascination with both musical and nonmusical sounds, his parents decided that he should become a violinist. Mannes' formal education consisted of four rather underprivileged years at a public school in New York, but his musical education was broad. Local theater and dance-hall musicians, Hermann Brody and Theodore Moses, were his earliest violin teachers, but he also studied with George Matska at the New York College of Music and with August Zeiss and Carl Richter

Nicolai, pupils of Ludwig Spohr. Further study was done in Berlin with Heinrich de Ahna and Karol Halíř, and in Brussels with Eugène Ysaÿe. As a boy Mannes was also a friend and informal student of the violinist John Douglas, a black man whose sympathetic and apparently selfless interest was a contributing factor to Mannes' later commitment to the welfare of blacks in American life and education.

From the age of fifteen, Mannes worked as a free-lance violinist in New York City, his engagements being mainly in theater and dance-hall orchestras of varying quality, with occasional opportunities to play under such noted conductors as Frank Damrosch and Anton Seidl. In 1891, Walter Damrosch, then in the process of forming the orchestra of the Symphony Society, which had been founded by his father, Leopold Damrosch, heard Mannes play and hired him for the forty-week season. Mannes remained with the New York Symphony Orchestra until 1911, and was its concertmaster from 1902. He accompanied some of the most famous virtuosi of the day, such as Ysaÿe and the pianist Ignace Paderewski, and worked under the conductors Gustav Mahler and Felix Weingartner, as well as Damrosch.

Mannes' activities as a violinist were not limited to orchestral playing. He was the founder and first violinist of the Mannes Quartet (1902–1904) and appeared as violin soloist in recital in the United States and Europe with his wife, pianist Clara Damrosch, a student of Busoni and daughter of Leopold Damrosch, whom he married on June 4, 1898. They had two children, writer Marya Mannes and pianist-educator Leopold Damrosch Mannes, who was also coinventor of the Kodachrome process of color photography.

In connection with his activities at the Music School Settlement, Mannes founded and conducted the Settlement Symphony. In 1904 he incorporated this group of young string players into the orchestra of the Symphony Club of New York, which he also conducted. These experiences proved valuable when, in February 1919, Mannes inaugurated a series of free concerts at the Metropolitan Museum of Art, conducting an orchestra of fifty-four musicians paid by the trustees of the museum. That year, John D. Rockefeller, Jr., attended one of these concerts and began financing a part of the series. Other backers were Mrs. Clarence Mackay, John A. Roebling, and the Juilliard School of Music.

Mannes conducted this series until 1949 and often appeared as a performer, using one of the Stradivarius violins owned by the Metropolitan Museum.

It was as an educator that Mannes made his most significant contributions to the musical life of his time. He helped to found the Music School Settlement, served as head of its string department, and was its director from 1901 to 1916. In 1912 he founded the Music Settlement for Colored People in Harlem, and four years later he and his wife founded the David Mannes Music School. Evincing Mannes' belief that a musical education should promote "not only the intense development of the potential professional, but [also] the efforts of those who want merely to enrich themselves through a better understanding or playing of music without the responsibilities of a career," the Mannes School flourished. It offered courses in harmony and counterpoint with Ernest Bloch, Rosario Scalero, and Hans Weisse, and master classes in piano with Alfred Cortot. This broad concept of musical education was reflected in the organization of the school, which included an extension division, preparatory and intermediate departments for the young, and, from 1953, a degree-granting college. In 1960 Mannes College merged with Chatham Square Music School and, on account of the increased net worth and endowment, was granted an "absolute," or degree-granting, charter by the state of New York. Mannes retired in 1949 but continued to be involved in the affairs of the college. He was honored at a scholarship-fund concert given by Dame Myra Hess, pianist, and Isaac Stern, violinist, on his ninetieth birthday. Mannes still made his daily rounds of the classrooms. He continued to be admired and loved not for his virtuosity or bravura, but for the enthusiasm that he brought to the study of music and for his exceptional gift of imparting it to others. He died in New York City.

[Mannes' autobiography is *Music Is My Faith* (1939). Many articles on Mannes and Mannes College are in *Musical America* and *Music Journal*. See also Walter Damrosch, *My Musical Life* (1923); Lucy Poate Stebbins and Richard Poate Stebbins, *Frank Damrosch* (1945); and *New York Times*, Apr. 15, 1956 (photograph) and Oct. 16, 1960 (merger of Mannes College with Chatham). Obituaries are in the *New York Times*, Apr. 25, 1959; *Musical America*, May 1959; and Marya Mannes, *Musical Clubs*, June 1959.]

RANDALL THOMPSON

MARQUAND, JOHN PHILLIPS (Nov. 10, 1893–July 16, 1960), novelist, was born in Wilmington, Del., the son of Philip Marquand, a civil engineer, and Margaret Fuller, the greatniece and namesake of the renowned transcendentalist. At the turn of the century the family moved to New York City, where Philip Marquand was set up in the bond business by his Newburyport, Mass., banker father, but was wiped out in the panic of 1907. In this crisis, Philip took an engineering job on the Panama Canal, while John was sent to Curzon's Mill, the family homestead outside of Newburyport to be brought up, as a poor relation, by two unmarried Marquand aunts. He attended Newburyport High School and entered Harvard College with the class of 1915.

Because of financial pressure he earned the A.B. in only three years. He then became a reporter on the *Boston Evening Transcript*. Having joined the Massachusetts National Guard, he spent three months as a private on the Mexican border in 1916 and the following year went to training camp at Plattsburg, N.Y., where he was commissioned a first lieutenant. After serving creditably in France as an artilleryman, he worked on the *New York Tribune* in 1919–1920 and as a copywriter at the J. Walter Thompson advertising agency before turning to fiction in 1921.

Marquand's first effort was a cloak-and-dagger novel, *The Unspeakable Gentleman*, set in early nineteenth-century Newburyport. In 1921 it was bought for serialization by the *Ladies' Home Journal* for $2,000, a sum that seemed immense after his weekly paycheck of $60 from advertising. A year later the book was published by Scribner's. The *Saturday Evening Post* and *Cosmopolitan* were soon competing for Marquand's short stories. He aimed at the popular market, which he captured over the next fifteen years with highly successful stories and half a dozen novels. Mr. Moto, the inscrutable Japanese detective of his spy thriller series, is the best remembered character.

On Sept. 8, 1922, Marquand married Christina D. Sedgwick in Stockbridge, Mass. They had two children and lived in Boston until their divorce in 1935. In that year Marquand bought an old house on Kent's Island, a peninsula jutting into the marshes of the Parker River in Newbury. This he regarded as home for the rest of his life.

Having achieved great popularity in writing for magazines of national circulation, Marquand in his forties found even greater success in serious literary creation. In the twenty-fifth report of the Harvard class of 1915 he wrote: "In 1936 I wrote a novel called *The Late George Apley*. When I showed it to my literary agent, his manner became sad and gentle. He passed it without comment to the lady who was his novel expert, and a day later she called me into her early American pine sanctum. She said she had always thought I might write a 'serious novel' some day, and now after all these years, what had I produced? A humorless fantasy. All that she could suggest, she said, was to put it away and to forget it as quickly as possible. It was published in 1937. In 1938 it won the Pulitzer Prize."

The instant success of this subtle, half-affectionate satire of the Boston he had known paved the way for some dozen novels, which would satirize other aspects of American life in the next twenty years. Marquand's power of mimicry, his gift for reproducing characteristic turns of speech with literal exactness, made him in conversation a superlative storyteller. With *The Late George Apley*, he clearly demonstrated his ability to transpose the spoken word to paper. He was thus able to abandon his commercial adventure stories for studies of places and people in which plot was subordinated to the presentation of human foibles. Apart from his highly accurate recollection of speech and choice of details, Marquand's most noteworthy literary device was his use of the flashback. The whole of his last book, *Timothy Dexter Revisited*, consists of a flashback to the Newburyport eccentric whose life had, thirty-five years earlier, inspired Marquand's only venture in biography, *Lord Timothy Dexter of Newburyport, Mass.* (1925).

Next to *The Late George Apley*, *Point of No Return* (1949), *Melville Goodwin, USA* (1951), *Thirty Years* (1954), and *Sincerely, Willis Wayde* (1955) are considered to be some of his strongest works. The trade sales of most of Marquand's later novels ran into six figures, while Philip Hamburger calculated in 1952 that book club and cheap editions had accounted for nearly four million copies. Unfortunately Marquand had greater success in shaping the lives of his characters than his own. He married Adelaide F. Hooker in New York on Apr. 17, 1937. They had two children but were divorced in 1958. Also, in spite of his phenomenal success, the memory of his childhood as a poor relation in Newburyport haunted Marquand; this type of preoccupation was shared by many of his characters.

Although he lived for long periods in Boston and New York, traveled extensively around the world, and dearly loved China, John Marquand nearly always set off in a novel from his Newburyport doorstep. The original doorstep not having been as high as his heart's desire, what a springboard he made of it! It was one of the paradoxes of his being that, having labored conscientiously and achieved a nationwide reputation, Marquand remained an Essex County man to the last—and rather an uneasy one at that. He was so diffident and delicately sensitive that at one moment his friends would marvel at his insight into them and their kind, and at the next instant they would be moved to wonder that John Marquand could seem so little at home with himself. But Essex County by tradition and experience and long-gathered affection was the true end of his journeys. It was there, at his home on Kent's Island, Newbury, that he died in his sleep of a heart attack.

[A *New Yorker* profile by Philip Hamburger, reprinted in 1952 as *J. P. Marquand, Esquire: A Portrait in the Form of a Novel*, is the best and most perceptive biography. Stephen Birmingham, *The Late John Marquand* (1972), although longer, is marred by errors of fact and interpretation. Reports of Marquand's Harvard class of 1915 contain valuable comments. Helen Howe, *The Gentle Americans* (1965), describes John and Christina Marquand as summer neighbors at Cotuit. Marquand contributed a thirty-page memoir to a project on the Book-of-the-Month Club done for the Oral History Collection of Columbia University in 1951.]

WALTER MUIR WHITEHILL

MARSHALL, GEORGE CATLETT, JR. (Dec. 31, 1880–Oct. 16, 1959), soldier and statesman, the only professional soldier to win the Nobel Prize for peace (1953), was born in Uniontown, Pa., the son of George Catlett Marshall, a well-to-do coke and coal merchant, and Laura Bradford. His great-great-grandfather, the Reverend William Marshall, was a brother of Thomas Marshall, father of Chief Justice John Marshall.

Marshall's father had accumulated a modest fortune by 1890. But unfortunate investments in real estate near Luray, Va., left him hard-pressed to pay his son's fees at Virginia Military Institute, which the boy entered in 1897. Ill-prepared academically, Marshall did poorly in his first year, but he graduated well above the middle of his class and was selected at the end of each year as the top cadet—first corporal, first sergeant, and first captain. The superintendent of Virginia Military Institute, in recommending him to President William McKinley in 1901, said that Marshall "was equal of the best" cadets who had graduated from that school.

After passing a competitive examination with high marks, Marshall took the oath as second lieutenant of infantry on Feb. 3, 1902, with date of rank from the act of Feb. 2, 1901, providing for new officers. On Feb. 11, 1902, he married Elizabeth Carter Coles. After a honeymoon in Washington, D.C., he was ordered to the Philippines, arriving just at the close of the Philippine Insurrection. Here, as a company officer and then as the only officer at an isolated post on the island of Mindoro, Marshall had his first taste of command. Returning to the United States in late 1903, he served at a small post in Oklahoma Territory and then helped to map part of West Texas. In 1906, Marshall studied at the Infantry-Cavalry School (soon renamed School of the Line) at Fort Leavenworth, Kans., and qualified for a second year at the Army Staff College by placing first in his class. After the second year he served for two years as an instructor in the Department of Military Engineering at the Fort Leavenworth Army Service Schools.

Marshall's solid foundation as a staff officer was laid in 1907–1912, when he was assigned to militia and regular units during summer maneuvers and given tasks of planning normally reserved for men of higher rank. It was this training that won him recognition and applause in the Philippines in 1914, when, as a first lieutenant, he was called on at the last moment to serve as acting chief of staff for the attacking force in important maneuvers.

Marshall's performance attracted the attention of the Philippine department commander, Major General J. Franklin Bell, former chief of staff of the U.S. Army, and of Bell's successor, Major General Hunter Liggett, for whom Marshall served as aide, 1915–1916. Liggett, who succeeded John J. Pershing as commander of First Army in France, in 1918 made Marshall his chief of operations. Bell requested Marshall as aide in 1916 at San Francisco and in 1917 at Governors Island, N.Y. At both headquarters he was assigned tasks in training and supply normally reserved for officers considerably higher in rank. For it was only on his way to the new post in California that he made captain. In 1917, Marshall joined the First Infantry Division, which was being organized as the first American field unit to go to France in World War I. After serving as training officer, he became chief of operations of the division and remained with it until the summer of 1918, when he was called to General Headquarters to help plan the battle in the St. Mihiel salient. While that battle was still in progress, he coordinated the withdrawal of French and Italian units from the Meuse-Argonne front and the movement forward of a large American force.

Marshall's share of the activity involved handling more than 400,000 men, an action that earned him the nickname "Wizard" in some of the newspapers and high praise from Pershing, who showed his appreciation by proposing Marshall for a star, later, by naming him his principal aide. The war ended before Marshall got his star; he would not reach that eminence until fifteen years later.

The years with Pershing (1919–1924) were valuable ones, since Marshall worked closely with his commander in outlining defense legislation presented to committees of Congress, visited most of the army posts and bases, and aided in the writing of Pershing's official reports.

From 1924 to 1927 Marshall served as executive officer of the Fifteenth Infantry Regiment at Tientsin, China, where he learned to speak rudimentary Chinese and became familiar with the thinking of the people. Several of his favorite officers, including Joseph W. Stilwell and Matthew B. Ridgway, were among those who served under him.

Particularly important among Marshall's assignments was that as assistant commandant in charge of instruction at the Infantry School, Fort Benning, Ga. (1927–1932). Sent there shortly after the death of his wife a few weeks following their return from China, he influenced ground-force doctrine and leadership by his bold rewriting of instruction manuals to gain simplicity and realism. More than 160 future generals—including Omar N. Bradley, Joseph Stilwell, J. Lawton Collins, Matthew Ridgway, and Walter Bedell Smith—were instructors or students at Fort Benning during that period. In October 1930 he married Katherine Tupper Brown, widow of a Baltimore attorney and mother of three children. In the next six years Marshall worked with National Guard units and with young men in the newly formed Civilian Conservation Corps (CCC). In the little more than a year during which he served as a battalion commander at Savannah, Ga., and a much shorter period as a regimental chief at Charleston, S.C., he built and developed camps for the CCC. From 1933 to 1936, Marshall directed instruction for the Illinois National Guard, and in 1936–1938, after he received his first star, he commanded the Fifth Infantry Brigade at Vancouver Barracks, in the state of Washington, and directed the CCC camps in that area. Few commanders knew better the problems and possibilities of young men who would be brought into the armed forces after 1940.

Summoned to Washington, D.C., as chief of the War Plans Division in the summer of 1938, Marshall was promoted a few months later to deputy chief of staff. He impressed President Franklin D. Roosevelt by his frankness and won the support of Harry Hopkins, the president's closest adviser, by his appraisal of what was needed for American defense. Marshall received his second permanent star and his four temporary stars when he became head of the army, succeeding General Malin Craig on Sept. 1, 1939. While Craig was on terminal leave (July 1–September 1), Marshall acted as chief of staff, succeeding to the full title a few hours after Hitler invaded Poland. Marshall became general of the army on Dec. 16, 1945, a rank that was made permanent in 1949.

As head of the U.S. Army until Nov. 20, 1945, when he asked to be relieved, he was the only top-level British or American political or military figure to hold the same post throughout World War II. Six feet tall, aloof, soft-spoken except when deeply angered, and moving with great self-confidence, Marshall won the confidence of Presidents Roosevelt and Harry S. Truman, gained the deep respect of Winston Churchill and the British and American chiefs of staff, and enjoyed excellent relations with Congress and the press. *Time* magazine, in proclaiming him Man of the Year in January 1944, declared that he had armed the republic.

In his two months as acting chief of staff, Marshall strove to bring the army up to its authorized strength under the Defense Act of 1920. His goal of 225,000 men was reached shortly after he became chief of staff. By the end of the war he commanded an American army and army air force of 8.3 million men. He frequently visited units in training, demanding realism in instruction and maneuvers and ruthlessly weeding out officers who lacked stamina, imagination, and the power to inspire men to action. In numerous appearances before committees of Congress, he warned early in 1940 that before the year ended the "phony war" in Europe might become a real

one. When he proved to be a true prophet, Congress provided more money that he could at once effectively use. Complicating his task was the fact that in addition to procuring and training men and increasing the production of war materials, the army had to find scarce weapons and munitions to aid Britain, China, and, after the summer of 1941, the Soviet Union. Before the end of 1940, Congress passed the Selective Service Act and nationalized units of the National Guard.

For planning purposes Marshall accepted a proposal by the chief of naval operations, Admiral Harold R. Stark, in late 1940, embodying the idea that if the United States was forced to fight simultaneously in the Atlantic and the Pacific, it would adopt a "Europe First" strategy. Discussions were held with British representatives in Washington early in 1941 and at the Anglo-American meeting at Argentia, Newfoundland, in August. Even after the Japanese attack on Pearl Harbor on Dec. 7, 1941, Marshall and his associates remained firm on the European attack. At home he demanded a complete reorganization of the War Department staff so that he could have a more effective command post. Marshall also was responsible for the appointment of Admiral William D. Leahy in the summer of 1942 as chairman of the joint chiefs of staff.

Marshall played a leading part in the great conferences and meetings with the president, the prime minister, and the British and American chiefs of staff from Argentia to Potsdam, becoming the chief advocate of the cross-Channel attack. Nevertheless, in 1942 and 1943 he accepted compromises. He was particularly aided in his efforts by the close friendship he developed with Field Marshal Sir John Dill, who headed the British mission in Washington from early 1942 until his death in late 1944. In preparation for the invasion of Europe, Marshall was responsible for the appointment of General Dwight D. Eisenhower, who had become chief of the War Plans Division in February 1942, to head American forces in the United Kingdom. He backed him for the chief command of Allied forces in the Mediterranean at the time of the North African invasion in November 1942. But it was assumed that Marshall would command the European invasion in 1944. At the Cairo and Teheran conferences in 1943, Roosevelt, who had initially insisted on Marshall's appointment, became disturbed at the thought of not having him in Washington. At first he agreed to leave the decision to Marshall, but when the chief of staff declined to make it, Roosevelt, saying he could not sleep well at night with Marshall out of Washington, appointed Eisenhower.

In the closing year and a half of the war, Marshall redoubled his efforts to step up production, to get necessary manpower, and to assure that during the main effort in Europe, General Douglas MacArthur would get support in the Pacific and supplies would flow to General Joseph W. Stilwell and his successor, Albert C. Wedemeyer, in China. But he made it clear that large units would not be committed on the Asian mainland. Near the end of the war in Europe, Churchill called Marshall "the true organizer of victory." A few days after Marshall's retirement on Nov. 20, 1945, President Truman read a citation saying that while millions of Americans had given their country outstanding service, General of the Army George Marshall had given it victory.

Marshall's retirement was interrupted almost at once by President Truman's request that he go to China as the president's special representative to secure a truce between warring Nationalist and Communist Chinese and to press for a coalition government. After a year of personal negotiations, Marshall had to acknowledge failure of his mission. He had already agreed to succeed James F. Byrnes as secretary of state. He took office in January 1947 and held it until early 1949, when he had a kidney removed and resigned for reasons of health.

As secretary Marshall reorganized the secretariat of the State Department and established a policy-planning staff, proving himself to be "a master of administration," in the words of a 1970 State Department study. He is best known for his role in developing the European Recovery Program, known as the Marshall Plan. He gave credit to a number of individuals for their contributions, suggestions, or actual drafting of the speech in which he set forth the plan during the day of the Harvard commencement, on June 5, 1947, but correctly believed that his nonpartisan stance and speeches given across the country had aided passage of the legislation.

Marshall took a leading role in the Council of Foreign Ministers meetings in Moscow in March–April 1947 and in London in November–December 1947; and he led the American delegation to the U.N. General Assembly at Paris from mid-September to mid-December 1948. He also took part in the Inter-American Conference for the Maintenance of Continental Peace and Security (1947), which resulted in the signing of the Rio Treaty of Reciprocal Assis-

tance, and the Ninth International Conference of American States at Bogotá (1948). This meeting arranged for the Pan American Union to be reorganized under the name Organization of American States.

Marshall's term was marked by the announcement of the Truman Doctrine, which was being discussed when the secretary left for Moscow in March 1947. Although he objected to some of the tough rhetoric in Truman's final draft, Marshall did not insist when he was told that the Congress would not grant assistance for Greece and Turkey without a warning against Soviet aggression.

In May 1948 Truman decided to recognize Israel's statehood within minutes of its proclamation of independence. Marshall was considering a compromise solution consisting of partition or a tripartite trusteeship when White House advisers pressed the president to recognize a state of Israel as soon as the British gave up their Palestine mandate. Believing that the way to such a step should be diplomatically prepared, Marshall protested against a decision made on a basis of domestic politics. In one of the few cases where the president went contrary to Marshall's advice, Truman decided to give prompt recognition to the new state.

A month later, on June 24, worsening relations between the Western occupation powers and the Soviet Union came to a head when Russian authorities in Berlin closed ground communications from the West into the former German capital. General Lucius Clay favored the sending of a convoy along the highway, but Marshall and Under Secretary Lovett advised against that course. Clay then proposed the Berlin airlift that proved successful.

During the summer of 1948, discussions were held with representatives of Canada and the Brussels Pact countries concerning a security organization for western Europe. These early negotiations were followed up by Secretary of State Dean Acheson, who signed agreements for the North Atlantic Treaty Organization. Later, Marshall as Secretary of Defense helped to implement the treaties.

In September 1950, after service as president of the American Red Cross, Marshall accepted Truman's offer of the secretaryship of the Department of Defense. Special congressional action was required to waive the requirement barring a professional military man from this position in his case. In his year in office Marshall helped to rebuild the strength of the army and to increase military production so that there would be a chance of victory. He was involved in President Truman's decision to remove General MacArthur from command of U.N. forces in the Far East in April 1951. Although Marshall had first advised against a removal at that time, he ended by giving his approval. In congressional hearings that followed, he strongly supported the civilian against military authority. In an effort to build up the army's manpower without recourse to a large professional army, Marshall made a strong but unsuccessful effort to have universal military training adopted. In September 1951, he retired. As a permanent five-star general, he remained on duty at the call of the president. Marshall was appointed by President Eisenhower in 1953 to head the U.S. mission at the coronation of Elizabeth II, and he was called on by the White House and the Pentagon for advice on military developments until near the end of his life.

Marshall's last months in office were overshadowed by the lengthy attack made on him in the Senate on June 14, 1951, by Senator Joseph McCarthy of Wisconsin in which his insistence on the cross-Channel attack, his failure to press for the capture of Berlin and Prague, his policy in China, and his part in the removal of MacArthur were all pictured as softness on Communism. Marshall was promptly defended by members of both parties in the Congress; and his Alma Mater proclaimed a Marshall Day on which he received the highest civilian decoration given by the Commonwealth of Virginia.

Marshall died in Washington, D.C., and was buried at Arlington National Cemetery. In 1964 the George C. Marshall Research Library was dedicated at Lexington, Va., by a group including President Lyndon B. Johnson, former President Eisenhower, former Secretary of Defense Robert A. Lovett, and General Omar N. Bradley.

In military affairs Marshall will be remembered as the individual who above all others built the U.S. Army and Army Air Force that contributed heavily to victory in World War II. No wartime commander so long enjoyed the trust and standing he held with the White House, with Congress, and with the public. His strength lay in his candor with Congress and the press, his refusal to play politics with military matters, and his firm insistence that the civilian power be superior to that of the military. In approving President Truman's action to remove General MacArthur from command in Korea in 1951, he spelled out for a congressional committee the limits of military authority.

As secretary of state Marshall gave his name and his strong backing to legislation that undertook to set Europe on the road to economic recovery. Although aware that such reconstruction was in the best interests of the United States, his first consideration was the defeat of hunger and misery in Europe. In his postwar career he tried to combine a policy of firmness toward the Soviet Union with an effort to promote peaceful relations. He embodied a happy combination of military and political leadership in one of the most violent decades in world history.

[The George C. Marshall Research Library, Lexington, Va., contains 250,000 of his personal papers; more than a million pages copied from official files of the Army, Defense, and State departments; files of photographs; 25,000 books and periodicals on Marshall and the period 1900–1951; articles about Marshall; and obituaries. The most extensive collection of interview material on General Marshall is in the Marshall Library. It consists of interviews with more than 350 people (more than half of the interviews are taped) brought together between 1956 and the present. Forty hours of twenty-nine interviews with Marshall are on tape, and notes are provided for at least fifteen hours of additional material. The holdings of the Columbia Oral History Collection contain numerous interviews that contain material pertaining to Marshall. Other interview collections containing material on Marshall are those at the Truman, Roosevelt, and Eisenhower libraries, the U.S. Army Military History Institute, and the Dulles project at Princeton University. Copies of notes on a large number of interviews—collected by Harry B. Price and assistants—from individuals associated with the Marshall Plan are in the Marshall Library. The collection includes notes on interviews with individuals in every Marshall Plan country.

The authorized biography, by Forrest C. Pogue, will consist of four volumes. Those now in print are *George C. Marshall: Education of a General, 1880–1939* (1963); *George C. Marshall: Ordeal and Hope, 1939–1942* (1966); *George C. Marshall: Organizer of Victory, 1943–1945* (1973). See also Mrs. George C. Marshall, *Together* (1946); William Frye, *George Marshall* (1947); Rose Page Wilson, *General Marshall Remembered* (1968); John Robinson Beal, *Marshall in China* (1970); Major H. A. DeWeerd, ed., *Selected Speeches and Statements of General of the Army George C. Marshall, Chief of Staff, U.S. Army* (1945); Joseph R. McCarthy, *America's Retreat from Victory* (1952); Joseph P. Hobbs, *Dear General, Eisenhower's Wartime Letters to Marshall* (1971); Alfred D. Chandler et al., *The Papers of Dwight David Eisenhower: The War Years* (1971); numerous volumes in the *U.S. in World War II* series, including in particular, Mark Watson, *Chief of Staff: Plans and Preparations* (1950); Maurice Matloff and Edward M. Snell, *Strategic Planning for*

Coalition Warfare, 1941–42 (1950); Maurice Matloff, *Strategic Planning for Coalition Warfare, 1943–1944* (1959); Ray Cline, *Washington Command Post: The Operations Division* (1951); and Forrest C. Pogue, *The Supreme Command* (1954) and *Marshall, Global Commander* (Harmon Lecture, 1968).

Special U.S. State Department Foreign Relations volumes dealing with the great conferences from Arcadia to Potsdam; Foreign Relations volumes for 1946 dealing with the China mission; and those dealing with the years 1947–1949, during which time Marshall was secretary of state, contain much of his correspondence and summaries of his statements at various meetings. A project is now underway at the Marshall Library to publish approximately seven volumes of Marshall's papers.]

FORREST C. POGUE

MASON, LUCY RANDOLPH (July 26, 1882–May 6, 1959), social worker and publicist for the Congress of Industrial Organizations (CIO), was born in Clarens, Va., the daughter of the Reverend Landon Randolph Mason, an Episcopalian minister, and of Lucy Ambler. Most of her childhood was spent in Richmond, Va. Influenced by her parents' religious commitment to social service, she considered becoming a missionary but decided that "religion can be put to work right in one's own community." Thus, even after she became a legal stenographer in 1904, she remained a volunteer worker for social service organizations concerned with labor and social legislation and interracial cooperation.

In 1914 Mason was able to combine her professional and volunteer careers by becoming industrial secretary for the Richmond Young Women's Christian Association (YWCA). After the death of her mother in 1918, she left full-time work to care for her ailing father. Nevertheless, she continued her volunteer work, becoming president of the Richmond Equal Suffrage League and, later, of the League of Women Voters.

The death of her father in 1923 allowed Mason to resume her professional career, as general secretary of the Richmond YWCA. Rather than confine herself to traditional "Y" activities, she used this post to continue her involvement in social issues, particularly working conditions and race relations. In 1931, for example, she spent two months traveling in the South, urging better child labor laws and shorter hours for women. On the basis of her trip, she wrote a pamphlet, *Standards for Workers in Southern Industry,* which was published and widely distributed by the National Consumers League (NCL), an organization founded in 1899 to combat sweatshop conditions.

Mason was becoming more widely known. And when, in 1931, the NCL began searching for a new general secretary to replace the gravely ill Florence Kelly, Mason emerged as a possible choice. Some, though, doubted that she had the stature for the job: "She is all right in her own bailiwick, but as a national figure would make no dent," NCL leader Clara Beyer commented. Molly Dewson, the chairman of NCL, shared these doubts but nevertheless urged Mason's selection because "She has personality, devotion to the industrial women, experience, prestige in her state and in the South . . . and is . . . a good speaker." Dewson's view prevailed, and Mason moved to New York in September 1932 to assume the leadership of the NCL.

In this post Mason energetically publicized labor conditions and testified often at National Recovery Administration code hearings. But the 1930's were a difficult period for the NCL; its finances were tight, and the New Deal seemed to be usurping some of its traditional functions. Ultimately, Mason decided it was an "impossible job" and, reinforced by a long-standing desire to return to the South, she left the NCL in 1937 for a post in Atlanta, as southeastern public relations officer for the newly organized CIO.

Oddly, it was this return to the South that made Mason an important national figure. For the next fourteen years she served as the uniquely effective CIO "roving ambassador to the South." With her impeccable southern credentials and her broad Virginia accent, the small, gray-haired, sweet-faced, bespectacled Mason could move in circles closed to most trade unionists. She traveled with missionary zeal from Charlotte, N.C., to McColl, S.C., to Tupelo, Miss., to Huntsville, Ala., to Ducktown, Tenn., preaching to leading citizens, newspaper editors, clergymen, and manufacturers on behalf of the fledgling southern union movement and against violations of the civil rights of textile, clothing, steel, mining, and communications organizers. Tough southern sheriffs who were harassing union organizers could be softened by mention of her Virginia lineage (George Mason, author of the Declaration of Rights, and Chief Justice John Marshall), her Confederate ancestors (including Robert E. Lee), or her Sunday-school teaching.

"Miss Lucy," as she was called, "was the one

CIO staff member who in the days of Operation Dixie could persuade a Southern sheriff to change his mind about running union organizers out of town," said the *AFL-CIO News*. When her mild southern voice failed to persuade them, she filed charges with the Department of Justice or sought presidential intervention through her regular correspondence with Eleanor Roosevelt.

By the 1940's, Mason's missionary work had made her a legend in the labor movement. In 1951 she retired and wrote her autobiography, *To Win These Rights*, which was published the following year. Mason, who never married, died in Atlanta, her dedication and religious idealism having altered some of the ingrained traditions of the South of which she was so much a part.

[Mason's personal papers have been deposited at Duke University. Obituaries are in *Atlanta Constitution*, May 7 and 9, 1959; *New York Times*, May 8, 1959; and *AFL-CIO News*, May 16, 1959. For her connection with the NCL, see the Molly Dewson Papers and Clara Beyer Papers at Schlesinger Library, Harvard University; and the NCL Papers at the Library of Congress.]

ROY ROSENZWEIG

MATAS, RUDOLPH (Sept. 12, 1860–Sept. 23, 1957), physician and surgeon, was born on a plantation near Bonnet Carre, La., the son of Narciso Hereu y Matas and Teresa Jorda, well-to-do Spaniards who had emigrated from Barcelona to New Orleans in 1857. Shortly after arriving in New Orleans, his father took two five-month courses at the Medical School of New Orleans and acquired degrees in pharmacy and medicine. A restless and flamboyant individual, Narciso Matas moved his family to Brownsville, Tex.; Matamoros, Mexico; Paris; Barcelona; and back to New Orleans. Rudolph attended schools in all of these places, and in the process became fluent in English, Spanish, and French. In 1875 he entered St. John Collegiate Institute in Matamoros and worked part-time in a pharmacy. In 1877 he enrolled in the medical department of the University of Louisiana (now Tulane University), and the following year was awarded a student residency at Charity Hospital.

In 1878 Matas was appointed clerk and interpreter to the Yellow Fever Commission sent to Cuba by the National Board of Health. While in Cuba he met Carlos Juan Finlay, the Cuban physician who first recognized the mosquito

Aedes aegypti as the vector of yellow fever. Finlay set forth his mosquito thesis at scientific meetings in Washington and Havana in 1881, but it received scant notice. Matas, the only physician to appreciate Finlay's idea, translated his paper and published it in the *New Orleans Medical and Surgical Journal* in 1882, eighteen years before Walter Reed and others demonstrated the validity of the mosquito theory.

Once Matas embarked upon his medical and surgical career, his rise to fame was rapid. In 1883, only two years after receiving the M.D. from the University of Louisiana, he became editor of the *New Orleans Medical and Surgical Journal*. Although he was an excellent physician, he had a natural aptitude for surgery. Despite the advent of anesthesia in 1846, surgery continued to lag behind medicine because of the omnipresent hospital fevers, the secondary infections that almost invariably negated the best efforts of surgeons. Matas came on the scene when antiseptic and aseptic techniques were drastically reducing secondary infections. At the start of his career the abdominal and thoracic cavities were sacrosanct and surgery on the brain was unthinkable. By the time he had practiced for twenty years, no section of the body was immune to the surgeon's knife.

Matas' interest in surgery and his activity in medical journalism and the local medical society led to his appointment in 1884 as demonstrator of anatomy at Tulane. Ten years later, against the wishes of the dean of the medical school, and partly in response to newspaper and public support, he was elected professor and chairman of the department of surgery. Only four years after his faculty appointment, Matas performed the operation that was to ensure his place in the history of surgery. The physicians of New Orleans had a long tradition of successfully treating aneurysms arising from trauma and pathological disorders, and vascular surgery became Matas' forte. In 1888 he was called to treat a young patient suffering from an aneurysm of the brachial artery resulting from a gunshot wound. After unsuccessfully trying compression, ligating the artery on the proximal and then on the distal side of the aneurysm, Matas made the bold decision to open it. On removing the clotted blood, he discovered three vessels supplying the aneurysm. Realizing the urgency of the situation, he disregarded traditional teaching and closed all three openings with fine silk sutures. The patient made an excellent recovery, and the operation, known as endoaneurysmorrhaphy, established Matas' fame.

In addition to many contributions in vascular surgery, Matas developed a catgut ring for making end-to-end sutures of severed intestines, developed an apparatus and technique (intralaryngeal insufflation) for preventing lung collapse following resection of the chest wall, contributed to the development of local and regional anesthesia (he was the first American to use spinal analgesia), and wrote on a wide range of medical and surgical topics.

On Jan. 20, 1895, Matas married Adrienne Goslee Landry, a widow with two children whom he had known for many years. He was an excellent teacher. In a day when the medical profession was not noted for its erudition, he was well educated, well read, and articulate. He had a retentive memory, and his ability to recall the writings of his predecessors enabled him to solve many unusual and unexpected problems arising in the course of surgery.

For most of the thirty years following his retirement in 1927 from the chair of surgery at Tulane, Matas continued his private practice. He began gathering materials for a history of medicine in Louisiana. Although beset by various ills in his early nineties, he remained clear of mind until 1956. He died in New Orleans. The bulk of his estate was willed to the Tulane University School of Medicine.

[The Howard-Tilton Library of Tulane University, New Orleans, has the Rudolph Matas Collection. His articles include "Traumatic Aneurism of the Left Brachial Artery . . . ," *Medical News*, Oct. 27, 1888; "Intralaryngeal Insufflation for the Relief of Acute Surgical Pneumothorax," *Journal of the American Medical Association*, June 9, 1900; and "Local and Regional Anesthesia," *American Journal of Surgery*, July and Aug. 1934. An account by Matas of his early life is in his introduction to Pedro Puliulacho, *Ulcers of the Legs* (1956). See also Alton Ochsner, "Dr. Rudolph Matas," *A.M.A. Archives of Surgery*, Jan. 1956; Isadore Cohn with Hermann B. Deutsch, *Rudolph Matas* (1960); and John Duffy, ed., *The Rudolph Matas History of Medicine in Louisiana*, vol. II (1962).]

JOHN DUFFY

MATTHES, GERARD HENDRIK (Mar. 16, 1874–Apr. 8, 1959), hydraulic engineer, was born in Amsterdam, the Netherlands, the son of Wille Ernest Matthes and Johanna van der Does. Matthes' parents immigrated into the United States in 1888, settling in Los Angeles, Calif.,

where the father became a businessman. Gerard and his twin brother remained in Europe to complete their education. They studied at private schools in the Netherlands and Switzerland, and graduated from gymnasium at Frankfurt-am-Main in 1891. That year both immigrated to the United States to enter the Massachusetts Institute of Technology (MIT).

Matthes graduated from MIT in 1895 and began his career as a surveyor of watercourses. He was an instrument man and draftsman for the town of Brookline, Mass., while surveying Boston Harbor and the Connecticut River for the Massachusetts State Board of Harbor and Land Commissioners. In 1896 he became a citizen.

After two years Matthes joined the U.S. Geological Survey as an assistant hydrographer. In that capacity he did stream gauging and irrigation studies. In 1902 he became district engineer in charge of the construction works in Comanche, Caddo, and Kiowa counties in the Oklahoma Territory. He had, the year earlier, taken time off to go to Sumatra with an MIT astronomical expedition. Matthes married Mary Mae Bewick on Mar. 3, 1904. They had one daughter.

Matthes became the assistant supervising engineer for the U.S. Reclamation Service in New Mexico and Idaho in 1905. His work mainly concerned irrigation projects. This position lasted two years. Matthes next worked for four years (1907–1911) as designing engineer, resident engineer, and superintendent of construction for the Colorado Power Company, which was developing the upper Colorado River.

In 1911, Matthes was appointed principal assistant engineer for the American Water Works and Guaranty Company, which was involved with power development of the Cheat River in West Virginia. Following this two-year stint he spent two years as a division engineer for the Pennsylvania Water Supply Commission. He then became a hydraulic engineer with the Miami Conservancy District, headquartered in Dayton, Ohio, doing flood control for the Miami River Valley.

Matthes joined the War Department in 1920 as an assistant engineer, with a principal assignment of surveying the Tennessee River. In this capacity he used aerial photographs to map the river, the first such use by the War Department. Sensing the potential of this technique, Matthes left federal service in 1923 to open a private consulting engineering practice in New York City. He returned to government work in 1929 as senior hydroelectric engineer, then principal engineer, in the Army Engineer Office at Norfolk, Va. In this capacity he studied rivers in Virginia and North Carolina. He also began his work as a consultant to other federal projects, an involvement that increased considerably as the New Deal expanded public works construction. In 1932, Matthes became principal engineer, head engineer, and consultant to the Mississippi River Commission in Vicksburg, Miss., an organization dedicated to flood control and improved navigation on the lower Mississippi River. He also was a consultant on flood control for the Tennessee Valley Authority in 1936, and head engineer and director of the U.S. Waterways Experiment Station in Vicksburg from 1942 to 1945. For this dual wartime service Matthes received the Gold Medal for Exceptional Civilian Service in 1944.

Matthes retired in 1945 but did not cease work. He created the Rocky Mountain Hydraulic Laboratory in Allens Park, Colo., a nonprofit research laboratory specializing in river and flood analysis. He also continued a private consultancy practice in New York City that extended to Latin America. He received a patent for a tetrahedral block revetment for riverbanks in 1946. Matthes died in New York City.

[Matthes' published works include the revision of Charles B. Breed and George L. Hosmer, *The Principles and Practice of Surveying*, vol. II (*Higher Surveying*, 7th edition, 1953). Of greater use to the reader are "Paradoxes of the Mississippi River," *Scientific American*, Apr. 1951; and "How Good Is Flood Control?" *Engineering News Record*, Nov. 1951. His obituary is in *New York Times*, Apr. 10, 1959.]

DWIGHT W. HOOVER

MAY, ANDREW JACKSON (June 24, 1875–Sept. 6, 1959), congressman, was born in Langley, Ky., the son of John May and Dorcas Conley. He was educated in Floyd County schools and taught in the common schools of Floyd and Magoffin counties before entering Southern Normal University Law School, Huntington, Tenn. He graduated in 1898, was admitted to the bar, and, soon after beginning the practice of law, entered politics. In 1901 May was elected Floyd County prosecuting attorney, and four years later he was reelected. On July 17, 1901, he married Julia Grace Mayo; they had three children. His terms as Floyd County attorney were followed, in 1925–1926, by service as a special judge of the circuit court of Johnson and Martin counties. During the intervening period he embarked on a business career, eventually becoming president of the Beaver Valley Coal Company.

In 1930, May was elected to Congress from the Tenth District of Kentucky. He was reelected to each succeeding Congress until 1946. His arrival in Washington, a full term before many other Democrats were elected in 1932, enabled May to gain coveted seniority. In the Seventy-third Congress (1933–1935) he was sixth-ranking Democrat on the House Military Affairs Committee; in 1938 he succeeded Lister Hill of Alabama as chairman of that committee.

Since he had not been elected to Congress as a New Deal Democrat, May did not always feel obliged to support President Franklin D. Roosevelt's policies. In 1933 he opposed Roosevelt's economy measures, and later led the opposition to the Tennessee Valley Authority (TVA). The journalist Arthur Krock once described May as a moderate, but it would be more accurate to view him as a moderate among southern Democrats and, as such, a conservative. His conservatism was reflected in his views on both domestic and foreign affairs. He spoke out forcefully against what he regarded as left-wing tendencies in the New Deal and in the late 1930's was an advocate of increased military expenditures.

From the beginning May was an opponent of TVA, referring to it as "a monstrosity out to gobble up the South." All enabling legislation for TVA had to pass through the Military Affairs Committee, a situation that put him in a strategic position to limit its growth. From 1933 to 1939 he was checked by the powerful pro-TVA faction in Congress, but in the latter year he won a victory over administration forces, sponsoring a bill passed by the House that put drastic curbs on TVA. This measure cut back a Senate-authorized $100 million bond issue to $61.5 million, limiting future TVA operations to certain counties in Alabama and Mississippi (in addition to areas it already served), and imposing on future agency activities restrictions that, according to TVA supporters, would completely wreck the "power yardstick" idea. May seems to have been motivated in part by fear that TVA would spread into Kentucky. He clearly stated the purpose of his bill by saying it "would go a long way in restoring confidence of the public in the future of the electric-utility industry."

May's bill was modified in conference committee, but TVA emerged more severely restricted than ever before. He continued to attack the TVA at every opportunity, charging that John M. Carmody, Federal Works Agency administrator, and David E. Lilienthal, TVA chairman, were leftists out to begin a utility war against private companies. May led the battle to force the people of the Tennessee Valley to compensate for the taxes lost when private utility companies in the area became government owned. In 1940 he again tried to hold up appropriations for the TVA and to place it under the jurisdiction of the General Accounting Office, but this attempt was defeated.

May gained prominence at the beginning of World War II as head of the powerful Military Affairs Committee. To bring the army up to full mechanized strength, he advocated diverting $500 million from river and harbor improvements and flood control programs to military expenditures. More and more after 1940 his views coincided with the preparedness and interventionist views of the Roosevelt administration. He first suggested relaxation—and finally, in late 1939, urged repeal—of the Johnson Debt Default Act, "since England is now fighting our battle," but his bill for repeal died with the introduction of the lend-lease bill. He tried to have this bill sent to his Military Affairs Committee for hearings, but it went instead to Foreign Affairs. He nonetheless remained a staunch supporter of the Lend-Lease Act, which was approved by Congress in March 1941.

May never hesitated to take a stand opposing or even embarrassing to the Roosevelt administration. In January 1942, after the attack on Pearl Harbor, he called for the court-martial of army and navy commanders in Hawaii, and went so far as to suggest that "when General Short and Admiral Kimmel come up for court-martial, I'm in favor of holding a shooting match." That same year he voted with three other Democrats and nine Republicans on the Military Affairs Committee to submit a report charging widespread inefficiency in war production.

But May's influence in Congress ended abruptly. Wartime bribery charges destroyed his public career. In 1946 a committee headed by Senator James M. Mead of New York began its investigation of war contracts. Repeatedly the committee tried to induce May to appear before it to answer questions about his association with a multimillion-dollar Illinois munitions combine headed by Henry M. Garsson. War contracts to

the Garsson brothers and their associates, obtained with May's influence, involved $78 million. May was under subpoena to appear when, on July 25, 1946, he suffered a heart attack. After a week or so in a hospital, he returned to Kentucky and ran for reelection, despite charges pending against him. He was defeated.

Late in 1946 the Mead Committee turned its investigation over to the Justice Department, and on Jan. 23, 1947, May and the Garsson brothers were indicted by a federal grand jury on charges of conspiracy to defraud the government. May pleaded not guilty to this and bribery charges, but testimony during the forty-seven-day trial revealed that he had received more than $53,000 in bribes and that some of the payments were made by the Garsson companies through an affiliate, the Cumberland Land Company in Prestonburg, Ky., of which May was an agent.

Witnesses at the trial included General Dwight D. Eisenhower, Secretary of State George C. Marshall, and Secretary of War Robert P. Patterson, who testified that May had come to him seeking wartime favors for the Garssons and their friends. On July 3, 1947, all three men were convicted on conspiracy charges, May of taking bribes, and the Garssons of furnishing them. Repeated appeals to higher courts failed; the Supreme Court refused for a second time to review the cases; and in December 1949, May began serving a sentence of eight months to two years. His request for reduction in sentence, based on poor health, was denied, as was an application for parole; but in September 1950 he was released from Ashland Federal Correctional Institute for his "outstanding institutional record."

In June 1952, a Kentucky court of appeals restored May to his standing as a lawyer, and he resumed practice in Prestonburg, where he spent his remaining years. He continued to protest his innocence but stated that he was not embittered by his experience. In December 1952, President Harry S. Truman granted him a full pardon, restoring his citizenship rights.

In view of the shadow cast on his reputation by his prison sentence, May retained a remarkable resilience, although he never tried to regain his former status in the public sector. In August 1950, Representative John McCormack, Democratic majority leader, called him "a great American," and Dewey Short, House Republican from Missouri, stated that he had "rendered a great and honorable service to his country during the war." May died in Prestonburg, Ky.

[Material on May is in Estes Kefauver and Jack Levin, *A Twentieth-Century Congress* (1947); and Sir Denis Brogan, *Politics in America* (1954). Both *Time* and *Newsweek* covered his indictment, trial, conviction, and release; see Tris Coffin, *Nation*, Aug. 3, 1946, on Mead Committee hearings. May's obituary is in *New York Times*, Sept. 7, 1959.]

MARIAN C. McKENNA

MAYBECK, BERNARD RALPH (Feb. 7, 1862–Oct. 3, 1957), architect, was born in New York City, the son of Bernhardt Maybeck and Elisa Kern, both of whom had emigrated from Germany during the political unrest of 1849–1850. His mother died when he was three years old, and his father later married Elizabeth Weiss.

Maybeck attended a German-American school in New York City and then a public high school. He entered the College of the City of New York to study languages and science, but the science courses were not to his liking. He therefore left school to follow his father's trade as a cabinetmaker, starting as an apprentice in the New York City firm of Pottier and Stymus, which specialized in custom furniture design and architectural interiors. His experiences in the shop kindled a desire to become a designer, so his father sent him to Paris to study. Maybeck passed the examinations in architecture at the École des Beaux Arts in the spring of 1882 and began his work in the atelier of Jules André. He developed a strong admiration for his patron and the teaching at the school that remained undiminished throughout his career.

In 1886 Maybeck returned to New York to work with John M. Carrere and Thomas Hastings (the latter had been his roommate in Paris) on their first commissioned works for Henry Morrison Flagler: the Ponce de Leon and Alcazar hotels in St. Augustine, Fla. Maybeck supervised the construction of the buildings. By 1888, though, he had decided to start an independent practice. He spent an unproductive year in Kansas City before moving to San Francisco, where he eventually found work in the office of A. Page Brown. He married Annie White on Oct. 29, 1890. They had two children.

Three young architects in Brown's office—Willis Polk, A. C. Schweinfurth, and Maybeck—are credited with initiating an architectural renaissance in the San Francisco Bay region. They introduced an unpretentious style of residential architecture directly expressive of its wooden construction.

In 1894, Maybeck began to teach drawing at the University of California. He gathered about him a group of engineering students, primarily interested in architecture, who later became leading practitioners in the area, among them John Bakewell, Arthur Brown, Harvey Wiley Corbett, Albert Landsburgh, and Julia Morgan. Maybeck was instrumental in the formation of the international competition for the Phoebe Hearst Architectural Plan for the University of California, and as its professional adviser he traveled throughout Europe in 1897 and 1898. Mrs. Hearst also commissioned Maybeck to design a large reception pavilion, Hearst Hall (1899), which he built as a demountable structure, employing large laminated wooden arches so that it could be moved to the campus when the university plan had been determined.

Maybeck resigned from the university in 1903 to devote full time to his practice. In the ensuing three decades he designed more than 200 projects. He worked with a small staff of which the principal members were his brothers-in-law Mark White, an engineer, and John White, an architect. Outstanding among Maybeck's work were simple residential designs that employed open planning and direct structural expression (G. H. Boke, Berkeley, 1902) and those using new materials such as reinforced concrete (A. C. Lawson, Berkeley, 1907). But his treatment of large, expensive residences was equally distinctive (L. L. Roos, San Francisco, 1909; A. E. Bingham, Santa Barbara, 1916).

Maybeck was an eclectic architect; he could use the vocabulary of the Gothic, Roman, baroque, or Tudor styles as an inspiration for unique formulation of space, light, and textures in contexts sensitively suited to modern life. He knew how to combine a traditional respect for individual craftsmanship with an adventurous use of the latest technological developments. In the First Church of Christ Scientist, Berkeley (1910), stenciled ornament, carved wood beams, and custom-forged fixtures harmonize with industrial steel sash, Transite facing, and reinforced concrete piers. Maybeck, unlike his contemporaries raised in the shadow of the École des Beaux Arts, was able to respect tradition and individuality without sham. He could turn the pomp of his time to winning fantasy in structures such as the Palace of Fine Arts (1915) in San Francisco and the Earle C. Anthony Packard Building (1928) in Oakland.

Costly craftsmanship was not essential to Maybeck's work because his inventiveness in the use of materials enabled him to design economically. He experimented with low-cost bungalows (1924) sheathed with gunny sacks dipped in lightweight concrete. His more modest work has, in fact, proved to be the most significant for architects of succeeding generations. In his simple houses and community projects he demonstrated how the individualism and human scale of the preindustrial age could be preserved without denying the economic and technical imperatives of modern society.

Maybeck's most significant work belongs to the time before World War I when a handful of visionaries—Louis Sullivan, Frank Lloyd Wright, Henry Mather Greene, and Charles Sumner Greene—were trying to stem the engulfing tide of architectural superficiality. This lonely and unrewarded struggle kept alive a spirit that could be rekindled in a later and more adventuresome generation. He died in Berkeley, Calif.

[Maybeck's drawings, office records, and correspondence are at the College on Environmental Design, University of California at Berkeley. See W. C. Hays, "Some Interesting Buildings at the University of California," *Indoors and Out*, May 1906; Sheldon Cheney, *New World Architecture* (1930); J. M. Bangs, "Bernard Ralph Maybeck, Architect, Comes Into His Own," *Architectural Record*, Jan. 1948; Winthrop Sargeant, *Geniuses, Goddesses and People* (1949); Esther McCoy, *Five California Architects* (1960); and Kenneth H. Cardwell, *Bernard Ralph Maybeck, Artisan, Architect, Artist* (1976).]

KENNETH H. CARDWELL

MAYER, LOUIS BURT (1885[?]–Oct. 29, 1957), motion picture producer and executive, was born in the vicinity of Minsk, Russia. The exact place and date of his birth are not known. On his marriage license he gave the year as 1882, but on his later application for naturalization he gave it as 1885 and, being unsure of the precise day, gave that as July 4. His parents' original family names likewise are unknown. The father's first name was Jacob, the mother's Chaya Sarah. The name Mayer may have been assumed when the impoverished family immigrated into the United States sometime in the late 1880's or, perhaps, when they removed to Saint John, New Brunswick, Canada, after an unfortunate and brief residence in New York City.

Louis grew up in Saint John, where he assisted his father first as a junk collector and later as a salvager of scrap metal from abandoned ships. His mother, a simple peasant woman, hawked live chickens from door to door. Always industrious and ambitious, Mayer received a modest public school education and occasionally traveled to Boston on business for his father. On Jan. 2, 1904, he moved to Boston on his own and found employment in the junk business. He lived in the South End, a ghetto area then similar to New York's Lower East Side, where he met Margaret Shenberg, daughter of a butcher and part-time cantor at the Emerald Street Synagogue. They were married on June 14, 1904.

Times were not good for junk merchants—or perhaps Mayer was not a very good one. He could barely make a living for his wife and newborn child, Edith. In 1907, he moved his family to New York City, where a second daughter, Irene, was born; but he soon became discouraged and returned to Boston, continuing to deal in junk. But now he began to be curious about a new form of enterprise, motion picture exhibition, which was then mainly confined to brief spots on vaudeville programs and in reconverted stores known as nickelodeons. Through a newly acquired friend who ran one, he heard of a vacant burlesque-vaudeville theater for rent in Haverhill, Mass. Borrowing and scraping together enough money to make a down payment on it, he took the place, rented some one-reel films from his Boston friend, and launched himself as a theater manager. He changed the name of his place from the Gem (known locally as the Germ) to the Orpheum and secured a financial foothold by successfully showing at Christmastime in 1907 Pathé's then-sensational *Passion Play*. This was the beginning of comparative prosperity for him. He became an American citizen on June 24, 1912.

The next year, inspired by his modest affluence and a swelling belief in his competence (Mayer was always cocky and boastful), he joined with a friend to conduct a general amusement business and took a season's lease on the Walnut Street Theater in Philadelphia to book touring Broadway companies at "popular" prices. At the same time, he installed a resident stock company at his theater in Haverhill. His inclination was now turning toward the more prestigious legitimate theater. But indifferent success in that area brought him back quickly to films, about which he was becoming sagacious. Along with his theaters in Haverhill, now increased to two, he opened a small distributing firm in Boston, handling the output of the newly formed Jesse Lasky–Samuel Goldfish (later Goldwyn)–Cecil B. DeMille producing company in the New England area. In 1915 he allied himself with a distributing combine called Alco, which was reorganized as Metro Pictures the following year. Mayer, appointed secretary of Metro, was branching out.

Also that year, he acquired for $50,000, which he borrowed from a group of Boston friends, the franchise for subsequent-run distribution in the New England area of D. W. Griffith's *The Birth of a Nation*. This turned out to be a bonanza, and with the money and assurance thus acquired Mayer was emboldened to go into film production. Audaciously, he persuaded the highly popular acting team of Francis X. Bushman and Beverly Bayne to make a serial for him, and shortly thereafter he lured the great star Anita Stewart away from the established Vitagraph Company and produced, with her in the lead, a drama, *Virtuous Wives*.

Its success, along with Stewart's insistence, induced Mayer to move to Hollywood, which was rapidly becoming the American filmmaking center after World War I. There he took modest space in what was known as the Selig Zoo on Mission Road, a studio-cum-menagerie where Colonel William Selig made animal-adventure films. Mayer was now full of braggadocio, energy, and brass, coupled with frequent private periods of shivering doubt and despair, which did not prevent him from pushing ahead. In rapid succession, he turned out several films with his big star, Stewart, and he also got Mildred Harris Chaplin, the notoriously estranged wife of Charlie Chaplin, to appear in several films. His distribution outlet was First National, but in 1923 he made a deal to do four pictures a year for Loew's, a strong nationwide theater chain whose head, Marcus Loew, had picked up, in 1920, the old Metro company to be a producing arm for the theaters. This alliance with Loew's was most propitious. In 1924, when Loew decided to buy the languishing Goldwyn Company (from which Samuel Goldwyn had been removed two years before) and merge his Metro outfit with it, he also drew Mayer's little unit into the merger and made him head of production for the new Metro-Goldwyn Company. (Mayer's name was not officially added until 1926.) Headquarters for the new combine was the former Goldwyn Studio in Culver City, and it was there that the induction was celebrated on Apr. 26, 1924.

Fortune smiled at the outset. Mayer had brought over with him in his producing unit Irving Thalberg, whom he had lured away from Universal to be his assistant. Thalberg soon proved to be a genius at supervising the studio's output of some forty films a year. Of these, fifteen a year were guaranteed by the so-called Mayer group. Three of the early pictures—*The Big Parade, The Merry Widow,* and *Ben Hur*—were smash hits. On a trip to Europe that first year, to shake up production of *Ben Hur* in Rome, Mayer manifested his extraordinary talent for picking potential star material by signing up Greta Garbo, then an inconspicuous Swedish actress. He also made a deal with William Randolph Hearst to bring the latter's protégé, Marion Davies, to his studio; but this arrangement was always suspected of having been intended as much to woo the powerful publisher as it was to get Davies, in order to nourish Mayer's taste for involvement in politics. He also got to know Secretary of Commerce Herbert Hoover by hiring his former secretary, Ida Koverman, who was a power in the Republican party in California.

The first of a series of crises within the Loew's company occurred in 1927–1928. After Marcus Loew died, Mayer discovered that his successor as president, Nicholas Schenck, was secretly negotiating with William Fox, head of the rival Fox theater and film company, to sell a controlling block of Loew's stock to him. Mayer, backed by Thalberg, became incensed and threatened to bolt the company. But the consummation of the deal was prevented by a combination of discouragements—a serious motor accident to Fox in July 1929, the stock market crash in October, and a Justice Department antitrust suit. However, the break between Mayer and Schenck, though plastered over, never healed.

Again trouble flared, beginning in 1933, when Thalberg, taken ill, was compelled to take a long leave. This put extra burdens of supervising production on Mayer. President Franklin D. Roosevelt, whom Mayer hated, inadvertently exacerbated difficulties by his "bank holiday," which froze studio funds. Because payrolls could not be met, friction between studio workers and management—already caused by the Great Depression—was aggravated. Mayer was able to weather it by urging the Academy of Motion Picture Arts and Sciences, which he had helped organize in 1927, to advise its members to accept pay cuts. And his friendship with Hearst was seriously strained by Hearst's unwillingness to support Hoover for the presidential nomination in 1936 and by Mayer's refusal to cast Marion Davies in the much-desired role of *Marie Antoinette*. Davies went to work for Warner Brothers, and Hearst's friendliness went with her.

Later the discord was palliated, and Mayer proved it in 1940 by trying vigorously to buy and suppress Orson Welles's film *Citizen Kane*, allegedly a veiled and unflattering biography of Hearst.

During Thalberg's absence, Mayer got David O. Selznick, who had married his daughter Irene, to produce several high-quality films at MGM. But with Thalberg's return and Selznick's departure to produce independently, Mayer found himself faced with grave problems. His rift with Thalberg, which had been widening over the past few years, became virtually a chasm as Thalberg kept himself apart, taking responsibility for only a few choice films each year. This forced Mayer to find other producers to turn out the thirty to forty films annually demanded by New York. To meet this difficulty Mayer instituted the "producer system" at MGM, delegating responsibility for blocs of pictures to eight or ten top producers, with Mayer in command of all. This system had its problems, mainly that of feuding within the ranks, but Mayer managed to control the situation and deliver an output of generally high-quality films, especially musicals and "family" dramas (for which he had a particularly strong taste) studded with star performers under contract at the studio whom he helped to develop.

In the decade or so following Thalberg's death in 1936, Mayer reached the peak of his productive eminence and power. He ruled the studio with an iron hand (although he said he would prefer to "rule with love"), he was deferred to by his peers in the community, and he was coddled by his Loew's associates in New York. MGM, large and freehanded with top artists, was known as the Tiffany of Hollywood.

Under these circumstances, it was not surprising that Mayer should have become expansive. He was making a great deal of money, averaging over a million dollars a year during the 1930's and 1940's. For several years he was listed by the Treasury Department as "the highest salaried man in the United States." On the advice of his doctors, he developed outside interests. In 1938, he began acquiring a racing stable, which he soon built into the best on the West Coast. He began to socialize more and was frequently seen in public in the company of various female stars and friends. In 1944, he left his wife, who divorced him in 1948. In December of that year he married Lorena Danker, a widow.

By that time, serious trouble had developed at MGM. Its films were not doing the expected business following World War II, in part because of the competition of television, and discontent was evident in the ranks. Schenck, always anxious and impatient, was increasingly critical of Mayer, charging him with neglecting his studio responsibilities. Mayer insisted on beefing up manpower and in 1947 employed Dore Schary, a former MGM writer and head of RKO studio, as vice-president in charge of production. At first, things seemed to go well, but soon Mayer and Schary were quarreling, enmities became intense, and Mayer was finally forced to resign in 1951.

For a few years he resumed his interest in horse racing, which he had been obliged to abandon in 1948, when with the studio's fortunes declining, he was charged by Schenck and the stockholders with spending too much time in that pursuit. He dabbled a bit in real estate. In 1952 he served briefly as chairman of the board of the Cinerama Productions Corporation, a company promoting wide-screen films that he had helped to finance. But his interest flagged. He likewise lost interest in politics after the election of President Dwight D. Eisenhower; the passing of his favorite, Senator Robert Taft; and the discrediting of Senator Joseph R. McCarthy, whom he had publicly endorsed. His final go at the film business came in 1957, when he became intensely involved in masterminding a complex but unsuccessful fight to get control of Loew's. Shortly thereafter Mayer died in Los Angeles.

Egotistical, strong-willed, and aggressive, Mayer was in the forefront of that group of men who, by their business acumen and by their sensitivity to mass-audience tastes, were able to build up the few large producing studios and guide their output during the so-called golden age of American films. Although his weaknesses worked against him when economic pressures set in and forced him out, he remains a legend in Hollywood.

[See Bosley Crowther, *The Lion's Share* (1957) and *Hollywood Rajah: The Life and Times of Louis B. Mayer* (1960); Benjamin B. Hampton, *A History of the Movies* (1931); David O. Selznick, *Memo* (1972); Bob Thomas, *King Cohn* (1967); and Norman Zierold, *The Moguls* (1969). The popular Arts Project of the Oral History Collection of Columbia University has considerable material about Mayer in memoirs by others.]

BOSLEY CROWTHER

MEES, CHARLES EDWARD KENNETH (May 26, 1882–Aug. 15, 1960), photographic scientist and industrial research administrator, was born in Wellingborough, England, the oldest of three children of Reverend Charles Edward Mees, a Wesleyan minister, and Ellen Jordan. A sickly child, Mees developed a keen enthusiasm for chemistry. His enthusiasm continued unabated during his studies at Kingswood School, Bath, and at Harrogate College, Yorkshire. From 1898 to 1900 he attended St. Dunstan's College, Catford, but pursued the study of chemistry independently in his fully equipped home laboratory.

In 1900, Mees received a scholarship to work at University College, London, with the physical chemist Sir William Ramsay. He and a fellow student from St. Dunstan's, Samuel E. Sheppard, jointly pursued research on their common enthusiasm, photography, and received the B.Sc. degree in 1903. They continued their collaborative work under Ramsay, substantially extending Ferdinand Hurter and Vero Charles Driffield's pioneering investigations of sensitometry and the kinetics of photographic development. This major contribution to the theory of the photographic process brought them the D.Sc. degree in 1906 and publication of their work as a book in 1907.

Although as a student Mees had been a follower of the Fabian socialist movement and an advocate of income redistribution plans, he now began to regard the cooperative efforts of science and industry to expand the pool of available resources as the solution to the social problem of poverty. Therefore, when Ramsay persuaded him to seek an industrial position, he joined the pioneer English dry plate firm of Wratten and Wainwright as joint managing director and partner. In 1909 he married Alice Crisp; they had two children.

At Wratten and Wainwright, Mees improved and introduced new products, and published numerous papers reflecting his continued investigations into color photography and the improved resolving power of photographic emulsions. Soon his technical accomplishments won him an international reputation. In 1912, when George Eastman of the Eastman Kodak Company was seeking a research scientist to establish and direct an industrial research laboratory for his Rochester photographic firm, he selected Mees.

Late in 1912, Mees assembled a staff of twenty researchers from England and America. He and Eastman agreed at the outset that nothing of major significance was to be expected from the laboratory for ten years. Possessing a positivist view of science, he emphasized measurement, experi-

ment, and the accumulation of data. Since only two or three academic institutions actively pursued photographic research, Mees saw the new laboratory as an institute for the scientific study of photography. Drawing upon his industrial experience and his limited observations of the pioneer industrial research organizations of William Rintoul of Nobel and William R. Whitney of General Electric, he established the laboratory as one that was "convergent," focusing on problems associated with subject photography. Yet, Mees also fostered an academic atmosphere within the laboratory, with self-directed research and the free flow of information. He employed the conference system of staff communication in order to ensure staff discussion and to lessen the possibility of director-dictated research.

During the first decade of operation, the staff quadrupled in size and expenditures increased sixfold. During that time the staff published nearly two hundred papers in leading scientific and technical journals, and introduced two important bibliographic tools for photography. The number of technical papers published by Mees declined as administrative duties demanded more of his energies, yet his forceful personality and power of expression carried influence. In 1919, Mees created a new development laboratory and became corporate director of research and development; four years later he was named a director of the company. Upon Eastman's retirement as president in 1925, Mees became one of the six officers of the management committee, the principal operating group of the company. In 1934 he was elected vice-president in charge of research and development.

Under Mees's direction the laboratory became not only the international center for photographic research but also the vital key to the continued dominance of the Eastman Kodak Company in worldwide photographic markets. It was central in the introduction of many new products and improvements, and Mees became an international spokesman for industrial research. He wrote the leading book on the theory and administration of industrial research, *The Organization of Industrial Research* (1920; 2nd ed., rev., 1950). He and his associates also compiled the definitive scientific treatise on photography, *The Theory of the Photographic Process* (1942; 4th ed., rev., 1977).

In 1947, Mees retired as director of the laboratory, but continued until 1955 as vice-president in charge of research and development. Although he made very significant contributions to the understanding of the photographic process, publishing about 250 articles and 10 books, his colleagues frequently mentioned his genius as director of the laboratory. His enthusiasm, imagination, and insight inspired and encouraged an unusually productive research staff that numbered nearly 750 when he retired. In 1955 he moved to Hawaii. He died in Honolulu.

[Mees's correspondence, papers, interviews, and Royal Society autobiography are at the George Eastman House, in Rochester, N.Y. Family correspondence is in possession of his grandson, Thomas Mees, and the Office of Corporate Information, Eastman Kodak Company. An autobiographical account and color portrait appear in his *From Dry Plates to Ektachrome Film* (1961). Accounts of his life and work are in *Biographical Memoirs of the Fellows of the Royal Society,* which contains a bibliography of Mees's publications, to which should be added "An Address to the Senior Staff of the Kodak Research Laboratories," 9 Nov. 1955 (1956); *Perspective,* 1961; and Reese V. Jenkins, *Images and Enterprise* (1975).]

REESE V. JENKINS

MENCKEN, HENRY LOUIS (Sept. 12, 1880–Jan. 29, 1956), journalist, editor, critic, and self-taught linguist, was born in Baltimore, Md., the son of August Mencken, co-owner of a cigar factory, and Anna Margaret Abhau. During most of his career he signed himself H. L. Mencken. His youngest brother was the engineer and writer August Mencken. Their paternal grandfather, Burkhardt Mencken, a native of Saxony, transmitted to his children and grandchildren his pride in ancestors famous throughout Europe in the seventeenth and eighteenth centuries as lawyers and university scholars. In *Happy Days 1880–1892* (1940) H. L. Mencken vividly portrayed his family's stable, secure life and the affluent, bourgeois German-American world that formed its cultural setting.

Harry (as Mencken was called) received his formal education at Knapp's Institute, a private school catering to middle-class German-Americans, and the Baltimore Polytechnic, a public high school. At an early age he began to read his father's books, and he soon became a regular user of the Enoch Pratt Free Library. Piano lessons provided the basis for his lifelong devotion to music as an amateur performer as well as a listener. While in high school he wrote verse, essays, and plays, and read widely in British and American literature. His keenness for chemistry anticipated

his later interest in the natural sciences and in medicine. He graduated in 1896 as valedictorian of his class.

Despite his ambition to begin at once as a newspaper reporter, Mencken deferred to his father's wishes and went to work in the family cigar factory. His father died early in 1899, and Mencken remained with the firm only until that July, when he became the youngest reporter on the *Baltimore Morning Herald.*

As Mencken noted in his lively *Newspaper Days, 1899–1906* (1941), veteran editors and reporters served as his advisers and instructors, and the city itself gave him "earfuls and eyefuls of instruction in a hundred giddy arcana, none of them taught in schools." Genial and convivial, with a relish for practical jokes, he fitted easily into the bohemian atmosphere that prevailed among his colleagues. His talent, energy, and promptness earned him rapid promotions and increases in pay. After stints as police reporter in the toughest parts of town and as political reporter at City Hall, he moved through the editorial hierarchy, holding jobs ranging from Sunday editor to city editor. On the *Evening Herald,* which replaced the *Morning Herald* in 1904, Mencken was soon promoted from city editor to managing editor. By 1906, when a financial crisis forced the *Evening Herald* to cease publication, he was editor in chief. After a brief interval as news editor of the *Baltimore Evening News,* he joined the *Baltimore Sun,* an association that was to last, with only an occasional interruption, until 1948.

Mencken's newspaper experience and his wide reading fortified the strong preferences and aversions that originated in his boyhood. He had been sent to Sunday school and confirmed in the Lutheran church, but he shared the skeptical, freethinking attitudes of his father and paternal grandfather. He found a fuller rationale for this homebred agnosticism in Darwinism and contemporary science as interpreted by Herbert Spencer and Thomas Henry Huxley. Mencken's faith in capitalism and its economic virtues, and his predilection for the managerial class, were reinforced by his reading of William Graham Sumner, Spencer's chief American disciple. Among the other attitudes that Mencken absorbed were a sympathetic response to an idealized version of eighteenth-century plantation society and a sense of belonging to a hereditary elite. In many of his early news reports, feature stories, editorials, reviews, and humor columns he either implied or stated his violent reaction, as a German-American, against the puritanism, blue laws, and temperance crusades sponsored by the dominant Anglo-Saxon culture. His love of liberty and his zest for iconoclasm and dissent undoubtedly fulfilled a temperamental need, but they were stimulated by his awareness that a tyrannical majority could exert its power to crush the rights of dissident individuals and minorities.

In the workshop of daily urban journalism, Mencken cultivated, much as Stephen Crane, Frank Norris, and Theodore Dreiser had done before him, the ability to see the life about him and interpret it vividly. Inspired by the *New York Sun* and by writers as diverse as Huxley, William Makepeace Thackeray, Rudyard Kipling, George Bernard Shaw, O. Henry, Mark Twain, Ambrose Bierce, George Ade, and James Huneker, he sought to achieve lucidity combined with a verve and color that expressed his individuality. As early as 1900 he was contributing occasional articles to out-of-town newspapers and verses and short stories to popular magazines. In 1903 his *Ventures Into Verse* was printed locally. Deciding that neither verse nor fiction was his forte, Mencken began to concentrate on essays and drama criticism. In *George Bernard Shaw* (1905) he aspired, on a more modest scale, to do for Shaw what Huxley had done for Darwin and what Shaw had done for Richard Wagner and Henrik Ibsen. By 1908, with his appointment as book reviewer of *Smart Set*, a New York monthly, and the publication of his *Philosophy of Friedrich Nietzsche*, which depicted the German thinker as "a thorough Darwinian," he had regular access to a national audience and had found his métier as "a critic of ideas."

In Baltimore, Mencken had a close circle of friends, some of them fellow members of the Saturday Night Club, which, from 1904 until the late 1940's, met to play classical music and afterward to talk and drink beer. As reviewer, and later as coeditor of *Smart Set* (1914–1923) with George Jean Nathan, the drama critic, he gained a following among intellectuals and writers throughout the country and became acquainted with many of them either personally or through correspondence. Frequent trips abroad, beginning in 1908, enabled him to speak more authoritatively about cultural trends in Europe.

In his reviews and other contributions to *Smart Set*, Mencken helped to keep alive and pass on to a younger generation the spirit of the aesthetic and moral rebellion of the 1890's. In some respects his efforts paralleled those of bohemian critics like James Huneker and Percival Pollard, but he combined their conception of the critic as artist with Huxley's idea of the iconoclastic truth-seeker. He defied the genteel assumption that American letters must be primarily Anglo-Saxon, optimistic, and morally uplifting. He ridiculed literary commercialism, dramatized the view that an essential function of art is to challenge accepted axioms, and conducted a boisterous onslaught against the "snouters" who favored literary censorship. Holding up Twain, Ade, Crane, Norris, and Dreiser as exemplars, he called on American writers to deal realistically or satirically with the life they knew.

World War I provoked Mencken into refurbishing his values and asserting them unequivocally against those of the dominant culture. This process is illustrated most directly in "The Free Lance," his column that appeared in the *Baltimore Evening Sun* from May 1911 to October 1915, but it is also evident in his other writings. He reacted so violently to the spread of pro-English sentiment and the downgrading of German-Americans in the public esteem that he temporarily became a partisan of Germany. While acknowledging that the first loyalty of German-Americans must be to the United States, he insisted that they had as much right as other citizens to voice their opinions. To the notion of Anglo-Saxon hegemony he opposed his own ideal of a national culture and a national literature that would reflect all the racial strains in the country. His *A Book of Prefaces* (1917), with its carefully revised estimates of Joseph Conrad, Dreiser, and Huneker and its trenchant essay "Puritanism as a Literary Force," was a summons to dissent that impressed young critics like Van Wyck Brooks and Randolph Bourne in New York and Burton Rascoe in Chicago. Of several other books Mencken compiled during the war years, the most important were *A Book of Burlesques* (1916), which displayed his talent for parody and deft satire, and the ironically titled *In Defense of Women* (1918).

In March 1917, when Mencken returned from service as war correspondent for the *Sun*, he felt the full force of the heightened anti-German hysteria. He was subjected to much personal harassment, and the *Sun* gave him no further assignments. Once America entered the war, he had to silence his determined opposition to Woodrow Wilson's administration; but, as shown by the enthusiasm with which he did the research for *The American Language* (1919), he continued to be as much attracted to the American scene as he was repelled by it. He also had enough faith in the American people to predict that they would jettison the repressive policies of the "archangel Woodrow" as soon as the conflict was over.

The disillusioned and questioning mood after the war made it possible for Mencken, together with the increasing number of recruits rallying to his cause, to bring this campaign to a successful conclusion. Through articles and reviews in the *Baltimore Sun* and *Evening Sun, Smart Set,* and other newspapers and magazines (including *Atlantic Monthly* and *Nation*), through *The American Language* and the first three series of *Prejudices* (1919–1922, with three more volumes added by 1927), he became a center of national controversy. He was accepted as a mentor by many young intellectuals who experienced revulsion against the war leaders and their aims, disgust with a business civilization, and skepticism about conventional morals and religion. They were uncertain about the future and in search of fresh values, while Mencken, having already undergone his time of testing, was more certain than ever about the essential rightness of his views. He graphically described the discrepancies between the ideals most Americans professed and the violation of individual rights revealed in the suppression of Dreiser's *The "Genius"* and of James Branch Cabell's *Jurgen,* and in the hounding of aliens during the "Red scare" of the 1920's. On topics ranging from prohibition and the Ku Klux Klan through all levels of American education, to Freudianism and sexual morality, he spoke out with vigor and assurance.

As an agent of literary revolt, Mencken was equally effective. *The American Language,* by demonstrating the distinctness of American and British usage, strengthened his efforts to define a native tradition. Its combination of sound scholarship with spirited exposition also enhanced his reputation in academic circles. On *Smart Set* he and Nathan searched aggressively for talent and developed enlightened editorial policies that went far to offset the shaky financing and small budget of the magazine. Through their efforts *Smart Set* became a major vehicle for modern short fiction. They introduced to the American public British authors as different as James Joyce, Aldous Huxley, and Somerset Maugham. They printed stories by many of the writers Mencken was praising in his reviews, including Cabell, Dreiser, Sherwood Anderson, Sinclair Lewis, Ben Hecht, Ruth Suckow, Willa Cather, and F. Scott Fitzgerald. Drama was represented by Eugene O'Neill. In poetry the two editors preferred the older to the newer modes, but they accepted work by Ezra Pound, Elinor Wylie, Sara Teasdale, Louis Untermeyer, and Edgar Lee Masters. Among the provocative essays by Mencken, "The Sahara of the Bozart" (*Prejudices: Second Series*) is worth singling out because the shock treatment it applied to the South helped to incite a revival of southern letters.

By 1923, when many young artists felt that they had absorbed his message and moved beyond him in their literary tastes, Mencken was turning away from literary and toward broadly cultural concerns. *American Mercury,* a monthly edited at first jointly with Nathan and then by Mencken alone, and backed by Alfred A. Knopf, who published Mencken's books, had a literary dimension but was designed chiefly to be a forum for extensive commentary on the gaudy, gorgeous spectacle of American life. First issued in January 1924 and reaching its peak circulation of 77,000 in 1927, the *Mercury,* contributors to which offered a wide spectrum of approaches and opinions, became one of the most striking journalistic phenomena of the decade. The "civilized minority" that it sought to guide, console, and entertain embraced every segment of the middle-class audience from college students to business leaders. With the onset of the Great Depression, the magazine began to falter, mainly because Mencken persisted in an economic conservatism that alienated many readers it had previously attracted. In 1932 he rather gingerly backed Franklin D. Roosevelt for president, but by early 1933 he was denouncing the New Deal's assertion of federal power and its spending programs. Late that year Mencken retired from the *Mercury,* but he still sniped at "Roosevelt Minor" in occasional magazine pieces and in his Monday articles in the *Baltimore Evening Sun.* In the time he could spare from editorial duties he had produced *Treatise on the Gods* (1930), which he followed with *Treatise on Right and Wrong* (1934).

During this period Mencken's private life underwent important changes. He had created a public image of himself as a determined bachelor valuing independence above all else, but in fact he was as loyal a family man as his father had been. He was content with the home over which his mother and sister presided, and found little incentive to marry. His mother's death in December 1925 left him with a feeling of emptiness that helps to account for his courtship of Sara Powell Haardt, a writer. They were married on Aug. 27, 1930. She died in 1935. Mencken, dismayed by the "cruel and idiotic world we live in," then rejoined his brother August at the old family home.

From the late 1930's well into the 1940's, Mencken's national reputation was in partial eclipse. Although his health was beginning to deteriorate, there was no letup in his output as amateur musician and music critic, social and political commentator, and scholar. He dismissed Hitler as an "idiot" and was not guilty of being, as some of his opponents charged, a proto-Nazi and anti-Semite. Yet at a time when Communism had a considerable vogue in the United States, he argued that Americans should be as fully aware of purges in the Soviet Union as of those in the Third Reich. He remained sympathetic to the German people and opposed American entry into World War II until the Japanese bombing of Pearl Harbor made it inevitable.

Many of the sketches later collected in three volumes of autobiography (1940–1943) appeared first in the *New Yorker*. Having already shepherded *The American Language* through two new editions in the 1920's, Mencken completed a fourth edition in 1936 and crowned the work with *Supplement I* (1945) and *Supplement II* (1948). He always rejoiced in having a ringside seat at national political conventions, and in 1948 he represented the *Sun* at the Democratic, Republican, and Progressive gatherings.

Not long after this strenuous tour of duty, Mencken's active career came to an abrupt end. On the evening of Nov. 23, 1948, he suffered a massive stroke. He recovered sufficiently to be physically active, but his memory and speech were partially impaired and he could no longer read or write. He spent the rest of his life in fretful retirement, relieved by August's attentive care, frequent visits from relatives and friends, and occasional outings.

Along with Dreiser, Edgar Lee Masters, Sherwood Anderson, and Sinclair Lewis, Mencken belonged to the older generation of leaders of the revolt of the 1920's. To many his name is synonymous with that decade, yet his tastes and values were shaped by conditions that prevailed before the turn of the century. As early as 1908 he was uprooting the tares and sowing the seed for the cultural flowering that followed World War I. While engaged in this process he earned distinction not only as a stylistically resourceful iconoclast but also as newspaperman, magazine editor, and pioneer student of the American vernacular. At his average as a writer, he was a master journalist who brought considerable knowledge and insight to bear upon a remarkably broad range of topics. At his best he was an artist whose "prejudices" were the themes of his art. A remark he made about Theodore Roosevelt applies with equal force to himself: "Life fascinated him, and he knew how to make his own doings fascinating to others."

Mencken could marshal evidence skillfully, as he did in *The American Language,* but in his social and literary commentary he was not so much concerned with logical proof as with showing "by his blasphemy that this or that idol is defectively convincing—that at least *one* visitor to the shrine is left full of doubts." Typically, while citing some facts he featured a wide variety of nonlogical appeals, shifting from simile and metaphor to vivid caricature, from a feigned ironic detachment to stereotyping and invective, from controlled ridicule to unrestrained vituperation. His style conveys the exhilaration of combat, his delight in "dancing with arms and legs" in defiance of the multitude. His affirmation of the right to dissent and the gusto and artistry with which he expressed it may well be the most enduring part of his legacy to each new generation of readers.

[The Enoch Pratt Free Library, Baltimore, houses the largest single collection of Mencken material, such as typescripts, clippings, and other memorabilia, and much of his personal library. Other major collections are in the New York Public Library, the Princeton University Library, and the University of Pennsylvania Library. Details are given in two compilations by Betty Adler: *A Descriptive List Of H. L. Mencken Collections in the U.S.* (1967) and *Man of Letters: A Census of the Correspondence of H. L. Mencken* (1969). Other books by Mencken include *Men Versus the Man* (1910), with Robert Rives La Monte; *The American Credo* (1920), with George Jean Nathan; *Notes on Democracy* (1926); *Making a President* (1932); *Minority Report* (1956); *Letters of H. L. Mencken* (1961), edited by Guy J. Forgue; and *The New Mencken Letters* (1977), edited by Carl Bode. An abridged edition of *The American Language*, with annotations and new material by Raven I. McDavid, Jr., appeared in 1963. Mencken edited *A Mencken Chrestomathy* (1949), a selection from his out-of-print writings. Anthologies of his writings edited by others are too numerous to list here.

Carl Bode, *Mencken* (1969), and Guy J. Forgue, *H. L. Mencken, l'Homme, l'Oeuvre, l'Influence* (1967; not yet available in English), are comprehensive well-documented biographies. Among other biographical and critical studies are Ernest A. Boyd, *H. L. Mencken* (1925); Isaac Goldberg, *The Man Mencken* (1925); Edgar Kemler, *The Irreverent Mr. Mencken* (1950); William R. Manchester, *Disturber of the Peace* (1951); Marvin K. Singleton, *H. L. Mencken and the American Mercury Adventure* (1962); Carl R. Dolmetsch, *The Smart Set* (1966); William H. Nolte, *H. L. Mencken: Literary Critic* (1966); Sara Mayfield, *The Constant Circle: H. L. Mencken and His Friends* (1968); Douglas C. Stenerson, *H. L. Mencken: Iconoclast From Baltimore* (1971); Fred C. Hobson, Jr., *Serpent in Eden: H. L. Mencken and the South* (1974); and Charles A. Fecher, *Mencken: A Study of His Thought* (1978). Reminiscences by August Mencken and by Alfred A. Knopf in the Columbia University Oral History Collection contain substantial material on Mencken. Further information is available in *H. L. M.: The Mencken Bibliography* (1961) and *H. L. M.: The Mencken Bibliography: A Ten-Year Supplement, 1962–1971* (1971), both compiled by Betty Adler; and current listings in *Menckenianna*, a quarterly journal. Obituaries may be found in the Jan. 30, 1956, issues of the *Baltimore Sun, New York Times*, and other newspapers.]

DOUGLAS C. STENERSON

MERCK, GEORGE WILHELM (Mar. 29, 1894–Nov. 9, 1957), chemical industry executive, was born in New York City, son of George Merck and Friedrike Schenck, a native of Antwerp, Belgium. His father, the son of the senior partner of Merck Chemical Works in Darmstadt, Germany, had come to New York in 1890 to manage the company sales office and warehouse, and when Merck and Company was incorporated in 1908, he became its president. The firm continued importing and also expanded the manufacturing of fine chemicals begun in 1903 at Rahway, N.J.

Merck spent his youth at Llewellyn Park in West Orange, N.J., attended Newark Academy and Morristown School, and received the B.A. from Harvard in 1915, having majored in chemistry. The outbreak of war in Europe thwarted his plans for graduate study in Germany and sent him to the Merck and Company laboratories, where he rotated through a series of jobs. When the United States entered the war, he became plant manager.

The war, cutting off German imports, brought prosperity to American chemical manufacturers. Merck's father, an American citizen since 1902, voluntarily gave 80 percent of the company stock, representing claims on the business by German members of the family, to the alien property custodian. (In 1919 all these shares were bought back by Merck and American financial interests friendly to him.) In 1918, Merck and Company was reorganized, with the father as president and the younger Merck as vice-president.

On Sept. 22, 1917, Merck married Josephine Carey Wall; they had two sons. The marriage ended in divorce, and on Nov. 24, 1926, Merck married Serena Stevens; they had three children. Merck became the president of Merck and Company in 1925. Two years later he merged the firm with a Philadelphia producer of fine chemicals, Powers-Weightman-Rosengarten Company, the expanded corporation being known as Merck and Company. The firm was esteemed for the quality of its pharmaceutical, photographic, reagent, and industrial chemicals. Its products included medicinal alkaloids such as morphine and quinine, for which the Mercks had long been famous in Germany.

Merck engaged in a continuing quest for new products and for increased sales. A pioneering and aggressive champion of the systematization of research, he opened enlarged laboratories in Rahway in 1933 and created a campus atmosphere in order to lure academic scientists who had scorned industrial research as inimical to pure science. The company introduced an interdisciplinary approach to research. Merck offered his scientists "the greatest possible latitude and scope in pursuing their investigations, the utmost freedom to follow leads promising scientific results no matter how unrelated to what one would call practical returns," as well as freedom to publish.

Merck research personnel and university scientists supported by the company made fundamental contributions to the chemotherapeutic revolution that began in the 1930's. Five outside scientists later received Nobel prizes for work done in collaboration with Merck. Several vitamins—B_1, B_2, B_6, pantothenic acid, and B_{12}—were first synthesized by Merck scientists, alone or in collaboration with other scientists, and Merck began large-scale production of virtually all vitamins needed in human nutrition. The company was also an early manufacturer of sulfa drugs, and the first penicillin used to treat an infection in the United States was made by Merck. But the company concentrated on trying to synthesize penicillin, which did not prove commercially practicable, rather than plunging into its production in fermentation plants. The discoverer of streptomycin, Selman Waksman, received support from Merck; at his request the company waived its contractual provision for "sole right" of commercial development, but it did become the leading producer of streptomycin. Merck scientists also had important roles in the discovery of cortisone and other corticosteroids.

In 1933, Merck helped draft the National Recovery Administration code for the basic chemical industry and became a member of the code authority. He served on the National Research Council Committee on Drugs and Medical Supplies (1942–1945) and was appointed by presidents Harry S. Truman (1951) and Dwight D. Eisenhower (1954) to the board of the National Science Foundation. Merck was president (1949–1952) of the Manufacturing Chemists' Association and director of such diverse organizations as the American Cancer Society, the American Foundation for Tropical Medicine, the National Industrial Conference Board, the National Conference of Christians and Jews, and the Save-the-Redwood League.

Merck's major responsibility outside his own company came during World War II. In 1942, President Franklin D. Roosevelt made him director of the War Research Service, a civilian agency charged with all biological warfare research and development. In 1944 this work was put within the Chemical Warfare Service of the War Department. Merck remained as special consultant to the secretary of war and was named chairman of the Biological Warfare Committee. After the war he received the Medal of Merit. His experience caused Merck to warn that biological warfare posed even graver threats to humanity than the atomic bomb.

Competition in the postwar drug industry proved extremely sharp. Hitherto Merck and Company had operated principally as a manufacturing chemist, supplying medicinal drugs to pharmaceutical firms that formulated, compounded, packaged, and resold the ingredients in finished form to physicians and pharmacists. Now the firms were producing drugs that, as single entities, were ready to be prescribed without further processing. Merck decided to abandon the traditional role of the company as ingredient supplier and to enter competition with its long-time customers. To strengthen entry by the firm into the new markets, Merck merged in 1953 with Sharp and Dohme, a long-established company with an excellent reputation among doctors and druggists, and with an experienced force of retail drug salesmen.

Merck was a vigorous, informal man with an easy smile. He possessed a tremendous capacity for work and an unusual ability to inspire his co-workers with the fervor of his own enthusiasm. He resigned the presidency in 1950, having become chairman of the board in 1949. He held the latter post until his death at West Orange, N.J.

[See G. W. Merck, "An Essential Partnership—The Chemical Industry and Medicine," *Industrial and Engineering Chemistry,* July 1935; William Haynes, *American Chemical Industry,* 6 vols. (1945–1954); *Time,* Aug. 18, 1952; Anon., "The Merck Tradition," *Medical Times,* Oct. 1958; and Tom Mahoney, *The Merchants of Life* (1959). Obituaries are in *New York Times,* Nov. 10, 1957; and *Chemical and Engineering News,* Nov. 25, 1957. Material from Merck and Company archives was furnished by Clyde Roche and Roy W. Walker; information was provided by John T. Connor, Albert W. Merck, and Max Tishler.]

JAMES HARVEY YOUNG

MERRILL, CHARLES EDWARD (Oct. 19, 1885–Oct. 6, 1956), stockbroker and investment banker, was born in Green Cove Springs, Fla., son of Charles Morton Merrill and Octavia Wilson. His father was a physician and drugstore proprietor in Green Cove Springs. Merrill attended a preparatory school affiliated with Stetson University and the Worcester Academy in Massachusetts before studying at Amherst College from 1904 to 1906. He played one summer of class-D minor league baseball. He also worked briefly for a newspaper in West Palm Beach. His first permanent job was in the New York City office of a textile firm. He rapidly rose to credit manager and then to assistant to the president. He later joined George Burr and Company, a commercial paper house, where he helped create a bond department and managed it until 1913. That year he left to become sales manager for Eastman, Dillon and Company.

In January 1914 Merrill established his own small investment banking firm. In 1915 he formed a partnership with Edmund Lynch and renamed the firm Merrill Lynch and Company. From 1915 to 1930 the firm was closely associated with underwriting the securities offered by numerous chain stores, including McCrory, Kresge, and J. C. Penney.

During World War I Merrill volunteered and served as a first lieutenant in the army, with the aviation division of the Signal Corps.

In 1926 his firm underwrote a large issue of securities for Safeway Stores, and Merrill became a large stockholder and director of this West Coast grocery chain. After the stock market crash in 1929, his reputation as a sound judge of security values was enhanced significantly when clients recalled his advice a year earlier to curtail their purchases of securities on borrowed funds because, in his opinion, the stock market was overpriced. In 1930 he temporarily retired from active participation in the brokerage and investment banking business. In 1932 Merrill was among the founders of *Family Circle,* the first magazine that depended on distribution through grocery stores.

Merrill returned to Wall Street in the early 1940's, and he was the key figure in the creation through merger of the nation's largest and most successful brokerage firm, known as Merrill Lynch, Pierce, Fenner, and Beane. As a senior partner, he urged the implementation of policies that altered drastically the relationship between the brokerage firm and its customers. He advocated the solicitation of accounts of unsophisticated, middle-class investors. The firm employed low-pressure sales representatives who were skilled in the techniques of public relations and offered customers generally reliable and basically conservative advice. To guarantee that salesmen were at least minimally familiar with investment techniques, Merrill Lynch inaugurated a training program for new employees. One goal was to improve the bad public image of stockbrokers as sleazy operators. Merrill strove to upgrade their status to a more professional level. The sales force was supported by a large number of security analysts whose opinions about stock values were now distributed free of charge to any customer or potential customer requesting information.

Simultaneously, Merrill Lynch launched in 1948 an aggressive advertising campaign, unprecedented in Wall Street history, which explained to the uninitiated investor, often in full-page advertisements, the mechanics of security transactions and discussed the principles of sound investment. Merrill hoped that by demystifying Wall Street operations and by advocating a conservative, nonspeculative investment program, thousands of new investors would be drawn into the stock market, and over the long run they would remain loyal customers of his firm. To encourage wide participation in the market, the firm also fought to maintain low commissions on small transactions. To inspire public confidence, the firm disclosed the extent of its own investment position in the stocks recommended by its security analysts and salesmen—another first.

This broad strategy of seeking out and servicing the typical middle-income investor in a more professional manner was extremely successful in the 1940's and 1950's, and it was instrumental in consolidating the position of Merrill Lynch as the leader in the brokerage field, with over a hundred offices in cities across the nation. By 1954 the firm alone handled around 10 percent of the round-lot transactions on the New York Stock Exchange and almost 18 percent of the odd-lot transactions popular with the small investor. Most important, the revolutionary new policies that the firm instituted were ultimately imitated by virtually every brokerage house on Wall Street, although none developed and maintained quite the same commitment to serving the requirements of the small investor.

Merrill ranks as one of the most important and innovative men in American finance in the twentieth century. In the brokerage field, he has no peer in all of American history.

Merrill was married three times: to Elizabeth Church on Apr. 12, 1912 (divorced in 1925); to Hellen Ingram on Feb. 19, 1925 (divorced in 1938); and to Kinta Des Mares on Mar. 8, 1939 (divorced in 1952). He had two children by his first wife and a son, James, by his second wife.

In his later years Merrill gave substantial sums to educational institutions and various charities, including Amherst College, Stetson University, and Harvard Medical School, where he was treated for heart disease. Merrill died in Southampton, N.Y. At his death his estate was valued at approximately $25 million. Most of the funds went to establish the Merrill Trust, which has made grants for educational, medical, religious, and general charitable purposes. In 1972 it listed assets of $64 million.

[Merrill's papers have never been collected; they are held by various family members and the main New York office of Merrill Lynch. The most reliable source of personal information remains the *New York Times* obituary of October 7, 1956. For an analysis of his role in American finance, see Martin Mayer, *Wall Street: Men and Money* (1955); Edwin Hoyt, *The Supersalesmen* (1962); and Robert Sobel, *The Big Board: A History of the New York Stock Market* (1965) and *Inside Wall Street,* (1977).]

EDWIN J. PERKINS

MERRILL, ELMER DREW (Oct. 15, 1876–Feb. 25, 1956), research taxonomist, administrator, and authority on the flora of the South Pacific and the Far East, was born in East Auburn, Me., the son of Daniel C. Merrill, a farmer, factory worker, and fisherman, and Mary Adelaide Noyes. Merrill was a twin. His parents and immediate ancestors were hardworking people with limited finances.

Merrill attended the village school, and oftentimes helped his maternal grandfather with various farming operations. He attended high school in Auburn, Me., graduating in 1894. At an early age he developed an interest in natural history, identifying local flora and collecting rocks and birds' eggs. He studied at the University of Maine and graduated with a B.S. degree in 1898. He spent the following year as assistant in natural science at the university. He received an M.S. degree in 1904. In 1899–1902 he worked as assistant agrostologist in the U.S. Department of Agriculture; in 1902 he went to the Philippines where he lived for the next twenty-two years. He served as professor of botany at the University of the Philippines and as director of the Bureau of Science in Manila. Merrill established a herbarium in the Philippines that contained more than 300,000 specimens and built up an extensive library. Both were destroyed by fire by the Japanese army one day before the liberation of Manila in 1946. Merrill devoted endless energy and time to his botanical programs, and he and his colleagues sent over 500,000 duplicates to foreign institutions. In 1906 the *Philippine Journal of Science* was established, with Merrill as editor. In May 1907 he married Mary Augusta Sperry in Manila. They had four children.

Merrill's contributions and achievements in the Philippines were many and eminent. The physical plant, the scientific programs, and the number of employees of the Bureau of Science grew considerably under his leadership. In 1912 he published his *Flora of Manila*. His *Enumeration of Philippine Flowering Plants* was published in four volumes (1923–1927). Merrill also published many significant papers on Malaysian botanical literature.

In 1923 Merrill became the dean of the College of Agriculture at the University of California. He founded the botanical journal *Hilgardia* and served as the director of the California Botanical Garden, Los Angeles, from 1926 to 1928. From 1930 to 1935 he was director of the New York Botanic Garden and professor of botany at Columbia University. His success at the gardens was great. During the Great Depression he took advantage of the Works Progress Administration and other government agencies in order to achieve his goals. He also continued his research and established the botanical journal *Brittonia*, serving as editor.

In 1935 Merrill moved to Harvard University as administrator of botanical collections and Arnold professor of botany. At Harvard his major efforts were the development of the great herbarium, plant research, and numerous plant expeditions. During 1935–1946 Merrill published profusely in the fields of economic and historical botany. In 1946 he retired from his administrative post at Harvard but continued as professor of botany, in spite of his failing health, until 1948.

In his postretirement period Merrill's major contribution was *The Botany of Cook's Voyages*, (1954), a study of theories of the origin and dispersal of useful plants. After this work, he went into a rapid physical decline. He died in Forrest Hills, Mass.

In addition to developing great schools, herbaria, libraries, and gardens, Merrill published more than 500 papers and books, two of the most important being the *Bibliography of Eastern Asiastic Botany* (with Dr. E. H. Walker, 1938) and *Index Rafinesquianus* (1949).

Merrill seemed to possess endless energy. He was blunt and frank of speech with a lasting Maine accent. He loved seeking new lands and looking for the unknown in the botanical world. A distinctive feature of Merrill's career was his lack of formal instruction in botany; his total botanical work was two one-semester courses as an undergraduate. However, the true taxonomist such as Merrill must be self-taught. Merrill emphasized to his students that time in the field, the herbarium, and the library was far more valuable than time in the classroom. Oftentimes it has been said that Merrill was satisfied to classify the plants that he dealt with and not go below the surface. Yet this characteristic allowed him to cover so large an area of the plant world as to earn him the epithet "the American Linnaeus." His international outlook in the botanical sciences made him a truly global botanist.

[The main biographical source is William J. Robbins with Lazella Schwarten, "Elmer Drew Merrill," *Biographical Memoirs, National Academy of Sciences,* XXXII (1958). See also Richard A. Howard, "Elmer Drew Merrill 1876–1956," *Journal of the Arnold Arboretum,* July 1956; and Richard Evans Schultes, "Elmer Drew Merrill—An Appreciation," *Taxon,* vol. 6, no. 4 (1957); the *American Philosophical Society Yearbook* (1956); *New York Times,* Feb. 26, 1956; and *Flora Malesiana Bulletin,* vol. 6, ser. 1.]

DANIEL S. KALK

MESSERSMITH, GEORGE STRAUSSER (Oct. 3, 1883–Jan. 29, 1960), diplomat, was born in Fleetwood, Pa., son of Charles A. Messersmith and Sarah S. C. Strausser. Whether through design or carelessness, Messersmith was peculiarly reticent about his background. Of his mother he said nothing at all, either in print or in his voluminous papers. He described his father simply as a "textile executive." Messersmith left no other reference to his parents or antecedents.

There are indications, though, that he may have been born to comfortable circumstances subsequently blighted by economic catastrophe. In the memoirs found among his papers, he wrote of being an "omnivorous" reader who by the age of eleven had "devoured" the works of the great English novelists, as well as countless adventure tales having exotic locales that instilled a desire to see and dwell in far places. He also mentioned being forced to leave school at age seventeen because of the pressing need to make a living. He had already graduated from Keystone State Normal School in Kutztown, Pa., and had done further academic work at Delaware State College, Newark, Del. He settled upon a teaching career, and until 1913 he held a series of teaching and administrative posts in the Delaware school system.

Late in 1913, about to marry and aware of the limitations of a career in secondary education, Messersmith deferred to his longings to see far places by taking, and passing, the Foreign Service examinations. On July 22, 1914, he married Marion Lee Mustard. They had no children.

From the beginning of his diplomatic career Messersmith revealed the flair for administrative work that had advanced him to the position of vice-president of the Delaware State Board of Examiners for Teachers. At his first post in Fort Erie, Canada, Messersmith had time to study the State Department regulations, which he found, out-of-date and a hindrance to efficient work. Thereafter he determined to make administrative reform a central feature of his work. Between 1914 and 1925 he served in consular posts at Fort Erie, Curaçao, and Antwerp. In 1925–1928 he was consul general for Belgium and Luxembourg at Antwerp, and in 1928–1930 consul general in Buenos Aires. He was appointed inspector of all Latin American consular and diplomatic posts in 1929.

In 1930, Messersmith went to Europe, first as consul general in Berlin, then as minister in Vienna from 1934 to 1937. He became an early and ardent opponent of Nazism, claiming in his memoirs that Adolf Hitler "frothed at the mouth" at the mention of his name, but that Hermann Göring had ordered that he not be molested. Messersmith also noted that he spent hours unsuccessfully urging his British diplomatic counterparts to abandon appeasement.

In 1937, Messersmith was transferred home to become assistant secretary of state for administration to reorganize the Department of State, a task that he performed efficiently. One of his chief attainments was to bring under State Department control those commercial and agricultural attachés who had formerly been assigned by, and responsible to, the departments of commerce and agriculture.

Messersmith began his ambassadorial career in 1940, in Cuba, where he proved to be an able executor of traditional Latin American policies, at one point pressing President Fulgencio Batista to pay a $7–$9 million bill to a bankrupt American construction firm that had collapsed as a result of Cuban nonpayment. At President Franklin D. Roosevelt's urging, Messersmith moved on to Mexico in 1942, where, among other assignments, he supervised the flow of strategic materials to the American war economy and worked to regain access to Mexican oil fields for both American and foreign oil companies, excluded since 1938.

Messersmith was no mere agent of American business interests. He honestly believed that the Mexican economy could prosper only if Mexican oil fields were thrown open to all competent exploiters, both American and European. And at one point he and Secretary of State Cordell Hull successfully resisted efforts by California oilman Edward Pauley, who worked, Messersmith claimed, through Secretary of the Interior Harold Ickes to force a flagrantly one-sided contract upon the Mexican government.

In April 1946, Messersmith was sent to Buenos Aires at the request of President Harry S. Truman and Secretary of State James Byrnes. Argentina had been accused of pro-Nazism during World War II, and some State Department officials had attempted to humble that country and exclude it from hemispheric affairs. Now Argentine adherence to an emerging hemispheric defense alliance was deemed vital, and Messersmith was sent to restore amicable relations.

Working closely behind the scenes with President Juan Perón, whom he liked, Messersmith helped to get the Argentine Congress to accept the 1945 Act of Chapultepec. He claimed that the Argentine government also worked diligently to suppress long-standing American suspicions that it was pro-Nazi by passing legislation aimed at German alien property and citizens. But to the antagonistic American press and a "wavering" Truman and Byrnes, the Argentineans did not move far enough, fast enough. Byrnes's successor,

George C. Marshall, seemed further to slight Messersmith's role; and in March 1947, when the ambassador criticized as inaccurate and hostile a State Department position paper on Argentina, he was asked for his resignation. He promptly submitted it, along with his resignation from the Foreign Service in June 1947.

Messersmith was soon elected chairman of the board of the Canadian-owned Mexican Power and Light Co., which was facing nationalization. He had become enamored of Mexico, believed that free enterprise was endangered in the postwar sweep of economic collectivism, and was attracted by the salary. He assumed office in 1947 and ran the company with great success until his retirement in 1955.

Throughout his later years Messersmith wrote at length, if disjointedly, about his Foreign Service career and left a rich collection for scholars. He served in several key Latin American posts at a time when world crises and emerging nationalism in the non-Western world decisively reshaped United States foreign policy. Messersmith's observations and recollections provide useful insights into how American diplomacy reacted, or failed to react, to rising political expectations and new economic demands of our Latin American neighbors at a crucial stage in our relations. A rather brusque, pedantic, hardworking man, who seldom played and had no real hobbies save reading detective stories, he died in Houston, Tex.

[The George S. Messersmith Papers are at the University of Delaware Library, Newark. A collection of his speeches during his diplomatic career was issued in pamphlet form by the U.S. Department of State Library, Washington, D.C., after earlier publication (1937–1939) individually by the government. See *Business Week,* Jan. 13, 1940; *Time,* July 22, 1940; U.S. Department of State, *Foreign Relations of the United States,* vols. on Germany (1930–1933), Austria (1934–1937), Cuba (1940), Mexico (1942–1946), and Argentina (1946–1947); and *New York Times,* Jan. 30, 1960. A number of memoirs in the Oral History Collection of Columbia University contain material on Messersmith, particularly that of Henry A. Wallace.]

LISLE A. ROSE

MEYER, EUGENE ISAAC (Oct. 31, 1875–July 17, 1959), investment banker, government official, and journalist, was born in Los Angeles, Calif., the son of Marc Eugene Meyer, a French Jewish immigrant, and Harriet

Newmark. He grew up in San Francisco and studied for one year (1892–1893) at the University of California. The family then moved to New York, where the elder Meyer had accepted a partnership in the international banking firm of Lazard Frères. After Meyer had earned an A.B. degree from Yale in 1895, and had studied languages and banking in Europe (1896–1897), he was employed as a clerk in his father's firm.

Despite his father's efforts to prepare a place for him at Lazard Frères, Meyer left that firm in 1901 and launched a brokerage business of his own. By shrewd investment of $600 given him by his father for not smoking, plus small earnings of his own, he had accumulated $50,000, with which he bought a seat on the New York Stock Exchange. His first major coup came in the financial panic of 1901. With pandemonium swirling around him, he coolly waited until the selling frenzy had run its course and then bought many stocks that others were dumping. In subsequent panics he repeated that strategy. His tactic of "running against the tide" and his statistical analyses of business ventures earned him a fortune estimated at $40 million to $60 million by the time he was forty. His influence had been strongly felt in the copper-mining and automobile industries, and he was the chief organizer of the Allied Chemical Company.

Meyer married Agnes Elizabeth Ernst on Feb. 12, 1910; they had five children, one of whom, Katharine Meyer Graham, became head of a communications empire including the *Washington Post, Newsweek,* and WTOP-TV.

As a young man Meyer worked out a plan of life designed to make him independent at age fifty, so that he could devote ten years to public service and then retire at sixty. When the United States entered World War I in 1917, he closed his business and became a dollar-a-year man in Washington. He was adviser to the Army on the purchase of shoes, and later to Bernard Baruch's Committee on Raw Materials (later the War Industries Board), where he was in charge of nonferrous metals. He was also a member of the National Commission on War Savings, and Secretary of War Newton Diehl Baker drafted him to investigate the lagging aviation industry.

Meyer's capacity for getting programs into motion led President Woodrow Wilson to name him director of the War Finance Corporation (WFC) in 1918. At the same time he managed a Treasury fund for stabilization of the bond market. After the war Meyer again directed the WFC, then transformed into an agency to aid farmers hit by the postwar depression. In 1927, President Calvin Coolidge named Meyer head of the Federal Farm Loan Board, with the special mission of cleaning up the scandals in that agency.

In 1930, President Herbert Hoover appointed Meyer governor of the Federal Reserve Board, a position he had often dreamed of holding because of his interest in reforming the shaky banking system. But during the Great Depression, with the economy collapsing and banks failing at an alarming rate, he could do little more than struggle through one emergency after another. When the epidemic of bank failures was at its peak, Meyer was a leading advocate of the Reconstruction Finance Corporation, patterned after the WFC, and was made its first director while still head of the Federal Reserve system.

Distaste for President Franklin D. Roosevelt's New Deal caused Meyer to leave public life in 1933. He bought the *Washington Post* at a public auction for $825,000. (In 1929 he had offered $5 million for the paper.) Despite the bargain price it proved to be a costly venture, with losses often exceeding $1 million a year. Meyer later confessed that in his first years as a publisher, he "made every mistake in the book." But he learned fast, and the *Post* eventually became one of the great newspapers of the world.

The idea around which Meyer built his paper was that journalism is a form of public service. He encouraged fair and trustworthy reporting and vigorous editorial comment divorced from politics and ideologies. Favored themes were international cooperation, constitutional government, civil liberties, and economic stability.

In June 1946, President Harry S. Truman asked Meyer to become the first president of the World Bank. He took the job reluctantly, turning over management of his paper to his son-in-law, Philip L. Graham, then assistant publisher. It proved to be an unhappy experience, and Meyer resigned that December, as soon as he had carried out his assignment to set up the bank. Back at the *Post* he became chairman of the board and Graham continued as publisher. The most notable achievements in this period were the purchase by the *Post* of television stations in Washington, D.C. (WTOP) and Jacksonville, Fla. (WJXT-TV), and of the *Washington Times-Herald*, in 1954. The *Post* thereby became the largest newspaper in the capital. Meyer died in Washington, D.C.

[Meyer's personal papers are in the Library of Congress Manuscript Division; with them are Sidney Hyman's uncompleted manuscript "Life of Eugene Meyer" and Dean Albertson's interviews with Meyer. In addition to his own memoir, done in 1938, many others in the Oral History Collection of Columbia University have material on Meyer, notably those of Chester Morrill and Henry A. Wallace. See also Agnes E. Meyer, *Out of These Roots* (1953); and Merlo J. Pusey, *Eugene Meyer* (1974). His obituary is in *Washington Post*, July 18, 1959.]

MERLO J. PUSEY

MILLER, GERRIT SMITH, JR. (Dec. 6, 1869–Feb. 24, 1956), mammalogist and museum administrator, was born in Peterboro, N.Y., the son of Gerrit Smith Miller and Susan Dixwell. The elder Miller was a cattle breeder and is credited with having formed the first organized football team in the United States. The Millers were wealthy, and young Gerrit was educated by tutors and in private schools. Shy and retiring from childhood, he showed less interest in playmates than in seeking animals outdoors, a pursuit that came easily on the family's large estate in central New York. His interest in animals was encouraged by his great-uncle Greene Smith, who, lived on the estate and owned a sizable collection of bird skins housed in a specially constructed building.

Miller entered Harvard in the fall of 1890 and received his B.A. in 1894. Following a brief trip to Europe with his aunt, he was employed in the fall of that year by C. Hart Merriam as a staff member of the Biological Survey in the U.S. Department of Agriculture. While working under Merriam, Miller completed several important monographic studies, one dealing with the taxonomy of American voles and lemmings, the other a revision of the North American *Vespertilionidae* (insectivorous bats). Miller was to return to the subject of bats in many subsequent publications. Merriam considered Miller one of his most competent subordinates but too much of a perfectionist because of his incessant revision of his articles and monographs. Miller for his part found Merriam overzealous as a supervisor and disagreed with some of the older man's assignments of specimens to taxonomic groups. Possessing independent means, Miller resigned in 1898. Shortly thereafter, in seeking more congenial employment, he established a lifelong professional connection. The U.S. National Museum hired him as assistant curator of mammals. In 1909, he became curator, and this post he held until his retirement in 1940.

In 1897, Miller married Elizabeth Eleanor Page, a widow much older than he with three children about his age. Scholarly and ambitious for her husband, she reinforced her husband's tendency to spend his time with his books and in other private pursuits.

Miller's lifelong efforts to categorize North American mammals began with his *Systematic Results of the Study of North American Land Mammals to the Close of the Year 1900* (with James A. G. Rehn, 1901). During the years 1907–1912, Miller produced his three most outstanding works: *The Families and Genera of Bats* (1907), *Catalogue of the Land Mammals of Western Europe (Exclusive of Russia) in the Collection of the British Museum* (1912), and *List of North American Land Mammals in the United States National Museum* (1912). *The Families and Genera of Bats* was the most exhaustive treatment accorded the subject to that time and was considered authoritative for many years; it is still consulted with profit by specialists, though parts of it currently need updating. *The Catalogue of the Mammals of Western Europe* was unquestionably Miller's most outstanding contribution to mammalogy. It was the definitive work on the subject for many years, though now quite out of date. In producing the book, Miller worked with some 12,000 specimens in the collections of the British Museum and U.S. National Museum. The magnitude of the task and Miller's passion for exactness necessitated his spending most of his time on this project from 1905 until 1911. In 1908, he was given a leave of absence from the museum for two and a half years, much of which he spent in Europe. Miller's influence upon the development of European mammalogy was considerable; he was instrumental in persuading colleagues there to make use of American methods of setting traps, preparing study skins, and collecting large series of specimens to determine the range of variation within species or subspecies. His *List of North American Land Mammals* grew in part out of his comparative work on European mammals. The *List* soon became the authority to which mammalogists turned when seeking information on taxonomic nomenclature. The work was twice revised and expanded, in 1923 and 1954, to include all North American mammals, the latter edition being prepared in collaboration with Remington Kellogg.

Miller's wife died in 1920, and in 1921 he married Anne Chapin Gates of New York City, whom he met on a trip to Hawaii. Under her influence he became more outgoing and sociable, but he was rarely able to get others to relax in his company. He habitually maintained his reserve and dignity, and many colleagues thought him cold and impersonal.

Miller's shyness made it virtually impossible for him to mix with the public or speak before groups in public. He was once persuaded against his better judgment to address a scientific group but found that he was unable to deliver his talk and had to be assisted from the meeting hall. With small groups of friends, he could be more relaxed. Miller had a variety of interests outside of mammalogy, including botany, art, paleontology, anthropology, and music. He had studied harmony and composition as a child and was unusually well informed about music. Since the majority of his scientific colleagues did not share his breadth of background and interests, Miller turned elsewhere for much of his intellectual stimulation.

Conversant in a number of European languages, particularly French, Miller translated some foreign mammal studies into English, most notably Herlauf Winge's *A Review of the Interrelationships of the Cetacea* (1921), originally published in Danish.

Miller's 400 publications exemplified his very high standards in mammalogy and ornithology and also in paleontology, botany, anthropology, and music. A many-sided individual whose wealth permitted him to indulge his varied intellectual interests to the fullest, he enjoyed a towering reputation among his scientific colleagues, though little known to the general public. For the last decade or so of his life, Miller was professionally inactive. His death in Washington followed by one month that of his second wife.

[Published material concerning Miller and his career is scanty. The single best source is "Gerrit Smith Miller, Jr.," with contributions by H. H. Shamel and others, in *Journal of Mammalogy,* Aug. 1954. See also *New York Times,* Feb. 26, 1956. Some of Miller's personal and official correspondence, notes, and manuscripts are in the archives of the Smithsonian Institution.]

KEIR B. STERLING

MILLIKIN, EUGENE DONALD (Feb. 12, 1891–July 26, 1958), lawyer, businessman, and politician, was born in Hamilton, Ohio, the son of Samuel Hunter Millikin, a dentist, and Mary Schelly. Millikin moved to Colorado at nineteen, partly for reasons of health, and enrolled at the University of Colorado. He took his law degree in 1913. As a young lawyer, he became active in

Republican politics; he managed the successful gubernatorial campaign of George A. Carlson and served as Carlson's executive secretary from 1915 to 1917. He joined the Colorado National Guard after the United States entered World War I. Sent to officers' training school and commissioned, he saw action in France, attended staff college at Langres, served in the army of occupation, and was mustered out as a lieutenant colonel.

Back in Denver in 1919, he plunged into business and law as a partner of Karl C. Schuyler. He was president of the Kinney-Coastal Oil Company, served as attorney for other oil firms, and became an authority on irrigation, mining, and oil matters. (One Schuyler-Millikin client was Harry M. Blackmer, whose links with the Continental Trading Company came to light in the Teapot Dome investigations.) Millikin managed Schuyler's winning 1932 campaign and acted as his unpaid assistant until Schuyler's sudden death in 1933. On Jan. 30, 1935, Millikin married his partner's widow, Delia Alsena Schuyler.

The death of Alva B. Adams left a Senate vacancy to which Governor Ralph Carr, a college friend, appointed Millikin on Dec. 20, 1941. The choice surprised even Millikin, and none of the newspapers had pictures of him in their files. Elected to the balance of the term in 1942 with 57 percent of the vote, Millikin was reelected in 1944 and 1950.

Although Governor Carr had called Millikin a "progressive Republican," his Senate career proved the contrary. One of the upper chamber's noted conservatives, he worked closely with Robert A. Taft and Arthur H. Vandenberg, the three constituting the triumvirate that dominated Republican Senate affairs from the mid-1940's on. Millikin headed the Republican Conference and, in the Republican-controlled Eightieth and Eighty-third Congresses, the Finance Committee. His power flowed not from seniority but from his talent as a conciliator; as Taft put it, "Gene doesn't make people angry." Democrats also held him in high regard. Observers were awed by the rapport between Millikin and Ed Johnson, his Democratic colleague from Colorado.

Millikin contributed sparingly to debate, but when he did speak, colleagues listened. His bald dome, "the Senate's finest head of skin," sheathed an acute intellect. It was a year and a half before his maiden speech, which eloquently and tersely damned an effort to cut off the salaries of three alleged "Reds" in the executive branch: the effort smelled, he said, "of ancient tombs in which liberty has been buried." He later jousted zestfully with liberal senators Hubert Humphrey and Paul Douglas on tax issues. Douglas called him the Senate's "wiliest debater" and likened him to a crocodile waiting to pounce on unwary orators. His dour mien belied his reputation as a raconteur. (Taft regretted how few of Millikin's ribald tales he could take home to his wife.) Though Millikin first came to national attention by piloting the Mexican Water Treaty through the Senate, he was soon marked as an isolationist. He voted for the United Nations Charter, the Marshall Plan, the North Atlantic Treaty Organization, and military assistance, yet he criticized administration efforts "to diaper every squalling problem all over the face of the earth" and voted against the Bretton Woods agreements, the Rio hemispheric defense pact (his was the sole nay vote), and the British loan. His hostility to the Fair Employment Practices Commission (FEPC), public housing, the full-employment bill, and aid to education and his support for the Taft-Hartley Act illustrated his conservatism in domestic affairs.

On the Interior Committee, Millikin strongly espoused Colorado's interest in irrigation. He was also a member of the Joint Committee on Atomic Energy, but he left his deepest impress on national policy in the area of taxation. A devout protectionist, he disliked the Reciprocal Trade Agreements Act. Yet, persuaded that the world situation made a precipitate change unwise, he helped fashion an accord with the administration in 1947: President Harry S. Truman accepted the principle of "peril points" and the "escape clause"; Congress did not dismantle the trade program and included these protectionist devices in its one-year renewal of the law in 1948. Millikin shepherded one-year extensions of the program through in 1953 and 1954; President Dwight D. Eisenhower won a three-year renewal in 1955. Millikin thus swallowed the principle of liberalized trade but sweetened it with protectionist condiments. "I do not war with history," he said in another context. "I cooperate with the inevitable."

Millikin played a key role in passage (over Truman's veto) of the 1948 tax cut. He also had charge of Eisenhower's 1953–1954 tax program: a short-term extension of the excess-profits tax, cuts in excise rates, and a major revision of the Internal Revenue Code yoked to an income tax reduction. Millikin's zeal for tax cuts was always tempered by his concern for balanced budgets.

In his final term, Millikin's health deteriorated. For years he suffered from painful arthritis; by

1955 it had immobilized even his head and neck and confined him to a wheelchair. In July 1956 he announced that he would not seek reelection. He died in Denver.

[There is no biography of Millikin, and there is only a small collection of papers, mostly speeches and clippings, at the University of Colorado Law Library. See Douglass Cater, " 'Mr. Conservative'—Eugene Millikin of Colorado," *Reporter,* Mar. 17, 1953; Beverly Smith, "The Senate's Big Brain," *Saturday Evening Post,* July 4, 1953; Richard Rovere, "Letter from Washington," *New Yorker,* Dec. 6, 1952. The *Denver Post* and *Rocky Mountain News* (for obituaries July 26 and 27, 1958, respectively) are helpful, as was the *Congressional Quarterly Almanac.* Also see Susan Hartmann, *Truman and the 80th Congress* (1971); Gary W. Reichard, *The Reaffirmation of Republicanism* (1975); R. A. Bauer, I. de Sola Pool, and L. A. Dexter, *American Business and Public Policy* (1964).]

RICHARD M. FRIED

MITROPOULOS, DIMITRI (Mar. 1, 1896–Nov. 2, 1960), conductor, pianist, and composer, was born in Athens, Greece, the son of Jean Mitropoulos, a leather merchant, and Angeliki Anagnostopoulos. He began to study the piano at the age of seven and entered the Athens Conservatory of Music, where he studied piano with Ludwig Wassenhoven and composition with the resident Belgian musician Armand Marsick. He graduated in piano in 1918 and in composition two years later. While still in his teens, Mitropoulos published several songs to Greek and French texts as well as religious works, among them a symphonic poem, *La mise au tombeau du Christ* (1916). He also wrote pieces of native derivation, such as *Fête crétoise* (1919) for piano, based on popular melodies of Crete. On May 20, 1919, his opera *Soeur Béatrice,* based on the play by Maurice Maeterlinck, was produced at the Athens Conservatory with considerable success. Camille Saint-Saëns, who was present at the performance, praised it highly in a review in the French press. On the strength of this accomplishment, Mitropoulos received a government stipend enabling him to go to Brussels, where he became a composition student of Paul Gilson. From 1921 to 1924 he studied composition and piano in Berlin, attending master classes in piano with Ferruccio Busoni.

Mitropoulos' talent for conducting emerged while he was serving as an opera coach at the Berlin Staatsoper, where he was noticed by Erich Kleiber and promoted to assistant conductor.

Mitropoulos then returned to Athens, where he conducted the orchestra of the Athens Conservatory, which later became the Greek State Orchestra. In 1930 he became professor of composition at the conservatory. The turning point of his career as a conductor was his appearance with the Berlin Philharmonic on Feb. 27, 1930, for which the pianist Egon Petri had been engaged as soloist in the Third Piano Concerto of Prokofiev. Petri suddenly became indisposed, and Mitropoulos volunteered to substitute, conducting—entirely by memory—from the keyboard. This extraordinary demonstration of dual prowess created a sensation. When Mitropoulos repeated this performance in Paris in 1932, Prokofiev commented that it was an "acrobatic salto mortale in a three-ring circus," adding that he himself would never have been able to duplicate it.

Mitropoulos impressed audiences and the Paris critics with his interpretations of diverse styles of music and his penetrating sense of subtle nuances of instrumental color. Florent Schmitt, the French composer and critic for *Le temps,* praised Mitropoulos for his inspired command of the orchestra and compared him to a priest officiating at the temple of Apollo at Delphi.

Mitropoulos' success in Berlin and Paris established his reputation as a conductor of the highest distinction. In 1934 he toured Italy, France, Belgium, Poland, and Russia. Invited by Serge Koussevitzky to make his American debut with the Boston Symphony Orchestra, he appeared on Jan. 20, 1936, in a difficult program that included the *Symphonia Domestica* of Richard Strauss. He conducted the entire program from memory and even dispensed with the score at rehearsals, an unexampled achievement. His practice of leading the orchestra without a baton was a procedure previously adopted by only a few conductors. Mitropoulos' gentlemanly regard for his players' sensitivities and his willingness to accept blame for minor contretemps, even when a player was patently at fault, endeared him to the Boston musicians, who rose to their feet to welcome him before the concert.

In 1937 Mitropoulos succeeded Eugene Ormandy as conductor and music director of the Minneapolis Symphony Orchestra. From the outset he showed his determination to promote modern music, including in his programs works by Schoenberg, Berg, Krenek, and then radical American composers such as Roger Sessions. Conflicts developed with the management of the orchestra, which favored programs of traditional music, and Mitropoulos resigned in 1949. He was then engaged as conductor of the New York Philharmonic jointly with Leopold Stokowski, having made his first appearance with the orchestra on Dec. 19, 1940, in a performance hailed by Olin Downes, music critic of the *New York Times*, as "incredibly exciting." In 1950 Mitropoulos became principal conductor and music director of the New York Philharmonic, and in 1955 he toured Europe with the orchestra. In 1958 Leonard Bernstein, who had been engaged two years earlier as associate conductor of the Philharmonic, succeeded Mitropoulos as music director. Mitropoulos had become an American citizen in 1946.

Mitropoulos also conducted notable opera performances, including Alban Berg's *Wozzeck* at La Scala in Milan on June 5, 1952; and in New York City on Dec. 15, 1954, Richard Strauss's *Salome* and the world premiere of Samuel Barber's *Vanessa* on Jan. 15, 1958, both at the Metropolitan Opera House.

Mitropoulos acknowledged his eclectic musical tastes, which embraced the full spectrum of classical, romantic, and modern music. His interpretations of works by Mahler, Bruckner, Debussy, Richard Strauss, and the Second Vienna School were particularly eloquent. He had virtually abandoned composition by 1938, after having produced songs, chamber music, incidental music for Greek tragedies, and minor works for orchestra or piano in a neoclassical style.

Mitropoulos never married. A man of modest habits, he cared little for formal honors and was known for his generosity in donating funds to humanitarian and other causes. During the civil strife in Greece in 1948, he ostentatiously sported a button proclaiming his sympathies with the leftist movement.

Mitropoulos died of heart failure during a rehearsal of Mahler's Third Symphony with the orchestra of La Scala in Milan. After his death the annual Mitropoulos Competition for young conductors was established in New York City.

[*Dimitri Mitropoulos–Katy Katsoyanis: A Correspondence, 1930–1960* (1973), provides a rich personal record in his own voice and includes a list of his compositions. See also David Brooks, *International Gallery of Conductors* (1951); Hope Stoddard, *Symphony Conductors of the U.S.A.* (1957); David Woolridge, *Conductor's World* (1970); David Ewen, *Musicians Since 1900* (1978), which contains an extensive article; and the clipping file on Mitropoulos, Lincoln Center Library of the Performing Arts, New York City.]

NICOLAS SLONIMSKY

MOODY, JOHN (May 2, 1868–Feb. 16, 1958), financial editor and publisher, was born in Jersey City, N.J., the son of Edmund Moody and Sarah Jane Nicholls. Edmund Moody, a clerk in the Adams Express Company, provided his family only a very modest home. John showed an early talent for writing, selling a story to the *Boy's World* for $3 when he was fourteen. He would probably have become a journalist if his father had not lost all of his savings in the stock market. John went to work as a clerk for a New York woodenware wholesaler at $3 a week when he was fifteen, and in 1890 his mother's cousin, George Foster Peabody, got him a job in the highly conservative Wall Street firm of Spencer Trask and Company. Beginning, he says, as a "stamplicker," Moody learned the young art of securities analysis and by 1900 was making a comfortable salary of $3,000 a year. On Apr. 5, 1899, he married Agnes Addison; they had two sons.

"Big business" in the modern sense had barely made its appearance by the 1890's. In 1900 the term still meant railroads, for although a few very large industrial (that is, manufacturing and mining) companies had emerged during the era of the trusts, companies like Standard Oil, American Sugar, and Carnegie Steel were still the exceptions. And while the railroads had been urging their stocks and bonds upon the investing public for over half a century, industrial firms raised their own expansion capital by plowing back their earnings. This was all about to change dramatically.

During the 1890's investment analysts like Moody were handicapped by the fact that reliable data on industrial companies, whose securities did sometimes come up for sale or purchase by his clients, was almost impossible to attain without special investigation. There was the *Manual of Statistics—Stock Exchange Handbook,* which Charles H. Nicoll had been publishing for over twenty years, but it listed no more than 400 industrial companies in all and in many cases provided little more than their addresses and the names of their officers and directors. It hardly touched out-of-town exchanges like Boston, which was second only to New York in importance, and the center of trading in the stocks of textile mills that had been America's first industrial companies. There was nothing in the industrials field to equal Henry Varnum Poor's *Manual of Railroads.*

It was Thomas F. Woodlock, editor of the *Wall Street Journal,* Moody said, who gave him the idea for a manual of industrial securities patterned after Poor's richly successful publication. With $5,000 raised largely through the efforts of a fellow worker, Eliphalet Nott Potter, Moody undertook to compile the first comprehensive manual of industrials. Worried lest the Poors add manufacturing and mining concerns to their already well-known manual of railroads, Moody called on the elder Poor and cautiously inquired about his intentions. Poor replied that he was not interested because those industrial companies would never amount to anything as a source of marketable securities.

Greatly relieved, and promising to stay out of the Poors' railroad province, Moody searched night and day for data on as many companies as he could. His midwestern correspondents disappointed him in his efforts to include such exchanges as St. Louis in his first volume, published in November 1900 as Moody's *Manual of Industrial and Miscellaneous Securities*. But its 1,100 pages and 1,800 entries contained data on several times as many companies as Nicoll's volume and included the Boston, Philadelphia, and Chicago exchanges. The first issue sold out in only three months, for, as Moody said, "We had appeared on the scene when new brokerage and banking houses were forming every day." And the demand soared with each passing year of the three decades of unbroken, unprecedented prosperity that had just begun.

Moody almost lost his business during the panic of 1907. Always something of a speculator, he had put money that was needed in the business into various unsuccessful small enterprises. Somehow, he said, he managed to pay off all his debts and find $100,000 with which to buy back the copyright to his manual. In 1905, the year Henry Varnum Poor died, he added railroad securities to his *Manual,* and by 1913 it was necessary to bring it out in two volumes, later increased to four. During these years Moody established *Moody's Magazine,* added an investors' advisory service, and published several technical treatises. He also wrote *The Truth About the Trusts* (1904), *The Railroad Builders* (1919), and *The Masters of Capital* (1921), of which the last two are titles in the Yale Chronicles of America series. In 1910 Poor's began to publish a manual of industrials of its own, and in 1919 the two companies merged.

Moody, whose program of self-education had been shunted aside by twenty years of unceasing work as a publisher, was now a rich man. Grasping the opportunity to give himself the education he never had, he and his family traveled

extensively in Europe, from which Moody reported frequently on the work of rebuilding war-torn France. An introspective person with a taste for the mystical, his search for religious faith was stimulated by the death of his older son in 1926. In 1931 he was confirmed in the Roman Catholic faith. A charming, energetic man of slight stature of English descent whom many people no doubt took for an Irishman, Moody was a valuable asset to the church, and died one of its most prominent laymen and a holder of the highest lay rank, Knight of the Holy Sepulchre.

Moody's name did not survive in the title of the company that publishes his manuals; a *New York Times* article of Mar. 1, 1941, announcing the merger of Poor's with Standard Statistics Company did not even mention him. But the manuals published by Standard and Poor's continue to bear the name Moody, and it is repeated in large letters on rows and rows of volumes in thousands of libraries. In 1957 Moody moved to La Jolla, Calif., where he died.

[See John Moody, *The Long Road Home* (1933) and *Fast by the Road* (1942); Thomas R. Navin and Marian V. Sears, "The Rise of a Market for Industrial Securities, 1887–1902," *Business History Review,* June 1955; and obituary, *New York Times,* Feb. 17, 1958.]
ALBRO MARTIN

MOORE, HENRY LUDWELL (Nov. 21, 1869–Apr. 28, 1958), economist, was born in Moore's Rest, Charles County, Md., the son of William Henry Moore and Alice Burch. He was educated in Scheib's Zion School and Milton Academy in Baltimore; and in 1889 he entered Randolph-Macon College in Virginia. He graduated with a B.A. degree in 1892. Moore was an excellent student. He began his graduate work at the Johns Hopkins University in 1892 and may have attended a series of lectures on mathematical economics (a field in which he later distinguished himself) offered by the visiting Simon Newcomb. In 1894–1895, Moore attended the University of Vienna, where he took courses in political economy taught by Carl Menger. Returning to Johns Hopkins in 1895, Moore received the Ph.D. degree in 1896 for a dissertation on Johann H. von Thünen's theory of the natural wage. At Johns Hopkins, Moore studied under John Bates Clark when the latter visited the university, and Clark became a good friend. Moore served as instructor at Johns Hopkins from 1896 to 1897. On June 16,

1897, he married Jane Armstrong Shafer of Richmond, Va.; they apparently had no children. In the same year he took the position of professor of economy at Smith College, although he continued to lecture at Johns Hopkins until 1898. Moore was brought to Columbia University in 1902 largely through the efforts of Edwin R. A. Seligman and served as adjunct professor of political economy from 1902 to 1906 and professor of political economy until his retirement in 1929.

Moore's primary contribution to economics lay in his work on the statistical estimation of economic relationships. The mathematical formulation of economic theory had been drawing increased attention since the publication of the work of León Walras in the 1870's. The statistical description of economic activity had a much longer history. Moore combined these two approaches and became a founder of the modern field of econometrics, which employs the tools of economic theory, mathematics, and statistical inference in the analysis of economic phenomena and the testing of theoretical hypotheses. He called this study statistical economics.

Beginning about 1901, Moore contrived for himself a course of study that included the examination of mathematical works by J. L. Lagrange, A. A. Cournot, Leonhard Euler, and others. In 1909 and 1913 he took courses in mathematical statistics and correlation with Karl Pearson at the University of London. By 1911, when he published *Laws of Wages: An Essay in Statistical Economics*, Moore had come to believe that it was possible to create an empirical complement to "pure" or theoretical economics because of advances in mathematical economics, statistical analysis, and the collection of economic data. In that book he tested some aspects of J. B. Clark's specific productivity theory using the new correlation analysis to determine the demand curve for labor from statistical data. Despite its somewhat crude economic theorizing, *Laws of Wages* was generally well received by the profession.

Moore's *Economic Cycles: Their Law and Cause* (1914) was less well received. It argued that economic cycles were caused by movements in the yield per acre of crops, which were in their turn caused by changing weather represented by cyclical changes in rainfall. The technical analysis was rather advanced for that time, but critics were less interested in this than in what they correctly discerned to be errors in some parts of its economic reasoning.

Forecasting the Yield and Price of Cotton (1917) was Moore's most successful book, partly, one supposes, because it clearly demonstrated the potential of the estimation and forecasting techniques he pioneered, without exhibiting much of the theoretical weaknesses of his other works. It described the elaborate system of informed observers used by the Department of Agriculture to estimate crop yields and its general inaccuracy. By relating crop yields to rainfall and temperatures in earlier months by the use of correlation analysis, Moore was much more successful in forecasting cotton crop yields. His work pointed the way for numerous statistical price-analysis studies.

Between 1919 and 1923, Moore did additional work on economic cycles, culminating in his *Generating Economic Cycles* (1932). But his contemporaries remained skeptical. His work on cycles per se had little or no impact upon modern economics. The last of his books (he also published over twenty articles) was *Synthetic Economics* (1929), in which he made the most complete formal statement of his approach and attempted the statistical derivation of both supply and demand functions.

Although not well understood when it was published, Moore's work had an impact upon agricultural economists, including Henry A. Wallace, because of its obvious relevance to agricultural prices and policy. Moore's most able student, Henry Schultz, helped to expand the work on statistical demand analysis. However, Moore's reputation as an economist was surprisingly limited in view of the seminal nature of his work. One reason for this was certainly the advanced level of his writing. Mathematical economics was still unfamiliar to most economists when Moore was attempting to give it an empirical dimension.

Another reason for Moore's lack of a wider reputation had to do with his personality. A modest and very private man, he wanted recognition but was extremely sensitive to criticism and completely unable to press his ideas aggressively upon the economics profession. He avoided intimacy with his colleagues as well as more formal requests for appointments to discuss his work, and he rejected invitations to give guest lectures or to attend professional meetings. His primary teaching areas were mathematical and statistical economics, but he disliked teaching undergraduates and even agreed to a reduction in his salary at Columbia between 1909 and 1918 for a corresponding reduction in his teaching duties.

Moore was plagued by poor health much of his life. In 1898, upon the advice of his physician, he requested and received a reduction in his teaching duties at Smith. His retirement from Columbia in 1929 came at his request after he had suffered a nervous collapse. From that time, he lived in virtual seclusion in Cornwall, N.Y., where he died.

[The Henry Ludwell Moore Papers are held by the Library of Columbia University. The best study of Moore's life and work is George J. Stigler, "Henry L. Moore and Statistical Economics," in *Essays in the History of Economics* (1965), which also contains a Moore bibliography and a list of reviews of his work by others. Joseph A. Schumpeter, *History of Economic Analysis* (1954), and Joseph Dorfman, *The Economic Mind in American Civilization*, vols. III and IV (1949), contain useful mateial.]

SIMEON J. CROWTHER

MOORE, JOSEPH EARLE (July 9, 1892–Dec. 6, 1957), physician and medical educator, was born in Philadelphia, the only child of Joseph Howard Moore, an executive with Spirella, a corset-manufacturing company, and Adelaide Marie Lovett.

When Moore was eight years old, his parents separated and his mother took him to Kansas City, Mo., where he attended public schools. In 1909 he entered the University of Kansas and received the B.A. degree in February 1914 after completing three years' work in the arts and sciences and two years in medicine. Following a summer session at the University of Chicago, he transferred to the Johns Hopkins Medical School in 1914 and graduated in 1916. The following year he became a resident house officer in medicine at the Johns Hopkins Hospital, and then, with the United States engaged in World War I, he entered the army as a first lieutenant.

On May 24, 1917, before sailing for France, he married Grace Douglas Barclay of Baltimore, a graduate of the School of Nursing of the Johns Hopkins Hospital. Moore served in France initially as a battalion medical officer attached to the British Expeditionary Forces and later joined the American Expeditionary Forces, attaining the rank of captain. During this service he was assigned to venereal disease control activities, which were under the general direction of Colonel Hugh H. Young, on leave from Johns Hopkins; and upon returning to Baltimore, he became associated with the syphilis division of the Johns Hopkins Medical School and Hospital.

The syphilis clinic at Johns Hopkins, the first of its kind in the country, had been established several years earlier for the purpose of centralizing the study and treatment of patients with this disease. Moore brought a new dynamism to the clinic, and under the joint leadership of himself on the clinical side and Alan M. Chesney on the experimental, it became perhaps the foremost center in the world for the study of syphilis. Moore became sole director of the clinic in 1929 and remained so until his death. He and his associates undertook many detailed and exhaustive studies to determine the most effective treatment for syphilis in its various stages and its effects on the nervous system. Moore was basically an internist and approached clinical syphilology from that perspective. His first major work, entitled *The Modern Treatment of Syphilis* (1933), became an authoritative text. When the effectiveness of penicillin against syphilis was demonstrated in 1943 and later established as the treatment of choice, Moore published *Penicillin in Syphilis* (1946), based on experience gained during World War II, which again became a standard work in its field. He served as consultant to the U.S. Public Health Service and the U.S. Army and was chairman of the venereal disease subcommittee of the National Research Council. He was awarded the Medal of Merit for his services during World War II. For several years after the war he served as chairman of the Syphilis Study Section of the National Institutes of Health, a group responsible for recommending grants for research in that field.

When the number of new syphilis cases declined with the widespread use of penicillin, Moore persuaded the Johns Hopkins authorities to convert the syphilis clinic to the study of other chronic diseases and initiated a series of painstaking investigations similar to those so successfully used in the syphilis studies.

Moore's main contributions to biomedical knowledge were his demonstration of the value of regular and long-term treatment of syphilis with established drugs, elucidation of the evolution of certain forms of neurosyphilis, and recognition of the occurrence of false positive serologic tests for syphilis in certain other chronic diseases. But his contributions to medicine and society greatly exceeded these accomplishments. He was an effective supporter of Thomas Parran in his move to bring the problem of syphilis out of the shadows. Moore communicated his zeal and enthusiasm for the discovery of better methods for the prevention and treatment of syphilis to many students and young physicians. He designed a graduate course on the study of syphilis that attracted physicians from North and South America and the United Kingdom. Many of these physicians later became leaders in the venereal disease control programs of their states and countries. One of his major accomplishments was the demonstration at Johns Hopkins of the feasibility of using an outpatient clinic as an effective clinical research facility.

Moore established the *American Journal of Syphilis*, which eventually became the *Journal of Chronic Diseases*, of which he was coeditor. He was a fluent speaker, an exceptionally effective committee chairman, and an excellent teacher, whose bibliography contains over 150 titles. In addition to maintaining a successful private practice throughout his career, Moore held senior academic appointments at both the Johns Hopkins School of Medicine and the School of Hygiene and Public Health. The outpatient clinic for research in chronic diseases at the Johns Hopkins Hospital is named in his honor.

His first wife died in 1954 leaving no children, and on Dec. 23 of that year he married Irene Mason Gieske of Baltimore. Moore died in Baltimore.

[See Moore's "Venereal Diseases," in E. C. Andrus et al., eds., *Advances in Military Medicine*, I (1948). On Moore's work, see Thomas H. Sternberg, Ernest B. Howard, Leonard A. Dewey, and Paul Padget, "Venereal Diseases," in Ebbe C. Hoff, ed., *Preventive Medicine in World War II*, V (1960); and Thomas B. Turner, *Heritage of Excellence: The Johns Hopkins Medical Institutions, 1914–1947* (1974).]

THOMAS B. TURNER

MOORE, (AUSTIN) MERRILL (Sept. 11, 1903–Sept. 20, 1957), poet and psychiatrist, was born in Columbia, Tenn., the son of John Trotwood Moore, a novelist and historian, and Mary Brown Daniel, who was also a writer and succeeded her husband after his death as Tennessee state librarian. In 1907 the family moved to Nashville, where Moore prepared for college at Montgomery Bell Academy. He went on to Vanderbilt University and earned the B.A. in 1924. While still in high school Moore had begun to write poems, and later, at Vanderbilt, he associated with Allen Tate, Donald Davidson, John Crowe Ransom, and other teachers and students seriously interested in poetry. He became the youngest member of the "Fugitives," a cohesive and influential literary group in Nashville, and

helped edit their poetry magazine, *The Fugitive*. He also contributed his own compositions, sonnets written at first under the pen name "Dendric." These poems lacked polish, but his lighthearted casualness of manner was a relief from the solemnity of much *Fugitive* verse. Nineteen numbers of the magazine were published (1922–1925) before it was discontinued.

Moore's father wanted him to work on a country newspaper, but Moore, while continuing to write poetry, decided on medicine as a career. In 1921 he entered Vanderbilt Medical School. Enormously energetic and industrious, Moore was considered brilliant but erratic and absentminded by his friends and colleagues. In 1928 he received the M.D. and began a one-year internship at St. Thomas Hospital in Nashville. In the tradition of Oliver Wendell Holmes, S. Weir Mitchell, and William Carlos Williams, Moore was to couple a medical career, spanning nearly three decades, with a productive literary life. "I am most interested in human personality and its problems," Moore wrote, "and it is on that common interest in my own life that medicine and poetry meet."

From 1929, when he moved to Boston, until 1935 he served at Boston City Hospital, Boston Psychopathic Hospital, and Massachusetts General Hospital.

On Aug. 14, 1930, Moore married Ann Leslie Nichol of Nashville, Tenn. They had four children. He began psychoanalytic training with William Herman in 1931 and associated with a group of leading neurologists and psychiatrists that included Tracy Jackson Putnam, Frederic Lyman Wells, Harry C. Solomon, and Stanley Cobb. From 1934 to 1938 he trained under Hanns Sachs, an early associate of Freud. In the 1930's and 1940's Moore taught neurology, neuropathology, and psychiatry at Harvard Medical School and was clinical associate in psychiatry there after 1950. He set up a private practice in Boston in 1935 and became an authority on the psychiatric aspects of alcoholism and suicide. He contributed more than 150 articles to medical journals.

In the period 1938–1940 Moore assisted Jewish physicians fleeing Nazi Germany. In World War II he was a major in the U.S. Army, serving as a psychiatrist in New Zealand and the South Pacific. Sent to China in 1946 with the rank of lieutenant colonel, he was responsible for the operation of medical services in the Nanking area and received high official commendations. After returning to civilian life, he resumed private practice in Boston and some of his previous teaching duties. In 1949 he described his work to Ralph Thompson of the *New York Times*: "Here in Boston I practice private medicine from one to six every afternoon, teach psychiatry at Harvard Medical School and work in the free clinics in the morning. That leaves only evenings off for writing."

Moore continued to turn out sonnets, often four or five each day. His energy and creativity amazed his medical colleagues, fellow poets, and literary critics; some of whom, like Yvor Winters, thought he wrote too much and too carelessly. "Mr. Moore's poems are obviously unrevised," Winters wrote. "The meters are a kind of rhymed and butchered prose, and the diction is for the most part very, very approximate, to speak as charitably as possible." The less austere Louis Untermeyer said, "Everything is here in rich disorganization, a genre picture, a case-history, a dream landscape, a seasoned philosophy, a story in journalese, a miniature drama, or the play of free association. . . . Many of the sonnets could be improved by a closer scrutiny of the material; many more are spoiled by flat phrases and feeble conclusions. But every other sonnet is, at least, printable; one of every ten is novel and arresting; and one out of twenty is distinguished by its power and depth."

Moore used only one form, the sonnet, but he used it freely. There are numerous meters and rhyme schemes in his poems, most of which have fourteen lines. He had a sharp gift of characterization. Some of his sonnets are poignant and penetrating, and others warm, witty, and whimsical. From his first book, *The Noise That Time Makes* (1929), Moore held to the views of his art expressed in the foreword to *Illegitimate Sonnets* (1950): "I like to experiment (or tamper if you prefer) with the sonnet form: I treat it roughly or kindly, as I please. . . . The sonnet has taken root in my subconscious mind so deeply that now when I am working on one I know when I have reached the end without consciously stopping to count the lines. . . . Like a dog playing with a bone, sometimes I gnaw the form, sometimes I merely sharpen my teeth on it; but I hope never to bury it."

Moore's longest work is *M: One Thousand Autobiographical Sonnets* (1938). His other volumes tend to be much shorter, ranging from the twenty-two pages of *Poems From 'The Fugitive'* (1936) and the thirty-nine pages of *Verse Diary of a Psychiatrist* (1954) to the seventy-two pages of *Clinical Sonnets* (1949). His steady production of poems ultimately filled thirty steel cabinets in a

building that Moore called a "sonnetorium" in the backyard of his residence in Quincy, Mass. He is said to have written more than 50,000 sonnets; more than 2,000 were published.

Moore described his writing as a "compulsive addiction" and as his own "occupational therapy." He made light of his literary work, particularly in the later years. "To tell you the truth, I am not a literary man," he told Harvey Breit of the *New York Times*. However, Moore's claim to lasting recognition probably rests more securely on his contribution to American literature than on his work in medicine, important as the latter was.

Moore somehow found time for hobbies. He was a spirited talker, an accomplished amateur conchologist, a photographer, and a strong long-distance swimmer who for several years competed in the marathon swim to the Boston Light. "I have never been very active in politics," he once said, "but I am what is generally called a Democrat." Moore died in Quincy, Mass.

[Moore's papers, comprising more than 130,000 items, are in the Library of Congress. Additional materials are in the Joint University Libraries, Nashville, Tenn. The principal bibliographical and critical source is Henry W. Wells, *Poet and Psychiatrist: Merrill Moore* (1955), which appraises 200 sonnets. See also Roy P. Basler, "Proteus as Apollo: The Poetry of Merrill Moore," *Literary Review*, Winter 1957–1958; Harvey Breit, "Talk With Merrill Moore," *New York Times Book Review*, July 15, 1951; Louise Cowan, *The Fugitive Group* (1959); Richard Eberhart, "Warmth and Ease and Charm and Aptitude," *Poetry*, June 1939; Edwin Honig, "Psychiatrist as Poet," *Poetry*, Apr. 1952; Fred B. Millett, *Contemporary American Authors* (1940); Merrill Moore, *The Fugitive* (1939); Ralph Thompson, "In and Out of Books," *New York Times Book Review*, Jan. 23, 1949; and Louis Untermeyer, "Merrill Moore: A Comment on His 'American' Sonnet," *Sewanee Review*, Jan.–Mar. 1935.]

WILLIAM McCANN

MORGAN, JULIA (Jan. 26, 1872–Feb. 2, 1957), architect, was born the daughter of Charles Bill Morgan and Eliza Woodward in San Francisco. The family was moderately well-to-do and esteemed the work ethic and education. Never married, she maintained close family ties throughout her life. Independent and determined, Morgan was one of the first women to enroll in the School of Engineering of the University of California at Berkeley. Her interest in architecture was stimulated by her apprenticeship in the atelier of Bernard Maybeck during her studies, and after receiving the B.S. in engineering in 1894, she went to Paris. After persistent effort she gained entrance to the École des Beaux Arts, the first woman to do so. Segregated from view by a physical screen, she studied in the atelier Chaussemiche. After receiving the *diplôme* in 1900, she remained in Paris briefly, reportedly working for a French architect, during which time she apparently designed a ballroom addition at Fontainebleau. Returning to the San Francisco Bay area in 1902, she became one of the earliest architects, and probably the first woman, to be licensed by examination in California; and in 1921 she became one of the first women admitted to the American Institute of Architects, testimony to her successful practice.

Upon her return from Paris, Morgan joined the office of John Galen Howard, then the newly appointed architect for the University of California campus at Berkeley. She contributed significantly to the design and construction of the university's Greek Theatre and the Hearst Memorial Mining Building. Already acquainted with Phoebe Apperson Hearst, mother of publisher William Randolph Hearst, from her Paris sojourn, Morgan's participation in the Howard firm led to closer ties with the Hearst family. Mrs. Hearst's ardent support of Mills College, Oakland, led to Morgan's involvement in its building program for more than a decade (the Mills College Bell Tower, 1904; the library, 1905; the gymnasium, 1911; the recreation building, 1916; dormitories, 1922; and the Ming Quong Home, 1925–1926) and subsequently her involvement in, and commitment to, architectural projects associated with the early development of American women's movements, such as the Young Women's Christian Association (YWCA).

She opened her own office in 1905, but from 1907 to 1909 she was in partnership with Ira W. Hoover. Several residences can be traced to the joint practice, but their quality is overshadowed by the more significant work from her own office, which she reestablished in 1910. Although she worked in association with Bernard Maybeck on Principia College in Elsah, Ill. (1932–1935), and the Hearst Gymnasium for Women at Berkeley (about 1935), she maintained an independent practice throughout most of her long career.

The YWCA's concern for the plight of young women in the early decades of the century's rapid urbanization generated an active program of housing and social services, and the Oakland YWCA (1913) was the first in a series of commissions for Morgan that continued for more than two decades, stretching from San Diego to San Francisco, from Honolulu to Salt Lake City. The temporary YWCA building at Berkeley also marked an innovative approach to building facilities in a period when architecture was synonymous with monumentality. Asilomar, the National Conference Meeting Ground for the YWCA, was established in 1913 at Pacific Grove, Calif.; and Morgan interpreted the YWCA's desire for a place of inspiration and intellectual expression through her choice of a rustic mode, the use of native materials, open design, and a camp setting in harmony with the environment. The many endowed buildings at Asilomar reflected an innovative, conservation-oriented approach.

In keeping with her personal and social philosophy, Morgan designed a number of women's residence halls and community clubhouses, which included not only the better-known Berkeley Women's City Club but the Emanu-El Residence Club and the Potrero Hill Neighborhood House in San Francisco, the Saratoga Foothill Club, the Sausalito Women's Club, and the Margaret Baylor Inn in Santa Barbara. Her practice extended to hospitals and nursing homes, including the San Francisco Ladies Protective and Relief Society Home, the Oakland Kings Daughters Home, the Rideout Memorial Hospital in Marysville, and the Marion Davies Foundation Hospital in West Los Angeles. Further evidence of the social content in her diverse practice is the educational structures she designed, of which the Katherine Delmar Burke School in San Francisco and the Lakeview Primary School in Oakland are only two. Her church commissions, reflecting a nonsectarian faith, spanned her entire career. Beginning with one of her most distinguished works, the St. John's Presbyterian Church in Berkeley (1907–1916), churches for Methodist, Baptist, Presbyterian, and interdenominational congregations were included in her repertoire of realized work. Among her largest commissions were the Berkeley Baptist Seminary and the Christian Science Principia College. Although her involvement with commercial design was relatively minor, early in her career she restored the structural integrity of, and went on to complete the construction of, the Fairmont Hotel following the San Francisco earthquake and fire of 1906.

The network of social ties begun in her college days led to a vast number of residential commissions, ranging from the modest Newhall Garage-Apartment in San Francisco to the sumptuous estate La Cuesta Encantada at San Simeon. The most notable examples in terms of design quality are the Berkeley house of her sister Emma North (1909) and Red Gate for Charles B. Wells in Oakland (1910). Her association with the Hearst family started with work on the Hacienda del Pozo de Verona at Pleasanton, continued with the Hacienda at Jolon, Wyntoon on the McCloud River, and the Hearst Ranch at Chihuahua, Mexico, and culminated in the vast twenty-year building program at San Simeon, now a California state monument.

Morgan's work has often been characterized as eclectic. Gothic, English Tudor, and Renaissance motifs are evident in many of the designs for her more affluent clients, such as the Chapel of the Chimes and the Williams Residence in Oakland and the Berkeley Women's City Club. The building program imposed by William Randolph Hearst's need to house a massive collection of European treasures and by his desire to provide a fantasy setting in which to receive celebrities and friends in the fields of politics and entertainment at the San Simeon and Wyntoon estates perpetuated the eclectic reputation perforce. But concurrent with, yet overshadowed by, the more flamboyant, much-publicized work ran a continuous stream of contributions to the pioneering architecture of the California school, most clearly revealed in St. John's Presbyterian Church, Saratoga Foothill Club, Asilomar, and the Joy houses in Berkeley. Attention to human scale, integrity with the landscape, clarity of detail, and the use of indigenous materials imbue these lesser-known works with a quality of warmth and a sense of fit. One of Morgan's remarkable gifts was her ability to cater simultaneously to the largesse of unlimited funds and the restrictions of a minimal budget imposed by her various clients. This ability to produce outstanding architecture with limited funds was a key factor in augmenting her reputation by word of mouth. She shunned publicity and was rarely published; when she closed her office in 1949, she destroyed most of the documents in it. Her life was her architecture and, credited with more than 700 projects, she remains the most prolific woman architect of the United States.

[Material on Morgan is in the Archives of the College of Environmental Design, University of California, Berkeley; and the Baldwin Memorial Archive of American Architects. See Walter L. Steilberg, "Some Examples of the Work of Julia Morgan," *Architect and Engineer of California*, 55 (1918), and "Examples of Women's Contributions to Architecture and Interior Decoration," *Christian Science Monitor*, Nov. 27, 1931; E. K. Thompson, "Early Domestic Architecture of the San Francisco Bay Region," *Journal of the Society of Architectural Historians*, Oct. 1951; "The Asilomar Story," *Monterey Peninsula Herald*, June 29 and July 2, 1956; Oscar Lewis, *Fabulous San Simeon* (1958); and W. A. Swanberg, *Citizen Hearst* (1961). Other sources include *American Architect*, Sept. 1934; *Architect*, 13 (1917); *Architect and Engineer*: Oct. 1907, Apr. 1908, Nov. 1909, Feb. 1910, Nov. 1918, Nov. 1919, Mar. 1921, and Apr. 1931; *Berkeley California Yearbook, 1930*; *Building Review*: Apr. 1919, Aug. 1922, and Dec. 1922; *Bulletin of the Berkeley Baptist Divinity School*, Feb. 1921; *California Arts and Architecture*, June 1931; *Fortune*, Oct. 1935; *Home and Grounds*, Feb. 1917; *New York Times Magazine*, July 21, 1929; and *Saturday Evening Post*, Mar. 2, 1940. Obituaries are in the *San Francisco Chronicle*, *San Francisco Examiner*, *Oakland Tribune*, and *Berkeley Daily Gazette*, Feb. 3, 1957.]

LABELLE PRUSSIN
PATRICIA VAUGHN ANGELL

MORLEY, CHRISTOPHER DARLINGTON (May 5, 1890–Mar. 28, 1957), writer and editor, was born in Haverford, Pa., the son of Frank Morley and Lilian Bird, both of English birth. Frank Morley, a distinguished English mathematician, had been invited to teach at Haverford College in 1887. Lilian Morley, a musician and poet, had worked at the English publishing house of Chapman and Hall, where she knew many of the most famous late Victorian writers. Taught to read by his mother, Christopher wrote his first story, "The Story of a Woodcutter," at the age of seven or eight.

In 1900 the family moved to Baltimore, where Frank Morley became professor of mathematics at the Johns Hopkins University. Christopher attended the Marston and Jefferson schools in Baltimore and spent much time in the Enoch Pratt Library. In 1906 he returned to Haverford College as an undergraduate. There he was elected to Phi Beta Kappa. Many of his pieces for the *Haverfordian* were later published in *Hostages to Fortune* (1925).

After graduating in 1910, he was awarded a Rhodes scholarship. At New College, Oxford, Morley read history for three years and published *The Eighth Sin* (1912), a collection of verse dedicated to Helen Booth Fairchild, an American whom he had met in England and married on June 3, 1914. They had four children.

In 1913 Morley returned to the United States

and embarked almost immediately upon the extremely varied career as a man of letters that occupied the rest of his life. At first he worked for Doubleday, Page and Company, where he became close friends with Frank Nelson Doubleday. The company remained his publisher for many years. In 1917 he became an editor of the *Ladies' Home Journal* and then a columnist for the *Philadelphia Evening Public Ledger.* In Philadelphia he published *Shandygaff* (1918), the first of his thirteen collections of essays; *Songs for a Little House* (1917), a collection of verse; the novel *Parnassus on Wheels* (1917); *The Haunted Bookshop* (1919), another novel; and five other volumes, culminating in *Travels in Philadelphia* (1920), which describes his wanderings about the city just before his return to New York.

This prodigious literary production foreshadowed what was to come, particularly during the following two decades, as Morley's passion for books, whether of his own creation or the work of others, combined with his tremendous energy and enthusiasm to make a positive and indelible impression upon the literature and the publishing business of his time. During his life he published eighteen volumes of fiction, sixteen of poetry, and thirteen of essays. Upon his move to New York in 1920, when he began his residency in Roslyn Heights, Long Island, he wrote and edited "The Bowling Green," a column in the *New York Evening Post,* until 1923; between 1924 and 1941 he served as a contributing editor of the *Saturday Review of Literature,* continuing "The Bowling Green" in that periodical until 1938 and writing the "Trade Winds" column until 1939. In 1926 he became a judge of the new Book-of-the-Month Club.

Morley's columns provided much of the substance of his volumes of essays and the foundation of his literary reputation. By 1927 he had reached the point in his career when Doubleday felt confident enough to publish the twelve-volume Haverford Collected Edition of his works. His enthusiasms multiplied: he promoted the works of little-known authors, among them William McFee, Joseph Conrad, Elinor Wylie, Sherwood Anderson, and dozens of others; he discovered Sir Arthur Conan Doyle and became a Sherlock Holmes fan, founding the Baker Street Irregulars in 1934; he ventured into play production in 1928 and again in 1940; and he lectured widely across the country and beyond. By 1931, when he published his fictionalized autobiography, *John Mistletoe,* he was perhaps the most widely known professional man of letters in the United States.

In 1939 Morley published his best-selling novel *Kitty Foyle,* which later achieved even greater popular acceptance as a film. Unfortunately the book's popularity and some of the sensational incidents in it and reactions to it have tended to obscure its merits, to the detriment of Morley's literary reputation. The novel was a significant literary and social document of the 1930's.

Between 1934 and 1937 Morley edited the eleventh edition of *Bartlett's Familiar Quotations* (1937); and during the years following the publication of *Thorofare* (1942) and his last novel, *The Man Who Made Friends With Himself* (1949), he edited the revised twelfth edition, which appeared in 1948. In both, Morley made substantial additions drawn from the literary accomplishments of his contemporaries.

In 1951 Morley suffered a massive stroke, the first of three which largely incapacitated him during the last six years of his life. Nevertheless, he continued his activities on a reduced scale, traveling, continuing as a judge for the Book-of-the-Month Club until 1954, and writing occasional essays for the *Saturday Review.* He died in Roslyn Heights. In a typical Morley gesture, a postmortem message to his friends appeared in the *New York Times* and the *New York Herald Tribune* on April 1, wishing them well and sending his love.

Morley's literary reputation has suffered since his death. His colleagues at the Book-of-the-Month Club published two posthumous volumes of his essays for the club news and his letters to members of the staff. A collection of his prefaces was published in 1970, and the Christopher Morley Knothole Association meets regularly. But he has received little critical attention. Although he published widely in every literary medium and occupied a central, influential role in the literary world of his time, he was not a major writer because, as he remarked, only part of his energy and interests "escaped into print" and his concern was less with his own creative work than with the world of literature. Nevertheless, he wrote well and his occasional experiments in writing remain interesting. His works are still readable, but his lifelong concern with literary promotion largely died with him. Unfortunately, the enthusiasm he brought to literary concerns is impossible to assess today, and his shortcomings as a literary artist preclude a serious reassessment of his place in American literary history.

[Important collections of Morley's papers are held by the University of Texas Library and the Haverford College Library. On his life and work, see Mark I. Wallach and Jon Bracker, *Christopher Morley* (1976), and Helen McK. Oakley, *Three Hours For Lunch* (1976). Morley is mentioned in several memoirs by others in the Oral History Collection of Columbia University.]

DAVID D. ANDERSON

MULFORD, CLARENCE EDWARD (Feb. 3, 1883–May 10, 1956), writer, was born in Streator, Ill., the son of Clarence C. Mulford and Minnie Grace Kline. He was educated at the public schools of Streator and at Utica, N.Y., following the family's move there. After graduating from high school, Mulford was given the choice of going to work or to college; he chose working on the *Municipal Journal and Engineer* in New York City. Then, in 1899, he became a clerk in the marriage license bureau at Borough Hall in Brooklyn.

At the age of eighteen Mulford sold his first story, "John Barrett," to *Metropolitan* magazine. It was a combination Western-detective story that shared first prize in a contest. Mulford had up to then never visited the West, but it was a region that fascinated him. Later he would state, "I have an extensive library of Western Americana, and have thrown away three times as many books as I retained. My card file of Western data, more than 17,000 cards, covers every activity of the West (except mining)."

Little did Mulford realize that he was creating a classic Western character when he published a series of connected stories about a ranch, the Bar 20, in Caspar Whitney's *Outing Magazine;* in 1907 the stories were collected in the book *Bar 20*. They centered on a rancher named William Cassidy, a Texan who drank whiskey, swore, gambled, engaged in gunplay in the manner of Wild Bill Hickok and John Wesley Hardin, and (in one book) was married. After Cassidy was wounded in the leg in a gunfight, he acquired the nickname "Hopalong." The book proved so popular that the character was continued in many others: *The Orphan* (1908), *Hopalong Cassidy* (1910), *Bar 20 Days* (1911), *The Coming of Cassidy* (1913), *The Man From Bar 20* (1918), *The Bar 20 Three* (1921), *Hopalong Cassidy Returns* (1924), *The Bar 20 Rides Again* (1926), *Hopalong Cassidy Takes Cards* (1937), and many more. The Cassidy series numbered twenty-eight books, but, in total, Mulford would write more than a hundred Western novels and short stories. He finally visited the region in 1920, but he never lived there and made only a few other

visits. Yet his hardcover books sold more than 1.5 million copies and were translated into German, Spanish, and Polish.

In 1934 Paramount Pictures decided to make a series of films with Cassidy as a hero. William Boyd was to be the villain, but he persuaded the producers to cast him as the hero instead. The films were most successful: sixty-six Hopalong Cassidy films were made. Mulford was appalled when he saw the result, calling the Cassidy in the movie "an absolutely ludicrous character." In these films Hopalong was a pasteboard character; he dispensed justice with a smoking six-gun, did not drink, and rarely did more than smile at women or help one in distress. Mulford saw only six of the movies. Later he sold the rights to the character to William Boyd.

With the royalties he earned from his writings, Mulford in 1926 moved to Fryeburg, Me., with his wife, Eva E. Wilkinson, whom he had married on Jan. 5, 1920. At Fryeburg, Mulford purchased fifty-five acres of land. On this estate, in addition to writing, he indulged his hobbies of building models of steamboats, stagecoaches, covered wagons, flatboats, and other modes of transportation, and of big-caliber revolver shooting. At one point he had the Colt firearms company specially make for him a pair of steel revolvers so strong as to allow chamber pressure that made marksmanship practical at 300 to 500 yards.

After World War II, Hopalong Cassidy became a great favorite not only in movies but also in the new medium of television, thereby earning Mulford hundreds of thousands of dollars in royalties. A stay-at-home person with modest spending habits, he used the money to establish the Clarence E. Mulford Trust Fund, a charitable and educational foundation intended to benefit worthy persons in the area around Fryeburg. About this same time he grew so angry over high income taxes that he quit writing altogether. In 1954 he gave his manuscripts, books, and card files to the Library of Congress, which valued the materials at $20,000 for tax purposes. Mulford stated bitterly, "If I'd sold the stuff, it would have cost me money. Give it away, and I make money."

Mulford was not a great writer and had little public recognition; Hopalong Cassidy always was far better known than his creator. However, he was extremely pleased that the Institute Littéraire et Artistique de France awarded him a laurette certificate, with gold medal, for his book *The Round-Up* (1933). Despite this recognition, his writings have not endured. They captured a market at a time when the public yearned to believe in a fictional West of superheroes. Mulford died at Fryeburg.

[The Mulford Collection is in the Library of Congress. See obituary in *Publishers Weekly*, May 21, 1956.]

ODIE B. FAULK

MUNRO, WILLIAM BENNETT (Jan. 5, 1875–Sept. 4, 1957), educator, was born in Almonte, Ontario, Canada, the son of John Mac-Nab Munro, a customs collector, and Sarah Bennett. He earned a B.A. in 1895, an M.A. in 1896, and an LL.B. in 1898 at Queens College, Kingston. He then attended Harvard University, where he was awarded another M.A. in 1899 and a Ph.D. in 1900. He completed his studies at the universities of Edinburgh and Berlin.

From 1901 to 1904 Munro was instructor of history and political science at Williams College. In 1904 he moved to the department of government at Harvard, where he rose from instructor to assistant professor, to professor of municipal government (1912) and Jonathan Trumbull professor of American history (1925). Munro left Harvard in 1929 to become Edward S. Harkness professor of history at the California Institute of Technology (CIT), where he remained until his retirement in 1945. Munro married Caroline Sanford Gorton on Feb. 19, 1913; they had one son.

Munro published *The Government of European Cities* in 1909. It was followed by volumes of political science and history the titles of which reflect Munro's catholic interests: *The Initiative, Referendum, and Recall* (1911), *The Government of American Cities* (1912), *Leading Cases on the Constitution of the United States* (ed.; 1913), *The Seigneurs of Old Canada* (1914), *Principles and Methods of Municipal Administration* (1916), *Crusaders of New France* (1918), *The Government of the United States, National, State, and Local* (1919), *Social Civics* (with C. E. Ozanne; 1922), *Municipal Government and Administration* (1923), *Personality in Politics* (1924), *Current Problems in Citizenship* (1924), *The Governments of Europe* (1926), *The Invisible Government* (1927), *American Influences on Canadian Government* (1929), *Makers of the Unwritten Constitution* (1929), *The Constitution of the United States* (1930), and *Municipal Administration*

(1934). Many of these books went through several editions and were used as texts by two generations of students, both in the United States and abroad. Munro also edited documents on the seignorial system in Canada, bibliographies on municipal government, and selections from *The Federalist*. In addition, he was a prolific lecturer and essayist.

Munro's writings were readable, direct, and dispassionate in tone. Their provocative and stimulating theses were praised by critics. Only his early books on municipal government and administration made substantial original contributions to scholarship, but these were pioneering works in "applied political science." They accelerated the study of this field at a time when most political scientists restricted their attention to classical concepts of government.

Munro's writing was marked by his attention to the functions of government as much as to its history and structure. Throughout could be seen his faith in democracy and his optimism about the ability of government to adapt to the demands of modern developments. Even Munro's scholarly books and college texts were written with the general reader in mind. He was recognized as a master at popularizing the topic of government.

Munro's eclectic academic pursuits did not absorb all of his energy. Between 1907 and 1921 he wrote editorials for the *Boston Herald*, and in 1917–1918 he chaired the Commission of Information and Data for the Massachusetts Constitutional Convention. He also served on many governmental commissions at the city level, especially during his Harvard years. During World War I, Munro, commissioned as a major in the U.S. Army, was attached to the training and instruction branch of the general staff. He was a charter member of the American Association of University Professors, a member of its earliest governing bodies, and its president from 1929 to 1931. He also served as president of the American Political Science Association in 1927. Munro was a fellow of the American Academy of Arts and Sciences, a trustee of the Henry E. Huntington Library and Art Gallery, and a member of the Harvard University Board of Overseers from 1940 to 1946. Following his retirement from CIT, he served as its treasurer and, later, as a member of its board of trustees. He died in Pasadena, Calif.

Since many of Munro's books and articles on municipal government appeared at a time when reformers were engaged in campaigns to purify urban politics and to introduce a higher degree of professionalism into city government, these writings, which argued the same causes from a scholarly perspective, served to inspire as well as to instruct those who were involved in these campaigns. Early in his career he became keenly interested in the National Municipal League, and he served it for many years as an officer and as a member of several of its key committees, including the one that wrote and repeatedly revised the league's model municipal charter.

Thousands of students heard Munro in his very popular courses; many more Americans, and others, were exposed to his advocacy of good government through his writings; still others were inspired by his unselfish service to his profession and community. Munro was a living example of the good citizen, whom he himself idealized in his teaching and writing.

[There is a small collection of Munro's papers in the Harvard University Archives. There are no significant writings about Munro, but obituaries can be found in the *New York Times*, Sept. 5, 1957; the *National Municipal Review*, Oct. 6, 1957; and the *American Political Science Review*, Dec. 1957. A likeness of Munro may be found in *Scientific Monthly*, Jan. 1932.]
DONN NEAL

MURRAY, WILLIAM HENRY DAVID (Nov. 21, 1869–Oct. 15, 1956), lawyer, congressman, and governor of Oklahoma, was born in a one-room, undressed pine house at Toadsuck on the north-central Texas frontier, the son of Uriah Dow Thomas Murray, who moved to Texas from Tennessee in 1852, and Bertha Elizabeth Jones, who died after childbirth in 1871. William and two older brothers lived with grandparents until their father married a widow, Mollie Green. Frequent childbearing and a not very successful husband possibly increased the stepmother's irritability, and the boys came to resent her. When William was twelve, the boys left home to make their own way. After picking cotton, cutting wood, and making brick, William found kindness and work with Ed Loper, a farmer, who taught him to "pay your debts, treat your neighbors right, tell the truth, vote the Democratic ticket, and drink your whiskey straight."

In brief periods of schooling Murray learned from *McGuffey's Readers* and a *Bluebook Speller* and practiced oratory and debate. After 1884 he attended various sessions of a kind of rural high school, College Hill Institute in Springtown,

Tex. Between terms he and brothers Henry and John sold books, mainly to farmers. After the Lopers moved to Buffalo, Tex., Murray rejoined them, and at nineteen he entered politics as a member of the Farmers' Alliance. He was an able speaker against high interest rates, high railroad rates, and low farm prices. He had served as a correspondent for the *Fort Worth Gazette* and in 1889 he began teaching at Millsap in western Parker County.

As a delegate to the state Democratic Convention in San Antonio in 1890 Murray became acquainted with the reform nominee for governor, James S. Hogg. Murray campaigned for Hogg then and again in 1892; and he benefited from lessons learned in the campaigns when he opposed a third party's spokesman, Harry Tracy, and the subtreasury plan. Murray spoke often of Hogg's example as an inspiration to him. He observed that large city newspapers tended to oppose the reform programs, and he became a reporter for the *Farmer's World* in July 1891. As secretary of two Farmers' Alliance meetings—the pro-Hogg meeting in July 1891 and the anti-subtreasury meeting in St. Louis—he observed the Farmers' Alliance division over Populism. In 1892 Murray was defeated in a race against George Jester, later lieutenant-governor, for a state senate seat but received strong support from farmers. An appointee of Governor Hogg, Murray was a delegate to the Pan-American Bi-Metallic Congress in October 1893.

While publishing the *Daily Corsicana News* and a farmers' weekly, the *Navarro County News,* in 1894, Murray read law with Judge John Rice. That year he lost a second try for a state senate seat to O. B. Colquitt, a rival Corsicana editor, later governor. Publishing revenues declined when Murray's support for William Jennings Bryan in 1896 caused gold Democrats to cut newspaper advertising. Admitted to the bar in 1897, he sold both papers and moved to Fort Worth to practice law. Disappointed at slow progress, Murray visited his father, who was living in Indian Territory, and in March 1898 settled in Tishomingo, the capital of the Chickasaws. At this point in his life many of Murray's principles were already fixed. An independent Democrat, he opposed Populist and Socialist third parties; but he declared some Populist ideas "right," and he championed the family farm and endeavored "to find 'truth' irrespective of its popularity."

In 1898 Douglas H. Johnston was the National party candidate for governor of the Chickasaws, favoring the opening of Chickasaw lands to individual ownership. Murray became secretary for the party, and Johnston's victory assured considerable legal work. As legal adviser to Johnston he drafted the new tax structure that required whites to help pay the tribal debt. On July 19, 1899, Murray married the governor's niece, Mary Alice Hearrell, a teacher, who was one-sixteenth Chickasaw; they had five children.

Murray was described as gaunt, being five feet, ten inches tall and weighing about 140 pounds. He had long arms and fingers, a lean face with steel-blue eyes and a handlebar mustache (the "walrus" came later). He accumulated extensive lands, experimented with diversified farming, and his success with alfalfa earned for him the nickname "Alfalfa Bill."

Possibly Murray's most important services to Oklahoma were related to his work on redrafting the Sequoyah constitution of 1905 and to his presidency of the constitutional convention. The results "reflected the most advanced social and political thinking of . . . the Progressive era."

As speaker in the first state legislature he urged a good school system, highway planning, and a strong judiciary. He failed to obtain the South Carolina dispensary plan for selling liquor but got a bank guaranty law, created a number of agriculture colleges, and passed the nine-foot-bedsheet-in-hotels law. He opposed Kate Barnard's child labor bill, saying the minimum working age of sixteen was too restrictive. At the Denver Democratic Convention in 1908 Murray supported Bryan. In 1910 he sought the governorship, but Ardmore banker Lee Cruce received the nomination. Two years later Murray supported Woodrow Wilson and won a seat in Congress.

Murray found the Washington atmosphere unfriendly. He told his wife it was "the hardest place to get anything done." He failed to add a bank guaranty clause to the Glass-Owen bill, and Glass opposed his rural-credits plan. Murray opposed Wilson on the Panama tolls issue and urged early intervention in Mexico, being concerned over Japanese influence there. In the summer of 1915 he earned over $4,000 as a popular Chautauqua orator, expounding "the Philosophy of the Plow." But he supported Wilson's preparedness program and lost his temper at the Oklahoma Democratic Convention in April 1917 when he was hissed for supporting Wilson's foreign policy. He was not returned to Congress in the 1916 election.

Giving up a race for governor in 1918, Murray and his sons farmed 1,100 bottom acres; high wartime prices enabled him to pay off old debts. Postwar developments alerted him to the declining role of American agriculture, and he feared that democracy would perish. After visiting several countries in South America, he obtained permission to create an agriculture colony in Bolivia's Chaco, settling with about seventy-five adults and children near an old mission at Aguagrande in 1924. Failure of the colony was caused by a lack of good water, homesickness, insects, and drought, while an impending war with Paraguay caused Indian workers to be drafted and mules commandeered. By August 1929 the Murrays were back home.

Oil had brought new wealth to Oklahoma. The Republican party had gained strength, and Democratic rural papers and oil man Roy Johnson of Ardmore urged Murray to seek the governorship in 1930. When the owner-editor of two Oklahoma City papers tried to picture Murray as hostile to industry and small business, Alfalfa Bill labeled them "the Twin Harlots of Fourth and Broadway" and spread his message in the *Blue Valley Farmer*. He was elected by 93,346 votes. As the Great Depression worsened, he urged tax relief to farmers and home owners, seeds for tenant farmers, reduced appropriations for the state university, consolidation of some state agencies, better collection of corporate and resources taxes, and an expanded highway program. When oil prices fell, Murray called a meeting of oil-producing states at Fort Worth in March 1931. In August he sent the National Guard to the oil fields to enforce production limitations; ultimately, an interstate oil compact was evolved. Failing to get the legislature to enact his program, he sought action by popular vote on initiated bills for a new income tax, free textbooks, amendments to escheat corporation lands if not sold in ten years, and a budget officer measure. These failed to pass in late 1931. Meanwhile, Murray found emergency relief for many unemployed.

In 1932 Murray campaigned in several states seeking the Democratic nomination for president. At the nominating convention, besides Oklahoma delegation votes, Murray received one vote from North Dakota, cast by his brother George. His attacks on Franklin D. Roosevelt were "cruel and vicious," including an unfortunate reference to Roosevelt's affliction.

After Roosevelt's election Murray was a New Deal critic. He did not run for governor in 1934 and his candidate was defeated by Congressman Ernest Marland, whose slogan was "Bring the New Deal to Oklahoma." Murray's governorship was "a partial success." He accomplished major tax reforms and equalized the tax burden. Corporations and individuals with higher incomes were compelled to pay more taxes, while farmers and home owners were relieved of heavy state property taxes. The Oklahoma Tax Commission and equalization boards proved to be lasting accomplishments. While higher education suffered, his supporters told of higher oil prices, free bridges, payroll warrants valued at par, and aid to the unemployed.

Support for Republican Alfred Landon in the 1936 presidential campaign cost Murray dearly in 1938 when he sought the office of governor on an economy platform. Opponents got President Roosevelt to speak at the Oklahoma City fairgrounds, where he called for more liberal officials and declared Murray "a Republican." Murray lost to Leon Phillips, 179,000 to 148,000 votes, declaring Roosevelt's charge cost him about 60,000 votes. More serious for his future happiness was the death of his wife in 1938.

He continued to speak out against Roosevelt and the New Deal and wrote many articles and books, which supplemented a declining farm income. His stamina obviously weakened, he joined the Democrats for Wendell Willkie in 1940 and tried unsuccessfully to be elected to Congress. He then joined Charles Lindbergh in opposing American entry into World War II. At seventy-three he had several operations on his eyes and wrote his three-volume *Memoirs*. He could not admit that defeats often reflected his own inadequacies. Riding a bus to Birmingham in July 1948, tattered and half-blind, he addressed the Dixiecrat convention, declaring that America's greatness was due to "Christian principles and the white man's brains." A lonely old man who had been progressive in racial matters became by the 1950's an embittered racist. He felt thwarted in his efforts to maintain "constitutional" government and a dominant agrarian society.

In January 1951 Alfalfa Bill administered the oath of governor to his son Johnston. While living with his oldest son, Massena, Murray suffered a stroke. He died in Oklahoma City.

[The National Archives has considerable material on the Bolivian adventure, and the University of Oklahoma Library has a substantial Murray collection. His *Memoirs of Governor Murray and True History of Oklahoma*, 3 vols. (1945), gives insights into lives of opponents and friends but should be used with caution. Keith L. Bryant, Jr., *Alfalfa Bill Murray* (1968), is an excellent, objective biography; and Gordon Hines,

Alfalfa Bill (1932), is a lively campaign biography for 1932. See also Edward E. Dale and Morris Wardell, *History of Oklahoma* (1948); and Ruth Overbeck Perez, "The Red River Bridges" (M.A. thesis, University of Texas, 1969).]

ROBERT C. COTNER

NATHAN, GEORGE JEAN (Feb. 14, 1882–Apr. 8, 1958), critic, editor, and author, was born in Fort Wayne, Ind., the son of Charles Naret Nathan, a lawyer, and Ella Nirdlinger. His father reputedly owned vineyards in France and a coffee plantation in Brazil, and had commercial interests in the United States. When Nathan was four, his family moved to Cleveland, Ohio, where he attended public schools and was tutored in languages and music. During high school he spent his summers with his father in Europe. After graduating from Cleveland High School, he entered Cornell University, from which he received the B.A. in 1904, distinguishing himself less in his studies than in dramatics, student publications, fencing, and tennis.

Nathan developed a passion for the theater at an early age, through the influence of a maternal uncle who was an impresario in Cleveland and Philadelphia. Another uncle, Charles Frederic Nirdlinger, who had adapted foreign plays for Broadway and had served as critic for several New York newspapers, helped Nathan obtain a job as a reporter for the *New York Herald* in 1905. In 1906, Nathan was hired to review the New York theater for two national magazines, *Bohemian* and *Outing*. These were the first of twenty such contracts with magazines and newspapers, the most important of which were with *Smart Set* (1908–1923), the *American Mercury* (1924–1930; 1940–1951), *Judge* (1922–1935), and the Hearst chain, including the *New York Journal-American* and King Features national syndicate (1943–1956). In 1915 he began reprinting (sometimes annually) his reviews and miscellaneous writings on the theater in books. These eventually ran to thirty-five titles. Thus, between his numerous journalistic contributions and these collections Nathan was probably the most widely published drama critic during the first half of the twentieth century.

Wide readership was only one measure of Nathan's importance to the development of the American theater. He was something of a theatrical celebrity himself—"The Dean of Broadway," whose opinions were courted and feared, and whose personal life, especially his alleged affairs with actresses, made good copy for gossip columnists. Nathan enjoyed such publicity, assiduously cultivating the image of an aloof, snobbish arch-cynic and an elegant bon vivant—the bane of playwrights, producers, and actors. In 1908 he rented a three-room flat in the Royalton Hotel, in the heart of the New York theater district. Thereafter he rarely left the metropolitan area, except for summer trips to review the European theaters. "The country," he said, referring to the United States west of the Hudson, "is where they grow cherries for use in Manhattan cocktails."

Yet Nathan was also a hardworking craftsman, striving to improve the theater according to his lights. "There are two kinds of dramatic critics: destructive and constructive. I am destructive," he boasted. At the outset he had much to destroy. American dramatic criticism was dominated by the pecksniffery of the octogenarian William Winter and the gentlemanly academicism of Brander Matthews. Broadway was enthralled by tawdry melodramas, at worst, or by such "realists" as David Belasco and Charles Klein, at best. Taking his cue from such European-influenced critics as James G. Huneker and Percival Pollard, Nathan adopted a Wildean pose of superaestheticism and a breezy style. He scorned the prudery, pedantry, and phony stagecraft he found on Broadway. Nathan smoothed the path for such important American playwrights as Eugene O'Neill, William Saroyan, and Tennessee Williams. He also promoted a number of modern European dramatists; he was on intimate terms with such salient figures as Edward Gordon Craig, Adolphe Appia, and Max Reinhardt, and he helped introduce their ideas into American theatrical productions. In 1934 he helped to found the New York Drama Critics' Circle, which offered prestigious annual awards, and from 1937 to 1939 he served as its president. He left half of his estate to establish an annual prize for outstanding contributions to American dramatic criticism.

In August 1914, Nathan and his colleague H. L. Mencken became coeditors of the monthly *Smart Set*, which they made into the liveliest, most iconoclastic, and arguably most important American literary periodical of its day. "The Magazine of Cleverness" was the vehicle of their critical opinions and bon mots. They lashed out at "Puritanism" (official and unofficial censorship and prohibition), provincialism, and democratic mediocrity. *Smart Set* also welcomed a genera-

tion of American writers struggling for recognition—including Ezra Pound, F. Scott Fitzgerald, Eugene O'Neill, and Sherwood Anderson—and an array of important British and Continental writers previously unpublished in the United States—including James Joyce, D. H. Lawrence, and Franz Wedekind. In 1923, Nathan and Mencken abandoned *Smart Set*. With the publisher Alfred A. Knopf they founded the *American Mercury*, a monthly that institutionalized in a more staid format the ideas they had developed in *Smart Set*. In 1925, Nathan resigned as coeditor over questions of policy, although he remained a contributing editor of the *Mercury* until 1930. In November 1932, with Ernest Boyd, James Branch Cabell, Theodore Dreiser, and Eugene O'Neill, Nathan founded the *American Spectator*, a monthly "literary newspaper." During the next three years Nathan, the managing editor, published essays of the highest quality by established writers. The Great Depression, though, was an inauspicious time for a venture that was, as one commentator remarked, "the last gasp of The Twenties." The group was forced to sell the *Spectator* in December 1935.

Nathan and Mencken frequently contributed fiction to *Smart Set* under fanciful pseudonyms ("Owen Hatteras" was their favorite). But Nathan's major effort in this genre—a roman à clef of the New York theater entitled *Monks Are Monks* (1929)—was both a critical and a popular failure. More successful were his plays, *The Eternal Mystery* (1913), *Heliogabalus* (with Mencken, 1920), and *The Avon Flows* (1937).

On June 19, 1955, while on a Caribbean cruise, the aging critic—a "professional bachelor" whose *The Bachelor Life* (1941) is a paean to misogyny—married Julie Haydon, an actress. In October 1957, Nathan, who, like Mencken, scoffed at "religious nonsense," and whose parents had been part Jewish, announced his conversion to Roman Catholicism. He died in New York City.

Because of his almost exclusive preoccupation with the theater, Nathan's reputation faded rapidly after his death. His vast legacy of reviews and his ruminations on critical theory are of little interest. But Nathan's pungent style is still entertaining, and his work reflects the attitudes and values of his time, an important era of American cultural history.

[The bulk of Nathan's papers are in the Cornell University Library, but there are also important letters in the Mencken collections of the New York Public

Library and the Enoch Pratt Free Library, in Baltimore. Aside from works mentioned in the text, Nathan's principal publications include *Europe After 8:15* (1914), with H. L. Mencken and Willard H. Wright; *Another Book on the Theater* (1916); *Mr. George Jean Nathan Presents* (1917); *The American Credo* (1920), with H. L. Mencken; *The Autobiography of an Attitude* (1925); *The Theater of the Moment* (1936); *The Morning After the First Night* (1938); and *The Theater Book of the Year* (annually, 1943–1951). There is no full-length biography of Nathan, although one is now in preparation by his widow and Thomas Quinn Curtiss. Nathan himself provided some reminiscences and autobiographical sketches in *The Intimate Notebooks of George Jean Nathan* (1932). There are important biographical chapters in Isaac Goldberg, *The Theater of George Jean Nathan* (1926); Constance Frick, *The Dramatic Criticism of George Jean Nathan* (1943); and Carl R. Dolmetsch, *The Smart Set: A History and Anthology* (1966); and introductory biographical essays in two anthologies of Nathan's writings: Charles Angoff, ed., *The World of George Jean Nathan* (1952); and Thomas Quinn Curtiss, *The Magic Mirror* (1960).]

CARL R. DOLMETSCH

NEELY, MATTHEW MANSFIELD (Nov. 9, 1874–Jan. 18, 1958), governor of West Virginia and U.S. congressman and senator from that state, was born on a farm near Groves, W.Va., the son of Alfred Neely, a doctor, and Mary Morris. He attended Salem College before enlisting in the infantry during the Spanish-American War. After the war he entered West Virginia University, where he excelled in oratory, earning the B.A. in 1901 and the LL.B. in 1902. On Oct. 21, 1903, he married Alberta Claire Ramage; they had three children. After practicing law for five years in Fairmont, W. Va., Neely won election as its mayor, on a prohibition platform (1908–1910). He next served (1911–1913) as clerk of the West Virginia House of Delegates. In 1913 he ran for the U.S. House of Representatives in a special election for the First District of West Virginia. His victory that year launched him on a career that saw him often a candidate, frequently a winner, and four times a loser.

After winning reelection to Congress three times, Neely was turned out in the Republican landslide of 1920. Two years later he won his first election for the U.S. Senate, only to be beaten six years later. In 1930 he again captured a Senate seat, held it against a challenge in 1936, and then abandoned it in 1941 after winning the governorship of West Virginia. In the Senate, Neely had established a reputation as a liberal New Dealer who was especially devoted to furthering the gains of organized labor. His move to the governorship seemed to be an effort to gain greater control of the state Democratic party (he was very organization- and patronage-minded) and to bring a New Deal–like program to West Virginia state administration. A United Mine Workers supporter, Neely called for laws protecting the right of collective bargaining, providing benefits for the needy blind and aged, eliminating the sales tax on basic foods, and providing higher salaries for teachers. He failed to get a state labor relations act, but in April 1944 he sent the state police into Weirton to protect organizers for the United Steel Workers who had been harassed by local police. He proclaimed his determination to "make West Virginia University as good for the poor as Yale is for the rich." Opponents accused him of injecting politics into university administration when he engineered the firing of its president.

Just as he had run for the governorship while a senator, so Neely ran for the Senate in 1942 before completing his term as governor. He lost but won election to the House of Representatives in 1944, only to lose for the last time in his House race two years later. Campaigning in Huntington, W.Va., with Neely in 1948, President Truman told a crowd, "If you don't elect this fellow, you don't know which side your bread's buttered on, I'll tell you that." Truman was returned to the presidency and Neely to the Senate.

Known as a shrewd and practical battler for liberal causes, Neely launched a vigorous fight in 1949 for repeal of the Taft-Hartley Labor Act and liberalization of immigration laws, which he assailed as "overtly discriminatory" against Catholics and Jews. He was a coauthor of the Displaced Persons Act of 1950. In August 1949 he became chairman of the Senate District of Columbia Committee, a position popularly known as the "unofficial mayor" of Washington, D.C. He immediately aligned himself with advocates of home rule for the city, slum clearance, its representation in Congress, and repeal of its sales tax. Neely was an outspoken critic of President Dwight D. Eisenhower, denouncing him as "the worst President we've ever had" and "Alice in Wonderland . . . taken in by the peddlers of special favors." He won reelection to the Senate in 1954.

An eccentric speaker with a rapid-fire delivery, Neely spiced Senate debate with scriptural quotations that suited his arguments. When a colleague inquired how he managed such great retention of biblical passages, Neely asserted that he eschewed nearly all social events in favor of reading the King James version of the New Testament, which he had gone through seven times. In 1955 he outraged many Americans by labeling President Eisenhower's church attendance as "hypocrisy" because Eisenhower had only begun attending services two weeks after his inauguration. To demands for a retraction, Neely retorted, "There is just as much chance of my apologizing as there is of the world coming to an end." The pugnacious Neely was no stranger to controversy. During a radio broadcast on which he defended President Roosevelt's race for a fourth term, he nearly came to blows with his antagonist. As his *New York Times* obituary observed, "Mr. Neely seldom forsook the role of the common man's David seeking out the Goliath of special interests." In 1949 he declared, "I'd rather be caught stealing sheep than voting for the sales tax." He characterized citizens of the District of Columbia as "shipwrecked on a voiceless, voteless island in the midst of the greatest ocean of democracy in the world." He branded the Eisenhower administration the "second everlasting monument to confusion," exceeded only by the Tower of Babel. Neely died in Washington, D.C.

[Neely's papers are in the West Virginia University Library. An obituary is in the *New York Times*, Jan. 19, 1958. For Neely as Bible reader, see Senator Richard L. Neuberger, "For Our Senators, Reading Time Is Stolen From Hours of Sleep," *New York Times Book Review*, July 21, 1957. Also see *Newsweek*, Nov. 16, 1942, July 3, 1944, and Apr. 11, 1955; *Time*, Aug. 17, 1942, and Apr. 11, 1955; *New Republic*, Oct. 25, 1948; *Commonweal*, Apr. 15, 1955; and *Business Week*, Jan. 29, 1949, and June 18, 1955.]

JORDAN A. SCHWARZ

NELSON, DONALD MARR (Nov. 17, 1888–Sept. 29, 1959), corporation executive, government official, and diplomat, was born in Hannibal, Mo., the son of Quincy Marr Nelson, a locomotive engineer, and Mary Ann MacDonald. His mother died when he was young, and Nelson was raised by his maternal grandmother. After attending elementary and secondary schools in Hannibal, he entered the University of Missouri, graduating in 1911 with a B.S. degree in chemical engineering. He then went to work in a Missouri agricultural experiment station.

His plans to continue graduate studies toward a Ph.D. were sidetracked permanently when, in 1912, he accepted employment as a chemist for Sears, Roebuck and Company, with which he remained until 1942. From the testing laboratories Nelson advanced to administrative posts; in 1921 he became manager of the men's and boys' clothing department, and he advanced to the post of general merchandise manager in 1927. Three years later he was appointed vice-president of merchandising and a company director. In 1939 he became executive vice-president and chairman of the executive committee. During this extended service with Sears, Roebuck and Company, Nelson had one brief experience in government: in 1934 he received a leave of absence to serve as assistant to Clay Williams, administrator of the National Recovery Administration.

In May 1940, Nelson accepted the first of a series of government appointments. Released by Sears, he reported to Secretary of the Treasury Henry Morgenthau, Jr., as acting director in charge of procurement, with the responsibility for aiding in the handling of requests by foreign governments for raw materials and manufactured products. The following month he was named chairman of the newly created National Defense Advisory Commission.

In January 1941, Nelson became part of the newly established Office of Production Management (OPM), as head of the Division of Purchases. The OPM was unwieldy and lacked authority. Furthermore, its leaders were divided regarding the urgency of war preparations and the extent of the need to curtail civilian production. Nelson favored as rapid an expansion of war production as possible. In July 1941, President Franklin D. Roosevelt created the Supply, Priorities, and Allocations Board (SPAB), which attempted to allocate the supply of materials among military, defense aid, and civilian needs. Nelson became executive director of SPAB and director of priorities. After Pearl Harbor it became apparent that the powers of SPAB were too limited to meet the needs of a nation at war.

President Roosevelt decided that American war production should be placed under one man, and at the suggestion of his adviser Harry Hopkins, he appointed Nelson as head of the new War Production Board (WPB) on Jan. 16, 1942. A major initial task of the WPB was to convert the economy from civilian to war production. This process included the redirection of the automobile industry to the manufacture of airplanes, tanks, and military vehicles. The WPB also was involved in the production of ships, including vessels for the navy and cargo craft. It had to deal with large companies and also brought small concerns into war production. Throughout the war the WPB handled the allocation of steel and sought to increase the supply of rubber by supporting the production of synthetic rubber and decreasing the unnecessary use of rubber. In addition it had to cope with the relationships between management and labor; in this connection Nelson pressed successfully for nationwide use of labor-management committees. He also made effective use of "dollar-a-year" men, a device initiated during World War I, in which prominent individuals served the government for a token fee.

Nelson headed the WPB until August 1944. By that time he had become embroiled in a bitter dispute with army leaders; one of the differences was over preparations for reconversion to a civilian economy when the war ended. Nelson accepted Roosevelt's offer of an assignment to accompany Major General Patrick J. Hurley on a special mission to the Soviet Union and China. Nelson conferred especially on economic matters with the leaders of these countries as President Roosevelt's personal representative and held cabinet rank.

In May 1945, Nelson returned to private life. He wrote a book on his war experiences, *Arsenal of Democracy* (1946). From June 1945 to February 1947 he was president of the Society of Independent Motion Picture Producers. In 1948 he became chairman of the board of Electronized Chemicals, and in 1950 he was elected president of Consolidated Caribou Silver Mines.

Nelson was married five times. His first wife was Estelle Lord, who died in 1923. He married Helen Wishart in 1926; they were divorced in January 1945. The following month Nelson married his former secretary, Marguerite S. Coulbourn, who died in February 1947. He married Edna May Rowell in November 1947; they were divorced in 1958. On Feb. 12, 1959, Nelson married Lena Peters Schunzel. He died in Los Angeles.

[The WPB did not keep its records centrally; rather, each organizational unit appears to have had its own files. After the war quantities of records were destroyed, in accordance with established procedures. Some 2,500 feet of the records of the WPB are in the National Archives. The files of the Chinese War Production Board, of which Nelson was a member, are in the Franklin D. Roosevelt Library in Hyde Park, N.Y. Published materials dealing with aspects of Nelson's career include Robert E. Sherwood, *Roosevelt*

and Hopkins (1948); Harry S. Truman, *Memoirs*, vol. I (1955); David E. Lilienthal, *Journals*, vol. I (1964); and Barbara W. Tuchman, *Stilwell and the American Experience in China, 1911–45* (1971).]

A. RUSSELL BUCHANAN

NEUBERGER, RICHARD LEWIS (Dec. 26, 1912–Mar. 9, 1960), newspaperman, author, and U.S. senator, was born in Portland, Oreg., the son of Isaac Neuberger, a restaurant owner, and Ruth Lewis. His father had come to the Pacific Northwest from Hainstadt, Germany, at the age of seventeen; his mother was the daughter of German immigrants. Neuberger attended the public schools of Portland and graduated from Lincoln High School in 1930. In high school he was drawn to journalism; became a sports reporter for the school newspaper; and met Lair H. Gregory, sports editor of the *Portland Oregonian*, who taught him the fundamentals of newspaper work. In the fall of 1931, after working as Gregory's assistant for a year, he entered the University of Oregon at Eugene to major in journalism.

As a student Neuberger showed more interest in campus activities and politics than in scholarship. When only a sophomore he was appointed editor of the *Oregon Daily Emerald*, the student newspaper, and quickly became a controversial crusader for, among other things, the abolition of the mandatory military training program and compulsory student fees. In 1933, after a trip to Germany, he published his first magazine article, "The New Germany," in the *Nation;* his first signed article in the *New York Times* appeared the following year. Aspiring to enter state politics and to advance the New Deal in Oregon, Neuberger abandoned his studies in the fall of 1934 to campaign for Peter Zimmerman, an independent liberal candidate for governor. Shortly thereafter, with deficient grades, he left the university without receiving a degree.

In January 1935, Neuberger returned to the *Oregonian* as a reporter and feature writer. At the same time he continued his free-lance writing. His articles appeared regularly in the *Nation, Harper's,* the *Saturday Evening Post, Current History,* the *New Republic,* and other magazines. In 1936 he was appointed *New York Times* correspondent for the Pacific Northwest and between 1936 and 1938 wrote three books of polemic, rather than particular literary, merit: *An Army of the Aged* (1936), written with Kelley

Loe, an exposé of the shortcomings of the Townsend Plan; *Integrity* (1937), a biography of George W. Norris, written with Stephen B. Kahn; and *Our Promised Land* (1938), an interpretive study of the Pacific Northwest.

Neuberger's articles and books, most of which dealt with the Pacific Northwest and western politics and conservation, served as his carefully constructed bridge to politics. Although unsuccessful in a bid for the state senate in 1936, he was elected to the legislative assembly as a Democrat from Multnomah County (Portland) in 1940. In July 1942 he enlisted in the U.S. Army as a second lieutenant, served as aide-de-camp to General James A. O'Connor during construction of the Alaska Military Highway, and was discharged with the rank of captain in August 1945, having produced reams of publicity for the project. On Dec. 20, 1945, he married Maurine Brown, a teacher of physical education and English. They had no children.

After the war Neuberger joined other liberal Democrats in an effort to break the traditional Republican monopoly on Oregon politics. In 1948 he was elected to the state senate; two years later his wife joined him in the legislature as a member of the legislative assembly. As the only husband-and-wife team in the legislature, the Neubergers were effective and popular; in 1952 both were overwhelmingly reelected. Meanwhile, Neuberger produced a large number of magazine articles and three more books: *The Lewis and Clark Expedition* (1951), *The Royal Canadian Mounted Police* (1953), and *Adventures in Politics* (1954). In 1954 he ran for the U.S. Senate. His victory, a milestone in efforts to rejuvenate Democratic state politics, marked the first time in forty years that Oregonians had sent a Democrat to the Senate.

Combative, outspoken, and at times brash, Neuberger mellowed in the Senate. He became less the ardent Democrat and more the nonpartisan. At the same time he strongly expressed the issues that had been central to both his political and his literary careers: conservation and political reform. Because of his tireless advocacy of Alaskan statehood, public power, and the preservation of natural and scenic resources, he became popularly known as "Mr. Conservation." His dedication to improvement of the legislative process prompted him to fight to eliminate the filibuster.

Four years into his Senate term, a routine physical examination revealed a malignant tumor. Following surgery in 1958 and extensive radiation treatment, he died in Portland of a cerebral hemorrhage. His wife succeeded him in the U.S. Senate.

Neuberger wrote in a colorful, vivid style— sometimes with exaggeration—and achieved recognition as the leading popular authority on the Pacific Northwest. He was also a facile public speaker.

[Neuberger's papers are at the University of Oregon. See also the papers of Wayne Morse at the University of Oregon. Among Neuberger's articles is "Running for Office: A Confession," *New York Times Magazine,* Sept. 7, 1940. Additional information is in Russ Sackett, "The Neubergers: Political Paradox," *Frontier,* Mar. 1953; A. Robert Smith, *The Tiger in the Senate* (1962), a biography of Wayne Morse; and the following magazine articles: *Time,* Nov. 15, 1954, and Mar. 21, 1960; *Harper's,* Feb. 1947; *New Yorker,* Nov. 27, 1954; and *Saturday Evening Post,* Dec. 16, 1960.]

ROBERT E. BURTON

NEUMANN, JOHN VON. See VON NEUMANN, JOHN.

NICHOLS, DUDLEY (Apr. 6, 1895–Jan. 5, 1960), motion picture scriptwriter, producer, and director, was born in Wapakoneta, Ohio, the son of Grant Byron Nichols and Mary Means. His father, a physician, wished the boy to become a surgeon, but Nichols developed a fascination with electricity. He experimented on his own and also worked on a crew that repaired high-tension power lines and as a ship's radio operator on the Great Lakes. In 1915 he entered the University of Michigan, where he studied electrical engineering and was employed as a student assistant in charge of the radio laboratory. At the outbreak of World War I, Nichols enlisted in the navy and set up a school for radio operators. Later, he was part of the North Sea Mine Laying Force. After the armistice he volunteered for minesweeping duty and invented a method of electrical protection for minesweepers for which he received the Distinguished Service Medal in 1920.

After the war Nichols took up journalism, having already published articles about his North Sea experiences. He spent the next ten years as a reporter, working first for the *Philadelphia Evening Public Ledger,* then the *New York Evening Post,* and finally (for five years) the *New*

York World. During this period he also studied at New York University and sailed again as a radio operator. In 1924 he married Esta Varez Gooch-Collings, a concert singer and pianist; they had no children. During 1927 he was a European correspondent for the *World*.

Although Nichols had gained a considerable reputation as a reporter, in 1929 he resigned, intending to sail to Spain to do research for a book. When he approached Winfield Sheehan, the head of Fox Studios, for letters of introduction, Sheehan persuaded him to become a screenwriter instead. Nichols achieved rapid success in his new field. His first film was *Men Without Women* (1930), directed by John Ford. Years later, Ford commented: "He had never written a script before, but he was very good, and he had the same idea I had about paucity of dialogue." This film began a long and fruitful collaboration with Ford that lasted, off and on, until 1947 and resulted in fourteen films. Many of these were critically acclaimed and several were financial successes. The Nichols-Ford films include *The Lost Patrol* (1934), *The Informer* (1935), *Mary of Scotland* (1936), *The Plough and the Stars* (1936), *Stagecoach* (1939), *The Long Voyage Home* (1940), and *The Fugitive* (1947).

During the 1930's, Nichols was a major force in the formation of the Screen Writers' Guild. When the Academy of Motion Picture Arts and Sciences voted a best-screenplay award to Nichols for *The Informer*, he did not attend the dinner or accept the award, explaining that because the guild had been "conceived in revolt against the Academy and born out of disappointment with the way it functioned against the employed talent in any emergency," to accept the award "would be to turn my back on nearly a thousand members of the Screen Writers' Guild." Nichols served two terms as the guild's president (1938–1939). He also wrote a play (with Stuart Anthony), *Come Angel Band*, which lasted for two performances on Broadway in 1936. Around this time, a reporter described him as "tall and slim, with a pink aquiline face and a maestro mop of prematurely gray hair."

Throughout his Hollywood career, Nichols struggled to retain his social conscience and artistic integrity. In 1939 he wrote the narration for *The 400,000,000*, a documentary about China, and in the same year publicly declared that Hollywood, "in its fear of losing profits by making enemies, in its mad desire to appease the prejudice of every group, has submitted to an ever-tightening censorship under which it becomes im-

possible to deal with reality. . . . The American cinema is strangling under a rope which it has helped to put around its own neck."

Nichols reached a peak of influence and respect during the 1940's, when he worked with such major directors as Ford, Fritz Lang, Jean Renoir, Howard Hawks, Leo McCarey, René Clair, and Elia Kazan. He wrote the final script of Ernest Hemingway's *For Whom the Bell Tolls*; the film, released in 1943, was reputedly Paramount's most expensive production to date. He also produced and directed two controversial films based on his own scripts, *Sister Kenny* (1946) and an adaptation of Eugene O'Neill's *Mourning Becomes Electra* (1947). With John Gassner he edited and wrote introductions for the anthologies *Twenty Best Film Plays* (1943; revised and condensed in 1959 as *Great Film Plays*), *Best Film Plays, 1943–44* (1945), and *Best Film Plays, 1945* (1946).

The 1950's marked a decline in Nichols' importance and activity. In 1953 he commented, "I don't have to do anything except sit down and grin at my past follies." A year later, he received the Screen Writers' Guild's highest award, the Laurel Achievement, voted to the writer "who has contributed most through the years to his craft and his Guild." Nichols' last screen credit was for *Heller in Pink Tights* (1960), directed by George Cukor. He died in Hollywood, Calif.

In his work Nichols sought to impose substance on the anti-intellectual Hollywood product and to circumvent the more obvious absurdities of censorship. His best and most personal work remains both dramatic and intelligent. He also gave considerable thought to the nature of the film medium, especially to the ways in which it differs from the stage, concluding that a scriptwriter must stress images over words. However, he was rarely able to follow his own advice, and today his weaknesses appear more obvious than his strengths: he tended to oversimplify characters into good and evil figures, to place them in scenes that allowed for speechmaking about social or a simplistic process of "redemption." But although Nichols' reputation has had been substantially deflated, his work reveals his sincerity, his integrity, and—viewed in the light of the period when he worked—his considerable courage.

[Brief biographical and career summaries appear in Roger Manvell, ed., *The International Encyclopedia of Film* (1972), and John M. Smith and Tim Cawkwell, eds., *The World Encyclopedia of the Film* (1972). More information can be found in Paul M. Jensen, "The Career of Dudley Nichols," *Film Comment* (Winter 1970–1971), reprinted in Richard Corliss, ed., *The Hollywood Screenwriters* (1972). Corliss analyzes four of Nichols' films in *Talking Pictures; Screenwriters in the American Cinema, 1927–1973* (1974). John Ford offers several comments on Nichols in Peter Bogdanovich, *John Ford* (1967). Obituaries appeared in the *New York Herald Tribune* and *New York Times*, Jan. 6, 1960, and in *Variety*, Jan. 13, 1960. The following scripts by Nichols have been published: *Stagecoach* in *Great Film Plays* and by Simon and Schuster Classic Film Scripts (1971); *The Informer* in *Theater Arts*, Aug. 1951; *It Happen Tommorrow* (excerpts) in *Theater Arts*, June 1944. Copies of various shooting scripts and drafts can be found in the University of Southern California at Los Angeles and the New York Public Library theater research collections.]

PAUL M. JENSEN

NICHOLS, RUTH ROWLAND (Feb. 23, 1901–Sept. 25, 1960), pioneer aviator, was born in New York City, the daughter of Erickson Norman Nichols and Edith Corlis Haines. Her father, a member of the New York Stock Exchange, had served as a Rough Rider under Theodore Roosevelt. She attended Miss Masters' School at Dobbs Ferry, N.Y., and graduated from Wellesley College in 1924. An average student, she devoted much time to athletics and dramatics.

In 1922, taking time out from college, Nichols learned to fly in Florida under the tutelage of Harry Rogers and received the first seaplane pilot's license ever issued to a woman by the Fédération Aéronautique Internationale. She was only the second woman to receive a pilot's license from the American government, and in 1927 received the second transport license issued to a woman. She worked briefly for the National City Bank in New York City, but after serving as a copilot for Harry Rogers on a nonstop flight from New York to Miami in 1928, she took a sales promotion position with the Fairchild Aviation Corporation. In 1929 she flew a Curtiss Fledgling to forty-six states in an attempt to set up a chain of aviation country clubs. The first was established at Hicksville, N.Y., but expansion plans were halted by the Great Depression.

Nichols' desire to accomplish feats that had never before been attempted led her to search for new records, which in turn led to six serious crashes. "When a person loves flying and understands it and knows the reason for an accident, there is no fear," she said. "I could hardly wait to be in the air again. That's just natural." In 1929 she and Amelia Earhart formed a women pilots' organization known as the "Ninety-Niners." In 1930, Nichols flew from Los Angeles to New York in thirteen hours and twenty-one minutes, cutting one hour off the mark set by Charles Lindbergh. She expressed an interest in flying around the world, but Clarence Chamberlin suggested that she fly solo across the Atlantic instead. With his support and several sponsors, she obtained a Lockheed Vega, a single-engine, high-wing monoplane. In March 1931, before her transatlantic attempt, she achieved the women's world altitude record of 28,743 feet, and in April 1931 set the women's world speed record of 210.754 miles per hour.

On June 22, 1931, Nichols took off from Floyd Bennett Field, N.Y., in her transatlantic effort, but crashed on landing at St. John, New Brunswick. She broke five vertebrae. Weather and lack of funds prevented another attempt. In October 1931 she flew from Oakland, Calif., to Louisville, Ky., corseted in a steel brace, and set a women's distance record of 1,977 miles after fourteen hours in the air. On Feb. 17, 1932, Nichols attained the diesel engine altitude record for men and women of 19,928 feet. In December of that year she became the first woman to serve as pilot for a passenger airline, flying for New York and New England Airways.

Nichols started a flying school for women at Adelphi College, Garden City, N.Y., in 1939 and was a director of Relief Wings, a humanitarian air service, from 1940 to 1949. During World War II she was a member of the Civil Air Patrol. From 1945 to 1947, Nichols was director of public relations for the White Plains Hospital. She was a special correspondent for UNICEF on a round-the-world tour in 1949, and received the title "world pilot." From 1952 to 1954 she was director of women's activities for Save the Children Federation in New York City; then, until 1956, she was director of the women's division of the United Hospital Fund; and in 1958, field director of the National Nephrosis Foundation, as well as pilot on a twenty-one-state tour. Nichols was the first woman in the United States to pilot a twin-engine jet executive aircraft, a Moraine Saulnier (1955), and three years later, at the age of fifty-seven, served as copilot of an air force supersonic jet that exceeded 1,000 miles per hour and reached an altitude of 51,000 feet. This was the highest altitude achieved by any woman in the world. She received the Lady Drummond Hay Trophy in 1958.

In 1960 Nichols, who had never married, suffered from depression and was placed under a doctor's care. She died in New York City after taking an overdose of barbiturates. Richard E. Byrd wrote of her, "There was a handful of women who shared in the hardships and perils of aviation pioneering. Two names that stand out, as I look back upon the late twenties and early thirties, were Amelia Earhart and Ruth Nichols."

[Some of Nichols' personal papers are held by the Ninety-Niners at Oklahoma City, Okla. Her autobiography is *Wings for Life*, Dorothy Roe Lewis, ed. (1957). References to her career are found in the *New York Times*, especially throughout 1931. Her obituary is in the *New York Times*, Sept. 26, 1960. See also Jean Adams and Margaret Kimball, *Heroines of the Sky* (1942); F. H. Ellis and E. Ellis, *Atlantic Air Conquest* (1963); and John Burke, *Winged Legend* (1970). The Aviation Project in the Oral History Collection of Columbia University contains a memoir by Nichols, completed just before her death.]

ERNEST A. McKAY

NOLL, JOHN FRANCIS (Jan. 25, 1875–July 31, 1956), Roman Catholic bishop, was born in Fort Wayne, Ind., the fifth of nineteen children of John George Noll, a laborer. His mother, Anna Ford, died when he was four. His father married Mary McCleary soon thereafter, and the boy was reared by his stepmother. Noll received his elementary education at the cathedral parish school in Fort Wayne. At thirteen he entered the preparatory seminary at St. Lawrence College, Mt. Calvary, Wis. In 1893 he went on to the major seminary at Mount St. Mary's of the West in Cincinnati, and on June 4, 1898, he was ordained a priest.

After brief temporary assignments as an assistant in various places, Noll was appointed pastor at Ligonier, Ind., in 1899. Over the next ten years he was transferred twice to other small-town pastorates, and in 1910 he took over St. Mary's Church in Huntington, Ind., a town some twenty miles southwest of Fort Wayne. He remained there as pastor until consecrated bishop of the diocese of Fort Wayne on June 30, 1925.

Anti-Catholic feeling was strong in the Midwest around 1900, and as a young priest Noll developed a special interest in apologetical work. His talent for putting the Catholic position into popular colloquial form was first displayed in a pamphlet written for his parishioners on the dangers of mixed marriages, the need for Catholic schools, and similar matters. Other priests re-

sponded favorably to sample copies of *Kind Words From Your Pastor* (1903), which subsequently went through twenty-four printings. The *Parish Monthly* followed a similar pattern. It was initiated in 1908 for the instruction and edification of Noll's congregation. He then offered it to other pastors, and it developed into a regular periodical. Its name was changed to *Family Monthly* in 1938; and by 1950 it had a circulation of 160,000 as *Family Digest*.

Noll's most significant contribution to Catholic apologetical journalism came in 1912 with the founding of *Our Sunday Visitor*. This weekly publication was intended to counteract the propaganda of *The Menace*, an anti-Catholic sheet published at Aurora, Mo. Subtitled *The Harmonizer, Our Sunday Visitor* was a newspaper in format, but more of a devotional magazine in content. It was distributed to Catholic pastors at a cost of one cent per copy, to be sold for a pittance or given away at church doors. By 1928 more than half the English-language Catholic churches in the country were receiving it. Although it had declined from the peak reached in the early 1960's, *Our Sunday Visitor* in 1974 had a circulation of more than 400,000 and served as the official publication for seven dioceses.

The Acolyte, a monthly founded in 1925 and renamed *The Priest* in 1945, was another product of Noll's literary energies. Besides contributing to these journals, he produced scores of pamphlets and ten book-length works. Aside from a volume on the history of the Fort Wayne diocese, his books and pamphlets were instructional, apologetic, or controversial in nature. By far the best known is *Father Smith Instructs Jackson*, an exposition of Catholic teaching in dialogue form. Published in 1913, this book has gone through some sixty printings and has been translated into half a dozen languages. There is also a Braille edition.

As bishop of Fort Wayne, Noll proved an energetic administrator and builder. He encouraged a number of religious orders to come to the diocese and was practically the cofounder of the Missionary Sisters of Our Lady of Victory, who carry on home missionary work from the motherhouse that Noll built for them at Huntington. He also established a minor seminary, built Catholic high schools in the largest cities of the diocese, created a diocesan Catholic charities organization, established fifty-four new parishes, and ordained more than 500 priests.

Noll was equally active on the national Catholic scene. He was an early worker in the Catholic Press Association and the Catholic Extension

Society. Appointed treasurer of the American Board of Catholic Missions in 1925, he held that position until his death. In 1930, Noll was elected to the administrative board of the National Catholic Welfare Conference, the official organization of the Catholic hierarchy of the United States. He served for eight years as secretary of its administrative board (1931–1934, 1942–1947); terms as chairman of the department of lay organizations (1934–1937, 1942–1947) partially overlapped his duties as secretary.

Noll was a member of the episcopal committee that organized the Legion of Decency (1934), the Catholic body that rated films for moral acceptability; and he was chairman of the Bishops' Committee on Obscene Literature, which established the National Organization for Decent Literature in 1938. From 1942 to 1950 he also served on the Bishops' Committee for Catholic Refugees. In the early 1950's he spearheaded the effort to complete construction of the National Shrine of the Immaculate Conception in Washington, D.C.

A man of the institutional church in a period of great growth and consolidation, Noll received recognition for his contributions by being granted the personal title of archbishop in 1953. He was a simple and affable man, known to the closest of his episcopal confreres as "Red." Despite his wide influence his career was remarkably localized in the area of his birth. He died at Fort Wayne and was buried from its cathedral, where he had been baptized, confirmed, ordained, and consecrated a bishop, and from which he had guided the Catholics of his diocese for thirty-six years.

[The Noll materials on deposit at the University of Notre Dame Archives consist mainly of newspaper clippings. Among Noll's more substantial works are *For Our Non-Catholic Friends, the Fairest Argument* (1917), *It Is Happening Here* (1936), *The Decline of Nations* (1940), and *Our National Enemy Number One: Education Without Religion* (1942). His *Diocese of Fort Wayne* (1940) contains a sketch of the author's episcopal career up to 1940. There is no scholarly biography, but Richard Ginder, *With Ink and Crozier* (1952), is an informative popular life of Noll. Clifford Stevens, "John Francis Noll: 1874–1956," *Homiletic and Pastoral Review*, Apr. 1975, is useful.]

PHILIP GLEASON

NORTON, MARY TERESA HOPKINS (Mar. 7, 1875–Aug. 2, 1959), congresswoman, was born in Jersey City, N.J., the daughter of Thomas Hopkins, a well-to-do contractor, and Marie Shea, both of whom were born in Ireland. She attended public and parochial schools, and had just graduated from Jersey City High School in 1892 when her mother died. As eldest daughter she managed the household for the next four years until her father remarried. Although her father opposed higher education for women, Mary Hopkins went to Packard Business College in New York City, graduating in 1896. For thirteen years she worked as a stenographer and secretary, finding life as an independent young businesswoman both pleasant and exhilarating. In April 1909 she married Robert Francis Norton, a widower who was an executive of a wholesale cooperage firm in Jersey City. This ended her business career.

The death of her only child in infancy turned Norton's energies in other directions. "The bottom dropped out of my world for a time," she remembered in her unpublished memoir, "something had to take the place of the children I could not have." After nearly two years as a recluse, she plunged into child-care work. She helped form the Queen's Daughters Day Nursery in the parish, and was elected secretary in 1913. Three years later she became president of the nonsectarian Day Nurseries Association of Jersey City, which cared for children of working women.

It was the notorious boss, Mayor Frank Hague of Jersey City, who encouraged Norton to enter politics. He never denied the accusation that he did this to bring respectability to his machine. When the Nineteenth Amendment, giving women the vote, was ratified in 1920, Hague urged Norton to organize the women of Jersey City and to serve as the Hudson County representative on the Democratic State Committee. She did so, and was elected vice-chairman of the committee in 1921, was chairman (1932–1935), and then vice-chairman again (1935–1943). In 1923 she was elected the first woman member of the Hudson County Board of Freeholders, the county governing board.

In 1924, with the endorsement of the Hague machine, Norton won election to the House of Representatives from the Twelfth (later Thirteenth) District of New Jersey, which comprised Bayonne and part of Jersey City. She was the first woman to be elected to Congress on the Democratic ticket and the first congresswoman from any eastern state.

In Congress, Norton was confronted with the conservative attitude of many male representatives who were often gallant but frequently unfair. Women, like independents, were discriminated against in committee assignments and excluded from the leadership. Genial and unassuming, she was cool, witty, and competent in debate. In one memorable exchange, Norton responded to a congressman who agreed to interrupt his remarks and "yield to a lady." "I'm no lady, I'm a member of Congress," she retorted, "and I'll proceed on that basis."

Norton had strong ideas about women and politics. Most women did not identify with female political candidates, she said, and for that reason neither the women in the electorate nor those in the Congress voted together as a group. She opposed the formation of a women's bloc in the House, saying her immediate task was to represent her own district. "It will probably take another generation," she wrote, "to make women realize their own power."

During her first decade in Congress, Norton became known as a "wet" and a loyal Democratic party regular from the urban Northeast. Although she insisted that Hague never asked her to vote against her conscience, she never voted against his interests. They apparently held similar views. As late as 1950 she helped Hague retain his seat on the New Jersey State Executive Committee.

Norton supported labor legislation and was the first member of Congress to introduce a bill to repeal the Eighteenth Amendment. She was one of a number of prominent Catholics who opposed the Gillett bill, which would have fostered the dissemination of birth-control information. At the Democratic National Convention in both 1928 and 1932, she worked for Al Smith's nomination. In March 1932, when the Democrats organized the Seventy-second Congress, Norton became head of the House Committee on the District of Columbia, the first woman to chair a major congressional committee. Since the committee governed the District of Columbia, she also became the first woman "mayor of Washington." She continued in that role until 1937.

Norton also was elected to a number of important Democratic party positions. In 1932 she became head of the New Jersey Democratic Committee, which had responsibility for federal patronage in the state. She was the first woman in either major party to be elected head of a state party organization. She retained that position until 1935 (she resigned the year after her husband died in 1934) and held it again from 1940 to 1944. She became a member of the Democratic National Committee in 1944 and in 1948 chaired the Credentials Committee at the Democratic National Convention.

In 1937, Norton succeeded to the chair of the House Labor Committee following the death of William P. Connery. A loyal New Dealer, she headed the committee for ten years. She successfully steered President Franklin D. Roosevelt's Wages and Hours Bill through the House in 1938, despite the opposition of Republicans and southern Democrats. With Roosevelt's support she succeeded in petitioning the bill out of the Rules Committee and led the floor fight for what became the Fair Labor Standards Act of 1938. In subsequent years Norton defended New Deal labor legislation against conservative attack. During World War II, however, many of the labor bills were removed from her jurisdiction and sent to the military and naval affairs committees. Norton charged that this resulted from discrimination against her personally. She also predicted that after the war women would be forced to leave jobs they had been handling capably.

When the Republicans gained a majority in Congress in the 1946 election, Norton resigned from the Labor Committee in protest against the new chairman, Fred A. Hartley of New Jersey. She helped to lead the unsuccessful fight against the Taft-Hartley Act of 1947. After the Democrats regained control of Congress in 1949, she became head of the House Administration Committee. Norton retired from Congress in 1951, having served for twenty-six years, longer than any other woman. For the next two years she worked as a special consultant on women in industry to the Department of Labor. In 1956 she moved to Greenwich, Conn., where she died.

Norton accepted a traditional and undistinguished role. Like the ward politicians that Jersey City had often sent to Congress, she remained a party regular. This was in keeping with the predominantly Catholic, working-class, urban northeastern district that she represented. She was an outsider to her colleagues on Capitol Hill because she was a woman, and to the Washington elite because of her background. "To snooty Washington society," Duff Gilford reported in 1929, "she is a business school graduate, Tammany, and Catholic, and hence unacceptable. But then, so was Al Smith, and Mrs. Norton is proud to be in any category with him."

Her political career was not much different from that of the average male member of Congress. Norton was neither a crusader nor a leader. No major piece of legislation bore her name. She served in the years after the suffrage movement had achieved its goal and before the reemergence of the women's movement in the 1960's. She worked hard, climbed up through the party and the congressional seniority systems, and mastered the skills of legislative politics. Yet as one of the first generation of women in Congress, Norton achieved a number of distinctions that made her historically significant. Her career helped to challenge prevailing stereotypes. She proved that a woman could win elections, retain the support of her constituency, and exert leadership in Congress. This was a valuable contribution toward the alteration of social norms and the legitimation of women in politics.

[A small collection of Norton's papers and scrapbooks, together with an unpublished memoir written in 1951 and entitled "Madame Congressman," is at the Rutgers University Library, New Brunswick, N.J. Among the articles written about her are Duff Gilford, "Gentlewomen of the House," *American Mercury*, Oct. 1929; *Time*, May 16, 1938; *U.S. News*, May 10, 1940; and Amy Porter, "Ladies of Congress," *Collier's*, Aug. 28, 1943. Obituaries are in *New York Times*, *New York Herald Tribune*, and *Washington Post*, Aug. 3, 1959. Information on her relationship with Hague is in Dayton D. McKean, *The Boss* (1940; repr. 1967); and Richard J. Connors, *A Cycle of Power* (1971). Capsule biographies of Norton and other congresswomen are in Hope Chamberlin, *A Minority of Members* (1973). Jeane J. Kirkpatrick, *Political Woman* (1974), provides a valuable conceptual study of women in Congress.]

JOHN WHITECLAY CHAMBERS II

NOVY, FREDERICK GEORGE (Dec. 9, 1864–Aug. 8, 1957), microbiologist, was born in Chicago. His father, a master tailor, and his mother, a milliner, were born in what is now Czechoslovakia, and came to the United States in 1864. Novy graduated with a B.S. from the University of Michigan in 1886, intending to pursue a career in chemistry. His first work after graduation, in the Department of Organic Chemistry at the University of Michigan, was on cocaine and its derivatives. In 1887, Victor C. Vaughan, professor of hygiene and physiological chemistry at the university, persuaded him to accept a position as instructor in that department.

Novy's first publication in bacteriological chemistry (1888), jointly with Vaughan, was on ptomaines and leucomaines. In the summer of 1888, he and Vaughan traveled to the Hygiene Institute in Berlin to study under Robert Koch, then the leading authority in bacteriology. On his return, Novy taught the first course on bacteriology to be offered at an American university. At the same time he undertook a program of research, the first concern of which was the development of techniques for the cultivation of pathogenic bacteria. Novy received the degrees of Sc.D. in 1890 and M.D. in 1891 from the University of Michigan. The latter year he married; from this marriage there were five children. In 1894 he published his first text on bacteriology, *Directions for Laboratory Work in Bacteriology*. In the same year he studied at the Pathological Institute in Prague. In 1897 he worked at the Pasteur Institute in Paris.

At Michigan, Novy made his first major discovery: the isolation of *Clostridium novyii*, an anaerobic bacillus capable of causing fatal septicemia in animals (1894). By 1900 he was an authority on bacteriology and communicable diseases. In 1901, in response to concern about a possible outbreak of bubonic plague in San Francisco, he served on a federal commission on the subject. Plague was indeed found; measures were adopted to prevent its spread; and provisions were established to avoid its recurrence. Novy also had been active on the Michigan Board of Health (1897–1899). Through his writings he attempted to give the general public an understanding of the role of bacteria in the generation of disease. He also was involved in the founding of a number of societies and journals specializing in bacteriology, including the Society of American Bacteriologists, of which he became president in 1904. By then he had become professor and head of the Department of Bacteriology at the University of Michigan.

Shortly after 1900, Novy began his work on trypanosomes and spirochetes. Once more he concentrated first on the development of methods for laboratory cultivation, a hitherto unsolved problem. His work on spirochetes, the etiological agents of relapsing fevers, led to the identification of a particular organism, the natural habitat of which is the blood of the rat, now called *Spirocheta novyi*.

Novy's work on trypanosomes led to a lengthy period of investigation of the artificial stimulation of resistance to trypanosome infections. This work culminated in the publication, with P. H. de Kruif and others, of nine papers on anaphylactic shock (1917). The authors showed clearly that there were changes in the blood of an animal caused by initial exposure to a trypanosomal antigen that, on a second exposure, could lead to a violent reaction, sometimes even to death. Novy and his colleagues ascribed this reaction to the formation of a highly potent trypanosomal poison that they called anaphylatoxin, but they were unable to proceed to a complete solution to the problem. The reactions observed by Novy are now ascribed to the production of histamines.

The last major research field in which Novy worked was the study of the metabolism of microorganisms, particularly the tubercle bacillus. In collaboration with Malcolm H. Soule, he published an account of the respiration of this organism and its dependence on the magnitude of the chemical potential of the oxygen in the host animal (1925).

Novy's later years were increasingly devoted to administrative matters. He was chairman of the Executive Committee of the University of Michigan Medical School from 1930 to 1933 and dean from then until 1935. Many honors were conferred on him, including election to the National Academy of Sciences in 1934.

His colleagues and former students at the University of Michigan continued Novy's work after his retirement. In fact, in 1953, eighteen years after his retirement, some tubes of dried rat blood, missing since 1920, were found and shown to contain a still-viable filterable agent that Novy had been investigating when the tubes were lost. Using Novy's carefully kept records from that era, workers were able to identify this filterable agent as a virus. Thus, Novy had been a pioneer virologist as well. This work was published in the *Journal of Infectious Diseases,* with Novy as one of the authors. He died at Ann Arbor.

Although he was a pioneer in many areas of microbiology, Novy regarded himself as simply a bacteriologist. His influence in the growth of microbiology in the United States, extending over more than fifty years, was immense. He was reputedly a stern taskmaster, exacting of himself and of others, but also a man of kindness and of wit.

[Obituaries are in *New York Times,* Aug. 10, 1957; and W. J. Nungester, *Science,* 1958. See also Ruth Good, "Frederick G. Novy: Biographic Sketch," *University of Michigan Medical Bulletin,* 1950; and Esmond R. Long, in *Biographical Memoirs. National Academy of Sciences,* 1959.]

C. G. B. GARRETT

OGBURN, WILLIAM FIELDING (June 29, 1886–Apr. 27, 1959), sociologist, statistician, and educator, was born in Butler, Ga., the son of Charlton Greenwood Ogburn, a planter and merchant, and Irene Florence Wynn. He received the B.S. degree from Mercer University in Georgia in 1905, his M.A. from Columbia Uni-

versity in 1909, and his Ph.D. also from Columbia in 1912. Ogburn began teaching at the Morton School for Boys (1905–1906) and served as assistant principal of the Darlington School in Rome, Ga. (1906–1908). Ogburn married Rubyn Reynolds in 1910; they had two sons.

He was appointed instructor in economics, politics, and history at Princeton in 1911. The next year he became professor of sociology and economics at Reed College (Portland, Oreg.), where he taught until 1917. After a year as professor of sociology at the University of Washington, he entered government service, becoming examiner and head of the cost-of-living department of the National War Labor Board (1918–1919) and special agent of the U.S. Bureau of Labor Statistics (1919).

Ogburn then returned to academic life as professor of sociology at Columbia University (1919–1927). He became professor of sociology at the University of Chicago in 1927 and remained there until retiring in 1951. In 1933 he was awarded the Sewell L. Avery distinguished service chair at the university. After retiring, he was visiting professor of sociology at Florida State University (1953–1959), lecturer at the University of Calcutta (1952), visiting professor at Nuffield College, Oxford (1952–1953), and professor of American history and institutions at the Indian School of International Studies at the University of Delhi (1956–1957). He died in Tallahassee, Fla.

Ogburn's teaching covered a wide range of courses, including economics, political science, history, and statistics as well as sociology. His research activities and publications also covered a wide range of topics. Moreover, he was able to bring into both his teaching and research his considerable acquaintance with the anthropological and psychoanalytic literature. His most important books were his *Social Change: With Respect to Culture and Original Nature* (1922), which went through eleven editions, and the two-volume report *Recent Social Trends in the United States* (1933). In the former work Ogburn set forth his conception of "cultural lag," which excited much discussion and criticism. He perceived that various elements of culture change at different rates and that many problems result therefrom. The latter work was the summary report of President Herbert Hoover's Research Committee on Social Trends, of which Ogburn was director of research. This report set a pattern followed by Ogburn in the annual series on social change, which he edited in the *American Journal of Sociology* from 1928 to 1935, with a number of follow-ups. That work foreshadowed the current interest in "social indicators" as a basis for public policy and action.

Over 170 of Ogburn's scientific publications have been organized and classified into thirteen categories by Otis Dudley Duncan in *William F. Ogburn on Culture and Social Change.* These categories reflect his diverse interests. His writings on "Sociology and the Social Sciences" cover the period from 1927 to 1959; on "Social Change," from 1922 to 1957; on "Interpretation of Social Trends," from 1929 to 1961; on "Technology," from 1922 to 1957; on "Economic Growth and Fluctuations," from 1919 to 1959; on "Standards of Living," from 1916 to 1935; on the "Family and Marriage," from 1923 to 1956; on "Population," from 1929 to 1959; on "Legislation and Voting," from 1912 to 1956; on "War and International Relations," from 1942 to 1949; on "Cities," from 1917 to 1960; on "Social Psychology," from 1919 to 1959; and on "Methods," from 1921 to 1955.

Although Ogburn's impact on sociology and other social sciences is difficult to evaluate definitely, it is possible to describe his most significant contributions. Like many pioneer social scientists, early in his career Ogburn was interested in social action and social reform. But he developed a keen interest in the scientific method and the importance of accumulating knowledge through research. He played a major role in converting the social sciences into quantitative empirical disciplines by introducing courses in statistics into social science curricula and using statistical techniques, advanced for his time, in his research. He also provided a seminal interpretation of social change and its consequences and, thereby, as he himself believed, clarified the process of social evolution. He exerted great influence on later sociologists and other social scientists through his influence on graduate students at Columbia University and the University of Chicago.

Ogburn's importance was widely recognized by his colleagues. He served as editor of the *Journal of the American Statistical Association* from 1920 to 1926. He was much in demand as a consultant to government agencies including the Consumers Advisory Board, NRA (National Recovery Administration) in 1933; the National Resources Committee (1935–1943); the Resettlement Administration (1936); and the Census Advisory Committee (1940–1953). He was president of the American Sociological

Society in 1929, president of the American Statistical Association in 1931, vice-president of the American Association for the Advancement of Science in 1932, chairman of the Social Science Research Council in 1937–1939, and president of the Society for the History of Technology in 1959.

[The major sources on Ogburn are his papers and selected materials in the Regenstein Library of the University of Chicago; and Otis Dudley Duncan, *William F. Ogburn on Culture and Social Change* (1964), which contains an excellent photograph of Ogburn on its cover (paperback). Obituary notices and memorial statements appeared in *New York Times,* Apr. 29, 1959; *Chicago Tribune,* Apr. 30, 1959; *Science,* Aug. 7, 1959; *American Journal of Sociology,* July 1959; *American Sociological Review,* Aug. 1959; *American Statistician,* June 1959; *Social Forces,* Oct. 1959; and *Wilson Library Bulletin,* June 1949.]

PHILIP M. HAUSER

OLDS, LELAND (Dec. 31, 1890–Aug. 3, 1960), economist and public official, was born in Rochester, N.Y., the son of George Daniel Olds, professor of mathematics at the University of Rochester, and of Marion Elizabeth Leland. In 1891 the family moved to Amherst, Mass., where George Olds assumed the chair of mathematics at Amherst College. In 1924 he became president of the college, succeeding Alexander Meiklejohn.

Olds entered Amherst in 1908. A serious young man, he early exhibited a concern for the welfare of workers, whom he regarded as victims of industrialization. Influenced by Henry George's *Progress and Poverty* and by Charles M. Sheldon's *In His Steps,* he sought to apply Christian principles to the amelioration of industrial problems. After receiving the B.A. in 1912, he worked in a social settlement in Boston; undertook graduate study at Harvard, Columbia, and Union Theological Seminary; served as pastor of a small Congregational church in Brooklyn; and spent a few months during 1918 in the army. He also did economic studies for the Council of National Defense and the National War Labor Board, where he began a long association with the labor attorney Frank P. Walsh.

In the early 1920's, Olds married Maud Agnes Spear; they had four children. The family lived in Northbrook, Ill., where Olds served on the school board, directed Boy Scout activities, and played cello in the local orchestra. Deceptively mild-mannered, he possessed a hard set of convictions about the wrongdoings of American capitalists, and a writing style midway between the muck-raking of the Progressive Era and the work of later radical journalists like I. F. Stone. Professionally, he continued to devote his energies to the labor movement in research tasks for the railway brotherhoods and as industrial editor of the Federated Press, a news service with an assortment of clients among labor journals. In this post, which he held from 1922 until 1929, he wrote some 1,800 articles, their content ranging from the nature and tendencies of industrial capitalism to the effects of particular business decisions and public policies. Blunt in tone, sharply critical of the values implicit in the "New Era" of American business, these articles were "certainly radical," as Olds himself acknowledged. Their radicalism and their appearance in Communist publications such as the *Daily Worker,* one of the many clients of the Federated Press, haunted Old years later, in the fear-ridden climate of the Cold War.

When the Federated Press ran short of funds in 1929, Olds's friendship with Frank P. Walsh took him to New York, as economic adviser to Community Councils of the City of New York, a group advocating the reform of public utility regulation. For Olds the utility issue embodied some of the principles for which he had been fighting for many years. With Walsh and others, he advised Governor Franklin D. Roosevelt on a legislative program aimed at reasserting public control over power resources and utility corporations. One result of this legislation was the creation of the Power Authority of the State of New York, and from 1931 until 1939 Olds served as its top-ranking staff member. In this position, and because of his influence with Roosevelt, he remained in the vanguard of the great power fight of the 1930's, a leader in the struggle for such reforms as the net-investment rate base, regulation by competition, uniform utility accounting, and public development of the St. Lawrence River.

In 1939, Roosevelt appointed Olds to the Federal Power Commission (FPC). To a remarkable degree he fitted the ideal of the early architects of regulatory agencies. An expert in the field of electric power, Olds had splendid credentials as a champion of the "public interest," and a confident sense of where that interest lay. Because of his experience as a journalist, he excelled in translating complex regulatory issues into everyday language. Olds served as chairman of the FPC during about half his tenure, which lasted a decade. He was proudest of his achievement in hammering out consensus, and

usually decisions by the five-member agency were unanimous. Olds's pursuit of harmony in this instance (and in others, such as his faith in cooperative economic enterprises) clashed with his equally sincere belief in market competition, and with his characteristic conviction that private interests and the "public interest" were usually antithetical. Known as a tireless worker and advocate of public power, Olds downplayed the public ownership controversy during World War II, and directed the resources of the FPC toward efficient use and development of power for the war effort.

During the war years, and more so afterward, Olds led the commission into ever deeper involvement in the regulation of the natural gas industry. It was this struggle that made him nationally famous, and that finally cost him his job. Originally aimed chiefly at pipelines, the Natural Gas Act of 1938 eventually affected prices at the wellhead, that is, the field prices at which gas was sold to wholesalers. In the midst of a major congressional debate over price regulation, embodied in the "Kerr Bill" of 1948, Olds and Commissioner Claude L. Draper completed a study that strongly contended that the FPC had both the authority and the duty to regulate wellhead prices. The opposing view, held by other members of the commission, was also thrust forward by powerful legislators from the gas-producing Southwest, including Senator Robert Kerr of Oklahoma and Senator Lyndon B. Johnson of Texas.

In 1949, when President Harry S. Truman appointed Olds to a third five-year term, the issue of his confirmation became a test of strength between advocates and opponents of wellhead price regulation. The confirmation subcommittee, chaired by Lyndon Johnson, heard witnesses who complained that Olds had changed his mind on the gas question, or that his new position was simply wrong. Equally damaging was the dramatic resurrection of his radical writings of the 1920's. Though "Red-baiting" efforts had been unsuccessful during Olds's 1944 confirmation hearings, the context had changed; the new hearings came during the year in which Communist forces triumphed in China, and only a few days after the Soviet Union exploded its first atomic bomb. Thus, despite Truman's support and the pleadings of prominent New Dealers and advocates of regulation, the Senate rejected Olds's appointment by a 53–15 vote. Some observers portrayed him as a martyr to anti-Communist hysteria. Others read object lessons on the fate of aggressive regulators. Lyndon Johnson's unbridled floor speech against Olds was one of the least creditable performances of his career.

After the confirmation fight Olds faded from public view, serving briefly as a federal adviser, then as a private consultant in his own business, Energy Research Associates. During the 1950's he occasionally published articles on energy and related topics. He died at Bethesda, Md.

[Olds's personal papers are in the Franklin D. Roosevelt Library, Hyde Park, N.Y. Representative articles include "The Temper of British Labor," *Nation,* Apr. 19, 1919; "Yardsticks and Birch Rods," *Harper's,* Nov. 1935; and "The Economic Planning Function Under Public Regulation," *American Economic Review,* May 1958. He also contributed to federal economic studies: *Inquiry on Cooperative Enterprise in Europe* (1937); and *Natural Gas Investigation . . . Report of Commissioner Leland Olds and Commissioner Claude L. Draper* (1948), which was instrumental in the Senate rejection of 1949. The fullest sources on Olds's career, other than his personal papers, are the records of his confirmation hearings before subcommittees of the Senate Committee on Interstate Commerce: *Leland Olds' Reappointment to Federal Power Commission: Hearings* (1944); and *Reappointment of Leland Olds to Federal Power Commission: Hearings* (1949). Joseph P. Harris, "The Senatorial Rejection of Leland Olds," *American Political Science Review,* Sept. 1951, is a good scholarly analysis of that episode. An obituary is in *New York Times,* Aug. 5, 1960. On the power issue consult Forrest McDonald, *Insull* (1962); Thomas K. McCraw, *TVA and the Power Fight, 1933–1939* (1971); and Philip J. Funigiello, *Toward a National Power Policy* (1973).]

THOMAS K. MCCRAW

OLMSTED, FREDERICK LAW (July 24, 1870–Dec. 25, 1957), landscape architect, planner, and conservationist, was born the son of Frederick Law Olmsted, Sr., a landscape architect, and Mary Cleveland Perkins Olmsted (his brother's widow) on Staten Island in New York. Named Henry Perkins at birth but renamed in childhood by his father, who intended that his son follow in his footsteps, "Rick" trained and studied under his father while attending Roxbury Latin School and then earned a B.A. at Harvard University in 1894.

As a sixteen-year-old he was taken to California to help his father, who was laying out the grounds for Stanford University; his later apprenticeship included work on the Chicago World's Columbian Exposition of 1893 and George W. Vanderbilt's Biltmore estate in Asheville, N. C., his father's last major project before retiring in 1895, at which time he turned his landscape architecture firm over to Frederick and John C. Olmsted, the son of Mary by her previous marriage to his younger brother, John. Under the name Olmsted Brothers they prospered and expanded at their Brookline, Mass., headquarters until in the early 1900's they headed by far the largest landscape architecture firm in the United States. Achieving competence in his own right, Frederick dropped the "Junior," causing thereafter much confusion in bibliographic nomenclature and even in the attribution of works to him and his father.

In 1898 Frederick was appointed landscape architect to the Boston Metropolitan Park Commision, a position he held until 1920; and in 1900, at the request of Harvard President Charles W. Eliot, he instituted the first curriculum in the United States for the study of landscape architecture as a profession. He also taught at Harvard from 1901 to 1914, having been appointed in 1903 to the Charles Eliot professorship established in honor of Eliot's son, who had been a partner in the Olmsted firm until his premature death in 1897. Frederick married Sarah Hall Sharples on Mar. 30, 1911; they had one child.

Olmsted's career was an amalgam of professional and public works in which he served as environmental designer, public and quasi-official servant, and member of numerous formal commissions and organizations dealing with urban park design, town planning, housing, recreation, landscape architecture, land development and management, national-park planning, and conservation. The beginning of his varied career really came in 1901 when President Theodore Roosevelt appointed him to the Senate Park Commission, a recommendation that his father's reputation undoubtedly influenced, along with the distinguished architects Daniel H. Burnham and Charles F. McKim. Their purpose was to "restore and develop the century-old plans of L'Enfant for Washington and to fit them to the conditions of today." Before beginning work the team traveled throughout Europe examining urban exemplars and precedents. This was a stimulating experience for Olmsted, who acted as design secretary, measuring and photographing subjects of interest. Not all the ideas put forward by the commission were adopted, but for Olmsted it marked the beginning of a long-term, felicitous association with those directing the physical growth of Washington, D. C. Perhaps more than any other person Olmsted is responsible for the appearance of the nation's capital, and especially for the coherent quality of the monuments that bespeak the symbols of national power. Not only was he, together with Olmsted Brothers, responsible in whole or in part for dozens of major landscape projects, such as the White House grounds, Lafayette Park, Washington Monument Gardens, the Jefferson Memorial, the National Arboretum, Washington Cathedral, portions of Rock Creek Park and its zoo, the Shrine of the Immaculate Conception, and other structures, but he was instrumental in the founding of the Fine Arts Commission, thereby assuring the urban and architectural controls necessary to protect the federal matrix. He thus continued the work begun by his father, who had designed, among other major early projects, the U.S. Capitol grounds and had recommended steps that resulted in the "greening" of Washington with trees and plantings.

Olmsted served on the Fine Arts Commission from 1910 to 1918 and during World War I with the War Industries Board's Commission on Emergency Construction and with the Town Planning Division of the U.S. Housing Corporation. Between 1926 and 1932 he was a member of the National Capital Park and Planning Commission. As a private consultant he directed the development of major residential complexes for the Roland Park Company of Baltimore, the Sage Foundation Home Company of Forest Hills, L.I. (Forest Hills Gardens), and Palos Verdes Estates in California. In these, as in many other projects, he had full responsibility, while in the manifold projects of the firm (10,000 jobs have been logged in the Brookline office, now known as Olmsted Associates, Inc.) he and his brother supervised and approved the work of draftsmen, plantsmen, and engineers.

Over the years Olmsted made many urban planning studies for cities such as Rochester, N.Y.; Pittsburgh; New Haven; Boulder, Colo.; and Newport, R.I.—work for which he further prepared himself in the early 1900's by study and travel in Europe. He devoted much time to two professional organizations, the American Society of Landscape Architects, which he helped found, and the American Institute of Planners, serving as president of both. Among the many works of landscape architecture he designed, one of the

most outstanding is Fort Tryon Park and the Cloisters in New York City. Here, the structure on a high rocky ridge is carefully blended into the extensive park grounds through which the paths curve and rise as the visitor approaches. Sited at the edges of the "natural" environment—artifice at its best—are terrace overlooks that take full advantage of the lower Hudson Valley views available from Manhattan.

Turning the firm over to his associates in 1950, Olmsted moved to California, where he devoted himself primarily to the conservation of natural lands and wilderness areas. In 1916 he had helped frame the legislation that established the National Park Service. He studied the Colorado River Basin for the Bureau of Reclamation, advising on conservation methods for these water resources. For the California State Park Commission he prepared a master plan for preservation of the redwoods and fought vigorously against the destructive exploitation of forest resources by private interests. From 1928 to 1956 he served on a committee of experts on plans and policies for Yosemite, closing a circle, for his father had served in 1864 as leader of the original commissioners of Yosemite, the first land set aside for public use in the United States. On his eighty-third birthday he attended the dedication of the Frederick Law Olmsted Grove of redwood trees purchased by friends in his honor in Prairie Creek Redwoods State Park, Humboldt County, Calif., a rare and fitting tribute. He died in Malibu, Calif.

During his lifetime Olmsted was believed to have surpassed the accomplishments of his father, who had slipped into almost total obscurity. Of course, the elder man has now emerged as a giant. The younger Olmsted did not seem to face, or perhaps recognize, the prototypical environmental challenges that came his father's way. He worked within the established framework. Nevertheless, he expanded the base and solidified the achievements of a profession that has no name even today ("geotecht" was Lewis Mumford's term for the elder Olmsted) but in whose pursuit of ordering the built environment he advocated and worked toward an ever more progressive and humanistic approach.

[An index of articles Olmsted wrote is in Columbia University's Avery Library Periodical File. Printed copies of his park and planning reports are stored at Olmsted Associates in Brookline, Mass. The bulk of Typescripts of published articles and occasional papers by Olmsted are held by his grandson, Dr. Stephen Gill the firm's professional papers from about 1857 to 1950 are in the Library of Congress Manuscript Division. of Atherton, Calif. Published biographical materials on Olmsted are sparse. Besides the obituary in the *New York Times,* Dec. 27, 1957, the best biographic summation is by E. C. Whiting and W. L. Phillips, "Frederick Law Olmsted—1870–1957, An Appreciation of the Man and His Works," *Landscape Architecture,* Apr. 1958, which also has a good photographic likeness. References to him appear in Laura W. Roper's biography of Olmsted Senior, *FLO* (1973); and in Elizabeth Stevenson, *Park-Marker: A Life of Frederick Law Olmsted* (1977). Pictorial highlights of the firm's work are shown in Joseph Hudak, "Nine Decades of Landscape Design," *Landscape Architecture,* Apr. 1955.]

WILLIAM ALEX

O'NEAL, EDWARD ASBURY, III (Oct. 26, 1875–Feb. 26, 1958), agricultural leader, was born on a plantation near Florence, Ala., the son of Edward Asbury O'Neal II, a lawyer, and of Mary Coffee. His paternal grandfather, Edward Asbury O'Neal, had been governor of Alabama from 1882 to 1886, and an uncle, Emmett Asbury, also had held that office.

After graduating from Washington and Lee University in 1898, O'Neal toured Europe for a year, then returned to assume management of the 1,900-acre cotton plantation near Florence that belonged to his family. On Nov. 23, 1904, he married Julia Camper; they had three children.

Although he was viewed by some as a southern aristocrat of the "old school," O'Neal's devout Presbyterianism seemed at times incongruous with his fondness for hard liquor and his proclivity for racy language. He was not a "dirt farmer," and he never concealed his contempt for barely profitable subsistence operations. His interest in scientific farm management prompted further study at the State Agricultural and Mechanical College at Auburn and the University of Illinois, and also attracted him to the modernizing program of the federal Agricultural Extension Service, established in 1914. In 1921, shortly after the American Farm Bureau Federation (AFBF) was established as a voluntary auxiliary organization to the extension service, O'Neal became president of the Lauderdale County chapter. In 1922 he became vice-president, and in 1923 president, of the Alabama Farm Bureau Federation. Farm politics, not farming, became his central interest for the rest of his life.

During the 1920's, O'Neal pressed for creation of a fertilizer production complex at the aban-

doned Muscle Shoals hydroelectric facility, located near his home. He was a late convert to George Norris' plan to utilize Muscle Shoals as a nucleus for a regional water-power and electric-power development that eventually took shape as the Tennessee Valley Authority. By 1925, O'Neal was recognized as spokesman within the AFBF for the minority faction of cotton producers in an organization dominated by corn and livestock producers of the Midwest. He served as national vice-president from 1924 to 1931.

O'Neal succeeded to the presidency of the AFBF (the only Southerner ever to hold the office) in 1931, on the eve of the most severe crisis in American agricultural history. He and his organization enthusiastically endorsed the agricultural reform program of the administration of Franklin D. Roosevelt, embodied in the acreage reduction and parity price goals of the Agricultural Adjustment Administration (AAA). With exaggerated pride, O'Neal credited the AFBF with having inspired the program. During the early New Deal years O'Neal, as spokesman for the AFBF, worked closely with the president and Secretary of Agriculture Henry A. Wallace. An effective lobbyist, he flexed the considerable political muscle of the AFBF to win added appropriations for farm programs, and he participated in restructuring the AAA following invalidation of the original act by the Supreme Court in 1936.

During O'Neal's long tenure as president of AFBF, he was an effective mediator who forged an alliance within AFBF between the cotton-producing Democratic farmers of the South and the Republican livestock producers of the Middle West. This cooperation had to overcome such obstacles as the conflict between the free-trade preferences of export-conscious cotton producers and the protectionist tendencies of Midwesterners. O'Neal engineered some of the subtle compromises that set price supports at a level acceptable both to cotton producers, who marketed their crop directly, and to corn producers, who fed most of their crop to livestock.

O'Neal considered his greatest achievement while president of AFBF to have been the increase in its membership from 276,000 when he assumed the presidency to 1,128,000 when he retired in 1946. Much of this increment was due to vigorous organizing activity in the South.

O'Neal also presided over a policy transformation that changed the AFBF from advocate to opponent of Democratic party farm policies. During World War II, AFBF backed higher price supports and objected to price ceilings that might curtail wartime profits of the large commercial producers who made up the bulk of its members. When the Agriculture Department sought, through the Farm Security Administration and other programs, to extend assistance and to create grass-roots organizations among poorer farmers, the AFBF, seeing a challenge to its rural hegemony, allied with conservative congressional farm interests to emasculate the programs. Fearful of wage increases not accompanied by corresponding gains in prices for commercial farmers, the AFBF in the later years of O'Neal's presidency took a militant stand against labor unions. By 1946, O'Neal's disenchantment with federal controls, and his increasing interest in international markets as a profitable outlet for the products of the large, mechanized farms that now dominated American agriculture, presaged the policy positions the AFBF would advocate consistently after 1950. A lifelong Democrat, O'Neal nevertheless urged farmers to elect Dwight D. Eisenhower as president in 1952. O'Neal died in Florence, Ala.

Appropriately, during one of the most critical periods of change in American agriculture, when depression policies of production limitation had to yield suddenly to wartime demands for production expansion, and when traditional family farming was being overwhelmed by the integrated, mechanized operations that characterize modern agriculture, the largest farm organization in the nation had as its leader an individual unswervingly committed to scientific commercial agriculture and to those programs that would augment and stimulate its growth and eventual dominance.

[Christiana McFadyen Campbell, *The Farm Bureau and the New Deal* (1962), is in large part a biography of O'Neal. There is additional personal information in "The Farm Bureau," *Fortune,* June 1944, an unsigned article that has been attributed to John Kenneth Galbraith, at one time an economist for AFBF. The Oral History Collection of Columbia University has a recollection by O'Neal, completed in 1952. Many other memoirs in the collection contain material on him, particularly those of Marvin Jones, Claude Wickard, and M. L. Wilson. O'Neal's obituary is in the *New York Times*, Feb. 27, 1958.]

JOHN L. SHOVER

OTT, MELVIN THOMAS ("MEL") (Mar. 2, 1909–Nov. 21, 1958), professional baseball player, was born in Gretna, La., the son of Charles

Ott, a worker at a nearby oil refinery who had once played semiprofessional baseball, and Caroline Miller. Ott was an all-around athlete at Gretna High School, playing football and basketball, and catching for the baseball team. He left school just before graduation, hoping to be signed by the New Orleans Pelicans of the Southern Association, but the owner rejected him as being much too small. He was then about five feet, six inches tall. (In his prime Ott stood five feet, nine inches tall and weighed between 160 and 170 pounds—by far the smallest of the great baseball sluggers.) Ott was soon playing for the Patterson Grays, a semiprofessional team owned by Harry Williams, a local lumberman. He was brilliant behind the plate and a bat, and Williams decided that the young man must be seen by his friend John J. McGraw, the awesome manager of the New York Giants.

With a one-way train ticket and his father's straw suitcase, Ott, just past sixteen years old, set out for New York in the summer of 1925. He immediately impressed a skeptical McGraw with the beauty and power of his batting. Ott's stance at the plate was uniquely unorthodox, and it was already his trademark. Swinging left-handed, he cocked his right leg stiffly about a foot off the ground as if he were goose-stepping; and thus poised, he lowered his bat slightly, then whipped it around in a perfect upward arc. "That kid's got the finest natural batting form I've ever seen," said McGraw, and almost immediately decided to groom Ott for big-league play. McGraw refused to send him to the minor leagues, afraid that somebody there would tamper with the youth's hitting stance. The Giants' manager also decided to convert Ott to outfielding, concerned lest his thick, muscular legs become knotted by the constant squatting that is the lot of catchers.

In 1926, Ott batted for the first time as a Giant, and struck out. But at the end of the season he was hitting .383 (in thirty-five games). His prowess as a slugger grew gradually. In 1927 he hit one home run; in 1928, eighteen; and in 1929—now the regular right fielder—he hit forty-two, the high of his career. The right-field stands at the Polo Grounds (only 257 feet from home plate at the foul line), into which Ott pulled so many of his homers, became known to fans as Ottville. Along with Bill Terry, the first baseman, and Carl Hubbell, the premier left-handed pitcher of the time, Ott was a Giant mainstay and fixture.

When Ott's playing days ended in 1947, he had hit 511 home runs—a lifetime record exceeded at the time only by Babe Ruth and Jimmy

Foxx. Moreover, he had batted in more runs (1,860), hit for more total bases (5,041), scored more runs (1,859), drawn more walks (1,708), and accumulated more extra bases (2,165) and extra base hits (1,071) than any player ever in the National League. His lifetime batting average was .304, his best year being 1930, when he hit .349. In eight different years he struck thirty or more home runs. Ott played in the World Series of 1933, 1936, and 1937. His homer in the tenth inning of the fifth game decided the World Series of 1933 against the Washington Senators. Ott also participated in eleven All-Star games.

As a fielder Ott made up for a certain lack of speed afoot with a powerful arm (he threw right-handed); the well-practiced technique of gauging in a flash a ball hit deep into his territory, and then, turning his back to it, sprinting to the spot where it would drop into his glove; and uncanny judgment of the carom of balls hit against the angled outfield fence of the Polo Grounds. Endowed with excellent reflexes, he also played splendidly at third base in several seasons.

When Bill Terry, who had succeeded McGraw as manager of the Giants in 1932, resigned in 1941, Ott was chosen to take over the club. The teams he fielded and on which he continued to play were decimated by the military draft, and their performance was generally disappointing. In July 1948 the flamboyant Leo Durocher, who had won fame as a Brooklyn Dodger, was appointed to replace Ott, who took a position in the Giants' front office. Subsequently he managed Oakland in the Pacific Coast League. In 1951 the Baseball Writers' Association elected him to the Baseball Hall of Fame.

Ott announced his retirement from baseball in 1955 and entered the construction business in Louisiana. But the lure of the game remained, and soon he returned as a broadcaster, first for the Mutual Broadcasting System and then for the Detroit Tigers.

In 1930 Ott had married Mildred Wattigny; they had two daughters. In mid-November 1958, Ott and his wife were critically injured in an automobile accident in Mississippi. Ott's condition improved for a few days; then his kidneys began to fail. Rushed to New Orleans for surgery, he died on the operating table.

As a player Ott was almost totally lacking in color. A modest, unassuming gentleman on the field and off, he was the target of Durocher's taunt "Nice guys finish last." But he was a revered national hero. A sportswriter dubbed him "Master Melvin" when he joined the Giants,

and he wore the nickname for years. To many people he was a living example of eternal youth: when he retired from active playing, he had spent twenty-two seasons with the Giants, a modern record for unbroken service with one team—and he was only thirty-nine years old. By then he was no longer the "boy wonder" from the bayous. Still, his place among the legendary sports figures of his era was secure; he was every boy's fantasy come alive: the child who came to the big leagues in the big city all alone, armed and assured only by his uncommon talent and determination, and who, without ever playing an inning in the minor leagues, won the adulation and respect of the crowds—and rewrote the baseball record book.

[Memorabilia and personal data are in the National Baseball Hall of Fame, Cooperstown, N.Y. The statistics of Ott's career are in *The Baseball Encyclopedia* (1969). A full-length biography is Milton J. Shapiro, *The Mel Ott Story* (1959). Evaluations of his playing are in Lee Allen and Tom Meany, *Kings of the Diamond* (1965); and *Time*, July 2, 1945 (a cover story that contains sequential photographs of Ott's batting swing). Obituaries are in the *New York Times* and the *New York Herald Tribune*, Nov. 22, 1958. The highlights of Ott's career in baseball can be traced in the pages of those newspapers.]

HENRY F. GRAFF

OTTLEY, ROI (Aug. 2, 1906–Oct. 1, 1960), journalist and author, was born in New York City as Vincent Lushington Ottley, the son of Jerome Peter Ottley, who had emigrated to New York City from the island of Grenada, and of Beatrice Brisbane. According to family legend he was born while his mother was employed by a family named Fitzroy who wanted the child named in their honor rather than for her native island of St. Vincent. His mother acceded by calling him Roy, a spelling he later gallicized.

Ottley's father, using savings accumulated from odd jobs, became a real estate broker in Harlem after World War I. Thus Roi witnessed the renaissance of art, music, and literature there and the Lenox Avenue parades of Marcus Garvey's Universal Negro Improvement Association. He grew up on "Strivers' Row" (138th Street between Seventh and Eighth avenues) in a townhouse that was fastidiously clean and orderly. Ottley and Adam Clayton Powell, Jr., the future congressman, played on the basketball team of the Abyssinian Baptist Church and made the rounds of the nightclubs in Harlem.

From his father, Ottley acquired the habits of keeping files and rising early that served him well as a free-lance writer. In the rush and disarray of journalism, he would be remembered as "one of the rare reporters who cleaned up after himself."

Ottley's formal education reflected a pragmatic bent. After graduating from Public School 5, he starred in basketball and track at Textile High School. A 1926 city sprinting championship won him a scholarship to St. Bonaventure College in Olean, N.Y., where he was a cartoonist and illustrator for the student newspaper. He showed greater promise as a writer, though, so in 1928 he enrolled in the journalism department at the University of Michigan. After leaving in 1929 without a degree, he briefly attended St. John's Law School in Brooklyn. As he saw a practical need, he later handpicked his courses: playwriting at Columbia University, article writing at the City College of New York, and Negro folk literature at New York University.

Ottley's newspaper career began in 1932 with a part-time job at the *Amsterdam News* in New York City. Between working for the New York City Welfare Department and distributing free meals at the Abyssinian Baptist Church, Ottley was a radio, theatrical, and sports columnist. In 1937, when he was editor of the sports and theatrical pages of the *Amsterdam News*, he was dismissed for his support of the fledgling New York Newspaper Guild. He then joined the Federal Writers Project of the Works Progress Administration, for which he compiled and edited manuscripts on the history of blacks in New York City. Much of this material was contained in his two popular histories of black American life, *New World A-Coming* (1943) and *Black Odyssey* (1948).

New World A-Coming was a World War II publishing phenomenon. Its forecast of postwar racial harmony came as a cool breeze during race riots in Detroit during the summer of 1943, in which thirty-four blacks and whites had been killed. On August 1, Harlem erupted, just as copies of the book were being read by reviewers. For alarmed whites, the good-spirited and crisply written overview of Harlem and the black American condition came as a revelation and a tonic. "The way to start to learn about Negroes," the *New York Post* critic wrote, "is to read Ottley's fine book." Launched by its publisher's $2,500 "Life in America" Prize, *New World* sold 50,000 copies and won the Ainsworth Award (1944) and the Peabody Award (1945). Ottley adapted the book for radio.

Ottley logged 60,000 miles in Europe, North Africa, and the Middle East as a wartime and postwar correspondent for the newspaper *PM*, *Liberty* magazine, and the *Pittsburgh Courier* in 1944–1945. In 1946 he returned to New York City, where he wrote and worked as a free-lancer. In 1950 he went to Chicago. The premise of his book *No Green Pastures* (1951)—that American blacks fared better economically than European blacks—was perceived by the novelist James Baldwin as "a reduction of black-white history to a kind of tableau of material progress." On Feb. 14, 1951, Ottley married Alice Dungey, the librarian for the black weekly newspaper *Defender*. They had one daughter. Two previous marriages, to Mildred M. Peyton and Gladys Tarr, had ended in divorce.

At his new home in the Hyde Park district of Chicago, Ottley wrote columns, editorials, and special features for the *Defender* and for *Ebony* magazine. Beginning in 1953, his by-lined articles appeared each Saturday and Sunday in the *Chicago Tribune*. These included a ten-part series on the migration of blacks to Chicago and scores of profiles of local and national personalities. The affable and handsome Ottley also conducted an interview program for radio station WGN, but he rarely spoke of himself. He left no biography or personal memoir.

Ottley's most valuable work, *The Lonely Warrior* (1955), was published in memory of Robert S. Abbott, founder of the *Defender*. Though authorized and subsidized by the newspaper, the biography is a lively and insightful account of a black man's rise to fortune, and is perhaps the most revealing book ever written about the black press. Following Ottley's death in Chicago, his only book of fiction, *White Marble Lady,* the story of an interracial marriage, was edited by his widow and published in 1965.

[An unpublished manuscript based on Ottley's travels as a war correspondent and *Chicago Tribune* clippings that his widow left to their daughter, Lynne Ottley Harris, are in the private collection of his brother, Jerome P. Ottley, Jr. The collection also includes a scrapbook that dates from the Ottley brothers' college days at St. Bonaventure. Ottley was coeditor, with William J. Weatherby, of *The Negro in New York* (1967), based on WPA materials that he deposited at the Schomburg Collection of the New York City Public Library in Harlem. Biographical sketches include "Ottley Sees New World A-Coming," *New York Post*, Apr. 7, 1944; and "What

Became of Roi Ottley?" *Sepia*, Sept. 1960. Obituaries are in *New York Times* and *Chicago Tribune*, Oct. 2, 1960; and *Amsterdam News* and *Defender*, Oct. 8, 1960.]

LUTHER P. JACKSON, JR.

OWSLEY, FRANK LAWRENCE (Jan. 20, 1890–Oct. 21, 1956), historian, was born on a farm in Montgomery County, Ala., the son of Lawrence Monroe Owsley and Annie Scott McGehee. His father was a teacher and farmer who rented land to sharecroppers, mostly blacks. Young Owsley was impressed with the many Confederate veterans who had been antebellum yeoman farmers, neither planters nor poor whites. This observation had great bearing on his later researches.

From 1906 to 1909 Owsley attended the Fifth District Agricultural School in Wetumpka, Ala., where the curriculum included two years of college. In 1911 he graduated from Alabama Polytechnic Institute at Auburn, returning a year later for a master's degree. At Auburn, Owsley was introduced to "scientific" history by Professor George Petrie, a product of Herbert Baxter Adams' famous seminar at the Johns Hopkins University. After a year of public school teaching and two years as instructor in history and Latin at Auburn, Owsley entered the University of Chicago's graduate school. William E. Dodd directed his work on a second master's degree, conferred in 1917. Dodd and Owsley shared a love for Jeffersonian agrarian values, an identification with the common man, and distrust of northern industrialists.

Following military service during World War I, Owsley taught briefly at Auburn and Birmingham-Southern College and in 1920 joined the history faculty at Vanderbilt University. On July 24, 1920, he married Harriet Fason Chappell; they had three children. His wife served as coauthor and research associate for many of his publications. In 1924 the University of Chicago awarded Owsley the Ph.D.

Owsley spent nearly three decades at Vanderbilt, where he was instrumental in developing the graduate program in history. A stimulating instructor, he excelled in training graduate students; Owsley directed almost forty doctoral dissertations and many masters' theses at Vanderbilt.

The opportunity to help establish a new Ph.D. program was a major factor in his decision to leave Vanderbilt in 1949 to accept the Hugo Friedman chair in southern history at the University of Alabama. He believed that professors often neglected their teaching responsibilities and became "selfish, conceited, narrow-minded doctrinaires who care nothing for the students—the personal element is missing" (Owsley to George Petrie, Feb. 25, 1921). Generations of his students appreciated this concern. They praised his warmth and exuberance, his wit and humor, and his ability to inspire and encourage. Neither dogmatic nor pretentious, Owsley encouraged students to disagree, to have fresh ideas. He was a colorful man, expansive in conversation, and prone to overstate and exaggerate for effect. Patient yet firm, he had the respect of students and colleagues alike.

Owsley wrote six books, thirty-four articles, and many reviews and review essays. His historical works developed a number of the most perceptive themes in the literature on the South. In *State Rights in the Confederacy* (1925) he attributed the Confederate defeat to the South's factious states' rights ideology rather than to overwhelming Union strength. Six years later he published *King Cotton Diplomacy*, a pioneer work based on research in previously unexamined European foreign-office records. Owsley criticized Confederate officials for withholding cotton from England and France, a policy that they hoped would forced recognition of the South. Differing with earlier writers, he argued that British neutrality resulted from "war profits," not from antislavery sentiment or dependence on northern wheat. *Plain Folk of the Old South* (1949) focused attention on the heretofore ignored southern middle class of yeoman farmers and herdsmen. Owsley revolutionized understanding of the subject by analyzing (with punch cards and calculators) statistics gleaned from manuscript census schedules, county tax records, and wills. He concluded that most plain folk were landowners who frequently lived alongside planters. This work and other studies by Owsley's students made it impossible any longer to describe the Old South's social structure as being composed simply of planters, slaves, and poor whites. This was Owsley's greatest contribution to southern historiography.

In his essays, too, Owsley sought to correct what he thought were incorrect interpretations of the South and its people. He loved the region's rural ethos and criticized what he termed the

North's carefully planned exploitation of the South. Owsley associated himself with the Nashville Agrarians and contributed "The Irrepressible Conflict" to their literary symposium, *I'll Take My Stand* (1930). This essay described the Old South as an agrarian society resisting the depredations of northern industrial capitalism. The North, he suggested, forced the South to secede. In a number of other essays Owsley applied this thesis to the twentieth century. He portrayed the South defending itself against the encroachments of northern corporate interests, often camouflaged in humanitarian garb. Owsley criticized bigness in industry, labor, and government and argued that the South's cultural heritage was threatened by "industrial insecurity and industrial insensitivity." So vigorously did Owsley defend the South that he was sometimes accused of being "choleric and impulsive to the point of fanaticism" (John L. Stewart, *The Burden of Time* [1965]). Shortly before his death, he admitted that he had been "deliberately provocative" in his polemical writings.

In 1940 Owsley was president of the Southern Historical Association. In 1956 he was a Fulbright lecturer at Cambridge University, where he studied Union diplomacy during the Civil War. Owsley died in Winchester, England, of a heart attack.

[Nineteen boxes of Owsley's private papers are deposited in the Joint University Libraries, Nashville. There are also Owsley letters in the Wendell Holmes Stephenson Papers, Duke University; William E. Dodd Papers, Library of Congress; Andrew Nelson Lytle Papers and Donald Davidson Papers, Joint University Libraries, Nashville; Robert Penn Warren Papers and *American Review* Papers, Yale University; and Allen Tate Papers, Princeton University. A representative group of Owsley's writings and a comprehensive bibliography appear in Harriet Chappell Owsley, ed., *The South: Old and New Frontiers—Selected Essays of Frank Lawrence Owsley* (1969). Not in this anthology is one of Owsley's most controversial essays: "Scottsboro, the Third Crusade: The Sequel to Abolition and Reconstruction," *American Review*, June 1933. Useful essays about Owsley are William C. Binkley, "Frank Lawrence Owsley, 1890–1956: A Memorial Foreword," *King Cotton Diplomacy*, revised ed. by Harriet Chappell Owsley (1959); M. E. Bradford, "What We Know for Certain: Frank Owsley and the Recovery of Southern History," *Sewanee Review*, 1970; Bernarr Cresap, "Frank L. Owsley and *King Cotton Diplomacy*," *Alabama Review*, Oct. 1973; and Edward S. Shapiro, "Frank L. Owsley and the Defense of Southern Identity," *Tennessee Historical Quarterly*, Spring 1977.

Fabian Linden leveled criticisms at the "Owsley School" in "Economic Democracy in the Slave South: An Appraisal of Some Recent Views," *Journal of Negro History*, Apr. 1946, and in a review of Herbert Weaver's *Mississippi Farmers, 1850–1860*, in *American Historical Review*, Jan. 1947. Owsley responded in *American Historical Review*, July 1947. Obituaries are in *Nashville Tennesseean*, Oct. 22, 1956, and *American Historical Review*, Jan. 1957.]

JOHN DAVID SMITH

PANGBORN, CLYDE EDWARD (Oct. 28, 1894–Mar. 29, 1958), aviator, was born in Bridgeport, Wash., the son of Max J. Pangborn, a farmer, and Francis Opal Lamb. In about 1896 the family moved to Idaho, where he graduated from St. Maries High School in 1914. He studied civil engineering at the University of Idaho for two and a half years. He also worked for the Forest Service and, in 1915, served as deputy sheriff of Shoshone County.

Pangborn enlisted as an army aviation cadet in the aviation section of the United States Army Signal Corps on Dec. 19, 1917. He proved to be an excellent airman during flight training at Eberts Field, Ark., and Love Field, Dallas, Tex. He received a reserve commission as a second lieutenant and pilot in the Army Air Service in November 1918, too late to see duty overseas. For a few months he was a flight instructor on Curtiss JN–4 "Jenny" training aircraft at Ellington Field, Houston, Tex., then was demobilized in March 1919.

Like many other war-trained airmen, Pangborn determined to make a career of aviation. He became one of many "barnstorming" pilots who made a living by exhibition flying and offering rides at county fairs and similar events. Flying his own Curtiss JN–4, he barnstormed throughout Washington, Oregon, Idaho, and California. In 1921 he and Ivan R. Gates formed the Gates Flying Circus. Between 1922 and 1928, Pangborn flew approximately 125,000 miles without injury. (During one flight he had to crawl from the cockpit to help a parachutist whose pull-out parachute was stuck in its container.) Like many barnstormers Pangborn was somewhat superstitious, refusing to fly unless he was wearing a particular soft chamois vest.

In 1929, Pangborn attempted to form a combination manufacturing concern and flying service, the New Standard Aircraft Corporation of

Paterson, N. J. The onset of the Great Depression ended his hopes, and he joined the Bergen County, N. J., police department as a pilot with the police rank of lieutenant. He returned to barnstorming in 1930, but the era of the barnstormer was rapidly drawing to a close.

In was natural, in the post-Lindbergh era, for former barnstormers to attempt record flights, and from 1927 through the mid-1930's long-distance flight records were set with almost commonplace regularity. Wiley Post and Harold Gatty set an around-the-world record of eight days, fifteen hours, and fifty-one minutes. Pangborn was certain that he could better this, and on July 28, 1931, less than a month after Post and Gatty's epic flight, he took off from Floyd Bennett Field, N.Y., with Hugh Herndon, Jr., in a Bellanca monoplane. They flew to England, Germany, and Russia, but delays forced them to abandon their attempt at Khabarovsk.

Next they determined to fly the Pacific. En route to Tokyo, Pangborn and Herndon passed over Japanese military fortifications, and upon landing they were tried as spies and fined $1,025 apiece. On Oct. 3, 1931, they took off from Samishiro Beach, Japan, in the first nonstop Pacific crossing by air. Forty-one hours and thirteen minutes after takeoff, with Pangborn at the controls, they landed at Wenatchee, Wash.

In 1932 Pangborn went to work for C. D. Chamberlin's flying school. He then demonstrated aircraft for the Fairchild Company in South America. In 1934 he teamed up with an equally famous aviator, Colonel Roscoe Turner, to fly a modified Boeing 247D twin-engine transport from London to Australia in the MacRobertson Race. On October 20 the 247D left London; it landed ninety-two hours, fifty-five minutes, and thirty-eight seconds later in Melbourne, having flown 11,325 miles. The race was won by a specially built De Havilland Comet racer, but the close finish of the 247D and another American transport indicated the beginning of American air transport ascendancy. The Pacific and MacRobertson flights marked the apex of Pangborn's career.

In 1935–1936, Pangborn demonstrated planes for the Burnelli Company and became chief test pilot for the Bellanca Aircraft Corporation. From 1937 until 1939 he promoted Burnelli interests throughout Europe. He married Swana Beauclaire Duval, a French dress designer, in 1937; they had no children. In 1939 they returned to the United States, where Pangborn assisted Americans wishing to enlist in the Royal Air

Force. He also helped to organize the Royal Air Force Ferry Command, and completed more than 170 ferry flights across the Atlantic and the Pacific.

After the war Pangborn demonstrated Burnelli's "Flying Wing" twin-engined transport in a vain attempt to win military production orders for this interesting airplane. From 1950 until his death, he ferried aircraft for private individuals and governments. He also served briefly as a test pilot for Lear Aviation, and he was responsible for reducing the drag and improving the performance of the Learstar executive business transport. During his career Pangborn accumulated more than 24,000 hours of flying time. He died in New York City.

Pangborn was a pioneer aviator whose background and entry into aviation were similar to those of many other early pilots, such as James H. Doolittle and Charles A. Lindbergh. Although he did not attain the stature of these men, he was recognized as a competent airman who sought to demonstrate the potential that the airplane offered society. He received a Harmon Aviation Trophy citation for 1931 and, shortly before his death, was selected to receive the Admiral William A. Moffett Maritime Aviation Trophy.

[Washington State University, Pullman, has a 100,000-item Pangborn Collection; the North Central Washington Museum Assn., Wenatchee, has a small exhibit relating to Pangborn. The National Air and Space Museum, Smithsonian Institution, has the Turner-Pangborn 247D on exhibit, and its library has some biographical material. See also Roland W. Hoagland, *The Blue Book of Aviation* (1932); Herbert Molloy Mason, Jr., *Bold Men, Far Horizons* (1966); Cecil R. Roseberry, *The Challenging Skies* (1966); Don Dwiggins, *The Barnstormers* (1968); William Rhode, *Bailing Wire, Chewing Gum, and Guts* (1970); National Air and Space Museum, *Aircraft of the National Air and Space Museum* (1976); Richard P. Hallion, *Legacy of Flight* (1977); and Carl M. Cleveland, *"Upside-Down" Pangborn: King of the Barnstormers* (1978). Pangborn's obituary is in *New York Times*, Mar. 30, 1958.]

RICHARD P. HALLION

PARKER, JOHN JOHNSTON (Nov. 20, 1885–Mar. 17, 1958), jurist, was born in Monroe, N.C., the son of John Daniel Parker, a struggling grocer, and of Frances Ann Johnston. Parker worked his way through the University of North Carolina at Chapel Hill, where he won numerous academic honors and prizes, became student government leader, and began a long oratorical career. He received the B.A. in 1907 and the LL.B. the following year. He married Maria Burgwin Maffitt on Nov. 23, 1910; they had three children.

Following a legal apprenticeship in Greensboro, N.C. (1908), Parker practiced in Monroe. In 1922 he moved to Charlotte, where, until 1925, he headed the firm of Parker, Stewart, McRae and Bobbitt. As special assistant to the federal attorney general (1923–1924), his prosecution of several war fraud cases evoked praise from Attorney General Harlan Fiske Stone and other high Justice Department officials.

Parker joined the Republican party in 1908, thereby casting his lot with the "lily-white" and anti-Bryan "business respectables" faction that sought to promote and represent the nascent commercial and industrial sector of the state. Through loyalty to and arduous efforts on behalf of the party organization, he climbed the political ladder: manager of John Motley Morehead's successful campaign for Congress (1908), Seventh District congressional nominee (1910), state attorney general candidate (1916), gubernatorial contender (1920), and member of the Republican National Committee and delegate-at-large to the Republican National Convention (1924). In his vigorous but losing 1920 campaign, he advocated protectionism and opposed American participation in the League of Nations. He favored state ratification of the woman's suffrage amendment, a workmen's compensation law, and protective legislation for women and children in industry. The traditional race-baiting strategy of the Democratic party impelled him to state in 1920 that the then largely disenfranchised "negro as a class does not desire to enter politics. The Republican Party of North Carolina does not desire him to do so."

President Calvin Coolidge appointed Parker to the U.S. Court of Appeals for the Fourth Circuit in 1925, and in 1930 President Herbert Hoover nominated him to be associate justice of the Supreme Court.

The appointment reflected political, sectional, and jurisprudential considerations. Parker's judicial record of 184 written opinions received little publicity, but his single decision in *United Mine Workers of America* v. *Red Jacket Consolidated Coal and Coke Company* (18 F.2d 839 [1927]) ignited massive opposition from organized labor and its allies. The opinion had modified the sweeping district court injunction against United Mine Workers organizing

efforts, but upheld that portion enjoining the union from "persuading" employees to break their nonunion contracts. Such "persuasion" indicated an "unlawful purpose" to interfere with production of bituminous coal prior to its shipment in interstate commerce, as proscribed by the Sherman Anti-Trust Act. Landmark Supreme Court decisions sanctioned both application of the Sherman Act (*United Mine Workers International Union* v. *Coronado Coal Company*, 268 U.S. 295 [1925]) and the scope of the injunction approved by Parker (*Hitchman Coal and Coke Company* v. *Mitchell*, 254 U.S. 229 [1917]; *American Steel Foundries* v. *Tri-City Trades Council*, 257 U.S. 184 [1921]. In addition the National Association for the Advancement of Colored People led a grass-roots lobbying campaign against the nomination. Although no evidence of racism appeared in Parker's judicial record, the association assailed him for his political statement of 1920. These and other factors caused a Senate confirmation defeat (41–39) on May 7, 1930. Parker continued unsuccessfully to seek a place on the Supreme Court, waging major efforts in 1941, 1942–1943, 1945, and 1954.

During his thirty-two years as appellate judge, Parker heard more than 4,000 arguments and wrote opinions in approximately 1,500 cases (found in volumes 8–253 of the *Federal Reporter, Second Series*). These opinions reflect his ability to grasp complicated issues of fact and law. He believed that society constitutes an organism, and law, the life principle of that organism. Law arises out of life through the process of reason in the natural law tradition. "Law is not a static thing," he said in *Marshall* v. *Manese* (85 F.2d 944, 948 [1936]), "bound down by prior decisions and legislative enactments. It . . . must change as the conditions of that life change." But judges are not legislators; as Sir William Blackstone asserted, they find law. Thus, for Parker there was constantly a tension between the dynamic and the static, between the need to do justice in individual cases and the imperative of harmonizing national decisional law. Where gaps or ambiguity existed in declared law, his opinions manifested humanitarianism, reliance upon the "rule of reason," presumption of the constitutionality of legislation, and belief that the Constitution was to be interpreted as a charter of government rather than as a contract.

Parker took a position against laissez-faire on the controversial relationship between government and the economy. The public welfare should not be left at the mercy of private individuals. Even in the 1920's he ordinarily upheld exercises of state police powers against challenges based on the due-process clause of the Fourteenth Amendment (*Suncrest Lumber Company* v. *North Carolina Park Commission*, 30 F.2d 121 [1929]) and the contract clause of the Constitution (*Carolina and Northwestern Railroad Company* v. *Town of Lincolnton*, 33 F.2d 719 [1929]). Important New Deal regulatory legislation generally passed early muster under Parker's broad conception of the general welfare clause (*Greenwood County, S.C.* v. *Duke Power Company*, 81 F.2d 986 [1936]); the commerce clause (*Virginian Railway Company* v. *System Federation No. 40*, 84 F.2d 641 [1936]; contra, *Burco Incorporated* v. *Whitworth*, 81 F.2d 721 [1936]); and the federal bankruptcy power (*Bradford* v. *Fahey*, 76 F.2d 628 [1935]).

Yet in regulating economic life, government must be a liberating, not an oppressive, force; it must act justly in taking privately owned property for public use (*United States* v. *Twin City Power Company*, 215 F.2d 592 [1954]) and in fixing prices of the products of such property (*Hope Natural Gas Company* v. *Federal Power Commission*, 134 F.2d 287 [1943]).

Major issues of civil liberties and civil rights came before Parker in the 1940's and 1950's. To the former he typically applied a version of the "clear and present danger" rule. *Barnette* v. *West Virginia State Board of Education* (47 F. Supp. 251 [1942]) voided a compulsory flag salute law; Parker balanced religious freedom of Jehovah's Witnesses against the compelling nature of the interest of the state in enforcement of a secular regulation. But when those asserting First Amendment rights were members of a Communist conspiracy, there was "nothing in the Constitution or in any sound political theory which forbids [government] to take effective action . . . to protect itself from being overthrown by force and violence. . ." notwithstanding the absence of a "clear and present danger" (*Frankfeld* v. *United States*, 198 F.2d 679, 682 [1952]; *Scales* v. *United States*, 227 F.2d 581 [1955]).

In criminal appeals Parker treated alleged procedural errors with the due-process-based "fair trial" rule (*Cary* v. *Brady*, 125 F.2d 253 [1942]) and labored to restrict the use of habeas corpus writs as vehicles of appeals from final decisions of high state courts (*Stonebreaker* v. *Smyth*, 163 F.2d 498 [1947]).

During Parker's last decade on the bench there was a rising volume of race relations litigation.

Disenfranchisement resulting from state "white primary" laws and practices were enjoined as clearly discriminatory under the Fourteenth and Fifteenth amendments (*Rice* v. *Elmore*, 165 F.2d 387 [1947]; *Baskin* v. *Brown*, 174 F.2d 391 [1949]). Outside the electoral process he strictly applied the "separate but equal" standard in the light of reason, striking down discriminatory municipal zoning ordinances (*City of Richmond* v. *Deans*, 37 F.2d 712 [1930]); public school-teachers' salary schedules (*Alston* v. *Norfolk School Board* 112 F.2d 992 [1940]); union collective bargaining and seniority strategies (*Brotherhood of Locomotive Firemen and Enginemen* v. *Tunstall*, 163 F.2d 289 [1947]; *Dillard* v. *Chesapeake and Ohio Railway Company*, 199 F.2d 948 [1952]). But in *Briggs* v. *Elliott* (98 F.Supp. 529 [1951]) Parker followed Supreme Court precedent and resisted finding segregated public schools unconstitutional per se. Reversed by the Supreme Court in *Brown* v. *Board of Education of Topeka*, Parker immediately complied. Hoping for "amicable adjustment" of the heated race question, he construed that decision as meaning "the Constitution does not require integration; it merely forbids discrimination . . ." (*Briggs* v. *Elliot*, 132 F. Supp. 776 [1955]).

Parker was administrator of his circuit as well as member of the policymaking Judicial Conference of the United States. From 1941 to 1958 he served on sixteen of its committees and chaired those on punishment for crime, court reporting, habeas corpus, pretrial, venue and jurisdiction, appeal from interlocutory orders, and administration of the criminal laws. His efforts aided drafting and enactment of the Administrative Office of the United States Courts Act (1939), the Federal Court Reporters Act (1944), the Federal Youth Corrections Act (1950), and the Interlocutory Appeals Act (1958). Parker also supported broad federal court jurisdiction under the diversity of citizenship clause found in Article III of the Constitution, as well as compensated counsel and public defenders for indigent defendants (provided by law long after his death).

Parker served as a member of the Council of the American Law Institute (1942–1958). As a leader in the American Bar Association (ABA) Section of Judicial Administration (chairman, 1937–1938; member of council, 1934–1938, 1942–1958; chairman of that section's Special Committee on Improving the Administration of Justice, 1940–1946), as a member of the Judicial Conference (1930–1958), and as judicial adviser to the United States high commissioner for

Germany (1949), he promoted judicial reforms intended to fortify an independent judiciary and protect that judicial function by means of judge-centered courts. His enduring legacy included negation of popular influence over courts, enhancement of institutional autonomy of the judiciary as a coordinate branch of government, advancement of intrajudiciary unification, simplification and centralization of procedures and administration, and assertion of control by judges over court proceedings.

Parker performed a wide variety of extrajudicial activities. They included long service on the board of trustees of the University of North Carolina (1921–1958). Governor Oliver Max Gardner appointed him to the North Carolina Constitutional Commission (1931–1932), the report of which embodied many of his long-held views on modern government administration. In 1943 he served on the presidentially appointed Advisory Board on Just Compensation to the War Shipping Administration. The board formulated guidelines for the agency in fixing compensation paid for requisitioned vessels.

During World War II, Parker advocated a world organization, free of old power politics, to enforce international law. Subsequently he became a strong defender of both the United Nations and collective security arrangements. On Sept. 24, 1945, President Truman commissioned him as alternate member for the United States of the International Military Tribunal at Nuremberg, Germany. There he contributed materially to development of the critical "conspiracy" issue in the judgment rendered by the court. As chairman of the ABA Committee on Offenses Against the Law of Nations (1946–1951) he perceived the Nuremberg trial as immeasurably strengthening the foundations of international law.

Parker was a devout and biblically knowledgeable Episcopalian. In November 1957 he became chairman of the General Crusade Committee of the Billy Graham Charlotte Crusade. "The great message of the Gospel," he declared then, "is that peace will be achieved not through political machinery or international negotiations ... but through the cleansing of the hearts of men and women throughout the world and instilling in them a sense of responsibility to Almighty God and to the ideals and standards of human brotherhood." Parker died in Washington, D.C.

[Parker's papers are deposited at the University of North Carolina, Chapel Hill. His writings include *Democracy in Government* (1940); *The American Constitution and World Order Based on Law* (1953); and many contributions to the *American Bar Association Journal*, the *American Law Institute Proceedings*, and various other law reviews. The only scholarly study of Parker is William C. Burris, "John J. Parker and Supreme Court Policy" (Ph.D. diss., University of North Carolina, Chapel Hill, 1965). Lengthy sketches of Parker's career are "John J. Parker: Senior Circuit Judge: Fourth Circuit," *American Bar Association Journal*, 1946, and memorial proceedings in *Federal Reporter, Second Series* (1958). Unpublished materials include Parker's personnel folder at the National Personnel Records Center, St. Louis, Mo.; and materials in the William Howard Taft, Calvin Coolidge, and Herbert Hoover papers, as well as in the Franklin D. Roosevelt, Harry S. Truman, and Dwight D. Eisenhower libraries, and the Arthur T. Vanderbilt Papers at Wesleyan University, Middletown, Conn. See also Richard L. Watson, Jr., "The Defeat of Judge Parker," *Mississippi Valley Historical Review*, 1963; Richard Kluger, *Simple Justice* (1966), esp. ch. 15; Peter Graham Fish, *The Politics of Federal Judicial Administration* (1973); and Francis Biddle, *In Brief Authority* (1962).]

PETER GRAHAM FISH

PARKINSON, THOMAS IGNATIUS (Nov. 27, 1881–June 17, 1959), lawyer and insurance executive, was born in Philadelphia, Pa., the son of John Henry Parkinson and Rose Fleming. After graduating from high school, he entered the University of Pennsylvania Law School, from which he received the LL.B., cum laude, in 1902. In that same year he began to practice law in Philadelphia. He moved to New York City in 1908 to serve as counsel to the Bureau of Municipal Research for the City of New York, and was admitted to the New York bar the following year. In 1911 Parkinson was appointed director of the Legislative Drafting Research Fund at Columbia University, where he served as professor of legislation from 1917 to 1935. On June 4, 1912, he married Georgia C. Weed; they had two sons. He was acting dean of the Columbia Law School in 1923–1924.

Parkinson's work as a consultant and as professor of legislation drew him into public service. He was committee counsel for legislative committees in New York and other states, helping to draft workmen's compensation and insurance laws, and to revise factory laws on the basis of recommendations of the Wagner Investigating Committee in 1913. Prior to and during World War I, he helped to develop and administer the federal War Risk Insurance Act. In 1919–1920 Parkinson was legislative counsel to the Senate Commerce Committee, which drafted the Transportation Act of 1920. During this era he also served as special assistant to the federal attorney general (1916), as major judge advocate in the War Department (1918–1919), and as chairman of the American Bar Association Committee on Legislation.

Parkinson joined the Equitable Life Assurance Society of the United States as a part-time adviser in 1920 and, in June of that year, was elected a second vice-president of the firm. He was promoted to executive vice-president in 1925 and, beginning in 1926, was acting president during the frequent absences of the incumbent president, William A. Day, who was in poor health. Day resigned as president in 1927, and Parkinson replaced him. He served as president until February 1953, when he became chairman of the board. He retired in February 1954.

Parkinson's tenure as president and chairman of the board was marked by both accomplishment and controversy. He engineered the recovery of the Vereinsbank deposit from Germany, the successful handling of significant litigation in Russia, and the liquidation of ill-advised foreign business ventures. He also is credited with providing strong leadership during the Great Depression. At the same time Parkinson came under attack for allegedly concentrating too much executive power in his own hands and for being unwilling to consult with the board of directors. He also was charged with having placed company advertising through an agency headed by one of his sons. No evidence was produced that the company or its policyholders suffered from his handling of the advertising. It also came out that legal fees were paid by Equitable to the firm of Milbank, Tweed, Hope and Hadley, in which another son was a partner. Again no misconduct was proved. The board of directors, under pressure from the New York superintendent of insurance, forced Parkinson into retirement and into severing all official connections with the company.

In February 1933 President-elect Franklin D. Roosevelt offered Parkinson the post of secretary of the Treasury. Parkinson apparently feared the consequences of the tinkering with the currency threatened by the New Deal, and he declined Roosevelt's offer. He became, in fact, an outspoken critic of New Deal monetary and fiscal experiments and policies, and was a leading insurance industry spokesman during the trying days of the Temporary National Economic Committee and the Securities and Exchange Commission investigation of life insurance companies (1938–1941). Parkinson died in New York City.

[Parkinson's papers are in the manuscript collections in the Equitable Archives, New York City. His address to the St. Louis Newcomen Society, " 'Equitable' of the U.S. What Henry B. Hyde Started in 1859!" (1950), includes the introduction of the speaker by Judge Frank A. Thompson. The most important source of information concerning his career is R. Carlyle Buley, *The Equitable Life Assurance Society of the United States, 1859–1964,* 2 vols. (1967). Also available is a briefer summary volume by Buley, *The Equitable Life Assurance Society of the United States, 1859–1959* (1959). His obituary is in *New York Times* and *Wall Street Journal,* June 18, 1959.]

ROBERT L. HUNGARLAND

PAUL, ELLIOT HAROLD (Feb. 13, 1891–Apr. 7, 1958), novelist, journalist, and editor, was born in Malden, Mass., the son of Howard Henry Paul, a varnish manufacturer, and Lucy Greenleaf Doucette. He was educated in the public schools of Malden and attended the University of Maine (1908–1909), but left the university to work with his brother as a surveyor and timekeeper on irrigation projects in Idaho and Wyoming. Upon returning to Boston, he worked on newspapers until 1917, when he enlisted in the 317th Field Signal Battalion. After serving in France, he was discharged as a sergeant. Paul worked as secretary of the Massachusetts Soldiers' and Sailors' Commission in 1919–1921 and then returned to France, where he began to write and served as correspondent for the Associated Press in the Ruhr. He was literary editor of the Paris edition of the *Chicago Tribune* in 1925–1926. He published the first serious assessment of Gertrude Stein's work, in the *Tribune*. In 1927 he was a founder and coeditor of *transition*, an international review, in the first issue of which were published an excerpt of James Joyce's *Work in Progress* (later retitled *Finnegan's Wake*) and the text of Stein's *An Elucidation,* a "meditation" on form, style, and grammar. In 1928 he left *transition,* and in 1930 he became literary editor of the Paris edition of the *New York Herald.*

In 1922, Paul published his first novel, *Indelible,* which was well received. He followed it with *Impromptu* (1923), *Imperturbe* (1924), and four other novels during that decade. He married Camille Nesbit Haynes in 1928; they had one son. The marriage ended in divorce. In 1931 Paul went to live at Santa Eulalia, Ibiza, in the Balearic Islands, remaining until 1936, when the town was attacked and nearly destroyed by the Nationalist forces in the Spanish Civil War. The experience resulted in his best-known book, *The Life and Death of a Spanish Town* (1937), which has been compared favorably with Sherwood Anderson's *Winesburg, Ohio.* After returning to New York, he published *The Last Time I Saw Paris* (1942), a moving book that treats his life on Rue de la Huchette as *Spanish Town* had treated Santa Eulalia.

These two books became part of a series of works that Paul called "Items on the Grand Account." These include *Linden on the Saugus Branch* (1947), *Ghost Town on the Yellowstone* (1948), *My Old Kentucky Home* (1949), and *Desperate Scenery* (1950). Ostensibly autobiographical, these accounts are largely concerned with people whom he knew and admired at various times and in various places. Like Sherwood Anderson's autobiography, though, they are unreliable for the biographer, as are the various accounts of his life that Paul furnished for standard reference sources. Like Anderson, he believed that facts must be filtered by the writer's imagination.

Paul's prolific literary production was the result of his theory that writing must be spontaneous. He refused to "torture" sentences. Among his works are the early impressionistic novels; a serious political novel, *The Governor of Massachusetts* (1930); and, after his return from Europe, a series of popular mystery novels, including *The Mysterious Mickey Finn* (1939), *Hugger-Mugger in the Louvre* (1940), *The Death of Lord Haw-Haw,* written under the pseudonym "Brett Rutledge" (1940); and *Fracas in the Foothills* (1940). Screenplays included *A Woman's Face* (1941), of which he was coauthor; *Our Russian Front* (1942), a documentary; and *Rhapsody in Blue* (1946). Collaborations with Luis Quintanilla and other photographers resulted in *All the Brave* (1939), *Paris* (1947), and other books. An accomplished musician who played the piano and the accordion, Paul organized an orchestra in Santa Eulalia and played several jazz concerts in the late 1930's. In 1940 he applied unsuccessfully for an appointment as a lighthouse keeper.

A large, unpredictable man of great energy, Paul married four times. His second wife was Flora Thompson Brown, whom he married in 1935; the third was Barbara Ellen Maycock, whom he married in 1945. He married the fourth, Nancy Dolan, in 1951. All of his marriages ended in divorce. In later years he referred to the latter two as his first and second wives.

A lifelong agnostic, Paul declared himself as such when he entered the Veterans Administration hospital at Providence, R.I., in April 1958, suffering from heart disease and arteriosclerosis. A few days later he was received into the Greek Orthodox Church, explaining that he had always found it attractive. He died in Providence.

Paul has never enjoyed a major literary reputation, although his work was admired by Gertrude Stein and others. *Life and Death of a Spanish Town* and *The Last Time I Saw Paris* quickly became minor classics, and his works generally received favorable reviews. A *New York Times* reviewer described Paul as "a vivid and sensitive recorder of nature, a warm-hearted viewer of human frailties, and a superb story-teller," but his work has received little serious scholarly attention. To most scholars he is little more than a footnote in the literary history of his time. But the vigor and breadth of his work and his varied experiences suggest that this condition may not be permanent. His role in the literary life of Paris in the 1920's was important, and his later work gives valuable insights into American popular taste during and after World War II.

[Substantial collections of Paul's manuscripts are in the Berg Collection of the New York Public Library and of his letters in Butler Library, Columbia University. Other works by Paul include *Lava Rock* (1928); *Low Run Tide* (1928); *The Amazon* (1929); *Concert Pitch* (1938); *Stars and Stripes Forever* (1939); *Mayhem in B-Flat* (1941); *Intoxication Made Easy* (1941), written with Luis Quintanilla; *With a Hay Nonny Nonny* (1942), written with Luis Quintanilla; *I'll Hate Myself in the Morning* (1945); *Summer in December* (1945); *Springtime in Paris* (1950); *Murder on the Left Bank* (1951); *The Black Gardenia* (1952); *Waylaid in Boston* (1953); *Understanding the French* (1954); *The Black and the Red* (1955); and *That Crazy American Music* (1957). No books about Paul have yet appeared, but he figures prominently in John Malcolm Brinnin, *The Third Rose* (1959). Reviews and appraisals of his work are in *Wilson Library Bulletin*, Oct. 1937; *New York Times Book Review*, Mar. 1, 1942, and Sept. 11, 1949; *Saturday Review of Literature*, July 24, 1948; and many other periodicals. His obituary is in *New York Times*, Apr. 8, 1958.]

DAVID D. ANDERSON

PECK, LILLIE (Dec. 28, 1888–Feb. 21, 1957), a leader in the settlement house movement, was born in Gloversville, N.Y., the daughter of Adolph L. Peck, a librarian who migrated to the United States from Vienna when he was twenty-two, and Clara Sperling. After graduating from the Gloversville school system, she attended Simmons College from 1907 to 1909 and again from 1910 to 1913, receiving a B.S. in household economics. She returned to Simmons for an additional semester in 1916. While at Simmons, Peck became involved in settlement house work. In 1912 she served as a volunteer at South End House in Boston and took a course at the Boston School of Social Work under Albert J. Kennedy, one of the pioneers of the early settlement movement.

Another important influence on Peck was Ellen W. Coolidge, a cousin of President Calvin Coolidge. In 1908, Coolidge and Robert A. Woods, head of South End House, had formed a city federation of Boston settlements, the Boston Social Union. In 1912, Peck became assistant secretary of the Boston Social Union (now the Boston Settlement Council). Later she replaced Coolidge as secretary. Peck and Coolidge also supported settlement cooperation on the national level when the National Federation of Settlements was formed in 1911.

The next step was international cooperation. After World War I, Peck joined Coolidge for a trip abroad, during which they visited settlement houses in most European countries and urged the European settlement workers to form national federations. These national federations formed the basis for the International Federation of Settlements, organized in 1922. Peck spent 1924–1926 on a National Federation of Settlements fellowship visiting settlements in Scandinavia, Germany, Austria, France, and England. Her purpose was to help the Europeans prepare for the Second International Conference of Settlements, held at Paris in 1926. In her autobiography settlement leader Helen Hall called Lillie Peck the "founder with Ellen Coolidge of the International Federation of Settlements."

Peck returned to the United States in 1926 to resume her position at the Boston Social Union, and in 1928 became assistant head worker of South End House. Two years later she moved to New York City, where she was assistant to her mentor, Kennedy, then head of University Settlement. She was also the unpaid assistant secretary, under Kennedy, of the National Federation of Settlements, devoting herself full-time to its affairs. In 1934 the National Federation formally hired Peck as its first paid executive secretary.

In this capacity Peck did much to strengthen the national settlement movement. Kennedy thought that when she took over, the federation was possibly heading for disintegration because of sectional feeling and a lack of communication. Peck helped to bind the settlement together through her correspondence and field visits. She also served as a consultant to local settlements. In addition, it was Peck's duty to make arrangements for the annual National Federation conferences. Her outstanding achievement in this regard was to arrange an integrated convention in the South in 1936. She did it by using construction camp dormitories at the Norris, Tenn., site of the TVA.

One of the reasons that Peck was chosen executive secretary of the National Federation was her belief that reform and social change activities were very much a part of the settlement idea. As secretary she frequently participated in meetings held to draft resolutions favoring various reforms. She was usually note taker, jotting down ideas and making sense out of the general stream of conversation. She also wrote letters to politicians and others on behalf of the reforms endorsed by the settlements. Furthermore, in her capacity as informal adviser to settlements, she tried to channel local houses into the mainstream of New Deal reform.

Peck's life-style and personality enhanced her effectiveness as secretary of the federation. She never married, and chose to live at Henry Street Settlement from 1933 until her death. During the late 1930's Helen Hall was head worker at Henry Street as well as president of the National Federation, and the proximity of the two contributed to their professional collaboration. Peck responded constructively to criticism, was sensitive to the needs of others, was eager to be of service, and had the ability to get people to cooperate. Like many settlement workers, she communicated easily with people at all levels of the social scale. Not only her professional life, but her personal life as well, revolved around settlements.

With little money, Peck ran the office of the federation almost single-handedly until 1944, when a second person was added to the staff. In 1945 the staff increased to three, and in 1947 to four. At that point Peck stepped aside for a younger professional, John R. McDowell.

Peck retained responsibility for the international work of the National Federation, assuming the title of secretary for international work in 1947, the year she was elected president of the International Federation of Settlements. During the 1949 Berlin blockade, the American military government hired her as a consultant for neighborhood centers in Berlin. After that the Arbeiter-Wohlfahrt and the Unitarian Service Committee asked her to organize a settlement house, which she did in Bremen, Germany, during 1951–1952. On her return to the United States, Peck served as the International Federation of Settlements representative to the United Nations Economic and Social Council. She continued in this role for the rest of her life. In addition she assisted the State Department in planning the itineraries of foreign social workers visiting the United States under various exchange programs. She was an honorary president of the International Federation of Settlements and active in its affairs until her death in New York City. More than anyone else, Lillie Peck helped to mold the individual settlement houses into a national and international movement.

[Peck's publications are "Intersettlement Arts," *Survey*, Dec. 11, 1920; "Where Beauty Dwells," *ibid.*, May 14, 1921; "Robert A. Woods," *Die Eiche*, no. 2, 1925; "International Conference of Settlements," *Social Worker* (Boston), Dec. 1927; "The Soziale Arbeitsgemeinschaft," *Neighborhood*, Jan. and Apr. 1928; "The American Girl and Her Club," *Signpost* (London), May 1930; "Stryker's Lane Community Center," *Neighborhood*, Sept. 1931; "Settlements Working Together Through the National Federation of Settlements, Inc.," *World Outlook*, Apr. 1936; "Bulwarks of Resistance," *Junior League*, Sept. 30, 1946. See also Helen Hall, *Unfinished Business in Neighborhood and Nation* (1971); and Judith Ann Trolander, *Settlement Houses and the Great Depression* (1975). Obituaries are in *New York Times*, Feb. 22, 1957; and Gloversville and Johnstown, N.Y., *Leader-Herald*, Feb. 22, 1957. The best manuscript source on Peck is the National Federation of Settlements and Neighborhood Centers Records, 1891–1965, in the Social Welfare History Archives of the University of Minnesota Library.]

JUDITH ANN TROLANDER

PEGRAM, GEORGE BRAXTON (Oct. 24, 1876–Aug. 12, 1958), physicist, was born in Trinity, N.C., the son of William Howell Pegram, a professor at Trinity College (now a part of Duke University), and of Emma Lenore Craven, daughter of George Braxton Craven, founder and first president of Trinity. He received the B.A. from Trinity in 1895 and taught in secondary schools in North Carolina from 1895 to 1900, when he received an assistantship in physics at Columbia University. Pegram remained at Columbia the rest of his life, playing a key role as teacher, researcher, and administrator, and helping to bring about the rise of America to greatness in physics.

Pegram received the Ph.D. from Columbia in 1903; his dissertation, with prophetic overtones for events that dominated the latter part of his life, was entitled "Secondary Radioactivity in the Electrolysis of Thorium Solutions." He became an instructor at Columbia in 1905. Two years later a Tyndall Fellowship from Columbia enabled him to travel to several laboratories in Europe and round out his education, as was necessary at that time for any aspiring American student of science. During his year abroad, Pegram studied at Berlin and Cambridge universities, and visited twenty university and governmental physics laboratories in Europe.

The Tyndall year proved to be important in Pegram's life in more ways than one. On his way to Europe, he met a young Wellesley graduate, Florence Bement, daughter of a wealthy Philadelphia art collector. Married on June 3, 1909, they had two sons.

Pegram moved rapidly up the academic ladder at a time when academic advancement was usually slow, becoming assistant professor of physics in 1909, associate professor in 1912, and a full professor in 1918. He assumed an increasing number of administrative roles. At Columbia he served as chairman of the physics department from 1913 to 1945, and was made acting dean of the School of Mines, Engineering and Chemistry in 1917 and dean in 1918, holding that post into 1930. He also became a member of the council of the American Physical Society in 1918, serving as treasurer from 1918 to 1957 and as president in 1941. Pegram also played one of the most important roles in organizing the American Institute of Physics, drafting the bylaws of the institute and serving as its secretary from its founding in 1931 until 1945, and as treasurer from 1938 until 1956.

Pegram was a quiet, relaxed administrator, who, after all had voiced their opinions, would sum up with a solution that generally satisfied even the most belligerent opponents. Despite his administrative talents, he had little taste for the duties of the deanship at Columbia and resigned in 1930 to devote full time to his work in physics. In 1936, however, his administrative burdens were once again increased when the dean of the Graduate Faculties died suddenly and Pegram was named to replace him.

Pegram's activities during World War I forecast his involvement in World War II. He played a major role in the establishment of the student army training corps and conducted antisubmarine research. After intensive study the Columbia group headed by A.P. Wills decided to concentrate on the use of sound waves for detecting and locating submarines. By February 1918 the apparatus was completed and tested at Key West, Fla., with sufficiently promising results that the Naval Experimental Station took over the work.

Soon after Pegram resigned as dean in 1930, the neutron was discovered and during the next few years Pegram and his group at Columbia were the first to reveal some of the major properties of neutrons and their interactions with other particles. Columbia became one of the world centers of neutron research. Pegram often did not put his name first in the by-lines of the papers that originated from this work.

In the late 1930's, Pegram learned of Enrico Fermi's desire to bring his family to the United States and invited Fermi to join the staff at Columbia. Two weeks after Fermi's arrival in January 1939, Neils Bohr brought news of the discovery of the fission of uranium under neutron bombardment. John R. Dunning, a member of Pegram's group at Columbia, soon demonstrated that energy could be released in microscopic amounts from uranium fission and that the isotope uranium 235 was the important isotope. Two groups were formed, one under Fermi to construct a "pile," a lattice structure of graphite and uranium, and one under Dunning to separate the isotope uranium 235 from its more abundant sister uranium 238.

Pegram's connection with the atomic project at Columbia was twofold. First, he assembled and coordinated the team of physicists who performed the crucial experiments and had operating responsibility for the role of Columbia as a major center of nuclear research. Second, he was a member of the advisory groups that originated the uranium project. The National Defense Research Committee (NDRC), formed in June 1940, awarded the first contract for the uranium project to Columbia along the lines recommended by

Pegram. In the summer of 1941 the NDRC was absorbed by the Office of Scientific Research and Development. The uranium project became the Uranium Section, with Pegram as vice-chairman. The decision to launch an all-out effort for the uranium project resulted in the formation of the Manhattan Project to take over and administer the engineering aspects.

Throughout the war Pegram headed the Columbia Committee on War Research, which directed various projects, of which those connected with undersea warfare were second in importance only to the atomic project. In 1941 he organized a group of scientists to begin a secret project that led to the invention and development of the magnetic airborne detector (MAD), which played a tremendous role in clearing the Atlantic of German submarines. When the war ended, he became chairman of the Columbia Committee on Government-Aided Research, serving in that capacity from 1945 to 1950 and again from 1951 to 1956. He was also vice-president of the university from 1949 to 1950, when he retired and became vice-president emeritus and special adviser to the president.

At the end of the war there were extensive discussions on how the research establishment spawned by the Manhattan District could continue to perform research for the benefit of the nation as a whole. Pegram was instrumental in the establishment of the Brookhaven National Laboratory in Upton, N.Y., in 1946. He was one of the five incorporating trustees of Associated Universities that operates the laboratory for the U.S. Department of Energy.

Pegram was a member of many scientific and Academic organizations, including the American Association for the Advancement of Science (vice-president in 1938), the American Association of Physics Teachers, the American Philosophical Society, the National Academy of Sciences, and the American Association of University Professors (president in 1930).

Pegram's health deteriorated steadily during the early 1950's. He died in Swarthmore, Pa. His honors included the Gold Cross of the Command of the Royal Greek Order of Phoenix and the first Karl T. Compton Gold Medal. The George B. Pegram Lectures at Brookhaven National Laboratory was initiated just before his death.

[Pegram's personal papers are available at the Department of Special Collections, Butler Library, Columbia University. His publications include "Radio-active Minerals," *Science,* 13 (1901); "Heat Developed in a Mass of Thorium Oxide Due to Its

Radioactivity," *Physical Review*, 27 (1908), with H. W. Webb; "Scattering and Absorption of Neutrons," *ibid.*, 43 (1933), with J. R. Dunning; "The Scattering of Neutrons by H_2O, H_2^7O, Paraffin, Li, B, and C, and the Production of Radioactive Nuclei by Neutrons Found by Fermi," *ibid.*, 45 (1934), with J. R. Dunning; "Interaction of Low Energy Neutrons With Atomic Nuclei," *ibid.*, 47 (1935), with J. R. Dunning, G. A. Fink, and D. P. Mitchell; "Thermal Equilibrium of Slow Neutrons," *ibid.*, 47 (1935), with J. R. Dunning, G. A. Fink, and D. P. Mitchell; "Experiments on Slow Neutrons With Velocity Selector," *ibid.*, 49 (1936), with J. R. Dunning, G. A. Fink, and E. Segrè; "On the Absorption of Neutrons Slowed Down by Paraffin at Different Temperatures," *ibid.*, 49 (1936), with P. N. Powers and G. A. Fink; "Distilling Apparatus for Separation of Isotopes," *ibid.*, 49 (1936), with H. C. Urey and J. Huffman; and "Some Experiments With Photoneutrons," *ibid.*, 50 (1936), with D. P. Mitchell, F. Rasetti, and G. A. Fink.]

W. W. Havens, Jr

PERLMAN, PHILIP BENJAMIN (Mar. 5, 1890–July 31, 1960), attorney and United States solicitor general, was born in Baltimore, Md., the son of Benjamin Perlman and Rose Nathan. He graduated from Baltimore City College in 1908, then continued his education at the Johns Hopkins University (1908–1909). In 1908 he launched a career in journalism, as a reporter for the *Baltimore American*. He continued in the same capacity with the *Baltimore Star,* and then the *Baltimore Evening Sun*, until 1913. Perlman graduated from the University of Maryland Law School in 1911 with an LL.B. and was admitted to the Maryland bar in the same year. He continued as a journalist, serving as the city editor of the *Baltimore Evening Sun* from 1913 to 1917.

In 1917, Perlman's career turned to public service and legal practice, which were to occupy the remainder of his life. That year he was appointed as an assistant in the Maryland State Law Department, and the following year he was named assistant attorney general. He served in that capacity until 1920, when he became secretary of the state. During his tenure as secretary of the state, Perlman maintained a private legal practice in Baltimore with the firm of Marbury and Perlman. His term ended in 1923, the same year that his edited work, *Debates of the Maryland Constitutional Convention of 1867,* was published. From 1923 to 1926, Perlman was solicitor of the city of Baltimore. In the latter year he left public office to return to legal practice, but served thereafter on several city and state commissions devoted to the arts or civic improvement. He was also a political adviser to state figures.

In 1947, President Harry S. Truman nominated Perlman for the post of solicitor general of the United States. During his service in that office, which lasted until April 1952, he argued sixty-one cases before the Supreme Court, winning more than two-thirds of them. During one term of the court he did not lose a single case. He vigorously represented government interests in the tidelands oil controversy and successfully defended the validity of the non-Communist employee loyalty oaths required by the Taft-Hartley Law, the contempt-of-Congress convictions of leading Communists, and the legality of rent control laws. His most notable defeat was suffered when he argued for the constitutionality of President Truman's seizure of the steel industry in 1952.

Perlman became most widely known for his opposition to racial discrimination. He strongly articulated the antidiscrimination views of the Truman administration and put pressure on government agencies to curtail discriminatory practices and policies. With Attorney General Tom C. Clark he prepared an amicus curiae brief for the case in which the Supreme Court in 1948 unanimously declared restrictive covenants in real estate to be unconstitutional. This brief was subsequently published as *Prejudice and Property* (1948). Perlman also argued for the abandonment of the "separate-but-equal" doctrine of *Plessy* v. *Ferguson,* a view the court later adopted.

Perlman served as acting attorney general from April to June 1952. He subsequently headed the President's Commission on Immigration and Naturalization that characterized the McCarran-Walter Act of 1952 as "an arrogant, brazen instrument of discrimination."

Perlman was also involved in Democratic party affairs. He was a delegate to the Democratic National Convention in 1932, 1940, 1948, 1952, and 1960. At the last of these he was cochairman of the Committee on Resolutions and Platform. For several years he worked on the Administrative Committee of the National Democratic Advisory Council. After leaving the President's Commission on Immigration and Naturalization, he returned to legal practice in Washington, D.C., with Perlman, Lyons and Emmerglick. Perlman, who never married, died in Washington, D.C.

[Perlman's career may most easily be reconstructed from accounts of his accomplishments in the *New York Times*. Debate on his confirmation as solicitor general occurred throughout July 1947, and was reported in both the *Times* and the *Hearings* of the Senate Judiciary Committee. His obituary is in *New York Times*, Aug. 1, 1960.]

ALAN STONE

PERLMAN, SELIG (Dec. 9, 1888–Aug. 14, 1959), labor economist, was born in Bialystok, Poland, the son of Mordecai Perlman and Pauline Blankstein. His father was a yarn spinner and jobber whose livelihood was steadily undermined by the encroaching factory system. The boy received religious and secular training in the local schools, and attended the Bialystok School of Commerce from 1900 to 1906. Barred from further education because he was a Jew, Perlman enrolled at the University of Naples with the intention of studying medicine. In Naples he struck up a friendship with Mr. and Mrs. William English Walling, prominent American socialists, who arranged for him to go to America in 1908 and to enroll at the University of Wisconsin.

At that time John Rogers Commons was making Wisconsin the leading American center for labor economics. He quickly recognized Perlman's exceptional promise and, while he was still an undergraduate, took him on as a research assistant. Thus, "by an unusual stroke of good luck," Perlman began a lifelong association with the Commons school and with the University of Wisconsin at Madison. He received the A.B. in 1910, the Ph.D. in 1915, and, after further service on Commons' research staff, a faculty appointment in 1919 and a full professorship in 1927. Perlman married Eva Shaber on June 23, 1918; they had two sons. She died in 1930, and on Aug. 22, 1930, he married her sister Fannie Shaber; they had two daughters.

Perlman grew up in the revolutionary ferment of the Pale of czarist Russia. Well-read in Karl Marx, Karl Kautsky, and Georgi Plekhanov, he came to America, as he later told his classes, filled with "certainty" about the dialectical laws of social development. His Marxist convictions soon gave way before the empirical approach of institutional economics, as a result of what he described as Commons' "method of deducing labor theory from the concrete and crude experience of the wage earners." From 1913 to 1915, Perlman served as a special investigator for the U.S. Commission on Industrial Relations. He then undertook to write a section of the monumental *History of Labor in the United States* that Commons was directing. Covering the period from 1876 to 1896, Perlman delved deep into the obscure history of the early Marxian socialists and

discovered them to have been the originators of the "pure and simple" unionism that shaped the American Federation of Labor. The evolution from socialism to trade unionism reversed the order of events expected by Marxist thinkers, and suggested to Perlman the idea that experience invariably pushed workers "towards collective control of their employment opportunities, but hardly towards similar control of industry."

Perlman's historical work, which appeared in the second volume of the *History* (1918), led to a decade of reflection about a theory of labor-movement development. Although operating within Commons' school of thought (Perlman always referred to his conclusions as the Commons-Perlman theory), he was actually fashioning a distinctive mode of analysis. Although both men were defenders of American trade unionism, Commons' point of reference was the hostile business environment, while Perlman's was an intrusive and dogmatic Left. Nor did Commons ever attempt a comprehensive theory of labor. Perlman, on the other hand, commanded languages, European history, and Marxist literature; he paid close attention to contemporary events abroad and in America; and he had a speculative bent that set him apart from other institutional economists. Workers everywhere, he believed, shared a common mentality that was based on a perceived scarcity of opportunity and that led to collective action intended, above all, to control the job.

The resultant labor movements were, in Perlman's view, "organic," genuine expressions of the "psychology" of the working class. The chief threat to job-conscious unionism derived from the intellectuals, the radical ideologues who viewed labor as "an abstract mass in the grip of an abstract force." In an elaborate comparative analysis Perlman argued that the fate of the labor movement was determined by the interaction of three factors: its own maturity, the vigor of the intellectuals, and "the resistance power of capitalism." It was in America, he concluded, that job-conscious unionism had triumphed most completely.

A Theory of the Labor Movement (1928) established Perlman as the leading labor scholar of his generation. This work, long in gestation, was the intellectual framework from which he did not deviate for the remainder of his career, notwithstanding the changes in the American labor movement and in its political and economic environment after 1929, or the scholarly criticism leveled against the *Theory* after its reissue in 1949. Perlman's creative energies went, rather, into the classroom. He was, by all accounts, an unusually gifted and dedicated teacher. His lectures were famous for their clarity, wide-ranging erudition, and lively presentation. Perlman was also for many years the main force in the School for Workers at the university. Off campus, he was comparatively inactive. A shy man, he rarely attended professional meetings or gave outside lectures and, except for membership in the Wisconsin Commission on Human Rights from its founding in 1947, took little part in government service or private work as a labor economist.

Perlman retired in 1959. That summer, while in Philadelphia as a visiting professor at the University of Pennsylvania, he died. By then the *Theory* had lost most of its force as an analytic formulation, but its characterization of American trade unionism as a job-conscious movement has endured. Equally enduring is the learning and wisdom Perlman imparted to generations of students.

[The State Historical Society of Wisconsin has a small collection of Perlman papers, and there are additional materials in several of its other collections. The Division of Archives of the University of Wisconsin has one file folder of Perlman's papers. In addition to the obituary in the *New York Times*, Aug. 15, 1959, there is a personal memoir by Edwin E. Witte, in *Industrial and Labor Relations Review (ILRR)*, Apr. 1960. Philip Taft, a former student, has assessments of Perlman's life and work in Industrial Relations Research Association (IRRA), *Proceedings*, 1959, and in *ILRR*, Jan. 1976, as well as a biographical account in *International Encyclopedia of the Social Sciences* (1968). IRRA, *Proceedings*, 1952, is devoted to an assessment of *A Theory of the Labor Movement*. The most thorough critique is G. A. Gulick and M. K. Bers, "Insight and Illusion in Perlman's Theory of the Labor Movement," *ILRR*, July 1953. A. L. Riesch Owen, *Selig Perlman's Lectures on Capitalism and Socialism* (1976), contains a student's lecture notes on Perlman's course as it was given in 1942, as well as a full bibliography of his writings and commentaries on him.]

DAVID BRODY

PERRY, RALPH BARTON (July 3, 1876–Jan. 22, 1957), philosopher and educator, was born in Poultney, Vt., the son of George Adelbert Perry and Susannah Chase Barton, both of whom were teachers. After attending the Franklin School in Philadelphia, he entered Princeton, from which he received the B.A. in 1896. Although he intended to study for the ministry, Perry decided first to pursue philosophy for a year at Harvard. That choice was decisive,

for it led him to become one of the foremost philosophers of his generation.

At the turn of the century, philosophy was in its heyday at Harvard. Teachers such as Josiah Royce, William James, and George Santayana greatly influenced Perry. He completed his M.A. and Ph.D. degrees in 1897 and 1899, one of a group of graduate students—Arthur O. Lovejoy, William Pepperell Montague, and John E. Boodin among them—who were to exert strong leadership in American philosophy during the first half of the twentieth century.

After brief stints as an instructor at Williams (1899–1900) and Smith (1900–1902) colleges, Perry returned to Harvard to teach philosophy in 1902. On Aug. 15, 1905, he married Rachel Berenson; they had two sons. Perry taught at Harvard for more than forty years, holding the Edgar Pierce professorship after 1930. He retired in 1946.

In addition to his teaching responsibilities, Perry's years at Harvard were filled with civic concerns and wide-ranging philosophical activities. During World War I he was a major in the army and served as executive secretary of the War Department Committee on Education and Special Training (1918–1919). In 1920 he was elected president of the eastern division of the American Philosophical Association. In 1921–1922 he was Hyde lecturer in France.

The James family gave Perry access to William James's unpublished papers in 1930. That opportunity resulted in Perry's two-volume *The Thought and Character of William James* (1935), for which he received the Pulitzer Prize in 1936.

Perry held strong political convictions. He supported the New Deal; and early on, he warned against the threat that Hitler and Nazism posed to world peace. With the outbreak of World War II, Perry became chairman (1940–1945) of the Committee of American Defense, Harvard Group, and in 1942–1945 he was chairman of the Universities' Committee on Postwar International Problems. He vigorously encouraged the formation and development of the United Nations.

In the academic years 1946–1947 and 1947–1948, Perry gave the Gifford lectures at the University of Glasgow; they became the basis for his *Realms of Value* (1954). A prolific writer, he published some two dozen books and 200 essays, their scope ranging from detailed epistemological argumentation to broad cultural analysis. Besides the works already mentioned, chief among his writings are *The Moral Economy* (1909); "The Ego-centric Predicament" (in *Journal of Philos-*

ophy [1910]); "A Realistic Theory of Independence," in E. B. Holt *et al.*, *The New Realism* (1912); *Present Philosophical Tendencies* (1912); *The Present Conflict of Ideals* (1918); *General Theory of Value* (1926); *Philosophy of the Recent Past* (1926); *Puritanism and Democracy* (1944); and *One World in the Making* (1945).

Perry is best known, though, for his scholarship and editorial work on William James. As a philosopher he was overshadowed by his three famous teacher-colleagues at Harvard, but that should not obscure the fact that his thought was original, creative, and distinguished. An outline of his views can be obtained by tracing some relations between his philosophy and that of Royce, James, and Santayana.

Absolute idealism was the reigning philosophical position during Perry's initial years at Harvard. Derived from Immanuel Kant and G. W. F. Hegel, and linked with the work of Thomas Hill Green and Francis Herbert Bradley in England, this school of thought equated reality with consciousness, thought, and will. It also claimed that an Absolute Knower is the source of all existence and the guarantee of the purpose, unity, and meaning of life. Royce expounded such ideas persuasively, but Perry was more attracted to James, who dissented. Specifically, Perry rebelled against a fundamental assumption of idealism: that being depends on knowing.

Banding together with William P. Montague, Edwin Bissell Holt, W. T. Marvin, Walter B. Pitkin, and Edward G. Spaulding, Perry became one of the "New Realists," a group dedicated to establishing an alternative theory of knowledge. His first writings, often polemical in character, reaffirmed versions of the commonsense belief that although the reality and structure of the world are knowable, they are by no means totally dependent on mind. In support of this "new realism," Perry appealed for greater logical rigor, more precise use of language, and extensive employment of the methods and results of science. His efforts helped to make those qualities dominant in American philosophy.

Questions in ethics concerned Perry even more than those in epistemology. His *General Theory of Value* remains a major American statement of a naturalistic theory of ethical judgment. Rooted in the psychology and pragmatism of William James, Perry's theory of value rested upon a now well-known principle: "Any object, whatever it be, acquires value when any interest, whatever it be, is taken in it."

Value has an irreducibly subjective component. It does not follow, though, that value is unanalyzable or purely emotive. Nor did Perry find that his understanding of value compromised his realistic epistemology. Interest can be investigated empirically, not least because its nature is to be directed toward some object different from itself. Indeed, the interest-object relationship, in which value exists, involves cognitive activity and expectancy as basic ingredients. It is possible, therefore, to explore whether individual value judgments are consistent with experience and to discern thereby whether interest in an object is accurately placed or misguided.

Perry went on to argue that normative judgments may, and must, be made in order to facilitate communal organization of interests. With a concern for human civilization and progress reminiscent of some of Santayana's writing, he held that one can adjudicate value disputes by using "the norm of harmonious happiness." This norm, elaborated in *Realms of Value*, assumes that conflict and its resolution are the points of departure for morality. Harmonious happiness can, and should, attract allegiance as an ideal because "it embraces all interests, is *to some extent* to everybody's interest, and thereby obtains a breadth of support exceeding that of any other good. Every person . . . has some stake in it." To underwrite such a norm, Perry urged, men and women must strive for moral education, democracy, and world unity.

One of his first books, *The Approach to Philosophy* (1905), emphasized Perry's "great desire that philosophy should appear in its vital relations to more familiar experiences." Whether his topic was "the ego-centric predicament" or "one world in the making," Perry believed that philosophy could make harmony and inclusiveness of interests more familiar and conflict among interests less so. From start to finish, his epistemological, moral, and social thought stayed true to that interest. It still provides insights of lasting value. Perry died in Cambridge, Mass.

[Helpful autobiographical comments are provided in Perry's "First Personal," *Atlantic Monthly*, Oct. 1946. The best available overview of his philosophy is "The New Realism of Ralph Barton Perry," in Andrew J. Reck, *Recent American Philosophy* (1964). See also Thomas E. Hill, *Contemporary Theories of Knowledge* (1961); Herbert W. Schneider, *Sources of Contemporary Realism in America* (1964); and Thomas Robischon's article on Perry in *The Encyclopedia of Philosophy* (1967).]

JOHN K. ROTH

PFAHLER, GEORGE EDWARD (Jan. 29, 1874–Jan. 29, 1957), radiologist, was born in

Numidia, Pa., the son of William H. Pfahler and Sarah A. Stein. After receiving a bachelor's degree in education from Bloomsburg State Normal School in 1894, he entered the Medico-Chirurgical College of Philadelphia, from which he graduated with the M.D. degree in 1898. Pfahler did his internship (1898–1899) and residency (1899–1902) at the Philadelphia General Hospital. He was then appointed clinical professor of symptomatology at the Medico-Chirurgical College, and served in that position until 1908. In 1909 he became the first clinical professor of radiology at the college, and was made a full professor two years later. The Medico-Chirurgical College and its faculty joined the University of Pennsylvania Graduate School of Medicine in 1916. Pfahler was appointed vice-dean for the department of radiology at the university in 1933. During these years he also maintained a private practice in Philadelphia, and served as a consultant in radiology at Misericordia, Hahnemann, General, and Woman's Medical College hospitals in that city.

Pfahler married Frances Simpson on Nov. 8, 1908. She died two years later, and on July 10, 1918, Pfahler married Muriel Bennett. There were no children from either marriage.

Pfahler began his work with X rays just four years after Wilhelm Roentgen announced their discovery in 1895, and just one year after the Curies made their discoveries about radium. His work was with both the diagnostic and the therapeutic uses of the rays. Pfahler published several hundred articles on various aspects of his research and practice, many of which were among the earliest on the medical use of X rays. Pfahler was president of the American Roentgen Ray Society in 1910, and the first president of the American College of Radiology in 1922–1923. He was also president of the American Electrotherapeutic Association (1912) and of the American Radium Society (1921–1922). He was a diplomat of the American Board of Radiology and a fellow of the American College of Physicians. He also devoted time to Philadelphia-area dermatological, cancer, and aid societies.

Pfahler was honored for his pioneer work in radiology with six gold medals: the Strittmatter Medal of the Philadelphia County Medical Society (1930), the gold medals of the American Radium Society, the American Roentgen Ray Society, the Radiological Society of North America, and the American College of Radiology (1935, 1937, 1951, and 1952, respectively), and the first gold medal of the Centre Antoine Bec-

querel in Paris (1955), an institution named for another early researcher in radiology.

Ironically, the nearly fifty years that Pfahler spent researching and applying X-ray techniques caused his disfigurement, poor health, and death. He died at Philadelphia, of leukemia caused by exposure to excessive amounts of radiation.

[Pfahler's major contributions to the literature of radiology appear in his many articles in medical journals; these can be located through *Index Medicus* for 1900–1956. Lengthy sketches of his life and medical activity appeared in *Radiology*, Apr. 1957; and *American Journal of Roentgenology, Radium Therapy and Nuclear Medicine*, May 1957. Short obituaries appeared in *New York Times*, Jan. 30, 1957; and *Journal of the American Medical Association*, Apr. 6, 1957.]

ELLEN GAY DETLEFSEN

PHIPPS, LAWRENCE COWLE (Aug. 30, 1862–Mar. 1, 1958), industrialist and United States senator, was born in Amityville, Pa., the son of William Henry Phipps, a Methodist minister, and Agnes McCall. When he was five years old, the family moved to Pittsburgh, where his father had accepted the call of a small congregation.

Phipps graduated from Pittsburgh High School in 1879 and went to work in the Carnegie steel mills as a weight clerk. Hardworking and extremely ambitious, he more than earned his dollar-a-day wage, and made sure that his immediate supervisors realized that fact. (Even as a day laborer he always identified his interests with those of management, carefully avoiding any contact with and showing no sympathy for the trade unionists active in the Carnegie mills.) Phipps was, in short, a model employee who quickly won the favor of his foreman, the plant superintendent, and those higher up in the Carnegie hierarchy of power ("Captain" William Jones and Charles Schwab), and eventually even of Andrew Carnegie, who considered Phipps "one of my young geniuses," an honor more rewarding in Pittsburgh than the Order of the Garter was in England. With that accolade always came a small percentage of the interest in the company partnership.

In 1885 Phipps married Isabella Hill Loomis, who died three years later, leaving two infant children. In 1897 he married Genevieve W. Chandler; they had two daughters. This marriage ended in divorce in 1904.

During the final, bitter struggle for power between Carnegie and his chairman of the board, Henry Clay Frick, Phipps sided with Carnegie and Schwab. When Frick was driven from the company in 1899, Phipps was rewarded with the position of vice-president and treasurer and an increased percentage of the partnership. Although that share was only 2 percent, it was enough to make him a very wealthy man when Carnegie sold his company (1901) for nearly half a billion dollars to the syndicate created by J. P. Morgan to form the United States Steel Corporation. Although only thirty-eight years old, Phipps retired from the industrial world.

He moved to Denver, Colo., where he invested his wealth in the Denver and Salt Lake Railway and the California Electric Power Company, which provided power to the Nevada goldfields and the farming districts of California. In 1911 he married Margaret Rogers, the daughter of Judge Platt Rogers of Denver; they had two sons.

Phipps quickly moved into the center of the political life of Colorado. In 1913 he was elected president of the Colorado Taxpayers' Protective League, which provided him with a base for assuming leadership of the most conservative faction within the Republican party. His greatly publicized gift of $11 million to found the Agnes Memorial Sanatorium for the treatment of tubercular patients and his appointment by President Woodrow Wilson to the National Finance Committee of the American Red Cross in 1917 identified him in the public mind with humanitarian causes. In 1918 he was elected to the U.S. Senate.

In the Senate, which liberals of the day called the "millionaire's club," Phipps was frequently the butt of attack by Southern Democratic Populists and Progressive insurgents within his own party. On at least two occasions the presiding officer had to reprimand fellow senators for impugning Phipps's motives for voting against legislation that would adversely affect his business interests. He served as chairman of the Senate Committee on Post Offices and Post Roads and of the Committee on Education. His major interests in the Senate were to push through a bill for the building of Hoover Dam and to provide appropriations for national highways. Some twenty years ahead of his time, he urged President Herbert Hoover in 1930 to sponsor the building of an interstate highway system as a means of easing the Great Depression by providing employment and stimulating industry, a proposal remarkably similar to the one that President Dwight D. Eisenhower would successfully advocate in the 1950's.

Phipps was not generally a proponent of an activist federal government. Calvin Coolidge was his political hero, and in the 1924 presidential campaign he attributed American prosperity and happiness to Coolidge's being in the White House and to the passage by Congress of a high protective tariff and a restrictive immigration bill. Phipps easily won reelection in 1924. Two years later, while serving as national chairman of the Republican Senatorial Campaign Committee, he was greatly embarrassed by losing control of the Republican party in Colorado. The more liberal faction of the party was able to defeat the junior senator, Rice W. Means, in the primary and to oust Phipps from his position as head of the party in Colorado because both men had sought and received the support of the Ku Klux Klan. Phipps was further chagrined by the gains made by the Democrats in the Senate, contrary to his loudly trumpeted prediction that the Republicans would win in every state outside the South.

Thereafter Phipps's political fortunes ebbed and, like Coolidge, he had the good sense to quit while still ahead. He refused to run for another term, in what would probably have been a hopeless contest. Although he served twice more as national committeeman from Colorado and was a delegate to the Republican National Convention in 1932 and 1936, he had little political influence within his state or the nation for the rest of his life. He died in Santa Monica, Calif.

[Papers relating to Phipps's career with Carnegie Steel are in the Andrew Carnegie Papers, Library of Congress, and in the United States Steel Corporation Archives, Pittsburgh, Pa. For material related to his career in the Senate, see two of his printed speeches, *Taxation in the District of Columbia* (1928) and *The Establishment of Air Mail Routes* (1930). His obituary is in *New York Times*, Mar. 3, 1958.]

JOSEPH FRAZIER WALL

PICK, LEWIS ANDREW (Nov. 18, 1890–Dec. 2, 1956), army officer and civil engineer, was born in Brookneal, Va., the son of George Washington Pick, a civil engineer for the Southern Railway, and Annie Crouch. After graduating from high school in nearby Rustburg, he entered Virginia Polytechnic Institute, from which he received the B.S. in 1914. For the next two years he was a civil engineer with the Southern Railway.

American entry into World War I permanently changed Pick's career. After completing officers' training in August 1917, he received a commission as a first lieutenant in the U.S. Army Corps of Engineers. In March 1918 he went to France as a company commander in the Twenty-third Engineers and took part in the Meuse-Argonne offensive. Pick was discharged in September 1919, then applied for a commission in the Regular Army. He was accepted as a second lieutenant in the Engineers on July 1, 1920, and was promoted to captain on the same date.

Pick first served with the Ninth Corps Area Engineers in San Francisco. In 1920 he was assigned to the Third Engineers in the Philippines. Until 1923 he commanded a company of Philippine Scouts in Rizal Province, Luzon; he also organized the first native engineer regiment, the Fourteenth Engineers. Pick then returned to the United States, and was graduated from the Engineer School at Fort Belvoir, Va., in 1924. In 1924–1925 he served as professor of military science and tactics at Alabama Polytechnic Institute in Auburn, Ala. On Dec. 15, 1925, he married Alice Cary; they had one son.

Pick served in the New Orleans Engineer District from 1925 to 1928, completing his tour as district engineer. During the Mississippi River flood of 1927, he was engineer assistant on the relief commission headed by Commerce Secretary Herbert Hoover. In 1928 he organized the ROTC unit at Texas A & M College. After heading the unit for four years, Pick served at the Command and General Staff School at Fort Leavenworth, Kans., as a student officer and then as an instructor until 1938. After graduating from the Army War College in Washington, D.C., in 1939, he was assigned to Cincinnati as executive officer to the Ohio River division engineer.

After the United States entered World War II, Pick was promoted to colonel. In April 1942 he was sent to Omaha, Nebr., as Missouri River division engineer. Between 1942 and 1943 he supervised more than $1.5 billion of military construction from Missouri to Montana.

Pick first gained national prominence for his flood-control activities and proposals. He directed the fight against the devastating Missouri River floods of 1943. Subsequently, at the request of Congress, he prepared a comprehensive water resources program for the Missouri River Basin. Pick proposed that the Corps of Engineers build a series of downstream levees and nearly two dozen major upstream multipurpose dams and storage reservoirs. These would provide not only flood control but also hydroelectric power, improved navigation, and water supply. But the Bureau of Reclamation, which also had extensive experience in flood control and irrigation, countered with its own plan, devised by W. Glenn Sloan, for numerous smaller dams and irrigation projects. The result was a compromise that included elements of both proposals and recommended 105 reservoirs in all. This Pick-Sloan Plan, adopted by Congress as part of the Flood Control Act of 1944, was a conservative alternative to proposed legislation that would have established a governmental Missouri Valley Authority for regional development.

Meanwhile, Pick had been assigned in October 1943 as commander of Advanced Section of the Army Service Forces in the China-Burma-India Theater of Operations. There he became famous as the builder of the Ledo Road, which ran from Ledo, Assam, India, to the old Burma Road. The latter, as the Japanese forces were pushed back, served as the main supply route for Allied troops in Burma and southwestern China. When Pick took over, only forty-two miles of the project had been built in the previous year, and construction had bogged down under monsoon rains and tropical disease. "The Ledo Road is going to be built—mud, rain, and malaria be damned!" Pick announced. And built it was—478 miles through some of the most rugged country in the world.

Construction involved cutting through dense jungle, bridging ten major rivers and 155 secondary streams, and traversing 100 miles of mountains so steep that at one point 200 hairpin curves were required within seven miles. Directing a force of nearly 90,000, including American and Chinese soldiers and Indian and Burmese laborers, Pick established sanitary measures and rigid discipline to ensure use of quinacrine to combat malaria, and began round-the-clock construction. Keeping his crews on the heels of the combat troops, he pushed the road ahead at an average rate of a mile a day.

Promoted to brigadier general in February 1944, Pick led the first convoy to go to China over the completed highway in January 1945. The Ledo Road, nicknamed "Pick's Pike" and known as the Stilwell Road (after General Joseph W. Stilwell) when linked with the old Burma Road, was hailed as "one of the greatest achievements in the history of military construction."

After the war Pick served for two months in the Office of the Chief of Engineers, then resumed his post as Missouri River division engineer from 1945 to 1949. Under his direction, development of the Pick-Sloan Plan began. Within the next decade many of its projects were completed.

During the winter of 1948–1949, Pick oversaw Operation Snowbound, an airlift relief program that aided blizzard-trapped residents of the Plains states.

Between March 1949 and February 1953, Pick capped his career. He was chief of army engineers during the Korean War and of the massive construction of American bases around the world that accompanied that conflict. He was promoted to major general in 1949 and to lieutenant general in 1951.

Pick retired in 1953. After settling in Auburn, Ala., he became director of industrial development for the state. He was also named chairman of the board of John J. Harte Company, an Atlanta architectural and engineering firm, and vice-chairman of the Georgia-Pacific Plywood Company. He died in Washington, D.C.

Pick was a man of relentless energy and indomitable will, but also was imaginative, pleasant-mannered, and soft-spoken. He rose through the military hierarchy despite the lack of a West Point background. His career illustrated the involvement of the Army Engineers in both civil works and military construction.

[Some of Pick's papers are in the possession of his widow in Auburn, Ala. Others are in the records of the Corps of Engineers, National Archives, Washington, D.C. His writings include "Missouri River Basin Development," *Military Engineer*, Mar.–Apr. 1948. Obituaries are in *New York Times* and *Washington Post*, Dec. 3, 1956. See also Karl C. Dod, *The Corps of Engineers: The War Against Japan* (1966); and Lenore Fine and Jesse A. Remington, *The Corps of Engineers: Construction in the United States* (1972), both volumes in the Office of the Chief of Military History series The U.S. Army in World War II.]

JOHN WHITECLAY CHAMBERS II

PINCHOT, CORNELIA ELIZABETH BRYCE (Aug. 26, 1881–Sept. 9, 1960), advocate of social legislation, was born in Newport, R.I., the daughter of Lloyd Stephens Bryce, owner and editor of the *North American Review* and United States minister to the Netherlands and Luxembourg, and of Edith Cooper, granddaughter of Peter Cooper. Because of her father's social and political connections, she was early accustomed to meeting eminent persons and arguing issues of the day. Theodore Roosevelt was said to have valued her friendship and views.

She married Gifford Pinchot on Aug. 15, 1914;

they had one son. With her husband she shared a determination to be effective in both private and public life. She had concluded that women must make their impress on politics, and had marched in woman suffrage parades; and in 1914, when her husband entered Pennsylvania politics, she began to work vigorously within the Republican party and on the speech-making and conference circuits to advance his interests, as well as her own.

Pinchot's earliest cause was the need to restore vitality to the individual vote. Women, she insisted, must take an interest in the primaries, in which party leaders were elected. They must contribute money to campaigns, and see that the money was legitimately spent. She was active in her husband's successful campaign for governor in 1923, and as a public figure in her own right she fought for enforcement of the Volstead Act. In 1926 she contributed $40,000 to her husband's unsuccessful attempt to win nomination as candidate for the U.S. Senate over Republican leader William S. Vare, and she herself made headlines by challenging Vare to public debate. In a letter published in 1926, addressed to a textile manufacturer, she urged recognition of the workers in his plant who were on strike for the right to join a union.

In 1928, Pinchot made her own bid for a seat in Congress, opposing the incumbent, Louis T. McFadden. She campaigned well, attracting audiences responsive to her clear, pointed statements. By then her controlled gestures—not unlike those of her husband—and her spare figure were well established in the public mind, as were her red hair and bright blue eyes. Although she was defeated, she continued to interest women's rights advocates, unionists, and others. So vigorously did Pinchot urge her views that she was rejected as a speaker in the presidential campaign of 1928 because of Herbert Hoover's opposing programs on such issues as water power and farm aid. In 1930 she was barred from speaking before the Pennsylvania Federation of Women's Clubs, then in conservative hands.

With the Great Depression and her husband's return to the governorship (1931–1935), Pinchot entered her most impressive period in public life. For a time she was, among women concerned with social issues, second in visibility only to Eleanor Roosevelt, with whom as a child she had gone to dancing school. Newsmen followed her as she went from picket line to picket line in her chauffeured limousine. Reporters and interviewers commented upon her manner, her clothes, and her liberal ideas, which were seen as just short of radical. Her two major causes were the conditions of women and children in industry and in the home. Her public statements were widely cited and influenced legislation, especially in Pennsylvania.

In February 1933, as the governor's wife, Pinchot gave a dinner for Eleanor Roosevelt and forty-eight others that entered into the lore of the era. The meal of soup, corn bread, cabbage rolls stuffed with salmon and rice, hamburger steaks, salad, and ice cream was reported as costing five and a half cents per person. In August of that year she was given a union card by the American Federation of Full Fashioned Hosiery Workers, whose cause she had supported.

Pinchot made another attempt to gain a congressional seat in 1932, but was defeated in the primaries by McFadden, a result that was seen as a blow to her husband's prestige. She remained newsworthy, being reported as intending to succeed Pinchot as governor if he should win the senatorship. In 1934 he made his final, unsuccessful attempt to reach the Senate. Characteristic was his wife's hiring of a horse-drawn sleigh on rollers, decorated with bells, in which she rode around the Philadelphia City Hall showing a placard that read "Voters—Don't let [opposing Senator David A.] Reed take you for another sleigh ride—vote for Pinchot."

Pinchot's relinquishing of the governorship took his wife substantially out of the news. She still made appearances, notably in connection with international peace, but her major work was done. She died in Washington, D.C.

[An overview of the times in which Pinchot made her career is in M. Nelson McGeary, *Gifford Pinchot* (1960). Elizabeth Frazer, "Mrs. Gifford Pinchot, Housewife and Politician," *Saturday Evening Post,* Aug. 26, 1922, provides views, descriptions, and photographs. "Mrs. Pinchot, Governor's Wife, Picket, and Politician," *Newsweek,* Feb. 3, 1934, is a journalistic sketch, as are accounts in *Literary Digest,* May 20 and Aug. 19, 1933. Her obituary is in *New York Times,* Sept. 10, 1960.]

LOUIS FILLER

PINZA, EZIO (May 18, 1892–May 9, 1957), operatic bass, was born in Rome, Italy, the son of Cesare Pinza, a carpenter, and Clelia Bulgarelli. His boyhood and early manhood were spent in Ravenna; there he attended the public schools and the University of Ravenna, where he studied engineering. While a student he supported himself by working as a carpenter's assistant and as a delivery boy for a bakery. When he was eighteen, Pinza left the university to become a professional bicycle rider. The realization that he was not destined for success as a cyclist led him to take up singing as a profession. He had had no vocal training, and his sole participation in the making of music had been as a member of an amateur choral group in Ravenna.

On a scholarship, Pinza studied voice with Ruzzi and Vezzani in Bologna. In the fall of 1914, he made his debut with a minor company in Soncino, as Oroveso in *Norma.* During World War I he served with the artillery in the Italian Alps, rising from private to captain, and received a bronze star for distinguished service.

After the war Pinza became a member of the Teatro Reale dell'Opera in Rome, where he made his debut as King Mark in *Tristan and Isolde* (1920). After two years in Rome, and additional experience as guest performer at opera houses in Naples, Ravenna, and Turin, he was engaged by La Scala in Milan, where he had his first significant successes. On Dec. 16, 1922, he appeared in the world premiere of Ildebrando Pizzetti's *Debora e Jaele* and, on May 1, 1924, in that of Arrigo Boito's *Nerone;* in both instances the conductor was Arturo Toscanini.

Pinza made his American debut at the Metropolitan Opera in New York City on Nov. 1, 1926, playing Pontifex in Gasparo Spontini's *La Vestale.* His success was immediate. He combined a voice of great expressiveness and sonority with a sure technique and boasted a majestic stage demeanor. He remained principal bass of the Metropolitan Opera company for the next twenty-two years; during that period he was heard 587 times in New York and 246 times on tour and performed fifty-one roles. His last Metropolitan Opera appearance was on Mar. 5, 1948, in one of his most highly acclaimed parts, that of Don Giovanni. During his Metropolitan Opera career he also distinguished himself in the title role in *Boris Godunov,* as Ramfis in *Aida,* Mephistopheles in *Faust,* Don Basilio in *The Barber of Seville,* Escamillo in *Carmen,* Raimondo in *Lucia di Lammermoor,* Sparafucile in *Rigoletto,* and Figaro in *The Marriage of Figaro.*

Pinza also sang at Covent Garden in London, the Vienna State Opera, the Paris Opéra, the San Francisco Opera, the Salzburg Festival, and in South America. He supplemented his opera career with successful appearances in recitals.

After leaving the Metropolitan Opera, Pinza carved an eminent career in the Broadway theater by playing the role of Émile de Becque in the Rodgers and Hammerstein musical *South Pacific,* which opened on Apr. 7, 1949. As the male star of this monumentally successful musical, Pinza became a matinee idol, a fact recognized by the motion-picture industry when it brought him to Hollywood in May 1950. His career on the screen was far less successful than that on the stage; both of his films, *Strictly Dishonorable* (1951) and *Mr. Imperium* (1951), were failures. He had done much better when called upon to sing an opera aria in the motion picture *Carnegie Hall* (1947), and he acquitted himself handsomely when singing an operatic segment in the screen biography of the impresario Sol Hurok, *Tonight We Sing* (1953).

In 1953, Pinza toured New England in Ferenc Molnár's *The Play's the Thing,* in which he had a nonsinging part. After 1953 he was often a guest performer on radio and television. He returned to Broadway in the successful musical *Fanny* in 1954. A heart attack in 1956 ended his career. He died a year later, in Stamford, Conn.

Pinza, a tall, handsome man with finely chiseled features and a beguiling smile, exuded charm offstage as well as on. He was married twice. His first wife was Augusta Cassinelli. Their daughter, Claudia, became an opera singer also. On Sept. 12, 1947, she appeared in San Francisco as Marguerite in *Faust.* Pinza sang Mephistopheles. After divorcing Augusta Cassinelli, Pinza married Doris Leak, a member of the Metropolitan Opera ballet corps, on Nov. 28, 1940. They had three children.

Apart from music, Pinza's interests lay mainly in sports. He enjoyed skiing, bicycling, boating, fishing, and attending boxing matches. He was also an excellent amateur photographer and a collector of Roman poison rings, pipes, and watches.

[See David Ewen, *Men and Women Who Make Music* (1949). See also *Theatre Arts,* Feb. 1938; *Vogue,* Apr. 15, 1939; and *Opera News,* Mar. 2, 1942.]

DAVID EWEN

POLLOCK, (PAUL) JACKSON (Jan. 28, 1912–Aug. 11, 1956), painter, was born in Cody, Wyo., the son of LeRoy Pollock and Stella May McClure. Never successful, LeRoy Pollock attempted ranching, farming, and surveying. The family lived in Wyoming, Arizona, and California; in 1928 they finally settled in Riverside, sixty miles outside Los Angeles. From 1923 to 1926 Pollock's eldest brother, Charles, worked in the layout department of the *Los Angeles Times,* while studying at the Otis Art Institute in Los Angeles. Thus Pollock heard serious talk about art. This exposure continued; and in 1926, when Charles registered at the Art Students League in New York, he still shared his experience through letters and publications sent home.

In the summer of 1927 Pollock and Sanford, his closest brother, worked at surveying along the northern rim of the Grand Canyon. It was hard work in rough surroundings; but Pollock was exhilarated by the scenery, the wildlife, and particularly the sense of endless space—aspects of nature with which he would always identify. Trying to be manly, and perhaps also trying to find a balance between his tender and aggressive tendencies, he also discovered alcohol. He not only drank heavily, but his system was allergic to alcohol; he became wild and hostile on comparatively small amounts of wine and beer. Pollock's problem with alcoholism was physiological and psychological.

In school—first at Riverside High School, then at Manual Arts High School in Los Angeles—Pollock was a rebellious student, primarily interested in art. He became friends with classmates of similar interests, among whom Philip Guston would also distinguish himself as a painter. Probably the most important influence on Pollock was Frederick John de St. Vrain Schwankovsky, an art teacher who introduced him to European modern art and also to Far Eastern religions and the contemporary teachings of Jiddu Krishnamurti, a poet and mystic whose meetings Pollock attended. In October 1929, after being dismissed from school because of a fight with his physical education instructor, he wrote to Charles and Frank (his brother who was studying literature at Columbia) that he knew only that he wanted to be "an Artist of some kind." By January, back at Manual Arts on probation, he wrote that his drawing "seems to lack freedom and rhythem it is cold and lifeless."

Pollock failed to graduate from Manual Arts, and in September 1930 he moved to New York City. He enrolled at the Art Students League with Charles's teacher Thomas Hart Benton, an academic painter who had abandoned all modern "isms" and returned to the values of High Renaissance and baroque art, superimposed on American regional subject matter. Pollock was soon doing exercises in foreshortening, perspective, and chiaroscuro. In 1944 he wrote: "My work with Benton was important as something against which to react very strongly, later on...." Yet for the next several years Benton was the single greatest influence on Pollock's life and artistic development. Copying Rubens, late Michelangelo, Tintoretto, and especially El Greco—all favorites of Benton's—was part of Pollock's training. Equally important was his personal contact with a "success," the successful role model his father had never been. At the time, Benton was working on a mural at the New School for Social Research, where José Clemente Orozco was also at work and where Pollock did some "action posing," assuming athletic postures. Except for a few works influenced by Albert Pinkham Ryder ("the only American master who interests me") and by the Mexican muralists Orozco, Rivera, and Siqueiros, almost everything Pollock did during the early 1930's was influenced by Benton.

Benton left the League temporarily in late 1932 to fulfill another major commission. Pollock stayed on at the League as a visiting member until 1935, but never again took classes with Benton. In 1933 he studied with the painter John Sloan and the sculptor Robert Laurent, but after Benton, Pollock was never again directly influenced by a teacher. He lived with his brother Charles from 1933 to the fall of 1934. During the Great Depression Pollock worked as a school janitor, then as a stone cleaner of public monuments for New York City's Relief Bureau. From 1934 to 1942 Pollock lived with Sanford and his wife in a small Greenwich Village apartment. In August 1935 he joined the easel division of the WPA Federal Art Project and earned an income of about $100 per month until the project ended in 1943. Pollock was required to complete one painting (for allocation to a public building) about every eight weeks. Fortunately his principal supervisor, Burgoyne Diller, a Mondrian-influenced, hard-edge abstractionist, was tolerant of Pollock's expressionistic explorations.

In early 1937 Pollock began psychiatric treatment for alcoholism. The following year he had a nervous breakdown, and was hospitalized for several months; he continued to see various therapists throughout his life. The most influential was Dr. Joseph L. Henderson, a Jungian with whom he worked in 1939 and 1940. Henderson encouraged him to bring in sketches to analyze during the sessions. Although Pollock's symbolism had become more personal than during the Benton period, there was still a considerable stylistic debt to the Mexicans, especially Orozco, and a new indebtedness to Picasso, particularly to his *Guernica*. Through therapy Pollock was moving toward a more private subject matter and was struggling to find the means of expressing it.

That final freeing would occur in the 1940's, through greater psychoanalytic awareness and by contact with many of the most important surrealists, including their leader André Breton, who fled from Europe to New York in 1941. That year John Graham—an influential underground painter and theoretician, whose aesthetic went beyond Picasso's cubism and approached Breton's automatist surrealism—organized "American and French Painting" for the McMillen Gallery in New York City. The exhibition opened in January 1942 and included Pollock's *Birth* and paintings by other Americans such as Lee Krasner and Willem de Kooning. Because of this exhibition with the established School of Paris painters, Pollock was reviewed for the first time in the art press. Also, he renewed his acquaintance with Krasner, who soon moved into his apartment.

In October 1942 Peggy Guggenheim, a copper heiress who had collected avant-garde art abroad, opened the predominantly surrealist Art of This Century Gallery in New York City. The young American painters William Baziotes and Robert Motherwell introduced Pollock to her and she asked all three and Ad Reinhardt to participate in an April show of collages. This led to Pollock's exhibition of the major painting *Stenographic Figure* in the "Spring Salon for Young Artists." By then he had assimilated aspects of Picasso, Matisse, and surrealism. His work contained some figurative and totemic elements, increasingly obscured by improvised "doodling," as he called it. In *Male and Female* (also painted in 1942 but not shown at the gallery until the fall of 1943) were already hints of the dripping and splattering—controlled accidents that were to become his trademark. Pollock's work was singled out as promising by Jean Connolly in the *Nation* (1943) and Robert Coates in the *New Yorker* (1943). Peggy Guggenheim commissioned Pollock to do a mural for her apartment, gave him a contract for $150 a month (against sales), and scheduled his first one-man show for November.

Pollock's November 1943 show was covered by many major newspapers and magazine art columns. The longest, most serious, though not totally affirmative, review was by Clement

Greenberg and appeared in the *Nation*. By the time of the next show Greenberg had become Pollock's greatest champion. Attention continued the following year: Pollock was interviewed in *Arts & Architecture* (1944); *The She-Wolf* was reproduced in *Harper's Bazaar*, and the original was purchased by the Museum of Modern Art and included in Sidney Janis' *Abstract & Surrealist Art in America;* and he had various group and traveling shows.

On Mar. 19, 1945, Pollock had his second one-man show at Art of This Century. This time Greenberg said Pollock was established "as the strongest painter of his generation and perhaps the greatest one to appear since Miró." Pollock and Krasner were sufficiently encouraged by public response to marry on Oct. 25, 1945, and to buy a house in Springs, Long Island. There Pollock continued his work—first in an upstairs bedroom of the old farmhouse, later in a barn moved to the property.

A 1946 exhibition at Art of This Century and the final one there in January 1947 consolidated Pollock's reputation as an "American surrealist"—rougher and more brutal than the Europeans, but still only a footnote to art history. In a spirit of confidence and maturity, perhaps influenced by the expansiveness of his new studio and country environment, Pollock began his most innovative paintings—totally abstract, frequently large-scale, freely dripped, overall images that suggest endless, cosmic space. When paintings such as *Cathedral* and *Full Fathom Five* were shown at Betty Parsons Gallery in January 1948, Pollock's reputation and the controversy surrounding his work grew, as it did when his paintings were shown at the Venice Biennale that year and in 1950. In the fall of 1948 he again entered treatment for alcoholism and began a two-year abstinence, at which time he did his greatest work. He produced about sixty paintings, almost all shown in two of Parsons' 1949 exhibitions. Thirty-two of these were at Betty Parsons Gallery in 1950, including his masterpieces *Lavender Mist, Autumn Rhythm,* and *One.* In these later paintings Pollock's vision is grand, his palette (mostly industrial enamels) original, his rhythmic impulse like a controlled "dance" across the canvas spread on the floor. On Aug. 8, 1949, *Life* published a two-page spread headed "Jackson Pollock: Is He the Greatest Living Painter in the United States?"; it showed him posed in front of *Summertime*. This publicity made him internationally famous and, as de

Kooning said, "broke the ice" for the American painters of his generation, variously called "abstract expressionists," "action painters," and "American-type painters."

After the artistic, if not financial, success of his 1948–1950 exhibitions, Pollock had a last show at Parsons in 1951. Included were mostly monumental black-and-white paintings, drawn with poured paint, and containing figurative elements unseen in his work since the surrealist period. Although the show was enthusiastically praised by Greenberg in *Partisan Review,* it was generally considered evidence of Pollock's decline. In 1952 he began working with color again; and although his productivity waned after 1953, his reputation as an established "modern master" grew. There were shows at the Sidney Janis Gallery in 1952, 1954, and 1955, containing such great paintings as *Blue Poles, Convergence,* and *Portrait and a Dream.*

A retrospective Pollock exhibition was being planned for fall 1956 at the Museum of Modern Art when he was killed in an automobile accident. That exhibition became a memorial show. Since then, his work has become increasingly institutionalized and his life, mythified. The prices of his works have soared. For example, *Blue Poles* was purchased just before Pollock's death for $6,000 and sold shortly thereafter for $32,000. In 1973 it was sold to the Australian National Gallery for $2 million.

[The only existing full-length biography is my *Jackson Pollock: Energy Made Visible* (1972). *Jackson Pollock: A Catalogue Raisonné of Paintings, Drawings, and Other Works,* 4 vols. (1978), edited by Francis V. O'Connor and Eugene V. Thaw, contains additional biographical material as well as 1,285 illustrations. Useful catalogues and monographs—all, unless otherwise noted, titled *Jackson Pollock*—include the Museum of Modern Art catalogue (1956), with introduction by Sam Hunter; Frank O'Hara, monograph (1959) for the Great American Artists series; Bryan Robertson's monograph (1960); Francis V. O'Connor, MOMA catalogue (1967); Bernice Rose, *Jackson Pollock: Works on Paper* (1969); and C. L. Wysuph, *Jackson Pollock: Psychoanalytic Drawings* (1970), which contains reproductions of work given by Pollock to Dr. Henderson. See also Harold Rosenberg, *The Tradition of the New* (1959), including his influential essay "The American Action Painters" (first published in 1952); Clement Greenberg, *Art and Culture: Critical Essays* (1961), including much of his writing on Pollock and particularly " 'American-Type' Painting" (first published in 1955 and, like Greenberg's other essays, revised for this collection); the ten-minute Hans

Namuth and Paul Falkenberg film (1951) of Pollock at work at the peak of his career, in which he completes *Number 29* (1950), an oil and collage on glass. A well-balanced general study of Pollock and his contemporaries is Irving Sandler, *The Triumph of American Painting: A History of Abstract Expressionism* (1970).]

B. H. FRIEDMAN

POST, EMILY PRICE (Oct. 3, 1873–Sept. 25, 1960), authority on etiquette, was born in Baltimore, Md., the daughter of Bruce Price, an architect, and Josephine Lee, daughter of a Pennsylvania coal baron. Born into a tradition of wealth and social position, she was trained to be "a lady" and to take her place in society. Through her family experiences, her German tutor, her education in private schools, and travel abroad, she learned to move easily and naturally in the highest social circles. Although she respected the code that molded people of her class, she was by no means bound to the position and was willing to rebel if she felt unnecessarily confined by Victorian standards.

Her parents moved to New York shortly after her tenth birthday, and there she received her finishing education at Miss Graham's, a private school famous for the high percentage of its students who moved into the top ranks of debutantes. She made her debut in 1891. The Gibson girl, who dominated the concept of a beautiful woman at that time, could have been modeled on Emily Price. She was tall and graceful, with a dazzling complexion and a crown of light brown hair.

On June 1, 1892, she married Edwin Main Post. They had two sons. Although the Posts came from similar social positions and enjoyed the round of social activities and trips abroad that accompanied their wealth and position, their relationship was not compatible. He was an avid yachtsman; she loathed sailing. They were divorced in 1906.

The Panic of 1903 had caused Edwin Post considerable financial loss, and the divorce settlement was not sufficient to allow Post to support her children as she wished. Under the social code of the period, it was acceptable for a woman to write for a suitable magazine, as long as money was not the major purpose of the undertaking. During a trip to Europe, Post had sent to her father a series of letters, entertaining as well as infor-mative, that showed both appreciation and slight ridicule of the ways of European royalty and the upper social classes. Her father showed the letters to George Barr Baker, editor of *Ainslee's* magazine; this led to her first novel, *The Flight of a Moth* (1904), based on her experiences in Europe. Post enjoyed both the writing and the $3,000 in royalties. She continued to write for *Ainslee's* as well as *Everybody's* while producing books: *Purple and Fine Linen* (1905), *Woven in the Tapestry* (1908), *The Title Market* (1909), *The Eagle's Feather* (1910), and *By Motor to the Golden Gate* (1916).

After several rebuffs Richard Duffy, of Funk and Wagnall's, suggested that Post write a book on etiquette. She scoffed. Etiquette to her was stupid and stuffy; she despised it and the people who took it seriously. But an appraisal of the type of material then being published on etiquette convinced her to undertake it. *Etiquette: The Blue Book of Social Usage* was published in 1922. Subsequent editions followed, and Emily Post became the social arbiter of middle-class America.

Primarily, Post contributed to the simplifying of manners. She thought that what was socially right was what was socially acceptable. Her basic rule was to make other persons comfortable; no well-mannered person would ever do anything to offend the sensibilities of others. "Etiquette is the science of living. It embraces everything. It is the code of sportsmanship and of honor. It is ethics."

Her book brought Post new careers in newspapers, in radio, and as founder of the Emily Post Institute, where "gracious living could be studied." Her newspaper column developed quite unexpectedly. Although she assumed her 250,000-word volume covered all topics in etiquette, readers began besieging her with requests for etiquette in a wide variety of unusual situations. She responded with the column. At the peak of her journalistic career, her column, distributed by the Bell Syndicate, was carried in more than 200 newspapers with a circulation of more than 6,500,000. Her advice on manners was sought by some 250,000 letter writers each year. Her book on etiquette sold more than 500,000 hardbound copies during the first twenty years. Radio broadcasts, which she began in 1929, further expanded her audience.

Post's other books include *Parade* (1925); *How to Behave—Though a Debutante* (1928); *The Personality of a House* (1930), her account of remodeling a home; *Children Are People* (1940); *Emily Post Cookbook* (1949), written with her son Edwin M. Post; and *Motor Manners* (1949).

The gracious dignity that Post brought to her advice on etiquette added greatly to the social mobility of the United States. The other person's comfort, rather than rigid adherence to rules, became the goal of American etiquette under Post's guidance. She died in New York City.

[See *New York Times*, Sept. 27, 1960; *Newsweek*, Aug. 11, 1958, and Oct. 10, 1960; *Life,* Oct. 10, 1960; and Edwin M. Post, *Truly Emily Post* (1961).]

WILLIAM E. AMES

POTTER, ELLEN CULVER (Aug. 5, 1871–Feb. 9, 1958), physician, social worker, and welfare administrator, was born in New London, Conn., the daughter of Thomas Wells Potter, a grocer, and Ellen Culver. She graduated from high school in 1890. Potter was a member of the Third Baptist Church, the missionary activities of which, in which she participated during her youth, influenced her later career in social service.

In 1893–1894, Potter studied at the Art Students' League in New York City. In the next few years she also attended the Academy of Art in Boston and art school in Norwich, Conn. In 1895 and 1896 she served at the Baptist-run Morning Star Mission in the Chinatown district of New York City, a typical urban mission that developed social services, including a medical dispensary. Carrying her art supplies with her in a little black bag as she performed her duties, she was often taken for a physician. According to her own accounts, these incidents persuaded her to study medicine.

After traveling to Europe in 1898 and 1899, Potter entered the Woman's Medical College of Pennsylvania in 1899, graduating in 1903. Two years later, having served her internship and residency at the Woman's Medical College Hospital, she entered private practice in Philadelphia, specializing in obstetrics and gynecology.

For the next fifteen years, while maintaining her private practice, Potter participated in the social justice progressive movement in Philadelphia. Between 1912 and 1918 she served as a public school medical inspector. Her career suggested the close relation between the Social Gospel and social justice progressive movements, and she encouraged women physicians to become medical missionaries. Potter served on the dispensary staffs of both the Howard and Ger-

mantown hospitals, and continued her affiliation with the gynecology and obstetrics departments at the Philadelphia General Hospital and the Woman's Medical College Hospital, where she was the nonresident medical director during World War I. Between 1918 and 1920 she supervised the Pennsylvania state program of the Social Hygiene Division of the War Department Commission on Training Camp Activities. This project sought to reduce the incidence of venereal disease and to promote abstinence from alcohol in and around military camps.

In 1920, Potter became head of the Division of Child Health in the Pennsylvania Department of Health. Under her leadership more than 200 local child hygiene stations were established. In October 1921 she organized the Bureau of Children in the Department of Public Welfare. The bureau conducted a much-needed study of nearly 150 institutions and agencies that cared for children, initiated regional conferences, and encouraged county systems of child care.

Potter was so popular among women's and social welfare organizations that she was named secretary of welfare by governor-elect Gifford Pinchot. When she took office early in 1923, Potter, who never married, became the first woman cabinet officer in Pennsylvania. She led her department to important gains in public welfare, transforming the unsanitary and corrupt state welfare and correctional institutions into models of efficiency, attracting top personnel in social work and business administration, and publicizing the need for social service reform through her writings and speeches.

After leaving office in 1927, Potter transferred her activities to New Jersey. In that same year she helped to develop the new North Jersey Training School at Totowa. She served as its medical director until 1928, when she became acting superintendent at the State Reformatory for Women at Clinton. From 1928 to 1930, Potter headed the New Jersey State Home for Girls at Trenton. In 1932 she was elected president of the Conference of Superintendents of Correctional Institutions for Women and Girls.

In 1930, Potter was appointed director of medicine for the New Jersey Department of Institutions and Agencies, a position she held for nineteen years. In this position she influenced many important programs, some of which ranged beyond the strict confines of her office. She worked to curb the evils of "black market" adoptions in the state, finally convincing the legislature to pass reform measures in the 1940's.

She also influenced the development of community mental health clinics.

Potter expanded her social welfare activities to the national level in the 1930's. During the Great Depression transiency increased markedly, and in 1932 she and other social workers established the National Committee on Care of Transients and Homeless, a voluntary agency that she chaired from 1933 until its demise in 1938. In 1933, as a consultant to the Federal Emergency Relief Administration, Potter influenced the establishment of the Federal Transient Service. After this program was dismantled in 1935, she led the Committee on Care of Transients and Homeless in urging a coordinated national policy similar to the coordinated movements she had headed in Pennsylvania and New Jersey.

Potter's activities decreased in the 1940's, but she continued to write and to speak, and she served as president of the National Conference of Social Work in 1945. The following year she was named deputy commissioner of the New Jersey Department of Institutions and Agencies, a post she held until she retired in 1949. She developed new interests, especially in the care of the chronically ill and the aged. Potter received numerous awards, including the first W. S. Terry, Jr., Award of the American Public Welfare Association (1948). She died in Philadelphia.

[There is no collection of Potter's letters and papers. But reprints of some of her articles, correspondence, and other materials are at the Medical College of Pennsylvania. Also consult the Gifford Pinchot Papers in the Library of Congress; the papers of the U.S. Children's Bureau at the National Archives, Washington, D.C., Record Group 102; the files of the Federal Emergency Relief Administration, National Archives, Record Group 69; the papers of the National Association of Social Workers and the papers of the Survey Associates, both at the Social Welfare History Archives Center, University of Minnesota, Minneapolis; the Franklin Delano Roosevelt Library, Hyde Park, N.Y.; and the Rutgers University Library, New Brunswick, N.J. There is no scholarly study of Dr. Potter. Except for James Leiby, *Charity and Correction in New Jersey* (1967), the publications in social welfare history do not mention her. See also Margaret Steel Moss, "Ellen C. Potter, M.D., F.A.C.P.," *Public Administration Review*, Summer 1941; Helen S. Hawkins, "A New Deal for the Newcomer" (Ph.D. diss., University of California, San Diego, 1975).]

PETER ROMANOFSKY

POWER, TYRONE (May 5, 1914–Nov. 15, 1958), actor, was born Tyrone Edmund Power in Cincinnati, Ohio, the son of Frederick Tyrone Power and Helen Emma Reaume. He came from a family of proud theatrical traditions, being the third member to bear the name Tyrone Power. His great-grandfather had been a famous Irish actor during the early part of the nineteenth century; his father was a noted Shakespearean; and his mother, using the name Patia Power, played with her husband in various Shakespearean productions. Power's childhood was spent in New York and California, where his parents were engaged in stage and screen work. He and his younger sister, Ann, lived with their mother in San Diego from 1917 to 1923 while his father toured. It was thought the climate there would bolster Tyrone's frail health. During that time he twice appeared in the annual San Gabriel Mission plays, performing with his mother.

The Power family moved back to Cincinnati in 1923. Patia Power began work there, teaching voice and dramatic expression at the Schuster-Martin School of Drama. Tyrone spent grades three to six at the Sisters of Mercy Academy and later enrolled at St. Xavier Academy. He attended the Preparatory School of the University of Dayton (1928–1929) and Purcell High School (1929–1931), both run by the Brothers of Mary. While in high school he was active in dramatics, was given speech arts training by his mother, and ended up playing the lead in his class play.

Following graduation in 1931, Power played a short season of small roles with a Shakespearean repertory company at the Chicago Civic Auditorium. His first professional appearance was in *The Merchant of Venice*, in which he played an old man. That same year his father had been hired for a film role, and Power went with him to Hollywood. But in December of 1931, while at work on *The Miracle Man*, the senior Power died. Tyrone and his mother and sister then moved to Santa Barbara.

Following his father's death, Tyrone made a tour of the various motion-picture casting offices. A friend of his late father's, the screen writer Arthur Caesar, boarded him for a time. Caesar was the first of several of his father's friends who helped the aspiring young actor. Two years later Power set out for New York, hoping to get employment on the stage, but he stopped off in Chicago to view the Century of Progress Exposition. He stayed in Chicago, where he did some

Circuit Theatre productions and a few radio shows. Then in 1935 he was given a part in a revival of the play *Romance,* starring Eugenie Leontovich, and which had an eight-week run at Chicago's Blackstone Theatre. Power finally went to New York when *Romance* closed. There he was again aided by family friends. Michael Strange, an author and former wife of John Barrymore, gave him a place to stay. Actress Helen Menken got him an interview with producer Guthrie McClintic. This led to a season of understudy, followed by a season of summer stock at West Falmouth, Mass. Then Power appeared with McClintic's wife, Katherine Cornell, in two plays, *Romeo and Juliet* (1935) and *Saint Joan* (1936). Film producer Darryl Zanuck then tested the lanky young actor, and in 1936 Power was signed to a seven-year motion-picture contract with Twentieth Century–Fox.

Power made four pictures during his first year. He gained the lead, as well as his first screen success, in *Lloyds of London* (1936). Fox undertook a campaign to make Power better known, including the many obligatory publicity romances. The studio was grooming him as its answer to such matinee idols as Errol Flynn and Robert Taylor.

By 1943 Power was a top box-office attraction, having appeared in some twenty films, including *In Old Chicago* (1938), *Alexander's Ragtime Band* (1938), *Suez* (1938), *Marie Antoinette* (1938), *Jesse James* (1939), *The Rains Came* (1939), *A Yank in the RAF* (1941), and *Crash Dive* (1943). During this period Power married the French movie star Annabella on Apr. 23, 1939. The marriage ended in divorce in 1948.

During World War II, Power joined the U.S. Marine Corps as a private and served from August 1942 to January 1946. He qualified for Officer Candidate School and was later commissioned as a second lieutenant. He received flight training and in February of 1945 was sent overseas, where he flew a number of dangerous missions in the South Pacific. He was discharged from the Marines with the rank of first lieutenant.

Back from the war, Power signed a new contract with Fox. In 1946 he played the leading role in the screen adaptation of Somerset Maugham's *The Razor's Edge.* The picture, one of Power's most memorable, gained him good reviews; Maugham himself described the acting as "perfect." That same year Power made a goodwill tour of South America. After giving a strong performance in *Nightmare Alley* (1947), he

appeared in a series of historical romances such as *Captain From Castile* (1947), *Prince of Foxes* (1949), and *The Black Rose* (1950). While these films provided little scope for acting, most critics agreed that Power was a fine performer in the swashbuckling tradition. On Jan. 27, 1949, he married the film actress Linda Christian; they had two daughters before the marriage ended in a stormy divorce in 1955.

Power returned once again to the stage in 1950 starring in such productions as *Mister Roberts* (1950), *John Brown's Body* (1953), and *The Dark Is Light Enough* (1955). During this same period other film roles came his way, including *Rawhide* (1951), *The Mississippi Gambler* (1953), and *The Long Gray Line* (1955).

Later Power played in *The Eddy Duchin Story* (1956), *The Sun Also Rises* (1957), and *Witness for the Prosecution* (1958). In this last film he gave one of his finest performances; it was also his last. Tyrone Power, like his father, was fatally stricken while acting. He suffered a heart attack on Nov. 15, 1958, in Madrid, while filming a dueling scene in *Solomon and Sheba.* He was buried with military honors at the Hollywood Memorial Park Cemetery. A large crowd attended, including Power's new bride of six months, the former Deborah Montgomery Minardos.

Power was part of the same film generation as Gable, Tracy, and Cooper; quite frankly, he was not their equal. But he was more than just a handsome matinee idol. He gave some fine and sensitive performances in difficult roles. Another actor, David Niven, said of him, "Ty was everybody's favorite person, and all agreed that he was that great rarity—a man who was just as nice as he seemed to be." But another matinee idol, Cesar Romero, summed up Tyrone Power best when he said, "He was a beautiful man. He was beautiful outside, and he was beautiful inside."

[There are two book-length studies of Power: the competent *Tyrone Power: The Last Idol* (1979) by Fred L. Guiles; and the sensational *The Secret Life of Tyrone Power,* by Hector Arce. Two good articles on his marriage to the glamorous Linda Christian are "Tyrone and Linda Get Married," *Life,* Feb. 7, 1949, and "Viva Ty! Viva Linda!" *Newsweek,* Feb. 7, 1949; a critical note on the marriage can be found in "Non-Catholic Marriage Is No Marriage," *Christian Century,* Feb. 9, 1949. A fine personal glimpse of Tyrone Power the man is given by a close friend and neighbor in David Niven, *Bring on the Empty Horses* (1975). Good obituaries are *New York Times,* Nov. 16,

1958; *Newsweek* and *Time*, Nov. 24, 1958; and "A Dashing Actor's Last Duel," *Life*, Dec. 1, 1958. A complete list of his films is in the *New York Times Directory of the Film* (1974).]

J. MICHAEL QUILL

PRATT, WILLIAM VEAZIE (Feb. 28, 1869–Nov. 25, 1957), naval officer, was born in Belfast, Maine, the son of Nichols Pratt, a merchant captain for British firms in China, and Abbie Jane Veazie. His early years were spent in China; at the age of six he began his education in Belfast and its environs. In 1885 he was appointed to the United States Naval Academy. Graduating sixth in the class of 1889, Pratt commenced forty-four years of active duty, during which he rose to the rank of admiral and to chief of naval operations (CNO), the highest post in the navy.

Pratt's first nine years after graduation were served mostly at sea as a junior officer. At the outbreak of the Spanish-American War, in April 1898, he joined the converted yacht *Mayflower* and then spent the war in the blockade of Cuba. At the end of the war, he transferred to the cruiser *Newark* and participated with distinction in the suppression of the Philippine Insurrection. In the summer of 1900 Pratt was appointed a mathematics instructor at the Naval Academy. On Apr. 15, 1902, he married Louise Miller Johnson; they had one son.

Between 1902 and 1911 Pratt advanced steadily in rank and served increasingly more responsible billets. In 1911, as a commander, he joined the faculty of the Naval War College in Newport, R.I. There he instructed and became a close friend of Captain William S. Sims, one of the most colorful and controversial figures in the navy. In 1913, Pratt became Sims's chief of staff in the Torpedo Flotilla of the Atlantic Fleet; the next year he took command of the flotilla flagship *Birmingham*. While working for Sims, Pratt became known as a skilled planner, tactician, and leader. A superb seaman, he was advanced to the rank of captain in 1915.

After serving on the Panama Canal Defense Board (1915) and studying at the Army War College, Pratt became assistant to the CNO, Admiral William S. Benson, in May 1917. Between May 1917 and January 1919, he demonstrated his outstanding administrative skills in Washington. For this service he received army and navy Distinguished Service medals and the

French Legion of Honor. As commander in chief of American naval forces in European waters, Sims testified that Pratt had been invaluable in assisting his mission. Admiral Benson, in recognition of Pratt's service, urged his promotion to rear admiral in 1918. After commanding the battleship *New York* (1919–1920) and the Destroyer Force, Pacific Fleet (1920–1921), he received his promotion in September 1921.

As a flag officer Pratt achieved distinction in both traditional and nontraditional areas. While a member of the General Board of the navy, he was assigned to staff duty with the American delegation to the Washington Naval Conference (November 1921–February 1922). His excellent service attracted the attention of President Warren G. Harding and Secretary of State Charles Evans Hughes. Within the navy Pratt quickly became recognized as an expert on limitation of naval forces. In 1925, 1927, 1930, and 1931–1932 he assisted the State Department as it planned for or participated in naval limitation conferences in Geneva or London. In 1930 President Herbert Hoover selected him to head the naval staff at the London Naval Conference. Distrusting naval limitation, most senior navy officers believed that Pratt had acted unwisely in supporting attempts to restrict naval growth. Between 1922 and 1932 he argued, before congressional committees and in published articles, that international limitation was a way to reduce the dangers of war and that the nation was in no danger so long as Congress built the fleet to the limits allowed by the 1922 and 1930 naval treaties. Unfortunately for him Congress permitted the navy to lag behind the construction being undertaken by Japan, Great Britain, Italy, and France.

As a rear admiral (1921–1927) Pratt was a member of the General Board (1921–1923), a battleship division commander in the Battle (Pacific) Fleet (1923–1925), and president of the Naval War College (1925–1927). Between September 1927 and September 1930, he served as a vice admiral commanding the Battleship Divisions, Battle Fleet (1927–1928); as an admiral, commander in chief, Battle Fleet (1928–1929); and from May 1929 to September 1930, as commander in chief, United States Fleet [CINCUS], the highest navy command afloat. While serving as Battle Fleet commander and as CINCUS, Pratt supported the development of the aircraft carrier as a major naval weapon. Always concerned about fleet training, he stressed gunnery and seamanship. Following his appointment as CNO in September 1930, Pratt reorganized the United States Fleet in order to emphasize training by ship type.

Pratt's years as CNO were difficult because of the Great Depression. Ship construction was almost halted and personnel reductions were heavy, promotions slow, and funds reduced. In his attempts to meet the required budgetary reductions and still maintain a credible national defense, he steadily lost the goodwill of the service. In February 1933 Franklin D. Roosevelt asked Pratt to continue briefly as CNO beyond his normal retirement date of March 1. On July 1, 1933, he retired to his home in Belfast.

Pratt remained prominent on the national scene until 1946. Through articles and speeches he continued to support the naval limitation movement until its demise in 1937 following Japanese denunciation of the Five Power Naval Treaty of 1922. With the outbreak of World War II, *Newsweek* magazine asked him to join its staff as a contributing naval specialist. In January 1940 he began writing a weekly analysis of naval events, and continued to do so until the spring of 1946. At the conclusion of his work for *Newsweek*, he again retired to Belfast. He died in Charleston, Mass.

[Pratt's papers are in the Naval History Division, Washington Navy Yard, and the Naval War College Collection, Newport, R.I. His views concerning naval limitation and international relations are in the thirteen articles that he published between 1922 and 1935. The most important of these are "Naval Policy and the Naval Treaty," *North American Review*, May 1922; "Some Considerations Affecting Naval Policy," *United States Naval Institute Proceedings*, Nov. 1922; "The Case for the Naval Treaty," *Current History*, Apr. 1923; "America as a Factor in World Peace," *Annals of the American Academy of Political and Social Science*, July 1923; "Disarmament and the National Defense," *United States Naval Institute Proceedings*, Sept. 1929; "Lest They Forget," *ibid.*, Apr. 1933; and "Pending Naval Questions," *Foreign Affairs*, Apr. 1935. See also Gerald E. Wheeler, "William Veazie Pratt, U.S. Navy," *Naval War College Review*, May 1969; and *Admiral William Veazie Pratt, U.S. Navy* (1974).]

GERALD E. WHEELER

PRENTIS, HENNING WEBB, JR. (July 11, 1884–Oct. 29, 1959), business executive and spokesman, was born in St. Louis, Mo., the son of Henning Webb Prentis, a high school principal, and Mary Morton McNutt. He completed high

school in three years and earned an A.B. from the University of Missouri in three years, graduating in 1903. He remained at the university until 1905, serving as secretary to the president, a position that initially paid $11 per week. In 1905, Prentis became secretary of the University of Cincinnati, where he also did graduate work in economics, earning an M.A. in 1907. In the latter year he became assistant to the manager of the insulation division of the Armstrong Cork Co. in Pittsburgh. On Sept. 2, 1909, he married Ida Bernice Cole. They had no children.

At Armstrong, Prentis became interested in the potential of advertising and spent a great deal of time selling management on its importance. In 1909 he wrote "Cork—Its Origins and Uses," the first piece of promotional literature published by Armstrong. He followed with "Engineer's Handbook on Corkboard Insulation," "selling helps" for retailers, and booklets on home decoration. In 1911, Prentis was appointed manager of the advertising department and initiated a three-year $50,000 national advertising campaign. The first national advertisement run by Armstrong appeared in the *Saturday Evening Post* in September 1917. Three years later Prentis was appointed general sales manager of the floor division. He continued to introduce new ideas, such as recruiting college graduates as salesmen. In a day when most salesmen were not college men, "Prentis' rah-rah boys" received some ridicule from competitors; but, more important, they developed into an outstanding sales force.

Prentis made a major contribution to the rationalization of wholesale distribution by establishing a principle that assured "even the smallest wholesaler a price proportionately lower than that given to the largest retailer, to compensate the wholesaler for the service he renders." This required published price lists, with discounts based on quantity purchased. "Open book" operations, as opposed to secret deals, were ridiculed by some competitors, but proved successful. Other innovations included inviting wholesalers to meet periodically with Armstrong policymakers and training sessions or courses for wholesalers, retailers, and salesmen. All of Prentis' early innovations were related to marketing, and it can be argued that the growth of the company was to a large degree a product of its marketing methods.

In 1926, Prentis was elected to the board of directors and made a vice-president of Armstrong; he became first vice-president in 1929 and, five years later, president.

As president Prentis put more emphasis on consumer goods; diversified by acquiring rubber, asphalt tile, and glass plants; and consolidated the insulation and building material divisions. He established a general personnel department in 1937 to deal with "the four specters that loom behind every man and woman who works for a living—. . . sickness, death, old age, and unemployment."

Prentis was a tireless participant in the debate of the 1930's between businessmen and New Dealers. (In his lifetime he delivered more than 700 speeches.) His central theme was the rise of big government, which he believed to be a serious threat to economic and personal freedom. Representative titles of his speeches are "The Price of Freedom," "The Roots of Liberty," and "The Tripod of Freedom." (The tripod consisted of constitutional representative democracy, political and religious liberty, and private free enterprise.) He was clearly one of the better-educated and more articulate conservative businessmen of his day, and became a popular spokesman for this particular viewpoint.

During the 1930's Prentis was a member of the National Advisory Council of the American Liberty League, of the United States Chamber of Commerce (director, 1938–1940), and of the National Association of Manufacturers (NAM) (director, 1936; president, 1940; chairman, 1941). As NAM president he inspired a "Declaration of Principles" and strengthened the educational and public information programs of the organization.

On the eve of World War II, Prentis recognized the vulnerability of Armstrong as a nonmetalworking firm and organized the conversion to contribute to wartime production demands. By April 1941 the company had a munitions division, and by the end of the war it had filled war production contracts worth more than $110 million. From April 1942 to January 1943 Prentis served as deputy director of the War Production Board for the Philadelphia region. Thus he became a part of the government that so often had been the target of his speeches.

After the war Prentis guided Armstrong through a period of expansion that included the construction of two more asphalt tile plants, a fiberboard plant, and a bottle closure plant. By 1950, when he was named chairman of the board, the record of growth during his tenure was impressive. Annual sales by Armstrong had climbed from $22 million in 1934 to $163 million, and annual earnings from $2 million to $10 million.

From 1950 until his death he played the role of elder statesman, serving on national and international committees, and delivering speeches.

The life of Prentis, a formal, hard-driving, self-made man who never wavered in his commitment to the basic tenets of free enterprise, the Republican party, and Calvinism, is so closely involved with the modern history of Armstrong Cork that it is hard to separate them. His major shortcoming was one common to many self-made men: the inability to comprehend human frailty. He died at Lancaster, Pa.

[It is believed that Prentis' personal papers were discarded after his death. His business correspondence and printed speeches are in the archives of Armstrong Cork, Lancaster, Pa. The NAM collection in the Eleutherian Mills Historical Library, Greenville, Del., contains papers and printed speeches related to Prentis' presidency of the NAM; his printed speeches are also in the Fackenthal Library, Franklin and Marshall College, Lancaster, Pa.

A brief biography is Armstrong Cork, *H. W. Prentis, Jr.* (1961). The only work by a professional historian is Thomas R. Winpenny, "Henning Webb Prentis and the Challenge of the New Deal," *Journal of the Lancaster County Historical Society,* 81 (1977). Herbert Kay, "To Live and Die for Armstrong," *Fortune,* Mar. 1964, is a favorable historical sketch. His obituary is in *New York Times,* Oct. 29, 1959.]

THOMAS R. WINPENNY

PRINGLE, HENRY FOWLES (Aug. 23, 1897–Apr. 7, 1958), journalist and biographer, was born in New York City, the son of James Maxwell Pringle, a pharmacist, and Marie Juergens. After graduating from high school, he served briefly in the army during World War I, but did not go overseas. In 1920 he graduated from Cornell University with a B.A. degree but was not fully determined upon a career, even though he had spent one summer working for the *New York Evening Sun* before his military service. He worked for the *Sun* until 1922, then for the *New York Globe* (1922–1924) and the *New York World* (1924–1927). On Sept. 26, 1926, Pringle married Helena Huntington Smith, a journalist, novelist, and, according to Pringle, "a mean and nasty critic." They had three children.

During the 1920's Pringle emerged as a latter-day muckraker. "His Master's Voice," his account of Ivy Lee, press agent for the Rockefellers, was a candid piece of reporting appropriate to the pages of the *American Mercury*. He did vignettes of Judge Eugene Gary, Mayor Jimmy Walker of New York City, and Judge Kennesaw Mountain Landis in much the same idiom. These sketches were collected under the title *Big Frogs* (1928). Though they were described as "libelous, untrue, inaccurate and mischievous," Pringle considered them "impartial and objective personality sketches." In any case, they revealed a considerable talent for character delineation, and the notice they won no doubt encouraged Pringle to look to biography as his likely métier. His study of Al Smith (1927) bore this out; it was a more substantial treatment of an individual than was to be found in *Big Frogs*, though it had some of the overtones of a campaign document.

Pringle's career took a prosperous turn in the 1930's. His *Theodore Roosevelt* (1931) won a Pulitzer Prize. In 1932 he joined the School of Journalism at Columbia University. At the close of the decade he brought out his most ambitious book, the two-volume *The Life and Times of William Howard Taft* (1939). He remained at Columbia until 1943, when he moved to Washington, D.C., to work for the Office of War Information. On May 23, 1944, his prior marriage having ended in divorce, Pringle married Katharine Douglas.

After the war Pringle wrote for the *New Yorker, Harper's, Collier's* and the *New York Times Book Review*. With his second wife he wrote a dual biography of Theodore Roosevelt and Woodrow Wilson, which was unfinished at his death.

Pringle is best, and most justly, remembered for *Theodore Roosevelt*. With wit and insight he portrayed Roosevelt as the inimitable Teddy: self-conscious of his place in history, self-confident of his claims to greatness, whimsical, opportunistic, occasionally cruel, and probably sincere. Pringle saw in Roosevelt a figure to notice more than someone to admire. He had arrived at this assessment not by relying on "psychographic dicta" but by recourse to "patient research." The biography was a devastating account in some ways, as was to be expected from a writer with muckraking tendencies. In any case, Pringle's verdict on Roosevelt was accepted by the reading public as well as by most professional historians. Indeed, *Roosevelt* was not seriously challenged for twenty-five years. If Roosevelt was fair game for Pringle's well-honed muckraking razor, this biography was, nonetheless, a serious effort to define Roosevelt in history based on a diligent and perceptive reading of the sources.

Pringle set himself the task of doing a large-scale account of William Howard Taft. Partly because of his own maturing as a writer and partly, no doubt, because of the subject, Pringle's biography of Taft was a more balanced and thoughtful piece of work than the Roosevelt study. He had unlimited access to the large collection of Taft papers. Moreover, he discovered in Taft a "tortured soul" whose life could best be understood from the inside rather than from the outside. This offered a more serious challenge to the biographer than the chiefly visible exploits of Teddy Roosevelt. Pringle's *Taft* lacked the excitement of his *Roosevelt*, but its reputation proved to be no less enduring.

By 1940, Pringle was established as a major biographer of twentieth-century public men. As such he expressed optimism about the future of biographical writing, observing that as long as people were curious about heroes and villains of the past, biography would continue to have a place in both history and literature. He set high ideals for himself as a writer of lives and expressed a becoming realism, admitting, in the foreword to *Roosevelt*, that it was impossible to eliminate all personal bias. He died at Washington, D.C.

[William Allen White, "Taft, T.R. and the G.O.P.," *Saturday Review of Literature*, Oct. 28, 1939, gives a perceptive analysis of Pringle the historian. A useful summary of his life and accomplishment is in his obituary, *New York Times*, Apr. 9, 1958.]

DAVID H. BURTON

PURDY, LAWSON (Sept. 13, 1863–Aug. 30, 1959), tax and zoning expert, was born in Hyde Park, N.Y., the son of James Souveraine Purdy, an Episcopal clergyman, and Frances Hannah Carter. He graduated from St. Paul's School, Concord, N.H., in 1880, and received a B.A. from Trinity College in 1884. Following his marriage to Mary Jenkins McCracken on Feb. 3, 1885, Purdy toured Europe and Asia Minor in 1885–1886. He then returned to Trinity College for an M.A., awarded in 1887. The couple had one daughter. His wife died in 1939, and Purdy married Hélène Schmitz Wexelsen on July 3, 1940. They had no children.

While employed as treasurer of the New York Bank Note Company (1891–1897), Purdy attended New York Law School, and was admitted to the bar in 1898. Like many other civic reformers of the early twentieth century, he was profoundly influenced by the single-tax doctrines of Henry George. He achieved national prominence as a tax authority and reformer while serving as secretary of the New York Tax Reform Association (1896–1906); president of the New York City Department of Taxes and Assessments (1906–1917); vice-president of the National Tax Association (1907–1912); and president of the National Municipal League (1916–1919). His leading achievement was the enactment of legislation of New York City that required publication of assessment rolls (1902) and the separate listing of land and total value of an assessed property (1906).

Purdy worked constantly to modernize the archaic and inequitable system of local and state taxation inherited from the preindustrial past. The ideal was always George's principle of land as the major revenue source, as opposed to taxes on income, labor products, or consumption. He advocated a "decent burial" for the personal property tax (a tax on possessions other than real estate). His vehement criticism was based on the blatant violation by that tax of the standards of efficiency and equity that governed his tax doctrines. Purdy insisted that a fair assessment of personal property was impossible, producing a patchwork system of undertaxation and overtaxation for most individuals. The personal property tax failed to meet two critical tests: that taxes be in proportion to ability to pay and, most important, "that taxes should be in proportion to the benefits received from government." Purdy's tax program also included elimination from state constitutions of archaic constraints upon the legislatures regarding taxation options; the apportionment of state taxes in proportion to local revenues; publication of assessment rolls; separate listing of land and building assessments; and a higher tax upon land than upon buildings.

Purdy was deeply involved in the enactment of the first comprehensive zoning law, in 1916. He had been a member of the advisory Heights of Buildings Commission in 1913 and vice-chairman of the Commission on Building Districts and Restrictions in 1914–1916; these commissions, appointed by the New York City Board of Estimate, laid the groundwork for the necessary enabling state legislation as well as the zoning law. His diplomatic and conciliatory skills, combined with his unquestioned knowledge of land and tax issues, helped to reassure New York business interests that zoning would stabilize and enhance, rather than undermine, property values.

Purdy's interest in zoning and taxation led inexorably to advocacy of city planning. Comprehensive planning would lead to development of the most efficient land use, thereby increasing property values, encouraging business activity, and providing a sound revenue base for the community. City planning and zoning would also contribute to better housing by controlling density and preventing indiscriminate land uses. These measures, supplemented by regulatory housing codes, would upgrade the quality of housing for all classes. Purdy served as secretary of the New York State Commission to Revise the Tenement House Law in 1927; its work led to the comprehensive Multiple Dwelling Law of 1929, an updating of the nationally influential New York State Tenement House Law of 1901.

After resigning the presidency of the Department of Taxes and Assessments, Purdy became general director of the New York Charity Organization Society (1918–1933). In the 1930's he served as an officer or trustee of numerous welfare and nonprofit organizations, including the Russell Sage Foundation, the Provident Loan Society, the Legal Aid Society, and the Seaman's Bank for Savings.

Purdy's career directs attention to key aspects of early twentieth-century social and municipal reform. It suggests, for example, the extent to which historians have underestimated the seminal influence of Henry George. If nothing else, George forced attention to tax issues and nurtured the antimonopoly crusade of the Progressive era. Purdy's career also exemplified the emergence of the reform professional or technician; like his friend Lawrence Veiller, the leading housing expert in the nation, Purdy embodied the ideal of reform as the province of the professional rather than of the prophet. He also personified the ameliorative objectives of Progressive reform. The Progressive movement was geared not to significant redistribution of power, income, or status but, rather, to the creation of a body of regulatory legislation designed to improve living and working conditions. It aspired to correct and limit the abuses of a capitalist economy, not to transform that economy.

Cultivated and urbane, Purdy was likened by one contemporary to a French statesman-ecclesiastic in modern dress. His undergraduate training—traditional and literary—triggered a lifelong involvement in cultural pursuits: literature, theology, Gothic architecture. Purdy died in Port Washington, N.Y.

[Purdy's reminiscences are in the Columbia University Oral History Project. His articles include

"Taxation of Personality," *Municipal Affairs,* June 1899; "Municipal Taxation," *Chicago Conference for Good City Government, Proceedings* (1904); "Outline of a Model System of State and Local Taxation," *Providence Conference for Good City Government, Proceedings* (1907); "The Assessment of Real Estate," *National Municipal Review,* Sept. 1919; "How Much Social Work Can a Community Afford?" *National Conference of Social Work, Proceedings* (1926); "The Housing of the Very Poor," *American City,* July 1928; and "Relief Taxes—Wise and Unwise," *American City, Apr. 1936.* For biographical information see *Municipal Affairs,* June 1899; *American* magazine, July 1911; *New York Times,* Sept. 1, 1959; and *American Journal of Economics and Sociology,* Oct. 1959.]

ROY LUBOVE

QUINN, ARTHUR HOBSON (Feb. 9, 1875–Oct. 16, 1960), educator, literary historian, and biographer, was born in Philadelphia, Pa., the son of Michael A. Quinn and Mary MacDonough. He received the B.S. from the University of Pennsylvania in 1894 and at once embarked upon a career at that institution, as instructor of mathematics (1894–1895) and then English (1895–1904). After a year studying modern philology at the University of Munich (1897–1898), Quinn received the Ph.D. at Pennsylvania in 1899. His academic climb was rapid, and he was appointed full professor in 1908. He married Helen McKee on May 31, 1904; they had five children.

Quinn had begun to write fiction shortly after his graduation, and his first book, *Pennsylvania Stories* (1899), dealt with undergraduate life. He later wrote of himself, "His contributions to fiction and verse, however, were checked somewhat by his scholarly duties, although he has occasionally written and published short stories." He organized and directed the first summer school at the university (1904), and served as dean of the undergraduate college from 1912 to 1922.

Although the subjects in which Quinn remained most interested had not fully attained academic respectability in the early years of the twentieth century, he gave the first graduate course in American literature in 1905 and the first course in American drama in 1918. A proselyte for the importance of native culture, he edited influential anthologies of American drama and other creative writing, and wrote histories of American fiction and drama that long remained standard reference works. Most notable of his editions are *Representative American Plays* (1917; revised 1953), *Contemporary American Plays* (1923), *The Literature of America* (with A. C. Baugh and W. D. Howe, 1929; revised 1938), *The Early Plays of James A. Herne* (1940), and *The Complete Poems and Tales of Edgar Allan Poe* (with E. H. O'Neill, 1946). At the time of its publication the last, though it skimped on the nonfiction prose, was the largest collection of Poe's writings in print; it also made a notable advance in textual accuracy.

Quinn's important contributions to the history of the American theater began with his article on early drama in volume I of the *Cambridge History of American Literature* (1917). He later served on councils dedicated to supporting the performing arts, notably that which organized the American National Theater in 1923. The capstone of his work in this field was the comprehensive two-part study *A History of the American Drama From the Beginning to the Civil War* (1923; revised 1943) and *A History of the American Drama From the Civil War to the Present Day* (2 vols., 1927; revised in 1 vol., 1936). The product of much original research (especially in the earlier periods) and of playgoing, these volumes remain highly useful for their play lists and bibliographies. Less comprehensive and now dated in some of its critical estimates is *American Fiction* (1936).

Quinn's secondary interest in fiction led him to undertake one of his most important contributions to scholarship, *Edgar Allan Poe* (1941). This study was an attempt rigorously to separate fact from the many legends that had grown up around Poe, and in preparing it Quinn exhumed significant new data—especially his revelation of the full extent of the forgeries committed by Poe's literary executor, Rufus W. Griswold. Jay B. Hubbell, a Poe authority, praised the volume as "on the whole the best life of Poe," but added: "A few readers have felt that Quinn was too ready to defend Poe against all comers, and some younger scholars have regretted that he did not employ the newer critical approaches." The *Poe Newsletter* of April 1968 concurred: "Fine as it is in many ways, [it] fails to capture some of Poe's more elusive qualities and is weak in its critical judgments."

In 1950, Quinn edited *A Treasury of Edith Wharton* and followed it the next year with his last major scholarly undertaking, general editorship of *Literature of the American People* (1951), to which he contributed "The Establishment of National Literature." The longest and most comprehensive one-volume history of American writing, it was honored by the Athenaeum Club of Philadelphia as the best book of 1951.

Quinn was named John Welsh centennial professor of history and English literature in 1939, a chair from which he retired in 1945. He continued as emeritus professor and special lecturer until his death in Philadelphia.

Quinn's anthologies served the needs of students for several decades, and he still merits recognition for solid contributions to the history of American drama and fiction. He was also a commentator on the current scene, writing letters to the *New York Times* drama editor, as his *Times* obituary recalled, that nearly always praised plays "he thought had been reviewed with sufficient admiration for their merits." This comment is significant, for it is not Quinn's historical scholarship but his critical judgments that have tended to date rapidly since his death.

[Biographical material on Quinn is not extensive. Most useful, besides the standard reference works, is his obituary in *New York Times*, Oct. 17, 1960. See also Jay B. Hubbell, ed., *Eight American Authors* (1956).]

J. V. RIDGELY

RADIN, PAUL (Apr. 2, 1883–Feb. 21, 1959), anthropologist and linguist, was born in Lodz, Poland, the son of Adolph M. Radin, a rabbi and Hebrew scholar skilled in modern and ancient languages, and Johanna Theodor. In 1884 the family migrated to Elmira, N.Y.

Radin acquired his father's skeptical liberalism and linguistic skills, learning Greek and Latin as well as Hebrew. He entered City College of New York at fourteen and, after graduation in 1902, enrolled at Columbia University to study zoology. But influenced by James H. Robinson, he turned to history. Between 1905 and 1907 Radin studied at Munich, substituting physical anthropology for zoology while continuing his historical interests, and at Berlin, where he concentrated on anthropology. In 1907 he returned to Columbia, where he worked under Franz Boas as well as Robinson. He finished Ph.D. work in 1911. As a student of Boas, Radin got to know anthropology's elder statesmen: A. L. Kroeber, Clark Wissler, Edward Sapir, Robert Lowie, Frank G. Speck, and Alexander Goldenweiser.

To finance his education after his father's death in 1910, Radin did translations and tutored in German at City College. On May 26, 1910, he married Rose Robinson. The next year he worked at the Bureau of American Ethnology. After spending 1912–1913 on a Columbia-Harvard fellowship, analyzing Zapotec linguistics, he joined Sapir at the Geological Survey of Canada, where he began publishing on the Ojibwa. Between 1908 and 1913 he also did fieldwork among the Winnebago.

Radin's varied interests can be seen in *The Sources and Authenticity of the History of the Ancient Mexicans,* published in 1920, the same year as his *Autobiography of a Winnebago Indian.* The intellectual atmosphere for this work came from Mills College and the University of California, where Radin worked with Kroeber and renewed a friendship with Lowie. Radin spent 1920 to 1924 in Europe, lecturing under W. H. R. Rivers at Cambridge but being attracted to Zurich and C. G. Jung. While *The Winnebago Tribe* (1923) appeared at this time, it seems primarily a seminal period for *Primitive Man as Philosopher* (1927), one of his best-known works.

In 1925 and 1926 Radin held fellowships for Ottawa Indian fieldwork and a final revision of *Crashing Thunder* (1926), which was first published as the first part of *The Autobiography of a Winnebago Indian.* In 1927 he went to Fiske for four years, finding time to collect life histories of former slaves. In 1931 he returned to the University of California, where his interests ranged from the Penutian language through minorities of San Francisco, especially the Italians, to original sources on Mexican history. His catalog for Spanish publications in the Sutro Library in San Francisco consisted of more than 1,000 pages. He also published a text, *Social Anthropology* (1932); a general review of the field, *Method and Theory of Ethnology* (1933); a revised edition of his 1927 overview of Middle and North America, *The Story of the American Indian* (1934); and a personal view of comparative religion, *Primitive Religion* (1937).

The years from 1931 to 1940 were spent in warm friendship with Kroeber and Lowie and saw a second marriage, to Doris Woodward. Radin disliked the formalities of the classroom, preferring to invite students into his home for broad-ranging give and take of ideas. One student, Cora DuBois, described the result: "For a man who entertained a fine impatience for the drudgery of schoolteaching, he has today a singularly wide and grateful circle of students whom he chose to instruct in his own informal and often caustic fashion."

Radin's range of linguistic and geographic interests was matched by his methods. He often argued that the task of the ethnographer was to record in detail what primitive peoples said of themselves while providing a minimum of critical evaluation. The Winnebago and Italian biographies illustrate the approach, as does *African Folk Tales* (1952); yet in reconstructing history Radin proposed grand waves of diffusion based on limited evidence, as in *The Story of the American Indian* and *Indians of South America* (1942). His reconstruction of culture in these two books exceeds much of what Kroeber did in North America, yet Radin frequently chided his colleague, claiming anthropology must never lose sight of the individual. Likewise, Radin explicitly rejected psychological interpretation and particularly Freudian theory, but some of his most insightful interpretations implicitly rest on psychoanalytic thought. Similarly, Radin advocated a purely historical method and would have rejected a Marxist label, but he stressed economics as basic for religion and in *Primitive Religion* and *The World of Primitive Man* (1953) Radin presented an evolutionary, rather than historical, framework.

In 1941 Radin left Berkeley for a position at Black Mountain College in North Carolina. The experimental and unstructured nature of the college appealed to him, but he was basically urban. In 1945, through support of Mary Mellon and the Bollingen Foundation, and later the Andrew Mellon Foundation, he was freed to write and edit, with occasional teaching at Kenyon College. In 1949 he lectured at four Swedish universities and at the Eranos Conferences in Ascona, Switzerland. These intermittent engagements led to four years of residence at Lugano, Switzerland, convenient for work and stimulation at the C. G. Jung Institute (Zurich) and for travel to lecture at Oxford and Cambridge. Bollingen support facilitated a series of papers on Winnebago folklore and religion, making Radin a major liaison between European and American ethnographers.

Radin's breadth of experience made him one of America's most cultivated scholars. It was altogether fitting he be best known for *Primitive Man as Philosopher*. Throughout his life he remained a man of thought, recognizing similar qualities in others in all cultures.

After publishing two widely read books, *The Trickster* (1956) and *The Evolution of an American Prose Epic* (1956), Radin left Switzerland in 1957 to become Samuel Rubin professor and then head of the department of anthropology at Brandeis University. He died in New York City.

[Radin's unpublished notes on Wintu, Winnebago, Ojibwa, and Huave linguistics are with the American Philosophical Society. Obituaries are by Harry Hoijer, *American Anthropologist*, Oct. 1959, with photograph; and J. David Sapir, *Journal of American Folklore*, Jan. 1961. Cora DuBois, "An Appreciation," in Stanley Diamond, ed., *Culture in History* (1960), provides biographical detail. Diamond extensively evaluates Radin's contribution in the 1960 paperback edition of *The World of Primitive Man*. Nancy Lurie sketches Radin's fieldwork among the Winnebago in "Two Dollars," in Solon Kimball and J. B. Watson, eds., *Crossing Culture Boundaries* (1972). Richard Werbner compiled Radin's bibliography for the Festschrift, *Culture in History* (1960).]

ERNEST SCHUSKY

RANKIN, JOHN ELLIOTT (Mar. 29, 1882–Nov. 26, 1960), congressman, was born near Bolanda, Miss., the son of Thomas Braxton Rankin, a schoolteacher, and Venola Modeste Rutledge. He attended public schools and the University of Mississippi at Oxford, from which he received his LL.B. in 1910. That year he started a law practice in Tupelo, Miss., which he maintained for the rest of his life. On Oct. 1, 1919, he married Annie Laurie Burrous: they had one daughter. From 1912 to 1915 Rankin was prosecuting attorney of Lee County, Miss. He served as a soldier in World War I.

Mississippi's First Congressional District sent Rankin to the U.S. House of Representatives in 1921, beginning a highly controversial career that lasted through 1952. In the House, he became identified with public power, veterans' interests, and a concept of "Americanism" that included white supremacy, anti-Semitism, union-baiting, and a wide-ranging xenophobia. His reputation for know-nothingness, his uninhibited language, and his fits of temper, which on one occasion resulted in a physical attack on a fellow congressman, tended to obscure his mastery of the workings of the House and his effectiveness in that body.

In 1933 he cosponsored, with Senator George W. Norris, the bill that created the Tennessee Valley Authority (TVA). As a representative of a rural constituency, Rankin championed programs to bring cheap electric power to rural areas, and it was largely through his efforts that virtually every farmhouse in his northeastern Mississippi district was enjoying cheap power within a few years after the creation of the TVA. Thereafter, he remained a strong advocate of the Rural Electrification Administration.

For most of his years in Congress, he was chairman or ranking minority member of the House Veterans Affairs Committee. Early in World War II he sponsored the amendment that raised the base pay of armed forces members to $50 a month, and he played an influential role in the formulation of the postwar G.I. Bill of Rights.

Increasingly, through the 1940's, Rankin's name came to be synonymous with the nation's nativist forces, as exemplified by the Committee on Un-American Activities, which had been established in 1938 "to investigate subversive and un-American propaganda." Although Rankin never served on the Dies Committee, he was one of its chief supporters in the House, and it was an adroit parliamentary maneuver of his at the outset of the 1945 session that turned the committee into a standing committee, with great latitude as to what it might investigate and how it chose to do its investigating. He was a prominent member of the new committee in its most celebrated years (1945–1948) and used his connections with veterans' organizations to rally support for it against recurrent attacks by liberals within his own party.

In addition to his legislative accomplishments in behalf of cheap power and veterans' benefits, Rankin's reputation rested on his impassioned fight against repeal of the poll tax, used throughout the South as a bar to black voters; against passage of the Fair Employment Practices Act, designed to open job opportunities to blacks; against repeal of the Chinese Exclusion Act, on the grounds that America would be flooded by yellow hordes; against labor organizers in general and Congress of Industrial Organizations organizers in particular. When, during World War II, the proposal was advanced that the American Red Cross cease labeling blood to indicate whether it had come from black or white veins, Rankin attributed it to a scheme by "the crackpots, the Communists and parlor pinks . . . to mongrelize the nation."

Small, thin, and white-haired, Rankin was a fiery debater who took special delight in baiting his Jewish colleagues with innuendoes that Jews were either international bankers or Communists. The flavor of his style can only be conveyed by examples. Here are two from his comments on the floor of the House in the mid-1940's: "Communism . . . hounded and persecuted the Savior during his earthly ministry, inspired his crucifixion, derided him in his dying agony, and then gambled for his garments at the foot of the cross. . . . These alien-minded communistic enemies of Christianity and their stooges are trying to get control of the press of this country. Many of our great daily newspapers have now changed hands and gone over to them. . . . They are trying to take over the radio. Listen to their lying broadcasts in broken English and you can almost smell them." And "it is not a disgrace to be a real Negro. As I said on this floor before, if I were a Negro, I would want to be as black as the ace of spades. I would want to go out with Negroes and have a real good time."

In 1946 Rankin made an unsuccessful try for his state's Democratic nomination for senator, and in 1949 he was dropped from the Un-American Activities Committee as punishment for supporting the States Rights party candidate for president against Harry S. Truman in the 1948 election. In 1952 he was defeated for renomination to the congressional seat that he had held for sixteen consecutive terms. By then he had become an anachronism, an embarrassment even to those who shared many of his views. He died in Tupelo, Miss.

[The *Congressional Record* and the hearings of the Committee on Un-American Activities for 1946–1949 document the quality of Rankin's oratory and the range of his prejudices. For his connections with the committee, see Robert K. Carr, *The House Committee on Un-American Activities* (1952), and Walter Goodman, *The Committee* (1968), which contains a striking picture of Rankin.]

WALTER GOODMAN

RAPAPORT, DAVID (Sept. 30, 1911–Dec. 14, 1960), psychoanalyst, was born in Munkács, Hungary, the son of Béla Rapaport, a merchant, and of Helen Balaban.

As a youth he was a leader of the Hashomer Hatzair, a politically radical Zionist youth movement, well known for his fiery oratory and on occasion one step ahead of the police. At eighteen Rapaport entered the University of Budapest, where he studied mathematics and physics. On Dec. 24, 1932, he married Elvira Strasser, who later became a professor of mathematics. They had two daughters. One year later the couple joined their group's kibbutz in Palestine, where Rapaport worked as a surveyor. After two years they returned to Hungary, where

Rapaport entered psychoanalysis for personal reasons and changed his field of study to psychology.

In 1938, Rapaport received a Ph.D. from the Royal Hungarian University. Soon thereafter he fled to America to escape the Nazi terror. After a brief period in New York City, he obtained a position at the Osawatomie State Hospital in Kansas, largely through the good offices of Lawrence S. Kubie, a New York psychoanalyst. At Osawatomie, Rapaport at once began research on the effect of Metrazol convulsions, the shock therapy of the time; and with help from Frank Fremont-Smith of the Josiah Macy, Jr., Foundation, he embarked on his first major theoretical study, *Emotions and Memory* (1942). In it he proposed a hierarchy of principles organizing the interrelationship of emotions and memory based on psychoanalytic, clinical and experimental psychological, and psychopathological data.

Rapaport had met Karl Menninger, chief of the Menninger Clinic at Topeka, Kans., in New York City. In 1940 he accepted a position at the clinic, and soon became chief psychologist and director of psychology training as well as director of research. He organized a training program and projects on perception, hypnosis, infant development, and the selection of psychiatric residents, in addition to continuing his studies of human thinking by way of a battery of diagnostic psychological tests.

Rapaport was able to show that though some diagnostic tests were especially useful in evaluating emotional functioning and others in evaluating intellectual functioning, all test responses shed light on both aspects of the personality. His *Diagnostic Psychological Testing* (1945–1946), revised and condensed by Robert Holt, is still standard in the field. Rapaport gradually became concerned that his energies were being dissipated in administration when what he really wanted to do was scholarly work in psychoanalytic theory. In 1948 he therefore accepted an opportunity to pursue such studies offered by Robert Knight, a former clinical director at the Menninger Clinic who had become the director of the Austin Riggs Center in Stockbridge, Mass..

At Riggs, Rapaport worked on systematizing psychoanalytic theory, in particular its metapsychology, the abstract level of theorizing in psychoanalysis, allegedly explanatory of its clinical theory. Although he was unusual among psychoanalytic theorists in not being a practitioner, his participation in the clinical milieu and regular attendance at case conferences led to an infusion of clinical considerations into his work.

After *Organization and Pathology of Thought* (1951), in which he presented and extensively annotated major papers in the field and then presented his formulation of the psychoanalytic theory of thinking, Rapport integrated the conceptual model of psychoanalysis and, later, the psychoanalytic theory of affect, ego psychology, developmental psychology, and motivation. He capped this work by *The Structure of Psychoanalytic Theory* (1959), which contains an extensive translation of psychoanalysis into the idiom of contemporary psychology. Indeed, none of his writings was confined by the parochial limits of psychoanalysis. He drew upon the work of the child psychologist Jean Piaget, upon ethology, and upon experimental psychology, both animal and human.

While at Riggs, Rapaport wrote relatively little on clinical topics. But it was there that he made his more original contributions, in contrast with his systematization of theory, notably in his studies of states of consciousness, ego autonomy, the superego, and the psychoanalytic theory of activity and passivity. He also taught theory at the Western New England Psychoanalytic Institute.

Though he lectured widely before psychoanalytic audiences and participated in the professional organizations of psychologists to some extent during the earlier part of his career in America, Rapaport essentially spent his time in his study. He was a founder of the Division of Clinical and Abnormal Psychology of the American Psychological Association, and in 1960 received its award for distinguished contribution to the field. In 1952 he was offered the chair of psychology at the Hebrew University in Jerusalem, but declined.

At about the same time Rapaport embarked on an ambitious experimental program designed to show, by the learning of word lists, how the psychoanalytic theory of attention cathexes and Freud's concept of consciousness as a sense organ could serve as the basis for a psychoanalytic theory of learning.

Rapaport died in Stockbridge of a heart attack. He was a man of wide-ranging interests, strong opinions, and powerful intellect. His goal was to understand the nature of human thought, and to that end he regarded Freudian psychoanalytic theory, especially as its drive psychology became expanded by ego psychology into a general psychology, as the most fruitful approach.

He asked how it is possible for man, influenced

by the Freudian id, to come to a veridical grasp of external reality. The metaphor of a bridge is singularly apt for Rapaport—between philosophy and psychology, psychology and psychoanalysis, id psychology and ego psychology, where he followed Heinz Hartmann, and individual and social psychology, where he followed Erik H. Erikson. He was an outspoken foe of behaviorist psychology and associationist learning theory because of their neglect of intrapsychic affective and drive motivations. On the other hand he regarded cognitive structures and their development in the learning process as crucial to the understanding of human thought.

Though he made no effort to develop a "school," Rapaport was enormously stimulating and a number of his students have achieved positions of prominence. He was a demanding teacher but drove no one harder than himself. His writings, which must be studied rather than simply read, are highly polished, spare, and intricately and carefully reasoned.

[Rapaport's principal papers and a complete bibliography are in *The Collected Papers of David Rapaport* (1967). Books not mentioned in text are *The Influence of Freud on American Psychology* (1964), with David Shakow; and *The History of the Concept of the Association of Ideas* (1974). Obituaries are by Robert Knight, in *Psychoanalytic Quarterly*, 30 (1961); and Merton M. Gill, in *Journal of the American Psychoanalytic Association*, 9 (1961).

A memorial volume is Robert Holt, ed., *Motives and Thought* (1967). See also Fred Schwartz and Richard Rouse, "The Activation and Recovery of Associations, "The *Psychological Issues* (1961); Fred Schwartz and P. Schiller, *A Psychoanalytic Model of Attention and Learning* (1970); and John Gedo, "Kant's Way," *Psychoanalytical Quarterly*, 42 (1973).]

MERTON M. GILL

RAULSTON, JOHN TATE (Sept. 22, 1868–July 11, 1956), lawyer, legislator, and judge, was born in Marion County, Tenn., the son of William Doran Raulston, a farmer, and Comfort Matilda Tate. He was educated in country schools, and attended Tennessee Wesleyan College and the University of Chattanooga while reading law in the office of William D. Spear, at Jasper. Although admitted to the bar in 1896, Raulston taught school for four years before beginning an independent practice in Whitwell. From 1902 to 1904 he served as a Republican in the state legislature. Thereafter he practiced law

with Alan S. Kelly, in South Pittsburg, until 1918. In August 1908, he married Estelle Otto Faller. They had one daughter. His wife died in 1916, and on Apr. 1, 1922, he married Eva Davis. The marriage was childless. In 1918 Raulston was elected judge of the seven counties in the Eighteenth District. He rode circuit until 1926.

Following World War I, attacks by William Jennings Bryan and others on the theory of evolution provoked into uproarious division and commotion the scientific and academic as well as religious communities. Raulston became involved in this controversy as the judge in the famous Scopes "monkey" trial. By 1925, various southern states had passed laws prohibiting the use of textbooks sympathetic to the theory of evolution. The Tennessee law, first to explicitly "prohibit the teaching of evolution in public schools," assessed penalties for its infringement of between $100 and $500. Upon learning that the American Civil Liberties Union had offered to finance a test case of the law, one George W. Rappelyea framed a case by asking the head of the Dayton school board and the county superintendent of schools to sue John T. Scopes, a substitute Rhea County high school teacher, for having taught the theory of evolution. Scopes acted from no motive other than testing the law in the name of academic freedom and freedom of thought.

John Randolph Neal and John L. Godsy, and later District Attorney General Arthur Thomas Stewart, served as defense counsel; Sue K. Hicks and Wallace C. Haggard, as prosecutors. When Bryan joined the latter, he elevated what might have been a petty local case into a national and even international affair; Clarence Darrow and Dudley Field Malone joined the defense specifically because he was on the other side.

On May 9, 1925, a preliminary hearing by three justices of the peace held that Scopes was "at least technically if not intentionally guilty." Two weeks later Raulston charged a grand jury "to ascertain whether or not the law has been violated." When the jury returned a true bill, he scheduled the trial to begin on July 10 so that it might be closed by the time school began in August. Although the question was Scopes's guilt, the defense hoped to discredit fundamentalist religion. Bryan's objective was equally clear. "If evolution wins in Dayton," he said, "Christianity goes. . . for the two cannot stand together."

In a hippodrome atmosphere concocted by Dayton's boosters and in a heat wave that drove the thermometer to over 100°, Raulston faced the defending "colonels" on one side and prosecuting "generals" on the other. In his opening, during which he read the law and also the first chapter of Genesis, he charged the jury to decide only whether Scopes had violated the law. The wisdom of the law was not at issue. He also cautioned that expression of emotion from spectators would not be permitted. To decide whether the defense could introduce testimony by theological scholars and scientists, he adjourned court until July 13, when he faced a motion to quash Scopes's indictment. Two days later he denied the motion. Although pressed by the defense to permit the submission of expert scientific testimony, he denied the request, whereupon Darrow mocked him. As Bryan's wife, Mary Baird Bryan, noted, "The judge . . . is a smiling man who tries to make everybody comfortable and happy and wants to do the fair thing. He has a difficult place to fill and has been so insulted by the opposition that were I in his place I would have clapped the gentlemen all in jail. . . ."

On July 20, Raulston cited Darrow for "contempt and insult." After Darrow apologized, he forgave him. But by permitting Bryan, a prosecution counsel, to sit as witness for the defense, he let Darrow expose Bryan's lack of scientific knowledge. Moreover, he denied Bryan a chance to rebut. Raulston charged the jury that if Scopes were found guilty he could be fined only from $100 to $500 and that if he were found guilty but no amount of fine were set, the fine would be $100. The jury found Scopes guilty but deferred to Raulston on the fine. He set it at $100. Because state law provided that no jury could assess a fine larger than $50, Raulston was considered to have made an error, which later enabled the state supreme court on appeal to dispose of the case on a technicality. Raulston at the time thought the antievolution law was properly framed. Later he questioned whether its ambiguous wording truly represented the intent of the legislature but still held that the state has the right to determine the curriculum for public instruction.

Failing of reelection as judge in 1926, Raulston resumed his law practice, eventually with the firm of Raulston, Raulston, and Swafford, with which he was associated until his retirement in 1952. Although he practiced both civil and criminal law, his forte was land law; in this connection he was retained by such large corporations as the U.S. Steel Corporation, Brush Creek Coal Company, Tennessee Coal, Iron and Railroad Company, and Nashville, Chattanooga, and St. Louis Railway Company.

A large, energetic man who dressed well,

Raulston neither drank, smoked, nor cursed. He worked hard, accumulated a sizable estate, and won a reputation for being penurious. He was president of the Marion County Bar Association from 1933 to 1952, a member of the Tennessee and American bar associations, and a thirty-second-degree Mason. He died in South Pittsburg, Tenn.

[Although Raulston lectured on the Scopes trial for several years, he wrote nothing about it. Silhouettes of Raulston and evaluation of his conduct of the trial appeared in all major newspapers during July 1925. Details are found in the official transcript, *State of Tennessee* vs. *Scopes* (n.d.), in the Tennessee State Archives and Library, Nashville. Varying only slightly from it is *The World's Most Famous Court Trial. Tennessee Evolution Case. A Complete Stenographic Report* (1925). An excellent abridgment is Leslie H. Allen, comp. and ed., *Bryan and Darrow at Dayton* (1925).

Autobiographical and biographical accounts include William Jennings Bryan and Mary Baird Bryan, *The Memoirs of William Jennings Bryan* (1925); Winterton C. Curtis, *Fundamentalism vs. Evolution at Dayton, Tennessee* (1956); Clarence Darrow, *The Story of My Life* (1932); Arthur Garfield Hays, *City Lawyer* (1942); and Scopes's own account in John T. Scopes and James Presley, *Center of the Storm* (1967).

Secondary works are L. Sprague de Camp, *The Great Monkey Trial* (1968); Paolo E. Coletta, *William Jennings Bryan III. Political Puritan, 1915–1925* (1969); Norman Furniss, *The Fundamentalist Controversy, 1918–1931* (1954); Ray Ginger, *Six Days or Forever?* (1958); Lawrence W. Levine, *Defender of the Faith* (1965); and Jerry R. Tompkins, *D-Days at Dayton* (1965). See also Donald Brod, "The Scopes Trial: A Look at Press Coverage After Forty Years," *Journalism Quarterly*, Spring 1965; Joseph Wood Krutch, "Tennessee: Where Cowards Rule," *Nation*, July 15, 1925; and "Tennessee's Dilemma," *ibid.*, July 22, 1925; and H. L. Mencken, "In Tennessee," *ibid.*, July 1, 1925.]

PAOLO E. COLETTA

RAYMOND, ALEXANDER GILLESPIE (Oct. 2, 1909–Sept. 6, 1956), cartoonist-illustrator, was born in New Rochelle, N.Y., the son of Alexander Gillespie Raymond and Beatrice Wallaz Crossley. After studies at Iona Preparatory School in New Rochelle from 1925 to 1928, Raymond took a position as a clerk for the Wall Street firm of Chisholm and Chapman, stockbrokers. After losing his job in the great stock-market crash of 1929, Raymond, encouraged by a neighbor, comic artist Russ Westover, creator of "Tillie The Toiler," enrolled in the Grand Central School of Art. While at art school he worked as a solicitor for the firm of mortgage broker James Boyd. On Dec. 31, 1930, he married Helen Frances Williams; they had five children.

Raymond had been drawing since early boyhood. In art school he learned the refinements of style that later gave him a reputation as a powerful draftsman. In 1930 he entered the comic art field at King Features Syndicate, first as an assistant to Russ Westover on the "Tillie" strip and later with Lyman Young on a strip called "Tim Tyler's Luck." For extended periods in 1932 and 1933 Raymond ghosted the "Tim Tyler" strip for the syndicate.

In 1934, as syndicate competition soared, Raymond was asked to develop a Sunday page composed of two new comic strips, "Flash Gordon" and "Jungle Jim." The two strips, created to compete with the already popular "Buck Rogers" and "Tarzan," established an immediate following, and both inspired radio and movie serials as well as comic books. In 1935 Raymond, in collaboration with mystery writer Dashiell Hammett, created another comic strip, "Secret Agent X-9," also for King Features.

"Flash Gordon" was inspired by the novel *When Worlds Collide*, by Philip Wylie and Edwin Balmer. It was the story of three people from Earth who take a spaceship to the distant planet Mongo, where they do battle with a villain called Ming the Merciless, emperor of Mongo. The three—Gordon, a handsome, blond polo player and Yale graduate; his girlfriend, Dale Arden; and a scientist, Dr. Hans Zarkov—played out their adventures "amid grandiose landscapes, in futuristic cities and the forsaken regions of the planet." "Flash Gordon," says Maurice Horn, "met with immediate success, establishing itself as the supreme science-fiction strip." From 1934 to 1944, Raymond combined brilliant draftsmanship and an articulation of realism. The strip inspired an even better-known movie serial with Buster Crabbe as Flash and Charles Middleton as Ming. During the 1930's and 1940's the strip provided the basis for a radio series, and in the 1953–1954 season it was also a television series.

In "Jungle Jim," Jim Bradley, an explorer, animal trapper, and adventurer, carried out swashbuckling adventures in an area defined only as "east of Suez." Along with his companion Kolu and a shady lady whom he reformed named Lil de Vrille, Jungle Jim fought villains of all description

with ferocity. The strip was hailed by one observer of comic art for its "striking elegance of line, a fine delineation of atmosphere and background, and a visual excitement which give [it] a highly polished gloss." Although "Jungle Jim" never surpassed "Tarzan" in popularity or in numbers of newspaper clients, it did become one of the highest-rated adventure strips and was widely imitated, mainly for its draftsmanship. Like "Flash Gordon," "Jungle Jim" became a comic book as well as radio and television serials. And in the 1940's and 1950's Columbia Pictures produced ten "Jungle Jim" movies starring Johnny Weissmuller, who had achieved fame as "Tarzan."

Like Raymond's two earlier strips, "Secret Agent X-9" was a competitor aimed at the "Dick Tracy" market. The inflexible and tough-minded secret agent battles crime with vigor, dash, and skill. In an era when a highly respected Federal Bureau of Investigation was battling the underworld, the strip found a responsive public. Raymond and Hammett both had left the strip by late 1935, passing their work on to other artists and continuity writers. The strip inspired a short-lived radio serial and two movie serials.

Toward the end of World War II, Raymond, a reserve officer in the U.S. Marine Corps, served as art director of the Marine Corps publicity office in Philadelphia and then saw combat duty as a public information officer and artist aboard the aircraft carrier U.S.S. *Gilbert Islands* off Okinawa, Balikpapan, Borneo, and Southern Japan. He returned to the United States with the permanent rank of major.

After the war Raymond looked for a new challenge. He found it in 1946, creating a fourth comic strip, "Rip Kirby," the story of a sophisticated and debonair criminologist. Kirby, like Raymond, was a former Marine Corps captain. The strip had more subtlety and less action than "Flash Gordon." Kirby, mature, intellectual, and witty, was the antithesis of Gordon and seemed to represent a new phase in Raymond's work. A Kirby comic book was later created, but the strip never achieved radio or television serialization, nor did it become a movie.

Raymond helped to refine realism in comic strips. As Coulton Waugh wrote in *The Comics*, "What is unique is the degree of realism achieved in the drawing, the conscientious clarity and brilliance of line. In its super-finish there is nothing to compare with it. . . . Raymond created the illusion of depth." Raymond also helped to fashion heroes who would have competitive appeal in feature syndication. And he was successful to a great degree, as the diversified spinoffs of his work (comic books, radio, television, and movies) seem to indicate. While "Flash Gordon" was a schoolboy's dream come to life, "Rip Kirby" showed the maturing of a hero who, unlike the blond Adonis Gordon, could wear glasses and lead a refined life. Raymond produced some of the most beautifully drawn comic strips in the history of American graphic humor. He was a creative technician more than a brilliant innovator, but the test of his work was its wide application and commercial success. He was president of the National Cartoonists Society from 1950–1952.

Raymond was killed in an automobile accident near Westport, Conn.

[See Stephen Becker, *Comic Art in America* (1959); Pierre Couperie and Maurice Horn, *A History of the Comic Strip* (1968); Maurice Horn, "The Adventure Strip," introduction to Alex Raymond, *Flash Gordon* (1967), and, as editor, *The World Encyclopedia of Comics* (1976), especially articles on Raymond and "Flash Gordon," "Jungle Jim," "Agent X-9" and "Rip Kirby"; Coulton Waugh, *The Comics* (1947); and the obituary, *New York Times*, Sept. 6, 1956.]

EVERETTE E. DENNIS

READ, CONYERS (Apr. 25, 1881–Dec. 23, 1959), historian, was born in Philadelphia, Pa., the son of William Franklin Read, a textile manufacturer, and Victoria Eliza Conyers. He attended Central High School in Philadelphia and then entered Harvard, where he earned the B.A. (1903), M.A. (1904), and Ph.D. in history (1908). Before taking the Harvard doctorate, he spent two years (1903–1905) at Oxford University (Balliol), earning a B.Litt (awarded in 1909). During 1908–1909 he did research work in several London archives and libraries. He married Edith Coulson Kirk of Philadelphia on June 10, 1910, at the end of his first year as an instructor in history at Princeton. They had three children.

In January 1911 Read became a history instructor at the University of Chicago, where he spent the next decade. He rose steadily through the academic ranks, reaching a full professorship in 1919. At the outbreak of World War I, he suffered from the deafness that afflicted him for the rest of his life, but he never allowed it to interfere with his work. Hence during the war he served with the Red Cross in Brittany.

Upon returning to the United States, Read took up an active role in the family textile mill, William F. Read and Sons, of which he had been a director since his father's death in 1916. Successively vice-president, general manager, and president of the mill, Read was responsible for a business that employed some 500 workers and operated 430 looms. He once said of his business career, "I was never really keen about it and therefore never very good at it." The business declined and was liquidated in 1933, the year Read became executive secretary of the American Historical Association, then a part-time post that lasted until 1941. In 1934 he was appointed professor of English history at the University of Pennsylvania. His first wife died in 1937, and on Mar. 25, 1939, he married Evelyn Plummer Braun, who later became a collaborator in his books.

In the late 1930's Read became increasingly concerned about the threat of German aggression. He chaired the Philadelphia branch of the Committee for the Defense of America by Aiding the Allies. During World War II, he served in Colonel William J. ("Wild Bill") Donovan's Research and Analysis Branch, which was soon transformed into the Office of Strategic Services. Read was chief of the British Empire Section and a member of the Board of Analysts in the OSS. After his return to academic life, he organized and chaired the Philadelphia branch of the Council on Foreign Relations. He continued to teach at the University of Pennsylvania until his retirement in 1951; in 1949 he had become president of the American Historical Association.

Read first became interested in history as a schoolboy. He went to Harvard to study it; the same impulse took him to Oxford. There he found a world so attractive that it was "near making an Englishman of me." His lifelong admiration and affection for England and Englishmen gave direction to his scholarship. While at Oxford he began work on a biography of Sir Francis Walsingham, secretary of state and effectually foreign minister to Elizabeth I. As early as 1909 Read edited the Bardon papers (a collection concerning the trial of Mary Queen of Scots), but it was not until 1925 that his three-volume *Mr. Secretary Walsingham and the Policy of Queen Elizabeth* was published. It was the most considerable piece of work on Elizabethan history since James Anthony Froude published his multivolume history of the mid-Tudor years; and it placed Read in the front rank of historians of England. Based on a sweeping command of all the manuscript sources and a meticulous use of evidence, it remains the magisterial study of English foreign policy in the crisis years before the Armada. It was followed by *Bibliography of British History, Tudor Period, 1485-1603* (1933), a comprehensive and authoritative compilation. At the time of his retirement he had begun work on another massive biography—that of William Cecil, Lord Burghley; the first volume appeared in 1955, and the second and final volume was complete although not in print when he died.

Read's career was an interesting blend of the nineteenth-century tradition of the gentleman-scholar and that of the twentieth-century academic professional. Relatively easy circumstances made it possible for him to spend a number of years at the beginning of his adult life immersing himself in the archival materials of Elizabethan history. Characteristically his first major work was published during the years when he was away from academia and fully involved in business. But Read's standards as an historian were rigorous. He rightly boasted that he had read every scrap of paper that Cecil had written. He was meticulous in trying to exclude his biases and preoccupations from his reconstruction of the English past. His works are rich, indeed exhaustive, in information but sparing and cautious in synthetic judgments. Only in his shorter work, *The Tudors* (1936), did he offer more sweeping judgments about the sixteenth century. Nevertheless, as he made clear in his presidential address of 1949, Read had a strong sense of the historian's social responsibility to his own age and to its problems. No historian was entitled to use his studies of the past as an excuse for withdrawal from the world. He practiced his preaching in his own career during World War II.

Read was a strong and self-assured person, a reflection of his wider experience in business and government. Endowed with a salty wit, he was forthright in speech and writing. He was a teacher much admired, who commanded the fullest respect and loyalty of his students, for he treated them as apprentices in a great art and as future colleagues in a serious enterprise.

[See *Conyers Read, 1881-1959* (privately published, 1963); *Harvard Class Notes,* class of 1905; and *American Historical Review* (1959).]

WALLACE T. MACCAFFREY

REDFIELD, ROBERT (Dec. 4, 1897–Oct. 16, 1958), anthropologist and educator, was born in Chicago, Ill., the son of Robert Redfield, who had risen to local prominence as a corporation lawyer, and Bertha Alexandra Dreier, the daughter of the Danish consul in Chicago. As a child he spent summers close to nature on land his great-grandfather had settled northwest of Chicago in 1833; winters, in the city among Danish-speaking kinfolk who kept alive a strong European tradition (reinforced by occasional trips abroad). The dual cultural heritage symbolized in this calendric cycle, however, produced no sense of conflict within the "inward facing" family in which Redfield spent a somewhat infirm and "overprotected" childhood—rather, by his own account, there was an "intense intimacy combined with a certain aloofness from the ordinary world."

After tutoring at home, he entered the University of Chicago Laboratory School (where his early natural history interests took a marked literary turn) in 1910, and in 1915 went on to the University of Chicago. In the spring of 1917, Redfield surprised his family by suddenly enlisting for service in France as an ambulance driver in the American Field Service. By the time his unit was disbanded that fall, Redfield had taken a "salutary beating" that left him "very much confused and disorganized" and something of a pacifist. Rejected by the draft because of a heart murmur, he spent a brief period at Harvard studying (and disliking) biology, and then joined his family in Washington, where he served as Senate office boy and worked in the code room at Military Intelligence. After the war Redfield, at his father's suggestion, decided to study law. In 1920 he received the Ph.B. cum laude from the University of Chicago; in 1921, the year of his father's death, he received the J.D.; and in 1922 he was admitted to the Illinois bar.

On June 17, 1920, Redfield married Margaret Lucy Park, the daughter of Robert E. Park, the leading figure of the "Chicago school" of urban sociologists and a major intellectual influence on Redfield's development. Dissatisfied with his job in his late father's law firm, Redfield went with his wife for a vacation in Mexico in the fall of 1923. While there he met some *indigenista* intellectuals, including the anthropologist Manuel Gamio, who was then combining archaeological research with the study of contemporary Mexican communities. Converted to anthropology, Redfield drew on a small inheritance to enter graduate study at Chicago in 1924, where Fay-Cooper Cole supervised his training, which included an archaeological dig in Ohio during the summer of 1925.

After a year as instructor of sociology at the

University of Colorado, Redfield won a Social Science Research Council fellowship to investigate the native cultural background of Mexican immigrants (whom he had previously studied in Chicago for Park's sociological practicum). In November 1926 he arrived with his family in Tepoztlán, a community near Mexico City that had long been a focus of *indigenista* interest, and that Redfield described as like "an experience in some earlier avatar." Although a flare-up of revolutionary violence forced the family's removal to Mexico City in February 1927, Redfield commuted to his fieldwork for four more months before returning to Chicago as instructor. He was promoted to assistant professor upon completion of his Ph.D. in August 1928. Save for summers teaching at Cornell (1928) and Stanford (1929), and later visiting professorships abroad, he remained at Chicago the rest of his life, ending his career as Robert M. Hutchins distinguished service professor (1953).

Although the published version of his doctoral dissertation was primarily a descriptive account of contemporary village life, Redfield's *Tepoztlán* (1930) was given an underlying theoretical coherence by a Parkian revision of the trait-distribution anthropology associated with Clark Wissler. Interpreting the diffusion of cultural traits as the communication of a new mentality, Redfield viewed Tepoztlán as an intermediate stage in the general process "whereby primitive man becomes civilized man, the rustic becomes the urbanite."

In 1930, Redfield undertook a long-term project in Yucatán for the Carnegie Institution that was more systematically structured by what came to be called the "folk-urban" hypothesis. Converting geographical distribution into historical sequence, he organized investigations in four communities "along the scale of modernization." By 1941, Redfield, accompanied sometimes by his wife and children, had spent more than two years at field sites in Yucatán and Guatemala, to which the project was extended in 1935. Resulting publications included an ethnography of *Chan Kom* (1934), by Redfield and Alfonso Villa Rojas, and Redfield's synthetic interpretation, *The Folk Culture of Yucatán* (1941), in which he argued that small, isolated, closely integrated folk communities underwent a regular process of disorganization, secularization, and individualization as they came into more frequent contact with heterogeneous urban society—or, as the Guatemalan data seemed to suggest, with the introduction of a money economy and externally imposed political authority.

Redfield's early work, with its emphasis on the harmonious integration of folk cultures, was heavily conditioned by his disillusionment with modern civilization during World War I. Although his service as adviser to the War Relocation Authority during World War II increased his sense of the gap between values and social behavior in modern American society, the threat of extinction by an unrestrained atomic technology led to a reaffirmation of the values of modern civilization and a reconsideration of the processes by which they had emerged. In *A Village That Chose Progress* (1950), Redfield emphasized the active role of Chan Kom in responding to the forces of change; and in his Messenger lectures at Cornell, *The Primitive World and Its Transformations* (1953), Redfield argued that the "technological order" was not simply the destroyer of primitive "moral orders," but had stimulated men to the conscious creation of new (and superior) standards of "truth and goodness."

By this time both Redfield's early fieldwork and the typological schema grounded upon it were coming under attack by other social scientists. Oscar Lewis' restudy of Tepoztlán, *Life in a Mexican Village* (1951), portrayed a community "burdened with suffering and torn with dissension." Other students of peasant societies also criticized the empirical and conceptual adequacy of the "folk society" notion. Although he insisted that his critics did not understand the use of "ideal types" in social science inquiry, Redfield responded to many of the issues raised by reworking his basic schema in *The Little Community* (1955) and in *Peasant Society and Culture* (1956). In each case he emphasized the place of such groupings within larger and more complex sociocultural systems.

Redfield's concern with the historical and structural relations of "little traditions" and "great traditions" was part of a larger attempt to develop a "social anthropology of civilizations." Funded by the Ford Foundation—to which his friend Robert Hutchins had gone in 1951—the project sought to coordinate research and to stimulate systematic comparative study as part of a "great conversation" of civilizations that might contribute to the establishment of a peaceful world community. Redfield's participation in the "study of civilizations from the bottom up" was limited to a brief trip to China in 1948 (constrained by the Communist revolution) and an abortive trip to India in 1955 (cut short by the onset of lymphatic leukemia). His developing thought on "world view," "ethos," and "the social organization of tradition" was never integrated in a volume on the methods of civilizational comparison that he was to have written with his co-worker Milton Singer. But the project did stimulate a great deal of research and publication by other scholars, and was a major factor in the development of modern Asian studies in the United States.

Redfield was basically a rather shy man. Even as an anthropological field-worker he was most comfortable when he could work out from the small world of his tightly knit family. He had, however, a deeply ingrained sense of noblesse oblige that tended to pull him outward into larger spheres of responsibility and discourse. For twelve years (1934–1946) he served as dean of the Division of Social Sciences at Chicago, where his capacity for balanced and incisive summations—the "Redfield statements"—helped to create a sense of integrated purpose among departments with strongly felt disciplinary identities. He was a frequent participant in the "Round Table" broadcasts, wrote numerous articles on civil liberties and educational policy, served as director of the American Council on Race Relations (1947–1950), and worked closely with the National Association for the Advancement of Colored People to end segregated education, most notably as expert witness in *Sweatt* v. *Painter* (1950). A member of the social Science Research Council from 1935 to 1943, and of the board of directors of the American Council of Learned Societies from 1952 to 1955, he was also honored by election to the presidency of the American Anthropological Association in 1944, by an honorary degree from Fisk University in 1947, and by the Viking Fund (1955) and Huxley Memorial (1956) medals. Despite his prolonged illness, he was active until shortly before his death in Chicago. He was survived by his wife and three of their four children.

When Redfield came upon the anthropological scene, American historical anthropology was already turning toward the study of processes of cultural integration in contemporary societies. His conceptual framework—structured in terms of an evolutionary polarity he traced back to Ferdinand Tönnies, Emile Durkheim, and Henry Maine—set Redfield apart from most anthropologists of the interwar generation. His early research contributed heavily to the development of social anthropology in Mexico, and may be regarded as the starting point of modern research on contemporary peasant societies.

Although some postwar neo-evolutionists were more inclined than Redfield to materialist determinism and causal analysis, his developing interest in the comparative study of values, and eventually in the universal aspects of human nature, articulated with a more general anthropological reaction against the prewar trend to cultural relativism. Focusing on the characteristic mental life of different social groups, and conceiving of culture as an "organized body of conventional understandings," Redfield also anticipated structural and semiotic viewpoints in cultural anthropology. Although his early orientation emphasized the scientific nature of anthropological inquiry, he later moved toward the humanistic end of the methodological continuum. Increasingly he came to see anthropology as a kind of dialogue "between the claims of the human whole . . . to communicate to us its nature as a whole" and "the disposition of science to take things apart and move towards the precise description of relationships." His own work was a constant struggle to develop "forms of thought" by which to encompass the "few kinds of integral entities" in which humanity presented itself "to the view of common sense."

An incisive critic of others' work, Redfield was not unaware that his concepts were often rather vaguely defined and not easily "operationalized." Although he tended always to see himself as somewhat marginal to his discipline, Redfield's attempt to refine the implications of his central evolutionary polarity secures him a permanent place in the history of American anthropology.

[Early biographical information and psychological data are in the materials collected by Anne Roe in a project on the psychological characteristics of American scientists, now on deposit in the American Philosophical Society; for the years from 1924 on, see the extensive collection of Redfield papers in the Regenstein Library, University of Chicago. Many of his essays were collected in *Papers of Robert Redfield*, Margaret Park Redfield, ed., 2 vols. (1962–1963).

A bibliography of Redfield's work is in the obituary by Fay-Cooper Cole and Fred Eggan, in *American Anthropologist*, n.s. 61 (1959). A discussion of his role in American anthropology by Milton Singer, Charles Leslie et al. is in J.V. Murray, ed., *American Anthropology* (1976). General background material is in George W. Stocking, Jr., "Ideas and Institutions in American Anthropology," in *Selected Papers From the American Anthropologist, 1921–1945* (1976).]

GEORGE W. STOCKING, JR.

REED, DANIEL ALDEN (Sept. 15, 1875–Feb. 19, 1959), congressman, was born and reared in Sheridan, N.Y., the son of Anson William Reed, a ship captain, and Alfreda Allen. After schooling in Sheridan and Silver Creek, N.Y., Reed enrolled at Cornell University in 1896. Owing to his father's death, he had to work his way through Cornell, from which he received the LL.B. in 1898. He was an all-America guard on the Cornell football team during his second year and also during his year of postgraduate work in law (1898–1899). Reed was admitted to the bar in 1900 and practiced in Silver Creek before becoming a counselor with the New York State excise department in 1903. In 1910 Reed resumed private practice, in Dunkirk, N.Y., where he maintained a home until his death. For over a dozen years following his graduating, Reed also coached football at several colleges, principally Cornell. He married Georgia Euretta Ticknor on Oct. 31, 1905; they had two children.

In 1915 Reed joined the American City Bureau, for which he organized chambers of commerce and campaigned for civic regeneration and rehabilitation in eastern and midwestern cities. He then spent two years (1916–1918) as executive director of civic activities in Flint, Mich. Throughout his life Reed was a popular speaker on civic betterment and community rebuilding. During World War I, he led drives for Liberty Loans, the Red Cross, and food conservation, and served (1917–1918) on Herbert Hoover's commission to study food needs and production in Europe.

In 1918 Reed was elected to the House of Representatives as a Republican, the first of his twenty-one consecutive terms; his tenure ultimately made him the senior Republican in Congress. His district, several predominantly agricultural counties in southwestern New York, was always "safe," but Reed never ran unopposed. He remained a minor figure in Congress through the 1920's, although he did chair (1926–1931) the Committee on Education. During the next quarter century, Reed earned the right to boast that he voted against more New Deal and Fair Deal measures than any other member of Congress; even many conservatives thought him inflexible.

Secretary of the Treasury Andrew Mellon's policies had convinced Reed that low taxes stimulate economic growth and restrain government spending. As chairman of the Republican Postwar Tax Study Committee in 1944, Reed made tax reduction party policy; he subsequently fought the tax increases of the Korean War era and asserted that a Republican-controlled government would lower taxes substantially.

When the Republicans gained control of the House after the elections of 1952, Reed became chairman (1953–1954) of the Ways and Means Committee, on which he had served since 1933. He immediately filed a bill, H.R. 1, to have the scheduled income tax reduction of about 11 percent take effect on July 1, 1953, rather than six months later.

Reed had not consulted with the Eisenhower administration before acting; but for months during early 1953 no one in the administration contradicted Reed or criticized H. R. 1, even after his committee had overwhelmingly approved it. Privately, however, the administration concluded that the budget had to be balanced before taxes could be cut, particularly in inflationary times. Eisenhower considered tax reduction a long-range, not an immediate, objective. He finally told Reed that the administration desired not only to defer the income tax cut until Dec. 31, 1953, but also to extend the excess profits tax for six months beyond June 30, 1953, when it was scheduled to expire. When Reed declined Eisenhower's invitation to cooperate, a celebrated confrontation ensued.

Reed resented being undercut by the administration, and Eisenhower's failure to confer with him during the early part of 1953 heightened his suspicions. More important, Reed held strong convictions about lower taxes, his party's promises to the voters, and the House's prerogatives on tax matters. He exploited the publicity that the entire affair had produced in order to advocate the income tax cut, even after Eisenhower, fearing for his future taxation and trade proposals if Reed prevailed, applied personal and indirect pressure. Reed still would not abandon H.R. 1 and refused to hold hearings on the excess-profits extension bill. But Eisenhower convinced the House leadership and influential congressional conservatives that the administration's course was the proper one. The leadership, stalling H.R. 1 in the Rules Committee, took the extraordinary step of having the House discharge the Ways and Means Committee from further consideration of the excess-profits bill and routed it to passage through the Rules Committee.

During the balance of his tenure as chairman, Reed guided most of Eisenhower's tax legislation through the House and generally supported the administration. In 1955, he surrendered his chairmanship to a Democrat and soon thereafter suffered a serious heart attack. He died in Washington, D.C.

Although a kindly man with a keen sense of

humor, Reed was also a vitriolic debater and a bombastic orator. In his political principles—an uncompromising advocacy of high tariffs, minimal government interference, and rigid economy—in his manner, and even in his appearance, Reed was frequently thought to typify the Old Guard Republicanism that in the 1950's seemed destined to be displaced by Eisenhower's "modern Republicanism."

[Reed's voluminous papers (1914–1960), which cover every part of his congressional career but little of his personal life, are housed at Cornell University's Regional History Collection. The papers consist of correspondence, newspaper clippings, printed materials, speeches, and photographs. The only full-length work on Reed is Peter B. Bulkley, "Daniel A. Reed: A Study in Conservatism" (Ph.D. diss., Clark University, 1972). *Current Biography*, XIV, 1953, 53–56, has the best contemporary account of Reed and his career. "Tax Cutter," *U.S. News and World Report*, Feb. 27, 1953; "People of the Week," *ibid.*, May 29, 1953; and "The Ways and Means of Dan Reed," *New York Times Magazine*, July 5, 1953, illuminate the Reed-Eisenhower dispute and document Reed's life and career. The *New York Times*, Feb 20, 1959, contains the best obituary.]

DONN NEAL

REVELL, NELLIE MacALENEY (1872– Aug. 12, 1958), journalist, publicist, and radio personality, was born in Springfield, Ill., the daughter of the editor and publisher of the *Springfield Republican*. She started her career on an opposition paper and was hired by her father after proving a worthy competitor for news. She married Joseph Revell; they had no children and were divorced. Revell left Springfield for Chicago, where she attracted attention as a writer for the *Chicago Journal*. Later in the decade she reported for the *Denver Post*, the *Seattle Post-Intelligencer*, the *San Francisco Chronicle*, and the *Chicago Times*. During this period she was as near to being a general assignment reporter as any woman could be in the decades of sensational reporting and frantic circulation drives. She learned to cover murder trials and to extract a full measure of emotion from the proceedings. But she wearied of this work, and left to become press agent for a circus. Contemporaries credited her attraction to the circus to her mother's family background, and Revell was said by acquaintances to have been "brought up on P. T. Barnum's lot."

New York was the center for American jour-nalism at the turn of the century, and an offer from the *New York World* to become its first woman reporter lured Revell from the Midwest. In New York her interests in both show business and journalism were nurtured. She refused to have anything to do with the woman's page and covered such pageantry as the coronation of Czar Nicholas II (1895) and Queen Victoria's funeral (1901).

Revell, reportedly the first woman to cover a prizefight, gibed at James J. Corbett when he objected to her plans: "If I don't come, neither will Bob Fitzsimmons. I don't think he has to anyway. He could lick you by mail."

She always threatened, "When you put my stuff on the woman's page, I quit." And she did so when she joined the *New York Evening Mail*, recently merged by Frank Munsey with the *New York Evening Telegram*, and her column was moved to the woman's page. Shortly after this Revell became press agent for Al Jolson. Her interest in press agentry for circuses also continued, so that in the years following she had as clients such Broadway stars as Lily Langtry, Norah Bayes, Lillian Russell, Elsie Janis, Eva Tanguay, and Will Rogers, as well as six circuses. Revell was head of publicity for the Keith-Orpheum motion-picture circuit and business manager of the Winter Garden.

In 1919, at the peak of her success, Revell's world collapsed. First, through an unfortunate investment, she lost her life's savings. Only weeks later a severe spinal ailment developed that placed her in the hospital for years. The collapse of several vertebrae left the doctors little hope that she would ever walk again, should she survive the long hospitalization.

While undergoing treatment, Revell published three books dealing with her battle for survival: *Right Off the Chest* (1925), *Fighting Through* (1925), and *Funny Side Out* (1925). All were written in the highly colorful and personal style that had served her well in her years as a journalist. Wit rather than profundity was her aim. Funds to pay her hospital and medical expenses were also raised by a testimonial performance at the Cohan and Harris Theater.

By 1930, Revell discarded the plaster cast that had encased her for years, lifted herself out of her wheelchair, and joined the National Broadcasting Company, where she became well known through her interviews with stage, screen, sports, and political figures. After her retirement in 1947, she continued to conduct a program called "Neighbor Nell."

Revell married Arthur J. Kellar, a press agent; they had one daughter. Revell died in New York City. Her own life, not unlike the highly emotional human-interest stories she frequently wrote for the sensational press, was marked with excitement, adventure, recognition, acquaintance with the famous, and years of life-threatening paralysis. She was one of the most colorful American journalists in the first half of the twentieth century. Her contribution lay not in the stylistic quality or profound thought of her writing, but in the wide range of activities that she undertook and in the spirit and courage with which she approached challenges in both her professional and private life.

[See Ishbel Ross, *Ladies of the Press;* Stanley Walker, *The City Editor; New York Times,* Aug. 14, 1958; *Newsweek,* Aug. 25, 1958; and *Wilson Library Review-Bulletin,* Oct. 1958.]

WILLIAM E. AMES

RHOADS, CORNELIUS PACKARD (June 20, 1898–Aug. 13, 1959), scientist, physician, and administrator, was born in Springfield, Mass., the son of George Holmes Rhoads, a physician, and Harriet Barney. He used the initials C. P. and was throughout his life called "Dusty" by friends and associates.

After early education in Springfield, Rhoads attended Bowdoin College and received his B.A. in 1920. In 1924 he was awarded his M.D. degree by Harvard Medical School. During the next year as a surgical intern at Peter Bent Brigham Hospital in Boston, he contracted pulmonary tuberculosis; the following year was spent in recovery and research at the Trudeau Sanatorium at Saranac Lake, N.Y. There he developed a lasting interest in and devotion to laboratory medicine. In 1926 he became an instructor in pathology at Harvard and an assistant pathologist at Boston City Hospital. In 1928 he joined the staff of the Rockefeller Institute for Medical Research in New York, where he served as associate and associate member of the institute and pathologist of its hospital. From 1933 to 1939 he was in charge of the institute's study of hematologic disorders.

Rhoads married Katherine Southwick Bolman on Sept. 9, 1936; they had no children.

On Jan. 1, 1940, Rhoads succeeded James Ewing as director of Memorial Hospital for Treatment of Cancer and Allied Diseases in New York. His service as director was soon interrupted by the war; he became chief of the Medical Division of the Army Chemical Warfare Service, with the rank of colonel. His later work on the development of the nitrogen mustard used in chemical warfare into a chemotherapeutic agent stemmed from his wartime service.

During the war he also came to realize the value of bringing many different disciplines of research to bear on a single problem, and he conceived the idea of an institute at which a concentrated attack could be made on cancer. He dreamed of an approach to the cancer problem in which fundamental differences between cancer cells and normal cells and differences in the endocrine metabolism of normal and cancer-bearing individuals would be sought, in which empirical attempts would be made to find drugs that would selectively damage the cancer cells without damaging vital normal cells, and in which biochemical and animal studies could be immediately translated into practical application in the patient.

At the end of the war, Alfred P. Sloan, Jr., provided the support that made the dream possible, and in 1948 the Sloan-Kettering Institute for Cancer Research was opened. Rhoads was director of the institute from its inception until his death. He remained director of Memorial Hospital until 1950 and was director of Memorial Center for Cancer and Allied Diseases from 1950 to 1952, when he became scientific director of the center. He served as professor of pathology at Cornell University Medical College from 1940 to 1952, when the Sloan-Kettering Division of Cornell University Medical College was created; at that time, he became professor of pathology in the division's Department of Biology and Growth.

Rhoads's contributions are recorded in more than 300 scientific publications. The first, written in 1926 with Dr. Fred Stewart, his longtime friend and associate, was concerned with the turberculin reaction, probably stemming from the Trudeau period. Early studies with Simon Flexner at the Rockefeller Institute resulted in a number of reports on aspects of immunity in poliomyelitis. His first papers on cancer (1928) concerned osteoblastomas and studies with leukemic blood. Nearly all his later publications related to various aspects of cancer, including many on the chemotherapy of cancer, in which he had a consuming interest and an abounding faith.

In 1948 the New York Cancer Committee awarded Rhoads the Clement Cleveland Medal, and in 1955 he received the American Cancer Society Award. For his wartime activities he was awarded the Legion of Merit. In 1956 he was a recipient of the Walker Prize of the Royal College of Surgeons and shortly before his death was made a chevalier of France's Légion d' Honneur. He died in Stonington, Conn.

The library at the Walker Laboratory of the Sloan-Kettering Institute for Cancer Research in Rye, N.Y., was officially designated the C. P. Rhoads Memorial Library in January 1961.

When he was posthumously honored with the Katherine Berkan Judd Award for outstanding contributions to cancer research, the citation stated, "The molding of the Sloan-Kettering Institute into one of international repute was but the summation of numerous and varied achievements. This especially required among his numerous abilities, those of the inquisitive scientist, the crusading educator, the dynamic administrator and his dauntless, untiring spirit of endeavor, all wrapped in the highest of motivation. It is safe to say that no one has contributed so much nor in so many ways to cancer research as did Dr. Rhoads."

[The Rhoads Memorial Library owns Rhoads's collected reprints (1927–1959), representing more than 300 scientific papers in 6 volumes. An early account of his work is contained in a feature article in the medicine section of *Time*, June 27, 1949. A more recent appreciation is Mary Woodard Lasker, "The Unforgettable Character of Dusty Rhoads," in *Reader's Digest*, Apr. 1965. Obituaries appeared in the *British Medical Journal*, Aug. 29, 1959; *Lancet*, Sept. 5, 1959; *Cancer Bulletin* (Texas), Nov.–Dec. 1959; *Cancer Research*, Apr. 1960 (by C. Chester Stock); and *Transactions of the Association of American Physicians*, 1960 (by W. B. Castle).]

ADELE SLOCUM

RICHARDS, VINCENT (Mar. 20, 1903– Sept. 28, 1959), tennis player, was born in New York City, the son of Edward A. Richards, a building contractor, and of Mary McQuade. He grew up in Yonkers, N.Y., where he began to play tennis at the age of eight. At twelve he participated in his first tennis tournament, and shortly thereafter he became a member of a boys' tennis team that represented New York in amateur play around the country. Richards graduated from Fordham Preparatory School in 1919, then studied for two years at Fordham University and for one year (1922) at the Columbia University School of Journalism.

Richards won twenty-seven national tennis titles in singles, doubles, and mixed doubles competition. He, William ("Big Bill") Tilden II, Richard Norris Williams II, and William M. Johnston were commonly recognized as the four outstanding players of the "golden era" of American amateur tennis—the period from 1920 to 1926, when the United States won seven consecutive Davis Cup championships.

Richards first achieved prominence in 1917, when he won the National Boys Outdoor Singles Tournament at age fourteen. He was then asked to play in a tournament against Tilden, who was his senior by ten years. Tilden won the contest, but was so impressed with Richards' quality of play that he asked him to be his partner in the adult competition for the national doubles championship. They took the doubles title in 1918. It was Tilden's first important national victory, and his fifteen-year-old partner captured the attention of the nation.

Richards and Tilden won the doubles again in 1921 and 1922, but their relationship was strained because of their intense rivalry for the national singles title, which Tilden invariably won. The partnership could not survive, and in 1925 and 1926, Richards teamed with Williams to capture the national doubles championships.

During this same period Richards had represented the United States on five winning Davis Cup teams, and had won the men's singles and doubles (with Francis T. Hunter) titles at the 1924 Olympic Games. Since the tennis event was held only at the 1924 Olympics, Richards and Hunter were the only male Olympic gold medalists in the sport.

In January 1924, Richards married Claremont Gushee; they had three children. From 1924 to 1927 he reported on tennis for the King Features Syndicate. The contract (for $8,000 per year) enabled Richards to devote most of his time to tennis, but he also wrote numerous articles on tennis and tennis players for national magazines and served (1925–1926) as an agent for the Equitable Life Assurance Society.

A major turning point in Richards' tennis career came in 1926, when the U.S. Lawn Tennis Association ruled that players could no longer receive pay for reporting on tournaments in which they were competing. The penalty for violation of the new rule was loss of amateur standing, and thus exclusion from championship competition. The ruling was undoubtedly a major factor in Richards' decision in October 1926 to turn professional, a move that stunned the sport and gave the original impetus to the development of professional tennis in the United States. Promoted by C. C. ("Cash and Carry") Pyle, a three-month tour made by Richards and five colleagues (two women and three men) proved popular and profitable. Richards' share of the purse was reported to have been $35,000. In September 1927 "big-time" professional tennis came into being when Richards and thirteen other top stars organized the Professional Lawn Tennis Association of the United States.

Richards won the professional singles title in 1927, and successfully defended it in 1928. Karel Kozeluh took the singles title from Richards in 1929, then teamed up with Richards to capture the professional doubles title that same year. After recapturing the singles title in 1930, Richards announced his retirement. He later said, "The money made right after an amateur turns professional is the cream, and what he makes afterward comes hard in comparison."

Shortly after retiring, Richards became general manager of the sporting goods division of the Dunlop Tire and Rubber Corporation. He remained with the corporation for the rest of his life, eventually becoming vice-president of the division. But by 1933 he was back in competition, winning the professional singles and doubles titles (the latter with Charles Wood). A triple fracture of the right arm suffered in an automobile accident in 1935 threatened to end his tennis career, but he gradually recovered and won the professional doubles title (with George M. Lott, Jr.) in 1937 and (with Fred Perry) in 1938. During World War II, Richards participated in exhibition tournaments to raise funds for government bond drives and for the Red Cross, and gave exhibitions to entertain American servicemen. Once more teaming up with Tilden, his former partner and adversary, he won the professional doubles championship in 1945. It was his last professional title.

After competing in the 1946 tournaments, Richards finally retired. For a time he broadcast tennis matches for the CBS television network, and in 1947 he accepted a one-year, nonsalaried appointment as the first commissioner of the World Professional Tennis League. He died in New York City.

Richards was five feet, nine inches tall, rather short for a tennis player, but he perfected a rifle-fire volley that contemporaries agreed made him one of the greatest volleyers of his era. His service was not first-class, and his ground strokes were markedly inferior to Tilden's, but in play at the net he was in a class by himself. One of the great players of the game, he was instrumental in making professional tennis a successful sport.

[Obituaries are in the *New York Times*, Sept. 29, 1959; *Time*, Oct. 12, 1959; and *Newsweek*, Oct. 12, 1959.]

GERALD KURLAND

RICHARDSON, SID WILLIAMS (Apr. 25, 1891–Sept. 30, 1959), philanthropist and oil executive, reputedly the second richest man in the United States during the middle third of the twentieth century, was born in Athens, Tex., the son of John Isidore Richardson and Nancy Bradley. The son of devout Baptists, he was named for Sid Williams, an itinerant minister.

Richardson's life story belongs somewhere between myth and fact. A poor boy, he left an estate variously valued from $400 million to $800 million, but as he said on occasion, "After the first hundred million, what the hell?" Much of his wealth lay in oil reserves still in the ground, which makes his wealth hard to estimate. But journalists never tired of trying. Since he disliked publicity, he gave no interviews, which only added to the myth. Again, as he liked to say, "You ain't learning nothing when you're talking."

Fired for laziness from his first job at the age of sixteen with a cotton compress, he proved to have anything but a lazy mind. He attended Baylor University and Simmons College (now Hardin-Simmons University) for about eighteen months in 1911–1912 before his money ran out. He then became a salesman for an oil well supply company, an oil scout, and a lease purchaser. In 1919 he became an independent oil producer in Fort Worth, where he lived for the remainder of his life.

Richardson was also interested in the cattle business, where his first business coup came early. With a combination of drought and tick infestation ruining the cattle industry around Athens, Tex., Richardson went to Louisiana, where he found "fat, red calves in the high Louisiana grass." Back home, he hastened to a department store and bought a loud, checked suit, an oxblood striped silk shirt, toothpick-toed shoes, and a checked cap. Then he borrowed money from the First National Bank of Athens and returned to Ruston, La. There he walked around town flashing bills and telling people, "I don't know anything about stock but pa and ma gave me this money and I think I'll buy me some calves." Figuring that some ignorant city dude had come to town, local cattlemen rushed to sell to him, cutting prices against each other until they were selling below the Louisiana market price, which in turn was below the Texas market price. Richardson shipped his cattle to Athens, took them to the town square on First Monday (a trades day in Texas), and sold them for three times their purchase price. Richardson now had his stake with which to tackle the burgeoning oil industry.

After 1919 Richardson's fortunes fluctuated widely, and he often remarked, "I've been broke so often I thought it was habit-forming." His first oil field was in Ward County in west Texas in 1932. In 1935 he helped bring in the rich Keystone field in Winkler County and three years later was active in developing the Slaughter field west of Lubbock. The next year he turned to Louisiana, where his holdings were sold after his death for nearly $22 million. He also owned a refinery at Texas City and a carbon-black plant at Odessa, Tex. With Amon Carter, publisher of the *Fort Worth Star-Telegram,* he owned the Hotel Texas in Fort Worth. He was an executive with the Texas State Network, a string of radio and television stations. By 1935 Richardson's wealth had grown so vast that his periodic flirtations with bankruptcy terminated, and his status as a multimillionaire became stabilized. At his death he probably controlled more oil reserves than any other individual in the United States and more than several of the major petroleum companies.

Richardson operated for years from a two-room "command post" in the Fort Worth Club, although he also maintained an office in a local bank building. In 1936 he purchased St. Joseph's Island off the Texas coast, a narrow spit of land accessible only by boat or airplane. Here he resided when he was not in Fort Worth, with his employees the only inhabitants of the island. In his Fort Worth headquarters he always kept five or six bags packed, so that he could travel at a moment's notice.

Richardson first came to national attention in 1954, when he teamed with another millionaire, Clinton Williams Murchison, then operating in Dallas. Robert R. Young, another Texan from the Panhandle area, was trying to gain control of the New York Central Railway from the Chase National Bank in New York. Lacking enough resources, Young turned to Murchison and Richardson, who purchased 800,000 shares from Cyrus S. Eaton's Chesapeake and Ohio Railway

for $20 million. Young then became head of the New York Central, an accession treated by Eastern journalists as a buccaneering coup by a trio of Texas brigands.

Attempts to interview Richardson on his part in the takeover were fruitless. "A man is getting in a hell of a shape if he can't buy something without people wanting to know what he's doing," he said. According to one possibly apocryphal anecdote, Young is supposed to have contacted Murchison, who then called Richardson to say that their fellow Texan was in trouble and needed $5 million from each. Richardson agreed to help. Later, when the sale of stock was about to be consummated, Murchison telephoned Richardson, asking him to deliver his promised $10 million. Richardson demurred. "You said five million" he allegedly said. "No, ten million," Murchison replied without blanching. "All right, I'll send over the ten million, but next time you call, Clint, don't mumble!"

In August 1957 the House Committee on Government Operations charged that the Army Engineers and Reclamation Bureau had changed its reservoir policy at Richardson's behest. According to the committee report, the engineers had been taking only flowage rights around shores of reservoirs, instead of buying land likely to be flooded periodically. Since Richardson owned a considerable portion of the Benbrook Reservoir near Fort Worth, he was therefore able to hold on to his land. A Department of the Interior assistant secretary claimed that the engineers' order was also detrimental to fish and wildlife development, and considerably diminished recreational values around reservoirs. According to the committee, Secretary of the Treasury Robert B. Anderson, former Secretary of the Army Robert T. Stevens, and—by implication—President Dwight D. Eisenhower himself had intervened in behalf of Richardson to get the army engineers to change to the new policy. The committee report was a one-day sensation that was quickly forgotten. The two Texas members of the committee, incidentally, were purposefully absent during the hearings.

Richardson was a lifelong Democrat but supported Eisenhower in 1952 and 1956. A principal reason was a long admiration for the general, dating back to an accidental meeting. The future commander of World War II troops had just been made a brigadier general and was en route to Washington for new orders when his plane was forced down in Dallas. He continued by train but was unable to get a berth immediately. Richardson, seeing his plight, invited Eisenhower to share Richardson's drawing room until the general could get his sleeping arrangements worked out. Richardson later visited Eisenhower when he was commander-in-chief of Allied troops in western Europe, and in 1948 tried to persuade Eisenhower to run for president on the Democratic ticket. Richardson's politics usually were moderate to mildly liberal, counter to the stereotype of right-wing Texas oil millionaires.

Richardson's down-home style is illustrated by the story of an invitation to luncheon at the White House during Eisenhower's administration. In Washington on business, he received an unexpected invitation from the president as transmitted by a White House operator. Richardson asked what was on the menu. The operator, somewhat taken aback, asked why he wanted to know. "Because," he answered blandly, "I might be able to get a better deal somewhere else in town." She assured him that though she did not know what the White House was serving that day, he undoubtedly would find no "better deal" anywhere else. Richardson accepted.

Richardson's philanthropies were largely private and characteristically little publicized until after his death. With Murchison he purchased the Del Mar Turf Club in California and assigned its profits to Boys, Incorporated, to combat juvenile delinquency. He established the Sid Richardson Foundation, which has provided millions of dollars for educational purposes. In 1964 the foundation gave $750,000 each to Richardson's two former schools, Baylor and Hardin-Simmons universities, and in 1969 it granted more than $2 million to the University of Texas to purchase an important history of science collection. When the University of Texas built its Lyndon B. Johnson Presidential Library complex, the building that provides quarters for the university's Institute of Latin American Studies, Texas Collection and Texas State Historical Association, and Lyndon B. Johnson School of Public Affairs was named Sid W. Richardson Hall.

Richardson died at his St. Joseph's Island compound. The Reverend Billy Graham officiated at his funeral. Contemporary journals estimated that the wealth of the "Billionaire Bachelor" was exceeded only by that of H. L. Hunt of Dallas.

Richardson was approachable and easy to meet for almost everyone except reporters. He never showed the arrogance of some other extremely wealthy self-made men and often remarked, "I'd rather be lucky than smart, 'cause a lot of smart people ain't eatin' regular." He was a superior collector of western art and had one of the more imposing private collections of paintings by Frederic Remington and Charles M. Russell. He was survived by two sisters, a nephew, and a niece.

[On Richardson and his career, see E. Harris, "The Case of the Billionaire Bachelor," *Look*, Nov. 30, 1954; "Billion-Dollar Team From Texas," *U.S. News and World Report*, Mar. 4, 1955; C. Amory, "Oil Folks at Home," *Holiday*, Feb. 1957; M. Parton, "Who Are America's Ten Richest Men?" *Ladies' Home Journal*, Apr. 1957; and obituary notices, *New York Times*, Oct. 1, 1959; and *Time* and *Newsweek*, Oct. 12, 1959.]

JOE B. FRANTZ

RICHBERG, DONALD RANDALL (July 10, 1881–Nov. 27, 1960), lawyer and government official, was born in Knoxville, Tenn., the son of John Carl Richberg, a German-born attorney of some prominence, and Eloise Olivia Randall, who came from old Vermont Yankee stock. A Chicago school principal, she later became a homeopathic physician.

Richberg grew up in Chicago in a substantial and highly achieving family. But it was not without its tensions. His parents separated for a number of years because of his mother's decision to study medicine. And Richberg's "strong ambitions and convictions" made his early married life unstable. In 1903 he married Elizabeth Herrick, sister of the novelist Robert Herrick. They separated in 1915 and were divorced in 1917. Richberg married Lynette Mulvey Hamlin in 1918 and was divorced again in 1924. On Dec. 24, 1924, he married Florence Weed. They had one daughter and were together until his death.

As a student at the University of Chicago, from which he received the B.A. in 1901, Richberg exercised his always strong, though never distinguished, literary bent, writing plays and poetry. After receiving the LL.B. in 1904 from Harvard Law School, he entered his father's law firm. Discussing "The Lawyer's Function" in the October 1909 issue of the *Atlantic Monthly*, Richberg held that the proper role of the attorney was to be a "harmonizer" rather than a "parasite" or "a mere businessman."

Like so many educated young men of his generation, Richberg found the Progressive movement an apt vehicle for his social moralism—and his personal ambition. In 1912 he served as counsel for the Illinois Progressive party, the beginning of his "role as one of the leading technicians in the service of reform for the next several decades." In 1913 and 1914 he directed the party's National Legislative Reference Bureau. Richberg found in the work "that combination of law and politics and social science which is rapidly creating a new professsion, which might be termed that of social counselor."

In 1915 Richberg was engaged to represent Chicago in its litigation against the People's Gas Light and Coke Company. Until 1927 he worked with some success to lower the gas rates charged the people of the city. In the same spirit he dealt with railroad problems during the 1920's. He was general counsel of the National Conference on Valuation of American Railroads, which sought to reduce the valuations on which railroad rates were based. From 1922 he was counsel for the shop craft and other railroad unions. He successfully argued the legality of the shopmen's strike of 1922, and played an important role in the drafting and passage of the Railway Labor Act of 1926. He served as counsel for the Railway Labor Executives' Association from 1926 to 1933. This was congenial work, for Richberg deeply believed that the ideal industrial commonwealth was one where labor and management bargained collectively, with a minimum of government intervention.

As a prominent railroad labor lawyer and executive chairman of the pro-FDR National Progressive League in 1932, Richberg had a strong claim on a place in the early New Deal. He assisted in the drafting of the Emergency Railroad Transportation Act in 1933 and worked with Hugh S. Johnson and Raymond Moley on the National Industrial Recovery Act. He was appointed general counsel of the National Recovery Administration (NRA) created under that act; supposedly, he was to be organized labor's spokesman in the NRA.

But Richberg was not content to speak for one interest group, nor did he accept a subordinate position to NRA head Hugh Johnson. In July 1934 President Roosevelt appointed him director of the Industrial Emergency Committee and of the National Emergency Council, which were designed to coordinate the New Deal's relief and recovery programs. With the appointment came Richberg's greatest public renown; the press spoke of him as "assistant President." But in fact Richberg's powers were minimal: policy remained firmly in Roosevelt's hands. He defended the NRA in the Schechter case, calling it a valid use of the government's power "to encourage and

to organize cooperation in doing good." In 1935, when the Supreme Court found the NRA unconstitutional, Richberg's prominence came to an end.

He supported Roosevelt in 1936 and assisted in the administration's attempt to limit the powers of the Supreme Court. But like Moley and other early New Dealers (and former Progressives), Richberg became increasingly critical of the widening range of the New Deal's social programs and its antibusiness, pro-labor tone. He returned to the practice of law, representing a number of corporate clients. From the late 1930's until his death he lived in Charlottesville, Va., teaching constitutional law at the University of Virginia Law School, working for restrictions on the power of labor unions of the sort that were incorporated into the Taft-Hartley Act, strongly criticizing the Truman administration, and opposing civil rights legislation.

Richberg's significance lies first in his career as a lawyer applying his technical expertise to the problems of a complex industrial society. Beyond this, he was representative of a distinct strand in twentieth-century American liberalism. He believed that government's primary role was to assure that the conflicting units of society— management and labor, public utilities and consumers—dealt with one another on reasonably equal terms. But the growth of the welfare state beginning in the 1930's alienated him, as it did a number of other old Progressives. Richberg's career exemplifies both the continuities of function (for example, the lawyer as social technician) and the discontinuities of ideology that have characterized the American response to socioeconomic change in the twentieth century.

[There are Richberg manuscript collections in the Library of Congress and the Chicago Historical Society. Serveral memoirs in the Columbia University Oral History Collection, especially that of Frances Perkins, have material on Richberg. Richberg's autobiographies are *Tents of the Mighty* (1930) and *My Hero* (1954). Thomas E. Vadney, *The Wayward Liberal* (1970), is a perceptive political biography and has a useful bibliographical note.]

MORTON KELLER

RINEHART, MARY ROBERTS (Aug. 12, 1876–Sept. 22, 1958), novelist and mystery story writer, was born in Pittsburgh, Pa., the daughter of Thomas Beveridge Roberts, a salesman and inventor, and Cornelia Gilleland. Educated in the public schools of Pittsburgh, she had her first writing success at fifteen, when she sold three stories to a local newspaper for a dollar each.

Her ambitions kindled by a neighborhood physician, C. Jane Vincent, Roberts aspired to become a doctor. Family finances would not permit her to go to medical school, so an uncle offered to pay her expenses. But she graduated from high school at age sixteen, two years too young to be admitted, and therefore entered the Pittsburgh Training School for Nurses when she turned seventeen.

On Apr. 21, 1896, four days after graduating, she married Stanley Marshall Rinehart, a physician who had initially attempted to discourage her from a career in nursing. They had three sons. Dr. Rinehart's practice flourished, and Mary Rinehart became a housewife, helping her husband and occasionally supplying emergency treatment.

Although she had known Willa Cather as a teacher in her high school, had written as a child, and had started but never finished one or two stories while in nurse's training, Rinehart had no literary ambitions. But, when the panic of 1903 wiped out family investments, she determined to attempt to help by writing. Her first story, based on an incident in her husband's practice, was sold to *Munsey's* magazine for $34. During her first year as a writer she sold forty-five items, primarily short stories, for a total of $1,842.50. Thus began a career that lasted until her death fifty-four years and sixty-two books later. Rinehart's first mystery novel, *The Circular Staircase* (1908), was published first as a serial in *Munsey's*. It has never been out of print. It was followed by *The Man in Lower Ten* (1909), which was almost as successful; *When a Man Marries* (1909), later made into the play *Seven Days*; and *The Window at the White Cat* (1910).

Rinehart then ventured into writing plays, collaborating successfully with Avery Hopwood on *Seven Days*, *Spanish Love*, *Cheer Up*, and *The Bat* (based on *The Circular Staircase*), which became her most successful mystery play. Performed in seven languages, it grossed several million dollars. She also wrote *The Avenger* (with her husband) and *The Breaking Point* and three other plays independently.

After spending much of 1913–1914 in Vienna, where her husband studied medicine, Rinehart began the popular series of "Tish" stories for the *Saturday Evening Post*. After the outbreak of war

in 1914, she determined to return to Europe and visit the front. In 1915, with a correspondent's credentials and support from the *Post*, she spent more than four months at and near the front, the first woman and one of the few correspondents to be permitted to do so. Upon her return she wrote an account of the experience, *Kings, Queens and Pawns* (1915).

After American entry into the war, Rinehart toured American army camps in a semiofficial capacity; afterward she wrote *The Altar of Freedom* (1917). At the end of the war she was in France with the Red Cross. Her husband served as a major in the Medical Corps.

In 1920, after Rinehart covered the Republican National Convention, the family moved to Washington, D.C., where Dr. Rinehart was associated with the Veterans Bureau until he resigned in disgust over the Harding scandals. Rinehart founded the publishing firm of Farrar and Rinehart, which later became Rinehart and Company; two of her sons were officers. Between 1920 and her husband's death in 1932, she wrote three mystery novels, four other novels, three "Tish" books, a play, at least eight romances, two collections of short stories, and two travel books, as well as her autobiography, *My Story* (1931; reissued, 1948). In 1934 she moved to New York City, where she died.

The last twenty-five years of Rinehart's life were marked by serious illness, including several heart attacks and surgery for cancer, but she continued to write almost until her death. Her last two books were mystery novels: *The Swimming Pool* (1952) and *The Frightened Wife* (1953).

Always proud of her craft, Rinehart was short with literary critics, who did not take her seriously. She attributed her success to playing fair with her readers. In her mystery stories, she pointed out, the initial crime was always the first of a series, and normally she told two stories simultaneously, a surface story and a hidden story that emerged periodically to provide clues for the reader. At the end the two merged into one.

[Collections of Mrs. Rinehart's papers are held in the R. H. Davis Collection at the New York Public Library; the Indianapolis Library; the Kriendler Collection, Rutgers University Library; the Moore Papers, Michigan Historical Collection; and the Pennsylvania Historical and Museum Collection. Her other principal works include *The Amazing Adventures of Letitia Carberry* (1911), "K" (1915), *Tish* (1916), *Long Live the King* (1917), *Twenty-three and One-half Hours' Leave* (1922), *The Red Lamp*

(1925), *Two Flights Up* (1928), *The Door* (1930), *Miss Pinkerton* (1932), *The State Versus Elinor Norton* (1934), *The Doctor* (1936), *The Great Mistake* (1940), *Haunted Lady* (1942), *The Yellow Room* (1945), *The Light in the Window* (1948), and *The Episode of the Wandering Knife* (1950). No biography of Mrs. Rinehart has yet appeared. Available is a pamphlet, by Dorothy C. Disney and Milton MacKaye, *Mary Roberts Rinehart (ca.* 1948). Essays about her work have appeared in the *New York Herald Tribune* "Books," Dec. 15, 1940; and the *New York Times Book Review*, Oct. 19, 1941.]

DAVID D. ANDERSON

RIVES, HALLIE ERMINIE (May 2, 1876–Aug. 16, 1956), novelist, was born at Post Oak Plantation, Christian County, Ky., the daughter of Colonel Stephen T. Rives and Mary Ragsdale. Her father, a well-to-do tobacco farmer who had served under General Robert E. Lee, was wounded in the battle of Antietam and confined in a Union prison for two years. Named for the heroine of the popular song "Listen to the Mockingbird," Hallie was tutored privately. At the age of fifteen she decided to be a writer after surreptitiously reading the controversial novel *The Quick or the Dead?* by Amélie Rives, her father's first cousin. A year later a short story, "The Treasure of a Feud," based on a Civil War incident told to her by her father, won a prize in a magazine contest. Her first novel, *Smoking Flax* (1897), a sensational story based on an actual lynching, was written when she was only seventeen.

Now determined on a writing career, Rives moved to New York to read and study writing and style, beginning with recent best-sellers. Her second novel, *A Furnance of Earth* (1900), a passionate love story, received mixed reviews. It was published by the Camelot Co., organized by the writer and diplomat Post Wheeler for that express purpose. *Hearts Courageous* (1902), a historical romance about Revolutionary Virginia and the Declaration of Independence, had as its central character Patrick Henry, a childhood hero. Rives finished the novel in six weeks; the title came to her in a dream the night she completed the book. The book was also published in Braille and was later dramatized.

Her next novel, *The Castaway* (1904), was a romantic treatment of the life of Lord Byron. She followed it with another successful novel, *Satan Sanderson* (1907), a melodramatic tale of

mistaken identity involving a popular minister who in his youth had sown wild oats. It was a best-seller and the source of both a successfull Broadway play and a screen production. *The Kingdom of Slender Swords* (1910), also a best-seller, was a romantic tale with luxuriant Japanese settings, florid language, and a villain who predicted atomic warfare. With a preface written by the Japanese minister of education, Baron Makino, it was one of the first Western novels to be translated into Japanese. *Valiants of Virginia* (1912) was a sentimental love story with a hero who discovered a new and rewarding life in rural Virginia on an estate inherited after his father's corporation failed. Filled with such dramatic events as a duel and a clock striking thirteen, the novel was also dramatized and made into a movie.

A temperance theme and prison settings characterized *The Long Lane's Turning* (1917), which was serialized in *Red Book* with the title "The Heart of a Man" and made into a movie. *The Magic Man* (1927), a love story having a hero who suffered amnesia and a scientist who experimented with atomic devices as well as re-creation of a human soul, also was made into a movie. *The Golden Barrier* (1934) described the effects of the Great Depression on the wealthy. Other Rives books include *Complete Book of Etiquette* (1926; 1934), *The Modern and Complete Book of Etiquette* (1939), and *John Book* (1947).

On Dec. 29, 1906, Rives married Post Wheeler in Tokyo, Japan, where he was second secretary in the American embassy. They had no children. The Wheelers lived in such great cities as Rome, St. Petersburg, London, and Rio de Janeiro, but also in Paraguay (1929–1933) and Albania (1933–1934), where Post Wheeler was United States minister. In their joint autobiography, *Dome of Many-Coloured Glass* (1955), the Wheelers wrote alternate chapters, describing the political and social background in the foreign service, as well as offering lively coverage of local customs and international events and gossip about dignitaries and lesser figures. The highly personal book charged that the State Department was run by a small, self-serving clique of hypocrites and sycophants. The Wheelers stated that, as critics, they were victims of pettiness, persecution, falsehood, and libel, and were punished with undesirable posts and assignments. They were close personal friends of such political figures as Theodore Roosevelt, William Howard Taft, and Speaker of the House Joseph G. Cannon.

Although now neglected and out of fashion,

several of Rives's novels were considered quite daring in their day and caused considerable controversy. The sales of *Hearts Courageous* were boosted by an aggressive promotional campaign that included personal appearances and publicity stunts. For the most part Rives's writing was characterized by a fast-moving narrative, vivid imagination, unrestrained prose, and shallow personalities. In her autobiography she described writing as "at one time an agony and a delight," with the "pleasure outweighing the pain."

Rives died in New York City.

[Biographies of Rives are in the *Wilson Library Bulletin*, Mar. 1956; and *New York Times*, Aug. 18, 1956 (her obituary).]

MARY SUE DILLIARD SCHUSKY

ROBERTS, KENNETH LEWIS (Dec. 8, 1885–July 21, 1957), author, was born in Kennebunk, Maine, the son of Frank Lewis Roberts, a businessman, and Grace Mary Tibbetts. He attended Cornell University, where he edited the campus humor magazine and received the B.A. in 1908. He was a reporter and columnist for the *Boston Post* from 1909 to 1917; he also contributed articles to *Life* (1915–1918) and *Puck* (1916–1917). Roberts married Anna Seiberling Mosser on Feb. 14, 1911; they had no children. During World War I he served as captain in the intelligence section of the U.S. Army Siberian Expeditionary Force, an episode that he recalled in several chapters of his literary reminiscences, *I Wanted to Write* (1949). In the 1920's Roberts served as Washington and foreign correspondent for the *Saturday Evening Post*, an association that secured his reputation as journalist and political commentator. His earliest books—such as *Europe's Morning After* (1921) and *Why Europe Leaves Home* (1922), an account of postwar immigration to the United States—were based on his journalistic pieces.

By the late 1920's a different literary interest had begun to assert itself. Roberts had long been curious about the lives of his ancestors, some of whom had settled in Maine as early as 1639. Other forebears, he found, had fought Indians, captained privateers, and served in the Revolution and the War of 1812. Seeking minute details about their daily activities, Roberts discovered that professional historians never supplied what he longed to know. Recalling the family tale that three of his relatives had served in the expedition that captured Louisburg from the French, Roberts posed the sort of questions that would become characteristic of his literary method: "How had they reached Louisburg? What had they done when they got there? What sort of equipment had they carried? What was the size of a regiment in those days? How were the men fed? Nobody knew the answer." In a series of historical novels grounded in a painstaking research not characteristic of the genre, Roberts would make sure that his readers learned the answers.

Arundel (1930), Roberts' first venture in revivifying the past, was largely composed in Porto San Stefano, Italy, where he maintained a part-time residence for many years. Revised with the aid of Booth Tarkington, a Maine neighbor and close friend, this account of Benedict Arnold's secret expedition against Quebec had only moderate sales despite some stir among reviewers about the "favorable" portrayal of the traditional archtraitor. A story of privateering, *The Lively Lady*, appeared in 1931; *Captain Caution*, another sea tale, was completed next but was not published until 1934. *Rabble in Arms* (1933), centered on the retreat from Lake Champlain and the defeat of Burgoyne at Saratoga, had generally good reviews; but sales were poor compared with the success of a quite different type of historical fiction, Hervey Allen's *Anthony Adverse*. Roberts reached an expanded audience with *Northwest Passage* (1937), a panoramic novel of Major Robert Rogers and his rangers; a Book-of-the-Month Club selection, it was also made into a film, about which Roberts was characteristically sulfurous because of its inaccuracies. *Oliver Wiswell* (1940), written from the viewpoint of a Loyalist during the American Revolution, predictably garnered such sneers as "the best-written historical novel I have ever read and the most outrageous apologia for Tory treachery since Munich." A final historical fiction, *Lydia Bailey* (1947)—ranging from Toussaint's uprising in Haiti to the Tripolitan war—was the selection of two book clubs and was turned into a Hollywood costume melodrama.

In his later years Roberts became obsessed with attempting to prove the efficacy of the divining rod in locating water and produced three tendentious books on the subject: *Henry Gross and His Dowsing Rod* (1951), *The Seventh Sense* (1953), and *Water Unlimited* (1957). Shortly before his death the author, who had almost always deplored Pulitzer Prize novels, received a special

Pulitzer citation for having "contributed to the creation of greater interest in our early American history." Roberts died at his home in Kennebunkport, Maine. His final book, *The Battle of Cowpens*, was issued posthumously in 1958.

Roberts was a man of often peculiar but always positively held opinions. His friend Ben Ames Williams emphasized his iconoclasm: "He is a hater of shams, pretensions, self-deceptions, fallacies; and he particularly hates the persistent distortion of history. In what would be for him the best possible world, every history would be written with a fine impartiality and by a neutral party. He is tireless in hunting out proof that Colonials during the Revolutionary period were (a) dauntless heroes, or (b) blovalating [sic] politicians and self-seekers; the choice depending on which misconception he is at the moment engaged in setting right. He is equally tireless in proving that all British and Tories were (a) cultivated and intelligent gentlemen abused by the Colonials or (b) tyrannical rascals abusing the Colonials. . . . It was characteristic of him that he began his career as a novelist by making the best possible case for Benedict Arnold."

In a more permissive literary climate, Roberts' historical fictions have something of an old-fashioned flavor. This is not to say that their author would have availed himself of greater freedom of speech or of narrative detail. Essentially he practiced a factual realism carefully curbed by his own sense of decorum; he would have taken as compliment a critic's observation that he never felt compelled to accompany a hero or heroine to bed or to the bathroom. His true forte was precise delineation of the details of the varied worlds through which his characters moved—not analysis of the furniture of their minds.

[Other works by Roberts include *For Authors Only* (1935), a collection of reprinted essays; *Trending Into Maine* (1938); and Marjorie Mosser's *Good Maine Food* (1939), for which he wrote the notes and introduction. *I Wanted to Write* (1949) contains autobiographical materials but is most useful as a record of the creation and reception of his fiction. His letters and manuscripts are scattered among a number of institutions. An anthology that includes selections from fiction and nonfiction is *The Kenneth Roberts Reader* (1945). James Playsted Wood found Roberts "The Most Unforgettable Character I Ever Met," *Reader's Digest*, Mar. 1959. Brief evaluations of Roberts' novels are in Ernest E. Leisy, *The American Historical Novel* (1950).]

J. V. RIDGELY

ROBINSON, GEORGE CANBY (Nov. 4, 1878–Aug. 31, 1960), physician and medical educator, was born in Baltimore, Md., the son of Edward Ayrault Robinson, a business executive, and Alice Canby. He received the A.B. from Johns Hopkins University in 1899. From 1899 to 1903 he attended the Johns Hopkins School of Medicine under the youthful and inspiring original faculty of that new institution, and received the M.D. in 1903. He then spent two years in pathology and two years as resident physician at the Pennsylvania Hospital, followed by a year in Europe, working in physiology in Friedrich Von Müller's clinic in Munich.

After returning to America, Robinson engaged briefly in private practice. In 1910 he accepted the invitation from Rufus Cole, who had been a resident at the Johns Hopkins Hospital during Robinson's student days in Baltimore, to be the first resident physician at the newly opened Hospital of the Rockefeller Institute. At the Institute Hospital he encountered an outstanding scientific atmosphere created by such men as Simon Flexner, Peyton Rous, Alexis Carrel, Jacques Loeb, Samuel J. Meltzer, and Donald Van Sykel. By 1913, when he left to become associate professor of medicine at Washington University in St. Louis, Robinson was thoroughly imbued with the scientific spirit as applied to the study of disease and was fully prepared to transplant this spirit to the schools of medicine with which he would later be associated. On Dec. 7, 1912, he married Marion Boise; they had two children.

In St. Louis, Robinson played a major role in organizing and constructing the teaching program in the department of medicine, particularly from 1917 to 1920, when he served first as acting dean and then as dean. His effectiveness in these posts led to his appointment in 1920 as dean and professor of medicine at Vanderbilt University, which had just received money for the building of a hospital and a medical school. While awaiting the opening of the Vanderbilt University School of Medicine, Robinson served as pro-tempore professor of medicine and director of the department of medicine at the Johns Hopkins School of Medicine for one year (1921–1922). When he left Vanderbilt in 1928, the school stood as a tribute to his outstanding skill in the organization of medical institutions and his ability to select gifted young faculty.

In 1928 Robinson became director of the newly created union of the Cornell University Medical College and New York Hospital. Again, he exercised his talents in the construction and organization of a new enterprise and in attracting a distinguished staff. It was a difficult time for the undertaking, however, because of the severe financial stringencies created by the Great Depression. Although all of his goals were not reached at the time, subsequent developments have demonstrated that Robinson's plans for that medical center were built on a sound foundation.

In October 1934, Robinson became visiting professor of medicine at the Peiping Union Medical College. After a year in China, he returned to the staff of the Johns Hopkins School of Medicine, where he embarked on the study (1936–1937) of what he called "the man within the patient." He had early recognized the importance of humanism in medicine, but for the next few years he devoted himself wholeheartedly to its study. His work resulted in the publication of *The Patient as a Person* (1939), a study of the social aspects of illness.

In 1941 Robinson was appointed national director of the blood donor service of the American Red Cross. For his accomplishments in this service, as well as for his other contributions to medicine, he was awarded the Medal of Merit in 1947. At the end of World War II, he retired from the Hopkins faculty and became executive secretary of the Maryland Tuberculosis Association. In 1955 he retired again. His memoirs were published as *Adventures in Medical Education* (1957).

Robinson was also editor in chief of the *Journal of Clinical Investigation* from its founding in 1924 until 1930 and served as president of the Association of American Physicians in 1933. He died in Greenport, N.Y.

Robinson's early studies were in the bacteriology of meningitis, but his principal research contributions were related to cardiovascular disease. He applied the technique of electrocardiography to the study of cardiac arrhythmias and developed a method for determination of the blood gases. His later work was mainly in occupational medicine and the relationship between doctor and patient.

Robinson lived during a period that has been widely acclaimed as the "heroic age in American medicine." He stands out as one of the principal architects responsible for the gigantic strides in medical education and research made during that period which marked the creation of medicine's scientific base. He contributed importantly in the four major areas of academic medicine—the care of patients, the pursuit of research, medical

education, and the administration of university medical schools and hospitals. He used his enormous talents and abilities with industry and generosity of spirit. He was perceptive in dealing with people and was keenly aware of the need to develop physicians of character in order to ensure a progressive increase in the quality of medical care.

[See C. S. Burwell, "George Canby Robinson," *Transactions of the Association of American Physicians,* 74 (1961); Robinson's memoirs, *Adventures in Medical Education* (1957); and A. McGehee Harvey, "G. Canby Robinson: Peripatetic Medical Educator," *Johns Hopkins Medical Journal,* 142 (1978), which contains a complete bibliography of his research contributions.]

A. McGehee Harvey

ROCKEFELLER, JOHN DAVISON, JR. (Jan. 29, 1874–May 11, 1960), industrialist and philanthropist, was born in Cleveland, Ohio, the son of John D. Rockefeller, founder of the Standard Oil combine, and Laura Celestia Spelman. The boy was reared to expect a life of serious hard work, religious observance, great financial responsibility, and social service. Both parents were devout Baptists of a strong fundamentalist cast, and Laura Spelman's mother had been a militant supporter of the Anti-Saloon League. The elder Rockefeller, while giving both time and money to his church, also set his son an example of ruthless devotion to efficiency, rational organization, and hard work that had made him the greatest moneymaker of the age of individual enterprise.

The Rockefellers lived in a comfortable middle-class house on Cleveland's Euclid Avenue, but it was at Forest Hill, their summer home outside Cleveland, that the family was happiest. "JDR, Jr.," as he later preferred to be called, had few playmates besides his sisters and the son of the caretaker. His father soon found that his business dictated a move to New York, and after several years in residential hotels the Rockefellers settled down in a spacious brownstone.

Rockefeller attended private schools in New York and had a private tutor during the long visits the family made to Cleveland. In 1893 he entered Brown University. He was popular with his classmates, who called him "Johnny Rock," and none of them, he was convinced, stood in awe of the great wealth that he would one day control. He later confessed that his college days had been the happiest of his life. Rockefeller was not a brilliant scholar, but he worked hard at his studies and was elected to Phi Beta Kappa. He graduated in 1897.

Rockefeller never developed an outstanding talent for business, nor did his father ever press him to do so. After college he entered the New York office of Standard Oil, where he performed miscellaneous tasks for his father. On Oct. 9, 1901, he married Abigail (Abby) Aldrich, daughter of Senator Nelson W. Aldrich of Rhode Island. They had six children, all of whom went on to notable careers.

In these years much of the mushrooming Rockefeller fortune was being channeled into the philanthropies that were the brainchildren of such Rockefeller aides as Abraham and Simon Flexner and Frederick T. Gates. But by far the larger part was being tranferred from petroleum, where it was being made, to industries more acutely in need of fresh capital. Pleased with his son's handling of the sale of Mesabi Range iron ore properties to J. P. Morgan in 1901, the elder Rockefeller gave him the responsibility for overseeing the management of the Colorado Fuel and Iron Company, in which he owned a 40 percent interest. The assignment brought JDR, Jr., the most devastating publicity of his life and plunged him deeply into the pressing national problem of labor-management relations.

The management of the Colorado Fuel and Iron Company had long blocked all attempts to unionize its miners. An even tougher breed than their eastern counterparts, the western miners were fully as determined to achieve company recognition of their right to bargain collectively. The result was a strike in 1914 that led management to close the mines and evict the miners' families from company-owned houses. The militant element among the unionists fomented confrontations between striking and nonstriking miners, the state militia was brought in, and soon the area around Ludlow, Colo., was a battleground on which more than forty people were killed in a series of skirmishes. One event has been transmogrified into the legend that company thugs and militiamen also shot and killed defenseless women and children. The truth is that two women and eleven children crawled into a cave to escape the gunfire and died of suffocation, but young Rockefeller, because of his stubborn support of a management that was trying to treat new problems with ancient remedies, came to be held responsible by the general public for the "Ludlow massacres."

The congressional investigations that followed did not hesitate to lay the responsibility for the disorders at Rockefeller's feet, and he quickly adopted a radically different policy. Canada's W. L. Mackenzie King, an expert on labor relations, conducted for him a thorough study of the problem and recommended a plan for employee representation. Rockefeller went to the mining camps, where his willingness to listen, and his many informal speeches in which he emphasized the responsibilities and the rights of both management and labor and appealed for a sense of mutual purpose between the two, helped to heal the wounds and provided for a modified "company union" arrangement that would last until the new era of labor ferment during the Great Depression.

A few years later he reprinted several of these speeches and magazine articles under the title *The Personal Relation in Industry* (1923). He demanded that capital realize that the men were working for more than mere wages and deserved a say in their destinies. He also adjured labor to recognize the many other claims on company income besides their wages. No businessman in the future, he asserted, would be free to consider profit the only motivating force in his affairs, while labor must recognize that low wages are not the result of large profits. "The most successful enterprises," he wrote, "have been those which have been so well organized and so efficient that the laborers were paid high wages, the consuming public enjoyed declining prices, and the owners realized large profits."

After World War I, Rockefeller devoted himself almost exclusively to public service and philanthropy. His leadership of the Interchurch World Movement in the early 1920's is often cited as the reason for its collapse, but that fatuous, bureaucratized structure was doomed from the start. Undiscouraged about the future of interfaith relations, he endowed Riverside Church, a non-sectarian church on New York's Riverside Drive, built it in stunning gothic style, and persuaded Dr. Harry Emerson Fosdick to become its first minister.

Never having tasted alcohol in any form (he returned the toast offered him by the burghers of Rheims, whose great cathedral he had helped restore after World War I, with a glass of Perrier water!), Rockefeller believed that outright prohibition was the only answer to excessive drinking, but when the "noble experiment" failed ignobly, he came out strongly for repeal of the Eighteenth Amendment. Meanwhile, he saw to it that the medical philanthropies grouped in the Rockefeller Foundation kept abreast of the exploding new sciences by organizing Rockefeller University. In Fort Tryon Park, at the northern end of Manhattan, he installed a great collection of medieval art in the Cloisters that still draws thousands of visitors even as the city itself decays. Having entered into a scheme to redevelop the rapidly growing midtown section of New York at the end of the 1920's, Rockefeller found himself after the beginning of the Great Depression with a long-term lease on several blocks of heavily taxed real estate. He plunged ahead with a striking plan to build skyscrapers that would house, among other enterprises, the new network radio industry. The result, Rockefeller Center, the construction of which spanned the depression and was not completed until after World War II, provided employment for thousands, became New York's number-one tourist attraction, and eventually revealed that the Rockefeller talent for making money was intact.

Project after project for preservation of historic sites, conservation of areas of natural beauty, and support of higher education followed. Williamsburg, colonial capital of Virginia, was restored and rebuilt when Rockefeller made a reality of the dream of the Reverend William A. R. Goodwin, a longtime resident of the area. It is one of America's most popular historic shrines. The spectacular regions around Jackson Hole, Wyo., and the Grand Tetons came under Rockefeller's protection. Brown, Dartmouth, the United Negro College Fund, the New York Public Library, and the library of the University of Tokyo, which had been leveled by the earthquake of 1923, were generously assisted.

Rockefeller had learned, like his father, that publicity was to be avoided because the newspapers would sensationalize even his most earnest remarks. He saw careless writers begin, after a time, to attribute his well-meant metaphor about snipping off excess rosebuds so that a few might grow to great size and beauty, to his father. But he maintained a quiet equanimity and in the bright glare of his talented sons was slipping into obscurity by 1946 when Senator Warren Austin, U.S. delegate to the United Nations (UN), announced that the UN's worried quest for a homesite in the United States had been solved with Rockefeller's gift of a $9 million plot of land on the East River in New York. He had long since abandoned religious fundamentalism and still believed that the future would prove the validity of his belief in world brotherhood. A slight, modest, good-looking, rather lonely man whose head could not be turned, Rockefeller proved that attainment of the golden mean owes nothing to money or to its lack. Abby Rockefeller died in 1948, and on Aug. 15, 1951, Rockefeller married Martha Baird Allen, a concert pianist and widow of one of his Brown classmates. His father died in 1937, but for the rest of his life, he insisted upon being called John D. Rockefeller, Jr., because, he said, there would always be only one John D. Rockefeller. He died in Tucson, Ariz.

[Raymond B. Fosdick, *John D. Rockefeller, Jr., A Portrait* (1956), is by Rockefeller's longtime legal adviser but is well balanced and contains many excerpts from revealing family letters. Nancy W. Newhall, *A Contribution to the Heritage of Every American: The Conservation Activities of John D. Rockefeller, Jr.* (1957), details one phase of his philanthropy. For examples of the paranoid attacks, one from the Left and one from the Right, that the Rockefellers have inspired, see Emanuel M. Josephson, *Rockefeller "Internationalist," The Man Who Rules the World* (1952), and Morris A. Bealle, *The House of Rockefeller* (1959). William Manchester, *A Rockefeller Family Portrait* (1958), is an even-tempered précis of others' works. Many of the transcripts in the Oral History Collection of Columbia University have references to Rockefeller, especially those of Flora Rhind on the Rockefeller Foundation and Horace M. Albright on conservation.]

ALBRO MARTIN

RODZINSKI, ARTUR (Jan. 2, 1892–Nov. 27, 1958), conductor, was born at Spalato, Dalmatia (now Split, Yugoslavia), the son of Josef Rodzinski, a Polish-born physician in the Austrian army, and Jadwiga Wiszmiewska. In 1897 the family moved to Lvov, Poland. There, as a teenager, Artur first became seriously interested in music and commenced piano lessons. Upon graduation from secondary school he attended the University of Lvov, where, at his father's insistence, he studied law and obtained the LL.D.

Music remained Rodzinski's first love, however. Deferred from World War I military service because of a postappendectomy infection, he enrolled at the Vienna Academy of Music, where he obtained a diploma after concentrated piano study with Georg von Lalewicz. In 1917 Rodzinski married fellow pianist Ilsa Reimesch; they had one son before being divorced.

In 1918 he returned to Lvov to undertake a career in music. After eking out a living for several months as a cabaret pianist, Rodzinski obtained a position as accompanist-coach at the Lvov Opera. There, in 1919, he conducted his first opera, *Ernani*. He was invited to Warsaw in 1920 and served five seasons as principal conductor of the Teatr Wielki Opera House, also appearing as guest conductor of the Warsaw Philharmonic Orchestra.

In 1925, while vacationing in Poland, Leopold Stokowski engaged Rodzinski as assistant conductor of the Philadelphia Orchestra commencing in the fall of 1926. His three-year apprenticeship under Stokowski proved to be of inestimable value: "What a taskmaster and what a hard school, [but] he taught me a lot!" During the 1928–1929 season Rodzinski conducted both the Philadelphia Orchestra and the Philadelphia Grand Opera concerts, and headed the orchestra department of the Curtis Institute of Music for the second consecutive year.

In 1929 Rodzinski was named conductor of the Los Angeles Philharmonic Orchestra, a position he held for four seasons. He became director of the Cleveland Orchestra in 1933, the same year he received American citizenship. On July 19, 1934, he married Halina Lilpop in Warsaw; they had one son. Rodzinski remained in Cleveland for ten seasons, during which time his reputation and that of the orchestra grew apace. On Jan. 31, 1935, Rodzinski directed the Cleveland Orchestra and a cast of Russian singers in the American premiere of Shostakovich's *Lady Macbeth of Mzensk* (later revised as *Katerina Ismailova*). Following a spectacular repeat performance in New York City on February 5, Rodzinski became a celebrity in the world of music.

During the summers of 1936 and 1937 Rodzinski conducted at the Salzburg Music Festival, the first American to do so. Also in 1937, at Arturo Toscanini's request, Rodzinski selected the membership and perfected the ensemble of the National Broadcasting Company Symphony Orchestra.

Although Rodzinski continued to enjoy artistic success in his last five Cleveland seasons, he became increasingly restive because of the limitations imposed by an economy-minded orchestra board. Consequently, in 1943 he eagerly accepted the post of musical director of the New York Philharmonic Orchestra. His four New York seasons represented the apex of Rodzinski's musical career.

But Rodzinski's New York tenure was endangered almost from the start because of his long-standing hostility toward orchestra manager Arthur Judson. By 1947 Rodzinski had become so resentful of Judson's alleged interference in the realms of the musical director that he requested the security of a multiyear "no strings attached" contract. A five-year contract was offered Rodzinski, but he deemed its provisions so restraining that he resigned in the middle of the 1946–1947 season to become director of the Chicago Symphony Orchestra.

Rodzinski's initial concerts were enthusiastically received in Chicago, but he soon clashed with the orchestra administration over the increased deficit resulting from his ambitious musical plans. Furthermore, he was suspected of feigning illness on several occasions. When he failed to conduct a January 1948 subscription concert, explaining that his physician had ordered complete rest (actually, according to his wife, Rodzinski had suffered a mild heart attack, which he kept secret), the orchestra board promptly announced that he would not be reengaged for the next season.

Upon completing the 1947–1948 Chicago season, Rodzinski embarked upon a ten-year guest-conducting odyssey that took him to various American and European music centers; to South America; to Cuba, as head of the Philharmonic Orchestra of Havana for the 1949–1950 season; and finally, to Italy, where he established residence in 1952. During his European exile Rodzinski conducted both opera and concerts. He enjoyed his greatest success at Florence, where, among other notable performances, he mounted the first production outside the Soviet Union of Prokofiev's *War and Peace*.

In the fall of 1958 Rodzinski returned to America to conduct two performances of *Tristan und Isolde* at the Chicago Lyric Opera. These were his last public appearances, for the energy expended completely debilitated a body ravaged by a decade of recurrent heart attacks. Rodzinski succumbed shortly thereafter in Boston.

Rodzinski was a striking podium figure, five feet, eleven inches tall, slender, with a profusion of coarse gray hair and myopic brown eyes peering intently through thick-lensed spectacles. A strict disciplinarian constantly in quest of perfection, he enjoyed a deserved reputation as an orchestra builder. He was justly renowned as an operatic conductor, of Wagner in particular. Rodzinski's many Columbia and Westminster recordings attest to his orchestral skill with Brahms, Tchaikovsky, and Richard Strauss and to his singular talent with the music of twentieth-century composers.

[Rodzinski discussed the art of conducting in Robert C. Marsh, "Artur Rodzinski and the Education of a Conductor," *Saturday Review*, Jan. 26, 1957; and his rehearsal techniques in Rose Heylbut, "Developing the Orchestra," *Etude*, Apr. 1945. Rodzinski's complex personality and stormy career are candidly described in Halina Rodzinski, *Our Two Lives* (1976), his widow's moving autobiography. A detailed account of Rodzinski's entire career may be found in Robert C. Marsh, *The Cleveland Orchestra* (1967). Howard Shanet, *Philharmonic: A History of New York's Orchestra* (1975), contains a well-balanced summary of Rodzinski's New York directorship, including complete program information for all of his concerts there. Brief biographical sketches are in David Ewen, *Dictators of the Baton* (1943); and Donald Brooks, *International Gallery of Conductors* (1951). The *New York Times*, Nov. 28, 1958, contains a full obituary.]

LOUIS R. THOMAS

ROGERS, EDITH NOURSE (Mar. 19. 1881–Sept. 10, 1960), United States congresswoman, was born in Saco, Maine, the daughter of Franklin Nourse, a prosperous woolens manufacturer in Lowell, Mass., and Edith Frances Riversmith. One of her ancestors, Rebecca Nourse (or Nurse), was hanged as a witch at Salem, Mass. She was educated at Rogers Hall School in Lowell, and at Madame Julien's School in Paris. On her return from France, she married John Jacob Rogers on Oct. 2, 1907. They had no children.

During World War I, Rogers joined the Women's Overseas Service League and went to Europe as a representative of that organization to inspect military field hospitals. She returned to the United States in June 1918, and until 1922 was a Red Cross volunteer at the Walter Reed Army Hospital in Washington, D.C. After the armistice she accompanied her husband, who had been elected to Congress in 1912, on an inspection of hospitals and ambulance stations in England and France. In recognition of her interest in veterans' affairs, President Warren G. Harding in 1922 named her his personal representative in charge of assistance for disabled veterans, an appointment renewed by presidents Calvin Coolidge (1923) and Herbert Hoover (1929). During these years Rogers served as a dollar-a-year inspector, visiting every military hospital in the United States; on her recommendations a number of reforms and improvements were made in their administration.

After her husband died in March 1925, Rogers ran in the special election to fill the vacancy caused by his death. She received more than 13,000 of the nearly 16,000 votes cast in the Republican primary, and on June 30, 1925, was elected to represent the Fifth Congressional District of Massachusetts, an area that included Lowell and consisted of farming, suburban, and industrial interests. She was the first woman to be elected to Congress from New England. At the time of her election, she declared: "I hope that everybody will forget as soon as possible that I am a woman. I have told my constituents that they may expect just the same service they obtained from my husband. I shall try to give my personal attention to every call on my office, and when I vote I shall try to represent them as accurately as my conscience will let me."

Although she had originally expected to stay in Washington for only a few years, Rogers was returned to office seventeen times. At the time of her death she was unopposed in her nineteenth campaign. Her thirty-five years of service in the House of Representatives was the longest of any woman.

In Congress Rogers continued to show a keen interest in veterans' problems. She served for many years on the House Committee on Veterans' Affairs, and twice chaired it. She secured passage of many private bills for pensions and disability allowances, and gained a reputation as the veterans' champion in Congress. She helped draft, and was a prime sponsor of, the G.I. Bill of Rights for veterans of World War II. She also introduced the legislation establishing the Women's Army Corps in 1942. Rogers was so popular with veterans' groups that during the war one group of soldiers adopted her as their company pin-up girl.

An energetic and vivacious woman, Rogers often irritated her Republican colleagues by taking an independent stance. In 1937, for example, she voted against the Neutrality Act (having been one of the early critics of Nazi persecution of minorities); she voted for the Selective Service Act in 1940; and later she supported the United Nations. She also backed a number of social service bills, and once said to a colleague after they had differed on such a measure: "I hope the vote did not disturb you. You know, I cannot refuse to spend mere money when I know that people need it."

A tireless and conscientious representative, Rogers normally took home large amounts of work, and used the telephone extensively to cut through bureaucratic red tape on behalf of her constituents. Throughout her long career she enjoyed immense popularity in her home district.

During her last year in office, Rogers found herself physically unable to carry out her duties. She missed the special session in the summer of 1960, and died in Boston, Mass. Contemporaries saw Rogers as "gay, vivacious, chatty and very feminine." She habitually wore a flower on her shoulder, and it became a sort of trademark. She took her role as dean of women representatives in Congress seriously; her dinners for new members at the beginning of each Congress became traditional.

[Rogers' obituary is in *New York Times,* Sept. 11, 1960. See also *Congressional Record,* 87th Cong., 1st sess., pp. 783–794.]

MELVIN I. UROFSKY

ROSENBERG, PAUL (Dec. 29, 1881–June 30, 1959), art dealer and collector, was born in Paris, France, the son of Alexandre Rosenberg and Mathilde Jellineck Rosenberg. His father, a successful dealer of antique furniture, also acquired paintings for sale, including those of the Impressionists. (He once bought Cézanne's *Man in a Blue Cap,* a purchase considered an act of pure folly by his wife.)

Paul Rosenberg attended the Collège Chaptal in Paris until he was eighteen. He then worked as a dealer with his father, beginning by assisting with purchases of antiques in England. In 1902 he settled in London with his own firm, which lasted three years. By 1911 he had opened a Paris art gallery with his father. They offered for sale some old master paintings, but mostly nineteenth-century artists, the Barbizon school, and the Impressionists. In 1914 he married Marguerite Loevi; they had a daughter and a son. Rosenberg served as an enlisted man in World War I but was discharged for reasons of health in 1916. After the war, Rosenberg established his own firm in Paris. He had difficulty at first, because established houses such as Georges-Petit, Durand-Ruel, Bernheim-Jeune, and others dominated the market, and the best art gravitated to them.

Rosenberg nevertheless developed a reputation as an astute dealer in modern art. He obtained an exclusive contract with Pablo Picasso, serving as his dealer from 1918 to 1940. In 1922 Georges Braque joined Rosenberg, as did Fernand Léger in 1926 and Henri Matisse in 1933. Rosenberg recognized the stature of these artists early in their careers.

His enthusiasm for Picasso led him to commission him to paint his wife. Picasso was not her favorite artist; she told him that she preferred the society portraitist, Boldini. Picasso therefore not only painted her seated on a decorative chair with her child on her knee, but also obliged with a small pastiche in the bravura Boldini style, with plumes, parasol, pearls and other jewelry and signed "Boldini." In 1921 Picasso made a line drawing of Paul Rosenberg after the manner of Ingres.

In 1935 Rosenberg opened a branch in London with his brother-in-law, Jacques Helft, an expert on French antique silver and the author of a monumental work on that subject. Rosenberg became known for the high quality of the exhibitions at his gallery as well as for superior catalogs. He sponsored the publication of two important *catalogues raisonnés,* one on Paul Cézanne by Lionello Venturi in 1936 and another on the art of Camille Pissarro by Pissarro's son Lucien and Venturi in 1939.

Rosenberg played an active role in the 1930's in opposing the Nazi government's sales of so-called *entartete kunst,* or "degenerate art," much of it by modern German masters such as Emil Nolde and Georg Grosz. Rosenberg waged an effective campaign among art dealers to boycott these sales, undoubtedly assisted by his position as president of the French Art Dealers' Association in Paris. Having thus aroused the animosity of the Nazis, when the German army invaded France in 1940 it was essential that the Rosenbergs leave before the Germans took Paris. Although he had most of his works of art transported to London and New York, his archives and records left behind were destroyed or dispersed by the Germans.

In 1940 Rosenberg established a gallery in New York City. After the war he never reestablished his European galleries, although he maintained close contact with the European art world and with members of his family in Paris.

In 1953 Rosenberg became an American citizen. Although most of the artists he represented were European, he began to exhibit Americans regularly, and he had under contract Max Weber, Karl Knaths, Abraham Rattner, and Marsden Hartley. Rosenberg did not represent surrealists because he considered the movement essentially literary; abstract painting, he thought, was out of the mainstream. The last artist he placed under contract was Nicolas de Staël. He had a high regard for American artists and predicted they would be an important international force, but he did not live to see their emergence in the 1960's and 1970's.

Rosenberg held benefit exhibitions nearly every year. He was very generous in giving art to museums in the United States as well as in Europe. He avoided publicity about himself and his family and never wrote a memoir, considering such an activity self-serving, vulgar, and irrelevant to his function as a dealer. A respected connoisseur, he believed that a dealer's main duty was to maintain high standards and to assure authenticity, and that much of his success was due to his policy of never trying to sell anything. "Great pictures sell themselves," he once said.

In November 1953, Rosenberg exhibited his private collection of paintings. Works by Picasso, Matisse, Renoir, Léger, Bonnard, and Braque were prominent. (He had begun to collect seriously about 1939.) The critic Henry McBride wrote that the collection was "destined ultimately to be a legacy and a safeguard for his family." Rosenberg died in Paris.

[On Rosenberg and his career, see "Dealer's Choice," *Time*, Dec. 7, 1953; Henry McBride, "Rosenberg and His Private Stock," *Art News*, Dec. 1953; and the obituary notice, *New York Times*, July 1, 1959.]

ROBERT REIFF

ROVENSTINE, EMERY ANDREW (July 20, 1895–Nov. 9, 1960), physician and anesthesiologist, was born in Atwood, Ind., the son of Cassius Andrew Rovenstine and Lulu Massena. The family ran a general store. After beginning high school in Atwood he transferred to Blue Island, a suburb of Chicago, where he lived with an uncle. During summer vacations he attended Winona State Teachers College in Indiana and was qualified to teach when he graduated from high school at seventeen. While teaching for a year at a one-room grammar school at Stony Point, Ind., he lived on his maternal grandmother's farm and made extra money by trapping.

In 1914 Rovenstine, an excellent baseball catcher, entered Wabash College on an athletic scholarship. He worked in an assortment of jobs and extracurricular activities on campus. During summer vacations he worked for the H. J. Heinz Company and played semiprofessional baseball. He graduated from Wabash with a B.A. in chemistry in June 1917 and enlisted in the Army Corps of Engineers, initially as a sergeant instructor in demolition. Then he was sent to France as a second lieutenant and reassigned to a courier detachment. Rovenstine later cited his experience as a dispatch rider, moving among wounded troops who were suffering from shock and pain, as a factor in his choosing a career in anesthesia.

After a few months with the Army of Occupation, Rovenstine was discharged in the summer of 1919. He then married Agnes Lane, whom he had met in college. He began teaching and coaching in Menominee in northern Michigan, working at extra jobs. In 1920 he took a similar teaching position in La Porte, Ind.

By 1923 he had saved enough money to pursue a career in medicine, and he entered the Indiana University medical school that year. He spent the first year on the Bloomington campus and the last three at Indianapolis Hospital. He received his M.D. in 1928 but spent an additional year as an intern before returning to La Porte to set up a general practice. Two years of a worsening economy and his own preference for specializing led him to decide to enter anesthesia training. While a medical undergraduate he had become interested in it through personal encouragement from Dr. Arthur E. Guedel. After taking a six-week course under Elmer I. McKesson of Toledo, Ohio, in 1930, he became in 1931 a resident under Dr. Ralph M. Waters at the University of Wisconsin, in what was probably the best anesthesia program in the nation.

Rovenstine was promoted to instructor in 1932; he became assistant professor in 1934. Mature, methodical, and diligent, he impressed Waters as especially promising. With Waters' strong backing he was chosen early in 1935 to head up a new anesthesia program at Bellevue Hospital and New York University (NYU) medical school. After only a few months in his new position, however, tragedy struck. He and his wife, Agnes, were living in a small Manhattan apartment, with little social life. One Sunday afternoon, while he was attending a professional football game, she committed suicide. Grief-stricken, Rovenstine threw himself into a frenzied work schedule, sleeping usually less than four hours a night. After only two years he was promoted to full professor and added the NYU College of Dentistry to his domain. By 1942 he had made Bellevue Hospital the showplace for anesthesia in New York City and the East.

Prolific writing, leadership in professional societies, and a flair for promotion brought him success and fame. In 1936 he was elected president of the American Society of Regional Anesthesia. In 1937 he was one of the nine founding members of the American Board of Anesthesiology. In 1938 he served as visiting professor of anesthesiology at the Radcliffe Infirmary, Oxford University, and in 1939 he served similarly at the University of Rosario, Argentina. From 1941 to 1946 he was a member of the National Research Council. With his passion for excellence, he often ruffled colleagues' feathers. Whenever accused of playing politics, "Rovey," as he was affectionately known to some friends, would reply, "Just an Indiana boy." In 1939 he married Jewel Sonya Gould, a successful businesswoman.

Rovenstine made several contributions to his specialty of anesthesia and to twentieth-century medicine. The first was his evangelistic crusade for autonomy and for high scientific standards in his specialty, achieved in 1938 when anesthesiology received affiliate status under the American Board of Surgery. Full legitimacy came with the creation of the American Board of Anesthesia in 1941. Another success came with Rovenstine's service on the Army Advisory Board in World War II, when he and others gained the right to supervise army hospital operating rooms. His other accomplishments include the design of anesthetists' instruments, such as forceps, angles, and connectors; the discovery of endotracheal and endobronchial anesthetic techniques and instruments; a system for collecting statistical data on each patient's anesthesia and surgery; and cyclopropane experiments. He wrote over 200 articles and 15 textbook chapters and also pioneered postgraduate seminars at NYU.

Rovenstine combined a capacity for hard work and a flair for promotion with the opportunities offered at Bellevue and NYU. Training some of the best anesthesiologists in the country, he extended the model Waters had developed at Wisconsin. Although a hard taskmaster in molding specialty physicians of scientific precision and human compassion, he provided an entrepreneurial devotion to his students' later advancement.

[A few letters, pamphlets, and reprints are located in the University of Wisconsin Archives, Ralph M. Waters Papers; the New York Academy of Medicine Library; and the NYU Medical Center Library. General folders of information, mainly on his early career, are available at the American Society of Anesthesiologists' Wood Library-Museum of Anesthesiology, in Park Ridge, Ill.

Among his publications of interest are "The Management of Pain in the Aged," *Geriatrics* I (1946), written with Emanuel M. Papper; and the report of the National Research Council's Division of Medical Sciences, Subcommittee on Anesthesia, *Fundamentals of Anesthesia* (1942). Rovenstine served as secretary of that group.

Taken together, three articles give the best survey of Rovenstine's life: the three-part series in the *New Yorker*, Oct. 25, Nov. 1 and 8, 1947; J. R. Miller, "Unknown Men in White," *This Week Magazine*, Nov. 23, 1947; and the tribute on his retirement, *Anesthesia and Analgesia*, July–Aug., 1960.

To place Rovenstine's technical achievements in perspective, see Thomas E. Keys, *The History of Surgical Anesthesia* (1945), and Albert Faulconer, Jr., and Thomas E. Keys, eds., *Foundations of Anesthesiology*, 2 vols. (1965); on the cyclopropane work as a model medical study, see H. P. Gutgesell, "Cyclopropane: The Early Days at Wisconsin," *Wisconsin Medical Journal*, May 1968.]

JAMES POLK MORRIS

RUBIN, ISIDOR CLINTON (Jan. 8, 1883–July 10, 1958), gynecologist, was born in Vienna, the son of Nehemiah Rubin and Froma Keller. The family migrated to New York City when Isidor was quite young. He attended City College and later the College of Physicians and Surgeons of Columbia University, from which he received the M.D. degree in 1905. He then entered on an internship and residency at Mt. Sinai Hospital that led ultimately to the position of house surgeon and terminated in 1909 when he returned to Europe for a year of postgraduate training. He visited Berlin, Dresden, Munich, and Paris but spent most of his time at the Frauenklinik in Vienna, where he studied under the famous surgeon J. Schottländer, with whom he developed a lasting friendship. Back in New York in 1910, he obtained gynecologic appointments at Beth Israel, Mt. Sinai, and Montefiore hospitals, while turning his special attention to the pathology of cancer of the cervix of the uterus. His first published paper, dated 1910, is still referred to as establishing clearly the entity now known as carcinoma in situ.

Elliot Philipp wrote, "Although Rubin had the gifts of a research worker he also had a great dexterity as an operator, and a wonderful gentleness and warmth of character that drew people to him; so inevitably he was taken from the laboratory to the clinical field and there became acutely aware of the misery of sterility. With determination and with a band of collaborators at Beth Israel and Mt. Sinai he set to work to unravel one problem after another. He did not casually stumble on his discovery that the ovum was conveyed to the uterus by the peristaltic waves of the Fallopian tubes."

Until 1914 Rubin experimented on cadavers and laboratory animals, using radio-opaque substances, but when he first carried out salpingography on a live subject, the substance proved to be too irritating and the procedure was temporarily discontinued. Later a gaseous medium, oxygen, was substituted and still later carbon dioxide, which was found to be relatively inert and therefore safer. In fact, it was not until Nov. 3, 1919, that Rubin performed the first successful test to determine the patency of the Fallopian tubes, thus creating a new eponym, the Rubin test. The original paper of fifty-three pages, illustrated by the author and now preserved in the New York Academy of Medicine, describes how the oxygen entered the peritoneal cavity and how its presence could be detected by the roentgenogram. Rubin's preliminary report, entitled "Nonoperative Determination of Patency of Fallopian Tubes in Sterility" (*Journal of the American Medical Association*, Apr. 10, 1920), created a sensation and made Rubin internationally famous.

In 1923 Rubin described a sudden acute pain in the shoulders as a reliable sign of ruptured ectopic pregnancy. Always anxious to relieve the distress of the patient in labor, he was among the first to advocate the use of hypnosis in delivery. Patients from all over the world now poured into his office, but like another Maimonides he reserved much of his time for the deserving poor.

Rubin was a teacher par excellence and took unusual interest in the young men under his supervision. V. B. Green-Armytage wrote, "He was generosity itself to postgraduates and I recall many a visit to his multicubicled office in Park Avenue where we would listen to him, surrounded by nurses, practitioners, as he passed from patient to patient. . . he was always quiet and efficient as he taught us how to work his beloved machine." Not only was he willing to share ideas for future research, but he experienced a sense of disappointment when some of his pupils failed to live up to his expectations. "Yet," according to Green-Armytage, "he detested bombast, hypocrisy and lack of truth and would not hesitate to criticize a work that he judged prematurely published or inadequately proved."

From 1937 to 1947 Rubin was clinical professor of obstetrics and gynecology at Columbia University. He also held a similar position at New York University and still later (1948) at New York Medical College. During the same decade he served as chief of gynecology at Mt. Sinai Hospital, retiring in 1946 to become consultant gynecologist and obstetrician, while retaining similar positions at Montefiore, Beth Israel, and Harlem hospitals.

Rubin was a founding fellow of the American Board of Obstetrics and Gynecology and the American Academy of Obstetrics and a fellow of the International College of Surgeons. He served as president of the American Gynecological Society; the American Association of Obstetricians, Gynecologists and Abdominal Surgeons; and the New York Obstetrical Society. He was also active in the American Society for the Advancement of Science and the U.S. Committee of the World Medical Association.

Rubin was also a prolific writer and, being a gifted draftsman, frequently provided illustrations for his own articles. He published no less than 132 articles in journals all over the world. In addition to his three major book publications, *Symptoms in Gynecology* (1923); *Uterotubal Insufflation* (1947); and, with Josef Novak, *Integrated Gynecology* (1956), Rubin had contributed chapters on sterility to Curtis' *System of Gynecology;* Lewis' *System of Surgery,* and the Davis *Cyclopedia of Medicine.* He also served on the editorial boards of the *International Journal of Fertility, Gynécologie Pratique, Excerpta Medica, Fertility and Sterility,* and the *Journal of Obstetrics and Gynecology.*

Rubin traveled widely to conferences and symposia, invariably accompanied by his wife, the former Sylvia Unterberg, whom he had married on Jan. 7, 1914. "I.C.," as he was affectionately called, received a hearty welcome wherever he went, and few physicians of modern times have been so widely honored by governments and learned societies. In 1949 an entire number of a Brazilian journal was dedicated to his honor. At least ten nations bestowed on him their highest decorations. Although not a trained linguist, he taught himself to deliver addresses in French and Spanish in addition to his native German. Rubin died in London. Undoubtedly the best-known gynecologist of his generation, Rubin is still regarded by many as the single most important contributor to the study of fertility in this century. The Rubin Lectures at Mt. Sinai Medical School preserve his memory.

[See *The Collected Papers of Dr. Isidor Clinton Rubin* (1954). Also see Harold Speert, "I. C. Rubin, A Gynecologic Eponym," *Journal of the Mount Sinai Hospital,* 25 (1958), which is very complete and contains a bibliography; and *ibid.*, Sept.–Oct., 1947. Obituaries are V. B. Green-Armytage and Elliot Philipp, *British Medical Journal*, 2 (1958); and *New York Times*, July 11, 1958.]

MORRIS H. SAFFRON

RUBLEE, GEORGE (July 7, 1868–Apr. 26, 1957), lawyer, socialite, and statesman, was born in Madison, Wis., the son of Horace Rublee, a Vermont-born newspaper editor and owner, a founder and state chairman of the Wisconsin Republican party, and minister to Switzerland, and of Kate Hopkins. Rublee lived in Switzerland until he was eight years old, when his father became editor and part owner of the *Milwaukee Sentinel*.

Rublee was the only member of Groton's first graduating class in 1886, received the A.B. from Harvard in 1890, and then spent two years in Europe. He earned the LL.B. at Harvard in 1895 and taught for one year at Harvard Law School. After two years of practice in Chicago, he moved to New York City in 1898 to practice with Victor Morawetz, a leading corporation lawyer. On Jan. 12, 1899, he married Juliet Barrett; they had no children. Shrewd investments made Rublee a fortune, and in 1900, at the age of thirty-two, he retired to the fashionable social life of Europe, where he became a favorite tennis partner of the king of Sweden.

Later he returned to the United States and joined the New York law firm of Spooner and Cotton. In 1910 he assisted Louis D. Brandeis in presenting the case against Secretary of the Interior Richard Ballinger before a Senate investigating committee. He supported Theodore Roosevelt for president in 1912, but after Woodrow Wilson's election he helped Brandeis draft financial legislation for the new administration. In 1913 he went to Washington as Brandeis's liaison with congressional committees.

Rublee wrote the key provision of the Federal Trade Commission Act of 1914. President Wilson had favored enactment of detailed definitions of prohibited corporate practices. Rublee feared that would lead to endless disputes and evasions, and that a better approach was to outlaw unfair practices in general terms and give the Federal Trade Commission (FTC) powers to determine whether a particular practice was unfair and to issue cease-and-desist orders. He persuaded a friend, Congressman Raymond B. Stevens of New Hampshire, to introduce a bill so drafted. In what Arthur S. Link called the "decisive event in the history of the anti-trust program," Wilson supported the Stevens bill and Rublee's draft was incorporated as section 5 of the Federal Trade Commission Act.

Wilson gave Rublee an interim appointment to the FTC, on which he served without pay for eighteen months (March 1915–September 1916). Senate Republicans objected to him on the ground that as a Progressive Republican he was more of a Wilson Democrat than a regular Republican. Also, he had opposed the election in 1914 of Senate Republican leader Jacob H. Gallinger of New Hampshire, where Rublee had a residence. Therefore, under traditional "senatorial courtesy" the Senate refused to confirm appointment of a nominee to whom his senator objected.

Nevertheless, Wilson made extensive use of Rublee's services. In 1916 he was appointed to a commission to report on the operation of the Adamson Eight-Hour Law, and in 1917 to the Commercial Economy Board of the Advisory Council of National Defense, to the Priorities Committee of the War Industries Board, and as special counsel to the Treasury Department. In 1918–1919 Wilson sent him to London as American delegate to the Allied Maritime Transport Council, which pooled and allocated shipping for war use. Here, in association with Jean Monnet and others, Rublee became enthusiastic about the prospects of a new world order and returned to America to fight for the League of Nations.

In 1921, Rublee joined the Washington law firm of Covington, Burling, Rublee, Acheson and Shorb, in which one of the partners was the future secretary of state, Dean Acheson. Rublee accompanied Ambassador Dwight Morrow to Mexico in 1928 and helped him settle disputes over properties owned by American citizens and the Roman Catholic Church. In 1930 he served as a referee for the government of Colombia in a dispute with foreign capitalists over oil holdings, and his decision for Colombia was accepted. He continued as adviser to Colombia until 1933.

In 1938, President Franklin D. Roosevelt appointed Rublee director of the Intergovernmental Committee on Refugees—the five members of which represented the United States, France, Britain, Scandinavia, and South America—which was to negotiate an agreement with the Nazi government that would allow the emigration of German Jews with their property. The Germans agreed to do so if the emigration was financed by a loan to Germany that would be repaid with extra exports of German goods. Discouraged by the unwillingness of other countries to accept either Jewish refugees or the German method of repayment, Rublee resigned in 1939.

In 1940, Secretary of State Cordell Hull appointed Rublee chairman of the Subcommittee for Political Problems of the Advisory Committee on Problems, which planned for the postwar world, but ill health severely limited his participation. In 1947–1948 he served as president of the Harvard Alumni Association. He died in New York City.

His friend and law partner, Dean Acheson, wrote that Rublee's life alternated between periods of "contented languor touched with melancholy" and "passionate . . . seizure which carried him to heights of brilliant and tireless effort." Perhaps, said Acheson, the "favor of fortune" prevented Rublee from acquiring the discipline to extend himself consistently to his full potential, but "few men have ever so absorbed the interest and devotion of their friends."

[Rublee told a part of the story of the FTC fight in "The Original Plan and Early History of the Federal Trade Commission," *Proceedings of the Academy of Political Science*, Jan. 1926. His oral history memoir, completed in 1951, is in the Oral History Collection at Columbia University. See also Dean Acheson, *Morning and Noon* (1965); and Arthur S. Link, *Wilson* (1956). An account of the refugee problem is in Joseph Tennenbaum, *Race and Reich* (1956). Obituaries are in *New York Times* and *Washington Post*, Apr. 27, 1957.]

WESLEY M. BAGBY

RUGG, HAROLD ORDWAY (Jan. 17, 1886–May 17, 1960), educator, engineer, and author, was born in Fitchburg, Mass., son of Edward Francis Rugg, a struggling carpenter, and Merion Abbie Davidson. Rugg attended the Fitchburg public schools and worked for two years in a local textile mill before entering Dartmouth College. He remained there for five years, receiving his B.S. in 1908 and a degree in civil engineering from Dartmouth's Thayer School in 1909.

After a brief period of employment with the Missouri Pacific Railroad, Rugg taught civil engineering for a little over a year at James Millikin University in Decatur, Ill. In 1911 he went to the University of Illinois to teach engineering and do graduate work in education and

sociology under William C. Bagley. On Sept. 4, 1912, Rugg married Bertha Miller, the first of his three wives. (His first two marriages were to end in divorce.) They had two adopted children.

Rugg took his Ph.D. in 1915 and in September of that year moved on to research and teaching in educational statistics and administration under Charles H. Judd at the University of Chicago. His work with Judd led, in turn, to an opportunity to serve during World War I with Edward L. Thorndike on the army's Committee on Classification of Personnel, the first group to make widespread use of intelligence and aptitude tests on adults.

Two of Rugg's colleagues on the committee, Arthur Upham Pope and John Coss, were instrumental in shaping his postwar career in education. Pope aroused Rugg's interest in the writings of Van Wyck Brooks, Waldo Frank, Randolph Bourne, and other contributors to the *Seven Arts* and the *New Republic;* Coss started Rugg thinking about an integrated social sciences curriculum by describing his own plans for merging the social sciences in an undergraduate course in contemporary civilization at Columbia University.

When the war ended, Rugg returned to Chicago to work for another year under Judd; but his conversations with Coss and Pope had persuaded him that his future lay in the social studies, and in January 1920 he left Chicago to pursue his new interests at Teachers College, Columbia University. He taught at Teachers College for the next thirty-one years.

At Columbia, Rugg continued his study of contemporary social criticism, canvassing the works of R. M. Tawney, Graham Wallas, Beatrice and Sidney Webb, Charles A. Beard, Harold Laski, and Thorstein Veblen. By the late spring of 1920 his transformation from educational technician into curriculum specialist in the social studies was well under way, and he was determined to convey the ideas encountered in his reading to the youth of the nation. The result was a controversial textbook series distributed in pamphlet form in the 1920's and published under the general title "Man and His Changing Society" (14 volumes) between 1929 and 1940. Eight of the books were written with Louise Krueger, who had become Rugg's second wife on Aug. 25, 1930. (They had one child.) The series, which was designed to portray American society accurately, including weaknesses as well as strengths, was widely used in the 1930's but by 1940 it had been labeled "subversive" by various conservative spokesmen, an action that precipitated one of the most sensational cases of textbook censorship in American educational history.

In 1938 Rugg's publisher, Ginn and Company, sold 289,000 copies of the textbooks. By 1940 total sales (including workbooks) had reached 5,500,000 copies, and the series was in use in some five thousand school systems. In the long run, however, the opposition of representatives of several patriotic and business organizations led a number of communities to officially ban the series and many others to quietly remove the books from their school libraries. By 1944 sales had dropped to 21,000, and Rugg had literally seen his efforts to teach critical thinking go up in smoke when his books were actually burned in Bradner, Ohio.

During the 1930's and early 1940's, Rugg was identified with a group of reformist educators, frequently referred to as "social reconstructionists," who were committed to the idea that the school should be utilized as an agent of social change. Within this group Rugg's own brand of reform was somewhat distinctive (largely because of the influence of Frank, Brooks, and Bourne) in that it encompassed not only the concept of social engineering but also the notion that the good society awaited the appearance of significant numbers of creative, cultured individuals. Rugg thought that the school, in addition to furnishing an accurate description of society, should provide ample opportunity for individual self-expression, which he assumed was an important element in character formation.

In the years after World War II Rugg concentrated on developing sound educational "foundations" by relating educational theory to the humanities and social sciences, on working out an adequate theoretical basis for teacher preparation, and on investigating the nature of the creative process. The last-named was actually a long-standing interest for Rugg, dating back to his early years at Columbia, when he had become acquainted with a number of writers and artists in the New York area.

Following his retirement in 1951, Rugg continued his intensive study of creativity for the nine remaining years of his life. He died in 1960 at his home in Woodstock, N.Y., which he had shared with his third wife, Elizabeth May Howe Page, since their marriage in 1947. They had no children.

One of the traits that set Rugg apart from most of his progressive colleagues was his versatility. At various points in his career he was associated with attempts to forge a science of education, with both the "child-centered" and "society-centered" wings of the progressive education movement, and with the earliest efforts to focus the attention of educators on the affective (as opposed to cognitive) dimensions of learning.

Intense, energetic, hard-driving, and somewhat combative (he seemed to thrive on the controversy that swirled around his textbook series), Rugg could generally be found in the forefront of educational developments. He was noted less for the originality of his thought than for his qualities of leadership, his teaching ability, and his skill in synthesizing for educational purposes the latest and most significant findings in a variety of disciplines. His influence was strongest in the field of curriculum design, where he pioneered in unifying the social sciences and developing methods of content selection based on research and experimentation. His textbook series, in which his curricular ideas were implemented, was one of the noteworthy achievements of the progressive era. It also provided Rugg with an opportunity—denied to other social reconstructionists—to have his views presented systematically in the nation's schoolrooms.

[Rugg's papers have not been made available, and there is no biography on him, although his *That Men May Understand* (1941) is a semiautobiographical work. The most comprehensive studies of Rugg's work are three doctoral dissertations: Elmer A. Winters, "Harold Rugg and Education for Social Reform" (University of Wisconsin, 1968); Virginia S. Wilson, "Harold Rugg's Social and Educational Philosophy as Reflected in His Textbook Series, 'Man and His Changing Society'" (Duke University, 1975); and Peter F. Carbone, Jr., "The Social and Educational Thought of Harold Rugg" (Harvard University, 1967), a revision of which was published in 1977. All three dissertations include extensive bibliographies of Rugg's writings and list numerous reviews of his books. His obituary is in *New York Times*, May 18, 1960.]

PETER F. CARBONE, JR.

RUML, BEARDSLEY (Nov. 5, 1894–Apr. 18, 1960), publicist, was born in Cedar Rapids, Iowa, the son of Wentzle Ruml, a physician, and Salome Beardsley, who was superintendent of the Cedar Rapids Hospital. His only sister, Frances, became dean of Radcliffe College. Ruml completed high school in three years and was active in student organizations at Dartmouth, from which he received the B.S. in 1915. Two years later he earned the Ph.D. in psychology and education at the University of Chicago. On Aug. 28, 1917, he married his fellow student, Lois Treadwell; they had three children.

Ruml was an instructor of applied psychology at the Carnegie Institute of Technology (1917–1918) and then helped devise tests of competence of soldiers in various trades useful in the army. After the armistice, and with several associates, he formed the Scott Company in Philadelphia to advise industries on personnel problems. In 1921 James R. Angell, president of the Carnegie Corporation, who had known Ruml at the University of Chicago, hired him as his assistant. After a year's experience Ruml became director of the Laura Spelman Rockefeller Memorial, established by John D. Rockefeller to promote the welfare of women and children. Ruml shifted from direct-benefit grants (to the Girl Scouts and Y.W.C.A., for example) to a policy of gifts to universities for fellowships in sociology, anthropology, psychology, and international relations.

In 1929 Ruml became a trustee of the Spelman Fund but the next year was in Washington as assistant to Arthur Woods, chairman of President Hoover's Emergency Commission for Unemployment. Here Ruml used his statistical skill to little purpose. At the invitation of President Robert Hutchins in 1931 he became dean of the social science division and professor of education at the University of Chicago. His effort at interrelating the social sciences was disappointed because the professors were too attached to their particular disciplines.

Ruml abandoned academic employment in 1934 to become treasurer of R. H. Macy and Company in New York City, where he was more listened to. A university associate commented that Ruml was "leaving ideas for notions," but the proposals he hatched for the business were profitable. He instituted an accounting device that encouraged the selling force to maximum effort. His "cash-time plan" enabled the store to do installment business without sacrificing its boasted policy of "6 percent less for cash." He was chairman of Macy's from 1945 to 1949 and continued as a director until 1951.

Ruml's activities surpassed his innovations for Macy's. As a director of the New York Federal Reserve Bank (1937–1947) and chairman during the last six years, he made original contributions to war and postwar finance. He was an active participant in the United Nations Monetary and Financial Conference held at Bretton Woods,

N.H., in 1944. Although a registered Republican, he voted three times for President Franklin D. Roosevelt and during the Great Depression originated the domestic allotment device, the basis of the New Deal's agricultural program.

Ruml is especially remembered for his pay-as-you-go income tax plan. When the United States entered World War II in 1941, he asked himself how young men who had forfeited excellent earnings to enter the armed services at $50 a month could meet the taxes on their higher income received the previous year. His solution was to "turn the tax clock forward" and make taxes current with income. This could be done by withholding taxes on wages and salaries at the source; taxes on other income for the current year would be estimated by the income receiver, subject to adjustment for overpayment or underpayment at the end of the year. Ruml presented the proposal in the summer of 1942 to the Senate Finance Committee. The Treasury opposed the plan, and the committee decisively rejected it.

In January 1943 President Roosevelt announced that he approved the principle and in his budget message asked Congress "to put our taxes as far as possible on a pay-as-you-go basis." Several plans were heatedly debated in the House Ways and Means Committee, in the committee of the whole, and in the press. Confusion existed in the minds of legislators and the public over "doubling up" of tax payments or greater or less "forgiveness" of taxes on 1942 income. Deploring the hassle, Ruml emphasized that the taxpayer would still pay on his taxable income every year until he died, stressing that any loss to the Treasury could—and would—be made up by an increase in rates over a span of years. In May 1943 Congress passed the Tax Payment Act, a modification of the Ruml plan. It canceled 75 percent of a year's income tax liability for forty million taxpayers whose tax was over $50, and 100 percent for four million people whose tax was below that figure.

In his speeches, books, and pamphlets Ruml looked forward to a postwar era in which old economic errors could be avoided. The burden of his advocacy was that "it is inescapable that the national state, through an explicit and implemented fiscal and monetary policy, must complement and supplement the activities of private business in the maintenance of high production and high employment." In spite of experience in the Great Depression, Ruml and other spokesmen of the National Planning Association and the Committee for Economic Development underestimated the role that government was to play in direct controls, subventions, and takeovers in important sectors of the economy.

Ruml advised officially on numerous cultural and other programs of the federal government. He urged industrial development in Puerto Rico. A director of many varied business enterprises, he was also a trustee of the National Bureau of Economic Research, Dartmouth College, and Fisk University.

Beardsley Ruml was made of fissionable material. His knowledge of society provided him with fertile means for promoting welfare in the economy. Although closely allied to business, he constantly drew on his academic equipment to the advantage of the public no less than of private enterprise. Warmhearted and informal, he harbored no desire to appear impressive. Indeed, he enjoyed surprising or mildly shocking with his intellectual sallies and, in social company, with his colorful clothes. His originality was accompanied by a becoming modesty. His writings and speech were straightforward. Six feet tall and weighing two hundred pounds, his refusal to find time for exercise may have shortened his life. He died in Danbury, Conn.

[Ruml's activities and ideas are described in his publications, which include *The Reliability of Mental Tests in the Division of an Academic Group* (1917); *The Pay-As-You-Go Income Tax Plan* (1942); *Government, Business, and Values* (1943); *Fiscal and Monetary Policy* (1944); *Tomorrow's Business* (1945); *Opportunity and Duty in Puerto Rico* (1949); *The Five Percent* (1951), written with Theodore Geiger; and *The Manual of Corporate Giving* (1952), of which he was coeditor with Geiger. His papers (1917–1959) are at the University of Chicago. Memoirs by Flora Rhind and by M. L. Wilson in the Oral History Collection of Columbia University include material on Ruml. See also "Ruml," *New Yorker*, Sept. 12, 1942; A. Porter, "Pay-As-You-Go Ruml," *Collier's*, Mar. 6, 1943; the obituary notice, *New York Times*, Apr. 19, 1960; and account of Ruml's memorial service, *ibid.*, Apr. 21, 1960.]

BROADUS MITCHELL

RUSSELL, HENRY NORRIS (Oct. 25, 1877–Feb. 18, 1957), astronomer, was born in Oyster Bay, N.Y., the son of Alexander Gatherer Russell, a Presbyterian minister who was a central figure in the reform of the catechism, and Eliza

Hoxie Norris. After spending his first twelve years in Oyster Bay, where he had been educated at home and at a local Dames' School, Russell was sent to live with his maternal aunt in Princeton, N.J., where he attended the Princeton Preparatory School and, three years later, Princeton University. In 1897 he graduated *insigne cum laude* ("with distinguished praise"), one of only two people ever to receive this honor. Three years later he received a Ph.D. with a dissertation on the orbit of the minor planet Eros, which had just been discovered and was causing great excitement as a probe with which one might gauge the scale of the solar system.

An unusual zeal for work, and consuming interests in both mathematics and astronomy, led Russell to pursue a double course load as a graduate student at Princeton, working with Henry Burchard Fine in mathematics and Charles Augustus Young in astronomy.

In 1902 Russell began postdoctoral study at King's College, Cambridge, to which he was attracted primarily by George Darwin and his work in orbit theory. He also attended lectures on planetary theory, on spherical harmonics, and on general topics by Arthur Robert Hinks. During the next year Russell worked with Hinks, supported by a Carnegie fellowship, to develop a program for the photographic determination of stellar parallaxes, one of the first of its kind. While engaged in the long observation project, Russell fell ill. In 1904 he had to return home, leaving the remaining observations to Hinks.

In 1905 Russell was appointed instructor in astronomy by Edgar O. Lovett, who had succeeded Young as chairman of the astronomy department at Princeton. He also began the long process of reducing his photographic parallax observations to find the distances and actual brightnesses of the stars involved. Upon his return to Princeton, he found a small, stable department interested in teaching and in observing double stars. The stability soon disappeared when Lovett left to become president of Rice University. Russell and Raymond Smith Dugan were put under the mathematics department, a situation that continued until Russell was appointed the chairman of the astronomy department in 1912.

On Nov. 24, 1908, Russell married Lucy May Cole, whom he had long known from summer vacations in Oyster Bay. They had four children.

Russell had long been keen on the analysis of double-star systems, contributing a technique for the reduction of visual pairs in 1898, a method for determining the densities of eclipsing pairs of the

Algol type in 1899, and a method for spectroscopic systems in 1904. He also included several double stars on his Cambridge parallax list, for without distances actual stellar masses could not be determined. Russell was also interested in stellar spectroscopy, a legacy from Young, under whom he had completed a visual spectroscopic survey of bright stars for his senior thesis in 1897.

As Russell continued to process his Cambridge parallaxes at Princeton, he acquired spectral data on his stars from Edward Charles Pickering of Harvard. Russell soon found a marked correlation between spectral type (considered a measure of color and temperature) and the actual stellar brightnesses he had found in his parallax work. This idea was not completely new, but had remained only a statistical inference until Russell's examination. Of greater interest to Russell was the realization that there were a few yellow and red stars that did not fit this relation. These were found to be of very high intrinsic brightness—as bright as or brighter than the bluest stars. The explanation, quickly surmised by Russell and later verified by his first graduate student, Harlow Shapley, was that these stars were of enormous volume.

Russell thought he was the first, by 1909–1910, to detect these giants, but in fact a Dane, Ejnar Hertzsprung, had made the suggestion a few years earlier. Hertzsprung and Russell were introduced to each other's work in late 1910, and both were delighted that they had come, by independent means, to what was a fundamental relationship in the study of the physical behavior of stars: the Hertzsprung-Russell diagram.

To Russell the existence of the red giants recalled a discarded theory of stellar evolution. He saw them as the initial stages of star formation, with subsequent stages arising from gravitational contraction and heating. By 1914 he drew upon almost every available observational source in stellar astronomy to create an empirical synthesis to support his view, which was widely discussed and debated. What Russell actually succeeded in doing was to set down firmly the reality of the diagram: that giant stars indeed exist. His interpretation—his theory of stellar evolution—has not stood the test of time.

Russell was aware of the problems that existed with his theory. Largely in response to the British theorist Arthur Stanley Eddington and to Meghnad Saha, who in 1920 provided a theoretical extension of the Bohr theory of the atom to explain the physical conditions necessary to produce the observed solar spectrum, Russell embarked upon a significantly different course of attack on the fundamental problems that confronted his evolutionary theory and stellar astronomy.

In a recollection of his career, Russell noted that his work could be briefly summed up:

1. The development of methods for calculating the orbits of eclipsing binary stars, and various practical applications.
2. The determination of dynamical parallaxes and the investigation of the masses of binary stars.
3. The application of physical principles to the study of the spectra of the sun, sunspots, and stars.
4. The application of these principles to a quantitative analysis of the atmospheres of the sun and stars.
5. The term-analysis of complex atomic spectra [National Academy of Sciences autobiographical sketch].

Russell felt that the first and the fifth areas were his most original, the latter work involving what is now known as Russell-Saunders coupling, which explains the spectral behavior of the alkaline earth elements. From the third and fourth areas came his monumental work, "On the Composition of the Sun's Atmosphere" (1929), which helped to establish hydrogen as the most abundant element in the solar atmosphere and produced an abundance picture that remains useful today.

His role as teacher might best be summed up in his two-volume text *Astronomy* (1926–1927), written with R. S. Dugan and J. Q. Stewart, which was the standard reference for almost three decades.

For many years Russell served as consultant to the staff at Mount Wilson Observatory and as a research associate in residence during summers. Later he held a similar post at Harvard. On many occasions he lectured on religion and science, and on the role of science in society. From his upbringing he held strong religious convictions and worked diligently toward their reconciliation with scientific knowledge. During World War I he contributed significantly to the development of air navigation.

Russell had ample opportunity to take administrative positions, and on several occasions was called to major observatory and institutional directorships. He declined them all, preferring freedom to work as he pleased, unencumbered by bureaucracy.

The enormous influence he gained as "Dean of American Astronomers" brought Russell awesome power within the discipline. While he could appear austere at a distance, to those who knew him best—his family and close associates—his passion for scientific truth translated into a love for life that knew virtually no bounds. He died at Princeton.

[The Henry Norris Russell Papers are at the Princeton University Library. Russell wrote a brief autobiographical sketch for the National Academy of Sciences; there is also an unpublished transcript of a talk by Russell (1954) before the astronomy department at Princeton. See F. J. M. Stratton, in *Biographical Memoirs of Fellows of the Royal Society*, 3 (1957); and Harlow Shapley, in *Biographical Memoirs. National Academy of Sciences*, 32 (1958). See also Bancroft W. Sitterly, "Changing Interpretations of the Hertzsprung-Russell Diagram, 1910–1940" in *Vistas in Astronomy*, 12 (1970); R. Szafraniec, "Henry Norris Russell's Contributions to the Study of Eclipsing Variables," *ibid.*; and Bruce C. Cogan, "Henry Norris Russell," in *Dictionary of Scientific Biography*, XII (1975).]

DAVID H. DEVORKIN

SACK, ISRAEL (Sept. 15, 1883–May 4, 1959), antiques dealer, was born in Kaunas, Lithuania, the son of Abraham Zak, a businessman. To the dismay of his parents, Sack left school at the age of fourteen and became an apprentice to a cabinetmaker. Two years later he received a diploma. His plan to work in England was interrupted when he was conscripted into the Russian army; but he escaped to Germany and then went to England, where he was employed as a woodworker in London and Birmingham. He decided to move to the United States; and on Nov. 15, 1903, he arrived in Boston, where he became a cabinetmaker's assistant.

Two years later Sack opened his own business in Boston, at 85 Charles Street. He successfully studied his customers' tastes and knew immediately, for instance, if a person wanted Chippendale or Queen Anne. He also repaired furniture for dealers and collectors, and visited other antique scouts during off-hours. On Jan. 6, 1910, he married Ann Goodman; they had four children.

Sack's skill as a cabinetmaker helped him develop an eye for quality in American antiques. He thought that the best American antiques were made by the finest craftsmen for the colonists of the seventeenth and eighteenth centuries. "I have nothing against ordinary antiques—only they don't interest me," he said. He also found remarkable rarities and capitalized on the acquisitive mentality of the millionaire collector. When Charles Street was widened, the city of Boston paid Sack $30,000; he was thus able to enlarge his inventory and move next door to 89 Charles Street. By this move he enlarged his showrooms and thereby became the major retailer of antiques in Boston.

With the growing regard for American antiques as superb models of preindustrial craftsmanship, Sack played a major role during the 1920's. He influenced the public's taste in antiques and helped both private collectors and public institutions amass their collections.

As early as 1881, *House Beautiful* had noted that "In Boston a polite internecine warfare has for some time raged between rival searchers after 'old pieces,' and the back country is scoured by young couples in chaises on the trail of old sideboards and brass andirons." It is not surprising that Sack and H. Eugene Bolles, another collector, explored remote areas of New England in search of "loot"—antiques considered too obscure and humble for museum curators or American art and history students. After helping the New London, Conn., manufacturer George Shephard Palmer acquire a significant collection, Sack bought back the collection in 1928. About 1909 Bolles sold his collection of early colonial period antiques to Mrs. Russell Sage. She gave it to the Metropolitan Museum, where it became an important part of the new wing. With the opening of this American Wing in 1924, the legitimacy of collecting American antiques was established.

With his business flourishing in the 1920's, Sack established branch shops in Marblehead, Mass., New London, Conn., and New York City. In 1923 Henry Ford bought the Wayside Inn (built in 1684) at Sudbury, Mass., and asked Sack to furnish it. Thereafter Ford was one of Sack's most important clients, buying historical items such as Longfellow furniture and an early eighteenth-century highboy that had belonged to Mary Ball Washington. In 1928 Sack was commissioned by John D. Rockefeller, Jr., to acquire American and English antiques for the Colonial Williamsburg collections; this project lasted two years.

By 1931 the antiques business in general and Sack in particular had begun to feel the debilitating effects of the Great Depression. In order to avoid bankruptcy, he had to sell Sack Period Hardware (reproductions of brass hardware) and drastically reduce his stock of antiques. In 1934 he moved his business to New York City and turned its management over to his three sons. Thereafter he concentrated his attention on the liquidation of estates and the commission business.

During the next decade, attitudes toward collecting changed and interest in antiques became much more broadly based. Sack remained fairly active in the field as a scholar-dealer of the highest order until 1955. He believed that the passing of time and the changing of styles only add to our understanding of the beauty and significance of the arts of the past. Throughout his life Sack appreciated America's cultural heritage; on one of his last excursions he visited the replica of the Mayflower at Plymouth, Mass. Sack died in Brookline, Mass.

[See "A Statement for Buyers of Antiques," *Antiques*, Mar. 1934; Israel's Sack's foreword to Albert Sack, *Fine Points of Furniture: Early American* (1950); "The Reminiscences of Mr. Israel Sack," Ford Motor Company Archives, Oral History Section, Oct. 1953; the obituary notice, *New York Times*, May 5, 1959; "In Memoriam," *Antiques*, June 1959; Roger Butterfield, "Henry Ford, the Wayside Inn, and the Problem of 'History Is Bunk,' " *Proceedings of the Massachusetts Historical Society*, 1965; *American Antiques From the Israel Sack Collection*, 5 vols. (1969–1974); and Marshall B. Davidson, "Those American Things," *Metropolitan Musuem Journal*, 1970.]

WENDELL GARRETT

SAKEL, MANFRED JOSHUA (June 6, 1900–Dec. 2, 1957), psychiatrist, was born in the Jewish community of Nadvorna, Austria (now Nadvornaya, Ukraine), the son of Mayer Sakel and Judith Golde Friedman. Little is known of Sakel's early life, except that he graduated from the First State College of Brno, Czechoslovakia, in 1920 and the medical faculty of the University of Vienna, where he received the M.D., in 1925. He continued as an associate physician at the Vienna Hospital until 1927, when he became a fellow at the Urban Hospital in Berlin.

That year Sakel became psychiatrist in chief at the Lichterfelde Hospital in Berlin, which specialized in the abstinence treatment for morphinism. Noting a resemblance between the excitation seen in hyperthyroidism and that seen in

morphine withdrawal, Sakel concluded that "there must be an overstimulation of the sympathetic part of the vegetative nervous system." Around 1928, he began using insulin as a "vagotonic antagonist" to the observed "sympathotonic overactivity." In the process he found that accidentally induced hypoglycemic shock actually seemed beneficial to his patients. As he later explained, Sakel thought at the time that insulin "abolished the phenomena of irritation . . . because the nerve cells were blocked and their function quantitatively affected." Starting with this observation, he then began considering how "to influence other states of excitation by means of insulin."

After the Nazis seized power in Germany, Sakel returned to Vienna in 1933 as a refugee and went to work as a volunteer assistant at the Vienna Psychiatric and Neurological Clinic. Julius Wagner von Jauregg had a young female schizophrenic patient who had not responded after a year of treatment. Sakel suggested using full insulin shock treatment. After the second shock the girl seemed very coherent, and although she had a relapse after a few days, a few more insulin shock treatments led to a complete recovery. Results with a second patient confirmed their first impression, and Otto Pötzl, director of the clinic, offered Sakel facilities for large-scale investigations.

Sakel reported his initial findings to the Vienna Medical Society on Nov. 3, 1933. He outlined four "phases" of treatment: (1) the introductory phase, during which increasing doses of insulin are given and the patient's personal reaction is evaluated; (2) the shock phase, which consists of provoking severe hypoglycemic shocks culminating in coma or convulsion as a result of the insulin dosage; (3) the rest and observation phase, when small or medium doses of insulin are administered; (4) the polarization phase, when preshock (similar to the introductory phase) doses of insulin are administered. Sakel also noted that the "gravity of the disease [schizophrenia] and the hopelessness of expecting a cure from any known therapy has justified my use of an apparently dangerous treatment." It is to Sakel's credit that he not only introduced one of the first successful pharmacologic treatments for schizophrenia, but also went to great lengths to make the initially dangerous treatment safe. A serialized article on his hypoglycemic method appeared in the *Wiener medizinische Wochenschrift*, November 1934–February 1935 and as a monograph entitled *Neue Behandlungsmethode der Schizophrenie* (1935).

In 1936 Sakel came to the United States to treat a private patient and was subsequently invited by the New York state commissioner of mental hygiene to conduct a training course on insulin coma therapy for physicians in the state hospital system. Several others in the United States had experimented with the treatment prior to Sakel's visit, but the studies conducted in New York gave impetus to the spread of his method and optimism.

Around 1937 Sakel modified his theory of how insulin coma therapy worked; for while the "assumption that insulin diminished the activity of the nerve cell was sufficient explanation of the sedative effect on excited states," it "did not serve to explain the mental changes during and after hypoglycemia." Sakel now suggested that "the hypoglycemia blockades the [newer and more aberrant] pathways which happen to be most active at a given time, so that the reactions to the same stimuli now come through [older neural] pathways which had previously been inactive." A special supplement to the *Schweizer Archiv für Neurologie und Psychiatrie* (1937), republished as a supplement to the *American Journal of Psychiatry* (1938), along with a republication of Sakel's earlier monograph as *The Pharmacological Shock Treatment of Schizophrenia* (1938), did much to spread these new views.

Sakel refused academic posts, preferring private practice. A near-fatal heart attack in 1946 restricted his career, and his last two books, *Schizophrenia* (1958) and *Epilepsy* (1958), were both published posthumously.

Sakel never married, but his relationship with Mimi Englander lasted for almost thirty years. He died of a heart attack in New York City.

[There is no collection of Sakel's papers. His most important works are *The Pharmacological Shock Treatment of Schizophrenia* (1935), first published in German and translated by Joseph Wortis (1938); "New Treatment of Schizophrenia," *American Journal of Psychiatry*, 1937; "Methodical Use of Hypoglycemia in Treatment of Psychoses," *ibid.*, 1937; "On the Significance of the Epilptic Convulsion as a Therapeutic Factor in the Pharmacological Shock Therapy of Schizophrenia," *Journal of Nervous and Mental Diseases*, 1938; "Nature and Origin of Hypoglycemic Treatment of Psychoses," *American Journal of Psychiatry*, 1938; and *Schizophrenia* (1958).

On his life and work, see Hans Hoff, "History of the Organic Treatment of Schizophrenia," in Max Rinkel and Harold Himwich, eds., *Insulin Treatment in Psychiatry* (1959); Joseph Wortis, "The History of Insulin Shock Treatment," *ibid.*; and Wortis' tribute to Sakel, *American Journal of Psychiatry*, 1958.]

ROBERT CHARLES POWELL

SARTON, GEORGE ALFRED LÉON (Aug. 31, 1884–Mar. 22, 1956), historian of science, was born in Ghent, Belgium, the only child of Alfred Sarton and Léonie Van Halmé. His father was one of the chief engineers and directors of the Belgian State Railways. His mother died when he was only a few months old. An isolated child, surrounded by servants, George had a prosperous but lonely upbringing. He attended the University of Ghent, where his pursuit of philosophy was soon abandoned in favor of the natural sciences. He studied chemistry (for which he won a gold medal), crystallography, and then mathematics. His 1911 D.Sc. dissertation on "Les principes de la mécanique de Newton" provided an early indication of the direction his interests were taking under the philosophical influence of Auguste Comte, Henri Poincaré, and Paul Tannery.

Visits to London led Sarton to the systematic exploration of the works of H. G. Wells, George Bernard Shaw, and the Fabians, whose ideas he found in refreshing contrast to the doctrinaire Marxism that he and his friends youthfully espoused. He met Eleanor Mabel Elwes, the daughter of a Fabian, agnostic, mining engineer. They were married on June 22, 1911. The couple settled in Wondelgem, near Ghent; their one daughter, May, who became a well-known writer, was born in May 1912. At about this time Sarton made the bold decision to found *Isis*, his revue dedicated to the history of science. He quickly recruited a distinguished editorial board, including his idol Poincaré, Svante August Arrhenius, Émile Durkheim, and Friedrich Wilhelm Ostwald.

Sarton was culturally oriented toward universal history and those progressivist philosophies that found their basis in positive science and their end in the imminent brotherhood of man. Yet in his thinking he was indebted to Condorcet as well as to Comte. The lines of English thought that led from Herbert Spencer to the Webbs were also important to his vision of the goals to be served by that new synthesis of knowledge to which the history of science was the essential key. High theory and a vigorous consistency were less urgent to him than sustained, appropriate action. Thus, throughout his life Sarton enjoyed the role of propagandist. Other roles were more nearly central to his mission. With a discipline to be created, a world to be won, the provision of tools, techniques, methodologies, and intellectual orientations lay uppermost in his mind. A cognitive identity for his new discipline was the primary goal, and his own pattern of work was the self-exemplifying model of appropriate scholarship.

Sarton's developing plans were rudely interrupted by the 1914 German invasion of Belgium. An impoverished refugee, he fled to London with his family. Finding no English opportunities in the history of science, he sailed for the United States in 1915. His early days in the United States were frustrating and his support precarious, but he arrived just as the history of science was reaching maturity in the United States. Under the impact of war, this new field was to become linked with the vision of a "new humanism." Sarton quickly became an acknowledged spokesman for the new humanism and, by the 1930's, the emerging leader of its uneasy bedfellow, the history of science.

Due to the intercessions of several influential scientists, Sarton was made a research associate in the history of science at the Carnegie Institution of Washington, D.C., on July 1, 1918. Nonetheless he took up permanent residence in Cambridge, Mass. He gave an annual lecture course at Harvard University in exchange for accommodations in Widener Library. Secure, and with no specific duties other than those he fashioned for himself, Sarton was at last free to develop his mission. He continued to edit Isis (placed on a firm footing in 1924 as the official journal of the newly founded History of Science Society). He worked religiously on its continuing series of critical bibliographies, for which he wrote perhaps 100,000 brief analyses. He founded Osiris in 1936 as a monographic companion to Isis. He occupied named lectureships at universities from Rhode Island to California. He published numerous propagandist and occasional pieces. Above all Sarton labored at the massive Introduction to the History of Science, the first volume of which was published in 1927. The Introduction was to be a further means of establishing standards in a field always threatened by the casual and dilettante. It was to contain twenty-odd volumes, surveying the field chronologically, by civilization and by science. He had completed only three massive volumes in five parts, covering the chronological survey down to A.D. 1400, when he reluctantly laid down this task in 1948. Although officially retired from the Carnegie Institution in 1949 and from Harvard in 1951, Sarton continued to work until his death at his home in Cambridge.

Sarton epitomized the history of science to both European and American audiences. In the years after World War II, when a growing cluster of teaching positions in the discipline appeared in the United States, he automatically served as the central reference point. He was the continuing propagandist for and the ideal type of the historian of science as researcher, scholar, and teacher. The international and the intensely personal aspects of his achievement also won increasing recognition. Among other honors, he was elected to the American Philosophical Society (1934), made honorary president of the History of Science Society (1938–1956), belatedly awarded a Harvard professorship (1940), and made president of the International Union of History of Science (1950–1956).

Sarton's immediate influence in the postwar years was that of the catalyst rather than that of the reactant. He had only a limited intellectual impact on the discipline he did so much to create. The positivistic cast of his thought and his belief in progress and in the moral virtue of science were antithetical to the idealistic and relativistic currents so powerful in recent Western thought. His holistic concerns and his emphasis on historical approaches through biography and bibliography did not capture the imagination of younger scholars or provide a powerful technique of analysis around which a research school could form. Sarton's influence endures in other ways. In founding a journal, in emphasizing critical bibliography, and above all in writing the Introduction, he was creating instruments for others to employ, not a finished product. His presence at Harvard was crucial to the later creation and legitimation of a department that is one of the world's major centers of the discipline. The history of science is now firmly institutionalized. It was Sarton's particular gift both to create necessary building materials and to act as the first deliberate architect of this field in America.

[Somewhere between 20,000 and 30,000 letters of Sarton's correspondence are preserved and indexed in the Houghton Library of Harvard University. Other major deposits of letters may be found at the California Institute of Technology (George E. Hale papers), the Carnegie Institute of Washington, Columbia University (David E. Smith papers), and Stanford University (F. E. Brasch Collection). Much of his correspondence exists in other public and private archives. Sarton wrote 15 books, over 300 articles and notes, and produced 79 critical bibliographies of the history of science. A sampling of his various writings appears in Dorothy Stimson, ed., Sarton on the History of Science (1962). A complete bibliography of his publications, with essays by colleagues, pupils, and friends, is in the memorial issue of Isis, 49 (1957). See also his daughter's delightful "Sketches for an Autobiography," published in May Sarton, I Knew a Phoenix (1969). The most recent study of his work is Arnold Thackray and

Robert K. Merton, "On Discipline-Building: The Paradoxes of George Sarton," in *Isis*, 63 (1972). The History of Science Society 59th Anniversary Issue of *Isis*, Dec. 1975, also contains relevant material.]

ARNOLD THACKRAY
ROBERT K. MERTON

SCHWARTZ, MAURICE (June 15, 1889–May 10, 1960), actor, director, and producer, was born Avrom Moishe Schwartz in Sudilkov, Ukraine, Russia, the son of Isaac Schwartz and Rosa Berenholtz. He was raised in the Orthodox Jewish faith and was educated in Hebrew school. His father, a hay merchant, immigrated with his family to America in 1900. Because young Schwartz had grown too tall to get passage to America at half fare, he had to be left behind in England. He worked in London in a rag factory, lost his job, roamed the streets, and slept in the subway until his father had earned enough money to return to London and bring him to America in 1902. Schwartz attended the Baron De Hirsch School in New York City until, at fifteen, he went to work in his uncle's rag factory.

A growing interest in the Yiddish theater, then at its height, awoke his ambition to become an actor. This desire found an outlet at the Delancey Street Dramatic Club. Amateur appearances led him to neglect his work, and after a quarrel with his father he went with a small troupe of Yiddish actors to Bridgeport, Conn. The venture was short-lived but led to subsequent engagements in several cities. In Cincinnati, Schwartz received eight dollars a week and an extra dollar as stage manager, a job he liked because it taught him the technical side of production. He soon rose from this position to that of director. A subsequent engagement in Chicago attracted attention from the critic Sholem Perlmutter, and with his recommendation Schwartz was engaged in 1911 at David Kessler's Second Avenue Theater in New York City. He remained there for seven years, and during this period, on Aug. 14, 1914, he married Anna Bordofsky.

In 1918, when Kessler quarreled with his manager and left the theater, Schwartz reorganized the troupe, opening that fall at the Irving Place Theater. Jacob Ben Ami, an actor in his cast, had been part of the Vilna Troupe in Poland, a group of idealistic amateurs who, under the guidance of the poet I. L. Peretz, toured Poland and Russia, performing only Yiddish plays of literary merit. In 1910 the Vilna Troupe performed in New York, creating an extraordinary impression with its stylized production of S. Ansky's *The Dybbuk*. Schwartz had been deeply impressed by their work. Now, on Ben Ami's advice, he produced *The Lonely Inn* by Peretz Herschbein and *Love's Crooked Ways* by David Pinski—both performed by the Vilna Troupe but not yet produced in America. The plays were acclaimed by critics but had no popular success. When Schwartz went back to his earlier repertoire, Ben Ami, disappointed, left the cast and, with the help of a manufacturer, formed his own company, calling it the Yiddish Art Theater.

An important part of the Yiddish public had been driven from the theater by the flood of cheap musicals and melodramas that followed the decline of the "Golden Era"—a period dominated by the playwright Jacob Gordin. The new plays, poetic studies of rural life in Poland, brought back this more discriminating audience and gave the Yiddish theater new impetus and direction. A more ethnic concept of Jewish life began to replace the heroic image of the earlier period. Praised by critics and supported by Jewish cultural organizations, Ben Ami had a very great success. Schwartz realized his mistake, and in 1920, when Ben Ami left the Yiddish theater to star on Broadway, Schwartz stepped in and renamed the company Maurice Schwartz's Yiddish Art Theater. Although it was Ben Ami who conceived of an art theater movement in America, it was Schwartz's personal force and organizational talent that carried it into the future.

During the next forty years Schwartz acted in and directed more than 150 plays, none of them claptrap musicals or melodramas. The repertoire included Yiddish translations of classics by Tolstoy, Ibsen, Strindberg, Schnitzler, Chekhov, Gogol, Molière, Shaw, and Lope de Vega, as well as studies of Jewish life by Sholem Aleichem, Sholem Asch, Osip Dymov, Moishe Nadir, Fishel Bimko, and Leon Kobrin. The Yiddish Art Theater toured the United States, Europe, South America, Canada, Mexico, and Israel, and fostered such talents as Paul Muni, Celia Adler, Joseph Buloff, Lazar Fried, Samuel Goldenberg, and Joseph Schoengold. In 1923, feeling the decline of Yiddish was eroding an audience no longer fed by masses of newly arrived immigrants, Schwartz produced and appeared in Leonid Andreev's *Anathema* in English on Broadway. This effort failed, and while he often thought of forming an Anglo-Jewish theater, his plans never materialized.

As an actor Schwartz had outstanding size and authority, and his presence on the stage was always powerful. He was at his greatest in comedy, and in certain Sholem Aleichem portraits he reached heights that remain unsurpassed. As a director his effects were often stylized and always impressive. He was both ambitious and innovative in this regard. In 1926 he opened the season in a new theater at Second Avenue and Twelfth Street called the Yiddish Art Theater with Wolf Goldfaden's *The Tenth Commandment*. The sets were by Boris Aronson and the choreography by Michael Fokine. Schwartz's production of I. J. Singer's mystic *Yoshe Kalb* (1932) won wide acclaim, and the play remained in his repertoire for thirty years. It was produced in a Hebrew translation in Israel and in Spanish in Argentina.

Supported by his niece, Miriam Riesel, Schwartz starred in the Yiddish film *Tevye* (1939), based on the Sholem Aleichem play. He later appeared in *Bird of Paradise* (1951) and in *Salome* (1953), starring Rita Hayworth. In 1947, during a tour of DP camps in Belgium, Schwartz and his wife adopted two Polish war orphans.

Schwartz died in Tel Aviv while making a theatrical tour of Israel. His body was brought back to the United States by the Yiddish Theatrical Alliance, and he was buried in the Mount Hebron Cemetery in New York City, resting place of many great figures of the Yiddish theater.

[Zalmen Zylbercweig, *Leksikon fun yidishn teater*, III (1958), in Yiddish, has a complete list of Schwartz's productions and details of his early life. See also *Who's Who in American Jewry*, III (1938), and IV (1955); and *Who's Who in the Theatre*, 12th ed. (1957). Documents, photographs, and letters concerning Schwartz are at the Institute for Jewish Research (YIVO), New York City. Lulla Rosenfeld, *Bright Star of Exile* (1977), contains autobiographical and critical material. The first chapter of Schwartz's autobiography, "Maurice Schwartz Relates," appeared in Yiddish in the *Jewish Daily Forward*, Nov. 22, 1941, and thereafter each Saturday and Wednesday for several months. See also J. Brooks Atkinson, "The Play," *New York Times*, Sept. 24, 1931; "The New Play," *ibid.*, Sept. 10, 1947; and "Yiddish Plays," *Variety*, Oct. 10, 1947.]

LULLA ROSENFELD

SCOTT, EMMETT JAY (Feb. 13, 1873–Dec. 12, 1957), educator and publicist, was born in Houston, Tex., the son of Horace Lacy Scott, a civil servant, and Emma Kyle. He graduated from the Colored High School in Houston at the age of fourteen, and was persuaded to go to Wiley University—a small Methodist school in Marshall, Tex.—by Reverend (later Bishop) Isaiah B. Scott, pastor of a Methodist church in Marshall and formerly a minister in Houston.

To help pay his expenses, Scott carried mail from the post office in Marshall to the campus, a mile away. Summers he worked in Houston. Returning to Marshall too late in 1889 to get his mail job, he chopped wood and fed the school hogs. Later he was a bookkeeper in the president's office. In 1890, after three years at Wiley, Scott's formal education ended.

Scott worked as a janitor in a Houston office building in 1890 and the next year became assistant janitor and messenger for the *Houston Post*. Executives noted his talents and assigned him increasing responsibilities. Once, when no reporter could be spared to cover commencement exercises at a black college, the editor sent Scott, who returned with a story worthy of a veteran reporter. In 1894, while a reporter on the *Post*, he also became associate editor of a new black newspaper in Houston, the *Texas Freeman*, soon taking over as editor. This newspaper became one of the most influential black journals in the Southwest.

Scott hitched his paper to the star of the leading black politician in the state, Norris Cuney. When Cuney retired, Scott sought another leader. His new "sun" was Booker T. Washington, founder of Tuskegee Institute. Washington's "Atlanta Compromise" speech of 1895 counseled blacks to stop agitating for rights in return for job opportunities. Some blacks disliked this bargain, but Scott wrote editorials praising the speech and also began a column of Tuskegee news; both moves caught Washington's eye. In 1897, Scott invited Washington to speak in Houston, hiring the largest hall and arranging a big turnout. Soon thereafter Washington hired Scott as his private secretary. Scott abandoned his newspaper work and moved to Tuskegee in September 1897. On Apr. 14, 1897, he had married Eleonora Juanita Baker, daughter of a newspaper editor; they had five children.

From 1897 to 1915, Scott was Washington's closest confidant and adviser. The two meshed so well that it is difficult to tell which of them composed some letters. Scott played a major role in the intrigues by which Washington dominated black organizations and media. He was chief architect of what Washington's arch rival, W. E. B. Du Bois, called the "Tuskegee Machine." Ironically, Washington and Scott took an idea of Du Bois's, and created the National Negro Business League (1900). Washington was president, but the league was actually administered by Scott, who was secretary from 1900 to 1922.

Working with Washington, Scott became increasingly well known. In 1905 the two wrote *Tuskegee and Its People.* Four years later President William Howard Taft appointed Scott to the American Commission to Liberia. Scott wrote a pamphlet and articles on his findings. In 1912 he was secretary of the International Conference on the Negro held at Tuskegee. After Washington's death in 1915, Scott continued as secretary of Tuskegee Institute, a post he had held since 1912. (Significantly, Robert R. Moton of Hampton Institute, not Scott, became president of Tuskegee.) In 1916, Scott and Lyman Beecher Stowe wrote a panegyric, *Booker T. Washington.* Most of Washington's followers, Scott included, were reconciled with Du Bois and his National Association for the Advancement of Colored People at the Amenia Conference that year.

Scott served from 1917 to 1919 as special assistant to Secretary of War Newton D. Baker, advising him on black soldiers and civilians. *Scott's Official History of the American Negro in the World War* (1919) resulted. *Negro Migration During the War* (1920) was done for the Carnegie Endowment for International Peace.

After the war Scott remained in Washington, where he became secretary-treasurer and business manager of Howard University in July 1919. At Howard, though, Scott did not find another star to follow; rather, he clashed with President Mordecai Johnson, who launched an attack on Scott in 1931 and reduced him to secretary of the university in 1933. But Scott, a small, light-skinned, impeccably attired man with delicate features and pince-nez glasses whom colleagues characterized as suave, skillfully withstood Johnson's further onslaughts and remained until his retirement in 1938. He had entered politics on an advisory committee for the 1924 Republican convention. He served on the public relations staff, as a specialist on blacks, for every Republican national convention from 1928 through 1948.

From 1939 to 1942, Scott was assistant publicity director of the Republican National Committee. He also advised the Republican national chairman on racial matters. During World War II, Scott was director of employment and personnel relations for Shipyard No. 4 of the Sun Ship Co. in Chester, Pa. (1942–1945). He also served from the 1920's to 1940's on civic groups,

including the national bodies of the Methodist home missions, the Young Men's Christian Association, the Southern Education Foundation, and the Federal Council of Churches. He died in Washington, D.C.

[The Emmett Jay Scott Papers are in the Morris A. Soper Library of Morgan State College, Baltimore. A great many Scott materials are in the Booker T. Washington Papers in the Library of Congress. See also unsigned editorial, "Making Good: From Obscurity to International Fame," *Southwestern Christian Advocate,* July 12, 1917; August Meier, *Negro Thought in America, 1880–1915* (1966); Rayford W. Logan, *Howard University* (1969); and Louis R. Harlan, *Booker T. Washington* (1972). Obituaries include the *Afro-American* (national ed.), Dec. 21, 1957; *Atlanta Daily World* and *Washington Post,* Dec. 13, 1957; and *New York Times,* Dec. 14, 1957.]

EDGAR ALLAN TOPPIN

SCOTT, W(ILLIAM) KERR (Apr. 17, 1896–Apr. 16, 1958), governor of North Carolina and United States senator, was born in Haw River, N.C., one of fourteen children of Robert Walter Scott and Elizabeth Hughes. In 1913 he graduated from public high school in Hawfields and entered North Carolina State College of Agriculture and Mechanic Arts at Raleigh (now part of North Carolina State University), where he received the B.S. degree in agriculture in 1917.

Shortly thereafter Scott volunteered for service in World War I as a private in the field artillery. Upon his discharge in 1918, he purchased a farm in Hawfields. He also acquired and operated the dairy farm that had been in his family since the mid-eighteenth century.

Scott had a Jeffersonian reverence for the land and was a believer in "moral agrarianism," the view that agriculture is more than a vocation, and that its preservation and prosperity are of fundamental importance to the stability of American society and the maintenance of democracy. He became known as "the Squire of Haw River," and his most dependable political supporters were rural North Carolinians whom he called "the branch-head boys." On July 2, 1919, he married his boyhood sweetheart, Mary Elizabeth White; they had three children.

Scott's services to agriculture included a year as an emergency food production agent of the Department of Agriculture. Alamance County employed him as farm agent from 1920 to 1930, and the North Carolina State Grange hired him as master from 1930 to 1933. In 1934 he became a regional director of the farm debt adjustment program of the Resettlement Administration.

In 1936 Scott was chosen state commissioner of agriculture; he was reelected to the post in 1940 and 1944. As commissioner he fought for soil conservation and improvement, reforestation, better roads, better health-care facilities, better schools and expansion of educational opportunities, eradication of animal diseases, rural electrification, and rural telephone lines. He was also chairman of the Tobacco Advisory Board, a member of the National Advisory Committee of Agricultural Research and Marketing, a member of the Special United States Commission to Mexico for Study of Hoof and Mouth Disease (1947), and president of the National Association of Commissioners, Secretaries, and Directors of Agriculture. For his many contributions to agriculture, *Progressive Farmer* named him "Man of the Year" in 1937; and in 1950 the North Carolina State Grange bestowed a similar honor.

In February 1948, Scott resigned his post as state commissioner of agriculture to seek the Democratic nomination for governor. He was nominated, and was elected in November 1948, serving from January 1949 to January 1953. Because of his rural background and his being the first nonlawyer to occupy the governorship in forty-eight years, he was considered a populist championing the rights of the people against special interests. He quickly initiated a politically liberal program designed especially to benefit those who had been shortchanged in the past. Highways were built and improved—half of them rural roads known colloquially as "Scott roads"; massive school construction programs were accomplished; health-care institutions were modernized and increased; ocean port facilities were completed; and rural electric and telephone services were expanded. (Scott also unsuccessfully attempted to have the closed-shop law repealed.) "He had the understanding of all men," said Senator Lyndon Baines Johnson of Texas regarding Scott's gubernatorial record, "whether they worked on the land in their overalls, in the factories, or in their blue serges in the counting houses."

Scott's national reputation as a southern liberal was enhanced by his rejection of the Dixiecrats and his support of President Harry S. Truman in 1948. In March 1949 he appointed a liberal Democrat, Frank P. Graham, president of the University of North Carolina, to fill a vacancy in the United States Senate. In 1952 he supported Adlai Stevenson for the Democratic presidential nomination. In the explosive area of race relations, Scott was a "liberal with the brakes on." Although a mild segregationist, he named the first black, H. L. Trigg, to the state board of education. In 1951 he instituted administrative reforms to equalize pay scales for black and white workers in state mental hospitals, and restricted a Ku Klux Klan membership drive in North Carolina. Scott also named the first woman to the State Superior Court and appointed a leader of the CIO to the state welfare board.

In 1954 Scott was elected to the United States Senate, running on a platform to reduce unemployment, to increase farm prices, and to destroy that "un-American thing that has come to be known the world over as 'McCarthyism.'" In the Senate he was a liberal on domestic issues and a cold warrior in the international arena. Unlike most freshman senators Scott was outspoken. He proposed a world food bank; he advocated equal rights for women; he introduced a resolution calling for a research program to ascertain whether smoking is a factor in lung cancer; he questioned the return by the Interior Department of public lands in Oregon to private timber and mining interests (the Al Serena case). He also called for another Franklin D. Roosevelt to "provide us with a leader who is bold, who is decisive, and who has imagination," to solve the problems of the space age and restore American prestige in the world. He died in Burlington, N.C.

[Brief accounts of Scott's life are found in *Congressional Record*, 85th Cong., 2, Sess., 15902–15936; and *New York Times*, May 30, 1954, and Apr. 17, 1958. See also *Congressional Record*, 85th Cong., 2 Sess., 3325, A-537, A-3656; V. O. Key, Jr., *Southern Politics in State and Nation* (1949); Hugh Talmage Lefler and Albert Ray Newsome, *The History of a Southern State: North Carolina* (1954); *Newsweek*, Apr. 28, 1958; *New York Times*, Jan. 4, 1955, and Apr. 19, 1958; Robert S. Rankin, *The Government and Administration of North Carolina* (1955); and *Time*, Apr. 28, 1958.]

RONALD A. MULDER

SEABURY, SAMUEL (Feb. 22, 1873–May 7, 1958), lawyer, jurist, and special anticorruption investigator and counsel, was born in New York City, the son of William Jones Seabury and Alice Van Wyck Beare. He was the namesake of his great-great-grandfather, the first Episcopal bishop in the United States, who was ordained by the Church of England and was named bishop in Connecticut in 1783. On his mother's side, he was a descendant of New England's governing Saltonstalls as well as the seafaring Beares. His father, William Jones Seabury, was rector of the Church of the Annunciation and professor of canon law at General Theological Seminary in New York City. The church family, of modest circumstances, provided great social recognition and background but minimal financial aid. Samuel Seabury's formal education began at a small private school in the Chelsea area, Wilson and Kellogg School, from which he graduated in 1890. He then clerked in the law office of Stephen P. Nash until he had enough funds to enter New York Law School. He graduated in June 1893 and was admitted to the New York bar on Mar. 16, 1894. He opened his own law office, and that same year he published his first law work, *Law Syllabus on Corporation Law*, a small pamphlet for law students.

Seabury was much influenced by Henry George's *Progress and Poverty*, and he visited the reformer at his Brooklyn home. Thereafter, he joined the Manhattan Single-Tax Club in 1894 and also became active in the Good-Government Club. In 1897 he was elected president of the Manhattan Single-Tax Club, devoting much time to the reform movement in politics and, at the same time, representing small-fee clients in criminal and civil courts. He ran on the Independent Labor ticket for the city court bench in 1899, with Republican backing, but lost to the dominant Democratic machine—the first of his anti-Tammany efforts. On June 6, 1900, he married Josephine Maud Richey; they had no children.

Supported by labor unions, single-taxers, and other reform groups, Seabury was elected a judge of the city court of New York as a candidate of the Citizens Union party. He was sworn in on New Year's Day, 1902, and became the youngest judge in New York. On the bench he remained politically active, taking a leadership role in the Municipal Ownership League and devoting himself to a favorite cause: public ownership of utilities and, especially, of the city's transit system. While on the city court, he wrote the booklet *Municipal Ownership and Operation of Public Utilities in New York City*.

In 1907 Seabury was sworn in as a justice of the state supreme court of New York, where he gained a reputation as a liberal. In the fall of 1913 the Progressive party nominated him for the state's highest court, the Court of Appeals, but he was defeated. The following year, backed by the Democrats, he became a member of the Court of Appeals, the only Progressive elected to the high bench. He continued to speak out on public issues, strongly supporting President Woodrow Wilson's nomination of Louis D. Brandeis for the U.S. Supreme Court. He resigned from the Court of Appeals upon receiving the Democratic nomination for governor in 1916. He aligned his state campaign with Wilson, but he was defeated because of the lack of support by Theodore Roosevelt's Progressives and Tammany Hall.

Seabury then returned to private practice but continued to be politically active during the 1920's and early 1930's. In 1928 he supported Alfred E. Smith for president. Then, in the summer of 1930, he was appointed referee to conduct an investigation of the magistrates' courts of New York City. The appointment had come after consultation with Governor Franklin D. Roosevelt. Thus began one of the greatest investigations of municipal corruption in the United States.

Under Mayor James J. Walker, Tammany corruption flourished. Judgeships were bought and sold; franchises to do business in the city involved political payments. In the course of the investigation, which took place in 1930–1931, Judge Seabury (as he was generally called) exposed payoffs and court fixing and the hold of political leaders on the bench. In the midst of this investigation Roosevelt appointed him commissioner to inquire into the conduct of the district attorney's office in New York County, again enabling him to show the workings of the corrupt criminal justice system. In the fall of 1931 the Joint Legislative Committee to Investigate the Affairs of the City of New York was formed, with Seabury as counsel. This led to a citywide investigation of the sheriffs and other bureaus and pockets of corruption. In the course of his cross-examination of Sheriff Thomas M. Farley of New York County, a new phrase was introduced into the political vocabulary: "little tin box." Sheriff Farley had one where money magically appeared. Finally, Judge Seabury confronted Mayor Walker himself on May 23, 1932. While the Mayor put on a good show, he was unable to explain the sources of his outside wealth, including nearly a quarter of a million dollars in a secret brokerage account. Walker was forced to resign, a stunning victory for Seabury against an official and Tammany Hall.

Thereafter, Seabury was instrumental in the election of Fiorello H. La Guardia as mayor. He remained a close adviser to the "fusion mayor" for three terms. He resumed his lucrative legal practice but continued to speak out on national and international issues. As president of the Association of the Bar of the City of New York (1939–1941), he advocated stricter legal ethics and created a new committee on national defense. His wife died in 1950, and his last years were marked by increased senility. His great achievement was the investigations that in municipal history bear his name.

[A full-length biography is Herbert Mitgang, *The Man Who Rode the Tiger: The Life and Times of Judge Samuel Seabury* (1963). See also Walter Chambers, *Samuel Seabury: A Challenge* (1932); William B. Northrop and John B. Northrop, *The Insolence of Office: The Story of the Seabury Investigations* (1932); and official Seabury Investigation Reports and Minutes of Public Hearings, 1930–1932. Many reminiscences in the Columbia University Oral History Collection have references to Seabury.]

HERBERT MITGANG

SEDGWICK, ELLERY (Feb. 27, 1872–Apr. 21, 1960), magazine editor and publisher, was born in New York City, the son of Henry Dwight Sedgwick, a lawyer, and Henrietta Ellery. At an early age he was sent to a private boarding school, where he was very unhappy. "I was an untalented boy," he later wrote, "biddable, reasonably unattractive, and most content when unnoticed." Sedgwick later attended the Groton School, where he was less dissatisfied and where he taught Latin and English in 1894–1896, after graduation from Harvard with the A.B. (1894). He next worked briefly as a reporter for the *Worcester* (Mass.) *Gazette* and in 1896 became an assistant editor of the *Youth's Companion*, beginning an editorial career that continued for more than forty years. In 1899, Sedgwick wrote a brief popular biography of Thomas Paine for Beacon Biographies, a series edited by Mark Antony De Wolfe Howe.

In 1900, Sedgwick went to *Leslie's Monthly* as editor. It was a "rickety periodical," Sedgwick said, "wedged in the ruck among also-rans, . . . without capital, without character, depending for its very life on an occasional hit." Although he did not consider himself a muckraker, Sedgwick looked for themes that would be "constructive" and popular. In 1903 he found one, the problem of railroad accidents. To Sedgwick and his

magazine, historian Louis Filler said, must go credit for a campaign that did much to bring government regulation of railroads. Although Sedgwick sometimes ran an appreciative article about a railroad executive, he often pointed to and deplored the injury and death rate among rail passengers and persuaded *Leslie's* readers to place the blame where he thought it belonged: on the railroad management.

On Sept. 23, 1904, Sedgwick married Mabel Cabot; they had five children. Mabel Sedgwick died in 1937. On May 1, 1939, Sedgwick married Isabel Marjorie Russell. They had no children.

While he was editor of *Leslie's*, Sedgwick was so pleased with an article by a young writer named H. L. Mencken that, in 1901, he offered him a job as an associate editor. Mencken declined, but a friendship between the two resulted. When Mencken started the *American Mercury* in 1923, he wrote to Sedgwick for advice. "Don't over-edit," Sedgwick said, "by doing so you will estrange your writers and rob the magazine of indispensable variety."

In 1906, Sedgwick left the *American Magazine* (it had recently succeeded *Leslie's*), worked for a year on *McClure's Magazine* and, briefly, for D. Appleton and Company as a book editor. In 1908 he was able to fulfill a lifelong ambition by arranging to buy, for $50,000, the venerable but ailing *Atlantic Monthly*. It had a circulation of only 15,000 copies a month, and its annual deficit was $5,000.

Within three years Sedgwick had the *Atlantic* in greatly improved financial condition. He early hit upon a successful editorial formula, based on his flair for social criticism and his awareness of political and economic changes in American life. Frederick Lewis Allen, a former editorial associate, described Sedgwick as an "odd mixture of primness, practicality, and wide-ranging enthusiasm," and said his method of editing was simple: "He keeps a sharp lookout for promising material among incoming manuscripts, never forgetting that even in an unpromising manuscript there may be the germ of a valuable feature." In 1922 the *New York Times Book Review* (Jan. 15) observed that the *Atlantic* "is not the staid magazine that refreshed our grandfathers. It has grown lively during recent years; it has moved with the times."

Sedgwick was the first American editor to publish a short story by Ernest Hemingway—"Fifty Grand" (July 1927)—and he frequently printed what he called "human documents"—personal confessions and firsthand accounts of adventures. He published the writing of Randolph Bourne, a voice of the new radical generation, as well as the radical prophecies of H. G. Wells. In 1926 he attacked Wall Street practices with penetrating articles by Harvard economist William Z. Ripley, and in March 1927 he attracted many readers by publishing Felix Frankfurter's discussion of the Sacco-Vanzetti trial. The following month, before the nomination of Alfred E. Smith for the presidency, Sedgwick printed an article by Charles C. Marshall, a New York lawyer, on the disabilities that Smith's opponents believed his Catholic faith imposed upon him. In reply Smith wrote a spirited affirmation, "Catholic and Patriot" (May 1927). By 1928 the circulation of the *Atlantic* had reached 137,000 a month.

Sedgwick discovered numerous writers, but he was an enthusiast and on a few occasions was taken in by those whose talent and authenticity were less impressive than he judged. For instance, "The Diary of Opal Whitely," the work of a young woman who claimed to be the daughter of Prince Henry of Orleans, was accepted as genuine by Sedgwick though serious doubts were later raised. Sedgwick printed a number of Robert Frost's poems, but the poet recalled a rejection note from the editor that read, "We are very sorry but at the moment the *Atlantic* has no place for vigorous verse."

In 1938, after thirty years as editor, Sedgwick resigned. He insisted the resignation was in no way related to two articles he had written that February for the *New York Times*, praising General Francisco Franco's regime in Spain and terming the conditions he found there "normal." The articles brought strong letters of protest to the *Times*, one signed by 63 members of the League of American Writers and one signed by more than 100 educators. The articles also caused the only sharp and prolonged disagreement on his own staff during his editorship. Sedgwick, who was occasionally irascible, always ran a tight ship and did not delegate editorial responsibilities often or easily.

In 1939, Sedgwick sold his controlling interest in the *Atlantic* for a sum of cash said to be the largest in the history of magazines until that time. In retirement he composed his memoirs, *The Happy Profession* (1946), in which he related anecdotes about his life and generously celebrated the accomplishments of friends and people with whom he had worked. A smoothly flowing narrative, the book was seasoned with wit and urbane comment. In *Atlantic Harvest* (1947) Sedgwick

put together an anthology of nearly fifty stories and articles by as many writers. The pieces included literary, scientific, and philosophical essays, as well as plays and short stories. He contributed a long introduction in which he discussed, in a relaxed, well-bred style, his performance as editor and compiler.

Sedgwick was short, thickset, and heavy-featured, and he had a taste for garishly checked suits and shirts of strange colors. He usually voted for Democratic candidates in national elections. In his later years he lived at his large estate in Beverly, Mass., but spent the winter in Washington, D.C., where he died.

[Sedgwick's papers, including his *Atlantic* correspondence and his personal letters, are at the Massachusetts Historical Society, Boston. An informative biographical-critical article is Frederick Lewis Allen, "Sedgwick and the *Atlantic*," *Outlook and Independent*, Dec. 26, 1928. See also Isaac Goldberg, *The Man Mencken* (1925); Leon Whipple, "The Revolution on Quality Street," *Survey*, Nov. 1, 1926; Frank Luther Mott, *A History of American Magazines, 1850–1865* (1938); Louis Filler, *Crusaders for American Liberalism* (1939); Guy J. Forgue, ed., *Letters of H. L. Mencken* (1961); and Gerald Gross, ed., *Editors on Editing* (1962). Obituaries are in *New York Times*, and *Boston Daily Globe*, Apr. 22, 1960; *Time*, May 2, 1960; and *Atlantic*, June 1960.]

WILLIAM McGANN

SENNETT, MACK (Jan. 17, 1880–Nov. 5, 1960), motion picture director, producer, and actor, was born Michael Sinnott in Richmond, Quebec, Canada, the son of John Sinnott and Catherine Foy, who operated a farm and small hotel in rural Quebec. Of Irish-Catholic heritage, Sennett lived a middle-class existence, attending various rural schools until he was seventeen, when the family moved to East Berlin, Conn. A poor student whose failure to master grammar and writing skills were to prove a lifelong handicap, Sennett went to work as an ironworker. A year later, the Sinnotts moved to Northampton, Mass., where the family lawyer, Calvin Coolidge, arranged for Mack to meet Marie Dressler, a Canadian actress who encouraged his ambition to become an actor.

After moving to New York City, Sennett landed minor roles in several notable musicals, including *A Chinese Honeymoon, Wang,* (1904), *Piff! Paff!! Pouff!!!* (1904), and *The Boys of Company B* (1907), a drama starring John Barrymore. But for nearly a decade leading stage roles eluded him. On his twenty-eighth birthday he joined the Biograph film company as an actor. From roles as a walk-on and extra he graduated to supporting parts and scenario writing in 1909, moved to leading roles in 1910, and became a director with *Comrades*, a one-reel film produced in March 1911. During that year, he formed the nucleus of a comedy stock company, enlisted the services of Henry Lehrman, Fred Mace, Mabel Normand, and Ford Sterling.

Although his Biograph comedies were popular with nickelodeon audiences, he and the company could not agree on a comic approach. Sennett therefore left Biograph in 1912 to form the Keystone Film Company in partnership with Adam Kessel and Charles Baumann, taking his small stock company with him. The first Keystone Comedies appeared in theaters in September 1912, and proved an immediate hit, quickly becoming the industry standard by which all other comedies were judged.

While motion picture comedy had existed for more than a decade before Keystone came into existence, its development had been a slow and tortuous process. Sennett alone seemed to have an innate understanding of what audiences of 1912 found funny. Combining a wide variety of techniques first used by others (especially the French), he evolved a purely American version of slapstick comedy by adding a touch of burlesque, comic improvisation, and a cutting technique known as "Keystone editing," in which every third or fourth frame of film was removed to speed up the action and movement.

By 1915, when Sennett moved release of his Keystone Comedies from Mutual to Triangle, he had developed the comic talents of Roscoe ("Fatty") Arbuckle, Chester Conklin, Al St. John, Mack Swain, and many others, yet had been completely frustrated by Charles Chaplin, whom he did not find humorous. In the process, his farcical comedies spawned a legion of imitators, and Sennett himself was referred to as "the king of comedy," an epithet he did nothing to discourage.

At Triangle, his comedies became longer and more sophisticated, containing more plot and characterization while taking on a more leisurely pacing. The Bathing Beauties joined his Keystone Kops as comic props, and talents such as those of Gloria Swanson, Phyllis Haver, and Bobby Vernon came to the fore. With the financial collapse of Triangle imminent in 1917, Sennett formed his own company to release through Paramount (1917–1919) and Associated First National (1920–1921) before contracting in

1923 with Pathé, where he made many of the best screen satires and parodies of the 1920's, using the gifts of Billy Bevan, Andy Clyde, Harry Langdon, and Ben Turpin.

Since audience tastes had become more sophisticated, Sennett's Pathé Comedies differed considerably from the frantic farces of Keystone and Triangle. Moving closer to the drawing room comedy styles of Al Christie and Hal Roach, his closest competitors, he relied upon fast-moving backgrounds, slow-moving mechanical gags, and many camera tricks to elicit laughter instead of the violent, bone-crushing indignities that his Keystone-Triangle Comedies had imposed upon their participants.

Although not his most inventive period, in the 1920's Sennett achieved his greatest financial success, despite a contraction of the short-subject market toward the end of the decade. When internal problems paralyzed Pathé in 1928, he began releasing talking comedies through Educational in 1929, utilizing the talents of W. C. Fields and Bing Crosby.

However, with the bankruptcy of Paramount-Publix, Sennett lost an estimated $15 million and retired from active participation in the industry in 1935. In 1938, the Academy of Motion Picture Arts and Sciences presented him with a special award for his contributions to screen comedy. Sennett spent the remainder of his life quietly, living at the Garden Court Apartments on Hollywood Boulevard until his death.

[Warm in its admiration and rich in colorful fabrications, Gene Fowler, *Father Goose* (1934), was the first full-length biography. Sennett's autobiography, *King of Comedy* (1954), written with Cameron Shipp, is a fascinating account of early Hollywood but contains many fabrications presented as fact, and its chronology is confused. Davide Turconi, *Mack Sennett*, in Italian (1961), and in French (1966), includes a filmography but still awaits an English translation. Ezra Goodman, *The Fifty-Year Decline and Fall of Hollywood* (1961), depicts Sennett in retirement. Kalton C. Lahue, *World of Laughter* (1966); *Kops and Custards* (1967), written with Terry Brewer; *Dreams for Sale* (1971); and *Mack Sennett's Keystone* (1971) are the most serious attempts to date to delve into the Keystone legend and the man who created it.

The Academy of Motion Picture Arts and Sciences' collection of Sennett's scripts, photographs, and correspondence remains closed to the public. The Aitken Collection, Wisconsin State Historical Society, Madison, contains photographs and business materials dealing with Keystone and Triangle.]

KALTON C. LAHUE

SERVICE, ROBERT WILLIAM (Jan. 16, 1874–Sept. 11, 1958), poet, was born in Preston, Lancashire, England, the son of Robert Service, a Scottish bank teller, and of Emily Parker, daughter of an owner of cotton mills. When Service was six, the family moved to Glasgow, Scotland, where he graduated from Hillhead High School. He attended a few university classes but left after a row with a professor. He then became an apprentice in the Commercial Bank of Scotland.

Finding banking too dull and confining, and having had his wanderlust roused by voracious reading, Service traveled to Canada on a tramp freighter in 1895 and made his way to British Columbia. Shortly thereafter his traveling brought him to Los Angeles, Calif., then a rough, young, brawling town. For the next several years Service wandered up and down the Pacific coast of the United States. To sustain his vagabond life-style he worked at various times as a logger, dishwasher, teacher, bank clerk, ranch hand, fruit picker, and even as a gardener for a bordello in San Diego.

Returning to Canada in 1901, Service took a steady position in Victoria, B.C., as a teller with the Canadian Bank of Commerce. The bank transferred him to Kamloops, B.C., then to Whitehorse and Dawson in the Yukon Territory. The experience led to his adventurous immersion in the ebullient, rough-and-ready frontier life that was the subject and setting of his most successful verse. After two years in Dawson, Service resigned his position but remained for seven years doing free-lance writing. During this time he observed the decline of the Klondike and Yukon gold rush and began to write the rhymes that made his fame and fortune.

Service's first book of verse was published (1907) in New York as *The Spell of the Yukon* and in Toronto as *Songs of a Sourdough*. Containing his two most popular poems, "The Shooting of Dan McGrew" and "The Cremation of Sam McGee," the book was a sensational success. The opening lines of "Dan McGrew" made Service perhaps the most popular household poet of his time in both America and Canada:

A bunch of boys were whoopin it up in the Malamute saloon; The kid that handles the music box was hitting a jag-time tune;
Back of the bar, in a solo game, sat Dangerous Dan McGrew,
And watching his luck was his light-o'-love, the lady that's known as Lou.

The book sold more than a million copies almost overnight. A sequel, *Ballads of a Cheechako* (1909), was nearly as successful; "sourdough" and "cheechako" became popular household words for "prospector" and "newcomer." Two more books appeared while Service remained in the Yukon: *The Trail of '98* (1910), an unsuccessful novel, and *Rhymes of a Rolling Stone* (1912), another success that returned to the vibrant mode of his first book.

In 1912, Service left the Yukon for good. After a brief stint as a correspondent reporting the war in the Balkans for the *Toronto Star*, he settled in France in 1913. That same year he married Germaine Bourgoin, a well-to-do Parisian; they had one daughter. Service bought a home in the coastal town of Lancieux, Brittany, that became his principal residence. He also maintained homes in Nice and Monte Carlo in later life. Despite his lengthy residence in France, his Canadian exploits, and the popular vision of him as an American rhymer, Service remained a British citizen throughout his life.

After he left the Yukon, Service continued to write with moderate success. During World War I he served as an ambulance driver with the American Red Cross, and later as an officer with an intelligence unit of the Canadian army. His Red Cross exploits resulted in a highly popular book of verses, *Rhymes of a Red Cross Man* (1916). But Service's later literary efforts failed to achieve much success. Nevertheless, he continued to write until his death. He produced several melodramatic novels, among them *The Poisoned Paradise* (1922), *The Roughneck* (1923), and *The House of Fear* (1927). He also wrote a health book, *Why Not Grow Young?* (1928), advocating a vegetarian diet, and two very anecdotal autobiographies, *Ploughman of the Moon* (1945) and *Harper of Heaven* (1948). None of these captured the popular fancy. After spending World War II in Hollywood, Calif., Service returned to France, where he published books of verse that included *Songs of a Sun-Lover* (1949), *Rhymes of a Roughneck* (1950), *Lyrics of a Low Brow* (1951), *Rhymes of a Rebel* (1952), *Carols of an Old Codger* (1954), and *Rhymes for My Rags* (1956). He died at his home in Lancieux.

For at least twenty years Service was clearly the most popular poet in the Americas. He never claimed to be a "poet," but only a "rhymer" and "inkslinger." Whatever the case, he chronicled the Yukon and Klondike gold rushes in hearty rhymes that captured the rough frontier. His best narrative verses reflected the earthy, vernacular character of the Far North through a fortunate mingling of romance and realism, of exaggeration and understatement, and of humor and pathos. Though his verse never achieved serious critical acclaim, it was the stuff of the people, the type of rhyme that they accepted. Several of his poems and ballads of frontier life and several of his characters, such as Dan McGrew, have rightfully become a genuine part of American folklore.

[Service's papers and manuscripts are scattered about, with no single sizable collection. The Lulu Fairbanks Collection in the University of Alaska Library does contain some significant correspondence. No major critical study exists. However, one significant biography, which also includes biographical references, is Carl J. Klinck, *Robert Service: A Biography* (1976). Obituaries are in *New York Times,* Sept. 13, 1958; and *Life,* Oct. 6, 1958.]

PETER P. REMALEY

SETON, GRACE GALLATIN THOMPSON (Jan. 28, 1872–Mar. 19, 1959), author and book designer, was born in Sacramento, Calif., the daughter of Albert Gallatin, a financier, and Clemenzie Angelia Rhodes. Albert Gallatin was associated with Collis P. Huntington and Mark Hopkins in the largest hardware, iron, and steel business on the Pacific Coast. The Gallatins were distantly related to Albert Gallatin, secretary of the treasury during the administrations of presidents Thomas Jefferson and James Madison.

When Grace was eight years old, her parents were divorced. Her mother later remarried, and Grace grew up in Detroit, Chicago, and the East. Her childhood was not a particularly happy one. She was educated privately and at the Packer Collegiate Institute in Brooklyn, N.Y.

In 1888, while in Paris with her mother, she began writing articles for the *San Francisco Call* and for the *Examiner,* under the pen name of Dorothy Dodge. She also contributed pieces to magazines in London, Paris, and New York.

While on board ship traveling to France with her mother in 1894, she met Ernest Thompson Seton, the artist and naturalist. They saw much of each other during the next two years in Paris, where he was studying painting. They were married on June 1, 1896, soon after their return to New York. They had an only child, the novelist Anya Seton. After living briefly in Tappan, N.Y.;

New Jersey; and New York City, the Setons made their home in Connecticut.

Although she continued to write occasional articles and two nonfiction books, *A Woman Tenderfoot in the Rockies* (1900) and *Nimrod's Wife* (1907), Seton spent the bulk of her time for several decades assisting her husband with his literary and lecturing enterprises. She accompanied him on many camping and field trips, was a crack shot, and, as her husband later wrote, "met all kinds of danger with unflinching nerve [and] was always calm and clear-headed." She also spent much time studying bookmaking, papermaking, and printing, and she largely designed the covers, title pages, and general appearance of some of Ernest Seton's earlier books. She also provided some editorial assistance and served as his literary agent, since he had little taste for business negotiations and she was more at home in cosmopolitan circles than he. She also doubled as publicity agent for his lecture tours, which became a regular and increasingly important source of family income.

During these years she was also increasingly involved in a variety of social activities, writers' organizations, and the women's rights movement. She was president of Pen and Brush (1898–1913), vice-president and later president of the Connecticut Woman Suffrage Association (1910–1920), and, with her husband, a founder in 1910 of the Girl Pioneers, which subsequently became the Camp Fire Girls.

Following the outbreak of World War I, Seton was engaged in relief work, raising funds for the purchase, equipping, and operation of six trucks for the Women's Motor Unit of La Bienêtre du Blessé in France, which she then directed for two years. She also wrote articles for the British Ministry of Information, undertook some work for the French Service de Santé Militaire, served as secretary of the Connecticut Division of the Women's Committee of the Council of National Defense, and sold Liberty Loan Bonds in Washington, D.C. She received three French decorations for her war services.

During the 1920's and 1930's, she traveled in Asia, Africa, and Latin America, spending much time in remote regions. She headed expeditions in northeastern India and Indochina. She wrote *A Woman Tenderfoor in Egypt* (1923), *Chinese Lanterns* (1924), and *Yes, Lady Saheb* (1925), works that reflected her interests not only in travel and exploration but in the role of women in various societies, the occult, Hinduism, metaphysics, theosophy, and Oriental mysticism. *Yes,*

Lady Saheb was adjudged the best book of the year by the League of American Pen Women in 1926. Her later books included *Log of the Look-See* (1932), *Magic Waters* (1933), *The Singing Traveller* (1947), and *The Singing Heart* (1957).

Seton was one of eight charter members of the Society of Women Geographers in 1925. The next year she visited Brazil as historian of the Field Museum Expedition. After completing that assignment, she continued on to Paraguay, Bolivia, and Peru, giving particular attention to the ancient civilizations of the region. She was much in demand as a lecturer on her travel experiences.

Seton had charge of an international conference of women writers of which she was the organizer at the Century of Progress Exposition (1933) and, in conjunction with the conference, arranged an exhibit of 3,000 books written by women in thirty-seven nations. This collection later became the core of the Biblioteca Feminina at Northwestern University's Deering Library.

Seton was a delegate to the Pacific Conference for Women in Honolulu (1928, 1931, 1934) and Vancouver, B.C. (1937). She actively supported the presidential candidacies of Herbert Hoover in 1928 and Thomas E. Dewey in 1944, and was instrumental in improving the status of women members of the Republican National Committee. Seaton served as an American representative to the International Council of Women Triennial Conference in Paris (1934). In 1938 she headed the United States delegation to the International Council of Women's Jubilee meetings in Edinburgh. From 1950 until 1955 she edited the *Poetry Booklet*.

Seton composed and published a number of songs, including "If You Were I and I Were You, Sweetheart," "Lotus Blossom," "Canton Boat Women," and "Lily of Arcady"; several song cycles; and a desert drama, *The Simoon*. Songwriting was not one of her major interests, but her work was charming.

Seton was short and plump. She was effective at handling people and an excellent organizer. A social being by nature, she possessed a fine sense of humor. Seton and her husband were frequently away from each other while traveling and lecturing. Divergent tastes and interests were among the factors that led to the dissolution of their marriage in 1935.

In her later years Seton suffered increasingly from arthritis. She usually spent the summer months at her home in Stamford, Conn., and after 1940, wintered in Florida. She died in Palm Beach.

[Seton's obituary is in the *New York Times*, Mar. 20, 1959.]

KEIR B. STERLING

SHERMAN, FREDERICK CARL (May 27, 1888–July 27, 1957), naval officer, was born in Port Huron, Mich., the son of Frederick Ward Sherman and Charlotte Esther Wolfe. Appointed to the U.S. Naval Academy in 1906, he performed well in athletics, especially sailing, and in scholarship, graduating twenty-fourth in the class of 1910. His initial sea duty (1910–1913) was in the Atlantic Fleet aboard the armored cruiser *Montana* and the battleship *Ohio*, and in the Pacific Fleet on the armored cruiser *Maryland.* In March 1912 Sherman received his commission as ensign. Transferring to submarine duty aboard the former monitor submarine tender *Cheyenne* early in 1914, he helped evacuate refugees from western Mexican ports in April and May in addition to tending Pacific Torpedo Flotilla subs. In April 1915 he began two and a half years in the West Coast-based submarines *H-3* and *H-2*, commanding the latter until its transfer to the Caribbean late in 1917. He married Fanny Jessop on Nov. 22, 1915; they had one son. In December 1917, Sherman, now a lieutenant commander, reported to Quincy, Mass., as prospective commanding officer of the sub *0-7*. Following its commissioning in April 1918, he patrolled the East Coast until the end of World War I. He was navigator of the battleship *Minnesota*, which returned American troops from Europe early in 1919.

Sherman's interwar duties were fairly routine: he rotated among shore billets at the Navy Department and elsewhere, submarine and destroyer commands, and shipboard service on heavy fleet units before finally establishing himself in naval aviation. He served in the Bureau of Engineering (1919–1921); commanded Submarine Division 9 (1921–1924); received instruction in the junior course of the Naval War College (1924–1925); had two tours of duty in the Division of Fleet Training, Office of the Chief of Naval Operations (1925–1926, 1931–1932); served as gunnery officer on the battleship *West Virginia* (1926–1929); and returned ashore to the Bureau of Navigation (1929–1931).

After a year as navigator of the cruiser *Detroit* (1932–1933), Sherman led Destroyer Divisions 8 (1933–1934) and 1 (1934–1935), then served as aide to the commandant of the Eleventh Naval District, Admiral W. T. Tarrant. During

1935–1936 he took flight training at Pensacola, Fla., where he was designated naval aviator at the age of forty-seven. His initial assignments were as executive officer of the aircraft carrier *Saratoga* (1936–1937), then of the Naval Air Station at San Diego, Calif. (1937–1938).

Promoted to the rank of captain in June 1938, Sherman commanded Patrol Wing 3 at Coco Solo, Canal Zone, for one year and took the Naval War College senior course prior to assuming command of the carrier *Lexington* on June 13, 1940. Based at Pearl Harbor, Hawaii, the ship was at sea near Midway on Dec. 7, 1941; its planes searched for the enemy fleet on succeeding days. Since the fleet needed experienced aviation officers to command in the early days of World War II, Sherman was a natural and popular choice—"a 'regular old sea dog' who had taken up air warfare with great zest; officers and men adored him," according to Samuel Eliot Morison. He was "explosive, zealous, demanding, showy, irritable due to [his] own ego and bad téeth problems; an intelligent, superb tactician, loving a good fight; though normally quiet and calm in battle, [he] took risks and preferred independent command . . ." (Reynolds, p. xiii). With his pet dog "Admiral Wags" at his side, Sherman took the *Lexington* into the first American offensive operations in the South Pacific and remained in demand for high combat command throughout World War II.

After the *Lexington* saw initial action against Japanese aircraft near Rabaul in February 1942, Sherman acted as task force air commander for successful long-range air strikes against Lae and Salamaua, New Guinea, in March. When the Japanese pushed southward toward Allied sea-lanes, the Battle of the Coral Sea ensued on May 4–8, the first carrier-to-carrier battle in history. Planes from the *Lexington* sank a Japanese light carrier before their own ship received the brunt of the Japanese air strikes. Hopelessly crippled, it had to be scuttled.

Immediately promoted to rear admiral, Sherman spent the summer at United States Fleet headquarters in Washington, then returned to the South Pacific in October. The following month he hoisted his flag on the carrier *Enterprise* as commander of Carrier Division 2 and spent the next six months supporting American operations in the Solomon Islands and experimenting with new carrier tactical formations. A favorite of South Pacific commander Admiral William F. Halsey, Jr., Sherman in July 1943 became commander of Carrier Division 1 aboard the *Saratoga*,

with which during November he covered Halsey's landings at Bougainville in the northern Solomons and neutralized Japanese fleet units at Rabaul. His task group participated in the invasion of the Gilbert Islands later in the month, with Sherman transferring to the *Bunker Hill* for the final air operations that neutralized Rabaul during December and January.

After a respite from combat as commander of fleet air for the West Coast, Sherman returned in August 1944 as commander of Carrier Division 1 and fast carrier task group commander in Task Force 58/38. With his flag aboard several different carries, he participated (August 1944–May 1945) in the Battle of Leyte Gulf, the Philippines and Iwo Jima operations, and the long Okinawa campaign, always advocating larger carrier tactical formations but seldom getting the opportunity to test his theories. Relieved of command in June 1945, he was promoted to vice admiral the next month and designated commander of the First Fast Carrier Force, Pacific (Task Force 58). The war ended just as he returned to sea. Sherman, "the only air admiral to lead fast carrier forces . . . almost continually, deserves special credit for advancing the multicarrier task formation and for his dynamic leadership at Rabaul, Leyte, and Okinawa. . . . A Halsey-type slugger and influenced by an explosive personality, Sherman was by any measure the best of the latecomer air admirals to command carriers in battle" (Reynolds, p. 389).

Sherman commanded the Fifth Fleet from January to September 1946, then retired early in 1947 with the rank of full admiral. He was a staff writer for the *Chicago Tribune* (1946–1948) and published a thin history of the wartime carriers, *Combat Command* (1950), which reflected little autobiographical content. Sherman, whose nickname was "Ted," died in San Diego.

[Biographical sketches of Sherman are the Navy Department official outline (1957) and the obituary in the *New York Times*, July 28, 1957. For Sherman's wartime service, see Samuel Eliot Morison, *History of United States Naval Operations in World War II*, vols. IV (1949), V (1949), VI (1950), XII (1958), and XIV (1960); and Clark G. Reynolds, *The Fast Carriers* (1968).]

CLARK G. REYNOLDS

SHIPSTEAD, HENRIK (Jan. 8, 1881–June 26, 1960), United States senator, was born in Burbank Township, Kandiyohi County, Minn., one of twelve children of a Norwegian Lutheran immigrant couple, Saave Shipstead and Christine Ellefson. Reared on a farm, he attended a one-room country school, enrolled briefly at the state normal school at St. Cloud, and in 1903 graduated from the Northwestern University school of dentistry. On Apr. 23, 1906, he married Lula Anderson; they adopted a son. He practiced dentistry in Glenwood, Minn., until 1920, when he opened an office in Minneapolis. Shipstead was mayor of Glenwood for two terms and in 1917 served in the state house of representatives. He lost election bids for Congress in 1918 and for governor in 1920. In 1922 he won election on the Farmer-Labor ticket to the United States Senate over incumbent Frank B. Kellogg. He was easily reelected in 1928, 1934, and 1940, but was defeated in his bid for a fifth term in 1946.

Tall, gray-haired, and well-built, Shipstead was fluent in Norwegian, Swedish, and Danish; throughout his life he spoke English with a slight Scandinavian accent. For years he was the Senate's lone member of the Farmer-Labor party but shifted to the Republicans before the election of 1940. He was a member of the Foreign Relations Committee throughout his twenty-four years in the Senate and served on the Agriculture and Forestry Committee for two decades. His positions on public issues generally were consistent with those of the earlier Populists and with the agrarian radical Non-Partisan League in which he had been active.

Although proudly independent, he regularly aligned on both domestic and foreign policy issues with other western progressives including Senators William E. Borah of Idaho, Hiram W. Johnson of California, Burton K. Wheeler of Montana, George W. Norris of Nebraska, Robert M. LaFollette of Wisconsin (father and son), and Gerald P. Nye of North Dakota. Those "Sons of the Wild Jackasses" spoke for the rural and small-town Middle West against dominance by eastern urban business and financial interests that, they said, controlled the domestic and foreign policies of the United States to advance their own "selfish interests" against those of the farmer and the "common man." Alienated from what a later generation would call the "eastern urban establishment," they spoke for an agrarian-based democracy and opposed concentrated power in the hands of big business or big government.

Shipstead sympathized with debtors against creditors, with farmers against industrialists, and with rural America against urban dominance. He supported "Fighting Bob" LaFollette for pres-

ident in 1924 and generally opposed the pro-business policies of Republican administrations in the 1920's. He approved much of President Franklin D. Roosevelt's New Deal in the 1930's, including relief measures and the reciprocal trade agreements program. Reflecting the interests of his Minnesota constituents, Shipstead urged approval of the St. Lawrence Seaway and a nine-foot navigational channel for the upper Mississippi River. Although critical of conservative Supreme Court rulings, he opposed Roosevelt's court-packing proposal in 1937 and his bid for a third term in 1940.

Like most western progressives, Shipstead was an isolationist in foreign affairs, opposing American involvement in alliances, world organizations, and "foreign" wars. He criticized American imperialism and "dollar diplomacy" in Latin America. Although not a pacifist, he wanted to limit American defense commitments to the Western Hemisphere. He blamed American imperialism and involvement abroad on big business and big finance, and on the politicians and parties that supported those interests. He opposed American membership in the World Court and League of Nations. He supported the neutrality legislation of the 1930's in order to restrict the interventionist proclivities of both big business and big government. After World War II erupted, Shipstead favored food relief for European peoples but opposed lend-lease and the other aid-short-of-war policies of the Roosevelt administration.

After the Japanese attack on Pearl Harbor, Shipstead supported the war but never abandoned his conviction that the United States could and should have stayed out of the conflict. In 1943 he was one of only five senators to vote against the Connally resolution calling for membership in a world organization after the war. And in 1945 he cast one of the two Senate votes against American membership in the United Nations.

Shipstead's continued devotion to rural and small-town values in an increasingly urbanized-industrialized America (and Minnesota), along with his unrepentant isolationism at a time when the United States was moving to an ever larger role in world affairs, doomed him to defeat in the election of 1946. After years of failing health, he died in Alexandria, Minn.

[Shipstead's papers are in the Minnesota Historical Society Library, St. Paul. The best political biography is an unpublished doctoral dissertation by Sister Mary René Lorentz, "Henrik Shipstead: Minnesota Independent, 1923–1946," (Catholic University of America, 1963). Martin Ross, *Shipstead of Minnesota* (1940), is a laudatory campaign biography.]

WAYNE S. COLE

SHUSTER, W(ILLIAM) MORGAN (Feb. 23, 1877–May 26, 1960), financier, lawyer, and publisher, was born in Washington, D.C., the son of William Morgan Shuster and Caroline H. von Tagen. He was educated in the Washington public schools and attended Columbian College and Law School, but was awarded no degree. He apparently read law and was admitted to the bar, but in 1898 he worked for the War Department as a stenographer in Cuba and then accepted a post as customs collector in the newly created Republic of Cuba (1899–1901). Next he was assigned to the Philippine Islands, where he reorganized customs and was collector from 1901 to 1906. His conduct in office led to his appointment to the Philippine Commission (the supreme governing agency) while he served as secretary of public instruction (1906–1909).

Shuster left the Philippines to practice law in Washington, where, owing to his experience in Manila, he was on good terms with President William Howard Taft, who had been the first American governor of the Philippines. His knowledge of international finance led him into à difficult assignment in Persia (now Iran) in 1911. A reform government sought neutral counsel in 1910 after Great Britain and Russia had agreed to respect Persian sovereignty while establishing "spheres of influence" where the two powers would hold extraterritorial rights. The Persian leaders, faced with a nearly empty treasury, turned to the United States for advice in selecting a team of experts who could restore some order to the fiscal system. Taft and Shuster conferred, and Shuster was appointed treasurer general by the Persian reformers, who hailed his arrival in Teheran (May 1911) as a portent of better times.

After investigating the staggering number of problems that had brought Persian finances to a crisis state, Shuster asked the national assembly to grant him almost dictatorial powers. To avoid involvement with other outsiders, he virtually ignored the Teheran diplomatic corps, ignored extraterritorial rights, and openly quarreled with the Belgian who ran the Persian customs service. The Russian diplomats, resentful of Shuster's selection, were critical of his brusqueness and took affront when he gave command of a special treasury police force to a British military attaché whose hostility toward the Russians was

well known. When Shuster directed the Persian police to seize the property of the ousted shah's brother, the Russian consulate blocked the action by sending a small cossack detachment to intervene (on the pretext that the Persian prince had defaulted on a Russian loan). Shuster countered with a larger treasury police force, and in the ensuing confrontation Russia claimed that two of its diplomats had been threatened by Persian sentries.

A Russian ultimatum followed, with demands for an apology for the alleged insult. When the Persian national assembly apologized, the Russians followed with a second ultimatum demanding Shuster's ouster. The assembly rejected this note, and Russian troops were attacked by Persian nationalists in two northern towns. In reprisal several prominent Persians were hanged by the Russians, who then began to advance on Teheran. A Persian commission was appointed to answer the ultimatum, and Shuster was the subject of debate in the House of Commons, where the British foreign secretary, Sir Edward Grey, conceded that Russia had demanded Shuster's dismissal and "the British Government had no objections to the Moscow demand." Grey said that the Anglo-Russian agreement should not be threatened, nor the two great powers "embroiled by the action of an individual, no matter how good his intentions were." Shuster's resignation was soon demanded.

On Christmas Day of 1911, Schuster was officially dismissed by the Persian cabinet, and in January he left Teheran much embittered by the experience, as his book *The Strangling of Persia* (1912) attested. In this book Shuster showed a broad knowledge of Persian history and politics, described the Russians and their friends as the real source of his problems, and lamented that his reform efforts to join Persian traditions with an honest and efficient modern nation had failed. In fact, Shuster had impressed many observers in Teheran, who admired his energy and integrity.

Shuster might have succeeded had he not tried to ignore the realities of the Anglo-Russian agreement. His public appeal in the midst of the crisis, through a letter to the *London Times* (printed Nov. 10–11, 1911), "was an entreaty in the name of truth and justice over the heads of the British government to the people" that backfired because it "outraged the diplomats' sense of decency." He left behind a reservoir of goodwill, as was proved by his being invited back to Persia in 1921 to complete the task he had barely begun.

Shuster had already found a new career. The

success of his book and a series of articles in *Century* magazine brought him to the attention of the executives of the Century Company. (Shuster had continued to write while retained by a New York-based bank to help solidify its Latin American operations.) In 1915, Shuster was invited to serve as president of Century, and he spent the remainder of his life in book publishing. (He was also the editor of *Century* magazine in 1920–1921.) When Century merged with Appleton and Company in 1933, Shuster became president of the resulting Appleton-Century organization. Fifteen years later he presided over the absorption of the F. S. Crofts Company and was president of Appleton-Century-Crofts until 1952, when he became chairman of the board. He held that position until his death.

Shuster married Pearl B. Trigg on Apr. 20, 1904; she died in 1942. He later married Katherine Kane; they had two daughters. He died in New York City.

[See Percy Sykes, *A History of Persia* (3rd ed., rev.; 1930); Firuz Kazemzadeh, *Russia and Britain in Persia, 1864–1914* (1968); and Robert A. McDaniel, *The Shuster Mission and the Persian Constitutional Revolution* (1974). His obituary is in *New York Times*, May 27, 1960.]

ROBERT A. RUTLAND

SIGERIST, HENRY ERNEST (Apr. 7, 1891–Mar. 17, 1957), medical historian, was born in Paris, the son of Ernest Heinrich Sigerist and Emma Wiskemann. His father, a native of Schaffhausen, Switzerland, was in the shoe business. When the young Henry was ten years old, his father became mortally ill and the family returned to Zurich, his mother's native city. After graduating from the Literaturgymnasium in Zurich, a public school that emphasized studies in Greek and Latin, he entered the University of Zurich in 1910 as a student of oriental philology, studying Arabic, Hebrew, and Sanskrit. In 1911 he spent nearly a year at University College, London. (He eventually knew fourteen languages, half of which he spoke fluently.) When he returned to Zurich, he decided to study medicine. His training at Zurich (M.D., 1917) was interrupted by nearly two years in the Medical Corps of the Swiss army. In the summer of 1914 he attended clinics at Munich, and at this time the idea of combining all his interests by pursuing the history of medicine occurred to him, although academic posts in the field were then almost nonexistent.

After World War I, Sigerist studied at the Leipzig Institute for the History of Medicine with the eminent historian Karl Sudhoff, who directed his research to philological studies of medieval and medical manuscripts. In 1923 he published *Studien und Texte zur frühmittelalterlichen Rezeptliteratur*, an analysis of early medical formularies, written as his *Habilitationsschrift* to become a privatdocent at Zurich in 1921. He became titular professor in 1924. On Sept. 14, 1916, he had married Emmy M. Escher; they had two daughters.

In 1923 Sigerist also published a critical edition of 549 Latin letters from Albrecht von Haller to Johannes Gesner that were in Zurich's Zentralbibliothek (*Albrecht von Hallers Briefe an Johannes Gesner, 1728–1777*). To his surprise in 1925 he was offered Sudhoff's chair of medical history at Leipzig, the major medico-historical research center in the world. There between 1925 and 1932 his manifold talents in research and organization unfolded. A brilliant lecturer and facile writer, he made medical history attractive to students and public alike. Without sacrificing scholarly standards and productivity he wrote general works like *Einführung in die Medizin* (1931), which was translated into six languages (English title, *Man and Medicine*, 1932) and *Grosse Aerzte* (1932; English ed., *Great Doctors*, 1933), sixty medical biographies used to interpret the evolution of modern medicine, considered by some his best work.

In post–World War I Germany, Sigerist's attention turned to the relationship between medicine and the social environment, the connection between poverty and disease, and the problems of providing medical care. When he was invited in 1931 to lecture in the United States, he used the opportunity to write a history of American medicine (*Amerika und die Medizin*, 1933) from what he first called the sociological point of view and later the social history of medicine. Similarly he observed medical conditions in the Soviet Union during the summers of 1935 and 1936 and wrote *Socialized Medicine in the Soviet Union* (1937).

During his highly successful lecture tour in the United States, Sigerist was invited to become professor of the history of medicine and director of the new Johns Hopkins Institute of the History of Medicine in Baltimore as William H. Welch's successor. The rising power of Hitler in Germany portended evil times and accelerated Sigerist's decision to move to America. Between the autumn of 1932 and 1947, when he resigned his Johns Hopkins chair, Sigerist's captivating personality and dynamic leadership shaped the future course of medico-historical studies and attitudes toward medical care in the United States. With the assistance of Owsei Temkin, whom he brought from Leipzig, and Ludwig Edelstein, a Berlin classicist, he raised the standards of medico-historical scholarship in America, founded the *Bulletin of the History of Medicine* (1933), and reorganized the American Association for the History of Medicine (founded 1925). Tactfully and persuasively he helped many amateurs, encouraged professionals, and made the Johns Hopkins Institute the mecca of medical historians throughout the world. A popular lecturer and enthusiastic advocate of socialized medicine, he both attracted and repelled, becoming a controversial figure in the medical community. His Terry Lectures at Yale University in 1938 (*Medicine and Human Welfare*, 1941) illustrated his intense concern with social problems, while his Messenger Lectures at Cornell University in 1940 (*Civilization and Disease*, 1943) demonstrated masterfully the interconnections of disease and the economic, social, religious, legal, philosophical, and cultural aspects of society. In 1944 he served as medical planning consultant to the governments of Saskatchewan, Canada, and India, and he helped to found the American-Soviet Medical Society, becoming the first editor of the *American Review of Soviet Medicine* (1943-1944). He became an American citizen in 1943.

During World War II, Sigerist struggled to keep his historical research going, although he was engulfed by administrative duties at the Johns Hopkins Institute and the Welch Medical Library, of which he had been named acting director. He became increasingly frustrated and embittered as his strength flagged, for he had begun to write an eight-volume social history of medicine as the culmination of his life's work. Finally in 1947 he resigned from Johns Hopkins and settled near Pura, Switzerland, overlooking Lake Lugano. When news of his resignation spread, he was offered chairs at Jena, Zurich, Berlin, and Leipzig. (In 1945 he had declined an offer to head an institute at the University of London.) He chose to affiliate with Yale Medical School as research associate with freedom to live in Switzerland.

But because of advancing cardiovascular disease he found it increasingly difficult to work, and only one volume and part of a second of his *History of Medicine* were completed (vol. I: *Primitive and*

Archaic Medicine, 1951; vol. II: *Greek Medicine*, 1961). He was able to give the Heath Clark Lectures at the University of London in 1952 (*Landmarks in the History of Hygiene*, 1956). After struggling bravely to recover from a cerebral hemorrhage in October 1954 that impaired his speech, he died in Pura, Switzerland, two and a half years later.

[Sigerist's Haller collection and many personal papers are in the Historical Library of Yale Medical School. The principal sources are *Henry E. Sigerist: Autobiographical Writings*, selected and translated by Nora Sigerist Beeson (1966); and Genevieve Miller, ed., *A Bibliography of the Writings of Henry E. Sigerist* (1966). Collections of his articles include Henry E. Sigerist, *The University at the Crossroads* (1946); Felix Marti-Ibañez, ed., *Henry E. Sigerist on the History of Medicine* (1960); and Milton I. Roemer, ed., *Henry E. Sigerist on the Sociology of Medicine* (1960). Articles by students and friends are in the Sigerist valedictory number of the *Bulletin of the History of Medicine*, Jan.–Feb. 1948, which includes remarks at a farewell dinner in New York, May 9, 1947, and a complete bibliography of the publications of the Johns Hopkins Institute, 1929–1947. See also the Sigerist issue of the *Journal of the History of Medicine and Allied Sciences*, Apr. 1958; and the addresses by Hopkins colleagues in *Bulletin of the History of Medicine*, July–Aug. 1957. A biographical article in *MD Medical Newsmagazine*, Sept. 1966, contains many excellent photographs.]

GENEVIEVE MILLER

SIMMONS (SZYMANSKI), ALOYSIUS HARRY (May 22, 1903–May 26, 1956), baseball player, was born in Milwaukee, Wis., the son of John and Agnes Szymanski. His father died in 1912, and Simmons' mother was forced to go to work to support the family.

After a successful career in amateur baseball, Simmons—who changed his name when he played—signed a contract with Aberdeen of the Dakota League. He was an immediate sensation, leading the league in hits and batting .365. In 1923, Simmons played for Shreveport in the Texas League, and hit .360. At the end of the season he played several games for the Milwaukee Brewers of the American Association. In 1924 the Milwaukee management sold him to the Philadelphia Athletics for $40,000.

Simmons, a right-handed outfielder, stood five feet, eleven inches tall and weighed 185 pounds throughout most of his major league career. He possessed a strong throwing arm and great speed. In 1925 he made more put-outs than any other outfielder in the American League. In 1928,

Simmons switched from center field to left field, where he again excelled. He led American League outfielders in fielding percentage in 1929, 1930, and 1937.

It was Simmons' batting that made him a star. Like many outstanding hitters he had an unorthodox batting stance. He stood deep in the batter's box, then stepped toward third base as he swung the bat. This style of hitting, called "putting your foot in the bucket," earned Simmons the nickname "Bucketfoot Al." Using a long bat, he could hit to all fields with power. He hit .300 or better in thirteen full seasons and had a lifetime average of .334. In 1930 and 1931, Simmons was the American League batting champion with averages of .381 and .390. He was particularly effective with runners on base, and drove in at least 100 runs in each of his twelve seasons. His lifetime total of 1,827 runs batted in is tenth best in baseball history. The best-known display of Simmons' ability to hit in crucial situations came in the seventh inning of a World Series game against the Chicago Cubs on Oct. 12, 1929. The Cubs led 8-0 when Philadelphia rallied to score ten runs in one inning. Simmons hit a home run and a single in the rally.

Two other factors insured that Simmons would have an enduring reputation. In the early 1920's the leaders of organized baseball increased the resiliency of the ball, which made it easier to hit home runs and to attain high averages. Many more runs were scored, and sluggers like Simmons and Babe Ruth became popular public figures. Equally important was the fact that Simmons played for the Philadelphia Athletics in 1929, 1930, and 1931. Managed by Connie Mack and led by Simmons, Mickey Cochrane, Jimmy Foxx, and Lefty Grove, this team is regarded as one of the best in baseball history. It won three consecutive American League pennants (1929–1931) and won the 1929 and 1930 World Series.

In 1929, Simmons was named the Most Valuable Player in the American League. In addition he was named by the Baseball Writers' Association as an outfielder on the *Sporting News* All-Star Major League Team in 1927, 1929, 1930, 1931, 1933, and 1934. He was elected to the Baseball Hall of Fame in 1953. Simmons was well aware of his value as a player and as an attraction to the fans. In the midst of the Great Depression, he forced a reluctant Philadelphia management to grant him a three-year contract for a total salary of $100,000.

When the Athletics failed to win the pennant in 1932 and attendance at their games declined dramatically, Simmons' high salary became a burden to the Philadelphia management. As a result he was sold to the Chicago White Sox with two other players for $150,000. He played well for the weak Chicago team in 1933 and 1934, but he suffered through his worst season in 1935. That winter he was sold to Detroit for $75,000. Simmons enjoyed his last fully productive season in 1936, but when Detroit failed to win its third consecutive pennant, the Tigers sold him to the Washington Senators for $15,000. After mediocre seasons in 1937 and 1938, he was sold to the Boston Braves for the 1939 season. In August 1939 the Cincinnati Reds purchased Simmons, who helped them win the pennant. The Reds then released him, and he signed with the Athletics as a player-coach. He remained in that capacity in 1940–1942 and 1944. In 1943 he played for the Boston Red Sox. From 1945 through 1949 he was a nonplaying coach for the Athletics. He finished his career in baseball as a coach for the Cleveland Indians in 1950.

Simmons married Dorris Lynn Reader on Aug. 6, 1934. The marriage was apparently not a happy one, and the couple was divorced in 1941. They had one son. After retiring from baseball, Simmons returned to Milwaukee, where he died. Simmons was one of the greatest players in baseball, outstanding both as a batter and as an outfielder.

[Short summaries of Simmons' career can be found in Thomas W. Meany, *Baseball's Greatest Hitters* (1950); Ira L. Smith, *Baseball's Famous Outfielders* (1954); Arthur Daley, *Kings of the Home Run* (1962); and Robert M. Broeg, *Super Stars of Baseball* (1971). His obituary is in the *Milwaukee Journal*, May 26, 1956.]

GORDON B. MCKINNEY

SIMON, RICHARD LEO (Mar. 6, 1899–July 29, 1960), publisher, was born in New York City, the son of Leo Leopold Simon, a milliner, and Anna Mayer. The family was intensely musical, and Simon early became an accomplished pianist. He attended the Ethical Culture School before entering Columbia University, from which he graduated in 1920. During World War I he served briefly as a second lieutenant in the infantry at Plattsburgh, N.Y.

Upon leaving college Simon went to work for William Grace and Co., sugar importers, but soon found more congenial employment as a piano salesman for the Aeolian Company. Among his potential customers was another young Columbia graduate, Max Lincoln Schuster, who edited a motor trade magazine and shared Simon's enthusiasm for the writings of Romain Rolland. Through their common interest in books and music, the two men became close friends and Simon was encouraged to enter book publishing. In 1921 he joined Boni and Liveright as a commission salesman; one year later he was sales manager.

Simon's obvious talent for solving marketing and distribution problems led him to consider founding his own publishing company, and in 1924 he and Schuster pooled savings of approximately $8,000 to establish Simon and Schuster. From the beginning the new firm shocked its more staid rivals by pursuing a policy of unabashed commercialism. Although the partners appreciated literary excellence and aesthetic values, they concentrated on the production of best sellers, the success of which depended primarily upon flamboyant advertising and a shrewd assessment of popular taste. They catered uncritically to market demand. Without a back list of authors, Simon later recalled, he and Schuster were forced to engage in "planned publishing"—a process by which they thought up marketable ideas and then commissioned writers to develop them into books.

Their first such venture set the tone for much of their subsequent publishing activity. Acting on the suggestion of an aunt, Simon employed the puzzle editors of the *New York World* to compile a book of crossword puzzles in 1924. This publication—the initial offering of the firm—appeared under the imprint of the Plaza Publishing Co. because, Schuster said, "We just did not want to be typed as game-book publishers at the start." But its instant popularity—50,000 copies were sold in three months—soon led to the publication of further volumes at regular intervals under the Simon and Schuster imprint.

Novelty items, including "how-to" books, remained a conspicuous feature of the Simon and Schuster book lists, along with a number of other made-to-order works that reflected the partners' enthusiasms and idiosyncrasies. Simon's addiction to music, bridge, and photography was largely responsible for the publication of books by such figures as Leopold Stokowski, Deems Taylor, Igor Stravinsky, Sidney Lenz, Charles H. Goren, Margaret Bourke-White, Henri Cartier-Bresson, and Werner Bischof, as well as Simon's own *Miniature Photography* (1937). He also introduced several noted German and Aus-

trian writers to the American public, including Felix Salten, Hans Fallada, and Arthur Schnitzler, whose *None but the Brave* he translated for publication by the firm in 1926. On Aug. 3, 1934, Simon married Andrea Louise Heinemann; they had four children.

Simon made his greatest contribution to the publishing industry by modernizing the methods of book promotion and distribution. He pioneered in the use of full-page newspaper advertisements, enclosed cards in his books to obtain reactions from readers, and launched massive prepublication campaigns to ensure the successful reception of doubtful works, such as Thomas Craven's *A Treasury of Art Masterpieces* (1939). That book, which relied exclusively upon color reproductions, was one of Simon's pet projects; the firm spent $60,000 on advertising it. The returns were gratifying; advance sales totaled 42,974 copies, and in a little over a year more than 100,000 copies were sold. The book became a model for the production of art books in America.

In addition to promoting books on an individual basis, Simon wrote a regular column entitled "From the Inner Sanctum" for the trade journal *Publishers Weekly*, from 1926 to 1935. With characteristic verve he praised the current titles of his firm, chided booksellers and the public for neglecting past offerings, apologized for unattractive book jackets, congratulated rivals on fortunate coups, and pontificated on the state of culture in general. Schuster wrote a similar column under the same title twice a week for the *New York Times*, in a complementary effort to stimulate reader interest.

The partners' persistent quest for new markets culminated in 1939 with their founding of Pocket Books, Inc., in association with Leon Shimkin, their business manager, and Robert F. de Graff. The new paperback concern filled a need for inexpensive, readily available reprints, sold through previously neglected outlets, such as newsstands and stationery stores. By 1944, when Simon and Schuster sold their business to Marshall Field Enterprises, the value of their investment in Pocket Books had risen twenty-five times over.

Although the terms of the merger permitted Simon to retain his executive position, the loss of genuine independence weighed upon him and gradually impaired his health and vitality. In 1957 he suffered two heart attacks and retired from the company. He died in North Stamford, Conn., an unhappy man who talked vaguely until the end of establishing a new publishing house of his own.

[There are unpublished letters from Simon in the Earnest Elmo Calkins Papers at Knox College, Galesburg, Ill. The memoir of M. Lincoln Schuster in the Oral History Collection at Columbia University is an important source on Simon. An obituary is in the *New York Times*, July 30, 1960. See also Bennett Cerf, "Trade Winds," *Saturday Review*, Sept. 10, 1960; and Charles A. Madison, *Book Publishing in America* (1966).]

MAXWELL BLOOMFIELD

SINCLAIR, HARRY FORD (July 6, 1876–Nov. 10, 1956), oil producer, was born in Wheeling, W.Va., the son of John Sinclair, a pharmacist, and Phoebe Simmons. In 1882 his father moved to Independence, Kans., where he operated a successful drugstore. Sinclair had an uneventful childhood; he attended the local public schools, and during 1897–1898 he studied pharmacy at the University of Kansas. He then returned to Independence to take over his father's shop. His career as a druggist was unsuccessful; by 1901 he had spent most of the money left by his father and he was forced to close the store. Many of his neighbors felt that Sinclair lacked a business sense.

Sinclair drifted for a few months before embarking on a new career. While hunting rabbits he accidentally discharged his rifle, and had to have one toe amputated. He was able to collect $5,000 from his insurance policy, and with this he purchased "mud silles," big logs that were used as foundations for oil derricks in the area. The venture proved profitable and he began to negotiate leases on oil-bearing lands. He became an oil lease broker and soon bought wells himself. Now prosperous, on July 20, 1903, he married Elizabeth Farrell; they had two children.

In 1905, on the advice of a friend, Sinclair invested all his money in the Kiowa Pool in Oklahoma. This turned out to be a big bonanza that netted him more than $100,000. By 1910 he was a millionaire, one of the most important independent oil producers in the Mid-Continent region. With strong financial backing from partners, he bought into such lucrative fields in Oklahoma as the Glenn Pool, Wann Field, Ponca City, and Flat Rock, and extended his operations to include the refining and marketing of petroleum.

Sinclair, however, dreamed of organizing his own integrated oil company. Differences with some of his partners also persuaded him to strike out on his own. In 1916 he went to New York City to secure financing. Combining all his producing properties, refineries, and a pipeline, he persuaded Wall Street bankers to float a $16 million bond issue for the new Sinclair Oil and Refining Corporation. This was one of the first large public offerings of corporate securities. With assets of $51 million the enterprise emerged as one of the new giants in the petroleum industry. In April 1917 Sinclair was appointed by President Woodrow Wilson as a member of the subcommittee on oil of the Committee on Raw Materials attached to the Council of National Defense.

After World War I, Sinclair did much to build his company into one of the nation's largest integrated oil corporations. Although he delegated authority extensively, his was a paternalistic enterprise in which he made all major decisions. His business judgments were usually impeccable. He beat out competitors in securing concessions in Costa Rica, Panama, Angola, and Portuguese West Africa, and he developed aggressive marketing strategies that bolstered his company's fortunes. His life-style was fitting for a business tycoon of the era. He owned a large estate on Long Island, a townhouse in New York, a racing stable that trained Kentucky Zev (winner of the Kentucky Derby in 1923), and a share of the St. Louis Browns baseball club.

In the 1920's, Sinclair attracted most notoriety by his alleged involvement in the scandals surrounding Teapot Dome. In 1923 a Senate investigating committee headed by Senator Thomas J. Walsh of Montana revealed that Secretary of the Interior Albert B. Fall had leased, without competitive bidding, the oil reserves at Teapot Dome, Wyo., to Sinclair, and the reserves at Elk Hills, Calif., to Edward L. Doheney, a friend. The moneys transferred were either loans or bribes. When Sinclair was called to testify, he refused to answer the questions of committee members and was held in contempt of the Senate. He was tried with Fall on a criminal conspiracy charge in 1927, but the case resulted in a mistrial. Later in the year Fall was tried separately, convicted of receiving a $100,000 bribe from Doheney, sentenced to prison, and fined $100,000. Sinclair was tried on criminal charges in 1928, but the jury acquitted him of attempted bribery although he again refused to testify. Moreover, in this trial he was accused of shadowing jurors and was held in contempt of court. Consequently, during 1929 he served nine months in prison for contempt of the Senate and for contempt of court. President Herbert Hoover ignored his plea for clemency.

Yet neither Teapot Dome, nor a jail sentence, nor the Great Depression diminished Sinclair's vigor, or his business or social status. In 1930 he made a reputed $28 million in a pipeline venture with John D. Rockefeller, Jr. He also increased his share of ownership in the Richfield Oil Company. With assiduity and skill he guided his own company through problems of the depression.

The outbreak of World War II inaugurated another spurt of growth for the Sinclair Oil Company. Sinclair enjoyed good repute, as evidenced by his appointment to the Petroleum Industry War Council in 1942, an important industry voice that helped to guide the secretary of the interior. By 1950 the assets of the Sinclair Oil Company exceeded $1.25 billion; it was the seventh largest integrated petroleum company in the United States, and fourteenth in *Fortune* magazine's list of the 500 largest industrial corporations in 1956. In his later years Sinclair transacted much of his business from his Park Avenue apartment in New York City, where he worked long and irregular hours. He left active management in 1949 and the company's board of directors five years later. Upon retirement he moved to Pasadena, Calif., where he died.

Sinclair's personal characteristics helped him to build a corporate empire. He was aggressive, ruthless, hard-working, and determined. Somewhat shy, and loath to step into the public limelight, he preferred to wield power from behind the scenes. In many ways he was like John D. Rockefeller, who personified big business leadership of the previous generation. Sinclair's success was due to a combination of shrewd business judgment, boundless energy, an uncanny ability to make the right decisions in the manifold phases of the industry, and a measure of good luck.

[Sinclair's manuscripts and correspondence are in company records. One of his close associates, W. L. Connelly, recorded his reminiscences in the rather incomplete *The Oil Business as I Saw It* (1954). Sinclair's role in the Teapot Dome affair is discussed in Burl Noggle, *Teapot Dome: Oil and Politics in the 1920's* (1962); J. Leonard Bates, *The Origins of Teapot Dome* (1963); and "Harry Ford Sinclair Looking Cool Among the Stream From Teapot Dome," *Current Opinion*, Apr. 1924. A brief survey of Sinclair's career and achievements is in R. Sheehan, "Harry Sinclair, His Hits and Misses," *Fortune*, Apr. 1956. Obituaries are in the *New York Times*, Nov. 11, 1956; *Newsweek*, Nov. 19, 1956; and *Time*, Nov. 19, 1956.]

GERALD D. NASH

SLICHTER, SUMNER HUBER (Jan. 8, 1892–Sept. 27, 1959), economist and leading interpreter of business institutions of the United States, was born in Madison, Wis., the son of Mary Lousie Byrne and Charles Sumner Slichter. His mother, an erstwhile grammar school teacher, was of Scottish and Irish ancestry. His father's family, apparently of Huguenot origin and of Swiss Brethren persuasion, immigrated to Pennsylvania from Switzerland or Alsace during the eighteenth century. Charles Sumner Slichter was a professor of applied mathematics and after 1920 dean of the Graduate School of the University of Wisconsin. He did some interesting theoretical work on underground water. Sumner Slichter's brothers also attained high achievements: one was professor of geophysics at the Massachusetts Institute of Technology and later director of the Geophysical Institute of the University of California; another was president of the Northwestern Mutual Life Insurance Company; and the third established and owned his own steel foundry in Milwaukee.

Slichter spent his boyhood in Madison during the heyday of the La Follette reform movement and in the immediate milieu of the University of Wisconsin, then led by such academic giants as Charles Van Hise, Frederick Jackson Turner, and John R. Commons. He retained a lifelong enthusiasm for the midwestern cultural tradition and regularly returned to his summer home on Lake Mendota.

Slichter studied at the University of Munich in 1910, when his family was abroad, but earned his B.A. (1913) and M.A. (1914) from the University of Wisconsin. He left Madison, purportedly in part because of a disagreement with Richard T. Ely over matters of curriculum, and took his Ph.D. in 1918 at the University of Chicago. His dissertation, "The Turnover of Factory Labor," was written for Harry Millis but was published in 1919 with an introduction by John R. Commons, who founded the "Wisconsin school" of institutional economics.

Slichter's first appointment was as instructor of economics at Princeton, where, he later noted, he found teaching less than fully congenial. After one year, he moved to Cornell as assistant professor and became professor in 1925. While at Cornell he wrote an elementary economics textbook, *Modern Economic Society* (1931). He also worked hard at improving his lecturing technique; apparently he had had something of a speech defect, which he significantly mastered. In 1930 he accepted an appointment as professor of business economics at the Harvard Business School. In 1940 he became Lamont University Professor at Harvard and thereafter divided his time between the Business School and the Department of Economics. That year, bothered by a charge that Harvard did too much for business and too little for labor, he created the Harvard Trade Union Fellowship project designed to offer short courses on administrative, economic, and social problems for trade union leaders.

Commons' influence on Slichter appears to have been strong. Both had a tremendous faith in the capacity of educational leaders to shape American economic institutions so that they would provide stability in the economic lives of the great majority of Americans. Slichter, like Commons, saw the professor's role as combining personal imagination and study with wise counsel to private groups (whether consumer, labor, or business) and particularly to government officials.

Much of Slichter's life was devoted to the study of the impact of working rules and working practices in the operation and growth of product and, particularly, factor markets. In 1941 his *Union Policies and Industrial Management* was published by the Brookings Institution. This careful survey of how industrial jurisprudence developed in a variety of industries represents the culmination of more than twenty years' observation, both intellectual and in the shop, of labor relations practices. Like Commons, Slichter had actually worked in the shop—as a machinist for a short time at the Deering works of the International Harvester Company in Chicago.

Although Slichter had a penchant for phrasing his ideas in rather formal language, what stands out in all of his work is the freshness of his eye with regard to the operation of the entrepreneurial market, the organization of the labor market, and the kind of impact that formal economic analysis had in handling changes in the American economy. His speeches to businessmen's organizations were, according to his view, developed along a formula: Tell them something they expect, and then tell them something they don't expect; tell them something they will like, then tell them something they won't like.

Slichter believed that there was an unfortunate modern tendency to denigrate the entrepreneurial spirit. He felt that with adequate attention to risk-taking, the American economy was, during his lifetime, not at its peak but merely at the threshold of its greatest period. Concerned about accounting systems that consistently overstated profits, he believed that the profit system was a dynamic element in economic growth that should be left free to encourage adaptation to changes in the product and in the factor markets. In his 1941

presidential address to the American Economic Association, he stressed the then unlikely theme that the American economy had little probability of permanent stagnation, a view markedly different from the presidential address given in 1938 by his Harvard colleague and fellow mid-westerner, Alvin H. Hansen.

During World War II, Slichter's optimism about the American economy led to his correct prediction that the postwar period would be one of boom rather than depression. This optimism, based on both intuition and careful empiricism, led him to worry about the functioning of the capital market. He was one of the first in this period to advocate "purchasing power bonds," a position he took long before indexation became a fashionable topic.

Slichter was also concerned about the growth of American unions. Although he accepted their desirability and inevitability, he had doubts about their developing sufficient social consciousness and responsibility. His advice to the governor and legislature of Massachusetts resulted in the passing in 1947 of the "Slichter Act," which permitted collective bargaining among state employees but denied them the right to strike.

Slichter was first president of the Industrial Relations Research Association. He was active in the Committee for Economic Development (a businessmen's research organization) and served for a lengthy period on the Labor Committee of the Twentieth Century Fund and the Labor Market Research Committee of the Social Science Research Council. He was associate chairman with Edward Stettinius of the Advisory Council on Social Security to the Senate Finance Committee (1947–1948). He testified regularly before congressional committees, particularly the Joint Economic Committee and the Senate Finance Committee.

Like his father, Slichter was an individualist in the midwestern tradition. He was a gentle person but one with a rather brusque manner. Similarly, his immense generosity with regard to time and interest was covered by a rather quizzical penny-pinching manner. These contradictions were more apparent than real, and his brusqueness and parsimony rarely interfered in most of his relationships as a scholar, adviser, and friend.

Slichter was a devoted family man; his wife, Ada Pence, whom he married on June 6, 1918, was the daughter of a one-time professor at the University of Wisconsin and later a member of the Interstate Commerce Commission. They had two sons. His last major project was *The Impact of*

Collective Bargaining on Management (1960), a book on industrial relations practices written with James J. Healy and E. Robert Livernash. When he became aware that his kidney condition was desperate he sent for his secretary in order to complete as much of the book as he had time to do in his remaining hours. He died in Boston, Mass.

[Two books give considerable insight into Slichter's personality, particularly as it involved his approach to economic matters. One was edited by his longtime colleague and friend, Professor John T. Dunlop (erstwhile secretary of labor); the other is a description of his father's household as it affected the University of Wisconsin and as it influenced Sumner Slichter's own views: John T. Dunlop, ed., *Potentials of the American Economy* (1961); and Mark H. Ingram, *Charles Sumner Slichter: The Golden Vector* (1972). Slichter's address to the American Economic Association was published as "The Conditions of Expansion," *American Economic Review*, Mar. 1942.]

MARK PERLMAN

SMILLIE, RALPH (July 8, 1887–Feb. 16, 1960), civil engineer, the son of James David Smillie and Anna C. Cook, was born in Montrose, Pa., and grew up in New York City. His father, an artist, had helped found the American Water Color Society in 1866.

Smillie received a B.S. degree from Yale University in 1909 and an engineering degree from Columbia University in 1912. He then returned to Yale to begin working toward an M.S. degree, which he received in 1915. Upon leaving Yale he secured a position with the New York subway system as a resident engineer in charge of steel plate construction. He left this position in 1917 to serve with the navy after the United States entered World War I.

After leaving the service in 1919, Smillie became an assistant engineer of design and later engineer of design for the Holland Tunnel, which connected New York City and New Jersey. Soon after receiving the appointment, he published an article in the *Engineering News-Record* offering a method for the simple determination of rivet pitch in metal-plate girders. The Holland Tunnel, completed in 1927, was the world's first to carry vehicular traffic beneath a river. While serving on the Holland Tunnel project, Smillie met and married the former Grace Cooley; they had three children.

Two years after the opening of the tunnel, Smillie became the transit engineer supervising a variety of projects for Newark, N.J. In 1933 he left Newark to become the engineer in charge of design for the Port of New York Authority. Smillie worked mainly on the construction of the Lincoln Tunnel, also connecting Manhattan and New Jersey, which opened in 1937. He remained with the Port Authority until 1945 and supervised the design work for a second Lincoln Tunnel tube under the Hudson.

In 1945 Smillie began a five-year stint as chief engineer for New York's Triborough Bridge and Tunnel Authority. The engineering for the construction of the Brooklyn-Battery Tunnel, which opened between lower Manhattan and the borough of Brooklyn in 1950, was his principal assignment while at Triborough.

After the opening of the tunnel, Smillie left the Authority to form his own consulting engineering firm, Smillie and Griffin. This company provided engineering services for a variety of important projects in the United States and abroad during the 1950's; these included tunnels for a highway from La Guaira to Caracas, Venezuela; highway approaches to New York City's Triborough Bridge; the third tube of the Lincoln Tunnel; bridge and tunnel projects in the states of Washington, Maryland, and Pennsylvania; a depressed limited-access highway in Boston; and a vehicular tunnel under the Fraser River in Vancouver, B.C.

Smillie died at his home in Essex Fells, N.J.

[Smillie's article, "Finding Rivet Pitch in Plate Girders Quickly," appeared in the *Engineering-News Record*, July 22, 1920. For the outlines of Smillie's career, see the obituaries in *New York Times*, Feb. 17, 1960; and *Civil Engineering*, Apr. 1960.]

ROY HAYWOOD LOPATA

SNELL, BERTRAND HOLLIS (Dec. 9, 1870–Feb. 2, 1958), businessman and congressman, was born in Colton, N.Y., the son of Hollis Snell, a lumberman, and Flora E. Kimball. Snell graduated from State Normal School in Potsdam, N.Y., in 1889, and then worked his way through Amherst College, graduating in 1894. He worked as a lumberjack and bookkeeper for the Racquette River Paper Company (Potsdam, N.Y.), where his father was a camp foreman. On June 3, 1903, he married Sara Louise Merrick; they had two daughters.

Snell's intelligence, perseverance, and willingness to work hard soon led to success in business. He became secretary and manager of the Racquette River Paper Company, and saved enough money to buy stock in the firm. He then organized the Canton Lumber Company in 1904 and became active as director or president of several pulp and milling operations. He built a power plant, organized the New York State Oil Company, which owned wells in Kansas, and purchased a cheese factory in New York City. He put money into insurance companies, orchards, banks, and a clothing firm. All of these ventures were profitable.

A lifelong Republican, Snell became a member of the New York State Republican Committee in 1914, a post he held until 1945. In 1915 he ran for Congress in the Thirty-first New York district. He won easily, and was reelected to the next eleven Congresses. In 1938, realizing that it would be many years before the Republicans would recapture the House of Representatives, he gave up his dream of becoming Speaker of the House and decided not to run again. On Jan. 3, 1939, he retired from the House of Representatives.

During his long career, Snell became an influential figure in the Congress and in the Republican party. He was a delegate to seven national Republican conventions, and in 1932 and 1936 he served as permanent chairman of these conclaves. During the 1920's, when the Republicans controlled the Congress, Snell chaired the powerful House Rules Committee. Speaker Nicholas Longworth, party whip John Q. Tilson, and Snell formed the triumvirate that "ruled" the House for nearly a decade. When accused of "gagging" the Democratic minority, Snell accurately predicted that if the Democrats ever regained control of the House, they would employ the same tactics. When Longworth died, Snell and Tilson fought a bitter six-month battle for the Republican leadership. Although Tilson had President Herbert Hoover's backing, Snell finally won, and during the 1930's acted as House minority leader.

A tough conservative (both allies and opponents called him "Hard-Boiled Snell"), Snell fought nearly all of the New Deal's programs. Recognizing that he could do little to impede President Franklin D. Roosevelt's early legislative proposals, Snell organized his followers into "truth squads." Each group would study a particular problem, and during the floor debate, would interrupt Democratic speakers to ask pointed, detailed, and often obscure questions designed to show the ignorance of the majority spokesmen on key issues.

Snell wore spats and expensive blue and brown suits, smoked good cigars, and rode in a chauffeured limousine. At a time when most congressmen still lived in Washington hotels, he maintained an apartment at 2400 16th Street, N.W., one of the most expensive buildings in the city. Despite his affluent style, Snell resented being thought of as a rich man. "I've got enough to live comfortably," he said. "But whatever I've got I've earned. I've done more hard labor in my time than most of the members of the House will ever do."

During his long service in the House, Snell was identified with only one major proposal. Beginning in 1917, he championed the idea of the St. Lawrence Seaway. Although never able to secure passage of the bill while in office, Snell lived to see Congress authorize the measure in 1954. Construction was nearly complete at the time of his death. Upon petition of the New York congressional delegation, President Dwight D. Eisenhower directed that the seaway lock at Grasse River be named after Snell.

After his retirement from Congress, Snell published the Potsdam *Courier-Freeman*, which he had purchased in 1934. He was involved in a variety of civic and educational enterprises in upstate New York. He died in Potsdam.

[For more information on Snell, see *Newsweek*, Jan. 27, 1934; the *New York Times*, Feb. 3, 1958; and U.S. Congress, Senate, *Congressional Record*, 85th Cong., 2nd sess., 1958, Vol. 104, pt. 2:1549.]

MELVIN I. UROFSKY

SPEAKER, TRIS E. (Apr. 4, 1888–Dec. 8, 1958), baseball player, was born in Hubbard, Tex., the son of Archie O. Speaker, a carpenter, and Nancy Jane Poer. Raised in the Texas cow country, Speaker fell from a horse at age ten and broke his collarbone and right hand. He soon learned to use his left so well that he would throw and bat left-handed throughout his career. As a teenager he attended the Fort Worth Polytechnic Institute, where he injured his left arm playing football. Reportedly, he declined the doctor's recommendation that the arm be amputated.

In 1906 Speaker joined the Cleburne baseball club of the North Texas League as a left-handed pitcher. After failing at that position, he was converted to an outfielder to make use of his hitting talents. In 1907 he was advanced to the Houston club. His hitting and defensive skills attracted the attention of the Boston Red Sox, who purchased his contract and brought him immediately to the major league club. His play in seven late-season games was undistinguished.

In 1908 Speaker was sent to the Red Sox minor league affiliate at Little Rock in the Southern Association. His .350 batting average there led to his recall to the major leagues, where he remained for twenty-two years. In 1909 he became a regular, joining Duffy Lewis and Harry Hooper to form what some authorities believe to be the greatest defensive outfield in the history of baseball.

Speaker soon established himself as one of the finest hitters and fielders in professional baseball. Popularly known as "Spoke" and the "Gray Eagle" (because of his prematurely graying hair), he batted over .300 in eighteen of the next nineteen years. Only the spectacular hitting of Ty Cobb of Detroit, who won twelve batting titles during Speaker's career, overshadowed Speaker's impressive consistency.

Competition from the outlaw Federal League forced the Boston club to grant Speaker a two-year contract for $36,000—reportedly the highest salary in baseball at that time. With the Federal League's demise after the 1915 season, Boston attempted to reduce Speaker's salary by half. He balked and was subsequently traded in 1916 to the Cleveland Indians in exchange for two players and $55,000—the highest sale price in baseball history until Babe Ruth was sold to the New York Yankees in 1920 for $125,000.

At Cleveland, Speaker was an instant success. He broke Cobb's nine-year hold on the batting title while batting .386, as well as leading the league in hits, doubles, and slugging percentage. Speaker's hitting prowess was remarkable. By 1979 he still led all major leaguers with 793 doubles, having led the league in that category on eight occasions. He also stood third on the all-time list with 3,515 hits, sixth with 223 triples, and seventh with a .344 lifetime batting average. Despite these statistics, it was his defensive work that merits Speaker a place alongside Babe Ruth, Ty Cobb, and Joe DiMaggio, the greatest outfielders. He led all outfielders with 452 lifetime assists, 139 double plays, and 7,463 total chances, and was second with 6,789 putouts. Speaker's range in the field was so great that he frequently played extraordinarily shallow centerfield, enabling him to participate in infield plays and catch base runners unawares. Still he was always prepared to dash into the center-field depths to catch, with apparent ease, balls hit well beyond the range of other fielders.

In July 1919 Speaker became player-manager of the Indians and in his first full season led the club to the World Series championship. His seven seasons as manager were marked by two second-place finishes and a third-place effort although competing with what was probably the greatest team in baseball history, the New York Yankees, led by Babe Ruth.

In 1926, the year after his marriage, Speaker was implicated, apparently unjustly, in a scandal involving the alleged fixing of a 1919 regular season game between the Indians and the Detroit Tigers. The allegations first came to light when Cobb and Speaker suddenly resigned as player-managers of Detroit and Cleveland, respectively. Soon thereafter Commissioner Kenesaw Mountain Landis revealed that the two had agreed to resign because of accusations that they had fixed a game. Coming as it did in the wake of the Chicago Black Sox scandal and the Teapot Dome affair, and involving two of the sport's biggest names, the scandal shocked the hero-conscious American public. Speaker denied any wrongdoing and indeed had three hits in the game that he was alleged to have thrown.

After an investigation Landis ruled that Cobb and Speaker were innocent of the charges. Both were restored to good standing but were made free agents by their teams. Speaker then signed with the Washington Senators where, in 1927, he hit .327. He was traded to the Philadelphia Athletics for his last season (1928), where he joined Cobb, who was also in his final year, in the outfield.

Speaker spent the 1929 and 1930 seasons as player-manager of the Newark Bears of the International League. In 1930, he batted .419 playing on a part-time basis. Soon thereafter he became a successful radio baseball announcer. He also purchased a part interest in the Kansas City Blues of the International League.

In the late 1930's Speaker served briefly as chairman of the Cleveland Boxing Commission. In 1937 he was elected to the National Baseball Hall of Fame, the seventh player so honored. From 1947 until his death, in Lake Whitney, Tex., Speaker was a coach of outfielders, batting instructor, and scout for the Cleveland Indians.

Speaker's buoyant personality won him widespread popularity both in baseball and outside the sport. He was almost six feet tall and weighed 193 pounds in his prime. He had large, powerful hands, and a voice "like rolling thunder."

[Speaker's statistics are in *The Baseball Encyclopedia* (1974). Harold Seymour, *Baseball*, Vol. II, *The Golden Age* (1971); and David Quentin Voigt, *American Baseball*, Vol. II, *From the Commission to Continental*

Expansion (1970), place his career within the perspective of baseball history. Lawrence S. Ritter, *The Glory of Their Times* (1966), provides interviews with two of his teammates and friends. J. G. Taylor Spink, *Judge Landis and 25 Years of Baseball* (1974), discusses in depth the Speaker-Cobb scandal and its resolution. There is a contemporary profile in *Literary Digest*, Dec. 11, 1920; and an obituary notice in the *New York Times*, Dec. 9, 1958. The National Baseball Hall of Fame, Cooperstown, N.Y., contains various memorabilia of Speaker's career.]

STEPHEN D. BODAYLA

SPRECKELS, RUDOLPH (Jan. 1, 1872–Oct. 4, 1958), manufacturer, banker, reformer, was born in San Francisco, Calif., the son of Claus Spreckels and Anna Christina Mangel, both of whom had emigrated from Germany. Rudolph suffered severely from asthma as a boy, and his formal education, limited to the public schools of San Francisco and some private tutoring, was often interrupted by this illness. His greatest interests were aroused when he heard his father and his older brothers discussing business. His father had become the principal sugar refiner on the West Coast, and in 1889 had built a new plant in Philadelphia in order to fight the American Sugar Refining Company, or "Sugar Trust." At the age of seventeen Rudolph went to work in his father's new refinery, where he observed the trust's tactics of industrial sabotage and espionage against would-be competitors, and learned to combat these tactics without resorting to them. He learned, in the later words of Lincoln Steffens, "the principles of business and—the lack of them." At twenty-two Spreckels forced the trust to buy the Philadelphia plant on his terms and to agree to stay out of the western part of the country.

In 1895 he married Eleanor J. Jolliffe. A year earlier he had become president of the Hawaiian Commercial and Sugar Company, owner of the great Spreckelsville plantation that his father had developed on the central plains of Maui. The plantation had not been prospering, but, in cooperation with his brother Claus Augustus ("Gus") Spreckels, he succeeded in putting it on a paying basis. When a family feud erupted in which the father and his older sons, John and Adolph, tried to drive the younger sons from control of the Hawaiian properties, Rudolph and Gus emerged victorious, but they then determined to sell the plantation to interests outside the family, at a large profit. In 1898 Rudolph thus

achieved his ambition of becoming a multimillionaire. "Perhaps I wanted to assert my independence of my father," he once recalled. "He always treated us in something of an authoritarian Prussian manner." Ultimately he received his father's forgiveness and even became the executor of his estate.

Spreckels then organized the First National Bank of San Francisco and the First Federal Trust Company. In 1900 he gained control of the San Francisco Gas Company, reorganized it, and eliminated many corrupt practices from its management. He had been repelled by corruption in business long before he became particularly concerned about it in politics, but in 1906 he became completely disgusted by a corrupt alliance between politics and big business that had taken hold of San Francisco. The political boss, Abraham Ruef, opportunistic and cynical captor of the so-called Union Labor Party, was receiving huge payments from public utility and other corporations under the guise of attorney's fees. Fremont Older, editor of the *San Francisco Bulletin*, had begun a crusade against the city machine, and Older and Spreckels became the original organizers of the San Francisco Graft Prosecution of 1906–1909. Older secretly persuaded President Theodore Roosevelt to lend the services of Francis J. Heney, then a special federal prosecutor of timber frauds in Oregon, and of William J. Burns, the chief detective in the Secret Service of the Treasury Department. Spreckels provided a quarter of a million dollars of his own money to pay the expenses of a San Francisco investigation and prosecution. Lincoln Steffens, author of *The Shame of the Cities* (1904), took part in the planning and strategy, and impressed Spreckels and Heney with his thesis that the wealthy captains of industry who paid bribes were guiltier and more dangerous than the politicians. Thus the prosecution granted immunity to the Union Labor members of the city-and-county board of supervisors to testify against those who had bribed them. Several leading executives of the street railway, gas, and telephone companies were indicted for bribery; but in the end only Boss Ruef went to prison. Most businessmen turned against the prosecution, and many tried to brand Spreckels as a traitor to his class.

Spreckels took a prominent part in the relief and reconstruction work after the San Francisco earthquake and fire of 1906. Although a progressive Republican and an admirer of Theodore Roosevelt, he supported Woodrow Wilson in

1912, but was said to have declined Wilson's offer of the ambassadorship to Germany in 1913, an action consistent with his repeated refusals to run for any public office. In 1924, after he had entered the field of radio manufacturing, Spreckels was charged with having ruined the Kolster Radio Corporation by making a huge profit through manipulation of its stock, but the case was thrown out of court. Throughout the 1920's he sponsored repeated but unsuccessful campaigns for a California state water and power project that would have put the state into competition with the monopolistic Pacific Gas and Electric Company, several of whose executives he detested. His campaigns for reform were often influenced in part by his feelings of personal hostility toward other leading men of business, and by his reluctance to lose a fight.

In 1929 Spreckels' fortune was estimated at $30 million, but he lost almost everything in the great crash. "Several financiers jumped out of their windows when they found themselves bankrupt," he told a reporter in 1958, "but I never lost a night's sleep over it." He saved his mansion in Hillsborough by selling it to his wife, who was wealthy in her own right. After her death in 1949, he moved to a small apartment in San Mateo, Calif., where he died.

[Lincoln Steffens, "Rudolph Spreckels, a Businessman Fighting for His City," *American Magazine*, Feb. 1908, reprinted as "Rudolph Spreckels, a Business Reformer" in Lincoln Steffens, *Upbuilders* (1968), is the most detailed account. See also Lincoln Steffens, *Autobiography* (1931); W. W. Cordray, "Claus Spreckels of California" (Ph.D. diss., University of Southern California, 1955); Jacob Adler, *Claus Spreckels; the Sugar King in Hawaii* (1966); and obituaries in the *San Francisco Chronicle, San Francisco Examiner*, and *New York Times*, Oct. 5, 1958.]

WALTON BEAN

STANLEY, AUGUSTUS OWSLEY (May 21, 1867–Aug. 12, 1958), lawyer, United States congressman and senator, was born in Shelbyville, Ky., the son of the Reverend William Stanley, a journalist and later a minister of the Christian or "Campbellite" Church, and Amanda Owsley. After attending local schools, he enrolled in the Kentucky Agricultural and Mechanical College in Lexington in 1886. He transferred to Centre College in Danville two years later and received the B.S. in 1889. After teaching for four

years, he was admitted to the bar in 1894 and practiced in Flemingsburg, Ky. In 1898 he settled in Henderson, Ky., where he married Sue Soaper on Apr. 29, 1903. They had three sons.

A dynamic orator, Stanley moved easily into the turbulent Democratic politics of Kentucky. As an antiprohibitionist, he opposed the dry faction led by Governor John C. W. Beckham. Service as a presidential elector for William Jennings Bryan in 1900 and well-received speeches led to a congressional race in the Second District in 1902. Following a narrow victory in the primary, he won the general election and began six consecutive terms (1903–1915) in the House of Representatives. He first gained national attention for supporting Kentucky tobacco growers against the Tobacco Trust between 1904 and 1909. Amid the Black Patch War, Stanley sought legislation to repeal a federal tax on tobacco.

Opposition to trusts led Stanley in 1910 to sponsor a congressional probe of the U.S. Steel Corporation. The Stanley Committee's hearings (1911–1912) dealt with such controversies as the steel corporation's acquisition of the Tennessee Coal and Iron Company in 1907. The hearings prodded the federal government to file an antitrust suit against U.S. Steel in 1911, and were, wrote Louis D. Brandeis, "a large factor in educating public opinion generally in regard to big business." The committee's majority report criticized the company's economic influence and offered proposals that rejected federal regulation in favor of legal restraints on corporate size. Many of Stanley's recommendations were included in the Clayton Antitrust Act of 1914.

Stanley sought his party's nomination for senator in the August 1914 primary against former governor Beckham and the incumbent governor James B. McCreary. The liquor question was the most important issue in a close election that Beckham won over Stanley by seven thousand votes. With his House career ended, Stanley ran for governor in 1915. Campaigning as a wet against statewide prohibition, he won the Democratic nomination in August 1915, running more than 37,000 ballots ahead of his major dry opponent in a field of four. Stanley then faced Republican Edwin Morrow in the general election. In what later was called an "eyelash finish," Stanley prevailed by 219,991 votes to Morrow's 219,521.

As governor, Stanley sought to reform Kentucky's tax system, to pass workmen's compensation laws, and to secure larger appropriations for higher education. When a mob in Murray, Ky., threatened to lynch a black prisoner in January 1917, Stanley dispersed the crowd, telling them that he came not "to snatch the accused from punishment but to save him from violence." During World War I, the state legislature passed a law barring the teaching of German in public schools, a measure that Stanley vetoed—"We are at war with an armed despotism, not a language." Stanley was not happy as governor, but he made a creditable record as state executive.

The death of Senator Ollie James in August 1918 opened Stanley's way to the Senate. He appointed an ally to James's unexpired term and secured the Democratic nomination for the general election in November. Stanley had the support of the Wilson administration, but his "German veto" and wet sentiments were a handicap. He won the election by only six thousand votes. He continued as governor until May 19, 1919, when he was sworn in as senator.

Republican control of the Senate limited Stanley's impact during his single term. He spoke out against what he believed to be abuses of civil liberties in enforcing prohibition, and denounced government centralization. "The most conspicuous 'progressive,' " he remarked in 1922, "is the most ingenious inventor of new ways and means of invading the vested rights of the States and the liberties of the citizens." He was renominated in 1924, but opposition from the Ku Klux Klan and prohibitionists, combined with a general Republican tide, cost him his seat.

After practicing law in Washington, D.C., for five years with Wilson's former secretary, Joseph P. Tumulty, Stanley was appointed in 1930 to the International Joint Commission, an agency that oversaw the boundary waters between the United States and Canada. He became the commission's chairman in 1933 and remained in office until February 1954, when the Eisenhower administration obtained his retirement. He died in Washington, D.C.

Stanley was a colorful and flamboyant figure in Kentucky affairs. Attacks on the Tobacco Trust and U.S. Steel gave him a reformist reputation during his years in the House, and he advanced progressive causes as governor. As his Senate career showed, however, his heart lay with older Democratic principles of limited government, states' rights, and economic conservatism. For several generations of Kentuckians, Stanley was "the silvertongued orator, the portly, almost bald storyteller," who animated state campaigns.

Upon his death, a newspaper accurately described him "as among the last and best of the old-fashioned Kentucky political orators."

[Stanley's papers are in the Margaret I. King Library, University of Kentucky; records relating to his governorship are in the Kentucky Historical Society, Frankfort. The University of Kentucky has the papers of Stanley's contemporaries Ollie James, Thomas R. Underwood, Samuel Wilson, and Urey Woodson; the Joseph P. Tumulty, Henry Watterson, Woodrow Wilson, and Robert W. Woolley collections at the Library of Congress illuminate his national career.

For material on Stanley, see U.S. House of Representatives, Committee on Investigation of United States Steel Corporation, *Hearings on Investigation of United States Steel Corporation*, 62nd Cong., 1st Sess. (1911–1912); Thomas Randolph, "The Governor and the Mob," *Independent*, Feb. 26, 1917; Paul Hughes, "Governor in Time of War, But Peace Is His Job Now," *Louisville Courier-Journal*, June 25, 1950; Thomas W. Ramage, "Augustus Owsley Stanley: Early Twentieth-Century Kentucky Democrat" (Ph.D. thesis, University of Kentucky, 1968), is a careful, thorough biography; David W. Levy and Melvin Urofsky, eds., *Letters of Louis D. Brandeis*, vols. II–III (1972; 2nd ed., 1973); and Thomas H. Appleton, Jr., "Prohibition and Politics in Kentucky: The Gubernatorial Campaign and Election of 1915," *Register of the Kentucky Historical Society*, Jan. 1977. See also the obituaries in the *New York Times*, Aug. 13, 1958; and *Louisville Courier-Journal*, Aug. 14, 1958.]

LEWIS L. GOULD

STARRETT, PAUL (Nov. 25, 1866–July 5, 1957), builder, was born in Lawrence, Kans., the son of William Aiken Starrett, a graduate of Princeton Theological Seminary who had immigrated to Kansas as a Presbyterian minister in 1864. His mother was Helen Martha Ekin. The elder Starrett supplemented his meager income by working as a farmer and a carpenter. He forsook his ministry, first to edit the *Lawrence Daily Journal* and then to study law. Starrett's mother sold pianos and ran the paper, but about 1880 she moved the family to Chicago, where she founded and edited the *Western Magazine*. The magazine failed, and Paul, then sixteen, quit school to go to work as a stockboy for a wholesale hardware firm. He then became a clerk in an insurance agency. After a short while as a salesman, he became discouraged and returned to office work, as a stenographer for a grain company. In poor health as a result of long hours of work and night school, he eagerly accepted the offer of an unsalaried job as clerk on his employer's ranch in New Mexico. When he returned to Chicago in 1888 he found a job with the architectural firm of Burnham and Root, where his older brother, Theodore, was a draftsman.

The enthusiasm and optimism of the late nineteenth-century American city permeated the offices of Burnham and Root, whose classic eclecticism was to dominate urban building in America for a generation. Deciding that he, too, would become an architect, Starrett enrolled in night classes at Lake Forest University. But, he later explained, "I couldn't *imagine* anything. I could copy, but I couldn't imagine. My mind was absolutely literal and matter-of-fact." Engineering seemed a logical alternative, and Starrett worked at its practical applications, performing the thousands of tedious calculations necessary to turn architectural drawings into bricks and mortar, steel and stone. Meanwhile, he spent his lunch hours watching the rebuilding of Chicago, where some of the world's first skyscrapers were rising.

Daniel H. Burnham soon told him that he was wasting his time doing engineering work. "You can hire people to do that," he said; "you Starrett boys are different. You have a genius for organization and leadership." It was as an architect's superintendent that Starrett learned construction methods. Burnham and Root were the chief architects of the World's Columbian Exposition of 1893, and Starrett superintended the construction of several of the classic temples that rose on the midway.

In 1894 Starrett directed the construction of Buffalo's Ellicott Square Building and was so disgusted at the contractor's incompetence that he decided to go into the business himself. Meanwhile he superintended construction of one of the first buildings influenced by the Chicago fair: Union Station in Columbus, Ohio, designed by his brother Theodore. But it was Harry S. Black, who had taken over the heavy construction company founded by George A. Fuller, who gave Starrett his big opportunity in 1897. Starrett turned a profit on a building in Baltimore that Black had decided was a losing proposition, and he did the same thing with the new Willard Hotel in Washington, D.C.

After Black put the Fuller Company into a promotional combine, U.S. Realty and Improvement Company, Starrett resigned, but when business difficulties led to Black's suicide, Starrett came back to head the firm. The famous buildings built by the firm over two decades

(1902–1922) included the Flatiron Building, Pennsylvania Station, General Post Office, the Hotel Pennsylvania, the Metropolitan Life Insurance Company Tower, the Hippodrome, and the Plaza Hotel in New York City; the Bellevue-Stratford Hotel in Philadelphia; and the Blackstone Hotel in Chicago. More than any other single firm, Starrett's company helped create the twentieth-century American city. Besides Burnham, he collaborated with such other major architects as Charles F. McKim, Stanford White, Henry J. Hardenbergh, Cass Gilbert, and Napoleon Le Brun.

On May 25, 1892, Starrett married Anna Therese Hinman, daughter of his former boss at the insurance agency. They had two daughters. His wife died in 1904. On June 8, 1920, he married Elizabeth Root; they had three sons.

In 1922 Starrett founded his own company, Starrett Brothers. He had failed to get the contract for New York's most celebrated skyscraper of the era, the Woolworth Building (1913), and considered it his biggest disappointment. But Starrett continued to change the skyline of New York with the New York Life Insurance Company Building (1928), the McGraw-Hill Building (1931), and Bank of Manhattan Company buildings. And 1931 saw the completion of the Starrett-built building that came to be the very symbol of New York City, the Empire State Building. The literal-minded master builder lived to see its utilitarian simplicity praised more highly than the classic entablatures of his youth, many of which were already being dismantled when he died, in Greenwich, Conn.

[Starrett's autobiography, written with Webb Waldron, is *Changing the Skyline* (1938). See the obituary notices, *New York Times,* July 6, 1957; *Engineering News-Record,* July 11, 1957; and *Architectural Forum,* Sept. 1957.]

ALBRO MARTIN

STEINMAN, DAVID BARNARD (June 11, 1886–Aug. 21, 1960), bridge engineer, was born in New York City, the son of Louis Kelvin Steinman, an immigrant factory worker, and of Eva Scollard. He grew up in lower Manhattan, close to the Brooklyn Bridge. Steinman entered the City College of New York (CCNY) at the age of thirteen, graduating in 1906 with highest honors. From there he moved to Columbia University, where he obtained C.E. and M.A. degrees in 1909 and a Ph.D. degree in 1911. His dissertation, "The Design of the Henry Hudson Memorial Bridge as a Steel Arch," was published shortly afterward. (The bridge itself was built twenty-five years later, to his design.)

In 1910, Steinman accepted a teaching appointment at the University of Idaho at Moscow; he rose to the rank of full professor four years later. His dissertation had come to the attention of Gustav Lindenthal, a bridge engineer, who was developing a design for the Hell Gate Bridge over the East River in New York. Lindenthal asked Steinman to become his assistant. Steinman agreed and returned to New York. On June 9, 1915, he married Irene Hofmann; they had three children.

Steinman worked with Lindenthal on the design of the Hell Gate Bridge, which was opened to traffic in 1917. In that year he became professor of civil and mechanical engineering at CCNY; at the same time he set himself up as an independent engineering designer and consultant. An opportunity presented itself at once. The Brazilian government proposed to select the design for the Florianópolis Bridge in an open competition. Holton D. Robinson, bridge engineer, asked Steinman to join him in submitting a design. Their design won the competition. Completed in 1926, the Florianópolis Bridge was at the time the longest suspension bridge in South America. Steinman and Robinson continued to design bridges together until Robinson's death in 1945.

Steinman's reputation brought an increasing flow of contracts to design bridges. In 1923, he founded the partnership of Steinman, Boynton, Fronquist and London. Over the next thirty years the firm designed more than 400 bridges throughout the world. The Carquinex Strait Bridge in California, of cantilever construction, was completed in 1927. In 1931, Steinman assisted Othmar H. Ammann, later his arch rival, in the design of the George Washington Bridge in New York City. Other important Steinman bridges during this period were the Sidney Harbor Bridge in Australia (1932), the Triborough Bridge in New York City (1936), and the Thousand Islands International Bridge linking the United States to Canada (1938).

Shortly after its construction reports came that the Thousand Islands Bridge was experiencing vertical heaving motions in a crosswind. Steinman solved the problem by adding pairs of inclined stays. Four years later the problem recurred on a much more serious scale in a bridge designed by Leon S. Moisseiff. The Tacoma Narrows Bridge, known, as soon as it was built, to be prone to torsional instabilities, broke apart in a strong wind and fell into the river in 1940.

Before the Tacoma Narrows disaster, Moisseiff had been commissioned to design a much longer suspension bridge, to be built across the straits of Mackinac in Michigan. When the project was revived after World War II, a committee was appointed to review the choice of architect. Two members of this committee were Ammann and Steinman, the most logical candidates to whom the task might be reassigned. They were unable to agree on their recommendations, and Ammann withdrew. The commission went to Steinman, and the Mackinac Straits Bridge was finally opened in 1957.

The design of the Mackinac Straits Bridge did not err on the side of flimsiness. It seems questionable, in fact, whether Steinman fully understood the problem of torsional oscillations. His paper "Rigidity and Aerodynamic Stability of Suspension Bridges," published by the American Society of Civil Engineers in 1943, pointed out the factors making for poor stability; but his remedy, as executed in the Mackinac Straits Bridge, was simply more steel. Later work, notably by Theodore von Kármán, using wind-tunnel modeling, showed how to reduce the effect of wind by means of different types of bridge cross section.

In 1948, Steinman was asked to assume responsibility for the modernization of the Brooklyn Bridge. Having grown up in its shadow, and been inspired by it to make bridge building his career, this was a labor of love for Steinman. He was careful to leave the external appearance of the bridge untouched. The project was completed in 1954.

Steinman wished to build a bridge between Brooklyn and Staten Island. The contract for what became the Verrazano-Narrows Bridge went instead to Ammann. Steinman designed a bridge to cross the Bosporus at Istanbul, Turkey, but the bridge constructed there in 1973 was not his. He conceived a bridge connecting Sicily to Italy at the Strait of Messina, but it was never built.

Steinman was a prolific writer. In addition to many technical articles, he wrote popular books on bridges and bridge building and two volumes of poetry. He died in New York City.

[Steinman's books include *Bridges and Their Builders* (1941), written with S. R. Watson; and *The*

Builders of the Bridge (1945). See also Joseph Gries, *Bridges and Men* (1963). Steinman's obituary is in *New York Times*, Aug. 23, 1960.]

C. G. B. GARRETT

STERN, KURT GUENTER (Sept. 19, 1904–Feb. 3, 1956), biochemist, was born in Tilsit, Germany, the son of John Kasper Stern and Sonia Goldberg. After studying in Berlin at the Werner-Siemens Realgymnasium, he attended the Friedrich-Wilhelms University in Berlin, where he received the Ph.D. in 1930. His doctoral work was done at the pathological institute of the university in the laboratory of Hans Kuhlman, the research dealing with proteases (protein-splitting enzymes) extracted from spleens of cattle. Two joint papers published in *Biochemische Zeitschrift* (1930) deal with extraction of the proteinases, their physicochemical properties, and their action is degrading various proteins.

On Dec. 24, 1931, Stern married Else E. Jacobi, who worked with her husband for a time and published several papers with him. They had one son.

Upon completion of his doctorate, Stern received a fellowship sponsored by Carl Duisberg, a prominent German chemical industrialist. The fellowship enabled Stern to spend the next year in the United States, where he worked in the laboratory of Leonor Michaelis at the Rockefeller Institute for Medical Research. This work dealt with the influence of heavy metals such as copper, mercury, iron, manganese, and selenium on the proteolytic action of tissue extracts on proteins such as casein, gelatin, and serum albumin. He showed that iron and manganese had an activating effect while mercury, copper, and selenium were inhibitory.

From 1931 to 1933 Stern worked as research chemist in the physiological chemistry laboratory of the Rudolf Virchow Hospital in Berlin, where he continued his studies on proteases. After the Nazis came to power in 1933, he was able to obtain a post as a visiting guest scientist in the Courtauld Institute of Biochemistry of the Middlesex Medical School in England. There he was associated with Ensor R. Holiday in work on the prosthetic group of the yellow enzyme discovered shortly before this in the Berlin laboratory of Otto Warburg. By spectroscopic study, Stern and Holiday identified a fragment of the group as an alloxazine derivative. This led to an elucidation of the chemical structure of the flavins and enabled Richard Kuhn in Heidelberg and Paul Karrer in Zurich independently to synthesize an extensive series of such compounds, leading to recognition of riboflavin as the substance then known as vitamin B_2.

In 1935 Stern was appointed lecturer in physiological chemistry at Yale University. In 1937–1938 he was Alexander Brown Coxe research fellow and then became assistant professor at Yale until 1942. In that year he became chief chemist with the Overly Biochemical Research Foundation. Two years later he was made adjunct professor of biochemistry at the Polytechnic Institute in Brooklyn, a position he held until his death while on a lecture tour in London. He had become a naturalized American citizen in 1946.

While at Yale, in association with Joseph L. Melnick, Stern became deeply interested in the Pasteur effect, an observation of Louis Pasteur who had noted in 1876 that glucose is metabolized much less extensively by yeast in the presence of free oxygen than under anaerobic conditions. In 1926 Warburg observed the linkage of respiratory and fermentation processes by a chemical reaction that was eventually referred to as the Pasteur reaction. Splitting of sugar by free oxygen in the presence of heavy-metal catalysts was inhibited by certain reagents leading, during the next two decades, to the search for the iron-containing substance associated with the Pasteur reaction. In 1941 Stern and Melnick reported the spectrum of the -carbon monoxide derivative of the Pasteur enzyme in the retina and in yeast. However, Stern's effort to shed further light on the Pasteur effect was unfruitful since the Pasteur reaction would prove to be more complex than had been surmised.

During much of his career, Stern was also interested in enzymes known as catalases. These enzymes have a role in cellular metabolism since they catalyze the breakdown of hydrogen peroxide—formed in certain steps in cellular respiration—to water and molecular oxygen. He first isolated catalases from blood cells and from animal liver and directed a large amount of research toward understanding their composition and properties. Utilizing the most advanced techniques of colloid chemistry, such as ultracentrifugation and electrophoresis, he was able to clarify the chemical and physical characteristics of these enzymes that have molecular weights in the neighborhood of 250,000 and contain four atoms of iron per unit.

Toward the end of his career Stern began to give attention to the chemistry of nucleoproteins—proteins associated with nucleic acids, the carriers of genetic information in the cell. His research was aimed toward understanding of the size and shape of chromosomal nucleoproteins and their bearing on gene structure, an objective which was, however, not readily responsive to the chemical approach but would ultimately be resolved by a combination of chemical information interpreted through X-ray crystallography.

Stern was deeply interested in application of scientific knowledge and obtained patents on the electrophoretic analysis of colloidal liquids and biological fluids; on the decolorization of soybean oil; and for the capacitron, a device for sterilizing food by destroying bacteria and viruses through disruptive effects on the deoxyribonucleic acid (DNA) of their cells or molecules. In his latest years he believed himself on the verge of successful results in the treatment of cancerous tissues by introduction of radioisotopes of rare earth compounds. He died in London.

[Stern's publications include *General Enzyme Chemistry* (1932), written with John Burdon S. Haldane, and *Biological Oxidation* (1939), with Carl Oppenheimer. For more information, see *Chemical and Engineering News,* Mar. 19, 1956; and *Chemical Abstracts,* passim, 1931–1958.]

AARON J. IHDE

STERNE, MAURICE (July 13, 1878–July 23, 1957), painter, draftsman, sculptor, and muralist, was born in Libau, Latvia, the son of Hirsch Zwi Sterne and Naomi Schlossberg. His father was trained as a rabbi but became a grain merchant. As a boy, Sterne was encouraged to read German literature, notably Goethe and Heine. Latvia, then under Russian rule, suffered from the oppressive authority of Czar Alexander III and the tyrannical police brutality of the Cossacks. Sterne's brother Michael was forced to flee to Germany because he was threatened by Cossack persecution for his liberalism. Sterne's father died when Sterne was seven, and his older brothers, Joel and Carl, and his sister Rosa had gone to Moscow. Soon after, Sterne and his mother joined them.

It was in Moscow that he was to have his first art experience, a visit to the Tretyakov Museum. He was so enchanted that he was determined to become an artist. He was enrolled in a trade school for locksmiths briefly but then was transferred to a more advanced polytechnical school. He was drawing on his own. Examples were submitted to the director of the Kommisarsky Art Academy,

who was so impressed that he offered a scholarship to the young artist. Sterne was not to avail himself of this opportunity, because in 1889 he, his mother, and sister Lena left for America to escape the increasing persecution of Jews. Michael Sterne was already there. The Sterne family moved into a house in New York's Lower East Side. Sterne took several menial jobs while learning English. At one point, he was working in a saloon and taking night classes at the National Academy of Design. He was to graduate from that institution in 1899, winning a number of awards. In 1904 he received a grant to study abroad, in Paris, where he saw the art of the impressionists and postimpressionists. He was particularly impressed by that of Cézanne. In Paris, he saw the painter Alfred Maurer, whom Sterne knew as a fellow student in New York, and made friends with collectors Leo and Gertrude Stein, painters Max Weber and Hans Purrmann, and the actress Alla Nazimova, with whom he had a brief affair. Sterne, generally conservative in art, rejected Matisse as a poor draftsman and Picasso as a charlatan. He believed that it was necessary to return to the nineteenth century in France, from Manet and Cézanne onward, and to develop a style of his own by avoiding what he considered the sensational and merely experimental.

Before the outbreak of World War I, Sterne traveled throughout Europe, particularly in France, Germany, Italy, and Greece. He haunted the museums. An exhibition of his etchings and drawings was held in Berlin in 1910. There he met Alard DuBois Reymond, who was to become Sterne's patron and support him in his travels to Egypt, India, Burma, and Bali. From 1912 to 1914 Sterne was in Bali, where he was fascinated by native rituals and folkways. He made several thousand paintings and drawings, many on rice paper with oil paint. The influence of Gauguin was seen in these works, which brought Sterne great acclaim in the United States and Europe. Before returning to America in 1915, he visited Italy and took up residence in Anticoli, where he was to establish a studio and art school in 1918. On Aug. 18, 1917, he married the heiress and author Mabel Dodge Luhan in Peekskill, N.Y. According to her, Sterne sympathized with the Germans during World War I. After a stormy four years of marriage, they divorced, and he married a dancer, Vera Segal, on June 3, 1923. There were no children.

In the mid-1920's, Sterne's reputation grew as he began to exhibit in Europe and America. In 1925 he was given the singular honor of being invited to submit a self-portrait to the Uffizi

Gallery, the first time an American was chosen. Sterne, for some reason, never complied. His 1926 show at the Scott and Fowles Galleries in New York was a sellout. In 1928 he won the Logan medal and a cash prize in a competition at the Art Institute of Chicago. He was similarly honored with prizes in competitive exhibitions at the Corcoran Gallery in Washington and the Carnegie Institute in Pittsburgh. In 1929 he was elected president of the Society of American Painters, Sculptors, and Gravers. He had invested in the stock market and suffered losses in the crash of 1929.

When Sterne was in Egypt and Greece during the first decade of this century, he developed an enthusiasm for sculpture and made his first attempts. He said that he wanted to emphasize contour and line rather than bulk and mass. Most critics consider his sculpture as minor in relation to his paintings and drawings. His major work in sculpture is the Rogers-Kennedy War Memorial in Worcester, Mass. He worked on this monumental piece for three years in Italy. In 1934–1936 the Sternes lived in San Francisco, where he taught painting at the California School of Fine Arts. In 1935 he was awarded a commission to do murals for the library of the Department of Justice Building. Sterne worked for five years on these murals. They were unveiled in 1941 to a generally unfavorable reception; however, his show at the Wildenstein Gallery in New York in 1947 was a critical success.

Toward the end of his life he was ill and aware of impending death. He spent much of his time working on his memoirs. Paintings of his went into the collections of the major museums, including the Metropolitan Museum of Art and the Whitney Museum of American Art. The town fathers of Anticoli, where Sterne had maintained his studio for nearly thirty years, honored him by naming a street after him. Sterne's reputation declined in the 1940's and 1950's. His work is generally considered academic and conventional.

[See his autobiography, *Shadow and Light: The Life, Friends and Opinions of Maurice Sterne*, Charlotte Leon Mayerson, ed. (1952).]

ROBERT REIFF

STEUBEN, JOHN (Oct. 31, 1906–May 9, 1957), union organizer, radical activist, and labor editor, was born Itzak Rijock in Brailov, Ukraine, Russia, and immigrated to the United States in 1923 with his father, Zalik, and other members of his family. As an adult he rarely used his family name, preferring Steuben, and occasionally adopting other pseudonyms such as Harold Schulsberg, John Stevenson, John Stevens, and David Brown, when engaged in covert organizing efforts. His friends, however, called him "Shorty" because of his five foot, one inch height.

Little is known of Steuben's early life. He is variously reported to have worked as a housewrecker, metal polisher, sheet metal worker, and machinist in his early days in New York City. In the early 1930's he became a full-time organizer for the Steel and Metal Workers Industrial Union, an affiliate of the Trade Union Unity League, the Communist-led union federation established in 1929. Having been a Communist party activist since the mid-1920's, Steuben in 1934 was chosen party section organizer for the steel-making region centered in Youngstown, Ohio. But he was never content with merely holding a party position; he preferred direct union organizing, disdaining party bureaucrats without practical field experience as mere "functionaries."

In accord with his primary commitment to union-building, when the Committee for Industrial Organization (CIO) set up the Steel Workers Organizing Committee (SWOC) in 1936, Steuben almost immediately resigned his party post (but not his membership) and became a full-time SWOC organizer. Given responsibility for the Youngstown Sheet and Tube Plant, he spent months quietly building the union, largely through house-to-house visits. His marriage to Frances Nagy, a Youngstown native, assured him of local credibility, and his engaging personality helped him to win converts.

The steel workers' organizing drive of 1936–1937 culminated in the hard-fought but unsuccessful "Little Steel" Strike against Bethlehem, Republic, Inland, and Youngstown Sheet and Tube in May 1937. Steuben played a leading role, particularly in the dramatic events of June 19, when two strikers were killed and forty-two injured in a riot at the entrance to the Republic mill in Youngstown. Steuben, recalled Harold Ruttenberg, a participant, "had taken control. He was the boss man, and he negotiated the settlements and the police withdrawal." In April 1938, however, he was purged from the SWOC's staff as part of the union's effort to cut cost—and Communist influence.

After his dismissal, Steuben returned to New York City. His study of the American labor movement in World War I was published as

Labor in Wartime (1940). Although he had little more than a sixth-grade education, he was widely respected for his erudition and gained a reputation as an expert on the American labor movement through his articles in the Communist press and his lectures at Communist party and workers' schools. Most of his writings, including *Strike Strategy* (1950), dealt perceptively with concrete problems facing labor organizers but lacked theoretical sophistication. Meanwhile, he continued to participate in unionizing drives, devoting much of his energy to the fledgling New York hotel unions.

This work was interrupted in 1943, when Steuben was naturalized and entered the army for a two-year stint that included a tour with the infantry in New Guinea. After a medical discharge, he resumed his hotel-organizing work and was elected secretary-treasurer of the Hotel Front Service Employees Union. In 1949, however, he lost his bid for leadership and left hotel union politics.

Having been divorced earlier, Steuben married another hotel organizer, Lee Candea, in 1950. That year he became editor of *March of Labor,* a new monthly aimed at left-wing trade unionists. His usual exuberance and dedication attracted talented volunteers who helped produce an "unusually slick and lively" labor publication. But the success of *March of Labor* was short-lived because of inadequate funds, Steuben's poor health, and the cold war climate. In June 1935 Steuben suffered the first of a series of crippling heart attacks, and by the spring of 1954 he was forced to retire from active work on the magazine. His physical decline, along with the demise of *March of Labor,* was accelerated by government harassment, ranging from denaturalization proceedings (1952), to surveillance by the FBI, and hearings before the House.

A staunch supporter of the Soviet Union, Steuben found his faith shaken by Khrushchev's revelations in February 1956 of excesses of Stalinism. He privately resolved to "live out my few remaining years in agony and silence." When the Soviet-installed Hungarian regime threatened to order the execution of strikers in January 1957, he felt compelled to speak out against this attack on "the inalienable right of free men to organize and strike." In a front-page interview in the *New York Times,* he told of his disillusionment with the Soviet government, and urged American Communists to "repudiate everything that smacks of Stalinism and chart a course on the basis of the true interests of American workers and the American people."

Steuben died in Flemington, N.Y. Despite his lifelong dedication to militant trade unionism, Steuben, wrote Len De Caux, a former co-worker, "got little tribute when he died—too soon after a side-switching statement to be shriven by his old side, or hailed by the other side."

[There is little published information on Steuben. The longest sketch is in Len De Caux, *Labor Radical* (1970). The House Committee on Un-American Activities, *Report on the March of Labor* (1954), contains much information but must be used with caution. Steuben's testimony before the U.S. Senate Subcommittee on Education and Labor, *Hearings on Violations of Free Speech and Rights of Labor* (1938), details his role in the "Little Steel" Strike; as do the memoirs of Harold Ruttenberg (May 12, 1968), in the Pennsylvania State University Oral History Project. Steuben's files in the Department of Justice and the FBI document government harassment. For further material, see *March of Labor,* Apr. 1953, June 1955, and Oct. 1955; *New York Times,* Jan. 19, 1957, and May 10, 1957 (obituary notice); and *Daily Worker,* May 10, 1957 (obituary notice).]

ROY ROSENZWEIG

STEWART, WALTER WINNE (May 24, 1885–Mar. 6, 1958), economist, was born in Manhattan, Kans., the son of Albert Alexander Stewart and Ella Winne. His interest in banking and monetary theory may have arisen from his childhood experiences. In the 1890's his father edited a Populist newspaper, *The Republic,* in Manhattan and was a close friend of Thomas Elmer Will, a "free silver" advocate and president of Kansas State Agricultural College. While in high school at Neosho, Mo., Stewart worked as a clerk in a local bank. In 1905 he entered the University of Missouri, from which he received a B.A. degree in 1909. There he studied economics with Herbert J. Davenport and E. H. Downey. Largely through the influence of Downey, Stewart was introduced to the institutional economics of Thorstein Veblen. After brief periods as instructor of economics at Missouri (1910–1911) and the University of Michigan (1911–1913) he returned to Missouri as an assistant professor of economics in 1913. In July 1912 Stewart married Helen Wynkoop, who had been a fellow student at Missouri. They had three children.

Stewart's intelligence and his attractive personality soon won him the respect and recognition of the academic, business, and governmental communities. He was offered the deanship of several universities, but decided to join Walton H. Hamilton as a professor of economics at Amherst College in 1916. As a member of the price section of the War Industries Board in 1918, Stewart wrote important papers showing the effectiveness of war-time price controls. His service during the war led him to believe that a reconstruction of economic theory was needed in order to provide an orderly transition to peacetime conditions. Given the complexity of modern industrial society, Stewart believed that an adequate analysis of economic problems required a union of the careful use of statistics and consideration of the specific institutional context within which economic decisions were made. Building on the statistical work of Wesley Clair Mitchell, Stewart collaborated with Edmund Ezra Day in pioneering means of measuring the physical volume of national production.

In the early 1920's Stewart established a reputation for his knowledge of the workings of the Federal Reserve System, particularly its potential for controlling the volume of credit and, thereby, prices and production. He warned, though, that the control over credit exercised by the Federal Reserve Board could not guarantee economic stabilization, for the actions of the board could be stymied by the decisions of the banking and business communities. If businessmen were pessimistic about the future, for example, lower interest rates might not induce them to increase investments.

In 1922 Stewart received the opportunity to put his central-banking theories into practice. He was appointed director of the Division of Analysis and Research (expanded in 1923 to Research and Statistics) of the Federal Reserve Board as well as economic adviser to the board. Under Stewart's direction the division gained worldwide recognition for the quality of its analytical and statistical reports. He understood, perhaps better than anyone else in the country, how actions of the Federal Reserve Board affected the performance of the economy as a whole. For more than twenty-five years his 1923 report to the board established the main guidelines for the actions of the Federal Reserve System.

Although Stewart left the Federal Reserve System in 1926 to become vice-president of Case, Pomeroy and Company, a private invest-ment house in New York City, he continued in public service. He appeared as an expert witness before many congressional committees and federal commissions. Concerned about the inflation of stock prices, he warned in the late 1920's against the extension of easy credit for speculation. In 1928–1930 he took a leave from his investment company to become the first economic adviser of the Bank of England. While in London and serving as the personal representative of Owen D. Young, the chairman of the group that subsequently drew up a plan for the readjustment of German reparations, Stewart helped draft the provisions for the Bank for International Settlements. Intended to facilitate the settlement of international transactions and to assist the central banks of the various nations, the bank served as a model for the vast international financial mechanisms of the post–World War II era.

In 1930 Stewart returned to New York as chairman of the board of Case, Pomeroy and Company, a position he held until 1937. In 1938 he became professor of economics at the Institute for Advanced Study at Princeton. From 1953 to 1955 he served on President Dwight D. Eisenhower's Council of Economic Advisers. In this position he advised cautious use of the fiscal and monetary powers of the federal government.

Throughout his career Stewart exemplified the ideal of an economist who lent his expertise to public service. He died in New York City.

[Important writings by Stewart include "Social Value and the Theory of Money," *Journal of Political Economy*, Dec. 1917; and *Prices of Iron, Steel, and Their Products*, War Industries Board Price Bulletin no. 33 (1919). The memoir of James P. Warburg in the Oral History Collection at Columbia University contains much material on Stewart. See also obituary in *New York Times*, Mar. 7, 1958; and Joseph Dorfman, *The Economic Mind in American Civilization* (1959).]

BENJAMIN G. RADER

STOKES, ANSON PHELPS (Apr. 13, 1874–Aug. 13, 1958), educator and clergyman, was born in New Brighton on Staten Island, N.Y., the son of multimillionaire banker Anson Phelps Stokes and Helen Louisa Phelps. After graduating from Yale University with a B.A. degree in 1896, Stokes spent a year traveling, mostly in the Far East. This early experience in the Orient helped sustain a lifelong interest in that part of the world, one result of which was the creation of the Yale-in-China Association. In 1897 Stokes entered the Episcopal Theological School in Cambridge, Mass., to prepare for the priesthood. Before he received his bachelor of divinity degree in 1900 (Yale granted him an honorary M.A. the same year), he agreed (1899) to serve as secretary of Yale University, but his clerical dimension found expression in his concurrent status as assistant rector (1900–1918) of St. Paul's Episcopal Church in New Haven. (While ordained to the diaconate in 1900, Stokes did not formally enter the priesthood until 1925.) On Dec. 30, 1903, he married Caroline Green Mitchell; they had three children, one of whom, Anson Phelps Stokes, Jr., was Episcopal bishop of Massachusetts from 1956 to 1970.

As Yale's secretary from 1899 to 1921, Stokes was instrumental in increasing Yale's endowment and property, in winning support for the university's professional schools, and in securing Yale's position as a major center of higher learning on the national and the international scene. He became in fact Yale's second in command; as such, he was deemed by many to be the logical successor to Arthur Twining Hadley as president. A deadlock in early balloting, however, led to the selection of James Rowland Angell. To leave him a free hand, Stokes resigned as secretary in 1921. In 1952 Yale awarded him its Medal for Distinctive Service, noting that Stokes "more than any man living is the architect" of the present-day university.

In 1924 Stokes began a second career as canon residentiary of the National Cathedral (Episcopal) in Washington, D.C. In his fifteen years in the national's capital, he gave himself without stint to varied social, cultural, and ecclesiastical causes. He worked with the poor, serving as president or trustee of the Family Service Association during virtually all of his tenure at the cathedral. In a pre-ecumenical age, he opened new doors between Protestants, Catholics, and Jews. He encouraged the development of an Institute for Government Research, out of which the Brookings Institute ultimately emerged. But above all he preached, worked, and wrote on behalf of better relationships between blacks and whites in America and around the world. In 1936 he published a brief biography of Booker T. Washington (based on his earlier sketch in the DAB), and he served for a time as trustee of Tuskegee Institute, the first fifty years of which he also recorded in a

Founder's Day historical address ("Tuskegee Institute: Its First Fifty Years," 1931). After one of his trips abroad, he offered his observations on race relations and education in *East and South Africa* (1934). During his Washington years and beyond, he guided the philanthropy of the Phelps Stokes Fund (established in 1911) toward improving the lot of African and American blacks. And in 1939, as he retired from the cathedral and the capital, he published *Art and the Color Line: An Appeal . . . to the . . . Daughters of the American Revolution to Modify Their Rules So As to Permit Distinguished Negro Artists Such As Miss Marian Anderson to Be Heard in Constitution Hall* (1939).

Upon retirement Stokes moved to the family farm in Lenox, Mass. There he gave himself to two long-cherished and ambitious projects. One, a sweeping history of western universities "from their origin to the present time," never came to fulfillment. But some eleven years after his retirement the second one did emerge. This monumental three-volume work, *Church and State in the United States* (1950), dominates the field like a colossus, guaranteeing to Stokes an enduring reputation for scholarship, fairness, balance, and comprehensiveness. In over 2,300 pages Stokes detailed the conflicts and tensions between the civil and the ecclesiastical estates from colonial beginnings to the middle of the twentieth century. Even his severest critic, Monsignor John Tracy Ellis, concluded that this painstaking study was absolutely essential to "every student of American religious history."

Other reviewers spoke of the work as being imbued with a remarkable spirit of charity. So indeed, it appears, was the whole man. Contemporaries testified as well to his moral courage, to his patient skill as mediator, to his selflessness and loyalty, and to what Rabbi Norman Gerstenfeld referred to as Stokes's membership in "that mystic congregation of the righteous." He saw all his activity—whether philanthropy, education, travel, ecumenism, theological reflection, historical analysis, or social service—as facets of what he called (following Phil. 1:5) "fellowship in the gospel." Following a long illness, he died in his home in Lenox, Mass.

[The major collection of papers for Canon Stokes is at Yale in the historical manuscripts collection, the archives, and the Alumni Office. Stokes's other works include *Historical Prints of New Haven . . .* (1910); *Christ, and Man's Latent Divinity* (1911); *What Yale Does for New Haven* (1911); *The Congressional "Pork*

Barrel" (1913); *University Schools of Religion* (1914); *Memorials of Eminent Yale Men* (1914); *The Question of Preparedness* (1916); *What Jesus Christ Thought of Himself* (1916); *Educational Plans for the American Army Abroad* (1918); *Yale and New Haven* (1920); *Confidential Memorandum Regarding the University Situation in Washington* . . . (1922); and *Negro Status and Race Relations in the U.S., 1911–1946* (1948) (Appendix 3 summarizes Stokes's many contributions). Biographical details may be found in Yale University News Bureau, *Yale Alumni Magazine,* release dated Aug. 14, 1958; *New Haven Register,* Aug. 14, 1958; and in the publication of the National Cathedral, the *Cathedral Age,* especially the Winter 1939–1940 issue. See also the obituary notice, *New York Times,* Aug. 15, 1958.]

EDWIN S. GAUSTAD

STOKES, THOMAS LUNSFORD, JR. (Nov.1, 1898–May 14, 1958), journalist, was born in Atlanta, Ga., the son of Thomas Lunsford Stokes and Emma Layton. His father was part owner of a department store; his mother died when he was fourteen. Stokes attended Boys High School in Atlanta for two years and the Peacock School for one year. In 1917 he entered the University of Georgia and studied English, history, and foreign languages. At the university Stokes was a debater, editor of the literary monthly, writer for the college newspaper, and the college correspondent for the Atlanta *Constitution* and the Atlanta *Georgian.* He obtained his B.A. in 1920.

The next year Stokes served his apprenticeship as a journalist for the Savannah *Press,* Macon *News,* and, finally, the Athens *Herald.* He accepted assignments as varied as the railroad and sports beat, or worked as state news or city editor. One of the last stories he covered in Georgia was the murder of a white woman, ostensibly by a mild-mannered black man, who was lynched despite his proclamations of innocence. This incident crystallized Stokes's decision to leave the South. He borrowed $200 from his father and headed for New York City, the mecca of aspiring newspapermen. But he got no farther than Washington, where he found a job with the United Press, taking telephone dictation from reporters. Stokes soon became a reporter for the agency.

Stokes's first big assignment was to cover the Washington Naval Conference in 1921. In the following years he shifted from the White House to the Capitol and various government agencies,

reporting stories ranging from the scandals of the Harding era to the presidential campaigns of 1924, 1928, and 1932. Stokes also served as copy editor. On Jan. 10, 1924, he married Hannah Hunt; they had two children.

Disillusioned with the conservative Republican policies of the 1920's, Stokes welcomed the New Deal with enthusiasm. His dispatches captured the spirit of the first "100 Days" of Franklin Roosevelt's presidency and won him appointment in 1933 as Washington correspondent for the New York *World Telegram,* a key paper of the Scripps-Howard chain. Three years later he became a national correspondent, reporting general politics and political campaigns for the Scripps-Howard Newspaper Alliance.

Stokes's growing popularity during the late 1930's stemmed from his lively style combined with the intelligence, mild cynicism, and compassion that many of the best correspondents seem to possess. Impressions of the presidents and the political scene from 1921 to 1935 were recorded in his reminiscences, *Chip Off My Shoulder* (1940). This work holds up surprisingly well; his analysis of Herbert Hoover's strengths and weaknesses displays an empathy and perspicacity seldom seen in the polarized Roosevelt era.

Although Stokes supported the New Deal reforms, he eventually found himself in the uncomfortable position of helping opponents of President Roosevelt. At the suggestion of his editor, he went to Kentucky in the late spring of 1938 to investigate the Works Progress Administration (WPA), a New Deal agency providing work relief for the unemployed. According to some reports, this WPA branch had been turned into a political organization to gain votes for Senator Alben W. Barkley, who was running for reelection in the Democratic primary. Stokes traveled 1,400 miles, interviewing dozens of officials, politicians, and relief workers. The eight stories he wired back detailed the sordid tale of how political leaders used state and federal employees for partisan purposes. The WPA in Kentucky, he concluded, was "a grand political racket in which the taxpayer is the victim."

These reports had far-reaching effects. Harry Hopkins and other New Deal stalwarts impugned Stokes's integrity, and the journalist felt himself a "pariah" among his peers for his action. Yet he could not, as they did, justify officeholders' political activity with the philosophy that the end justifies the means. The Senate sent an investigator to Kentucky who discovered even more extensive political use of the WPA than Stokes had uncovered. As a result, Congress passed the Hatch Act (1938), which restricted the political activity of federal officeholders (it was repealed in 1977). For his accomplishment, Stokes was awarded the Pulitzer Prize for the most distinguished reporting of 1938.

In December 1944 Stokes left Scripps-Howard to join the United Feature Syndicate as a Washington political columnist. Two months earlier he had been chosen by a poll of Washington correspondents for the *Saturday Review of Literature* Award because of his "reliability, fairness and ability to analyze the news." In 1947 he won the Raymond Clapper Award of the White House Correspondents Association. The citation praised him for "willingness to tackle controversial issues, for going after tough national questions in the best journalistic tradition, for the fairness in reporting both sides of controversial questions." This award must have been particularly satisfying, as it was Clapper who had taught the young Stokes, fresh from Georgia, "all about politics and what makes it tick." Stokes died in Washington, D.C.

[In addition to *Chip Off My Shoulder*, Stokes wrote *The Savannah* (1951), a study of the Savannah River as the heartstream of the old South. His articles appeared in such magazines as *The Nation, Look, Colliers', Forum*, and *Common Sense*. See *PM*, Oct. 8, 1945; and his obituary, *New York Times*, May 15, 1958.]

SYDNEY WEINBERG

STONE, ABRAHAM (Oct. 30, 1890–July 3, 1959), physician and birth-control activist, was born in Russia, the son of Miron Stone, a merchant, and Amelia Chamers. In 1905 his parents sent him to live with relatives in New York City. He became a naturalized United States citizen in 1915. He attended New York University, receiving his M.D. in 1912. He served his internship and residency at the Knickerbocker, St. Mark's, and Bellevue hospitals in New York and began the private practice of urology in 1915. He was lieutenant in the army medical corps from 1917 to 1920.

On Aug. 17, 1917, he married Hannah Mayer, a Bellevue hospital pharmacist. Hannah Stone went to medical school while Abraham was in the army. She became a gynecologist and joined Stone in his private practice upon his return from service. They had one daughter, who became a physician and also married a physician.

Stone was appointed instructor in urology at the New York Postgraduate Medical School in 1923, a position he held until 1927. He also served as chief urologist for the Union Health Center from 1929 to 1950 and was on the faculties of the New School for Social Research and the New York University-Bellevue medical school until his death.

The major focus of his career, however, emerged in 1921, when the Stones attended the First International Birth-Control Congress in New York and met the pioneering Margaret Sanger. The three quickly allied themselves for the cause of promoting both the practice of and research in birth-control methods. Hannah Mayer Stone became the first director of the Margaret Sanger Research Center, and after her death in 1941, Abraham Stone became its director.

In 1931, Stone became director of the marriage consultation center of the Community Church of New York and began to write extensively on a number of issues involving human sexuality, contraception, marriage counseling, and fertility. *A Marriage Manual*, written jointly with his wife, quickly became a classic, appearing subsequently in six English editions as well as in several foreign languages.

Practical Birth-Control Methods, by Norman E. Himes, "with the medical collaboration of Abraham Stone, M.D.," was published in 1938, with subsequent editions in 1940, 1945, and 1949. A revised edition, *Planned Parenthood: A Practical Guide to Birth-Control Methods*, by Abraham Stone and Norman E. Himes, appeared in 1951.

Stone's *The Premarital Consultation: A Manual for Physicians*, written with Lena Levine, was published in 1956. He also wrote many articles and served as editor of the *Journal of Contraception* from 1935 to 1940. He was editor of *Human Fertility* from 1940 to 1948 and served on the editorial board of *Fertility and Sterility* from 1949 until his death.

In 1947 Stone received the Albert and Mary Lasker Award of the Planned Parenthood Federation of America. He traveled extensively, lecturing and consulting for the United Nations and for other agencies, and was vice-president of both the Planned Parenthood Federation of America and the International Planned Parenthood Federation. He was also founder (1942) and president of the American Association of Marriage Counselors.

Stone died in New York City. Alan Gutt-macher, a fellow physician and colleague in the birth-control movement, wrote that "he was the peripatetic World Ambassador for family life."

[There are Abraham Stone papers in the Margaret Sanger collections of both the Library of Congress and the Sophia Smith Collection on the History of Women at Smith College, Northampton, Mass. Stone's articles in medical journals may be located through *Index Medicus.* There are lengthy biographical sketches in *Current Biography,* Mar. 1952; and *Fertility and Sterility,* (Sept.–Oct. 1959), with portraits. Brief obituary notices appeared in the *New York Times,* July 4, 1959; and *Journal of the American Medical Association,* Sept. 26, 1959.]

ELLEN GAY DETLEFSEN

STONG, PHIL(LIP DUFFIELD) (Jan. 27, 1899–Apr. 26, 1957), author, was born near Pittsburg, Iowa, the eldest of three sons of Benjamin Jacob Stong, and Ada Evesta Duffield. Stong, a merchant, later moved his business to the nearby Van Buren County seat, Keosauqua, where he became postmaster.

Phil Stong was educated in the Keosauqua schools and at Drake University, where he received (1919) a B.A. in journalism. He taught at Biwabik, Minn., for the academic year 1919–1920. That fall he enrolled at Columbia University to pursue an M.A. but soon wearied of all but Carl Van Doren's writing classes. From the fall of 1921 to December 1923 he taught at Neodesho, Kans. In January 1924 he went to Drake to teach debate and journalism, but a part-time reporting job for the *Des Moines* (Iowa) *Register* soon led to full-time employment. All this is told with typical Stong lightheartedness in *If School Keeps* (1940). In that book he credits his editor, Harvey Ingham, and a teacher, Lewis Worthington Smith, with showing him how to eliminate "the more florid terms and locutions" from his writing.

On Nov. 8, 1925, Stong married Virginia Maude Swain, whom he had met at Drake and who also worked for the *Register.* She too became a novelist; her *The Hollow Skin* (1938) and *Dollar Gold Piece* (1942) were warmly received by critics.

From 1925 to 1932 Stong worked in New York City successively as a wire editor for the Associated Press, a copy editor for North Amer-ican Newspaper Alliance, a staffer for *Liberty* and *Editor and Publisher,* Sunday feature editor of the *World,* and as an advertising writer for Young and Rubicam. In 1932, after twelve failures, his thirteenth book-length manuscript, *State Fair,* was published and became a Literary Guild selection. It was filmed three times, in 1932, 1945, and 1961.

Stong wrote forty books, two anthologies, and many magazine stories and articles. In *State Fair, Village Tail* (1934), *Week-End* (1935), *Career* (1936, filmed 1939), *The Rebellion of Lennie Barlow* (1937), *The Long Lane* (1939), *The Princess* (1941), *One Destiny* (1942), *Return in August* (1953, a sequel to *State Fair)* and *Blizzard* (1955) Stong used Keosauqua as his background, calling the area "Pittsville." *Buckskin Breeches* (1937), *Ivanhoe Keeler* (1939, a sequel), *Jessamy John* (1947), and *Forty Pounds of Gold* (1951) are historical novels; some of these are based on his Grandfather Duffield's journals. *Farmer in the Dell* (1935) is Hollywood froth. He also wrote *Hawkeyes: A Biography of the State of Iowa* (1940), a lighthearted account; *Gold in Them Hills, Being an Irreverent History of the Great 1849 Gold Rush* (1957); and *Horses and Americans* (1939), a serious account of the horse in America.

The best of his twenty children's books are *The Hired Man's Elephant* (1939), which won the *New York Herald Tribune* Award in 1939; *Farm Boy* (1934); *High Water* (1937); *Honk the Moose* (1935); and *No-Sitch! the Hound* (1936). His others include *Young Settler* (1938), *Cowhand Goes to Town* (1939), *Captain Kidd's Cow* (1941), *The Iron Mountain* (1942), *Marta of Muscovy* (1945), and *Mississippi Pilot* (1954). He also wrote the text for a photographic book, *County Fair* (1938).

Stong's books were a welcome relief during the Depression and war years from what he called the "Sheep Dip" school of literature and what a critic called the "Devil take the farm" novel. Though he had no children, his children's books show an obvious liking and understanding of his readers. But another critic's judgment that "those who had hoped he might contribute more profoundly to American literature felt he had betrayed his talents" is today's accepted judgment about his work. He died of a heart attack at Washington, Conn., while working on his forty-third book.

[The Special Collections of the University of Iowa Libraries and the Drake University Library are sources for biography and bibliography, books, manuscripts, and photographs. See also *New York Times,* Apr. 27, 1957, the obituary; *Palimpsest,* Dec. 1957; Frank Paluka, *Iowa Authors, a Bio-Bibliography of Sixty Native Writers* (1967); Clarence A. Andrews, *A Literary History of Iowa;* and George Mills, "Phil Stong's Legacy," *Des Moines Register,* Aug. 11, 1974.]

CLARENCE A. ANDREWS

STOUFFER, SAMUEL ANDREW (June 6, 1900–Aug. 24, 1960), sociologist and statistician, was born in Sac City, Iowa, the son of Samuel Marcellus Stouffer, and Irene Holmes. His father was editor and owner of the Sac City *Sun.* Stouffer received his B.A. in 1921 from Morningside College in nearby Sioux City, Iowa, and did graduate study in English at Harvard, receiving the M.A. in 1923. On June 10, 1924, he married Ruth McBurney; they had three children. Because of his father's illness, he became editor and manager of the family newspaper from 1923 to 1926. It was only after this early career that he began graduate training in sociology at the University of Chicago, from which he received the Ph.D. in 1930. The clarity of his later sociological writing and his ability to direct large research staffs and to edit and produce *Studies in Social Psychology in World War II* (1949–1950), which is his greatest monument, rests upon his original foundation in English, journalism, and practical management.

Because of Stouffer's monumental studies and other later works, he was understandably seen as a methodologist who made major contributions to the development and use of a particular quantitative method of social research, the sample survey. However, his earlier career shows that he was no narrow methodologist confined to a single technique of inquiry. His scientific contributions were wide-ranging.

Stouffer's teachers at the University of Chicago had emphasized the use of case studies and qualitative description; most of them disparaged statistics and the quantitative method. A notable exception was the sociologist William Fielding Ogburn, a pioneer in the use of statistics and diverse, large-scale records for social research and especially for the study of social change. Just as Ogburn became research director of *Recent Social Trends in the United States* (1933) and then coordinated a large staff to produce a series of specialized monographs and a two-volume comprehensive description of American society, so, too, did Stouffer later make similar contributions.

His scientific stance parallels Ogburn's: reformist in purpose and empiricist in approach, insisting on verified evidence for the advancement of social science and the solution of social problems, but searching for it laboriously and ingeniously in all sources and places, rather than relying on one standard tool or type of data. Stouffer's title for his selected papers, *Social Research to Test Ideas* (1962), fits the man. His fundamental principles were stated and his practices, implied in his prefatory remarks: "Too much has been promised, too fast, by some social scientists, especially by those unchastened by the arduous, meticulous, and unrewarding labor of empirical testing of ideas."

Stouffer's quantitative training at Chicago also was influenced by Louis Thurstone, the psychologist, statistician, and pioneer in the development of instruments or scales by which such subjective features as social attitudes, previously vaguely described in qualitative terms, could be precisely scorned or measured. The quintessential Stouffer is revealed in his doctoral dissertation, "An Experimental Comparison of Statistical and Case-History Methods of Attitude Research" (1930). Scores of a large group of individuals on a Thurstone scale measuring attitudes toward prohibition were compared with, or validated against, elaborate evidence from life histories that the individuals wrote about the development and present state of their views on drinking and prohibition laws. The claims of the two methods were thus tested empirically and in the style that became characteristic of Stouffer: by replication, or a multiplicity of tests applied to the two kinds of data. The theory and method of measurement of subjective entities remained a life-long interest, to which Stouffer returned during the wartime studies. He then sponsored and collaborated in the work of Louis Guttman and Paul F. Lazarsfeld, each of whom had developed a sophisticated new method for scaling attitudes. After the war the "H-technique" that he developed simplified the intricate procedures for developing Guttman scales and increased their utilization by others.

In 1930 Stouffer began his academic career as instructor in statistics at the University of Chicago. He spent 1931–1932 at the University of London on a postdoctoral fellowship, studying with the English statisticians Karl Pearson and Ronald A. Fisher. Upon his return he was assistant professor and then professor of social statistics at the University of Wisconsin (1932–1935), before rejoining the University of Chicago faculty as professor of sociology

(1935–1946). During this period he published a series of papers in statistics; but substance, social problems, and sociological theory always remained in mind. The Great Depression had led to the formation of a committee under Ogburn's chairmanship to study the social and psychological effects of unemployment. Stouffer became director of the staff writing monographs on aspects of the general problem, and he and Lazarsfeld were coauthors of *The Family in the Depression* (1937).

During this period Stouffer's main substantive work was in the field of demography. When the Carnegie Commission sponsored a "comprehensive study of the Negro in the United States," to be directed by the Swedish scholar Gunnar Myrdal, many American experts were commissioned to prepare the monographs that Myrdal would need as background. Stouffer was coauthor of "Negro Population and Negro Population Movements: 1860–1940," but his larger contribution to this classic study is little known. Myrdal went back to Sweden in April 1940 at the invasion of Norway and was unable to return to the United States for almost a year. Stouffer became the director in his absence and, as Myrdal remarks, "unselfishly devoted all his talents . . . to the task of bringing the research to completion by September 1940, and he succeeded."

In those early years, the sample survey—a method designed to yield direct large-scale evidence on the subjective world through questioning of representative samples about their inner life—had not yet become established. Men like Stouffer had to use available records of related objective facts, treating them as indirect indicators of the missing subjective datum. For example, in studying whether there was a trend toward "impulsive" marriage during the depression, he examined whether the ceremony occurred in a community other than the residence of the bride and groom, official historical records of such facts being available in certain states. That era produced men who had to think in clever but disciplined ways, increasing their powers of abstraction and sensitivity about the relationship between inner experience and outward action.

So when the survey era came to pass and the day dawned in late 1941 when Stouffer became the professional director of the Research Branch Information and Education Division of the United States Army that conducted several hundred surveys and other social psychological studies of soldiers, he was ideally suited for the task. He plunged into it with characteristic enthusiasm, carried on the work until 1946, and brought to it his elaborate technical skills, experience in managing large research staffs, and concern about social problems.

The surveys yielded systematic, comprehensive evidence on the attitudes, emotions, and conduct of men drawn into military institutions, enduring the ordeal of war, and returning to civilian life. Since the surveys display that distinctive hallmark, replication, and other methodological safeguards, the findings can be trusted. They are an almost priceless gift to social scientists. Stouffer put it mildly: "If by some miracle a cache should be found of manuscript materials telling of the attitudes toward combat of a representative sample of, say, a hundred men in Stonewall Jackson's army, the discovery would interest Civil War historians." Stouffer's total cache covers the attitudes of a half-million soldiers, and the patterns that were documented led to new theorizing in social psychology, notably to the concept of "relative deprivation." The soldiers who were worse off, paradoxically, expressed more satisfaction than those who in fact were better off: it all depended on whom one compared himself with and their relative positions. The processes underlying the choice of particular "reference groups," or points of comparison when reexamined and codified, in turn led to Robert K. Merton's and Alice Kitt's classic "Contributions to the Theory of Reference Group Behavior" (1950), a central theory in modern social psychology.

In 1946 Stouffer went to Harvard as director of the Laboratory of Social Relations, in addition to professor of sociology, where he remained until his death. He worked with a group of former colleagues condensing the wartime studies, published in 1949–1950 in four volumes; he conducted a series of experiments related to the theory of social roles and role conflict; and two major contributions to the growth and use of survey methods were added in those years. The joint committee of the National Research Council and Social Science Research Council, of which he was chairman, sponsored studies of critical methodological problems of survey research that led to monographs on interviewing and sampling procedures. In 1954 Stouffer directed a national survey to test whether McCarthyism had ramified so far as to produce widespread fear and political intolerance. Here, Stouffer used his special knowledge of population trends to project the findings into the future, in a valuable blending of demography and survey method that was characteristic of much of his work.

Stouffer died in New York City. After his death, Herbert Hyman wrote: ". . . the writings cannot convey his style of work. They are too pallid a representation. How passionately Sam could attack a table, or an IBM machine, and not only in the darkest hours of night, but all through the next day as well." With such a joyful companion, such arduous labor was for Stouffer's colleagues a merry chase.

[Stouffer's writings include *Research Memorandum on the Family in the Depression* (1937), written with Paul F. Lazarsfeld; *Studies in Social Psychology in World War II,* 4 vols. (1949–1950), of which he was editor; "A Technique for Improving Cumulative Scales," *Public Opinion Quarterly,* Summer 1952, of which he was coauthor; and *Communism, Conformity, and Civil Liberties* (1955). A complete bibliography of his works is included in his *Social Research to Test Ideas* (1962), which also contains an appraisal by Lazarsfeld. On his life and work, see Herbert H. Hyman, "Samuel A. Stouffer and Social Research," and Philip M. Hauser, "On Stouffer's *Social Research to Test Ideas,*" *Public Opinion Quarterly,* Fall 1962. For detailed commentary on the wartime surveys, see Robert K. Merton and Paul F. Lazarsfeld, eds., *Continuities in Social Research* (1950), which includes the Merton and Kitt "Contributions to the Theory of Reference Group Behavior." Other sources include President's Committee on Social Trends, *Recent Social Trends in the United States,* 2 vols. (1933); Gunnar Myrdal, *An American Dilemma* (1944); Herbert H. Hyman et al., *Interviewing in Social Research* (1954); and Frederick F. Stephan and Philip J. McCarthy, *Sampling Opinions* (1958).]

HERBERT H. HYMAN

STRAUS, ROGER W(ILLIAMS) (Dec. 14, 1891–July 28, 1957), industrialist and philanthropist, was born in New York City, the son of Oscar Solomon Straus and Sarah Lavanburg. Shortly before Roger's birth his father had begun work on a biography of the founder of Rhode Island, for whom he named his son.

Some of Straus's earliest memories were of Constantinople, where his father served as American minister. Oscar Straus, a graduate of Columbia Law School, was able to give up the practice of law and devote his life to public service with the financial help of his father-in-law (a merchant banker) and his two older brothers, Isidor and Nathan (who bought the firm of R. H. Macy and Co. and built it into the largest de-

partment store in the world). While Roger was in preparatory school at Lawrenceville, N.J., his father served as secretary of commerce and labor in Theodore Roosevelt's cabinet and while he was attending Princeton, his father ran (unsuccessfully) for governor of New York on the Bull Moose ticket.

On Jan. 12, 1914, Straus married Gladys Eleanor Guggenheim, daughter of Daniel, the most prominent of the Guggenheim brothers. They had three children.

Although there were twenty-four third-generation Guggenheims, only two were inclined to a business career. Harry, Gladys' older brother, was interested in the family copper mine in Chile; and Edmond, a cousin, represented the family on the board of Kennecott Copper Corporation. From the beginning of his marriage Straus was groomed to represent the Guggenheim family at American Smelting and Refining Company (ASARCO), of which his father-in-law was president.

During World War I, Straus was assigned to the Military Intelligence Division of the General Staff and was sent on a six-month tour of duty as an assistant intelligence officer in Siberia. On his return to ASARCO, he became a member of its executive committee and, following his father-in-law's retirement in 1919, served as assistant to the new president, Simon Guggenheim.

Simon continued his older brother's strategy of managing ASARCO as a processing segment of the wider family interests. He tried to extend the ASARCO processing expertise overseas, particularly to Russia and southern Africa, but without success, although an Australian investment at Mount Isa later proved profitable. Straus came to be critical of the Guggenheim strategy as a result of his experience as an ore buyer. Such was the strength of his conviction that he was able to challenge the Guggenheim strategy and overturn it.

As a processing specialist ASARCO was dependent on the purchase of ores from others; throughout the 1930's the critically important ore-buying function was Straus's principal responsibility. Because the smaller mining companies were not surviving and the larger ones (except Kennecott) were developing their own processing capabilities, Straus foresaw the time when ASARCO should have its own mines as an assured source of supply.

When Straus became president in 1941, he vigorously espoused mining projects. Many of his board members and executives opposed the projects on the grounds that they required too much capital and involved too much risk. Guggenheim family members, led by Edmond, objected on the ground (later justified) that such moves would hasten entry into processing by Kennecott. By overcoming such opposition Straus moved ASARCO from a processing specialist toward a diversified and integrated minerals enterprise.

Handsome and gregarious, Straus had few enemies even among opponents. He delegated technical matters to his vice-presidents and kept himself informed of the widely dispersed ASARCO facilities through extensive travel, usually with his wife.

As befitted someone named after Roger Williams, Straus had a lifelong interest in furthering religious tolerance. In 1928 he helped to organize, and provided the seed money for the establishment of, the National Conference of Christians and Jews. Until his death he served as one of its three cochairmen.

A staunch member of the liberal wing of the Republican party, Straus became a personal friend, intimate adviser, and financial supporter of Thomas E. Dewey in all of Dewey's campaigns for public office. Three months after his retirement from ASARCO and four months after being named chancellor of the New York State Board of Regents, Straus died in Liberty, N.Y.

[At the time of his death, Straus and his secretary were working on his personal papers. Distraught by grief, the secretary burned nearly the entire collection. Most of his writings are published speeches: *Religious Liberty—Civilization's Barometer* (1935); *The American Way*, proceedings edited by Newton D. Baker, Carlton J. H. Hayes, and Straus (1936); *Religious Liberty and Democracy* (1939). See also Harold Loeb, *The Way It Was* (1959). A cover article was published by *Business Week*, Nov. 24, 1956. His obituary is in *New York Times*, July 29, 1957.]

THOMAS R. NAVIN

STRITCH, SAMUEL ALPHONSUS (Aug. 17, 1887–May 27, 1958), bishop of Toledo, archbishop of Milwaukee, and cardinal-archbishop of Chicago, was born in Nashville, Tenn., the son of Garrett Stritch and Catherine Malley. His father had emigrated from Ireland in the 1870's and was office manager of Sycamore Mills in Nashville.

Stritch was a precocious student, completing primary grades in his parish school at the age of ten and high school at fourteen. He received the B.A. from St. Gregory's Preparatory Seminary, Cincinnati, in 1904, then continued his preparation for the priesthood in Rome, residing at the North American College and taking classes at the College of Propaganda Fide. He received doctorates in both philosophy (1906) and theology (1910) within six years and, on May 21, 1910, with a special dispensation from Pope Pius X, was ordained a priest three months before his twenty-third birthday.

Stritch returned to Nashville that same year, served for a brief period as assistant in his home parish, and was then transferred to St. Patrick's Church in Memphis, where within a year he was named pastor. He was recalled to Nashville and appointed secretary to Bishop Thomas Byrne in 1916. The following year he was named chancellor of the diocese and supervisor of diocesan schools. In November 1921, at the age of thirty-four, he was consecrated bishop of Toledo, the youngest bishop in the American hierarchy.

Stritch remained in Toledo for nine years. He established Mary Manse College in 1922, opened the first diocesan teachers' college in the nation two years later, and had new high schools built in Toledo and Tiffin. He centralized the missionary and charitable activities of the diocese, built more than twenty churches, and began construction of the Holy Rosary Cathedral in 1926.

On Aug. 26, 1930, Stritch was appointed archbishop of Milwaukee, the first priest of non-German ancestry to hold that appointment and the youngest archbishop in the Roman Catholic Church in America. During his ten-year tenure he had three new high schools built, established four new colleges, encouraged the expansion of Catholic Youth Organization activities, and urged increased participation of the laity in the work of the Church through Catholic Action. He focused major attention during the 1930's on the needs of the poor, sharing his resources with less fortunate dioceses throughout the country, rescuing several of his parishes from financial failure, and undertaking annual fund-raising campaigns for local charity. "As long as two pennies are ours," he often remarked, "one of them belongs to the poor."

Transferred to Chicago after the death of George Cardinal Mundelein and formally installed in March 1940, Stritch continued the same kinds of works he had emphasized in Toledo and Milwaukee. He had nearly 100 new grade and high schools built, opened special educational facilities for the handicapped, and was a major benefactor of the Lewis Memorial Maternity Hospital and the Stritch School of Medicine at Loyola University. In the field of Catholic Action, membership in the archdiocesan Holy Name Society quadrupled; the Cana Conference, a program of spiritual renewal for married and engaged couples, was established in 1944; and the Christian Family Movement, founded in Chicago that same year, soon expanded into more than ninety dioceses. The Young Christian Students, the Young Christian Workers, the Catholic Guild for the Blind, the Catholic Council on Working Life, and the Bishop's Resettlement Committee (to assist war refugees) were all established at Stritch's inspiration. The number of persons assisted through Catholic Charities during his tenure increased from 34,000 to more than 400,000 annually. Concerned for minorities, Stritch encouraged the establishment of the Cardinal's Committee for the Spanish-Speaking, the St. Therese Chinese Catholic Mission, and the Catholic Interracial Council.

Stritch twice served as chairman of the Administrative Board of the National Catholic Welfare Conference, was vice-chancellor and chancellor of the Catholic Church Extension Society, and was chairman of the bishops' committee on Pope Pius XII's Peace Plan in 1941. He received an award in 1956 from the George Washington Carver Institute for his work in bettering race relations and the Pro-Hungaria Medal from the Knights of Malta for his work with refugees in 1957. On Feb. 18, 1946, he was elevated to the Sacred College of Cardinals by Pope Pius XII.

After eighteen years as archbishop of Chicago, Stritch was called to Rome in early 1958 and appointed pro-prefect of the Sacred Congregation for the Propagation of the Faith, the first American ever named to head a department of the Roman Curia. During the voyage to Rome, he suffered an occlusion of the major artery of his right arm and underwent surgery for the removal of the arm shortly after his arrival. He then suffered a stroke and died in Rome.

Stritch was short and, in his later years, slightly overweight. He had a gentle, kindly personality and a sincere interest in others. He was also an excellent financier and able administrator of the most populous Catholic diocese in the world. Traditional and even conservative in his theological views, he was permissive of innovations by others and was a defender of the rights of workers and minorities. Stritch spoke out against both Nazi and Communist tyranny, and championed the United Nations and American foreign aid through the Marshall Plan. In a city famed for its politicians, he remained nonpolitical. A man of sincere but unobtrusive piety, Stritch had a deep concern for the less fortunate, and was called by many the Cardinal of the Poor.

[The major collection of Stritch's papers is in the archives of the Archdiocese of Chicago, St. Mary of the Lake Seminary, Mundelein, Ill. A popular biography is Marie Cecilia Buehrle, *The Cardinal Stritch Story* (1959). Shorter biographical sketches are Thomas B. Morgan, *Speaking of Cardinals* (1946); Brendan A. Finn, *Twenty-Four American Cardinals* (1947); and Francis Beauchesne Thornton, *Our American Princes* (1963). See also Dan Herr, "Prince Among Men," *The Sign*, Jan. 1957. The archdiocesan newspapers of Milwaukee and Chicago, the *Catholic Herald Citizen* and the *New World*, contain much information on Stritch's activities and addresses.]

THOMAS E. BLANTZ

STROHEIM, ERICH VON. See VON STROHEIM, ERICH.

STURGES, PRESTON (Aug. 29, 1898–Aug. 6, 1959), playwright, motion picture director, and producer, was born in Chicago, Ill., the son of Edmund Biden and Mary D'Este Dempsey. In 1901 he was adopted by Solomon Sturges, his mother's third husband, and became known as Preston Sturges. Much of his childhood was spent in France and he attended Lycée Janson in Paris (1907–1911), L'École des Roches in Normandy (1911–1913), and La Villa in Lausanne, Switzerland (1913–1914). From 1914 to 1915 he attended Irving Preparatory School in New York City. The next year he worked for F. B. Keech and Company, a New York stock brokerage firm.

During World War I, Sturges served with the Signal Corps of the United States Army. He attended the United States School of Military Aeronautics in Austin, Tex., and was stationed at Millington, Tenn., and Arcadia, Fla., in 1918. A member of the 63rd Air Squadron, he was commissioned a second lieutenant in the air reserve when he was discharged in 1919. From 1919 to 1925 he worked in his mother's cosmetic firm, "Maison Desti," where he invented "kissproof" lipstick. In 1922 he married Estello De Wolfe Mudge, whom he later divorced. They had no children.

Sturges' first job in the theater was as assistant stage manager for Brock Pemberton, a Broadway producer. In 1928 a ruptured appendix immobilized Sturges for several weeks and he took up playwriting. That same year he wrote and produced *The Guinea Pig*. A speedy worker, he claimed that he wrote the play *Strictly Dishonorable*, which appeared in 1929, in five days. A mixture of sweet and brazen sentiments that charmed both the sophisticated and unsophisticated, the play was one of the smash hits of the decade. Other plays include *Recapture* (1930) and *Well of Romance* (1930). Sturges believed that a successful dramatist must have his characters express conflicting opinions. "The playwright has all opinions or is not a playwright," he wrote. "His characters must disagree from the beginning. When they agree the play is over." In 1930 he married Eleanor Post Hutton, granddaughter of C. W. Post, the cereal magnate, but the marriage was annulled in November 1932 on the ground that his previous divorce was not valid in New York State.

By 1932 Sturges had squandered profits of about $300,000 from his plays. He went to Hollywood to start again as a screenwriter. A man of great ingenuity, he thought of himself as a modern American humorist working in film. He dictated his stories and rarely had more than a rough idea of the plot when he began. His raffish and satiric themes usually attacked human foibles. Among his films were *Child of Manhattan* (1932), *The Green Hat (1933)*, *Thirty Day Princess* (1934), *Diamond Jim* (1935), *Hotel Haywire* (1936), *Easy Living* (1937), *If I Were King* (1938), and *Remember the Night* (1939). On Nov. 7, 1938, he married Louise Sargent; they had one son. They were divorced in 1947.

Sturges sold *The Biography of a Bum* to Paramount Pictures for $10 on the condition that he could direct the film. "When a picture gets good notices, everyone but the writer is the prince. So I decided that I was going to be one of the princes." As *The Great McGinty* (1940) it made machine politics the theme of a searing comedy and received an Academy Award for best screenplay. Sturges also wrote and directed *Christmas in July* (1940), which spoofed high-pressure advertising and pleaded for job opportunities for young people so that they could show their merit; *The Lady Eve* (1941), a commentary upon the susceptibility of the gullible male to the treacherous female; *The Miracle of Morgan's Creek* (1943); *Sullivan's Travels* (1941); *The Palm Beach Story* (1942); and *Hail the Conquering Hero* (1944). In 1946 he formed a brief partnership with Howard Hughes, and produced and directed *The Sin of Harold Diddlebock* (1946), starring Harold Lloyd.

The style of Sturges' films drew upon Keystone comedies in their harum-scarum, pantomimic action that required a fast pace. He studiously worked to attain visual locomotion, and his combination of sobriety, slapstick, and satire resulted in scenes of energetic yet controlled confusion. Despite an insouciant personal manner and reputation for elegant eccentricity, he was precise and efficient on the set. He showed endless patience, never lost his temper, recognized good performances by extras as well as stars, and departed from typecasting. It was said that as a producer Sturges had the advantage of never hiring any director but himself, and as a director he never changed any of the author's ideas. On Aug. 15, 1951, he married Anne Margaret Nagle, thirty-two years younger than himself; they had two sons. In 1953 he wrote *Carnival in Flanders*, and in 1956, *The Birds and the Bees*. His popularity, however, had waned. Although noted for his geniality, he managed to alienate all the major studios and was out of work in the latter part of the 1950's. His wit seemed to be at odds with both the Hollywood system and society. He also suffered heavy financial losses by investing in a restaurant enterprise, The Players, in Hollywood. In Paris he wrote and directed *The French They Are a Funny Race* (1957). Sturges died of a heart attack at the Algonquin Hotel in New York City while writing an autobiography entitled "The Events Leading Up to My Death."

[For more information on Sturges, see *New York Herald Tribune*, Nov. 4, 1932; Mar. 2, 1941; Jan. 25, 1942; May 19, 1957; and Aug. 7, 1959. In the *New York Times*, see Nov. 8, 1938; Mar. 2, 1941; Feb. 1, 1942; and Bosley Crowther, "When Satire and Slapstick Meet," Aug. 27, 1944. See also the *New York World-Telegram*, Nov. 6, 1940; the *Boston Post*, Mar. 19, 1944; Frank Nugent, "Genius With a Slapstick," *Reader's Digest*, Mar. 1945; Noel F. Busch, "Preston Sturges," *Life*, Jan. 7, 1946; *New York Post*, Aug. 7, 1959; *New York Daily News*, Aug. 9, 1959; *Variety*, Aug. 12, 1959; and Michael Budd, "Notes on Preston Sturges and America," *Film Society Review*, Jan. 1968.]

ERNEST A. McKAY

SULLAVAN, MARGARET (May 16, 1909–Jan. 1, 1960), actress, was born in Norfolk, Va., the daughter of Cornelius Hancock Sullavan, a produce broker, and Garland Councill. Her interest in acting began at age six, when she gave performances in the parlor of her home. She attended the Walter Herron Taylor School and Chatham Episcopal Institute (now Chatham Hall), where she participated in productions of *A Midsummer Night's Dream* and *Bab, the Sub Deb*. After graduating from Chatham in 1927, Sullavan enrolled at Sullin's College in Bristol, Va., but stayed for only a year.

Her parents' resistance to her dramatic inclinations did not inhibit her driving desire to act. In 1928 they agreed to let her study dance in Boston, but she enrolled instead at the E. E. Clive Dramatic School in that city. She worked her way through school by selling books in the Harvard Cooperative Store. In the summer of 1929 she joined the University Players Guild, a community theater group in Falmouth, Mass., where she met Henry Fonda. Returning to Norfolk, Sullavan made her social debut before the Norfolk German Club but returned the following summer for another season with the University Players. After playing the lead in *Strictly Dishonorable* with a company that had been touring the South, she again returned to the University Players, who were in Baltimore beginning a season of stock. On Dec. 25, 1931, Sullavan married Henry Fonda. They were divorced in less than a year.

Sullavan's first role on Broadway was in *A Modern Virgin* (1931), produced by Lee Shubert. (She often remarked that she got the role because of a case of laryngitis. Her husky voice, she thought, reminded Shubert of Helen Morgan and Ethel Barrymore.) She began working on the voice that Shubert and the critics liked and "after several months of mistreating my vocal cords I found it stuck." Although *A Modern Virgin* and her next four plays, *If Love Were All* (1931), *Happy Landing* (1932), *Chrysalis* (1932), and *Hey Ho, Everybody* (1932), were failures, critics praised Sullavan's performances. One reviewer wrote, "someday someone will find a real part for her —and then —!"

That part came in March 1933 when she replaced Marguerite Churchill in *Dinner at Eight*. Her performance won her a contract from Universal Pictures to appear in *Only Yesterday*, and she became a film star overnight. Working in Hollywood, however, was not like working on Broadway. Acting in the movies, she said, was "just like ditch-digging," and she tried in vain to

be released from her contract with Universal. Stubborn, and with a mind of her own, Sullavan shunned the Hollywood life-style. Some of her antics during this period included arriving barefoot for fashion portraits, explaining that her feet would not show, driving an old, rented Ford, and defying studio officials' requests that she straighten a crooked tooth. Such actions led Hollywood to label her "eccentric."

During the next three years, under contract to Universal, Sullavan starred in *Little Man, What Now?* (1934), *So Red the Rose* (1935), *Next Time We Love* (1936), and *The Moon's Our Home* (1936). Her affair with William Wyler allegedly evolved on the set of *The Good Fairy*, which Wyler directed. According to Howard Sharpe, Wyler reprimanded her for disrupting the progress of the picture. The quarrel ended with a dinner date and on Nov. 25, 1934, they were married. This marriage also terminated in divorce two years later.

During her years in Hollywood, Sullavan became a great star. David Shipman wrote that she "was an enchantress pitched in temperament and magnetism somewhere between two Hepburns" [Audrey and Katharine]. Yet, according to Shipman, her lack of self-confidence caused her to be one of the most "temperamental and difficult of stars." When her contract with Universal expired, Sullavan returned to New York, where she took an unstarred part in *Stage Door* (1936). She refused her producer's offer to put her name in lights on the marquee on the grounds that she had not yet earned stardom in the theater.

On Nov. 15, 1936, during the run of *Stage Door,* she married her agent Leland Hayward. She left the play to have her first child, Brooke Hayward, born in 1937. They had two other children. Sullavan continued to make films during these years: *Three Comrades* (1938), *The Shopworn Angel* (1938), *The Shining Hour* (1938), *The Shop Around the Corner* (1940), *Mortal Storm* (1940), *So Ends Our Night* (1941), *Back Street* (1941), and *Appointment for Love* (1941). In 1943 Sullavan again returned to Broadway and achieved what many critics consider her greatest triumph in *The Voice of the Turtle*, written and directed by John Van Druten. Both the play and Sullavan won Donaldson Awards. Critics acclaimed her as "an eloquent symbol of wartime romance," and Van Druten described her "almost embarrassing directness." But after leaving *The Voice of the Turtle* in December 1944, Sullavan did not appear again on Broadway until November 1952, when she appeared in *The Deep Blue Sea*. Her marriage to Hayward ended in divorce in 1947, and on Aug. 30, 1950, she married Kenneth Arthur Wagg, a British industrialist. That same year she starred in *No Sad Songs for Me*, her last film. After appearing in *Sabrina Fair* (1953), she starred on Broadway in *Janus* (1955) but withdrew for health reasons. Another such incident occurred in the fall of 1956. Having made several television appearances, including a performance in the first broadcast of "Studio One" in 1948, Sullavan was scheduled to star in the role of Sister Mary Aquinas on a CBS television broadcast but never arrived on the set. Three days later she issued a public apology, claiming that she felt unable to give the role "the kind of performance" it deserved. Shortly thereafter she spent several weeks in a sanitarium that specialized in the treatment of neuroses.

Her return to the stage in 1959 resulted from her reading the script of *Sweet Love Remember'd*, a play about a woman in her mid-thirties who was fiercely in love with her dead husband. "I read the play on Wednesday and on Thursday I knew I wanted to be in it desperately," she explained. "I haven't been as anxious to go to work in a play since I was young and just beginning." While on a pre-Broadway tour with the show, Sullavan died in New Haven, Conn., of accidental barbiturate poisoning. A copy of the script was found beside her. Hollywood gossip labeled her death a suicide, after evidence surfaced that she had grown increasingly hard of hearing. (She left her temporal bones to science.) Whether or not her death was deliberate remains in question.

[There are family pictures of Sullavan in *Life*, June 17, 1940. See also *Who's Who in the Theatre*, 12th ed. (1957); "Husky Voice Silenced," *Newsweek*, Jan. 11, 1960; "Missed Cues," *Time*, Jan. 18, 1960; David Shipman, *Great Movie Stars: The Golden Years* (1970); and Brooke Hayward, *Haywire* (1977).]

HELEN S. STRITZLER

SULLIVAN, JOHN FLORENCE. See ALLEN, FRED.

SUMMERS, EDITH. See KELLEY, EDITH SUMMERS.

SWANTON, JOHN REED (Feb. 19, 1873– May 2, 1958), anthropologist and folklorist, was born in Gardiner, Maine, the son of Walter Scott Swanton and Mary Olivia Wor-

cester. After the death of his father, he and his two brothers were raised by his mother, grandmother, and great-aunt in modest circumstances and under a strict moral code. His mother inculcated in him a Swedenborgian faith that caused him conflict with his scientific studies. At an early age he showed a studious bent; he began writing a world history in a notebook at ten. Reading William Hickling Prescott's *Conquest of Mexico*, especially the section on the pyramids of Teotihuacán, kindled his interest in anthropology. After preparing at a high school in Chelsea, Mass., he entered Harvard University in 1892, and there received a B.A. in 1896, an M.A. in 1897, and a Ph.D. in 1900 in anthropology.

As an undergraduate Swanton found stimulation outside the classroom in folklore, joining a small society organized by his friend Roland Dixon. As a graduate student he dutifully undertook archaeological digs in Maine, New Jersey, and the Southwest. But it was the two years (1898–1900) in New York while at Columbia University and the American Museum of Natural History under the tutelage of Franz Boas that directed his interests to the ethnological fields in which he achieved his major work.

Upon attaining his doctorate, Swanton joined the Bureau of American Ethnology in the Smithsonian Institution, and from 1900 to 1944, when he retired, he devoted himself to field research and reports on North American Indian tribes. The bureau had been established by congressional act in 1873 for the sole purpose of investigating the conditions of the American Indian, and this nonacademic work perfectly suited Swanton. An elf of a man, as a colleague described him, Swanton suffered from extreme shyness, and any public appearance gave him anguish. He poured his energies into his research and writings, which reached 167 publications, a number of them full-length monographs, collections, and dictionaries. He published chiefly in the *Annual Reports* and *Bulletins* of the Bureau of American Ethnology and major professional journals such as the *American Anthropologist*, the *Journal of American Folklore*, and the *International Journal of American Linguistics*.

Following the lead of Boas, Swanton first undertook fieldwork among Tlingit and Haida Indians of the Pacific Northwest Coast in British Columbia and Alaska. In papers on their social organization, he supported the antievolutionism view of Boas and contended that the family structure and the system of patrilineal descent were the result of gradual diffusion. By 1913 he had shifted his fieldwork to the Indians of Oklahoma and Texas, but he had also begun researches into the area he was to make distinctively his own, the southeastern tribes of the United States. During the colonial period these tribes had been dominated by the Spanish, English, and French, and had intermarried with whites and blacks. Little remained of their organization and cultural traditions, so that fieldwork, in the words of the anthropologist A. L. Kroeber, "was like working over tailings instead of following a fresh vein." Swanton fleshed out the limited fieldwork opportunities with extensive library investigations, according to the technique of ethnohistory, which he largely developed. His major works, *Indian Tribes of the Lower Mississippi Valley and Adjacent Coast of the Gulf of Mexico* (1911) and *Indians of the Southeastern United States* (1946), as well as other, more limited studies, represent in good part an assemblage of passages from earlier travelers and observers who enjoyed contact with the region's 150 or so tribes before they disintegrated. To these excerpts Swanton added the observations and recollections of living Indians. He included photographs of some of his informants, among them the last speakers of the Chitimacha, Tunica, Atakapa, and Natchez languages.

Because of the nonscientific character of the early chronicles and the fragmentary nature of the informants' knowledge, these ethnohistorical treatments fall short of the demands of the field anthropologist, but they did salvage and reconstruct in part the historical cultures of these tribes. Swanton recognized the shortcomings of his sources, but he made little effort to analyze critically the documents he reprinted.

In none of his work did Swanton develop full-fledged theories or hypotheses. He was content to collect, record, edit, reprint, and amass specific data. The substantial compendium he prepared in 1952 on *The Indian Tribes of North America* he called a mere "gazetteer of present knowledge" about the location of Indian tribes, and he contrasted it with the interpretive examination by Kroeber in *Cultural and Native Areas of Native North America*, which dealt with matters of environmental and historical relationships. In his folklore collections, such as *Haida Texts and Myths* (1905) and *Myths and Tales of the Southeastern Indians* (1929), Swanton presented the oral tales, with representative linguistic texts, fully and meticulously recorded, but without any attention to the tellers and their narrative skills, to the social setting, or to the meaning and dispersion of the tales, points stressed by folklorists today.

Swanton let his materials speak for themselves and declined to speculate. Thus, he relates without commentary an account of a Sitka shaman who, through his spirit, paralyzed the arms of a big American marine about to cut the Indian's hair. So with his linguistic materials, as in the dictionaries of the Biloxi, Ofo, Choctaw, and Atakapa languages, he collated the lexical items painstakingly but abstained from abstract discussion.

The ancient history of America should be studied, Swanton had written in 1910, along three lines of inquiry: among living peoples, in the science called ethnology; through archaeological explorations; and by the examination of early narratives descriptive of the Indians. In 1935, in recognition of his historical knowledge, he was named chairman of the commission to celebrate the four hundredth anniversary of the DeSoto expedition, and he later prepared a report of that commission. Swanton's concept of ethnology included tribal customs, language, and folklore, and he published extensively on all three areas. Later scholars consider his *Social Condition, Beliefs, and Linguistic Relationship of the Tlingit Indians* (1908) and *Source Material on the History and Ethnology of the Caddo Indians* (1942) as exemplary of his ethnological, archaeological, historical, and linguistic multiple approach.

A private side of Swanton's thought, his Swedenborgian belief in human communication with the spirit world and in a meaningful life after death, jarred with his scientific training and caused him inner anxieties. In an unpublished manuscript of 1944, "An Anthropologist Looks Backward and Forward," he wrote, "Those who believe that ultimate knowledge can be attained by scientific methods alone are in for a disillusionment." He accepted the existence of miracles in nature. The confirmation of extrasensory perception in the experiments of J. B. Rhine emboldened Swanton to speak against materialism, naturalism, and atheism. He once wrote, "I cordially loathe from the ground up the entire competitive system, a system which rewards dessert about as intelligently as a Ouija board."

In his personal life Swanton considered his greatest success the marrying of Alice Barnard on Dec. 16, 1903; they had three children. In spite of his modesty and withdrawn nature, he possessed a cheerful disposition and enjoyed quoting Gilbert and Sullivan at length. A number of professional honors came to Swanton, among them the Viking Fund Medal in General Anthropology, the Loubat Prize, and election to the National Academy of Sciences. He was elected president of the American Anthropological Association and of the American Folklore Society. A volume of *Essays in Historical Anthropology of North America* was published in 1940 in honor of his completion of forty years with the Bureau of American Ethnology. Photographs confirm the verbal descriptions of a gentle, studious soul who could have passed for a missionary. Yet Swanton could assume and vigorously defend a position, as in his response, with Roland Dixon, to Robert H. Lowie's denial of any historical value in native American traditional history. Swanton's primary role was to provide building blocks and reference works for later, theory-minded anthropologists. He died in Newton, Mass.

[Two manuscripts of personal thoughts and recollections by Swanton are deposited in the Anthropology Archives of the Smithsonian Institution. One is his "An Anthropologist Looks Backward and Forward," and the other is "Notes Regarding My Adventures in Anthropology and with Anthropologists," in which he recalls with a surprisingly light touch his years at high school, college, graduate school, and the Bureau of American Ethnology. An excellent, judicious, and comprehensive appraisal by a former bureau associate with whom Swanton worked on the *Handbook of North American Indians* is Julian H. Steward, "John Reed Swanton," *Biographical Memoirs. National Academy of Sciences* (1960), with a photograph and a bibliography of Swanton's publications. Another assessment during his lifetime was A. L. Kroeber, "The Work of John R. Swanton," *Essays in Historical Anthropology of North America* (1940). An obituary with some personal reminiscences by William N. Fenton appeared in *American Anthropologist*, 61:4 (1959).]

RICHARD M. DORSON

SWEENEY, MARTIN LEONARD (Apr. 15, 1885–May 1, 1960), lawyer and congressman, was born in Cleveland, Ohio, the son of Dominic Sweeney and Anne Collery. He received his early education in the Cleveland public schools and at St. Bridget's elementary school. His father, who had been an active Democrat for many years, died in 1897, and Sweeney began working to help support his mother and four brothers and sisters. From 1903 to 1908 he worked on the ore docks for the Central Furnace Company. During this period he was active in the Longshoremen's Union, having been elected secretary of his local at the age of eighteen. In 1909 Sweeney was discharged because he refused to sign a "yellow dog" contract.

Sweeney then became a salesman to support himself while he attended law school at Baldwin-Wallace College in Cleveland. His union activities provided Sweeney with a foundation for a political career that began with his election to the state legislature in 1913 as a representative from Cuyahoga County. But his prolabor stance in the state legislature cost him official party endorsement for reelection. In 1914 he received the LL.B. from Baldwin-Wallace College and began the practice of law in Cleveland. He married Marie Carlin in 1921; they had four children.

Sweeney was elected judge of the municipal court of Cleveland in 1923; in 1929 he was reelected. During these years he was an outspoken opponent of prohibition and active in such fraternal organizations as the Ancient Order of Hibernians and the Fraternal Order of Eagles.

In 1931 Sweeney was elected to the U.S. House of Representatives from the Ohio Twentieth Congressional District. He served in the House from 1931 until 1942. An early supporter of Franklin D. Roosevelt, Sweeney worked on Roosevelt's behalf at the Democratic Convention in Chicago in 1932. A maverick in politics, he broke with Cleveland Mayor Ray T. Miller in order to support Roosevelt, ran unsuccessfully for mayor of Cleveland in 1933 as an independent, and survived an attempt by the local Democratic organization to defeat him in the congressional primary in 1934.

Sweeney's congressional career was checkered. He was a consistent supporter of such labor legislation as the Norris-La Guardia Act and the Wagner Act, but he was not a New Dealer. Early in the New Deal he introduced the Nye-Sweeney bill, which proposed to give Congress the exclusive rights to regulate the currency. He called for an investigation of maladministration in the Home Owners Loan Corporation. He supported the Townsend Plan for old age pensions, and he supported Father Charles Coughlin and his National Union for Social Justice, appearing with him in demonstrations in New York and Detroit. Sweeney backed Father Coughlin's candidate, William J. Lemke of North Dakota, in the presidential campaign of 1936. Nevertheless, he was reelected to Congress in 1934 and 1936 without the support of the Democratic party. He asserted that his victory in 1936 was a mandate for him to pursue an independent course.

Sweeney's congressional carreer was perhaps most noteworthy for his strict isolationism. In

1936 he opposed a resolution of condolence to England upon the death of King George V. His anglophobia stemmed from his passionate loyalty to Ireland, where many of his relatives still lived. He consistently voted against all legislation such as lend-lease, which he believed would lead America into war. In 1939 he suggested ironically that Washington streets be given new English names in preparation for the visit of King George VI. While the king was at the White House, Sweeney sent him a telegram asking for the repayment of England's World War I war debt. In 1940, after Sweeney had delivered a speech accusing Roosevelt of seeking to draw America into war, Congressman Beverly M. Vincent of Kentucky called him a traitor, and the result was a well-publicized exchange of punches on the floor of the House.

After being elected as an independent in 1934 and 1936, Sweeney patched up differences with local Democratic chiefs and was easily reelected in 1938. New differences appeared, however, in 1940, and he encountered opposition in his reelection bid. Despite victory, his strength was ebbing. In 1942 he was defeated. Sweeney did not seek reelection to Congress.

In 1944 Sweeney entered the Democratic gubernatorial primary. He was endorsed by the reactionary Gerald L. K. Smith. He ran a poor second to Frank J. Lausche. For the rest of his life he practiced law in Cleveland, where he died.

Sweeney was a politician of fierce independence and deep conviction. His career was shaped by strong identification with urban workers and intense ethnic loyalty. Labor advocate, ardent wet, isolationist, and Irish patriot, he was a colorful politician of a type that has been both the strength and the despair of the Democratic party.

[The Sweeney Papers, which consist mainly of copies of speeches, campaign literature, and a scrapbook of newspaper clippings, are located at the Western Reserve Historical Society in Cleveland. See also obituaries in the *New York Times* and the *Cleveland Plain Dealer*, May 2, 1960.]

NELSON L. DAWSON

SWOPE, GERARD (Dec. 1, 1872–Nov. 20, 1957), engineer and business executive, was born in St. Louis, Mo., the son of Isaac Swope and Ida Cohn. His father, a German Jew, had emigrated from Saxony in 1857 and by 1872 was a relatively prosperous manufacturer of watchcases. Swope attended public schools and early exhibited an interest in mathematics and electricity, a bent that led to his education as an electrical engineer. While pursuing his degree at the Massachusetts Institute of Technology, he also spent a summer in Chicago, studying exhibits at the World's Columbian Exposition and working in a General Electric shop.

After graduating with a B.S. in 1895, Swope joined the Western Electric Company, beginning as a helper in the motor department and rising by 1913 to become vice-president in charge of all domestic sales and all operations abroad. Although in the engineering department for a time, he made his mark primarily as a salesman, organizer, and negotiator. Henry Ford once called him the world's best salesman, and by 1913 he had already become a corporate troubleshooter and innovator of the first rank. Short, wiry, and imperious, he impressed others with his intense energy and command of detail, his cool but penetrating analysis of complex problems, and his ability to bring order out of chaos. Largely through his initiative, Western Electric became a pioneer in market research, cost analysis, institutional advertising, and statistically based sales planning.

While rising in business, Swope also became keenly interested in the "social problem." From 1897 to 1899 he lived and worked at Hull House in Chicago and later was active in a number of urban reform causes. Such interests were also enhanced by his marriage on Aug. 20, 1901, to Mary Dayton Hill, a social worker whom he had met at Hull House. By 1913 they had five children and were living on a country estate, but much of their social life remained tied to the world of reform.

Between 1913 and 1922 Swope undertook three tasks that enhanced his reputation as an organizational genius. The first involved a systematic reorganization of Western Electric's foreign interests, an assignment that led to extensive travel in Europe and Asia. The second, undertaken as a dollar-a-year man during World War I, involved an overhauling of the Army Supply Service. And the third, on which he embarked in 1919, involved a rebuilding of General Electric's operations abroad. As the first president of International General Electric, a GE subsidiary, Swope became the prime mover behind an intricate series of corporate reorganizations and multinational business agreements, and in association with such foreign statesmen as Walther Rathenau of Germany and Louis Loucheur of France he took a keen interest in European reconstruction.

In 1922, when Charles Coffin retired as head of General Electric, Swope became president and Owen D. Young chairman of the board, thus forming the most celebrated managerial team of the 1920's. By 1929 the two had become firmly associated with the decade's "new capitalism," especially with corporate welfare and employee representation programs, mass marketing of consumer durables, and the recognition of managerial responsibility to workers, customers, and the industry as a whole. Swope also helped to organize and direct the National Electrical Manufacturers Association, and, hoping to develop a parallel industrial union, he encouraged labor leader William Green to organize the industry's workers. There was, however, no follow-up on the invitation.

In September 1931, with the economy mired in depression, Swope's vision of an organized capitalism became the basis for the much publicized Swope Plan. All major firms, he proposed, should be organized into mandatory trade associations, and under federal supervision these should regulate economic activity and provide social insurance programs. The plan met with much initial criticism. But Swope's approach was adopted in the National Industrial Recovery Act of 1933, and Swope himself served on such implementing agencies as the Industrial Advisory Board, the National Labor Board, and the Business Advisory and Planning Council. In late 1933 he also set forth a second plan calling for greater industrial self-government, but this did not win administration support.

Unlike most businessmen, Swope continued to support the New Deal after 1934. He served on the advisory agencies that developed the social security system, on a commission studying industrial relations abroad, as an alternate on the Defense Mediation Board, and briefly, in 1942, as assistant secretary of the Treasury. At the same time, he remained active in developing private welfare programs, particularly as head of the community chest campaigns, instigator of new profit-sharing arrangements at General Electric, and founder of the National Health and Welfare Retirement Association. His interest in urban problems also persisted. Following his retirement from business in 1939, he served as chairman of the New York City Housing Authority and later helped to develop cooperative housing.

From 1942 to 1944, while his successor Charles E. Wilson served on the War Production Board, Swope returned to the presidency of General Electric. And following a second retirement, he remained active in such causes as health insurance

and foreign aid. In 1951, as chairman of the Institute of Pacific Relations, he staunchly defended the organization against congressional critics, and late in life he became a supporter of the Zionist cause. He died in New York City.

Seen in perspective, Swope stands as a major architect of what defenders call "enlightened capitalism" and critics label "corporate liberalism." His exploits at General Electric became legendary, and his activities outside the company left major imprints on managerial philosophy, business practice, and national institutions.

[Swope's oral history memoir and a collection of his papers are at Columbia University. Swope's oral reminiscences of the New Deal are available at the Franklin D. Roosevelt Library. Other relevant manuscript materials can be found in the Owen D. Young papers, Van Hornesville, N.Y.; and in the National Archives, especially Record Groups 9 and 40.

Swope's writings include *Selected Addresses of Gerard Swope and Owen D. Young* (1930); *Stabilization of Industry* (1931); and *The Futility of Conquest in Europe* (1943). Significant articles and addresses appeared in *Annals of the American Academy of Political and Social Science*, Mar. 1931; *Atlantic Monthly*, Mar. 1938, June 1940, Dec. 1950; *General Electric Review*, May 1925, Oct. 1931; *Industrial Management*, Nov. 1923, Dec. 1926; *Mechanical Engineering*, Jan. 1939; *New York Times Magazine*, Oct. 1, 1950; *Survey*, Mar. 1, 1924, Sept. 1943; *System*, Apr. 1923; *Vital Speeches*, May 1, 1938; and *World's Work*, Mar. 1927.

The only full-length biography, a journalistic rather than a scholarly work, is David G. Loth, *Swope of G.E.* (1958). Short biographical sketches and fragmentary biographical data can be found in John Franklin Carter, *The New Dealers* (1934); Dorothea Fisher, *American Portraits* (1946); Trentwell M. White, *Famous Leaders of Industry* (1931); see also *American Magazine*, Sept. 1926; *Electrical Engineering*, Nov. 1942; *Fortune*, Mar. 1938, Jan. 1940, May 1947; *Iron Trade Review*, Nov. 25, 1926; *New York Times Magazine*, Oct. 19, 1947; and the obituary notice, *New York Times*, Nov. 21, 1957.

Also useful on Swope's activities are Beulah Amidon, "Out of the House of Magic," *Survey*, Dec. 1, 1930; J. George Frederick, ed., *The Swope Plan* (1931); John Raymond Hall, *Tomorrow's Route* (1932); *Steel*, Nov. 6, 1933; *Public Utilities Fortnightly*, Dec. 7, 1933; Theodore K. Quinn, *Giant Business* (1953); and D. Thompson, "Special Law Passed for Zionist," *American Mercury*, Jan. 1959.]

ELLIS W. HAWLEY

SWOPE, HERBERT BAYARD (Jan. 5, 1882–June 20, 1958), journalist, was born in St. Louis, Mo., the son of Isaac Swope (formerly

Schwab), a German immigrant who had set up a watchmaking business in St. Louis, and Ida Cohn. In his first year at Central High School Swope was expelled for unruly behavior, but he was read-mitted and graduated. A high-spirited, uncon-ventional, adventurous boy, he tried his gentle father's authority. After his father's death Swope made a trip to Germany on his share of the meager inheritance, returned to do odd jobs, and then drifted into his lifework on newspapers. He was a reporter on the *St. Louis Post-Dispatch*, the *Chicago Tribune*, the *Morning Telegraph* (in New York), and then for several years on the *New York Herald*. He also worked as a theatrical press agent, and led a glittering although impecunious life as a young man-about-town in New York. In 1909 Swope became a reporter for Ralph Pulitzer's *New York World*, which sold for a penny and had a circulation of 350,000. He remained with that paper for nineteen years as reporter and editor. He used the *World* as his entrée into society, where he cut a swashbuckling, news-tracking, news-making figure. He married Margaret Honeyman Powell on Jan. 10, 1912, with H. L. Mencken as their only attendant.

Swope quickly built a reputation as a resource-ful, aggressive reporter. Among his scoops was his tour de force exposé of the police corruption behind the murder of a gambler named Herman Rosenthal. This was a classic case of participatory journalism; he not only wrote the story but also helped track down the suspects.

Swope made two trips to Europe during World War I to get an objective view of Germany. After the second visit he wrote a long series of articles for which, in 1917, he received the first Pulitzer Prize for reporting. Swope's only book, *Inside the German Empire* (1917), consisted of these arti-cles. When the United States entered the war, Swope became an assistant to his close friend Bernard Baruch, whom President Woodrow Wilson had appointed chairman of the War In-dustries Board. Swope later went to Paris to report on the Versailles Peace Conference. He championed Wilson's early role, and magnified the president's influence in Europe, but he was dis-illusioned by the later compromises, especially the reparations clauses, the text of which he obtained, probably from Secretary of State Robert Lansing, then out of favor with Wilson, and published. Harold Nicolson, on David Lloyd George's staff at the time, noted in his diary that Swope was "the star turn in the American journalistic world" and added, "He bursts with boost."

On his return Swope became executive editor of the *World*, at a salary of $54,000 a year plus 2 percent of the profit from the morning and Sunday editions. He held the post from 1920 to 1928. His first headline was on Warren G. Harding's presidential victory over James M. Cox; his last was about Franklin D. Roosevelt's inauguration as governor of New York. Swope's imagination, never exactly dormant, ran riot. His favorite crusades illustrated his credo that editing a paper was a combination of drama, furor, and public service. He knew the *World* could not compete with the *New York Times* in breadth of coverage, so he relied on selected in-depth treatments. "Pick the best story of the day and hammer the Hell out of it," was his injunction to reporters. Slum landlords, subway service, and the League of Nations were subjects of his "crusades." His cherished project was the "Op Ed" (opposite editorial) page, which featured columnists and reviewers including Heywood Broun, William Bolitho, Franklin P. Adams, Deems Taylor, and Laurence Stallings, and became the model for all later "Op Ed" pages.

During his reign at the *World*, Swope cut a wide swath in politics, bringing the Democra-tic Convention to New York City in 1924. The same year he pushed Governor Al Smith for the presidency. Swope was triumphant when Smith was nominated in 1928, and crestfallen when he was defeated. Later he served as go-between in bringing Smith's nominal support to Roosevelt in 1932. Mencken believed he was "far more a politician than a newspaperman," but Mencken was wrong. Swope never cared much about the substance of political issues; Smith and Roosevelt, despite the chasm between them, were much alike to him. He saw politics as analogous to his favorite sport, horse racing: both entailed excitement, competitiveness, drama, betting, identification, and success. Aside from that, Swope viewed his political role as part of his editorial role and his personal role in the world of publicity: together they formed a single image.

"What I try to do," Swope told Broun, "is to give the public part of what it wants and part of what it ought to have whether it wants it or not." His "chiefest occupation" was "evaluating an event in terms of public reaction." He also claimed, "My whole capital is my knowledge of things and my acquaintance with people." These remarks show his limitations as well as strengths.

Swope's decision to resign from the *World* seemed both sudden and arbitrary: he didn't want to be "a hired boy any longer," he told his wife. Yet its sources were deeper. When Herbert Pulitzer assumed control of the *World* papers, his decisions seemed arbitrary to Swope. The price increase from two cents to three cents proved disastrous for readership and advertising revenue, and the return to two cents did not help much. Worst of all, the profits, while they lasted, were drawn out instead of being plowed back into strengthening the papers. Actually, Swope never left newspaper work; when he heard the *Washington Post* was for sale, he tried to buy it—and failed. This happened again when the news leaked out that the Pulitzers wanted to sell the *World* papers. Swope became entangled in a maze of schemes to raise the money for the purchase, pinning his highest hopes on William Randolph Hearst. That too fell through, and the papers were sold to Roy Howard for $5 million in 1931, and merged with his *New York Telegram*.

From then on, Swope's life was anticlimactic. He continued to live lavishly and entertain on a grand scale at his fabled Sands Point, N.Y., home, designed by Stanford White and decorated by Lady Mendl. (Scott Fitzgerald had used Swope's rented house at Great Neck as the setting for his *The Great Gatsby*.) He continued to play high-stakes poker with the moguls he cultivated; he proved to be an "elegant" chairman of the New York Racing Commission (1934–1945); he rarely missed a theater first night. But he had no heart for it all. To live on the level he was accustomed to, he took a public relations job. But he had little pride in the work and was ashamed of the fees he got.

Swope took great pride in a number of his friendships, especially the one with Baruch, which was a kind of symbiosis between very self-centered, very vain, but also very able and affectionate friends. Swope felt he had added to Baruch's public stature by his public relations advice: Baruch felt grateful but also behaved as if Swope's help was somewhat onerous. Baruch's term "cold war," as well as the opening sentence of his U. N. speech on the atomic bomb—"We are here to make a choice between the quick and the dead"—were actually Swope's words. It was characteristic of Swope that he wanted the world to know the origin of these words.

Swope was a brilliant reporter and a memorable and creative editor, but his chief impact on journalism consisted of the public-spirited crusade, the "Op Ed" page, and a stylish approach to daily liberal journalism. In life he was a great legend maker, and his greatest legend was himself. He died in New York City.

[Some of Swope's correspondence is in the Library of Congress Manuscript Division and in the Franklin D. Roosevelt Library, Hyde Park, N. Y. There is also material in the Oral History Collection of Columbia University. See also Swope's *Journalism* (1924). Elv J. Kahn, Jr., *The World of Swope* (1965), gives a detailed account of Swope and includes a good bibliography. An obituary is in the *New York Times*, June 21, 1958.]

MAX LERNER

TALBOTT, HAROLD ELSTNER (Mar. 31, 1888–Mar. 2, 1957), business executive and government official, was born in Dayton, Ohio, the son of Harry Elstner Talbott and Katharine Houk. His father, a civil engineer and construction contractor, was also active in the paper, electric power, and banking businesses. Talbott's principal commitment was to the H. E. Talbott Company, a construction firm, which Harold joined in 1910, following his studies at the Sheffield Scientific School of Yale University. The younger Talbott had oversight of hydroelectric and industrial construction.

During the ensuing decade the Talbotts joined other ambitious Dayton businessmen, including Edward Deeds of National Cash Register and the inventor Charles Kettering, in investing in the automotive and aviation industries. Known as the "Dayton group," they established the Dayton Metal Products Company, which prospered on Allied war orders. Together with Detroit automobile executives, they organized the Dayton-Wright Aeroplane Company in time to win enough government contracts to make it the nation's largest producer of military aircraft during World War I.

Talbott's experience in aviation led to his appointment in 1918 as a major in the Army Air Service with the assumption that he would be assigned to duty in France with specific responsibilities for aircraft maintenance and repair. But the war ended before he could leave the United States. For the next few years he prospered in the family construction firm and gained wider business contacts as several of the Dayton-based companies with which he was associated were absorbed into the growing General Motors Corporation. Talbott himself moved to New York City in 1924. On Aug. 11, 1925, he married Margaret Thayer of Philadelphia. They had four children.

Although Talbott had substantial investments in such concerns as Chrysler and Electric Auto-Lite, he remained close to the aviation industry, which by the late 1920's had begun to attract the close attention of Wall Street investors. Talbott served in 1932 as chairman of the board of North American Aviation, an expanding holding company that controlled firms in both the manufacturing and transportation sides of the industry. His experience in the aviation business earned him appointment in early 1942 as chief of the War Production Board's Aircraft Production Division. The difficulties of rapid expansion in output led to a reorganization that soon cost Talbott his influence, and he resigned within a year.

After World War II, Talbott, while retaining his extensive business interests, devoted more of his time to Republican politics. In 1940 he had chaired presidential candidate Wendell Willkie's eastern finance committee. Thereafter he became associated with Thomas E. Dewey of New York, a rising political star; and as one of the insiders who organized Dewey's presidential campaign in 1948, he headed the Republican finance committee. He was involved from the start in General Dwight D. Eisenhower's campaign four years later.

In December 1952, Eisenhower appointed Talbott secretary of the air force. In what was known as a businessman's administration, Talbott was considered an able administrator and served as a vigorous partisan of the air force. Although hampered by multibillion dollar budget cuts imposed by Secretary of Defense Charles E. Wilson, Talbott guided the air force in its expansion, while improving it in equipment and personnel as it fully entered the supersonic era. He won wide respect in Congress and among air force professionals for his efforts on behalf of the service.

Yet ironically his career as air force secretary ended with recrimination in the summer of 1955. Although he had sold his million-dollar stock holdings in defense-related industries at the time of his appointment, Talbott was permitted to retain a partnership in P. B. Mulligan and Company, a young but increasingly profitable New York clerical efficiency and management engineering firm. On occasion, he solicited business for it. His activity on its behalf became the subject of a lengthy investigation, the first phase of which was headed by Robert F. Kennedy, then counsel to the Senate Permanent Subcommittee on Investigations. Although Talbott had some bipartisan support for his position that no impropriety had been intended (since the accounts he sought were from firms having no substantial direct defense contracts), senators Wayne Morse and Estes Kefauver led a vigorous attack upon him that became an embarrassment to the Republicans. In

August 1955 the president, who was reputed to regard Talbott as a close friend, readily accepted his reluctantly proffered resignation in a widely quoted "Dear Harold" letter.

Talbott died while vacationing at Palm Beach, Fla. Few Americans had more lengthy and varied involvement with the organizational and financial aspects of the development of the aviation industry, especially with its role in the defense complex. It is in this context that Talbott most deserves to be remembered.

[Talbott's correspondence is scattered among various collections, chiefly at the Eisenhower Library and, for official matters, at the National Archives. On the Dayton-Wright Company, which wound up at the center of a controversy over favoritism in the awarding of contracts, see Grover Loening, *Our Wings Grow Faster* (1935), and Henry Ladd Smith, *Airways* (1942), which take a negative view of the organization; and Howard Mingos, *The Birth of an Industry* (1930), which accents the positive. Elsbeth E. Freudenthal, *The Aviation Business* (1940), helps clarify the dramatic changes in the industry following Lindbergh's flight to Paris. *Aviation Week* (1952–1955) has numerous brief articles on or referring to Talbott's tenure as secretary of the air force. The *New York Times* mentions Talbott numerous times over a period of some twenty-five years and has a lengthy obituary notice, Mar. 3, 1957. See also the clipping file of the *Dayton Journal-Herald*.]

LLOYD J. GRAYBAR

TALMADGE, NORMA (May 2, 1897–Dec. 24, 1957), film actress, was born in Jersey City, N.J., the daughter of Frederick Talmadge, an advertising salesman, and Margaret Talmadge. She grew up in Brooklyn, N.Y., in modest circumstances. She and her two sisters were movie-struck, far more interested in the nearby Vitagraph studio than in Erasmus Hall High School, which they nominally attended. Talmadge, slight, brown-haired, and dewy-eyed, began her career by posing for nickelodeon song slides and, at fourteen, started work at Vitagraph. In *The Household Pest* (1910) she first appeared on the screen, although only the back of her head was visible. In *Tale of Two Cities* (1911) she had a minor ingenue role, and in *Under the Daisies* (1913) she played her first lead. A crude prototype of her later successes, the film told the story of a young country girl, ruined in the big city, who returned to her home to die.

At Vitagraph, Talmadge received her real education. She played every kind of part, from a teenager to a grandmother. She was also called upon to serve as a seamstress and to make up extras. She learned much about acting from her idols, Florence Turner and Maurice Costello, leading members of the Vitagraph stock company; and she acquired, above all, the discipline of hard work. During her five years there she appeared in more than 100 films, her salary slowly rising from $25 a week to $250.

The Battle Cry of Peace (1915), a full-length feature designed to promote wartime recruiting, first brought Talmadge to prominence. It also brought her a salary offer of $400 a week from National Pictures Company in Hollywood. Her career at National failed to materialize, but she made two films for Fine Arts and soon afterward was placed under contract by the Triangle Film Corporation headed by Thomas Ince, Mack Sennett, and D. W. Griffith. She appeared under their aegis in seven inconsequential pictures, none of them directed by Griffith. Her sister Constance was luckier. She too had served an apprenticeship at Vitagraph, and her performance as a mountain girl in Griffith's *Intolerance* (1916) launched her on a highly successful film career.

Returning to the East in 1916, Talmadge met Joseph M. Schenck, the manager of the Loew's Theater Circuit; she married him on Oct. 20, 1916. Under his shrewd guidance she founded her own film studio in New York City and in 1917 completed her first film, *Panthea*. Its success was instantaneous. As in *Under the Daisies*, she loved and she suffered. "I love to portray women with fire in their blood and true wholesome romance in their hearts," she later wrote. She found an audience at once, and for five years she continued to suffer, in boudoirs and in palaces, in contemporary dress and in costume, usually with Eugene O'Brien as her leading man.

In 1922, Talmadge moved her studio to Hollywood, where she continued to make films that appealed primarily to women. *Smilin' Through* (1922) proved perhaps the most successful of these, with its skillful blend of high romance and the supernatural. *Secrets* (1924) had an almost equal appeal. Only in *Kiki* (1926), her one excursion into comedy, did she fail to please her public. Second only to Mary Pickford in popularity, she had no rival as "the lady of the great indoors."

The glitter of Talmadge's private life was equally satisfying to her army of fans. Like Constance and her other sister, Natalie, who married Buster Keaton, Talmadge lived in the opulent style expected of Hollywood royalty during the 1920's. She worked hard, though, and

between 1922 and 1930 reputedly earned more than $5 million.

With the advent of sound pictures Talmadge's career, like that of her sister Constance, came to an end. Critics complained that in *New York Nights* (1930), her first talkie, she sounded like a student of elocution. They complained again that in *Dubarry, Woman of Passion* (1930), she sounded like a teacher of elocution. After these two failures Talmadge retired from film making. She had never wanted a stage career, but in 1932 she made a number of vaudeville appearances with George Jessel, whom she married on Apr. 23, 1934, after her divorce, earlier that month, from Schenck. Following the advice of Schenck and her strong-willed mother, Talmadge had invested her salary well, largely in California and Florida real estate, and in spite of the simultaneous collapse of her career and the stock market, she remained rich. Her marriage to Jessel ended in divorce in 1939. Seven years later she marrried Carvel M. James, a physician. Plagued by arthritis during the last years of her life, she lived in Las Vegas, Nev., for much of the time, confined to a wheelchair. She died there, leaving an estate of more than $3 million in addition to extensive land holdings.

Moviegoers today have little opportunity to evaluate Talmadge's talents. Her still extant version of *Camille* (1927) survives only in a fragmentary state, but it gives a glimpse of Talmadge at the height of her career. Her performance shows her to be an affecting actress and, to a surprising extent, it justifies the high reputation she once enjoyed.

[On Talmadge and her work, see Norma Talmadge, "Closeups," and other articles in the *Saturday Evening Post*, Mar. 3 and Apr. 4, May 7 and 21, and June 25, 1927; Margaret Talmadge, *The Talmadge Sisters* (1924); Rudi Blesh, *Keaton* (1966); Jack Spears, *Hollywood* (1970); George Jessel and John Austin, *The World I Lived in* (1975). See also clippings in the Lincoln Center Theater Collection. An obituary is in *New York Times*, Dec. 25, 1957.]

WILLIAM W. APPLETON

TATUM, ART (Oct. 13, 1910–Nov. 5; 1956), jazz pianist, was born in Toledo, Ohio, the only child of a mechanic from North Carolina. From birth he was blind in one eye and could see only large objects or smaller ones held very close to his other eye. At the age of three he reputedly played on the family organ a hymn that he had heard at his mother's choir practice. Although he played piano for several years before he received any formal training, the first instrument he studied was the violin, when he was thirteen; only later did he take piano lessons. He made his first appearance at sixteen before a large audience on an amateur program at a Toledo radio station. As a result, he was hired as a staff pianist by radio station WSPD in Toledo and given a fifteen-minute morning program that so impressed the National Broadcasting Company (NBC) that it was sent out on NBC's Blue Network.

In 1932 the singer Adelaide Hall, who had heard him when she was appearing in Toledo, brought him to New York as her accompanist. Tatum made his first records that year as her accompanist and the following year cut his first solo records. He remained in New York for two years, playing officially at the Onyx Club, a musicians' hangout on New York's West Fifty-second Street (then known as "Swing Street") and unofficially at after-hours clubs in Harlem, an atmosphere he particularly enjoyed because of the opportunities for "cutting" contests in which Tatum could unleash his virtuoso prowess in competition with other pianists.

His playing was an intricate tapestry of changing keys, musical lines that he slyly twisted as they were about to reach a seemingly inevitable climax, rapid juggling of several figures simultaneously, an implied beat, a rocking caress, and sudden tremendous bursts of stride piano, all performed with seemingly offhand ease. He owed relatively little to other pianists, although there were occasional touches in his work of Earl Hines, Teddy Wilson, and particularly Fats Waller. Tatum readily admitted his debt to Waller. "Fats, man—that's where I come from," he once said, adding, "Quite a place to come from."

Waller was also fond of Tatum. When Tatum entered a club one night while Waller was playing, Fats stopped his performance, stood up, and declared, "Ladies and gentlemen, I play piano. But God is in the house tonight."

Other jazz musicians also stood in awe of Tatum's technique, but, as Dan Morgenstern, a jazz historian, has pointed out, technique was merely the vehicle through which he expressed himself. "What others could imagine, Tatum could execute," Morgenstern said. "And what he could imagine went beyond the wildest dreams of most musical mortals."

"He leaves you with a sense of futility," said Everett Barksdale, a guitarist who frequently played with Tatum. "What you've studied years to perfect, he seems able to perform with such ease."

In the mid-1930's Tatum settled in Chicago at the Three Deuces, where he led a small band, building such a reputation that he was invited to play in London in 1938. On his return, he embarked on a solo career, a reasonable move, according to Billy Taylor, one of his disciples, "because he was a whole band in himself."

In 1943 he formed a trio (with Lloyd "Tiny" Grimes on guitar and Slam Stewart on bass) that for the next two years was one of the top attractions on Fifty-second Street. By the late 1940's his popularity had declined. Some critics claimed that Tatum's playing had become too florid, but Billy Taylor attributed Tatum's alleged floridity to the fact that "he heard so much." Tatum wanted to "fill in all the other things he could hear besides just a normal piano part."

By 1950, however, Tatum was once again appearing with great success in concerts and at clubs. In 1953, 1954, and 1955 Norman Granz, the impresario of "Jazz at the Philharmonic," recorded Tatum in four marathon sessions during which Tatum played more than 200 selections, from which Granz drew thirteen long-playing records entitled "The Genius of Art Tatum." In 1955 he married Geraldine, his second wife.

By this time Tatum was already suffering from the illness that led to his death. He had been a heavy drinker all his life, and that, combined with his fondness for all-night sessions, weakened him. He died of uremia in Los Angeles.

A year before his death, the esteem in which Tatum was held by his peers was made apparent when the *Encyclopedia of Jazz* asked 126 jazz pianists to name their prime influence: 78 named Art Tatum.

[On Tatum and his career, see Roger D. Kinkle, *The Complete Encyclopedia of Popular Music and Jazz, 1900–1950* (1974); Nat Shapiro and Nat Hentoff, eds., *Hear Me Talkin' to Ya* (1955); Nat Shapiro and Nat Hentoff, eds., *The Jazz Makers* (1957); Arnold Shaw, *The Street That Never Slept* (1971); Rex Stewart, "Genius in Retrospect," *Down Beat*, Oct. 20, 1966; Barry Ulanov, *A History of Jazz in America* (1957); and John S. Wilson, *The Collector's Jazz: Traditional and Swing* (1958).]

JOHN S. WILSON

TAYLOR, FRANCIS HENRY (Apr. 23, 1903–Nov. 22, 1957), museum director, was born in Philadelphia, Pa., the son of William

Johnson Taylor, a former president of the College of Physicians of Philadelphia and president of the Library Company of Philadelphia, and Emily Buckley Newbold. He prepared at the Kent (Conn.) School for the University of Pennsylvania, from which he was graduated in 1924. While an undergraduate, Taylor decided to specialize in the humanities. After graduation he taught English at the Lycée de Chartres while following courses at the Sorbonne in Paris. (He had spoken French from childhood.) He then did graduate work at the universities of Paris and Florence, the Institut d'Estudis Catalans in Barcelona, and the American Academy in Rome.

Returning to the United States, in 1926–1927 Taylor was a Carnegie fellow at the Graduate College in Princeton. From 1927 to 1931 he served as assistant and then curator of medieval art and as editor at the Philadelphia Museum of Art. On Nov. 3, 1928, he married Pamela Coyne, a fellow Philadelphian; they had four children.

Taylor's unique talents were revealed when he became director of the Worcester Art Museum in Massachusetts in 1931 at the exceptionally young age of twenty-eight. In this post he demonstrated his broad conception of the role of the museum in the community. His purchase of works of art in every field and from every period and the outstanding exhibitions he staged with brilliant showmanship reflected his wide knowledge of art history and underlined his driving purpose to build bridges between scholarly understanding and public awareness. As he wrote in the *Atlantic Monthly*, "The American Museum is after all not an abandoned European palace, a solution for storing and classifying the accumulated national wealth of the past, but an American phenomenon, developed by the people, for the people, and of the people." He made the Worcester Museum the liveliest and best of its kind in the nation. Taylor's accomplishments there and his fresh, invigorating approach to his profession in general led to his being chosen in 1939 as the fifth director of the Metropolitan Museum of Art in New York. From the start he was heavily burdened by problems arising from a depressed economy, by the imminence of war, and then by America's entry into the global struggle. At that point the most important parts of the museum's vast holdings had to be moved to a place of safety, temporary exhibitions had to be improvised, and the general public still had to be served day by day. In the midst of the pressures these difficulties imposed, Taylor laid bold plans for the reconstruction of the musuem and the modernization of its program.

With the coming of peace these plans were energetically pursued. At a time when many great European collections had not yet been returned to their permanent quarters from emergency storage, he undertook a series of international loans on an unprecedented scale. The Metropolitan organized unique exhibitions of art treasures, never before seen in this country, from Great Britain, France, Germany, Austria, Holland, and Japan.

Taylor recognized the rewarding possibilities of associating the relevant aspects of industry with museum activities. One outstanding result of this vision was the incorporation of the Costume Institute into the general structure of the Metropolitan. In effect, he so altered the concept of an art museum's usefulness to society that a generation later it is hard to recall the prewar American museum world. As is often the case with those who spend themselves setting new patterns, many of his innovations were left to be fully realized by others in years to come.

During his administration, attendance at the museum soared, membership almost tripled, the endowment was almost doubled, gallery space was substantially enlarged, and, among other developments, a newly constructed auditorium (with every provision to facilitate television broadcasting when that medium was still in its early stages) was almost immediately booked to capacity with musical and educational events. Taylor also found time for government service before and during the war, bringing to many foreign countries a better understanding of the United States and its cultural resources. After the war, he published *The Taste of Angels* (1948), a history of art collecting from Rameses to Napoleon. His worldwide contributions to the arts and humanities were recognized with awards from a half-dozen foreign nations.

Francis Taylor was inevitably a controversial figure. His temper was volatile, but his spirit was charitable. He was a man of impressive bulk, with striking features that lent him an air of command. His energy was boundless. He could not tolerate cant or preciosity. He had a ready, pungent wit and was quick to puncture any sign of pomposity in those about him. Yet he wore his erudition and his academic honors with ease and grace. His conversation was salted by an irrepressible and bawdy sense of humor that could brighten the most solemn occasion. In 1954 he decided to resume his old post at Worcester, and left the Metropolitan in 1955. He died in Worcester just three years later, following a kidney operation. An obituary in the *Worcester Telegram* rightly observed that America had lost "one of the rarest and most delightful personalities of this age."

[See *New York Times* and *New York Herald Tribune,* Jan. 12, 1940; *Worcester Art Museum News Bulletin and Calendar,* Jan. 1940; *Metropolitan Museum of Art Bulletin,* Feb. 1940; *Art Digest,* Feb. 1, 1940; *New York Times,* Dec. 14, 1954; *New York Herald Tribune,* Dec. 15, 1954; *Metropolitan Museum of Art Bulletin,* Jan. 1955; *Worcester Telegram, New York Times,* and *New York World-Telegram and Sun,* Nov. 23, 1957; *Saturday Review,* Dec. 12, 1957; *College Art Journal,* 1958; *Metropolitan Museum of Art Bulletin* and *Art News,* Jan. 1958; Century Association, *Year-Book, 1958*; and the archives of the Metropolitan Museum of Art.]

MARSHALL B. DAVIDSON

TAYLOR, MYRON CHARLES (Jan. 18, 1874–May 6, 1959), financier and diplomat, was born in Lyons, N.Y., the son of William Delling Taylor, a well-to-do landowner, and Mary Morgan Underhill. (One of Taylor's remote maternal ancestors, John Underhill, had gone into exile from the Massachusetts Bay Colony for his heretical views and had later settled in Locust Valley, L.I., on a farm that two and a half centuries later became Myron Taylor's country estate.) Taylor graduated with an LL.B. from Cornell University in 1894. Admitted to the New York bar the following year, he began the practice of law in the firm of De Forest and De Forest. He became an expert in corporation law and was soon handling legal matters for various textile companies. On Feb. 21, 1906, he married Anabel Stuart Mack; they had no children.

It was in the textile industry that Taylor made his initial fortune and first attracted the attention of Wall Street. Abandoning the practice of law, he devoted his full attention to the reorganization and development of several textile concerns, in all of which he eventually held a controlling interest. His success brought him offers to serve as director from several of the nation's most important banking and railroad companies: the First National Bank of New York, the First Security Company, the New York Central, and the Atchison, Topeka and Santa Fe. By 1923 he had divested himself of most of his textile interests

and was devoting his full time to banking and railroad directorships.

By nature somewhat reserved and aloof, Taylor shunned publicity, and when it was announced in 1927 that he would become chairman of the finance committee of U.S. Steel, the press called him "the man nobody knows." Quite obviously some important people did know him and appreciated his remarkable talents in finance management. Most notable among Taylor's sponsors were J. Pierpont Morgan, who broke a long-standing rule of not holding office in a corporation and agreed to become chairman of the board of U.S. Steel only if Taylor were made finance chairman; and George F. Baker, chairman of the First National Bank and the largest single stockholder in U.S. Steel.

When Taylor assumed the position of finance chairman, the company had a bonded indebtedness of $400 million. Within three years he had reduced it to $60 million and led the company to a financial position that enabled it to survive the Great Depression. In 1932 Morgan stepped aside and Taylor assumed full executive power in the company. As chief executive officer from 1932 to 1938, Taylor kept the mills open and the company solvent even though production plummeted to only 17 percent of capacity. He reduced wages but refused to cut jobs; instead, he instituted in 1930 a program of sharing work so that every employee kept a job even if for only two or three days a week. The company also made credit available to its employees at a nominal rate of interest and in 1932, during the worst year of the depression, spent over $16 million in direct relief to employees as partial compensation for their reduced work time and wages.

At first cautiously and later enthusiastically a supporter of the New Deal relief and recovery programs, Taylor played an important role in drawing up the first steel code under the National Recovery Act. Unlike many other leaders in the industry, he supported the administration's labor legislation. In 1937 he dramatically broke U.S. Steel's nonunion policy, established following the Homestead Strike of 1892, and signed a labor contract with the CIO. The nation's largest steel company was now unionized, and the other steel companies eventually had to follow its lead. In 1938 Taylor resigned as chairman of the board. His six-year term as chief executive was one of the most significant in the history of the company. He represented the new type of managerial leader, not the flamboyantly aggressive competitor, such as Andrew Carnegie, but rather the company lawyer, the skilled negotiator and diplomat who worked best through committees but ultimately exercised power at least as effectively as any of his predecessors.

In his many private meetings with President Franklin D. Roosevelt, Taylor had won the president's confidence and friendship. Almost immediately following his retirement from U.S. Steel, Roosevelt selected him to head the American delegation to an international conference on refugees held at Evian-les-Bains, France, in the summer of 1938. Although frequently frustrated by the cautious approach of the professional diplomats, Taylor was able to accomplish the little that could be done by international agreement to aid the thousands of refugees fleeing from Hitler's regime. With the outbreak of World War II, Roosevelt selected Taylor for perhaps the most sensitive diplomatic assignment in neutral Europe, to serve as his special representative with ambassadorial rank to the Vatican. Although the president carefully timed this announcement for Christmas Eve 1939, the Christmas spirit in no way lessened the storm of criticism that met this appointment. American Baptists in particular viewed resumption of diplomatic relations with the papacy, closed since 1867, as a dangerous violation of the doctrine of separation of church and state. But Roosevelt, not needing Senate confirmation of a personal representative, stuck by his decision. For the next two years, until Mussolini closed Rome to him in 1942, Taylor was an invaluable informant on Vatican, Italian, and German activities.

With the liberation of Rome in 1944, Taylor returned to the Vatican and, despite continuing criticism, served both Roosevelt and later President Harry S. Truman there as special envoy. He also headed a special commission for American relief to Italy under the auspices of the president's War Relief Control Board. A close friendship developed between Taylor and Pope Pius XII. In 1941 the Taylors had presented the pope with their Florentine villa, Schifanoia. In 1946, Taylor was made a papal nobleman, receiving the Grand Cross of the Order of Pius. Taylor resigned as special envoy to the Vatican in 1949 but retained his ambassadorial rank and continued to serve Truman on special missions to various church leaders throughout Europe until 1953.

Taylor and his wife gave nearly $5 million to Cornell University. He was also a generous contributor to the Metropolitan Museum of Art and served as director of the board for many years.

The day after his death, in New York City, the *New York Times* wrote: "His was, indeed, a useful life." This was the kind of simple understatement of fact that Taylor himself would have most appreciated.

[Some of Taylor's own papers covering his diplomatic service (1939–1947) are in the Franklin D. Roosevelt Presidential Library, Hyde Park, N.Y. Other papers are in the U.S. Steel Corporation archives, Pittsburgh, Pa. Taylor's writings include "Spreading Work to Avoid Lay-offs," in *Addresses Given Under the Auspices of the President's Emergency Commission for Unemployment* (1931); introduction and explanatory notes to *Wartime Correspondence Between President Roosevelt and Pope Pius XII* (1947); and the privately printed *Correspondence Between President Truman and Pope Pius XII* (1953). Taylor is conspicuous in several memoirs in the Oral History Collection of Columbia University, particularly in that of Frances Perkins. For biographical articles and studies, see the *New York Times*, Dec. 28, 1927; Dec. 24, 1939; and May 7, 1959; Ida T. Bacci, "United States–Vatican Relations and the Taylor Mission" (M.A. thesis, American University, 1949); and U.S. Steel Corporation, *Myron C. Taylor: An Appreciation* (1956).]

JOSEPH FRAZIER WALL

TAYLOR, WILLIAM CHITTENDEN (Mar. 3, 1886–Nov. 2, 1958), industrial chemist, was born in San Francisco, Calif., the son of William Taylor, Jr., and Carrie Louise Chittenden. His father was one of the last clipper ship captains, and during his youth Taylor sailed eleven times "around the Horn" on voyages between California and the East Coast, in addition to making several trips around the world. Ultimately he rose from apprentice seaman to first mate. Much of his early education was obtained from his mother while on shipboard, but he also attended the California School of Mechanic Arts and the Boston English High School. He entered the Massachusetts Institute of Technology in 1904, and graduated four years later with the B.S. degree, ranking first in his class.

Late in 1908, Taylor was appointed assistant chemist at the newly established research laboratory of the Corning Glass Works, Corning, N.Y. He left in 1909 for a brief stint as a chemist with the U.S. Agricultural Experiment Station in Mayagüez, P.R., but returned to the Corning Glass Works in 1910 and remained with that firm for the rest of his career. By 1923 he had risen to the rank of chief chemist, followed by promotions to director of glass technology (1939), and vice-president and director of manufacturing and engineering (1947). Upon his retirement in 1954, he became honorary vice-president and general technical adviser.

Taylor's career spanned a period of revolutionary change in glassmaking. When it began, glass was still melted in small pots and blown by hand; by the time it ended, continuous melting of raw materials in massive furnaces, followed by rapid blowing, pressing, or drawing by machines, was characteristic. Taylor contributed significantly to this transformation. During his career he obtained thirty-two patents; typical was one awarded to him in 1935 for stirring molten glass in continuous tank furnaces. He was prominent in developing improved bulbs for incandescent electric lighting and vacuum tubes for radios. He also played a major role in perfecting glass with chemical characteristics permitting the transmission or absorption of specific wavelengths in the visible, ultraviolet, and infrared spectra, thereby opening up many new scientific and technological applications.

Taylor achieved most recognition for his role, along with Eugene C. Sullivan, in the development of borosilicate glass, highly resistant to heat and corrosion. After numerous experiments in search of a chemically stable mixture of silica sand and boric oxide, success was achieved in 1912 with a material that was first used in lamp globes and battery jars. This was of special value for the safer operation of railroads because it dramatically reduced the shattering of signal lanterns when heated glass came in contact with cold rain or snow.

Another important application was soon suggested by a new member of the research team, Jesse T. Littleton, who urged that the material would make good baking vessels because it absorbed radiant heat, whereas most metal containers reflected it. This idea, tested successfully by Littleton's wife, resulted by 1915 in an improved type of ovenware marketed under the trade name of Pyrex.

During World War I Corning was quick to exploit the market for beakers, test tubes, and other glassware requiring high resistance to chemical attack, which American laboratories had previously obtained from Germany. Later the chemical and food-processing industries began to use large quantities of piping made of borosilicate glass, which also proved to be a superior material for insulators on telephone and electrical power

lines. During the mid-1930's the same versatile material was used in making the 200-inch mirror for the Hale Telescope of the Mt. Palomar Observatory.

In 1928 Taylor, together with Sullivan, had won the Potts Medal of the Franklin Institute for the development of heat-resistant glass; in 1929 he received the Perkin Medal of the Society of Chemical Industry. In 1940 the National Association of Manufacturers presented him with its Pioneer of Industry Award.

Taylor married Alice C. Pratt on Dec. 29, 1909. They had two children. Taylor served for a time as an alderman of the city of Corning, and he played a leading role in the Sea Scout movement. Those who knew him well described him as "a man of gentle wit and humor." He died at Corning, N.Y., just four days after he, Sullivan, and Littleton had received the plaudits of numerous scientists and engineers at a dinner marking the fiftieth anniversary of the founding of the Corning research laboratories.

[The public relations department of Corning Glass Works maintains a file of information on Taylor's career. Obituaries of Taylor are in *Corning* (N.Y.) *Leader, New York Herald Tribune,* and *New York Times,* Nov. 3, 1958. See also Eugene C. Sullivan, "William Chittenden Taylor," *Glass Industry,* June 1959; and Corning Glass Works, *Sand and Imagination* (1959).]

W. DAVID LEWIS

TCHELITCHEW, PAVEL (Sept. 21, 1898–July 31, 1957), painter and theater designer, born in Moscow, the son of Fyodor Tchelitchew and Nadezhda Permyakov, wealthy aristocrats. They provided their son with a private education with tutors. As a child, he was fascinated with the book illustrations of Gustave Doré. His lifelong interest in the fantastic began in germinal form in his earliest work. In 1918 the family was forced to flee its estate in the aftermath of the Bolshevik Revolution. They settled in Kiev, where Pavel entered the school of painting and theater design operated by Alexandra Exter, a student of Fernand Léger. He also took private lessons with Basil Tchakrigine and Isaac Rabinovitch, two artists who worked in the constructivist-cubist manner. He also worked on theater projects and designed posters.

In the fall of 1920 he left Russia by way of

Istanbul and Sofia, for Berlin, where he lived for two years, executing theater sets for the ballet and opera. Then he moved to Paris, where he began to shed his cubist-derived style and return to the representational. At first he painted landscapes but soon turned to portraiture, producing self-portraits and interpretations of such friends as Nicolas Nabokov, Glenway Wescott, Margaret Anderson, and Allen Tanner. He favored a palette of pale blues and fuchsias. One of these portraits and a still life were represented in the 1925 Salon d'Automne, where they attracted the attention of Gertrude Stein. She searched him out and invited him to her apartment, where he saw her superb collection. He was much moved by her blue- and pink-period Picassos. These thereafter influenced his choice of subject, manner of representing the figure, and use of color.

In 1926 Tchelitchew exhibited at the Galerie Druet in Paris with other figurative painters, including Christian Bérard, Kristians Tonnys, the Russian expatriates Eugene Berman and Léonide, and others. As a group that reaffirmed the centrality of the human figure in art, they offered a clear alternative to cubist abstraction, much expressionist painting, and most surrealism. Their work was often mysterious and dreamlike; one critic called it "neo-romantic." Tchelitchew was considered the *"chef-d'école."*

From about 1930 onward Tchelitchew developed a vocabulary of techniques and approaches to representation that was to give his art its particular stamp. Although he never joined the surrealist movement, like certain surrealists, Salvador Dali and Max Ernst in particular, he experimented with double imagery. Confronting such a work, the beholder would recognize some objects at once but identify others only upon further reflection. He also introduced exaggerated perspective and foreshortening. He would, for instance, show a reclining figure with the feet very close to the beholder so they would appear abnormally large. Thus, he projected a troubled state of mind, as if nature were being viewed by the mentally disturbed.

Between 1929 and 1932 Tchelitchew painted a series of circus figures, several conspicuously tattooed; tennis players; and bullfighters. He was winning great recognition. In 1928 he had his first one-man show, in London, and two years later, another in Paris. In the 1930's he painted portraits of socialites and such celebrities as Helena Rubinstein (attaching real sequins to the portrait); his lifelong companion and secretary, the poet Charles-Henri Ford; Lincoln Kirstein; and

Dame Edith Sitwell, whom he had met through Gertrude Stein and who did much to establish his reputation in England. He was given his first one-man show in the United States in 1934, at the Julien Levy Gallery in New York City.

Tchelitchew settled in America in 1938 and became an American citizen. In 1942 the Museum of Modern Art put on a large retrospective exhibition of his work and acquired *Hide and Seek* (1940–1942), a work considered by many to be his masterpiece. It and *Phenomena* (1936–1938; Moscow, Tretykov State Gallery) were conceived as two parts of a triad representing Hell, Purgatory, and Paradise.

Phenomena reveals a broad, deep landscape peopled with a wide assortment of circus freaks and similarly distorted beings of the artist's invention. Most are peering out of the canvas. The color is shrill and spectral. When first shown in London, this painting scandalized the critics. *Hide and Seek* is an "interior landscape" that makes the most of multiple-image metamorphosis and complex and ambitious use of perspective. It is more lyrical and mysterious than *Phenomena*. One critic attacked its "shrill saccharine color and gelatinous symbolism." Tchelitchew was working on plans for the third stage, the celestial, when he died.

In the 1940's he also painted a number of male heads composed entirely of illumined, glowing, transparent tubing against a dark ground. These recall the anatomical drawings of exposed nervous systems by Vesalius, but they also seem hallucinated and illusory.

Throughout his career, Tchelitchew designed sets and costumes for the ballet, collaborating with Diaghilev, Balanchine, and others. A list of ballets on which he worked includes *Ode* (1929), *L'Errante* (1933), *Orpheus* (1936), *St. Francis* (1938), *Ondine* (1939), *Balustrade* (1941), and *Apollon Musagète* (1942). In 1949 he was given a large retrospective exhibition in Buenos Aires. In 1952 he left the United States to settle in Frascati, Italy. In his last years his health deteriorated, and he was in financial difficulties. His work slowed down as he became increasingly depressed. He died in Rome.

[See James Thrall Soby, *Tchelitchew, Paintings, Drawings,* exhibition catalog, Museum of Modern Art (N.Y.), 1942; special Tchelitchew number of *View 2,* May 1942, with articles by Lincoln Kirstein, James Thrall Soby, Parker Tyler, and William Carlos Williams; Lincoln Kirstein, ed., *Pavel Tchelitchew, Drawings* (1947); Lincoln Kirstein, *Pavel Tchelitchew,* exhibition catalog, Gallery of Modern Art (N.Y.), 1964; Parker Tyler, *The Divine Comedy of Pavel Tchelitchew* (1967).]

ROBERT REIFF

TERMAN, LEWIS MADISON (Jan. 15, 1877–Dec. 21, 1956), psychologist, was born on a farm in Johnson County, Ind., the son of James Terman and Martha Cutsinger. Terman stayed at home until he was fifteen, working on the farm in season and attending a one-room school in the winters. His father had a good collection of books, including the *Encyclopaedia Britannica*, and Terman became a voracious reader, fiercely ambitious for more education. Between periods of teaching in a rural school, he attended Central Normal School at Danville, Ind., from which he received the B.A. in 1898. He then, when he was still only twenty-one, became principal of a nearby township high school. At the end of his first year in that post he married Anna B. Minton; they had two children.

Terman was still eager for further education, however, and resolved to become a psychologist. After two years at Indiana University, Terman went to Clark University, in Worcester, Mass., from which he received the Ph.D. in 1905. It was at Clark that he became interested in mental testing, seeing the possibilities it provided for the study of intellectually gifted children, a subject that had fascinated him from his early adolescence. For his dissertation he constructed a massive battery of tests that he gave to seven bright and seven dull children. The results convinced him that well-designed tests could differentiate between children with great intellectual promise and those who lacked it.

Terman's health had never been robust, and his family medical history placed him at severe risk from tuberculosis. In 1905, when he was twenty-eight, it became clear that he had contracted the disease. On urgent medical advice, he accepted a high school principalship in the benign climate of San Bernardino, Calif.; the following year he moved to a faculty position at Los Angeles State Normal School, where he remained until 1910. There he found stimulating colleagues (including the young Arnold Gesell) who supported him in his decision to construct an American version of Alfred Binet's French-language intelligence test. In 1910 he accepted an appointment in the Department of Education at Stanford University and at once began the arduous work of constructing new test items to add to Binet's. Then came the equally demanding process of standardizing his new test. The result was the famous Stanford-Binet test, the standard intelligence test in English-speaking countries for the next thirty years, which Terman described in *The Measurement of Intelligence*, published in 1916.

The immediate success and wide usefulness of the test brought Terman national fame among psychologists as well as educators. When intelligence tests were needed by the army in World War I, Terman was called to Washington, commissioned a major, and employed in the construction of the Army Alpha and Beta tests. Returning to Stanford in 1919, he began his famous study of gifted children. He selected about 1,500 ten-year-old California youngsters who had intelligence quotients of 140 or over, measured on a scale of Terman's own design on which an average child has an IQ of 100. With a corps of assistants, he made an intensive case study of each subject and published the statistical description of the group in the first volume of his *Genetic Studies of Genius* (1925). This study continued to be the central focus of Terman's work throughout the rest of his life; he carried out successive follow-ups at five- or ten-year intervals and reported the results in subsequent volumes of the series.

In 1922 Terman was appointed head of Stanford's psychology department, a position he retained until his retirement in 1943. With the aid of a new endowment fund he soon developed a very strong faculty, proving to be as skillful at administration as at test construction. His election to the presidency of the American Psychological Association and to the National Academy of Sciences followed shortly. During the 1920's he was coauthor of the Stanford Achievement Tests, and in the 1930's he applied his talent for testing to the measurement of masculinity-femininity and to the study of marital happiness, rightly believing that these fields needed the same objectivity and quantification of methods that he had brought to intelligence and school achievement. At the time of his death, at Stanford, he was at work on volume V of the *Genetic Studies of Genius*; the volume was completed by his long-time research associate, Melita Oden.

Terman was rather slight in build, with reddish hair, a soft voice, and a warm and engaging smile. He was a shy man, whose outward warmth masked an inner retiringness—social interaction seemed more fatiguing to him than to most men. He was intensely ambitious, however, in almost the Horatio Alger tradition. Despite his frail health he was a tireless worker, eager for achievement, and not reluctant to accept honors and money. With all his gentleness, he could be a fierce fighter for his ideas—when, in the early 1920's, some humanists attacked mental measurement he responded with vitriolic satire and he was likewise intemperate a decade later, when research at the State University of Iowa called into question his lifelong belief in the heritability of intelligence. Beneath a quiet and modest exterior there was a true passion for accomplishment.

Terman's ambition was well fulfilled. The Stanford-Binet test brought mental measurement to scientific maturity, while his study of gifted children destroyed the myth of the weakness, insanity, and early deterioration of highly intelligent school-age children (indeed, it showed that high IQ is often concomitant to other good qualities, including both physical and mental health). His work on masculinity-femininity laid much of the groundwork for the modern application of psychometrics to personality study. Terman was fundamentally a pure empiricist, with little interest in theory—and on occasion he substituted belief for theory, as demonstrated by his early nativistic position concerning the inheritance of intelligence. His chief interest throughout his career was the art and science of mental measurement.

[Terman wrote "Trails to Psychology," in C. Murchison, ed., *A History of Psychology in Autobiography* (1932), an autobiography that emphasizes his professional activities. See also E. G. Boring, "Lewis Madison Terman, 1877–1956," *Biographical Memoirs. National Academy of Sciences* (1959), with a good photograph and with a complete bibliography of Terman's writings by Melita Oden; E. R. Hilgard, "Lewis Madison Terman (1877–1956)," *American Journal of Psychology*, Sept. 1957, an evaluation of scientific achievements, together with quotations from two of Terman's unpublished autobiographical papers and assessment of his accomplishments as a teacher and administrator; M. V. Seagoe, *Terman and the Gifted* (in press), a full-length authorized biography by a former student; and R. R. Sears, "L. M. Terman, Pioneer in Mental Measurement," *Science*, May 15, 1957, a brief evaluation of Terman's contribution to mental measurement.]

ROBERT R. SEARS

THAYER, TIFFANY ELLSWORTH (Mar. 1, 1902–Aug. 23, 1959), novelist, actor,

and advertising scriptwriter, was born in Freeport, Ill., the son of Elmer Ellsworth Thayer and Sybil Farrar. His parents were actors and were divorced when Thayer was five. He lived with his father in Rockford, Ill., until 1916, when he ran away to join his mother in Chicago. After dropping out of high school in his third year, he worked for a commercial artist and, in 1917, as a copyboy on the *Chicago Record-Herald*.

Thayer emulated the careers of his parents by joining a dramatic and operatic stock company in Oak Park, Ill. From 1918 to 1922 he played in theaters in Illinois, Indiana, and elsewhere in the Midwest, mostly in one-night stands. He had roles in *Her Unborn Child* and *Up the Ladder* and, in 1918, appeared with Lillian Kingsbury in *The Coward*. However, he was not notably successful as an actor and worked as a newspaper reporter between theatrical seasons. For a time he clerked in bookshops specializing in old and rare books in Chicago and managed bookshops in Cleveland and Detroit.

In 1926 Thayer moved to New York City, still hoping to achieve fame on the stage. His savings ran out before he could find a role, and he took a job as an advertising copywriter. He at once showed extraordinary competence in this field and continued to work in it for the rest of his life, even after achieving financial success as a novelist.

Written during evenings and weekends in 1928 and 1929, Thayer's first novel, *Thirteen Men*, was published in May 1930. Soon afterward, he sailed for Europe. On his return to New York that fall, he found that he had produced a best-seller. In the novel twelve of the characters are members of the jury deciding the fate of the thirteenth man, Frank Miller, a young intellectual who had murdered thirty-eight people. The stories of their lives are narrated, one reviewer wrote, " with speed, humor and verve. They are smart and smutty, and sometimes both the smartness and the smut pall, but not badly." These observations apply appropriately to most of Thayer's more than twenty other novels, some of which were published under the pseudonyms Elmer Ellsworth, Jr., and John Doe. Nearly all of them—including *Call Her Savage* (1931), *Thirteen Women* (1932), *An American Girl* (1933), *One Woman* (1933), and *The Old Goat* (1937)—are ribald, gaudy, and spiced with facetious sexual episodes. In their mild salacity they resembled the novels of Maxwell Bodenheim, Thorne Smith, and Ben Hecht, who once referred to Thayer as "a fellow pornographer."

Thayer, who prided himself on his understanding of feminine psychology, wrote with gusto and always seemed capable of doing better work than he actually did. Critic Burton Rascoe wrote of *Thirteen Men* that "the author has one of the most promising talents I have observed among newcomers in fiction." However, Thayer had no literary pretensions. "To hell with literature," he told interviewer Rochelle Girson in 1956. It may have been this attitude and declaration that inspired Ezra Pound's remark to Donald Hall in a *Paris Review* interview that "People who have lost reverence have lost a great deal. That was where I split with Tiffany Thayer." Thayer had befriended Pound and his daughter Mary and worked (1957–1958) for Pound's release from St. Elizabeth Hospital in Washington, D.C.

From 1930 Thayer was advertising manager of the Literary Guild. In 1931 he founded the Fortean Society honoring Charles Fort, a critic of science and expounder of unconventional theories of scientific phenomena. Other members included Alexander Woollcott, John Cowper Powys, and Ben Hecht. Thayer was permanent secretary of the society and editor of its magazine, *Doubt*.

In the mid-1930's Thayer spent time in Hollywood as a scenarist and part-time actor. Always insisting that he would rather act than write, he appeared in a mediocre film and "scored a personal triumph," he believed, in a stage revival of *Whistling in the Dark*. He returned to New York and from 1938 to 1948 worked as a radio advertising writer for J. Walter Thompson Agency. After 1948 he wrote for the advertising firm of Sullivan, Stauffer, Caldwell, and Bayles for six months and spent the other half of the year writing at Nantucket, Mass.

In 1939 Thayer began a prodigiously long and ambitious story of the Renaissance in Italy with the aim of discovering the reasons for the Mona Lisa's enigmatic smile. The first three of twenty-one projected volumes were published in 1956 as *Mona Lisa: The Prince of Taranto*. Many reviewers were impressed with the enormous extent of the author's research and with his narrative skill, but some were repelled by the immense cargo of "venery, chicanery, and intrigue" that Thayer's inflated prose was able to support. Thomas Caldecot Chubb, writing in the *New York Times*, said the book "as a sheer piece of work" is "amazing and unforgettable." Thayer's own favorite book was *Rabelais for Boys and Girls* (1939), a bowdlerized version.

Thayer, who insisted throughout life that his marital status was "nobody's business," was married three times. His widow was the former Kathleen McMahon. He had no children. Of average size (five feet, seven inches), he described himself as an "atheist, an anarchist,—in philosophy a Pyrrhonean." He prized rare books and was an expert collector of first issues of odd and curious magazines, an interest he discussed learnedly in 1930 in one of his few magazine articles. Thayer died of a heart attack at Nantucket, Mass.

[In addition to the books cited above, Thayer wrote *The Illustrious Corpse* (1930); *The Greek* (1931); *Eye-Witness!* (1931); *Three-Sheet* (1932); *Kings and Numbers* (1934); *The Cluck Abroad* (1935); *One-Man Show* (1937); *Little Dog Lost* (1938); and *Tiffany Thayer's Three Musketeers* (1939); and he edited *33 Sardonics I Can't Forget* (1946), a collection of short stories. Thayer discussed his magazine collection in "Volume One, Number One," *Bookman*, Dec. 1930. On his life and career, see Rochelle Girson, "That Dirty Boy," *Saturday Review of Literature*, June 9, 1956; J. K. Hutchens, "Meet Nelson Algren and Tiffany Thayer," *New York Herald Tribune Book Review*, June 10, 1956; Lewis Nichols, "A Talk With Tiffany Thayer," *New York Times Book Review*, June 10, 1956; *Newsweek*, June 11, 1956; *Time*, June 11, 1956; Mary de Rachewiltz, *Discretions* (1971); C. David Heymann, *Ezra Pound: The Last Rower* (1976); and Donald Hall, *Remembering Poets* (1978).]

WILLIAM McCANN

THEOBALD, ROBERT ALFRED (Jan. 25, 1884–May 13, 1957), naval officer, was born in San Francisco, Calif., the son of George Theobald and Hattie Caroline Yoell. His father had come from England as a young man, and worked for an insurance company. Theobald was educated in the public schools of San Francisco, then enrolled at the University of California in 1902 to study mining engineering. On a dare from a friend, he took the competitive examinations for the service academies, and in 1903, unable to obtain a preferred appointment to West Point, he entered the United States Naval Academy. He graduated ninth (in a class of eighty-six) in 1907. Commissioned an ensign in 1908, he made the world cruise with the "Great White Fleet" aboard the *Wisconsin* from 1907 to 1909. On Oct. 2, 1909, Theobald married Helen Reeves Berry. They had two children. His wife died in 1938, and on May 24, 1941, he married Elizabeth Burnham Dartnell. They had no children.

Theobald

The next two decades brought assignments in which Theobald impressed his superiors with his ability and intellectual acumen. In 1910–1913 he served aboard the *Nebraska*, and from 1913 to 1915 he was stationed at Annapolis. In 1915 he assumed command of a destroyer, and a year later he commanded a destroyer landing force at Montecristi in the Dominican Republic intervention. During World War I, Theobald was gunnery officer on the *New York*, flagship of the American battleship squadron attached to the British Grand Fleet. In 1919 he became executive officer of the Navy Postgraduate School, but left this post in 1921 for two years of destroyer command with the Asiatic Fleet. In 1924 he was appointed head of the Postgraduate School. He returned to sea duty in 1927 as executive officer of the *West Virginia*. From 1930 to 1931 he attended the Naval War College.

During the 1930's Theobald emerged as one of the most promising officers in the navy. After leaving the War College, he was successively assigned to the War Plans Division of the Navy Department and as chief of staff and aide to the commander of destroyers, Battle Force. In 1935 he returned to the Naval War College as a member of the advanced class, and from 1936 to 1938 he was in charge of the Strategy Division at the college. Students at the college during these years would long remember his fiery debates with Captain Richmond K. Turner, a strong air power enthusiast, over the proper weight the navy should give to air war and the role that air power would have in the event of war in the Pacific. Following his second tour at the War College, Theobald commanded the *Nevada* and served briefly on the staff of the commander in chief, United States Fleet, as a member of the General Board, and as commander of a cruiser division. In June 1940 he was promoted to rear admiral, and three months later he became commander of a destroyer flotilla with the Pacific Fleet, a post he held until the Japanese attack at Pearl Harbor in December 1941.

The promise that Theobald displayed in his rise to flag rank did not materialize into a major role in World War II. After serving briefly as commander of destroyers, Pacific Fleet, he was named commander of the North Pacific Force in May 1942. From the outset Theobald and Major General Simon Bolivar Buckner, Jr., commander of army forces in the Alaskan sector, differed on strategy for the Aleutians campaign. The small size of his force and a proclivity for focusing on the possible perils of an undertaking inclined

Theobald to be cautious in moving against the Japanese, while Buckner favored an aggressive strategy. Matters were worsened by a personality clash with Buckner and disputes with Brigadier General William O. Butler, commander of the Eleventh Air Force, and Lieutenant General John L. DeWitt, head of the Western Defense Command. These problems with his army counterparts and their negative effect on army-navy cooperation, along with Theobald's undisguised feeling that he had been consigned to a backwater of the war, irritated Admiral Chester W. Nimitz, commander of the Pacific Fleet, and in January 1943, Theobald was reassigned as commandant of the First Naval District and the Boston Navy Yard. He was relieved of all active duty in October 1944, and retired in February 1945.

In retirement Theobald immersed himself in the Pearl Harbor controversy. He had helped Admiral Husband E. Kimmel, a close friend and commander of the Pacific Fleet, prepare for the hearings of the Roberts Commission in the weeks following the attack, and was convinced that Kimmel and Lieutenant General Walter C. Short, commander of the Hawaiian Department, had been made scapegoats for the Japanese success. In *The Final Secret of Pearl Harbor* (1954) he claimed that Kimmel and Short were purposely not alerted to the threat of attack because of a plot by President Franklin D. Roosevelt who invited the attack to unify the United States behind a direct part in the war. Theobald also wrote a biweekly column for a Beverly, Mass., newspaper and gave numerous speeches on world affairs. He died in Boston.

Theobald, known as "Fuzzy" to his friends, was a portly man with a wide, square face. He possessed a quick mind that at times prompted him to be caustic and insulting. He is remembered as one of Roosevelt's harshest critics in the Pearl Harbor controversy.

[Theobald's papers are deposited at the Hoover Institute on War, Revolution and Peace at Stanford University. In addition to writing *The Final Secret of Pearl Harbor*, Theobald provided an introduction, annotations, maps, and an appendix for Andrieu d'Albas's *Death of a Navy* (1957). The basic biographical survey of Theobald is on file with the U.S. Naval Academy Alumni Association. On Theobald's years at the Naval War College, see George Carroll Dyer, *Amphibians Came to Conquer*, 2 vols. (1972). On his service during World War II, see Samuel Eliot Morison, *The United States Navy in World War II*, 15 vols. (1947–1962); Louis Morton, *The War in the Pacific—Strategy and*

Command (1962); Brian Garfield, The Thousand-Mile War (1969); and E. B. Potter, Nimitz (1976). An obituary is in New York Times, May 14, 1957.]

JOHN KENNEDY OHL

THOMAS, JOHN CHARLES (Sept. 6, 1891–Dec. 13, 1960), baritone, was born in Meyersdale, Pa., the son of Milson Thomas, a Methodist preacher, and Anna Dorothea Schnaebel. Milson Thomas took the family around the countryside, where he preached at camp meetings, and young John would join his parents in singing at these gatherings.

After early schooling received in the towns they visited, he finally attended Conway Hall in Carlysle, Pa., where he excelled in football and track. In 1908 he ran a mile in five minutes and cleared the high-jump bar at 5 feet, 10½ inches.

His father had hoped young Thomas would choose the ministry, but instead John enrolled at the Mount Street College of Homeopathy in Baltimore (1907–1909). Then, reportedly after he flipped a coin to decide on a medical or a musical career, he enrolled at the Peabody Conservatory of Music in Baltimore (1910–1913); his voice teachers were Blanche Blackman and Adelin Fermin. His first appearance on stage took place at a Peabody performance of Trial by Jury, in which he played the judge. In 1912 he was engaged to sing Passion in Everywoman, with music by George W. Chandwick, in London, Ontario. Subsequent musical comedy appearances included The Passing Show of 1913 for the Schuberts and Franz Lehar's Alone at Last in 1915. His first leading role in New York was in The Peasant Girl in 1915. Then came Sigmund Romberg and Emerich Kalman's Her Soldier Boy in 1916 and Romberg's 1917 Maytime, opposite Peggy Wood. Thomas's rugged physique, wavy blond hair, and smile of a born comedian, plus the beautiful quality of his voice, made him a matinee idol. Thomas married Ruby Rothnour on Oct. 11, 1913; ten years later they were divorced.

Thomas was not satisfied with stardom in light opera. He kept up his vocal training and made his concert debut at Aeolian Hall on Dec. 2, 1918. In 1922 he studied with the legendary Jean de Reszke in Europe. In that year he sang at Royal Albert Hall with Luisa Tetrazzini. In 1923 he starred in a movie called Under the Red Robe with William Powell and Anna Rubens. On Mar. 5, 1924, he married Dorothy May Kaehler.

Thomas's opera debut was as Amonasro in Aida with the Washington Opera on Mar. 3, 1925. On Aug. 1, 1925, he made his debut as Herod in Massenet's Hérodiade at the Théâtre de la Monnaie in Brussels and was subsequently engaged in a three-year contract. In 1930 his first appearance at a major opera house was in San Francisco in Salome, with Maria Jeritza.

Thomas's career with the Chicago Opera began in November 1930, when he made his debut as Tonio in I Pagliacci. His success was enormous, causing the biggest demonstration at the house since the debut of Amelita Galli-Curci. His debut at the Metropolitan Opera came in February 1934. He sang Germont père in La Traviata with Tito Schipa and Rosa Ponselle. Other roles included Scarpia in Tosca and Amonasro in Aida.

From 1927 on, he sang on the radio in shows such as "The Maxwell House Show Boat," "The Ford Sunday Evening Hour," "The Westinghouse Hour," and "The Bell Telephone Hour." He also made many recordings, the bulk of them on the RCA Victor Red Seal label.

Thomas had a unique ability to reach many levels of listener taste. He was at heart a showman, judging from the many enthusiastic reviews and reports of his concert stage persona. His concert programs were a mixture of serious and light-hearted fare; one often sees music of Schumann, Verdi, and Fauré listed with Guion's Home on the Range. His diction in any language was superb, and he stopped at nothing (including grimaces, grunts, and even whistles) to put the material across. In review after review, mention is made of sold-out houses. A champion of American concert composers, he chose large portions of his programs from the English-language repertoire.

His colleague from 1933 to 1945 was the pianist Carroll Hollister. Early in their collaboration Thomas asked Hollister if he could do a whole concert from memory. Hollister did their concerts without music from then on. It became a trademark of a John Charles Thomas–Carroll Hollister recital.

Thomas spent long periods of the year on his 101-foot yacht, The Masquerader, where he did much of his rehearsing with Hollister. On one such occasion, in the 1930's, he received the manuscript directly from Albert Hay Malotte for his new setting of "The Lord's Prayer." Thomas ran through it and said "Wow! This'll be a hit! It's got great lyrics!" He would often go directly from his yacht, sometimes barefoot, to the radio studio to do his program. His relaxed approach reflected a lack of patience with rules of etiquette, and his temper could be short when faced with red tape or bureaucracy. Newspaper reports of a feud Thomas had with the Federal Radio Commission in 1936 regarding their censure of his saying "Good night, Mother" at the close of his radio programs show him at his feisty best. "Thomas said yesterday that the Federal Radio Commission had told him the 'Good night, Mother' at the conclusion of his broadcasts constituted a personal communication, banned on the air. Mr. Thomas said he told the commission it was either 'Good night, Mother' or 'Goodbye, Broadcasting.' Thomas won the argument."

This stubbornness was expressed with much humor in a painting of him in his debut as Tonio in *I Pagliacci* at the Brussels Opera which hung in Thomas's living room. In a 1940 *New York Post* interview, Thomas explained the story behind this painting. Thomas is shown on stage in costume, with his left foot inside the prompter's box. The prompter apparently thought the newly arrived American needed help with his French lines and was "yelling his head off. I was afraid he would drown me out, so I stepped on his hand ["very, very lightly," he insisted later] to keep him from turning the pages of the score."

Thomas made his farewell concert tour in 1952–1953. He sang in about fifty cities. From 1954 until his death, he lived in Apple Valley, Calif. He continued broadcasting and recording hundreds of ballads and religious selections with piano and with orchestra. He even managed a radio station in Los Angeles.

In 1940 Virgil Thomson expressed succinctly the secret of Thomas's musical greatness: "He reminds one at the same time of Chauncey Olcott and of John McCormack. The first, because of his combination of personal charm with dramatic power. The second, because of his high perfection in the kind of easily floated melody-with-or-naments that used to be called, when singers still had enough control to master it, bel canto. . . . Gifted so rarely and schooled so soundly, everything he touches becomes, in a different way, and for a different public, beauty." Thomas died in Apple Valley.

[See Charles I. Morgan, "John Charles Thomas," *The Record Collector*, vol. 25 (1979), which gives a complete discography and a very detailed and dated career listing. There is no full-length biography.]

ROBERT WHITE

THOREK, MAX (Mar. 10, 1880–Jan. 25, 1960), surgeon, was born in Hungary, the son of Issac Thorek and Sarah Mahler. His father practiced medicine as a *feldsher*, or physician without academic training; while his mother was one of the first midwives to receive official training at the University of Budapest. In 1897 he was sent to the gymnasium in Budapest; but later that year a wave of anti-Semitic violence in his hometown resulted in the death of his younger brother, and the family immigrated to the United States. They settled in Chicago at the invitation of an uncle who, however, provided little financial support.

Thorek began earning money as a violinist in a traveling orchestra. After beginning medical studies at the University of Chicago, he earned tuition money by playing a snare drum in the university band. He completed the last two years of the curriculum at Rush Medical College, where he received his M.D. in 1904. Among the teachers with whom he came into contact were Frank Billings, Jacques Loeb, and the surgeon John Benjamin Murphy. Most important to Thorek personally was the support of the dean of students, C. B. H. Harvey.

Thorek served his internship in obstetrics at the Marcy Home in Chicago, which specialized in sending physicians out to assist at births in homes of the indigent. Thorek began his private practice in 1904, renting an office in the impoverished West Side area that he had come to know as an immigrant. Through intimate contact with patients from the many ethnic groups in Chicago, Thorek became proficient in a number of languages. On Apr. 16, 1905, he married Fannie Unger; they had one son.

During this period, Thorek also worked for five years at the gynecological clinic of Henry Banga, first as assistant and later as associate. But while he continued to have a strong interest in the diseases of women, he made an early decision to practice general surgery. Highly energetic and aggressive, Thorek did not want to spend years as a surgeon's assistant in an established hospital and so proceeded to start his own. With financial help from fellow physician Solomon Greenspahn, the American Hospital (now Thorek Hospital and Medical Center) was established in 1911, with Thorek as chief surgeon; in 1917 it was moved to a new building on the North Side. Its services were open to all regardless of ability to pay.

Thorek made numerous contributions to medical literature. Some of his earliest work was in mammoplasty and surgical reconstruction of other parts of the female body. Thorek was allegedly the first to succeed in reimplanting the nipple onto a breast treated with plastic surgery. His techniques were later described in *Plastic Surgery of the Breast and the Abdominal Wall* (1942).

In 1921, Thorek met the Franco-Russian surgeon Serge Voronoff, whose success in gonadal transplantation had received much publicity. Inspired also by the work of the Viennese physiologist Eugen Steinach, Thorek began his own experiments to test the popular claims that such operations could induce a dramatic rejuvenescence in both apes and humans. In 1923 he concluded that success was limited to a "reactivation," or "a partial synthetic reanimation of performance," rather than a complete restoration of youthful performance. He summarized his findings in *The Human Testis* (1924).

Thorek also became known for a procedure perfected in 1933 that reduced the mortality rate in gallbladder surgery. Rather than attempt to remove the entire gallbladder (which can cause excessive loss of bile and blood), Thorek proposed that the part of the roof that is attached to the liver be left in place and then destroyed by electrocoagulation. During a visit to Europe in 1937, Thorek delivered a paper on the technique at a congress in Vichy.

Thorek also held academic positions, including assistant professor of diseases of women at Michael Reese Hospital in Chicago (1905–1909) and professor of clinical surgery at Loyola University (1908–1912) and at Cook County School of Medicine (1934–1960).

Often a controversial figure in the medical world, Thorek is best remembered as the founder of the International College of Surgeons, organized in Geneva in 1935 with the help of Albert Jenter. This came about partly due to his strong disagreement with the policies of the American College of Surgeons, which was founded in Chicago in 1913 and never admitted Thorek as a member, and partly due to his desire for an organization of broader, international scope. Thorek became permanent secretary-general of the college and editor in chief of its *Journal* from its founding in 1938 until his death, in Chicago.

[The best source remains Thorek's autobiography, *A Surgeon's World* (1943). The *Journal of the International College of Surgeons*, Feb. 1960, has tributes and a bibliography. Thorek's books, besides those mentioned above, include a translation of Fedor Krause's *Surgery of the Brain and Spinal Cord* (1912); *Surgical*

Errors and Safeguards (1932); *Modern Surgical Technic* (1938); and *The Face in Health and Disease* (1946).]
RICHARD Y. MEIER
RONNIE BETH BUSH

TIBBETT, LAWRENCE MERVIL (Nov. 16, 1896–July 15, 1960), baritone, was born Lawrence Mervil Tibbet in Bakersfield, Calif., the son of William Edward Tibbet, a sheriff, and Frances Ellen Mackenzie. He grew up in Long Branch, Calif., where after his father's death his mother ran a hotel and where he received his elementary schooling. While attending the Manual Arts High School in Los Angeles, he acted in school plays, sang in the glee club, appeared as soloist with a church choir, and acquired fundamental instruction in voice and piano. After graduating from high school in 1915, he acted with several professional companies in Los Angeles, among them the Tyrone Power Shakespearean Players.

Tibbett saw service in the navy during World War I. Four days after his discharge, on May 19, 1919, he married Grace Mackay Smith, and a year later they had twin sons. Singing now became Tibbett's sole source of income, as a member of a male quartet that he had formed. They sang at weddings, funerals, and church services. Tibbett also sang at the Grauman Theater in Hollywood and as a member of a light-opera company. In September 1923 he assumed his first operatic role: Amonasro in Verdi's *Aida* at the Hollywood Bowl.

In California he continued his vocal studies with Basil Ruysdael and Joseph Dupuy. In 1923, with financial support from the writer Rupert Hughes, he went to New York to continue his training with Frank La Forge and Ignaz Zitomirsky, supporting his family by singing in a church in New Rochelle. A successful audition at the Metropolitan Opera that year brought him a contract; his debut with that company took place on Nov. 24, 1923, in a minor role, that of Lovitsky, in Mussorgsky's *Boris Godunov*. (A typographical error on the program that evening led him from that point on to spell his last name with two *t* 's.) He continued appearing in lesser parts without attracting much interest until Jan. 2, 1925, when he was hastily recruited to substitute for an indisposed singer as Ford in Verdi's *Falstaff*. His powerful dramatic interpretation of that role, together with his full command in using the resources of his voice, brought down the house, inspiring at one time a sixteen-minute ovation. This performance was reported on the front page of the *New York Times*, which pointed out that this was the first time in Metropolitan Opera history that an American-born singer, without any foreign training, had created such a furor.

During the next quarter of a century he firmly solidified his reputation by his successful realizations of Neri in Giordano's *La Cena della Beffe* (1926), the title role in *Simon Boccanegra* (1932), Amonasro in *Aida* (1928), the elder Germont in *La Traviata* (1925), and Iago in *Otello* (1937). Appearances in the world premieres of American operas were also of consequence: as Eadgar in *The King's Henchman* (1927) and as Colonel Ibbetson in *Peter Ibbetson* (1931), both by Deems Taylor; as Brutus Jones in Louis Gruenberg's *The Emperor Jones* (1933); as Wrestling Bradford in Howard Hanson's *Merry Mount* (1934); and as Guido in Richard Hageman's *Caponsacchi* (1937). His remarkable versatility was further demonstrated by the fact that, in addition to the traditional French and Italian repertory and the premieres of American operas, he was also successfully cast in Wagner's *Tannhäuser* (1926) and *Lohengrin* (1927) and Ernst Krenek's *Johnny spielt auf!* (1929). His twenty-fifth anniversary as a member of the Metropolitan Opera was commemorated in January of 1949 in Benjamin Britten's *Peter Grimes*; and his last appearance on the stage of the Metropolitan was on Mar. 24, 1950, in Mussorgsky's *Khovanchina*. By then he had been heard 396 times in New York and 163 times on tour.

He enjoyed success abroad as well, beginning with his first tour of Europe in the spring of 1937, when he made his debut at Covent Garden in London as Scarpia in Puccini's *Tosca*, following which (on June 24, 1937) he appeared in the title role of Eugene Goossens's *Don Juan de Mañara*, a world premiere. In Stockholm, still in 1937, he was presented with the Litteris et Artibus medal by King Gustav, an honor rarely conferred on a foreigner. In Vienna he was acclaimed as "a great, outstanding artist, amazing in the scope of his talents."

Tibbett also enjoyed a long and fruitful career as a recitalist; as a performer on radio; on television, where he became a pioneer in the presentation of televised operas; and in motion pictures. On the screen he was starred in *The Rogue Song* (1930), *The New Moon* (1930), *The Southerner* (1931), *Cuban Love Song* (1931), *Metropolitan* (1935), and *Under Your Spell* (1936).

After his retirement from opera Tibbett continued to appear in concerts, on television, and, in 1956, in the Broadway musical *Fanny* when he replaced Ezio Pinza as César.

Tibbett divorced his wife in 1931, and on Jan. 1, 1932, he married Jennie Marston Burgard; they had a son.

Tibbett was one of the founders of the American Guild of Musical Artists (AGMA) in 1936, serving as president from 1940 to 1952 and as honorary president from 1952 on. During World War II he served on the executive committee for camp shows for the United Service Organization (USO) and made numerous appearances for the armed forces and at Red Cross and war bond drives. He was invited to sing at the inauguration ceremonies of Calvin Coolidge, Herbert Hoover, and Franklin Delano Roosevelt. He received a gold medal for diction from the American Academy of Arts and Letters in 1933. He died in New York City, where he had been operated on for a head injury sustained many years earlier.

[See Tibbett's autobiographical "Along the Glory Road," *American Magazine*, Aug–Nov. 1933; Oscar Thompson, *The American Singer* (1937; repr. 1969); David Ewen, *Men and Women Who Make Music*, rev. ed. (1949); the obituary notice by R. Sabin, *Musical America*, Aug. 1960; and *Opera News*, Oct. 29, 1960.]

DAVID EWEN

TILSON, JOHN QUILLIN (Apr. 5, 1866–Aug. 14, 1958), lawyer and majority leader of the U.S. House of Representatives, was born in Clear Branch, Tenn., the son of William E. Tilson and Katharine Sams. Tilson's first education was from itinerant preachers and travelers to his mountain home. His formal education was pursued at public and private schools in Flag Pond (in his native Unicoi County) and also at Mars Hill, N.C. In 1888 Tilson attended Carson-Newman College in Jefferson City, Tenn. He then worked his way through Yale University, receiving the B.A. in 1891. Two years later he received his LL.B. degree from Yale. He was admitted to the bar in 1897 and the following year began to practice law in New Haven, Conn. During the Spanish-American War, he served as a second lieutenant in the Sixth United States Volunteer Infantry.

Following the war, Tilson resumed his legal practice. He was elected to the Connecticut House of Representatives as a Republican in

1904. Rising quickly in that body, he served as speaker in the 1907–1908 term. He then challenged the Connecticut Republican leadership by defeating the candidate backed by Republican National Committeeman J. Henry Roraback in the 1908 congressional campaign. In the November election that year, Tilson won a seat in the Sixty-first Congress.

On Nov. 10, 1910, Tilson married Marguerite North. They had three children. He won reelection to Congress in 1910, but in 1912, the year of the Taft-Roosevelt split, he lost to a Democrat. Two years later, however, Tilson regained the seat. He served eight consecutive terms (1915–1931) in the House of Representatives and was Republican majority leader in the Sixty-ninth, Seventieth, and Seventy-first congresses. After World War II, Tilson's differences with Roraback and the Connecticut Republican leadership continued. Their lack of backing cost him a bid for the U.S. Senate in 1924, and they declined to support his vice-presidential candidacy at the 1928 Republican national convention.

Meanwhile, as Republican majority leader from 1925 until 1931, Tilson, along with Speaker Nicholas Longworth and New York Representative Bertrand H. Snell, dominated the proceedings of the House of Representatives. He worked closely with Republican presidents Calvin Coolidge and Herbert Hoover, managed the congressional campaign committee, and directed the Republican party speakers' bureau. Following Longworth's death in 1931, Tilson sought to succeed him as speaker, but was defeated by Snell.

Tilson did not seek reelection to Congress in 1932, claiming that he sought a more lucrative employment. He chose to open law offices in Washington, D.C., and New Haven. In 1932 he was a delegate to the Republican National Convention in Chicago. An expert in parliamentary law, Tilson lectured on that topic at Yale Law School. In 1935 he wrote the *Manual of Parliamentary Law and Procedure*.

He later served as chairman of the board of Save the Children Federation, and was cited by the British, Italian, and French governments for service to children following World War II. Tilson died in New London, N.H., where he had been a summer visitor for many years.

[Although no full-length biographical sketch on Tilson exists, additional information can be found in *New York Times*, Aug. 15, 1958.]

HARVARD SITKOFF

TIMME, WALTER (Feb. 24, 1874–Feb. 12, 1956), physician, neurologist, and endocrinologist, was born in New York City, the son of Frederick J. E. Timme, a Lutheran minister, and Emma Wirth. He attended public schools and took private lessons in piano, organ, and voice. After he graduated from the City College of New York in 1893, he entered the College of Physicians and Surgeons of Columbia University. Following graduation in 1897, Timme practiced general medicine in Manhattan. In 1898 he joined the staff of the Vanderbilt Clinic, focusing on the new specialties of neurology and endocrinology.

In 1910 Timme joined the staff of the newly formed Neurological Institute of New York. From 1912 to 1913 he took graduate courses at the University of Berlin and, upon his return, was appointed chief neurologist at the Vanderbilt Clinic. A pioneer in patient care, research, and teaching neurology in the United States, he became military director of the Institute for Neurological Research during World War I, training a hundred medical officers in neuropsychiatry, emphasizing the anatomy, physiology, and pathology of the nervous system. This descriptive approach omitted the mental component later recognized as significant during wartime.

After World War I endocrinology captured wide interest. From 1918 to 1937 Timme headed a separate neuro-endocrine department at the Neurological Institute, as endocrinology, the study of the relation of the body's internal secretions to growth, development, and disease, explored normal and abnormal growth and appearance. Since impressive cures sometimes occurred through supplemental therapy, the public clamored for more information. Because there were few governmental restrictions on the drug marketplace, Timme began in 1916 to participate in the Association for the Study of Internal Secretions, which promoted research in the new field, monitored endocrine product purity, and protected the public from charlatans. Timme's work included associate editorship of the association's journal, *Endocrinology*. His major contribution was his work on pluriglandular endocrinologic disturbances—that is, dysfunction in one or more glands, causing complex feedback effects. In 1918 he first described publicly the syndrome named for him, ovarian and adrenal insufficiency leading to compensatory hypopituitarism.

Timme also contributed to neurology. In 1920 he founded, and served as the first president of, the Association for Research in Nervous and Mental

Diseases. Its method, which he labeled "intensive ante-mortem study," consisted of selecting a disease entity in advance, identifying available experts, and convening in New York each December for a symposium. The organization continues to fulfill his goal: "a unified and inspired all-American group of neurologists and psychiatrists" sharing current information on neurological disease.

Timme's successes should be viewed against the context of the years of his work. During intense investigation of endocrinology's relationship to human genetics, growth, and development, moral and racial biases existed that sometimes distorted scientific ideas for social purposes. Timme was courageous and farsighted in dealing with most of the issues and problems that the new knowledge generated and usually supported a reasoned approach to reform when public concern overlapped with his fields. In 1923 he called for new definitions nationally of the racial aspects of disease and in 1928 joined others at the state level in suggesting that legalizing hard drugs on the open market would reduce crime and needless public expenditure. In the latter year he discussed mongolism, a newly recognized form of idiocy, reminding Americans that mongoloids were only part of a neglected 1.5 million feebleminded people and urging attention to scientific rather than racial or moral views of such diseases.

Appeals to the public by Timme and his colleagues, however, sometimes reflected biases of the 1920's that curtailed patient rights. In 1928, while heading a campaign to raise $2 million for the Neurological Institute, Timme cited his seventeen years of research on feeblemindness and argued that endocrinopathic inheritance of hypoplastic body characteristics correlated directly with subsequent criminal activity. His predictions of benefits from the early identification, isolation, and therapeutic alteration of such individuals did not withstand subsequent scientific scrutiny.

On June 27, 1901, Timme married Ida Helen Haar. They lived in a large country residence overlooking the Hudson, and Timme commuted to his Manhattan office. In 1937 Timme retired from the Neurological Institute and the position he had held since 1929 as professor of clinical neurology at Columbia. Ida Timme died in 1940. On July 28, 1951, Timme married Anne Cecil Auwell. He died in St. Petersburg, Fla.

Timme's career reflects the overlapping development of neurology, endocrinology, and psychiatry in the early twentieth century. Like others in this era of evolving academic medicine, he contributed to patient care, teaching, administration, and research. Functioning without large government or foundation support and amidst a field of public interest, his moderate calls for reform based on research breakthroughs aided reason in tempering bias and placed demands for government control over patients into perspective. The syndrome named for him, his articles, his text *Lectures in Endocrinology* (1928; 2d ed., 1932), and his brainchild, the Association for Research in Nervous and Mental Diseases, were major contributions to American medicine.

[Material on Timme can be found at the Neurological Institute Library of Columbia-Presbyterian Medical Center, the library of the New York Academy of Medicine, and the New York Public Library. Timme's first published description of the syndrome named for him was "A New Pluriglandular Compensatory Syndrome," *Endocrinology*, July–Sept. 1918. In addition to his text, Timme published at least twenty-five original articles, contributed chapters to six books, and served on the editorial boards of the Association for Research in Nervous and Mental Diseases and the Association for the Study of Internal Secretions. J. Lawrence Poole, *The Neurological Institute of New York, 1909–1974* (1975), describes Timme's contributions to the group. Charles A. Elsberg, *The Story of a Hospital: The Neurological Institute of New York, 1909–1938* (1944), lists Timme in various places without much evaluation. For a summary of his participation as a founder of the endocrinology group, see F. M. Pottenger, "The Association for the Study of Internal Secretions: Its Past, Its Future," *Endocrinology*, June 1942.]

JAMES POLK MORRIS

TINKHAM, GEORGE HOLDEN (Oct. 20, 1870–Aug. 28, 1956), United States congressman and big game hunter, was born in Boston, Mass., the son of George Henry Tinkham and Fannie Ann Holden. He was educated in Boston public and private schools, graduated from Harvard College in 1894, and spent two years at the Harvard Law School. On Jan. 1, 1897, he began studying law in the offices of Carver and Blodgett in Boston and was admitted to the bar in 1899. A wealthy man, he never married but devoted his life to politics and foreign travel.

From 1897 to 1914 Tinkham was a member of the Republican ward and city committee in Boston, and during 1897 and 1898 served on the seventy-five-man Boston Common Council. He was appointed public administrator by Governor Roger Wolcott in 1899, was a member of the Boston Board of Aldermen and county commissioner (1901–1902), and served in the Massachusetts Senate (1910–1912). In 1914 he was elected to Congress.

Tinkham began his long career in the House of Representatives on Mar. 4, 1915, serving fourteen consecutive terms, from the Sixty-fourth to the Seventy-seventh Congress. He was rigidly isolationist, opposing America's entry into both the League of Nations and the World Court; and in 1939, when a member of the House Foreign Affairs Committee, he declined an invitation to a British embassy garden party in honor of King George and Queen Elizabeth, declaring that "the United States is not the pawn and ally of the British Empire." Tinkham was a strong advocate of civil rights, and in 1929, after a fight of more than a decade, he succeeded in getting an amendment added to the apportionment-census bill, by which the provisions of the Fourteenth Amendment would be enforced to deny states representation in Congress to the extent that they excluded blacks from voting. He was a vigorous foe of prohibition and hurled some of his sharpest epithets against the Anti-Saloon League. He also insisted on the separation of church and state, and his battles against the lobbying of the Federal Council of Churches of Christ in America and the Board of Temperance, Prohibition and Public Morals of the Methodist Episcopal Church received nationwide attention. In 1937 Methodist Bishop James J. Cannon, Jr., sued him for half a million dollars on charges of libel, but lost.

During the 1930's Tinkham opposed Adolph Hitler and Franklin D. Roosevelt's New Deal with equal enthusiasm, saying: "I come from Plymouth Rock, and I am against all dictators, by whatever name they may be known, and against unnecessary interference with the liberties of the individual and the regimentation of his life and affairs."

Although Tinkham's congressional district included Beacon Hill and the fashionable Back Bay (where he lived), it also embraced the South End rooming houses and the "three-decker" tenements of Roxbury and Jamaica Plain. His constituency was a mixture of Yankee, Jewish, black, and German, with a large proportion of Irish Catholics. Over the years few of his constituents went away from his Boston office disappointed. Whether they were selling tickets to a church whist party or needed coal, clothing, a wooden leg, spectacles, a job, or only a handout, he satisfied their needs, mostly with his own money. Following his first election to Congress, he never felt the need to campaign again; usually he spent the period before elections abroad, returning only to cast his own ballot. His hold on his congressional district was so strong that in the 1936 Democratic landslide he ran ahead of President Roosevelt by more than 4,500 votes.

Tinkham's bushy beard.was the cartoonists' delight. For most of his career in Washington he was one of only two members of Congress with beards (the other was Senator J. Hamilton Lewis of Illinois, who was known as "the other Smith Brother.") The *Boston Herald* said of him: "Fifty years from now Bostonians of the Tenth will be voting for him as southern mountaineers voted for Andrew Jackson half a century after he had joined the great non-political majority." He decided to retire from Congress when the lines of his district were altered in 1942.

During his world travels over the years, Tinkham met the leading statesmen and diplomats of Europe and was entertained by viceroys, governors, and potentates in the most remote corners of Asia. In 1929 he made the first airplane flight from Bangkok to Angkor-Wat in a Siamese army plane. In 1934 his plane crashed in Moscow, but he escaped uninjured. He once shot seventeen leopards in six days in British East Africa, and his apartment at the Arlington Hotel in Washington was filled with big game trophies and curios. His gifts to the Boston Museum of Fine Arts ran the gamut from a ninth-century Javanese stone head to twentieth-century tapestries and vestments for Java, Indonesia, Tibet, India, and Russia. He died in Cramerton, N.C., where he had lived in retirement with his sister. He left $2 million to the Judge Baker Guidance Center in Boston, the largest single grant ever given in the field of child psychology up to that time.

[See the Quinquennial File, Harvard University Archives; Class Secretary's Files, Class of 1894, Harvard University Archives; and the archives in the Asiatic and Textile departments, Museum of Fine Arts, Boston, See also the *Boston Transcript*, Aug. 5, 1920; *Boston Herald*, Dec. 6, 1920, Jan. 5, 1929; *Boston Transcript*, Nov. 12, 1932; *Boston Herald*, Sept. 23, 1934, Feb. 14, 1937, Feb. 7, 1939; *Boston Transcript*, May 24, 1939; and *Boston Herald*, Apr. 28, 1942, Sept. 7, 1956. Obituaries are in *Boston Globe*, Aug. 29, 1956; *Boston Herald*, Aug. 29, 1956; and *Boston Traveler*, Aug. 29, 1956.]

JOHN T. GALVIN

TODD, MIKE (June 22, 1909–Mar. 22, 1958), theatrical and motion picture producer, was born Avrom Hirsch Goldbogen in Minneapolis, Minn., the son of Chaim Goldbogen and Sophia Hellerman, who had come to the United States from Poland in 1906. He spent his early years in Bloomington, Minn., where his father, an impoverished rabbi, operated a general store to support his large family. By the time he was seven, Avrom was selling newspapers, working at carnivals, and playing the cornet in a boys' band. When he was twelve, the family moved to Chicago, where his father was appointed to a small synagogue.

In Chicago, Goldbogen was an apprentice pharmacist, then, at fourteen, began his career as a promotor, arranging "must vacate" and "lost our lease" sales for small merchants. While a student at Tulle High School, he organized a prefabricated home company and was soon engaged in constructing apartment buildings. On Feb. 14, 1927, he married Bertha Freshman; they had one son. Goldbogen went to Hollywood in 1927, reputedly after having made and lost a million dollars as a builder and real estate operator. He constructed some of the earliest soundproof stages there, making and losing another fortune before he was twenty.

Returning to Chicago, Goldbogen wrote radio sketches for the comedy team of Olsen and Johnson and created his own vaudeville revue, *Bring on the Dames*. At the Century of Progress Exposition in 1933, he produced a flame dance in which a girl dressed as a moth had her costume gradually singed off by real flames. Then, having legally changed his name to Michael Todd, he moved to New York City to become a theatrical producer. Todd's first two Broadway shows were unsuccessful. *Call Me Ziggy* opened in 1937 and closed after three performances. His production of *The Man from Cairo* (1938) was another fiasco. But, using his persuasive personality to gather backers for another venture, he more than recouped his earlier losses with his 1939 production of *The Hot Mikado*, a jazz version of Gilbert and Sullivan's operetta starring dancer Bill Robinson. He soon moved *The Hot Mikado* to the New York World's Fair, where it became as great a money-maker as the other three attractions he had there: *Gay New Orleans*; Gypsy Rose Lee's revue, *Streets of Paris*; and *Dancing Campus*, which featured name bands and a floor that could hold 12,000 jitterbugs.

In 1942 Todd presented his first major Broadway attraction, *Star and Garter*, a musical starring Gypsy Rose Lee. Its success enabled him to finance another lavish musical, Cole Porter's *Something for the Boys* (1943), starring Ethel Merman. In the same year Todd presented *The Naked Genius*, written by Miss Lee and directed by George S. Kaufman. Although it did well at the box office, Todd withdrew the play when a survey revealed that only 44 percent of the audience liked it. He produced another successful musical, *Mexican Hayride*, with songs by Porter, in 1944. It was followed by *Pick-up Girl*, a well-received social drama about delinquent girls that was produced in London, and by *Catherine Was Great*, starring Mae West.

Todd's biggest money-maker, *Up in Central Park* (1945), is representative of his relationship with the public and the critics. Opening on Broadway in January, it received unfavorable reviews but ran for 504 performances and made more than $2 million. Todd also produced it successfully at the Hollywood Bowl and sold the movie rights to Universal Pictures for $100,000. One of the first full-scale musical comedies to tour American military bases, it quickly achieved great success as a USO Camp Show.

During World War II, Todd was a civilian consultant to the Special Services Division of the army. He went to Europe in 1945 to provide entertainment for American soldiers. Recruiting talent from among the troops, he produced various shows, including a military version of *Hamlet*. Late in 1945 Todd brought his *Hamlet* to Broadway, where it was staged in nineteenth-century costume and ran for 131 performances.

In 1946 Todd presented comedian Bobby Clark's version of Molière's *The Would-Be Gentleman*. This was followed by a straight play, *January Thaw*, which was not well received. At one point that year he had four productions—*Up in Central Park, Hamlet, The Would-Be Gentleman*, and *January Thaw*—running on Broadway at the same time. In the same year his first wife died. On July 5, 1947, Todd married actress Joan Blondell; they were divorced in 1950.

Summing up his philosophy regarding Broadway shows, Todd said: "I believe in giving the customers a meat and potatoes show. Dames and comedy. High dames and low comedy—that's my message." The success of two of his next shows—*As the Girls Go* (1948) and *Peep Show* (1950)—illustrates his generally perceptive understanding of what many Broadway audiences liked: the former ran for 420 performances; the latter, for 276. Yet *The Live Wire*, a Garson

Kanin comedy presented by Todd in 1950, closed after only twenty-eight performances.

Todd was one of the founders of the company that produced the Cinerama three-dimensional film process. Selling his interest before its first production was presented, he worked with Brian O'Brien and scientists at the American Optical Company to develop a new film process called Todd-AO. Using a single camera and projector, Todd-AO achieved multidimensional effects by means of sixty-five millimeter film and a full-stage curved screen. The first film to use this process was *Oklahoma*. Todd's own *Around the World in 80 Days*, also in Todd-AO, was a worldwide commercial success and received the Academy Award for the best film for 1956.

Todd, always the epitome of the fast-talking, boyishly exuberant, and high-living impresario, married actress Elizabeth Taylor on Feb. 2, 1957; they had one daughter. He died in a plane crash near Grants, N.M.

[See *New York Times Magazine*, May 13, 1945; *Saturday Evening Post*, June 9, 1951; *Theatre Arts*, July 1953; *New Yorker*, Jan. 15, 1955; and Art Cohn, ed., *Michael Todd's Around the World in 80 Days Almanac* (1956); and *The Nine Lives of Michael Todd* (1958). Obituaries are in the *Chicago Tribune* and *New York Times*, Mar. 23, 1958.]

L. MOODY SIMMS, JR.

TOLLEY, HOWARD ROSS (Sept. 30, 1889–Sept. 18, 1958), agricultural economist, was born in Howard County, Ind., the son of Elmer E. Tolley, a farmer, and Mollie Grindle. Tolley studied at Marion (Ind.) Normal College during the 1905–1906 school year. From 1906 to 1911 he taught at Indiana high schools and attended Indiana University, graduating in 1910, with a major in mathematics.

On May 8, 1912, Tolley married Zora F. Hazlett, a graduate of Marion Normal College. They had three sons, all of whom became economists. The same year Tolley went to work as a mathematician at the Coast and Geodetic Survey in Washington, D.C. Three years later he began a long association with the Department of Agriculture.

After one year with the Bureau of Plant Industry, Tolley moved in 1916 to the Office of Farm Management at the invitation of William Jaspon Spillman, who was anxious to start researching the quantitative and analytical aspects of farm management. Beginning in 1921, Tolley informally studied farm management and agricultural economics under the tutelage of Secretary of Agriculture Henry Cantwell Wallace.

When the Bureau of Agricultural Economics (BAE) was created in 1923, Tolley helped to shape its research program, which generated both data and techniques for analyzing agricultural problems. He was a leader in the development of multiple-correlation and input-output studies. The agricultural outlook work within the BAE was largely his creation. In September 1928 Tolley was elevated to assistant chief of the BAE.

In March 1930 Tolley left the BAE to help organize and develop the newly established Giannini Foundation for Agricultural Economics at the University of California (Berkeley). While Tolley is listed as director of the foundation from 1930 to 1936, he was under considerable pressure from the administration of Franklin D. Roosevelt to return to Washington and assist with the formation of New Deal agricultural programs. Initially he served as economic adviser and assistant to Chester C. Davis, administrator of the Agricultural Adjustment Administration (AAA). In that capacity Tolley's principal concern was with marketing agreements for fruits and vegetables, a task made difficult by the grower groups seeking special advantages. Tolley was next appointed chief of the Program Planning Division of the AAA (1933–1935). In that capacity he played a leading role in developing a long-run, conservation-oriented approach that was written into the Soil Conservation and Domestic Allotment Act of 1936.

When the AAA was declared unconstitutional in 1936, the work of the Program Planning Division simplified the transition of the AAA to an agricultural program acceptable to the court. When Chester Davis resigned in June of that year, Tolley became administrator and resigned his directorship at the Giannini Foundation. Two years later he transferred back to the BAE and served as its chief until 1946. In the period before the war, Tolley helped Secretary of Agriculture Henry A. Wallace, son of his chief in the 1920's, change the emphasis of the BAE from research to long-run planning. Tolley also helped develop the county planning committee approach to local agricultural problems.

Throughout the 1930's Tolley supported the concept of an "ever-normal granary" to put agriculture on a sound and stable basis. He argued that this would double the national inventory of grain and achieve "stabilizing prices." Wallace accepted the argument and erected government granaries to store surplus harvests as insurance against lean years. Tolley also reasoned that the financial and physical problems of agriculture were interdependent, and that increased soil fertility was the farmers' main hope for a brighter financial future. To that end he advocated a quota system for planting specific crops and urged farmers to restrict the acreage they planted. His advocacy of cash grants to farmers under the federal price support plan aroused controversy but did not lessen his reputation as the "soil wizard" of the New Deal. At his death the *Washington Post* noted that Tolley "... helped to plant and nurture the seeds of agricultural policy that during the last 25 years have grown into programs which are now as familiar a part of the American farm scene as a silo."

During World War II, in addition to his duties in the BAE, Tolley served in the Office of Price Administration and represented the United States at many international agricultural conferences. He was economic adviser to the United States delegates at the Hot Springs (Va.) Conference of 1943, which led to the creation of the Food and Agriculture Organization of the United Nations (FAO), and he served as a member of the interim commission that drafted a constitution and program for the FAO. In 1946 Tolley became chief economist of the Economics and Statistics Division of the FAO. Like his situation at the BAE more than two decades earlier, this position offered him the challenge of pioneering an agricultural research and service program.

When the FAO moved to Rome in 1951, Tolley resigned to become a staff assistant to Chester Davis, who had been appointed a vice-president of the Ford Foundation. Tolley was in charge of the Washington office of the foundation until 1954. After his retirement he served as an adviser to the Planning Board of Pakistan (1955) and as a consultant to many organizations, particularly the National Planning Association in Washington.

Tolley was a dominant figure in the development of agricultural economics and American agricultural policy. He wrote *The Farmer, Citizen at War* (1943) and numerous articles and bulletins, many published in the *Journal of Farm Economics*. Tolley edited the *Journal* between 1927 and 1929, and was president of the American Farm Economics Association, which published it, in 1933. Tolley died in Alexandria, Va.

[A memorial to Tolley appeared in *Journal of Farm Economics*, Feb. 1959. There are also good obituaries in the *New York Times*, Sept. 20, 1958, and *Washington Post*. The Oral History Collection at Columbia University has a memoir done by Tolley in 1954. Extensive references to him appear in other volumes in the same collection, especially those by M. L. Wilson, Jesse Tapp, Claude Wickard, and O. C. Stine.]

Louis P. Cain

TOLMAN, EDWARD CHACE (Apr. 14, 1886–Nov. 19, 1959), psychologist, was born in West Newton, Mass., the son of James Pike Tolman, a successful industrialist, and Mary Chace. With a deep sense of New England propriety, his father felt that sons of a "lower-upper" family should not aspire to Harvard, and insisted that his two sons go to the Massachusetts Institute of Technology instead, of which he was a graduate and trustee. Both initially went to MIT, where Edward received his B.S. in electrochemistry in 1911. He then braved Harvard for his M.A. (1912) and for his Ph.D. in psychology (1915) in the then joint department of philosophy and psychology. He was influenced at Harvard by the philosophers Josiah Royce and Ralph Barton Perry, the philosopher-psychologist Edwin B. Holt, and the experimental psychologists Hugo Münsterberg and Herbert S. Langfeld. From Robert M. Yerkes he learned the possibilities within the studies of animal behavior, and, after reaching California, he devoted most of his research career to that area, which had already been named comparative psychology. His graduate study at Harvard included a summer in Germany, where he spent a month with Kurt Koffka and became receptive to gestalt concepts. He married Kathleen Drew on Aug. 30, 1915; they had three children.

Tolman's first academic appointment was as instructor of psychology at Northwestern University (1915–1918). He spent the remainder of his professional career at the University of California at Berkeley, as instructor (1918–1920), assistant professor (1920–1923), associate professor (1923–1928), and professor of psychology (1928–1954). He received several honorary degrees and was a member of the National Academy of Sciences, the American Philosophical Society, and the American Academy of Arts and Sciences. He was president of the American Psychological Association in 1937 and received its Distinguished Scientific Contribution Award in 1957.

Tolman's impact on psychology dates largely from his major book, *Purposive Behavior in Animals and Men* (1932), in which his summarizations of a brilliant set of experiments with the white rat—the book was dedicated to that useful animal—were fitted into a highly original theoretical scheme. It was "behavioristic" only in the sense that it was based on observations that could be open to others rather than depending upon introspection, or on what he characterized as trying to make science out of "raw feels." His behaviorism was at odds with the contemporary behaviorism of John B. Watson because it was molar (holistic) rather than molecular (reductionistic), and stressed the goal-directed or purposive nature of behavior as against a more mechanistic interpretation of stimulus-response sequences patterned upon reflex behavior.

In rejecting introspection, early behaviorism had largely negated higher mental processes through an emphasis on peripheral activity, as in interpreting thought according to implicit movements of the speech apparatus. Tolman converted this to a truly cognitive psychology, with an emphasis upon knowing the environment instead of merely learning how to move about in it. He did this in part by developing the concept of intervening variables, which he introduced in his presidential address before the American Psychological Association in 1937.

The basic idea is that behaviorism could be preserved by using only observable behavior to produce the data points derived from experiments, but then going on to infer intervening processes that gave order to these observations. For example, if the observed behavior demonstrated that the animal appeared to be following a map rather than merely repeating a learned movement sequence—taking a shortcut, for example, in familiar territory—then it may be inferred that the behavior is being directed by an intermediate or intervening process that contains maplike information, perhaps a "cognitive map." Learning may consist in knowing what-leads-to-what instead of following a learned movement pattern.

These ideas were supported by a variety of experiments, of which those on latent learning, place learning, and vicarious trial-and-error (VTE) are representative. The latent learning experiments demonstrated that the rat might have learned more than what showed in his movements, and hence was latent instead of manifest. If permitted to explore a maze without food at the end, its movements were relatively random, and the rat wandered into blind alleys off the true path. Once fed at the end of the maze, however, the rat quickly adopted the true path and avoided the blinds, demonstrating that it knew what-led-to-what. The place-learning experiments showed that a rat fed at a particular place on a table in the midst of other tables and trestles could find its way to that place by an economical route if placed at a totally new starting point; hence it had learned spatial relationships instead of movement sequences. The VTE experiments, later in the experimental program, showed vacillation at a choice point, as though the animal were trying out alternatives in abbreviated form, by "looking-back-and-forth" rather than by "running-back-and-forth." This behavior was called vicarious because it replaced the more complete trial-and-error behavior that had been prominent in the prior accounts of learning by Edward L. Thorndike and others. Here, then, was vestigial behavior that lent support for the cognitive interpretation. By proposing cognitive explanations that were coherent with objective experimentation, Tolman provided the background for an upsurge of interest in cognitive psychology that became prominent in the United States in the two decades after his death.

Tolman was a most humane and sensitive person whose influence is incompletely described by his scientific achievements. His students, while remaining deeply loyal to him, show few signs of scientific discipleship; it was somehow his personal qualities that most affected them. These qualities were clearly shown in 1949 in a controversy at the University of California over a loyalty oath that seemed to him an infringement of academic freedom. He resigned rather than sign it and led the movement against it, ultimately winning the fight and having his professorship restored in 1953. The following year he became professor emeritus. Eight months before his death he was awarded an honorary LL.D. from the university to which he had given most of his life. President Clark Kerr's citation ended with these words: "A man of tolerance and humor, dedicated to rigorous methods of scientific psychology and at the same time hospitable to all imaginative and original ideas. A great teacher who inspired generations of students and colleagues to high creative effort." Tolman died in Berkeley, Calif.

[Tolman's papers (1915–1957) are in the Archives of the History of American Psychology at the University of Akron. His major book, *Purposive Behavior in Animals and Men* (1932), was reprinted in 1949. *Drives Toward War* (1942), begun as an essay on motivation strongly influenced by Freud's views, was published with an altered title as a consequence of World War II. His major papers were published as *Collected Papers in Psychology* (1951), reprinted in 1958 as *Behavior and Psychological Man.*

Biographical materials include an autobiography in Edwin G. Boring et al., *A History of Psychology in Autobiography*, IV (1952); and accounts by Richard S. Crutchfield, *American Journal of Psychology*, Mar. 1961; and Benbow F. Ritchie, *Biographical Memoirs. National Academy of Sciences*, 37 (1964), with portrait and bibliography. For a summary of his views on the learning process and his influence upon later theorists, see Ernest R. Hilgard and Gordon H. Bower, "Tolman's Sign Learning," which is chapter 5 of their *Theories of Learning*, 4th ed. (1957).]

ERNEST R. HILGARD

TORREY, CHARLES CUTLER (Dec. 20, 1863–Nov. 12, 1956), Bible scholar and Semitist, was born at East Hardwick, Vt., son of Joseph Torrey, Jr., a Congregational clergyman, and Maria Thorpe Noble. After graduation from Bowdoin College in 1884, Torrey taught for a year (1884–1885) at the Auburn (Me.) High School; in 1885, appointed tutor in Latin at Bowdoin, he continued his studies there and was awarded the M.A. degree in 1887. He then entered Andover Theological Seminary, where, under George Foot Moore, he studied Semitic philology, notably sacred texts in Hebrew, Aramaic, and Arabic. He was graduated from Andover in 1889.

Awarded a fellowship by Andover for further study in Europe, Torrey entered the University of Strasbourg, where his graduate training was under the guidance of the greatest Semitic philologist at that time, Theodor Noeldeke. In 1892 he received the Ph.D. with a dissertation entitled *The Commercial-Theological Terms in the Koran.*

From 1892 to 1898 Torrey served as instructor and professor of Semitic languages at Andover, and from 1898 until 1900 was professor of biblical theology and history. He was then named professor of Semitic languages and literatures at Yale University, but immediately left to spend a year (1900–1901) in Jerusalem, where he established and was first director of the American School of Archaeology (later the American School of Oriental Research). The results of the

excavation he carried out at Sidon during that year were edited and published by him in 1920.

His Jerusalem sojourn also enabled Torrey to nurture his interest in epigraphy and numismatics; many of the papers on those and similar subjects that he contributed to scholarly publications—especially to *Journal of the American Oriental Society*, of which he was coeditor from 1900 to 1917—are still valuable and influential. In 1901 Torrey assumed the duties of his professorship at Yale, where he remained until retirement in 1932. He married Marian Edwards Richards, daughter of a professor of mechanical engineering at Yale, on June 16, 1911; they had one daughter.

Torrey's gifts were manifested in an astonishing number and variety of directions. Seemingly frail in physique, he excelled at college in both baseball and tennis; he was a fine fisherman and hiker, a keen amateur mycologist, and a better than average flutist. A capable administrator, he was for many years chairman of the department of Semitic and biblical languages, literature and history at the Yale Graduate School, and curator of coins at the Yale University Library. Above all, he was a brilliant and original scholar, and a gifted teacher who more by example than by precept fostered in his students his own uncompromising standards in searching out, and freely and fearlessly stating, the truth. The range of his intellectual interests and the scope of his teaching transcended the fields in which his scholarly contributions ranked as authoritative; he was, for example, a connoisseur and an accomplished declaimer and interpreter of Arabic and Persian poetry.

Torrey's most important and influential books and monographs were *The Composition and Historical Value of Ezra-Nehemiah* (1896); *Ezra Studies* (1910); *The Composition and Date of Acts* (1916); *The History of the Conquest of Egypt, North Africa and Spain* (1922); *The Second Isaiah* (1928); *Pseudo-Ezekiel and the Original Prophecy* (1930); *The Jewish Foundation of Islam* (1933); *The Four Gospels: A New Translation* (1933; 2nd ed., 1947); *Our Translated Gospels* (1936); *Documents of the Primitive Church* (1941); *The Apocryphal Literature: A Brief Introduction* (1945); *The Lives of the Prophets* (1946); *The Chronicler's History of Israel* (1954); and *The Apocalypse of John* (1958).

His strikingly original views on the sacred texts he studied, brilliantly set forth on the basis of searching and careful assessments of the evidence, were almost always controversial, and were vigorously, though not always justly, contested. Although few of his solutions to the higher critical problems of the texts he investigated have won wide acceptance, the problems themselves have for the most part remained moot. Indeed, because Torrey posed such problems so sharply and definitively, *Ezra Studies, Pseudo-Ezekiel,* and *The Jewish Foundation of Islam* have been reissued, each with a "prolegomenon" in which the scholarly discussion subsequent to Torrey's work is reviewed and brought up to date. His works thus remain heuristically valuable and stimulating.

Torrey died in Chicago, where he had retired to live with his daughter.

[Torrey's more important papers include "The Bilingual Inscription from Sardis," *American Journal of Semitic Languages and Literatures,* Apr. 1918; "The Letters Prefixed to Second Maccabees," *Journal of the American Oriental Society,* June 1940; "Notes on the Greek Texts of Enoch," *ibid.,* Mar. 1942; "Medes and Persians," *ibid.,* Jan. 1946; "Wellhausen's Approach to the Aramaic Gospels," *Zeitschrift der Deutschen Morgenländischen Gesellschaft,* Fall 1951; "The Aramaic Period of the Nascent Christian Church," *Zeitschrift für die Neutestamentliche Wissenschaft,* 44 (1952–1953). On Torrey, see Millar Burrows, "A Sketch of Charles Cutler Torrey's Career," *Bulletin of the American Schools of Oriental Research,* Dec. 1953; *New York Times,* Nov. 13, 1956; and H. A. Wolfson, "Charles Cutler Torrey," *Speculum,* July 1957. See also F. Rosenthal, *Die aramaistische Forschung seit Th. Nöldeke's Veröffentlichungen* (1939).]

ISAAC RABINOWITZ

TOSCANINI, ARTURO (Mar. 25, 1867–Jan. 16, 1957), conductor, was born in Parma, Italy, the son of Claudio Toscanini, a tailor, and Paola Montani. Despite his poverty, the father often attended opera performances in Parma, occasionally taking Arturo with him. At grade school Arturo received some piano instruction, for which he demonstrated such talent that in his ninth year he was transferred to the Parma Conservatory. There, for nine years he studied the cello and composition and soon came to be known throughout the school as "the Genius." Toscanini made his conducting debut on May 25, 1884, at the conservatory by performing one of his own compositions, an Andante and Scherzo for Orchestra. In 1885 he was graduated with highest ratings in cello, piano, and composition.

After leaving the conservatory, Toscanini was employed for about a year as cellist by the orchestra of the Parma Opera and the Parma Municipal Orchestra. In 1886 he was engaged for the orchestra touring South America with an Italian opera company. When, on June 25, 1886, in Rio de Janeiro, the scheduled conductor was unable to perform *Aida,* Toscanini was called upon as a substitute, even though up to then he had never led a professional opera or symphonic performance. To the amazement of all, he conducted the opera from memory made necessary by his nearsightedness. Without the benefit of a single rehearsal, he produced what one local critic described as the best *Aida* he had ever heard. On the strength of this remarkable exhibition, Toscanini was made principal conductor of that touring company, called upon to perform eight operas, all directed from memory.

Toscanini's professional debut in Italy took place on Nov. 4, 1886, with a performance of Alfredo Catalani's *Edmea* in Turin. Between 1887 and 1899 he was frequently heard in both opera and symphonic performances throughout Italy. In 1892, in Turin, he performed his first Wagnerian opera, *The Flying Dutchman.* He was chosen by Leoncavallo to conduct the world premiere (May 21, 1892) of his opera *I Pagliacci* at the Teatro Dal Verme. In 1895 Toscanini led the first Italian production of Wagner's *Die Götterdämmerung.* On Feb. 1, 1896, also in Turin, he directed the world premiere of Puccini's *La Bohème.* In May of 1898 he performed forty-three orchestral concerts in a two-month period at the International Exposition of Turin.

On June 21, 1897, Toscanini married Carla De Martini, a ballerina. They had three children: Walter, who ultimately became Toscanini's manager; Wanda, who married the piano virtuoso Vladimir Horowitz; and Wally, who became the Countess Castelbarco.

In 1898 Toscanini was named principal conductor of La Scala in Milan. During three years in Milan he shattered the insularity of the La Scala repertory by emphasizing the music of Wagner, as well as that of other German composers, and Russian and French operas, all rarely, if ever, heard in Italy at that time. He also brought to the stage of La Scala new Italian operas by Leoncavallo, Mascagni, Franchetti, and others.

The persistence of the audience in demanding an encore by its beloved tenor, Giovanni Zenatello, in violation of Toscanini's edict against encores, sent the conductor into such a rage that he resigned from La Scala in 1903. But in 1906 he was back at this post for another two-year period.

By then Toscanini had established his identity as one of the world's greatest conductors. Opposed to the romantic liberties in which so many of his conducting colleagues indulged, Toscanini became the literalist determined to carry out every demand of each score he conducted as strictly and as meticulously as he could. Various elements in Toscanini's art fused to put his performances in a class by themselves: his capacity to concentrate on minutiae without losing sight of the grand design; a wonderful feeling for the rhythmic pulse; personal dynamism; a gift for bringing a soaring singing line to lyrical pages; an uncommon capacity for achieving a transparency of orchestral structure; a commanding knowledge of the symphonic and operatic literature (all of which he committed to memory); and a seemingly infallible musical intuition. Contemporary composers of works that he introduced were lavish in their praises of his capacity to penetrate to the essence of their artistic intentions, and familiar works emerged under his baton as if reborn, glowing in their pristine beauty.

In his untiring pursuit of perfection, he became a despot, tyrannical in his demands on those who performed under him. He often subjected musicians to stinging insults; and he was given to childish tantrums and violent outbursts of temper. Orchestra members feared and often resented him; nevertheless few conductors of the twentieth century commanded such hero worship from musicians.

Mounting disagreements with the La Scala management over artistic policies led Toscanini to resign once again, in 1908. He went to New York to conduct the Metropolitan Opera, making his American debut with *Aida* on Nov. 16, 1908. He remained seven years. But after the outbreak of World War I, he returned to Italy, conducting for war charities and performing at patriotic rallies and even directing a military band. After the war, with the reopening of La Scala in 1920, he became not only its principal conductor but also artistic director. This "Toscanini epoch" at La Scala, which lasted until 1929, contributed one of the most luminous chapters in the history of that world-renowned opera house. Among his new productions perhaps the most significant was the world premiere of Puccini's last opera, *Turandot*, on Apr. 25, 1926.

Toscanini paid a return visit to the United States during the winter of 1920–1921 to conduct performances with the visiting La Scala orchestra. On Jan. 14, 1926, he appeared as a guest conductor of the New York Philharmonic. A season later he assumed the post of associate conductor with that orchestra and in 1933 that of musical director. A Toscanini cult soon developed in New York, one with few parallels in the history of musical performances. Under his baton the Philharmonic became one of the world's foremost orchestras. With Toscanini at its head, it made its first tour of Europe in the spring of 1930. Toscanini led his final concert with the New York Philharmonic in New York on Apr. 29, 1936. Meanwhile, in 1930 he had become the first foreign conductor to be heard at the summer Wagner festival at Bayreuth, Germany. Between 1935 and 1938 he appeared regularly at the summer festivals at Salzburg, Austria.

In 1937 Toscanini became conductor of the NBC Symphony, organized for him by the NBC radio network. During the next seventeen years, he elevated the orchestra to the front rank of the world's symphonic organizations, one known not only through its broadcasts but also through tours of South America and the United States and a comprehensive library of symphonic and operatic recordings for RCA Victor.

From the beginning of the rise of fascism in Italy, Toscanini was outspoken in his opposition. Every effort by Mussolini to win him over to fascism proved futile. When, on May 14, 1931, Toscanini refused to perform the Fascist hymn, *Giovinezza*, at one of his concerts he was bodily attacked by Blackshirts. Several years later, Toscanini was placed under house arrest because of his renewed attacks on fascism and nazism. Finally allowed to leave Italy and to return to the United States to fulfill his obligations with the NBC Symphony, Toscanini vowed never again to return as long as the Fascists were in power. His home for the remainder of his life was Villa Pauline at Riverdale, N.Y. But he never gave up his Italian citizenship.

His hostility to nazism was no less articulate or intransigent. He was among the first musicians to express his rage and disgust at the Nazi policy of "cleansing" German musical life of Jewish influences. In retaliation, Nazi storm-troopers made a public display throughout Germany of destroying Toscanini recordings. Toscanini refused to return to Bayreuth, where he was scheduled for performances during the summer of 1933. After the Anschluss, he would no longer appear at Salzburg either. As a further sign of his anti-Nazi sentiments, he went to Palestine to conduct the then newly organized Palestine Symphony Orchestra (the present-day

Israel Philharmonic), made up of Jewish émigré musicians from Germany. His first concert took place in Tel Aviv on Dec. 26, 1936. He accepted no fee for his services and insisted upon paying his own travel expenses.

During World War II Toscanini gave concerts for the benefit of the United Service Organization (USO), the sale of war bonds, the Red Cross, and the armed forces. He made for the Office of War Information a film performance of Verdi's *Hymn of the Nations,* in the text of which he altered one phrase to read "Italy—betrayed." He conducted a special concert in New York to commemorate the surrender of Italy that he named "Victory Concert—Act I." He followed it in subsequent years with two additional concerts celebrating V-E Day and V-J Day.

The end of World War II and the overthrow of fascism in Italy brought Toscanini back to his native land. He conducted several concerts with the La Scala orchestra to reopen an auditorium that had then just been partially restored after having been bombed during the war. His initial concert, on May 11, 1946, was a highly emotional event that attracted world attention.

Early in life, Toscanini said that when his fabulous memory failed him he would call it a day. It finally faltered early in January 1954. Just before a rehearsal with the NBC Symphony of a concert presentation of Verdi's *Un Ballo in Maschera,* he was unable to remember some of the opera's text. At an all-Wagner concert on April 4 several measures in the "Bacchanale" from *Tannhäuser* eluded him. He continued conducting till the end of the concert without any further mishaps. In the closing measures of the final composition, the Prelude to *Die Meistersinger,* his baton fell to the floor. Then he walked slowly from the stage and refused to acknowledge the ovation of the studio audience. Though he subsequently was involved in several recording sessions, he never again conducted a concert. He lived thereafter in retirement at his home in Riverdale, where he died. Following funeral services at St. Patrick's Cathedral in New York, his body was transported to Italy to be buried in the family tomb in Milan's central cemetery.

[See Samuel Chotzinoff, *Toscanini: An Intimate Portrait* (1956); David Ewen, *The Story of Arturo Toscanini* (1951, revised 1960); George R. Marek, *Toscanini* (1975); Harvey Sachs, *Toscanini* (1978);

Howard Taubman, *The Maestro: The Life of Arturo Toscanini* (1951).]

DAVID EWEN

TOWNLEY, ARTHUR CHARLES (Dec. 30, 1880–Nov. 7, 1959), organizer and president of the Nonpartisan League, was born near Browns Valley, Minn., the son of Fitch R. Townley, a farmer, and Esther J. Cross. Following graduation from high school in Alexandria, Minn., he taught in a country school for about two years and then began farming with his brother, Covert, near Beach, N.D. He soon joined others in acquiring land for large-scale wheat farming near Cheyenne Wells, Colo., but the venture failed. While in Colorado he met, and in 1911 married, Margaret Rose Teenan. They had one foster daughter.

Townley's return to Beach in 1907 marked the beginning of an extensive flax-raising enterprise that initially proved highly successful. But in 1912, when he was being termed the "flax king of the Northwest," early frost and a depressed market brought disaster, and Townley was bankrupted. Embittered, he became an organizer for the Socialist party, at which he proved to be unusually talented. In 1914 he was an unsuccessful candidate for the legislature on the Socialist ticket, and soon therafter left the party to promote his plan for a new type of farmers' political movement.

Discontent was rife among upper Midwest farmers, who (with considerable justice) believed themselves exploited by the grain traders and railroads. Townley's idea was for an organization that would cut across party lines but would use the relatively new instrument of the direct primary to nominate farmer-endorsed candidates in the major parties, mainly the Republican party in North Dakota. He proposed a simple and direct program: state ownership of terminal elevators, flour mills, packinghouses, and cold storage plants; state inspection and grading of grain; exemption of farm improvements from taxation; state hail insurance; state rural credit banks, operated at cost.

Townley proved to be an organizing genius and a remarkably persuasive "stump speaker" whose mastery of sarcasm, scorn, and ridicule, and vitriolic attacks on "Big Biz," roused enthusiastic responses. Beginning with a lone farm-to-farm canvass, within a few months he had scores of commission-paid organizers throughout the state signing up dues-paying members for his new Nonpartisan League (NPL). In 1916, a little more than a year from the start of organizing efforts, the league succeeded in nominating and electing a governor, all but one other state officer, and a large majority of the lower house of the legislature. Two years later the NPL swept all state offices and obtained a more than two-thirds majority in both houses of the legislature. The platform was speedily enacted, and soon United States senators and congressmen were also elected.

Townley never sought public office under league auspices, but he remained its president and dominating influence, wielding tremendous power. After 1918 organizing spread to adjoining states, and what had become the National Non-partisan League soon played a role in the politics of thirteen states; but only in Minnesota, other than the state of its birth, did it become a major force. In Minnesota it was the immediate ancestor of the highly successful Farmer-Labor party.

During the six years of league ascendancy, Townley acquired some status as a national political figure, and was widely attacked as a dangerous "leftist" radical. When the league fell from power in 1921–1922, victim of internal dissension, heavily financed opposition, and spurious charges of "pro-Germanism" during World War I, Townley went down with it, although he had lost effective control some months earlier. His ninety-day jail sentence in Minnesota in 1921, on the dubious charge of "conspiring to discourage enlistments," did not help.

Townley never again found a successful outlet for his abilities. He tried organizing the National Producers Alliance, then promoting unproductive oil well drilling efforts in North Dakota. In the early 1930's he advocated a moratorium on all interest payments and helped to organize the Farm Holiday Association. For a time he edited the *Farm Holiday News.*

Townley was repeatedly a candidate for public office in various places and under different party labels, securing moderate support the first two times but thereafter sinking to the status of nuisance candidate: for a North Dakota congressional seat in 1930; for an at-large congressional seat in Minnesota on the Farmer-Labor ticket in 1932; for governor of Minnesota in 1934; for the United States Senate in North Dakota in 1944, 1956, and 1958, first as a Republican and subsequently as an independent.

Townley's wife died in 1944; their foster daughter, the following year. For a time in the late 1940's he is said to have lived near New Effington, S.D., with a group concerned with faith healing and speaking in tongues. During the McCarthy era of the 1950's he found that anti-communism was a marketable commodity, and much of his time was devoted to lecturing on the subject, taking up collections to pay his way. The man once excoriated as a "left-wing radical" now became a "right-wing radical." He apparently secured financial backing from individuals (and perhaps organizations) fighting the Farmers Union, and his virulent attacks, including claims that the North Dakota Farmers Union was Communist-dominated, led to libel suits against him.

In his last years Townley sold insurance. He was traveling about the state, collecting funds to fight the libel suits, when his car crashed into a truck near Makoti, N.D., and he was killed instantly. Although he died almost unknown, his Nonpartisan League helped shape the politics of an entire region for generations, and its patterns of operation became a guide for many later political movements.

[No biography of Townley has been written, and he preserved no personal papers. The principal work on the Nonpartisan League is Robert L. Morlan, *Political Prairie Fire* (1955). See also Edward C. Blackorby, *Prairie Rebel* (1964); Andrew A. Bruce, *Non-Partisan League* (1921); Usher L. Burdick, *History of the Farmers' Political Action in North Dakota* (1944); Theodore Christianson, *Minnesota* (1935); Lewis F. Crawford, *History of North Dakota* (1931); William Watts Folwell, *A History of Minnesota* (1926–1931); Paul R. Fossum, *The Agrarian Movement in North Dakota* (1925); Herbert E. Gaston, *The Nonpartisan League* (1920); William Langer, *The Nonpartisan League* (1920); Russel B. Nye, *Midwestern Progressive Politics* (1951); Theodore Saloutos and John D. Hicks, *Agricultural Discontent in the Middle West, 1900–1939* (1951); and O. M. Thomason, *The Beginning and the End of the Nonpartisan League* (1920). The National Nonpartisan League papers, in the library of the Minnesota Historical Society, contain limited information on Townley. Useful obituaries appeared in the *Fargo* (N.D.) *Forum,* Nov. 8, 1959; and the *Minneapolis Tribune,* Nov. 13, 1959.]

ROBERT L. MORLAN

TOWNSEND, FRANCIS EVERETT (Jan. 13, 1867–Sept. 1, 1960), physician and originator of the Old Age Revolving Pension Plan, was born near Fairbury, Ill., the son of George Warren Townsend, a farmer, and Sarah Ann Harper. He completed two years of college preparatory work at Franklin (Neb.) Academy before accompanying a brother to southern California (1887) in a brief, abortive effort to cash in on the first land boom in the Los Angeles area. He returned to Franklin in 1890 to finish school and then moved to his own farm in northwestern Kansas. Townsend did not prosper. Forced off his land in 1898, he sought work in the Colorado Rockies as an itinerant laborer and a mucker in the mines. Drifting back to Kansas, he sold cook stoves to farm families, finally saving enough to enroll at Omaha Medical College in 1899.

Townsend, the oldest member of his graduating class, worked his way through medical school as grocery salesman and college accountant. After graduation in 1903, he moved to Belle Fourche, S.D., in the Black Hills. His practice included cowhands and miners, ranchers and adventurers living throughout the rough frontier area. On Oct. 30, 1906, he married Wilhelmina ("Minnie") Mollie Brogue, a widowed nurse. They had three children and an adopted daughter. In 1917 Townsend answered the call for medical men to serve in the army. After the war he returned to the Black Hills, but was stricken almost immediately with acute peritonitis. Certain that he could not survive another South Dakota winter, he took his family to Long Beach, Calif., in 1919.

Townsend lived in southern California for the rest of his life. For fourteen years he labored in obscurity. His health remained a problem; aggressive young doctors and established older ones limited his practice, and soon he was struggling to earn money for necessities. When the Great Depression struck California, most of his savings were wiped out. Good fortune smiled briefly when he was appointed assistant health officer of Long Beach. The job carried him through the depression and afforded the opportunity to see how cruelly it had ravaged many older Americans. When Townsend suddenly lost his job through a local political upheaval, he found himself again in grave financial straits. It was in this setting that he conceived his celebrated plan.

Gaunt and white-haired, Townsend was an old man when he decided to arouse the nation. His deep-set eyes, smudge of a moustache, and lantern jaw were set off by the high, stiff collar that he always wore above his threadbare clothes. He was old and poor, but—as he said later—he had seen a

vision and he was a committed man. His vision was of the elderly American population permanently free from economic privation. The method of liberating the elderly would be a pension of $200 per month, disbursed monthly by the federal government, to every citizen aged sixty and over. The government could raise the huge sums needed through a 2 percent "turnover tax" to be levied on every business transaction. Although the plan would cost more than $20 billion per year, Townsend advertised it as a boon not only for the aged but for all Americans. He decided that spending the $200 within thirty days should be made mandatory, thus stressing the "revolving" aspect of the proposal: the $24 billion paid to the elderly would stimulate the entire economy as the old people spent money on food, clothing, shelter, and all manner of consumer goods. The "velocity effect" of the pension money, he said, would sweep away the depression.

The Townsend Plan was announced in a letter written for the "People's Forum" column of a Long Beach newspaper in September 1933. Within three months the idea had been transformed into a social movement. Local Townsend Clubs were organized; Townsend claimed 3,000 such units by January 1934. The *Townsend National Weekly* was published with the income from sales of pamphlets, songs, buttons, badges, tire covers, and other items marketed by shrewd younger managers attracted to Townsend's staff. By late summer 1935, Townsend headquarters claimed a membership of 2.25 million in 7,000 clubs.

Townsend's simple idea was attacked by economists as a cruel hoax, one critic observing that "What the Townsendites are really demanding is a revision of the science of arithmetic by law." But hundreds of thousands found comfort in the plan, and community in a movement that not only promised economic security but also offered commitment, involvement, and identification for many lonely older people.

Townsend was affected by his meteoric rise to fame. The cheering throngs, the plane trips, the adulatory letters made him feel, he confessed, that "he had been chosen by God to accomplish this mission." Feted as a new messiah at two national conventions of his followers, he insisted in 1936 that "Our movement will make as deep and mighty changes in civilization as did Christianity." Thus he was vulnerable to the flattery and schemes of others who had plans to save America.

When Townsend came under attack by the New Deal and faced congressional investigators who charged he was profiting from the plight of others, he made a temporary alliance with the Reverend Gerald L. K. Smith, national organizer of Huey Long's Share Our Wealth Society, another hyperinflationary panacea of the mid-1930's. Smith and Townsend joined the Reverend Charles E. Coughlin, leader of the National Union for Social Justice, in Coughlin's newly organized Union party.

The Townsend Plan had become a political force. Townsend asked his supporters to vote only for candidates friendly to his pension idea. But his interest in the new third party waned as its leaders pulled in different directions throughout the acrimonious 1936 campaign. When the Union party received only 10 percent of the predicted 9 million votes, Townsend abandoned it.

Nevertheless, he continued to attack President Franklin D. Roosevelt, even after passage of the Social Security Act (1935). He insisted that social security was a palliative designed to buy off old people who might otherwise join the Townsend Movement. Nevertheless, Roosevelt commuted the jail sentence Townsend received for contempt of Congress in 1937, when he refused to answer questions asked by a Senate committee that was investigating alleged corruption in the Townsend Plan. In later years Townsend continued his leadership of the movement, publishing his newspaper and maintaining a national headquarters. He tried to modernize his plan and to remove the stigma of naive utopianism it had acquired. He no longer called for pensions of $200 per month. But the return of prosperity killed the movement. Townsend was still on the road, addressing crowds of older people, a few months before he died in Los Angeles.

[Townsend materials can be found in the Franklin D. Roosevelt Papers, Franklin D. Roosevelt Library, Hyde Park, N.Y., official file 1542. The library of the University of Oregon at Eugene contains the minute books of the Townsend National Recovery Plan and the Townsend Foundation; the proceedings of the national conventions of the movement; and pamphlets, newspapers, and other material published by Townsend's organization. Townsend's autobiography is *New Horizons* (1943). He sought to explain his pension plan in *The Townsend National Recovery Plan* (1934); and *Old Age Revolving Pensions* (1934). See also Abraham Holtzman, *The Townsend Movement* (1963); and David H. Bennett, "The Year of the Old Folks' Revolt," *American Heritage*, Dec. 1964. Critical contemporary views of Townsend's pension scheme and his movement are

Richard L. Neuberger, "The Townsend Plan Exposed," *Nation*, Oct. 30, 1935; Nicholas Roosevelt, *The Townsend Plan* (1936); Stuart A. Rice, "Is the Townsend Plan Practical?" *Vital Speeches of the Day*, Jan. 27, 1936; and Donald R. Richberg, "The Townsend Delusion," *Review of Reviews*, Feb. 1936. Townsend defends his plan in Russell Owen, "Townsend Talks of His Plan and Hopes," *New York Times*, Dec. 29, 1935.]

DAVID H. BENNETT

TOWNSEND, WILLARD SAXBY, JR.

(Dec. 4, 1895–Feb. 3, 1957), labor leader, was born in Cincinnati, Ohio, the son of Willard Townsend, contractor, and Cora Beatrice Townsend, who were cousins. He attended public schools in Cincinnati and graduated from Walnut Hills High School in 1912. His first job in the industry that would be the foundation of his life's work came in 1914, when he became a redcap at the Union Station in Cincinnati. In 1916 he joined the army and served with the American Expeditionary Forces during World War I. After the war he took a prominent role in organizing a Cincinnati company of the Ohio National Guard and eventually rose to first lieutenant. He also studied chiropody at the Illinois School of Chiropody and practiced the profession for a short while.

After running unsuccessfully for city councilman in Cincinnati, Townsend moved to Canada to continue his education. While there, he took a premedical course at the University of Toronto for two years. In 1924 he received a degree in chemistry from the Royal College of Science in Toronto. He supported himself while studying by working as a dining-car waiter and redcap on the Canadian National Railways. Townsend thus went to Texas, where he spent several years as a schoolteacher. In 1929 he moved to Chicago. In Oct. 1930, he married Consuello Mann; they had one son. He also began work as a redcap with the Chicago and Northwestern Railroad.

During the early 1930's, Townsend initiated efforts to organize redcaps, a group that lacked job security and received abysmally low pay. As late as 1938, according to the Interstate Commerce Commission (ICC), few received wages from their employers. Their livelihoods came from tips given by the passengers whose baggage they carried. Wages ranged from a token $1 a year to $10 per month, while tips averaged from $1 to $3 a day. Labor organizers had to overcome both the resistance of management and the hostility that blacks felt toward organized labor in general.

Chicago was the ideal location for one interested in organizing railroad service employees. It was a major terminus, but perhaps more important, from an organizational standpoint, it was also the center of activity of A. Philip Randolph's and Milton P. Webster's efforts to organize the Brotherhood of Sleeping Car Porters (BSCP). Much publicity surrounded their activities, and Townsend observed their work and profited from their experience.

In 1936 Townsend called representatives of various local redcap groups together in Chicago to discuss forming a national union. That group founded the International Brotherhood of Red Caps, with Townsend as president. After withstanding a leadership challenge the following year, Townsend solidified his position in the union, becoming its perennial president. In 1940 the union changed its name to the United Transport Service Employees (UTSE) and two years later obtained a charter from the Congress of Industrial Organizations (CIO). Townsend then gained a seat on the CIO Executive Council, thus becoming the highest-ranking black labor leader in the country and the first ever to become a vice-president in the national labor movement. Randolph had long labored in the ranks of the American Federation of Labor, but that branch of the labor movement did not elevate him to national office until 1957.

Townsend was a dashing and energetic agent for both this union and the CIO. In 1938, following a procedure the BSCP had pioneered in 1927, he successfully appealed to the ICC to have redcaps declared employees of railroads, and thus eligible to bargain collectively under railway labor legislation. He then negotiated contracts that improved redcaps' wages and working conditions. Townsend's major work with the CIO was on the Committee to Abolish Racial Discrimination, a post to which he was appointed in 1942; he served as secretary in 1943. He worked also as a liaison between the American labor movement and labor organizations abroad. In 1947 and 1952 he represented the CIO at conferences in Japan. He wrote a pamphlet, *Trade Union Practices and Policies,* which was translated into Japanese to instruct Japanese workers on the purposes of trade unionism.

Townsend, a conservative, was devoutly anti-Communist. His denunciation of a tobacco workers' union as a Communist front actually worked against the labor movement when North Carolina workers, fearful of Communism yet unwilling to support the group Townsend endorsed, voted for nonrepresentation in a jurisdictional dispute in 1947. On another occasion he showed his conservatism when he supported Walter Reuther of the United Automobile Workers (UAW) in his stance that it was unnecessary for the UAW to have a black vice-president. Townsend called such a demand on the part of black UAW members "racism in reverse." Townsend's support of white trade union leaders may have stemmed from his own precarious position among blacks. Numerous black journalists decried the lack of results achieved by the Committee to Abolish Racial Discrimination, and Townsend confronted healthy competition from leaders of the BSCP, an older and stronger union that wanted jurisdiction over the workers he represented.

Nevertheless, Townsend's activities in organized labor led to positions of influence in black leadership circles. He became a prominent figure in Chicago politics. He performed important functions on racial matters for the Chicago Urban League and the mayor of Chicago, and he lent his considerable prestige to fund-raising campaigns for Hampton Institute and served on its board of trustees. As late as 1951 he earned a degree from the Blackstone Law School. He died in Chicago.

[There is to date no full study of Townsend's career. His personal and professional papers are at AFL-CIO headquarters, Washington, D.C., and at headquarters of the Brotherhood of Railway, Airline and Steam Ship Clerks, Freight Handlers, Express and Station Employees in Homewood, Ill. See also Philip S. Foner, *Organized Labor and the Black Worker: 1619–1973* (1974). Obituaries are in *AFL-CIO News,* Feb. 9, 1957; *Time,* Feb. 18, 1957; and *American Federationist,* Mar. 1957.]

WILLIAM H. HARRIS

TUCKER, HENRY ST. GEORGE (July 16, 1874–Aug. 8, 1959), Episcopal minister and bishop, was born in Warsaw, Va., one of thirteen children of Beverley Dandridge Tucker, Episcopal bishop for the diocese of southern Virginia, and Anna Maria Washington. He was educated at Norfolk Academy, the University of Virginia (M.A., 1895), and the Theological Seminary of Virginia (B.D. and D.D., 1899).

In 1899, the year of his ordination as a deacon and priest of the Episcopal church, Tucker was sent to a mission station at Sendai, Japan. Shortly thereafter he was sent to Hirosaki to administer the Aomori prefecture. In his church at Hirosaki—a converted pool hall—he soon began delivering his sermons in Japanese, a language in which he eventually came to feel more fluent than English.

In 1902 Tucker was appointed president of St. Paul's College, a missionary school in Tokyo. Six years later he met Mary Lillian Warnock, daughter of an Atlanta physician, who was visiting Japan with her sister, a missionary. They were married on Apr. 18, 1911, and had two sons.

Tucker was named missionary bishop of Kyoto in 1912. When the United States entered World War I, he volunteered as a major in the American Expeditionary Force and spent the war in Siberia, where he had charge of civilian refugee work for the Red Cross. At the end of the war, he returned to Kyoto, where he remained until 1923. He then was appointed professor of pastoral theology at the Theological Seminary of Virginia.

Tucker became bishop coadjutor of Virginia in 1926 and full bishop of the diocese of Virginia the following year. He was also elected in that year to the National Council of the Protestant Episcopal Church. When the triennial Episcopal Convention met at Cincinnati in 1937, to select a new presiding bishop, it rejected the three nominees on the official slate and chose Tucker. The convention also greatly enhanced the power and prestige of the office, previously little more than ceremonial. The presiding bishop would henceforth function as the executive and administrative head of the church in addition to his continuing role as the spiritual leader.

Tucker did not hesitate to speak out on the issues of the day, particularly the developing international crisis of the late 1930's. Shortly after his installation he publicly deplored Japanese aggression against China, but noted that Western nations, including the United States, had provided bad examples to the Japanese and that most world governments "don't pay attention to Christian principles" in their activities. In 1938 he condemned the Munich Pact, by which England and France tried to appease Hitler, as "concessions to methods far from Christian."

In October 1941, at the Cathedral of St. Peter and St. Paul in Washington, D.C., Tucker assumed the newly created chair for the presiding bishop of the Protestant Episcopal Church. The occasion was historic, *Newsweek* noted, for it elevated Tucker "to the highest ecclesiastical rank any presiding bishop has ever enjoyed." The following year Tucker became the most important Protestant spokesman in America with his election as president of the Federal Council of the Churches of Christ in America.

Although Tucker originally opposed American entry into World War II, he soon came to identify the Axis powers as anti-Christian forces and to call for their defeat, even at the cost of American intervention. During the war he spoke out forcefully and often, insisting (for example) that the Allies adhere to Christian principles even in the heat of battle. He was particularly outspoken in condemnation of Hitler's liquidation of European Jews. He also anticipated the eventual Far East peace terms by calling upon the Allies to allow Japan to retain the emperor after the war as a stabilizing factor.

Tucker retired in December 1946 to a life of contemplation and the writing of a memoir of his years as a missionary. He died in Richmond, Va. Throughout his career as a spokesman for Protestant Americans, he had condemned anti-Semitism at home and abroad, and had insisted that blacks must be granted full civil rights. And he did so with marked grace and true Christian charity.

[Tucker's autobiography is *Exploring the Silent Shore of Memory* (1951). He also wrote *Reconciliation Through Christ* (1910); *Providence and the Atonement* (1934); and *History of the Episcopal Church in Japan* (1938). Obituaries are in the *New York Times* and the *Richmond* (Va.) *Times-Dispatch* and *News-Leader*, Aug. 9, 1959. Also see the biographical sketches in *Newsweek*, Nov. 3, 1941; and *Time*, Dec. 21, 1942.]

RICHARD F. HAYNES

VANCE, HAROLD SINES (Aug. 22, 1890–Aug. 31, 1959), industrialist, automobile executive, and government official, was born in Port Huron, Mich., the son of Samuel W. Vance, a lawyer and circuit court judge, and Carrie Sines. After his father's death when Harold was in his teens, Vance worked and read law with his father's partner, and sought unsuccessfully an appointment to West Point. His real interest was in mechanical things, and in 1910 he took a job as a mechanic's apprentice at 15 cents an hour in the machine shop of the Everitt-Metzger-Flanders (EMF) Company in Port Huron.

EMF was a combination of several small automobile and parts manufacturing firms, which in turn was absorbed into the Studebaker Corporation in 1912. In the larger organization Vance rose rapidly because he showed a talent for resolving complicated problems and a willingness to make decisions. He became purchasing agent for Studebaker in 1915. He spent eight months in 1918 on a wartime assignment as production engineer with Bethlehem Steel and then returned to Studebaker as assistant to the president. In 1922 he was put in charge of export sales and a year later became general sales manager. That year he married Agnes M. Monaghan. They had four children.

Vance had thus compiled a record of competence in areas beyond his mechanical talents, but his principal interests and greatest skills continued to be in production and engineering. Consequently, when Albert R. Erskine, president of Studebaker, reorganized the company in 1926 in order to carry out an ambitious program of expansion, he made Vance vice-president in charge of manufacturing. (Other features included making Paul G. Hoffman vice-president in charge of sales and concentrating all production in South Bend, Ind.) At this time Studebaker's prospects appeared bright. It was the country's third largest automobile manufacturer, although it would lose that position a year later when Chrysler acquired Dodge.

However, Erskine's ambitions outran his judgment. He made unsound acquisitions, and he grossly underestimated the severity of the Great Depression. Studebaker went into receivership in 1933, and Erskine committed suicide. The company would have gone out of business completely but for heroic efforts by Hoffman and Vance, who were made receivers. They did so well that Studebaker was again showing a profit by the end of 1933 and was discharged from receivership two years later. In the reconstituted company Hoffman became president and Vance chairman of the board. They worked in such close cooperation that it is impossible to assign credit to either one separately for the rehabilitation of Studebaker. Hoffman, as salesman and promoter, was more visible.

The Studebaker revival continued through World War II and for a few years afterward. The company was the first motor vehicle manufacturer to return to peacetime production, a feat that can certainly be attributed to Vance's talents. It came after a second intermission for government service; in World War II he worked with the War Production Board. Vance became president of Studebaker in 1948, switching jobs with Hoffman when the latter took time off to administer the Marshall Plan.

By 1950 the postwar seller's market for motor vehicles was gradually vanishing, and all the independent firms found their existence increasingly threatened. Their only solution was to merge in order to try to achieve the economies of scale that gave the "Big Three" their competitive advantage. After a good deal of maneuvering, Studebaker finally merged with Packard in 1954 as the Studebaker-Packard Corporation. Vance became chairman of the executive committee of Studebaker-Packard, but he held this post for only a year. He appears to have consented to the merger only because of a catastrophic decline in Studebaker sales that began in 1953.

In any case, he was becoming more involved in public service. In 1951 he became a lay trustee of the University of Notre Dame, which conferred an honorary LL.D. on him in 1954. From 1952 to 1955 he was consultant to the Office of Defense Mobilization, and in the latter year President Dwight D. Eisenhower appointed him to the Atomic Energy Commission (AEC) for what was supposed to be a five-year term. As a member of the AEC, Vance was very strongly interested in industrial applications of atomic energy and was a vigorous advocate of the development of nuclear power for the generation of electricity. In 1957 he was given a Lord and Taylor Award for his contributions to the peaceful uses of nuclear energy. Just before his death he had exchanged letters with Carlos P. Romulo, then Philippine ambassador to the United Nations, regarding a grant to the Philippine Republic for the construction of a nuclear research reactor. Vance died in Washington, D.C.

[A sketch of Vance's life can be found in his obituary in the *New York Times*, Sept. 1, 1959. Stephen Longstreet, *A Century on Wheels* (1952), has a considerable amount of information on his business career. References to his early career appear in John B. Rae, *American Automobile Manufacturers: The First Forty Years* (1959).]

JOHN B. RAE

VANDERBILT, ARTHUR T. (July 7, 1888–June 16, 1957), lawyer and jurist, was born in Newark, N.J., the son of Lewis Vanderbilt, a railway executive, and Alice H. Leach. Vanderbilt attended Wesleyan University, obtaining the B.A. in 1910, and then Columbia Law School, where he received the LL.B. in 1912. He married Florence Josephine Althen in Newark on Sept. 12, 1914. They had five children.

Vanderbilt opened his own law office in Newark in 1915 and maintained a practice there for the next thirty-two years. He established a reputation as an extremely capable attorney, a "lawyer's lawyer," whom others often brought in as counsel to a case. He also became involved in government reform, teaching, and professional activities within the bar.

Active in Republican politics, Vanderbilt became president of the Essex County Republican League in 1919 and from that base fought the political machine of Jersey City boss Frank Hague. In 1938 he represented the American Bar Association when that organization intervened in a civil liberties case in the U.S. Court of Appeals. Norman Thomas, the Socialist leader, had been barred from speaking in Jersey City under a Hague ordinance severely restricting public gatherings and had sued to have the measure declared unconstitutional. Although the New Jersey state courts upheld the statute, the federal courts ultimately found it in violation of constitutional guarantees of freedom of speech and assembly.

Vanderbilt began teaching at the New York University (NYU) Law School in 1914 and rose to full professor by 1919. In 1943 he was chosen as dean of the school, a position he held until 1948. He became a nationally recognized expert on judicial administration and reform. He wrote or edited several volumes on legal administration, including *Cases and Materials on Administrative Law* (1947), *Minimum Standards of Judicial Administration* (1949), and *Cases and Materials on Modern Procedure and Judicial Administration* (1952).

His philosophy of court reform was best summed up in his William H. White Lectures at the University of Virginia, published as *The Challenge of Law Reform* (1955). There he argued somewhat hyperbolically that criminals, gangsters, and corrupt officials were no more dangerous to their communities than judges and lawyers who clung to outmoded legal procedures and fought against any and all changes in procedural law and administration because they were comfortable with the established way of doing things.

Vanderbilt's concern with judicial reform was far from academic. He chaired the New Jersey

Judicial Council (1930–1940), the National Conference of Judicial Councils (1933–1937), and the U.S. attorney general's commission on administrative procedures (1938–1939). He secured the creation of the Office of Administrative Director of the Federal Courts. Elected president of the American Bar Association in 1937, he led that group's campaign for reform of the federal court system. From 1938 to 1946 he chaired the advisory committee to the U.S. Supreme Court on federal rules of criminal procedure, and he played a major role in the reorganization of the federal courts initiated by the Supreme Court and the attorney general's office. While dean of NYU Law School, he established the Law Center Forum, where judges and attorneys could meet with scholars, businessmen, and labor leaders to work on common problems related to the courts.

Vanderbilt's greatest opportunity to effect court reform came in September 1948, when he took up his duties as chief justice of the New Jersey Supreme Court, after having served as a judge of the circuit court since the previous November. He now resigned from NYU Law School and from his practice, and devoted all his time and energy to overhauling New Jersey's antiquated court system, one of the worst in the nation.

As chief justice, Vanderbilt instituted an annual national conference of judges, lawyers, and legislators to review and revise court procedures in order to make them more flexible and less technical. He recognized that courts constituted a big business and insisted that they should be run with efficient, businesslike methods. Every case should be handled promptly and on its merits, he asserted, rather than on the basis of procedural technicalities. He worked hard to upgrade the lowest courts, especially the municipal courts, because they were closest to the people and because if a case were heard properly and efficiently there, it would help clear away the backlog clogging the appellate courts.

Vanderbilt also recognized that no legal reform could succeed unless the people understood the arguments and supported the proposed measures. As chief justice—indeed, for many years before—he carried this message to the people in numerous speeches and articles; one of the last pieces he wrote warned that no matter how great the need for judicial reform, it could only succeed through an aroused public opinion.

Vanderbilt's campaign proved extremely effective. He reduced the different types of New

Jersey courts from seventeen to seven and cut the waiting time on cases significantly. Much of his success was made possible by New Jersey's new state constitution, which was adopted in 1947 and in the drafting of which Vanderbilt had played a major role. His activities were also winning him increased national recognition, and there was talk that he was in line for nomination to the U.S. Supreme Court when he died of a massive heart attack on his way to work.

[The Vanderbilt Papers are in the Collection on Legal Change, Wesleyan University. See also his *Selected Writings*, 2 vols. (1965). On his life and work, see J. H. Spingarn, "Order in the Courtroom," *Harper's*, May 1956; Arthur T. Vanderbilt II, *Changing Law: A Biography of Arthur T. Vanderbilt* (1976); and the obituary in the *New York Times*, June 16, 1957.]

MELVIN I. UROFSKY

VAN DRUTEN, JOHN WILLIAM (June 1, 1901–Dec. 19, 1957), playwright, was born in London, England, the son of Wilhelmus Van Druten, a Dutch banker, and Eve Van Druten, a Londoner of Dutch parentage. After attending University College School in London, (1911–1917), Van Druten wished to make a career of writing; but his father insisted upon an immediately practical profession, and Van Druten chose the law. For five years he worked in a London law firm; he also received the LL.B. from the University of London in 1923. Finding that he preferred the academic side of the profession to practice, he was a special lecturer in English law and legal history at the University College of Wales, in Aberystwyth, from 1923 to 1926.

During his years of legal training, Van Druten had been striving to establish himself as a writer by contributing to *Punch* and other periodicals. His first play, *The Return Half*, was produced by the Ex-Students' Club of the Royal Academy of Dramatic Art in 1923, with the then-unknown John Gielgud in the leading role. His next play, *Young Woodley*, established him as a professional playwright. The work had been banned by a British censor on the grounds that it disparaged the English public school system; brought to New York, it had a successful Broadway run in 1925 but was not produced in London until 1928. Van Druten turned this play into his first novel, under the same title (1929). Following this success, Van Druten made a lecture tour of the United States,

to which he would make many more visits before settling in California; he became a naturalized citizen in 1944. He was a lifelong bachelor.

From the late 1920's to his death Van Druten had equally successful careers as playwright, screenwriter, and director, but his three later novels—*A Woman on Her Way* (1930), *And Then You Wish* (1936), and the partially autobiographical *The Vicarious Years* (1955)—added little to his stature. He once estimated his successes in the theater at about fifty percent of his prolific output. Productions of the 1920's and 1930's included *Diversion* (1927), *After All* (1929), *London Wall* (1932), *There's Always Juliet* (1931), *Behold, We Live* (1932), *Somebody Knows* (1932), *The Distaff Side* (1933), *Most of the Game* (1935), and *Gertie Maude* (1937). The following decade saw the staging of *Leave Her to Heaven* (1940) and *Old Acquaintance* (1940) before Van Druten had a major critical and popular success in *The Voice of the Turtle* (1943), a play about a soldier on a weekend visit to New York City that neatly captured a wartime mood. *I Remember Mama*, based on stories by Kathryn Forbes about a Norwegian-American family, was a hit of 1944; it was followed by *The Mermaids Singing* (1945), *The Druid Circle* (1947), and *Make Way for Lucia* (1948), based on novels by E. F. Benson. Van Druten remained in top form in his last years, producing a popular comic fantasy, *Bell, Book and Candle* (1950), and a skillful and moving dramatization of Christopher Isherwood's Berlin stories, *I Am a Camera* (1951).

Van Druten's Hollywood career, which began with the screen adaptation of *Young Woodley* (1930), included the scenarios for *Night Must Fall* (1937), a thriller based on a play by Emlyn Williams; *Parnell* (1937); *Raffles* (1939); *Johnny Come Lately* (1943); and (with others) *Gaslight* (1944), for which Ingrid Bergman won an Academy Award. A number of his own plays were also filmed. Van Druten directed most of his later works as well as the Rodgers and Hammerstein musical *The King and I* (1951).

For many years Van Druten lived on a ranch in Indio, Calif., in the Coachella Valley, where he died at the age of fifty-six. During this period he had turned to the study of religion, following an accidental injury to his arm that had taken him to a Christian Science practitioner. He discussed his views in various religious magazines and in a final volume of reminiscence, *The Widening Circle* (1957), in which he wrote that we "have to keep reminding ourselves, jolting our minds and our attention back to the oneness of God and the world, seeing and holding them as one. Of all the things that I have learned in religion, this seems to me the most important one."

Van Druten's best plays were well made, amusing and often touching, and characterized by natural-sounding dialogue that made them favorites of exponents of the realistic school of acting. In his manual *Playwright at Work* (1953) he acknowledged: "I am still bound by the conventions of the fourth wall, and the pretense that the play really is happening somewhere." He added, "That will ultimately change, I think. We shall move forward to another kind of play"—but he confessed that he could not foresee what kind it would be. His credo, which describes a theater more ambitious than the one he wrote for, is a revealing expression of the questing spirit that was characteristic of him as he grew older and more widely read in philosophical and religious literature: "If the author can still feel a new wonder about life, and its sadness, its humor and fascination, then he will be able to communicate that wonder to the audience, and if his wonder is a keen and new and vivid thing, it will emerge as beauty. I would say that the real wonder, an awareness of standing among great mysteries, is the clue to those plays which have truly moved us."

[Autobiographical reminiscences are in *The Way to the Present* (1938) and *The Widening Circle* (1957). *Playwright at Work* (1953) includes a portrait. See also the *New York Times* obituary notice, Dec. 20, 1957. There is no full-length biographical or critical study. Lloyd R. Morris has written about him in *Postscript to Yesterday* (1947).]

J. V. Ridgely

VEBLEN, OSWALD (Jan. 24, 1880–Aug. 10, 1960), mathematician, was born in Decorah, Iowa, the son of Andrew Anderson Veblen and Kirsti Hougen. The social scientist Thorstein Veblen was an uncle. Andrew Veblen taught mathematics, physics, and other subjects at Luther College in Decorah (1877–1881) and at the State University of Iowa (1883–1905).

Following early schooling in Iowa City, Veblen received the B.A. from the State University of Iowa in 1898. After a one-year assistantship at Iowa and a year of study at Harvard, which awarded him a second B.A., he earned the Ph.D. in mathematics at the University of Chicago in 1903; he remained there for two more years. In 1905 Woodrow Wilson, then president

of Princeton University, brought Veblen to Princeton as one of fifty "preceptors" hired to enhance the scholarship and level of instruction of the faculty. Veblen was promoted to full professor in 1910, and was appointed Henry Burchard Fine professor of mathematics in 1926. Meanwhile, in 1908, he had married Elizabeth Mary Dixon Richardson, a young Englishwoman he had met while she was visiting her brother, Owen Willans Richardson, then teaching physics at Princeton. They had no children. (Owen Richardson was awarded the Nobel Prize for physics in 1928.)

During World War I, Veblen served as a captain and a major in the Army Ordnance Department. He was in charge of range firing and ballistics at a proving ground, and in 1923–1924 served in the office of the chief of ordnance. He was an exchange professor at Oxford in 1928–1929, and lectured at Göttingen, Berlin, and Hamburg in 1932. In the latter year he became the first professor in the Division of Mathematics of the newly founded Institute for Advanced Study at Princeton, where he remained until he retired in 1950. Veblen's health deteriorated in the later years of his life—he became partially blind and suffered from a strained heart—but was cheerful and mentally keen to the end. He died in Brooklin, Me.

Veblen's reputation was based mainly on his contributions to geometry and its applications, and on his devoted service to mathematics and mathematicians. His first book, *Introduction to Infinitesimal Analysis* (1907), written with N. J. Lennes, was for years the only text that offered American students a careful introduction to the theory of real functions. His second book, *Projective Geometry* (1910–1918), volume I of which was written with J. W. Young, was the culmination of his dissertation, *A System of Axioms for Geometry* (1904), and a dozen other papers. His work was characterized by precise definitions, rigorous proofs, postulational development, and clarity of exposition. His *Analysis Situs* (1922) was a meticulous approach to the branch of mathematics now called topology and an inspiration for further investigations.

About the time *Analysis Situs* appeared, Veblen's interest began to shift from pure geometry to differential geometry and its applications to physics, notably the theory of relativity; he wrote many papers and four books in these fields: *Invariants of Quadratic Differential Forms* (1927); *Foundations of Differential Geometry* (1932), written with J. H. C. Whitehead; *Projektive Relativitätstheorie* (1933); and

Geometry of Complex Domains (1936), written with Wallace Givens. These works exhibit the same careful development found in his earlier articles and books. All his books, the first four in particular, were for many years the standard texts at American universities.

Veblen was more than a gifted mathematician; he was a sincere person with a deep devotion, almost religious in its nature and intensity, to mathematics and to people in mathematics. A simple, quiet man with a warm smile, who spoke and thought slowly and deliberately, he had remarkable judgment and great force of character. He encouraged excellence in scholarship, and was intolerant of sham and frivolity. He was instrumental in building up the Princeton University department into a world center of mathematics, and more than anyone else he was responsible for gathering the faculty of the Institute for Advanced Study. The National Research Council inaugurated its program of granting postdoctoral fellowships in mathematics in 1924 at his suggestion, and for years he was one of a three-member committee that selected the recipients. He used his influence to relocate many foreign mathematicians after Hitler came to power. Veblen was chairman of the Physical Science Division of the National Research Council in 1923–1924 and, in the same year, president of the American Mathematical Society. He was also president of the 1950 International Congress of Mathematicians.

[Deane Montgomery, "Oswald Veblen," *Bulletin of the American Mathematical Society*, Jan. 1963, contains a complete listing of Veblen's published works. His obituary is in the *New York Times*, Aug. 11, 1960.]
JAMES SINGER

VEILLER, LAWRENCE TURNURE (Jan. 7, 1872–Aug. 30, 1959), social worker and housing expert, was born in Elizabeth, N.J., the son of Philip Bayard Veiller and Elizabeth du Puy. Philip Veiller was a broker and the owner of syrup factories in Brooklyn and Illinois. As a result of family migrations connected with his father's business activities, Lawrence attended public and private schools in Chicago, Newton, Mass., and New York City. At the age of fourteen he entered the City College of New York, from which he received the B.A. in 1890. Veiller married Amy Hall in 1897; they had no children.

Veiller's interest in social issues was aroused during his college years by exposure to the writings of such English critics as Thomas Carlyle and John Ruskin. During the 1890's he worked as a volunteer for the University Settlement and Charity Organization Society of New York (COS). Direct contact with the poor convinced him that better housing was the key to social melioration. As a plan examiner in the city buildings department later in the decade, he acquired expertise in the technicalities of housing construction and finance.

Veiller's career as the nation's leading housing reformer was launched in 1898, when he persuaded the COS to establish a Tenement House Committee. He served as its executive officer until 1907, when the committee was absorbed into a broader Department for the Improvement of Social Conditions, which Veiller headed until 1935.

Veiller rose to national prominence in 1900–1901 as secretary of the New York State Tenement House Commission. This appointment enabled him to display the unique combination of talents that transformed the housing reform movement in the United States: political strategist, propagandist and lobbyist, technical adviser, legislative draftsman, and administrator. The commission's bill, devised by Veiller, led to the enactment of the New York State Tenement House Law of 1901, which prohibited further construction of the worst forms of low-income, multifamily housing in New York City. Veiller was also instrumental in the creation of the Tenement House Department of New York City, responsible for enforcement of the drastically revised housing code. He then organized the new department as its deputy commissioner in 1903–1904.

After 1900 Veiller frequently acted as consultant to citizen groups or official agencies considering housing legislation. In order to provide focus for the nationwide housing movement, he established the National Housing Association and served as director from 1911 to 1936. Also of national significance were the three volumes he published on the objectives and tactics of housing reform: *A Model Tenement House Law* (1910); *Housing Reform: A Hand-Book for Practical Use in American Cities* (1910); and *A Model Housing Law* (1914; rev. ed., 1920). In these various ways, Veiller influenced the content of most of the local and state housing legislation in the first two decades of the twentieth century.

If Veiller raised the housing reform movement in the United States to a new level of effectiveness and organization, he also helped ensure that it would be limited mainly to a strategy of regulatory legislation. Thus he consistently opposed emulation of European subsidy or public housing programs. His influence diminished in the 1920's, when it became apparent that while regulatory legislation might prevent the worst housing from being built, it could not ensure an adequate supply of good housing at low cost.

Closely related to the housing reform movement of the early twentieth century was the advocacy of zoning legislation. Veiller's contributions in this field included participation on the New York City Advisory Committee on the Height, Size and Arrangement of Buildings, whose report of 1913 served as the basis for the nation's first comprehensive zoning law in 1916. Veiller also prepared the Standard Zoning Law for the United States Department of Commerce in 1921. A long-time secondary interest concerned court reform, particularly the magistrate and children's court frequently encountered by the tenement population. He served as secretary of the COS Committee on Criminal Courts from 1911 to 1936 and was a member of the New York Citizens' Crime Commission from 1937 to 1940. He died in New York City.

Veiller's career signified a change in the nature of the social reform process. The moral imperatives of the nineteenth-century reformer, often religious in inspiration, were receding in favor of the bureaucratized technician and administrator. In the housing field, the transition was embodied in the contrast between Jacob Riis and Lawrence Veiller.

[Two valuable manuscript sources are Veiller's reminiscences, Oral History Collection, Columbia University; and a set of letters and documents on microfilm, also at Columbia. Veiller's most important publications include the three works cited above, as well as Robert W. DeForest and Lawrence Veiller, *The Tenement House Problem: Including the Report of the New York State Tenement House Commission of 1900* (1903). Veiller's role in the housing movement can be traced in the annual reports of the Charity Organization Society of New York, beginning in 1898. One of Veiller's most original contributions to housing reform is discussed in "The Tenement-House Exhibition of 1899," *Charities Review*, Mar. 1900. His views on the social consequences of substandard housing are expressed in "The Housing Problem in American Cities," *Annals of the American Academy of Political and Social Science*, Jan.–June 1905. For a detailed analysis of his career, see Roy Lubove, *The Progressives and the Slums* (1962).]

ROY LUBOVE

VON NEUMANN, JOHN (Dec. 28, 1903–Feb. 8, 1957), mathematician, theoretical physicist, and economist, was born in Budapest, Hungary, the son of Max von Neumann, a well-to-do banker, and Margaret Kann. While he was attending the Lutheran High School in Budapest, his mathematics teacher, L. Ratz, recognized von Neumann's abilities, provided books for him to read, and tutored him privately. However, because of the scarcity of positions for mathematicians in Hungary, it was decided that he should study chemistry. After attending the University of Berlin (1921–1923), he received the Ph.D. in chemistry at the Technische Hochschule in Zurich in 1926. That year he was also granted the Ph.D. in mathematics from the University of Budapest. Von Neumann was a Rockefeller fellow at the University of Göttingen (1925–1926) and then taught mathematics at the University of Berlin (1927–1929) and at the University of Hamburg (1929). His associations at Göttingen with Max Born, Lothar Nordheim, and David Hilbert stimulated his interest in quantum mechanics as well as mathematical logic. The former interest led him to provide a mathematically rigorous formulation of the foundations of quantum mechanics and also to one of his most important mathematical contributions, the spectral theory of unbounded self-adjoint operators in Hilbert space. His work in mathematical logic, although of great significance and ingenuity, was largely superseded by the contributions of Kurt Gödel. Nevertheless, his abiding interest in the subject greatly influenced his thinking in other areas, including computer theory.

On Jan. 1, 1930, von Neumann married Marietta Kövesi, the daughter of a prominent Budapest physician. Their daughter, Marina, became a member of the President's Council of Economic Advisors. That year he spent a term at Princeton University as visiting professor of mathematical physics. In 1931 he received an appointment to a professorship, first on a part-time basis and then full time. In 1933 he left the university and joined the staff of the Institute for Advanced Study, in Princeton, of which he remained a member until his death. Von

Neumann's first marriage ended in divorce, and on Dec. 18, 1938, he married Klári Dán. They had no children.

Despite his devotion to his adopted country, of which he became a citizen in 1937, von Neumann maintained close connections with relatives and friends in Hungary as well as with the Hungarian scientific community. His correspondence with the foremost Hungarian theoretical physicist of his time, R. Ortvay, was published in 1975; and he also published papers in Hungarian journals.

Recognizing the inevitability of armed conflict with Nazi Germany, von Neumann contributed to the realization of this danger by his American colleagues and also to the defense of the United States. Beginning in 1940 he was a member of several governmental agencies at various times, including the technical advisory panel on atomic energy of the Department of Defense and the weapons evaluation group of that department; he also served as chairman of the nuclear weapons committee of the U.S. Air Force scientific advisory panel. From 1943 to 1945 he worked in Los Alamos, N.M., on the development of the atomic bomb. A frequent visitor to the Aberdeen Proving Ground, he became a close associate of Robert H. Kent; and his contributions to research at that institution helped to remedy the insulation of the academic community from those working on national defense. His continuing interest in defense problems resulted in several published papers, mostly in collaboration with Kent. His early interest also resulted in an understanding of the nature of shock waves that was far superior to that of most physicists who later joined the defense effort. His suggestion to use converging shock waves to detonate the nuclear explosive was of decisive importance. His realization of the practical importance of obtaining solutions to nonlinear differential equations stimulated his interest in the presently accepted means of obtaining such solutions with computers.

After the war, von Neumann returned to the Institute for Advanced Study, where he served as director of the Electronic Computer Project from 1945 to 1955. He was largely responsible for the development and construction of the mathematical analyzer, numerical integrator, and computer (MANIAC), completed at the institute in 1952. The fastest and most accurate computer of its kind at that time, it was instrumental in speeding the work in the completion and testing of the hydrogen bomb later that year. From October 1954 until his death, von Neumann was a member of the U.S. Atomic Energy Commis-

sion. Lewis Strauss, chairman of the commission, commented: "If he analyzed a problem, it was not necessary to discuss it further. It was clear what had to be done." Von Neumann's *Theory of Games and Economic Behavior* (1944), written with Oskar Morgenstern, is the founding block of econometrics and of many mathematical studies of economics.

[The best review of von Neumann's contributions to science can be found in a booklet published as *Bulletin of the American Mathematical Society,* 64, pt. 2 (1958). His most remarkable books are *Mathematische Grundlagen der Quantenmechanik* (1932); *Theory of Games and Economic Behavior* (1944), written with O. Morgenstern; and *The Computer and the Brain* (1958). His articles include "Beweis des Ergodensatzes und des H-Theorems in der neuen Mechanik," *Zeitschrift für Physik* (1929); "Uber die Widerspruchfreiheitsfrage der axiomatischen Mengenlehre," *Journal für die reine und angewandte Mathematik* (1929); "Allgemeine Eigenwertstheorie Hermitischer Funktionaloperatoren," *Mathematische Annalen* (1929); and "Blast Wave Calculation," *Communications on Pure and Applied Mathematics,* VII (1955), written with H. H. Goldstine.]

EUGENE P. WIGNER

VON STROHEIM, ERICH (Sept. 22, 1885–May 12, 1957), film director and actor, was born in Vienna, Austria. He asserted that his full name was Erich Oswald Hans Carl Maria Stroheim von Nordenwald and that his father, Frederick von Nordenwald, was a major in the Imperial army. His mother, Johanna Bondy, was the sister of Emil von Bondy, an Imperial counselor.

Von Stroheim's claim to aristocratic status has been questioned. An alleged birth certificate stating that his parents were Jewish has been published in the British film magazine *Sight and Sound,* together with speculations about his family and social position.

Von Stroheim was educated at a preparatory boarding school and at the Mariahilfe Military Academy, from which he was graduated as a second lieutenant in 1901. Although trained for an army career, he had a keen interest in the arts, had a gift for sketching, was a good amateur musician, and read widely. His own future writing was particularly influenced by the "Young Vienna" group of 1900.

During the Bosnian campaign of 1908, von Stroheim served in the field and came under fire from Serbian irregulars. Upon returning to Vienna, he soon found himself crushed by debts. His family agreed to settle his obligations on condition that he leave Austria. He was given a one-way ticket to the United States, a small sum was deposited for him in a New York bank, and he sailed from Bremen in November 1909.

In New York City von Stroheim took menial employment and wrote for the German-language press. He also served for two years in the U.S. cavalry during this time but refused a commission in the Mexican army. As an agent for a hat firm he traveled to San Francisco in 1912. There in 1913 he married Margaret Knox, who helped him perfect his English and collaborated with him in writing stories and plays. They were divorced in 1914. Von Stroheim then worked as a railroad section hand and as a handyman at a Lake Tahoe inn. A chance acquaintance at the resort read his play *Brothers* and promised to finance its production in Los Angeles. He then obtained a job as an ostler, and arrived in Los Angeles in charge of a carload of horses for a riding stable. The play had a single, disastrous performance on a vaudeville program. Von Stroheim then began to haunt the casting agencies for film work. D. W. Griffith chose him from the "extra" pool to play a black Confederate soldier in *The Birth of a Nation*, which led to other bit parts and stunt-man assignments.

John Emerson, a director on Griffith's staff, hired von Stroheim as his assistant. The new assignment took him to New York City, where von Stroheim married May Jones, a theatrical costume designer, in 1917; they had one son. Later that year they were divorced, and in 1919 he married Valerie Germonprez. They had one son.

Von Stroheim acted in the Griffith spectacles *Intolerance* (1917) and *Hearts of the World* (1918) and in Emerson's productions, and was typecast as the dastardly Prussian officer of war propaganda films. While playing this customary role at Universal Studios he met Carl Laemmle, president of the company. Von Stroheim recounted a scenario he had written, and Laemmle offered to buy it. But von Stroheim insisted that only he could direct it and play its leading role. He was so persuasive that Laemmle agreed. The resulting film was *Blind Husbands* (1919), in which von Stroheim portrayed an Austrian lieutenant attempting to seduce the wife of an American doctor holidaying in the Tyrol. The great success of the film made von Stroheim a star and a directorial talent to be reckoned with. He followed it with the popular *The Devil's Passkey* (1920),

which he wrote and directed, but in which he did not appear. It concerned an American couple, a playwright and his pretty wife, bewildered by the continental mores and temptations of Paris.

Next came a glittering, luxurious spectacle, *Foolish Wives* (1922), advertised by Laemmle as "the first million dollar motion picture." Von Stroheim played an émigré czarist officer preying on wealthy, idle women. A sensational success, it was banned in some cities in the United States.

Von Stroheim next wrote and directed *Merry-go-Round,* a tale of prewar Vienna. Irving Thalberg, a young executive appointed production chief at Universal, became alarmed at the mounting costs of the filming and abruptly dismissed von Stroheim. *Merry-Go-Round* was completed in 1923 by Rupert Julian, who received sole directorial credit although he had followed von Stroheim's carefully planned shooting script.

The Goldwyn Studio then offered von Stroheim an enticing contract, promising him an absolutely free hand, a high salary, and his own choice of subjects. He prepared an adaptation of Frank Norris's novel *McTeague,* giving it the title *Greed.* Opposed to the star system, he cast its important roles with little-known players, such as ZaSu Pitts, Gibson Gowland, and Jean Hersholt. He trained his players in a school of acting. He could draw unsuspected qualities from typed stars—for example, Mae Murray, John Gilbert, and Gloria Swanson. Von Stroheim was determined to make *Greed* a naturalistic epic after the manner of Émile Zola. To emphasize its realism the entire film was shot on locations in the mean streets of San Francisco, in Oakland parks, and in the Mojave Desert.

Meanwhile, the Goldwyn Company had merged with the Metro Company, and Louis B. Mayer—with Thalberg as his aide—had been placed in charge of production at the Metro-Goldwyn-Mayer (MGM) studios. Von Stroheim's first version of *Greed* was in forty-two reels and ran for nine hours. He proposed that it be released in two—or possibly three—sections, but Mayer rejected this unconventional plan. Eventually the film was turned over to a hack studio cutter who slashed it down to ten reels. In this unsatisfactory condition it was released in December 1924, with scant success. Since then it has been hailed as a masterpiece.

For MGM von Stroheim directed his own adaptation of Franz Lehar's operetta *The Merry Widow* (1925), with Mae Murray and John

Gilbert. A film of wide appeal, it is reported to have earned more than $5 million. In 1926 American critics voted von Stroheim the best director of the year. He also became an American citizen in that year.

Resenting the supervision of Mayer and Thalberg and embittered by their destruction of *Greed*, von Stroheim broke his contract with MGM. Pat Powers, an independent producer, offered to finance his next film, *The Wedding March*, another drama of Vienna on the eve of World War I. Von Stroheim played the principal role. He engaged a screen novice, Fay Wray, to play the abandoned heroine and ZaSu Pitts to portray the crippled bride.

The production was of stunning opulence. *The Wedding March* was before the cameras for seven months (June 1926–January 1927), after which Powers, anxious to profit from his investment immediately, halted the shooting. Only a few bridging scenes remained unrealized and the enormous footage was divided into two separate films: *The Wedding March* and *Honeymoon*. *The Wedding March* opened in New York in October 1928, to mixed reviews. It was a commercial success both at home and abroad, but producers were wary about the expense of his productions. Von Stroheim forbade the release of *Honeymoon* in the United States, since he had had no hand in its editing, but it was shown later in Europe and South America.

Early in 1928, when *The Wedding March* was being edited by others, Joseph P. Kennedy, the Boston financier who had become involved in films, engaged von Stroheim to write and direct a film for Gloria Swanson. His script, entitled *Queen Kelly*, carried its heroine from a convent school in a German principality to a German colony in East Africa, where she had inherited a hotel at a jungle outpost. The Hays censorship office disapproved of certain episodes, which were eliminated from the shooting script, but during filming von Stroheim slyly restored them in slightly modified form. This procedure, and the fact that *Queen Kelly* was being shot as a silent film after the firm establishment of the "talkies," caused Kennedy and Swanson to discontinue its production when it was three-fourths completed. Swanson later assembled its first half and released it abroad.

Von Stroheim directed only one other film, *Walking Down Broadway* (1933), for the Fox studios. Using a play by Dawn Powell, von Stroheim, with Leonard Spigelgass as his col-

laborator, gave a story of provincials seeking their fortunes in New York some characteristic revisions. The finished film, judged unmarketable by studio officials, was never released. A few scenes were incorporated into a reworking of its scenario known as *Hello, Sister* (1933).

Rejected as a director, von Stroheim returned to acting, appearing as a mad music-hall ventriloquist in James Cruze's *Great Gabbo* (1929); as a fanatically realistic movie director in *The Lost Squadron* (1931); as a treacherous German diplomat in India in *Friends and Lovers* (1931) with Laurence Olivier and Adolphe Menjou; and as a sadistic novelist in *As You Desire Me* with Greta Garbo in an adaptation of the Pirandello play (1931). He also took roles in minor films of the "poverty row" studios and at one point—1934—was reduced to being a wardrobe consultant at MGM. In 1935 he went bankrupt and moved to the MGM story department. (A script he wrote at this time, "Between Two Women," set in a city hospital, was filmed in 1937 after he had success in the French cinema.) In Hollywood he was viewed as a passé figure, a defeated survivor of the irresponsible 1920's, when he had imposed his reckless, ruinous dictatorship on million-dollar productions. The Mayer-Thalberg system of production control by then had been adopted by all the major studios.

In 1936, von Stroheim was invited to Paris to play opposite Edwige Feuillère in a World War I espionage film, *Marthe Richard*. He scored a resounding success as the disabled German officer in Jean Renoir's *Grand Illusion* (1938). Renoir allowed him full liberty to rewrite and embroider the role of the aristocratic soldier. After *Grand Illusion* he starred in a series of popular French films and was scheduled to direct a film, but the plan was interrupted by the outbreak of war. He returned to Hollywood to play in *I Was an Adventuress* (1940), in *So Ends Our Night* (1940), and (as General Rommel) in *Five Graves to Cairo* (1943). In early 1941 he opened in Baltimore in the comedy *Arsenic and Old Lace* and toured until the end of 1942, when he replaced Boris Karloff in the Broadway production.

In 1945, von Stroheim returned to France and made several films there, including a screen version of Strindberg's *Dance of Death* (1948). In 1949, at the request of Billy Wilder, he came back to Hollywood for his last appearance in an American film, *Sunset Boulevard* (1950), in which he played a director who has become the butler of a former movie queen, Gloria Swanson. To celebrate this reunion of Miss Swanson and her quondam director, an excerpt from *Queen Kelly* was included in *Sunset Boulevard.*

During the early 1950's von Stroheim acted in French films, among them Sacha Guitry's *Napoleon*, in which he portrayed Beethoven. He devoted much time to writing, still hoping he might have the opportunity to direct again. He prepared several scenarios in his customary exacting fashion. His novel *Paprika* (1935) had had good sales in the United States and England, and was translated into French, Dutch, and Portuguese. He wrote a two-volume novel in French, *Les Feux de la Saint-Jean* (1951–1954), and followed it with *Poto-Poto* (1956), from an unrealized screenplay. He was preparing to write his memoirs when he died at Maurepas, Seine-et-Oise, France.

Von Stroheim was one of the great creative artists of the cinema. He learned the technique of film-making during his apprenticeship under Griffith; but while Griffith, with his sentimental Victorianism, was old-fashioned by the end of World War I, von Stroheim came forward as the new master of American cinematography in the early 1920's. He introduced a bolder treatment of sex, much of it influenced by continental writers Émile Zola, Guy de Maupassant, and Arthur Schnitzler.

Von Stroheim considered himself a Zolaesque realist, though in his films realism—as in Zola—was often stylized into a sort of surrealism of Strindberg's nightmare visions, while the drab and dull were touched up with grotesque, humorous detail. His fabled extravagances, much exaggerated by publicity agents and journalists, his demand that all detail be convincing regardless of expense, lent depth to his films. His often graphic reproduction of the sordid was imitated by other directors—Josef von Sternberg, King Vidor, and William Wyler—and his treatment of sexual relationships influenced Luis Buñuel. His masterful direction has seldom been equaled. Sergei Eisenstein cited him as "The Director." His indifference to money was an inborn trait, causing both his exile from Austria and his exile from direction in Hollywood.

[Biographies are Peter Noble, *Hollywood Scapegoat* (1951; repr. 1979); and Thomas Quinn Curtiss, *Von Stroheim* (1971). Two books of stills, with informative text, are by Herman Weinberg: *The Complete "Greed"* (1973) and *The Complete "Wedding March"* (1975). See also Denis Marion, "Stroheim, the Legend and

the Fact," in *Sight and Sound* (London), Winter 1961–1962, which includes an alleged birth certificate of von Stroheim's and argues that the director-actor misrepresented his origins.]

THOMAS QUINN CURTISS

WADSWORTH, ELIOT (Sept. 10, 1876–May 29, 1959), financier, philanthropist, and assistant secretary of the Treasury, was born in Boston, Mass., the son of Oliver Fairfield Wadsworth and Mary Chapman Goodwin. He attended Hale's School in Boston and received the B.A. degree from Harvard University in 1898.

After graduation Wadsworth worked briefly for the Planters' Compress Company in East Boston and then joined the electrical engineering firm of Stone and Webster in Boston, becoming a partner in 1907. He retired at the end of 1916 because of pressing war work, but continued on the board of directors.

Wadsworth spent considerable time in Russia and eastern Europe between 1914 and 1916 in his work for the European Relief Commission of the Rockefeller Foundation and the American Red Cross. His activities brought him the Distinguished Service Medal from President Woodrow Wilson and decorations from the Belgian and Polish governments.

In 1916, Wadsworth began a lifelong connection with the Red Cross, when he accepted appointment as vice-chairman of the Central Committee, a post he held until 1919. He served as a member of the Central Committee from 1921 to 1942, as national treasurer from 1921 to 1926, and as chairman of the Retirement Board from 1937 to 1956. He represented the United States at Geneva in 1929, at the Conference for Rewriting the Red Cross Convention and in the drafting of the new Prisoners of War Convention.

In 1919, Wadsworth became chairman of the Executive Committee of the Harvard Endowment Fund, helping to raise $15 million dollars within two years. He served as president of the Harvard Alumni Association from 1920 to 1926. He also sat on the Board of Overseers of Harvard for twelve years, becoming president of the board in 1929. On July 10, 1922, he married Nancy Whitman Scull. They had one daughter.

As assistant secretary of the Treasury from 1921 to 1925, during the administrations of Warren Harding and Calvin Coolidge, Wadsworth represented the United States at the Paris conference in 1923 to discuss costs of maintaining American forces in Germany. He also served as secretary to the World War Foreign Debt Commission from 1923 to 1925, in particular, negotiating with the British regarding their debt refunding agreement.

Wadsworth was a member of the Massachusetts legislature from 1926 to 1932 and chairman of the Board of Commissioners of the Sinking Fund for the City of Boston from 1926 to 1929 and from 1934 to 1940. From 1933 to 1939 he was president of the Boston Chamber of Commerce, also acting as director of the Chamber of Commerce of the United States from 1934 to 1940, and as chairman of the American section of the International Chamber of Commerce from 1937 to 1945.

In the fall of 1930, President Herbert Hoover sent Wadsworth to Santo Domingo to investigate conditions after a major hurricane. Hoover also appointed him, in 1931, as chairman of the Committee on Cooperation with National Groups and Associations within the president's Organization on Unemployment Relief, an effort to fight the Great Depression. In 1932, Wadsworth represented American investors on the League Loans Commission in London. In the 1940's he was treasurer and trustee for the Carnegie Endowment for International Peace; and in 1950 President Harry S. Truman appointed him a member of the Loyalty Review Board of the Civil Service Commission, a post he retained until 1953. Wadsworth died in Washington, D.C.

[Wadsworth's career and travels are chronicled in the reports of the Harvard class of 1898, especially the twenty-fifth, fortieth, and fiftieth anniversary issues. Obituaries appear in the *Boston Traveler*, May 29, 1959; and *New York Times* and *Boston Herald*, May 30, 1959.]

     SUSAN ESTABROOK KENNEDY

WALKER, FRANK COMERFORD (May 30, 1886–Sept. 13, 1959), politician, postmaster general, and lawyer, was born in Plymouth, Pa., the son of David Walker, a miner and merchant, and Ellen Comerford. The eleventh of fourteen children, he grew up in the frontier mining town of Butte, Mont., where his father had sought his fortune in 1889 and died of silicosis in 1901. With middle-class status acquired, the children were raised and educated in the Catholic faith that meant so much to Ellen Walker. Frank attended Gonzaga University in Spokane, Wash., from 1903 to 1906 and took the LL.B. at Notre Dame in 1909. After returning to Butte, he entered practice with his brother Thomas, won election to the state legislature in 1912, and married Hallie Victoria Boucher on Nov. 11, 1914. They had two children. After spending only one term in the legislature, Walker returned to his law practice before serving as a first lieutenant in World War I. Although his firm prospered, Walker moved to New York City in 1924 to aid in managing the growing theatrical enterprises of his uncle, Michael E. Comerford, in Pennsylvania and New York.

In New York, the citadel of Irish-Catholic political activism, Walker's taste for the game returned. Having amassed a modest personal fortune, he was first attracted to the career of his coreligionist, Alfred E. Smith. After Smith's defeat in 1928, Walker became an enthusiast and financial backer of Franklin D. Roosevelt. By early 1931 he was a key member of the Roosevelt for President Club and launched a successful drive for funds, contributing $20,000 personally and soliciting large donations from Joseph P. Kennedy and others. After Roosevelt's nomination in 1932, Walker became treasurer of the Democratic National Committee.

Roosevelt appreciated Walker's support and called upon him for various services during the next twelve years. In July 1933 Walker became secretary of the president's executive council to coordinate activities of the new emergency agencies with existing government bureaus. When the president established the National Emergency Council in December 1933, Walker assumed the position of executive secretary and served until December 1935, refereeing the struggle between Harold Ickes and Harry Hopkins over who would become master of federal relief spending.

Even before Hopkins pushed ahead with the Works Progress Administration, Walker happily returned to New York and resumed his financial career. But the respite was temporary. He reappeared to raise funds for the 1936 campaign but again faded from the Washington scene until 1940. At that time he became an early and vigorous proponent of a third term for Roosevelt. Faced with the defection of James Farley as postmaster general, Roosevelt turned to Walker as a replacement. On Aug. 31, 1940, he became postmaster general and served until June 30, 1945. During the 1940 campaign he solicited support from leading Catholic prelates. In July

1944, he was involved in the decision to promote the vice-presidential candidacy of Harry Truman. Walker also served from January 1943 until January 1944 as chairman of the Democratic National Committee.

During World War II Walker originated V-mail: streamlined mail delivery through the use of microfilm and helicopter service to the troops. He became a major news item in December 1943, when the Post Office revoked the second-class mailing privileges of *Esquire* on the grounds of obscenity. The magazine finally obtained reinstatement in June 1945, when the United States Appeals Court overturned Walker's order.

With Roosevelt's death in April 1945, Walker's political career came to an end. After resigning from the Cabinet, he served as an alternate delegate to the first United Nations General Assembly meeting in December 1945. The appointment was criticized by Senator William Fulbright, who considered Walker poorly qualified and publicly questioned his knowledge of foreign affairs. Even without such criticism Walker had every reason to return to private life. He had always considered politics a hobby, and his commitment was more to Roosevelt than to government. His business and social responsibilities had grown enormously over the years. He ran the Comerford Corporation, was director of several banks in the East, and worked extensively in Catholic education and charities. At the time of his death, in New York City, he had made important contributions as a fund raiser for and lay trustee of Notre Dame.

Walker has not been given much credit by historians for his New Deal work, although his outstanding personal qualities, and especially his loyalty and honesty, have been acknowledged. Even such chronic faultfinders as Ickes and Hopkins admired his fairness. But his shyness and dilettantish approach presented problems in a cast of political activists.

Walker's significance must be sought not in New Deal legislation, although he did contribute to both the Banking Act of 1933 and the National Housing Act of June 1934, but in the added political dimension that he brought to the president. Roosevelt needed a man such as Walker as an honest broker and frequently used him to perform distasteful chores involving Ickes, Farley, and James Byrnes. A progressive in politics, Walker believed in the system of middle-class democracy. Despite his misgivings about the class bias of some New Dealers, Walker kept open the lines of communication between the president and his moderate business supporters. He played the same role with Catholics through his influence with the hierarchy. He promoted an honorary degree for Roosevelt from Notre Dame, thereby undermining the criticism of Father Charles Coughlin, and played amateur diplomat with Maryknoll missionaries seeking to promote a reconciliation with Japan in early 1941.

[The Frank C. Walker papers are in the University of Notre Dame Archives; the major emphasis is on Democratic party finances from 1932 to 1945, but several documents also deal with Walker's role in the aborted negotiations with the Japanese in 1941. The Franklin Roosevelt Library, Hyde Park, N.Y., has material in President's Personal Files 258 and 1126, and Official File 1952; the collection is rather thin. Perhaps the best scholarly treatment of Walker (to 1935) is Paul L. Simon, "Frank Walker, New Dealer" (Ph.D. thesis, Notre Dame University, 1965). There is scattered information in Bernard F. Bonahoe, *Private Plans and Public Dangers* (1965); and in the published memoirs of James Farley, Edward Flynn, Cordell Hull, Samuel Rosenman, Harold Ickes, and Marrimer Eccles. See also the obituary notice, *New York Times*, Sept. 14, 1959.]

GEORGE Q. FLYNN

WALSH, EDMUND ALOYSIUS (Oct. 10, 1885–Oct. 31, 1956), Roman Catholic clergyman, educator, and author, was born in Boston, Mass., the son of John Francis Walsh, a policeman, and Catherine Josephine Noonan. He attended schools in Boston and Dorchester, and then Boston College High School, where he was a good student and a member of the track team.

In 1902 Walsh entered the Society of Jesus at its novitiate in Frederick, Md. Seven years later, having completed undergraduate studies at Woodstock College, Md., he was assigned to teach at Georgetown Prep in Washington, D.C. After three years he went to the National University at Dublin and to London University for further study of the classics. In September 1913, Walsh began theological studies at Innsbruck, Austria, but the outbreak of World War I in 1914 forced him to complete his theology course at Woodstock College, where he received the M.A. and was ordained in 1916. After a further year of study, he returned to Georgetown University and, in May 1918, became dean of the College of Arts and Sciences.

Almost immediately Walsh was appointed by the War Department to a board of five educators who were to coordinate studies for the Students' Army Training Corps, and served as its educational director for the New England area. This experience convinced him that American education gave insufficient attention to the study of international relations, diplomacy, and foreign languages. In 1919 he established the School of Foreign Service at Georgetown to meet these needs. Despite his numerous absences from the campus, the school remained Walsh's major interest until his death. He served as its regent until 1952, regularly taught in the program, and took every opportunity to advance its work. In 1920 he completed his doctorate at Georgetown and in 1924 became vice-president of the university.

In February 1922, Walsh was summoned to Rome and directed to survey famine conditions in Russia and, if possible, to arrange an affiliation of the proposed Papal Relief Mission with the American Famine Relief Mission already operating in the Soviet Union. Walsh arranged the affiliation, and became director of the Papal Relief Mission and a member of the American mission. In addition he was named Vatican representative for safeguarding the interests of the Catholic Church in Russia. Dealing first with the famine, Walsh directed the activities of the dozen other members of his band in Moscow, Petrograd, Rostov, and the Crimea, and soon was feeding 150,000 children a day.

With the relief operation in full swing, Walsh turned to the safeguarding of clergy and church property in Russia. Despite strenuous efforts, he had little success in deflecting or delaying Soviet aims with respect to religious liberty. His experience convinced him that the antipathy of the Russian leadership to religion and to the humanistic values of the West would prove dangerous. Walsh took it as his task to alert Americans to the danger: he introduced a course called "Russia in Revolution" at the School of Foreign Service, built the Russian holdings of the school, and began to lecture widely on the Russian experiment and its implications. His first book, *The Fall of the Russian Empire* (1928), was not so much a chronicle of the last years of the Romanovs as a study of the methodology and philosophy of the Bolsheviks. *The Last Stand* (1931) analyzed the first Five-Year Plan and its relation to the ultimate aims of the Soviet government.

From 1926 to 1931 Walsh was president of the Catholic Near East Welfare Association. In 1929 he served with Ambassador Dwight Morrow and Miguel Cruchaga on a special commission in Mexico that facilitated a relaxation of tensions between the Mexican government and the Catholic Church. In 1931, as papal legate, he established the basis upon which the American College in Baghdad was founded by the Society of Jesus in 1932. In 1934 he published *Ships and National Safety*, a brief argument for the redevelopment of the American merchant marine. In 1935 and 1939 he was a visiting lecturer at the Academy of International Law, The Hague, and in 1942 became a consultant to the War Department.

After World War II, Walsh served as a civilian consultant to the chief American counsel, Robert H. Jackson, at the Nuremberg war crimes trials, and in 1947–1948 was visitor general of the Society of Jesus in Japan, where he recommended reorganization of its missions and educational efforts. In 1949 he published *Total Power*, an analysis of the anatomy and abuse of power as illustrated by the rise and fall of the Nazi movement. *Total Empire*, his study of communist geopolitical aims, strategy, and tactics, appeared in 1951. Until 1952 he continued to lecture widely under private auspices and at such institutions as the Army War College and the National Police Academy. Walsh was a member of President Harry S. Truman's commissions on universal military training and on religion and welfare in the armed forces, and served on the Academic Advisory Board of the U.S. Merchant Marine Academy. In 1949 he established the Institute of Languages and Linguistics at Georgetown.

Walsh's lectures and publications and the influence of the School of Foreign Service were such that in 1952 the *Christian Century* could assert that no "other Roman Catholic . . . has had an impact on the policy of the United States government since World War I to compare with" Walsh's. For the last four years of his life Walsh was an invalid, frequently hospitalized but always planning a return to his work. He died in Washington, D.C. In 1958 the School of Foreign Service was named in his honor.

[Walsh's papers are at Georgetown University. A biography is Louis J. Gallagher. S.J., *Edmund A. Walsh, S.J.* (1962). His obituary is in *New York Times*, Nov. 1, 1956.]

J. F. Mahoney

WALSH, EDWARD AUGUSTINE (May 14, 1881–May 26, 1959), baseball pitcher, called Big Ed, was born in Plains, Pa., in the heart of coal country. In 1902, after a brief period at the University of Pennsylvania, Walsh signed with the Wilkes-Barre team of the Pennsylvania State League. Because a miners' strike made it a financial burden for fans to go to games, the league folded; but Walsh's catcher, Frank Burke, wrote C. J. Danaher, a stockholder in the Meriden club of the Connecticut League, and Danaher offered Walsh $125 a month to play there. Walsh demanded $150 a month and got it. He joined the Chicago White Sox in 1906. Though only a rookie, he became one of the team's leaders, winning nineteen games and leading the "Hitless Wonders," as the punchless team was called, to the American League pennant.

In the 1906 World Series against the Chicago Cubs, Walsh won two games, striking out seventeen batters in the fifteen innings he pitched. That year the series ended in a four-two victory for the White Sox. Pitching between 1906 and 1913 during the "dead ball" era, Walsh won 194 games for the weak-hitting White Sox. He shut out the opposition 58 times, and his career earned-run average, 1.82 runs per nine innings, is a major league record.

Walsh was one of a handful of successful spitball pitchers. He learned to throw the pitch from teammate Elmer Stricklett when Walsh joined the White Sox in 1906. Stricklett himself learned to throw it from its discoverer, George Hildebrand. It was this pitch that made Walsh a star. In Larry Ritter's *The Glory of Their Times* (1966), Detroit Tiger Hall of Famer Sam Crawford described what it was like facing Walsh: "I think that the ball disintegrated on the way to the plate, and the catcher put it back together again. I swear, when it went past it was just the spit that went by."

At six feet, one inch and 190 pounds, Walsh was a strong right-hander who never seemed to tire. Twice he pitched and won both games of a doubleheader (1908), allowing just one run in the two games. On Aug. 27, 1911, Walsh threw a no-hit game against the Boston Red Sox. A detailed account of the game is given in James T. Farrell's 1936 novel *A World I Never Made*.

After Walsh's successful rookie year in 1906, he won twenty-eight games, and in 1908 he compiled one of the greatest single-season records in the history of the game. That year Walsh won forty games. Only Jack Chesbro, with forty-one wins in 1904, has won more. Walsh finished 40-15 in 1908, pitching in sixty-six games, completing fifty-two of them, and pitching 464 innings, a major league record for innings pitched in a season. In 1908 Walsh was earning a salary of $3,500, but Chicago owner Charles Comiskey at the end of the season rewarded Walsh's excellence with a $3,500 bonus.

Walsh's forty wins were not enough for the White Sox to win the pennant in 1908, however. The team was in the race until the final week, when on Oct. 2, in one of the classic games of baseball history, Cleveland star pitcher Addie Joss defeated Walsh 1-0 to end Chicago's pennant chances. Walsh allowed four hits and one run on an error and a wild pitch. Joss pitched a perfect game, retiring all twenty-seven White Sox batters.

After Walsh won twenty-seven games each in 1911 and 1912, his arm gave out in 1913. That year he appeared in only sixteen games, winning eight of them. His career effectively was over, though he fought to stay in baseball as a player. Walsh was traded in 1917 to the Boston Braves, with whom he was but 0-1. He pitched in the minor leagues in 1919 and 1920.

After spending 1922 as an American League umpire, Walsh rejoined the White Sox as a coach from 1923 to 1925 and from 1928 to 1930. In 1926 he coached baseball at the University of Notre Dame. Walsh's two sons briefly played major-league baseball. Ed, Jr., had a short career with the White Sox, and Robert spent one year on the Yankee roster, though he did not win any games. Ed Walsh died in Pompano Beach, Fla.

[The statistics on Walsh are in the *Baseball Encyclopedia* (1969); it must be noted that the *Encyclopedia*, which updated players' records using a computer, credits Walsh with only thirty-nine wins in 1908. However, Hall of Fame records credit him with forty. Memorabilia and news clippings are in the National Baseball Hall of Fame, Cooperstown, N.Y. Information on Walsh can be found in Robert Smith, *Baseball's Hall of Fame* (1965); Ken Smith, *Baseball's Hall of Fame* (1958); and Harold Seymour, *Baseball, The Golden Age* (1971). An obituary of Walsh is in the *New York Times*, May 27, 1959.]

PETER J. GOLENBOCK

WARBASSE, JAMES PETER (Nov. 22, 1866–Feb. 22, 1957), surgeon and sociologist, was born in Newton, N.J., the son of Joseph Warbasse, a merchant, and Harriet Delphine Northrup. Among his mother's ancestors was a sister of Benjamin Franklin. James received an excellent education at the Newton Collegiate Institute, from which he graduated in 1885. Considered too young to proceed directly to medical school, he spent a year at home, working by day and studying at night in his father's well-stocked library. Here he absorbed the writings of Darwin, Huxley, Tyndall, Paine, and Ingersoll, developing the liberal trend of thought that was to characterize him throughout life.

At Columbia University's College of Physicians and Surgeons Warbasse attracted the attention of the surgeon Lewis Stephen Pilcher, then editor of the *Annals of Surgery*. Pilcher encouraged the eager young man to write by giving him books to review and also stimulated his interest in the historical aspects of medicine. Warbasse, who was to become a prolific writer, later acknowledged the release obtained from putting his thoughts on paper, thus satisfying "an inward desire for expression—to do things." Following graduation with the M.D. in 1889, he interned for two years at the Methodist Episcopal Hospital of Brooklyn and then left for a year of postgraduate study in Europe. He studied at Göttingen under the pathologist Johannes Orth and the surgeon Franz König, but what proved ultimately to be of even greater importance was the fact that at Göttingen Warbasse received his first direct introduction to the cooperative movement, which was to play such a vital role in his subsequent career. Later he continued to Vienna, where he spent several months under Theodor Billroth, then the most famous surgeon in Europe.

After returning to the United States in 1892, Warbasse joined the staff of the Methodist Hospital as assistant attending surgeon, where he set up the first American laboratory devoted exclusively to the pathology and bacteriology of surgical diseases, including cancer. He also received an appointment in 1903 at the German (now Wyckoff Heights) Hospital, of which he became chief surgeon in 1906. His practice was interrupted in 1898 by army service in the Spanish-American War. The horrors of combat seem to have accentuated an antimilitary bias that Warbasse claimed was characteristic of his family and that made him a lifelong pacifist. After the war he began to take a more active interest in organized medicine, serving the Kings County Medical Society as censor, chairman of the historical commission, and directing librarian (1905–1908). During this period he was also editor of the *New York State Journal of Medicine*.

In the meantime, on Apr. 15, 1903, Warbasse had married Agnes Dyer; they had six children. Charming and intelligent as well as wealthy, she entered closely into the sociological subjects that were already beginning to take up much of Warbasse's thoughts. They began a serious study of the radical movements of the period.

Warbasse admitted that he "was naturally in-

clined to look into something that somebody condemned." This inquisitiveness led him to study labor unionism, the IWW, socialism, the single-tax system, and anarchism. For one reason or another none of these proved entirely satisfying. At the same time he was becoming increasingly disenchanted with the economics of the medical profession as then practiced. He felt that medicine, the noblest of all pursuits, should be as deeply involved with the ills of society as with those of the body, and should speak out more vigorously against the laissez-faire tenets of contemporary capitalism. What was the point of operating on an individual, only to send him back to quarters where disease and malnutrition were rampant? Warbasse's voice was one of the first to be raised (1907) against the then popular, though often unnecessary, operation of appendectomy. This position, taken long before the antibiotic era, reflects the caution with which Warbasse regarded all surgical procedures. In "Are There Too Many Doctors?" (1912), he excoriated the profession for exploiting disease for mercenary reasons. Two years later the *Journal of the American Medical Association*, perhaps unaware of the controversial aspects of the subject, printed "The Socialization of Medicine," an article by Warbasse. His thoughts were best expressed in the following statement: "The knowledge and skill which have the power of preventing disease, relieving suffering, and prolonging life should be available to all. They should not be purchaseable by some and denied to others, nor bestowed as a charity upon any. Health and life are too precious to be at the mercy of trade and barter."

Such statements did not tend to endear him to the conservative medical establishment, and Warbasse began to consider withdrawing entirely from the practice of surgery. Having decided that the cooperative movement was the one most sympathetic to his own beliefs, in 1916 he became the first president of the Cooperative League of America, a position he was to hold for twenty-five years. A year earlier his wife, the largest stockholder of the Dennison Manufacturing Company, had shown complete sympathy with her husband's advanced views by turning over this $6 million concern to employee control.

During World War I Warbasse banded together with Roger Baldwin, Max Eastman, Lilian Wald, John Haynes Holmes, and others to form the American Union Against Militarism. Because of his radical views he was suspended from membership in the Kings County Medical Society on Apr. 17, 1918. Soon afterward he renounced his profession, having had the satisfaction of seeing published his successful three-volume *Surgical Treatment* (1918–1919).

Now fully launched on his crusade to improve society, Warbasse traveled widely, speaking in every state of the union. His *Cooperative Democracy* (1923) ran through five editions and was translated into several languages.

Warbasse refused to become discouraged at a lack of response that would have discouraged a less resilient person. After a disillusioning trip to the Soviet Union in 1924, he strongly resisted the attempts of the Communists to infiltrate American liberal movements. In 1933 he was invited by President Frank L. Babbitt, Jr., of the Long Island College of Medicine to give the first course in medical sociology ever taught. Designed to give the future physician "a broad conception of his relation to human affairs and social conditions," these lectures led to *The Doctor and the Public* (1935), directed to the profession, and *Cooperative Medicine* (1936), intended for the layman. During his later years Warbasse remained true to his liberal convictions, supporting the Spanish insurgents, civil liberties, birth control, the right to abortion, workmen's compensation, women's liberation, and similar causes.

After the death of his wife in 1945, Warbasse reduced his activities and became more deeply introspective. But his final decade showed little evidence of physical or mental decay. He continued to travel, to ski, and to chop wood. He wrote incessantly. In 1956 he produced the autobiographical *Three Voyages. North Star* (1958), written in the last year of his life, was the final summation of his credo. He died at Woods Hole, Mass. His name is memorialized in the Amalgamated Warbasse Houses of Brooklyn, a mammoth project containing over 2,500 apartments.

[On Warbasse and his career, see the *New York World*, Apr. 12, 1915; the *New York Times*, Jan. 7, 1933; James Peter Warbasse, *Three Voyages* (1956); the obituary notices, *New York Times*, Feb. 24, 1957; and *Journal of the American Medical Association*, June 15, 1957; Warbasse's autobiographical *North Star* (1958); and Frank L. Babbitt, Jr., "Doctors Afield, James P. Warbasse," *New England Journal of Medicine*, Feb. 6, 1958, the best account by a close associate.]

MORRIS H. SAFFRON

WARNER, EDWARD PEARSON (Nov. 9, 1894–July 12, 1958), aeronautical engineer and international civil servant, was born in Pittsburgh, Pa., the son of Robert Lyon Warner and Ann Pearson. His father, an electrical engineer, moved the family to Cambridge, Mass., when Warner was young. He attended the Volkmann School in Boston, and at an early age displayed a capacity for arithmetic and numbers that awed and impressed his contemporaries throughout his professional lifetime. Interested in flight while still a schoolboy, he and a friend built a glider with which they won a soaring meet at Boston in 1911. Warner provided the design and technical detail, leaving his friend to do the actual piloting.

Warner graduated from Harvard with honors in 1916, and received a B.S. degree from the Massachusetts Institute of Technology (MIT) the next year. While completing course work for the M.S. at MIT in 1919, he was also an instructor in aeronautical engineering. Warner became the chief physicist for the National Advisory Committee for Aeronautics (NACA) in 1919–1920 and served as the NACA technical attaché in Europe in 1920. As chief physicist he also designed and supervised the construction of the first wind tunnel used by NACA, and began a series of technical reports and writings for NACA publications.

Warner returned to MIT in 1920, as associate professor of aeronautical engineering; he had been promoted to professor by 1926. He was a rapid-fire lecturer, highly professional and somewhat aloof in his relationships with students, and possessed of a prodigious knowledge of mathematics. He could work complex formulas in his head. His students at MIT included a number of aeronautical pioneers: General James Doolittle, and such significant aviation designers as Leroy Grumman and James McDonnell. Warner also served on the President's Aircraft Board in 1925, beginning a long commitment to private and public policy studies activities.

Warner left MIT to become assistant secretary of the navy for aeronautics in 1926, and for the next three years he played a leading role in the development of naval aviation as an integral arm of the American military capability. As editor of *Aviation* magazine (published by McGraw-Hill) from 1929 to 1934, his technical expertise and firsthand experience in the development of aeronautical policy helped make the publication into the leading American aviation journal of the day. He married Joan Potter in 1931; they had two children.

While continuing as editor of *Aviation*, Warner also became editorial assistant to the president of McGraw-Hill Publications and helped organize the Institute of the Aeronautical Sciences (which became the American Institute of Aeronautics and Astronautics in 1963). In 1929 he was appointed a member of the National Advisory Committee for Aeronautics, a position he held until 1945. Warner also was active in the Society of Automotive Engineers, serving as president in 1930.

In 1934–1935, Warner was again drawn into public service as vice-chairman of the Federal Aviation Commission, appointed by President Franklin D. Roosevelt to analyze the problems in American airmail service. For the next three years Warner worked as a consulting engineer, becoming deeply involved in drawing up preliminary specifications for a four-engine airliner designed by the Douglas Aircraft Company, a concept that later evolved into the famous DC-4. In the course of this design work, Warner developed a highly significant scientific technique of quantitative measurement and specification. Beginning with descriptions of desirable flying qualities for transport aircraft, as given by pilots, Warner converted these ideas into engineering language that could be incorporated into basic design specifications. The concept spurred further flying-quality research by NACA and was incorporated into airworthiness regulations for air transports.

In 1938, Warner was economic and technical adviser to the Civil Aeronautics Authority, which became the Civil Aeronautics Board (CAB). He was appointed a member in 1939, serving as vice-chairman in 1941 and again from 1943 to 1945. His technical background and vast experience in aeronautical subjects eminently qualified him to do a great deal of work in the formulation of guidelines for certification and regulation of airmen, aircraft, and flight operations. These concerns complemented an abiding interest in flight safety, dating back to his early activities with the Society of Automotive Engineers.

During Warner's tenure on the CAB, he became involved with international aspects of aviation operations, serving as a liaison between the CAB and the War Department and the Department of the Navy, and making trips to Alaska and the Caribbean. In 1941, Warner was a member of the W. Averell Harriman commission to England; he assisted in working out details of the lend-lease program involving aircraft. Warner made other wartime trips, including another visit to England in 1944, when he accompanied Assistant Secretary of State Adolf A. Berle to discuss the nature of international air

transport activities following the conclusion of World War II. This mission led directly to the creation of the International Civil Aviation Conference in November 1944, convened to discuss international air transport operations in the postwar period.

From 1945 to 1947, Warner headed the interim council of the International Civil Aviation Organization (ICAO), which became an agency of the United Nations. Under Warner's presidency (1947–1957) ICAO grew from twenty-six member nations to a total of seventy. Its activities included the setting forth of standards for navigational services, meteorology, air traffic control and communications, and a host of regulations defining operational activities of both airmen and aircraft. During this period ICAO developed a network of meteorological observation stations throughout the north Atlantic and updated, revised, and renegotiated a series of international conventions dealing with aeronautical activities.

Because of his aeronautical knowledge, as well as his broad understanding of the economic, social, and political ramifications of international aviation, the members of ICAO repeatedly elected Warner as its president until his retirement in 1957. During the ceremonies surrounding his departure, colleagues from many nations attested to Warner's fairness and objectivity in conducting affairs of the ICAO. He died at Duxbury, Mass.

In the development of aviation, few men exercised as much influence as Warner in his diverse roles as teacher, researcher, author, bureaucrat, editor, publicist, engineer, planner, administrator, and internationalist.

Between 1926 and 1931, Warner wrote or was coauthor of several outstanding books dealing with aeronautical theory and design. His *Airplane Design* (1927), named the best aviation publication of the year by the Aero Club of France, and *The Early History of Air Transportation* and *Technical Development and Its Effect on Air Transportation* (1938), are outstanding and lucid summaries of the state-of-the-art of the day. In addition to technical papers and articles for NACA and *Aviation*, he wrote many newspaper pieces, and published articles in the *Yale Review*, *Air Affairs*, and *Foreign Affairs*. He delivered the Wilbur Wright memorial lecture to the Royal Aeronautical Society of London (1943), and received the Daniel Guggenheim Medal for achievement in aeronautics (1950), the gold medal of the Fédération Aéronautique Internationale (1952), and the Wright Brothers

Memorial Trophy of the National Aeronautic Association (1956).

[T. P. Wright, "Edward Pearson Warner," *Journal of the Royal Aeronautical Society,* Oct. 1958, cites remarks on Warner's career and personality from many acquaintances and associates. See also Henry Ladd Smith, *Airways Abroad* (1950); ICAO *Bulletin,* Apr. 18, 1957; and G. Edward Pendray, ed., *The Guggenheim Medalists* (1964). An obituary is in *New York Times,* July 13, 1958.]

ROGER E. BILSTEIN

WARNER, HARRY MORRIS (Dec. 12, 1881–July 25, 1958), motion picture executive, was born in Krasnosielce, Poland, the son of Benjamin Warner and Pearl Eichelbaum. (Harry Warner always listed the Americanized name of the village, Krasnashiltz. In 1881 Poland contained three villages with that approximate spelling; Warner probably came from the one in eastern Poland.) Benjamin Warner, a poor cobbler, immigrated to the United States during the 1880's to escape persecution as a Jew. He sent for his wife and four children sometime between 1887 and 1890. The family first settled in Baltimore. There Harry Warner attended elementary school for two years at most. The family then moved frequently as Benjamin Warner sought better jobs, finally settling in Youngstown, Ohio, in 1895. The family by then included seven children. In Youngstown, Benjamin Warner opened a shoe repair shop and later operated other small retail operations. The older sons added to the family income: Harry began as an apprentice cobbler and later became a salesman for Armour and Company, the meat packers. In 1898 he set up a bicycle shop.

In 1903 the teenaged Sam Warner began touring eastern Ohio presenting motion pictures. Soon his brothers Harry, Albert, and Jack, and his sister Rose joined the enterprise. (The specific dates for these early activities are unknown. The best data comes from the official histories provided by Warner Bros. Pictures in later years.) During this period the brothers' division of labor evolved: Harry supervised and handled all financial matters, Albert negotiated sales and controlled advertising, Jack produced the show (and later the movies themselves), and Sam managed the technical end. In 1905 the Warner brothers opened their first permanent theater, a nickelodeon, in New Castle, Pa. To ensure a constant supply of films, Harry Warner organized a

company to distribute motion pictures, the Duquesne Amusement Supply Company. This exchange (in industry terminology) was one of the earliest.

On Aug. 20, 1907, Harry Warner married Rea Levinson. They had three children, and in 1927, after Sam Warner's death, assumed the guardianship of his only child.

The company prospered until 1912, when the monopolistic Motion Picture Patents Company forced the brothers to sell. The Warners then began producing low-cost features and serials, which they distributed through small, independent firms. Gradually the Patents Company lost power, and opportunities for the Warners increased. In 1917 they produced their first major success, a feature-length film, *My Four Years in Germany.* Immediately Harry moved all production to Hollywood. In 1923 Warner Bros. Pictures, Inc., was formed with Harry as president. Thereafter Warner devoted most of his time to corporate activities. His chief hobby was horse breeding and racing. For many years he owned an important California stable.

During the early 1920's the American motion picture industry was dominated by three firms: Loew's, Famous Players, and First National. Harry Warner reasoned that Warner Bros. must either expand or be absorbed by one of these three. As a first step, in 1925 he negotiated the takeover of the Vitagraph Corporation. Next, with the help of Wall Street's Goldman Sachs and Company, Warner Bros. moved into international distribution. It also purchased important theaters in major American cities and initiated motion pictures with sound. Warner moved slowly and conservatively toward full production of sound pictures. First Warners produced short filmed recordings of popular vaudeville acts, then all-talking shorts, and finally all-talking narrative feature-length films. Warner Bros.' first sound movie show opened on Aug. 6, 1926. Nearly two years passed before Warners had its major "talkie" hits: *Lights of New York* and *The Singing Fool.* During 1928 and 1929 Warners absorbed the 250-theater Stanley chain and the First National studio.

Harry's expansionary policies had paid off. By 1930 Warner Bros. was America's second largest film company, with assets of $230 million; controlled 800 theaters; maintained exchanges in seventy foreign countries; and operated fifty-one subsidiaries, including holdings in the radio, music publishing, and phonograph industries.

Warner Bros. survived the Great Depression in relatively good shape and prospered throughout

World War II. During the 1930's Warners produced many important films, but became famous for its gangster films (*Little Caesar, The Public Enemy*), its musicals (*Gold Diggers of 1933, 42nd Street*), and its social consciousness films (*I Am a Fugitive from a Chain Gang, They Won't Forget*). Its most noted stars included James Cagney, Bette Davis, Edward G. Robinson, Pat O'Brien, Ida Lupino, and Humphrey Bogart. During the late 1930's and throughout World War II, Harry Warner spoke out strongly in favor of pro-American, anti-Nazi films while his fellow movie moguls remained silent. Warner Bros. films such as *Watch on the Rhine, Destination Tokyo,* and *Air Force* realistically portrayed the war effort. And these films made money; the corporation generated, on average, $10 million profit (before federal taxes) each year between 1935 and 1945.

Warner nevertheless worried constantly about the company's finances. He tried to run it like an assembly-line factory and minimized costs wherever he could. Competitors outspent Warners two-to-one for feature films. Harry's cost-conscious attitude helped the brothers retain control of Warner Bros. Pictures during the Great Depression but caused several bitter strikes and well-publicized contract disputes.

In 1948 the Justice Department won an antitrust case against the major movie companies, including Warner Bros. (*United States* v. *Paramount Pictures et al.,* 334 U.S. 131). Warner Bros. was ordered to sell its theaters. By 1953 the Stanley-Warner circuit had taken over the bulk of Warner's movie houses. Consequently, in 1951 Warner and his brother Albert decided to retire. They announced that their shares of Warner Bros. stock, a controlling interest, would be sold. Since television and suburban living had caused movie attendance to decline significantly after World War II, they found it difficult to locate acceptable buyers. Finally, in 1956, they sold nearly all of their stock for $16.5 million to a syndicate headed by Serge Semenenko, a Boston banker. This transaction caused a major split between Harry and Jack Warner, who succeeded him as president of the company. Harry remained on the company's board of directors until his death in Bel Air, Calif.

[Extensive manuscript materials can be found in *Koplar (Scharaf et al., Interveners)* v. *Warner Bros. Pictures, Inc. et al.,* 19 F. Supp. 172 (1937), on deposit at the Regional National Archives in Philadelphia. As an executive Harry Warner wrote little for the public record. What he did is quite useful: "Future Developments," in Joseph P. Kennedy, ed., *The Story of the Films* (1927); "Warners—Past and Future," *Variety,* June 25, 1930; and statements in *New York Times,* May 19, 1943, p. 16.

Four sources traditionally provide the basic material for accounts of Harry Warner's life: Fitzhugh Green, *The Film Finds Its Tongue* (1929); Frederic M. Thrasher, *Okay for Sound* (1946); Jack L. Warner, *My First Hundred Years in Hollywood* (1964); and "Warner Brothers," *Fortune,* Dec. 1937. Information can also be found in the following: Frederick Van Ryn, "Warner Brother Number One," *Liberty,* Oct. 31 and Dec. 12, 1942; and Hermine R. Isaacs, "Presenting the Warner Brothers," *Theatre Arts,* Feb. 1944. Obituaries in the *New York Times,* July 26, 1958, and *Variety,* July 30, 1958, are complete.]

DOUGLAS GOMERY

WARREN, HENRY ELLIS (May 21, 1872–Sept. 21, 1957), inventor and entrepreneur, was born in Boston, Mass., the son of Henry Warren and Adelaide Louise Ellis. In 1894 he received the B.S. from the Massachusetts Institute of Technology. After working as an electrical engineer with the Saginaw Valley Traction Company in Michigan, he returned to Boston in 1902 and joined the Lombard Governor Company, where he made a number of inventions, including an improved governor for water-driven turbines. On Jan. 19, 1907, he married Edith B. Smith and settled in Ashland, Mass. They had no children. He acquired ownership of the Lombard Governor Company in 1937 and was president from then until his death. Having become interested in local politics, Warren served as an Ashland selectman from 1907 to 1909 and as a member of the Ashland Forestry Commission from 1937 until his death.

Sometime before 1914 Warren had become interested in the problem of devising a reliable, accurate electric clock that could be synchronized to the frequency of distributed alternating-current power (60 cycles per second in the United States). His proposal to base such a clock on a synchronous electric motor had been suggested as early as 1895. Warren's contributions were to design a specific mechanism for the purpose and to establish a manufacturing facility to produce it.

Warren considered it important that any electric clock be self-starting. To accomplish this, and to ensure that the motor began to revolve in the desired direction, one of the pole pieces was "shaded," that is, provided with copper rings, in which eddy currents could build up, thereby delaying the growth of the magnetic field. This arrangement allowed the rotor to be brought up to synchronism from rest, while ensuring that it did not slip thereafter. The clock would then keep time as faithfully as the power supply was maintained at 60 cycles per second. In order to manufacture his clock, Warren founded the Warren Clock Company (subsequently renamed Warren Telechron) in 1912. By 1918 it was selling in mass quantities what came to be called the Warren synchronous clock. Electric clocks were not new at this time. In some, the mechanism was directly driven by an electric motor. In others, a pendulum or balance wheel was activated by periodic pulses. There were slave clocks controlled electrically through wiring from a central master clock. Warren's invention made available for the first time an electric clock that was cheap, reliable, and accurate. It also pointed the way toward the use of fractional horsepower motors in self-contained equipment for other domestic uses. The principle of Warren's clock is still in use in electric clocks.

Warren's invention and promotion of the synchronous clock led directly to a twenty-year association with the General Electric Company. Prior to the introduction of the synchronous clock, standards of power frequency control were quite lax: several percent variation from nominal was quite common, and there had been little motivation to improve it. (Translated into time, a 1 percent variation in frequency would amount to a clock error of nearly fifteen minutes per day.) Warren therefore had a decided interest in improving the quality of power frequency control. While aware of the potential profit in Warren's invention, General Electric also realized that improved frequency control would be increasingly important if individual power companies were to be linked in regional distribution networks. In 1919, therefore, General Electric invited Warren to become a consulting engineer. Soon thereafter, he devised a master clock for controlling the power frequency of the generating stations. Thanks to this invention, the power frequency control had by 1939 been substantially improved, with the result that clock errors had been brought down to a second or two per day. General Electric acquired a 50 percent interest in Warren Telechron in 1929 and bought full control fifteen years later.

Warren's other inventions included fire control mechanisms and tracking devices for astronomical telescopes. Financially secure, War-

ren later developed a number of other interests, including farming, and ran his house in Ashland as a working dairy farm. He was active in the Boy Scouts and in the Salvation Army. He died in Ashland, Mass.

[See Frank Hope Jones, *Electrical Timekeeping*, 2nd ed. (1949); and the obituary notice, *New York Times*, Sept. 22, 1957.]

C. G. B. GARRETT

WARREN, LEONARD (Apr. 21, 1911– Mar. 4, 1960), operatic and concert singer, was born in New York City, the son of Russian Jewish immigrants, Sol Warenoff and Sara Kantor. After graduating from Evander Childs High School, he worked for his father, a wholesale fur dealer. However, he found little satisfaction in the business world and within a few years, even though he had no prior musical training and received scant encouragement from his parents, he began studies with Will J. Stone at the Greenwich House Music School.

In 1935 Warren joined the Radio City Music Hall Glee Club at a salary of $35 a week and commenced intensive vocal study with Sidney Dietch. Three years later, on Mar. 26, 1938, he was a cowinner in the nationwide Metropolitan Opera Auditions of the Air competition. A $5,000 gift from George A. Martin, president of the Sherwin-Williams Company, which sponsored the auditions, enabled him to give up his job at the Music Hall for further musical study in Italy. In Milan he worked with Riccardo Picozzi and Giuseppe Pais. He also met Agatha Leifflen, a graduate of New York's Institute of Musical Art, whom he subsequently married on Dec. 27, 1941.

Returning to New York in the fall of 1938, Warren performed for the first time at the Metropolitan Opera House in a Sunday evening concert on November 27. He made his official operatic debut on Jan. 13, 1939, as Paolo in Verdi's *Simon Boccanegra*. During the next four years Warren was cast primarily in English, French, and German roles. It became increasingly apparent, however, that Italian opera was his forte, and he specialized in that repertory from the fall of 1943 on.

As the scope and difficulty of his roles increased, Warren worked assiduously to overcome two handicaps, a complete lack of dramatic experience and an inability to learn new music quickly. Diligent observance of fellow performers and three years of private coaching with Giuseppe de Luca improved Warren's stage presence immensely. This, together with a detailed nine- to twelve-month preparation of each new role, resulted in such a complete mastery of a part that, according to Warren, not a "single tone, a single gesture" was delivered without total confidence.

Consequently, by the late 1940's Warren had become one of the world's foremost Verdi baritones, enthusiastically acclaimed for his Amonasro, Count di Luna, and Iago, and especially for his moving portrayal of Rigoletto, a role he eventually sang eighty-eight times with the Metropolitan alone. In the 1950's Warren enjoyed a like success in other Verdi operas as well as in Leoncavallo's *I Pagliacci* and Puccini's *Tosca*.

Although under annual contract to the Metropolitan Opera Company, for which he sang 633 performances (twenty-six roles) in twenty-two seasons, Warren appeared with the San Francisco Opera Company for seven seasons and with the Chicago Opera Company from 1944 through 1946. In addition, he performed at the Teatro Colón in Buenos Aires in 1942, 1943, and 1946 and at the Teatro Municipal in Rio de Janeiro during the summers of 1942–1945. He also sang at the Cincinnati Summer Opera in 1940; at Mexico City's Teatro Nacional in 1948; in Havana, Cuba, in June 1953; with the La Scala Opera, Milan, in December 1953; at Moscow's Bolshoi Theatre in 1958; and at operatic festivals in Canada and Puerto Rico.

During his career Warren also sang on numerous radio shows and made frequent television appearances, including the first operatic concert ever televised, on Mar. 10, 1940. He concertized extensively throughout North America, appearing both in song recitals and with major symphony orchestras. In 1944 he sang several ballads in the motion picture *When Irish Eyes Are Smiling*.

A perfectionist, Warren constantly restudied and refined even his most renowned roles. No detail of makeup, costume, or staging escaped his critical scrutiny. As a result, he was frequently embroiled in temperamental confrontations with his co-workers because "he tells other singers how to sing, conductors how to conduct, directors how to direct . . . " (*New York Times*, Oct. 25, 1959).

Temperament notwithstanding, Warren was highly esteemed by musicians, critics, and the public. His voice was rich in timbre, poignantly expressive, and beautifully controlled from a low

G upward through two and a third octaves to a thrilling B flat. Warren's ability to crescendo and decrescendo his upper notes was unmatched; his enunciation both in English and Italian, superb. His artistry has been preserved on a number of RCA Victor records. These include nine operas and several single albums devoted to operatic highlights, sea chanties, and concert songs.

Warren was a stocky man, five feet, eleven inches tall and weighing 215 pounds. His hair and eyes were brown, his complexion dark. Despite his success, his general manner and life-style were quite unpretentious. For recreation he enjoyed model railroading, cruising on the waters of Long Island Sound, fishing, and tinkering with mechanical objects.

At the peak of his career, Warren suffered a massive cerebral hemorrhage and died onstage at the Metropolitan Opera House during a performance of Verdi's *La Forza del Destino*.

[No detailed, full-length account of Warren's life has been published. Full casts and dates of all Warren performances at the Metropolitan Opera House are catalogued in William H. Seltsam, *Metropolitan Opera Annals: A Chronicle of Artists and Performances* (1947) and its supplements (1957, 1968). Similar information pertaining to the Met operas Warren performed outside New York City from 1939 through 1956 is available in Quaintance Eaton, *Opera Caravan* (1957). Further highlights and critical evaluations of his operatic performances may be found in Irving Kolodin, *The Metropolitan Opera, 1883–1966* (1966), as well as in the monthly issues of *Musical America* and the *Musical Courier*.

Several Warren interviews are in print: *Opera News*, Jan. 23, 1950, and Mar. 23, 1959; *Music Journal*, July–Aug. 1956; and *Etude*, Mar. 1949.

Satisfactory biographical sketches of Warren may be found in *Newsweek*, Dec. 13, 1948; *Musical America*, Dec. 1, 1956; David Ewen, ed., *Living Musicians*; *First Supplement* (1957); and, particularly, the British publication *Opera*, June 1960. Warren's obituary appears in the *New York Times*, Mar. 5, 1960; *Time*, Mar. 14, 1960; and *Musical America* and *Musical Courier*, Mar. 1960.]

LOUIS R. THOMAS

WATSON, JOHN BROADUS (Jan. 9, 1878–Sept. 25, 1958), psychologist and advertising executive, was born near Greenville, S.C., the son of Pickens Butler Watson and Emma Kezia[h] Roe. According to family stories Watson's father, a "high-tempered" southerner, had fought in the Civil War as a youth and had then been unable to settle down, wandering about the countryside engaging in the sawmill business. He was seldom at home. The family was dominated by John's mother and his oldest brother, Edward. They lived in genteel poverty, employing only one servant. As a boy, Watson learned the routines of farming. He attended public schools in Travelers Rest, White Horse, and Greenville. Watson's mother and brother were fanatically devoted to a very harsh, literal Baptist faith that dominated events in the home. (John Broadus, after whom Watson was named, was a well-known evangelist of that area and era.) Watson reacted violently against this upbringing, although while his mother was alive he tried to hide the extent of his dissent and she tended to overlook "lapses" by this son, who was her favorite. He later regretted that he had permitted himself to be baptized. For most of his adult life swearing, drinking, and other behavior in defiance of nineteenth-century evangelical standards were of major importance to him.

At the age of sixteen, Watson entered Furman University, where he studied psychology with Gordon B. Moore. As a student he was able but argumentative. He completed his courses in 1899, qualifying for the M.A. In 1899-1900 he taught as principal of Batesburg (S.C.) Institute. In the fall of 1900, Watson left to do graduate work in psychology at the University of Chicago, where he had relatives and where Moore had studied.

He arrived in Chicago with only fifty dollars in his pocket and sustained himself by a number of odd jobs, including waiting on tables, helping care for psychology department apparatus, and caring for the white rats of neurologist H. H. Donaldson. The family funds that saw him through Furman were no longer forthcoming, and until the 1920's Watson keenly felt his constant need for money. He always regretted that lack of funds prevented him from obtaining medical training.

Despite his rejection of religion, Watson brought with him to Chicago many traditional attitudes from his South Carolina rearing. Although not given to athletics, for example, he nevertheless proudly pictured himself as a fighter. In fact, he was courteous and extraordinarily charming, winning friends and support easily. And he was consumed with the desire to make a name for himself. He first gained national press coverage when his research on his doctoral dissertation engaged antivivisectionists against him, and for decades his provocative—though professional—statements showed that he retained some of his combative character.

At Chicago, Watson worked with Donaldson,

functional psychologist James Rowland Angell, and Jacques Loeb, an experimental physiologist and mechanistic materialist. He also studied philosophy with John Dewey, George Herbert Mead, and James H. Tufts. Watson later pretended contempt for philosophy, but he was quite able to defend himself in that field. Neurology and physiology became his interests, and he took the Ph.D. in 1903, when only twenty-five. He stayed on at Chicago as assistant in the psychology department for a year (1903-1904) and then was advanced to instructor. His eight years at Chicago were happy, except for occasional anxiety about his work and his continued inability to gain financial security. On Dec. 26, 1903, he was married secretly to Mary Ickes, younger sister of Harold Ickes, who later became secretary of the interior. On Oct. 1, 1904, they were married again, publicly. They had two children.

Watson's doctoral dissertation was a study of the psychological development of the white rat, an animal just being established as a major laboratory subject. The research launched his career as a specialist in animal psychology. From the beginning he found that his training at home as carpenter and handyman was of great use in designing and building experimental apparatus. After taking his doctorate he continued working with rats, studying their adaptation to new conditions and the correlation of the body weight of postpartum rats with the weight of the nervous system, a quantitative endeavor utilizing surgical techniques learned from the physiologist William H. Howell at Johns Hopkins in the spring and summer of 1904. Watson also tested the reactions of rats learning to run through mazes. He investigated imitation among monkeys. He carried out some classic experiments in color discrimination.

In 1907, Watson won support from the Carnegie Institution of Washington and spent three months in the Dry Tortugas, studying the behavior of noddy and sooty terns. By that time he was one of the leading figures in experimental and animal psychology. By 1906 he was preparing the annual summary of comparative psychology literature for the *Psychological Bulletin*. In 1907 he was named professor of comparative and experimental psychology at Johns Hopkins University.

During his last year at Chicago (1907-1908), Watson was rethinking what he was doing. In 1904 he had been impressed by a paper in which James McKeen Cattell stressed control of human beings as the goal of psychology and rejected the introspective techniques then used in investigations of human mental functioning. Watson for several years talked with his colleagues about the direction that his thought was taking, but they discouraged him. Finally, in 1907–1908, he began to develop his idea that animal psychology could serve as the basis for human psychology, and he embodied his beliefs in a lecture presented at three different professional forums. At that point he was concentrating on comparative psychology, stressing that scientists should not attribute mental content to animals but, rather, adhere to objective observation of their behavior.

Within the next four years Watson perfected a behavioristic theory of the higher thought processes based upon stimulus-response patterns of implicit speech mechanisms. He then had a fully developed human psychology emphasizing the objective study of human adaptation and behavior. Unlike many of his friends and teachers, including Loeb and Herbert Spencer Jennings, Watson did not attempt to describe the physiological processes involved in thinking, but only the observable changes in behavior after the presentation of an environmental stimulus. Except for his emphasis on adaptation, this new psychology represented a substantial shift in viewpoint from the conventional mentalism that Watson had been taught and taught for years.

At Johns Hopkins, Watson was free, as he put it, to "work without supervision," and he soon developed a fully equipped laboratory. Eventually he worked in the medical school psychiatric clinic headed by Adolf Meyer, who himself had a biological approach to human thought and behavior. Watson worked with his friend Robert M. Yerkes on color vision and experimented on learned and instinctive behavior in various animals. He again studied birds in the Tortugas in 1910, 1912, and 1913. He continued to gain professional recognition and was increasingly drawn into editing duties for the group of *Psychological Review* publications (1908) and the *Journal of Animal Behavior* (1911). William James, before his death in 1910, stated that Watson could be trusted in professional affairs, and others showed similar confidence.

In the winter of 1912–1913, Watson gave some lectures at Columbia University, one of which, "Psychology as a Behaviorist Views It," was published in *Psychological Review* (1913). That paper was Watson's manifesto, designed to make psychology both scientific and useful by following the model of good animal experimentation, which did not depend upon an inferred consciousness in the experimental subject, but only reactions to stimuli. It created a sensation: a number of psychologists, especially the younger ones, felt that Watson spoke for them and the way that psychology was developing. He seemed to promise them both objectivity and social significance.

In 1915, Watson became president of the American Psychological Association. In his presidential address he brought the idea of conditioned reflexes into his psychological schema. Soon thereafter he added a psychopathology, acknowledging the importance of the work of Sigmund Freud.

For many years both psychologists and intellectuals knew and talked about this new departure, behaviorism, and sought applications for it not only in psychology but also in such fields as sociology and literature.

From August 1917 to November 1918, Watson served in the army, working mostly with air corps personnel problems. After returning to Johns Hopkins he concentrated on a line of experiments that he had begun earlier in a very tentative fashion, trying to discover what instincts humans have when born. He utilized infants just as he earlier had used animals, and concluded that inheritance had little, and environment much, to do with behavior. Watson's plans for far more extensive infant studies—a "baby farm," perhaps, for controlled experiments—were shattered in 1920 by divorce proceedings that were widely publicized and caused the university to ask for his resignation. Shortly thereafter, on Dec. 31, 1920, he married Rosalie Rayner, a former graduate student. They had two sons.

Because of the circumstances of his divorce, Watson now found academia closed to him, although he lectured during the 1920's at the New School for Social Research in New York City. He took a position with the J. Walter Thompson advertising agency in New York. After a period of training, he became an account executive and, in 1924, one of four vice-presidents of the company. He later claimed that he had to use the established standards and procedures of advertising, and was not successful in introducing psychological or conditioning theory into his new work. But he did work on early consumer surveys for the agency. Watson became successful and felt financial ease for the first time. Among his important accounts were Norwich Pharmaceutical Company, Baker's Coconut, Maxwell House Coffee, Sharpe and Dohme, General Motors Overseas, and Pond's, for the last of which he inaugurated a famous and successful testimonial campaign. At one point his office in the agency was responsible for annual billings of $11 million.

For some years Watson hoped to return to psychology, and he tried to spend evenings on scientific matters. But his prosperity and the harshness with which academics excluded him made his feelings ambiguous. In 1922 he wrote to Yerkes: "I have lost interest in university work. If I could get the baby work going I would be willing to starve to death." Instead of addressing an academic audience, Watson gave popular lectures and published popular articles and books. In effect he acted as an evangelist or advertiser for the behavioristic viewpoint. His most important influence came in the rapidly expanding field of advice on child rearing. His dicta not to cuddle or spoil infants, but to condition them to lead independent lives, appeared in his own publications and in writings of other child-rearing experts of the 1920's and later.

After his wife died in 1935, Watson found his life increasingly circumscribed, and he was very much less in the public eye. In 1936 he left J. Walter Thompson for William Esty and Company, again as vice-president. There he worked mostly on drug and cosmetic accounts, including Hind's Honey and Almond Cream, Dorothy Gray, and Tussy. He retired in 1945. To the end of his life he kept busy working on farming and building projects in rural Connecticut. He died in New York City.

Watson's popularizing accelerated the growth of environmentalism in all aspects of American thought. In psychology he had very few immediate followers, but by taking an extreme position in favor of objective behavioral studies, he provided an ideal for two generations of younger psychologists who moved the discipline substantially toward behaviorism. In particular, he helped bring animal experiments into the mainstream of psychology by emphasizing that behavioral reactions are common to man and beast and can be studied in either one. Half a century later his belief that habits can be conditioned was still cited—if only symbolically—by proponents of behavioral psychotherapy and educational techniques.

[The largest body of Watson's correspondence is in the Robert M. Yerkes Papers, Yale University Medical Library. Bibliographies of his published works are in *The Psychological Register*, II (1929); and *Author Index to Psychological Index, 1894 to 1935, and Psychological Abstracts, 1927 to 1958* (1960), V.A. more complete list is in possession of the family. Autobiographical accounts are "The Origin and Growth of Behaviorism," *Archiv für systematische Philosophie und Sociologie*, 30 (1927); and in Carl Murchison, ed., *A History of Psychology in Autobiography*, III (1936). See also Kenneth McGowan, "The Adventure of the Behaviorist," *New Yorker*, Oct. 6, 1928; Gustav Bergmann, "The Contribution of John B. Watson," *Psychological Review*, 63 (1956); Albert E. Goss, "Early Behaviorism and Verbal Mediating Responses," *American Psychologist*, 16 (1961); David Bakan, "Behaviorism and American Urbanization," *Journal of the History of the Behavioral Sciences*, 2 (1966); Lucille Terese Birnbaum, "Behaviorism" (Ph.D. diss., University of California, Berkeley, 1966); and John C. burnham, "On the Origins of Behaviorism," *Journal of the History of the Behavioral Sciences*, 4 (1968).]

JOHN C. BURNHAM

WATSON, THOMAS JOHN (Feb. 17, 1874–June 19, 1956), industrial entrepreneur and business executive, was born in East Campbell, a rural area near Corning, N.Y., the son of Thomas Watson and Jane Fulton White, who had left Northern Ireland in the middle of the nineteenth century. His father operated a small lumber business. The local Methodist church was the center of the religious and social life of the family. Young Watson, a shy lad, attended a one-room public school and later the Addison Academy at Painted Post, N.Y. Although his father wanted him to attend Cornell University or study law, he studied accounting and business for a year at the Miller School of Commerce in Elmira. Completing his education in the spring of 1892, he was soon engaged as a bookkeeper for a butcher shop in Painted Post.

That summer Watson, bored with bookkeeping, became a traveling salesman for a local supplier of pianos, organs, sewing machines, and caskets. Displaying industry and persistence, he was a highly successful "drummer." After two years he moved to the wider horizons of Buffalo. Eventually he sold stock shares for a Buffalo building-and-loan company. Brimming with entrepreneurial ambition, he planned a retail chain of butcher markets, but when his stock partner absconded with the funds, he had to abandon his plans.

In 1895 Watson obtained a sales position with John Range in the Buffalo office of the National Cash Register (NCR) Company. This association shaped his career. NCR was a strong and growing company. At a time when the emergence of a national market fostered large-scale enterprise, NCR stood as the dominant corporation in a rapidly growing industry. By 1899 Watson was the top cash register salesman in the Buffalo region. Consequently, he was promoted to agent of the sales office in Rochester, a region of tough competition. Within four years he and his staff were doing so well that John Henry Patterson, the brilliant president of NCR, summoned Watson to the home office to head a secret new division that quietly acquired control of the secondhand cash register business. During the next decade Watson stood near the executive center of NCR. He suffered the insecurity of working with the volatile Patterson, whose executive suites served as the training ground for a number of major automobile executives of the coming generation. Despite Patterson's eccentricities, Watson learned lessons in entrepreneurship, evangelical salesmanship, executive decision-making, and paternalism.

In the fall of 1907 Patterson dismissed NCR's sales manager. Watson fell heir to the position. With Patterson in Europe or New York much of the time, Watson's department flourished. During this period Watson introduced the slogan THINK and at Patterson's order THINK signs blanketed the offices of NCR. The ability of NCR to dominate the industry—by superior salesmanship, questionable tactics, or direct acquisition of competing firms—led not only to mushrooming sales and profits but in 1912 to the filing of an antitrust suit charging thirty of the executives with conspiracy in restraint of trade. Watson was included.

While under this cloud, Watson met Jeannette M. Kittredge, the daughter of a prominent Dayton industrialist. On Apr. 17, 1913, two months after the jury had found Watson and others guilty and the judge had sentenced them to a year in jail, Watson and Kittredge were married. They returned from their honeymoon to live in the summer house that Patterson had given them for a wedding gift. While Watson's appeal was being prepared, his growing prominence and independence in the company prompted Patterson to dismiss him.

Watson promptly obtained the position of general manager of the Computing-Tabulating-Recording Company (CTR), a holding company formed in 1911 from the Tabulating Machine Company, International Time Recording Company, Dayton Scale Company, and Bundy Manufacturing Company. With the new combine Watson maintained a low profile, deferring to powerful financial figures in the company such as Charles R. Flint and George W. Fairchild and trying to end management conflicts among the divisions. He joined the faltering enterprise with a guarantee of a percentage of the profits in addition to a salary in cash and stock. The percentage and stock features later made him an extremely wealthy man.

Within a year of joining CTR, Watson's conviction was overturned by the Appeals Court on a technicality. (NCR later signed a consent decree, but Watson refused to sign and no further action was taken against him.) At once CTR made him president. During these years with CTR, the Watsons had four children.

The first decade of Watson's service witnessed major changes in the direction and financial integrity of CTR. Increasing emphasis was placed on the tabulating machine division, an area previously influenced strongly by the engineer Herman Hollerith, who had developed the first commercial tabulating machines for the national census of 1890. At the risk of angering Hollerith, Watson promoted independent product research, and by 1919 CTR had pulled ahead of the competition in tabulating equipment. Soon profits from this division exceeded those of the time-recording, scale, and food-cutting divisions. Much of Watson's success came from his emphasis on sales organization and his use of many of the sales techniques employed at NCR. These included Hundred Percent Clubs for salesmen exceeding their quotas and Watson's evangelical talks at circus-style sales meetings.

In 1924 Watson assumed full command of the company. He placed new emphasis on international markets, establishing factories in France and Germany and changing the company's name to International Business Machines (IBM). In a decade sales and dividends tripled and the value of the stock increased fivefold.

During the late 1920's and the 1930's Watson continued to emphasize tabulating machinery. In 1933 he sold the floundering scale division and acquired the Electromatic Typewriter Company. Despite the Great Depression, Watson gambled, keeping tabulating machine employees at work and storing parts in warehouses. When the New Deal introduced programs such as the National Recovery Administration (NRA) and social security, requiring detailed accounting, IBM readily met the demand for machines. With the government as the company's largest customer by 1935, IBM had under lease about 85 percent of all tabulating equipment. Despite the Great Depression, the company's profits increased. By 1934 Watson's $364,432 salary was the largest in the nation.

Watson's relations with his employees was generous but paternalistic. IBM provided liberal wages and fringe benefits, including a stock purchase plan and company country clubs. Yet, Watson imposed on his "family" a standardized dress code. A teetotaler, he prohibited drinking and demanded a strict code of behavior. Because of the generous company benefits and its dominant position in the industry, unions were unable to organize the employees.

Increasingly Watson's attention turned to national and international affairs. He voiced strong support for Roosevelt and the New Deal. Like many leaders of large corporations, he advocated the NRA and became identified with liberal national planning councils such as the Department of Commerce's Business Advisory Council and, later, the Committee for Economic Development. He is reputed to have declined the posts of secretary of commerce and ambassador to Britain.

Watson's political and economic positions were not always consistent or broadly profound. During the 1930's he moved from the presidency of the U.S. Chamber of Commerce to a strong commitment to the International Chamber of Commerce. At the time of Watson's inauguration as president of that organization in 1937 in Berlin, Adolf Hitler presented him with the Order of Merit of the German Eagle with Star. After a private conference with Hitler, he spoke highly of the chancellor and, later, of Mussolini.

In the early 1940's Watson turned his personal energies and those of his company to the war effort. He contributed his contractual percentage of the company's war profits to employee benefits and provided special bonuses for former employees serving in the armed forces. The company produced about forty military ordnance items, and its gross sales increased from $41 million in 1939 to $142 million in 1945. Moreover, IBM developed new military uses for tabulating machines and closer relations with university research centers, ultimately leading to IBM's participation in a major technological revolution: the emergence of the computer.

Although large mechanical calculators had been built at MIT between 1925 and 1940, the first automatic calculator, Mark I, was built during World War II. In this joint enterprise Howard Aiken of Harvard University developed the de-

sign and IBM supplied the engineering and money. While other groups in the United States and abroad were active, a team at the University of Pennsylvania developed the first electronic computer, ENIAC. This team developed in 1951 the first commercial computer with a stored program, UNIVAC, which IBM's chief competitor, Sperry-Rand, marketed.

Despite his research ties with Columbia and Harvard, Watson had built IBM on the basis of strength in marketing and production, not on pioneering research. Hence, in the 1950's, as first the vacuum tube and then the transistor quickly altered computer capabilities, the company found itself challenged technically. Only with the ending of Watson's leadership did IBM place strong internal emphasis upon research.

Watson continued his advocacy of internationalism after the war, strongly supporting the United Nations. The range of his public activities was reflected in his entry in *Who's Who in America*, reputed to be the longest in the volume. As trustee of Columbia University; a confidant of its president, Nicholas Murray Butler; and a great admirer of General Dwight D. Eisenhower, Watson was largely responsible for Eisenhower's appointment as successor to Butler at Columbia in 1948. He later supported Eisenhower for president, but very quietly, because of pending antitrust suits against IBM.

The charges were based on IBM's large market share in punch cards and machines. Watson, feeling self-righteous about the company's behavior, feared being "tinged" in the public eye. The controversy caused by his refusal to sign the court-mandated consent decrees diverted the company's energies in the early 1950's as it fought to survive and then lead the electronic computer revolution.

Following periods of apprenticeship, Watson's two sons, Thomas, Jr., and Arthur, were appointed in 1952 as president and general manager of international activities, respectively. Yet, as Watson approached his eightieth year, he continued to dominate policy. After a dramatic verbal clash late in 1955 with his father, Thomas, Jr., went defiantly to the federal courthouse to sign the antitrust consent decree. The torch of leadership officially was passed on May 8, 1956. Five weeks later Watson died in New York City.

[Substantial manuscript material relating to Thomas J. Watson, including personal correspondence, financial records, and transcripts of IBM executive meetings and conferences, are preserved by IBM.

Watson's writings include *As a Man Thinks* (1936); *Human Relations* (1949); and *Men, Minutes and Money* (1927). IBM material is not generally available to the public; however, a commissioned, book-length biography by Thomas Graham Belden and Marva Robins Belden, *The Lengthening Shadow* (1962), was based on it. A popular, more critical biographical account is William Rodgers, *THINK: A Biography of the Watsons and IBM* (1969). Both biographies have substantial bibliographies. Many reminiscences in the Oral History Collection of Columbia University refer to Watson.

Important histories of computers that have materials on Watson and IBM include two popular accounts: Jeremy Bernstein, *The Analytical Engine, Computers—Past, Present and Future* (1963), and Jerry M. Rosenberg, *The Computer Prophets* (1969). An authoritative scholarly history is Herman H. Goldstine, *The Computer from Pascal to von Neumann* (1972).]

REESE V. JENKINS

WAYMACK, WILLIAM WESLEY (Oct. 18, 1888–Nov. 5, 1960), journalist and government official, was born in Savanna, Ill., the son of William Edward Waymack and Emma Julia Oberheim. His father's Virginia family, after losing its possessions in the Civil War, had migrated to western Illinois. His father served the Chicago, Milwaukee and St. Paul Railroad as a car foreman. Waymack began elementary school at Savanna, but before completing the eighth grade went to Mt. Carroll, Ill., to live with his mother's parents. After graduating from high school he worked as a section hand and did other jobs in the Savanna area.

Beginning in 1908, Waymack worked his way through Morningside College in Sioux City, Iowa. During his senior year, he was the college correspondent for the *Sioux City Journal*. He graduated with the B.A. in 1911 and on June 27 of that year he married Elsie Jeannette Lord of Savanna. They had one son. Waymack then went to work as a reporter on the *Journal*. Exceptional capacity and energy soon impressed his superiors, who in 1914 established him in the somewhat competing posts of city editor and chief editorial writer. He held these positions until 1918, when he joined the Cowles newspaper organization in Des Moines to write editorials for the morning *Register* and the evening *Tribune*. Three years later he was moved to the managing editor's desk, which he administered until 1929. After a period of ill health, he was chosen a director of the publishing company and placed in charge of the

editorial sections in 1931. They remained his responsibilities until 1946.

Waymack's editorials were characterized by forthrightness and constructive ideas. Thus he became a spokesman for Iowa's farm belt similar to what William Allen White was for Kansas'. His editorial pages were addressed in particular to "farm tenancy," already a problem in the 1920's and worsened in the 1930's by the Great Depression. Showing that by 1936 some 40,000 Iowa farmers had become tenants or had been forced off the land altogether, Waymack calculated the costs in human as well as economic terms. He sought to hold down the annual "massive" March 1 migration of farmers (before the crop-planting season) by which, he said, everyone lost—tenant, landlord, and "the social soundness of Iowa." From 1930 he lived on a 275-acre farm at Adel, twenty miles west of Des Moines. There he experimented with crops and livestock and demonstrated his convictions about owner–tenant relations.

But Waymack's horizon extended beyond the rural Middle West to the sharecropping South, the industrial East, and on to the international scene. At a time when his region was regarded as isolationist, Waymack campaigned for a wider, more effective role for the United States in global affairs. He supported freer world trade and called for entrance of the United States into the League of Nations. He believed that a free democracy had an obligation as well as opportunity to demonstrate its superiority over the postwar dictatorships. He also advocated wage and price controls to combat inflation.

Second in the Pulitzer Prize competition for editorial writing in 1936, Waymack received the top award a year later for his commentaries on "man and the land," which were described as possessing "a sweep, a depth and a history-dominating quality as well as a sense of national prophecy." In 1938 he was given the first-place editorial award of Sigma Delta Chi, a professional journalistic society.

Although Waymack could hold unswervingly to a policy when convinced of its correctness, he was a foe of cant and dogma and sponsored open exchange of viewpoints on political, economic, social, and religious issues. He avoided easy labels but defined conservatism as "nostalgia for the never never land that never was."

In October 1946 Waymack gave up his newspaper responsibilities to accept appointment by President Harry S. Truman to the newly created Atomic Energy Commission. He served for two formative, exploratory years before retiring because of ill health. The *New York Herald Tribune* wrote that at the time of Waymack's service "the future course of the atom was in such shadowy form that the AEC officials spent their time making tentative guesses about the future rather than disagreeing violently about it."

Although unusually busy, Waymack participated in dozens of local, state, regional, and national movements, organizations, programs, and causes. He regularly put editorials into action by leading or joining in meetings as a "public-spirited doer." While many other editors would have avoided Waymack's course as exceeding a journalist's proper function, Waymack saw it as fulfillment. His own newspaper characterized him as having "one of those rare minds which stir and invigorate and challenge." He contributed "clarity, force and drive" to a long range of activities "from local welfare to the development of the atom for peaceful purposes."

From 1941 to 1959 Waymack was a trustee of the Carnegie Endowment for International Peace, and he was a director of the Twentieth Century Fund from 1942 until his death. He was a director of the Federal Reserve Bank in Chicago, a member of the War Labor Board, a member of the National Council for NATO, an adviser to the State Department after the bombing at Pearl Harbor, and a national committeeman for the American Civil Liberties Union. He was a pioneer advocate of radio and television as potential instruments for education and was among the first users of aviation, which he enthusiastically promoted. He died in Des Moines.

[See the *Des Moines Register*, Oct. 6, 1957, and Nov. 6, 8, and 12, 1960—the last reprints a tribute from the *New York Herald Tribune; Des Moines Tribune*, Nov. 7, 1960; and George S. Mills, *Things Don't Just Happen* (1977). The assistance of David Kruidenier is gratefully acknowledged.]

IRVING DILLIARD

WEHLE, LOUIS BRANDEIS (Sept. 13, 1880–Feb. 13, 1959), lawyer, author, and public servant, was born in Louisville, Ky., the son of Otto A. Wehle and Amy Brandeis, a sister of Louis Dembitz Brandeis. His father emigrated from Vienna in 1867 and settled in Louisville, where in 1868 he entered the practice of law with his future brother-in-law, Louis Brandeis. His mother's family emigrated from Prague in 1849.

Wehle attended both academic and manual-training high schools in Louisville before entering Harvard University, where he received the B.A. in 1902, the M.A. in 1903, and the LL.B. in 1904.

Admitted to the Kentucky bar, Wehle joined his father in Louisville as a partner in the firm of Wehle and Wehle. He practiced law there between 1904 and 1917, gaining considerable experience as counsel for contractors on local, state, and national public works projects. On May 17, 1911, he married Mary Gray Patterson Liddell; they had three children.

With the beginning of American participation in World War I, Wehle joined the legal committee of the General Munitions Board, the function of which it would be to organize the drafting of emergency production contracts for the War Department. Thus began a brief but active period of public service that continued until the Republican victory in the elections of 1920. Wehle also served briefly on the legal committees of the War Industries Board and the Council of National Defense.

In June 1917, as special assistant to Secretary of War Newton Baker, Wehle was instrumental in negotiating and drafting a written agreement between Baker and Samuel Gompers, president of the American Federation of Labor, with respect to adjustment of labor disputes in the building of cantonments. This agreement became a model for such arrangements in other areas of wartime production, greatly minimizing the possibility of strikes in crucial industries. Wehle's success in labor negotiations led to his appointment as counsel to both the Cantonment Labor Adjustment Commission and the Federal Shipbuilding Labor Adjustment Board. Wehle also served as a counsel to the Emergency Fleet Corporation from August 1917 until March 1919, when he was appointed general counsel for the War Finance Corporation. There he acquired expertise in the areas of foreign trade and international law that subsequently influenced his career.

Wehle returned to the private practice of law in 1921 and maintained offices in New York and Washington. Between 1927 and 1935, he was associated with J. Markham Marshall in the law firm of Marshall and Wehle. After Marshall's death, in 1935, Wehle practiced independently for the rest of his life.

At Harvard, Wehle had coedited the *Harvard Crimson* with Franklin D. Roosevelt, beginning a friendship that continued until the latter's death. During World War I, Wehle and Roosevelt, who was then assistant secretary of the navy, worked together on matters concerning labor relations in the shipbuilding industry. In the autumn of 1919, they discussed the possibility that Roosevelt might run for vice-president on the Democratic ticket. Wehle proposed this to the Democratic National Campaign Committee and worked for Roosevelt's nomination. He later assisted Roosevelt in the unsuccessful presidential campaign of 1920. When Roosevelt became the Democratic candidate for president in 1932, Wehle attempted to enlist the support of organized labor. During the New Deal he served as a member of the White House Conference on Power Pooling in 1936 and was chief of the U.S. Foreign Economic Administration's mission to the Netherlands during World War II. In 1953 Wehle described his public career and relationship with Roosevelt in *Hidden Threads of History: Wilson Through Roosevelt*. He died in New York City.   .

[Wehle's papers, at the Franklin D. Roosevelt Library, Hyde Park, N.Y., cover aspects of his family and personal life, law practice, and public career between 1877 and 1958. A frequent contributor to law journals, Wehle wrote "The International Administration of European Inland Waterways," *American Journal of International Law*, Jan. 1946; "The U.N. By-Passes the International Court as the Council's Adviser," *University of Pennsylvania Law Review*, Feb. 1950; and "Comparative Law's Proper Task for the International Court," *ibid.*, Oct. 1950. For family background, see Josephine Goldmark, *Pilgrims of '48* (1930). See also the obituary notice, *New York Times*, Feb. 14, 1959.]

CHARLES S. WARD

WEIR, ERNEST TENER (Aug. 1, 1875–June 26, 1957), steel manufacturer, was born in Pittsburgh, Pa., the son of James Weir and Margaret Manson. Little is known of his family or childhood. His proudest boast was "I was born a commoner. I'm still a commoner. No one has ever given me anything." His father, a day laborer, died when Weir was fifteen, and he began work as a $3-a-week office boy in the Braddock Wire Company. The following year, he became a clerk for the Oliver Wire Company. Alarmed at the ever-increasing wire production in Pittsburgh, Weir decided that there was no future in that business. "I concluded that at the rate we were going, we would in a few years have made enough wire to last civilization for a long time." In 1899, with characteristic resolve, he left the Oliver Wire Company, where his future advancement

was assured, and became chief clerk at the American Tin Plate Company. In 1901 he married Mary Kline of Pittsburgh. They had one daughter and twin sons.

In 1903 Weir became plant manager and then superintendent of the Monessen Tin Plate Mills, subsidiaries of the American Tin Plate Company. Two years later, he was ready to strike out on his own. With a group of associates, including his brother David, James R. Phillips, and John Charles Williams, he purchased a bankrupt tinplate mill in Clarksburg, W.Va. In a short time the renamed Phillips Sheet and Tin Plate Company was prospering enough to allow the young partners to expand. In 1909 they bought 400 acres of land on the Ohio River twenty miles north of Wheeling and began building a new tinplate mill and the industrial town of Weirton. This plant continued to expand, and in 1913 a mill for the production of strip steel was built. It became the first plant of the Weirton Steel Company, which was incorporated in 1918 with a capitalization of $30 million.

Weir first achieved nationwide notoriety immediately after World War I, when he closed his profitable Steubenville, Ohio, plant rather than negotiate with the striking workers. In October 1919, at the Weirton plant, 185 Finnish workers, accused of being Communists, were forced by a local vigilante group to kneel in the public square and kiss the American flag. They were then run out of town. Weir issued a formal order to all of his plants never again to hire a Finn. This incident was an appropriate introduction of Weir to the American public, for throughout his long career in industry he remained an implacable foe of unions and an outspoken advocate of "American rugged individualism."

Weir was one of the first steel manufacturers to realize that the future of the industry lay not with railroads but with automobiles. He sought and got contracts with Detroit, including a major contract with Henry Ford. And he raised the capital necessary to expand production and fill these contracts by selling stock directly to the public. "I went to the opposite side of Wall Street from J. P. Morgan and Company. I wanted $40 million for 25 years at a time when that money looked like the national debt. . . . I got it not from Wall Street but from Main Street."

In September 1929, Weir joined forces with the Great Lakes Steel Corporation of Detroit and the M. A. Hanna Company subsidiaries of Cleveland to form the National Steel Company. It was not an auspicious moment for a new venture;

but following the stock market crash the next month, while every other steel company was cutting back on production, Weir boldly planned expansion—a $25 million plant in Detroit to be followed by a $40 million plant in Gary, Ind. National Steel quickly became the fifth largest producer of steel in America, second only to U. S. Steel in terms of ore resources in Minnesota and Michigan.

Although the Great Depression ultimately forced Weir to limit his plans for plant expansion, National Steel was the only major steel producer to show a profit in every year from 1930 to 1935. Insisting that the cure was infinitely worse than the disease, Weir became one of the nation's most outspoken critics of the New Deal. Claiming that his workers were fully satisfied with their own company-sponsored union, he refused to comply with Section 7 (a) of the National Recovery Act, which called for free elections for union representation within plants. Taken to court by the government, Weir emerged triumphant when a federal district judge in Wilmington, Del., declared Section 7 (a) null and void as applied to a manufacturing plant. It was one of the New Deal's earliest setbacks in the courts, and before the government could appeal this ruling, the U. S. Supreme Court, in a separate case, declared the entire National Recovery Act unconstitutional in 1935.

Weir's victory was short-lived, however. Changes in membership resulted in the Supreme Court's upholding the National Labor Relations Act, which Weir had claimed was grossly unconstitutional. Forced to bow to the dictates of government and to the lead taken by Big Steel, Weir admitted union elections into his plants. He himself retreated ever further into reactionary politics. One of the early and most ardent supporters of the Liberty League, he urged his fellow industrialists to become more active in politics in order to save the nation from what he considered socialistic dictatorship. He obeyed his own preaching by seeking and obtaining the position of chairman of the Republican National Finance Committee in 1940.

In the midst of his difficulties with the government and the top leaders in his own industry, Weir was also beset by personal problems. On Jan. 12, 1925, following the death of his first wife, he had married Mrs. Aeola Dickson Siebert. In 1941 she divorced him on the grounds of desertion. On Dec. 11, 1941, he married Mary E. Hayward. They had one son. During and immediately after the war, he continued to crit-

icize the government, freely giving interviews and making speeches whenever he had an opportunity. His name was frequently linked to such ultraright-wing organizations as American Action, established to counteract the political influence of the CIO Political Action Committee. He felt some measure of vindication when Congress passed the Taft-Hartley Act over President Harry S. Truman's veto in 1947 and when the Supreme Court declared the president's seizure of the nation's steel mills in 1952 unconstitutional.

In April 1957, Weir granted his last interview. Something of an anachronism as the last founder of a major steel plant who was still active, he gave no indication of any diminution of energy. Nor had his political and economic views been in any way affected by wars or depression. "There is only one word to describe Mr. Weir," the reporter commented. "He is indisputably a rugged individualist." He died in Philadelphia, Pa., and left an estate appraised at $10.6 million.

[Weir stressed his faith in the free enterprise system in his only book, *Progress Through Productivity* (1952). See also his testimony before the U.S. Senate Committee on Education and Labor, 74th Cong., 2d sess., 1936 and 76th Cong., 3rd sess., 1941. His last interview was published in the *New York Times*, Apr. 25, 1957; see also the obituary notice, *ibid.*, June 27, 1957; and "John Charles Williams," *National Cyclopaedia of American Biography*, 27, (1939).]

JOSEPH FRAZIER WALL

WELCH, JOSEPH NYE (Oct. 22, 1890–Oct. 6, 1960), lawyer, was born in Primghar, Iowa, the son of William Welch, a farmer and handyman, and Martha Thyer, who had been a hired girl on his brother's farm. He recalled "the blessing of being poor and totally unaware of it." Pushed by his mother, "Josie" excelled in school. After clerking for two years in a real estate office, he entered Grinnell College, from which he was graduated Phi Beta Kappa in 1914.

Ever since his boyhood, when he had frequented the courthouse, Welch had been attracted to the law. Armed with a scholarship, he headed for Harvard Law School; ranking second in his class, he won another. In 1917 he took his law degree and, on Sept. 20 of that year, married Judith Hampton Lyndon of Washington, Ga. They had two sons. Welch then attended Army Officer Candidate School, but was not commissioned until after Armistice Day. He served briefly with the legal division of the U.S. Shipping Board.

In 1919, Welch joined the Boston firm of Hale and Dorr. He became a partner in 1923 and a senior partner in 1936. He practiced civil law, especially antitrust, libel, estates, wills, and tax cases. An esteemed trial lawyer, he headed the trial department of the firm. He developed an engaging, self-effacing courtroom style. Puckishly, he pointed out that he lost his most noted case, a $7 million tax dispute involving the Chicago stockyards. Though active in bar and legal associations, Welch was not a joiner; he preferred to spend time with his family.

Welch's comfortable existence was interrupted in April 1954 by a call to serve as special counsel to the Department of the Army in its confrontation with Senator Joseph R. McCarthy. Hearings were held before the Special Subcommittee on Investigations of the Government Operations Committee to unravel a snarl of charges. The army claimed that McCarthy and two aides, especially Roy M. Cohn, had exerted improper pressures to obtain preferential treatment for G. David Schine, a consultant to McCarthy's subcommittee who had faced induction into the military. McCarthy riposted that the army had held Private Schine hostage to blunt McCarthy's investigation of subversive employees at the Fort Monmouth Signal Corps laboratories. Although he was a Republican who was known to several members of the Eisenhower administration, Welch had never been politically active: the circumstances of his selection are obscure.

If Welch expected the probe to resemble a trial, he was soon disabused. The thirty-six days of hearings, before television cameras that beamed them to 20 million viewers, were political theater in which legal standards of relevancy and materiality went for naught. Welch showed his acumen nonetheless. He sensed that the famous "cropped photo" of Army Secretary Robert T. Stevens and Schine had been doctored and that the "FBI document" introduced into the hearings was a carbon "copy of precisely nothing." The army principals had not acquitted themselves very well in their testimony, but Welch was ready with vigorous interrogation when Cohn and McCarthy took the stand. Projecting a bemused, urbane, Dickensian image, he proved to be a master of the weapon of humor. His deft thrusts aroused in McCarthy a strong aversion to the man he termed "a clever little lawyer."

On June 9, 1954, Welch goaded McCarthy into what became the dramatic climax of the hearings. As Welch ragged Cohn about the need to oust Communists from defense installations "by sundown," McCarthy lashed out at this "phony" solicitude and noted that Welch had tried to "foist" Frederick G. Fisher, Jr., a member of Hale and Dorr, upon the subcommittee despite Fisher's membership "for a number of years . . . of an organization which was named, oh, years and years ago, as the legal bulwark of the Communist party." Explaining the innocence of the episode, Welch added: "Little did I dream you could be so reckless and so cruel as to do an injury to that lad . . . . I like to think I am a gentleman, but your forgiveness will have to come from someone other than me." McCarthy bored in again but Welch, verging on tears, cut him off, as forbidden applause reverberated through the room.

The hearings ended June 17, a victory for neither side; legal issues had long since been muddled. The Fisher episode, by juxtaposing two divergent characters, may have epitomized what McCarthyism meant, and contributed to the indeterminate, but profound, decline in McCarthy's stature. The Boston lawyer personified a felicitous contrast to the senator. If too modest, Welch was near the truth in saying, "The people made me into what they needed."

Welch hoped to return to his accustomed obscurity, but it was not to be. Fame opened up a new career. His theatrical talents led him back to television in 1956 as narrator of a much-praised series of "Omnibus" programs on the constitutional history of the nation. Appearances on other shows followed, and in 1959 Welch played the judge in the movie *Anatomy of a Murder*. He received excellent notices.

Welch marveled that his later years could yield such joy and adventure. They were saddened only by the death of his wife in 1956. He married Agnes Rodgers Brown, a family friend, on July 13, 1957. He died at Hyannis, Mass.

[The Welch Papers are at the Boston Public Library. With Richard Hofstadter and the "Omnibus" staff he wrote *The Constitution* (1956), a compendium of his first three television programs. The Karl E. Mundt Papers, Dakota State University, Madison, S.D., are useful on the hearings. For the latter, see U.S. Senate, 83rd Cong., 2nd Sess., Special Subcommittee on Investigations, Committee on Government Operations, *Special Senate Investigation on Charges and Counter-charges Involving: Secretary of the Army Robert T. Stevens, John G. Adams, H. Struve Hensel and Senator Joe McCarthy, Roy M. Cohn and Francis P. Carr* (1954).

See also Michael Straight, *Trial by Television* (1954); and Robert Griffith, *The Politics of Fear* (1970). Less reliable are Charles E. Potter, *Days of Shame* (1965); and Roy Cohn, *McCarthy* (1968). Obituaries are in *Boston Globe*, Oct. 6–7, 1960; and *New York Times*, Oct. 7, 1960.]

RICHARD M. FRIED

WELKER, HERMAN (Dec. 11, 1906–Oct. 30, 1957), lawyer and U.S. senator, was born at Cambridge, Idaho, the son of John Thornton Welker, a farmer, and Ann Zella Shepherd. Welker graduated from Weiser High School and then attended the University of Idaho at Moscow. While in college he sustained himself by herding sheep, washing dishes, and helping on a ranch. After graduation he attended the university law school, from which he received the LL.B. in 1929. While still in law school he was appointed prosecuting attorney of Washington County. On Sept. 12, 1930, Welker married Gladys Pence. They had one daughter. He remained in western Idaho, practicing law and farming, until 1935, when the lure of Hollywood attracted him to southern California. He built up a successful law practice throughout the West and proudly numbered entertainers among his clients. In 1943 Welker enlisted in the air force. While in the military he decided to return to Idaho and pursue a political career.

Welker built up a law practice in Payette, and in 1948 was elected to the Idaho state senate. His state legislative experience proved to be a springboard for higher political goals. In 1950 he entered the Republican primaries as a candidate for the United States Senate. A handsome man with prematurely gray hair, Welker possessed a fine platform presence. He faced numerous contenders in the Republican runoff. Welker ignored his Republican opponents and campaigned against the Democratic incumbent, Glen H. Taylor, an outspoken critic of the cold war who had bolted the Democrats in 1948 and run for vice-president on the Progressive ticket. Welker hammered away at the "soft on communism" theme that was developing throughout the nation in 1950. D. Worth Clark, a conservative Democrat, challenged Taylor in the Democratic primary and defeated him. Taylor blamed Welker, who easily won the Republican nomination.

In his campaign against Clark, Welker's main theme centered on the "Red scare." Utilizing the tactics made famous by Senator Joseph R. McCarthy of Wisconsin, he defeated Clark by nearly 45,000 votes.

Welker was a straight-line conservative and usually voted the will of the Republican party as a senator. When the Republicans got control of the Senate in 1952, Welker obtained assignments on the judiciary, agriculture, and District of Columbia committees. Most important, he was put on Senator McCarthy's Internal Security Subcommittee of the Judiciary Committee. It was as a member of this subcommittee that Welker earned the title of "Junior McCarthy." He worked hard at looking for subversives throughout the government. His motives were probably both political and patriotic. He did believe that there were Communist agents employed by the federal government, and he felt that the Republican party could clean them out.

His desire to cleanse the United States of leftists brought Welker back to Idaho in 1954. Taylor had won the Democratic senatorial nomination, and the incumbent Republican, Henry Dworshak, was barely holding on to a slight lead in the polls. Welker devised a successful scheme to discredit Taylor among the Idaho electorate. At the very time the full Senate was considering the censure of Senator McCarthy, Welker called the Internal Security Subcommittee into special session. Although he was the only senator in attendance, he listened to testimony by a number of former Communists, including Herbert Philbrick, Matthew Cvetic, and John Lautner. They testified that Taylor and the 1948 Progressive party were Communist-controlled and -inspired. According to Welker, Taylor knew this to be the case, yet he ran. Welker and Cvetic then flew to Idaho and campaigned against Taylor. Dworshak was the easy winner.

Welker stoutly defended McCarthy on the Senate floor but was unable to stop the censure move. The discrediting of McCarthy had an effect on Welker's credibility in Idaho. Although he was renominated in 1956, a young Democratic attorney, Frank Church, had little difficulty in defeating him. During Welker's last year in the Senate, and especially during the campaign, it was apparent that he was having health problems. He collapsed on two occasions and at times found it difficult to form sentences correctly.

After his defeat Welker intended to return to Boise and practice law, but in 1957 he was operated on twice in Washington, D.C., for a brain tumor. He died following the second operation.

[Most of Welker's senatorial papers were destroyed or lost after the family returned to Idaho. There are numerous references to him in the papers of Henry Dworshak and of Governor Len B. Jordan, both at the Idaho State Library in Boise. The *Idaho Daily Statesman* has many references to Welker and contains a full obituary. Most accounts of McCarthyism have some information on Welker. The best of these is Robert Griffith, *The Politics of Fear* (1971).]

F. ROSS PETERSON

WEST, OSWALD (May 20, 1873–Aug. 22, 1960), governor of Oregon, was born near Guelph, Ontario, the son of John Gulliver West and Sarah McGregor. His family moved to Salem, Oreg., in 1877. As a boy, West worked for his father, who was a butcher and livestock broker. He attended grammar school through the eighth grade in Salem and in Portland, and at the age of fifteen became an office boy in the Ladd and Bush Bank at Salem. He was later promoted to clerk and teller. West prospected for gold in Alaska in 1899, without notable success, and returned to his bank job later that year. In 1900 he became a teller for the First National Bank in Astoria. One of his duties was carrying saddlebags of gold and cash, on horseback, from Salem to Astoria. On Sept. 22, 1897, he married Mabel Hutton; they had three children.

West's public career began in September 1903, when Governor George E. Chamberlain appointed him state land agent. In this office, he performed with skill, efficiency, and seemingly tireless energy. His exposures of forgeries and bogus transactions enabled Oregon to recover more than 900,000 acres of state land fraudulently obtained by speculators. He was instrumental in the passage of a revised land law with criminal penalties for fraud.

Appointed to the Oregon Railroad Commission in 1907, West helped secure more rigid safety standards and lower freight and passenger rates. In the process, he cultivated an image of a progressive reformer. The *Portland Oregonian* praised his "aggressive spirit" and "efforts to establish a better order of things."

By 1910, there was considerable public interest in West as a gubernatorial candidate. He resisted initially and tried to persuade Mayor Harry Lane of Portland to enter the race. When Lane declined, West became the Democratic candidate. He conducted a nonpartisan campaign, partly because he was a political maverick but also because the Republicans held a registration advantage of more than three-to-one. He vowed to defend the "Oregon System" of government, with its initiative, referendum, and direct-primary laws, which were then under attack by conservatives. "No corporation nor individuals," he promised, "nor machine nor combination of men, will have the slightest claim on me." A major turning point came when Senator Jonathan Bourne, a progressive Republican, endorsed him. West defeated Republican incumbent Jay Bowerman by 6,102 votes.

West's administration was probably the most progressive in Oregon's history. In 1911 he turned back real estate interests that were threatening to ruin Oregon's coastline, by declaring the state beaches a public highway. "No local selfish interest should be permitted," he said, ". . . to destroy or even impair this great birthright of our people." He established a state conservation commission, an office of state forester, a bureau of forestry, and a fish and game commission. He blocked efforts to turn national forest lands over to private interests. Theodore Roosevelt described West in a 1911 article in *Outlook* magazine as "more keenly appreciative of how much this natural beauty should mean to civilized mankind, than almost any other man I have ever met holding high political position."

In addition, West pushed through such social reforms as minimum wage, workmen's compensation, and widows' pension laws. In 1913 he established an industrial welfare commission to protect women and children workers. He was a strong advocate of prison reform, creating a parole board and modifying an indeterminate-sentence law. He opposed capital punishment but lost a referendum to abolish the death penalty.

An early supporter of woman's suffrage, West campaigned successfully in 1912 for an initiative giving Oregon women the vote. He expanded the Railroad Commission into the Public Utilities Commission, with wider authority, and formed the state's first highway commission, which authorized construction of a new system of roads. As is often the case with strong executives, West had a stormy relationship with the legislature and in 1911 he vetoed seventy-two bills.

West decided not to seek reelection in 1914, but he did campaign for a constitutional amendment making Oregon a dry state. The prohibition amendment passed and West became a stalwart dry. In 1918 West ran for the U.S. Senate after Secretary of the Treasury William G. McAdoo had helped persuade him to run. Although he campaigned as a Wilson loyalist, the president refused to support him because of West's close ties with Senator George Chamberlain, a leading administration critic. West was defeated by Republican Senator Charles L. McNary, whom he had earlier appointed to the Oregon Supreme Court.

West, a self-educated lawyer, practiced law in Portland upon leaving the governorship but remained politically active for many years. He attended the 1924 Democratic convention as a McAdoo supporter and in 1926 was elected Democratic national committeeman. He opposed the nomination of Alfred E. Smith in 1928 because of Smith's advocacy of the repeal of prohibition, and gave him only nominal support in the campaign. In 1930 West was defeated for reelection as national committeeman. He regained some influence in 1932 as an early supporter of Franklin D. Roosevelt.

Like many other reformers of the Progressive era, West became a conservative critic of the New Deal. Yet he continued to support Roosevelt and the Democratic party. In his law practice, West represented private utilities and he fought public power in the Pacific Northwest. His strident attacks on younger, more liberal Democratic leaders left him isolated from the mainstream of his party. He curtailed most public activities after a heart attack in 1945 but became a prolific writer for Oregon newspapers about the early history of the Northwest.

Tall, of medium build, and with craggy features, West spoke with a clipped voice and often used his acerbic wit to advantage in speeches. He died in Portland, Oreg.

[The West papers at the University of Oregon Library include some correspondence, an extensive collection of clippings, and photographs; a smaller but useful collection is at the Oregon Historical Society. His role in Oregon politics is covered in Robert E. Burton, *Democrats of Oregon* (1970); and George S. Turnbull, *Governors of Oregon* (1959). West's "Reminiscences and Anecdotes: The McNarys and Lanes," *Oregon Historical Quarterly*, Sept. 1951, is useful autobiographical material. Howard A. De-Witt, "Charles L. McNary and the 1918 Congressional Election," *ibid.*, June 1967, includes an account of West's campaign.]

STEVE NEAL

WEST, ROY OWEN (Oct. 27, 1868–Nov. 29, 1958), secretary of the interior and Repub-

lican party leader, was born in Georgetown, Ill., the son of Pleasant West and Helen Anna West. His father combined insurance with the lumber business. West received his early education in Georgetown, then attended DePauw University, where he received the B.A. and LL.B. degrees in 1890. He was awarded the M.A. degree at DePauw three years later. Upon completing his education, West moved to Chicago to practice law. There he met Charles S. Deneen, a lawyer and future leader of the Deneen (later Deneen-West) faction of the Illinois Republican party. A close association developed between them, with "never a written understanding and never a misunderstanding."

West quickly won prominence in Chicago politics. In 1894 he became assistant county attorney, and from 1895 to 1897 he was city attorney for Chicago. On June 11, 1898, he married Louisa Augustus; they had one son. Also in 1898 he commenced five consecutive terms, lasting to 1914, as a member of the Cook County Board of Review. By 1900, West, Deneen, and William Lorimer, a member of the U.S. House of Representatives, dominated the Cook County Central Committee, although the parting of the ways between the first two and Lorimer was not far off. West in 1902 formed a law partnership with Percy B. Eckhart, son of a wealthy and influential Chicago miller whose backing he enjoyed. His law office was part of the suite occupied by Frank O. Lowden, who was ambitious for political power.

His wife died in 1901, and on June 8, 1904, West married Louise McWilliams; they had one daughter. In the gubernatorial campaign of 1904, West acted as Deneen's campaign manager. Deneen won the nomination over Lowden and the election. (He was governor of Illinois from 1905 to 1913.) West then became chairman of the Republican State Central Committee, serving until 1914. During these years Lorimer, now a United States senator, embarrassed Illinois Republicans when he was accused of election fraud. Deneen and West were credited with helping oust Lorimer from the Senate in 1912.

West's influence in the Republican national organization grew steadily. In 1908, 1912, 1916, and 1928 he was a delegate to the Republican National Convention. He succeeded Lowden as the Illinois member of the Republican National Committee in 1912, holding this position until 1916 and again from 1928 to 1932. After Lowden became governor of Illinois in 1917, he cultivated West by consulting him about patronage. When

Lowden aspired to the Republican presidential nomination in 1920, West traveled through New England at his own expense, seeking support for him. Early that year he took charge of Lowden's New York headquarters. But in 1928, when Lowden again sought the nomination, West was an enthusiastic supporter of Herbert Hoover.

In 1924, West successfully directed the primary campaign that eventuated in the election of Deneen to the United States Senate. That same year he had become secretary of the Republican National Committee, administering a budget system instituted by President Calvin Coolidge, with whom he worked closely. On July 20, 1928, Coolidge appointed West secretary of the interior to succeed Hubert Work, who had resigned in order to become chairman of the Republican National Committee. The surprise appointment was construed as recognition of West's ability, friendship with the president, and substantial service to the party, but also as a move to strengthen the party in Chicago, where the Democratic presidential candidate, Alfred E. Smith, held a strong lead.

West's tenure as secretary of the interior lasted until March 1929. It was marked by his quick grasp of the varied responsibilities of his office. His annual report, released in early December, set forth a policy of conservation of natural resources, and won praise as "a remarkable inventory of the nation's wealth" contained in the public domain. His appointment was made while the Senate was in recess; and upon convening in December, it determined, through the Public Lands Committee, to hold hearings about West's fitness to hold the cabinet post. At a time when the issue of public power companies was at the fore, West's connection with the Chicago utilities magnate Samuel Insull came into question. An attorney for Insull and a heavy investor in his companies, West had previously acknowledged his family holdings in the Insull empire.

At the committee hearing, where Senator Thomas James Walsh, who had investigated the naval oil leases made by a former secretary of the interior (the Teapot Dome scandal), questioned him sharply, West testified that he had sold his Insull stock and had opposed Insull in political conflicts in Illinois. By a vote of nine to four, the committee recommended confirmation. On the Senate floor Senator George Norris, pointing out that the secretary of the interior was ex officio a member of the Federal Power Commission, which ruled on applications for power-plant sites, vigorously objected to confirmation. Senate

confirmation on January 21, by a vote of fifty-three to twenty-seven, led to another controversy. Though the vote had been taken in secret session, a press association released details of the vote. The release angered some members, and prompted Norris and others to attack the practice of considering nominations behind closed doors. On June 18, 1929, the Senate, by a vote of sixty-nine to five, altered its rules, declaring that in the future all business would be in open session unless a majority of the Senate determined that a nomination or treaty required secrecy.

West's term expired with the end of the Coolidge administration. President Hoover offered him the ambassadorship to Japan, which he declined. On Deneen's death in 1940, West became chief of the faction known as the National Republican Party. During World War II he returned to public service, acting as special assistant to the attorney general of the United States. He heard the cases of conscientious objectors until 1952.

Nearly six feet tall, slender in build, both reserved and disarming in manner, and loyal to his friends, West had a quiet devotion to his party and church. He favored minimal government interference in the economy, and was an enemy of corruption. From 1914 to 1950 he was a trustee of DePauw University, serving as board president from 1924 to 1950. He was instrumental in securing more than $10 million in gifts for his alma mater. He died in Chicago.

[See U.S. Senate, Public Lands and Surveys Committee, *Nomination of Hon. Roy O. West to Be Secretary of the Interior* (1928); William T. Hutchinson, *Lowden of Illinois*, 2 vols. (1957); and Richard Lowitt, *George W. Norris* (1971). Obituaries are in *New York Times* and *Chicago Tribune*, Dec. 1, 1958.]

JAMES A. RAWLEY

WESTON, EDWARD HENRY (Mar. 24, 1886–Jan. 1, 1958), photographer, was born in Highland Park, Ill., the son of Edward Burbank Weston, a physician, and Alice Jeanette Brett. His mother died before he was five, and much of his upbringing, especially after his father remarried, was left to his sister, May (Mary Jeanette), who was nine years older. As a child, Weston showed little interest in academic subjects. In the summer of 1902 his father gave him a Kodak Bulls-Eye #2 box camera. Soon he was saving every penny in order to buy a secondhand view camera and tripod with which to take better landscape photographs in and around Chicago.

When Weston dropped out of high school in 1903, a place was secured for him with Marshall Field and Company, where in three years he advanced from errand boy to salesman. But the joys of exploring with his camera and developing and printing his own negatives at home had become his major enthusiasms. In 1906, while visiting his sister in California, Weston decided not to return to Chicago. After working as a railroad surveyor, he bought an old postcard camera to take from door to door, offering his services as an all-purpose family photographer.

To increase his technical competence, Weston attended the Illinois College of Photography in 1908; he finished the course in six months, but a technicality deprived him of a diploma. Returning to southern California, he worked as a printer for other portrait photographers. On Jan. 30, 1909, he married Flora May Chandler, the daughter of a wealthy Los Angeles family. They had four sons: Edward Chandler, Theodore Brett, Laurence Neil, and Cole. The marriage, however, was not always happy.

In 1911 Weston built and opened his own studio, surrounded by a garden, in Tropico (now Glendale), Calif., where his sister and her husband, John H. Seaman, resided. Before long, customers from the Hollywood movie colony began to find their way to his rustic workplace. Through a troubled affair with Margrethe Mather, lasting on and off from about 1912 to 1920, Weston was introduced to the latest, most advanced ideas in all the arts. The period from 1914 to 1917 was one of considerable success as his spontaneous, soft-focus, outdoor portraits of children and dancers won many awards. He gave many demonstrations of his "high-key" techniques and in 1917 was elected to the London Salon, pictorial photography's highest honor.

But growing dissatisfaction with artificiality of any kind led to a profound change of direction in Weston's career. From 1919 to 1921 he sent no work to public exhibitions, and, as part of the process of ridding himself of the romantic overtones and self-conscious aestheticism of the pictorial movement, he destroyed in a bonfire many of his earlier photographs along with three years of entries in his daybook, a kind of diary he had begun to keep in 1917. His new work involved experiments with semiabstract fragments of nudes or natural forms, seen in close-up or taken at unusual angles with an 8 × 10 view camera.

In March 1922 Tina Modotti took some of Weston's new, sharp-focus contact prints to Mexico City, where they were enthusiastically received. In October of that year, Weston went east, stopping to see his sister, who was then living in Ohio, and taking his first industrial photographs of the Armco Steel plant, before going on to New York in November to meet Alfred Stieglitz, Paul Strand, and Charles Sheeler, the leading exponents of "straight" photography.

In August 1923 Weston went to live in Mexico with Tina Modotti, taking his son Chandler along. He opened a studio first in Tacubaya and then in Mexico City, where he met the leaders of the Mexican Renaissance—including Diego Rivera, David Alfaro Siqueiros, and José Clemente Orozco. After several months in 1925, when he shared a studio in San Francisco with his friend, Johan Hagemeyer, Weston went back to Mexico for another year, traveling with Modotti and another son, Brett, while photographing marketplaces, bars, sculpture, landscapes, and clouds. He returned to Glendale in November 1926.

Building on the dramatic power of his Mexican portrait heads and still lifes, Weston began a series of extreme close-up studies of shells and vegetables. Cypress roots, eroded rocks, and twisted seaweed became major themes in his work during the years he shared a studio with Brett in Carmel (1929–1934). He was invited, along with Edward Steichen, to organize the American section of the Deutsche Werkbund "Film und Foto" exhibition held in Stuttgart in 1929; and he was given his first one-man shows in New York (1930) and San Francisco (1931). Together with Ansel Adams and Willard Van Dyck, he was a leading member of the Group f64, an informal association founded in 1932 and disbanded in 1935 that promoted the principles of "pure" photography.

Having turned his attention from small details to larger forms and broader vistas in the early 1930's, Weston made his famous series of nudes and sand dunes at Oceano, Calif., in 1936. The following year he was the first photographer to be awarded a Guggenheim Fellowship. The $2,000 stipend, renewed in 1938, allowed him to travel throughout the southwest and northwest, making more than 1,500 exposures.

After divorcing his wife, Flora, in 1938, Weston married Charis Wilson on Apr. 24, 1939. They lived in a house, built by his son Neil, on Wildcat Hill in Carmel, not far from Point Lobos, where he began photographing again. A trip through the southern and eastern states to collect photographs for a special edition of Walt Whitman's *Leaves of Grass* was cut short by America's entry into World War II.

In 1946 a major retrospective of Weston's work was held at the Museum of Modern Art in New York City. Stricken with Parkinson's disease, Weston took his last negative at Point Lobos in 1948. Thereafter he supervised his sons, Brett and Cole, and his darkroom assistant, Dody Warren, as they produced several sets of prints from 1,000 selected negatives. He died in Carmel.

[Portfolios of Weston's photographs published during his lifetime include Merle Armitage, ed., *The Art of Edward Weston* (1932); and *Fifty Photographs: Edward Weston* (1947). Weston and Charis Wilson collaborated on *California and the West* (1940), using ninety-six of his Guggenheim Fellowship photographs; and on *The Cats of Wildcat Hill* (1947). Walt Whitman's *Leaves of Grass*, 2 vols. (1942), published by the Limited Editions Club, includes fifty of Weston's photographs. Ansel Adams edited *Edward Weston: My Camera on Point Lobos* (1950).

Nancy Newhall, comp., *The Photographs of Edward Weston* (1946), is the first monographic treatment and includes a chronology, list of exhibitions, and bibliography. Newhall also edited *The Daybooks of Edward Weston*, 2 vols. (1961–1966), which provides the most intimate glimpse of his art and life in the 1920's and 1930's. Telling excerpts from the daybooks were reprinted in Nancy Newhall, *Edward Weston, Photographer* (1965). *Edward Weston: Fifty Years* (1973), contains an illustrated biography by Ben Maddow; and the exhibition catalog, *Edward Weston's Gifts to His Sister* (1978) by Kathy Kelsey Foley, provides additional information about the Weston family relationships. *The Photographer* (1947), produced by the United States Information Agency, is the only film in which Weston himself appeared.]

ELLWOOD C. PARRY III

WHEELER, (GEORGE) POST (Aug. 6, 1869–Dec. 23, 1956), diplomat and author, was born in Owego, N.Y., the son of Henry Wheeler and Mary Sparks. His father, a Methodist clergyman and writer, was born in England. His mother served the Woman's Christian Temperance Union as its national evangelist. Educated at home by a governess, he also attended public schools and graduated from William Penn Charter School in Philadelphia. He received the B.A. from Princeton in 1891 and remained there as a teaching fellow, earning the D. Litt. in 1893. He then continued his studies at the University of Pennsylvania and at the Sorbonne. While in Paris he established a syndicated newspaper column, presenting feature topics for newspapers in eleven major American cities.

In 1895 Wheeler returned to New York. He worked first as editor of the *New York Press*, where he helped to popularize the term "yellow journalism" when he used it as a caption for an editorial deploring the sensationalism and vulgarity of the circulation war between William Randolph Hearst and Joseph Pulitzer. He also began to write poetry (later published as *Love-in-a-Mist* [1901] and *Poems* [1902]), short stories, and articles. He also published *The Writer* (1893) and *Reflections of a Bachelor* (1897). From 1897 to 1900, at the height of the gold rush, Wheeler explored the Alaskan frontier and the Yukon. In 1900 he founded the Camelot Publishing Company in New York and, under its imprint, issued and promoted a best-selling novel, *A Furnace of Earth* (1900), by Hallie Erminie Rives. They were later married and had no children.

Wheeler began his diplomatic career in 1906 as second secretary to the United States Embassy at Tokyo. He subsequently was secretary to the embassies at St. Petersburg (1909–1911), Rome (1912–1913), and Tokyo (1914–1916). He was also counselor of the legation at Stockholm (1917–1921) and of the embassies at London (1921–1924), Madrid (1925), and Rio de Janeiro (1929). In 1929 he was appointed envoy and minister to Paraguay and, in 1933, minister to Albania, where he served until his retirement in November 1934.

Wheeler was considered the first American career diplomat. His assignment by President Theodore Roosevelt in 1906 followed his taking the first examination given by the State Department for admission to the Foreign Service. In his first term in Tokyo he became absorbed with the events and ultimate conspiracy that led to the fall of the Russian fortress, Port Arthur, to the Japanese in 1905. Gathering data from informants, Wheeler traveled to Korea in search of additional facts and eventually set forth the bizarre details in *Dragon in the Dust* (1946).

Wheeler was traveling by train in Austria when World War I broke out in 1914. Caught with other aliens, he was sent to Berlin, where he took charge of American refugees fleeing Germany. From Berlin he and his group of approximately 100 Americans entrained to Esbjerg, Denmark, from which they made safe passage across the minefilled North Sea to Hull, England, their Danish vessel being the first to come from

Europe after the declaration of war. While chargé d'affaires in Japan he handled negotiations concerning military matters. All correspondence between the Japanese government and the governments of the Central Powers was channeled through him. He was also responsible for some 3,000 prisoners of war taken by the Japanese at the collapse of the German fortress at Tsingtau. While minister to Paraguay, Wheeler conducted two years of negotiations between the Paraguayan government and the Commission of Neutrals in Washington growing out of the Chaco War between Paraguay and Bolivia.

Throughout his diplomatic career Wheeler continued to write. In St. Petersburg he was attracted to Russian folklore and published a collection of twelve folktales, *Russian Wonder Tales* (1912), each story illustrated with a painting by Ivan Bilibin commissioned by the czar. His other collections included *Albanian Wonder Tales* (1936), illustrated by Maud and Miska Petersham, and *Hawaiian Wonder Tales* (1953). Fascinated by life in India, he wrote *Hathoo of the Elephants* (1943), a jungle adventure story, and *India Against the Storm* (1944). His abiding interest in geography was reflected in *The Golden Legend of Ethiopia* (1936), the love story of the Queen of Sheba and King Solomon, and *The Sacred Scriptures of the Japanese* (1952). During his tenure in Japan, Wheeler began a continuing study of *hanashika* tales, which had been handed down in the oral tradition by professional storytellers. He assembled and collated approximately five hundred legends in ten volumes entitled *Ho-Dan-Zo, Storehouse-of-Ten-Thousand-Jewels*. The work was not published due to a shipping error involving customs clearance at the time of Pearl Harbor, but a posthumous one-volume collection, *Tales From the Japanese Storytellers* (1964), appeared under the editorship of Harold G. Henderson.

On Dec. 29, 1906, Wheeler married the novelist Hallie Erminie Rives in Tokyo. Throughout their careers they kept diaries and scrapbooks highlighting the ups and downs of their life abroad. In their joint autobiography, *Dome of Many-Coloured Glass* (1955), they wrote alternate chapters describing their life in the foreign service. In candid and lively prose they revealed that although their service overseas was a series of adventures, it was also filled with frustration and disappointment. The book was an indictment of the Foreign Service. Charging that a controlling clique favored friends and associates with desirable assignments and other preferential treatment, the Wheelers accused the service of "rampant favoritism and nepotism, craft, falsehood, sycophancy and chicanery." They claimed that they had been placed on the cabal's blacklist and received only minor assignments in less important posts.

In fact, Wheeler held the grade of counselor of embassy for a longer period than any previous officer in the foreign service, before his promotion to minister. His career was interrupted by ill health, and at one time he had a two-year hiatus while waiting for a suitable assignment. The nadir came in 1913, when he was recalled to Washington and officially requested to resign from the diplomatic service by Secretary of State William Jennings Bryan. Wheeler fought the ouster and won, being completely cleared and reinstated in 1914.

A lifelong Republican, Wheeler developed many political friendships, including those with Theodore Roosevelt, William Howard Taft, William E. Borah, Joseph G. Cannon, and Sumner Welles. In retirement Wheeler continued to travel and write. He died in Neptune, N.J.

[In addition to the Wheelers' autobiography, *Dome of Many-Coloured Glass* (1955), see the obituary notice, *New York Times*, Dec. 24, 1956.]

MARY SUE DILLIARD SCHUSKY

WHEELWRIGHT, MARY CABOT (Oct. 2, 1878–July 19, 1958), anthropologist, was born in Boston, Mass., the daughter of Andrew Cunningham Wheelwright, a merchant, and Sarah Perkins Cabot. Her formal education was minimal, but she played the piano and studied singing. Wheelwright knew and loved the Maine coast, and could navigate under sail. Although her early years were spent chiefly in New England, she accompanied her parents to California in 1897 and toured France with them in 1906. After her father's death in 1908, she and her mother traveled in western Europe (1909) and in Greece and Egypt (1912).

For forty years Wheelwright remained the dutiful Victorian daughter, devoting herself to good works, particularly a settlement-house music school in the South End of Boston. Since she was dyspeptic, gawky, and opinionated, she did not attract suitors; but after her mother's death in 1917, she conquered her shyness and set out to see the world. Wheelwright went to New Mexico with her cousin Evelyn Sears, riding and camping with cowboy guides. She became so attached to the Southwest that in 1923 she bought the Los Luceros Ranch near Alcalde, N.M. She visited remote places in Spain and the eastern Mediterranean, buying Son Batle, a beautiful farm on Mallorca, in 1931. After acquiring these houses she left Boston and bought a tiny shipmaster's cottage on Sutton's Island, Maine. Wheelwright loved everything about the Maine coast. In 1928, when *British Ballads From Maine* was about to be published without tunes, she brought a musicologist from North Dakota to Maine at her expense. In a month he took down 199 old airs that greatly enriched the publication. Despite her sketchy education she had an instinctive feeling for what ought to be done, and the energy and means to see that it was done.

Wheelwright had great curiosity about the most unlikely things. In New Mexico, despite the barrier of language, she won the friendship of a famous Navajo medicine man, Hasteen Klah, whom she first met when snowbound on the Navajo reservation. With his help she learned to appreciate the Navajo religion, began to collect the record of its ceremonies, and in 1936 founded the Museum of Navajo Ceremonial Art at Santa Fe, N.M. For the museum she provided a building modeled on a Navajo ceremonial hogan.

The symbolic paintings in colored sands that are an essential element of Navajo ceremonies are rubbed away at the conclusion of the rite of which they form a part. Their designs and meaning thus remain only in the medicine man's head. To insure the preservation of the most important of these, Klah wove thirteen blankets to perpetuate his designs for the Hail and Night chants. These, plus hundreds of watercolor and casein copies of sand paintings from other ceremonies, are preserved in the museum, as are sound recordings of chants and many ceremonial objects. Wheelwright went to India in 1940 to search for symbols comparable with those in Navajo rites. She also studied symbolism in primitive religions in many parts of the world, producing a study published by the Peabody Museum at Harvard University (1956).

Although she continued to summer in Maine, Wheelwright concentrated all her resources on the Museum of Navajo Ceremonial Art. (Being the victim of a prudent Boston family trust, she had a handsome income for life but no control of the capital. This protection against fortune-hunting suitors made it impossible for her to endow the museum as she would have wished.) On the twentieth anniversary of the museum in

1956, the chairman of the Navajo Tribal Council sent a message thanking Wheelwright "for undertaking with courage what could only be accomplished in the most intangible awareness of spiritual tranquility and symbolic beauty. She has accomplished this and she has done it well. The Navajo people will be forever grateful to her for this achievement of building the things of the spirit into visible and physical form in the Museum of Navajo Ceremonial Art.

Wheelwright died at Sutton's Island. Her museum continues under a board of trustees, who in 1976 changed its name to the Wheelwright Museum, an act that she would have deprecated.

[Wheelwright's papers are preserved at the Wheelwright Museum. Her publications include *Navajo Creation Chant* (1942); *Water and Hail Chants* (1946); "Notes on Corresponding Symbols in Various Parts of the World," part 3 of "A Study of Navajo Symbolism," *Peabody Museum Papers*, 32, no. 3 (1956); and *Great Star Chant and Prayers, and Coyote Chant* (1957). See also Phillips Barry, Fannie H. Eckstorm, and Mary Winslow Smyth, *British Ballads From Maine* (1929). L. Vernon Briggs, *History and Genealogy of the Cabot Family 1475–1927*, II (1927), gives the family background. Walter Muir Whitehill, *Independent Historical Societies* (1962), describes the museum, and prints the text of the 1956 tribute of the Navajo Tribal Council. Helen Howe, *The Gentle Americans* (1965), describes Wheelwright among the "mighty maidens" who were friends of her father, M. A. De Wolfe Howe.]

WALTER MUIR WHITEHILL

WHITE, BENJAMIN FRANKLIN (Feb. 3, 1873–May 20, 1958), driver, breeder, and trainer of harness horses, was born in Whitevale, Ontario, Canada. His father was a miller. White drove his first race at Markham, Ontario, in 1888. Five years later he began working as a groom at Cicero J. Hamlin's Village Farm at East Aurora, N.Y., near Buffalo. Hamlin's breeding farm dominated the Grand Circuit of harness racing during the late 1890's and early 1900's. White worked under the legendary trainer Edward ("Pop") Geers, the "Silent Man from Tennessee," eventually becoming Geers's first assistant. He became head trainer at Village Farm in 1903, when Geers resigned to return to Tennessee, and he raced the Village Farm stable in its final racing season. In 1905 the horses at Village Farm were sold because of the ill health of Hamlin, who died that year. Seymour Knox, the wealthy gelatin manufacturer, purchased many of Hamlin's horses and hired White as trainer. White remained with Knox until his death in 1915.

In 1915 White was hired by the Pasttime Stable to replace Billy Andrews as head trainer. While at Pasttime he drove Volga to victory in the Junior Horse Review Futurity, the Horseman Futurity, the Junior Kentucky Futurity, the Champion Stallion Stake, the Horse Review, and the Kentucky Futurity (1916). He broke the two-minute barrier for the mile with Lee Axworthy on Sept. 15, 1916, and drove him to the trotting stallion title. Within a few years Pasttime Stable was dissolved, but White continued to train for Frank Ellis, one of the former owners. In 1920 he trained during the winter in Orlando, Fla., and was instrumental in developing Orlando into an important winter training ground for harness racing. The city-owned track was later named the Ben White Raceway.

During the 1920's and 1930's, White was to harness racing and training what Babe Ruth was to baseball, Red Grange to football, and Jack Dempsey to boxing. Among the trotters he developed and rode in the 1920's were Lee Worthy, Lee Axworthy, Volga E, Alma Lee, and Ruth M. Chenault. He drove Mr. McElwyn, Sumatra, and Main McElwyn to world records during the 1920's, and he developed and trained Iosola's Worthy, winner of both the Hambletonian and the Kentucky Futurity of 1927.

White drove in his first Hambletonian in 1926, coming in third with Charm. In 1933 White won his first Hambletonian at Goshen, N.Y., with Mary Reynolds. That same year he also won the Kentucky Futurity with Meda.

The most memorable years in White's career were 1935–1939, when he was associated with the bay filly Rosalind. White had given the horse as a yearling to his ill son, Gibson, in the hope that this would restore the boy's health. White had bred her and trained her, and in 1936 he drove her to seven victories and one second place in her eight starts, including victories in the Kentucky Futurity and the Hambletonian. In 1939 Rosalind won the Transylvania, one of the three major harness races along with the Hambletonian and the Kentucky Futurity. During five years of competition, she was the all-time champion trotting mare, winning twenty-four of thirty-six races and establishing seven world records, including a 1:56.75 mile. White won his last Kentucky Futurity in 1937 with Twilight Song, defeating the supposedly invincible Dean Han-

over. He won his third Hambletonian with The Ambassador in a startling upset in 1942. The Ambassador's first victory, it was at the longest odds until then in Hambletonian history.

The greatest colt White ever drove was Volo Song, which never lost on a mile track. White drove him to victory in 1942 in the Junior Kentucky Futurity and, the next year, to victories in the Review Futurity, the Matron, and the Hambletonian. White's last Hambletonian was in 1949, when he drove William Wells. He trained and drove more winners of major harness races than anyone else in history. During his career White drove in nineteen Hambletonians, winning four; he also won seven Kentucky Futurities, six Matron Stakes, and four Review Futurities. His success earned him the title "Dean of Colt Trainers."

White was not a spectacular and flamboyant driver. He rarely used the whip and hardly ever took extravagant chances. Instead, he relied on a masterful judgment of pace, an incisive knowledge of his horse, and an acute perception of the location of the other horses in the race. One of his major influences was in turning the emphasis in harness racing toward speed among the two- and three-year-old trotters.

White spent the last years of his life in Orlando, operating a training stable with his son, who had become a driver and a trainer. Together they developed True Boy and Madison Hanover. Although in failing health late in his life, White remained active in the sport virtually to the end. He died in Orlando, Fla.

[The most complete summary of White's life is in *Harness Horse*, May 28, 1958. *Hoof Beats*, June 1958, contains a brief obituary. Marguerite Henry, *Born to Trot* (1950), for juvenile readers, discusses Rosalind and Gib White. Philip Pines, *The Complete Book of Harness Racing* (1970), has brief biographies of Ben White, C. J. Hamlin, and Edward F. Geers, as well as the dates and times of White's record-setting performances. The *New York Times*, May 21, 1958, has a brief obituary.]

EDWARD S. SHAPIRO

WHITE, CLARENCE CAMERON (Aug. 10, 1880–June 30, 1960), violinist, composer, and music educator, was born in Clarksville, Tenn., the son of James William White and Virginia Caroline Scott. He grew up in Oberlin, Ohio, where his father was a doctor. Apparently at an early age he showed an interest in and a talent for music. After a year (1894–1895) at Howard University, he studied at the Oberlin Conservatory of Music, from which he graduated in 1901.

White then went to Boston for advanced studies in violin with private tutors. In 1903 he became a teacher at the Washington Conservatory of Music while also performing as a concert violinist. On Apr. 24, 1905, White married Beatrice Louise Warrick; they had two sons. In 1908 he went to England, where he appeared as a guest artist and studied for a time with the noted black composer Samuel Coleridge-Taylor. He returned to the United States in 1910. From 1910 to 1923 he ran a music studio in Boston.

In 1924 White was named director of music at West Virginia State College, a position he held for six years. During the mid-1920's he produced some of his most popular works: *Bandanna Sketches; Cabin Memories*, for solo voice and piano; and *From the Cotton Fields*, for violin and piano. His *Forty Negro Spirituals* was published in 1927.

White began work on *Ouanga*, a three-act opera based on Haitian history, in 1928. The libretto, written by John Frederick Matheus, a colleague of White's at West Virginia State, was based on the life of Jean Jacques Dessalines, the slave who helped to lead his people in revolt and became emperor of Haiti at the beginning of the nineteenth century. Having won the Harmon Foundation Prize for distinguished service to music in 1928, White used the award of $400 to spend a few months in Haiti, studying native folk music and observing the voodoo ceremonies of the peasants. In 1930 he received a Julius Rosenwald fellowship that enabled him to study for several years in Paris with Raoul Laparra, whose operas were produced in both France and the United States. In 1932, *Ouanga*, which means "voodoo spell" or "voodoo charm," won the David Bisham Medal, presented annually by the American Opera Society of Chicago for the best operatic work by an American.

From 1932 to 1935, White was music director at Hampton Institute. He served as a music specialist with the National Recreation Association from 1937 to 1942, organizing community music groups. In 1940 he published *Traditional Negro Spirituals*, his arrangements of twenty spirituals for concert and community choruses. His first wife died in 1942, and on Dec. 26, 1943, he married Pura Belpré. *Ouanga* was staged for the first time in 1949, when it was presented by the Burleigh Music Society of South Bend, Ind.

Generally well received, it was performed many times thereafter.

In 1951 White published "Lonesome Road," "This Train," and "Tambour," a Haitian dance for symphonic band. The following year he completed Concertino in D Minor for violin, *Four Caribbean Dances* for piano, and an opera for college workshops entitled *Carnival Romance*. In 1954 he won the Edward B. Benjamin Award for "tranquil music" with his orchestral work *Elegy*, a piece written some years earlier in memory of his first wife. The Benjamin award was established by a New Orleans industrialist to encourage American composers to produce "short, tranquil and reposeful music." *Elegy*, a smoothly flowing work that was one of seventy-two entries in the Benjamin competition, was given its premier performance on Mar. 16, 1954, by the New Orleans Philharmonic-Symphony Orchestra. On Apr. 8, 1954, Kermit Moore, in an appearance at Salle Plevel in Paris, introduced White's *Fantasie* for cello.

White's anthem, "If I Had a Hammer," was included in the hymnal of the Central Conference of American Rabbis (1955). In the same year White completed *Dance Rhapsody* and *Poeme* for orchestra, and a piece commissioned by Kermit Moore for cello and piano. His *Spiritual Suite* for four clarinets was released in 1956. The premiere of his *Poeme* for orchestra took place in January 1958, during the Festival of American Music at Hunter College. One of White's last works, completed in 1959, was *Heritage*, a "musical statement" for soprano or tenor, speaking and mixed choruses, and orchestra. The text for this piece was written by the poet Countee Cullen.

During his lengthy career as a composer, White compiled an imposing list of published and unpublished works for violin, voice, cello, clarinet, piano, orchestra, band, and choral groups. His violin pieces in particular were popular program numbers, and were performed by such accomplished concert artists as Fritz Kreisler and Albert Spalding. White died in New York City.

[See *Musical Courier*, July 1949, Oct. 15, 1949, and Apr. 1, 1954; *Violins and Violinists*, Nov.–Dec. 1949 and May–June 1950; *Pan Pipes*, Jan. 1952, Jan. 1953, Jan. 1955, Jan. 1956, Jan. 1957, Jan. 1958, and Jan. 1960; and *Time*, Mar. 29, 1954. Obituaries are in *New York Times*, July 2, 1960; *Violins and Violinists*, July–Aug. 1960; and *Musical America*, Aug. 1960.]

L. MOODY SIMMS, JR.

WHITE, JOSEPH MALACHY (Oct. 14, 1891–Feb. 28, 1959), composer, lyricist, and singer known as "The Silver-Masked Tenor," was born in New York City, the son of John White, a typographer, and Rose Anne Lackave. His mother came from an American theatrical family and was a cousin of Wilton Lackave, famous for his characterization of Svengali in *Trilby*. White was educated in New York public schools and sang as a boy soprano in various New York churches. He made his first appearance on stage at the age of ten as "a village urchin" in a play called *Checkers*. His first vocal teacher was Charles Abercrombie, and he worked with E. Presson Miller throughout most of his career. In 1910, he joined Denman Thompson's Old Homestead Quartet. From 1914 to 1917 he was entertainer at Billy Gallagher's Film Café and, in the summer of 1916, manager of the Swan Lake Casino. His first recording test took place in the Edison studios in 1915, but nothing was issued at that time. Edison, who insisted on personally passing on every record, was not impressed. White's first release was "Molly Brannigan," issued in January 1917. That year he also recorded for Columbia as J. Malachy White and enlisted in the 102nd Engineers, 27th Division. He made ten record sides for Columbia, some of which were announced in the catalog supplements with pictures of White in uniform. One announcement read: "J. Malachy White, be it known, sings the good old Irish songs in the good old American uniform." On one occasion, during war service abroad, he was called out of the trenches to sing for Field Marshall Douglas Haig and King Albert I of Belgium.

In 1919, White joined Neil O'Brien's Minstrels as soloist and between 1921 and 1923 toured the United States on the Klaw and Erlanger circuit. A pioneer broadcaster, he was the first singer heard in England on a transatlantic broadcast, from the WJZ studio in Newark, N.J., on July 4, 1922. On Oct. 8, 1924, he married Maureen Burns. They had six children, one of whom, Robert, also became a singer. That year he joined Joseph Knecht and his B. F. Goodrich Silvertown Orchestra as vocalist.

One day Phillips Carlin, the announcer, in a jocular mood, told his radio audience that the members of the orchestra, in honor of the Silvertown cord tires that they advertised, all played silver instruments and that the tenor soloist always wore a silver mask. The announcement created a sensation, and fan letters poured in. From then on, "The Silver-Masked Tenor" was the mystery man of Station WEAF. For many years White never sang publicly without a mask, even though on radio he was invisible to the audience. This was perhaps the earliest radio publicity stunt, and it paid off handsomely. Not until his connection with the orchestra ended in 1930 was his identity revealed. Ben Gross, the radio critic, recalls in his memoirs, "Some letter writers to newspapers guessed he was John McCormack, the great Irish tenor, and a few women even accused him of being their long-lost husbands."

The mask became a part of White's act, and he retained it long after his Silvertown days were over. By then he had become one of radio's major stars. "I shall always remember," writes Gross, "his performance on a night in 1933, when NBC moved from 711 Fifth Avenue to its studios in Radio City. Joe sat atop a heap of chairs and desks on the last vanload of furniture leaving the old quarters, broadcasting via short wave over a portable microphone. He sang *Kathleen Mavourneen*, the beginning of the song going out in the air from the Fifth Avenue building and its end from the towering RCA structure in Rockefeller Center."

White's most successful records were made for the Victor label, beginning in September 1925, when the new electrical process was being introduced. His first release coupled "Brown Eyes, Why Are You Blue?" and "A Kiss in the Moonlight." His records, both with dance band and as soloist in Irish ballads and popular songs, were big sellers throughout the 1920's. After 1930 he went on the RKO vaudeville circuit, appearing all over the United States and Canada, but he continued to sing regularly on the radio.

White's career ended in April 1943, when he slipped and broke his leg, which then had to be amputated. For the remainder of his life he remained active as a vocal coach. Jim Walsh, writing in *Hobbies* magazine, recalled meeting White in 1940. At this time White was "a stocky, short, rather florid man with a friendly manner . . . casually dressed . . . a friendly, down-to-earth fellow . . . as plain as an old shoe." Among the works that White published as composer or lyricist are "In Flanders," "Bells of Killarney," "Maureen Mavourneen," "Say That You Care for Me," "Hold Me in Your Arms," "Roses in the Moonlight," "Drifting in the Moonlight," and "McGuire's Musketeers." He died in New York City.

[On White and his career, see Ben Gross, *I Looked*

and I Listened (1954); Jim Walsh, "Joe White, 'The Silver-Masked Tenor,' " *Hobbies,* Mar. 1973; and the obituary notice, *New York Times,* Mar. 1, 1959.]

PHILIP LIESON MILLER

WHITE, LEONARD DUPEE (Jan. 17, 1891–Feb. 23, 1958), political scientist and historian, was born in Acton, Mass., the son of John Sidney White and Bertha Dupee. White attended Dartmouth College, receiving the B.S. in 1914 and the M.A. in 1915. That summer he began doctoral work at the University of Chicago, and in the fall he embarked upon his teaching career as an instructor in government at Clark University. On June 17, 1916, he married Una Lucille Holden, also of Acton, Mass.; they had one daughter.

From 1918 to 1920 White taught political science at Dartmouth and then moved to the University of Chicago as an associate professor of political science. He received his Ph.D. from Chicago in 1921 and became a full professor in 1925. When he retired in 1956 he was Ernest DeWitt Burton Distinguished Service Professor of Public Administration.

Within the field of government, White was primarily interested in public administration. He was one of the first to teach this subject in a university classroom, and even in the early 1920's was becoming a leader among the political scientists who shared this interest. His *Introduction to the Study of Public Administration,* first published in 1926 and revised in 1939, 1948, and 1955, was the first, and for many years the preeminent, textbook in this field.

During his early years at Chicago, White's progress was influenced and aided by the work of his chairman, Charles E. Merriam, who was building up one of the outstanding political science departments in the United States. Merriam was active in Chicago politics, a leader of the American Political Science Association, and a founder of the Social Science Research Council (1923). In some measure all of these activities influenced White's career.

In 1929 President Hoover, drawing on the resources of the SSRC, created the Committee on Social Trends. Merriam was the vice-chairman. White, as a member of the committee, reported on the expansion of American government in a chapter on "Public Administration" in the committee's report, *Recent Social Trends in the United States* (1933). It was also published the

same year in a longer form as *Trends in Public Administration,* one of a series of monographs that resulted from the work of the committee.

Meanwhile, White was also involved in Chicago civic affairs. He served on the Chicago Citizens' Police Committee (1929–1931) and on the Chicago Civil Service Commission (1931–1933). In this work he became a friend of Harold L. Ickes. In 1934, when Franklin Roosevelt needed to appoint a Republican to the United States Civil Service Commission, Ickes, then secretary of the interior, recommended White, and the president concurred.

As a commissioner, White was primarily responsible for developing a system of junior civil service examinations, for college graduates only, intended to draw better-educated persons into governmental careers. To help government employees provide better service and advance professionally, he worked with American University to develop a program of in-service training for them. He resigned from the commission in 1937 to return to teaching. Two years later, however, Roosevelt appointed him to the President's Committee on Civil Service Improvement, on which he served until 1941. A few years after that, when the problem of investigating the loyalty of government employees had become acute, White was a member of the Civil Service Commission's Seventh Regional Loyalty Board (1948–1950) and of the Commission's Loyalty Review Board (1950–1952).

White worked with both of the Hoover Commissions on the Organization of the Executive Branch of the Government, the first in 1948–1949 and the second in 1953–1955. In both cases he helped to prepare the report on personnel management, which advocated the creation of a career executive program. It was initiated by executive order in 1957 to help identify, retain, and advance government employees who should be moved into positions of greater responsibility.

In all this work, White was expressing a concern for the quality of governmental service, chiefly with reference to personnel problems. The conditions of the times had tended, in the 1920's, to depreciate public service, and thereafter to place more demands and greater responsibility on government. White grappled with the problems inherent in this situation, both as a public official and as a researcher and writer. Two early studies examined *The Prestige Value of Public Employment in Chicago* (1929) and *Further*

Contributions to the Prestige Value of Public Employment (1932). In numerous articles he discussed practical problems of administration, such as ways of encouraging better-qualified people to go into government service, keeping them in the service, and developing and utilizing their talents most effectively. Although a lifelong Republican, White considered the Taft-Hartley Act's prohibition on all strikes in government service too extreme, and he regarded the loyalty tests of the Truman administration as more reasonable than those of the Eisenhower era. Besides writing many articles, he helped establish the *Public Administration Review* and served as its first editor (1940–1941).

White's conviction that the United States could benefit from the experience of other nations led him to write *The Civil Service in the Modern State* (1930), *Whitley Councils in the British Civil Service* (1933), and a portion of *Civil Service Abroad* (1935). Above all, he came to conclude that Americans should understand their own national experience in this field. As he had been a leader in developing the contemporary study of public administration, White became a pioneer in the historical study of American public administration. His four volumes in this field—*The Federalists* (1948), *The Jeffersonians* (1951), *The Jacksonians* (1954), and *The Republican Era, 1869–1901* (1958)—were widely acclaimed; the first volume won the Woodrow Wilson Prize of the American Political Science Association; the third, the Bancroft Prize for distinguished writing in American history; and *The Republican Era* received the 1959 Pulitzer Prize in history. White's final scholarly undertaking was to serve as editor of the widely scattered papers of James Madison. His death prevented his completing this project, but his guidelines and procedures set the pattern for the series.

White was a member of the University of Chicago faculty for thirty-six years. Although his influence in the university was somewhat restricted by his philosophical disagreements with President Robert Maynard Hutchins, he was the chairman of the Political Science Department from 1940 to 1948 and was the chief architect of the university's faculty senate. He was president of the American Political Science Association in 1944 and of the American Society for Public Administration in 1947. Colleagues remembered him as a man of reserve, but of great goodwill, warmth, and complete integrity. He died in Chicago, Ill.

[Some of White's papers are in the Regenstein Library of the University of Chicago, but there is neither a general collection of his papers nor a complete list of his publications. Helpful commentaries on his career and some of his writings include Franklin G. Connor, "Leonard D. White, Public Administration Pioneer," *Personnel Administration*, July–Aug. 1958; John Gaus, "Leonard Dupee White, 1891–1958," *Public Administration Review*, Summer 1958; Herbert Storing, "Leonard D. White and the Study of Public Administration," *Public Administration Review*, Mar. 1965; and two anonymous articles: "Leonard D. White, Architect of Modern Civil Service," *Good Government*, Mar.–Apr. 1958; and "The Career Executive Program," *ibid.*]

MAURICE M. VANCE

WHITESIDE, ARTHUR DARE (Sept. 15, 1882–June 17, 1960), president of Dun and Bradstreet, was born in East Orange, N.J., the son of Newton Elkanah Whiteside, a jewelry manufacturer, and Elizabeth Hankins. After leaving Princeton University in 1904, Whiteside worked in the credit department of a New York City bank. Two years later, he joined the National Credit Office, a commercial credit-reporting agency that specialized in the textile trade. On Feb. 12, 1909, he married Edith E. Davidson; they had one daughter. He became president of National Credit in 1912 and thereafter greatly expanded its business, largely by developing a highly trained staff whose reports were of exceptionally high quality. According to one estimate, Whiteside tripled the volume of National Credit in the years from 1922 to 1930.

The Great Depression was crucial to Whiteside's career, as it provided the immediate cause for fundamental changes in the several business enterprises engaged in commercial credit reporting. In addition to specialized agencies, such as Whiteside's National Credit Office, there existed since the mid-nineteenth century two large general agencies: R. G. Dun and Company and the Bradstreet Company. By 1930 it was evident to Whiteside and others that the declining economy could not sustain the competition and duplication of effort of these several agencies.

Whiteside played a major role in the consolidation of three major commercial-credit agencies into one company, Dun and Bradstreet, Incorporated. First, as president of National Credit, he initiated long and difficult negotiations with the owners of R. G. Dun and Company, a family-held trust. As a consequence, in December 1930 R. G. Dun was incorporated and merged with National Credit, with Whiteside as the new president. Whiteside quickly exerted vigorous and effective leadership in the new company. Some of this effort was largely depression-era morale boosting, such as refinishing office equipment and cleaning the exterior of the headquarters building. More important, in 1931 and 1932, Whiteside introduced changes that significantly improved the quality of R. G. Dun and Company's services. These changes included the development of continuous service, whereby subscribers automatically received updated credit information on businesses of interest to them; expansion from four to six of the number of annual editions of the printed credit-rating or reference book; and more thorough training of reporters in the preparation of analytical credit reports, of the kind Whiteside had introduced at National Credit.

Whiteside's innovations and improvements helped make R. G. Dun and Company much stronger than the Bradstreet Company. Indeed, Whiteside believed that Bradstreet could not long survive and that its elimination was a necessary step for the future prosperity of R. G. Dun. As president of R. G. Dun, Whiteside negotiated purchase of all the assets of Bradstreet, with Bradstreet shareholders paid in shares in the new company, Dun and Bradstreet, Incorporated, formed in March 1933. Bradstreet representatives received three seats on the board of directors, but management of the new company was composed entirely of Dun managers, with Whiteside continuing as president.

These changes were accompanied by friction and conflict, usually with Whiteside at the center. Believing that his company's survival was at stake, Whiteside acted forcefully—and perhaps ruthlessly at times—and ultimately succeeded in creating a business that would grow dramatically in the post-Depression years.

Whiteside also devoted his energies to government service. Although a lifelong Republican, he worked in three Democratic administrations. During World War I he served briefly with the War Industries Board. During the New Deal he was a division administrator in the National Recovery Administration, where he emphasized the negative effects of unrestricted competition and the necessity for price stability. He left government service in 1935 but returned to Washington during World War II, serving in 1941 with the Office of Production Management and from April 1943 to February 1944 with the War Production Board as vice-chairman in charge of civilian requirements. In 1947 President Truman appointed Whiteside to the Air Policy Committee.

After World War II, Whiteside began to see the need for a new business strategy at Dun and Bradstreet. As traditional methods and channels of marketing and distribution changed, he argued that the company could no longer rely solely on supplying credit information in advance of sale but had to diversify and provide more general information and services. But Whiteside's declining health prevented vigorous leadership toward expansion and diversification. He remained in office long enough to preside over the opening in 1951 of the new headquarters building at 99 Church Street in New York City but retired in November 1952. He continued in an advisory role with the company for several years and served on the board of directors until his death, in New York City.

[The most useful source is a lengthy unpublished history and memoir by a former employee and associate, Owen A. Sheffield, "Dun & Bradstreet, Inc. . . .: A Private History," a copy of which is in the company's New York City office. The history and general problems of commercial credit reporting are treated in Roy A. Foulke, *The Sinews of American Commerce* (1941); and James H. Madison, "The Evolution of Commercial Credit Reporting Agencies in Nineteenth-Century America," *Business History Review*, Summer 1974. See also the obituary notice, *New York Times*, June 18, 1960. Periodicals providing useful information include *Fortune*, Feb. 1931 and Sept. 1933; *Business Week*, Mar. 8, 1933; *Dun & Bradstreet Weekly Review*, Mar. 4, 1933; and *Time*, Apr. 26, 1943. Whiteside's role in the National Recovery Administration is treated in Elis W. Hawley, *The New Deal and the Problem of Monopoly* (1966).]

JAMES H. MADISON

WHITNEY, WILLIS RODNEY (Aug. 22, 1868–Jan. 9, 1958), chemist and research director, was born in Jamestown, N. Y., the son of John Jay Whitney, owner of the Jamestown Wood Seat Chair Co., and Agnes Reynolds. He read widely, enjoyed outdoor pursuits, and learned both the craft of chairmaking and the use of a microscope. Undergraduate work at the Massachusetts Institute of Technology (MIT) under chemist Arthur A. Noyes helped him choose chemistry as a career. Upon graduation with the B.S. (1890), he accepted an assistant instructorship in sanitary chemistry at MIT.

On June 26, 1890, Whitney married Evelyn Jones of Jamestown; they had one daughter. He studied physical chemistry under Wilhelm Ostwald at the University of Leipzig from 1894 to 1896. After receiving the Ph.D. there, he returned to MIT as instructor of theoretical chemistry.

Whitney was an outstanding teacher and a good, but not a first-rank, researcher. His specialties were the chemistries of solutions, colloids, and corrosion. His most important paper, "On the Corrosion of Iron" (1903), helped to establish that the principles governing the rusting of iron are the same as those governing the operation of an electric battery.

In 1896, Whitney declined an employment offer from the chemist Arthur D. Little. But he and Noyes took a subsequent consulting job, devising a process for reclaiming alcohol and ether at the Boston plant of the American Aristotype Co. Success of this project (returns to Whitney alone exceeded $20,000) was followed in October 1900 by an offer from Edwin W. Rice, Jr., vice-president of the General Electric (GE) Co., of a research position in Schenectady, N. Y. Whitney agreed to take on a self-directed research program there for three days a week.

Overcoming some initial skepticism, Whitney quickly proved that chemical research techniques (such as use of an electric furnace) could be highly useful in the electrical industry. By 1904 he was directing a staff of forty-one. In May of that year he moved to Schenectady and began devoting full time to GE.

Although Whitney patented forty inventions (including the GEM lamp filament [1904], a major commercial success), his main contributions were indirect. He did much of his work through his associates at the GE research laboratory, who included chemist Irving Langmuir and physicists William D. Coolidge, Albert W. Hull, and Saul Dushman. Not the least of his achievements was creating an institution responsive to the business needs of GE, yet with enough scientific freedom to attract top people.

Outgoing and optimistic, Whitney had a paternalistic managerial style. "Come in, rain or shine," read a sign above his always open door. He daily toured the laboratory, leaving administrative details to his capable aide, Laurence A. Hawkins. His private life was simple, spent largely pursuing such hobbies as collecting arrowheads or studying the habits of turtles.

Although Whitney urged experiment and distrusted scientific dogma, his social and political views were conventional. He accepted public duties (serving, for example, on the Naval Consulting Board [1917–1919]) but did not seek them. He preached a creed of continuous and positive change through research and its technological applications in numerous speeches and articles from 1910 through 1929.

Nevertheless, the center of Whitney's attention remained on the GE Research Laboratory, which he sought to develop into a unique institution on the boundry of science and industry. His success in doing this task has often been misinterpreted by those who see him as a champion of "pure" research. Actually he was a follower of Francis Bacon in his insistence on the usefulness of science. Within GE he made the full resources of his laboratory available for the solution of such practical problems as the perfection of the hermetically sealed refrigerator and the solution of mechanical problems of steam turbines.

Also like Bacon, Whitney was a complete empiricist with a distrust of theoretical science. In the 1920's this enabled him to contribute unorthodox engineering concepts of much practical value (such as his highly successful 1921 suggestion to improve the efficiency of electrical generators by running them in a hydrogen atmosphere), but it also weakened the research laboratory by preventing it from participating fully in the theoretical advances that led ultimately to modern solid-state and nuclear physics. Nevertheless outstanding pure science, such as Irving Langmuir's Nobel Prize-winning work in surface chemistry, was possible under Whitney's policies.

Evaluating Whitney's contributions to the achievements of his laboratory associates is virtually impossible, since he recorded few of his many suggestions and encouraging hints. Their major inventions during his 1904–1932 tenure as director of research included tungsten filaments for light bulbs, the modern X-ray tube, electronic devices for radio and industrial processes, improved metals and mechanical devices for the electrical industry, and the "gas-filled" lamp. Many of the practices he established have become basic to the research and development function in American industry, especially his policy of a heavy concentration on development work while granting wide research freedom to scientists of proven ability.

Whitney was named a vice-president of GE in 1928. The business downturn of 1929–1932 caused a cutback in GE research expenditures. At the same time his never-robust health worsened. He sank into a deep depression, and in 1932 retired as director of research. Under a reduced work schedule his health and spirits recovered. He retained the honorary title of vice-president of research until 1941, and from 1933 through 1954 he maintained an office at the research lab and carried out experimental studies, most notably in the use of electromagnetic radiation in medical therapy. He ceased active work in 1954, and died in Schenectady.

[Whitney's personal papers for 1910–1937 are in the Schenectady Archives of Science and Technology, Union College, Schenectady, N. Y. Other papers and most of his laboratory notebooks are in the General Electric Research and Development Center in Schenectady. A full bibliography of his published works is in C. Guy Suits, "Willis Rodney Whitney, 1868–1958," *Biographical Memoirs. National Academy of Sciences*, 34 (1960). John Broderick, *Willis Rodney Whitney* (1945), and Virginia Westervelt, *The World Was His Laboratory* (1965), are anecdotal and adulatory biographies. Sketches by close associates include Laurence A. Hawkins, "American Contemporaries—Willis Rodney Whitney," *Industrial and Engineering Chemistry*, 25 (1933); A. W. Hull, "W. R. Whitney, the Man and His Contribution to Science," *Science*, Sept. 18, 1958; and William D. Coolidge, "Willis R. Whitney," address to GE Research Lab staff (1958), on file in Communications Branch, GE Research and Development Center, Schenectady, N.Y.]

GEORGE WISE

WILDER, LAURA INGALLS (Feb. 7, 1867–Feb. 10, 1957), author, was born in Pepin, Wis., the daughter of Charles Philip Ingalls and Caroline Lake Quiner. Her father, a farmer, often took odd jobs such as carpentry and hotel management to supplement the family income. Laura's family traveled extensively during her childhood: by prairie schooner from Wisconsin to Kansas and Missouri and then, when she was four, back to Wisconsin. Three years later they moved to southwestern Minnesota. In 1876 the Ingalls moved to eastern Iowa and then returned to Minnesota before traveling west to the Dakota Territory. Life was hard, and the family nearly starved during the blizzards of the winter of 1880–1881.

Although an industrious child, Ingalls was unable to attend school during most of her childhood and was largely self-taught. At the age of fifteen she received a license to teach in the Dakota Territory. To help her family pay for special education for her blind sister, Mary, she began teaching in a one-room schoolhouse twelve miles from their home and boarded in an unhappy and discordant household. During this time she became acquainted with Almanzo Wilder, who often drove her home for weekends in his sleigh. They were married on Aug. 25, 1885, and had one daughter.

The Wilders' early married life and struggles to raise crops are described in *The First Four Years* (1971). After living in Dakota and then western Florida, in 1894 they settled in the Ozarks, where they cleared land and built a house. Eventually, they had "200 acres of improved land, a herd of cows, good hogs, and the best laying flock of hens in the country." For many years they did the farm work themselves but later rented or sold most of their land. The Rocky Ridge Farm in Mansfield, Mo., is now a museum included in the National Register of Historic Places.

Before writing novels, Wilder had been for twelve years home editor of the *Missouri Realist*, poultry editor of the *St. Louis Star*, and a contributor to *Country Gentleman*, *McCall's*, and other periodicals. She began writing, at the age of sixty-five, at the urging of her daughter, who encouraged her to record her experiences as a pioneer. *Little House in the Big Woods* (1932), the first of her eight *Little House* books, described her early life in Wisconsin and received immediate acclaim for its accurate and vivid descriptions of frontier life. It was followed by *Farmer Boy* (1933), covering Almanzo Wilder's childhood; *Little House on the Prairie* (1935), set in Indian territory in Kansas; *On the Banks of Plum Creek* (1937), set in Minnesota; *By the Shores of Silver Lake* (1939), *The Long Winter* (1940), and *Little Town on the Prairie* (1941), set in the Dakota Territory; and *These Happy Golden Years* (1943), which won a prize in the *New York Herald Tribune* Book Festival that year. *The First Four Years*, discovered among her manuscripts, was probably written in the 1940's.

Written for a progressively older readership of approximately eight to fourteen years, Wilder's novels follow the chronology of her own life. They vividly depict farm life, showing clearly the work ethic, thrift, sacrifice, love, courage, and values of pioneer days. Many of her stories may be considered how-to books; in them she described setting snares, baking bread, cooking, and other practical details of rural life. An accurate record of an important phase of American social history, her books show a sympathetic insight into the spirit of the independent pioneers, interweaving the beauty and danger of the world of nature, the family's dreams, and her father's steadfastness and integrity. Over two million copies of her books have been sold.

Wilder was described by Irene V. Lichty, curator of the Laura Ingalls Wilder Home and Museum, as "a very modest, unassuming little lady (she was barely over five feet tall)—pretty and well groomed, neatly but never over dressed." Her hobbies included cooking—she was famous for her gingerbread—needlepoint, and horseback riding.

A popular television series, "Little House on the Prairie," based on her books, began in September 1974. In 1954 the Laura Ingalls Wilder Award was established by the Children's Library Association (a division of the American Library Association) for "substantial and lasting contribution" to children's literature. Wilder herself was the first recipient. Earlier editions of her books were illustrated by Helen Sewell and Mildred Boyle; later ones, by Garth Williams. She died in Mansfield, Mo.

[Wilder's books are the primary source for her life history. For a summary of her novels and a chronology, see Donald Zochert, *Laura* (1976). Other sources include M. Cimino, "Laura Ingalls Wilder," *Wilson Library Bulletin*, Apr. 1948; and the obituary notice, *New York Times*, Feb. 12, 1957. See also Irene Smith, "Laura Ingalls Wilder and the *Little House* Books," *Horn Book*, Sept. 1943; and W. J. Jacobs, "Frontier Faith Revisited," *ibid.*, Oct. 1965. The Dec. 1953 issue of *Horn Book* includes several articles on Wilder and her books.]

OLIVIA H. GOULD

WILDER, RUSSELL MORSE (Nov. 24, 1885–Dec. 16, 1959), medical clinician, scientist, and educator, was born in Cincinnati, Ohio, the son of William Hamlin Wilder and Ella Taylor. His father moved the family to Chicago in 1892, where he ultimately became head of the department of ophthalmology at Rush Medical College.

Wilder received the B.S. from the University of Chicago in 1907 after a course of studies that included a year in Heidelberg. He then enrolled in Rush Medical College, where one of his first assignments was to prepare a detailed exposition on the pancreas. This contributed to Wilder's great interest in that organ, to which he devoted many years of study, especially through clinical investigations of patients with diabetes mellitus.

Wilder also worked in Chicago and in Mexico as a volunteer assistant to Howard Taylor Ricketts, who was studying typhus fever. Ricketts' earlier experience with Rocky Mountain spotted fever had led him to undertake this investigation. The two diseases, as this work showed, are caused by organisms of the same family, now known as *Rickettsiae*. Ricketts and Wilder worked together from the autumn of 1909 until Ricketts' death in May 1910. Wilder then returned to Mexico to complete the work and saw their papers on typhus through publication. On Mar. 18, 1911, Wilder married Lucy Elizabeth Beeler; they had two sons.

In 1912, Wilder obtained both the Ph.D. from the University of Chicago and the M.D. from Rush Medical College (receiving the Benjamin Rush gold medal with the M.D.). He worked in the laboratory of John Ulric Nef from 1912 to 1913. Wilder held an internship at Presbyterian Hospital in Chicago until 1914, then studied for eight months in Vienna. He returned to Chicago shortly after the outbreak of World War I.

In 1915, Wilder took up a residency at Presbyterian Hospital under Frank Billings, professor of medicine at Rush, and simultaneously became a fellow of the Otho S. A. Sprague Institute. He remained in this position until 1917, participating in research into carbohydrate metabolism with Rollin T. Woodyatt and other colleagues. With Woodyatt he investigated the rate of utilization of ketones and glucose, thus further pursuing his interest in diabetes. This work was interrupted by service in World War I when his commission in the Medical Reserve Corps was activated in 1917. Wilder served with the American Expeditionary Forces in France as head of the medical service at Evacuation Hospital No. 2 and, later, as medical gas officer for the Second Army. In 1919 he was appointed associate in medicine and a member of the staff of the Mayo Clinic in Rochester, Minn., an association that continued until his retirement in 1950. In 1929–1931 he was chairman of the department of medicine at the University of Chicago. From the time of his return to the Mayo Clinic and Mayo Foundation in 1931 until his retirement, he was professor of medicine and department chairman.

Wilder's knowledge about metabolic diseases, particularly diabetes, was recognized in 1922; he was one of a handful of physicians invited to make the first clinical investigations of insulin after its discovery and the initial trials with patients. Wilder did not only excel in the scientific approach to diabetes. He recognized the need for educating the diabetic patient, and with the dietitians Mary A. Foley and Daisy Ellithorpe he published *A Primer for Diabetic Patients* (1921). This work, issued in revised editions for more than four decades, helped thousands of diabetics to live longer and healthier lives.

But Wilder was principally a clinician, and his clinical work brought him the reputation of being an innovator and a keen observer. In 1927, for example, he and three colleagues published "Cancer of the Islands of the Pancreas: Hyperinsulinism and Hypoglycemia," an elegant, detailed paper on the first recorded instance of organic hyperinsulinism, a condition caused by cancer of the insulin-producing cells of the pancreas. Although this patient died of cancer, it was soon found that benign tumors can cause a similar disorder. Many patients have been cured surgically of this disease.

With various colleagues Wilder studied diseases of the thyroid, pituitary, and adrenal glands, and problems of nutrition. In addition to his work on obesity, in 1938 he proposed to the Council on Food and Nutrition of the American Medical Association that milling companies be encouraged to add thiamine to white flour. This work, as well as nutritional surveys carried out for the Newfoundland government in 1944, occupied Wilder during World War II.

Modesty and willingness to give credit to all involved in a project were two especially appealing facets of Wilder's character. For instance, he arranged for the Mayo Clinic to assign the royalties earned by the book for diabetics to create the Mary Agnes Foley Fund (in the name of one of the dietitians who worked on it) that would assist needy diabetic patients. Wilder died in Rochester, Minn.

[In collaboration with colleagues, Wilder wrote "The Relation of Typhus Fever (Tabardillo) to Rocky Mountain Spotted Fever," *Archives of Internal Medicine*, Apr. 1910; "Prolonged and Accurately Timed Intravenous Injections of Sugar," *Journal of the American Medical Association*, Dec. 11, 1915; "Clinical Observations on Insulin," *Journal of Metabolic Research*, Nov.–Dec. 1922; "Carcinoma of the Islands of the Pancreas," *Journal of the American Medical Association*, July 30, 1927. Biographical accounts of

Wilder appear in *Perspectives in Biology and Medicine*, Spring 1958; *Proceedings of the Institute of Medicine of Chicago*, 23 (1960); *Transactions of the Association of American Physicians*, 73 (1960); *Diabetes*, Sept.–Oct. 1960; and *Journal of Nutrition*, July 1961.]

CHARLES G. ROLAND

WILLARD, FRANK HENRY (Sept. 21, 1893–Jan. 11, 1958), comic artist, was born in Anna, Ill., the son of Francis William Willard and Laura Kirkham. His father, who was a dentist, thought that Frank should aspire to medicine or the law, but the youth's ambitions were not professional. After being "tossed out of the local high school for something or other," he had a similar experience at the Union Academy of Southern Illinois, also in Anna. He tried a run of odd jobs that included working at a mental hospital and operating a sandwich stand at county fairs, where he was fascinated by the ballyhoomen, tattoo artists, and other carnival types. In 1909 his father moved to Chicago. Later the family followed and Frank was a claim tracer in a department store. He attended night classes at the Illinois Academy of Fine Arts in 1913.

In the summer of 1914 Willard noted that the outbreak of World War I caught the *Chicago Tribune* temporarily lacking the services of a political cartoonist. He drew a caricature of the God of War as a chauffeur touring the battlefields with Death and Devastation as passengers. He entitled it "Touring Europe" and sold it to the managing editor of the *Tribune* for $15. When his cartoon appeared prominently on the front page, four columns wide, Willard left the department store and "spent the day walking around looking at *Tribune*s on the news stands." He also volunteered a cartoon on the White House death of Mrs. Woodrow Wilson.

Certain that he had been ordained to be a political cartoonist, Willard continued as a freelance cartoonist while seeking a steady position. Since there was no full-time opening on the *Tribune*, he applied at the *Chicago Herald*, only to be rejected as lacking in education and experience. Willard then proposed drawing a comic strip, and it was accepted. Employed in 1914 at $20 a week, he produced "City Life," "Mrs. Pippin's Husband," and a children's attraction, "Tom, Dick and Harry." He stayed with the *Herald* until he was drafted into the army in October 1917. Assigned to the Eighty-sixth Division as an infantryman, he was transferred in

May 1918 to its road-building engineers, and served with the Allied Expeditionary Forces from September 1918 to July 1919.

After settling in New York City, Willard drew a strip called "The Outta Luck Club," the "Penny Ante" series, and an occasional cartoon for the King Features Syndicate (1920–1923). In 1923 he married Priscilla Mangold; they had two children. A new venture in journalism at the time was a picture-style tabloid, the *New York Daily News,* begun in 1919. Its publisher, Joseph M. Patterson, wanted a different comic strip for his new readership—one that would be frankly "low life-roughneck." Willard heard about this desire and went to see him. After discussing the chief figure, a tough fellow utterly without manners, they searched for a name. Patterson suggested Moonshine, slang for the illegal whiskey currently circulating, then shortened it to Moon. Next he looked under "Plumbers" in a classified telephone directory and happened onto the firm of Mullins Brothers. With that, Moon Mullins was conceived.

Willard did the rest. He developed an uninhibited, impolite denizen of poolrooms who looked and acted the part—with banjo eyes; cigar stump issuing from a face half-slaphappy, halfinsolent; a derby hat worn defiantly indoors as well as outside; baggy, checked trousers; and showing no sign of interest in gainful employment. Moon Mullins made his bow on June 14, 1923, and Willard forthwith joined the Chicago Tribune–New York News Syndicate.

There was a good deal of Frank Willard in Moon, including a deliberate similarity in appearance and a sharing of generally low-level preferences, although both were completely at home in more refined company. One of the characters who came into the strip was Moon's delinquent but likeable little brother, Kayo, who slept in a bureau drawer. Kayo was Willard's embellished recollection of his own boyhood in Anna. Other inhabitants of Moon's world were Uncle Willie, a former hobo; his wife, Mamie, who more or less ran the boarding house for the social-climbing Lady Plushbottom, née Emmy Schmaltz, and her outwardly bookish husband, Lord Plushbottom; Mushmouth, the chauffeur; and Little Egypt, the burlesque queen. It was a cast that appealed, as one publisher put it, "to the highest of the highbrows and the lowest of the lowbrows."

Production of the strip was a series of ordeals for Willard, who made a rule of procrastination. Instead of building a backlog and turning out a

strip a day, he would wait until hard pressed by the syndicate for a week's work at a time. Then he shut himself up with his drawing materials, wearing a heavy sweat shirt, smoking cigars, and drinking coffee. Sharing these hotbox sessions, which ran as long as thirty-six hours, was Willard's friend and co-worker from 1930, Ferd Johnson. A combination of Willard and Moon, Johnson took over in emergencies during their long association. A devotee of tennis and golf, Willard sometimes followed tournaments around the country, and on such occasions Moon Mullins issued from hotel rooms. Willard also created a four-panel Sunday feature, "Kitty Higgins," which ran from 1930 to the early 1960's. Willard's $100,000 gross salary made him one of the highest paid among comic artists of his time.

While working in New York Willard lived near Greenwich, Conn., and maintained a summer home at Poland Springs, Me., but for most of his career Los Angeles was his home. On Jan 7, 1933, he married Marie O'Connell. After his death, in Los Angeles, the comic strip, then appearing in 250 newspapers with a circulation of 15,000,000, was carried on by Ferd Johnson.

[On Willard and his career, see Herb Galewitz, ed., *Great Comics* . . . (1972); Clive Howard, "The Magnificent Roughneck," *Saturday Evening Post,* Aug. 9, 1947; Martin Sheridan, *Comics and Their Creators* (1942); Coulton Waugh, *The Comics* (1947); and Willard's article, "Moon Mullins and Me," *Collier's,* May 7, 1949. There are obituary notices in the *Chicago Tribune, New York Daily News,* and *New York Times,* Jan. 13, 1958.]

IRVING DILLIARD

WILLS, HARRY (May 15, 1889 [?]–Dec. 21, 1958), boxer, was born in the waterfront slums of New Orleans, La. His exact date of birth is uncertain, although most authorities believe that he was born in 1889. At an early age Wills went to work on the New Orleans docks, where he developed the physique and stamina for his later career. As a youth he frequented the New Orleans horseracing tracks, and his earliest athletic ambition was to be a jockey.

Wills began boxing at age sixteen in dingy gymnasiums in New Orleans. He won his first recorded fight, against Kid Ravarro in 1910, by a first-round knockout. From 1911 through 1921 he fought throughout the United States, Panama, and Cuba, winning fifty-six bouts, losing only four, with twenty-seven no-decisions or no-contests. Thirty-two of his victories were by knockouts. During this period he had sixteen recorded fights with the legendary black heavyweight Sam Langford, winning five and losing only twice. In 1916 he married a former model and Sunday school teacher.

By 1920 Wills had become the unofficial black heavyweight champion, known as the "Brown Panther" because of his agility and grace. He fought at two hundred and twenty pounds, was six feet, two inches tall, and had a reach of eighty-four inches. He was exceptionally strong and had great endurance.

Wills's career was at its height between 1922 and 1927, when he was a leading contender for a shot at the heavyweight championship held by Jack Dempsey. It was at this time that Paddy Mullins, Wills's manager, claimed that Wills had been born in 1892 in order to quiet any arguments that he was past his prime. Wills and Dempsey signed a contract in July 1922 for a bout, but in February 1923 the New York State Boxing Commission declared that Dempsey would not be allowed to fight Wills in New York. Wills's petition to overturn this decision was denied by the commission in September 1923.

Neither Jack Kearns, Dempsey's manager, nor Tex Rickard, the czar of the boxing promoters, wanted a Dempsey–Wills fight. Rickard had promoted the Jack Johnson–Jim Jeffries fight in 1910, when Johnson became the first American black heavyweight champion. Rickard was charged with having allowed the white race to be humiliated by Jeffries' defeat and was blamed for the race riots that followed the fight. Rickard did not want any repetition, and the boxing authorities in New York feared that a Dempsey–Wills fight would lead to similar riots. Rumors circulated that Al Smith, the governor of New York, as well as political figures in Washington, opposed a Dempsey–Wills bout. Wills fought other leading contenders during 1922 and 1923, winning nine fights and losing two. His most important bout was on Sept. 11, 1924, against the Argentinian Luis Angel Firpo before 80,000 fans in Jersey City. Although the official decision was a draw, most observers believed that Wills had won decisively. Not only were his $150,000 earnings the biggest purse of his career, but his strong showing against Firpo, as well as his second-round knockout of Charley Weinert in New York in July 1925, intensified pressure on the Dempsey camp to give Wills a chance. Wills publicly accused Dempsey of cowardice and challenged him to fight. Finally Wills signed a

contract with Floyd Fitzsimmons, a Midwest promoter, to fight Dempsey in 1926. The bout never took place, and Wills pocketed his $50,000 advance. It was the most famous American boxing match that never took place.

By 1926 even the New York State Boxing Commission believed Wills to be the logical contender for the championship and ruled that Demsey could not fight anyone for the title in the state except the "Black Menace." But Dempsey, under the influence of Rickard and Kearns, continued to avoid Wills and was forced to go outside of New York to fight. In September 1926 he was upset in Philadelphia by Gene Tunney. But Wills always believed Dempsey's claim that he was eager to fight the black challenger. Although Wills was optimistic about his own chances, most boxing authorities share Dempsey's opinion that Wills would have been easily defeated. Both Wills and Dempsey agreed that racism was the only possible reason for the bout not to have occurred.

Tunney's defeat of Dempsey ended any possibility that Wills would fight for the championship. On Oct. 12, 1926, Wills fought Jack Sharkey, a fast, young, and aggressive battler. Sharkey gave Wills a fearful beating, winning every round before Wills was disqualified in the thirteenth round. The fight ended Wills's career as a prominent boxer. On July 13, 1927, he was knocked out in the fourth round by the obscure Spanish fighter Paulino Uzcudun. Wills's last fight was on Aug. 4, 1932, when he knocked out little-known Vinko Jankassa in the first round.

Officially, Wills fought one hundred and two times, winning sixty-two, forty-five by knockouts, while losing only eight. Wills claimed that he had actually fought over two hundred bouts. For much of his career he was limited to black opponents. (All told, he fought Sam Langford twenty-two times.) During his lifetime Wills fought and defeated every leading black heavyweight except Jack Johnson.

Both during and after his boxing career Wills was famous for month-long fasts during which he lost from thirty to forty pounds by refusing to eat, drinking only water, sleeping a maximum of five hours per day, and walking twelve miles a day. He claimed these fasts drained the "impurities" from his body.

After retiring from the ring, Wills went into the real estate business in New York City. With his wife's help, he had saved much of his boxing earnings of approximately half a million dollars. He purchased six apartment houses, including a thirty-family apartment house in Harlem, where he died. Wills was elected to the boxing hall of fame in 1970.

[A complete list of Wills's official fights is in the *1976 Ring Boxing Encyclopedia and Record Book* (1976). A brief analysis of his career is Jersey Jones, "The Legend That Was Harry Wills," *Ring,* Mar. 1959, with photographs. The *New York Times,* Dec. 22, 1958, has a brief obituary notice. Jack Dempsey gives his side of the controversy in his autobiography, *Round by Round* (1940), and in *Dempsey by the Man Himself* (1960). Wills's challenge to Dempsey is in " 'If Dempsey's Afraid, Let Him Say So' Says Harry Wills," *Collier's,* Mar. 20, 1926. Al-Tony Gilmore discusses the furor surrounding Jack Johnson in *Bad Nigger!* (1975).]

EDWARD S. SHAPIRO

WINSLOW, CHARLES-EDWARD AMORY (Feb. 4, 1877–Jan. 8, 1957), bacteriologist and public health expert, was born in Boston, Mass., the son of Erving Winslow, a merchant and publicist, and Catherine Mary Reignolds, an English actress who played Shakespearean heroines and popularized Ibsen's plays in America. Early displaying a brilliance and creativity, he learned German, French, and rhetoric from his mother. After graduating from the English High School in Boston in 1894, he entered the Massachusetts Institute of Technology. While an undergraduate he translated *Heimath* by Hermann Sudermann, a play that was a particular favorite of his mother's. It was published in 1896 as *Magda.*

Winslow grew up at a time when the profession later called public health was emerging in America. Numerous epidemics brought to official attention the issues of safe water, of sewage and waste disposal, and of sanitary production of milk. The pioneer investigator of these matters in Massachusetts was William Thompson Sedgwick, the head of the department of biology at MIT. Winslow was inspired by Sedgwick and the possibilities of this new field. Most of Sedgwick's students were preparing for careers in medicine, but Winslow specialized in biology and bacteriology. He received his B.S. in 1898, and spent another year with Sedgwick as a graduate student, making a notable investigation of the action of freezing on the typhoid bacillus and the importance of ice as a vehicle for disease. This served as his M.S. essay (1899), and was published in 1902 in the *Memoirs of the American Academy of Arts and Sciences.*

Winslow was appointed an assistant in Sedgwick's department (1900–1901) and then served as an instructor in sanitary bacteriology from 1902 to 1905. In 1904 he wrote, with Samuel C. Prescott, *The Elements of Water Bacteriology,* a pioneering text. His own *Elements of Applied Microscopy* appeared in 1905. He was appointed assistant professor of sanitary biology (1905–1910) at MIT, where he was also biologist in charge of the sanitary research laboratory (1903–1910).

In 1903 Winslow became head of MIT's sewage experiment station. He was associated with the station for seven years and prepared a number of special studies, including an investigation on the purification of Boston's sewage. He also carried through an extensive study on the *Coccaceae,* in which his assistant was a student named Anne Fuller Rogers. They were married on May 19, 1907, and had one daughter.

Winslow's reputation soon became widespread. Encouraged by Sedgwick, he spent a sabbatical at the University of Chicago as a visiting assistant professor of bacteriology (1910). Shortly thereafter, he accepted an appointment as associate professor of biology at the College of the City of New York (1910–1914).

Although he published over fifty journal articles during his four years at CCNY, Winslow seemed to prefer the challenging work as a curator of public health at the American Museum of Natural History, a position he held concurrently. As curator, he prepared imaginative public health exhibits and arranged for public lectures and seminars. The first exhibition of the Hall of Public Health in 1913 contained models of a giant house fly and other insects involved in the dissemination of disease. Winslow served as curator from 1910 to 1922. In 1915 he left CCNY to become director of the division of publicity and health education in the New York State Department of Public Health. There he worked under Hermann M. Biggs, the new commissioner of public health. Like Sedgwick, Biggs aroused in Winslow a fierce dedication and loyalty. He became Biggs' confidant and, thirteen years later, his biographer.

Under Biggs, Winslow developed innovative health promotion exhibitions and programs, edited *Health News* and *Health Hints,* and helped to coin the department's motto ("Public Health Is Purchasable. Within Natural Limitations a Community Can Determine Its Own Death Rates").

The New York experience, as teacher, curator, consultant, and public servant, was a happy one for Winslow. But in 1915 he accepted an appointment as the first Anna M. R. Lauder Professor of Public Health at the Yale University Medical School. This was the first public health department that was an integral unit in a medical school. When Winslow accepted the Lauder chair, there was a shortage of health officers who had been trained both as doctors and as public health professionals. He attempted to imbue medical students with the "preventive" spirit. He established a program in which nonmedical bacteriologists, engineers, and social workers were trained for positions as public health scientists and administrators. He also designed a program in which medical students could obtain a combined M.D.–D.P.H. degree in five years; but whereas he was increasingly successful in training professional public health workers, who then staffed the nascent municipal and state health department, not a single Yale medical student enrolled for the joint degree.

Winslow's research in this period considered the bateriological, epidemiological, and statistical effect of various factors on the incidence of communicable diseases and problems of industrial hygiene, particularly those related to ventilation and dust hazards. In 1916 he became the first editor of the *Journal of Bacteriology*, the official organ of the Society of American Bacteriologists. Winslow recognized the need for his department to serve as the catalyst for reform, and his health surveys and reports led to substantial improvement in the organization of public health services throughout Connecticut. After the creation of a State Department of Public Health in 1917, Winslow was the first member appointed to the Board of Health.

In 1917 Winslow was named chairman of the New York State Commission on Ventilation, serving in this capacity from 1917 to 1923 and 1926 to 1931. In 1932 he became director of the John B. Pierce Laboratory of Hygiene in New Haven, which promoted research in the field of heating, ventilation, and sanitation. Winslow and his team designed a number of experiments on the physiological effects of various atmospheric conditions and on the partition of heat loss from the human body. In a related area, he championed adequate housing and shelter. "Good health," he wrote when he became chairman of the American Public Health Association's (APHA) Committee on the Hygiene of Housing (1936), "means vigor and efficiency and satisfaction in living. Bad housing is profoundly detrimental to health." In 1938 he became chairman of the New Haven Housing Authority, and he published scores of technical papers and reports, including one that considered the proper height of kitchen sinks. A housewife with a sore back, he reasoned, was just as much a public health concern as the sanitary removal of sewage.

Winslow was elected to the American Public Health Association in 1902, and was involved with its programs and policies until his death. In 1920 he was appointed the first chairman of APHA's Committee on Municipal Health Department Practice, a position he held for fifteen years. The committee (which in 1925 became the Committee on Administrative Practice) collected important data concerning actual health department administrative practices and prepared an appraisal form from which actual health services in a given community could be measured objectively. He saw more clearly than most others that public health was mutable and continuously expanding. In 1926, in an address as president of APHA, "Public Health at the Crossroads," he stressed the emerging role of the physician. The health officer of the 1900's might or might not have been a physician, but his major tasks then were engineering and bacteriological. There was a need for prompt public health measures ranging from prevention, early diagnosis, control, treatment, and rehabilitation for the recently studied heart diseases, cancers, and mental illnesses. Those who assumed that prevention was the task of the state and treatment the responsibility of the private physician were deluding themselves. Individual practitioners could not affect the change. Only society could provide the machinery necessary to achieve optimum health for all.

Winslow called for organized health services, public health clinics, and health insurance. But since many health officers served at the sufferance of local medical societies, they were fearful of attempts to link them with plans for state medicine or with programs falsely labeled "socialistic" or "bureaucratic."

The economics of medical care became another of Winslow's interests. In 1926, he helped organize the Committee on the Costs of Medical Care. He became chairman of the executive board and was the guiding force behind its twenty-seven major surveys. He helped to draft its final report, *Medical Care for the American People* (1932), which called for the development of group practice and group payment of health care and for the expansion and coordination of public health and medical services. He was perplexed with the reception of the report by the American Medical Association (AMA), which responded to it with disdain, bombast, and then indifference.

Gradually, the federal government assumed national leadership for both communitywide and personal health services. At the National Health Conference in 1938, Winslow spoke in support of "a coordinated, completely interlocking, dovetailing health program." The AMA, however, would have nothing to do with a federal program. As a result of the conference and the continued intransigence of the medical profession, Winslow advocated action by the federal government. He also advocated medical care programs within the APHA, and supported national health insurance. In 1944 Winslow became editor of the *American Journal of Public Health*. By the time failing eyesight forced his retirement from the journal in 1954, he had written a prodigious number of brilliant editorial essays, each a gem of erudition and clear thinking.

Winslow was also deeply involved with international health. In 1917 he was a member of an American Red Cross mission to Russia, and in 1921 he became general medical director of the League of Red Cross Societies in Geneva, Switzerland. From 1927 to 1930 he served as expert health assessor on the League of Nations health committee, and he later was a member of the league's committee on the hygiene of housing. In the 1950's he served as consultant to the World Health Organization. Winslow's *Cost of Sickness and the Price of Health* (1951) was a social and economic analysis of health and a framework for a truly preventive national health program and program of technical assistance, "in which the more fortunate areas may cooperate with those of less advanced development." His philosophy is most apparent in his address to the Fifth World Health Assembly: "We are all 'members one of another.' The stable world order of which we dream can be built only on the foundation of member states in every one of which there is at least a reasonable hope of progress toward freedom from disease and want as well as from fear."

Winslow produced numerous journal articles and monographs on historical medical topics, including "The Epidemiology of Noah Webster" (1934), *The Conquest of Epidemic Disease* (1943), and *Man and Epidemics* (1952). His other books were *Healthy Living* (1917); *A Pioneer of Public Health—William Thompson Sedgwick* (1924), with E. O. Jordan and G. C. Whipple; *The Life of Hermann M. Biggs* (1929); *Health on the Farm*

and in the Village (1931); *A City Set on a Hill* (1934); and *Health Under the "El"* (1937), with Savel Zimand.

An energetic man, Winslow walked two miles to and from work daily. While on nature walks over the summer, he would pack a lunch in a rucksack, stuff a book in a pocket, and hunt up plant specimens and insects. He also collected rare books, usually those with historical medical or public health titles. During the school term, his seminar met in his home. Students would sit before the fireplace, sip tea, and present their research papers and abstracts of recently published journal articles. Winslow then commented critically, revealing his crisp analytic mind and wealth of knowledge. Winslow's writings (numbering more than 600 titles), lectures, and penetrating participation in councils throughout the world have been reflected in great achievements in public health and have assured his position as the predominate figure of the public health campaign in this century. He died in New Haven.

[The C.-E. A. Winslow Papers are in the Contemporary Medical Care and Health Policy Collection of Manuscripts and Archives, Yale University Library. The *Yale Journal of Biology and Medicine* (1947), dedicated in his honor, has a bibilography of his writings up to 1946. Articles about Winslow include Ira V. Hiscock, "Charles-Edward Amory Winslow, February 4, 1877–January 8, 1957," *Journal of Bacteriology*, 73 (1957); "Charles-Edward Amory Winslow, 1877–1957," *American Journal of Public Health*, 47 (1957); John F. Fulton, "C.-E. A. Winslow, Leader in Public Health," *Science*, 125 (1957); and Reginald M. Atwater, "C.-E. A. Winslow: An Appreciation of a Great Statesman," *American Journal of Public Health*, 47 (1957). On Winslow's contribution to epidemiology and medical care, see Roy M. Acheson, "The Epidemiology of Charles-Edward Amory Winslow," *Journal of Epidemiology*, 91 (1970); and Arthur J. Viseltear, *Emergence of the Medical Care Section of the American Public Health Association 1926–1948; A Chapter in the History of Medical Care in the United States* (1972).]

ARTHUR J. VISELTEAR

WISLOCKI, GEORGE BERNAYS (Mar. 25, 1892–Oct. 22, 1956), anatomist, was born in San Jose, Calif., the son of Stanislaus Wislocki, a Polish army officer who died shortly before the birth of his son, and Lily C. Bernays. He received his education partly in America and partly in Europe, spending five years at a *Hochschule* in Heidelberg and graduating from Washington

University in St. Louis with a B.A. in 1912. He then attended the Johns Hopkins University Medical School and received his M.D. in 1916. After graduating he remained at Johns Hopkins as assistant in anatomy. During World War I he served as a first lieutenant in the Army Medical Corps. On returning from army service he went to Harvard as Arthur T. Cabot Fellow in charge of the Laboratory of Surgical Research but returned to the anatomy department at Johns Hopkins in 1920, where he remained for eleven years. In 1931, having become associate professor, he returned to Harvard, where he became, in turn, Parkman Professor of Anatomy (1931–1941), James Stillman Professor of Comparative Anatomy (1941–1956), and Hersey Professor of Anatomy (1947–1956). On Feb. 13, 1931, he married Florence Clothier, who was also a physician. They had four children.

Although primarily a placentologist, Wislocki did not limit himself to this field; anything that could throw light on the working of human cells was grist for his mill. His interest in placentation began early in his career with a series of comparisons of the placenta of sloths and anteaters; but underlying these detailed observations on structure, there were always latent, and often patent, questions of function and physiological significance, and phylogenetic and evolutionary implications.

By 1931, Wislocki's commitment to descriptive studies of the placenta had become more explicit. He was now a recognized authority on this subject; and monographs together with more than 175 shorter papers, clarifying the function of this complex organ and establishing its variations among mammals, began to flow from his pen. His output of original work, all of which testifies to his clarity of thought and powers of precise exposition, has been exceeded by that of few placentologists.

Wislocki played a notable role in establishing the course of the blood flow to the pituitary gland in the monkey, the uniqueness of which aroused interest in its physiologic and endocrinologic implications. His concept of a hypophyseoportal system (in the hypophyseopetal sense) opened a new perspective on hormone transport and the functional interdependence of the central nervous system and the system of endocrine glands. This must be regarded as the starting point of one of the most important advances in our knowledge of the pituitary, namely, that relating to the control of its secretion. That he should also extend his study to cetaceans was characteristic of the man and entirely in keeping with his interest in comparative and functional anatomy.

A natural outcome of Wislocki's interest in sex organs and pituitary-gonad relationships was his study of gonad and antler cycles in the Virginia deer. By a combination of careful histological observation and ingenious experimental manipulation he showed that the cycles are subject to regulation by light, operating through the anterior pituitary, and that the ripening and shedding of the antlers are controlled by the concentration of testosterone in the body. During this period he also investigated the circulation and development of the blood vessels of the brain, and especially the intricacies of the hematoencephalic barrier.

Besides these research activities, Wislocki was also interested in the newer techniques of microscopy, and many pioneering studies in histochemistry, cytochemistry, and electron microscopy were carried out in his department. He never tired of learning something new, whether it be a method of vital staining, microinjection, the use of tetrazolium salts, or electron microscopy. Yet these were only methods by which to gain particular ends. The basic problem was always the biological one of how things are constructed and how they work, whether spermatozoa, megakaryocytes, teeth, sweat glands, mammary glands, muscle fibers, fetal gonads, developing embryos, or placentas.

Wislocki's influence as the founder of a school of placentologists and histochemists is evident in the long list of his students and co-workers. As a teacher he was at his best with small groups; in formal lectures he was less effective. About his own work he was always modest and reticent. He disliked committee work, yet when he undertook it himself it was carried out efficiently. Scientifically and intellectually Wislocki was a man of major stature. Physically he was tall, handsome, and well-built. Until he smiled his face was often stern and rather sad. At the age of fifty-two and again at sixty-two, he suffered serious myocardial infarctions, and in between bladder cancer had begun to plague him. He endured these illnesses with courage and a complete absence of self-pity. His work, which brought him much happiness and satisfaction, was imbued with his rich humanity and, conversely, his scientific outlook dominated his whole life. It was his aim to impress on people that the pursuit of science is a rewarding and exciting adventure. He proved his point by the example of his own life.

Wislocki was a member of the National Academy of Sciences and the American Academy of Arts and Sciences. From 1923 to 1931 he was associate editor of the *Bulletin of the Johns Hopkins Hospital* and, from 1939 to 1946, of the *American Journal of Anatomy*. He died in Milton, Mass.

[See the obituary notices in the *New York Times*, Oct. 23, 1956; and *Journal of the American Medical Association*, Dec. 29, 1956. For family genealogy, see Thekla Bernays, *Augustus Charles Bernays* (1912).]

E. C. AMOROSO

WITTE, EDWIN EMIL (Jan. 4, 1887–May 20, 1960), labor economist, was born near Watertown, Wis., the son of Emil Witte, a moderately successful farmer and minor local official, and Anna Yaeck. Witte earned the B.A. (1909) and Ph.D. (1927) from the University of Wisconsin. On Sept. 2, 1916, he married Florence Elizabeth Rimsnider, a librarian; they had three children. Witte's entire academic career was spent at the University of Wisconsin. Starting as lecturer in economics in 1920, he became professor in 1933 and was chairman of the department from 1936 to 1941 and from 1946 to 1953. He retired emeritus four years later.

Witte's boyhood had been Pietistic and centered on the Moravian church. As an adult he gave little time to religion (although formally a Methodist), yet he retained a kind of piety: not smoking, for instance, disinclination toward parties, and an almost fastidious devotion to straightforward honesty and conscientious hard work. But his adult outlook was a secular one, shaped by the idealistic side of Wisconsin progressive government and, more particularly, by the economist John R. Commons, his true mentor in both graduate studies and career. Witte thoroughly imbibed a faith that democratic government could serve the public welfare well—if only officials worked in a spirit of service, and if public-minded experts (including university professors) brought care and rationality to policy, law, and institutions.

Commons was a pioneer in "institutional" economics. Drawing more from German historical economists than from English classicists, he emphasized the actual conditions, customs, usages, precedents, and laws that determine real, as opposed to theoretical, economic decisions. Witte avoided theoretical models even more than did Commons and extended his teacher's practical emphases. Commons was famous for investigations of industrial conditions and for proposing and helping to design and implement laws, especially in Wisconsin, to cover working conditions, labor disputes, and industrial-accident and unemployment compensation. Witte gave further working form to Commons' and others' progressive-era ideas. For instance, Commons in 1911 had been chief designer of the Wisconsin Industrial Commission; in 1912 Witte began to work intermittently for it, serving as secretary from 1917 to 1922. From 1922 to 1933 he was chief of the Wisconsin Legislative Reference Library, established to provide lawmakers with quickly accessible, reliable information and expert bill-drafting service. Thereafter, while a university professor, he continued to serve state and federal government in a host of advisory roles. He was highly skilled in legislative technique and very sensitive to political procedures.

For such qualities President Franklin D. Roosevelt's advisers chose him in July 1934 for perhaps the most important post of his life, executive director of a cabinet-level Committee on Economic Security that formulated the nation's basic social-welfare law, the Social Security Act (1935). Others had done more than Witte to advance the ideas of social insurance and federal involvement in welfare; but few reformers had his grasp of legislative technique, and too many had become embroiled in divisive debates, for example, over the broad pooling of unemployment insurance funds. Yet Witte's role was not merely that of neutral technician; he helped give U.S. social security its chief character. With strong faith in state government and lifelong skepticism of Washington, for example, he doubted the constitutionality of direct federal administration; and he continued to question its wisdom, later opposing the federalization of unemployment insurance.

Politically cautious, Witte was less perturbed than many fellow reformers when certain groups were at first excluded from old-age insurance, or when the bill did not impose rigorous federal standards on participating state welfare programs. He did not consider systematically the macroeconomic implications of social security financing; even in later years, after the impact of Keynesian thinking, he thought much more in terms of guaranteeing individual workers' benefits than of transfer of wealth or of large money flows through the national treasury. Consequently he favored quasi-actuarial financing—not only in 1935, but throughout his continuing service to the Social Security Administration in advisory roles.

Apart from social insurance, Witte delved deeply into labor mediation and its law. His most substantial book was *The Government in Labor Disputes* (1932), a careful description of public policy, court decisions, and legislation. In 1928 he helped draft the Norris-LaGuardia Anti-Injunction Act (1932). Among other mediation activities, he served the National War Labor Board, beginning in 1943 as director of the regional board in the key war-production district of Detroit and continuing in 1944 and 1945 in Washington as a full-time "alternate" member of the national board. From 1948 to 1953 he was a member first of a key presidential commission and then of the major national panel overseeing labor relations in atomic energy installations. In 1956 Witte was elected to the presidency of the American Economic Association. Although he had made no great contribution to economic theory, he had demonstrated an unsurpassed ability to translate key ideas into working practices, laws, and institutions. An uncommon number of his students by that time held significant posts throughout government. He died at Madison, Wis.

[Witte's vast collection (approximately 300 boxes) of papers (1914–1961), including diaries, correspondence, research files, class notes, government reports, and clippings, is in the Manuscripts Division of the State Historical Society of Wisconsin. See also the collected papers of John R. Commons, Arthur Altmeyer, Wilbur J. Cohen, and Willian H. Davis, in the same location; papers of the Industrial Commission of Wisconsin, the Legislative Reference Library, and other state agencies, at the Legislative Reference Madison, Wis.; and the collections of the 1934–1935 Committee on Economic Security, the 1937–1938 Social Security Advisory Council, and the World War II National War Labor Board, at the National Archives, Washington, D.C. The Social Security series in the Oral History Collection of Columbia University has substantial material on Witte, especially in contributions by Isidore Falk, Murray Latimer, and Herman Somers.

Witte's principal writings include *The Government in Labor Disputes* (1932); several articles on labor relations published in *Harvard Business Review* in 1945, 1946, and 1948; *Marathon Corporation and Seven Labor Unions* (1950), written with Robben W. Fleming; and *Historical Survey of Labor Arbitration* (1952). *Social Security Perspectives*, Robert J. Lampman, ed. (1962), an excellent sampling of Witte's lifetime writings, includes a comprehensive bibliography of his works.

The definitive biography is Theron F. Schlabach,

Edwin E. Witte: Cautious Reformer (1969), with a full bibliography. On Witte's social security work, see his own account, *The Development of the Social Security Act* (1962); U.S. Committee on Economic Security, *Social Security in America* (1937); Arthur Altmeyer, *The Formative Years of Social Security* (1966); and Charles McKinley and Robert W. Frase, *Launching Social Security* (1970).]

THERON F. SCHLABACH

WOLL, MATTHEW (Jan. 25, 1880–June 1, 1956), labor leader, was born in Luxembourg, the son of Michael Woll and Janette Schwartz. His father owned and operated an iron foundry until 1891, when he moved his family to Chicago, where they settled on the predominantly Irish South Side. Woll attended Chicago public schools until his fifteenth year, when he was apprenticed to a photoengraver. In 1899, Woll married Irene C. Kerwin; they had two sons. She died in 1945 and he later married Celenor Dugas, an artist. At the age of twenty-one he began studying law at night at the Lake Forest (Ill.) College of Law, graduating in 1904. He never practiced law, since while he was a law student, he had become involved in the affairs of the Chicago local of the International Photo-Engravers Union of North America. In 1906, while attending his first convention, he was elected general president of the union.

Although the president of a small union, Woll became one of the more important labor leaders in American history. He became closely associated with Samuel Gompers, whose ideas he generally shared. Many considered him Gompers' heir apparent, but following Gompers' death in 1924, the two largest American Federation of Labor (AFL) affiliates elected William Green as his successor. If this was a blow, Woll never showed it, nor did he slacken his activity and interest in the AFL. He had been elected eighth vice-president of that body in 1919, thereby becoming a member of the Executive Council.

Woll served as general president of the International Photo-Engravers Union until 1929. He was also a vice-president of the Union Label Trades Department and chairman of the AFL Standing Committee on Education and Social Security. From 1925 to his death he was associated with the Union Labor Life Insurance Co. For a time he edited *American Photo-Engraver*, the official publication of his union, and he was the author of *Labor, Industry and Government* (1935), and, with William English Walling, *Our Next Step—a National Economic Policy* (1934).

From the beginning of his career, Woll showed a strong interest in foreign affairs. He was a fraternal delegate to the British Trade Union Congress in 1915 and in 1916, and he was one of three delegates who defended the League of Nations against a slashing attack by Andrew Furuseth, the leader of the sailors, at the AFL convention in 1919. (At the same convention he also took the floor to reply to charges that the revolutionary Mexican government was persecuting the Catholic church; he was himself a Catholic.)

Woll, like many other labor leaders, was strongly biased against the Communist party. He opposed dictatorship and denial of human rights. Nor did he think socialism a proper means of solving the problems in the United States, although he defended the right of European workers to follow that path. In 1927 he was appointed by AFL president Green to a committee formed, at the request of the International, to investigate the strike in the ladies' garment industry, called by the Communist-controlled Joint Board, that almost destroyed the union. He was also appointed by the AFL to look into the Communist takeover of the Furriers Union. He served on the committee appointed in 1937 to work out a peace agreement with the Committee for Industrial Organization (the original name of the CIO) and on the War Labor Board in World War II. A tentative agreement was rejected by John L. Lewis. The agreement did not differ essentially from the one negotiated in 1955, which ended the division in the labor movement.

When the AFL affiliated with the International Federation of Trade Unions in 1937, Woll was sent as a delegate. He was also a delegate to the Oslo conference of the International Labor Organization in 1938. Four years earlier he was on the committee to carry out a boycott of German goods, as a protest of the persecution of democrats, trade unionists, and Jews; in 1943 he was appointed chairman of the newly created AFL standing committee on foreign affairs.

In 1944, Woll became president of the Free Trade Union Committee organized by the AFL for the promotion of "free and democratic trade unions" throughout the world. The International Federation of Trade Unions had been disbanded, and the World Federation of Trade Unions organized in its place. Although the trade union centers of democratic countries were represented, except for the AFL the Communists controlled the administrative apparatus and were working feverishly to win over the labor movements of the occupied European countries. Working closely with Jay Lovestone, the secretary of the Free Trade Union Committee, and its European representative, Irving Brown, Woll hoped to counter the Communist thrust and, at the same time, to assist in the revival of free trade unionism in Europe. He helped bring about the withdrawal of the democratic trade union centers from the World Federation and the eventual formation of the International Confederation of Trade Unions. At the close of World War II, Woll worked to provide aid to German and Austrian union leaders. He also fought for the return of the property confiscated from the Weimar Republic unions to those emerging during the occupation. He called for a revision of the policy of dismantling German industry for reparations payments to the Soviet Union, and argued that the retention of industry would enable Germany to meet its reparations obligations. He defended code termination for German industry as long as it was the desire of the German workers, and argued for offering full partnership in the community of nations to a democratic Germany. His contributions were recognized by Germany when he was awarded the Order of Merit by Chancellor Konrad Adenauer in 1953.

Woll was concerned that the postwar European labor movement not be split on denominational lines, and on a visit to the Vatican appealed to Pope Pius XII to issue a suggestion against the Catholic labor organizations. He attacked the occupation authorities in Austria for their attitude to the civilian employees, and the protests brought a change in policy. He opposed the appointment of former Nazis to high posts in industry, attacked French colonial policy in Tunisia, supported the Atlantic Pact, and pleaded with Secretary of State Dean Acheson to maintain a token force in Korea. The last suggestion was rejected by the State Department, which was confident that the agreement with North Korea would be observed. He also supported the emerging Japanese trade union movement.

[See Philip Taft, *The A.F. of L. in the Time of Gompers* (1957); *The A.F. of L. from the Death of Gompers to the Merger* (1959); *Organized Labor in American History*; *Defending Freedom*; Walter Galenson, *The CIO Challenge to the AFL*, proceedings of the conventions of the American Federation of Labor, 1906–1955; and *American Federationist*, especially 1918–1935. Numerous memoirs in

Columbia University Oral History Collection have references to Woll.]

PHILIP TAFT

WOYTINSKY, WLADIMIR SAVELIE-VICH (Nov. 12, 1885–June 11, 1960), statistician, economist, and public official, was born in St. Petersburg, Russia, the son of Savely J. Woytinsky, a mathematics professor, and Wilhelmina Berman. After being educated by tutors and at a St. Petersburg high school, he studied economics at the University of St. Petersburg from 1904 to 1908. Woytinsky was a brilliant and precocious student. While still in high school he wrote *Market and Prices* (1906), published with an introduction by Mikhail Tugan-Baranovsky, an internationally known authority on business cycles.

The eruption of the Revolution of 1905 plunged Woytinsky into radical politics. He joined the Bolshevik wing of the Social Democratic party and became a leader of a student strike and then of a general strike in St. Petersburg. He was arrested several times and finally, in 1908, sentenced to four years at hard labor and exiled to Irkutsk, the capital of Eastern Siberia. In June 1916, while living in Irkutsk, he married Emma Shadkan in an unofficial ceremony performed by a rabbi; they had no children.

Theirs was an intellectual as well as a personal partnership. She collaborated with him on so many of his later books and articles that they were frequently compared with the English social scientists Sidney and Beatrice Webb, a comparison that Emma Woytinsky, at least, did not find flattering.

With the success of the February Revolution, Woytinsky returned to St. Petersburg (then Petrograd) in March 1917. There he became a member of the executive committee of the Petrograd Soviet and coeditor of the newspaper *Izvestiia*. He tried to take a centrist position in the conflicts between Bolsheviks and Mensheviks, but he considered Lenin a demogogue and was increasingly alienated from the Bolshevik group. Later in 1917, Woytinsky went to Riga, on the Baltic front, as a war commissar. When the Bolsheviks seized power in November, he was arrested, thrown into the Fortress of Peter and Paul in Petrograd, and charged with counterrevolutionary conspiracy and mutiny. "A storm of madness and bestiality is over us," Woytinsky

wrote at this time. In January 1918 he was released without trial. Fearing rearrest, he and his wife fled to Tiflis, in Georgia, where the Menshevik Social Democrats were still in control. Briefly he was editor of the socialist paper *Bor'ba* ("Struggle").

From 1919 to 1921, Woytinsky served on diplomatic missions for the Republic of Georgia in Rome and Paris. In 1922 he moved to Berlin, where he did free-lance editing and wrote his memoirs of the two Russian revolutions for a Russian émigré publisher. Two years later he conceived of a "statistical book covering everything that can be measured." The result was the monumental *Die Welt in Zahlen* ("The World in Figures"), which was published in seven volumes between 1925 and 1928. This work, written with the assistance of his wife and the German statistician Ladislaus von Bortkiewicz, covered, as the title implies, the whole world. The volumes dealt with population, national wealth, labor, agriculture, industry, commerce, and government finances. Political and cultural statistics were also included, and historical materials, where available, were added to the current data. Woytinsky combined statistics and excellent graphs and charts, which he designed and drafted himself, with descriptive text and analysis. He wrote in a manner intelligible to ordinary readers as well as specialists. A perhaps overly enthusiastic reviewer for a German literary periodical called one of the volumes "a novel in figures."

Die Welt in Zahlen established Woytinsky's reputation. He began to write extensively on questions of international economics. In 1929 he accepted a post as statistician for the General German Federation of Labor (ADGB). Woytinsky revised and extended its system for collecting unemployment statistics, which were the basis for the official government unemployment figures.

The onset of the Great Depression caused a rapid increase in unemployment in Germany and focused attention on Woytinsky's work. He gave much thought to the problem and devised a plan to stimulate the economy by a public works program and by increasing bank credits. This "active economic policy" (*aktive Konjunkturpolitik*) was described in his *Internationale Hebung der Preise als Ausweg aus der Weltkrise* ("International Raising of Prices as a Way out of the World Crisis," 1931).

Because Woytinsky's proposal seemed to involve currency inflation, it was anathema to most Germans, who could not forget the runaway inflation the nation had endured in the early 1920's. German Socialist party leaders were as alarmed by his inflationary ideas as most others. He became very depressed and pessimistic. But by 1931, with unemployment soaring, the ADGB leaders were ready to endorse his plan. With Fritz Baade, an economist who was a member of the Reichstag, and Fritz Tarnow, a union official, Woytinsky drafted an official union statement, the Woytinsky-Tarnow-Baade (W-T-B) Plan, which was a condensation of his thinking. But the rise of Hitler to power put an end to the W-T-B Plan, along with the free German labor unions. Ironically, Hitler's antiunemployment policy bore many similarities to what Woytinsky had proposed.

Woytinsky resigned from the ADGB when its leaders decided against resisting the Nazis. They went along, he recalled scornfully, "like a group of captives dragged behind the chariot of the conqueror." He then fled the country, escaping arrest by only a few hours. After a brief period in Switzerland and in Paris, where he helped develop a scheme similar to the W-T-B Plan for the French unions, the Confédération Générale du Travail, he worked from 1934 to 1935 in Geneva for the International Labor Office (ILO). His *Three Sources of Unemployment* (1935) and *The Social Consequences of the Economic Depression* (1936) were written under ILO auspices.

Soviet objections to Woytinsky prevented his obtaining a permanent post with the ILO. For years Emma Woytinsky had been urging that he leave Europe for America. Finally, in October 1935, he agreed, and they immigrated to the United States. After years of being driven, through no fault of their own, from one country to another, America seemed a place of refuge. They became about as uncritical admirers of the nation as was possible for people of their intelligence. "After our long wandering," Woytinsky wrote, "we at last became part of a great country."

Woytinsky worked first on the Central Statistical Board in Washington, having been employed at the suggestion of the economist Wesley Clair Mitchell. His job entailed the modernization of government employment statistics. After a few months he moved to the Committee on Social Security of the Social Science Research Council, for which he studied the supply of and demand for labor in the United States. He analyzed such problems as labor turnover and wage differentials in various industries. He also maintained what he called an "informal" connection

with the Social Security Board, doing research on various topics, mostly of his own choosing.

After he became a citizen in 1941, Woytinsky's position with the Social Security Board was regularized. He urged shifting the social security system to a pay-as-you-go basis whereby "each generation . . . would support the old people who had been economically active in the preceding generation." This idea roused much conservative opposition, but was later adopted. In addition, Woytinsky did research on the unemployment insurance part of the social security system, developing methods of making long-range estimates of the cost of insurance under differing economic conditions.

During World War II, Woytinsky worked on problems related to the allocation of scarce labor. Later he made a detailed study of demobilization and postwar economic prospects. He concluded that a serious depression was "out of the question." His report on this subject was not published, but it was read in government circles during the latter stages of the war and was generally thought to be wrongheaded. Events proved his judgment to have been correct.

In 1957–1958 Woytinsky again lectured for the State Department, this time in Latin America. His last five years were devoted mostly to writing his memoirs, which were published after his death under the title *Stormy Passage* (1961). He died in Washington, D.C.

and Production (1953) and *World Commerce and Governments* (1955). In the course of their work on this project they returned to Europe in 1950, a trip that confirmed Woytinsky's pride in being an American. In 1955 and 1956 Woytinsky made a protracted lecture tour throughout the Far East under State Department sponsorship. His *India* (1956) was a result of this trip.

In 1957–1958 Woytinsky again lectured for the State Department, this time in Latin America. His last five years were devoted mostly to writing his memoirs, which were published after his death under the title *Stormy Passage* (1961). He died in Washington, D.C.

Woytinsky's fate was similar to that of many European liberals who spent their last years in the United States. He was by all accounts a person of enormous energy and enthusiasm, one who gave willingly of his time and knowledge to friends and colleagues. He lived through most of the major revolutions of the twentieth century, each time fighting on the side of the angels, each time defeated by antidemocratic extremists. Yet he emerged from each upheaval cheerful and unbowed, his principles unshaken, ready to begin life again in a new place, even though it meant working and thinking in a new language. "He wrapped the smallest happenings . . . in a mantle of fun," his wife recalled after his death.

That a person of Woytinsky's temperament and abilities should have had to endure so many uprootings through no fault of his own is a commentary on early twentieth-century European society. His career also provides a good example of how much European political refugees have contributed to modern America. He was typical of these refugees too in his affection for what he called "the promised land I discovered at the end of my stormy passage."

[Emma S. Woytinsky, ed., *So Much Alive* (1962), contains essays dealing with all aspects of Woytinsky's career, written by his associates, and an exhaustive bibliography of his writings. Emma Woytinsky's autobiography, *Two Lives in One* (1965), contains many personal details and copious extracts from the Woytinskys' letters and diaries. See also *New York Times*, June 13, 1960.]

JOHN A. GARRATY

WRIGHT, FIELDING LEWIS (May 16, 1895–May 4, 1956), governor of Mississippi (1946–1952) and vice-presidential candidate for the States' Rights party ("Dixiecrats") in 1948, was born in Rolling Fork, Miss., the son of Henry James Wright and Fannie Clements. He attended the Webb School in Bell Buckle, Tenn., then earned a law degree from the University of Alabama. He married Nan Kelly, his childhood sweetheart, on July 16, 1917; they had two children. Wright was admitted to the Mississippi bar and, with an uncle, began a practice that was interrupted by his enlistment as a private in the U.S. Army. He served in France from September 1918 to July 1919, then returned to Mississippi to practice law, play semiprofessional baseball, and organize and captain Company B of the 106th Engineers of the Mississippi National Guard—a commission he resigned in 1928, when he was elected to the Mississippi state senate.

The bifactionalism in the Mississippi Democratic party had historically pitted the "black belt" Mississippi Delta planters against the Populist highland whites. Wright represented the former in the tradition of "business progressivism" that opposed the racial demogoguery of

Governor Theodore Bilbo and championed the attraction of industry to Mississippi, the construction of farm-to-market roads, increased expenditures for education (including black schools), and levying a sales tax to bolster the imperiled credit rating of the state. He could not run for reelection in 1932 because Sharkey, his home county, shared its senator with an adjacent county on an alternating basis, so he was elected state representative instead. He worked so closely with Speaker Thomas Bailey that when Bailey's successor as speaker died in 1936, Wright's colleagues unanimously elected him to fill the vacancy. At the end of his second term in the Mississippi house (1940), Wright retired from politics and returned to private practice in Vicksburg. In 1943, Bailey ran for governor and Wright was nominated and elected lieutenant governor on the same ticket. When Bailey died in November 1946, Wright became acting governor. In 1947 he was elected to a full four-year term as governor.

In his inaugural address on Jan. 20, 1948, Wright sounded a call for revolt against President Harry S. Truman and the national Democratic party for encouraging the proposals of the Committee on Civil Rights, especially in regard to black voting and employment rights and federal protection from lynching that the Truman-appointed committee had called for in October 1947. Wright regarded the proposals as "aimed to wreck the South and our institutions," and called for a break with the national Democratic party because "vital principles and eternal truths transcend party lines, and the day is now at hand when determined action must be taken."

On Feb. 2, 1948, Truman nevertheless recommended that Congress enact some of the proposals. Wright carried his crusade to the meeting of the Southern Governors' Conference in Wakulla Springs, Fla., where a committee chaired by South Carolina Governor J. Strom Thurmond was appointed to persuade Truman (who refused to meet with them) and Democratic national chairman J. Howard McGrath to back away from the civil rights proposals. In May, Wright sponsored a states' rights conference of "all true white Jeffersonian Democrats" in Jackson, Miss. He was temporary chairman and Thurmond was keynote speaker. When the Democratic National Convention nominated Truman for president, Wright staged a walk-out of the Mississippi delegation and called for a states' rights Democratic convention in Birmingham, Ala., where on July 17 he was nominated for the vice-presidency and Thurmond for the presidency.

The Dixiecrat strategy was to deny Truman a majority of 266 electoral votes and throw the election into the House of Representatives, but the party got on the ballot in only thirteen states and won only the thirty-nine electoral votes (1,176,125 popular votes) of South Carolina, Mississippi, Alabama, and Louisiana, and one from Tennessee. Unlike the "Hoovercrat" bolt of 1928, which was an Upper South revolt against Catholic Al Smith, the Dixiecrat revolt was primarily a Deep South protest by racially conservative "black belt" whites. Wright failed in a gubernatorial comeback bid in the 1955 Democratic primary. He died in Rolling Fork, Miss.

[There is no biography of Wright, nor a major repository of his manuscripts, but the Mississippi Department of Archives and History in Jackson holds a scrapbook on the 1948 election, correspondence concerning paroles and pardons, and political correspondence with the first state Democratic national committeewoman, Henrietta Henry. On the 1948 election, see Emile B. Ader, *The Dixiecrat Movement* (1955); Barton J. Bernstein, "The Ambiguous Legacy: The Truman Administration and Civil Rights," in Barton J. Bernstein, ed., *Politics and Policies of the Truman Administration* (1970); and Richard S. Kirkendall, "Election of 1948," in Arthur M. Schlesinger, Jr., and Fred L. Israel, eds., *History of American Presidential Elections,* vol. IV (1971). An obituary is in the *New York Times,* May 5, 1956.]

HUGH DAVIS GRAHAM

WRIGHT, FRANK LLOYD (June 8, 1867–Apr. 9, 1959), widely considered the greatest American architect because of the strong originality of his works, the impressive number of them (about 1,000 all told), and the consistent, radical principles of architecture he affirmed, was born at Richland Center, Wis., the son of William Russell Cary Wright, a musician and minister, and Anna Lloyd-Jones, a schoolteacher born in Wales. In 1876 his mother visited the Philadelphia Centennial Exposition and brought back educational toys designed by Friedrich Froebel, the German kindergarten pioneer. The elementary solids and primary colors, and their interplay, awakened Wright's creativity; *"form becoming feeling,"* he later wrote in his autobiography.

In 1878 the Wrights returned to Wisconsin from Massachusetts. Wright worked seasonally on his uncles' farms for the next nine years, becoming robust and keenly aware of the earth and its creatures. When he was seventeen, Wright's father was granted a divorce and left the family. In 1886, rather irregularly schooled, Wright registered as a special student at the University of Wisconsin, where he earned his way helping the dean of engineering; architecture was not taught there. Then, or soon after, Wright read books that influenced him enduringly: John Ruskin, records of Mayan architecture, Eugène Viollet-le-Duc's *Dictionnaire raisonné de l'architecture française,* and Owen Jones's *Grammar of Ornament.* Also in that year, on a corner of their farmland, the Lloyd-Jones family built a small chapel designed by J. L. Silsbee, newly arrived from the East. Through him Wright became acquainted with the shingle style (an American adaptation of English fashions) and with the art of architectural rendering.

Early in 1887, Wright, despite counsel, went to Chicago and found work with Silsbee. In about a year he moved to a busier office, Adler and Sullivan, as chief assistant to the "designing partner," Louis H. Sullivan. Wright was immediately involved in the design of commercial structures now considered masterpieces: the Auditorium, Wainwright, and Schiller Theater buildings; Sullivan became Wright's ideal. On June 1, 1889, Wright married Catherine Lee Tobin; they had six children. He borrowed from Adler and Sullivan to buy property in Oak Park, a suburb of Chicago. Wright's mother and a sister moved into an existing house, and next door he designed and built a new one for his family. Wright often worked long evenings at home; sometimes, surreptitiously, he did houses on his own. When Sullivan learned this, he was outraged. By 1893 Wright was in practice alone.

In *An Autobiography* (1932) Wright said that in these years he began to formulate the principles that ruled his work. Describing them, Wright used terms that need elucidation:

Organic architecture. Just as he saw human life to be part of the whole natural order, so Wright conceived architecture to be an organic part of human life, produced by it and reacting on it. He considered this his essential insight. Wright did not imagine that buildings should be designed to look like organisms; instead, his architecture was intended to let individuals evolve, and to link people to each other, to their world, and to nature in a productive cycle. Thus organic architecture could lead to an organic society.

The architecture of democracy. To Wright an organic society meant a democracy of free individuals; his phrase indicated architecture as a factor of this society.

The nature of materials. This was Wright's affirmation of the doctrine that a material (wood, stone, glass, or metal) should be used deliberately to demonstrate its character and the method of its handling. Wright read this in Ruskin and Viollet-le-Duc, and observed its application in American works.

Plasticity. Learning from Sullivan's ornamentation that surfaces can be made richly expressive, Wright emphasized the textures and colorings of his materials. Exploring the potentials of surfaces, he discovered that wall and ceiling planes could be placed so as to mold space without confining it. Wright called this "plasticity."

Continuity. Wright began to study space in its own right. After 1930, when he fully grasped the concept of spatial continuity, his insights matured. The architectural expression of space necessarily arose from the treatment and placement of matter, yet matter was kept subservient. Henceforth continuous, organized space became the chief instrument of Wright's art.

By 1900, Wright's designs were original and unified. His aims and expressive means were shared with a group of local architects known as the Prairie School; Wright was its acknowledged star. His residences provided separate zones for sociability, for privacy, and for services. One or two floor levels usually sufficed, cellars and attics were eliminated, and plans were boldly simplified. Each design was anchored at its vertical core, a central chimney; nearby rose the stairs. Spaces spread outward along clear axes, screened by bearing walls. Wide, sloping roofs sheltered walls and bands of windows; these usually were ornamented in toned, geometric patterns softening the harsh prairie light. Among Wright's more than fifty Prairie-style houses many were modest, like the Hickox house in Kankakee, Ill., or those designed for and published by the *Ladies' Home Journal*, works of 1900. They could be large and generously landscaped, like his masterwork, the Coonley estate at Riverside, Ill., or the grand project for the McCormicks at Lake Forest of 1907 and 1908. In 1908, Wright built a neat, small house with a balconied, two-story living room for his bookkeeper, Isabel Roberts; he varied this design for half a dozen clients.

Wright developed his first big commercial commission, the Larkin Building in Buffalo (1904), most inventively. The five-story brick structure housed executives and clerical staff of a mail-order business; the top level was devoted to employees' rest and recreation. An oblong glass-roofed space occupied the center of the building, its light balancing the clerestory light on wide working balconies. Air conditioning and sound absorption were provided. The metal furniture was composed of adjustable standard parts. Stairways were isolated in fireproof corner towers, and ducts were designed for ready access. These practicalities were united in lively but quiet harmony; nevertheless the Larkin Building, a pioneering masterwork of business architecture, was demolished in 1949.

In 1906 Wright built a small church, Unity Temple, in Oak Park; it is now designated a National Historic Landmark. It consists of a 400-seat auditorium linked to an annex used for instruction and social gatherings. The whole is made of inexpensive, massive concrete with reinforced beams boxing skylights over the square main room. Clerestories balance the top light. Street noises are well muffled, and inside traffic is skillfully screened from the congregation seated on a main level and in balconies; from every seat there is a sense of closeness to the speaker.

Wright's work now was often exhibited and published; his 1901 talk, "The Art and Craft of the Machine," considered a manifesto of modern architecture, was delivered several times. In 1905 Wright and his wife accompanied friends to Japan. Wright had admired Japanese art for at least a decade, and during this trip he formed a notable collection of wood-block prints.

The year before, Wright designed a modest home for the E. H. Cheneys in Oak Park, and his attachment to Mamah Cheney deepened. His wife did not keep pace with his artistic interests, and he felt stifled by the suburbs and by the cliquish Prairie School. Wright's dissatisfaction grew, and late in 1909, after the German publishing firm Wasmuth indicated its readiness to produce a monograph on his work, Wright went abroad. Mrs. Cheney met him en route, although neither was divorced. In Berlin the pair registered at a hotel as man and wife; the *Chicago Tribune* quickly published the news. Despite simmering scandal, Wright arranged with Wasmuth to publish two books. The first, which appeared in 1910, was a sumptuous double portfolio presenting Wright's buildings and projects from 1893 to 1909. With his son Lloyd and young Taylor Willey, Wright redrew 100 renderings and plans for these plates. The second book, published in 1911, reproduced good photographs of buildings and plans. Both books influenced architects in Germany, Holland, and France but were little noticed in America.

Wright returned to Oak Park late in 1910. Mrs. Cheney got a divorce, but Catherine would not free Wright. At the end of 1911 Wright announced publicly that he and Mamah Cheney would settle in Wisconsin (on land his mother gave him). There Wright created his new environment, called Taliesin after the Welsh bard. Unlike anything suburban, it was farmstead, studio, and Pieria all in one. Soon remarkable designs began to appear from it, including a children's center where John Dewey's teachings could be pursued and a system for partially prefabricated, low-cost houses and apartment blocks. Wright proposed a reinforced-concrete office skyscraper for downtown San Francisco, efficiently slab-shaped, half again as high as any then standing. In 1913 a group of Japanese investors, after searching widely, appointed Wright the architect for a new, Western-style hotel in central Tokyo, to serve official as well as commercial purposes. Wright had become world-famous.

While Wright was developing the hotel, Edward Waller, Jr., son of an old client, asked him to design an indoor-outdoor, dining-and-concert complex for Chicago, to be built immediately. The plan was conventionally symmetrical, but the structure and the generally abstract murals and sculpture were novel and colorful. Just before the opening of the building, known as Midway Gardens, Wright was called to the telephone; Taliesin was burning. On the train to Madison, Wright found E. H. Cheney, whose two children were visiting their mother. At Taliesin the full horror hit both men. An insane cook-houseman, newly employed, had sealed the dining room at mealtime, set the building on fire, and then axed anyone who tried to escape; seven were murdered including Mamah and the children. The murderer hid, was caught, and killed himself. Wright's private world was destroyed.

Dazed, Wright began to rebuild Taliesin. In this state he was approached by a worldly, monied, and hypersensitive woman. From 1915 to 1923 Miriam Noel was Wright's companion in Tokyo, Taliesin, and California. Something within her worsened steadily; Wright could not help her, and in time she became bent on destroying him.

Building the hotel involved Wright in crisis after crisis, yet he stood his ground and a dreamlike structure arose, rich, comfortable, and efficient. Other Japanese commissions were drawn up; some were realized (most, like the hotel, have vanished). In 1923 the structurally innovative Imperial Hotel, completed the year before, survived a major earthquake and fire; Wright's technical mastery was apparent.

About 1915 Wright met Aline Barnsdall, patroness of experimental art, who hoped to develop an artists' colony with studios, theaters, and a central residence for herself. In 1919 she bought a hilly olive grove in Los Angeles, Calif. From 1920 to 1922 the handsome Barnsdall house, two studio homes, and some minor adjuncts were built to Wright's designs. (The Barnsdall house, somewhat changed, is now open to the public.)

Barnsdall's wealth came from oil, as did that of E. L. Doheny, who, in 1921, had Wright design the development of extensive mountain property east of Pasadena, Calif. Doheny fell in the Harding administration's scandals, but some of Wright's grand drawings for him survive. Automobile roads span ravines, spiral around crests, and occasionally bud into fantastic aeries that, like the roadway itself, seem natural outgrowths of the native rock. All this construction, roads and homes alike, is of concrete blocks, some patterned; steel reinforcing rods are luted into the vertical and horizontal joints, creating a strong, composite mass readily erected by unskilled labor. In 1923 Wright used reinforced block construction in four notable homes still standing in Pasadena and Hollywood.

Wright's private life was changing rapidly. Late in 1922 he was finally divorced from Catherine and his mother died the following February. In November 1923 he married Miriam Noel, but she left him six months later. Louis Sullivan, reconciled with Wright for a decade, died in April 1924 poor and frustrated; Wright grieved over him. Late in 1924 Wright met Olgivanna Lazovich, with whom he remained for the rest of his life. She was twenty-six, born in Montenegro, and separated from the father of her seven-year-old daughter.

In 1924 Wright projected skyscraper headquarters for A. M. Johnson, president of an insurance company. The frame was of concrete; the skin, of metal and glass; the standardized, movable partitions and office furniture of sound-insulated metal were all well ahead of current practice. Then Gordon Strong wished to sell home sites on Sugar Loaf Mountain near Washington, D.C.; in 1925 Wright proposed a spiral drive to a lookout on the mountain top where further features were considered, restaurant, radio mast, or planetarium (then a great novelty). For New York City he devised a huge interfaith cathedral in steel and glass, a 1,500-foot-high tepee.

Amid these fantasies Wright's spirit was buoyed by Olgivanna Lazovich and the daughter she bore him. Wright was attacked by his second wife; accusations, legal actions, and intrusions, one followed the other. An accidental fire badly damaged Taliesin. In 1926 Olgivanna Lazovich's former husband joined forces with Mrs. Wright in legal maneuvers that involved the children. Bankers and other creditors succeeded in taking possession of Taliesin (temporarily) and Wright's art collections; the harassment lasted far into 1927. By August 1927, Miriam Noel gave Wright a divorce, and a group of Wright's prominent friends formed a corporation to handle his debts in return for his earnings over a period of years. Wright drew living expenses and some security returned to his existence. Wright and Olgivanna were married on Aug. 25, 1928.

The Wrights spent the winter of 1928–1929 in the Arizona desert, where a new client planned to develop a large, luxurious resort. In the vibrant desert sunlight Wright perceived sharp edges as dotted lines and the mountains, rocks, and cacti appeared to be formed in thirty-degree angles. This angle dominated the beautiful drawings of the resort; it also combined with Wright's more habitual right angles especially happily in studio towers planned for St. Mark's in the Bowery, New York City.

Most enterprises of 1929 were abruptly canceled by the stock market crash; from 1929 to 1936 only one modest house of Wright's was built (1934). He survived by lecturing and by publishing articles and books. Olgivanna had set him to writing *An Autobiography,* often evocative and engaging. It first appeared in 1932, as did *The Disappearing City,* the earliest of several books in which Wright wrote of automobile travel heralding a new way of life and of the country gas station as a new commercial nucleus, indicating dispersed populations and decay in city centers.

In 1932 the Wrights opened Taliesin and its acres to apprentices wishing to share an organic way of life by operating farm, house, and drafting room and paying what they could; some thirty men and women were accepted. Throughout the winter of 1934–1935 Wright and his apprentices worked on a complex display of an ideal community called Broadacres, neither urban nor rural, embodying the values that guided Taliesin.

This was exhibited in New York City in 1935, later traveling throughout the country. Its impact on Depression-battered citizens was dramatic; here was a plausible vision of a new and saner life.

In 1935–1936 Wright designed two of his best-known works, Fallingwater, a home in Mill Run, Pa., and the Johnson's Wax administrative center in Racine, Wis. After their construction Wright was acclaimed in publications and exhibitions from 1938 until World War II; at seventy he had begun a new cycle of activity. Fallingwater's enduring popularity is due to its superb coordination with a shaggy, cascaded, mountain site; it is now open to the public. The unprecedented spaces and structure of the Johnson building are monumental and provide a convenient, cheerful office environment. Before these two commissions were finished, two more of import were begun. The Hanna house at Palo Alto, Calif. (now owned by Stanford University), was Wright's first executed building planned on hexagonal modules; the quiet flow of space is exhilarating. Far simpler, a small house for Herbert Jacobs and his family cost $5,000; it was the first realization of a type called Usonian (suggesting United States) homes, which Wright built in grand variety over the next two decades. Wright's prodigious architectural center and winter residence, Taliesin West, near Scottsdale, Ariz. (1938), has been changed since his death.

A very small Usonian house for two school-teachers, built in 1939 at Okemos, Mich., was one of his masterpieces. That year Wright lectured at London University; the talks, published as *An Organic Architecture,* include some of his best statements. The next year an exhibition held at the Museum of Modern Art, New York, resulted in the basic study of Wright's architecture, Henry-Russell Hitchcock's *In the Nature of Materials* (1942).

Polygons, arcs, and spirals were used increasingly by Wright in his last years. At the same time many of the buildings that issued from his drafting room were based on plans and forms previously mastered. More apprentices were at work, yet any design that bore his signature bore his controlling touch. In 1943 the Jacobs family needed a larger house; Wright gave them another prototype, often repeated with variations. An arc of enclosed space, oriented to the sun, curves around a shallow, excavated circular court; the removed earth is banked against the outer, weather wall. Insulation and insolation are teamed with an organized play of space. At this time Wright made his first designs for a public museum to present

Solomon Guggenheim's collection of nonrepresentational paintings and sculpture. Wright used his time-tested scheme of a central, skylit well, circular now; the diffused, central light was balanced by direct clerestory light that edged an enveloping spiral ramp containing exhibition and walkway space. Movable radial partitions were planned to give increased display surface and, more important, to allow a rhythmic sequence of subspaces along the ramp, variable to suit the art exhibited. Wartime shortages led Guggenheim to postpone construction.

Wright's last decade opened with a large exhibition, presented in Philadelphia before a triumphal tour of Europe. His greatest spatial design, the Guggenheim Museum, was at last begun, but not completed until after his death. He died in Phoenix, Ariz. Wright's revolutionary idea can be comprehended only by examining his designs. Another masterwork of Wright's, built after his death but kept close to the original concept, is the Marin County Civic Center near San Francisco, Calif. Wright's only building for government, it unites complex services with essential highway and parking facilities free of urban congestion. Ingenious air conditioning saves energy, making large interior spaces practicable. In seventy years of practice, over 400 of Wright's designs were built, and more than three-quarters of these still stand, witnesses to a unique career.

[The fundamental archive of Wright drawings and correspondence is closely held by the Frank Lloyd Wright Foundation; a diversified collection of documents is accessible in Avery Memorial Library at Columbia University, New York City.

Robert L. Sweeney, *Frank Lloyd Wright, an Annotated Bibliography* (1978), contains 2,095 carefully researched entries. Henry-Russell Hitchcock, *In the Nature of Materials* (1973), reprinted with a special foreword and a selected, up-to-date bibliography, is the chief reliable record of Wright's architecture. However, works later than 1941 are not listed in this book; supplementary data, not always dependable, are to be found in Olgivanna Lloyd Wright, *Frank Lloyd Wright, His Life, His Work, His Words* (1966). William Allin Storrer, *The Architecture of Frank Lloyd Wright* (rev. ed., 1978), records the extant buildings of Wright.]

EDGAR KAUFMANN, JR.

WRIGHT, RICHARD NATHANIEL (Sept. 4, 1908–Nov. 28, 1960), author, was born in a sharecropper's cabin at Roxie, near Natchez,

Miss., the first child of Ella Wilson, a country-schoolmistress, and Nathaniel Wright, the son of one of the few local freedmen to have retained the land they had acquired after the Civil War. Wright's father deserted his family when Richard was five. His mother became a housemaid, struggling to raise her sons as they all moved from Natchez to Memphis and then to Arkansas. A paralytic stroke left her disabled and the boys at the mercy of their mother's family for support. After a brief stay in an orphanage, Wright knew poverty, hunger, and the somewhat repressive education of a grandmother whose strict religious beliefs led her to curb his attempts at reading and writing fiction. In June 1925, he completed the ninth grade at the Smith-Robinson School in Jackson, Miss. He soon left for Memphis, where he worked for an optical company and discovered, along with the rigors of Jim Crow, a sustaining intellectual influence in the writings of H. L. Mencken and the American naturalists.

Wright left for Chicago in December 1927, and was soon followed by his family. There he worked as a porter, dishwasher, and substitute clerk at the post office; he sold insurance, cleaned floors at the Michael Reese Hospital, and was periodically unemployed. He started attending the left-wing John Reed Club, where he met white artists and writers, in 1932, and joined the Communist party the same year. He published revolutionary poems in such little magazines as *Left Front*, which he coedited; Jack Conroy's proletarian *Anvil; New Masses; International Literature;* and *Partisan Review*. Hired by the Illinois Federal Writers' Project in 1935, he worked for the Chicago unit of the Federal Negro Theater. A dynamic member of the black Southside Writers' Club, he composed forceful short stories of racial oppression and *Lawd Today*, a humorous novel about lower-class black life in Chicago that was rejected by publishers then but was published posthumously in 1963.

In June 1937, Wright went to New York City, where he helped launch *New Challenge* magazine and became the Harlem editor of the *Daily Worker*. "Fire and Cloud," one of the novellas he had submitted for the *Story* magazine contest open to W.P.A. writers, won first prize, and Harper's published it, together with three of his other stories, as *Uncle Tom's Children* (1938). He then completed *Native Son* (1940), partly on a Guggenheim fellowship. A powerful novel of ghetto life and resentment of white oppression and paternalism, it became a Book-of-the-Month Club selection and a best-seller. In August 1939

Wright married Dhimah Rose Meadman, a ballet dancer. They spent the following summer in Mexico, where he worked on a still unpublished novel dealing with black female domestics. The couple separated in the fall of 1940.

Wright collaborated with Paul Green on a stage adaptation of *Native Son*, which, produced by John Houseman and staged by Orson Welles, ran successfully on Broadway in the spring of 1941. On Mar. 12, 1941, he married Ellen Poplar and settled in Brooklyn Heights. They had two children. In 1941, he wrote the text, along Marxist concepts but in very poetic prose, of *Twelve Million Black Voices*, "a folk history of the Negro in the United States," with photographs selected from the files of the Security Farm Administration. He then completed "The Man Who Lived Underground," an existentialist and surrealistic novel later included in *Eight Men* (1961) in novella form. He worked on several projects aimed at fighting segregation, discrimination, and racism: a television series, an ethnic magazine, an anthology of social essays—but without success.

Since 1941, Wright had been dissatisfied with the Communist party, mostly because it tended to curb his freedom as a writer and soft-pedaled the fight against segregation for the sake of a united front against fascism. He gradually became estranged from party activities and in 1944, responding to attacks from erstwhile friends, published "I Tried to Be a Communist," relating his Chicago experiences, in the *Atlantic Monthly*. These episodes were part of the final section of his autobiography, *American Hunger*, which, on his editor's advice, he agreed to restrict to the first sections at the time. *Black Boy* (1945), the story of Wright's life prior to his arrival in Chicago, became another best-selling Book-of-the-Month Club choice. Wright lectured extensively, served on the American Council on Race Relations, and was active in the social field, helping Frederic Wertham found the Lafargue Clinic, which provided free psychiatric treatment for Harlem blacks.

In the summer of 1945, Wright went .to Canada and then to Paris, as a guest of the French government, in May 1946. He was welcomed by Gertrude Stein, met Jean-Paul Sartre, Simone de Beauvoir, and the existentialists, and enjoyed the free atmosphere and cultural and intellectual contacts of the city. Having again met with discrimination and racism on his return to America, he established permanent residence in Paris in August 1947. Active in existentialist circles and in

the political Rassemblement Démocratique Révolutionnaire, which opposed both the Stalinists and the Marshall Plan, he sponsored the Gary Davis movement for peace and world citizenship, founded the French-American Fellowship to combat discrimination, and helped French, African, and West Indian intellectuals launch the magazine *Présence africaine*.

While busy with a number of projects, including the rather unsuccessful filming of *Native Son* in Buenos Aires in 1950–1951, Wright went through a long period of metaphysical questioning. He turned increasingly toward Africa and the Third World. It took him seven years to complete *The Outsider* (1953), a major philosophical novel with a detective plot, in which he rejected both communism and fascism as societal models and concluded that it was impossible for the individual to live beyond good and evil without human solidarity. Meanwhile, Wright wrote *Savage Holiday* (1954), a short nonracial novel exploring psychoanalytical themes of guilt and violence.

Largely on the advice of the Pan-Africanist militant George Padmore, who shaped his thinking regarding Africa, Wright spent the summer of 1953 in the Gold Coast, then on the eve of acquiring independence under the leadership of Kwame Nkrumah. The results of his social observations, political reflections, and emotional reactions to the culture of his ancestors were published in 1954 as *Black Power*, "a record of reactions in a land of pathos." Wright did not spare British colonialism, and he advocated a mobilization of African energies in the struggle against neocolonialism. While engaged in research for a study of Spain, Wright was again attracted by Third World issues. He went to Indonesia in April 1955 to report on the Asian-African Conference, held at Bandung, Indonesia. His impressions, published in 1956 as *The Color Curtain*, stressed the importance of racial and religious factors in the thinking of leaders of former colonial countries, and it ended with an appeal to the generosity and good sense of Europe.

In September 1956, at the First Congress of Black Artists and Writers in Paris, Wright presented a paper, "Tradition and Industrialization," advocating an end to tribal customs and religious traditions that shackled individual freedom and thus hampered the struggle against colonialism. For several years he lectured on that subject, on the plight of Third World elites, on the psychological reactions of oppressed people, and on Afro-American literature. These lectures were collected in 1957 in *White Man, Listen!*, a last call to the West. In the meantime, Wright explored the sexual and emotional "heathen" roots of Western religion and culture in his controversial *Pagan Spain* (1957).

Returning to fiction, he planned a trilogy that would center on Fishbelly, a black youth in an oppressive Mississippi environment. He planned to describe the lingering effects of his conditioning in the free atmosphere of Paris and to explore his relationship to his African heritage. Only the first novel, *The Long Dream*, and the second (the still unpublished "Island of Hallucinations") were completed. Largely autobiographical, *The Long Dream* (1958) evokes childhood memories and offers in the character of Tyree Tucker the most positive image of a black father depicted by Wright. Set in the Deep South of the 1940's, it seemed outdated; critics claimed that Wright had been away too long and had lost touch with the Afro-American reality. With other black exiles in Paris, he was the object of sniping from magazines like *Time* for "living amid the alien corn." Involved in disputes between black expatriates, he felt spied on and threatened, possibly for exposing the work of agent provocateurs in the Afro-American colony. He thought of living in London, but despite the backing of former Minister of Defense John Strachey, he was refused permission to reside in Great Britain in 1958. During the summer of 1959 he fell ill from amoebic dysentery caught in the tropics and spent most of his time at the American Hospital of Paris, writing haiku.

That year, he wrote an adaptation of a folk comedy by Louis Sapin, *Daddy Goodness*, which was performed by a United States Information Service drama group and successfully revived by the Negro Ensemble Company in New York City in the late 1960's. An adaptation of *The Long Dream* by Ketti Frings closed in February 1960 after five performances on Broadway. Although sick again, Wright continued to lecture on the racial situation, especially for the French radio. He put together a collection of short stories written over three decades, *Eight Men*, which includes two radio plays, "Man, God Ain't Like That" and "Man of All Works," and "Big Black, Good Man," written in the humorous and satirical vein of *Lawd Today*. The volume appeared posthumously in 1961. Wright was recovering at the Clinique Eugène Gibez, in Paris, when he died of a heart attack.

Wright's literary reputation has been secure since the publication of *Native Son* and *Black Boy*, and, as a black novelist, he enjoys international fame equaled only by that of Ralph Ellison and James Baldwin. His critical analysis of modern societies and championship of Third World liberation made him one of the most meaningful Afro-American writers. His career, themes, and intellectual and spiritual development mirror an important chapter of Afro-American history, the transition from parochial southern agrarianism to mass, urbanized society first on a national scale, then in wider, global perspective. Both his achievement and his experience illuminate the black experience, both in its specificity and as a symbol for the awakening of modern humanity. His quest for the survival of individual freedom against the dictates of totalitarian systems lends his ideology a dimension that is more broadly humanistic than political.

[Wright's papers, including unpublished manuscripts, correspondence, and memorabilia, are at the Beinecke Library, Yale University. Michel Fabre, *The Unfinished Quest of Richard Wright* (1973), is a critical biography listing all pertinent sources as well as publications by and about Wright. See also Constance Webb, *Richard Wright, a Biography* (1968). Full-length studies of Wright's works are David Bakish, *Richard Wright* (1973); Robert Bone, *Richard Wright* (1969); Russell Brignano, *Richard Wright* (1970); Keneth Kinnamon, *The Emergence of Richard Wright* (1972); Dan McCall, *The Example of Richard Wright* (1969); and Edward Margolies, *The Art of Richard Wright* (1969). To these should be added Richard Abcarian, ed., *Richard Wright's Native Son, a Critical Handbook* (1970); Houston Baker, ed., *Twentieth Century Interpretations of Native Son* (1972); David Ray and Robert M. Farnsworth, eds., *Richard Wright: Impressions and Perspectives* (1973); John H. Reilly, ed., *Richard Wright: The Critical Reception* (1978); and Ellen Wright and Michel Fabre, eds., *A Richard Wright Reader* (1978).]

MICHEL FABRE

YERKES, ROBERT MEARNS (May 26, 1876–Feb. 3, 1956), animal psychologist, was born in Breadysville, Pa., the son of Silas Marshall Yerkes, a farmer, and Susanna Addis Carrell. His early life illustrates how Protestant farm boys were often recruited into the newly forming urban white-collar and professional classes. Yerkes's family was extended, not nuclear, in structure—and middle-income Presbyterian. Grinding farm work and a strong religious atmosphere made him an intense, hard-working, and highly motivated person. He was often shy in social relationships, except with family and professional intimates.

Personal experiences pushed the adolescent Yerkes from his father's occupation of farming to an uncle's profession of medicine. At sixteen, after eight years of rural schooling, he went to nearby Collegeville, where he lived with his uncle, Dr. Edward A. Krusen, in order to attend Ursinus Academy and College. In his junior biology and philosophy classes Yerkes discovered Darwinism, which caused him to question religious doctrines for the first time. He received the A.B. in 1897. An anonymous loan enabled Yerkes to attend Harvard instead of Jefferson Medical College in Philadelphia.

At Harvard, a sophisticated milieu very different from bucolic Bucks County, Yerkes studied with the distinguished zoologists Edward L. Mark, Charles B. Davenport, and William E. Castle, taking the A.B. in 1898 and the A.M. in 1899, both degrees in zoology. These teachers, philosopher Josiah Royce, and psychologist Hugo Münsterberg inspired Yerkes to abandon medicine for the riskier career of psychological researcher. He became committed to the liberal, skeptical, rationalistic, and cosmopolitan intellectual atmosphere of Harvard, discovering, as rural people in such settings often do, social relationships defined by occupational, not familial, ties and a new world of secular culture and science. Evolutionary science replaced Presbyterianism thereafter in Yerkes's mind; he hoped the former would help professional men construct a science of man leading to social control. In 1902 he completed the Ph.D. under Münsterberg with a thesis on sensory reaction in jellyfish, and became instructor in animal psychology at Harvard on a half-time research appointment.

The next fifteen years at Harvard were busy and fruitful, although not easy financially. On Sept. 15, 1905, Yerkes married Ada Watterson, a botanist; they had two children. He was promoted to assistant professor in 1908. Yerkes supplemented his meager salary by extra teaching and as consultant (1913–1917) to the Boston Psychopathic Hospital. He also published nine books and some eighty articles, and constantly broadened his intellectual horizons and capacities—studying the behavior of diverse species, eugenics, abnormal psychology, and mental testing.

Yerkes assumed that "mind" was psychobiologically innate and had evolved; he studied the stages of the evolution of mind, or genetic psychology, from jellyfish to the presumed races of man. He invented imaginative laboratory apparatus and the point-scale intelligence test as an alternative to the more famous Simon-Binet mental age intelligence test, and he owned and edited, with the Johns Hopkins behaviorist John B. Watson, the *Journal of Animal Behavior* (1911–1919).

Yerkes began systematic primate work in 1915. His election as president of the American Psychological Association (APA) in 1916 reflected both his rising reputation and the dominant influence of experimentalists over more traditional philosophical psychologists in the affairs of the APA and of the psychology profession. Informed that the path to a Harvard professorship lay in education, not animal psychology, Yerkes resigned in April 1917 to head the new psychology department at the University of Minnesota.

American entry into World War I pushed Yerkes into government for the next seven years. A Wilsonian Democrat, he applied his science to contemporary public issues. At Yerkes's suggestion the Office of the Army Surgeon General created the Division of Psychology (which Yerkes commanded as major) to classify recruits for jobs in the mushrooming army. Yerkes functioned effectively, despite suspicion among regular officers of the mental testing program and the usual wartime chaos.

He resigned from both the army and the University of Minnesota in April 1919, to become chairman of the Research Information Service of the National Research Council in Washington, D.C. Yerkes's most interesting work with the council involved research on human sexual behavior and on immigration. He organized the Committee for Research in Problems of Sex in 1921, remaining a member until 1947. The committee sponsored several important studies, including those of Alfred Kinsey. Yerkes also chaired the Committee on Scientific Problems of Human Migration (1922–1924), which sought to stimulate large-scale research on the intelligence of American ethnic groups.

The Social Science Research Council deftly preempted much of the work of this committee, but Yerkes became involved, at least by implication, in the public and scientific controversies over the army test results and immigration restriction. These experiences in Washington made him long to return to university life. In 1924 he became research professor at Yale and, five years later, research professor of comparative psychobiology. He retired in 1944.

Yerkes's successes at Yale in establishing

primate research intellectually and institutionally were his most important scientific achievements. His primate work focused on ideation and problem solving (intelligence), not sensory perception and habit formation (which had dominated his pre-1915 nonprimate work). He published several enduring works, including *The Great Apes* (1929) in collaboration with his wife. He studied gorillas and especially chimpanzees; after the Scopes trial he named one chimp Darwin and another William Jennings Bryan. Yerkes created, with foundation assistance, the Yale Laboratories of Primate Biology, in Orange Park, Fla. (1929). He was director until 1941. Thereafter Harvard and Yale jointly operated the facility as the Yerkes Laboratory of Primate Biology.

Yerkes remained vigorous until disabled by a stroke in 1954, serving as a consultant to the government and research organizations and writing an unpublished intellectual autobiography. He died in New Haven, Conn.

Yerkes's life was significant in several respects. He literally launched comparative psychology as a field of experimental research in America. He was an important promoter of scientific institutions in the age of the graduate universities—typical of the new class of professional university scientists in America. His life offers, furthermore, important insights about secularization, the white-collar and professional classes, and the new culture of science. Yerkes's life and work, like those of thousands of other natural and social scientists, are eloquent testimony to the pervasive influence of evolutionary science and ideas in twentieth-century, middle-class American culture.

[The Robert Mearns Yerkes Papers, located at the Historical Division, Yale University Medical Library, New Haven, Conn., include his unpublished autobiography, 425 typescript pages, entitled "The Scientific Way." He also provided an account for Carl Murchison, *A History of Psychology in Autobiography*, II (1932). Yerkes's important books were *The Dancing Mouse* (1907); *Methods of Studying Vision in Animals* (1911), written with J. B. Watson; *A Point Scale for Measuring Mental Ability* (1915), written with R. S. Hardwick and J. W. Bridges (2nd ed., 1923); *The Mental Life of Monkeys and Apes* (1916); *Psychological Examining in the United States Army* (1921), written with others; *Almost Human* (1925); *Chimpanzee Intelligence and Its Vocal Expressions* (1925), written with B. W. Learned; *The Mind of a Gorilla* (3 vols.; 1927–1928); *Modes of Behavioral Adaptation in Chimpanzee to Multiple-Choice Problems* (1934); *Oes-*

trus, Receptivity, and Mating in Chimpanzee (1936); and *Chimpanzees, a Laboratory Colony* (1943). Obituaries of Yerkes include Edwin G. Boring, "Robert Mearns Yerkes," *Yearbook. American Philosophical Society* (1956); Robert M. Elliott, "Robert Mearns Yerkes (1876–1956)," *American Journal of Psychology*, 69 (1956); *New York Times*, Feb. 5, 1956, p. 86; Leonard Carmichael, "Robert Mearns Yerkes, 1876–1956," *Psychological Review*, 64 (1957); "R. M. Yerkes, Psychobiologist," *Science*, 126 (1957); and Ernest R. Hilgard, "Robert Mearns Yerkes, May 26, 1876–February 3, 1956," *Biographical Memoirs. National Academy of Sciences*, 38 (1965). The last obituary has a complete bibliography. Secondary accounts that treat Yerkes are Edwin G. Boring, *A History of Experimental Psychology* (1950); Loren Baritz, *The Servants of Power* (1960); Daniel J. Kevles, "Testing the Army's Intelligence," *Journal of American History*, 55 (1968); Hamilton Cravens and John C. Burnham, "Psychology and Evolutionary Naturalism in American Thought, 1890–1940," *American Quarterly*, 23 (1971); and Hamilton Cravens, *The Triumph of Evolution* (1978).]

HAMILTON CRAVENS

YOUNG, MAHONRI MACKINTOSH (Aug. 9, 1877–Nov. 2, 1957), sculptor, painter, etcher, and teacher, was born in Salt Lake City, Utah, the son of Mahonri Moriancumer Young and Agnes Mackintosh. His grandfather, Brigham Young, led the Mormons to Salt Lake City in 1847. His father, one of Brigham Young's fifty-six children, owned the Deseret Woolen Mills, and the family lived on a farm near the factory.

In 1884 Young's widowed mother sold the family business and moved to Salt Lake City. Young attended public schools, but quit at the beginning of his freshman year of high school. As a youth in Utah, he learned to whittle from his father, to model clay from the sculptor Cyrus Dallin, and to draw from academician J. T. Harwood. He was inspired by the published drawings of Charles Dana Gibson; the subject matter of Frederic Remington; salon catalogs from Paris; issues of *Harper's*, *Scribner's*, and *Century*; and John Gadsby Chapman's *American Drawing Book*. Young became portrait and sketch artist for the *Salt Lake Tribune* during the 1890's and worked in its engraving shop. In 1899 he studied at the Art Students League in New York. In Chicago and in New York he visited museums for the first time, being especially impressed by paintings by Rembrandt and Jean Millet.

In 1901 Young went to Paris to study painting and drawing with Jean Paul Laurens and modeling with Charles Raoul Verlet at the Académie Julian. He traveled to Florence, Rome, and Venice during the summer. The quality of Young's small bronze figures of men laboring and at rest, exhibited in 1902 at the American Art Association, was recognized by artists and critics. He continued formal study at the Académie Delacluse and with Jean-Antoine Injalbert at the Académie Colarossi.

In Paris in 1903 a thumb injury prevented Young from modeling clay, and he started to experiment with watercolors; two were exhibited at the spring salon (1904). He built an impressive library of books on art and the American West, and clipped and filed periodical articles and photographs.

Young employed themes typical of realists: figures (cowboys, Indians, laborers, dancers, and athletes), landscapes, animals, and interior scenes. His style was based upon close observation of his subjects. "Here is a man who kindles before the actual thing; who can give the kick of a horse, the frolic of a goat, . . . the stride of a squaw," wrote C. Lewis Hind in *International Studies,* April 1918.

Young was close to Leo and Gertrude Stein during the pivotal years of their support of vanguard artists, but he eschewed modernist primitivism, anatomical distortion for expressive purposes, and abstraction. He also modified the quest for idealized beautiful forms favored by academicians. He stressed actuality, simplification, anatomical study, and compositional structure.

On Feb. 19, 1907, Young married Cecelia Sharp, daughter of Mormon Bishop John Sharp. They had two children. She died in 1916. Young divided his time between a studio/apartment in New York City and a country studio in Connecticut. Between 1912 and 1918, he traveled three times to the Southwest to observe and sketch Apache, Navajo, and Hopi Indians. The resulting sculptures were deposited at the American Museum of Natural History in 1916 and 1924.

In 1911 the National Academy of Design in New York awarded Young the Helen Foster Barnett Prize for his bronze statuette *Bovet Arthur—A Laborer.* He was elected academician and exhibited there regularly. His first one-man exhibition of sixty-five works, held at the Berlin Photographic Company, New York City, in 1912, included drawings, watercolors, and sculpture, and was well received by critics.

Young's granite and marble Sea Gull Monument was erected in Salt Lake City in 1913. It commemorated the gulls that devoured the grasshoppers that threatened the first crops of the Mormons in 1848. The relief panels on the base were fine and original solutions to the technical and artistic problems involved. They were exhibited in New York at the celebrated Armory Show of 1913, which Young helped to organize. At the Panama-Pacific Exposition in San Francisco in 1915, Young was awarded a silver medal for his bronze figures of laboring men. One-man exhibitions were held at the Macbeth Gallery (1914), the Sculptors' Gallery (1918), Scott and Fowles (1919), and the Whitney Studio Club (1919).

Intermittently between 1916 and 1943, Young taught printmaking, painting, illustration, and sculpture at the Art Students League. He worked in Paris in 1923 and from 1925 to 1927. The Rehn Galleries exhibited his bronze sculptures of prizefighters in 1928, and his prints were on view at the Smithsonian Institution in 1930. Young's etchings were lightly scratched landscapes with a deep focal point to render a sense of the wide spaces of the American West.

Young married Dorothy Weir on Feb. 17, 1931. The following year he won first prize at the Olympic Games Exhibition, Los Angeles, for his sculpture *Knockdown.* He had one-man exhibitions at the Corcoran Gallery of Art in Washington, D.C. (1932), Kraushaar Galleries in New York City (1935, 1940, and 1948), and the Addison Gallery of American Art in Andover, Mass. (1940). Young was represented at the 1939 New York World's Fair by two monumental statues, *Industry* and *Agriculture,* installed in the Hall of Special Events.

A second monumental sculpture inspired by his Mormon heritage, *This Is the Place,* was erected at the entrance to Emigration Canyon near Great Salt Lake in 1947. Young also did the marble statue of Brigham Young (1950) for Statuary Hall in the United States Capitol.

Young's writings provide insight into his goals and methods. In the *Encyclopaedia Britannica* (1932, 1946, 1952) he expressed biases against excessively vigorous modeling and the technique of direct carving. He died in Norwalk, Conn.

Young is represented in the following museum collections: Metropolitan Museum of Art, Whitney Museum of American Art, Brooklyn Museum, and American Museum of Natural History, New York City; Newark, N.J., Museum, Cleveland Museum of Art, Toledo Museum of Art, and Dayton Art Institute in Ohio; Frank M. Hall Collection of the University of

Nebraska and Joslyn Art Museum, Omaha, Neb.; Rhode Island School of Design in Providence; and Brookgreen Gardens, S.C.

A posthumous one-man exhibition of Young's work from the Brigham Young University Art Collection was shown in Provo, Utah, and at Knoedler Galleries in New York City in 1969.

[Brigham Young University, Provo, Utah, is the chief repository of maquettes, models, sculptures, paintings, drawings, and etchings by Young, as well as of his private collection of works by other artists, his library, and archival material. Clippings files at the Whitney Museum of American Art, the Metropolitan Museum of Art, and the New York Public Library contain reviews and exhibition catalogs and some unpublished material. Young wrote "Sculpture Technique: Modeling, Theory" and "Frederic Remington" for the *Encyclopaedia Britannica* (1932, 1946, 1952).

Critical opinion includes Lester J. Lewine, "The Bronzes of Mahonri Young," *International Studio*, Oct. 1912; Guy Pene duBois, "Mahonri Young—Sculptor," *Arts and Decoration*, Feb. 1918; "An Art . . . Epitomizing the West," *Touchstone*, Oct. 1918; and Jane Watson, "News and Comments," *Magazine of Art*, Oct. 1940.

Young received significant treatment in *American Artists Group Handbook* (1935); *Index of Twentieth Century Artists* (1934–1936); Beatrice Gilman Proske, *Brookgreen Gardens Sculpture* (1968); and Wayne Craven, *Sculpture in America* (1968).

The most comprehensive exhibition catalogs, which serve as the only monographs, were published by the Addison Gallery of Art (1940) and Brigham Young University and the Knoedler Galleries (1969). Obituaries are in the *New York Times* and *New York Herald Tribune*, Nov. 3, 1957.]

ROBERTA K. TARBELL

YOUNG, ROBERT RALPH (Feb. 14, 1897–Jan. 25, 1958), railway executive, was born in Canadian, Tex., the son of David John Young, a banker, and Mary Arabella Moody. His mother died when he was ten, and Robert was raised by his father, a strict man who did not particularly care for his rather precocious son. Young was sent to Culver Military Academy in Indiana, from which he graduated at the head of his class in 1914. Then he entered the University of Virginia, where he became more interested in social life than studies; he dropped out before the end of his second year. Rather than work for his father, Young took a job as a common laborer at the E. I. du Pont powder plant at Carney's Point, N.J. Soon after—on Apr. 27, 1916—he married Anita Ten Eyck O'Keeffe, the sister of the artist

Georgia O'Keeffe. They had one daughter. He worked his way up to the treasurer's office, and there learned about finance. His grandfather had just died and left Robert an inheritance of $5,000. He used this money to speculate in securities, and lost it all. But in the process Young became interested in Wall Street, and thus found one of his major occupations, that of a stock speculator and manipulator.

In 1922 Young took a job at General Motors, where his financial acumen enabled him to rise to the post of assistant treasurer by 1928. He became a protégé of John J. Raskob, the head of the company, and left General Motors soon after to manage Raskob's finances when Raskob took a leave of absence to manage Al Smith's presidential campaign as chairman of the Democratic National Committee. But the two men argued in early 1929 when Young predicted a stock market crash and Raskob disagreed. Young went off on his own, sold stocks short, and made a fortune in the 1929 market collapse.

In 1931 Young purchased a seat on the New York Stock Exchange, and in alliance with Allan P. Kirby (a retail merchant) made large purchases of Alleghany Corporation common stock. The Guaranty Trust Company also wanted control of Alleghany, a holding company that owned large blocks of stock in the Chesapeake and Ohio (C and O), the New York, Chicago and St. Louis (the "Nickel Plate"), and other lines. A prolonged struggle began, with Young assuming the posture of the defender of the small stockholders. In the process he learned about railroad operations and considered creating a true transcontinental line, an ambition that had eluded the giants of the golden age of railroads in the late nineteenth century.

Young assumed the chairmanship of both Alleghany and the C and O. After World War II he attempted to obtain a central position at the Pullman Company, and when this failed, he turned to the New York Central. Young purchased New York Central shares through Alleghany and the C and O, and in 1947, in control of 400,000 shares, he demanded seats on the board. The Central responded with a publicity campaign, in which Young was characterized as an irresponsible plunger who meant to milk the line dry. In addition, the board of directors filed a complaint with the Interstate Commerce Commission, noting that Young's position at the C and O would compromise any office he might hold at the Central, since there would then be de facto interlocking directorates.

Young responded by writing a series of advertisements, which appeared throughout the country from 1947 on. In them he attacked mismanagement not only at the Central but throughout the nation, and promised to end it once he obtained power. "A Hog Can Cross the Country Without Changing Trains—But You Can't" was the most famous of his advertisements, in which Young noted that although freight shipments could go from coast to coast without changing cars, passengers had to transfer at Chicago, St. Louis, or New Orleans. He offered the Cincinnati terminal of the C and O as a connecting point for any western road willing to use it and the C and O rolling stock. The Central had terminals in Chicago and St. Louis, and he proposed to do the same with them if and when he assumed command.

Young and the management of the New York Central entered into a series of proxy wars in the late 1940's. They ended in a Young victory in 1954. He then stepped down as chairman of the C and O to take the same post at the Central. Young selected Alfred Perlman of the Denver and Rio Grande Railroad as the new president of the Central, with a mandate to improve passenger service and seek mergers so as to create a national rail corporation. But the western lines were not interested in uniting with the Central, then close to bankruptcy, although the Pennsylvania wanted talks, in the hope of decreasing competition.

Meanwhile, Young suffered fits of depression. His daughter had died in a plane crash in 1940, and he never fully recovered from the blow. Continued economic troubles at the Central, compounded by a recession and the inability to make good his promises, led to further gloom. The nature of the industry and the unwillingness of the federal government to sanction a unitary rail system compounded all of this, and in one of his dark moods Young committed suicide in Palm Beach, Fla.

[The only biography of Young is Joseph Borkin, *Robert R. Young, the Populist of Wall Street* (1969). Also see Joseph R. Daughen and Peter Binzen, *The Wreck of the Penn Central* (1971). An obituary is in *New York Times*, Jan. 26, 1958. Magazine articles on Young include John Brooks, "The Great Proxy Fight," *New Yorker*, July 3, 1954; and "How Young Got the Votes," *Fortune*, Aug. 1954.]

ROBERT SOBEL

ZAHARIAS, MILDRED ("BABE") DIDRIKSON (June 26, 1914–Sept. 27, 1956), athlete and Olympic champion, was born in Port Arthur, Tex., the daughter of Ole Didrikson and Hannah Marie Olsen. Her father and mother were from Norway, where her mother had been an outstanding skier and skater. Her father was a ship's carpenter and cabinetmaker. The family, who spelled their name Didriksen, moved to Beaumont, Tex., when Mildred was three.

Times were often difficult for the large Didrikson family, and as an adolescent Mildred worked at many part-time jobs, including sewing gunny sacks at a penny a sack. Her father, a firm believer in physical conditioning, built a weight-lifting apparatus out of a broomstick and some old flatirons. Mildred, called "Baby" in her early years, was always competitive, interested in sports, and eager to play boys' games with her brothers. After hitting five home runs in one baseball game, "Baby" became "Babe" (Babe Ruth was then in his heyday), a nickname that remained with her for the rest of her life.

At the age of fifteen, Babe was the high-scoring forward on the girls' basketball team at Beaumont Senior High School. She attracted the attention of Melvin J. McCombs, coach of one of the best girls' basketball teams in the nation. In February 1930, McCombs secured a job for her with the Employers Casualty Company of Dallas, and she was soon a star player on its Golden Cyclones. She returned to Beaumont in June to graduate with her high school class. The Golden Cyclones won the national championship the next three years, and she was All-American forward for two of those years.

Didrikson soon turned her attention to track and field. At the National Women's AAU Track Meet in 1931, she won first place in eight events and was second in a ninth. In 1932, with much more interest in the meet because of the approaching Olympics, she captured the championship, scoring thirty points; the Illinois Women's Athletic Club, which entered a team of twenty-two women, placed second with twenty-two points. Babe then went to the Olympics. Women were allowed to enter only three events, but she broke four world's records; she won the javelin throw, with 143 feet, 4 inches, and won the 80-meter hurdles, twice breaking the previous world record (her best time was 11.7 seconds). She made a world record high jump, but the jump was disallowed and she was awarded second place. The noted sports writer Paul Gallico remarked, "On every count, accomplishment, temperament, personality, and color, she belongs to the ranks of those story-book champions of our age of innocence." Gallico also referred to her as "the most talented athlete, male or female, ever developed in our country."

Didrikson began playing golf in 1931 or 1932. According to Gallico, in 1932, in her eleventh game of golf, she drove 260 yards from the first tee and played the second nine in 43. She herself stated that she entered her first golf tournament in the fall of 1934. Although she did not win, she captured the qualifying round with a 77. In April 1935, in the Texas State Women's Championship, she carded a birdie on the par-5 thirty-first hole, to win the tournament two-up. In the summer of 1935 she was declared a professional because of an unauthorized endorsement. She accepted the decision and for several years traveled about the country giving golf exhibitions. She also appeared on the vaudeville circuit with a number of different acts. She was the only woman on the Babe Didrikson All-American basketball team and played a few games with the House of David baseball team. It was during these years that she pitched an inning for the St. Louis Cardinals in an exhibition game with the Philadelphia Athletics. She excelled at almost everything she tried: when only sixteen she won a prize for a dress that she had made, at the Texas State Fair; she could type eighty-six words a minute; she could throw a baseball from deep center field to home plate—once a throw of hers was measured at over 300 feet.

In January 1938, Didrikson met George Zaharias, a professional wrestler often billed as "The Crying Greek from Cripple Creek," at the Los Angeles Open. She was attracted to this hulk of a man who could drive a golf ball farther than she. On Dec. 23, 1938, they were married. They had no children. Urged by her husband, she applied for reinstatement as an amateur golfer in 1941 and was reinstated in January 1943. Utilizing her tremendous powers of concentration, her almost unlimited self-confidence (She once wrote: "My main idea in any kind of competition always has been to go out there and cut loose with everything I've got. I've never been afraid to go up against anything. I've always had the confidence that I was capable of winning out."), and her patience, she began to take up golf seriously. She would drive as many as 1,000 balls a day, take lessons for five or six hours, and play until her hands were blistered and bleeding. In 1947, Zaharias became the first American woman to win the British Ladies' Amateur Championship, at Gullane, Scotland. On one hole she stroked a drive so far that a spectator whispered,

"She must be Superman's sister." That August she announced that she was turning professional. For the next six years she dominated women's golf.

Zaharias had a cancer operation in April 1953, and it was feared she would never be able to return to competition. Three and a half months later, though, she played in competition. The next year she won the United States Women's Open by twelve strokes. In 1955 she had a second cancer operation. She died in Galveston, Tex. In the last months of her life she and her husband established the Babe Didrikson Zaharias Fund to support cancer clinics and treatment centers. Zaharias was the greatest woman golfer of all time, the winner of seventeen successive golf tournaments in 1946–1947, and of eighty-two tournaments between 1933 and 1953. The Associated Press voted her "Woman of the Year" in 1936, 1945, 1947, 1950, and 1954. In 1950 the AP acclaimed her the "Woman Athlete of the Half Century." The skinny, shingle-headed teenager, a shy and socially immature girl who could win at sports but usually antagonized her fellow competitors, became a poised, well-dressed, graceful, and popular champion, the darling of the galleries, whose drives whistled down the fairways and whose comments won the hearts of the spectators.

Paul Gallico paid perhaps the finest tribute to her: "Much has been made of Babe Didrikson's natural aptitude for sports, as well as her competitive spirit and indomitable will to win. But not enough has been said about the patience and strength of character expressed in her willingness to practice endlessly, and her recognition that she could reach the top and stay there only by incessant hard work."

[There is much material in periodicals about Zaharias, but a lot of it is fanciful, and must be checked carefully. She herself exploded many of the myths written about her in her best-selling autobiography, *This Life I've Led* (1955), reprinted in the *Saturday Evening Post*, June 25–July 23, 1955. Among the better magazine articles are "Whatta Woman," *Time*, Mar. 10, 1947; "The Babe in Britain," *Time*, June 23, 1947; "What a Babe!" *Life*, June 23, 1947; "Big Business Babe," *Time*, June 11, 1951; "Personality," *Time*, Feb. 2, 1953; "Tell Everybody Hello," *Newsweek*, Apr. 20, 1953; Paul Gallico, "Farewell to the Babe," *Reader's Digest*, Jan. 1957. An obituary is in *New York Times*, Sept. 28, 1956. A sensitive and revealing biographical essay is in Paul Gallico, *The Golden People* (1965).]

RALPH ADAMS BROWN

ZILBOORG, GREGORY (Dec. 25, 1890–Sept. 17, 1959), psychoanalyst and psychiatric historian, was born in Kiev, Russia, the son of Moses Zilboorg and Anne Braun. After graduating from the local *Realschule,* he served (1915–1916) in the medical corps of the czar's army. After graduation from the Faculty of Medicine in St. Petersburg, he worked at the Psychoneurological Institute of that city under Vladimir Bekhterev, the founder of the school of "psycho-reflexology." He participated in the Russian Revolution of March 1917 and served as secretary to the minister of labor in the governments of Prince Georgi Lvov and Alexander Kerensky. Following the Bolshevik Revolution he fled Russia, arriving in the United States in 1919. On Dec. 14, 1919, he married Ray Leibow; they had two children.

Zilboorg supported himself by lecturing, writing, and translating for the theater. After graduating from the Columbia University College of Physicians and Surgeons in 1926, he worked for five years on the staff of the Bloomingdale Hospital. He spent 1929–1930 at the Berlin Psychoanalytic Institute, where he was analyzed by Franz Alexander. From 1931 on, he engaged in psychoanalytic practice in New York City.

Until 1941, Zilboorg was mainly concerned with the study of certain syndromes of the schizophrenic reaction from the psychoanalytic perspective. He described patients suffering from postpartum psychosis as affected by ambivalence toward motherhood, sadistic tendencies toward men, and inclination to marry later in life. Zilboorg found in many cases of suicide both strong unconscious hostility and an unusual inability to love others, at times related to lack of a normal loving relationship with parental figures.

In 1941 he first described "ambulatory schizophrenia" (later described by Hoch and Polatin as "pseudoneurotic schizophrenia" or, even later, as "borderline" cases) as typical of patients inclined to wander about and clinically presenting free associations and anxiety; such patients were amenable to psychotherapy, inasmuch as their strict superegos could be modified through identification with the therapist. He translated the German originals of Franz Alexander and Hugo Staub's *The Criminal, the Judge and the Public* (1931) and Otto Fenichel's *Outline of Psychoanalysis* (1934).

Zilboorg's primary importance, however, lies in his many studies on the history of psychiatry. His unusually broad humanistic background was a great asset in this work. His most original contribution was *The Medical Man and the Witch During the Renaissance,* which he delivered as the Noguchi lectures at the Institute of the History of Medicine of the Johns Hopkins University in 1935. This work broke new ground mainly in stressing the misogynic and sexually oriented importance of the *Malleus maleficarum* (1486), which remained for almost two centuries the manual for prosecution of alleged witches; in attempting to translate into modern terminology the signs described in the women accused of witchcraft and to minimize the belief in the role of the devil held by some enlightened men by considering it a *façon de parler* (an endeavor for which he was later criticized by many); and in presenting the pioneering views of the Dutch physician Johann Weyer, author of *De praestigiis daemonum* (1563), whom he called "the founder of modern psychiatry."

Zilboorg's lively *History of Medical Psychology* (1941) has enjoyed continuing popularity. It was the first comprehensive history of psychiatry by a psychiatrist. In it Zilboorg argued that the "medical" aspect of psychology was the only one leading to the understanding of the mentally ill.

The book described two psychiatric revolutions. The first was the *pietas literata,* a successful blending of scholarship and social action, of such Renaissance figures as Juan Luis Vives, Weyer, and Paracelsus; the second, Freud's discovery of the unconscious. In retrospect, Zilboorg's volume is impressive for his view of the entire history of psychiatry from Freud's early psychoanalytic perspective of the unconscious (rather than from the perspective of the ego, as in the later psychoanalytic literature) and for his outspoken defense of individualism. The book ends with the statement "The history of psychiatry is essentially the history of humanism."

Zilboorg remained faithful to this view. He never revised the volume, in spite of criticism and advances in the field. Later he published a translation of Paracelsus' *The Diseases That Deprive Man of His Reason* (1941) and wrote on the history of psychiatry in Russia. In 1946 he divorced his wife and, on Aug. 19, 1946, married Margaret Stone. They had three children.

In 1944, on the occasion of the centennial of the founding of the American Psychiatric Association, he was associate editor of *One Hundred Years of American Psychiatry,* for which he wrote the chapter "Legal Aspects of Psychiatry." In *The Psychology of the Criminal Act and Punishment* (1954), a series of lectures that he delivered as

Isaac Ray lecturer at Yale University, he made a strong case for the clinical evaluation of the total personality of the criminal and for a candid inquiry into the unconscious motivations of judges.

In his monograph *Sigmund Freud* (1951) Zilboorg stressed Freud's discovery of the dynamic power of the unconscious, the role of free associations (which, according to Zilboorg, Francis Galton had anticipated in 1879), and the importance of applying psychoanalytic understanding to literature. He paid particular attention to Freud's defense of humanism.

Zilboorg's religious development was interesting. Born of Orthodox Jewish parents, he later joined the Episcopal Church and, in 1954, the Roman Catholic Church. As early as 1939 he submitted that the opposition to psychoanalysis was mainly due to Freud's disregard for the two basic human beliefs—immortality and free will. In *Mind, Medicine and Man* (1943), a collection of essays on various aspects of psychoanalysis, Zilboorg wrote: "The central point of Freud's fascination was man's great capacity for love." Love was the common point of contact between religion and psychoanalysis. Freud "confused the ideational content of religion with its ritualistic expression, its psychological elements with its institutional aspects."

Zilboorg wrote on religious as well as on humanistic issues for many years. He submitted that Freud had a personal conflict with religion; he criticized Freud for having called only religion a neurosis, and not other cultural phenomena (myths, songs, folklore, dreams); and he maintained that in Freud, intuition and psychophysical determinism, a mystic as well as a materialistic trend, coexisted. Moreover, Zilboorg stated that the sexual restrictions posed by religion are older than the monotheistic religions criticized by Freud, that reaching ascetic ideals presupposes a level of mature sexuality in which unconscious neurotic struggles are overcome; and he pointed to the fundamental difference between psychoanalysis and confession. He argued that psychoanalysis, though never directly involved in philosophical issues, can contribute to the understanding of religious life.

For Zilboorg psychoanalysis developed "officially without moral values not because it rejected these values but because it carried them implicitly and inherently as everything human carries them. The trouble with psychology was that it had degenerated into "scientism," the overestimation of man's importance.

In an existential vein Zilboorg made reference to a "disease which I might call the disease of substitute restlessness—a form of living without really participating in the wholeness of life"; yet he did not find a solution to it in the new socially oriented psychoanalytic schools (so-called "Neo-Freudian") that he considered "as defenses against Freudian classical empiricism." Nor, as he put it in his last paper, was the future of the synthesis of psychoanalysis, psychiatry, and medicine clear in the United States.

Zilboorg was a charter member of the New York Psychoanalytic Institute (1931) and a cofounder of *Psychoanalytic Quarterly* (1932). He also served as training analyst for many years. Aside from his positions as professor of psychiatry at the College of Medicine of the State University of New York and at the New York Medical College, he was Gimbel lecturer at the University of California in 1947 and first academic lecturer at the annual meeting of the American Psychiatric Association in 1957. He also served as director of research for the Committee for the Study of Suicide and as chairman of the Consulting Delegation on Criminology to the United Nations.

Zilboorg had an extremely forceful personality. He was a nonconformist, a master of the written and spoken word, a linguist and a scholar, and a champion of individualism, both admired and rejected because of his tremendous ability to love. Among his contemporaries Zilboorg elicited "admiration, usually unexpressed; antipathy, usually openly expressed; envy, disguised; and occasionally loyalty and affection." He died in New York City.

[See Zilboorg's "Post-partum Schizophrenias," *Journal of Nervous and Mental Diseases*, 68 (1928), 370–383; "Ambulatory Schizophrenias," *ibid.*, 94 (1941), 201–204; *Sigmund Freud: His Exploration of the Mind of Man* (1951); "Scientific Psychopathology and Religious Issues," *Theological Studies*, 14 (1953), 288–297; *Freud and Religion: A Restatement of an Old Controversy* (1958); and "A Psychiatric Consideration of the Ascetic Ideal," in his *Psychoanalysis and Religion* (1962), edited by Margaret Stone Zilboorg.

On Zilboorg and his work, see F. J. Braceland, "In Memoriam: Gregory Zilboorg," *American Journal of Psychiatry*, 116 (1960), 671–672; and the obituary notice, *New York Times*, Sept. 18, 1959.]

GEORGE MORA

ZNANIECKI, FLORIAN WITOLD (Jan. 15, 1882–Mar. 23, 1958), sociologist and philosopher, was born in Swiatniki, Poland, the son of

Leon Znaniecki, a noble landowner, and Amelia Holtz. After graduation from a Warsaw gymnasium, he enrolled at the university of Warsaw as a student of literature, but was expelled after a year for rebellious activities against Russian authorities. From 1904 to 1909 he studied at the universities of Geneva and Zurich and at the Sorbonne in Paris. At the latter, under the influence of Henri Bergson and Lucien Lévy-Bruhl, he changed his interest from literature to philosophy. On Sept. 1, 1906, he married Emma Szwejkowska; they had one son. In 1909 he returned to Poland and in 1910 obtained the Ph.D. degree at the Jagiellonian University of Krakow with a dissertation entitled *Zagadnienie wartości w filozofii* ("The Value Problem in Philosophy").

Because of his activities in behalf of Polish independence, Znaniecki could not obtain an appointment at a university in occupied Poland. He therefore accepted a position in 1911 as director of the Polish Emigrant Protective Association. In this capacity he met W. I. Thomas, professor of sociology at the University of Chicago, who had come to Poland in search of material for his study of immigration problems in the United States. Impressed by the vast amount of material on Polish immigration and by Znaniecki's knowledge of Polish culture and peasant life, Thomas decided to make the Polish immigrant the chief subject of his planned investigation and to employ Znaniecki as his chief collaborator. The outbreak of the war in 1914 threatened the continuity of this collaboration, so Znaniecki moved to Chicago in order to carry on the research. His wife died, and on Apr. 26, 1916, he married Eileen Markley; they had one daughter. While assisting Thomas he lectured at the University of Chicago on Polish history and institutions (1917–1919).

In 1918 the first two volumes of Znaniecki and Thomas' *The Polish Peasant in Europe and America* were published. Volumes III–V appeared in 1919–1920, and a second edition, combining the five volumes into two, in 1927.

The core problem of this monumental study was the nature of the patterns of change in the structure of an immigrant community and the conditions that brought about the change. Znaniecki provided the detailed description and analysis of peasant culture in Poland. He also translated the personal documents, such as letters and biograms, used in the report and wrote the extensive "Methodological Note" that preceded it. The theoretical framework was the outcome of the fortunate meeting of two creative minds and the unhampered interchange of ideas to which each of the authors contributed an equal share. Znaniecki has described this collaboration in an article in *Sociology and Social Research* (1948).

The publication of *Polish Peasant* heralded a new era in the history of sociology. It was the first comprehensive study of a community and the first to use personal records as data. A source of new ideas and practices, it profoundly affected the handling of the immigration problem in the United States. Furthermore, the study introduced a new sociological approach by promoting the recognition of the significance of subjective factors in the analysis of human actions.

Deeply convinced of the originality and creative potential of the new approach, Znaniecki decided to make its theoretical and empirical development his main goal. In 1919 he published *Cultural Reality*, an attempt to formulate his basic philosophical ideas. In 1920 he was appointed to a professorship at the newly created University of Poznan in Poland. In 1922 Znaniecki succeeded in establishing the first department of sociology in Poland. He created the Polish Institute of Sociology and drew around him brilliant students who became his co-workers. In 1930 a new journal, *Przeglad socjologiczny* ("Sociological Review"), appeared under his editorship. The institute made an intensive investigation of Polish social life, using the method of collecting personal life histories (biograms) written as entries in a prize contest. It collected hundreds of autobiographies of workers, peasants, professionals, delinquents, and other types. Of the resulting monographs, Joseph Chalasinski's four-volume study *Mlode pokelenie chlopow* ("The Young Generation Peasant," 1938), is outstanding. Znaniecki also persuaded the Polish government to adopt the biogram method of obtaining data.

Znaniecki's own researches dealt primarily with problems of education. In 1928–1930 he published *Socjologia wychowania* ("The Sociology of Education"). His approach was innovative. He viewed educational processes as sociological events to be analyzed in terms of theories of personal relationships, group formation, and, above all, in the articulation of social roles in the process of socialization.

Znaniecki spent 1932–1934 as visiting professor of sociology at Columbia University, where he studied the effect of social change on education in the United States. This period proved to be the happiest and most fruitful of his career. He was greatly stimulated by close contacts with colleagues and graduate students, and by the intellectual ferment prevailing at the time in sociological theory (such as physicalism versus humanism). Znaniecki offered a thorough and systematic presentation of his views in *The Method of Sociology* (1934).

The world of nature, he argued, and the world of culture are completely incommensurable. The objects of nature exist in and by themselves. Cultural objects exist only with reference to human beings. They have a reality of their own only as objects of experience and interest of the members of some social group. Cultural objects can be understood only with regard to the function they fulfill in the human sphere. They are human values, inseparable from their meaning. For this reason the techniques of the natural sciences are inapplicable to the study of the cultural realm. There can be no theory of the natural origin of culture, or of a direct causal influence of the natural environment upon civilization; there can be no biological interpretation of conscious activities, no theory of the uniformity of human nature or of the influences of racial characteristics upon culture.

The development of culture is governed by its own laws of coexistence and change, the discovery of which is the task of the cultural sciences. Each cultural science deals with a particular class of human values (aesthetic, intellectual, technical, juridic, religious, hedonistic, symbolic, social) and corresponding classes of special activities. Sociology is one of these cultural sciences. It is not a general science; it is not the science of culture as a whole or of society in its generic sense. It is a special discipline (Znaniecki was the first after Georg Simmel to emphasize this point) concerned with human interactions.

Social activities and social values are the basic elements of which social systems are formed. Znaniecki distinguished four such basic systems in ascending order of complexity: social relations, social roles, social groups, and societies. The chief task of sociology is the discovery of the laws governing the formation, the maintenance, and the changes of these systems.

Znaniecki returned to Poland in 1934. He resumed the direction of the Polish Institute and at the same time embarked upon the arduous task of systematizing sociological knowledge. In 1936 he published *Social Actions*, which was to serve as the introduction to his planned systematic sociology. It described the fifteen patterns of social action that Znaniecki considered to be universally operative.

Znaniecki lectured again in the 1939 summer session at Columbia University. As a result he was abroad when Germany invaded Poland. This saved his life, for his name was high on the list of intellectuals slated for execution. The Nazis killed many of his students, destroyed the Institute of Sociology, and burned all the research material collected over the years.

While at Columbia, Znaniecki lectured on the role of creative individuals in human history. The lectures were later published as *The Social Role of the Man of Knowledge* (1940).

In 1941 Znaniecki accepted a professorship at the University of Illinois, where he taught until 1950. He continued his work on systematic sociology, but only fragments remained at his death. These were published posthumously by his daughter, Helena Znaniecka-Lopata, as *Social Relations and Social Roles* (1965). While teaching at Illinois, Znaniecki completed *Modern Nationalities* (1952) and *Cultural Sciences, Their Origin and Development* (1952); in the latter he offered the most complete formulation of his view on the nature and tasks of the science of man. In 1953, Znaniecki was elected president of the American Sociological Association. He died at Urbana, Ill.

[Major writings by Znaniecki not in the text are *Humanizm i poznanie* ("Humanism and Knowledge," 1912); *Upadek cywilizacji zachodniej* ("The Fall of Western Civilization," 1921); *The Laws of Social Psychology* (1925); "The Object Matter of Sociology," *American Journal of Sociology*, 32 (1927); *Ludzie teraźniejsi a cywilizacja przyszłości* ("Modern Man and the Civilization of the Future," 1931); "Social Groups as Products of Participating Individuals," *American Journal of Sociology*, 44 (1939); "Social Organization and Institutions," in G. Gurvitch and W. Moore, eds., *Twentieth Century Sociology* (1945); "Basic Problems of Contemporary Sociology," *American Sociological Review*, 19 (1954). See also Herbert Blumer, *An Appraisal of . . . Polish Peasant in Europe and America* (1939); Theodore Abel, "The Nature and Use of Biograms," *American Journal of Sociology*, 53 (1947); A. Kwilecki, ed., *Florian Znaniecki and His Role in Sociology* (1955), in Polish; Pitirim A. Sorokin, *Sociological Theories of Today* (1966); Robert Bierstedt, ed., *Florian Znaniecki on Humanistic Sociology* (1969); Alvin Boskoff, *Theory in American Sociology* (1969); L. A. Coser, *Masters of Sociological Thought* (2nd ed., 1977).]

THEODORE ABEL

ZUPPKE, ROBERT CARL (July 2, 1879–Dec. 22, 1957), football coach, was born in Berlin, Germany, the son of Franz Simon

Zuppke, a jeweler, and Hermine Bocksbaum. In 1881 the Zuppkes migrated to Milwaukee, Wis., where Robert attended public school and, for two years, Milwaukee Normal School. Skill at drawing and painting came to the fore in his school years, and he was a member of the art staff of the Milwaukee Normal yearbook in 1901. Zuppke then entered the University of Wisconsin at Madison, where he earned the Ph.B. degree. He was too short and light to win a letter in football, but he played with the scrubs. In basketball speed and agility made up for lack of size, and he received his letter with a championship team. After graduating in 1905, Zuppke spent a year doing commercial art work in New York City. He then took a position as athletic director and football coach at Muskegon (Mich.) High School, where he also taught history. Art continued to be of increasing interest, as indicated by his enrollment in a summer course at the Chicago Art Institute (1904).

Zuppke's four years at Muskegon (1906–1910) determined the direction of his career. Going next to the high school at Oak Park, Ill., he compiled a record so phenomenal that after three years the athletic directors of Northwestern, Purdue, and the University of Illinois all made him offers. Impressed by its athletic director, George Huff, he accepted a salary of $2,700 a year and went to the University of Illinois as head football coach. His beginning season, 1913, was notable for the surprise scoreless tie to which Zuppke's players held powerful Purdue. Since Zuppke had no experience as a university coach, this feat attracted wide attention. In his second season Zuppke's team won the conference championship. Almost before the football world of the Middle West recovered from that shock, Illinois captured a second conference title in 1915. What went into the record books as one of the biggest upsets in football history was scored by "the little Dutchman's" team in 1918. Minnesota, which had defeated Chicago 49–0, Wisconsin 54–0, and Iowa 67–0, was turned back by Illinois, 14–9. Zuppke teams also won conference championships in 1918, 1919, 1923, 1927, and 1928.

Zuppke was a persistent innovator. He either devised or contributed to the development of the huddle, the screen pass, the spiral pass from

center, the "flea flicker" pass, and other plays and strategies. He was also credited with originating spring practice. Coaches throughout the country watched Illinois to see what its coach would come up with next. As a consequence a procession of brilliant football players converged on Champaign-Urbana. Harold ("Red") Grange, "the Galloping Ghost" of the 1920's, was the most spectacular among many. No other decade in Zuppke's coaching career was so successful as his first, when his teams took four titles in seven seasons. And when his teams were not in first place, they were regularly close to the top.

Zuppke's last years as coach were controversial ones. Championships eluded his teams. A plan to remove him took form in 1938. He survived, but the athletic director, Wendell S. Wilson, was dismissed. In 1941 his team lost all its conference games. Just before the final game Zuppke announced his retirement. His twenty-nine-year record was 131 victories, 81 defeats, and 12 ties. His teams were recognized as national champions in 1914, 1919, 1923, and 1927.

Zuppke often filled positions such as commissioner of sports programs at the Century of Progress Exposition at Chicago (1933–1934) and the New York World's Fair (1939–1940). He chaired the $2 million campaign for the University of Illinois War Memorial Stadium (1922–1923). In 1942 he coached the All-Star Football Team. He was president of the American Football Coaches Association (1924–1925). In 1951, Zuppke was elected to the National Football Hall of Fame. He was married twice: on June 27, 1908, to Fanny Tillotson Erwin, who died in 1936; and on Sept. 10, 1956, to Leona Ray. He died in Champaign.

Zuppke never lost interest in painting. His landscapes and other works were exhibited in New York City, Chicago, Milwaukee, Toledo, Davenport, Iowa, and elsewhere. Arizona was a favorite setting, and he passed many happy hours putting its desert scenes and moods onto canvas.

[A Zuppke collection was established at the University of Illinois. Zuppke wrote *Football Technique and Tactics* (1922) and *Coaching Football* (1930). See *Milwaukee Journal*, Oct. 31, 1940. An obituary is in *New York Times*, Dec. 23, 1957.]

IRVING DILLIARD

INDEX GUIDE
TO THE
SUPPLEMENTS

INDEX GUIDE

TO THE SUPPLEMENTS

Index Guide to the Supplements

Index Guide to the Supplements

Index Guide to the Supplements

Index Guide to the Supplements

Index Guide to the Supplements

Index Guide to the Supplements

Index Guide to the Supplements

Index Guide to the Supplements

Index Guide to the Supplements

740

Index Guide to the Supplements

Index Guide to the Supplements

Index Guide to the Supplements

Index Guide to the Supplements

Index Guide to the Supplements

Index Guide to the Supplements

Index Guide to the Supplements

Index Guide to the Supplements

Index Guide to the Supplements

Index Guide to the Supplements

Index Guide to the Supplements

Index Guide to the Supplements

Index Guide to the Supplements

Index Guide to the Supplements

Index Guide to the Supplements

Index Guide to the Supplements

Index Guide to the Supplements

Index Guide to the Supplements

Index Guide to the Supplements

Index Guide to the Supplements

Index Guide to the Supplements

Index Guide to the Supplements

Index Guide to the Supplements

Index Guide to the Supplements

Index Guide to the Supplements

Index Guide to the Supplements

Index Guide to the Supplements

Index Guide to the Supplements

Index Guide to the Supplements